INDIA

After GANDHI

THE HISTORY *of the* WORLD'S
LARGEST DEMOCRACY

For IRA, SASHA, *and* SUJA

lights on my coast

HARPER ● PERENNIAL

Frontispiece illustration: Indians marching to join Gandhi's funeral procession, New Delhi, 31 January 1948; by Henri Cartier-Bresson, courtesy of Magnum.

Grateful acknowledgment is made to V. Narayana Rao for permission to reprint the translation of Mohiuddin on page 636, from *Hibiscus on the Lake: Twentieth-Century Telugu Poetry from India,* copyright © 2003, published by University of Wisconsin Press.

A hardcover edition of this book was published in 2007 by Ecco, an imprint of HarperCollins Publishers.

HarperCollins books may be purchased for educational, business, or sales promotional use. For information please write: Special Markets Department, HarperCollins Publishers, 10 East 53rd Street, New York, NY 10022.

FIRST HARPER PERENNIAL EDITION PUBLISHED 2008.

Designed by Kate Nichols

Library of Congress Cataloging-in-Publication Data is available upon request.

ISBN 978-0-06-095858-9

08 09 10 11 12   WBC/RRD   10 9 8 7 6 5 4 3 2 1

"Finally, here is a history of democratic India that is every bit as sweeping as the country itself. . . . One of the many strengths of *India After Gandhi* is the wealth and breadth of its sources. . . . [A] magisterial work." —Edward Luce, *Financial Times* (London)

"It is a formidable undertaking to write in a single volume a history of this vast country. . . . [I]t is as comprehensive, balanced, and elegantly crafted as any reasonable reader could expect. . . . The publisher described this book as a 'must-read for anyone interested in India.' Such hyperbole usually needs to be taken with a barrow load of salt. Add the word 'contemporary' before 'India' and in this case, it is well justified." —Philip Ziegler, *The Spectator*

"[An] insightful, spirited, and elegantly crafted account of India since 1947." —*The Times Literary Supplement* (London)

"[A] dazzling book. Its prose is always attractive, and it has a sure chronological organization. The different regions get a fair and balanced treatment, which is not always the case in such histories. Besides memoirs, monographs, essays, and contemporary newspapers, Guha has also examined important archival collections." —Sanjay Subrahmanyam, *London Review of Books*

"Guha is a scholar of astounding energy and ingenuity, and his book triumphantly dismisses an often-made plea: that India's contemporary history cannot be written because (as a result of government pigheadedness) the sources are not available. He seems to have visited every archive from Alabama to Allahabad, Calcutta to California, delving into a sea of private correspondence, news reports, pamphlet ephemera, as well as state papers. The result is a fascinating, kaleidoscopic narrative." —Sunil Khilnani, *The Daily Telegraph* (London)

"Guha has produced a superb, gloriously detailed book that is essential reading for anybody with a serious interest in modern India. . . . A brilliant and beautifully balanced book. It is impeccably researched and documented, but Guha is no dry-as-dust academic historian. He presents his facts objectively but never hides his patriotism or cosmopolitan Nehruvian ethos. He avoids self-congratulation and celebrates the survival of democratic India without overlooking the nation's countless failings and shortcomings." —*The Independent* (London)

"Ramachandra Guha's weighty account of the struggle to forge a democratic nation out of discord and disparity is a riveting narrative. . . . *India After Gandhi* is a balanced and unfailingly insightful work."
                                            —*The Sunday Times* (London)

"Huge and absorbing. . . . No brief review could convey the astonishing range of this remarkable and capacious book. Having clearly done an enormous amount of research, Guha marshals his facts and figures brilliantly, fleshing them out with well-chosen anecdotes. . . . Guha provides an epilogue that is both optimistic and unexpectedly moving. . . . There will undoubtedly be other books covering the extraordinary and exhilarating story of post-independence India, but it is hard to imagine there will be a better one."   —*Sunday Telegraph* (London)

"Choosing 'the more primitive techniques of a narrative historian' over 'the methods of statistical social science', Guha gives us a lucid and lively chronicle of independent India's adventurous engagement with democracy. His choice of techniques is fully vindicated in a book that is, from beginning to end, a genuine pleasure to read. With an eye for detail and a knack for finding the most telling anecdotes, Guha presents a grand panorama of the unfolding of sixty years of India's political history. It is a book worthy of a diamond jubilee."
                                            —*The Indian Express* (Mumbai)

"Guha's book is a tour de force on at least four counts. First, the sources he uses are new and would well be considered 'scoops.' . . . Second, the style he adopts is easy flowing, conversational. . . . His writing is always marked by clarity and is remarkably free of obfuscation. . . . Third, the scope of what he has taken on could have deterred anybody, but Guha is able to pull it off. . . . Fourth, the substance of what he says has great relevance. . . . Guha has a wide conception of history and does not confine himself to 'big' history—the stuff of politics and personalities. He writes brilliantly on 'small' history as well—the history of people [as] reflected in sports, in films and music, and in numerous popular protests and agitations."
                                            —*Outlook* (New Delhi)

"Combining academic rigor with the readability of a thriller, *India After Gandhi* is a breathtaking survey of India's attempts to stay united and democratic since 1947."   —*Time Out* (Mumbai)

"[T]he scholarship that has gone into this volume is astounding. To my mind, this is the most well-researched book on Indian politics since independence produced by a single author. The reader can safely trust Guha's facts as well as his accounts of debates and controversies over contentious topics. . . . His presentation is always careful, well-informed, and fair."

—Partha Chatterjee, *The Book Review* (New Delhi)

"India's colorful history spans millennia, but arguably its most vivid era began in 1947, when the newly independent nation embarked on the unprecedented experiment of democracy. Its survival as a unified country . . . is one of the greatest stories of our time. It is also one of the least understood. . . . Guha's new book provides important clues on how a democracy is built and sustained—making it mandatory reading."
—*Time Asia*

Sujata Keshavan

About the Author

RAMACHANDRA GUHA was born in Dehradun in 1958 and educated in Delhi and Calcutta. He has taught at the universities of Oslo, Stanford, and Yale, and at the Indian Institute of Science. He has been a Fellow of the Wissenschaftskolleg zu Berlin and also has served as the Indo-American Community Chair Visiting Professor at the University of California at Berkeley.

After a peripatetic academic career, with five jobs in ten years on three continents, Guha settled down to become a full-time writer, based in Bangalore. His books cover a wide range of themes, including a global history of environmentalism, a biography of an anthropologist-activist, a social history of Indian cricket, and a social history of Himalayan peasants. His entire career, he says, seems in retrospect to have been an extended (and painful) preparation for the writing of *India After Gandhi*.

Guha's books and essays have been translated into more than twenty languages. The prizes they have won include the UK Cricket Society's Literary Award and the Leopold-Hidy Prize of the American Society of Environmental History.

ALSO BY RAMACHANDRA GUHA

*The Unquiet Woods: Ecological Change and
Peasant Resistance in the Himalaya*

*Savaging the Civilized: Verrier Elwin,
His Tribals, and India*

Environmentalism: A Global History

The Use and Abuse of Nature
(with Madhav Gadgil)

An Anthropologist among the Marxists and Other Essays

The Picador Book of Cricket
(editor)

*A Corner of a Foreign Field:
The Indian History of a British Sport*

RAMACHANDRA GUHA

AN ecco BOOK

HARPER ● PERENNIAL

NEW YORK ● LONDON ● TORONTO ● SYDNEY ● NEW DELHI ● AUCKLAND

India is a pluralist society that creates magic with democracy, rule of law and individual freedom, community relations and [cultural] diversity. What a place to be an intellectual! . . . I wouldn't mind being born ten times to rediscover India.

ROBERT BLACKWILL,
departing U.S. ambassador, in 2003

Nobody could be more conscious than I am of the pitfalls which lie in the path of the man who wants to discover the truth about contemporary India.

NIRAD CHAUDHURI,
The Autobiography of an Unknown Indian, 1950

CONTENTS

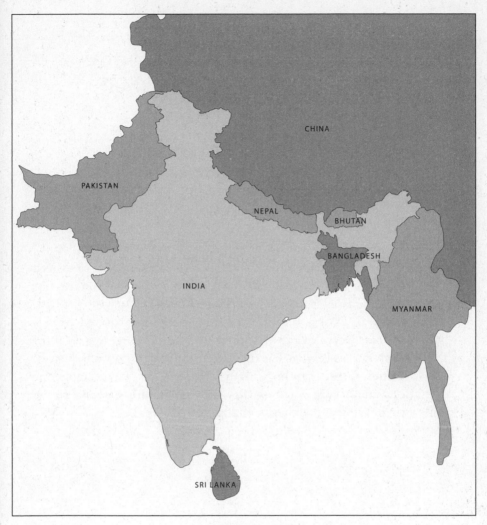

India and Its Neighbourhood

A NOTE ON PLACE NAMES

In recent years, the names of several towns and cities in India have been modified or changed—thus, Bombay has become Mumbai, Madras has become Chennai, and Calcutta has become Kolkata. Likewise, the Bangladeshi capital, Dhaka, was for much of the period covered by this book known as Dacca, while the Chinese capital, Beijing, was until the 1980s referred to as Peking. The usage in this book conforms to historical convention rather than linguistic precision. Thus, for example, the capital of Maharashtra is referred to as Bombay until we come to the time when its name was officially changed to Mumbai.

CAST OF PRINCIPAL CHARACTERS

ABDULLAH, SHEIKH MOHAMMED (1905–1982), Kashmiri leader and politician.

AMBEDKAR, B. R. (1892–1956), leader of the low castes and first law minister of independent India.

DESAI, MORARJI (1896–1995), first non-Congress prime minister of India, 1977–1980.

GANDHI, INDIRA (1917–1984), prime minister of India, 1966–1977, 1980–1984.

GANDHI, MOHANDAS K., also known as Mahatma Gandhi (1869–1948), commonly regarded as the Father of the Nation, no relation to Indira, Rajiv, or Sanjay Gandhi.

GANDHI, RAJIV (1945–1991), prime minister of India, 1984–1989, son of Indira Gandhi.

GANDHI, SANJAY (1946–1980), Congress party politician, son of Indira Gandhi.

GANDHI, SONIA (1946–), Congress party politician, wife of Rajiv Gandhi.

GOLWALKAR, M. S. (1906–1973), leader of the Hindu radical organization the Rashtriya Swayamsewak Sangh.

NAMBOODIRIPAD, E. M. S. (1909–1998), first Communist chief minister of an Indian state (Kerala).

NARAYAN, JAYAPRAKASH (1902–1979), socialist and social worker.

NEHRU, JAWAHARLAL (1889–1964), prime minister and foreign minister of India, 1947–1964, father of Indira Gandhi and grandfather of Rajiv and Sanjay Gandhi.

PATEL, VALLABHBHAI (1875–1950), home minister and deputy prime minister of India, 1947–1950.

PHIZO, A. Z. (1913–1991), Naga separatist leader.

RAJAGOPALACHARI, CHAKRAVARTI (1878–1972), first Indian governor general, and founder of the free-market Swatantra party.

SHASTRI, LAL BAHADUR (1902–1966), prime minister of India, 1964–1966.

VAJPAYEE, ATAL BEHARI (1924–), first non-Congress prime minister to complete a full term in office, 1998–2004.

Prologue

UNNATURAL NATION

I

BECAUSE THEY ARE SO MANY, and so various, the people of India are also divided. They appear to have always been so. In the spring of 1827, the poet Mirza Asadullah Khan Ghalib set out on a journey from Delhi to Calcutta. Six months later he reached the holy Hindu city of Banaras. Here he wrote a poem called "Chirag-i-Dair" ("Temple Lamps"), with these timeless lines:

> Said I one night to a pristine seer
> (Who knew the secrets of whirling Time),
> "Sir, you well perceive,
> That goodness and faith,
> Fidelity and love
> Have all departed from this sorry land.
> Father and son are at each other's throat;
> Brother fights brother. Unity
> and Federation are undermined.
> Despite these ominous signs
> Why has not Doomsday come?
> Why does not the Last Trumpet sound?
> Who holds the reins of the Final Catastrophe?"[1]

Ghalib's poem was composed against the backdrop of the decline of the Mughal Empire. His home territory, the Indo-Gangetic Plain, once ruled by a single monarch, was now split between contending chiefdoms and armies. Brother was fighting brother; unity and federation were being undermined. But even as he wrote, a new (and foreign) power was asserting its presence across the land. The British had steadily acquired control of the greater part of the subcontinent, until in 1857 large sections of the native population rose in revolt, in what the colonialists then called the Sepoy Mutiny, and Indian nationalists later referred to as the First War of Independence.

Some of the bloodiest fighting was in Ghalib's home town, Delhi, still nominally the capital of the Mughals, and in time to become the capital of the British Raj as well. His own sympathies were divided. He was the recipient of a stipend from the new rulers, yet a product of Mughal culture and refinement. He saw, more clearly than the British colonialist did then or the Indian nationalist does now, that it was impossible here to separate right from wrong, that horrible atrocities were being committed by both sides. Marooned in his home, he wrote a melancholy account of how "Hindustan has become the arena of the mighty whirlwind and the blazing fire." "To what new order can the Indian look with joy?," he asked.[2]

An answer to this question was forthcoming. After the events of 1857, the Crown took over control of the Indian colonies. A sophisticated bureaucracy replaced the somewhat ad hoc and haphazard administration of the old East India Company. New districts and provinces were created. The running of the state was overseen by the elite cadre of the Indian Civil Service, supported by departments of police, forests, irrigation, etc. Great energies (and monies) were spent on building a railway network that criss-crossed the land. This contributed enormously to the unity of British India, as well as to its stability, for now the rulers could quickly move troops to forestall any repeat of 1857.

II

By 1888, the British were so solidly established in India that they could look forward to, if not a thousand-year Raj, at least a rule that extended well beyond their own lifetimes. In that year a man who had helped put the Raj in place gave a series of lectures at Cambridge, which were later published in book form under the simple title *India*. This was Sir John Strachey. Strachey had spent many years in the subcontinent, ultimately becoming a member of the Governor-General's Council. Now, in retirement in England, he set his Indian experience against the background of recent political developments in Europe itself.

Large chunks of Strachey's book are taken up with an administrative history of the Raj: of its army and civil services, its land and taxation policies, and the peculiar position of the "native states." This was a primer for those who might work in India after leaving Cambridge. But there was also a larger theoretical argument, to the effect that "India" was merely a label of convenience, "a name which we give to a great region including a multitude of different countries."

In Strachey's view, the differences between the countries of Europe were much smaller than those between the countries of India: "Scotland is more like Spain than Bengal is like the Punjab." In India, the diversities of race, language, and religion were far greater. Unlike those in Europe, these "countries" were not "nations": that is, they did not have a distinct political or social identity. This, Strachey told his Cambridge audience, "is the first and most essential thing to learn about India— that there is not, and never was an India, or even any country of India possessing, according to any European ideas, any sort of unity, physical, political, social or religious."

There was no Indian nation or country in the past; nor would there be one in the future. Strachey thought it "conceivable that national sympathies may arise in particular Indian countries," but

> that they should ever extend to India generally, that men of the Punjab, Bengal, the North-western Provinces, and Madras, should ever feel that they belong to one Indian nation, is impossible. You might with as much reason and probability look forward to a time when a single nation will have taken the place of the various nations of Europe.[3]

Strachey's remarks were intended as a historical judgement. At the time, new nations were vigorously identifying themselves within Europe, on the basis of a shared language or territory, whereas none of the countries that he knew in India had displayed a comparable national awakening. But we might also read his comments as a political exhortation, intended to stiffen the will of those in his audience who would end up in the service of the Raj. For the rise of every new "nation" in India would mean a corresponding diminution in the power and prestige of the British Empire.

Ironically, even as Strachey spoke his verdict was being disputed by a group of Indians. These had set up the Indian National Congress, a representative body that asked for a greater say for natives in the running of their affairs. As the name suggests, this body wished to unite Indians across the divisions of culture, territiory, religion, and language, and thus to construct what the colonialist thought inconceivable—a single Indian nation.

Very many good books have been written on the growth of the Indian National Congress, on its development from debating club through mass movement to political party, on the part played by leaders such as Gokhale, Tilak, and (above all) Gandhi in this progression. Attention has been paid to the building of bridges between linguistic communities, religious groupings, and castes. These attempts were not wholly successful, for low castes and especially Muslims were never completely convinced of the Congress's claims to being a truly national party. Thus when political independence finally came in 1947, it came to not one nation, but two—India and Pakistan.

This is not the place to rehearse the history of Indian nationalism.[4] I need only note that from the time the Congress was formed right up to when India was made free—and divided—there were sceptics who thought that Indian nationalism was not a natural phenomenon at all. There were, of course, British politicians and thinkers who welcomed Indian self-rule, and, in their own way, aided its coming into being. (One of the prime movers of the Indian National Congress was a colonial official of Scottish parentage, A. O. Hume.) Yet there were many others who argued that in India, unlike France or Germany or Italy, there was no national essence, no glue to bind the people and take them purposively forward. From this perspective stemmed the claim that it was only British rule that held India and the Indians together.

Among those who endorsed John Strachey's view that there could never be an independent Indian nation were writers both famous and obscure. Prominent in the first category was Rudyard Kipling, who had spent his formative years in—and was to write some of his finest stories about—the subcontinent. In November 1891, Kipling visited Australia, where a journalist asked him about the "possibility of self-government in India." "Oh no!" he answered: "They are 4,000 years old out there, much too old to learn that business. Law and order is what they want and we are there to give it to them and we give it them straight."[5]

Whereas Kipling laid emphasis on the antiquity of the Indian civilization, other colonialists stressed the immaturity of the Indian mind but reached the same conclusion: that Indians could not govern themselves. A cricketer and tea planter insisted, after forty years here:

Chaos would prevail in India if we were ever so foolish to leave the natives to run their own show. Ye gods! What a salad of confusion, of bungle, of mismanagement, and far worse, would be the instant result.

These grand people will go anywhere and do anything if led by us.

Themselves they are still infants as regards governing or statesmanship. And their so-called leaders are the worst of the lot.[6]

Such views were widely prevalent among the British in India, and at home as well. Politically, the most important of these "Stracheyans" was undoubtedly Winston Churchill. In the 1940s, with Indian independence manifestly around the corner, Churchill grumbled that he had not become the king's first minister in order to preside over the liquidation of the British Empire.

A decade previously, he had tried to revive a fading political career on the plank of opposing self-government for Indians. After Gandhi's "Salt Satyagraha" of 1930, the British government began speaking with Indian nationalists about the possibility of granting the colony Dominion status. This was vaguely defined, with no timetable set for its realization. Still, Churchill described the idea as "not only fantastic in itself but criminally mischievous in its effects." Since Indians were not fit for self-government, it was necessary to marshal "the sober and resolute forces of the British Empire" to forestall any such possibility.

In 1930 and 1931, Churchill delivered numerous speeches designed to work up, in most unsober form, the constituency opposed to independence for India. Speaking to an audience at the City of London in December 1930, he claimed that if the British left the subcontinent, then "an army of white janissaries, officered if necessary from Germany, will be hired to secure the armed ascendancy of the Hindu." Three months later, speaking at Albert Hall on "Our Duty to India"—with his kinsman the duke of Marlborough presiding—Churchill argued that "to abandon India to the rule of the Brahmans [who in his opinion dominated the Congress party] would be an act of cruel and wicked negligence." If the British left, he predicted, then the entire gamut of public services created by them—the judicial, medical, railway, and public works departments—would perish, and India would "fall back quite rapidly through the centuries into the barbarism and privations of the Middle Ages."[7]

III

A decade and a half after Winston Churchill issued these warnings, the British left India. A time of barbarism and privation did ensue, the blame for which remains a matter of much dispute. But then some sort of order was restored. No Germans were necessary to keep the peace. Hindu ascendancy, such as it was, was maintained not through force of arms but through regular elections based on universal adult franchise.

Yet, throughout the sixty years since India became independent, there has been speculation about how long it would stay united, or maintain the institutions and processes of democracy. With every death of a prime minister has been predicted the replacement of democracy by military rule; in every failure of the monsoon has been anticipated countrywide famine; in every new secessionist movement has been seen the disappearance of India as a single entity.

Among these doomsayers there have been many western writers: after 1947, these were as likely to be American as British. Notably, India's existence has not just been a puzzle to casual observers or commonsensical journalists; it has also been an anomaly for academic political science, according to whose axioms cultural heterogeneity and poverty do not make a nation, still less a democratic one. That India "could sustain democratic institutions seems, on the face of it, highly improbable," wrote the distinguished political scientist Robert Dahl, adding: "It lacks all the favourable conditions." "India has a well-established reputation for violating social scientific generalizations," wrote another American scholar, adding, "Nonetheless, the findings of this article furnish grounds for skepticism regarding the viability of democracy in India."[8]

The pages of this book are peppered with forecasts of India's imminent dissolution, or of its descent into anarchy or authoritarian rule. Here, let me quote only a prediction by a sympathetic visitor, the British journalist Don Taylor. Writing in 1969, by which time India had stayed united for two decades and gone through four general elections, Taylor yet thought that

> the key question remains: can India remain in one piece—or will it fragment? . . . When one looks at this vast country and its 524 million people, the 15 major languages in use, the conflicting religions, the many races, it seems incredible that one nation could ever emerge.
>
> It is difficult to even encompass this country in the mind—the great Himalaya, the wide Indo-Gangetic plain burnt by the sun and

savaged by the fierce monsoon rains, the green flooded delta of the east, the great cities like Calcutta, Bombay and Madras. It does not, often, seem like one country. And yet there is a resilience about India which seems an assurance of survival. *There is* something which can only be described as an Indian spirit.

I believe it no exaggeration to say that the fate of Asia hangs on its survival.[9]

The heart hoped that India would survive, but the head worried that it wouldn't. The place was too complicated, too confusing—a nation, one might say, that was *un*natural.

In truth, ever since the country was formed there have also been many Indians who have seen the survival of India as being on the line, some (the patriots) speaking or writing in fear, others (the secessionists or revolutionaries) with anticipation. Like their foreign counterparts, they have come to believe that this place is far too diverse to persist as a nation, and much too poor to endure as a democracy.

IV

In the last decade of the last century, I became a resident of Ghalib's native city. I lived, however, not in the old walled town where his family haveli, or mansion, still stands, but in New Delhi, built as an imperial capital by the British. As in the poet's day, Indian was fighting Indian. On my way to work, I had to pass through Rajpath (formerly Kingsway), the road whose name and location signal the exercise of state power. For about a mile, Rajpath runs along flat land; on either side are spacious grounds meant to accomodate the thousands of spectators who come for the annual Republic Day parade. The road then ascends a hill and reaches the majestic sandstone buildings known as the North and South Blocks, which house the offices of the government of India. The road ends at the great house where the viceroy of British India once lived.

By the time I moved to New Delhi the British had long departed. India was now a free and sovereign republic—but not, it seemed, an altogether happy one. Signs of discord were everywhere. Notably, on Rajpath, the grounds meant to be empty except on ceremonial days had become a village of tents, each with colourful placards hung outside it. One tent might be inhabited by peasants from the Uttarakhand Himalaya, seeking a separate province; a second by farmers from Maharashtra, fighting for a higher price for their produce; a third by residents of the southern

Konkan coast, urging that their language be given official recognition by inclusion in the Eighth Schedule of the constitution of India.

The people within these tents and the causes they upheld were ever-changing. The hill peasants might be replaced by industrial workers protesting retrenchment; the Maharashtra farmers by Tibetan refugees asking for Indian citizenship; the Konkani-speakers by Hindu monks demanding a ban on cow-slaughter.

In the early 1990s, these tents were summarily dismantled by a government worried about the impression made on foreign visitors by such open expression of dissent. Rajpath was cleared of encroachments, and the lawns were restored to their former glory. But the protesters regrouped and relocated. They now placed themselves a mile to the northwest, next to the Jantar Mantar observatory in Connaught Place. Here they were away from the eyes of the state, but directly in view of the citizens who daily passed through this busy shopping district. In 1998 the police decided this would not do either. The shanties were once again demolished, but, as a newspaper report put it, "as far as the authorities are concerned, only the venue has changed—the problem persists. The squatters are merely to be shifted to an empty plot at the Mandir Marg–Shankar Road crossing, where they are likely to draw less attention."[10]

When I lived in Delhi, in the 1990s, I wished I had the time to walk on Rajpath every day from January 1 to December 31, chronicling the appearance and disappearance of the tents and their residents. That would be the story of India as told from a single street, and in a single year. The book that is now in your hands follows a different method. Its narrative extends over six decades, from 1947 to the present. However, like the book that I once intended to write—based on a year spent walking up and down Rajpath—this too is a story, above all, of social conflicts: of how these arise, how they are expressed, and how they are sought to be resolved.

These conflicts run along many axes, among which we may—for the moment—single out four as pre-eminent. First, there is *caste*, a principal identity for many Indians, defining whom they may marry, associate with, and fight against. The Portuguese word *casta* conflates two Indian concepts: jati, the endogamous group one is born into; and varna, the place this group occupies in the system of social stratification mandated by Hindu scripture. There are four varnas, with the former "untouchables" constituting a fifth (and lowest) stratum. Into these varnas fit the 3,000 and more jatis, each challenging those, in the same region, that are ranked above it, and being in turn challenged by those below.

Second, there is *language*. The constitution of India recognizes twenty-two languages as "official." The most important of these is Hindi, which in one form or another is spoken by upwards of 400 million people. Others include Telugu, Kannada, Tamil, Malayalam, Marathi, Gujarati, Oriya, Punjabi, Bengali, and Assamese, each of which is written in a distinct script and boasts of many million native speakers. Naturally, national unity and linguistic diversity have not always been seen to be compatible. Indians speaking one tongue have fought with Indians who speak another.

A third axis of conflict is *religion*. A vast majority of the billion-plus Indians are Hindus. But India also has the second largest population of Muslims in the world—about 140 million (only Indonesia has more). In addition, there are substantial communities of Christians, Sikhs, Buddhists, and Jains. Since faith is as fundamental a feature of human identity as language, it should scarcely be a surprise that Indians worshipping one kind of God have sometimes quarrelled with Indians worshipping another.

A fourth axis of conflict is *class*. India is a land of an unparalleled cultural diversity and also, less appealingly, of enormous social disparities. There are Indian entrepreneurs who are fabulously wealthy, owning huge homes in London and New York. Yet fully 26% of the country's population—that is, about 300 million individuals—are said to live below the official poverty line. In the countryside, there are deep inequalities in landholding; in the city, wide divergences in income. Not unexpectedly, these asymmetries have inspired many movements of protest and opposition.

These axes of conflict operate both singly and in combination. Sometimes, a group professing a particular faith also speaks a separate language. Often, the low castes are the subordinate classes as well. And to these four axes one should perhaps add a fifth that cuts across them: *gender*. Here, again, India offers the starkest contrasts. A woman served as prime minister for a full fifteen years, yet in some parts female infanticide is still very common. Landless labourers are paid meagre wages, the women among them the lowest of all. Low castes face a social stigma, the women among them most of all. And the holy men of each religion tend to assign their women an inferior position in this world and the next. As an axis of discrimination, gender is even more pervasive than the others, although it has not so often expressed itself in open and collective protest.

As a laboratory of social conflict the India of the twentieth century has been—for the historian—at least as interesting as the Europe of the nineteenth. Here, as well as there, the conflicts have been produced by a conjunction of two truly transformative processes of social change: industrialization and the making of modern nation states. In India the scope for contention has been even greater, given the diversity of competing groups across religion, caste, class, and language. Conflicts are also more visible here, since, unlike nineteenth-century Europe, contemporary India is a democracy based on adult suffrage, with a free press and a largely independent judiciary. At no other time or place in human history have social conflicts been so richly diverse, so vigorously articulated, so eloquently manifest in art and literature, or addressed with such directness by the political system and the media.

One way of summarizing the history of independent India—and the contents of this book—would be through a series of "conflict maps." We might draw a map of India for each decade, with the conflicts then prevalent marked in various colours depending on their intensity; blue for those that democratically advance the interests of a particular group; red for those that more aggressively, yet still non-violently, ask for a major change in the law; and black for those that seek the destruction of the Indian state by arms.

Reading these maps chronologically, one would find major variations across the decades, with red areas becoming black, black areas becoming red, and blue and red areas becoming white—that being the colour of those parts of India where there appears to be no major conflict at all. These maps would present a vivid kaleidoscope of changing colours. But amid all the changes the discerning viewer would also see the two things that remain constant. The first is that the shape of the map does not change through all its iterations. This is because no part of India has sucessfully *left* India. The second is that at no time do the blue, red, and black areas, taken together, anywhere approximate the extent of the white areas. Even in what were once known as its "dangerous decades," much more than 50% of India was comfortably at peace with itself.

The press nowadays—quality and tabloid, pink and white, Indian and western—is chock-full of stories of India's economic success, reckoned to be greatly at odds with its past history of poverty and deprivation. However, the real success story of modern India lies not in the domain of economics but in that of politics. The saluting of India's "software boom" might be premature. We do not yet know whether this boom will lead to a more general prosperity among the masses. But that India is still a single nation after sixty testing years of independence, and that it is still largely democratic—these are what should compel our deeper attention. A recent statistical analysis of the relationship between democracy and development in 135 countries found that "the odds against democracy in India were extremely high." Given its low levels of income and literacy, and its high levels of social conflict, India was "predicted as [a] dictatorship during the entire period" of the study. Since, in fact, it was a democracy for that entire period (barring two years) there was only one way to characterize India: as "a major outlier."[11]

To explain this anomaly, or paradox, one needs perhaps to abandon the methods of statistical social science—in which India will always be the exception to the rule—in favour of the more primitive techniques of the narrative historian. The forces that divide India are many. This book pays due attention to them. But there are also forces that have kept India together, that have helped transcend or contain the cleavages of class and culture, that—so far at least—have nullified the many predictions that India would not stay united and not stay democratic. These moderating influences are far less visible; it is one aim of this book to make them more so. I think it premature to identify them now; they will become clearer as the narrative proceeds. Suffice it to say that they have included individuals as well as institutions.

V

The "period of Indian history since 1947," writes the political theorist Sunil Khilnani, "might be seen as the adventure of a political idea: democracy." Viewed thus, independent India appears as the "third moment in the great democratic experiment launched at the end of the eighteenth century by the American and French revolutions." Each of these experiments "released immense energies; each raised towering expectations; and each has suffered tragic disappointments." Although the Indian experiment is the youngest, says Khilnani, "its outcome may well turn out to be the most significant of them all, partly because of its sheer human scale, and partly because of its location, a substantial bridgehead of efferverscent liberty on the Asian continent."[12]

As an Indian, I would like to think that democracy in India will turn out to be "more significant" than comparable experiments in the West. As a historian, I know only that it is much less studied. There are hundreds, perhaps thousands, of books on the French and American revolutions: biographies of their leaders famous and obscure, studies of the social background of those who participated in them, assessments of their deepening or degradation in the decades and centuries that followed. By contrast, the works by historians on any aspect of Indian democracy can be counted on the fingers of one hand—or, if one is more open-minded, two.

The educationist Krishna Kumar writes that "for Indian children history itself comes to an end with Partition and Independence. As a constituent of social studies, and later on as a subject in its own right, history runs right out of content in 1947. . . . All that has happened during the last 55 years may filter through the measly civics syllabus, popular cinema and television; history as formally constituted knowledge of the past does not cover it."[13]

If, for Indian children, history comes to an end with independence and partition, this is because Indian adults have mandated it that way. In the academy, the discipline of history deals with the past, while the disciplines of political science and sociology deal with the present. This is a conventional and in many ways logical division. The difficulty is that in the *Indian* academy the past is defined as a single, immovable date: 15 August 1947. Thus, when the clock struck midnight and India became independent, history ended, and political science and sociology began.

In the decades since 1947, the present has moved on. Political scientists studied the first general elections of 1952, and then the next one five years later. Social anthropologists wrote accounts of Indian villages in the 1950s, and then some more in the 1960s. The past, however, has stayed fixed. By training and temperament, historians have restricted themselves to the period before independence. A vast literature grew—and is still growing—on the social, cultural, political, and economic consequences of British colonialism. A even vaster literature grew—and it too is still growing—on the forms, functions, causes, and consequences of the opposition to colonial rule. Leading that opposition was the social reformer, spiritualist, prophet, and political agitator Mohandas Karamchand Gandhi.

Gandhi was, and is, a man greatly admired by some and cordially detested by others. Much the same could be said of the monumental edifice he opposed, the British Raj. The British finally left India in August 1947; Gandhi was assassinated by a fellow Indian a bare five and a half months later. That the demise of the Raj was followed so quickly by the death of its most celebrated opponent has had a determining influence on the writing of history. One cannot say whether if Gandhi had lived on much longer, historians would have shown greater interest in the history of free India. As it turned out, by custom and convention Indian history is seen as "ending" on 15 August 1947—although Gandhi's biographers are allowed a six-month extension. Thus many fine, as well as controversial, books have been written on the last, intense, conflict-filled years of British India. That great institution, the British Raj, and that great individual, Mahatma Gandhi, continue to be of absorbing interest to historians. But the history of *independent* India has remained a field mostly untilled. If history is "formally constituted knowledge of the past," then for the period since 1947 this knowledge practically does not exist.

And yet, as this book shows, the first years of freedom were as full of dramatic interest as the last years of the Raj. The British had formally handed over power, but authority had to be created anew. Partition had not put an end to Hindu-Muslim conflict, nor independence to class and caste tension. Large areas of the map were still under the control of the maharajas; these had to be brought into the Indian Union, by persuasion or coercion. Amid the wreckage of a decaying empire a new nation was being born—and built.

Of his recent history of postwar Europe, Tony Judt writes that "a book of this kind rests, in the first instance, on the shoulders of other books." He notes that "for the brief sixty-year-period of Europe's history since the end of the Second World War—indeed, for this period above all—the secondary literature in English is inexhaustible."[14] The situation in India is all too different. Here the gaps in our knowledge are colossal. The republic of India is a union of twenty-eight states, some larger than France and Germany. Yet not even the biggest or most important of these states have had their histories written. In the 1950s and 1960s India pioneered a new approach to foreign policy, and to economic policy and planning as well. Authoritative or even adequate accounts of these experiments remain to be written. India has produced entrepreneurs of great vision and dynamism—but the stories of the institutions they built and the wealth they created are mostly unwritten. Again, there are no proper biographies of some of the key figures in our modern history: such as Sheikh Abdullah or Master Tara Singh or M. G. Ramachandran, "provincial" leaders each of whose province is the size of a large European country.

Unlike a history of postwar Europe, a history of postwar India cannot simply rest on the shoulders of other books on more specialized subjects. In matters big and small, it must fill in the blanks with materials picked up by the author himself. My first mentor, a very wise old civil servant named C. S. Venkatachar, once told me that every work of history is "interim": to be amplified, amended, contested, and overthrown by works written in its wake. Despite the range of subjects it covers, this book cannot hope to have treated any of them comprehensively. Individual readers will have their own particular complaints: some might object, for instance, that I have not said enough here about tribals, others that I should have written even more pages on Kashmir.

My own hopes for this book are best expressed in the words of Marc Bloch, writing about another country in another time:

> I could liken myself to an explorer making a rapid survey of the horizon before plunging into thickets from which the wider view is no longer possible. The gaps in my account are naturally enormous. I have done my best not to conceal any deficiencies, whether in the state of our knowledge in general or in my own documentation. . . . When the time comes for my own work to be superseded by studies of deeper penetration, I shall feel well rewarded if confrontation with my false conjectures has made history learn the truth about herself.[15]

VI

The great Cambridge historian F. W. Maitland liked to remind his students that "what is now in the past was once in the future." There could be no better maxim for the historian, and especially the historian of the recent past, who addresses an audience with very decided views on the subjects about which he presumes to inform them. An American historian of the Vietnam War is read by those who have mostly made up their minds on whether the war was just or not. A French historian of the student movement of 1968 knows that his readers will have forceful, if mutually contradictory, opinions about that particular upsurge.

Those who write contemporary history know that they are not addressing a passive reader of the text placed in front of him. The reader is also a citizen, a *critical citizen*, with his own political and ideological preferences. These preferences direct and dictate how he looks at the past, and at leaders and lawmakers most particularly. We live with the consequences of decisions by modern politicians, and often assume that an alternative politician—someone modelled on oneself—would have made better or wiser decisions.

The further back we go in time, the less of a problem this is. The historian studying the eighteenth century seeks to interpret and understand that time, and so, following him, does his reader. The biographer of Jefferson or Napoleon can count on more *trusting* readers—they do not presume to know the things those men did, or wish they had done something different. Here, the reader is usually happy to be led and guided by the expert. But the biographer of Kennedy or De Gaulle is not so fortunate. Some, perhaps many, of his potential readers already know the "truth" about these men, and are less willing to hear alternative versions of the truth, even if these be backed by hundreds of footnotes.

The contemporary historian thus faces a challenge from his readers, which his more backward-looking colleagues escape. But there is also a second, and perhaps less commonly acknowledged, challenge. This is that *the historian is himself a citizen*. The scholar who chooses to write on the Vietnam War already has strong views on the topic of his research. The scholar who writes on the American Civil War would have less strong views, and the one who writes on the Revolutionary War has weaker views still. For the historian as well as the citizen, *the closer one gets to the present, the more judgemental one tends to become*.

In writing this book I have tried to keep Maitland's maxim always in front of me. I have been driven by curiosity rather than certainty, by the wish to understand rather than the desire to pass judgement. I have sought to privilege primary sources over retrospective readings, so that I can interpret an event of 1955 in terms of what was known in 1955 rather than in 2005. This book is, in the first instance, simply an attempt to tell the modern history of one-sixth of humankind. It is an account, as well as an analysis, of the major characters, controversies, themes, and processes in independent India. However, the manner of the telling has been driven by two fundamental ambitions: to pay proper respect to the social and political diversity of India, and to unravel the puzzle that has for so long confronted scholar and citizen, foreigner as well as native—why is there an India at all?

PART I

PICKING UP *the* PIECES

1

FREEDOM *and* PARRICIDE

> The disappearance of the British Raj in India is at present, and must for a long time be, simply inconceivable. That it should be replaced by a native Government or Governments is the wildest of wild dreams. . . . As soon as the last British soldier sailed from Bombay or Karachi, India would become the battlefield of antagonistic racial and religious forces . . . [and] the peaceful and progressive civilisation, which Great Britain has slowly but surely brought into India, would shrivel up in a night.
>
> J. E. WELLDON, former bishop of Calcutta, writing in 1915

> I have no doubt that if British governments had been prepared to grant in 1900 what they refused in 1900 but granted in 1920; or to grant in 1920 what they refused in 1920 but granted in 1940; or to grant in 1940 what they refused in 1940 but granted in 1947—then nine-tenths of the misery, hatred, and violence, the imprisonings and terrorism, the murders, flogging, shootings, assassinations, even the racial massacres would have been avoided; the transference of power might well have been accomplished peacefully, even possibly without Partition.
>
> LEONARD WOOLF, writing in 1967

I

FREEDOM CAME TO INDIA on 15 August 1947, but patriotic Indians had celebrated their first "Independence Day" seventeen years before. In the first week of January 1930, the Indian National Congress passed a resolution fixing the last Sunday of the month for countrywide demonstrations in support of *purna swaraj*, or complete independence. This, it was felt, would both stoke nationalist aspirations and force the British to seriously consider giving up power. In an essay in his journal *Young India*, Mahatma Gandhi set out how the day should be observed: "It would be good if the declaration [of independence] is made by whole villages, whole cities even. . . . It would be well if all the meetings were held at the identical minute in all the places."

Gandhi suggested that the time of the meeting be advertised in the traditional way, by drumbeats. The celebrations would begin with the raising of the national flag. The rest of the day would be spent "in doing some constructive work, whether it is spinning, or service of 'untouchables,' or reunion of Hindus and Mussalmans, or prohibition work, or even all these together, which is not impossible." Participants would take a pledge affirming that it was "the inalienable right of the Indian people, as of any other people, to have freedom and to enjoy the fruits of their toil," and that "if any government deprives a people of these rights and oppresses them, the people have a further right to alter it or abolish it."[1]

The resolution to mark the last Sunday of January as Independence Day was passed in the city of Lahore, where the Congress was holding its annual session. It was here that Jawaharlal Nehru was chosen president of the Congress, in confirmation of his rapidly rising status within the Indian national movement. Nehru was born in 1889, twenty years after Gandhi, was a product of Harrow and Cambridge, and had become a close protégé of the Mahatma. He was intelligent and articulate, knowledgeable about foreign affairs, and particularly appealing to the young.

In his autobiography, Nehru recalled how "Independence Day came, January 26th, 1930, and it revealed to us, as in a flash, the earnest and enthusiastic mood of the country. There was something vastly impressive about the great gatherings everywhere, peacefully and solemnly taking the pledge of independence without any speeches or exhortation."[2] In a press statement that he issued the day after, Nehru "respectfully congratulate[d] the nation on the success of the solemn and orderly demonstrations." Towns and villages had "vied with each other in showing their enthusiastic adherence to independence." Mammoth gatherings were held in Calcutta and Bombay, but the meetings in smaller towns were well attended too.[3]

Every year after 1930, Congress-minded Indians celebrated 26 January as Independence Day. However, when the British finally left the subcontinent, they chose to hand over power on 15 August 1947. This date was selected by the viceroy, Lord Mountbatten, as it was the second anniversary of the Japanese surrender to the Allied forces in the Second World War. He, and the politicians waiting to take office, could not wait until the day some others would have preferred—26 January 1948.

So freedom finally came on a day that resonated with imperial pride, rather than nationalist sentiment. In New Delhi, capital of the Raj and of free India, the formal events began shortly before midnight. Apparently, astrologers had decreed that 15 August was an inauspicious day. Thus it was decided to begin the celebrations on 14 August, with a special session of the Constituent Assembly, the body of representative Indians working toward a new constitution.

The function was held in the high-domed hall of the erstwhile Legislative Council of the Raj. The room was brilliantly lit and decorated with flags. Some of these flags had been placed inside picture frames that until the previous week had contained portraits of British viceroys. Proceedings began at 11 p.m., with the singing of the patriotic hymn "Vande Matram" and a two-minute silence in memory of those "who had died in the struggle for freedom in India and elsewhere." The ceremonies ended with the presenting of the national flag on behalf of the women of India.

In between the song and the flag presentation came the speeches. There were three main speakers that night. One, Chaudhry Khaliquzzaman, was chosen to represent the Muslims of India; he duly proclaimed the loyalty of the minority to the newly freed land. A second, the philosopher Sarvepalli Radhakrishnan, was chosen for his powers of oratory and his work in reconciling East and West: appropriately, he praised the "political sagacity and courage" of the British who had elected to leave India while the Dutch stayed on in Indonesia and the French would not leave Indochina.[4]

The star, however, was the first prime minister of free India, Jawaharlal Nehru. His speech was rich in emotion and rhetoric, and has been widely quoted since. "At the stroke of the midnight hour, when the world sleeps, India will awake to life and freedom," said Nehru.[5] This was "a moment which comes but rarely in history, when we step out from the old to the new, when an age ends, and when the soul of a nation, long suppressed, finds utterance."

This was spoken inside the columned Council House. In the streets outside, as an American journalist reported,

bedlam had broken loose. Hindus, Muslims, and Sikhs were happily celebrating together. . . . It was Times Square on New Year's Eve. More than anyone else, the crowd wanted Nehru. Even before he was due to appear, surging thousands had broken through police lines and flowed right to the doors of the Assembly building. Finally, the heavy doors were closed to prevent a probably souvenir-hunting tide from sweeping through the Chamber. Nehru, whose face reflected his happiness, escaped by a different exit and after a while the rest of us went out.

No event of any importance in India is complete without a goof-up. In this case, it was relatively minor. When, after the midnight session at the Constituent Assembly, Jawaharlal Nehru went to submit his list of cabinet ministers to the governor general, he handed over an empty envelope. However, by the time of the swearing-in ceremony the missing piece of paper was found. Apart from Prime Minister Nehru, it listed thirteen other ministers. These included the nationalist stalwarts Vallabhbhai Patel and Maulana Abul Kalam Azad, as well as four congressmen of the younger generation.

More notable perhaps were the names of those who were not from the Congress. These included two representatives of the world of commerce and one representative of the Sikhs. Three others were lifelong adversaries of the Congress. These were R. K. Shanmukham Chetty, a Madras businessman who was one of the best financial minds in India; B. R. Ambedkar, a brilliant legal scholar and an "untouchable" by caste; and Shyama Prasad Mookerjee, a leading Bengal politician who belonged (at this time) to the Hindu Mahasabha. All three had collaborated with the rulers while the congressmen served time in British jails. But now Nehru and his colleagues wisely put aside these differences. Gandhi had reminded them that "freedom comes to India, not to the Congress," urging the formation of a cabinet that included the ablest men regardless of party affiliation.[6]

The first cabinet of free India was ecumenical in ways other than politically. Its members came from as many as five religious denominations (with a couple of atheists thrown in for good measure), and from all parts of India. There was a woman, Rajkumari Amrit Kaur, as well as two untouchables.

On 15 August, the first item on the agenda was the swearing in of the governor general, Lord Mountbatten, who until the previous night had been the last viceroy. The day's programme read:

8:30 a.m.	Swearing in of Governor-General and Ministers at Government House
9:40 a.m.	Procession of Ministers to Constituent Assembly
9:50 a.m.	State Drive to Constituent Assembly
9:55 a.m.	Royal Salute to Governor General
10:30 a.m.	Hoisting of National Flag at Constituent Assembly
10:35 a.m.	State Drive to Government House

6:00 p.m.	Flag ceremony at India Gate
7:00 p.m.	Illuminations
7:45 p.m.	Fireworks display
8:45 p.m.	Official Dinner at Government House
10:15 p.m.	Reception at Government House

It appeared that the Indians loved pomp and ceremony as much as the departing rulers did. Across Delhi, and in other parts of India, both state and citizens joyously celebrated the coming of independence. Three hundred flag-raising functions were reported from the capital alone. In the country's commercial hub, Bombay, the mayor hosted a banquet at the posh Taj Mahal Hotel. At a temple in the Hindu holy town of Banaras, the national flag was unfurled by, significantly, a Muslim. In the north-eastern hill town of Shillong, the governor presided over a function at which the flag was raised by four persons—a Hindu boy and girl and a Muslim boy and girl, for "symbolically it is appropriate for young India to hoist the flag of the new India that is being born."

When the first, so to say fantastical, Independence Day had been observed on 26 January 1930, the crowds were "solemn and orderly" (as Nehru observed). But in 1947, when the real day of independence came, the feelings on display were rather more elemental. To quote a foreign observer, everywhere, "in city after city, lusty crowds have burst the bottled-up frustrations of many years in an emotional mass jag. Mob sprees have rolled from mill districts to gold coasts and back again. . . . [T]he happy, infectious celebrations blossomed in forgetfulness of the decades of sullen resentment against all that was symbolized by a sahib's sun-topi."

The happenings in India's most populous city, Calcutta, were characteristic of the mood. For the past few years the city had been suffering from a cloth shortage, which now miraculously ended in a "rash of flags that has broken out on houses and buildings . . . , on cars and bicycles and in the hands of babes and sucklings." Meanwhile, in Government House, a new Indian governor was being sworn in. Not best pleased with the sight was the private secretary of the departing British governor. He complained that "the general motley character of the gathering from the clothing point of view detracted greatly from its dignity." There were no dinner jackets and ties on view: there were only loincloths and white Gandhi caps. With "the throne room full of unauthorized persons," the ceremony was "a foretaste of what was to come" after the British had left India. Its nadir was reached when the outgoing governor of Bengal, Sir Frederick Burrows, had a white Gandhi cap placed on his head as he went to leave the room.

II

In Delhi, there was "prolonged applause" when the president of the Constituent Assembly began the meeting by invoking the father of the nation—Mohandas Karamchand Gandhi. Outside, the crowds shouted *Mahatma Gandhi ki jai*. Yet Gandhi was not present at the festivities in the capital. He was in Calcutta, but did not attend any function or raise a flag there either. The Gandhi caps were on display at Government House without his knowledge or permission. On the evening of 14 August, he was visited by the chief minister of West Bengal, who asked him what form the celebrations should take the next day. "People are dying of hunger all round," answered Gandhi. "Do you wish to hold a celebration in the midst of this devastation?"[7]

Gandhi's mood was bleak indeed. When a reporter from the leading nationalist paper, the *Hindustan Times*, requested a message on the occasion of independence, Gandhi replied that "he had run dry." The British Broadcasting Corporation (BBC) asked his secretary for help in recording a message from the one man the world thought really represented India. Gandhi told them to talk to Jawaharlal Nehru instead. The BBC were not persuaded: they sent the emissary back, adding, as an inducement, the fact that this message would be translated into many languages and broadcast around the globe. Gandhi was unmoved, saying, "Ask them to forget I know English."

Gandhi marked 15 August with a twenty-four-hour fast. The freedom for which he had struggled so long had come at an unacceptable price. Independence had also meant partition. The last twelve months had seen almost continuous rioting between Hindus and Muslims. The violence had begun on 16 August 1946, in Calcutta and had spread to the Bengal countryside. From there it moved on to Bihar, then to the United Provinces, and finally to the province of Punjab, where the scale of the violence and the extent of the killings exceeded even the horrors that had preceded them.

The violence of August-September 1946 was, in the first instance, instigated by the Muslim League, the party that fuelled the movement for a separate state of Pakistan. The Muslim League was led by Mohammad Ali Jinnah. Jinnah was an austere, aloof man, and yet a brilliant political tactician. Like Nehru and Gandhi, he was a lawyer trained in

England. Like them, he had once been a member of the Indian National Congress, but he had left the party because he felt that it was led by and for Hindus. Despite its nationalist protestations, argued Jinnah, the Congress did not really represent the interests of India's largest minority, the Muslims.

By starting a riot in Calcutta in August 1946, Jinnah and the Muslim League hoped to further polarize the two communities, and thus force the British to divide India when they finally left. In this endeavour they richly succeeded. The Hindus retaliated savagely in Bihar, their actions supported by local Congress leaders. The British had already said that they would not transfer power to any government "whose authority is directly denied by large and powerful elements in the Indian national life."[8] The bloodshed of 1946–1947 seemed to suggest that the Muslims were just such an element, who would not live easily or readily under a Congress government dominated by Hindus. Now "each communal outbreak was cited as a further endorsement of the two nation theory, and of the inevitability of the partition of the country."[9]

Gandhi was not a silent witness to the violence. When the first reports came in from rural Bengal, he set everything else aside and made for the spot. This seventy-seven-year-old man walked in difficult terrain through slush and stone, consoling the Hindus, who had much the worse of the riots. In a tour of seven weeks he walked 116 miles, mostly barefoot, addressing almost 100 village meetings. Later, he visited Bihar, where the Muslims were the main sufferers. Then he went to Delhi, where refugees from the Punjab had begun to pour in—Hindus and Sikhs who had lost all in the carnage. They were filled with feelings of revenge, which Gandhi sought to contain, for he was fearful that it would lead to retributory violence against Muslims who had chosen to stay behind in India.

Two weeks before the designated day of independence, the Mahatma left Delhi. He spent four days in Kashmir, and then took a train to Calcutta, where, a year after it began, the rioting had not yet died down. On the afternoon of 13 August he set up residence in a Muslim-dominated neighbourhood, Beliaghata, in "a ramshackle building open on all sides to the crowds," to see whether "he could contribute his share in the return of sanity in the premier city of Calcutta."

Gandhi decided simply to fast and pray on 15 August. By the afternoon, news reached him of (to quote a newspaper report) "almost unbelievable scenes of fraternity and rejoicing" in some of the worst-affected areas of Calcutta. "While Hindus began erecting triumphal arches at the entrance of streets and lanes and decorating them with palm leaves, banners, flags and bunting, Muslim shopkeepers and householders were not slow in decorating their shops and houses with flags of the Indian Dominion." Hindus and Muslims drove through the streets in open cars and trucks, shouting the nationalist slogan *Jai Hind*, to which "large, friendly crowds of both communities thronging the streets readily and joyfully responded."[10]

Reports of this spontaneous intermingling seem to have somewhat lifted the Mahatma's mood. He decided he would make a statement on the day, not to the BBC, but through his own preferred means of communication, a prayer meeting. A large crowd—10,000 according to one report; 30,000 according to another—turned up to hear him speak at the Rash Bagan Maidan in Beliaghata. Gandhi said he would like to believe that the fraternization between Hindus and Muslims on display that day "was from the heart and not a momentary impulse." Both communities had drunk from the "poison cup of disturbances"; now that they had made up, the "nectar of friendliness" might taste even sweeter. Who knows, perhaps as a consequence Calcutta might even "be entirely free from the communal virus for ever."

That Calcutta was peaceful on 15 August was a relief—and also a surprise, for the city had been on edge in the weeks leading up to Independence. By the terms of the Partition Award, Bengal had been divided, with the eastern wing going to Pakistan and the western section staying in India. Calcutta, the province's premier city, was naturally a bone of contention. The Boundary Commission chose to allot it to India, sparking fears of violence on the eve of independence.

Across the subcontinent, there was trouble in the capital of the Punjab, Lahore. This, like Calcutta, was a multireligious and multicultural city. Among the most majestic of its many fine buildings was the Badshahi Mosque, built by the last of the great Mughal emperors, Aurangzeb. But Lahore had also once been the capital of a Sikh empire, and was more recently a centre of the Hindu reform sect, the Arya Samaj. Now, like that of all other settlements in the Punjab, its fate lay in the hands of the British, who would divide up the province. The Bengal division was announced before 15 August, but the Punjab Award had been postponed until after that date. Would Lahore and its neighbourhood be alloted to India, or to Pakistan?

The latter seemed more likely, as well as more logical, for the Muslims were the largest community in the city. Indeed, a new governor had already been appointed for the new Pakistani province of West Punjab, and had moved into Government House in Lahore. On the evening of 15 August he threw a party to celebrate his taking office. As he later recalled, this

> must have been the worst party ever given by anyone. . . . The electric current had failed and there were no fans and no lights. The only light which we had was from the flames of the burning city of Lahore about half a mile away. All around the garden, there was firing going on— not isolated shots, but volleys. Who was firing at who, no one knew and no one bothered to ask.[11]

No one bothered to ask. Not at the governor's party, perhaps. In Beliaghata, however, Mahatma Gandhi expressed his concern that this "madness still raged in Lahore." When and how would it end? Perhaps one could hope that "the noble example of Calcutta, if it was sincere, would affect the Punjab and the other parts of India."

III

By November 1946, more than 5,000 people had died in the rioting. As an army memo mournfully observed: "Calcutta was revenged in Noakhali, Noakhali in Bihar, Bihar in Garmukteshwar, Garmukteshwar in ????."[12]

At the end of 1946, one province that had escaped the rioting was the Punjab. In office there were the Unionists, a coalition of Muslim, Hindu, and Sikh landlords. They held the peace uncertainly, for ranged against them were the militant Muslim Leaguers on the one side and the no less militant Sikh political party, the Akali Dal, on the other. Starting in January, episodic violence broke out in the cities of the Punjab. These accelerated after the first week of March, when the Unionists were forced out of office. By May, the centre of violence had shifted decisively from eastern India to the north-west. A statement submitted to the House of Lords said that 4,014 people were killed in riots in India between 18 November 1946 and 18 May 1947. Of these, as many as 3,024 had died in the Punjab alone.[13]

There were some notable similarities between Bengal and Punjab, the two provinces central to the events of 1946–1947. Both had Muslim majorities, and thus were claimed for Pakistan. But both also had many million Hindus. In the event, both provinces were divided, with the Muslim majority districts going over to East or West Pakistan, while the districts in which other religious groups dominated were alloted to India.

But there were some crucial differences between the two provinces as well. Bengal had a long history of often bloody conflict between Hindus and Muslims, dating back to (at least) the last decades of the nineteenth century. By contrast, in the Punjab the different communities had lived more or less at peace—there were no significant clashes over religious issues before 1947. In Bengal, large sections of the Hindu middle class actively sought partition. They were quite happy to get rid of the Muslim-dominated areas, and make their home in or around the provincial capital. For several decades now, Hindu professionals had been making their way to the west, along with landlords who sold their holdings and invested the proceeds in property or businesses in Calcutta. By contrast, the large Hindu community in the Punjab was dominated by merchants and moneylenders, bound by close ties to the agrarian classes. They were unwilling to relocate, and hoped until the end that somehow partition would be avoided.

The last difference, and the most telling, was the presence in the Punjab of the Sikhs, the third leg of the stool. They were absent in Bengal, where it was a straight fight between Hindus and Muslims. Like the Muslims, the Sikhs had one book, one formless God, and formed a close-knit community of believers. Sociologically, however, the Sikhs were closer to the Hindus. With the Hindus they had a *roti-beti rishta*—a relationship of interdining and intermarriage—and also a shared history of persecution at the hands of the Mughals.

Forced to choose, the Sikhs would come down on the side of the Hindus. But they were in no mood to choose at all, for there were substantial communities of Sikh farmers in both parts of the province. At the turn of the twentieth century, Sikhs from eastern Punjab had been asked by the British to settle western areas, newly served by irrigation. In a matter of a few decades the Sikhs had built prosperous settlements in these "canal colonies." Why should they leave now? Their holy city, Amritsar, lay in the east, but Nankana Sahib (the birthplace of the founder of their religion) lay in the west. Why should they not enjoy free access to both places?

Unlike the Hindus of Bengal, the Sikhs of Punjab were slow to comprehend the meaning and reality of partition. At first they doggedly insisted that they would stay where they were. Then, as the possibility of division became more likely, they claimed a separate state for themselves, to be called "Khalistan." This demand no one took seriously—not the Hindus, not the Muslims, and least of all the British.

The historian Robin Jeffrey has pointed out that at least until August 1947, the Sikhs were "more sinned against than sinning." They had been "abandoned by the British, tolerated by the Congress, taunted by the Muslim League, and, above all, frustrated by the failures of their own political leadership."[14] The peculiar (not to say tragic) situation of the Sikhs best explains why, when religious violence finally came to the Punjab, it was so accelerated and concentrated. From March to August, every month was hotter and bloodier than the last. Nature cynically lent its weight to politics and history, for the monsoon was unconscionably late in coming in 1947. And, like the monsoon, the boundary award was delayed as well, heightening the uncertainty.

The task of partitioning Bengal and the Punjab was entrusted to a British judge, Sir Cyril Radcliffe. He had no prior knowledge of India; this was deemed an advantage. However, he was given only five weeks to decide on the lines he would draw in both east and west. This was, to put it mildly, a very difficult job. He had, in the words of W. H. Auden, to partition a land "between two people fanatically at odds/with their different diets and incompatible gods," with "the maps at his disposal . . . out of date," and "the Census Returns almost certainly incorrect."[15]

Radcliffe arrived in India in the first week of July. He was assigned four advisers for the Punjab: two Muslims, one Hindu, and one Sikh. But since these fought on every point, he soon dispensed with them. Still, as he wrote his nephew, he knew that "nobody in India will love me for the award about the Punjab and Bengal and there will be roughly 80 million people with a grievance who will begin looking for me. I do not want them to find me."[16]

On 1 August, a Punjab Boundary Force was set up to control the violence. The force was headed by Major General T. W. ("Pete") Rees, a Welshman from Abergavenny. Under him were four advisers of the rank of brigadier: two Muslims, one Hindu, and one Sikh. In his first report, Rees predicted that the boundary award "would please no one entirely. It may well detonate the Sikhs."[17] This was said on 7 August; on 14 August, the commander-in-chief of the British Indian army, Field Marshal Sir Claude Auchinleck, observed that

the delay in announcing the award of the Border Commission is having a most disturbing and harmful effect. It is realised of course that the announcement may add fresh fuel to the fire, but lacking the announcement, the wildest rumours are current, and are being spread by mischief makers of whom there is no lack.[18]

The rains still held off, and the temperature was 100 degrees (Fahrenheit) in the shade. This was especially trying to Muslims, both soldiers and civilians, observing the dawn-to-dusk fast on the occasion of Ramadan, which that year fell between 19 July and 16 August. Rees asked his Muslim driver why the monsoon had failed, and the driver replied, "God too is displeased."

The boundary award was finally announced on 16 August. The award enraged the Muslims, who thought that the Gurdaspur district should have gone to Pakistan instead of India. Angrier still were the Sikhs, whose beloved Nankana Sahib now lay marooned in an Islamic state. On both sides of the border, brutality escalated. In eastern Punjab, bands of armed Sikhs roamed the countryside, seeking out and slaying Muslims wherever they were to be found. Those who could escape fled over the border to West Punjab, to further contribute to the cycle of retribution and revenge. Muslims from Amritsar and around streamed into the (to them) safe haven of Lahore. The "stories of these Refugees, oriental and biblical in exaggeration are indeed founded on very brutal fact, and they do not lack handless stumps etc., which they can and do parade before their fellow Muslims in Lahore and further west."

According to Pete Rees's own figures, from March to the end of July, the casualties in the Punjab were estimated at 4,500 civilians dead and 2,500 wounded. But in the month of August alone, casualties as reported officially by the troops were estimated at 15,000 killed, and the general admitted that the actual figure "may well have been two or three times the number."

The Indian prime minister, Jawaharlal Nehru, was deeply worried about the troubles in the Punjab and their wider repercussions. In the last fortnight of August he visited the province three times, talking to people on either side of the border and making aerial sorties. Nehru did not think that there was "anything to choose between the brutality of one side or the other. Both sides have been incredibly inhuman and barbarous."[19] The adjective that Rees himself used for the savagery was "pre-medieval." In truth, it was also medieval and modern. For the arms used by the rioters "varied from primitive axe, spear, and club to the most modern tommy-gun and light machine-gun."

On 2 September, the Punjab Boundary Force was disbanded. It had not been especially effective anyway. It was hampered by the problem of dual authority: having to report to civilian officers in the absence of martial law. With the exit of the Punjab Boundary Force, responsibility for law and order was now vested in the governments of India and Pakistan. The riots continued, as did the two-way exodus. West Punjab was being cleansed of Hindus and Sikhs; East Punjab was being emptied of Muslims. The clinical even-handedness of the violence was described by the Punjab correspondent of the respected Madras-based weekly, *Swatantra*. He wrote of seeing

> an empty refugee special steaming into Ferozepur Station late one afternoon. The driver was incoherent with terror, the guard was lying dead in his van, and the stoker was missing. I walked down the platform—all but two bogies [carriages] were bespattered with blood inside and out; three dead bodies lay in pools of blood in a third class carriage. An armed Muslim mob had stopped the train between Lahore and Ferozepur and done this neat job of butchery in broad daylight.
>
> There is another sight I am not likely to easily forget. A five-mile-long caravan of Muslim refugees crawling at a snail's pace into Pakistan over the Sutlej Bridge. Bullock-carts piled high with pitiful chattels, cattle being driven alongside. Women with babies in their arms and wretched little tin-trunks on their heads. Twenty thousand men, women and children trekking into the promised land—not because it is the promised land, but because bands of Hindus and Sikhs in Faridkot State and the interior of Ferozepur district had hacked hundreds of Muslims to death and made life impossible for the rest.[20]

Ten million refugees were on the move, by foot, by bullock cart, and by train, sometimes travelling under army escort, at other times trusting to fate and their respective gods. Jawaharlal Nehru flew over one refugee convoy that had 100,000 people and stretched for ten miles. It was travelling from Jalandhar to Lahore, and had to pass through Amritsar, where there were 70,000 refugees from West Punjab "in an excited state." Nehru suggested bulldozing a road around the town, so that the two convoys would not meet.[21]

This was without question the greatest mass migration in history. "Nowhere in known history ha[d] the transfer of so many millions taken place in so few days." They fled, wrote an eyewitness, through heat and rain, flood and bitter Punjab cold. The dust of the caravans stretched low across the Indian plains and mingled with the scent of fear and sweat, human waste and putrifying bodies. When the cloud of hate subsided the roll of the dead was called and five hundred thousand names echoed across the dazed land—dead of gunshot wounds, sword, dagger and knife slashes and others of epidemic diseases. While the largest number died of violence, there were tired, gentle souls who looked across their plundered gardens and then lay down and died. For what good is life when reason stops and men run wild? Why pluck your baby from the spike or draw your lover from the murky well?[22]

The trouble in the province was made worse by the noticeably partisan attitude of the governor of West Punjab, Sir Francis Mudie. He was "inveterate against the Congress." Mudie thought he "could govern himself. Thus he thwarts his Cabinet, above all in their attempts to bridge the gulf between West and East Punjab, and therefore between Pakistan and India." Tragically, no Pakistani politician was willing to take on religious fanaticism. Whatever their private thoughts, they were reluctant to speak out in public. As for Pakistan's new governor general, Mohammad Ali Jinnah, his headquarters were in the coastal city of Karachi (the country's capital), and he had "only visited Lahore in purdah and most carefully guarded." This timidity was in striking contrast to the brave defence of their minorities by the two pre-eminent Indian politicians. Indeed, as a British observer wrote, "Nehru's and Gandhi's stock has never been so high with the Muslims of West Punjab."[23]

Meanwhile, trouble had flared up once more in Bengal. There were reports of fresh rioting in Noakhali. In Calcutta itself, the peace was broken in Gandhi's own adopted locality, Beliaghata. Here, on 31 August, a Hindu youth was attacked by Muslims. Retaliatory violence followed, and spread. By dusk on 1 September more than fifty people lay dead. That night, Gandhi decided he would go on a fast. "But how can you fast against the *goondas* [hooligans]?" asked a friend. Gandhi's answer, according to an eyewitness, was as follows: "I know I shall be able to tackle the Punjab too if I can control Calcutta. But if I falter now, the conflagration may spread and soon. I can see clearly two or three [foreign] Powers will be upon us and thus will end our short-lived dream of independence." "But if you die the conflagration will be worse," replied the friend. "At least I won't be there to witness it," said Gandhi; "I shall have done my bit."[24]

Gandhi began his fast on 2 September. By the next day, Hindu and Muslim *goondas* were coming to him and laying down their arms. Mixed processions for communal harmony were taken out in different parts of the city. A deputation of prominent politicians, representing the Congress, the Muslim League, and the locally influential Hindu Mahasabha, assured Gandhi that there would be no further rioting. The Mahatma now broke his fast, which had lasted three days.

The peace held, prompting Lord Mountbatten to remark, famously, that one unarmed man had been more effective than 50,000 in Punjab. But the Mahatma and his admirers might have treasured as much this tribute from *The Statesman*, a British-owned paper in Calcutta that had long opposed Gandhi and his politics:

> On the ethics of fasting as a political instrument we have over many years failed to concur with India's most renowned practitioner of it. . . . But never in a long career has Mahatma Gandhi, in our eyes, fasted in a simpler, worthier cause than this, nor one calculated for immediate effective appeal to the public conscience.[25]

On 7 September, having spent four weeks in Beliaghata, Gandhi left for Delhi. He hoped to proceed further, to the Punjab. However, on his arrival in the capital he was immediately confronted with tales of strife and dispossession. The Muslims of Delhi were frightened. Their homes and places of worship had come under increasing attack. Gandhi was told that no fewer than 137 mosques had been destroyed in recent weeks. Hindu and Sikh refugees had also forcibly occupied Muslim homes. A Quaker relief worker reported, "The Muslim population of Delhi of all classes—civil servants, businessmen, artisans, tongawallahs, bearers—had fled to a few natural strongholds"—such as the Purana Qila, the great high-walled fort in the middle of the city; and the tomb of the Mughal emperor Humayun. In the Purana Qila alone there were 60,000 refugees, huddled together in tents, "in the corners of battlements and in the open, together with their camels and tongas and ponies, battered old taxis and luxury limousines."[26]

Gandhi now put his Punjab programme in abeyance. He visited the camps in the capital and outside it. In the plains around Delhi lived a farming community called the Meos, Muslims by faith, but who had adopted many of the practices and rituals of their Hindu neighbours. In the madness of the time this syncretism was forgotten. Thousands of Meos were killed or driven out of their homes, whether these lay in Indian territory or in the princely states of Alwar and Bharatpur.[27]

Through September and October, writes his biographer D. G. Tendulkar, Gandhi "went round hospitals and refugee camps giving consolation to distressed people." He "appealed to the Sikhs, the Hindus and the Muslims to forget the past and not to dwell on their sufferings but to extend the right hand of fellowship to each other, and to determine to live in peace." He "begged of them all to bring about peace quickly in Delhi, so that he might be able to proceed to both East and West Punjab." Gandhi said "he was proceeding to the Punjab in order to make the Mussalmans undo the wrong that they were said to have perpetrated there [against the Hindus and the Sikhs]. But he could not hope for success, unless he could secure justice for the Mussalmans in Delhi."[28]

Gandhi also spoke at a camp of the Rashtriya Swayamsevak Sangh (RSS). Founded by a Maharashtrian doctor in 1925, the RSS was a cohesive, motivated body of young Hindu men. Gandhi was impressed by their discipline and absence of caste feeling, but less so by their antagonism to other religions. He told the RSS members that "if the Hindus felt that in India there was no place for any one except the Hindus and if non-Hindus, especially Muslims, wished to live here, they had to live as the slaves of the Hindus, they would kill Hinduism." Gandhi could see that the RSS was "a well-organized, well-disciplined body." But, he told its members, "its strength could be used in the interests of India or against it. He did not know whether there was any truth in the allegations [of inciting communal hatred] made against the Sangha. It was for the Sangha to show by their uniform behaviour that the allegations were baseless."[29]

Unlike Gandhi, Jawaharlal Nehru was not inclined to give the Sangh the benefit of the doubt. "It seems to me clear," he told his home minister, Vallabhbhai Patel, "that the R. S. S. have a great deal to do with the disturbances not only in Delhi but elsewhere. In Amritsar their activities have been very obvious." Nehru's feelings about the RSS stemmed from his deeper worries about the communal situation. He thought that there was "a very definite and well-organised attempt of certain Sikh and Hindu fascist elements to overturn the Government, or at least to break up its present character. It has been something more than a communal disturbance. Many of these people have been brutal and callous in the extreme. They have functioned as pure terrorists."[30]

The worry was the greater because the fanatics were functioning in "a favourable atmosphere as far as public opinion was concerned." In Delhi, especially, the Hindu and Sikh refugees from Pakistan were calling for blood. But the prime minister insisted that India must be a place where the Muslims could live and work freely. An Englishman on the governor general's staff wrote in his diary:

> [T]o see Nehru at close range during this ordeal is an inspiring experience. He vindicates one's faith in the humanist and the civilised intellect. Almost alone in the turmoil of communalism, with all its variations, from individual intrigue to mass madness, he speaks with the voice of reason and charity.[31]

At the initiative of Gandhi and Nehru, the Congress now passed a resolution on the "rights of minorities." The party had never accepted the "two-nation theory": forced against its will to accept partition, it still believed that "India is a land of many religions and many races, and must remain so." Whatever the situation in Pakistan was, India would be "a democratic secular State where all citizens enjoy full rights and are equally entitled to the protection of the State, irrespective of the religion to which they belong." The Congress wished to "assure the minorities in India that it will continue to protect, to the best of its ability, their citizen rights against aggression."[32]

However, the RSS was actively sceptical about this viewpoint. Its *sarsanghchalak*, or head, was a lean, bearded science graduate named M. S. Golwalkar. Golwalkar was strongly opposed to the idea of a secular state that would not discriminate on the basis of religion. In the India of his conception:

> The non-Hindu people of Hindustan must either adopt Hindu culture and language, must learn and respect and hold in reverence the Hindu religion, must entertain no idea but of those of glorification of the Hindu race and culture . . . in a word they must cease to be foreigners, or may stay in the country, wholly subordinated to the Hindu nation, claiming nothing, deserving no privileges, far less any preferential treatment—not even citizens' rights.[33]

On Sunday, 7 December 1947, the RSS held a large rally at the Ramlila Grounds in the heart of Delhi. The main speech was by Golwalkar. As the *Hindustan Times* reported, he denied that the RSS aimed at the establishment of a Hindu Raj, but nevertheless insisted: "We aim at the solidarity of the Hindu society. With this ideal in view, the Sangh will march forward on its path, and will not be deterred by any authority or personality."[34]

The authorities being alluded to were the Congress party and the government of India; the personalities, Nehru and Gandhi, toward whom there was much hostility among the refugees sympathetic to the RSS. Gandhi's meetings were disrupted by refugees who objected to readings from the Koran, or who shouted slogans asking why he did not speak of the sufferings of those Hindus and Sikhs still living in Pakistan. In fact, as Tendulkar writes, Gandhi "was equally concerned with the sufferings of the minority community in Pakistan. He would have liked to be able to go to their succour. But with what face could he now go there, when he could not guarantee full redress to the Muslims in Delhi?"

With attacks on Muslims continuing, Gandhi chose to resort to another fast. This began on 13 January and was addressed to three different constituencies. The first constituency was the people of India. To them he simply pointed out that if they did not believe in the two-nation theory, they would have to show in their chosen capital, the "eternal city" of Delhi, that Hindus and Muslims could live in peace and brotherhood. The second constituency was the government of Pakistan. "How long," he asked it, "can I bank upon the patience of the Hindus and the Sikhs, in spite of my fast? Pakistan has to put a stop to this state of affairs" (that is, the driving out of minorities from their territory).

Gandhi's fast was addressed, finally, to the government of India. It had withheld Pakistan's share of the "sterling balance" that the British owed jointly to the two dominions, a debt incurred on account of Indian contributions to the Second World War. This amounted to 550 million rupees, a fair sum. New Delhi would not release the money, as it was angry with Pakistan for having recently attempted to seize the state of Kashmir. Gandhi saw this as unnecessarily spiteful. And so he made the ending of his fast conditional on the transfer to Pakistan of the money owed to it.

On the night of 15 January the government of India decided to release the money owed the government of Pakistan. The next day, more than 1,000 refugees signed a declaration saying that they would welcome back the displaced Muslims of Delhi and allow them to return to their homes. But Gandhi wanted more authoritative assurances. Meanwhile, his health rapidly declined. His kidneys were failing, his weight was dropping, and he was plagued by nausea and headaches. The doctors issued a warning: "It is our duty to tell the people to take immediate steps to produce the requisite conditions for ending the fast without delay."

On 17 January, a Central Peace Committee was formed under the leadership of the president of the Constituent Assembly, Rajendra Prasad. Other congressmen were among its members, as were representatives of the RSS, the Jamiat-ul-Ulema, and Sikh bodies. On the morning of 18 January they took a joint declaration to Gandhi, which satisfied him enough to end his fast. The declaration pledged "that we shall protect the life, property and faith of Muslims and that the incidents which have taken place in Delhi will not happen again."[35]

Would the "miracle of Calcutta" be repeated in Delhi? The leaders of the militant groups seemed chastened by Gandhi's fast. But their followers remained hostile. On previous visits to Delhi Gandhi had stayed in the sweepers' colony; this time, however, he was put up at the home of his millionaire follower G. D. Birla. While his fast was on, bands of refugees marched past Birla House, shouting, "Let Gandhi die." Then, on 20 January, a Punjabi refugee named Madan Lal threw a bomb at Gandhi in Birla House, while he was leading a prayer meeting. It exploded at some distance away from him; luckily, no one else was hurt either.

Gandhi was undaunted by the attempt on his life. He continued meeting people, angry refugees included. On 26 January, he spoke at his prayer meeting of how this day had been celebrated in the past as Independence Day. Now freedom had come, but its first few months had been deeply disillusioning. However, he trusted that "the worst is over," that Indians would work collectively for the "equality of all classes and creeds, never the domination and superiority of the major community over a minor, however insignificant it may be in numbers or influence." He also permitted himself the hope "that though geographically and politically India is divided into two, at heart we shall ever be friends and brothers helping and respecting one another and be one for the outside world."

Gandhi had fought a lifelong battle for a free and united India; and yet, at the end, he could view its division with detachment and equanimity. Others were less forgiving. On the evening of 30 January he was shot dead by a young man at his daily prayer meeting. The assassin, who surrendered afterwards, was a Brahman from Poona named Nathuram Godse. He was tried and later sentenced to death, but not before he made a remarkable speech justifying his act. Godse claimed that his main provocation was the Mahatma's "constant and consistent pandering to the Muslims," "culminating in his last pro-Muslim fast [which] at last goaded me to the conclusion that the existence of Gandhi should be brought to an end immediately."[36]

IV

Gandhi's death brought forth an extraordinary outpouring of grief. There were moving tributes from Albert Einstein, who had long held Gandhi to be the greatest figure of the twentieth century; and from George Orwell, who had once thought Gandhi a humbug but now saw him as a saint. There was a characteristically flippant reaction from George Bernard Shaw—"It shows you how dangerous it is to be good"—and a characteristically petty one from Mohammad Ali Jinnah, who said that the death of his old rival was a loss merely to "the Hindu community."

However, the two most relevant public reactions were from Gandhi's two most distinguished, not to say most powerful, followers, Vallabhbhai Patel and Jawaharlal Nehru. Patel, who was now home minister in the government of India, was a fellow Gujarati who had joined Gandhi as far back as 1918. He was a superb organizer and strategist who had played a major role in making the Congress a national party. In the Indian cabinet, he was second only to the prime minister, Jawaharlal Nehru. Nehru had come to Gandhi a couple of years later than Patel, and could converse with him in only two of his three languages (Hindi and English). But he had a deep emotional bond with the Mahatma. Like Patel, he generally called Gandhi *bapu*, "father." But he was, in many ways, the favourite son (dearer by far than the four biological children of the Mahatma), and also his chosen political heir.

Now, in an India caught in the throes of civil strife, both men told the nation that while their master had gone, his message remained. Speaking on All India Radio immediately after Gandhi's death, Patel appealed to the people not to think of revenge, but "to carry the message of love and non-violence enunciated by Mahatmaji. It is a shame for us that the greatest man of the world has had to pay with his life for the sins which we have committed. We did not follow him when he was alive; let us at least follow his steps now he is dead."[37] Speaking at Allahabad after immersing Gandhi's ashes in the Ganga, Nehru observed that "we have had our lesson at a terrible cost. Is there anyone amongst us now who will not pledge himself after Gandhi's death to fulfil his mission . . . ?" Indians, said Nehru, had now "to hold together and fight that terrible poison of communalism that has killed the greatest man of our age."[38]

Nehru and Patel both called for unity and forgiveness, but as it happened the two men had recently been involved in a bitter dispute. In the last fortnight of December, Nehru had planned to visit the riot-hit town of Ajmer. At the last minute he called off his trip, and sent his personal secretary instead. Patel took serious offence. He felt that since the Home Ministry had sent its own enquiry team to Ajmer, a tour by the prime minister's underling implied a lack of faith. Nehru explained that he had been forced to cancel his own visit because of a death in the family, and had thus sent his secretary—mostly so as not to disappoint those who had expected him to come. But in any case, as the head of government he had the right to go wherever he wished whenever he wished, or to send someone else to represent him. Patel answered that in a cabinet system the prime minister was merely the first among equals; he did not stand above or dominate his fellow ministers.

The exchange grew more and more contentious, and at one point both men offered to resign. Then it was agreed that they would put their respective points of view before Gandhi. Before a suitable time could be found the Mahatma began his last fast. The next week Patel was out of Delhi, but the matter lay very much on his mind, and Nehru's. Indeed, on 30 January, Gandhi met Patel just before the fateful prayer meeting, and asked that he and Nehru sort out their differences. He also said he would like to meet both of them the next day.

Three days after Gandhi's assassination, Nehru wrote Patel a letter which said that "with Bapu's death, everything is changed and we have to face a different and more difficult world. The old controversies have ceased to have much significance and it seems to me that the urgent need of the hour is for all of us to function as closely and co-operatively as possible." Patel, in reply, said that he "fully and heartily reciprocate[d] the sentiments you have so feelingly expressed. . . . Recent events had made me very unhappy and I had written to Bapu . . . appealing to him to relieve me, but his death changes everything and the crisis that has overtaken us must awaken in us a fresh realisation of how much we have achieved together and the need for further joint efforts in our grief-stricken country's interests."[39]

Gandhi could not reconcile, in life, Hindu with Muslim, but he did reconcile, through his death, Jawaharlal Nehru with Vallabhbhai Patel. It was a patch-up of rather considerable consequence for the new and very fragile nation.

2

THE LOGIC *of* DIVISION

It was India's historic destiny that many human races and cultures
should flow to her, finding a home in her hospitable soil, and that
many a caravan should find rest here. . . . Eleven hundred years of
common history [of Islam and Hinduism] have enriched India
with our common achievements. Our languages, our poetry, our
literature, our culture, our art, our dress, our manners and
customs, the innumerable happenings of our daily life, everything
bears the stamp of our joint endeavour. . . . These thousand years
of our joint life [have] moulded us into a common nationality. . . .
Whether we like it or not, we have now become an Indian nation,
united and indivisible. No fantasy or artificial scheming to
separate and divide can break this unity.

MAULANA ABUL KALAM AZAD, Congress presidential address, 1940

The problem in India is not of an intercommunal but manifestly
of an international character, and must be treated as such. . . . It
is a dream that Hindus and Muslims can evolve a common
nationality, and this misconception of one Indian nation has gone
far beyond the limits, and is the cause of most of our troubles,
and will lead India to destruction, if we fail to revise our actions
in time. The Hindus and Muslims belong to two different
religious philosophies, social customs, and literature. They
neither intermarry, nor interdine together, and indeed they belong
to two different civilizations which are based mainly on conflicting ideas and conceptions. Their aspects on and of life are
different.

M. A. JINNAH, Muslim League presidential address, 1940

I

DID INDIA HAVE to be partitioned? When the British left, could
they not have left a single country behind? Ever since 1947
such questions have been asked. And in the process of being
answered, they bring forth a supplementary question—*why* was India
partitioned?

The nostalgia for an undivided India has been manifest mostly among people on the Indian side of the border. But there has sometimes also been a sense of loss in what has become Pakistan. Indeed, on 15 August 1947 itself, a veteran Unionist politician wrote of how he wished he

> could do anything to save the unity of the Punjab. . . . It is heartbreaking to see what is happening. . . . It is all due to the policy of liquidating and quitting before any real agreement has been arrived at. . . . The fixing of a date for transferrence of power ruled out any adjustment and vivisection was the only course left. . . . We will have to start afresh [but] there is hardly any hope of building things on old lines as communal hatred and mutual destruction are now uppermost in everybody's mind.[1]

Why could not the unity of Punjab, or of India, be saved? Three rather different answers have been offered. The first blames the Congress leadership for underestimating Jinnah and the Muslims. The second blames Jinnah for pursuing his goal of a separate country regardless of human consequences. The third holds the British responsible, claiming that they promoted a divide between Hindus and Muslims to perpetuate their rule.[2]

All three answers, or should one say accusations, carry an element of truth. It is true that Nehru and Gandhi made major errors of judgement in their dealings with the Muslim League. In the 1920s, Gandhi ignored Jinnah and tried to make common cause with the mullahs. In the 1930s, Nehru arrogantly and, as it turned out, falsely, claimed that the Muslim masses would rather follow his socialist credo than a party based on faith. Meanwhile, the Muslims steadily moved over from the Congress to the League. In the 1930s, when Jinnah was willing to make a deal, he was ignored; in the 1940s, with the Muslims solidly behind him, he had no reason to make a deal at all.

It is also true that some of Jinnah's political turns defy any explanation other than personal ambition. He was once known as an "ambassador of Hindu-Muslim unity" and a practitioner of constitutional politics. Even as he remade himself as a defender of Islam and Muslims, in his personal life he ignored the claims of faith. (He liked his whisky and, according to some accounts, his ham sandwiches too.)[3] However, from the late 1930s on he began to stoke religious passions. The process was to culminate in his calling for Direct Action Day, the day that set off the bloody violence and counter-violence that finally made partition inevitable.

Finally, it is also true that the British did welcome and further the animosities between Hindus and Muslims. In March 1925, by which time the anti-colonial struggle had assumed a genuinely popular dimension, the secretary of state for India wrote to the viceroy: "I have always placed my highest and most permanent hopes upon the eternity of the Communal Situation."[4] In England, the growth of liberal values placed a premium on the sovereignty of the individual; but in the colonies, the individual was always seen as subordinate to the community. This was seen in government employment, where care was taken to balance Muslim and Hindu jobs; and in politics, where the British introduced communal electorates, so that Muslims voted exclusively for other Muslims. Most British officials were predisposed to prefer Muslims, for, as compared to Hindus, their forms of worship and ways of life were not entirely alien. Overall, colonial policy deepened religious divisions, which helped consolidate the white man's rule.

Congress's short-sightedness, Jinnah's ambition, Britain's amorality and cynicism—all these might have played their part, but at least by the early 1940s partition was written into the logic of Indian history. Even if the British had not encouraged communal electorates, the onset of modern electoral politics would have encouraged the creation of community vote banks. Muslims were increasingly persuaded to think of themselves as, indeed, Muslims. As late as 1927 the Muslim League had a mere 1,300 members. By 1944, it had more than 500,000 members in Bengal alone (Punjab had 200,000). Muslims of all classes flocked to the League. Artisans, workers, professionals, businessmen—all rallied to the call of "Islam in danger," fearing the prospect, in a united India, of a "Brahman Bania Raj."[5]

The call for Pakistan was first made formally by the Muslim League in March 1940. The Second World War had postponed the question of Pakistan (as of Indian independence more generally). After the war a Labour government came to power in Great Britain. Unlike the Conservatives, the Labour party "regarded itself as morally committed to speed up the process of independence for India." On the subject of India, the prime minister, Clement Atlee, showed "a decisiveness and passion unusual during his career."[6]

Some leading Labour politicians had close ties to Congress. These included Sir Stafford Cripps, who at the beginning of 1946 was sent as part of a three-member cabinet mission to negotiate the terms of Indian independence. Cripps, and other Labour leaders, would have liked to leave behind a united India for the Congress to govern and guide. But a note prepared for the mission in December 1945 showed how unlikely this would be. Its author was Penderel Moon, a brilliant Fellow of All Souls and sometime member of the Indian civil service. Moon pointed out that "there is more likelihood of obtaining Hindu consent to Division than Muslim consent to Union." From the British point of view, "to unite India against Muslim wishes would necessarily involve force. To divide India against Hindu wishes would *not* necessarily involve force; and at worst the force required is likely to be less. The Hindus of Madras, Bombay, U. P, and C. P. may loudly lament their bretheren in Bengal and the Punjab being torn from the embrace of Mother India, but they are not likely to have the will or the power to undertake a Crusade on their behalf."[7]

The next few months bore out the cold wisdom of these remarks. Early in 1946, elections were held to the various provincial assemblies. These were conducted on a franchise restricted by education and property. Only about 28% of the adult population was eligible to vote—but this, in a land the size of British India, still amounted to some 41 million people.[8]

The world over, modern democratic politics has been marked by two rather opposed rhetorical styles. The first appeals to hope, to popular aspirations for economic prosperity and social peace. The second appeals to fear, to sectional worries about being worsted or swamped by one's historic enemies. In the elections of 1946, the Congress relied on the rhetoric of hope. It had a strongly positive programme, promising land reforms, workers' rights, and the like. The Muslim League, on the other hand, relied on the rhetoric of fear. If Muslims did not get a separate homeland, the League told the voters, then they would be crushed by the more numerous Hindus in a united India. The League, sought, in effect, a referendum on the question of Pakistan. As Jinnah put it in a campaign speech, "elections are the beginning of the end. If the Muslims decide to stand for Pakistan in the coming elections half the battle would have been won. If we fail in the first phase of our war, we shall be finished."

The leader's message was energetically carried by the cadres. In Bihar, the provincial Muslim League asked the voters to "judge whether the bricks of votes should be used in the preparation of a fort of 'Ram Raj' or for the construction of a building for the independence of Muslims and Islam." A League election poster in Punjab offered some meaningful pairs of contrasts: *din* (the faith) versus *dunya* (the world); *zamir* (conscience) versus *jagir* (property); *haqq-koshi* (righteousness) versus *sufedposhi* (office). In each case, the first item stood for Pakistan, the second for Hindustan.

League propaganda also urged voters to overcome sectarian divisions of caste and clan. "Unite on Islam—Become One," declared one poster. The Muslims were asked to act and vote as a single *qaum*, or community. A vital role was played by student volunteers, who traversed the countryside, canvassing votes from house to house.

The election results were a striking vindication of the League's campaign. As Table 1 shows, across India, in province after province, the Congress did exceedingly well in the general category. But the Muslim seats were swept by the League, fighting on the single issue of a separate state for Muslims. In the General Constituencies, the Congress won 80.9% of the votes, whereas in the seats reserved for Muslims the League garnered 74.7% of the votes.

TABLE 1: PROVINCIAL ASSEMBLY ELECTION RESULTS, 1946

	PROVINCE SEATS	TOTAL MUSLIM SEATS	SEATS WON BY CONGRESS	SEATS WON BY MUSLIM LEAGUE
Madras	215	29	165	29
Bombay	175	30	125	30
Bengal	250	119	86	114
U.P.	228	66	153	54
Punjab	175	86	51	75
Bihar	152	40	98	34
CP and Berar	112	14	92	13
Assam	108	34	58	31
NWFP	50	36	30	17
Orissa	60	4	47	4
Sind	60	34	22	28
Total	1,585	492	927	429

Source: Sho Kuwajima, *Muslims, Nationalism and the Partition: 1946 Provincial Elections in India* (New Delhi: Manohar, 1998).

After the results had come in, the Muslim League's paper, *Dawn*, proclaimed:

> Those who have been elected this time to the Legislatures have been charged by the voters with the duty . . . of winning Pakistan. Within and outside the Provincial and Central Assemblies and Councils that and that alone is now the "priority job." The time for decision is over; the time for action has come.

This was written on 7 April 1946. Three days later, Jinnah convened a meeting in Delhi of the 400 legislators elected on the Muslim League ticket. This convention reiterated the call for an independent Pakistan. However, in early May, Jinnah attended a conference in Simla, where attempts were being made by the cabinet mission to find a unitary solution. Through the next two months various drafts were passed around, allowing for one nation state but with provinces having the option to leave if they so desired. The Congress and the League could not agree on the conditions under which provinces would join or leave the projected union. Another sticking point was Jinnah's contention that the Congress could not nominate a Muslim as one of its representatives to the talks.[9]

Jinnah bargained hard, knowing now that he had Muslim popular sentiment behind him. By the end of June 1946 it was clear that no settlement could be reached. The cabinet mission returned to London. The League leaders met on 29 July and affirmed that "the time has now come for the Muslim nation to resort to direct action in order to achieve Pakistan and assert their just rights and to vindicate their honour and to get rid of the present slavery under the British and contemplated future of Caste Hindu domination."

Two weeks later was Direct Action Day, and the beginning of the end of the dream of a united India.

II

Gandhi was not alone in choosing to mark the day of Indian independence, 15 August 1947, as a day of mourning rather than celebration. Across the border, in Pakistan, where independence had come a day earlier, the poet Faiz Ahmad Faiz wrote:

This leprous daybreak, dawn night's fangs have mangled—
This is not that long-looked-for break of day,
Not that clear dawn in quest of which those comrades
Set out, believing that in heaven's wide void
Somewhere must be the stars' last halting-place,
Somewhere the verge of night's slow-washing tide,
Somewhere the anchorage for the ship of heartache.[10]

The lament here was not so much for the fact of partition as for its bloody costs. At least by the end of 1945, and possibly earlier, some form of Pakistan had seemed inevitable. It could not now be stopped by the magnanimity of Congress or by a sudden show of modesty on the part of Jinnah. But the poet's lament impels us to ask one further question—if partition had to happen, did it necessarily have to cause so much loss of life?

To answer this, we need to briefly rehearse the events of the last six months of the Raj. On 20 February 1947, the Labour government in London announced that the British would quit India by June 1948, and that the viceroy, Lord Wavell, would be replaced. On 22 March the new viceroy, Lord Mountbatten, took office. Over the next few weeks he discussed the terms of the British withdrawal with the relevant parties. He found that most leaders in Congress were coming around to the inevitability of partition. They saw that the "immediate independence of the major part of India was preferable to the postponement of the independence of the whole of India."[11] Gandhi made a last-ditch effort to save unity, by asking Jinnah to head the first government of free India. But this offer did not have the backing of Congress, and in any case Jinnah did not accept it.

On 2 May, the viceroy's chief of staff, Lord Ismay, was sent to London with a plan for partition. He obtained the cabinet's approval, but the plan had to be redrafted several times on his return, so as to satisfy both Congress and the League. (At one stage, Jinnah, brazen to the last, asked for an 800-mile-long corridor through India, to link the eastern and western wings of Pakistan.) The revised plan was taken by Mountbatten to the British cabinet.

All this took the better part of a month. On 3 June, Mountbatten, back from London, announced the partition plan over All India Radio. He was followed on the microphone by Nehru, Jinnah, and Baldev Singh (speaking for the Sikhs). The next morning the viceroy addressed a press conference in the Legislative Assembly building. Here, he suggested for the first time that the British would leave not by June 1948 but by the middle of August 1947, that is, in less than ten weeks.

The decision to dramatically shorten the time frame of the British withdrawal was made by Mountbatten himself. His biographer, Philip Ziegler, has justified the decision in the following words:

> Once the principle of partition had been accepted, it was inevitable that communalism would rage freely. The longer the period before the transfer of power, the worse the tension and the greater the threat that violence would spread. Today it was the Punjab, tomorrow Bengal, Hyderabad, or any of the myriad societies in the sub-continent where Hindu and Muslim lived cheek by jowl. Two hundred thousand could have become two million, even twenty million.[12]

In fact, at the time Ziegler wrote (in 1985) the toll of the violence related to partition was estimated at 1 million dead; some later scholars have suggested that the figure is closer to 2 million. How many would it have been if the British had left, as planned, in June 1948? In a blistering attack on Mountbatten's reputation, Andrew Roberts accuses him of softness and vacillation—"whenever he had to exhibit toughness, Mountbatten took the most invertebrate line possible"—of being unwilling to crack down effectively on communal violence, and, more specifically, of understaffing the Punjab Boundary Force and not supplying it with air cover. Unlike Ziegler, Roberts is convinced that the "over-hasty withdrawal" led "to more rather than fewer deaths."[13]

Some contemporary observers also felt that the decision to undo in two months flat an empire that had been built over two centuries was poorly conceived. In the summer of 1947, the man occupying the hottest of hot seats was the governor of the still undivided Punjab, Sir Evan Jenkins. In early May, Jenkins wrote to the viceroy, urging him to "reconsider the terms of any early announcement embodying a solution of the Indian political problem. In the Punjab we are going to be faced with a complete refusal of the communities to co-operate on any basis at all. It would clearly be futile to announce a partition of the Punjab which no community would accept."[14] The decision was made regardless, and the governor was left with the task of maintaining law and order while the Punjab was divided. On 30 July, he wrote to Mountbatten that the prospect of independence with partition evoked anger rather than enthusiasm. The Muslims had hoped for the whole of the Punjab, whereas the

Sikhs and Hindus were fearful that they would lose Lahore. "It would be difficult enough," archly commented the governor, "to partition within six weeks a country of 30 million people which has been governed as a unit for 98 years, even if all concerned were friendly and anxious to make progress."[15]

Jenkins did in fact ask several times for more troops and for a "Tactical reconnaissance squadron." One reason there weren't enough troops to deal with rioters was that the British, the rulers, feared they would be attacked as soon as the decision to leave was made public. This feeling was widespread among all groups of Europeans in India: officers, priests, planters, and merchants. In the summer of 1946, a young English official wrote to his family that "we shall virtually have the whole country against us (for long enough at all events to wipe out our scattered European population) before the show becomes, as inevitably it will, a communal scrap between Hindus and Muslims."[16]

To make the protection of British lives a top priority was pretty much state policy. In February 1947 the governor of Bengal said that his "first action in the event of an announcement of a date for withdrawal of British power . . . would be to have the troops 'standing to' and prepare for a concentration of outlying Europeans at very short notice as soon as hostile reactions began to show themselves."[17] In fact, in the summer of 1947 white men and women were the safest people in India. No one was interested in killing them.[18] But because of their insecurity, many army units were placed near European settlements, instead of being freed for riot control elsewhere.

The instinct of self-preservation also lay behind the decision to postpone the Punjab boundary award until after the date of independence. On 22 July, after a visit to Lahore, Lord Mountbatten wrote to Sir Cyril Radcliffe asking him to hurry things up, for "every extra day" would lessen the risk of disorder. The announcement of the boundary award *before* independence would have allowed movements of troops to be made in advance of the transfer of power. The governor of Punjab was also very keen that the award be announced as soon as it was ready. As it happened, Radcliffe was ready with the award on 9 August. However, Mountbatten now changed his mind, and chose to make the award public only after 15 August. His explanation for the delay was strange, to say the least: "Without question, the earlier it was published, the more the British would have to bear responsibility for the disturbances which would undoubtedly result." By the same token, "the later we postponed publication, the less would the inevitable odium react upon the British."[19]

As a rule, one must write of history only as it happened, not as it might have happened. Would a more extended time frame—an announcement in April 1947 that the British would quit in a year—have allowed for a less painful process of division? Would more active troop deployments and an earlier announcement of the Radcliffe award have led to less violence in the Punjab? Perhaps. Or perhaps not. As it turned out, the most appropriate epitaph on the last days of the Raj was provided by the Punjab official who told a young social worker from Oxford: "You British believe in fair play. You have left India in the same condition of chaos as you found it."[20]

While the debates continue to rage about the causes of partition, somewhat less attention has been paid to its consequences. These were quite considerable indeed—as this book will demonstrate. The division of India was to cast a long shadow over demography, economics, culture, religion, law, international relations, and party politics.

3

APPLES *in the* BASKET

The Indian States are governed by treaties. . . . The Indian States,
if they do not join this Union, will remain in exactly the same
situation as they are today.

Sir STAFFORD CRIPPS, British politician, writing in 1942

We shall have to come out in the open with [the] Princes sooner or
later. We are at present being dishonest in pretending we can
maintain all these small States, knowing full well in practice we
shall be unable to.

LORD WAVELL, viceroy of India, writing in 1943

I

FEW MEN have been as concerned with how history would portray them as Lord Mountbatten, the last viceroy and governor general of India. As a veteran journalist once remarked, Mountbatten appeared to act as "his own Public Relations Officer."[1] An aide of Mountbatten's was more blunt, calling his boss "the vainest man alive." The viceroy always instructed photographers to shoot him from six inches from above the eyeline, as a friend, the actor Cary Grant, had told him that this way the wrinkles didn't show. When Field Marshal Montgomery visited India, and the press clamoured for photos of the two together, the viceroy was dismayed to find that Monty wore more medals than himself.[2]

All together, Mountbatten had a personality in marked contrast to that of his predecessor. A civil servant who worked under Lord Wavell noticed that "vanity, pomposity and other such weaknesses never touched him," another way of saying that Wavell did not look to, or care about, how history would judge him.[3] Yet Wavell should get most of the credit for initiating the end of British rule in India. While sceptical of the political class, he was yet deeply sympathetic to Indian aspirations.[4] It was he who set in motion the discussions and negotiations at the end of the war, and it was he who pressed for a clear timetable for withdrawal. But

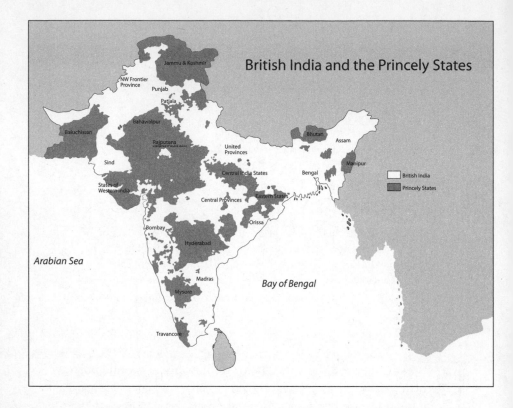

it was left to his flamboyant successor to make the last, dramatic gestures that announced the birth of the two new nations.

After Mountbatten left India, he worked hard to present the best possible version of his tenure as viceroy. He commissioned or influenced an array of books that sought to magnify his successes and gloss over his failures. These books project an impression of Mountbatten as a wise umpire, successfully mediating between squabbling schoolboys: whether India and Pakistan, the Congress and the Muslim League, Mahatma Gandhi and M. A. Jinnah, or Jawaharlal Nehru and Vallabhbhai Patel.[5] Mountbatten's claims are taken at face value: sometimes absurdly, as with the suggestion that Nehru would not have included Patel in his cabinet had it not been for Mountbatten's recommendation.[6]

Curiously, Mountbattten's real contribution to India and Indians has been rather underplayed by his hagiographers. This was his part in solving a geopolitical problem such as no newly independent state had ever faced (or is likely to face in the future). For when the British departed from the subcontinent, they left behind more than 500 distinct pieces of territory. Two of these were the newly created nations of India and Pakistan; the others were the assorted chiefdoms and states that made up what was known as "princely India." The dissolution of these units is a story of extraordinary interest; told from a partisan point of view in V. P. Menon's fifty-year-old book, *The Story of the Integration of the Indian States*, but not told elsewhere, or since.[7]

II

The princely states were so many that there was even disagreement as to their number. One historian puts them at 521; another at 565. There were more than 500, at any rate, and they varied very widely in size and status. At one end of the scale were the extensive states of Kashmir and Hyderabad, each the size of a large European country: at the other end, tiny fiefdoms or *jagirs* of a dozen or fewer villages.

The larger princely states were a product of the *longue durée* of Indian history as much as of British policy. Some states made much of having resisted the waves of Muslim invaders who swept north India between the eleventh and sixteenth centuries. Other states owed their history to association with these invaders: for instance, the Asaf Jah dynasty of Hyderabad began life in the early eighteenth century as a vassal state of the great Mughal Empire. Yet other states, such as Cooch Behar in the east and Garhwal in the Himalayan north, were scarcely touched by Islamic influence.

Whatever their past history, these states owed their present shape and powers to the British. Starting as a firm of traders, the East India Company gradually moved toward a position of overlordship. It was helped by the decline of the Mughals after the death of Aurangzeb in 1707. Indian rulers were seen by the Company as strategic allies, useful in checking the ambitions of their common enemy, the French. The Company forced treaties on these states, which recognized it as the "paramount power." Thus, while legally the territories the various nawabs and maharajas ruled over were their own, the British retained the right to appoint ministers and control succession, and to extract a large subsidy for the provision of administrative and military support. In many cases, the treaties also transferred valuable areas from the states to the British. It was no accident that except for the states of Kathiawar and two chiefdoms in the south, no Indian state had a coastline. The political dependence was made more acute by economic dependence, with the states relying on British India for raw materials, industrial goods, and employment opportunities.[8]

The larger native states had their own railroad, currency, and stamps, vanities allowed them by the Crown. Few had any modern industry; fewer still had modern forms of education. A British observer wrote in the early twentieth century that, taken as a whole, the states were "sinks of reaction and incompetence and unrestrained autocratic power sometimes exercised by vicious and deranged individuals."[9] This, roughly, was also the view of the main nationalist party, the Congress. From the 1920s, it pressed the princes to at least match the British in allowing a modicum of political representation. Under the Congress umbrella rested the All India States Peoples Conference, to which in turn were affiliated the individual *praja mandals* (peoples' societies) of the states.

Even in their heyday the princes had a bad press. They were generally viewed as feckless and dissolute, overfond of racehorses and other men's wives and holidays in Europe. Both the Congress and the Raj thought that they cared too little for mundane matters of administration. This was mostly true, but there were exceptions. The maharajas of Mysore and Baroda both endowed fine universities, worked against caste prejudice, and promoted modern enterprises. Other maharajas kept going the great traditions of Indian classical music.

Good or bad, profligate or caring, autocratic or partly democratic, all the princes found themselves facing a common problem by the 1940s: their future in a free India. In the first part of 1946, British India had a definitive series of elections; but these left the princely states untouched. As a consequence, there was a "growing antipathy towards princely governments."[10] Their constitutional status, however, remained ambiguous. The cabinet mission of 1946 focused on the Hindu-Muslim question, or the question of a united India versus Pakistan; it barely spoke of the states at all. Likewise, the statement of 20 February 1947, formally announcing that the Raj was to end, also avoided the issue. On 3 June the British announced both the date of their final withdrawal and the creation of two Dominions—but this statement also did not make clear the position of the states. Some rulers began now "to luxuriate in wild dreams of independent power in an India of many partitions."[11]

Now, just in time, came the wake-up calls.

III

In 1946–1947, the president of the All India States Peoples Conference was Jawaharlal Nehru. His biographer notes that Nehru "held strong views on this subject of the States. He detested the feudal autocracy and total suppression of popular feeling, and the prospect of these puppet princes . . . setting themselves up as independent monarchs drove him into intense exasperation."[12] The prospect was encouraged by the officials of the Political Department, who led the princes to believe that once the British left they could, if they so wished, stake their claims to independence.

On their part, the princes disliked and even feared Nehru. Fortunately, the Congress had assigned the problem of the states to the pragmatic administrator Vallabhbhai Patel. Through the spring of 1947 Patel threw a series of lunch parties, where he urged his princely guests to help the Congress in framing a new constitution for India. This they could do by sending delegates to the Constituent Assembly, whose deliberations had begun in Delhi in December 1946. At the same time, Patel wrote to the more influential diwans (chief ministers), urging them to ask their rulers to come to terms with the party that would now rule India.[13]

One of the first princes to come over to Patel's side was the maharaja of Bikaner. His diwan was K. M. Pannikar, a widely respected historian who, more clearly than other people, could see that the "Vasco da Gama epoch of Asian history"[14] was swiftly coming to an end. The forces of nationalism were irresistible; if one did not compromise with them, one would be swept away. Accordingly, in the first week of April 1947 Bikaner issued a public appeal to his fellow princes to join the Constituent Assembly. Their entry into the assembly, he said, would "make quite clear to everyone that the Indian Princes are not only working for the good of their States and for their mother country but are above all patriotic and worthy sons of India."[15]

The first chiefdom to join the Constituent Assembly, back in February, was in fact the state of Baroda. After Bikaner's appeal a dozen states joined, many of them from Rajasthan. Pannikar and Bikaner had "led the Rajput princes in a fresh act of traditional obeisance to Delhi, where in place of Mogul or British, a Pandit now rules. They have made a compact with Congress—probably, from their point of view, rightly."[16]

Several states in Rajasthan, Bikaner included, would share a border with Pakistan; this fact, and ancient memories of battles with Muslim kings, predisposed them to an early compromise with Congress. But other states in the hinterland were less sure of how far Delhi's writ would run after the British left. Might not the situation revert to that of the eighteenth century, when the peninsula was divided up among dozens of more or less sovereign states?

On 27 June, a new States Department was set up by the government of India. This replaced the old Political Department, whose pro-prince, anti-Congress tenor had caused so much mischief.[17] Patel would be the minister in charge. As his secretary, he chose V. P. Menon, a small, alert, and ferociously intelligent Malayali from Malabar. Unusually for a man in his position, Menon had come up from the ranks. Far from being a member of the elite Indian civil service—as other secretaries to government were—he had joined the government of India as a clerk and steadily worked his way up. He had been reforms commissioner and constitutional adviser to successive viceroys, and had played a key role in drafting the Indian Independence Bill.

His peers in the civil service derisively called him *"babu* Menon," in reference to his lowly origins. But in fact, as British Raj gave way to Congress Raj, there could have been no better man to supervise this most tricky aspect of the transition. Menon's first act was to urge the British government not to support fanciful claims to independence. "Even an inkling that H. M. G. would accord independent recognition," he told London, "would make infinitely difficult all attempts to bring the States and the new Dominions together on all vital matters of common concern."[18]

Menon was also ideally placed to mediate between his old boss, Mountbatten, and his new boss, Vallabhbhai Patel. Between them they worked on a draft Instrument of Accession, whereby the states would agree to transfer, to the Congress government, control of defence, foreign affairs, and communications. On 5 July, Patel issued a statement appealing to the princes to accede to the Indian Union on these three subjects and join the Constituent Assembly. As he put it, the "alternative to co-operation in the general interest" was "anarchy and chaos." Patel appealed to the princes' patriotism, asking for their assistance in raising "this sacred land to its proper place among the nations of the world."[19]

On 9 July, Patel and Nehru both met the viceroy, and asked him "what he was going to do to help India in connection with her most pressing problem—relations with the [princely] States." Mountbatten agreed to make this matter "his primary consideration." Later that same day, Gandhi came to meet Mountbatten. As the viceroy recorded, the Mahatma "asked me to do everything in my power to ensure that the British did not leave a legacy of Balkanisation and disruption on the 15th August by encouraging the States to declare their independence."[20]

Mountbatten was being urged by the Congress trinity to bat for them against the states. This he did most effectively, notably in a speech to the Chamber of Princes delivered on 25 July, for which the viceroy was decked out in all his finery, with rows of military medals pinned on his chest. He was, recalled an adoring assistant, "in full uniform, with an array of orders and decorations calculated to astonish even these practitioners in Princely pomp."[21]

Mountbatten began by telling the princes that the Indian Independence Act had released "the States from all their obligations to the Crown." They were now technically independent, or, to put it another way, rudderless, on their own. The old links were broken, but "if nothing can be put in its place, only chaos can result"—chaos that "will hit the States first." He advised them to forge relations with the new nation closest to them. As he brutally put it, "you cannot run away from the Dominion Government which is your neighbour any more than you can run away from the subjects for whose welfare you are responsible."

The Instrument of Accession the princes were being asked to sign would cede away defence—but in any case, said Mountbatten, the states would, by themselves, "be cut off from any source of supplies of up-to-date arms or weapons." It would also cede away external affairs, but the princes could "hardly want to go to the expense of having ambassadors or ministers or consuls in all these foreign countries." And it would cede away communications, but this was "really a means of maintaining the life-blood of the whole sub-continent." The offer by Congress, said the Viceroy, left the rulers "with great internal authority" while divesting them of subjects they could not deal with on their own.[22]

Mountbatten's talk to the Chamber of Princes was a tour de force. In my opinion it ranks as the most significant of all his acts in India. It finally persuaded the princes that the British would no longer protect or patronize them, and that independence for them was a mirage.

Mountbatten had prefaced his speech with personal letters to the more important princes. Afterwards he continued to press them to sign the Instrument of Accession. If they did so before 15 August, said the viceroy, he might be able to get them decent terms with the Congress. But if they did not listen, then they might face an "explosive situation" after Independence, when the full might of nationalist wrath would turn against them.[23]

By 15 August virtually all the states had signed the Instrument of Accession. Meanwhile, the British had departed, never to return. Now the Congress went back on the undertaking that if the princes signed up on the three specified subjects, "in other matters we would scrupulously respect their autonomous existence."[24] The *praja mandals* became active once more. In Mysore state, a movement was launched for "full democratic government." Three thousand people courted arrest.[25] In some states in Kathiawar and Orissa, protesters took possession of government offices, courts, and prisons.[26]

Vallabhbhai Patel and the Congress party cleverly used the threat of popular protest to make the princes fall into line. They had already acceded; now they were being asked to *integrate*, that is, to dissolve their states as independent entities and merge with the Union of India. In exchange, they would be allowed to retain their titles and would be offered an annual allowance in perpetuity. If they desisted from complying, they faced the threat of uncontrolled (and possibly uncontrollable) agitation by subjects whose suppressed emotions had been released by the advent of Indian independence.[27]

Through the latter part of 1947, V. P. Menon toured across India, cajoling the princes one by one. His progress, wrote the *New York Times*'s correspondent in New Delhi,

> could be measured from the ensuing series of modest newspaper items, each series running about like this:
> First, a small headline, "Mr. V. P. Menon Visits State of Chhota Hazri";
> Then, in the Governor-General's daily Court Circular, a brief notice, "H. H. the Maharajah of Chhota Hazri has arrived";
> And soon, a banner headline, "CHHOTA HAZRI MERGED."[28]

As this account makes clear, the groundwork was done by Patel and V. P. Menon; but the finishing touch was applied by Mountbatten, a final interview with whom was sometimes a necessary concession to princely vanity. The governor general also visited the more important chiefdoms, where he saluted their "most wise and Statesmanlike decision" to link up with India.[29]

Mountbatten dealt with the symbolism of the princes' integration with India, V. P. Menon with the substance. In his book, Menon describes in some detail the tortuous negotiations with the rulers. The process of give and take involved much massaging of egos, for one ruler claimed descent from Lord Rama and another from Sri Krishna, while a third said his house was immortal, as it had been blessed by the Sikh gurus.

In exchange for their land, each ruler was offered a "privy purse," its size determined by the revenue earned by the state. The bigger, more strategically placed states had to be given a better deal, but relevant too were such factors as the antiquity of the ruling dynasty, the religious halo that might surround it, and their martial traditions. Apart from an annual purse, the rulers were allowed to retain their palaces and other personal properties and, equally significantly, their titles. The maharaja of Chhota Hazri would still be the maharaja of Chhota Hazri, and he could pass on the title to his son as well.[30]

To reassure the princes, Patel sought to include a constitutional guarantee with regard to the privy purses. But, as V. P. Menon pointed out, the pay-off had been trifling compared with the gains. In addition to securing the political consolidation of India, the integration of the states was, in economic terms, a veritable steal. By Menon's calculation, while the government would pay out some 150 million rupees to the princes, in ten years the revenue from their states would be at least ten times as much.[31]

Acquiring the territory of the states was followed by the scarcely less difficult job of administrative integration. In most states, the land revenue and judicial systems were archaic, and there was no popular representation of any kind. The States Ministry transferred officials trained in British India to put the new systems in place. It also oversaw the swearing-in of interim ministries before full-fledged elections.

Patel and Menon took more than one leaf out of the British book. They played "divide and rule," bringing some princes in on their side early, and unsettling the rest. They played on the childlike vanity of the maharajas, allowing them to retain their titles and sometimes giving them new ones. (Thus several maharajas were appointed governors of provinces.) But, like the British in the eighteenth century, they kept their eye firmly on the main chance: material advantage. As Patel told the officials of the States Ministry, "we do not want their women and their jewellery—we want their land."[32]

In a mere two years, 500 autonomous and sometimes ancient chiefdoms had been dissolved into fourteen new administrative units of India. This, by any reckoning, was a stupendous achievement. It had been brought about by wisdom, foresight, hard work, and not a little intrigue.

IV

When Vallabhbhai Patel had first discussed the problem of the states with Mountbatten, he had asked the viceroy to bring in "a full basket of apples" by the date of independence. Would Patel be satisfied with a bag of 560 instead of the full 565? the viceroy asked. The Congress strong-man nodded his assent.[33] As it turned out, only three states gave trouble before 15 August, and three more after that date.

Travancore was the first state to question the right of the Congress to succeed the British as the paramount power. This state was strategi-cally placed, at the extreme southern tip of the subcontinent. It had the most highly educated populace in India, a thriving maritime trade, and newly discovered reserves of monazite, from which is extracted thorium, used in the production of atomic energy and atomic bombs. The diwan of Travancore was Sir C. P. Ramaswamy Aiyar, a brilliant and ambi-tious lawyer who had been in his post for sixteen years. It was com-monly believed that he was the real ruler of the state, whose maharaja and maharani were like putty in his hands.

As early as February 1946, Aiyar had made clear his belief that after the British left, Travancore would become a "perfectly independent unit," as it had been before 1795, when it first signed a treaty with the East India Company. In the summer of 1947 he held a series of press conferences, seeking the cooperation of the people of Travancore in his bid for independence. He reminded them of the antiquity of their ruling dynasty and of Travancore's sinking of a Dutch fleet in the year 1741 (this was apparently the only naval defeat ever inflicted by an Asian state on a European power). This appeal to a glorious regional past was meant to counter the pan-Indian nationalism of the present. For the Congress had a strong presence in the state, as did the Communist party of India. Still, the diwan insisted that from 15 August 1947 on, "Tra-vancore will become an independent country." "There was no particu-lar reason," he defiantly added, "why she should be in a worse position than Denmark, Switzerland, and Siam."

Interestingly, Travancore's bid for independence was welcomed by Mohammad Ali Jinnah. On 20 June he sent Aiyar a telegram indicating that Pakistan was "ready to establish relationship with Travancore which will be of mutual advantage." Three weeks later the diwan wrote to the Madras government, saying that Travancore was taking steps to "maintain herself as an independent entity." It was, however, ready to sign a treaty between the "independent Sovereign State" of Travancore and the "Dominion Governments" of both India and Pakistan.

On 21 July, the diwan of Travancore had an appointment to meet the viceroy in Delhi. The evening before, he met a senior British diplo-mat, whom he told that he hoped to get recognition from the British government. If India refused to supply Travancore with textiles, he asked, would the United Kingdom step in? Aiyar had, it seems, been encouraged in his ambitions by politicians in London, who saw an independent Travancore as a source of a material crucial to the coming cold war. In fact, the government of Travancore had already signed an agreement with the British government for the supply of monazite. In London, the minister of supply advised his government to avoid making any statement that would "give the Indian Dominions leverage in combating Travancore's claim for independence." Since this state had the "richest known deposit of monazite sand," said the minister, from the British point of view "it would be an advantage if Travancore retained political and economic independence, at least for the time being."

On 21 July, Aiyar had his scheduled interview with Mountbatten. They were together for more than two hours, which were spent by the diwan in an excoriating attack on Gandhi, Nehru, and the Congress. After he "had worked off his emotional upset," the Viceroy "let him go and sent V. P. Menon to work on him." Menon urged him to sign the Instrument of Accession, but the diwan said he would prefer to negotiate a treaty with India instead.

Aiyar returned to Travancore, his mind still apparently firm on independence. Then, while on his way to a music concert on 27 July, he was attacked by a man in military shorts, knifed in the face and on the body, and taken off for emergency surgery. (The would-be assassin turned out to be a member of the Kerala Socialist party.) The consequences were immediate, and from the Indian point of view most gratifying. As the viceroy put it in his weekly report to London, "The States Peoples organisation turned the heat on and Travancore immediately gave in." From his hospital bed, Aiyar advised his maharaja to "follow the path of conciliation and compromise," which he, "being autocratic and overdecisive," had not himself followed. On 30 July, the maharaja sent a telegram to the viceroy announcing his decision to acede to the Indian Union.[34]

A second state that wavered on the question of accession was Bhopal. It lay in Central India and had the not unusual combination of a mostly Hindu population and a Muslim ruler. Since 1944 the nawab of Bhopal had served as chancellor of the Chamber of Princes. He was known to be a bitter opponent of the Congress, and correspondingly close to Jinnah and the Muslim League. When, after the war, the British made clear their intention to leave India, the prospect filled the nawab with despair. He saw this as "one of the greatest, if not the greatest, tragedies that has ever befallen mankind"—for now the "States, the

Moslems, and the entire mass of people who relied on British justice . . . suddenly find themselves totally helpless, unorganised and unsupported." The only course left to the nawab now was to "die in the cause of the Moslems of the world."

These lines are from a letter of November 1946, written to the political adviser to Lord Wavell. Four months later Wavell was replaced as viceroy by Lord Mountbatten, who, as it happens, was an old polo-playing buddy of the nawab of Bhopal. Their friendship went back twenty-five years; Mountbatten once claimed that the nawab was his "second-best friend in India."[35] But it was soon clear that they now stood in different camps. In the middle of July 1947 Mountbatten wrote to Bhopal, as he had written to all other princes, advising him to accede to India. He got a long and self-confessedly "sentimental" letter in reply. It began with a profession of "unbroken and loyal friendship" with the Crown, a link now being broken by unilateral action by the British government. And to whom had the British delivered Bhopal and his colleagues? The hated party of Gandhi and Nehru. "Are we," asked Bhopal angrily, "to write out a blank cheque and leave it to the leaders of the Congress party to fill in the amount?"

After accusations of betrayal, the letter issued a warning. In India, said the nawab, the main bulwarks against the "rising tide of Communism" were men of property. The Congress had already stated its intention to liquidate landlords. To that party's left stood the Communist party of India, which controlled the unions of transport workers; if they so chose, the communists could paralyse and starve the subcontinent. "I tell you straight," said Bhopal to his friend, "that unless you and His Majesty's Government support the States and prevent them from disappearing from the Indian political map, you will very shortly have an India dominated by Communists. . . . If the United Nations one day find themselves with 450 million extra people under the heel of Communist domination they will be quite justified in blaming Great Britain for this disaster, and I naturally would not like your name associated with it."

Bhopal hinted that he, like Travancore, would declare his indepedence; in any case, he would not attend the meeting of the Chamber of Princes scheduled for 25 July. On 31 July, Mountbatten wrote back to Bhopal inviting him once more to sign the Instrument of Accession. He reminded Bhopal of what he had said in the speech: that no ruler could "run away" from the Dominion closest to it. And he shrewdly turned the argument about communism on its head. Yes, he told Bhopal, there was indeed such a threat, but it would best be met if the Congress and the princes joined hands. For men like Patel were "as frightened of communism as you yourself are. If only they had support from all other stable influences such as that of the Princely Order, it might be possible for them to ward off the communist danger."[36]

By this time Bhopal had received reports of the meeting of 25 July. He had heard of the terrific impression his old friend had made, and also of the increasing tide of accessions by his fellow princes. And so he capitulated, asking only for a small sop to his pride. Would the viceroy press Patel to extend the deadline by ten days, so that Bhopal's accession would be announced *after* 15 August, instead of before? That, he said "would enable me to sign our death warrant with a clear conscience." (In the event, Patel said he could not make any exceptions; so Mountbatten said that if Bhopal would sign the Instrument of Accession on 14 August, he would keep it under lock and key and hand it over to Patel only after 25 August.)[37]

A case more curious still was that of Jodhpur, an old, large state with a Hindu king as well as a largely Hindu population. At a lunch hosted by Mountbatten in mid-July, the young maharaja of Jodhpur had joined the other Rajput princes in indicating his willingness to accede to India. But soon afterwards someone—it is not clear who—planted the idea in his head that since his state bordered Pakistan, he might get better terms from that Dominion. Possibly at Bhopal's initiative, a meeting was arranged between him and Jinnah, the Muslim League leader. At this meeting, Jinnah offered Jodhpur full port facilities in Karachi, unrestricted import of arms, and a supply of grain from Sindh to his own famine-stricken districts. In one version, Jinnah is said to have handed the maharaja a blank sheet and a fountain pen and said, "You can fill in all your conditions."

If Jodhpur had defected to Pakistan, this would have opened up the possibility that states contiguous to it—such as Jaipur and Udaipur—would do likewise. However, K. M. Pannikar got wind of the plan and asked Vallabhbhai Patel to intervene. Patel contacted Jodhpur and promised him free import of arms too, as well as adequate grain. Meanwhile, his own nobles and village headmen had told the maharaja that he could not really expect them to be at ease in a Muslim state. The ruler of an adjoining state, Jaisalmer, also asked him what would happen if Jodhpur joined Pakistan and a riot broke out between Hindus and Muslims. Whose side would he then take?

And so the maharaja of Jodhpur also came around, but not before a last-minute theatrical show of defiance. When presented with the Instrument of Accession in the anteroom of the viceroy's office, Jodhpur took out a revolver and held it to the secretary's head, saying, "I will not accept your dictation." But in a few minutes he cooled down, and signed on the line.[38]

V

Among the states that had not signed up by 15 August was Junagadh, which lay in the peninsula of Kathiawar in western India. This, like Bhopal, had a Muslim nawab ruling over a chiefly Hindu population. On three sides Junagadh was surrounded by Hindu states or by India, but on the fourth side—and this distinguished it from Bhopal—it had a long coastline. Its main port, Veraval, was 325 nautical miles from the Pakistani port city (and national capital) of Karachi. Junagadh's ruler in 1947, Mohabat Khan, had one abiding passion: dogs. His menagerie included 2,000 pedigreed canines, sixteen of which were hounds specially deputed to guard the palace. When two of his favourite hounds mated, the nawab announced a public holiday. On their "marriage" he expended 300,000 rupees, or roughly 1,000 times the average annual income of one of his subjects.

Within the borders of Junagadh was the Hindu shrine of Somnath, as well as Girnar, a hilltop with magnificent marble temples built by, and for, the Jains. Both Somnath and Girnar attracted thousands of pilgrims from other parts of India. The forests of Junagadh were also the last refuge of the Asiatic lions. These had been protected by Mohabat Khan and his predecessors, who discouraged even high British officials from hunting them.[39]

In the summer of 1947 the nawab of Junagadh was on vacation in Europe. While he was away, the existing diwan was replaced by Sir Shah Nawaz Bhutto, a leading Muslim League politician from Sind who had close ties to Jinnah.[40] After the nawab returned, Bhutto pressed him to stay out of the Indian Union. On 14 August, the day of the transfer of power, Junagadh announced that it would accede to Pakistan. This it was legally allowed to do, although the accession made little sense geographically and also flew in the face of Jinnah's "two-nation" theory, since 82% of Junagadh's population was Hindu.

Pakistan sat on the nawab's request for a few weeks, but on 13 September it accepted the accession. It seems to have done this in the belief that it could then use Junagadh in bargaining to secure Jammu and Kashmir. That state too had not acceded to either Dominion by 15 August. It had a Hindu maharaja and a majority Muslim population: in structural terms, it was Junagadh in reverse.

The acceptance by Pakistan of Junagadh's accession enraged the Indian leaders. Touched in a particularly tender spot was Vallabhbhai Patel, who came from the same region and spoke the same language (Gujarati) as the residents of Junagadh.[41] His first response was to secure the accession of two of Junagadh's tributary states: Mangrol and Babariawad. Their Hindu chiefs claimed that they had the right to join India; the nawab of Junagadh denied this, claiming that as his vassals they had to first seek his consent. The Indian government went with the vassals, and sent in a small military force to support them.

In the middle of September V. P. Menon went to Junagadh to negotiate with the nawab. But the ruler would not see him, feigning illness. Menon had to make do with meeting the diwan instead. He told Sir Shah Nawaz that from a cultural and geographical point of view Junagadh really should join India. Sir Shah Nawaz did not dispute this, but complained that local feelings had been inflamed by the "virulent writings in the Gujarati Press." He said that he personally would favour deciding the issue by a referendum.[42]

Meanwhile, a "provisional government of Junagadh" was set up in Bombay. This was led by Samaldas Gandhi, a nephew of the Mahatma, who was a native of the kingdom. This "government" became the vehicle of popular agitation in Junagadh. In panic, the nawab fled to Karachi, taking a dozen of his favourite dogs with him. The diwan was left holding the baby. On 27 October Sir Shah Nawaz wrote to Jinnah that while "immediately after accession [to Pakistan], His Highness and myself received hundreds of messages chiefly from Muslims congratulating us on the decision, today our bretheren are indifferent and cold. Muslims of Kathiawar seem to have lost all their enthusiasm for Pakistan."

Ten days later, Sir Shah Nawaz informed the Indian government that he would like to hand over the administration of Junagadh. The formal transfer took place on 9 November. Back in Delhi, however, Mountbatten was cross that he had not been consulted before the chiefdom was taken over. Partly to placate him, but also to establish its own legitimacy, the Indians then organized a plebiscite. A referendum held on 20 February 1948 resulted in 91% of the electorate voting for accession to India.[43]

VI

The state of Hyderabad also had a Muslim ruler and a mostly Hindu population, but it was a prize greater by far than Bhopal or Junagadh. Hyderabad ran right across the Deccan plateau, in the centre of the subcontinent. Its area was more than 80,000 square miles; its population was more than 16 million, distributed among three linguistic zones: Telugu, Kannada, and Marathi. Hyderabad was surrounded by Central Provinces in the north, by Bombay in the west, and by Madras in the south and east. Although landlocked, it was self-sufficient with regard to food, cotton, oilseeds, coal, and cement. Gasoline and salt, however, had to be imported from British India.

Hyderabad began as a Mughal vassal state in 1713. Its ruler was conventionally known as the nizam. Of its population, 85% were Hindus, but Muslims dominated the army, police, and civil service. The nizam himself owned about 10% of the land of the state; much of the rest was controlled by large landowners. From his holdings the ruler earned 25 million rupees a year in rent, while another 5 million rupees were granted him from the state treasury. There were some very rich nobles, but the bulk of the Muslims, like the bulk of the Hindus, worked as factory hands, artisans, labourers, and peasants.[44]

In power in 1946–1947 was the seventh nizam, Mir Usman Ali, who had ascended to the throne as far back as 1911. He was one of the richest men in the world, but also one of the most miserly. He rarely wore new clothes, his preferred mode of dress being unironed pyjamas, a shirt, and a faded fez. He "generally drove in an old, rattling, tin-pot of a car, a 1918 model; he never offered any kind of hospitality to a visitor."[45]

This nizam was determined to hang on to more than his personal wealth. What he wanted for his state, when the British left, was independence, with relations forged directly between him and the Crown. To help him with his case he had employed Sir Walter Monckton, a King's Counsel who was one of the most highly regarded lawyers in England. (Among Monckton's previous clients was King Edward VIII, whom he had advised during his abdication.) For Monckton's services the nizam was prepared to pay a packet: as much as 90,000 guineas a year, it was rumoured. In a meeting with the viceroy, Monckton "emphasized that His Exalted Highness would have great difficulty in taking any course likely to compromise his independent sovereignty." When Mountbatten suggested that Hyderabad should join the Constituent Assembly, the nizam's lawyer answered that if India pressed too hard his client might "seriously consider the alternative of joining Pakistan."[46]

The nizam's ambitions, if realized, would virtually cut off the north of India from the south. And, as the constitutional expert Reginald Coupland pointed out, "India could live if its Moslem limbs in the north-west and north-east were amputated, but could it live without its midriff?" Vallabhbhai Patel put it more directly, saying that an independent Hyderabad constituted a "cancer in the belly of India."[47]

In this face-off between the nizam and the government of India, each side had a proxy. The Indians had the Hyderabad State Congress, formed in 1938, which pressed hard for representative government within the state. The nizam had the Ittihad-ul-Muslimeen, which wished to safeguard the position of Muslims in administration and politics. Another important actor was the Communist Party of India, which had a strong presence in the Telengana region of the state.

In 1946–1947 all three voices grew more strident. The State Congress demanded that Hyderabad fall into line with the rest of India. Its leaders organized street protests, risking arrest. Simultaneously, the Ittihad was being radicalized by its new leader, Kasim Razvi, a lawyer who had been trained in Aligarh and believed passionately in "Muslim pride." Under Razvi the Ittihad had promoted a paramilitary body called the Razakars, whose members marched up and down the roads of Hyderabad, carrying swords and guns.[48]

In the countryside, meanwhile, there was a rural uprising led and directed by the communists. Across Telengana, large estates were confiscated and redistributed to land-hungry peasants. The insurrectionists first seized all holdings in excess of 500 acres, then brought the limit down successively to 200 and then 100 acres. They also abolished the institution of forced labour. In the districts of Nalgonda, Warangal, and Karimnagar the communists ran what amounted to a parallel government. More than 1,000 villages were "practically freed from the Nizam's rule."[49]

On 15 August, the national flag was raised by Congress workers in different parts of Hyderabad state. The offenders were arrested and taken off to jail.[50] On the other side the Razakars grew more truculent. They affirmed their support for the nizam's declaration of independence, and printed and distributed handbills that proclaimed: "Free Hyderabad for Hyderabadis" and "No pact with the Indian Union."[51]

The nizam's ambitions were encouraged by the Conservative party—the Tories—in England. Sir Walter Monckton was himself a prominent Tory; and he had written to his party leaders to support his client's case. Monckton claimed that the Congress practiced a kind of "power politics," which was an "exact replica of those in which Hitler and Mussolini indulged." Since Mountbatten was hand in glove with Nehru and Patel, it was up to the Tories to "see to it that if this shameful betrayal of our old friends and allies cannot be prevented, at least it does not go uncastigated before the conscience of the world."[52]

To see the nizam's Hyderabad as Poland and the Congress as the equivalent to Hitler's Nazis boggles the imagination. But even Winston Churchill allowed himself to be persuaded of the analogy, perhaps because he had a long-standing dislike for Mahatma Gandhi. Speaking in the House of Commons, Churchill argued that the British had a "personal obligation . . . not to allow a state, which they had declared a sovereign state, to be strangled, starved out or actually overborne by violence." The party's rising star, R. A. Butler, weighed in on Churchill's side, saying that Britian should press for the "just claims of Hyderabad to remain independent."[53]

The nizam, and more so the Razakars, also drew sustenance from the support of their cause from Pakistan. Jinnah had gone so far as to tell Lord Mountbatten that if the Congress "attempted to exert any pressure on Hyderabad, every Muslim throughout the whole of India, yes, all the hundred million Muslims, would rise as one man to defend the oldest Muslim dynasty in India."[54]

The nizam now said he would sign a treaty with India, but not an Instrument of Accession. In late November 1947 he agreed to sign a "Standstill Agreement," under which the arrangements made between Hyderabad and the British Raj would be continued with its successor government. This bought both parties time: the nizam to reconsider his bid for independence, the Indians to find better ways of persuading him to accede.

Under this agreement, the nizam and the Indian government deputed agents to each other's territory. The Indian agent was K. M. Munshi, a trusted ally of Vallabhbhai Patel. In November, the nizam had appointed a new diwan, Mir Laik Ali, a wealthy businessman who was known to be sympathetic to Pakistan. Laik Ali offered some Hindu representation in his government, but it was seen by the state congress as too little, too late. In any case, by now the real power had passed on to the Razakars and its leader, Kasim Razvi. By March 1948 the membership of the Ittihad had reached 1 million, a tenth of whom were being trained in arms. Every Razakar had taken a vow in the name of Allah to "fight to the last to maintain the supremacy of Muslim power in the Deccan."[55]

In April 1948, a correspondent of The Times of London visited Hyderabad. He interviewed Kasim Razvi and found him to be a "fanatical demagogue with great gifts of organization. As a 'rabble-rouser' he is formidable, and even in a tête-à-tête he is compelling."[56] Razvi saw himself as a prospective leader of a Muslim state, a sort of Jinnah for the Hyderabadis, albeit a more militant one. He had a portrait of the Pakistani leader prominently displayed in his room. Razvi told an Indian journalist that he greatly admired Jinnah, adding that "whenever I am in doubt I go to him for counsel which he never grudges giving me."

Pictures of Razvi show him with a luxuriant beard. He looked "rather like an oriental Mephistopheles."[57] His most striking feature was his flashing eyes, "from which the fire of fanaticism exudes." He had contempt for the Congress, saying "we do not want Brahmin or Bania rule here." Asked which side the Razakars would take if Pakistan and India clashed, Razvi answered that Pakistan could take care of itself, but added: "Wherever Muslim interests are affected, our interest and sympathy will go out. This applies of course to Palestine as well. Even if Muslim interests are affected in hell, our heart will go out in sympathy."[58]

The Razakars saw the battle between Delhi and Hyderabad in Hindu-Muslim terms. The Congress, on the other hand, saw it as a clash between democracy and autocracy. In truth, it was a bit of both. Caught in the crossfire were the citizens of Hyderabad, for whom the months after August 1947 were a time of deep insecurity.[59] Some Hindus began fleeing the state for the adjoining districts of Madras. Meanwhile, Muslims from the Central Provinces were flocking to Hyderabad. Mostly illiterate, these Muslims had heard fearful reports of attacks on their co-religionists in Bengal and Punjab. But they did not seem to realize that in Hyderabad too they would be a minority. Perhaps, as an independent observer put it, "these emigrating Muslims have more trust in the Nizam's troops and Arabs to protect them than in the Union provincial administration." In turn, these Muslims from the Central Provinces were said to have thrown out Hindus from their houses in Hyderabad, aided by the nizam's men. It was even claimed that there was a plan to make Muslims a majority in the state: apparently, Hindu neighbourhoods in cities like Aurangabad, Bidar, and Hyderabad had come to "present a deserted appearance."[60]

Through the spring and summer of 1948 the tension grew. There were allegations of gunrunning from Pakistan to Hyderabad—in planes flown by British mercenaries—and of the import of arms from eastern Europe. The prime minister of Madras wrote to Patel saying he found it difficult to cope with the flood of refugees from Hyderabad. K. M. Munshi sent lurid reports of the nizam's perfidy, of his "fixed idea" of independence, of his referring to the government of India as "the scoundrels of Delhi," of "the venomous propaganda being carried out day and night through speeches, Nizam's radio, newspapers, dramas etc., against the Indian Union."[61]

For the moment, the Indians temporized. In June 1948, V. P. Menon and Laik Ali held a series of meetings in Delhi. Menon asked that the state introduce representative government and promise a plebiscite on accession. Various exceptions were proposed to protect the nizam's dignity; these included the retention of troops. None were found acceptable. Meanwhile, the respected former diwan of Hyderabad, Sir Mirza Ismail, attempted to mediate. He advised the nizam not to take Hyderabad's case to the United Nations (as Laik Ali had threatened to do), to get himself out of the clutches of the Razakars, and to accede to India. Hyderabad, Mirza Ismail told His Exalted Highness, "must realize the weakness of its own position."[62]

On 21 June 1948 Lord Mountbatten demitted the office of governor general. Three days previously, he had written to the nizam urging him to compromise, and go down in history "as the peace-maker of South India and as the Saviour of your State, your dynasty, and your people." If the nizam stuck to his stand, however, he would "incur the universal condemnation of thinking people."[63] The nizam chose not to listen. But with Mountbatten gone, it became easier for Patel to take decisive action. On 13 September a contingent of Indian troops was sent into Hyderabad. In less than four days it had full control of the state. Those killed in the fighting included forty-two Indian soldiers and some 2,000 Razakars.

On the night of 17 September, the nizam spoke on the radio, his speech very likely written for him by K. M. Munshi. He announced a ban on the Razakars, and advised his subjects to "live in peace and harmony with the rest of the people in India." Six days later he made another broadcast, saying that Razvi and his men had taken "possession of the State" by "Hitlerite" methods and "spread terror." He was, he claimed, "anxious to come to an honourable settlement with India but this group . . . got me to reject the offers made by the Government of India from time to time."[64]

Whether by accident or design, the Indian action against Hyderabad took place two days after the death of Pakistan's governor general. Jinnah had predicted that 100 million Muslims would rise if the nizam's state was threatened. That didn't happen, but in parts of Pakistan feelings ran high. In Karachi a crowd of 5,000 marched in protest to the Indian High Commission. The high commissioner, an old Gandhian, came out on the street to try to pacify them. "You cowards," they shouted back, "you have attacked us just when our Father has died."[65]

In June, a senior Congress leader had told the nizam that if he made peace with the Indian Union, His Exalted Highness of Hyderabad might even become "His Excellency the Ambassador of the whole of India at Moscow or Washington."[66] In the event, that offer was not made, perhaps because his dress or his style of entertainment, or both, did not seem fitting for a diplomatic mission. But he was rewarded for his final submission by being made *rajpramukh*, or governor, of the new Indian state of Hyderabad.

Two years after the end of the ancien régime, the journalist Khwaja Ahmad Abbas of Bombay visited Hyderabad. He found that in the window of the 100-year-old photo studio of Raja Deendayal, pictures of the city's "liberator," Colonel J. N. Chaudhuri of the Indian Army, had eclipsed portraits of the nizam. Now, in Hyderabad, the white Congress cap was "the head-gear of the new ruling class, and inspire[d] the same awe as the conical Asafjahi dastaar (ready-to-wear turban) did before the police action."[67]

VII

In August 1947, an experienced British official who had served in the subcontinent published an article with the portentous title "India and the Future." British India had just been divided into two new nations, and the writer asked, "Will the division stop there?" Or would the subcontinent break up "into innumerable, small, warring States"? Pakistan seemed inherently unstable; there was every chance that its northwestern parts would become an independent "Pathanistan." Nor was India necessarily more stable. Thus "many competent observers believe that [the province of] Madras will ultimately secede into virtual independence." As for the princely states, the smaller and more vulnerable ones would have no option but to join India. But "the big States of the South, . . . notably Hyderabad, Mysore and Travancore—are in an altogether different position. They could, if necessary, preserve an independent existence, and the recent threats of the Congress Party are not likely to deter them from deciding this matter solely on consideration of their own advantage."

The "ultimate pattern of India," this prophet concluded, "is likely to consist of three or four countries in place of British India, together with a Federation of South Indian States. This will be, approximately speaking, a return to the pattern of sixteenth century India."[68]

Given the odds, and the opposition, the integration of these numerous and disparate states was indeed a staggering achievement. The job was done so smoothly and comprehensively that Indians quite quickly

forgot that this was once not one country but 500. In 1947 and 1948 the
threat of disintegration was very real, what with "honey-combs of intrigue" such as Bhopal and Travancore and "strategic points of assault"
such as Hyderabad. But a mere five years after the last maharaja had
signed away his land, Indians had "come to take integrated India so
much for granted that it requires a mental effort today even to imagine
that it could be different."[69]

The position of the Indian princes in the Indian polity "afforded no
parallel to or analogy with any institution known in history." Yet, through
"peaceful and cordial negotiations" the chiefdoms had dissolved themselves and had become "hardly distinguishable from the other democratic
units comprising the [Indian] Union."

The words are from a booklet issued by the government of India in
1950. The self-congratulation was merited, for 500 "centres of feudal autocracy" had, with little loss of life, been "converted into free and democratic units of the Indian Union." The "yellow dots on the map" that marked
these chiefdoms had now "disappeared. Sovereignty and power have been
transferred to the people." "For the first time," the booklet went on, "millions
of people, accustomed to living in narrow, secluded groups in the States, became part of the larger life of India. They could now breathe the air of freedom and democracy pervading the whole nation."

This being an official booklet, the credit for the job was naturally
given to the man in charge. "What the British pro-consuls failed to
achieve after two centuries of ceaseless efforts," wrote the publicists,
"Sardar Vallabhbhai Patel accomplished through his persuasive appeal
to the nobler feelings of the Princely Order."[70]

Patel's guiding hand was indeed wise and sure; another congressman,
even (or especially) Nehru, might not have supervised the princes' extinction with such patience and foresight. But Patel could scarcely have done
the job without V. P. Menon, who made hundreds of trips to the chiefdoms, chipping away at their rulers. In turn, Menon could have done little without the officials who effected the actual transition, creating the
conditions for financial and social integration with the rest of India.

In truth, both politicians and bureaucrats had as their indispensable
allies the most faceless of all humans: the people. For some decades,
many people of the princely states had been clamouring for the rights
granted to the citizens of British India. Many states had vigorous and
active *praja mandals*. The princes were deeply sensible of this; indeed,
without the threat of popular protest from below, they would not have
ceded power so easily to the Indian government.

In the unification of India Vallabhbhai Patel had plenty of helpers. Most of them are now unknown and unhonoured. One who is not completely forgotten is V. P. Menon, who was both the chief draughtsman of princely integration and its first chronicler. Let us listen now to the lesson he drew from the process:

> To have dissolved 554 States by integrating them into the pattern of the Republic; to have brought order out of the nightmare of chaos whence we started, and to have democratized the administration in all the erstwhile States, should steel us to the attainment of equal success in other spheres.[71]

We shall, in time, turn our attention to those "other spheres" of nation-building. But we have first to investigate the case of the princely state that gave the Indian Union the most trouble of all. This particular apple stayed perilously placed on the rim of the basket; never in it, but never out of it either.

4

A VALLEY BLOODY
and BEAUTIFUL

My love of the mountains and my kinship with Kashmir
especially drew me to them, and I saw there not only the life
and vigour and beauty of the present but also the memoried
loveliness of ages past. . . . When I think of India, I think of many
things . . . [but] above all, of the Himalayas, snow-capped, or
some mountain valley in Kashmir in the spring, covered with new
flowers, and with a brook bubbling and gurgling through it.

JAWAHARLAL NEHRU, writing in 1946

I

THERE WERE MORE THAN 500 princely states that joined the
Indian Union. Of these the most important was, and is, the state of
Jammu and Kashmir. At 84,471 square miles, it was even larger
than Hyderabad. However, its population was more thinly spread: it had a
little over 4 million people in all. The state was marked by a great deal of
cultural heterogeneity. There were five main regions. The province of
Jammu, abutting Punjab, had low hills and large areas of arable land. Before partition the Muslims were in a slight (53%) majority; but with the
wave of panicky migrations that year Jammu came to be dominated by
Hindus. In contrast, the Valley of Kashmir, which lay to Jammu's north,
had a substantial Muslim majority. The Valley was, by common consent,
one of the most beautiful parts of India, and its lakes and slopes were visited in the summer by wealthy tourists from Delhi and the Punjab. It was
also home to sophisticated craftsmen working with silk, wool, wood, and
brass, making exquisite artifacts exported to all parts of India and beyond.
In both Jammu and the Valley, there was also a fair sprinkling of Sikhs.

To the Valley's east lay the high mountains of Ladakh, bordering
Tibet, and peopled mostly by Buddhists. Further west lay the thinly populated tracts of Gilgit and Baltistan. The people here were mostly Muslim,
but from the Shia and Ismaili branches of Islam, rather than (as was the
case in the Valley) from the dominant Sunni tradition.

These disparate territories were not brought under a single state until the nineteenth century. The unifiers were a clan of Dogra Rajputs from Jammu, who conquered Ladakh in the 1830s, acquired the vale of Kashmir from the British in the 1840s, and moved into Gilgit by the end of the century. And thus the state of Jammu and Kashmir came to share borders with Afghanistan, Chinese Xinjiang (Sinkiang), and Tibet. Only a very narrow tract of Afghan territory separated it from the Soviet Union.[1]

Its location gave the state a strategic importance quite out of proportion to its population. This importance multiplied after 15 August 1947, when Kashmir came to share borders with both the new Dominions. The anomaly of a Hindu ruler with a mostly Muslim population was compounded by an accident of geography: that unlike the other disputed chiefdoms, such as Junagadh and Hyderabad, Kashmir was contiguous with both India and Pakistan.

The maharaja of Kashmir in 1947 was a man named Hari Singh, who had ascended the throne in September 1925. He spent much of his time at the racetrack in Bombay or hunting in the vast and plentifully stocked jungles of his domain. In one other respect he was typical of his ilk. As his fourth and youngest queen complained, he "never meets the people—that's the trouble. He just sits surrounded by fawning courtiers and favourites, and never really gets to know what is going on outside."[2]

For much of his rule, the maharaja's bête noire was a Muslim from the Valley, Sheikh Mohammed Abdullah. Born in 1905, the son of a shawl merchant, Abdullah graduated with a master's degree in science from the Aligarh Muslim University. Despite his qualifications, he was unable to find a government job in Kashmir, for the state administration was dominated by Hindus. Abdullah began to question "why Muslims were being singled out for such treatment. We constituted the majority and contributed the most towards the State's revenues, still we were continually oppressed. . . . Was it because a majority of Government servants were non-Muslims? . . . I concluded that the ill-treatment of Muslims was an outcome of religious prejudice."[3]

Denied a job by the state, Abdullah became a schoolteacher. He started a reading club and spoke out on behalf of his fellow subjects. His was an inspiring presence: he was six feet four inches tall and was a witty and compelling orator. Although he smoked the odd cigarette, he did not drink. He visited the mosque every Friday and had a deep knowledge of the Koran.[4]

In the summer of 1931, Abdullah was chosen as part of a delegation of Muslims who hoped to place their case before the maharaja.[5] Before they could meet with him, an activist named Abdul Qadir was arrested and put on trial. This led to a clash between protesters and the police, in which twenty-one people died. This was followed by a wave of communal violence in the Valley, in which many Hindu shops were looted and burned.

The next year, 1932, an All Jammu Kashmir Muslim Conference was formed to give shape to the growing opposition to the maharaja. Among its leading lights were Sheikh Abdullah and Ghulam Abbas, a lawyer from Jammu. Six years later, Abdullah took the lead in transforming the organization into a National Conference, which would also include Hindus and Sikhs. The new body asked for representative government based on universal suffrage.

At about this time, Abdullah also made the acquaintance of Jawaharlal Nehru. They hit it off instantly. Both were impulsive, and they both had strong views, but fortunately these were the same—a commitment to Hindu-Muslim harmony and to socialism. The National Conference grew closer to the Indian National Congress, alienating some of its members, most notably Ghulam Abbas, who left the party and sought to organize Kashmiri Muslims on their own. This was the beginning of a bitter rivalry with Sheikh Abdullah, a feud which was as much personal as ideological.

In the mid-1940s, Abdullah was winning this popularity contest hands down. He was, recalled one contemporary, "greatly loved by the people of Kashmir at the time."[6] He had been in and out of jail since 1931; and in 1946 he was incarcerated once more, after he asked the Dogra dynasty to "quit Kashmir" and hand over power to the people. In the ensuing unrest, more than twenty people died. The maharaja declared martial law and had the sheikh sentenced to three years imprisonment for "sedition." This particularly angered Jawaharlal Nehru, who dashed to the state in his friend's defence. Nehru was prevented from entering by the maharaja's men, who stopped him at the border and sent him back to British India.[7]

Now that it was clear that the British would soon leave the subcontinent, Hari Singh's prime minister, Ramchandra Kak, encouraged him to think of independence for his state. On 15 July 1946, the maharaja stated that the Kashmiris would "work out our own destiny without dictation from any quarter which is not an integral part of the State."[8] In November, the British resident in Srinagar observed that the

Maharaja and Kak are seriously considering the possibility of Kashmir not joining the [Indian] Union if it is formed. On a previous occasion Kak hinted to me that Kashmir might have to stay out of the
Union in view of the antagonism likely to be displayed by a Congress
Central Government towards Kashmir. The Maharaja's attitude is, I
suspect, that once Paramountcy disappears Kashmir will have to
stand on its own feet, that the question of loyalty to the British Government will not arise and that Kashmir will be free to ally itself with
any power—not excluding Russia—she chooses.[9]

The idea of independence had taken strong hold over the maharaja. He
loathed the Congress, so he could not think of joining India. But if he
joined Pakistan, the fate of his Hindu dynasty might be sealed.[10]

In April 1947 a new viceroy took over in New Delhi. As it turned
out, he was an old acquaintance of Maharaja Hari Singh's; they had
served together on the staff of the prince of Wales when the prince visited India in 1921–1922. In the third week of June 1947, after the decision was made to divide India, Lord Mountbatten set off for Kashmir,
"largely to forestall Nehru or Gandhi from doing so."[11] Mountbatten
wanted to make his own assessment of where the state might be going.
In Srinagar, the viceroy met Kak and advised him to tell the maharaja to
accede to either Dominion—but to accede. The prime minister defiantly
answered that Kashmir intended to stay independent.[12] The viceroy then
arranged for a private meeting with the maharaja. On the appointed
day, the last of the viceroy's visit, Hari Singh stayed in bed with an attack of colic: this most probably was a ruse to avoid what would certainly have been an unpleasant encounter.[13]

Nehru now told Mountbatten that "your visit to Kashmir was from
my particular point of view not a success"; he wanted to go there and
break the political deadlock himself. Gandhi also wished to go. Hari
Singh, expectedly, wanted neither.[14] As it turned out, Nehru was busy
with other matters, so the Mahatma went instead. At the maharaja's request, he addressed no public meetings in his three days in Srinagar. But
he met delegations of workers and students, who demanded Abdullah's
release and Prime Minister Kak's dismissal.[15]

On 15 August, Jammu and Kashmir had not acceded to either India
or Pakistan. It offered to sign a "Standstill Agreement" with both countries, and to allow the free movement of peoples and goods across borders. Pakistan signed the agreement, but India said it would wait and
watch. However, in the middle of September the rail service between

Sialkot in West Punjab and Jammu was suspended, and trucks carrying goods for the state were stopped on the Pakistan side of the border.[16]

As relations with Pakistan deteriorated, the maharaja dismissed two prime ministers in quick succession. First Kak was replaced with a soldier named Janak Singh; then he in turn gave way to a former judge of the Punjab high court, Mehr Chand Mahajan, who had better relations with the Congress bosses. Of these, the two top bosses were crucial: the prime minister, Jawaharlal Nehru (who was himself an ethnic Kashmiri); and the home minister and minister of states, Vallabhbhai Patel. Notably, while Nehru always wanted Kashmir to be part of India, Patel was at one time inclined to allow it to join Pakistan. His mind changed on 13 September, the day the Pakistani government accepted the accession of Junagadh—for "if Jinnah could take hold of a Hindu-majority State with a Muslim ruler, why should the Sardar not be interested in a Muslim-majority State with a Hindu ruler?"[17]

On 27 September 1947, Nehru wrote a long letter to Patel about the "dangerous and deteriorating" situation in the state. He had heard that Pakistan was preparing to send infiltrators "to enter Kashmir in considerable numbers." The maharaja and his administration could hardly meet the threat on their own: hence the need for Hari Singh to "make friends with the National Conference so that there might be this popular support against Pakistan." Releasing Abdullah, and enlisting the support of his followers, would also help "bring about the accession of Kashmir to the Indian Union."[18]

On 29 September, Sheikh Abdullah was released from prison. The next week, in a speech at the great Hazratbal Mosque in Srinagar, Abdullah demanded a "complete transfer of power to the people in Kashmir. Representatives of the people in a democratic Kashmir will then decide whether the State should join India or Pakistan." A popular government in Kashmir, he added, "will not be the government of any one community. It will be a joint government of the Hindus, the Sikhs and the Muslims. That is what I am fighting for."[19]

Pakistan naturally expected Kashmir, with a Muslim majority, to join it. India thought that the religious factor was irrelevant, especially since the leading political party, the National Conference, was known to be non-sectarian. By early October, as Patel wrote to Nehru, there was no "difference between you and me on matters of policy relating to Kashmir": both wanted accession.[20] What were the feelings of the Kashmiris themselves? Shortly after Abdullah's release, the British commander of the state forces noted that "the vast majority of the Kashmiris have no strong bias for either India or Pakistan." However, while there was "no well organized body in Kashmir advocating accession to Pakistan," the "National Conference has been pro-Congress and anti-Pakistan."[21]

As for Maharaja Hari Singh, he still clung to the dream of independence. On 12 October, the deputy prime minister of Jammu and Kashmir said in Delhi that

> We intend to keep on friendly relations with both India and Pakistan. Despite constant rumours, we have no intention of joining either India or Pakistan. . . . The only thing that will change our mind is if one side or the other decides to use force against us. . . . The Maharaja has told me that his ambition is to make Kashmir the Switzerland of the East—a State that is completely neutral.[22]

II

The only thing that will change our mind is if one side or the other decides to use force against us. Two weeks after these words were spoken, a force of several thousand armed men invaded the state from the north. On 22 October, they crossed the border that separated the North-West Frontier Province from Kashmir, and briskly made their way toward the capital, Srinagar.

Most of these raiders were Pathans from what was now a province of Pakistan. This much is undisputed; but what is not so certain is why they came or who was helping them. These two questions lie at the heart of the dispute over Kashmir; sixty years later, historians still cannot provide definitive answers to them. One reason for this uncertainty is that the northern extremity of Kashmir was both obscure and inaccessible. No railways or roads penetrated these high mountains. No anthropologists had come here, nor had any journalists. There are thus no independent eyewitness accounts of what came to be known as the "tribal invasion of Kashmir."

There are, however, plenty of accounts that are biased in one direction or the other. At the time, and later, Indians believed that the tribals were pushed across the border by Pakistan, which also supplied them with rifles and ammunition. The Pakistanis disclaimed any involvement in the invasion—they insisted that it was a "spontaneous" rushing of Pathan Muslims to the aid of co-religionists persecuted by a Hindu king and a Hindu administration.[23]

There was, indeed, discontent in one part of Kashmir. This was the district of Poonch, to the west of the capital, Srinagar. Until 1936, Poonch was ruled by a subsidiary clan of the Dogra ruling family. But in that year the district came directly under the control of the maharaja in Srinagar. The loss of autonomy hurt, as did the new taxes imposed by the king. There were cesses on individual goats, sheep, and cattle and a tax on entering the forest. Hardest hit were the pastoralists of Poonch, almost all of whom were Muslim.[24]

During the Second World War many Muslims from Poonch served in the British army. They came back, as demobilized soldiers tend to do, as highly conscious political beings. The rule of the maharaja of Kashmir had already been challenged in the Valley by Sheikh Abdullah and his party. To that was now added the independent challenge of the men of Poonch.

On 14 August, several shops and offices in Poonch had flown Pakistani flags, indicating their allegiance to Pakistan rather than to the still unaffiliated state of Kashmir. In the following weeks clashes between Dogra troops and local protesters were reported. By the beginning of September, dozens of Poonch men had equipped themselves with rifles, obtained from "informal sources in Pakistan." They had also established a base in the Pakistani town of Murree; here were collected arms and ammunition to be smuggled across the border to Kashmir. Pakistani accounts acknowledge that both the prime minister, Liaqat Ali Khan, and a senior leader of the Punjab Muslim League, Mian Iftikharuddin, knew and sanctioned assistance to the Poonch rebels. Overseeing the operation was Abkar Khan, a colonel in the Pakistani army. Khan had collected 4,000 rifles from army supplies and diverted them for use in Kashmir. More fancifully, he had adopted the nom de guerre General Tariq, after a legendary medieval Moorish warrior who had fought the Christians in Spain.[25]

In Poonch, Muslim officials and soldiers had left their jobs in the state administration and joined the rebels. So by the end of September, there were intimations of a serious conflict between a dissenting district and the government of Maharaja Hari Singh. But although there were clashes here and there, there was no major eruption, no head-on battle. Poonch bordered West Punjab; Pakistani cities like Rawalpindi were easily reached from there. However, the North-West Frontier Province is some distance to the west. Did the raiders from that province hear of the insurrection brewing in Poonch? Or were they planning to come anyway?

For these questions too one cannot supply uncontested answers. All we know for certain is that after the Pathan raiders crossed the border on 22 October, they made remarkably swift progress in their march southward. "The principal characteristics of the tribal invasion," writes the historian Michael Brecher, "were the surprise tactics of the tribesmen, the absence of the most rudimentary defence by the Kashmir State Army, and the pillage, loot and rapine of the tribesmen inflicted on Hindus and Muslims alike." Or, as a British social worker familiar with Kashmir laconically put it, the invading Pathans had sensed "an opportunity of gaining both religious merit and rich booty."

Once in Kashmir, the tribesmen moved quickly down the Jhelum valley. Their first stop was the town of Muzaffarabad, on the Kishanganga, just seven miles from the border. A battalion of the Jammu and Kashmir infantry was stationed here, but it was split down the middle, with half the men, Muslims from Poonch, now asserting their disenchantment with the maharaja. The garrison fell, but not before a few men escaped and phoned Srinagar to report what had happened. This allowed the acting commandant of the state forces, Brigadier Rajinder Singh, to gather a couple of hundred men and rush toward Uri, a town that lay roughly halfway between Srinagar and Muzaffarabad.

The raiders were also on their way to Uri. Brigadier Rajinder Singh got there first and, as a precaution, blew up the bridge that linked the town to the north. This held up the invaders for forty-eight hours, but they were eventually able to cross the river and decimate the brigadier's men. From Uri they made their way to Mahuta, the site of the power plant that supplied electricity to the Valley. At the plant they turned off the switches, plunging Srinagar into darkness.[26]

It should not surprise us that estimates of the number of invaders vary. According to some estimates there were as few as 2,000; according to others, these were as many as 13,000. We do know that the invaders had rifles and grenades, and that they travelled in trucks. Their incursion into Kashmir was openly encouraged by the prime minister of the North-West Frontier Province, Abdul Qayyum. The British governor, Sir George Cunningham, turned a blind eye. So did the British officers who were serving with the Pakistani army. As Jinnah's American biographer observes, "trucks, petrol, and drivers were hardly standard tribal equipment, and British officers as well as Pakistani officials all along the northern Pakistan route they traversed knew and supported, even if they did not actually organize and instigate, the violent October operation by which Pakistan seems to have hoped to trigger the integration of Kashmir into the nation."[27]

Once the Mahuta power plant fell on 24 October, the raiders headed down the open road to Srinagar. Along the route was the town of

Baramula. Here, for the first time, we can draw on eyewitness accounts of what happened. A British manager of a timber firm in Baramula saw the raiders come, "well supplied with lorries, petrol, and ammunition. They also have both two and three inch mortars." This manager was relieved of the 1,500 rupees he had just drawn from the bank.

The next target was the Convent of Saint Joseph's. Here the visitors smashed the machinery in the hospital and shot and wounded the mother superior. A colonel who lived in the same compound was killed outright. According to one report, the nuns were then lined up to be shot, but an Afridi who had studied in a convent school in Peshawar stopped his men from applying the finishing touches.[28]

"There can be no doubt that for those in the way, Pathans on the warpath are bad news." So writes one historian of the Kashmir dispute, Alastair Lamb. He tells us that apart from the attack on the convent, the Pathans also burned shops owned by Hindus and Sikhs. Lamb says they did "what might be expected from warriors engaged on what they saw as a *jihad*, a holy war."[29] However, at Baramula the greed of the tribesmen triumphed over religious identity, for here they "invaded the houses of the peace-loving Kashmiri Moslems as well. They looted and plundered the latter's houses and raped their young girls. Shrieks of terror and agony of those girls resounded across the town of Baramula."[30]

The incidents at Baramula were a strategic and propaganda disaster for the invaders. They showed that "once the first fanaticism of jehad had passed, there was left only the incentive of loot." There was now a "stampede to stuff the lorries full of the spoils of the Kashmir bazaars and send them back to their homes in Waziristan."[31] By stopping to steal and rape, the raiders had lost sight of their principal objective: the capture of Srinagar. And by attacking Muslims as well as Hindus, they had undermined their claim that they were fighting a holy war. It especially hurt that among those they killed were apolitical Christian priests doing "good works," and that a British correspondent was around to take down the testimony of those who survived.[32]

On 24 October, when the tribesmen were en route from Uri to Baramula, Maharaja Hari Singh sent a telegram to the Indian government asking for military assistance. The next morning the goverment's Defence Committee met in New Delhi and decided to depute V. P. Menon for an inspection on the spot. Menon flew to Srinagar later that day; when he landed at the airport, he was "oppressed by the stillness of a graveyard all around. Over everything hung an atmosphere of impending calamity." He went straight to M. C. Mahajan's house, and learned that the raiders were in Baramula, less than fifty miles away. He also met the maharaja, and advised him to move to the safety of Jammu.

On the morning of 26 October Menon flew back to Delhi, accompanied by the prime minister of Kashmir. There was another meeting of the Defence Committee. In attendance, apart from Mountbatten, Nehru, and Patel, was Sheikh Abdullah, who happened to be in Delhi that day. Both he and Mahajan urged that India immediately send troops to push back the invaders. Mountbatten suggested, however, that it would be best to secure Hari Singh's accession to India before committing any forces to his defence.

Menon now flew to Jammu, where the maharaja had taken refuge. On his arrival at the palace he "found it in a State of utter turmoil with valuable articles strewn all over the place." The maharaja was asleep, recovering from the all-night drive from Srinagar. He was woken up, and agreed to accede at once. Menon took the signed Instrument of Accession back with him to Delhi.[33]

At dawn on 27 October, the first plane left Delhi for Srinagar with troops and arms aboard. In all, twenty-eight Dakotas flew to Srinagar that day. In the following days, more than 100 planes took off from Delhi for the Valley, carrying soldiers and supplies and bringing back refugees and the wounded.[34]

Some of the planes that flew to Srinagar on 27 October belonged to the army or the air force. Others were commandeered by the government of India from private airlines. As an officer who flew in one of these passenger planes recalled, "the luxury fittings were ripped out, comfortable chairs pulled out of their fixtures, and within minutes fully-armed troops clambered aboard—as many as could fit in." They flew over the Punjab, seeing "long strings of refugee caravans below them," with "an odd house or village still smouldering." They landed in Srinagar airport to "the sound of small-arms and machine-gun fire."[35]

With his troops in the Valley, the Indian prime minister breathed a sigh of relief. "If we had vacillated and delayed by a day," wrote Nehru to his sister, "Srinagar might have been a smoking ruin. We got there in the nick of time." The Indian prime minister thought that they had succeeded

in warning off Pakistan from Kashmir. We have agreed that the future of Kashmir must be determined by the people. Meanwhile, Sheikh Abdulla is being entrusted with the formation of a Ministry. For my part, I do not mind if Kashmir becomes more or less independent, but it would have been a cruel blow if it had become just an exploited part of Pakistan.[36]

The view from the other side was all too different. The news that Indian troops had landed in Srinagar infuriated the governor general of Pakistan. Jinnah first fortified himself with several brandies, and then ordered his generals to march their troops into Kashmir.[37] His British commander-in-chief refused to follow the order. So, for the moment, the Pakistani troops kept out of the conflict, although their officers remained in close contact with the raiders.

When the Indian troops landed in Srinagar the maharaja had already left. There was not much sign of his administration, either. The police were nowhere in sight; substituting for them were volunteers of the National Conference, who stood guard at street corners and bridges, and generally supervised the movement of men and goods. A journalist who had covered the violence in the Punjab confessed that he was "not prepared for the incredible sights of amity and indeed fraternity that I saw in Srinagar. Hindus and Sikhs moved about with complete unself-consciousness among Muslims who constituted the vast majority of the population of the town; they marched shoulder to shoulder with them down Srinagar's streets as volunteers engaged in a common task."[38] Another reporter recalled the happy relationship between the National Conference and the army, as symbolized by the drives taken together by Sheikh Abdullah and the divisional commander, Major General Thimayya.[39]

As the Indians prepared to push back the raiders, Lord Mountbatten flew to Lahore on a peace mission. On 1 November 1947, he had a contentious meeting with Jinnah, at which he was told that if India gave up its claim to Kashmir, Pakistan would relinquish its claim to the other disputed state, Junagadh. Jinnah described Kashmir's accession to India as based on "fraud and violence." Mountbatten suggested that the violence had come from raiders who were Pakistani citizens; he knew for a fact that Maharaja Hari Singh wanted independence, and had been forced to accede to India only after his state was attacked. Jinnah countered by saying that the maharaja had brought this upon himself by his ill-treatment of Muslims in Poonch.[40]

In Kashmir, meanwhile, the Indian army had thrown a protective ring around Srinagar. There were now 4,000 troops in position, armed with machine guns. The safety of the city had been secured.[41] And with

Srinagar no longer vulnerable, the Indians began to clear other parts of the Valley of infiltrators. Baramula was taken on 8 November, and four days later Mahuta was captured, just in time to save the power plant from being blown up. The town of Uri fell the next day.[42]

With the onset of winter, the military operations were temporarily suspended. Attention now returned to the internal affairs of Kashmir. Mahajan was still prime minister, but he was being actively assisted by National Conference leaders. On 11 November, Nehru wrote to Hari Singh asking him to place "full confidence" in Sheikh Abdullah—that is, to formally make Abdullah head of the administration instead of Mahajan. The "only person who can deliver the goods in Kashmir is Sheikh Abdullah," insisted Nehru. "He is obviously the leading popular personality in Kashmir. The way he has risen to grapple with the crisis has shown the nature of the man. I have a high opinion of his integrity and general balance of mind. He has striven hard and succeeded very largely in keeping communal peace. He may make any number of mistakes in minor matters, but I think he is likely to be right in regard to major decisions."[43]

Mahatma Gandhi was equally impressed with Sheikh Abdullah. In the last week of November 1947 Abdullah visited Delhi, where he accompanied Gandhi to a meeting held on the birthday of the founder of the Sikh faith, Guru Nanak. As Gandhi told the gathering:

> You see Sheikh Abdullah Saheb with me. I was disinclined to bring him with me, for I know that there is a great gulf between the Hindus and the Sikhs on one side, and the Muslims on the other. But the Sheikh Saheb, known as the Lion of Kashmir, although a pucca Muslim, has won the hearts of both, by making them forget that there is any difference between the three. . . . Even though in Jammu, recently, the Muslims were killed by the Hindus and Sikhs, he went to Jammu and invited the evil-doers to forget the past and repent over the evil they had done. The Hindus and the Sikhs listened to him. Now the Muslims and the Hindus and the Sikhs . . . are fighting together to defend the beautiful valley of Kashmir.[44]

For Gandhi as well as Nehru, Sheikh Abdullah had become a symbol of secularism, a practitioner of interfaith harmony whose deeds in Kashmir were a stirring refutation of the two-nation theory. On the other hand, the Pakistani prime minister, Liaqat Ali Khan, contemptuously dismissed Abdullah as a "quisling." On 27 November, Khan met with Nehru in Delhi, with Mountbatten as an umpire. When a plebiscite was suggested as a way out of the impasse, Khan stated that first "an entirely new administration should be set up in Kashmir, which the people of Pakistan would accept as impartial."[45]

By now, Nehru was of the opinion that India must come to some "rapid and more or less final decisions about Kashmir with the Pakistan Government." Continuing military operations would mean "grave difficulties and suffering for the people of the State." In a letter to Maharaja Hari Singh, Nehru outlined the various forms a settlement could take. There could be a plebiscite for the whole state, to decide which Dominion it would join. Or the state could survive as an independent entity, with its defence guaranteed by both India and Pakistan. A third option was a partition, with Jammu going to India and the rest of the state to Pakistan. A fourth option was for Jammu and the Valley to stay with India, with Poonch and beyond being ceded to Pakistan. Nehru himself inclined to this last alternative. He saw that in Poonch "the majority of the population is likely to be against the Indian Union." But he was loath to give up the vale of Kashmir, a National Conference stronghold whose population seemed to be inclined toward India. From the Indian point of view, Nehru said to the maharaja,

> it is of the most vital importance that Kashmir should remain within the Indian Union. . . . But however much we may want this, it cannot be done ultimately except through the goodwill of the mass of the population. Even if military forces held Kashmir for a while, a later consequence might be a strong reaction against this. Essentially, therefore, this is a problem of psychological approach to the mass of the people and of making them feel they will be benefited by being in the Indian Union. If the average Muslim feels that he has no safe or secure place in the Union, then obviously he will look elsewhere. Our basic policy must keep this in view, or else we fail.[46]

This letter of Nehru's is much less well known than it should be. Excluded (for whatever reason) from his own *Selected Works*, it lies buried in the correspondence of Vallabhbhai Patel, to whom he had sent a copy. It shows that, contrary to received wisdom, the Indian prime minister was quite prepared to compromise on Kashmir. Indeed, the four options he outlined in December 1947 remain the four options being debated today.

III

On 1 January 1948, India decided to take the Kashmir issue to the United Nations. This was done on the advice of the governor general, Lord Mountbatten. Since Kashmir had acceded to it, India wanted the UN to help clear the northern parts of what it said was an illegal occupation by groups loyal to Pakistan.[47]

Through January and February the Security Council held several sessions on Kashmir. Pakistan, represented by the superbly gifted orator Sir Zafrullah Khan, was able to present a far better case than India. Khan convinced the delegates that the invasion was a consequence of the tragic riots across northern India in 1946–1947; it was a "natural" reaction of Muslims to the sufferings of their fellows. He accused the Indians of perpetrating "genocide" in east Punjab, forcing 6 million Muslims to flee to Pakistan. The Kashmir problem was recast as part of the unfinished business of partition. India suffered a significant symbolic defeat when the Security Council altered the agenda item from the "Jammu and Kashmir Question" to the "India-Pakistan Question."

Pakistan now suggested the withdrawal of all armed forces in the state, and the holding of a plebiscite under an "impartial interim administration." Ironically, Pakistan had rejected the idea of a plebiscite in the case of Junagadh. Jinnah's position then was that the will of the ruler would decide which Dominion a princely state would join. India instead referred the matter to the will of the people. Having done this in Junagadh, India could not so easily duck the question in Kashmir. However, the Indian government insisted that a plebiscite could be conducted under a National Conference administration, whose leader, Sheikh Abdullah, was the "most popular political leader in the State."[48]

So said Sheikh Abdullah himself, when he spoke at the United Nations on 5 February 1948. His language, recalled one observer, "was blunt, direct, and devoid of diplomatic language." "There is no power on earth which can displace me from the position which I have [in Kashmir]," he told the Security Council. "As long as the people are behind me I will remain there."[49]

A striking feature of the UN discussions on Kashmir was the partisanship of the British. Their representative, Philip Noel-Baker, vigorously

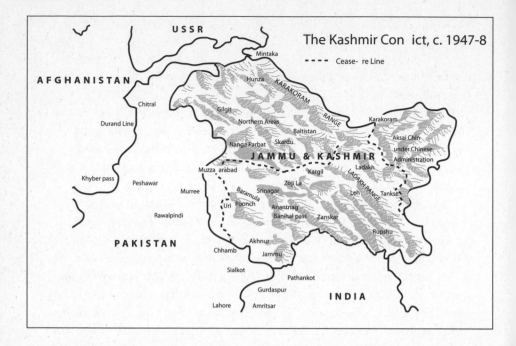

supported the Pakistani position. The British bias was deeply resented by
the Indians. Some saw it as a hangover from before independence, a conversion from support of the Muslim League to support of Pakistan. Others thought it was in compensation for the recent creation of the state of
Israel, after which there was a need to placate Muslims worldwide. A
third theory was that in the ensuing struggle with Soviet Russia, Pakistan would be the more reliable ally. Pakistan was also better placed,
with easy access to British air bases in the Middle East.[50]

In the first week of March 1948, the editor of the *Sunday Times*
wrote to Noel-Baker that

> in the world struggle for and against Communism, Kashmir occupies
> a place more critical than most people realise. It is the one corner at
> which the British Commonwealth physically touches the Soviet Union.
> It is an unsuspected soft spot, in the perimeter of the Indian Ocean
> basin, on whose inviolability the whole security of the Common-
> wealth and indeed world peace depend.[51]

By now, Nehru bitterly regretted going to the United Nations. He was
shocked, he told Mountbatten, to find that "power politics and not ethics"
were ruling an organization which "was being completely run by the

Americans," who, like the British, "had made no bones of [their] sympathy for the Pakistan case."[52] In the cabinet, pressure grew for renewing hostilities, for throwing out the invaders from northern Kashmir. But was this militarily feasible? A British general with years of service in the subcontinent warned that

> Kashmir may remain a "Spanish Ulcer." I have not found an Indian familiar with the Peninsular War's drain on Napoleon's manpower and treasure: and I sometimes feel that Ministers are loath to contemplate such a development in the case of Kashmir—I feel they still would prefer to think that the affair is susceptible of settlement, in a short decisive campaign, by sledge-hammer blows by vastly superior Indian forces which should be "thrown" into Kashmir.[53]

Meanwhile, in March 1948 Sheikh Abdullah replaced Mehr Chand Mahajan as the prime minister of Jammu and Kashmir. Then, in the middle of May, when the snows had melted, the war recommenced. An infantry brigade advanced north and west from Uri. It took the town of Tithwal but met with sharp resistance en route to the key town of Muzaffarabad.[54]

On the other side of an ever-shifting line of control, Pakistan had sponsored a government of Azad ("Free") Kashmir. It had also created an Azad Kashmir army, manned from these parts of the state and helped and guided by officers of the Pakistani army. These forces were skilful in their use of the terrain. In the late summer of 1948 they took the towns of Kargil and Dras and threatened the capital of Ladakh, Leh, which is at an altitude of 11,000 feet. However, an Indian air force squadron was successful in bringing supplies to Leh. The air force also brought relief to the town of Poonch, in the west, whose surroundings were under the control of the raiders.[55]

The two armies battled on through the later months of 1948. In November both Dras and Kargil were recaptured by the Indians, so Leh and Ladakh were safe for the moment. In the same month the hills around Poonch were also cleared. However, the northern and western parts of Kashmir were still in the control of Pakistan. Some Indian commanders wanted to move on, and asked for the redeployment of three brigades from the plains. Their request was not granted. For one thing, winter was about to set in. For another, the offensive would have required not merely troop reinforcements but also massive air support.[56] Perhaps it was as well that the Indian army halted its forward movement. As a scholar closely following the Kashmir question commented

at the time, "either it must be settled by partition or India will have to
walk into West Punjab. A military decision can *never* be reached in
Kashmir itself."[57]

At the United Nations, a Special Commission had been appointed
for Kashmir. Its members made an extensive tour of the region, visiting Delhi, Karachi, and Kashmir. In Srinagar they were entertained
by Sheikh Abdullah at the famous Shalimar Gardens. Later, Abdullah
had a long talk with one of the UN representatives, the Czech diplomat and scholar Josef Korbel. He dismissed both a plebiscite and independence, arguing that the "only solution" was the partition of Kashmir.
Otherwise, said Abdullah, "the fighting will continue; India and Pakistan will prolong the quarrel indefinitely, and our people's suffering
will go on."

In Srinagar, Korbel went to hear Abdullah speak at a mosque. The
audience of 4,000 listened "with rapt attention, their faith and loyalty
quite obvious in their faces. Nor could we notice any police, so often
used to induce such loyalty." The commission then visited Pakistan,
where they found that it would not consider any solution which gave the
vale of Kashmir, with its Muslim majority, to India.[58]

IV

By March 1948 Sheikh Abdullah was the most important man in the
Valley. Hari Singh was still the state's ceremonial head—now called
Sadr-i-riyasat—but he had no real powers. The government of India
completely shut him out of the UN deliberations. Their man, as they saw
it, was Abdullah. Only he, it was felt, could "save" Kashmir for the Indian
Union.

At this stage, Abdullah himself was inclined to stress the ties between Kashmir and India. In May 1948 he organized a week-long "freedom" celebration in Srinagar, to which he invited the leading lights of
the Indian government. The events on the calendar included folk songs
and poetry readings, the remembrance of martyrs, and visits to refugee
camps. The Kashmiri leader commended the "patriotic morale of our
own people and the gallant fighting forces of the Indian Union." "Our
struggle," said Abdullah, "is not merely the affair of the Kashmir people, it is the war of every son and daughter of India."[59]

On the first anniversary of Indian independence, Abdullah sent a
message to the leading Madras weekly, *Swatantra*. The message sought

to unite north and south, mountain and coast, and above all Kashmir and India. It deserves to be quoted in full:

> Through the pages of SWATANTRA I wish to send my message of fraternity to the people of the south. Far back in the annals of India the south and north met in the land of Kashmir. The great Shankaracharya came to Kashmir to spread his dynamic philosophy but here he was defeated in argument by a Panditani. This gave rise to the peculiar philosophy of Kashmir—Shaivism. A memorial to the great Shankaracharya in Kashmir stands prominent on the top of the Shankaracharya Hill in Srinagar. It is a temple containing the Murti of Shiva.
>
> More recently it was given to a southerner to take the case of Kashmir to the United Nations and, as the whole of India knows, with the doggedness and tenacity that is so usual to the southerner, he defended Kashmir.
>
> We in Kashmir expect that we shall continue to receive support and sympathy from the people of the south and that some day when we describe the extent of our country we shall use the phrase "from Kashmir to Cape Comorin."[60]

Swatantra, for its part, responded by printing a lyrical paean to the union of Kashmir with India. "The blood of many a brave Tamilian, Andhra, Malayalee and Coorgi," it said, "has soaked into the fertile soil of Kashmir and mixed with the blood of the Kashmiri patriots, cementing for ever the unity of the North and the South." Sheikh Abdullah's Eid perorations, noted the journal, were attentively heard by many Muslim soldiers from Kerala and Tamil Nadu. In Uri, sixty miles from Srinagar, there was a grave of a Christian soldier from Travancore, which had the Vedic swastika and a verse from the Koran inscribed on it. There could be "no more poignant and touching symbol of the essential oneness and unity of India."[61]

Whether or not Abdullah was India's man, he certainly was not Pakistan's. In April 1948 he described that country as "an unscrupulous and savage enemy."[62] He dismissed Pakistan as a theocratic state and the Muslim League as "pro-prince" rather than "pro-people." In his view, "Indian and not Pakistani leaders . . . had all along stood for the rights of the States' people."[63] When a diplomat in Delhi asked Abdullah what he thought of the option of independence, he answered that it would never work, as Kashmir was too small and too poor. Besides, said Abdullah, "Pakistan would swallow us up. They have tried it once. They would do it again."[64]

Within Kashmir, Abdullah gave top priority to the redistribution of land. Under the maharaja's regime, a few Hindus and fewer Muslims had very large holdings, with the bulk of the rural population serving as labourers or as tenants at will. In his first year in power, Abdullah transferred 40,000 acres of surplus land to the landless. He also outlawed absentee ownership, increased the tenant's share from 25% to 75% of the crop, and placed a moratorium on debt. His socialistic policies alarmed some elements in the government of India, especially as he did not pay compensation to the dispossessed landlords. But Abdullah saw this as crucial to progress in Kashmir. As he told a press conference in Delhi, if he was not allowed to implement agrarian reforms, he would not continue as prime minister of Jammu and Kashmir. Asked what he would do if reactionary elements got the upper hand in the central government, Abdullah answered: "Don't think I will desert you, even if you desert me. I will resign and join those people in the Indian Union who will also fight for economic betterment of the poor."[65]

At this press conference, Abdullah also made some sneering remarks about Maharaja Hari Singh. He pointed out that the maharaja had run away from Srinagar when it was in danger. In April 1949, Abdullah won a major victory when Hari Singh was replaced as *sadr-i-riyasat* by his eighteen-year-old-son, Karan Singh. The next month, Abdullah and three other National Conference men were chosen to represent Kashmir in the Constituent Assembly in Delhi, in a further affirmation of the state's integration with India.[66] That summer the Valley opened itself once more for tourists. As a sympathetic journalist put it, "every tourist who goes to Kashmir this summer will be rendering as vital a service to Kashmir—and to India—as a soldier fighting at the front."[67]

In the autumn came a visitor more important than a million tourists—Jawaharlal Nehru. Nehru and Abdullah took a leisurely two-hour ride down Srinagar's main thoroughfare, the river Jhelum. As their barge moved on, commented the correspondent of *Time* magazine, "hundreds of *shikaras* (gondolas) milled around; their jampacked passengers wanted a good look, and they pelted Nehru with flowers." Thousands watched the procession from the riverbanks, setting off firecrackers from time to time. "Carefully coached schoolchildren" shouted slogans in praise of Nehru and Abdullah. Seizing the chance, merchants had hung out their wares, alongside banners which advertised "best Persian and Kashmiri carpets."

"All the portents," concluded *Time*, were that "India considered that the battle for Kashmir had been won—and that India intended to keep the prize."[68]

V

The battle for Kashmir was, and is, not merely or even mostly a battle for territory. It is, as Josef Korbel put it half a century ago, an "uncompromising and perhaps uncompromisable struggle of two ways of life, two concepts of political organization, two scales of values, two spiritual attitudes."[69]

On one side was the idea of India; on the other side, the idea of Pakistan. In the spring of 1948 the British journalist Kingsley Martin visited both countries to see how Kashmir looked from each. Indians, he found, were utterly convinced of the legality of the state's accession, and bitter in their condemnation of Pakistan's help to the raiders. To them the religion of the Kashmiris was wholly irrelevant. The fact that Abdullah was the popular head of an emergency administration was "outstanding proof that India was not 'Hindustan' and that there are Muslims who have voluntarily chosen to come to an India which, as Nehru emphasised, should be a democracy in which minorities can live safely and freely."

When Martin crossed the border he found "how completely different the situation looks from the Pakistan angle." Most people he met had friends or relatives who had died at the hands of Hindus and Sikhs. The dispute, for the Pakistanis, had started with the rebellion in Poonch, which in India had been "largely and undeservedly forgotten." In Karachi and Lahore, the people were "completely sympathetic" to the raiders from the frontier who, in their eyes, were fighting "a holy war against the oppressors of Islam."[70] Martin's conclusions were endorsed by the veteran Australian war correspondent Alan Moorehead. On a visit to Pakistan he too found that the conflict over Kashmir was looked on "as a holy Moslem war. . . . Some of them, I have seen, talk wildly of going on to Delhi. Everywhere recruiting is going on and there is much excitement at the success of the Moslems."[71]

The fragility of the Pakistani state and of its ideology was personified in the ambiguous identities of its main leaders. The governor general, M. A. Jinnah, was a Gujarati who had married a Parsi. The prime minister, Liaqat Ali Khan, was an aristocrat from the United Provinces who was married to a Christian. Neither was, in any sense of the term, a practising Muslim. The top civil servants of Pakistan were, like Jinnah and Liaqat, *mohajirs*, migrants whose ancestral homes were on the Indian side of the border. The ruling class had no roots in what was now their state. This, one suspects, made them even more fervent in their desire to make Kashmir part of Pakistan.

However, the new Indian nation state was not so robust either. Its insecurity was manifest in its anointing, as a secular hero, a Muslim officer who had died fighting in Kashmir. True, unlike the Pakistani army, the Indian army was drawn from men of all religions. Among its senior commanders were a Sikh, a Parsi, and two Coorgs, these last from a south Indian hill community that likes to see itself as "not-Hindu." Yet the commander who was to be venerated most was a Muslim—Brigadier Usman. Usman was educated in Allahabad and Sandhurst, and chose to stay with India at the time of partition. It was claimed that Pakistan had designated him a Kaffir, and that the Azad Kashmir government had put a price of 50,000 rupees on his head, dead or alive.

In January–February 1948, Brigadier Usman and his men repulsed a fierce attack on Nowshera. In July of that year he died in action. An Indian journalist wrote that "a precious life, of imagination and unswerving patriotism, has fallen a victim to communal fanaticism. Brigadier Usman's brave example will be an abiding source of inspiration for Free India."[72] He was publicly mourned by Congress leaders, from Jawaharlal Nehru downward. The tributes that poured in praised not merely his bravery but also his character: he was, the Indian public was told, an army officer who was withal "a vegetarian, a non-smoker, and a tetotaller." His body was brought back from Kashmir to Delhi and buried with full military honours. His grave was placed next to that of Dr. M. A. Ansari, a legendary nationalist Muslim of the previous generation.[73] One might say that Brigadier Usman was to the Indian army what Sheikh Abdullah was to Indian politics: a symbol of its putatively inclusive secularism, an affirmation of its being, if it was anything at all, the Other of a theologically dogmatic and insular Pakistan.

Both sides had invested men and money in the battle for Kashmir. More crucially, they had invested their respective ideologies of nationhood. The clash of ideologies was captured in a debate on the future of Kashmir organized by a leading Bombay weekly. The protagonists were both young Muslim journalists, but one was Indian and the other Pakistani. Both were asked to answer the question: Which way would the Kashmiris vote if the United Nations did succeed in holding a plebiscite?

Speaking on India's behalf was the gifted novelist and scriptwriter Khwaja Ahmad Abbas. One-fourth of Kashmir's population, he said, were squarely behind Sheikh Abdullah and his National Conference—these were the politically conscious, "progressive" elements. Another one-fourth were just as resolutely opposed to Abdullah—these were "fully indoctrinated by the Pakistan ideology." Half the voters were undecided—they could go either way. These were attracted to the person of Abdullah, but also "susceptible to the cry of Islam in Danger." When the day of reckoning came, Abbas thought, the memories of the raiders' brutalities and the appeal of the progressive ideology of secularism would tilt the balance in favour of India. However, if India "wanted to make absolutely sure of a comfortable and convincing majority," then the maharaja and his dynasty had to be removed, and Abdullah allowed to fully implement his economic programme.[74]

The next week, Abbas was answered by Wares Ishaq, a journalist based in Karachi. He thought that the pull of religion would ensure a Pakistani victory in any plebiscite in Kashmir. Islam, he argued, was not just a religion but a culture and a way of life. There was only one circumstance in which the Kashmiris would disregard the call of the faith—if India actually lived up to its claim of being a secular state. However, after the death of Mahatma Gandhi, the position of minorities was fraught with danger. In particular, wrote Ishaq, the lifting of the ban on the Hindu chauvinist body, the Rashtriya Swayamsevak Sangh, "has finally convinced Muslims all over India, and specially in Kashmir, that their position in India will always be that of a downtrodden minority." Thus, when the crunch came, the bulk of the Kashmiris would vote to join "the Islamic comity of nations."[75]

VI

One might say of the conflict of 1947–1948 that it had only losers. The indecision—with neither nation succeeding in getting the whole of the state—hurt both sides then, and it hurts them now. Hence the prevalence and persistence of conspiracy theories. On the Indian side, the finger is pointed at the British governor general, who dragged the case to the UN; and at the British general in command of the Indian army, who is believed to have stopped his troops from going into northern Kashmir.[76] But the Pakistanis blame Mountbatten too; they think he conspired with Sir Cyril Radcliffe to gift the district of Gurdaspur to the Indians, so as to allow them a road into Kashmir.[77] And they chastise their own government for not helping the raiders even more. A senior civil servant lamented in 1998:

> [T]he only chance of Pakistan obtaining Kashmir was by a blitzkrieg, combining the call of jihad, speed, and surprise, to present the enemy with a fait accompli before it could recover from the shock. The tribal invasion was well-conceived as the only means to counter the Indian designs and compensate for Pakistan's military weakness. . . . The one single element which decided the issue against Pakistan was the faulty leadership of the tribal horde. . . . This was the only mistake, and a decisive one at that, for which those who organized the invasion . . . should bear responsibility.[78]

This book will return to Kashmir at regular intervals. But let me end this investigation of the dispute's origins with some prophetic statements made at the time. The quotations below come from observers speaking not in 1990 or 2000, but in the very early years of the conflict.[79]

Kashmir is the one great problem that may cause the downfall of India and Pakistan (Henry Grady, United States ambassador to India, January 1948).

So long as the dispute over Kashmir continues it is a serious drain on the military, economic and, above all, on the spiritual strength of these two great countries (General A. G. L. McNaughton, UN mediator, February 1950).

So vital seems its possession for economic and political security to Pakistan that her whole foreign and defence policy has largely revolved around the Kashmir dispute. . . . Far more than the Punjab massacres, which, though horrible, were short-lived, it is the Kashmir dispute which has poisoned every aspect of Indo-Pakistan relations (Richard Symonds, British social worker and author, 1950).

Kashmir is one situation you could never localize if it should flare up. It would influence the whole Muslim world. [It is] potentially the most dangerous in the world (Ralph Bunche, senior UN official, February 1953).

5

REFUGEES *and the* REPUBLIC

Refugees are [being] sent all over India. They will scatter
communal hatred on a wide scale and will churn up enormous ill-
will everywhere. Refugees have to be looked after, but we have to
take steps to prevent the infection of hatred beyond the necessary
minimum which cannot be prevented.

C. RAJAGOPALACHARI, governor of Bengal, writing on 4 September 1947

May the blood that flowed from Gandhiji's wounds and the tears
that flowed from the eyes of the women of India everywhere they
learnt of his death serve to lay the curse of 1947, and may the
grisly tragedy of that year sleep in history and not colour present
passions.

C. RAJAGOPACHARI, writing on 20 March 1948

I

IN THE INDIAN IMAGINATION Kurukshetra occupies a special place.
It was the site of the bloody battles described in the epic *Mahabharata*. According to the epic, the fighting took place on an open
plain north-west of the ancient city of Indraprastha (now known as
Delhi). The plain was called Kurukshetra, a name it retains to this day.

Several thousand years after the *Mahabharata* was composed, the
place of its enactment became the temporary home of the victims of another war. This, too, was fought between closely related kin: India and
Pakistan, rather than Pandava and Kaurava. Many of the Hindus and
Sikhs fleeing West Punjab were directed by the government of India to a
refugee camp in Kurukshetra. A vast city of tents had come up on the
plain, to house waves of migrants, sometimes up to 20,000 a day. The
camp was initially planned for 100,000 refugees, but it came to accommodate three times that number. As an American observer wrote, "the
army worked miracles to keep the tents rising ahead of the last refugees." The new inhabitants of Kurukshetra consumed 100 tons of flour
daily, along with large quantities of salt, rice, lentils, sugar, and cooking

oil—all provided free of charge by the government. Helping the state in this effort was a network of Indian and foreign social workers, the United Council for Relief and Welfare (UCRW).

The refugees had to be housed and fed, and also clothed and entertained. With winter approaching, the "Government soon recognized that the evenings and nights were hardest to bear." So the UCRW commandeered film projectors from Delhi and set them up in Kurukshetra. Among the movies shown were those Disney specials, Mickey Mouse and Donald Duck. With large cloth screens allowing for two-way projection, crowds of up to 15,000 could watch a single show. This "two-hour break from reality," commented a social worker, "was a life-saver. The refugees forgot their shock experiences and misery for two golden hours of laughter. Yes, they who had been bruised and beaten, were homeless and wounded, could laugh. Here was hope."[1]

Kurukshetra was the largest of the nearly 200 camps set up to house refugees from West Punjab. Some refugees had arrived before the date of transfer of power, among them prescient businessmen, who had sold their properties in advance and migrated with the proceeds. However, the vast majority came after 15 August 1947, and with little more than the clothes on their backs. These were the farmers who had "stayed behind till the last moment firmly resolved to remain in Pakistan if they could be assured of an honourable living." But when, in September and October, the violence escalated in the Punjab, they had to abandon that idea. The Hindus and Sikhs who were lucky enough to escape the mobs fled to India by road, rail, and sea, and on foot.[2]

Camps like Kurukshetra were only a holding operation. The refugees had to be found permanent homes and productive work. A journalist visiting Kurukshetra in December 1947 described it as a city in itself, with 300,000 people, all "sitting idle like mad." "The one thought that dominates the peasant-refugees of Kurukshetra," he wrote, is " 'Give us some land. We will cultivate it.' That is what they shouted. These land-hungry peasants told us that they did not very much care where land was given to them provided [it] was cultivable. Their passion for land appeared to be elemental."[3]

As it happened, a massive migration had also taken place the other way, into Pakistan from India. Thus, the first place to resettle the refugees was on land vacated by Muslims in the eastern part of the Punjab. If the transfer of populations had been "the greatest mass migration" in history, now commenced "the biggest land resettlement operation in the world." As compared with 2.7 million hectares abandoned by Hindus and Sikhs in West Punjab, there were only 1.9 million hectares left behind by Muslims in East Punjab. The shortfall was made more acute by the fact that the areas in the west of the province had richer soils, and were more abundantly irrigated. Indeed, in the late nineteenth century, hundreds of Sikh villages had migrated en masse to the west, to cultivate land in the newly created "canal colonies." There they had made the desert flourish; but one day in 1947 they were told that their garden now lay in Pakistan. So, in just two generations, these dispossessed Sikhs found themselves back in their original homes.

To begin with, each family of refugee farmers was given an allotment of 4 hectares, regardless of its holding in Pakistan. Loans were advanced to buy seed and equipment. While cultivation began on these temporary plots, applications were invited for permanent allotments. Each family was asked to submit evidence of how much land it had left behind. Applications were received from 10 March 1948 on; within a month, more than 500,000 claims had been filed. These claims were then verified in open assemblies consisting of other migrants from the same village. As each claim was read out by a government official, the assembly approved, amended, or rejected it.

As expected, many refugees were at first prone to exaggeration. However, every false claim was punished, sometimes by a reduction in the land allotted, and in extreme cases by a brief imprisonment. This acted as a deterrent; still, an officer closely associated with the process estimated that there was an overall inflation of about 25%. To collect, collate, verify, and act on the claims a Rehabilitation Secretariat was set up in Jalandhar. At its peak about 7,000 officials worked there; they came to constitute a kind of refugee city of their own. Most of these officials were accommodated in tents, serviced by makeshift lights and latrines, and by temporary shrines, temples for Hindus and gurdwaras for Sikhs.

Leading the operations was the director general of rehabilitation, Sardar Tarlok Singh of the Indian civil service. A graduate of the London School of Economics, Tarlok Singh used his academic training to good effect, making two innovations that proved critical in the successful settlement of the refugees. These were the "standard acre" and the "graded cut."

A standard acre was defined as that amount of land which could yield ten to eleven maunds of rice. (A maund is about 40 kilograms.) In the dry, unirrigated districts of the east, four physical acres were equivalent to one standard acre; but in the lush "canal colonies," one physical acre was about equal to a standard acre. The innovative concept of the standard acre took care of the variations in soil and climate across the province.

The idea of the graded cut, meanwhile, helped overcome the large discrepancy between the land left behind by the refugees and the land now available to them—a gap that was close to 1 million acres. For the first ten acres of any claim, a cut of 25% was implemented—thus one got only 7.5 acres instead of ten. For higher claims the cuts were steeper: 30% between ten and 30 acres, and on upward, so that those having more than 500 acres were taxed at the rate of 95%. The biggest single loser was a woman named Vidyawati, who had inherited (and lost) her husband's estate of 11,500 acres, spread across thirty-five villages of the Gujranwala and Sialkot districts. In compensation, she was alloted a mere 835 acres in a single village of Karnal.

By November 1949, Tarlok Singh and his officials had made 250,000 allotments of land. These refugees were then distributed equitably across the districts of East Punjab. Neighbours and families were resettled together, although the re-creation of entire village communities proved impossible. Refugees were invited to protest against their allotments; close to 100,000 families asked for a review. A third of these objections were acted on; as a result, 80,000 hectares changed hands once again.

In exchange for their well-watered lands in the west, these refugees were given impoverished holdings in the east. With the implementation of graded cuts, they also had less land. But with characteristic ingenuity and enterprise, they set to work, digging new wells, building new houses, planting their crops. By 1950 a depopulated countryside was alive once again.[4]

Yet a sense of loss persisted. The economy could be rebuilt, but the cultural wrongs of partition could never be undone—not in, or by, either side. The Sikhs once more had land to cultivate, but they would never get back much-loved places of worship. These included the gurdwara in Lahore where lay buried their great warrior-chieftain, Ranjit Singh; as well as Nankana Sahib, the birthplace of the founder of the faith, Guru Nanak.

In April 1948 the editor of the Calcutta *Statesman* visited Nankana Sahib, where he met the few Sikhs permitted by Pakistan to stay on as guardians of the shrine. A few months later he visited the centre of the Ahmediya sect of Islam, the town of Qadian, in the Indian Punjab. The great tower of the Ahmadiya Mosque was visible from miles around, but within its precincts there now lived only 300 of the faithful. Otherwise, the town had been taken over by 12,000 Hindu and Sikh refugees. In both Qadian and Nankana Sahib there was "the conspicuous dearth of daily worshippers, the aching emptiness, the sense of waiting, of hope and . . . of faith fortified by humbling affliction."[5]

II

Most of the migrants from West Punjab were farmers; but there were also many who were artisans, traders, and labourers. To accommodate them the government built new townships. One, called Faridabad, was twenty miles south of the nation's capital, Delhi. Among the groups active in Faridabad was the Indian Cooperative Union (ICU), an organization headed by Kamaladevi Chattopadhyaya, a socialist and feminist who had been closely associated with Mahatma Gandhi.

The residents of Faridabad were mostly Hindu refugees from the North-West Frontier Province. A social worker named Sudhir Ghosh encouraged them to construct their own homes. However, the government wished to build the houses through its Public Works Department (PWD), notorious for sloth and corruption and widely known as the "Public Waste Department" and as "Plunder Without Danger." In protest a group of refugees besieged the prime minister's house in Delhi. They were a "nuisance" to Nehru, who encountered them as he went to work every morning, but at least they made him "think furiously of the problems" facing the refugees. In a typically Indian compromise, the refugees were allowed to build about 40% of the houses, with the PWD constructing the rest.

In Faridabad, the ICU organized cooperatives and self-help groups, setting up shops and small production units. To power these, and to light the homes, a diesel plant was erected at short notice. This plant lay in a shed in Calcutta, where it had come as part of German war reparations. No one wanted it in Calcutta, so it was sent to Faridabad instead. Sudhir Ghosh located the German engineer who had built the plant and persuaded him to come from Hamburg to India. He came, but to his dismay no cranes were available to erect the plant. So he trained the men in Faridabad to operate fifteen-ton jack screws, which helped raise the equipment inch by inch. In ten months the plant was ready. In April 1951, Nehru himself came to commission it, and as he "pressed the button, the lights came on and lifted the spirits of all in Faridabad. The township had power in its hands to fashion its industrial future."[6]

Meanwhile, thousands of refugees had made their homes in Delhi itself. Until 1911, it had been Muslim in character and culture. In that year, the British shifted their capital here from Calcutta. After 1947, New Delhi became the seat of the government of free India. Urdu-speaking Muslims went away to Pakistan, many unwillingly; while Punjabi-speaking Hindus and Sikhs came in their place. They set up house, and shop, wherever they could. In the middle of the city was Connaught Circus, a majestic shopping arcade designed by R. T. Russell. Had Russell ever seen what became of his creation, he would perhaps have been "spinning in his grave like a dervish." In 1948 and 1949, "stalls and push-carts of every size and shape" had been set up along the pavements. Thus, "what was once a shaded walk where the shopper could stroll at leisure, inspecting the goods on offer and not meeting an insistent salesman, unless he or she went into a store, has become pandemonium. . . . All in all, the exclusive shopping district of New Delhi, which in pre-independence days catered to the élite and wealthy, is now just a glorified bazaar."[7]

Almost 500,000 refugees came to settle in Delhi after partition. They flooded the city, "spreading themselves out wherever they could. They thronged in camps, schools, colleges, temples, *gurdwaras*, *dharam-shalas*, military barracks, and gardens. They squatted on railway platforms, streets, pavements, and every conceivable space." In time, these squatters built houses on land alloted to them in the areas west and south of Lutyens's Delhi. Here arose colonies that to this day are dominated by Punjabis: *nagars* or townships named after Patel, Rajendra (Prasad), and Lajpat (Rai), Hindu Congress leaders they particularly admired.

Like their counterparts who had settled on the farms of East Punjab, the refugees in Delhi displayed much thrift and drive. In time they came to gain "a commanding influence in Delhi," dominating its trade and commerce. Indeed, a place that was once a Mughal city and then a British city had by the 1950s emphatically become a Punjabi city.[8]

III

Like Delhi, the city of Bombay also had its culture and social geography transformed by the partition. By July 1948 there were 500,000 refugees in Bombay, arriving from Sind, Punjab, and the North-West Frontier. The refugees further intensified what was already the most acute of Bombay's problems: the housing shortage. Almost 1 million people were now sleeping in the streets. Slums were growing apace. In crowded tenements, people lived fifteen or twenty to a room.[9]

One journalist reported that the total losses of Sindh refugees were 4 billion to 5 billion rupees, since at home they had owned large areas of land, dominated the public services, and controlled business and trade. Whereas the Punjabi refugees now had East Punjab as their own, to fulfil there "the essentials of an independent corporate existence and the attributes of an autonomous Government," the Sindhis had nothing similar on which to rebuild.[10] Some looked beseechingly or angrily to the state; others took matters into their own hands. Thus in Bombay, it was "a sight to see even little Sindhi boys hawking pieces of cloth in the thoroughfares of the city. They have got salesmanship in their blood. That is why the Gujaratis and Maharashtrians have not taken kindly to the Sindhi invader. Even little urchins from the backwoods of Sind are able to make a living by selling trinkets in suburban trains."[11]

There were five refugee camps in Bombay. Their condition left much to be desired. The Kolwada camp had 10,400 people living in barracks. The average space alloted to each family was 36 square feet. There were only twelve water taps in the entire camp; there were no doctors; there was only one school, and no electricity. The place was run in dictatorial fashion by a man named Pratap Singh. In April 1950 a minor riot broke out when some tenants, protesting against their living conditions, refused to pay rent. Pratap Singh had them served with an eviction order, and when they resisted, called in the police. In the ensuing fight, a young man was killed. The journalist reporting the story appropriately called the residents of the camp "inmates"; as he noted, "other inmates [were] huge cat-sized ugly rats, bugs, mosquitoes, and snakes."[12]

The refugees from Sindh spread across the towns and cities of western India. Apart from Bombay, there were substantial communities in Pune and Ahmedabad. A social psychologist visiting them in the autumn of 1950 found the Sindhis deeply dissatisfied. The "complaints of crowded, filthy quarters, inadequate water, insufficient rations, and above all, insufficient support from the government, are almost universal." A refugee in Ahmedabad said that "we are eating stuff which we used to throw away in Pakistan for the birds to eat." Others complained of ill-treatment by the local Gujaratis and were particularly hostile toward the Muslims. And they fulminated against the Indian state, although they exonerated Nehru himself. "Our government is useless," they said. "All are thieves collected together. Only Pandit [Nehru] is all right; the rest are all worthless and self-serving. The Pandit himself says what he can do; the rest of the machinery does not work."[13]

IV

The influx of refugees also transformed the landscape of India's third great metropolis, Calcutta. Before partition, the more prosperous Hindu families of eastern Bengal had begun moving with their assets to the city. After partition the immigration was chiefly of working-class and farming families. In the Punjab, the exodus happened in one big rush; but in Bengal it was spread out. However, in the winter of 1949–1950 there was a wave of communal riots in East Pakistan, which forced many more Hindus across the border. In previous years about 400,000 refugees came into West Bengal; in 1950 the number jumped to 1.7 million.

Where did these people seek refuge? Some stayed with relatives. Others made a home in the city's railroad stations, where their beds, boxes, and other accessories lay spread out on the platforms. Here "families lived, slept, mated, defecated and ate on the concrete amidst flies, lice, infants and diarrhoea. Victims of cholera would lie exhausted staring at their vomit, women were kept busy delousing each other, beggars begged." Still others lived on the street, "with the stray cattle, like the stray cattle, drinking gutter-water, eating garbage, sleeping on the curb."[14]

So wrote the *Manchester Guardian's* correspondent in India. In truth, the refugees were a good deal less passive than this description suggests. Early in 1948 a "large number of refugees, disgusted with their miserable existence at Sealdah station, occupied the Lake military barracks, Jodhpur military barracks, the Mysore House and other large unoccupied houses and military barracks at Shahpur, Durgapur, Ballygunge Circular Road and Dharmatala. Almost overnight these deserted houses swarmed with refugee men, women and children. These were deliberate acts of trespass."[15]

Whereas some refugees took possession of empty houses, others colonized vacant land along roads and railway lines, as well as freshly cleared shrub jungle and recently drained marshes. The squatters "would stealthily enter these plots at night, and under cover of darkness rapidly put up makeshift shelters. They would then refuse to leave, while offering in many instances to pay a fair price for the land."[16]

It was the government of West Bengal which forced the refugees, willy-nilly, to take the law into their own hands. For one thing, there had been no mass migration in the other direction—as there had been in the Punjab—leaving untended fields and farms for the refugees to be settled in. For another, the government liked to believe—or hope—that this influx was temporary, and that when things settled down the Hindus would return to their homes in the east. Buttressing this belief was the claim that the Bengalis were somehow less "communal-minded" than the Punjabis. Here, the Muslim spoke the same language and ate the same food as his Hindu neighbours; thus he might more readily continue to live cheek-by-jowl with them.

This latter argument was vigorously rejected by the refugees themselves. For them there was no going back to what they saw as an Islamic state. They found support for their views in the person of the historian Sir Jadunath Sarkar, arguably the most influential Bengali intellectual of his generation. Addressing a mammoth public meeting of refugees, held on 16 August 1948, Sarkar compared the migration of East Bengal Hindus to the flight of French Huguenots in the time of Louis XIV. He urged the people of West Bengal to absorb and integrate the migrants, and thus to nourish their culture and economy. With the help of the refugees, Sarkar said, "we must make our West Bengal what Palestine under Jewish Rule will be, a light in darkness, an oasis of civilisation in the desert of medieval ignorance and obsolete theocratic bigotry."[17]

In September 1948 an All Bengal Refugee Council of Action was formed. Marches and demonstrations were organized demanding that the refugees be given fair compensation and citizenship rights. The leaders of the movement aimed to throw "regimented bands of refugees in the streets of Calcutta and to maintain a relentless pressure on the Government. . . Processions, demonstrations and meetings, traffic jams, brickbats and teargas shells and [police] *lathis* coming down in showers, burning tramcars and buses, and occasional firings—these became the hallmark of the city."[18]

Displaced from their homes by forces outside their control, refugees everywhere are potential fodder for extremist movements. In Delhi and the Punjab, the radical Hindu organization Rashtriya Swayamsevak Sangh (RSS) very early on got a foothold among the migrants. In Bengal, its sister organization, the Hindu Mahasabha, also worked hard at giving a religious colour to the problem. The Bengali Hindus, these organizations said, "have been made sacrificial goats in the great Yajna of India's freedom." In asking them to return to East Pakistan, the government was guilty of "appeasement" and of abetting "genocide." While the state asked them to submit, what the refugees needed was a stiff dose of "the virility of man." "One only wishes," wrote an angry Hindu in March 1950, that "a Sivaji or a Rana Pratap emerged from their ranks."[19]

This invocation of medieval Hindu warriors who had fought Muslim kings found more response in Delhi and the Punjab. In Bengal, however, the communists most sucessfully mobilized the refugees. It was the communists who organized the processions to government offices, and it was they who orchestrated the forcible occupation of fallow land in Calcutta, land to which the refugees "had no sanction other than organized strength and dire necessity." Thus in different parts of the city grew numerous impromptu settlements, "clusters of huts with thatch, tile or corrugated iron roofs, bamboo mat walls and mud floors, built in the East Bengal style."[20]

By early 1950 there were about 200,000 refugees in these squatter colonies. In the absence of state support, the refugees "formed committees of their own, framed rules for the administration of the colonies and organised themselves into a vast united body."[21] A "South Calcutta Refugee Rehabilitation Committee" claimed to represent 40,000 families who, in their respective colonies, had constructed a total of 500 miles of road, sunk 700 tube wells, and started forty-five high schools as well as 100 primary schools—all at their own expense and through their own initiative. The committee demanded that the government make these colonies "legal" by formally bringing them under the Calcutta municipality, that it similarly regularize private plots and school buildings, and that it help develop markets and arrange loans.[22]

Those who spoke for these migrants frequently complained about the preferential treatment given to the Punjabi refugees. A team of Bengali social workers visiting north India found the camps there "of a superior kind." The houses were permanent, with running water and adequate sanitation; whereas in west Bengal the refugees had to make do with "decaying bamboo hutments" where "lack of privacy and of kitchen space is notorious." Cash and clothing allowances were also higher in the north.[23]

On the whole, the resettlement process was far less painful in the Punjab. By the early 1950s, the refugees in the north had found new homes and new jobs. But in the east the insecurity persisted. So long as the Bengali refugees remained "unsettled and unemployed," wrote one correspondent in July 1954, "economic and political discontent will grow; the Communists will succeed in exploiting their grievances."[24]

V

Unquestionably the main victims of partition were women: Hindu, Sikh, and Muslim. As the respected Sindhi congressman Choitram Gidwani put it, "in no war have the women suffered so much." Women were killed, maimed, violated, and abandoned. After independence the brothels of Delhi and Bombay came to be filled with refugee women, who had been thrown out by their families because of what someone else had done to them—against their will.[25]

In the summer of 1947, as the violence in the Punjab spread from village to village, Hindus and Sikhs in the east of the province abducted and kept Muslim women. On the other side the compliment—if it may be called that—was returned, with young Hindu and Sikh girls seized by Muslim men. However, after the dust had settled and the blood had dried, the governments of India and Pakistan agreed that these captured women must be returned to their original families.

On the Indian side, the operation to recover abducted women was led by Mridula Sarabhai and Rameshwari Nehru. Both came from aristocratic homes, and both had sturdily nationalist credentials. Their work was encouraged and aided by Jawaharlal Nehru, who took a deep personal interest in the process. In a radio broadcast to the refugees, the prime minister spoke especially "to those women who are the victims of all these hardships." He assured them that "they should not feel that we have any hesitation whatsoever in bringing them back or that we have any doubts about their virtue. We want to bring them back with affection because it had not been their fault. They were forcefully abducted and we want to bring them back respectfully and keep them lovingly. They must not doubt that they will come back to their families and be given all possible help."[26]

The abducted women were tracked down singly, case by case. When a person had been located, the police would enter the village at sunset, after the men had returned from the fields. An "informer" would lead them to the home of the abductor. The offender would usually deny that the woman in his possession had been seized. After his objections were overcome—sometimes by force—the woman would be taken away, at first to a government camp, and then across the border.[27]

By May 1948 some 12,500 women had been found and restored to their families. Ironically, and tragically, many of the women did not want to be rescued, for after their seizure they had made some kind of peace with their new surroundings. Now, as they were being reclaimed, these women were deeply unsure about how their original families would receive them. They had been "defiled" and, in a further complication, many were pregnant. These women knew that even if they were accepted, their children—born out of a union with the "enemy"—would never be. Often, the police and their accomplices had to use force to take the women away. "You could not save us then," said the women; "what right have you to compel us now?"[28]

VI

Compounding the refugee crisis were serious shortages of food. After the end of the war imports of grain were steadily on the rise, increasing from about 0.8 million tons in 1944 to 2.8 million four years later. On the eve of independence, a politician travelling through the district of East Godavari found men and women surviving on tamarind seeds, palmyra fruits, and the bark of the *jeelugu* tree—these were boiled together into gruel that caused bloating, diarrhoea, and sometimes death. The following year, the rains failed in the western province of Gujrat, leading to an acute shortage of water and fodder. Wells and riverbeds ran dry, and cattle and goats died of hunger and disease.[29]

In some places farmers were starving, and in other places they were restive. In the uncertainty following the Indian takeover of Hyderabad, the communists moved swiftly to assume control of the Telengana region. They were aided by a pile of .303 rifles and Mark V guns left behind by the retreating Razakars. The communists destroyed the palatial homes of landlords and distributed their land to tillers of the soil. Dividing themselves into several *dalams*, or groups, each responsible for a number of villages, the communists asked peasants not to pay land revenue, and enforced law and order themselves.[30] In districts such as Warangal and Nalgonda, their work at getting rid of feudalism won the Reds much support. A congressman visiting the area admitted that "every housewife silently rendered valuable assistance to the communists. Innocent looking villagers extended active sympathy to the communists."[31]

Their successes in Hyderabad had encouraged the communists to think of a countrywide peasant revolution. Telengana, they hoped, would be the beginning of a Red India. The party unveiled its new line at a secret conference held in Calcutta in February 1948. The mood was set by a speaker who said that the "heroic people of Telengana" had shown the way "to freedom and real democracy"; they were the "real future of India and Pakistan." If only the communist cadres could "create this spirit of revolution among the masses, among the toiling people, we shall find reaction collapsing like a house of cards."[32]

At the meeting in Calcutta, the party elected a new general secretary, with P. C. Joshi giving way to B. T. Ranadive. Ranadive was solemn and studious, unlike the playful, and lovable Joshi. (Both, notably, were upper-caste Hindus—as was typical of communist leaders of the day.)[33]

Joshi was a friend of Nehru who urged "loyal opposition" to the ruling Congress party. He argued that after the murder of Gandhi the survival of free India was at stake. He supervised the production of a party pamphlet whose title proclaimed, "We Shall Defend the Nehru Government" (against the forces of Hindu revivalism). Ranadive, however, was a hardliner who believed that India was controlled by a bourgeois government beholden to the imperialists. Now, in a complete about-face, the party described Nehru as a lackey of American imperialism. The pamphlet printed by the former general secretary was pulped. Joshi himself was demoted to an ordinary member, and a whole series of charges were levelled against him. He was called a reformist who had encouraged the growth of "anti-revolutionary" tendencies in the party.[34]

The new line of the Communist Party of India was that Nehru's government had joined the Anglo-American alliance in an "irreconcilable conflict" with the "democratic camp" led by the Soviet Union. The scattered disillusionment with the Congress was taken by B. T. Ranadive as a sign of a "mounting revolutionary upsurge." From his underground hideout, he called for a general strike and peasant uprisings across the country. Communist circulars urged their cadres to "fraternize with the revolutionary labourers in the factories and the students in the streets," and to "turn your guns and bayonets and fire upon the Congress fascists." The ultimate aim was to "destroy the murderous Congress government."[35]

Ranadive and his men took heart from the victory of the communists in China. In September 1949, shortly after Mao Zedong had come to power, Ranadive wrote him a letter of congratulation, saying that "the toiling masses of India feel jubilant over this great victory. They know it hastens their own liberation. They are inspired by it to fight more determinedly and courageously their battle for ending the present regime [in India] and establishing the rule of People's Democracy."[36] The Indian communists were also urged on by Russian theoreticians, who believed that "the political regime established in India is similar in many respects to the anti-popular, reactionary regime which existed in Kuomintang China."[37] The embassy of the Soviet Union in Delhi itself had a large staff, so that (in the words of a senior civil servant) the Indian "communist movement [was] receiving first class direction on the spot."[38]

The communists had declared war on the Indian state. The government responded with all the force at its command. As many as 50,000 party men and sympathizers were arrested and detained. In Hyderabad the police arrested important leaders of communist *dalams*, although Ravi Narayan Reddy, "the father of the Communist movement in Deccan, [was] still at large." The military governor, J. N. Chaudhuri, launched a propaganda war against the Communists. Telugu pamphlets dropped on the villages announced that the nizam's private lands would be distributed to the peasantry. Theatrical companies touring the villages presented the government case through drama and pantomime. In one play, Chaudhuri was portrayed as a Hindu deity; the Communists were portrayed as demons.[39]

The propaganda and the repression had their effect. Membership in the Communist party dropped from 89,000 in 1948 to 20,000 two years later. The government's counteroffensive had exposed the "lack of popular empathy it experienced for its unbridled revolutionism." It appears that the Communist party had grossly underestimated the hold of the Congress over the Indian people.[40]

Even as the communists were losing their influence, a band of extremists gathered strength on the right. This was the Rashtriya Swayamsevak Sangh (RSS). After the murder of Mahatma Gandhi in January 1948, the RSS was banned by the government. Although not directly involved in the assassination, the organization had been active in the violence in the Punjab, and had much support among disaffected refugees. Its world view was akin to Nathuram Godse's; and there was a widespread rumour that RSS men had privately celebrated his killing of the Mahatma. Writing to the Punjab government two weeks after Gandhi's death, Nehru said that "we have had enough suffering already in India because of the activities of the R. S. S. and like groups. . . . These people have the blood of Mahatma Gandhi on their hands, and pious disclaimers and disassociation now have no meaning."[41]

So the RSS was banned, and its cadres were arrested. However, after a year the government decided to make the organization legal once more. Its head, M. S. Golwalkar, had now agreed to ask his men to profess loyalty to the constitution of India and the national flag, and to restrict the activities of the RSS "to the cultural sphere abjuring violence or secrecy." Golwalkar promised the home minister, Vallabhbhai Patel, that "while rendering help to the people in distress, we have laid our emphasis on promoting peace in the country." Patel himself had mixed feelings about the RSS. While deploring their anti-Muslim rhetoric, he admired their dedication and discipline. In lifting the ban, he advised the RSS "that the only way for them is to reform the Congress from within, if they think the Congress is going on the wrong path."[42]

After the RSS was made legal, Golwalkar made a "triumphal" speaking tour across the country, drawing "mammoth crowds." The RSS, wrote one observer, "has emerged from its recent ordeal with a mass support that other parties, not excluding the Congress, might well envy and guard against, while it is yet time, unless they wish to see the country delivered to a Hindu irredentism that will lead it to certain disaster." The RSS was the Hindu answer to the Muslim League, "imbued with aggressively communal ideas, and with the determination that there must be no compromise with the ideal of a pure and predominant Hindu culture in Bharat-Varsh."[43]

Like the communist B. T. Ranadive, Golwalkar was an upper-caste Maharashtrian. Both men were relatively young—in their early forties—and both commanded the loyalty of hundreds of cadres a good deal younger than themselves. The RSS and the communists likewise drew on the energy and idealism of youth, and on its fanaticism too. In the early years of Indian independence, these two groups were the most motivated opponents of the ruling Congress party.

At the helm of the Congress was the prime minister Jawaharlal Nehru. In confronting the radicals of left and right, Nehru had two handicaps. First, he was a moderate, and the middle ground is generally not conducive to the kind of stirring rhetoric that compels men to act. Second, he and his colleagues were far older than their political rivals. In 1949 Nehru himself was sixty, an age at which a Hindu male is supposed to retire from the workaday world and take *sanyas*.

Nehru saw the RSS as the greater of the two threats. Others in his government, notably Vallabhbhai Patel, disagreed. Intriguingly, M. S. Golwalkar had written to Patel offering help in battling the common enemy—the communists. "If we utilize the power of your Government and the cultural strength of our organization," he wrote, "we will be able to get rid of the [communist] menace very soon."[44] This idea of a joint front appealed to Patel; indeed, it may have been one reason he contemplated absorbing the RSS within the Congress.

As it happened, members of the RSS were not admitted to the Congress. But Golwalkar remained at large, free to present his views to those who chose to hear them. In the first week of November 1949, he addressed a crowd of 100,000 at Shivaji Park in Bombay. A reporter in attendance described him as "a man of medium height with a sunken chest, long uncut and unkempt hair and a flowing beard." He looked for all the world like a harmless Hindu ascetic, except that "the black piercing eyes deep in the sockets gave the [RSS] Chief the typical look of a black magician about to pull out a blood curdling trick." Before he spoke, Golwalkar was presented with garlands by clubs specializing in bodybuilding and the martial arts. The speech itself "waxed hot" on the virtues of Hindu culture. As the reporter put it, "He had a cure-all for the ills of the nation: Make Golwalkar the Fuehrer of All India."[45]

A week later Jawaharlal Nehru came to speak in Bombay. The venue was the same: Shivaji Park, an oasis of green grass in the heart of the densely packed, middle-class, chiefly Marathi-speaking housing colonies of central Bombay. Nehru used the same microphone as Golwalkar, one supplied by the Motwane Chicago Telephone and Radio Company. But his message was emphatically different, for he spoke of the need to maintain social peace within India as well as peace between warring nations abroad.

Nehru's talk was delivered on his sixtieth birthday, 14 November 1949. He could not have wished for a better present: the abundant affection of his countrymen. The prime minister was due to arrive in Bombay at 4:30 p.m. An hour before his plane landed at Santa Cruz airport, "people started closing their shops and stopped working so that they might be able to see Pandit Nehru. They jammed the sidewalks and the streets long before the open maroon car carrying Panditji sped by. As he passed by a tumultuous waving and rejoicing was noticed."

An hour later, after a wash and a change of clothes, Nehru arrived at Shivaji Park. Here, "a record crowd [had] stampeded the vast maidan grounds to hear him. More than six lakhs [600,000] assembled that memorable evening. There was one seething mass of humanity; men, women and children who had come . . . to hear him for they still had faith in his leadership and ability to show the way in these hard and try-ing times ahead of us."[46]

A hundred thousand people had come to hear Golwalkar espouse the idea of a Hindu theocratic state for India. But in this Maharashtrian stronghold, six times as many people came to cheer as the prime minister defended democracy against absolutism, and secularism against Hindu chauvinism. In this contest between competing ideas of India, Jawaharlal Nehru was winning hands down: for the time being, at any rate.

VII

Like the integration of the princely states, the rehabilitation of refugees was a political problem unprecedented in nature and scope. The migrants into India from Pakistan, wrote one of their number, were "like the fallen autumn leaves in the wind or bits of stray newspaper flying hither and thither in the blown dust." For "those who have come away safe in limb and mind are without any bearings and without any roots."[47]

The refugees who came into India after independence numbered close to 8 million. This was greater than the populations of small Euro-pean countries like Austria and Norway, and as much as the population of a continent such as Australia. These people were resettled with time, cash, effort, and—not least—idealism.

There was indeed much heroism and grandeur in the building of a new India. There were also errors and mistakes, loose ends that re-mained untied. Pain and suffering were involved in the extinguishing of the princely order, and in the resettlement of the refugees. Yet both tasks were, in the end, accomplished.

Notably, the actors in this complicated and tortuous process were all Indian. This, at least on the British side, was completely unanticipated. A former governor of Bengal had written in 1947:

The end of British political control in India will not mean the depar-ture of the British, as individuals, from India. It will not be possible for many years ahead for India to do without a large number of Brit-ish individuals in government service. They will remain under con-tract to the Government of India and to the governments of the Provinces and States in a wide range of administrative, legal, medical, police and professional and technical appointments. It will be many years before India will be able to fill, from amongst her own sons, all the many senior positions under the government that the administration of her 400 million people makes necessary.[48]

Actually, that help was not asked for; nor was it needed. Admittedly, the rulers had left behind a set of functioning institutions: the civil service, the police, the judiciary, and the railroads, among others. At independence, the government of India invited British members of the ICS to stay on; but with only a few exceptions, they all left for home, along with their colleagues in the other services. Thus it came to be that the heroes remembered in these pages were all Indians: politicians like Nehru and Patel, bureaucrats like Tarlok Singh and V. P. Menon, social workers like Kamala Devi Chattopadhyaya and Mridula Sarabhai. So too were the countless others who were unnamed then and continue to be unknown now: the officials who took in and acted on applications for land allotment, the officials who built houses and ran hospitals and schools, the officials who sat in courts and secretariats. Also overwhelmingly Indian were the social workers who cajoled, consoled, and cared for the refugees.

Albert Mayer, an American architect who worked in India in the early years of independence, has written with feeling of the calibre and idealism of those around him. "The number and kinds of people I've seen, their ability, outlook, energy, and devotion; the tingling atmosphere of plans and expectation and uncertainty; and yet the calm and self-possession—what it adds up to is being present at the birth of a nation."[49]

In the history of nation-building only the Soviet experiment bears comparison with the Indian. There too, a sense of unity had to be forged between many diverse ethnic groups, religions, linguistic communities, and social classes. The scale—geographic as well as demographic—was comparably large. The raw material the state had to work with was equally unpropitious: a people divided by faith, and ridden by debt and disease.

India after the Second World War was much like the Soviet Union after the First World War. A nation was being built out of its fragments. In this case, however, the process was unaided by the extermination of class enemies or the creation of gulags.

6

IDEAS *of* INDIA

In Governance are realised all the forms of renunciation; in
Governance are united all the sacraments; in Governance are
combined all knowledge; in Governance are centred all the
Worlds.

The *Mahabharata*

Constitutional morality is not a natural sentiment.
It has to be cultivated. We must realize that our people
have yet to learn it. Democracy in India is only a
top-dressing on an Indian soil, which is essentially
undemocratic.

B. R. AMBEDKAR

I

WITH 395 ARTICLES and twelve schedules, the constitution of India is probably the longest in the world. It went
into effect in January 1950, having been framed over a
period of three years, between December 1946 and December 1949.
During this time its drafts were discussed clause by clause in the Constituent Assembly of India. In all, the assembly held eleven sessions,
which consumed 165 days. In between the sessions the work of revis-
ing and refining the drafts was carried out by various committees and
subcommittees.

The proceedings of the Constituent Assembly of India were printed
in eleven bulky volumes. These volumes—some of which exceed 1,000
pages—are testimony to the loquaciousness of Indians, but also to their insight, intelligence, passion, and sense of humour. The volumes are a little-
known treasure trove, invaluable to the historian, and also a potential
source of enlightenment to the interested citizen. In them we find many
competing ideas of the nation, of what language it should speak, what political and economic system it should follow, and what moral values it
should uphold or disavow.

II

From the early 1930s, the Congress had insisted that Indians would frame their own constitution. In 1946 Lord Wavell finally gave in to the demand. The members of the Constituent Assembly were chosen on the basis of that year's provincial elections. However, the Muslim League boycotted the early sessions, making it effectively a one-party show.

The first meeting of the Constituent Assembly was held on 9 December 1946. A sense of anticipation was in the air. The top congressmen, such as Nehru and Patel, sat on the front benches. But to show that it was not in principle a one-party show, known opponents of the Congress, such as Sarat Bose of Bengal, were also given seats in front. A nationalist newspaper noted that "nine women members were present adding colour" to a scene dominated by Gandhi caps and Nehru jackets.[1]

Apart from the members sent by the provinces of British India, the Constituent Assembly also had representatives of the princely states, sent as these states joined the Indian Union one by one. Of the members of the Assembly, 82% were members of the Congress. However, since the party was itself a broad church they held a wide range of views. Some were atheists and secularists; others "technically members of the Congress but spiritually members of the R. S. S. and the Hindu Mahasabha."[2] Some were socialists in their economic philosophy, others defenders of the rights of landlords. Aside from the diversity within it, the Congress also nominated independent members of different castes and religious groups, and ensured the representation of women. It particularly sought out experts in the law. Thus "there was hardly any shade of public opinion not represented in the Assembly."[3]

This expansion of the social base of the assembly was in part an answer to British criticism. Winston Churchill, in particular, had poured scorn on the idea of a Constituent Assembly dominated by "one major community in India," the caste Hindus. In his view, the Congress was not a truly representative party, but rather a mouthpiece of "actively organised and engineered minorities who, having seized upon power by force, or fraud or chicanery, go forward and use that power in the name of vast masses with whom they have long since lost all effective connection."[4]

The process was made more participatory by asking for submissions from the public at large. There were hundreds of responses, a sampling of which gives a clue to the interests the lawmakers had to take account of. Thus the All India Varnashrama Swarajya Sangh (based in Calcutta) asked that the Constitution "be based on the principles laid down in ancient Hindu works." The prohibition of cow-slaughter and the closing down of abatoirs was particularly recommended. Low-caste groups demanded an end to "ill treatment by upper caste people" and "reservation of separate seats on the basis of their population in legislature, government departments, and local bodies, etc." Linguistic minorities asked for "freedom of speech in [the] mother tongue" and the "redistribution of provinces on linguistic basis." Religious minorities asked for special safeguards. And bodies as varied as the District Teachers Guild of Vizianagaram and the Central Jewish Board of Bombay requested "adequate representation" of their kind "on all public bodies including legislatures etc."[5]

These submissions testify to the baffling heterogeneity of India, but also to the precocious existence of a "rights culture" among Indians. They were many; they were divided; above all, they were vocal. The constitution of India had to adjudicate among thousands of competing claims and demands. The task was made no easier by the turmoil of the times. The Constituent Assembly met between 1946 and 1949, against a backdrop of food shortages, religious riots, refugee resettlement, class war, and feudal intransigence. As one historian has put it, "Fundamental Rights were to be framed among the carnage of Fundamental Wrongs."[6]

III

The Constituent Assembly had more than 300 members in all. In his history of the constitution, Granville Austin identifies twenty as being the most influential. Of these, as many as twelve had law degrees. These included those Congress stalwarts Jawaharlal Nehru, Vallabhbhai Patel, and Rajendra Prasad.

Nehru's first major speech in the assembly was on 13 December 1946, when he moved the "Objectives Resolution." This proclaimed India as an "independent sovereign republic," guaranteeing its citizens "justice, social, economic and political; equality of status; of opportunity, and before the law; freedom of thought, expression, belief, faith, worship, vocation, association and action, subject to law and public morality"—all this while assuring that "adequate safeguards shall be provided for minorities, backward and tribal areas, and depressed and other backward classes." In moving the resolution, Nehru invoked the spirit of Gandhi and the "great past of India," as well as modern precedents such as the French, American, and Russian revolutions.[7]

Nine months later Nehru spoke again in the same columned hall, at midnight, when he asked Indians to redeem their tryst with destiny. In between, on 22 July 1947, he had moved a resolution proposing that the national flag of India be a "horizontal tricolour of saffron, white and dark green in equal proportion," with a wheel in navy blue at the centre. On this occasion Nehru led a chorus of competitive patriotism, with each subsequent speaker seeking to see in the colours of the flag something special about his own community's contribution to India.[8]

The speeches of symbolic importance were naturally made by Nehru. Just as naturally, the bulk of the backroom work was done by Vallabhbhai Patel. A consummate committee man, Patel played a key role in the drafting of the various reports. It was Patel, rather than the less patient Nehru, who worked at mediating between warring groups, taking recalcitrant members on his morning walks and making them see the larger point of view. It was also Patel who moved one of the more contentious resolutions: that pertaining to minority rights.[9]

The third congressman of importance was the president of the Constituent Assembly, Rajendra Prasad. He was nominated to the office on the second day and held it with dignity until the end. His was an unenviable task, for Indians are better speakers than listeners, and Indian politicians especially so. Prasad had to keep the peace between quarrelsome members and (what was as difficult) keep to the clock with men who sometimes had little sense of what was trifling and what significant.

Outside this Congress Trinity the most crucial member of the assembly was the brilliant low-caste lawyer B. R. Ambedkar. Ambedkar was law minister in the Union government, and also chairman of the Drafting Committee for the constitution. Serving with him were two other formidable minds: K. M. Munshi, a Gujarati polymath who was a novelist and lawyer as well as freedom fighter; and Alladi Krishnaswami Aiyar, a Tamil who for fifteen years had served as advocate general of the Madras presidency.

To these six men one must add a seventh who was not a member of the assembly at all. This was B. N. Rau, who served as constitutional adviser to the government of India. In a long career in the Indian civil service Rau had a series of legal appointments. On the basis of his learning and experience, and a fresh study tour of western democracies, Rau prepared a series of notes for Ambedkar and his team to chew on. Rau, in turn, was assisted by the chief draughtsman, S. N. Mukherjee, whose "ability to put the most intricate proposals in the simplest and clearest legal form can rarely be equalled."[10]

IV

Moral vision, political skill, and legal acumen were all brought together in the framing of the Indian constitution. This was a coming together of what Granville Austin has called the "national" and "social" revolutions.[11] The national revolution focused on democracy and liberty—which the experience of colonial rule had denied to all Indians—whereas the social revolution focused on emancipation and equality, which tradition and scripture had withheld from women and low castes.

Could these twin revolutions be brought about by indigenous methods? Some people advocated a "Gandhian constitution," based on a revived panchayat raj system, with the village as the basic unit of politics and governance. This was sharply attacked by B. R. Ambedkar, who held that "these village republics have been the ruination of India." Ambedkar was "surprised that those who condemn Provincialism and communalism should come forward as champions of the village. What is the village but a sink of localism, a den of ignorance, narrow-mindedness and communalism?"[12]

These remarks provoked outrage in some quarters. The socialist H. V. Kamath dismissed Ambedkar's attitude as "typical of the urban highbrow." The peasant leader N. G. Ranga said that Ambedkar's comments showed his ignorance of Indian history. "All the democratic traditions of our country has (sic) been lost on him. If he had only known the achievements of the village panchayats in Southern India over a period of a millenium, he would not have said those things."[13] However, the feisty female member from the United Provinces, Begum Aizaz Rasul, "entirely agreed" with Ambedkar. As she saw it, the "modern tendency is towards the rights of the citizen as against any corporate body and village panchayats can be very autocratic."[14]

Ultimately, the individual, rather than the village, was chosen as the unit. In other respects, too, the constitution was to look toward Euro-American rather than Indian precedents. The American presidential system was considered and rejected, as was the Swiss method of directly electing cabinet ministers. Several members argued for proportional representation (PR), but this was never taken very seriously. Another former British colony, Ireland, had adopted PR, but when the constitutional adviser, B. N. Rau, visited Dublin, de Valera himself said that he wished the Irish had adopted the British "first-past-the-post" system of elections and the British cabinet system. These, he felt, made for a strong government. In India, where the number of competing interest groups was immeasurably larger, it made even more sense to follow the British model.[15]

The lower house of the Indian Parliament, as well as the lower houses in
the provinces, were to be chosen on the basis of universal adult franchise.
After much discussion, Parliament, as well as most provinces, decided
also to have a second chamber to act as a check on excesses of democratic zeal. Its members were chosen through indirect election, in the
case of the upper house of Parliament by the state legislatures.

While the cabinet was headed by a prime minister, the head of state
was a president elected by a college comprising the national and provincial legislatures. The president would be the commander-in-chief of the
armed forces, and had the power to refer bills back to Parliament. This
was a post of "great authority and dignity," but, like the British monarchy, one with "no real power."[16] (In the provinces, a governor nominated
by the central government played a role comparable to the president's.)
The constitution provided for an independent election commission, and
an independent comptroller general of accounts. To protect the judiciary
from party politics, judges were to be appointed by the president in consultation with the chief justice; and their salaries were not decided by
Parliament but charged directly to the treasury. The supreme court in
Delhi was seen both as the guardian of the social revolution and as the
guarantor of civil and minority rights. It was endowed with broad ap-
pellate jurisdiction—any civil or criminal case involving an interpretation of the constitution could be referred to it.

The constitution mandated a complex system of fiscal federalism.
With some taxes (for instance, customs duties and company taxes) the
Centre retained all the proceeds; with others (such as income taxes and
excise duties), it shared the proceeds with the states; with still others
(e.g., estate taxes), it assigned the proceeds wholly to the states. The states,
meanwhile, could levy and collect certain taxes on their own: these included land and property taxes, the sales tax, and the hugely profitable
tax on bottled liquor.

These financial provisions borrowed heavily from the Government
of India Act of 1935. The "conscience of the Constitution"[17] meanwhile,
was contained in Parts III and IV, outlining a series of Fundamental
Rights and Directive Principles. The Fundamental Rights, which were
enforceable in a court of law, derived from the negative obligations of
the state not to encroach on or stifle personal liberty, and the positive
obligation to protect individuals and groups from arbitrary state action.
The rights defined included freedom and equality before the law, the
cultural rights of minorities, and the prohibition of such practices as untouchability and forced labour.[18] The Directive Principles, which were

not justiciable, derived from the positive obligations of the state to provide for a more fulfilling life for the citizen. They were a curious amalgam. Some principles were a concession to the socialist wing of the Congress, others (such as the ban on cow-slaughter) to the party's conservative faction.[19]

To the unprejudiced eye, the constitition was an adaptation to Indian ends of western principles. Some patriots did not see it that way. They claimed that it was Indians who had invented adult suffrage. T. Prakasam spoke about an inscription on a 1,000-year-old Conjeevaram temple that mentioned an election held with leaves as ballot papers and pots as ballot boxes.[20] This kind of chauvinism was not the preserve of the south alone. The Hindi scholar Raghu Vira claimed that ancient India was "the originator of the Republican system of government" and "spread this system to the other parts of the world."[21]

Those who had looked closely at the provisions of the constitution could not thus console themselves. Mahavir Tyagi was "very much disappointed [to] see nothing Gandhian in this Constitution."[22] And K. Hanumanthaiya complained that while freedom fighters like himself had wanted "the music of *Veena* or *Sitar*," what they had got instead was "the music of an English band."[23]

V

The constitution of India sought both to promote national unity and to facilitate progressive social change. There was a fundamental right to propagate religion, but the state reserved to itself the right to impose legislation aimed at social reform (such as a uniform civil code). The Centre had the powers, through national planning, to redistribute resources away from richer provinces to poorer ones. The right of due process was not allowed in property legislation—another instance in which the social good as defined by the state took precedence over individual rights. Land reform laws were on the anvil in many provinces, and the government wanted to close the door to litigation by disaffected moneylenders and landlords.

Fundamental Rights were qualified and limited by needs of social reform, and also by considerations of security and public order. There were provisions for rights to be suspended in a "national emergency." And there was a clause allowing for "preventive detention" without trial. A veteran freedom fighter called this "the darkest blot on this Constitution." Having spent ten years of his own life in "dungeons and condemned cells in the

days of our slavery under the British," he knew "the tortures which detention without trial means and I can never reconcile myself to it."[24]

The constitution showed a certain bias toward the rights of the Union
of India over those of its constituent states. There was already a unitary
system in place, imposed by the colonial power. The violence of the times
gave a further push to centralization, now seen as necessary both to forestall chaos and to plan for the country's economic development.

The constitution provided for three lists of subjects: union, state,
and concurrent. The subjects in the first list (union) were the preserve of
the central government, while those in the second list (state) were vested
with the states. As for the third list (concurrent), here the Centre and the
states shared responsibility. However, many more items were placed exclusively under "union" than in other federations; and more were placed
under "concurrent" than the provinces wanted. The Union of India also
had control of minerals and key industries. And Article 356 gave the
Centre the power to take over a state administration on the recommendation of the governor.[25]

Provincial politicians fought hard for the rights of states—for fewer
items to be put under "concurrent" and "union." They asked for a greater
share of tax revenues. And they mounted an ideological attack on the
principle itself. A member from Orissa said that the constitution had "so
centralised power, that I am afraid, due to its very weight, the Centre is
likely to break." A member from Mysore thought that what was proposed was a "unitary" rather than "federal" constitution. Under its provisions "democracy is centred in Delhi and it is not allowed to work in
the same sense and spirit in the rest of the country."[26]

Perhaps the most eloquent defence of states' rights came from K. Santhanam of Madras. He thought that the fiscal provisions would make
provinces "beggars at the door of the Centre." In the United States, both
the federal government and the states could levy "all kinds of tax," but
here, crucial sources of revenue, such as the income tax, had been denied to the provinces. Besides, the Drafting Committee had tried "to
burden the Centre with all kinds of powers which it ought not to have."
These included "vagrancy," which had been taken away from the states
and put on the "concurrent" list. "Do you want all India to be bothered
about vagrants?" asked Santhanam sarcastically. As he put it, rather than
place an excessive load on the central government, "the initial responsibility for the well-being of the people of the provinces should rest with
the Provincial Governments."[27]

The next day, a member from the United Provinces answered these charges. Hearing Santhanam, he wondered whether it was not "India's age-old historical tendency of disintegrating that was speaking through these stalwarts." A strong Centre was an absolute imperative in these "times of stress and strain." Only a strong Centre would "be in a position to think and plan for the well being of the country as a whole."[28]

Members of the Drafting Committee vigorously defended the unitary bias of the constitution. In an early session, B. R. Ambedkar told the House that he wanted "a strong united Centre (*hear, hear*) much stronger than the Centre we had created under the Government of India Act of 1935."[29] And K. M. Munshi argued for the construction of "a federation with a centre as strong as we can make it."[30] In some matters Munshi was close to being a Hindu chauvinist; but here he found himself on the same side as the Muslims, for the horrific communal violence of 1946 and 1947 bore witness to the need for a strong Centre. In the words of Kazi Syed Karimuddin, "everybody is not Pandit Jawaharlal Nehru" (in respect of his commitment to harmony between Hindus and Muslims). There were "weak and vacillating executives in all the Provinces," said Karimuddin. Thus "what we want today is a stable Government. What we want today is a patriotic Government. What we want today is a strong Government, an impartial and unbending executive, that does not bow before popular whims."[31]

VI

Much attention was paid by the Constituent Assembly to the rights of the minorities. The first extended discussion of the subject took place ten days after partition. Here, a Muslim from Madras, B. Pocker Bahadur, made a vigorous plea for the retention of separate electorates. "As matters stand at present in this country," he said, it was "very difficult" for non-Muslims "to realise the needs and requirements of the Muslim community." If separate electorates were abolished, then important groups would be "left feeling that they have not got an adequate voice in the governance of the country."[32]

The home minister, Sardar Patel, was deeply unsympathetic to this demand. Separate electorates had in the past led to the division of the country. "Those who want that kind of thing have a place in Pakistan, not here," thundered Patel, to a burst of applause. "Here, we are building a nation and we are laying the foundations of One Nation, and those who choose to divide again and sow the seeds of disruption will have no place, no quarter, here, and I must say that plainly enough."[33]

There were, however, some Muslims who from the start were opposed to separate electorates. These included Begum Aizaz Rasul. It was "absolutely meaningless" now to have reservation on the basis of religion, she said. Separate electorates were "a self-destructive weapon which separates the minorities from the majority for all time." The interests of the Muslims in a secular democracy were "absolutely identical" with those of other citizens.[34]

By 1949, Muslim members who had at first demanded separate electorates came around to Rasul's point of view. They sensed that reservation for Muslims "would be really harmful to the Muslims themselves." Instead, the Muslims should reconstitute themselves as voting blocs, so that in constituencies where they were numerous, no candidate could afford to ignore them. They could even come to "have a decisive voice in the elections" because "it may be that an apparently huge majority may at the end . . . find itself defeated by a single vote." Therefore, "the safety of the Muslims lies in intelligently playing their part and mixing themselves with the Hindus in public affairs."[35]

A vulnerable minority even more numerous than the Muslims were the women of India. The women members of the Constituent Assembly had come through the national movement, and were infected early with the spirit of unity. Thus Hansa Mehta of Bombay rejected reserved seats, quotas, or separate electorates. "We have never asked for privileges," she remarked. "What we have asked for is social justice, economic justice, and political justice. We have asked for that equality which alone can be the basis of mutual respect and understanding and without which real co-operation is not possible between man and woman."[36] Renuka Roy of Bengal agreed: unlike the "narrow suffragist movement[s]" of "many so-called enlightened nations," the women of India strove for "equality of status, for justice and for fairplay and most of all to be able to take their part in responsible work in the service of their country." For "ever since the start of the Womens' Movement in this country, women have been fundamentally opposed to special privileges and reservations."[37]

The only voice in favour of reservation for women was a man's. This was strange; stranger still was the logic of his argument. From his own "experience as a parliamentarian and a man of the world," said R. K. Chaudhuri,

I think it would be wise to provide for a women's constituency. When a woman asks for something, as we know, it is easy to get it and give it to her; but when she does not ask for anything in particular it becomes very difficult to find out what she wants. If you give them a special constituency they can have their scramble and fight there among themselves without coming into the general constituency. Otherwise we may at times feel weak and yield in their favour and give them seats which they are not entitled to.[38]

VII

There would be no reservation for Muslims and women. But the constitution did recommend reservation for untouchables. This was in acknowledgement of the horrific disabilities they had suffered, and also a bow toward Mahatma Gandhi, who had long held that true freedom, or Swaraj, would come only when Hindu society had rid itself of this evil. It was also Gandhi who had made popular a new term for "untouchables": Harijans, or children of God.

The constitution set aside seats in legislatures as well as jobs in government offices for the lowest castes. It also threw open Hindu temples to all castes, and asked for the abolition of untouchability in society at large. These provisions were very widely welcomed. Muniswamy Pillai of Madras remarked that "the fair name of India was a slur and a blot by having untouchability. . . . [G]reat saints tried their level best to abolish untouchability but it is given to this august Assembly and the new Constitution to say in loud terms that no more untouchability shall stay in our country."[39]

As H. J. Khandekar of the Central Provinces pointed out, untouchables were conspicuously under-represented in the upper echelons of the administration. In the provinces, where they might constitute as much as 25% of the population, there was often only one Harijan minister, whereas Brahmans, who made up only 2% of the population, might command two-thirds of the seats in the cabinet. Khandekar suggested that despite the public commitment of the Congress, "except for Mahatma Gandhi and ten or twenty other [upper-caste] persons there is none to think of the uplift of the Harijans in the true sense."

This member eloquently defended the extension of reservation to jobs in government. He alluded to the recent recruitment to the Indian administrative service, the successor to the ICS. Many Harijans were interviewed but rejected, on the grounds that their grades were not good enough. Addressing his upper-caste colleagues, Khandekar insisted:

> You are responsible for our being unfit today. We were suppressed for thousands of years. You engaged in your service to serve your own ends and suppressed us to such an extent that neither our minds nor our bodies and nor even our hearts work, nor are we able to march forward. This is the position. You have reduced us to such a position and then you say that we are not fit and that we have not secured the requisite marks. How can we secure them?[40]

The argument was hard, if not impossible, to refute. But some members warned against the possible abuse of the provisions. One thought that "those persons who are clamouring for these seats, for reservation, for consideration, represent a handful of persons, constituting the cream of Harijan society." These were the "politically powerful" among these groups.[41] For the left-wing congressman Mahavir Tyagi, reservation did not lead to real representation: "no caste ever gets any benefit from this reservation. It is the individual or family which gets benefits." Instead of caste, perhaps there might be reservation by class, such that "cobblers, fishermen and other such classes send their representatives through reservation because they are the ones who do not really get any representation."[42]

VIII

The first report on minority rights, made public in late August 1947, provided for reservation for untouchables only. Muslims were denied the right, as in the circumstances was to be expected. However, one member of the Constituent Assembly regretted that "the most needy, the most deserving group of Adibasis has been completely left out of the picture."[43]

The member was Jaipal Singh, himself an Adibasi, albeit of a rather special kind. Jaipal was a Munda from Chotanagpur, the forested plateau of south Bihar peopled by numerous tribes all more or less distinct from caste Hindu society. Sent by missionaries to study in Oxford, he made a name there as a superb hockey player. He obtained a blue, and went on to captain the Indian team that won the gold medal in the Olympic Games of 1928.

On his return to India, Jaipal did not, as his sponsors no doubt hoped, preach the gospels, but came to invent a kind of gospel of his own. This held that the tribals were the "original inhabitants" of the subcontinent—hence the term *adibasi* or *adivasi*, which means precisely that. Jaipal formed an Adivasi Mahasabha in 1938, which asked for a separate state of "Jharkhand," to be carved out of Bihar. To the tribals of Chotanagpur he was their *marang gomke*, or "great leader." In the Constituent Assembly he came to represent the tribals not just of his native plateau, but of all of India.[44]

Jaipal was a gifted speaker, whose interventions both enlivened and entertained the House. (In this respect, the church's loss was unquestionably politics' gain.) His first speech was made on 19 December 1946, when, in welcoming the Objectives Resolution, he provided a masterly summation of the *adivasi* case. "As a jungli, as an Adibasi," said Jaipal,

> I am not expected to understand the legal intricacies of the Resolution. But my common sense tells me that every one of us should march in that road to freedom and fight together. Sir, if there is any group of Indian people that has been shabbily treated it is my people. They have been disgracefully treated, neglected for the last 6,000 years. The history of the Indus Valley civilization, a child of which I am, shows quite clearly that it is the newcomers—most of you here are intruders as far as I am concerned—it is the newcomers who have driven away my people from the Indus Valley to the jungle fastness. . . . The whole history of my people is one of continuous exploitation and dispossession by the non-aboriginals of India punctuated by rebellions and disorder, and yet I take Pandit Jawahar Lal Nehru at his word. I take you all at your word that now we are going to start a new chapter, a new chapter of independent India where there is equality of opportunity, where no one would be neglected.[45]

Three years later, in the discussion on the draft constitution, Jaipal made a speech that was spirited in all senses of the word. Bowing to pressure by Gandhians, the prohibition of alcohol had been made a Directive Principle. This, said the *adivasi* leader, was an interference "with the religious rights of the most ancient people in the country." Drink was part of their festivals, their rituals, indeed their daily life. In West Bengal "it would be impossible for paddy to be transplanted if the Santhal does not get his rice beer. These ill-clad men . . . have to work knee-deep in water throughout the day, in drenching rain and in mud. What is it in the rice beer that keeps them alive? I wish the medical authorities in this country would carry out research in their laboratories to find out what it is that the rice beer contains, of which the Adibasis need so much and which keeps them against all manner of diseases."[46]

The Constituent Assembly had convened a subcommittee on tribal rights headed by the veteran social worker A. V. Thakkar. Its findings, and the words of Jaipal and others, sensitized the House to the tribal predicament. As a member from Bihar observed, "the tribal people have been made a pawn on the chess-board of provincial politics." There had been "exploitation on a mass scale; we must hang down our heads in shame."[47] "We" referred to Hindu society as a whole, which had sinned against *adivasis* by either ignoring them or exploiting them. It had done little to bring them modern facilities of education and health; it had colonized their land and forests; and it had brought them under a regime of usury and debt. And so, to make partial amends, tribals would also have seats in the legislature and jobs in government "reserved" for them.

IX

The most controversial subject in the Constituent Assembly was language: the language to be spoken in the House, the language in which the constitution would be written, the language that would be given the singular designation "national." On 10 December 1946, while the procedures of the House were still being discussed, R. V. Dhulekar of the United Provinces moved an amendment. When he began speaking in Hindustani, the chairman reminded him that many members did not know the language. This was Dhulekar's reply:

> People who do not know Hindustani have no right to stay in India. People who are present in this House to fashion a constitution for India and do not know Hindustani are not worthy to be members of this Assembly. They had better leave.

The remarks created a commotion in the House. "Order, order!" yelled the chairman, but Dhulekar continued:

> I move that the Procedure Committee should frame rules in Hindustani and not in English. As an Indian I appeal that we, who are out to win freedom for our country and are fighting for it should think and speak in our own language. We have all along been talking of America, Japan, Germany, Switzerland and the House of Commons. It has

given me a headache. I wonder why Indians do not speak in their own language. As an Indian I feel that the proceedings of the House should be conducted in Hindustani. We are not concerned with the history of the world. We have the history of our own country of millions of past years.

The printed proceedings continue:

> The Chairman: Order, order!
> Shri R. V. Dhulekar (speaking still in Hindustani): I request you to allow me to move my amendment.
> The Chairman: Order, order! I do not permit you to proceed further. The House is with me that you are out of order.[48]

At this point Jawaharlal Nehru went up to the rostrum and persuaded Dhulekar to return to his seat. Afterwards, Nehru told the errant member of the need to maintain discipline in the House. He told him that "this is not a public meeting in Jhansi that you should address 'Bhaio aur Behno' [brothers and sisters] and start lecturing at the top of your voice."[49]

But the issue would not go away. In one session, members urged the House to order the Delhi government to change all car license plates from English to Hindi.[50] More substantively, they demanded that the official version of the constitution be in Hindi, with an unofficial version in English. This demand the Drafting Committee did not accept, on the grounds that English was better placed to incorporate the technical and legal terms of the document. When a draft constitution was presented for discussion, members nevertheless asked for a discussion of each clause in Hindi. To adopt a document written in English, they said, would be "insulting."[51]

It is necessary, at this point, to distinguish between "Hindustani" and "Hindi." Hindustani, the lingua franca of much of northern India, was a unique amalgam of Hindi and Urdu. Hindi, written in the Devanagari script, drew heavily on Sanskrit, whereas Urdu, written in a modified Arabic script, drew on Persian and Arabic. From the nineteenth century on, as Hindu-Muslim tension grew in northern India, the two languages began to move further and further apart. On the one side, there arose a movement to root Hindi more firmly in Sanskrit; on the other, to root Urdu more firmly in the classical languages from which it drew. Especially in the literary world, a purified Hindi and a purified Urdu began to circulate.[52]

Through all this, the language of popular exchange remained Hindustani. This was intelligible to speakers of Hindi and Urdu, but also to the speakers of most of the major dialects of the Indo-Gangetic plain: Awadhi, Bhojpuri, Maithili, Marwari, and so on. However, Hindustani, Hindi, and Urdu were all virtually unknown in eastern and southern India. The languages spoken there were Assamese, Bengali, Kannada, Malayalam, Oriya, Tamil, and Telugu, each with a script and a sophisticated literary tradition of its own.

Under British rule, English had emerged as the language of higher education and administration. Would it remain in this position after the British left? The politicians of the north thought that it should be replaced by Hindi. The politicians and people of the south preferred that English continue as the vehicle of inter-provincial communication.

Jawaharlal Nehru himself was concerned about this question. In a long essay of the late 1930s he expressed his admiration for the major provincial languages. Without "infringing in the least on their domain" he thought there must still be an all-India language of communication. English was too far removed from the masses; so he opted instead for Hindustani, which he described as a "golden mean" between Hindi and Urdu. At this time, with partition not even a possibility, Nehru thought that both scripts could be used. Hindustani had a simple grammar and was relatively easy to learn, but to make it easier still, linguists could evolve a Basic Hindustani after the fashion of Basic English, to be promoted by the state in southern India.[53]

Like Nehru, Gandhi thought that Hindustani could unite north with south, and Hindu with Muslim. It, rather than English, should be made the *rashtrabhasha*, or national language. As he put it, "Urdu diction is used by Muslims in writing. Hindi diction is used by Sanskrit pundits. Hindustani is the sweet mingling of the two."[54] In 1945 he engaged in a lively exchange with Purushottamdas Tandon, a man who fought hard, not to say heroically, to rid Hindi of its foreign elements. Tandon was vice-president of the All India Hindi Literature Conference, which argued that Hindi with the Devanagari script alone should be the national language. Gandhi, who had long been a member of the Conference, was dismayed by its chauvinist drift. Since he believed that the Nagari and Urdu scripts should both be used, perhaps it was time to resign his membership. Tandon tried to dissuade him, but, as Gandhi put it, "How can

I ride two horses? Who will understand me when I say that *rashtrabha-sha*=Hindi and *rashtrabhasha*=Hindi+Urdu=Hindustani?"[55]

Partition more or less killed the case for Hindustani. The move to further "Sanskritize" Hindi gathered pace. One saw this at work in the Constituent Assembly, where early references were to Hindustani but later references were all to Hindi. After the division of the country the promoters of Hindi became even more fanatical. As Granville Austin observes, "The Hindi-wallahs were ready to risk splitting the Assembly and the country in their unreasoning pursuit of uniformity."[56] Their crusade provoked some of the most furious debates in the House. Hindustani was not acceptable to south Indians; Hindi was even less so. Whenever a member spoke in Hindi, another member would ask for a translation into English.[57] When the case was made for Hindi to be the sole national language, it was bitterly opposed. These remarks, by T. T. Krishnamachari of Madras, are representative:

> We disliked the English language in the past. I disliked it because I was forced to learn Shakespeare and Milton, for which I had no taste at all. . . . [I]f we are going to be compelled to learn Hindi . . . I would perhaps not be able to do it because of my age, and perhaps I would not be willing to do it because of the amount of constraint you put on me. . . . This kind of intolerance makes us fear that the strong Centre which we need, a strong Centre which is necessary will also mean the enslavement of people who do not speak the language of the Centre. I would, Sir, convey a warning on behalf of people of the South for the reason that there are already elements in South India who want separation . . . , and my honourable friends in U. P. do not help us in any way by flogging their idea [of] "Hindi Imperialism" to the maximum extent possible. Sir, it is up to my friends in U. P. to have a whole-India; it is up to them to have a Hindi-India. The choice is theirs.[58]

The assembly finally arrived at a compromise: "the official language of the Union shall be Hindi in the Devanagari script"; but for "fifteen years from the commencement of the Constitution, the English language shall continue to be used for all the official purposes of the Union for which it was being used immediately before such commencement."[59] Until 1965, at any rate, the notes and proceedings of the courts, the services, and the all-India bureaucracy would be conducted in English.

X

Mahatma Gandhi had once expressed his desire to see an untouchable
woman installed as the first president of India. That did not happen, but
some compensation was at hand when an untouchable man, Dr. B. R.
Ambedkar, was asked to serve as the chairman of the Drafting Committee of the Constituent Assembly.

On 25 November 1949, the day before the assembly wound up its
proceedings, Ambedkar made a moving speech summing up the work.[60]
He thanked his fellow members of the Drafting Committee, thanked
their support staff, and thanked a party of which he had been a lifelong
opponent. Without the quiet work in and outside the House by the Congress bosses, he would not have been able to make order out of chaos.
"It is because of the discipline of the Congress Party that the Drafting
Commitee was able to pilot the Constitution in the Assembly with the
sure knowledge as to the fate of each article and each amendment."

In a concession to patriotic nostalgia, Ambedkar then allowed that
some form of democracy was not unknown in ancient India. "There was
a time when India was studded with republics." Characteristically, he
invoked the Buddhists, who had furthered the democratic ideal in their
bhikku sanghas, which applied rules akin to parliamentary procedure—
votes, motions, resolutions, censures, and whips.

Ambedkar also assured the House that the federalism of the constitution in no way denied states' rights. It was mistaken, he said, to think
that there was "too much centralization and that the States have been reduced to Municipalities." The constitution had partitioned legislative and
executive authority, and the Centre could not on its own alter the boundary of this partition. In his words, "the Centre and the states are co-equal
in this matter."

Ambedkar ended his speech with three warnings about the future.
The first concerned the place of popular protest in a democracy. There
was no place for bloody revolution, of course, but in his view there was
no room for Gandhian methods either. "We must abandon the method
of civil disobedience, non-cooperation and satyagraha." Under an autocratic regime, there might be some justification for them, but not now,
when constitutional methods of redressal were available. Satyagraha
and the like, said Ambedkar, were "nothing but the Grammar of Anarchy and the sooner they are abandoned, the better for us."

The second warning concerned the unthinking submission to charismatic authority. Ambedkar quoted John Stuart Mill, who cautioned

citizens not "to lay their liberties at the feet of even a great man, or to trust him with powers which enable him to subvert their institutions." This warning was even more pertinent here than in England, for

> in India, Bhakti or what may be called the path of devotion or hero-worship, plays a part in its politics unequalled in magnitude by the part it plays in the politics of any other country in the world. Bhakti in religion may be the road to the salvation of a soul. But in politics, Bhakti or hero-worship is a sure road to degradation and to eventual dictatorship.

Ambedkar's final warning was to urge Indians not to be content with what he called "mere political democracy." India had gotten rid of alien rule, but it was still riven by inequality and hierarchy. Thus, once the country formally became a republic on 26 January 1950, it was

> going to enter a life of contradictions. In politics we will have equality and in social and economic life we will have inequality. In politics we will be recognizing the principle of one man one vote and one vote one value. In our social and economic life, we shall, by reason of our social and economic structure, continue to deny the principle of one man one value. How long shall we continue to live this life of contradictions? How long shall we continue to deny equality in our social and economic life? If we continue to deny it for long, we will do so only by putting our political democracy in peril.

XI

The Constituent Assembly of India was convened on 9 December 1946. Eight months previously, a new constitution had been presented for approval to the Japanese parliament, the Diet. This document had been almost wholly written by a group of foreigners. In early February 1946, twenty-four individuals—all Americans, and sixteen of them military officials—met in a converted ballroom in Tokyo. Here they sat for a week, before coming up with a constitution they thought the Japanese should adopt. This was then presented as a fait accompli to the local political leaders, who were allowed to "Japanize" the draft by translating it into the local tongue. The draft was also discussed in the Diet, but every amendment, even the most cosmetic, had to be approved beforehand by the American authorities.

The historian of this curious exercise writes that "no modern nation ever has rested on a more alien constitution."[61] The contrast with the Indian case could not be more striking. One constitution was written in the utmost secrecy; the other was drafted and discussed in the full glare of the press. One was finalized at breakneck speed, and written by foreigners. The other was written wholly by natives, and emerged from several years of reflection and debate. In fairness, though, one should admit that despite their different provenances, both constitutions were, in essence, liberal humanist credos. One could equally say of the Indian document what the American supervisor said of the Japanese draft, that "it constitutes a sharp swing from the extreme right in political thinking— yet yields nothing to the radical concept of the extreme left."[62]

Granville Austin has claimed that the framing of the Indian constitution was "perhaps the greatest political venture since that originated in Philadelphia in 1787." The outlining of a set of national ideals, and of an institutional mechanism to work toward them, was "a gigantic step for a people previously committed largely to irrational means of achieving other-wordly goals." For this, as the title of the last section of Austin's book proclaims, "the credit goes to the Indians."[63]

PART II

NEHRU'S INDIA

7

THE BIGGEST GAMBLE
in HISTORY

We are little men serving great causes, but because the cause is
great, something of that greatness falls upon us also.
                                    JAWAHARLAL NEHRU, speaking in 1946

India means only two things to us—famines and Nehru.
                                    American journalist, speaking in 1951

I

IN THE FIRST YEARS of freedom, the ruling Congress party faced
threats from without and within. As rebels against the Raj the nationalists had been self-sacrificing idealists; but as governors they came
rather to enjoy the fruits of office. As a veteran journalist from Madras put it, "in the post-Gandhian war for power the first casualty is decency."[1] *Time* magazine commented that after independence was achieved,
the Congress "found itself without a unifying purpose. It grew fat and
lazy, today harbors many time-serving office-holders [and] not a few
black-marketeers."[2] An influential weekly in Bombay remarked that
"from West Bengal to Uttar Pradesh, along the Gangetic Valley, the Congress is split. The old glamour of the premier political organization is fading, factions are becoming more acute and the party's unpopularity is
increasing."[3]

There were party factions at the district level as well as at the provincial level. However, the most portentous of the cleavages was between
the two biggest stalwarts, Pandit Jawaharlal Nehru and Sardar Vallabhbhai Patel. These two men, prime minister and deputy prime minister
respectively, had major differences in the first months of independence.
Gandhi's death made them come together again. But in 1949 and 1950
the differences resurfaced.

In character and personality Nehru and Patel were certainly a study
in contrasts. The prime minister was a Brahman from an upper-class

background whose father had also been a prominent figure in the nationalist movement. His deputy, on the other hand, was from a farming caste, and a descendant of a sepoy mutineer of 1857. Nehru loved good food and wine, appreciated fine art and literature, and had travelled widely abroad. Patel was a non-smoker, a vegetarian, a teetotaller, and on the whole "a hard task master with little time for play." He got up at 4 a.m., attended to his correspondence for an hour, and then went for a walk through the dimly lit streets of New Delhi. Besides, "a grave exterior and a cold and cynical physiognomy [made] the Sardar a really tough personality." In the words of the *New York Times*, he was "leather tough."

There were also similarites. Both Nehru and Patel had a daughter as housekeeper, companion, and chief confidante. Both were politicians of conspicuous integrity. And both were fierce patriots. But their ideas did not always mesh. As one observer rather delicately put it, "the opposition of the Sardar to the leftist elements in the country is one of the major problems of political adjustment facing India." He meant that Patel was friendly with capitalists while Nehru believed in state control of the economy; that Patel was more inclined to support the West in the emerging cold war; and that Patel was more forgiving of Hindu extremism and harsher on Pakistan.[4]

In late 1949, Nehru and Patel had a serious disagreement. In the new year, India would transform itself from a Dominion, where the British monarch was head of state, to a full-fledged republic. Nehru thought that when the governor generalship became a presidency, the incumbent, C. Rajagopalachari, should retain the job. "Rajaji" was an urbane scholar with whom the prime minister then got along very well. Patel, however, preferred Rajendra Prasad, who was close to him, and who also had wider acceptance within the Congress party. Nehru had assured Rajaji that he would be president; but much to his annoyance, and embarrassment, Patel got the rank and file in Congress to put Prasad's name forward instead.[5]

The original date of Indian independence, 26 January, was chosen as the first Republic Day. The new head of state, Rajendra Prasad, took the salute in what was to become an annual and ever more spectacular parade. Three thousand men of the armed forces marched before the president. The artillery fired a thirty-one-gun salute, while Liberator planes of the Indian air force flew overhead. Gandhi's India was announcing itself as a sovereign nation state.[6]

Round one had gone to Patel. A few months later commenced round two, the battle for the presidency of the Indian National Congress. For this post Patel had put forward Purushottamdas Tandon, a veteran congressman from the United Provinces—indeed, from the prime minister's own hometown, Allahabad. Tandon and Nehru were personal friends, but hardly ideological bedfellows. The presidential candidate was "a bearded, venerable orthodox Hindu . . . who admirably represented the extreme communalist wing of the [Congress] party." He was, in sum, "a personification of political and social anachronisms," an "anti-Muslim and pro-caste Hindu" who stood "for the resurrection of a dead culture and a long extinct system of society."[7]

Nehru had previously criticized Tandon for his desire to impose Hindi on regions of India that did not know the language. He was particularly upset when Tandon addressed a conference of refugees and spoke of revenge against Pakistan. India, Nehru believed, needed a healing touch, a policy of reconciliation between Hindus and Muslims. The election of Tandon as president of the premier political party, the prime minister's own party, would send all the wrong signals.

When the election for the congressional presidency was held in August 1950, Tandon comfortably won. Nehru now wrote to Rajagopalachari that the result was "the clearest of indications that Tandon's election is considered more important than my presence in the Govt. or the Congress." "All my instincts," he said, "tell me that I have completely exhausted my utility both in the Congress and Govt." The next day he wrote again to Rajaji, saying: "I am feeling tired out—physically and mentally. I do not think I can function with any satisfaction to myself in future."[8]

Rajaji now tried to work out a compromise between the two factions. Patel was amenable, suggesting a joint statement under both their names, in which he and Nehru would proclaim their adherence to certain fundamentals of Congress policy. The prime minister, however, decided to go it alone. After two weeks of contemplation he had decided to exchange resignation for truculence. On 13 September 1950 he issued a statement to the press deploring the fact that "communalist and reactionary forces have openly expressed their joy" at Tandon's victory. He was distressed, he said, that the "spirit of communalism and revivalism ha[d] gradually invaded the Congress, and sometimes affects Government policy." But unlike Pakistan, India was a secular state. "We have to treat our minorities in exactly the same way as we treat the majority," insisted Nehru. "Indeed, fair treatment is not enough; we have to make them feel that they are so treated." Now, "in view of the prevailing confusion and the threat of false doctrine, it has become essential that the Congress should declare its policy in this matter in the clearest and most unambiguous terms."[9]

Nehru felt that it was the responsibility of the Congress and the government to make the Muslims in India feel secure. Patel, on the other hand, was inclined to place the responsibility on the minorities themselves. He had once told Nehru that the "Muslim citizens in India [had] a responsibility to remove the doubts and misgivings entertained by a large section of the people about their loyalty founded largely on their past association with the demand for Pakistan and the unfortunate activities of some of them."[10]

On the question of minorities, as on other matters of philosophy and policy, Nehru and Patel would never completely see eye to eye. Now, however, in the aftermath of the bitter contest for the Congress presidency, Patel did not press the point, for he knew that the destruction of their party might very well mean the destruction of India. He told congressmen who visited him to "do what Jawaharlal says" and to "pay no attention to this controversy." On 2 October, while inaugurating a women's centre in Indore, he used the occasion—the anniversary of Gandhi's birth—to affirm his loyalty to the prime minister. He described himself in his speech as merely one of the many non-violent soldiers in Gandhi's army. Now, that the Mahatma was gone, "Jawaharlal Nehru is our leader," said Patel. "Bapu [Gandhi] appointed him as his successor and had even proclaimed him as such. It is the duty of all Bapu's soldiers to carry out his bequest. . . . I am not a disloyal soldier."[11]

Such is the evidence placed before us by Patel's biographer, Rajmohan Gandhi. It confirms in fact what Nehru's biographer (Sarvepalli Gopal) had expressed in feeling: that what forestalled "an open rupture" between the two men "was mutual regard and Patel's stoic decency."[12] Patel remembered his promise to Gandhi to work along with Jawaharlal. And by the time of the controversy over the Congress presidency he was also a very sick man. It was from his bed that he wrote a handwritten letter greeting Nehru on his birthday, 14 November. A week later, when the prime minister visited him at his home, Patel said: "I want to talk to you alone when I get a little strength. . . . I have a feeling that you are losing confidence in me." "I have been losing confidence in myself," answered Nehru.[13]

Three weeks later Patel was dead. It fell to the prime minister to draft the cabinet resolution mourning his passing. Nehru singled out his devotion to a "united and strong India," and his "genius" in solving the complicated problem of the princely states. To Nehru, Patel was both comrade and rival; but to their compatriots he was "an unmatched warrior in the cause of freedom, a lover of India, a great servant of the people and a statesman of genius and mighty achievement."[14]

II

Vallabhbhai Patel's death in December 1950 removed the one congressman of equal standing with Nehru. No longer were there two power centres within India's ruling party. However, the prime minister still had to contend with two somewhat lesser rivals; the president of the Congress, Purushottamdas Tandon; and the president of the republic, Rajendra Prasad. Nehru's biographer says of Prasad that he was "prominent in the ranks of medievalism."[15] That judgement is perhaps excessively harsh on a patriot who had sacrificed much in the cause of Indian freedom. Nonetheless, it was clear that the prime minister and the president differed on some crucial subjects, such as the place of religion in public life.

These differences came to a head in the spring of 1951, when the president was asked to inaugurate the newly restored Somnath temple in Gujarat. Once fabled for its wealth, Somnath had been raided several times by Muslim chiefs, including the notorious eleventh-century marauder Mahmud of Ghazni. Each time the temple was razed it was rebuilt. Then the Mughal Emperor Aurangzeb ordered its total destruction. It lay in ruins for two-and-a-half centuries, until Sardar Patel visited it in September 1947 and promised help in its reconstruction. Patel's colleague K. M. Munshi then took charge of the rebuilding.[16]

When the president of India chose to dignify the temple's consecration by his presence, Nehru was appalled. He wrote to Prasad advising him not to participate in the "spectacular opening of the Somnath temple [which] . . . unfortunately has a number of implications. Personally, I thought that this was no time to lay stress on large scale building operations at Somnath. This could have been done gradually and more effectively later. However, this has been done. [Still] I feel that it would be better if you did not preside over this function."[17]

Prasad disregarded the advice and went to Somnath. To his credit, however, his speech there stressed the Gandhian ideal of interfaith harmony. True, he nostalgically evoked a golden age when the gold in India's temples symbolized great wealth and prosperity. The lesson from

Somnath's later history, however, was that "religious intolerance only foments hatred and immoral conduct." By the same token, the lesson of its reconstruction was not to "open old wounds, which have healed to some extent over the centuries," but rather to "help each caste and community to obtain full freedom." Asking for "complete religious tolerance," the president urged his audience to "try to understand the great essence of religion," "that it is not compulsory to follow a single path to realize Truth and God." For "just as all the rivers mingle together in the vast ocean, similarly different religions help men to reach God."[18]

One does not know whether Nehru read the speech. In any case, he would have preferred for Prasad not to go at all. The prime minister thought that public officials should never *publicly* associate with faiths and shrines. The president, on the other hand, believed that they should be equally and publicly respectful of all. Although he was a Hindu, said Prasad at Somnath, "I respect all religions and on occasion visit a church, a mosque, a dargah and a gurdwara."

Meanwhile, the growing Hindu tint of the Congress had led to the departure of some of its most effervescent leaders. In 1948, a group of brilliant young congressmen had left to start the Socialist party. Now, in June 1951, the respected Gandhian J. B. Kripalani left to form his Kisan Majdoor Praja Party (KMPP), which stood for the interests of farmers, workers, and other toiling people. Like the socialists, Kripalani claimed that the Congress under Purushottamdas Tandon had become a deeply conservative organization.

As it happened, the formation of the KMPP strengthened Nehru's hand against Tandon. The Congress, he could now say, had to move away from the reactionary path it had recently taken, and reclaim its democratic and inclusive heritage. In September, when the All India Congress Committee (AICC) met in Bangalore, Nehru forced a showdown with Tandon and his supporters. The rank and file of the party were increasingly concerned with the upcoming general elections. And as a southern journalist pointed out, it was clear that the AICC would back the prime minister against Tandon, if only because "the Congress President is no vote-getter." By contrast, "Pandit Nehru is unequalled as a vote-catcher. On the eve of the general elections, it is the votes that count and Pandit Nehru has a value to the Congress which none else possesses."[19]

That indeed, is what happened in Bangalore, where Tandon resigned as president of the Congress, with Nehru being elected in his place. As head of both party and government, "Nehru could now wage full war against all communal elements in the country."[20] The first battle in this war would be the general elections of 1952.

III

India's first general elections were, among other things, an act of faith. A newly independent country chose to move straight into universal adult franchise, rather than—as was the case in the West—at first reserve the right to vote to men of property, with the working class and women granted the right much later. India became free in August 1947, and two years later set up an Election Commission. In March 1950 Sukumar Sen was appointed chief election commissioner. The next month the Representation of the People Act was passed in Parliament. In proposing the act, the prime minister, Jawaharlal Nehru, expressed the hope that elections would be held as early as the spring of 1951.

Nehru's haste was understandable, but it was viewed with some alarm by the man who had to make the election possible. It is a pity we know so little about Sukumar Sen. He left no memoirs, and few papers. He was born in 1899 and was educated at Presidency College and at London University, where he was awarded a gold medal in mathematics. He joined the Indian civil service (ICS) in 1921, and served in various districts and as a judge before being appointed chief secretary of West Bengal, from where he was sent on deputation as chief election commissioner.

It was perhaps the mathematician in Sen that made him ask the prime minister to wait. For no officer of state, certainly no Indian official, has ever had such a stupendous task placed in front of him. Consider, first of all, the size of the electorate: 176 million Indians aged twenty-one or more, of whom about 85% could not read or write. Each one had to be identified, named, and registered. The registration of voters was merely the first step. For how did one design party symbols, ballot papers, and ballot boxes for a mostly illiterate electorate? Then, sites for polling stations had to be identified, and honest and efficient polling officers recruited. Moreover, along with the general election there would be elections to the state assemblies. Working with Sukumar Sen in this regard were the election commissioners of the different provinces, also usually ICS men.

The polls were finally scheduled for the first months of 1952. An American observer justly wrote that the mechanics of the election "present a problem of colossal proportions."[21] Some numbers will help us understand the scale of Sen's enterprise. At stake were 4,500 seats—about 500 for Parliament and the rest for the provincial assemblies. Some 224,000 polling booths were constructed and equipped with 2 million steel ballot boxes, requiring 8,200 tons of steel. To type and collate the electoral rolls by constituencies 16,500 clerks were appointed on six-month contracts. About 380,000 reams of paper were used for printing the rolls. To supervise the voting, 56,000 presiding officers were chosen. They were aided by 280,000 "lesser" staff members; and 224,000 policemen were put on duty to stop violence and intimidation.

The elections and electorate were spread out over an area of more than 1 million square miles. The terrain was huge, diverse, and—for the project at hand—sometimes horrendously difficult. In remote hill villages, bridges had to be specially constructed across rivers; in small islands in the Indian Ocean, naval vessels were used to take the rolls to the booths. A second problem was social rather than geographical: the reluctance of many women in northern India to give their own names—they wished to register themselves as A's mother or B's wife. Sukumar Sen was outraged by this practice, a "curious senseless relic of the past," and directed his officials to correct the rolls by inserting the names of the women "in the place of mere descriptions of such voters." Nonetheless, some 2.8 million women voters had finally to be struck off the list. The resulting furore over their omission was considered by Sen to be a "good thing," for it would help end the prejudice by the next elections, when the women could be reinstated under their own names.

In western democracies, most voters could recognize the parties by name, but in India pictorial symbols were used to make recognition easier. Drawn from daily life, these symbols were easily recognisable: a pair of bullocks for one party, a hut for a second, an elephant for a third, a clay lamp for a fourth. A second innovation was the use of multiple ballot boxes. On a single ballot, an illiterate Indian elector might make a mistake; thus each party had a ballot box with its symbol marked in each polling station, so that voters could simply drop their paper in it. To avoid impersonation, Indian scientists had developed a variety of indelible ink which, applied on the voter's finger, stayed there for a week. A total of 389,916 phials of this ink were used in the election.[22]

Through 1951, the Election Commission used films and the radio to educate the public about this novel exercise in democracy. A documentary on the franchise and its functions, and the duties of the electorate, was shown in more than 3,000 movie theatres. Many more Indians were reached through All India Radio, which broadcast numerous programmes on the constitution, the purpose of adult franchise, the preparation of electoral rolls, and the process of voting.[23]

IV

It is instructive to reflect on the international situation in the months leading up to India's first general election. Elsewhere in Asia, the French were fighting the Vietminh, and UN troops were thwarting a North Korean offensive. In South Africa, the Afrikaner National Party had disenfranchised the Cape Coloureds, the last non-white group to have the vote. America had just tested its first hydrogen bomb. Maclean and Burgess had just defected to Russia. The year 1951 had witnessed three political assassinations: of the king of Jordan; of the prime minister of Iran; and of the prime minister of Pakistan, Liaqat Ali Khan, shot dead on 16 October, nine days before the first votes were cast in India.

Most intriguingly, the polls in India were to coincide with a general election in the United Kingdom. The old warhorse Winston Churchill was seeking to bring his Conservatives back into power. In the United Kingdom the elections were basically a two-party contest. In India, however, there was a dazzling diversity of parties and leaders. In power was Jawaharlal Nehru's Indian National Congress, the chief legatee and beneficiary of the freedom movement. Opposing it were a variety of new parties formed by some greatly gifted individuals.

Prominent among parties of the left were J. B. Kripalani's KMPP and the Socialist party, whose leading lights included the young hero of the "Quit India" rebellion of 1942, Jayaprakash Narayan. These parties accused the Congress of betraying its commitment to the poor. They claimed to stand for the ideals of the old, "Gandhian" Congress, which had placed the interests of workers and peasants before those of landlords and capitalists.[24] A different critique was offered by the Jana Sangh, which sought to consolidate India's largest religious group, the Hindus, into one solid voting bloc. The party's aims were well expressed in the symbolism of its inaugural meeting, held in New Delhi on 21 September 1951. The session began with a recitation from the Vedas and a singing of the patriotic hymn, "Vande Matram." On the rostrum, the party's founder, Shyama Prasad Mookerjee, sat alongside other leaders, behind them a white background [with] pictures of Shivaji, Lord Krishna persuading the remorse-striken Arjuna to take up arms to fight the evil forces of the Kauravas on the battle-field of Kurukshetra, Rana Pratap Singh and of an earthern deepak, in saffron. From the Pandal was hung banners inscribed with "Sangh Shakth Kali Yuge," a dictum taken from [the] Mahabharat, professing to tell the people who attended the convention that in the age of Kali there was force only in [Jana] Sangh.[25]

The imagery was striking: it was taken from the Hindu epics but also invoked Hindu warriors who had later fought the Muslim invader. But who, one wonders, represented the evil enemy, the Kauravas? Was it Pakistan, the Muslims, Jawaharlal Nehru, or the Congress party? All figured as objects of hatred in the speeches of the Sangh's leaders. The party stood for the reunification of the motherland through the absorption (or perhaps conquest) of Pakistan. It suspected the Indian Muslims as a problem minority, which had "not yet learnt to own this land and its culture and treat them as their first love." The Congress party was accused of "appeasing" Muslims, whose patriotism was uncertain.[26]

S. P. Mookerjee had once been a member of the Union cabinet. So had B. R. Ambedkar, the great untouchable lawyer who, as the law minister, helped draft the Indian constitution. Ambedkar had resigned from office to revive the Scheduled Caste Federation in time for the elections. In his speeches he sharply attacked the Congress government for doing little to uplift the lower castes. Freedom had meant no change for these peoples: it was "the same old tyranny, the same old oppression, the same old discrimination." After freedom was won, said Ambedkar, the Congress had degenerated into a dharmashala, or rest home, with no unity of purpose or principles, and "open to all, fools and knaves, friends and foes, communalists and secularists, reformers and orthodox and capitalists and anti-capitalists."[27]

Still further to the left was the Communist Party of India (CPI). As we have seen, in 1948 many activists of the CPI had gone underground, to lead a peasant insurrection that they hoped would expand into a countrywide revolutionary upsurge on the Chinese model. But the police and in some places the army had cracked down hard. Now, the communists came overground in time to fight the elections. The Telengana struggle, said the party's general secretary, had been withdrawn "unconditionally." A temporary amnesty was granted, and the militants put away their arms and went out seeking votes. This abrupt change of roles produced dilemmas no text by Marx or Lenin could help resolve. Thus a woman communist running for a seat in Bengal was not sure whether to wear crumpled saris, to signify her identification with the poor, or wash and iron them, to better appeal to the middle class. And a parliamentary candidate in Telengana (where the peasant revolt had been most intense) recalled his confusion at being offered a drink by a senior official: he said yes and gulped down the offering, only to be hit by a "reeling sensation" in his head as it turned out to be whisky rather than fruit juice.[28]

The election campaign of 1951–1952 was conducted through large public meetings, door-to-door canvassing, and the use of visual media. "At the height of election fever," wrote a British observer, "posters and emblems were profuse everywhere—on walls, at street corners, even decorating the statues in New Delhi and defying the dignity of a former generation of Viceroys." A novel method of advertising was on display in Calcutta, where stray cows had "Vote Congress" written on their backs in Bengali.[29]

Speeches and posters were used by all parties, but only the communists had access to the airwaves—not those transmitted by All India Radio, which had banned party propaganda; but those of Moscow Radio, which relayed its programmes via stations in Tashkent. Indian listeners could, if they wished, hear that the non-communist parties in the election were "corrupt stooges of Anglo-American imperialists and oppressors of the workers."[30] For the literate, a weekly in Madras had helpfully translated an article from *Pravda* that called the ruling Congress "a government of landowners and monopolists, a government of national betrayers, truncheons and bullets," and announced that the alternative for the "long-suffering, worn-out Indian people" was the Communist party, around which "all progressive forces of the country, everyone who cherishes the vital interests of his fatherland, are grouping."[31]

Adding to the list (and interest, and excitement) were regional parties based on affiliations of ethnicity and religion. These included the Dravida Kazhagam in Madras, which stood for Tamil pride against north Indian domination; the Akalis in Punjab, the main party of the Sikhs; and the Jharkhand party in Bihar, which wanted a separate state for tribal people. There were also numerous splinter groups on the left, as well as two Hindu parties more orthodox than the Jana Sangh: the Hindu Mahasabha and the Ram Rajya Parishad.

The leaders of these parties all had years of political service behind them. Some had gone to jail in the nationalist cause; others in the communist cause. Men like S. P. Mookerjee and Jayaprakash Narayan were superb orators, with the ability to enchant a crowd and make it fall in line behind them. On the eve of the election, the political scientist Richard Park wrote that "the leading Indian parties and party workers are surpassed by those of no other country in electioneering skill, dramatic presentation of issues, political oratory, or mastery of political psychology."[32]

Some people might celebrate this diversity as proof of the robustness of the democratic process. Others were not so sure. Thus a cartoon strip in *Shankar's Weekly* lampooned the hypocrisy of the campaign. It showed a fat man in a black coat canvassing among different groups of voters. He told an emaciated farmer that "land for peasants is my aim." He assured a well dressed young man that "landlords' rights will be protected." At one place he said that he was "all for nationalization"; at another he insisted that he would "encourage private enterprise." He told a woman in a sari that he stood for the Hindu Code Bill (a reform aimed principally at enhancing the rights of women), but said to a Brahman with a pigtail that he would "safeguard our Ancient Culture."[33]

V

These varied parties all had one target: the ruling Congress. Its leader, Jawaharlal Nehru, had just successfully come through a challenge to his leadership of the party. With the death of Vallabhbhai Patel, Nehru was also the dominant presence in the government. But he faced problems aplenty. These included angry refugees from East and West Pakistan, not yet settled in their new homes. The Andhras in the south and the Sikhs in the north were getting restive. The question of Kashmir was, in the eyes of the world, still unresolved. And independence had not as yet made any dent in the problems of poverty and inequality: a state of affairs for which, naturally, the ruling party was likely to be held responsible.

One way of telling the story of the election campaign is through newspaper headlines. These make interesting reading, not least because the issues they express have remained at the forefront of Indian elections ever since. "MINISTERS FACE STIFF OPPOSITION" read a headline in Uttar Pradesh. "CASTE RIVALRIES WEAKEN BIHAR CONGRESS" read another. From the north-eastern region came this telling line: "AUTONOMY DEMAND IN MANIPUR." From Gauhati came this one: "CONGRESS PROSPECTS IN ASSAM: IMPORTANCE OF MUSLIM AND TRIBAL VOTE." Gwalior offered "DISCONTENT AMONG CONGRESSMEN: LIST OF NOMINEES CREATES

WIDER SPLIT." A headline in Calcutta ran: "W. BENGAL CONGRESS CHIEF BOOED AT MEETING" (the hecklers being refugees from East Pakistan). "NO HOPES OF FREE AND FAIR ELECTION," started a story datelined Lucknow: this being the verdict of J. B. Kripalani, who claimed that state officials would rig the polls in favour of the ruling party. And the city of Bombay offered, at three different moments in the campaign, these quite timeless headlines: "CONGRESS BANKS ON MUSLIM SUPPORT"; "CONGRESS APATHY TOWARDS SCHEDULED CASTES: CHARGES REITERATED BY DR. AMBEDKAR"; and "FOURTEEN HURT IN CITY ELECTION CLASH." But there was also the occasional headline that was of its time but emphatically not of ours—notably one in *The Searchlight* of Patna which claimed: "PEACEFUL VOTING HOPED [FOR] IN BIHAR."

Faced with wide-ranging opposition from outside, and with some dissidence within his own party, Jawaharlal Nehru took to the road and, on occasion, the plane and the train as well. From 1 October he commenced a tour which a breathless party functionary later described as comparable to the "imperial campaigns of Samudragupta, Asoka and Akbar" as well as to the "travel[s] of Fahien and Hieun Tsang." In nine weeks Nehru covered the country from end to end. He travelled 25,000 miles in all: 18,000 by air; 5,200 by car; 1,600 by train; and 90 by boat.[34]

Nehru kicked off his party's campaign with a speech in the Punjab town of Ludhiana on Sunday, 30 September. The place he chose was significant, as was the thrust of his talk, in which he declared "an all-out war against communalism." He "condemned the communal bodies which in the name of Hindu and Sikh culture were spreading the virus of communalism as the Muslim League once did." These "sinister communal elements" would if they came to power "bring ruin and death to the country." He asked his audience of half-a-million to "keep the windows of our mind open and let in fresh breeze from all corners of the world."

The sentiment was reminiscent of Gandhi, and indeed Nehru's next major speech was delivered in Delhi on the afternoon of 2 October, the Mahatma's birthday. To a mammoth crowd, he spoke in Hindustani about the government's determination to abolish both untouchability and landlordism. Once more, he identified communalists as the chief enemies, who "will be shown no quarter," and "overpowered with all our strength." His ninety-five-minute speech was punctuated with loud cheers, not least when he made this ringing declaration: "If any person raises his hand to strike down another on the ground of religion, I shall fight him till the last breath of my life, both at the head of the Government and from outside."

Wherever he went Nehru spoke out strongly against communalism. In S. P. Mookerjee's native Bengal he dismissed the Jana Sangh as the "illegitimate child of the R. S. S. and the Hindu Mahasabha." To be sure, he touched on other themes as well. In Bihar he deplored the "monster of casteism." In Bombay he reminded his audience that a vote for Congress was also a vote for its foreign policy of principled neutralism. In Bharatpur and Bilaspur he deplored the impatience of his left-wing critics, whose ends he shared but not their means: as he put it, "we can build the edifice of Socialism brick by brick only." In Ambala he asked the women to cast off their purdah and "come forward to build the country." In many places he expressed his admiration for the best among his opposition: for men such as Ambedkar, Kripalani, and Jayaprakash Narayan, who had once been his colleagues in the party or in government. "We want a number of [such] men with ability and integrity," he said. "They are welcome. But all of them are pulling in different directions and doing nothing in the end." He was particularly sorry to find himself in opposition to the Socialist party, which, he said, "contains some of my old intimate friends whom I admire and respect." These sentiments were not shared by his daughter, Indira Gandhi, who in her own speeches alleged that the socialists were funded by American dollars.[35]

In the course of his campaign Nehru "travelled more than he slept and talked more than he travelled." He addressed 300 mass meetings and countless wayside ones. He spoke to about 20 million people directly, and an equal number had a darshan, eagerly flanking the roads to see him as his car whizzed past. Those who heard and saw Nehru included miners, peasants, pastoralists, factory workers, and agricultural labourers. Women of all classes turned out in large numbers for his meetings. Sometimes there would be a sprinkling of hostile spectators in the crowd. In parts of north India, supporters of Jana Sangh shouted out at Nehru's rallies that he was not to be trusted, as he ate beef. Coming across a group of communists waving the hammer and sickle, Nehru asked them to "go and live in the country whose flag you are carrying." "Why don't you go to New York and live with the Wall Street imperialists?" they shot back.[36]

But for the most part the people who came to hear Nehru were sympathetic, and often adulatory. This summation in a Congress booklet exaggerates, but not by very much:

Almost at every place, city, town, village or wayside halt, people had waited overnight to welcome the nation's leader. Schools and shops closed: milkmaids and cowherds had taken a holiday; the kisan and his helpmate took a temporary respite from their dawn-to-dusk programme of hard work in field and home. In Nehru's name, stocks of soda and lemonade sold out; even water became scarce. . . . Special trains were run from out-of-the-way places to carry people to Nehru's meetings, enthusiasts travelling not only on foot-boards but also on top of carriages. Scores of people fainted in milling crowds.[37]

The independent press provided many instances of the popular mood. When Nehru spoke in Bombay, a procession, mainly of Muslims, marched to Chowpatty to the accompaniment of pipes and cymbals. It was headed by a pair of bullocks and a plough (the Congress symbol). Everywhere, crowds started gathering in the early morning for talks scheduled for the afternoon; almost everywhere, barricades were broken in "the enthusiasm to catch a glimpse of Mr Nehru." After a speech in Delhi, Nehru was met as he came off the dais by a famous wrestler, Massu Pahalwan, who offered him a gold chain and remarked: "This is only a token. I am prepared to give my life for you and the country." The media were much taken with a Telugu-speaking woman who went to listen to Nehru speak in the railroad town of Kharagpur. As the prime minister lectured on, she was stricken by labour pains. Immediately, a group of fellow Andhras made a ring around her: the baby was safely delivered, no doubt while the midwives had an ear cocked to hear what their hero was saying.

The extraordinary popular appeal of the Indian prime minister is best captured in the testimony of a confirmed Nehru-baiter, D. F. Karaka, editor of the popular Bombay weekly *Current*. He was in the vast crowd at Chowpatty beach, one of 200,000 people gathered there, many standing in the sea. Karaka noted—no doubt to his regret—"the instant affinity between the speaker and his audience." This is how he reported Nehru's speech:

He had come to Bombay after a long time, he told them. Many years.

He paused and looked at them with that wistful look he specialises in. In that pause, ominous for his political opponents, a thousand votes must have swung in his favour.

Yes, he felt a personal attachment to the city.

Pause.

Two thousand votes.

It was like coming home.

Pause.

Five thousand votes.

In Bombay he had passed some of the happiest moments in his life. Yes, the happiest.

Five thousand votes. . . .

He remembered those great moments so vividly. And some of the saddest moments too—the sad, hard days of the [freedom] struggle.

Ten thousand votes for the Congress.

Pause. "By looking at the people who have struggled together with me in the fight for freedom, I derive freedom and strength," he said.

The affinity was complete.

Twenty thousand votes!

Pause.

A deep, sorrowful, soulful look in the fading twilight hour; with the air pregnant with emotion. . . . He told the gathering that he had taken upon himself the role of a mendicant beggar. Amidst cheers, he said: "if at all I am a beggar, I am begging for your love, your affection and your enlightened co-operation in solving the problems which face the country."

Thirty thousand votes were sure for Nehru.

Pause.

A stir in the audience. A tear on the face of the man or woman sitting on the beach or standing on the shore. Two tears, a *sari*-end wiping them gently off a woman's face. She would give her vote to Nehru no matter what anyone else said. Memories of Gandhi came back to the people—the days when Nehru stood beside the Mahatma. Nehru . . . was the man he left to us as his political heir.

Fifty thousand votes! a hundred thousand! Two hundred thousand![38]

The crowds were moved by Nehru; and he, in turn, was moved by them. His own feelings are best captured in a letter he wrote to one who with both delicacy and truth can be referred to as his closest woman friend. "Wherever I have been," he told Edwina Mountbatten,

vast multitudes gather at my meetings and I love to compare them, their faces, their dresses, their reactions to me and what I say. Scenes from past history of that very part of India rise up before me and my mind becomes a picture gallery of past events. But, more than the past, the present fills my mind and I try to probe into the minds and hearts of these multitudes. Having long been imprisoned in the Secretariat of Delhi, I rather enjoy these fresh contacts with the Indian people. . . . The effort to explain in simple language our problems and our difficulties, and to reach the minds of these simple folk is both exhausting and exhilarating.

As I wander about, the past and the present merge into one another and this merger leads me to think of the future. Time becomes like a flowing river in continuous motion with events connected with one another.[39]

VI

One place even Nehru didn't get to was the *tahsil* of Chini in Himachal Pradesh. Here resided the first Indians to cast their vote in a general election—a group of Buddhists. They voted on 25 October, days before the winter snows shut their valleys off from the world. The villagers of Chini owed allegiance to the Panchen Lama in Tibet, and were ruled by rituals adminstered by local priests. These included *gorasang*, a religious service to celebrate the completion of a new house; *kangur zalmo*, a ceremonial visit to the Buddhist library at Kanam; *menthako*, "where men, women, and children climb hills, dance, and sing"; and *jokhiya chug simig*, the exchange of visits between relatives. Now, although they didn't as yet know it, was added a new ritual, to be performed at five-year intervals: voting in a general election.[40]

Coincidentally, it was also on 25 October 1951 that polling began in the general elections in the United Kingdom. Here the first voters were Buddhist peasants in a Himalayan valley; there the first voters were "milkmen, charwomen and all-night workers returning home from work."[41] However, in Britain the results of the election were known the next day—Labour had been swept out of power, with Winston Churchill returning as prime minister. In India, the first voters had to wait for months before learning the results, because the rest of the country went to the polls later, in January and February 1952.

The highest voting percentage, 80.5, was recorded in the parliamentary constituency of Kottayam, in present-day Kerala; the lowest, 18.0, in Shahdol in what is now Madhya Pradesh. For the country as a whole, about 60% of registered voters exercised their franchise; this is an impressive figure, given the high level of illiteracy. A scholar from the London

School of Economics noted that a young woman in Himachal walked several miles with her bent mother to vote: "for a day, at least, she knew she was important."[42] A weekly based in Bombay marvelled at the high turnout in the forest districts of Orissa, where tribals came to the voting booths with bows and arrows. One booth in the jungle reported more than 70% voting; but evidently Sukumar Sen got at least some things wrong, for the neighbouring booth was visited only by an elephant and two panthers.[43] The press especially highlighted the aged who turned up to vote: a 110-year-old-man in Madurai who came propped up on either side by a great-grandson, a ninety-five-year-old-woman in Ambala, deaf and hunchbacked. There was also a ninety-year-old Muslim in rural Assam, but he had to return disappointed, as he was told by the presiding officer that "he could not vote for Nehru." Another nonagenarian, in rural Maharashtra, cast his vote for the assembly elections, but fell down and died before he could vote for Parliament. And there was a vindication of Indian democracy in the electoral roll of Hyderabad, where among the first who voted was the nizam himself.

One place where there was especially brisk polling was Bombay. Delhi was where the rulers lived, but the island metropolis was India's financial centre. It was also a very politically aware city. All together, 900,000 residents of Bombay, or 70% of the city's electorate, exercised their democratic right on election day. The workers came in far greater numbers than the fashionable middle class. Thus, reported the *Times of India*, "in the industrial areas voters formed long queues long before the polling stations opened, despite the particularly cold and dewy morning. In contrast to this, at the W. I. A. A. Club [in Malabar Hill], which housed two polling stations, it appeared as if people straggled in for a game of tennis or bridge and only incidentally to vote."

The day after Bombay went to the polls it was the turn of the Mizo Hills. With regard to both culture and geography there could not have been a greater contrast. Bombay had a great density of polling stations: 1,349 in all, in only ninety-two square miles. At the other extreme lay this tribal area bordering East Pakistan and Burma: here there were a mere 113 booths spread over more than 8,000 square miles of territory. The people who lived in these hills, said one scribe, "have not known any queues hitherto except those in battle arrays." But they had nonetheless "taken a strong fancy" to voting, reaching their booths by walking for days on "perilous tracks through wild jungles, camping at night on the way amid song and community dances around the fire." And so 92,000 Mizos, who "have through the centuries decided an issue with their arrows and spears, came forward to give their decision for the first time through the medium of the ballot."

An American woman photographer on assignment in Himachal Pradesh was deeply impressed by the commitment shown by the election officials. One official had walked for six days to attend the preparatory workshop organized by the district magistrate; another had ridden four days by mule. They went back to their distant stations with sewn gunnysacks, containing ballot boxes, ballots, party symbols, and electoral lists. On election day the photographer chose to watch at an obscure hill village, Bhuti. Here the polling station was a schoolhouse that had only one door. Since the rules prescribed a separate entry and exit, a window had been converted into a door, with improvised steps on either side to allow the elderly and ailing to step out after voting.[44]

At least in this first election, politicians and the public were both (to quote the chief election commissioner) "essentially law-abiding and peaceful." There were only 1,250 election offences reported. These included 817 cases of "impersonation of voters," 106 attempts to take ballot papers out of a polling station, and 100 instances of "canvassing within one hundred yards of a polling station." Some of the last of these offences were doubtless committed unknowingly by painted cows.[45]

VII

Polling for the general election ended in the last week of February. When the results came in, the Congress party had won comfortably. It secured 364 out of 489 seats in Parliament and 2,247 out of 3,280 seats in the state assemblies. But, as critics of the Congress were quick to point out, there was a serious discrepancy between the percentage of seats won and the percentage of votes polled. This was because in most constituencies there were half a dozen or more candidates; the person who received the most votes won, even if—as was usually the case—more than 50% of the electorate had voted for other candidates or parties. Thus, for Parliament as a whole, Congress had received 45% of the vote and won 74.4% of the seats; the corresponding figures for the states were 42.4% and 68.6%. Even so, as many as twenty-eight Congress ministers had been defeated in the elections. These included such influential men as Jai Narayan Vyas in Rajasthan and Morarji Desai in Bombay. More striking still was the fact that a communist, Ravi Narayan Reddy—he who drank his first glass of whisky during the campaign—won by the largest margin, larger even than Jawaharlal Nehru's.

One of the more notable defeats was that of the Scheduled Caste leader, B. R. Ambedkar. Opposing him in his Bombay constituency was a obscure milkman named Kajrolkar. The gifted Marathi journalist P. K. Atre popularized the following slogan:

> *Kuthe to Ghatnakar Ambedkar,*
> *Aani Kuthe ha Lonivikya Kajrolkar?*

Roughly translated, this meant:

> *Where is the (great) constitution-maker Ambedkar*
> *And where the (obscure) butter-seller Kajrolkar?*[46]

Yet, in the end, the prestige and hold of the Congress, and the fact that Nehru made several speeches in Bombay, carried Kajrolkar to victory. As one wag remarked, even a lamppost running on the Congress ticket could have been elected. Or, as a political scientist more dispassionately put it, the election was won on "Nehru's personal popularity and his ability to express the aspirations of a newly independent India in a vivid and forceful manner."[47]

On the eve of the election, Sukumar Sen suggested that it constituted "the biggest *experiment* in democracy in human history." A veteran editor in Madras was less neutral; he complained that "a very large majority [will] exercise votes for the first time: not many know what the vote is, why they should vote, and whom they should vote for; no wonder the whole adventure is rated as the biggest *gamble* in history."[48] And a recently dispossessed maharaja told a visiting American couple that any constitution sanctioning universal suffrage in a land of illiterates was "crazy." "Imagine the demagoguery, the misinformation, the dishonesty possible," said the maharaja, adding, "The world is far too shaky to permit such an experiment."[49]

Sharing this scepticism was Penderel Moon, a fellow of All Souls College, and a former ICS man who had chosen to stay on in India. In 1941, Moon had spoken to the graduating students of Punjab University about the unsuitability of western democracy to their social context. Now, eleven years later, he was the chief commissioner of the hill state of Manipur, and had to depute election officers and supervise the polling and the counting. As the people of Manipur went to the polls on 29 January, Moon wrote to his father that "a future and more enlightened age will view with astonishment the absurd farce of recording the votes of millions of illiterate people."[50]

Just as sceptical was the *Organiser*, a weekly published by the revanchist Hindu group, the RSS. The *Organiser* hoped that Jawaharlal Nehru "would live to confess the failure of universal adult franchise in India." It claimed that Mahatma Gandhi had warned against "this precipitate dose of democracy," and that the president, Rajendra Prasad, was "sceptical about this leap in the dark." Yet Nehru, "who has all along lived by slogans and stunts, would not listen."[51]

There were times when even Nehru had second thoughts about the universal franchise. On 20 December 1951, he took a brief leave of absence from the campaign to address a UNESCO symposium in Delhi. In his speech, Nehru accepted that democracy was the best form of government, or self-government, but still wondered whether

> the quality of men who are selected by these modern democratic methods of adult franchise gradually deteroriates because of lack of thinking and the noise of propaganda. . . . He [the voter] reacts to sound and to the din, he reacts to repetition and he produces either a dictator or a dumb politician who is insensitive. Such a politician can stand all the din in the world and still remain standing on his two feet and, therefore, he gets selected in the end because the others have collapsed because of the din.

This was a rare confession, based no doubt on Nehru's recent experiences on the road. A week later, Nehru suggested that it might be better to have direct elections at the lower levels—say, within the village and district—and indirect elections for the highest levels. As he put it, "direct election for such a vast number is a complicated problem and the candidates may never come into touch with the electorate and the whole thing becomes distant."[52]

Nehru had an unusual capacity—unusual among politicians, at any rate—to view both sides of a question. In this case he could see the imperfections of the process even while being committed to it. However, by the time the final results were in, and the Congress had emerged as the unchallenged ruling party, his doubts had disappeared. "My respect for the so-called illiterate voter," he said, "has gone up. Whatever doubts I might have had about adult suffrage in India have been removed completely."[53]

The election itself also set to rest the doubts of the new American ambassador to India, Chester Bowles, who assumed his post in Delhi in the fall of 1951. He confessed that he was "appalled at the prospect of a poll of 200 million eligible voters, most of whom were illiterate villagers." He "feared a fiasco," even, as the *Madras Mail* put it, "the biggest farce ever staged in the name of democracy anywhere in the world." But a trip through the country during the election changed his mind. Once, he had thought that poor countries needed a period of rule by a benevolent dictator as preparation for democracy. But the sight of many parties contesting freely, and of untouchables and Brahmans standing in the same line, persuaded him otherwise. He no longer thought literacy was a test of intelligence, no longer believed that Asia needed a "series of Attaturks" before it would be ready for democracy. Summing up his report on the elections, Bowles wrote: "In Asia, as in America, I know no grander vision than this, government by the consent of the governed."[54]

A visiting Turkish journalist focused on the content of the election rather than its form. He admired Nehru's decision not to follow other Asian countries in taking the "line of least resistance" by developing "a dictatorship with centralisation of power and intolerance of dissent and criticism." The prime minister had "wisely kept away from such temptations." Yet the "main credit" "goes to the nation itself. 176,000,000 Indians were left all alone with their conscience in face of the polling box. It was direct and secret voting. They had their choice between theocracy, chauvinism, communal separatism and isolationism on the one side; secularism, national unity, stability, moderation and friendly intercourse with the rest of the world on the other. They showed their maturity in choosing moderation and progress and disapproving of reaction and unrest." So impressed was this observer that he took a delegation of his countrymen to meet Sukumar Sen. The chief election commissioner showed them samples of ballot boxes, ballot papers, and symbols, as well as the plan of a polling station, so that they could work to resume the interrupted progress of democracy in their own country.[55]

In one sense the Turkish journalist was right. There were indeed 176 million heroes, or at least 107 million—those among the eligible who actually took the trouble to vote. Still, some heroes were more special than others. As the respected sociologist D. P. Mukerji of Lucknow pointed out, "great credit is due to those who are in charge of this stupendous first experiment in Indian history. Bureaucracy has certainly proved its worth by honestly discharging the duties imposed on it by a honest Prime Minister."[56]

The juxtaposition is important, and also ironic. For there was a time when Nehru had little but scorn for the bureaucracy. As he put it in his autobiography, "few things are more striking to-day in India than the progressive deterioration, moral and intellectual, of the higher services, more especially the Indian Civil Services. This is most in evidence in the superior officials, but it runs like a thread throughout the services."[57] This was written in 1935, when the objects of his derison had the power to put him and his like in jail. And yet, fifteen years later, Nehru was obliged to place the polls in the hands of men he would once have dismissed as imperialist stooges.

In this respect, the elections of 1952 were a script written jointly by historical forces that had long been opposed to each other: British colonialism and Indian nationalism. Between them these forces had now given this new nation what could fairly be described as a jump-start to democracy.

8

HOME *and the* WORLD

Pandit Nehru is at his best when he is not pinned down to matters of detail.

Economic Weekly, 28 July 1951

I

NOT LONG after the elections of 1952, Nirad C. Chaudhuri wrote an essay on Jawaharlal Nehru in a popular magazine. The writer was (by this time) a moderately well known Indian, but his subject still towered over him, as well as everybody else. Nehru's leadership, remarked Chaudhuri, "is the most important moral force behind the unity of India." He was "the leader not of a party, but of the people of India taken collectively, the legitimate successor to Gandhiji." As Chaudhuri saw it, "Nehru is keeping together the governmental machine and the people, and without this nexus India would probably have been deprived of stable government in these crucial times. He has not only ensured co-operation between the two, but most probably has also prevented actual conflicts, cultural, economic, and political. Not even Mahatmaji's leadership, had it continued, would have been quite equal to them.

"If, within the country, Nehru is the indispensable link between the governing middle-classes and the sovereign people," continued Chaudhuri, "he is no less the bond between India and the world." He served as "India's representative to the great Western democracies, and, I must add, their representative to India. The Western nations certainly look upon him as such and expect him to guarantee India's support for them, which is why they are so upset when Nehru takes an anti-Western or neutral line. They feel they are being let down by one of themselves."[1]

Through his long tenure as prime minister, Nehru served simultaneously as foreign minister of the government of India. This was natural, for among the Congress leadership he alone had a genuinely international perspective. Gandhi was universalist in outlook but had hardly ever travelled abroad. The other Congress leaders, such as Vallabhbhai Patel, were determinedly inward-looking. Nehru, on the other hand, "had always been fascinated by world trends and movements."[2]

Through the interwar period, Nehru remained a close observer of and occasional participant in European debates. In 1927 he visited Soviet Russia, and in the next decade he travelled widely over the European continent. In the 1930s, he played an active part in mobilizing support for the Republican cause in Spain. He became a pillar of the progressive left, speaking often in public in England and France. His name and fame in this regard were aided by the publication and commercial success of his *Autobiography*, which appeared in London in 1936.[3]

Representative of Nehru's ideas is a speech he delivered on "Peace and Empire" at Friends House, Euston, in July 1938. He began by speaking of "Fascist aggression" but went on to see fascism as merely another variant of imperialism. In Britain the tendency was to distinguish between the two. But in Nehru's mind there was little doubt that those who "sought complete freedom for all the subject peoples of the world" had to oppose both fascism and imperialism.

The crisis of the times, said Nehru, had promoted a "growing solidarity of the various peoples" and a "feeling of international fellowship and comradeship." His own talk ranged widely around the hot spots of the world. He spoke of Spain, of Abyssinia, of China, of Palestine, and most sensitively of Africa. The "people of Africa deserve our special consideration," he pointed out, for "probably no other people in the world have suffered so much, and have been exploited so much."[4]

In the late summer of 1939, Nehru planned a trip to India's great Asian neighbour, China. He had been in friendly correspondence with Chiang Kai-shek, for, as he told a colleague, "more and more I think of India and China pulling together in the future." He hoped to go by air to Chungking, spend three weeks travelling in the hinterland, and return home via the Burma Road. But the war in Europe put paid to the tour.[5]

After the "Quit India" movement of 1942, Nehru was jailed. When he was released, in July 1945, his energies were at first devoted to the endgame of empire. Then, after it became clear that India would soon be free, his thoughts turned once more to foreign affairs. In a radio broadcast of September 1946 he identified the United States, the Soviet Union, and China as the three countries most relevant to India's future. The next year he spoke in the Constituent Assembly, saying that India would be friends with both the United States and the Soviet Union, rather than become a camp follower of one power "in the hope that some crumbs might fall from their table." As he put it, "we lead ourself."[6]

An early articulation of what came to be known as "non-alignment" is contained in a letter written by Nehru to K. P. S. Menon in January 1947, as Menon prepared to take up his assignment as India's first ambassador to China. "Our general policy," said Nehru,

> is to avoid entanglement in power politics and not to join any group of powers as against any other group. The two leading groups today are the Russian bloc and the Anglo-American bloc. We must be friendly to both and yet not join either. Both America and Russia are extraordinarily suspicious of each other as well as of other countries. This makes our path difficult and we may well be suspected by each of leaning towards the other. This cannot be helped.[7]

Nehru saw Indian independence as part of a wider Asian resurgence. Past centuries might have belonged to Europe, or to the white races in general, but it was now time for coloured and previously subordinated peoples to come into their own.

A remarkable initiative in this regard was the Asian Relations Conference, held in New Delhi in the last week of March 1947. As many as twenty-eight countries sent representatives—these included India's close neighbours (Afghanisthan, Burma, Ceylon, and Nepal), the still colonized nations of southeast Asia (such as Malaya, Indonesia, and Vietnam), China and Tibet (which sent separate delegations), seven Asian "republics" of the Soviet Union, and Korea. The Arab League and a Jewish delegation from Palestine were also represented. As a western journalist covering the event recalled, for a week the city of Delhi "was filled with the most intricate variety of people, strange in costume and countenance—brocades from South-East Asia, bell-bottoms from the Eastern Soviet Republics, braided hair and quilted robes from Tibet, ... dozens of curious languages and polysyllabic titles. One way and another, as we kept reminding one another, this multitude represented nearly half the population of the world."[8]

The conference was held in the Purana Qila, a large, somewhat run-down, yet still majestic stone structure built by Sher Shah Suri in the sixteenth century. The opening and concluding sessions were open to the public and attracted large crowds—20,000 by one estimate. The official language was English, but interpreters were provided for the delegates. The speakers were on a raised podium; behind them was mounted a huge map of the continent, with ASIA written atop it, in neon lights. The inaugural address was by Nehru. "Rising to a great ovation," he said that "after a long period of quiescence," Asia had "suddenly become important in world affairs." Its countries could "no longer be used as pawns by others."[9] However, as the journalist G. H. Jansen recalled, Nehru's speech "was not directly or strongly anti-colonial. 'The old imperialisms are fading away,' he said. With an almost contemptuous wave of the hand he did something worse than attack them; he pronounced a valediction."[10]

After Nehru had his say, each participating country, in alphabetical order, sent a speaker to the podium. This took two whole days, after which the meeting broke up into thematic round tables. There were separate sections on "national movements for freedom"; "racial problems and inter-Asian migration"; "economic development and social services"; "cultural problems"; and "status of women and women's movements."

The conference concluded with a talk by Mahatma Gandhi. He regretted that the conference had met not in the "real India" of the villages but in the cities that were "influenced by the West." The "message of Asia," insisted Gandhi, was "not to be learnt through the Western spectacles or by imitating the atom bomb. . . . I want you to go away with the thought that Asia has to conquer the West through love and truth."[11]

Gandhi made an appearance, but this was really Nehru's show. His admirers saw it as confirmation of his status as the authentic voice of resurgent Asia. His critics were less generous. In its account of the conference, the Muslim League newspaper, *Dawn*, complained about how

> skilfully he [Nehru] has worked himself into some sort of all-Asian leadership. That is just what this ambitious Hindu leader had intended—to thrust himself upon the Asian nations as their leader and through his attainment of that prestige and eminence to further the expansionist designs of Indian Hinduism.[12]

II

Nehru had been often to Europe before independence. His first trip to the United States, however, took place two years after he had assumed office as prime minister. The United States had not loomed large in Nehru's political imagination. His *Glimpses of World History*, for example, devotes far less space to it than to China or Russia. And what he says is not always complimentary. American capitalism had led to slavery, gangsterism, and extremes of wealth and poverty. J. Pierpont Morgan owned a yacht costing 6 million pounds, yet New York was known as "Hunger Town." Nehru admired Franklin Delano Roosevelt's attempts at regulating the economy, but he was not hopeful that these would succeed: "American Big Business is held to be the most powerful vested interest in the modern world, and it is not going to give up its power and privileges merely at the bidding of President Roosevelt."[13]

Before Nehru's trip to America in late 1949, an enterprising reporter at *Time* magazine went through his writings. The exercise revealed that he had "simply never given the subject [of America] much thought. As a British university man, he has perhaps looked down snobbishly at American deficiency in culture. As a sentimental socialist, he has ticked off the U. S. as unrivalled in technology but predatory in its capitalism."[14]

Nehru's feelings were widely shared. Like British aristocrats, the Indian elite tended to think of America and Americans as uncouth and uncultured. The views of P. P. Kumaramangalam, scion of an illustrious south Indian family, are representative. His father, Dr. P. Subbaroyan, was a rich landlord and an influential politician who later served in Nehru's cabinet. The son studied at Sandhurst and his siblings at Oxford and Cambridge. These, a brother named Mohan and a sister named Parvathi, went on to become leading lights of the Communist party of India and were thus predisposed to dislike America. But in this respect their brother who was an army officer outdid them. After Indian independence he was sent for training to the artillery school at Fort Sill in Oklahoma. From here he wrote to a mentor in Madras:

> This country is not one that I will ever get fond of. I have not got a
> very high opinion of them. The people that I have to deal with are
> very kind, hospitable and have been very good to the two of us. But
> somehow I feel there is a trace of artificiality in that and also it is the
> result of trying to impress one. They I think are very jealous of the old
> world and its background and culture and this results in an aggressive
> inferiority complex. As for their state of morality there is none. People
> seem to delight in trying to outwit each other by any means mainly
> crooked. The politicians are racketeers and big business have a tight
> grip on everything in the country. The small country tradesman and
> the farmer I think have their hands pretty securely tied by the big
> men. I do hope our country proceeds with caution and doesn't get
> entirely under the influence of the [United] States.[15]

Americans, for their part, had their own prejudices about India. They admired Gandhi and his struggle for national independence, but their knowledge of the country itself was scant. As Harold Isaac once pointed out, for Americans in the postwar years there were really only four kinds of Indians: (1) *fabulous* Indians, the maharajas and magicians coupled with equally exotic animals like tigers and elephants; (2) *mystical* Indians, a people who were "deep, contemplative, tranquil, profound"; (3) *benighted* Indians, who worshipped animals and many-headed gods and lived in a country that was even more heathen than China; and (4) *pathetic* Indians, plagued by poverty and crippled by disease—"children with fly-encircled eyes, with swollen stomachs, children dying in the streets, rivers choked with bodies." Of these images perhaps the last two predominated. It was no accident that the book on the subcontinent best known in America was Katherine Mayo's *Mother India*, which Gandhi had described as a "drain inspector's report."[16]

Nehru in part shared the prejudices of Indians, and he was sensible of the American ones. But for this first high-level encounter between the youngest democracy and the richest, he was willing to put them aside. In August 1949, as he prepared for his trip, Nehru was uncharacteristically nervous. "In what mood shall I address America?" he asked his sister Vijayalakshmi Pandit. "How shall I address people etc.? How shall I deal with the Government there and businessmen and others? Which facet of myself should I put before the American public—the Indian or the European. . . . I want to be friendly with the Americans but always making it clear what we stand for."[17]

Nehru spent three weeks in America, delivering a speech a day to audiences as diverse as the United States Congress and a congregation at a chapel in Chicago. He was awarded an honorary doctorate by Columbia University, and listened to by a crowd of 10,000 at the University of California at Berkeley. He displayed the common touch, being photographed with a taxi driver in Boston; but also made clear his membership in the aristocracy of the intellect—as in a much publicized visit to Albert Einstein in Princeton.

Addressing Congress, Nehru spoke respectfully of the founders of America, but then counterposed to them a great man of his own. This was Gandhi, whose message of peace and truth had inspired independent India's foreign policy. The Mahatma, however, "was too great for the circumscribed borders of any one country, and the message he gave may help us in considering the wider problems of the world." For what

the world most lacked, said Nehru, was "understanding and appreciation of each other among nations and peoples."

This was diplomatically put, but elsewhere Nehru spoke more directly. At Columbia University, he deplored the desire to "marshal the
world into two hostile camps." India, he said, would align with neither,
but pursue "an independent approach to each controversial or disputed
issue." In his view, the main causes of war were the persistence of racism
and colonialism. Peace and freedom could be secured only if the domination of one country or one race over another was finally brought to an
end.[18]

The American press was impressed with the Indian prime minister.
The *Chicago Sun Times* went so far as to say that "in many ways Nehru
is the nearest thing this generation has to a Thomas Jefferson in his way
of giving voice to the universal aspirations for freedom of people everywhere."[19] The *Christian Science Monitor* described him as a "world titan." When he left, a columnist observed in the *St. Louis Post Dispatch*
that "Nehru has departed from us, leaving behind clouds of misty-eyed
women."[20] Even *Time* magazine admitted that while Americans were
still not sure what Nehru stood for, "they sensed in him, if not rare
truth, a rare heart."[21]

However, one set of people did not warm to the visitor from India—
the mandarins of the State Department. Nehru had several long discussions with the secretary of state, Dean Acheson, but these went nowhere.
In his memoirs Acheson wrote about Nehru's visit dismissively and with
some despair. In their talks he had found Nehru "prickly," arrogant ("he
talked to me . . . as though I was a public meeting"), and too ready to
pounce on the faults of others (notably the French and Dutch colonialists)
without recognizing any of his own. When Acheson broached the subject
of Kashmir, he got "a curious combination of a public speech and flashes
of anger and deep dislike of his opponents." All together, he found Nehru
"one of the most difficult men with whom I have ever had to deal."[22]

Other American officials were more sympathetic to Nehru. One was
Chester Bowles, who was ambassador in New Delhi from 1951 to 1953.
Observing Nehru at work in his own environment, Bowles was visibly
impressed by his commitment to democracy, democratic procedure, and
the rights of minorities. Dean Acheson, and many other Americans, divided the world into two categories: friends and foes.[23] That was not a
reading that Bowles endorsed. He insisted that "it is immature and ri-
diculous for us [Americans] to jump to the conclusion that because he
[Nehru] is not 100 per cent for us, he must be against us."[24]

During Bowles's tenure India and the United States drew closer. The United States sent experts and equipment to help with Indian programmes of agricultural development. But the popular mistrust persisted. A writer from Delaware, touring the subcontinent in the early 1950s, came across many educated Indians for whom the United States was a country "isolated by gross faults, stewing alone in the unthinkable sins of materialism, imperialist ambitions, war mongering, political corruption, spiritual and cultural poverty, racial discrimination and injustice."[25]

The mutual distrust deepened after 1953, when the Republicans found themselves back in power after twenty years out of it. Toward the end of that year, William F. Knowland, the Republican leader in the Senate, undertook a six-week world tour. After he returned home he told *U.S. News and World Report* that Jawaharlal Nehru did not represent all the nations or peoples of Asia. Said Senator Knowland emphatically, "Certainly Nehru does not speak for the Republic of Korea, for Japan, for Free China or Formosa, for Thailand, Viet Nam, Laos or Cambodia. He certainly does not speak for Pakistan. The only countries he might be able to speak for with some authority, or at least represent their views, would be India itself, Indonesia which is also neutralist in outlook and perhaps Burma."[26]

These views were shared by the new secretary of state, John Foster Dulles. Dulles was the coldest of cold warriors, whose foreign policy was dominated by his obsession with communism. In the battle against the Soviet Union Dulles was prepared to disregard the internal political systems of other nations. Dictators who toed the American line were to be preferred to democrats who didn't: "if he is a bastard, at least he is our bastard," Dulles is famously supposed to have said.

Dulles and Nehru disliked each other from the start. The American claimed that "the concept of neutrality is obsolete, immoral, and shortsighted." Those who professed it were, in effect, crypto-communists. Nehru, naturally, did not take kindly to this interpretation. As the Australian diplomat Walter Crocker wrote, the Indian prime minister did not miss the irony that

> as regards the sanctity of the Free World and the Free Life proclaimed by Dulles, he, damned by Dulles, was carrying India through a gargantuan effort towards Parliamentary Democracy, the rule of law, freedom and equality for all religions, and social and economic reforms, while among the countries which Dulles praised and subsidized because they

were "willing to stand up and be counted" as anti-Communist were effete or persecuting tyrannies, oligarchies and theocracies, sometimes
corrupt as well as retrograde.[27]

Dulles further offended Indian sensibilities when he suggested that
Portugal—a trusted ally of the United States—could keep its colony,
Goa, as long as it chose to. However, Dulles's decisive contribution to
relations between the United States and India was the military pact he
signed with Pakistan in February 1954. As one historian drily remarked, "Mr. Dulles wanted pacts. . . . Pakistan wanted money and
arms."[28]

Almost from the time of Indian independence, the United Kingdom
had seen Pakistan as a potential ally in the cold war—as, in fact, a "strong
bastion against Communism." By contrast, India was seen as being soft
on the Soviet Union. Winston Churchill himself was greatly impressed by
the argument that Pakistan could be made to stand firm on Russia's eastern flank, much as the reliable western client Turkey stood firm on the
west. The brilliant young Harvard professor Henry Kissinger endorsed
this idea—in his view, the "defense of Afghanistan [from the Soviets] de-
pends on the strength of Pakistan."[29]

For Republicans like Dulles, the fight against communism was paramount. Hence the tilt toward Pakistan, which he saw as a key member
of a defensive ring around the Soviet Union. From bases in Pakistan,
American planes could strike deep into Soviet central Asia. Dulles's view
was seconded by Vice President Richard Nixon, and their combined efforts ultimately prevailed over President Eisenhower, who was worried
about the fallout in India of any formal alliance with Pakistan.[30]

American military aid to Pakistan ran to about $80 million a year.
The United States also encouraged the Pakistanis to join the anti-Soviet
military alliances in central and south-east Asia known respectively as
CENTO and SEATO. Two months before Dulles signed his pact with
the Pakistanis, an American missionary who had worked for years in
the subcontinent warned that "to weigh Pakistan militarily over and
against India, would alienate India."[31] It certainly did, although there
were other strains on Indo-American relations as well. In the ongoing
conflicts of the cold war—as in Korea and Indochina—India was seen
as being too neutral by far. Nehru's vigorous canvassing for recognition
of the People's Republic of China, and his insistence that it be given the
permanent seat in the Security Council then occupied by Taiwan, was

also not taken kindly by Washington. An increasing number of Americans felt that Nehru had "entered the arena of world politics as a champion challenging American wisdom."[32]

Perhaps he had. As Nehru wrote to the industrialist G. D. Birla in May 1954, "I do not think that there are many examples in history of a succession of wrong policies being followed by a country as by the United States in the Far East during the past five or six years. They have taken one wrong step after another. . . . They think that they can solve any problem with money and arms. They forget the human element. They forget the nationalistic urges of people. They forget the strong resentment of people in Asia against impositions."[33]

Birla himself was rather eager for the two countries to forge better relations. In October 1954 he visited the United States and spoke to a cross section of influential people. He even had half an hour with John Foster Dulles, who complained that India "misrepresented them as warmongers and so on and so forth."[34] In February 1956 Birla visited the United States again on a bridge-building mission. He asked Nehru for advice, and got a sermon. "Dulles's statement about Goa has angered everybody here," said the prime minister. "Indo-American relations are much more affected by this kind of things than by the aid they may give. Then there is the American military aid to Pakistan, which is a constant and growing threat to us and, in effect, adds to our burdens much more than the actual aid they give to us."[35]

The next month, John Foster Dulles was bold enough to visit New Delhi. The record of his talks with the Indian government is still secret, but we do have the proceeedings of a press conference he addressed. Here, the secretary of state was subjected to a series of hostile questions. He was asked why he said that Goa was an integral part of Portugal. Dulles did not deny this, but did say that he was for a "peaceful solution" of the controversy. Then the talk turned to military aid to Pakistan, and the possibility that it might lead to an escalation of the conflict in Kashmir. Dulles answered, defensively, that "the arms supply to Pakistan is not designed in any way to be a threat to India." When the questioner persisted, Dulles angrily remarked that "we do not feel that because there is a dispute over Kashmir . . . Pakistan should be unarmed so that it could not resist Soviet Communist aggression." The secretary of state then threatened to walk out if any more questions were asked on Goa or Kashmir.[36]

India and the United States did seem to have much in common—a democratic way of life, a commitment to cultural pluralism, and (not least) a nationalist origin myth that stressed a struggle against the British oppressor. But on questions of international politics they resolutely differed. America thought India soft on communism; India thought America soft on colonialism. In the end, that which divided them seemed to overwhelm that which united them, in part because of the personal chemistry—or rather, the lack thereof—between the key players on either side.[37]

III

Jawaharlal Nehru had visited the Soviet Union two decades before he toured North America. Arriving by train from Berlin, he reached the Russian frontier on 7 November 1927, the tenth anniversary of the Bolsheviks' seizure of power. "Lenin worship" was abundantly on display. There were red flags and busts of the Bolshevik hero everywhere. Nehru went on to Moscow, a city which impressed him both with its physical grandeur and with its apparent social levelling. "The contrasts between extreme luxury and poverty are not visible, nor does one notice the hierarchy of class or caste."

Nehru wrote an account of his trip; its tone is unfailingly gushing, whether he is speaking of peasant collectives, the constitution of the Soviet Union, the presumed tolerance of minorities, or economic progress. A visit to Lenin's tomb prompted a reverie on the man and his mission, ending with a ringing endorsement of Romain Rolland's claim that the Bolshevik leader was "the greatest man of action in our century and at the same time the most selfless." Nehru was taken to a model prison, which he thought illustrative of the "better social order and humane criminal law" of the socialist system.

Compared with bourgeois countries, Nehru concluded, the Soviet Union treated its workers and peasants better, its women and children better, and even its prisoners better. The credulousness of the narrative is made complete by its epigraph—Wordsworth on the French Revolution: "Bliss was it in that dawn to be alive/But to be young was very heaven."[38]

Nehru's biographer points out that he visited the Soviet Union "in the last days of its first, halcyon period. If his reaction was idealistic, it was partly because there was still some idealism in the air."[39] This is true, after a fashion; there was still a glow about Lenin (whose own intolerance was not yet widely known outside Russia), and the Siberian death camps and the extermination of kulaks lay in the future. And of course other such endorsements were provided by western fellow travellers during the 1920s. Like them, Nehru had come intending to be impressed; and he was.[40]

It was above all the Soviet economic system that most appealed to Nehru. As a progressive intellectual of his time, he thought state ownership more just than private property, and state planning more efficient than the market. His *Glimpses of World History* contains an admiring account of the Soviet Union's five-year plans. Yet at no time was he attracted by the Bolshevik model of armed revolution or by the one-party state. His training under Gandhi predisposed him toward non-violence; and his exposure to western liberalism made him an enthusiast for electoral democracy and a free press.

After Indian independence, relations with the Soviet Union were at first frosty. This was because the Communist party of India, with Moscow's blessing, had attempted to overthrow the state, but the insurrection failed. Later the Soviet Union thawed, and sought to woo India away from the western camp. In 1951, while the American Congress debated a request for food aid from India, the Soviet Union—unencumbered by democratic procedure—offered to send 50,000 tons of wheat at once. India's efforts at mediating in the Korean conflict were also appreciated by Moscow. Previously, Asian states had been judged by their suitability for communism; but (as with Dulles's America) the cold war made the Soviet Union's ideology more flexible. It no longer mattered if a country was socialist; what was crucial was whether it was on one's side.[41]

The culmination of this change was the reception given to Jawaharlal Nehru when he visited the Soviet Union in 1955. "Wherever Nehru went in the Soviet Union," wrote one observer, "there were large crowds to greet him. In all the factories workmen gathered in thousands to have a glimpse of him." At Moscow University, "the students left their classes and gave him a great ovation." (One of the students was Mikhail Gorbachev; years later, he was to recall in his memoirs the impact made on him by Nehru's idea of a moral politics.[42]) On the last day of his stay the Indian prime minister was to speak at a public meeting in Gorky Park. But the crowd turned out to be far greater than anticipated, so the speech was shifted to the stadium of the Dynamo Moscow football team.[43]

Six months later, the Soviet leaders Bulganin and Khrushchev came for a return visit. The Indians in turn pulled out all the stops. Before the visitors arrived in Delhi, loudspeakers exhorted the people to turn out in large numbers, in gratitude for the reception the Russians had given

Nehru. There were indeed spectacular turnouts in all the cities the two men visited. There were several reasons for this enthusiasm: curiosity about the exotic and foreign, the Indian love of a good show, and not least the deep vein of anti-western feeling and of vicarious pride in Russia's challenge to the United States. The crowds were biggest in radical, anti-imperialist Calcutta, where students and factory workers made up a good proportion of the 500,000 people who came out to cheer the Soviet leaders. But even New Delhi was ablaze with illumination. "The brightly lit Delhi Stock Exchange vied with the Communist Party office in a challenge of festive lights."[44]

In their three weeks in India, Bulganin and Khrushchev visited steel mills and hydroelectric plants, and spoke at public meetings in no fewer than seven state capitals. The most significant of these, without question, was the capital of Jammu and Kashmir state, Srinagar. Here they made clear that they accepted the Valley as being part of the Indian Union, and the Kashmiris as being one of the "talented and industrious peoples of India."[45] Nothing could have sounded sweeter to Indian ears.

IV

On the eve of Nehru's departure for Moscow in 1955, an Indian critic had worried that he would be taken in by his hosts. For "like many another sensitive nature, accustomed in its late twenties and early thirties to regard the Soviet Union as truly Progressive, the Prime Minister seems never to have quite got over the vision of those days. Despite all that has happened since then, the Soviet [Union] still retains for him some of that enchantment. To its virtues he continues to be very kind, to its vices and cruelties, he is almost blind."[46]

The writer was A. D. Gorwala, a western-leaning liberal. There were others like him, Indians who believed that India should ally itself more strongly with the democracies in the cold war.[47] But these were most likely outnumbered, and certainly outshouted, by Indians who suspected the United States and favoured the Soviet Union. One reason for this was that while the United States was loath to ask its European allies to end their empires in Asia and Africa, the Russians spoke frequently about the evils of racism and colonialism.[48]

Nehru at first tried hard to avoid taking sides in the cold war. But, as he often said, this non-alignment was not merely an escape; it had a positive charge. A third bloc might come to have a salutary moderating effect on the hubris of the great powers. We have spoken already of the

Asian Relations Conference in 1947. Another such effort, in which Nehru played an important part, was the Afro-Asian conference, held in the Indonesian town of Bandung in 1955.

Only countries that had independent governments were invited to Bandung. Twenty-nine sent delegations, including India and China. Four African nations were represented (the others were still under the colonial yoke); and Iran, Iraq, Saudi Arabia, and Syria all came. The participants discussed methods of cultural and economic cooperation, and the conference committed itself firmly to the end of colonial rule. As President Sukarno of Indonesia observed, "how can we say that colonialism is dead so long as vast areas of Asia and Africa are unfree?"[49]

Nehru considered the Bandung Conference "a great achievement"; it "proclaimed the political emergence in world affairs of over half the world's population. [But] it presented no unfriendly challenge or hostility to anyone." As he told the Indian Parliament on his return, the historic links between Asian and African countries had been sundered by colonialism; now, as freedom dawned, they could be revived and reaffirmed.[50]

This last protestation was in answer to a charge that Bandung and the like were, in essence, anti-western. How "non-aligned," in fact, was non-alignment? In India, its ideals were put to the test in the second half of 1956. In July of that year Gamal Abdel Nasser nationalized the company that managed the Suez Canal. Britain (whose strategic interests were most threatened by the action) reacted by asking for international control over the canal. Nehru, who knew both parties well, tried hard to mediate. But he failed, and ultimately, in late October, the British, in collusion with the French and the Israelis, undertook a military invasion of Egypt. This act of neocolonial aggression drew worldwide condemnation. Finally, under American pressure, the Anglo-French alliance was forced to withdraw.[51]

Soon after the invasion of Egypt, Soviet tanks rolled into Budapest. A popular revolt had overthrown the Soviet client regime in favour of a more representative government, and Moscow reacted brutally to restore the status quo. Its action, like that of the British and the French in the Middle East, was viewed as an unacceptable infringement of national sovereignty.

Indian commentators saw the invasions of Egypt and Hungary as wholly comparable. Both were "acts of international brigandage" by powers that had permanent seats in the UN Security Council—and both had "spread a wave of cynicism throughout the world." As a journal in

Madras pointed out, "the independence of Egypt threatened the oil resources of the Anglo-French nations," It continued:

> The independence of Hungary would not only threaten the supply of
> uranium so essential for the maintenance of the Red Army in top
> form, but would cause a dangerous rift in the Soviet empire. London
> could not countenance the first and Moscow could not tolerate the
> second. Hence their acts of naked aggression which amounts to a sav-
> age exhibition of the predatory animal instinct.[52]

Nehru had criticized the Anglo-French intervention as soon as it
happened.[53] But now, when the United Nations met to discuss a resolution calling on the Soviet Union "to withdraw all of its forces without
delay from Hungarian territory," India, represented by V. K. Krishna
Menon, abstained. This caused great resentment in the western world,
and exposed the Indian government to a charge of applying a double
standard.[54]

There was also much domestic criticism of India's stand. There was
an angry debate in Parliament, and some in the press deplored "our
shameful sycophancy to the Soviet rulers." "By kowtowing to Russia we
have abdicated our moral pretensions," wrote one journalist. It was
speculated that the government may have been influenced by its uncertain hold over Kashmir, since one of the UN resolutions it had abstained
from asked for an internationally supervised plebiscite in Hungary.[55]

Later research has revealed that Nehru was actually deeply unhappy
about the Soviet invasion. He had sent several private messages to Moscow urging the Soviet Union to withdraw its troops. Afterwards, India
spoke out in public too, but the damage had been done. It was compounded when Nehru stood by Krishna Menon's original abstention, on
the grounds that insufficient information was available at the time.[56]

The fiasco over Hungary undermined Nehru's international credibility. Non-alignment was seen by some people as meaning "fierce condemnation of the Western bloc when its actions are wrong," but "equivocal
language when the Soviet bloc goes off the rails."[57] The episode also exposed the prime minister to the charge of putting personal loyalty over
national purpose—for while Nehru privately deplored what Krishna Menon had done, he stood by him in public.

Krishna Menon was an old friend of Nehru's, and in his own way
a remarkable man. He had been educated at the London School of
Economics, and was also the first editor of Penguin Books' prestigious

non-fiction imprint, Pelican. In the 1930s he had worked tirelessly in canvassing British support for Indian independence. But he also found time to act as an unofficial spokesman and literary agent for Nehru. After independence, he was rewarded with the high commissioner's job in London. Here he worked very hard, but he also made enemies, through his arrogance and by frequently advertising his friendship with the prime minister.[58]

After returning from London, Krishna Menon was made a cabinet minister without portfolio. He became a sort of roving ambassador, representing India at the UN and at disarmament meetings in Geneva. A man of forceful opinions, he was controversial in his homeland and outside it. The "lucidity of his intellect," wrote one journalist who knew him well, "is sometimes clouded by passions and resentments." Since his "likes and dislikes are stronger than would seem quite safe for a man in his position," it did seem "strange that a man who carries such a storm around with him should have been used for delicate diplomatic missions."[59]

Even before Hungary there had been adverse comment about the prime minister's reliance on Krishna Menon. In the Congress, there were many who were uncomfortable with his pro-communist leanings.[60] And the western press hated him; a newspaper in New York, for instance, noted the "lack of loveableness" in this "least tactful of diplomats."[61]

But Nehru would continue to stand by Menon. As early as 1953, it was being noticed in Delhi that the prime minister "turns blue when anyone criticises his diplomatic pet, Mr. Krishna Menon." This blindness was to cost Nehru dearly with regard to Hungary in 1956. But he still would not discard Menon. Why? A helpful answer is provided by Alva Myrdal, who was Sweden's ambassador in India at the time, and knew Nehru well. The prime minister, concluded Myrdal, "knew Menon's shortcomings but kept listening to him because of his brilliance. Menon was the only genuine intellectual foil Nehru had in the government," the only man with whom he could discuss Marx and Mill, Dickens and Dostoevsky.[62]

V

Let us now turn to India's relationship with its larger and even more populous neighbour, China. The two civilizations had long been linked by trade and culture. More recently, each had keenly watched the other's struggle against European domination. The Congress, and Nehru, had a particular regard for the Kuomintang leader Chiang Kai-shek, who had urged the Americans to in turn urge the British to grant the Indians independence.

In 1949, however, the Kuomintang were overthrown by the communists. What would relations now be like? To indicate continuity, India retained its ambassador to Beijing, the historian K. M. Pannikar. In May 1950, Pannikar was granted an interview with Mao Zedong, and came away greatly impressed. Mao's face, he recalled later, was "pleasant and benevolent and the look in his eyes is kindly." There "is no cruelty or hardness either in his eyes or in the expression of his mouth. In fact he gave me the impression of a philosophical mind, a little dreamy but absolutely sure of itself." The Chinese leader had "experienced many hardships and endured tremendous sufferings," yet "his face showed no signs of bitterness, cruelty or sorrow." Mao reminded Pannikar of his own boss, Nehru, for "both are men of action with dreamy, idealistic temperaments," and both "may be considered humanists in the broadest sense of the term."[63]

This would be laughable if it were not so serious. Intellectuals have always been strangely fascinated by powerful men; George Bernard Shaw wrote about Lenin in much the same terms. Yet Shaw was an unaffiliated writer, responsible only to himself. Pannikar was the official representative of his government. What he said and believed would carry considerable weight. And here he was representing one of history's most ruthless dictators as dreamy, soft, and poetic.

In October 1950, not long after Mao met Pannikar, China invaded and annexed Tibet. China had long claimed suzerainty over Tibet, and in the past had often exercised control over it. But there had also been periods when Tibet was genuinely independent, as in the four decades before the communist invasion. Tibet and China, after all, had sent separate, independent delegations to the Asian Relations Conference in 1947.

Nehru was now placed in an unenviable position. India had close relations with Tibet, economic as well as cultural. But a newly free and still vulnerable India could scarcely go to war on Tibet's behalf. Speaking in Parliament a few weeks after China's action, Nehru hoped that the matter would be resolved peacefully. He explained that he believed that although China had historically exercised some kind of "suzerainty" over Tibet, this did not amount to "sovereignty." He added that he did not see how Tibet could at all be a "threat" to China.[64]

Privately, Nehru thought "the Chinese acted rather foolishly" in annexing Tibet. There was "a strong feeling here [in India] of being let down by them." Still, thought the prime minister, "we have to be careful not to overdo" criticisms of a neighbouring country that was also emerging from the shadows of European domination.[65]

Other members of the government urged a stronger line. The home minister, Vallabhbhai Patel, for instance, was convinced that the Chinese had made a dupe out of Pannikar. They had lulled him into a "false sense of confidence" which led him to completely overlook the plans for the invasion. But now that the deed was done, it behooved India to be vigilant. Writing to Nehru on 7 November, Patel warned that "China is no longer divided. It is united and strong." "Recent and bitter history," said Patel,

> also tells us that communism is no shield against imperialism and that the Communists are as good or as bad imperialists as any other. Chinese ambitions in this respect not only cover the Himalayan slopes on our side but also include important parts of Assam. . . . Chinese irredentism and Communist imperialism are different from the expansionism or imperialism of the Western Powers. The former has a cloak of ideology which makes it ten times more dangerous. In the guise of ideological expansion lies concealed racial, national or historical claims.

Patel urged Nehru to be "alive to the new danger" from China, and to make India "defensively strong." He then outlined a series of steps to enhance security. He thought that in view of the "rebuff" over Tibet, India should no longer advocate China's entry into the UN. Finally, he argued that the latest developments should prompt a fresh reconsideration of "our relationship with China, Russia, America, Britain and Burma." Patel seemed here to be hinting that India should reconsider its policy of non-alignment in favour of an alliance with the West.[66]

This latter shift was advocated more vigorously by the journalist D. F. Karaka. Like Patel, Karaka was appalled by Pannikar's carelessness. (Apparently, the ambassador had not heard of the Chinese invasion until it was announced on All India Radio.) The annexation of Tibet had shown that the Himalaya were no longer impregnable. And the Indian army lacked the equipment or training to take on a determined and focused enemy. Thus, concluded Karaka, "whatever may be our past unhappy relations with Britain, however much may be our fear of American

Imperialism spreading in Asia, we have to decide now whether we will continue with this policy of neutrality and endanger our frontiers, or whether we will take the lesser risk and make a military pact with the United States and with Great Britain."[67]

Nehru would not deign to take notice of journalists like Karaka. But he did answer Patel, in a note on the subject circulated to the cabinet. He thought it a pity that Tibet could not be "saved." Yet he considered it "exceedingly unlikely" that India would now face an attack from China; it was "inconceivable" that the Chinese would "undertake a wild adventure across the Himalayas." He thought that "the idea that communism inevitably means expansion and war, or to put it more precisely, that Chinese communism means inevitably an expansion towards India, is rather naive." Regardless of the events in Tibet, India should still seek "some kind of understanding" with Beijing, for "India and China at peace with each other would make [a] vast difference to the whole set-up and balance of the world."[68]

A month later Patel died. Now there was no real opposition to a policy of "understanding" with China. The two countries shared a long border; a thousand miles of mostly unmarked and unsurveyed territory. On India's west, the border ran along the Buddhist-dominated district of Ladakh in Jammu and Kashmir state, which touched the Chinese provinces of Tibet and Sinkiang. On the east, the border was defined by the McMahon Line, drawn on the crest of the Himalaya, as a result of a treaty signed by the British and Tibet in 1914. In the middle, the two countries touched each other near the watershed of the Ganges River, which divided Tibet from the Indian state of Uttar Pradesh.

The border in the centre was relatively uncontentious, whereas in the two extremes the situation was more problematic. The Chinese regarded the McMahon Line in particular as an imperialist imposition. For the moment they let the matter pass, and focused on getting India's goodwill, necessary at this time as a bridge to the western world. In the summer of 1952 a government delegation led by Vijayalakshmi Pandit visited Beijing. Mrs. Pandit had served as India's ambassador to Moscow; more to the point, she was Nehru's adored younger sister. She met Mao once and Chou En-lai twice, and was profoundly impressed by both. Mao, wrote Mrs. Pandit to her brother, was "quiet [and] precise," with a "great sense of humour." His appearance in public called Gandhi to mind. As with the Mahatma, "the public doesn't just applaud him, they worship him. There is both love and adoration in the glances of those who look at him. It is moving to see." As for Chou En-lai, he "is a great statesman and possesses abundant vitality and charm. He is polished and has a sense of humour which is terribly infectious. One has to join in his laughter—and he laughs often. He makes one feel at home in a moment and his conversation loses nothing in translation."

The letter did strike an oddly ambivalent note. "We have been wined and dined," wrote Mrs. Pandit, "and have spoken of friendship and culture and peace until I am getting a little tired." And she wasn't sure whether the "great helmsman" reminded her more of Gandhi or of Stalin. For while "Mao gives the impression of being kind and tolerant and wise," the "tolerant part struck me almost as if it might be a pose as it is reminiscent of the Russian leaders particularly Stalin. He uses the same gesture in greeting and has the same technique with the public." Still, what stood out was "the great vitality of the people and the dedicated manner in which they are working. The oppression one feels in Moscow is absent here. Everybody seems happy and determined to make the country prosperous."[69]

Mrs. Pandit seems to have reacted to China in 1952 much as her brother reacted to Russia in 1927. Perhaps this dawn might not turn out be a false one after all. So Nehru was inclined to think, too. Soon, romanticism was to be reinforced by realpolitik. The United States began to tilt markedly toward Pakistan, giving New Delhi one more reason to befriend Peking. In a wide-ranging agreement signed in April 1954, India officially recognized Tibet as being part of China. The joint declaration outlined five principles of peaceful coexistence (*panch sheel*), which included mutual non-aggression and respect for each other's territorial integrity.[70]

One person who did not welcome this agreement was the former secretary general of the Foreign Ministry, Sir Girija Shankar Bajpai. Writing to a colleague, Bajpai warned that communist China was no "different from Russian Communism in its expansionist aims." The current thinking in New Delhi was "the naturalness of indefinite continuance of indefinite peace and friendship between China and us." Bajpai feared that "those on whom the P[rime] M[inister] now relies most for advice completely and vehemently reject any possibility of a change in what appears to be China's present policy of peace with its Asian neighbours."[71]

It is unlikely that this warning reached Nehru, and even if it had he would most likely have disregarded it. Toward the end of 1954 he visited China for the first time. As in Russia six months later, huge crowds were mobilized to greet the visitor, who appreciated this "tremendous emotional response from the Chinese people." Nehru had discussions with Chou En-lai about border questions, and with Mao about the world situation. He also pressed the case for Tibetan autonomy, the Chinese assuring him in the Dalai Lama's presence that the Buddhist state would have a status which "no other province enjoyed in the People's Republic of China."[72]

On his return from China Nehru addressed a mammoth public meeting on the maidan in Calcutta. A million people heard him affirm that "the people of China do not want war"; they were too busy uniting their country and getting rid of poverty. He spoke admiringly of the spirit of unity in China, the absence of the provincial and sectarian interests that bedevilled India. As for the "mighty welcome" he had received in the People's Republic, this was "not because I am Jawaharlal with any special ability, but because I am the Prime Minister of India for which the Chinese people cherish in their hearts the greatest of love and with which they want to maintain the friendliest of relations."[73]

Two years later the compliment was returned, when Chou En-lai visited India. With him were the Dalai and Panchen Lamas, who had been invited as part of the celebrations of the 2,500th anniversary of the Buddha's birth. On a drive through the countryside the Dalai Lama escaped his Chinese minders and travelled with Nehru. A revolt was brewing in Tibet against the occupiers, he said; he himself was strongly tempted to seek asylum in India. If that was not possible, at least India could send a consul to Lhasa who was not pro-Chinese and not pro-communist. When Nehru asked Chou about the situation in Tibet, the Chinese leader conceded that there had been "unfortunate incidents" there, and promised to look into them.[74]

So there the matter rested. The Dalai Lama went back to Lhasa, and India and China continued to be brothers in arms; as a slogan of the time went, *Hindi-Chini bhai-bhai*. The man most responsible for this was the charming Chou. He impressed Nehru, of course, but also a man more cynical by far, the veteran politician C. Rajagopalachari. "Rajaji" had lunch with the Chinese prime minister, and later wrote to a friend that "frankly my impression was very favourable. Apart from the general thawing of all communists the Chinese Premier is I believe a good type of man and trustworthy."[75]

In public India and China expressed undying friendship, but on the ground each was working to protect its own strategic interests. India was more concerned with the eastern sector; China with the western one. The British had drawn the McMahon Line to protect the prosperous tea estates of the province of Assam from a putative raid down the Himalaya. There was an "inner line" at the foot of the hills, beyond which no one could venture without a permit. Between this and the border lay some 50,000 square miles of densely forested territory, inhabited by many self-contained and self-administered tribes, each too small to be called a state, each too remote to be subservient to another, bigger state. Some of the tribes were Buddhist, and there was also an old Buddhist monastery at Tawang. This paid tribute to Tibetan authorities and was "ecclesiastically subject" to Lhasa.

By the treaty of 1914, the British persuaded the Tibetans to relinquish control over Tawang. As one colonial official argued, it was necessary to get this "undoubtedly Tibetan territory" into British India, "as otherwise Tibet and Assam will adjoin each other and, if Tibet should again come under Chinese control, it will be a dangerous position for us."[76]

Other tribes living between the "inner" and "outer" lines were beyond Tibetan influence. These, like the Buddhists, became Indian citizens by default in August 1947, when the new government inherited the borders bequeathed to it by the British. Slowly, New Delhi moved to fill in the administrative vacuum that the British had left behind. In February 1951 a small force accompanied by a political officer visited Tawang, and instructed the lamas that they need no longer pay tribute to Lhasa. Officials also began to fan out into what was now called the North-East Frontier Agency (NEFA). An Indian Frontier Administrative Service (IFAS) was formed, whose recruits were coached on how best to deal with the sometimes truculent tribes. The coach was the British-born anthropologist Verrier Elwin, who was now an Indian citizen and a confidant of Nehru's.[77]

The Chinese, for their part, focused on expanding their footprint in the western sector. Here, too, the adjoining Indian territory, known as Ladakh, was, like Tibet, Buddhist. However, it had been an independent state as early as the tenth century. And for the past 150 years it had been part of the principality of Kashmir, whose own allegiance was to the Indian side of the border.

Between northeast Ladakh and Sinkiang, on the Chinese side, was an elevated tableland, Aksai Chin, "absolutely bare" for the most part, with

only occasional patches of "scant herbage."[78] In the past, Ladakhi pastoralists had used Aksai Chin for grazing and salt collection. By an agreement of 1842 this area was identified as being part of Kashmir. This was
confirmed by the British, who were worried that the Russians, their adversary in the "Great Game," might use the plateau to advance heavy artillery into British India.

That didn't happen, but after 1950 the Chinese saw in the same flat
terrain a route to their troublesome province of Tibet from the Sinkiang
town of Yarkand. Peking sent surveyors to scout the land, and in 1956
began building a road across Aksai Chin. By October 1957 the road was
ready, equipped to carry ten-ton military trucks with arms and personnel from Yarkand to Lhasa.

We owe this information to accounts published much later. At the
time, the Chinese activities in the west, and the Indian activities in the
east, were carried on out of each other's gaze. To the world at large, and
to their own citizens, the two Asian neighbours were bound by an exemplary relationship of friendship and cooperation.

VI

 "If there were ever two countries where every prospect promised broth-
erly understanding and friendship," wrote a Bombay newspaper in January 1952, "these two are India and Pakistan. Every possible kind of tie
exists between them; the tie of race, the ties of language, of geography,
economy and culture."[79]

Yet India's relations with Pakistan were poisoned from the start. The
country had been divided against a backdrop of violence, and the mutual
suspicion and hostility persisted. In the winter of 1949–1950 there was a
wave of communal riots in East Pakistan. Several hundred thousand Hindus crossed over the border into India. Nehru now suggested to his Pakistani counterpart, Liaqat Ali Khan, that they together visit the affected
areas to bring about peace. His offer was declined; but Khan agreed to
come to Delhi and sign an agreement binding both countries to the humane treatment of their respective minorites. However, the "Nehru-Liaqat"
pact failed to stem the tide of refugees. There was much anger among Hindus in West Bengal, some of whom even wanted the government to go to
war with Pakistan on their behalf.[80]

The two main conflicts were about elemental human needs: land and
water. The first, which this book has already mentioned and to which it

will return, related to the unresolved status of Kashmir. The second pertained to the fair use of the Indus and its five main tributaries. These rivers ran from east to west, that is, from India toward Pakistan. The Indus and the Jhelum entered Pakistan before any major extraction was possible, but the other four rivers ran for many miles in Indian territory. This made it possible for India to regulate their flow and impound water before the rivers reached Pakistan.

After partition, the governments of East and West Punjab signed a "Standstill Agreement" whereby water continued to flow uninterrupted. When this agreement lapsed, in April 1948, India stopped the waters of the Ravi and the Sutlej from flowing west. The Indians claimed that no fresh agreement had been signed, but it was widely believed that the action was revenge for Pakistan's backing of the invasion of Kashmir. The drying up of their canals created panic among the farmers of West Punjab. Within a month a new agreement was signed, and the water supply was restored. However, the building of the Bhakra-Nangal dam, on the Indian side of the Sutlej River, prompted fresh protests by Pakistan.

Both sides now sought a more permanent solution. Pakistan asked for the matter to be referred to international arbitration, which India at first refused. The World Bank stepped in to play the role of peacemaker. Knowing the recalcitrance of both sides, the bank offered a surgical solution—the waters of three rivers would go to Pakistan, and the waters of the other three rivers to India. This proposal was made in February 1954; it took another six years for the two sides to finally sign it.[81]

With the Indus, as with Kashmir or any other topic under the subcontinental sun, agreement was made more difficult by domestic politics. An Indian or Pakistani head of government who promoted dialogue was invariably accused of selling out to the other side. An early example of this was the trade war of 1949–1951, prompted by the devaluation of the Indian rupee. Pakistan stopped the shipment of jute in protest; India retaliated by refusing to supply coal.[82] The conflict was resolved only when, in February 1951, Nehru agreed to recognize the par value of the Pakistani rupee. His decision was welcomed by chambers of commerce, but bitterly opposed by politicians of all stripes. The consensus in New Delhi was that "India has been completely defeated." A congressman reported that the feeling in the party office was that "such a humiliation could not have been possible if Sardar Patel were alive." A refugee leader remarked: "The real question to be considered now is to find out the next issue on which Jawaharlal will surrender to Pakistan—Kashmir, or more probably Evacuee Property." A spokesman for the Hindu Mahasabha said: "In order to become a world leader, Nehru can go to the extent of surrendering the whole of India to Pakistan." And an organizer for the RSS claimed: "This shows what is to come next. More appeasement and surrenders if the masses do not check Nehru."[83]

On the Pakistani side, any concession to India was likewise seen by opposition politicians as appeasement of the enemy. At the popular level, however, the feelings about the other side were distinctly mixed. Nationalist ideology drove them apart; but mass culture brought them back together again. It was not just that they ate the same food and lived in the same kinds of homes. They also had the same sense of fun. Indian film stars were widely admired in Pakistan; and Pakistani cricketers were given a rousing reception when they played in India.

This ambivalence is captured in an exchange printed by the Karachi newspaper *Dawn* in 1955. A woman who had recently visited her relatives in India wrote of her experiences while travelling in a train from Amritsar to Ambala. When people heard she was from Pakistan, she was set upon by passengers who were refugees from Sindh and West Punjab. Apparently, "some of the non-refugee Hindu passengers remonstrated, but the refugee Hindus and Sikhs brushed aside their remonstrance, saying that the non-refugees could not realise the suffering of the refugees from Pakistan." This account of Indian animosity provoked several letters recounting the warmth and hospitality offered on the other side of the border. A man advised any future traveller to India to "indulge in Amroods and Pans [guavas and betel leaf] which are at their best these days instead of indulging in such talks as tend to injure the growing Indo-Pak accord." A woman correspondent complained that such "misstatements" created bitterness and precluded "amity between India and Pakistan." This last ideal was then endorsed by the original letter writer, with this telling caveat: "I wish, however, that as a Pakistani, which I suppose she is, she had the delicacy of stating 'Pakistan and India' instead of 'India and Pakistan.'"[84]

VII

Indian foreign policy was opposed to the continuance of colonial rule anywhere. This, naturally, implied reclaiming the pieces of the motherland that were still under the control of foreigners. When the British left in

1947, the Portuguese stayed on in Goa and their other possessions in India, and the French remained in control of three slivers of land in the south—most importantly the port of Pondicherry—as well as the eastern enclave of Chandernagore.

In June 1949, the population of Chandernagore voted by an overwhelming majority to merge with India. The election had elicited a resounding display of patriotism, with posters representing a mother in Indian dress reaching out to reclaim a child clad in western apparel. A year later the territory was transferred. But the French hung on to their slices of south India. In the spring of 1954 the situation became "increasingly tense"; there was a vigorous pro-merger movement in Pondicherry, and there were daily demonstrations in front of the French consulate in Madras. On 1 November the French finally handed over their territories, and the Indians celebrated with a spectacular display of fireworks. The following January, the annual Republic Day parade for the first time featured a float from Pondicherry, with girls singing French songs.[85]

In welcoming back these fragments, Jawaharlal Nehru praised the governments of both countries for their "tolerance, good sense and wisdom," in solving the problem of French India "with grace and goodwill."[86] These remarks were intended above all for the Portuguese, who, however, were not listening. They were determined to hang on to Goa as long as they could. As the transfer of Pondicherry was being finalized, the Portuguese dictator, Antonio de Oliveira Salazar, spoke on national radio of their Indian colonies as belonging to "the Portuguese Nation by injunction of History and force of Law." "Goa constitutes a Portuguese community in India," he insisted. "Goa represents a light of the West in lands of the Orient." It had to be retained, so that it might "continue to be the memorial of Portuguese discoveries and a small hearth of the spirit of the West in the East."[87]

Well before independence, there was a Goa Congress Commitee in operation; its activists included resident Goans as well as exiles in Bombay. They argued that conditions were far worse in Goa than in British India; race prejudice was rife; and human rights were wholly absent. In 1946, the left-wing congressman Rammanohar Lohia visited the territory and exhorted the people to rise against the rulers. A wave of strikes and protests followed; these were crushed by the authorities. On 15 August 1947, the Indian tricolour was hoisted here and there, but the protesters were quickly taken away by the police.[88]

Apart from Goa, the Portuguese also held several smaller territories up the Konkan coast. One was Daman, which had a garrison of 1,500 soldiers from Portuguese East Africa. This abutted the Indian province of Bombay, which after independence had prohibited the sale and consumption of alcohol. There was now a flourishing trade in the smuggling of liquor. On Sunday evenings, the frontier between Daman and Bombay was "strewn with pilgrims to Bacchus, wending their way back to the land where they belong, back to Bharat, land of scarcity and austerity."[89]

Alcoholics apart, most politically conscious Indians were outraged by Portugal's attitude regarding its colonies. Nehru at first moved slowly, hoping that the matter would be resolved by dialogue. But his hand was being forced by radicals of the Socialist party, who began a series of satyagrahas to compel Goa to join the union. In July 1954 a group of activists from Bombay seized the tiny enclave of Dadra. The next month the somewhat bigger enclave of Nagar-Haveli also fell without a fight. Then, 1,000 volunteers attempted to cross over to Daman on Independence Day. They were stopped by the Indian police, whereupon they telegraphed the prime minister for support. Nehru wired back saying that such a showdown would not "help our cause."[90]

The socialists were only temporarily deterred. A year later a group led by N. G. Goray entered Goa shouting slogans. They walked several miles into the territory before being attacked by the police. Several protesters were badly injured. The satyagrahis were put in Fort Aguada prison, where they spent twenty months before being released. During these protests in 1954 and 1955, the Portuguese arrested more than 2,000 people.[91]

VIII

For Jawaharlal Nehru, foreign policy was a means of making India's presence felt in the world. After independence he personally supervised the creation of the Indian foreign service (IFS), transferring to it able officers from the ICS and making new appointments from among the young. A job in the IFS had a nearly unique combination of idealism and glamour; it also offered the chance of personal contact with the prime minister. One IFS officer recalled how, early in 1948, he was called into Nehru's office, and showed a map of the world. The prime minister's eyes ranged over the map, and his fingers pointed to places north, south, east, and west. "We will have forty embassies!" Nehru exclaimed. "We will have forty missions!"[92]

Five years later, when India did have forty missions, Nehru wrote them all a letter of congratulation. The "prestige of India has greatly increased" since independence, he said; "we have always avoided playing a flashy role in international affairs. . . . Gradually, an appreciation has grown in other countries of our own sincerity of purpose even though there has been disagreement." He asked all those representing India abroad—"from the Head of the Mission to the humblest employee"—to "feel and work as a happy family, cooperating with each other. . . . We are all partners in a great adventure, and are all partners and comrades in the same undertaking."[93]

Although presented and carried out as a collective enterprise, this particular adventure had "made by the prime minister" stamped all over it. In 1950, one of his most intelligent and least sycophantic cabinet ministers spoke of how Nehru was becoming "the biggest man in the world, overtopping the U. S. A. men, the U. K. men and every other man." Through its leader, a country "without material, men or money—the three means of power"—was "now fast coming to be recognised as the biggest moral power in the civilized world, . . . her word listened to with respect in the councils of the great."[94] Even opposition politicians appreciated what Nehru had done for India's international standing. Non-alignment seemed to them a creative application of Gandhian principles in world affairs. Confidence in its viability was strengthened when India was called on to play an important mediatory role in the conflicts and civil wars of the time.

Intelligent foreigners also praised Nehru's non-alignment. When the great publishing firm Feltrinelli of Milan began operations in 1955, one of the first two books it published was Nehru's *Autobiography*, which it praised both for "consistent and coherent anti-Fascism" and as an authentic voice of "the countries that were emerging from colonial domination . . . to take their place forcefully in the global political system."[95] And from the Swedish embassy in New Delhi, Alva Myrdal wrote to her husband, Gunnar, that Nehru was "naturally playing an authoritative, not to say world-historical role without the slightest tendency to Caesarism. Isn't it true that he is perhaps the only person we have seen reach a high and powerful position without taking on new self-importance?"[96]

Such was Nehru's standing among the people of the front-line states in the cold war, those who stood between the United States and the Soviet Union. In 1955 non-alignment still had about it a glow and a moral halo. The next year brought the invasion of Hungary, and the beginning of westerners' disillusionment with Nehru. It took longer for him to lose the enchanted support of his countrymen.

9

REDRAWING *the* MAP

Some want to revive the tradition of Shivaji and to hoist the
Bhagwa Jhanda in Samyukta Maharashtra; others wish to extend
the economic empire of the Bombay and Ahmedabad millionaires
all over Maha-Gujarat. Provincial prejuidices, rivalries and
jealousies are being revived on all sides and everyone seems
anxious to separate from, rather than unite with the others. The
Assamese want this bit of land cut off from Bengal, the Bengalis
want a slice of Bihar, the Telugus are discontented in Orissa, the
Tamilian minority wants to cut itself off from Travancore.

The left-wing writer K. A. ABBAS, in January 1951

I

THE LEADING INDIAN NATIONALISTS had long been sensible of
the power of the mother tongue to rouse and move. India was a
land of many languages, each with its distinct script, grammar,
vocabulary, and literary traditions. Rather than deny this diversity, the
Congress sought to give space to it. As early as 1917, the party had committed itself to the creation of linguistic provinces in a free India. A separate Andhra circle was formed in that year, a separate Sindh circle the
following year. After the Nagpur Congress of 1920, the principle was extended and formalized, with the creation of provincial Congress committees by linguistic zones: the Karnataka Pradesh Congress Committee
(PCC), the Orissa PCC, the Maharashtra PCC, etc. Notably, these did
not follow, and were often at odds with, the administrative divisions of
British India.

The linguistic reorganization of the Congress was encouraged and
supported by Mahatma Gandhi. When independence came, in August
1947, Gandhi thought that the states of the new nation should be defined
on the basis of language. On 10 October 1947 he wrote to a colleague:
"I do believe that we should hurry up with the reorganization of linguistic provinces. . . . There may be an illusion for the time being that different languages stand for different cultures, but there is also the possibility

[that with the creation] of linguistic provinces it may disappear. I shall write something [about it] if I get the time. . . . I am not unaware that a class of people have been saying that linguistic provinces are wrong. In my opinion, this class delights in creating obstacles."[1]

Jawaharlal Nehru also appreciated the linguistic diversity of India. In an essay of 1937, he wrote that "a living language is a throbbing, vital thing, ever changing, ever growing and mirroring the people who speak and write it." And "our great provincial languages are no dialects or vernaculars, as the ignorant sometimes call them. They are ancient languages with a rich inheritance, each spoken by many millions of people, each tied up inextricably with the life and culture and ideas of the masses as well as the upper classes. It is axiomatic that the masses can only grow educationally and culturally through the medium of their own language."[2]

That was Nehru's view in 1937; but by 1947 he was having other thoughts. The country had just been divided on the basis of religion: would not dividing it further on the basis of language merely encourage the break-up of the Indian Union? Why not keep intact the existing administrative units, such as Madras, which had within it communities of Tamil, Malayalam, Telugu, Kannada, Urdu, and Konkani speakers; and Bombay, whose peoples spoke Marathi, Gujarati, Urdu, Sindhi, Gondi, and other tongues? Would not such multilingual and multicultural states provide exemplary training in harmonious living? In any case, should not the new nation unite on the secular ideals of peace, stability, and economic development, rather than revive primordial identities of caste and language?

Nehru gave voice to these reservations in a speech to the Constituent Assembly three months after independence. Although the Congress had once promised lingustic provinces, he said, the country now faced "a very critical situation resulting from partition." Now "disruptionist tendencies had come to the fore"; to check them, one had to underline "the security and stability of India. . . . The first essential therefore is for India as a whole to be strong and firmly established, confident in her capacity to meet all possible dangers and face and meet all problems. If India lives, all parts of India also live and prosper. If India is enfeebled, all her component elements grow weak."[3]

The creation of linguistic provinces, then, had to be deferred until such time as India was strong and sure of herself. Nehru seems to have persuaded even Gandhi of this, for in November 1947 the Mahatma was writing that "the reluctance to enforce linguistic redistribution is perhaps justifiable in the present depressing atmosphere. The exclusive spirit is ever uppermost. No one thinks of the whole of India." Gandhi now thought that the reorganization of provinces should be postponed until a calmer time, when communal strife had died out and been replaced by "a healthy atmosphere, promoting concord in the place of discord, peace in the place of strife, progress in the place of retrogression and life in the place of death."[4]

As ever, Gandhi stressed the need to take "one step at a time." But the principle itself he would not surrender. In a prayer meeting held on 25 January 1948, Gandhi returned to the subject of lingustic states. "The Congress had decided some twenty years ago," he recalled, "that there should be as many provinces in the country as there are major languages." Now it was in power, and in a position to execute that promise. Gandhi thought that if new provinces were formed on the basis of language, and if "they are all placed under the authority of Delhi there is no harm at all. But it will be very bad if they all want to be free and refuse to accept central authority. It should not be that Bombay then will have nothing to do with Maharashtra and Maharashtra with Karnataka and Karnataka with Andhra. Let all live as brothers. Moreover if linguistic provinces are formed it will also give a fillip to the regional languages. It would be absurd to make Hindusthani the medium of instruction in all the regions and it is still more absurd to use English for this purpose."[5]

Within a week Gandhi was dead. And the men in power had other, more urgent matters to attend to. Millions of refugees from East and West Pakistan had to be found homes and gainful employment. An undeclared war was on in Kashmir. A new constitution had to be decided on. Elections had to be scheduled, economic policies framed and executed. For now, the creation of new provinces had to wait, perhaps indefinitely.

Nehru's reluctance to impose divisions of language on the recent division by religion had the support of both Vallabhbhai Patel and C. Rajagopalachari. The latter insisted that "further fissiparious forces" had to be checked forthwith.[6] And Patel worked hard within the Constituent Assembly to reverse the official Congress position. Under his direction, the assembly appointed a committee of jurists and civil servants to report on the question. This committee recognized the force of popular sentiment—the "strong appeal" that the demand for linguistic sentiments made on "many of our countrymen"—but concluded that in the prevailing unsettled conditions "the first and last need of India at the present moment is that it should be made a nation. . . . Everything which helps the growth of nationalism has to go forward and everything which throws obstacles in its way has to be rejected or should stand over. We have applied this test to linguistic provinces also, and judged by this test, in our opinion [they] cannot be supported."[7]

This verdict caused dismay in large sections of the Constituent Assembly. Most congressmen who spoke Marathi insisted on a separate Maharashtra state. Party members who claimed Gujarati as their mother tongue likewise wanted a province of their own. Similar were the aspirations of congressmen who spoke Telugu, Kannada, Malayalam, or Oriya. To calm the clamour, a new committee was appointed. Both Nehru and Patel served on it; the third member was the party historian and former Congress president, Pattabhi Sitaramayya.

This committee, known as the JVP Commitee after the initials of its members, revoked the seal of approval that the Congress had once put on the principle of linguistic provinces. It argued that "language was not only a binding force but also a separating one." Now, when the "primary consideration must be the security, unity and economic prosperity of India," "every separatist and disruptive tendency should be rigorously discouraged."

II

To quote one authority, Robert King, the report of the JVP Committee was a "cold-water therapy." It "slowed things for a while."[8] But the fires soon started up again. In 1948 and 1949 there was a renewal of movements aimed at linguistic autonomy. There was the campaign for Samyukta or Greater Karnataka, aiming to unite Kannada-speakers spread across the states of Madras, Mysore, Bombay, and Hyderabad. Complementing this was the struggle for Samyukta Maharashtra, which sought to bring together Marathi-speakers in a single political unit. The Malayalis wanted a state of their own, based on the merger of the princely states of Cochin and Travancore with Malabar. There was also a Mahagujarat movement.

In a class of its own was the struggle for a Sikh state in the Punjab. This brought together claims of language as well as religion. The Sikhs had been perhaps the main sufferers from partition. They had lost their most productive lands to Pakistan. Now, in what remained of India, they had to share space and influence with the Hindus.

Around 1950, the Hindus were roughly 62% of the population of the Indian Punjab, and the Sikhs about 35%. However, these figures masked a major regional divide. The eastern half of the province was a chiefly Hindi-speaking region, with Hindus being about 88% of the population. The western half was a Punjabi-speaking region, with Sikhs constituting a little over half the population.

The division by religion did not perfectly map division by language. All Sikhs had Punjabi as their first language, and so did many Hindus. However, the Hindus were prone to view Punjabi as merely a local dialect of Hindi, whereas the Sikhs insisted it was not just a language in its own right, but also a holy one. The Sikhs wrote and read Punjabi in the Gurmukhi script, whose alphabet they believed to have come from the mouth of the guru.[9]

Since the 1920s, the interests of the politically conscious Sikhs had been represented by the Akali Dal. This was both a religious body and a political party. It controlled the Sikh shrines, or gurdwaras, but also contested elections. The long-time leader of the Akali Dal was Master Tara Singh, an important, intriguing figure, who (like many such figures in Indian history) has yet to find a biographer.

Tara Singh was born in June 1885, as a Hindu. This fact should not unduly surprise us, since the first-generation convert is often the most effective—not to say fundamentalist—of religious leaders. He studied at the Khalsa College in Amritsar, excelling academically and also on the soccer field, where his steadfastness as a defender earned him the sobriquet Patthar, "the rock." Rather than join the colonial government, he became headmaster of a Sikh school in Lyallpur, acquiring the title "master."[10]

In the 1920s Tara Singh joined the movement to rid the Sikh shrines of the decadent priests who then ran them. In 1931 he became the head of the Shiromani Gurdwara Prabandhak Committee, a position with vast authority and influence, not least over money. For the next thirty years he was the most resolute and persistent defender of the Sikh community, or *panth*. He was able to project himself as "the only consistent and long-suffering upholder of the Panth as a separate political entity, as the one Sikh leader who relentlessly pursued the goal of political power territorially organized for the Sikh community, and as a selfless leader without personal ambition."[11]

Before 1947 Tara Singh insisted that the Sikh *panth* was in danger from the Muslims and the Muslim League. After 1947 he said it was in danger from the Hindus and the Congress. His rhetoric became more robust as the general elections of 1951–1952 approached. He inveighed against Hindu domination and proclaimed that "for the sake of religion, for the sake of culture, for the sake of the Panth, and to keep high the flag of the Guru, the Sikhs have girded their loins to achieve independence."[12]

Tara Singh was arrested several times between 1948 and 1952, for defying bans on public gatherings and for what were seen as "inflammatory" speeches. Hundreds of his supporters went to jail with him. He had strong support among the Sikh peasantry, particularly among the upper-caste Jats. Tara Singh's use of the term "independence" was deliberately ambiguous. The Jat peasants wanted a Sikh province within India, not a sovereign nation. They wanted to get rid of the Hindu-dominated eastern Punjab, leaving a state where they would be a comfortable majority. But by hinting at secession Tara Singh put pressure on the government, and simultaneously convinced his flock of his own commitment to the cause.

Not all Sikhs were behind Tara Singh, however. The low-caste Sikhs, who feared the Jats, were opposed to the Akali Dal. Some Jats had joined the Congress. And in a tendentious move, many Punjabi-speaking Hindus identified Hindi as their mother tongue in the census of 1951.

But the biggest blow to Tara Singh was the general election itself. In the Punjab assembly, which had 126 seats, the Akalis won a mere fourteen.

III

Without question the most vigorous movement for linguistic autonomy was that of the Telugu-speakers of the Andhra country. Telugu was spoken by more people in India than any other language besides Hindi. It had a rich literary history, and was associated with such symbols of Andhra glory as the Vijayanagara Empire. While India was still under British rule, the Andhra Mahasabha had worked hard to cultivate a sense of identity among the Telugu-speaking peoples of the Madras presidency, who, they argued, had been discriminated against by the Tamils. The Mahasabha was also active in the princely state of Hyderabad.

After independence, the speakers of Telugu asked the Congress to implement its old resolutions in favour of linguistic states. The methods they used to advance their case were various: petitions, representations, street marches, and fasts. In a major blow to the Congress, the former chief minister of Madras, T. Prakasam, resigned from the party in 1950 over the issue of statehood. Cutting across party lines, the Telugu-speaking legislators in the Madras Assembly urged the immediate creation of a state to be named "Andhra Pradesh." In the monsoon of 1951 a congressman turned swami named Sitaram went on hunger strike in support of this idea. After five weeks he gave up the fast, in response to an appeal by the respected Gandhian leader Vinoba Bhave.[13]

The case for Andhra was now put to the test of universal adult suffrage. During his campaign tour in the Telugu-speaking districts, Jawaharlal Nehru was met at several places by protesters waving black flags and shouting, "We want Andhra."[14] The official party paper wrote in dismay that "the Congress President witnessed demonstrations by protagonists of an Andhra State, with slogans, placards and posters. At some places he smiled at them, at others he was enraged by their behaviour."[15] The signs were ominous, and indeed despite its successes elsewhere the Congress did very poorly here. Of the 145 seats from the region in the Madras legislative assembly, the party won only forty-three. The bulk of the other seats were won by parties supporting the Andhra movement. These included the communists, who won as many as forty-one seats.

The election results encouraged the revival of the Andhra movement. Toward the end of February 1952, Swami Sitaram began a march through the Telugu-speaking districts, drumming up support for the struggle. He said the creation of the state "could not wait any longer." Andhras "were ready to pay the price to achieve the same." The swami urged all Telugu-speaking members of the Madras assembly to boycott its proceedings till such time as the state of their dreams had been carved out.[16]

The agitating Andhras hated two people in particular: the prime minister and the chief minister of Madras, C. Rajagopalachari. Both had gone on record as saying that they did not think that the creation of Andhra was a good idea. Both emphasized that even if, against their will, the state came into being, the city of Madras would not be part of it. This enraged the Andhras, who had a strong demographic and economic presence in the city, and who believed that they had as good a claim to it as the Tamils.[17]

On 22 May, Nehru told Parliament that "for some years now our foremost efforts have been directed to the consolidation of India. Personally, I would look upon anything that did not help this process of consolidation as undesirable. Even though the formation of linguistic provinces may be desirable in some cases, this would obviously be the wrong time. When the right time comes, let us have them by all means."

As K. V. Narayana Rao has written, "this attitude of Nehru appeared too vague and evasive to the Andhras. Nobody knew what the right time was and when it would come." Impatient for an answer, the Andhras intensified their protest. On 19 October 1952, a man named Potti Sriramulu began a fast unto death in Madras. He had the blessing of Swami Sitaram, and of thousands of other Telugu-speakers.[18]

Sriramulu was born in Madras in 1901, and studied sanitary engineering before taking a job with the railroads. In 1928 he suffered a double tragedy, when his wife died along with their newborn child. Two years later he resigned his position to join the Salt Satyagraha. Later, he spent some time at Gandhi's Sabarmati ashram. Later still, he spent eighteen months in jail as part of the individual satyagraha campaign of 1940–1941.

An adulatory study published in 1985 by the Committee for History of Andhra Movement claimed that Potti Sriramulu's stay at Mahatma Gandhi's ashram "was epoch-making. For here was a seeker full of love and humility, all service and all sacrifice for his fellow-humanity; and here also was a guru, the world-teacher, equally full of affection, truth, *ahimsa* and kinship with *Daridra Narayana* or the suffering poor. While at Sabarmati, [Sriramulu] . . . did his tasks with cheer and devotion, and won the affection of the intimates and the approbation of the Kulapati [Gandhi]."[19]

Gandhi did regard Sriramulu with affection but also, it must be said, with a certain exasperation. On 25 November 1946 the disciple had begun a fast unto death to demand the opening of all temples in Madras province to untouchables. Other congressmen, their minds more focused on the impending freedom of India, urged him to desist. When he refused, they approached Gandhi, who persuaded him to abandon the fast. The Mahatma then wrote to T. Prakasam that he was "glad that the fast of Sreeramulu ended in the happy manner you describe. He had sent me a telegram immediately he broke his fast. I know he is a solid worker, though a little eccentric."[20]

Potti Sriramulu had called off that fast of 1946 at Gandhi's insistence. But in 1952 the Mahatma was dead; and in any case, Andhra meant more to Sriramulu than the untouchables once had. This fast he would carry out till the end, or until the government of India relented.

On 3 December, Nehru wrote to Rajagopalachari: "Some kind of fast is going on for the Andhra Province and I get frantic telegrams. I am totally unmoved by this and I propose to ignore it completely." By this time Sriramulu had not eaten for six weeks. As his ordeal went on, support for the cause grew. Hartals were called in many towns. The sociologist André Béteille, travelling to Madras from Calcutta at this time, recalls having his train stopped at Vizag by an angry mob shouting slogans against Rajaji and Nehru.[21]

Nehru now had to recognize the force of popular sentiment. On 12 December he wrote again to Rajaji, suggesting that the time had come to accept the demand for Andhra. "Otherwise complete frustration will grow among the Andhras, and we will not be able to catch up with it." Two days later Rajaji cabled the prime minister in desperation: "We might prevent more mischief if you summon repeat summon Swami Sitaram to Delhi. He is now in Madras hanging round the fasting gentleman, Sriramulu. The entire mischief starts from this focus, as the Andhra boys are highly emotional and prone to rowdyism. If you invite Sitaram for a talk, the atmosphere may change and probably the mischief may dwindle away."[22]

By now it was too late. On 15 December, fifty-eight days into this fast, Potti Sriramulu died. Now all hell broke loose. "The news of the passing away of Sriramulu engulfed entire Andhra in chaos." Government offices were attacked, and trains were stopped and defaced. The damage to state property ran into millions of rupees. Several protesters were killed when the police fired on them.[23] Nehru had once claimed that "facts, not fasts" would decide the issue. Now, faced with the prospect of widespread and possibly uncontrollable protest, the prime minister gave in. Two days after Sriramulu's death, he made a statement saying that a state of Andhra would come into being.

Over the next few months, the Telugu districts of Madras Province were identified for separation. The division of the province, wrote the chief minister, was "accompanied by a lot of bad language, bad behaviour and distrust and anger."[24] Suppressing his feelings, Rajagopalachari attended the ceremonies for the new state of Andhra at Kurnool on 1 October 1953. Also in attendance—as the chief guest—was that other erstwhile enemy of the Andhras, Prime Minister Jawaharlal Nehru.

IV

The formation of Andhra Pradesh grated on the prime minister. "You will observe," wrote Jawaharlal Nehru grimly to a colleague in the cabinet, "that we have disturbed the hornet's nest and I believe most of us are likely to be badly stung."[25]

As Nehru had feared, the creation of Andhra intensified similar demands by other language groups. Somewhat against its will, the government of India appointed a States Reorganization Commission (SRC) to "make recommendations in regard to the broad principles which should govern the solution of this [linguistic] problem." Through 1954 and 1955 the commissioners travelled across India. They visited 104 towns and cities: interviewed more than 9,000 people; and received as many as 152,250 written submissions.

One of the longer and more interesting submissions was by the Bombay Citizens' Committee. This was headed by a leading cotton magnate, Sir Purushottamdas Thakurdas; and within its ranks were other prominent industrialists such as J. R. D. Tata. On its masthead were many of the city's most successful lawyers, scholars, and doctors.

The Bombay Citizens' Committee had a one-point agenda—to keep the city out of the state of Maharashtra. To make its case, it printed an impressive 200-page book, replete with charts, maps, and tables. The first chapter was historical, showing how the city was settled by successive waves of settlers from different linguistic communities. This chapter claimed that there had been little Maharashtrian immigration before the end of the nineteenth century. Even now, the Marathi-speakers were only 43% of the city's population. The second chapter spoke of Bombay's importance in the economic life of India. It was the premier centre of industry, finance, and foreign trade. It was India's window to the world: more planes flew in and out of it than all other cities combined. The third and fourth chapters were sociological, demonstrating the multilingual and multicultural character of the city. To quote a European observer, Bombay was "perhaps the most motley assemblage in any quarter of this orb"; to quote another, it was "a true centre of the diverse varieties and types of mankind, far surpassing the mixed nationalities of Cairo and Constantinople." The fifth chapter was geographical, an argument for Bombay's physical isolation, with the sea and the mountains separating it from the Marathi-speaking heartland.

The first settlers were Europeans; the chief merchants and capitalists were Gujaratis and Parsis; the chief philanthrophists were Parsis. The city was built by non-Maharashtrians. Even among the working class, Marathi-speakers were often outnumbered by north Indians and Christians. To the Bombay Citizens' Committee, it was clear that "on the grounds of geography, history, language and population or the system of law, Bombay and North Konkan cannot be considered as a part of the Mahratta region as claimed by the protagonists of Samyukta Maharashtra."[26]

Beneath the veneer of cosmopolitanism there was one language group that dominated the "save Bombay" movement: the Gujaratis. If Bombay became the capital of a Greater Maharashtra state, the politicians and ministers would be mostly Marathi-speaking. The prospect was not entirely pleasing to the Gujarati-speaking bourgeoisie, whether Hindu or Parsi. It was they who staffed, financed, and basically ran the Bombay Citizens' Committee.[27]

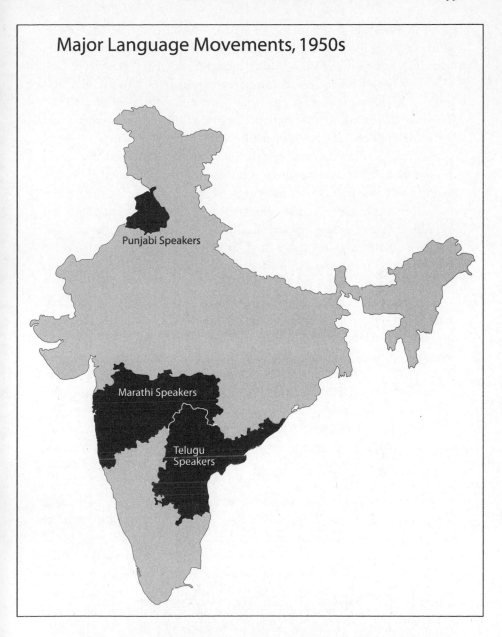

Major Language Movements, 1950s

Punjabi Speakers

Marathi Speakers

Telugu Speakers

Nehru himself was somewhat sympathetic to the idea of keeping Bombay out of the control of a single language group, and so was the Marathi-speaking M. S. Golwalkar—a rare meeting of minds between the prime minister and the RSS leader. Both thought that the creation of linguistic states would "lead to bitterness and give rise to fissiparous tendencies endangering the unity of the country."[28] In May 1954 Golwalkar spoke in Bombay at the invitation of the Anti-Provincial Conference, which saw linguistic demands as a manifestation of "the menace of provincialism and sectionalism." "Multiplicity breeds strife," thundered Golwalkar. "One nation and one culture are my principles." To see oneself as Tamil or Maharashtrian or Bengali was to "sap the vitality of the nation." He wished them all to use the label "Hindu." Here, he diverged from Nehru, who of course wished them all to be "Indian."[29]

But just as other congressmen did not see eye to eye with Nehru on this question, there were members of RSS who diverged from their leader. As early as 1946, there was a Samyukta Maharashtra Parishad in operation. In its ranks were Maharashtrians of all political persuasions: left and right; secular and communal; Brahman, Maratha, and Harijan. The Parishad sought a state that would unite Marathi-speakers dispersed across many different political units. In their minds, however, there was no doubt that such a state could have only one capital: Bombay.

The president of the Samyukta Maharashtra Parishad was the veteran congressman Shankarrao Deo; its secretary and chief theoretician was the celebrated Cambridge-trained economist D. R. Gadgil. In Gadgil's opinion, although Bombay could still be the major port and economic centre of Maharashtra, there must be a "compulsory decentralization" of the city's industries. Another ideologue, G. V. Deshmukh, was more blunt. Unless Bombay city became part of their state, he said, Maharashtrians would have to remain content with "playing the part of secondary brokers to brokers, secondary agents to agents, assistant professors to professors, clerks to managers [and] hired labourers to shopkeepers."[30]

To answer the Citizens' Committee of the Gujaratis, the Samyukta Maharashtra Parishad prepared an impressive 200-page document of its own. The first part mounted a theoretical defence of the principle of linguistic states. These, it argued, would deepen federalism, by bringing together speakers of the same language in one consolidated, cohesive, unit. Thus, "a linguistic province with its administration in the language of the common people, would make it possible for the people to feel and understand the working of democracy and the need to participate in it."

Coming specifically to their own state, the document claimed that "society all over the Marathi country is remarkably homogeneous." There was the same configuration of castes; there were the same deities, saints, folklore, and legends. That the Marathi-speakers were at present spread out over three political units—Hyderabad, Bombay state, and the Central Provinces—was an accident of history that needed urgently to be undone.

A new, unified, state of Maharashtra had to be created, argued the Parishad, and with Bombay as its capital. For the land on which this island city stood had long been inhabited by speakers of the Marathi language. While the sea lay to Bombay's west, the territory to its north, south, and east was dominated by Marathi-speakers. The city itself was the main centre of the Marathi press, of publications in the Marathi language, and of the Marathi drama. Economically, Bombay depended heavily on its Marathi hinterland, from which it drew much of its labour and all its water and power. Bombay's routes of communication all lay through Maharashtra. In sum, it was "unthinkable to form a State of Maharashtra which has not Bombay as its capital and it would render impossible the working of a State of Maharashtra, if any attempt was made to separate the city of Bombay from it." To the argument that the city did not have a Marathi-speaking majority, the Parishad answered that there were more people speaking this language than any other. In any case, it was in the nature of great port cities to be multilingual. In Burma's capital, only 32% of the population spoke the national language, but "nobody yet dared to suggest that Rangoon should be considered as non-Burmese territory."[31]

Bombay was surrounded by Marathi-speaking districts; it must be the capital of a new state of Maharashtra. So argued the Samyukta Maharashtra Parishad. But the Citizens' Committee claimed that Bombay had been nurtured mostly by non-Maharashtrians, and must therefore be constituted as a separate city state. Could the two sides meet? In June 1954 Shankarrao Deo visited Sir Purushottamdas Thakurdas to discuss a compromise. Deo said that no negotiation was possible on the core demand—Bombay as capital of Maharashtra—but that they could work together to retain "the same autonomous character of the metropolitan city, ensuring its cosmopolitan life; its trade, commerce and industry, etc." Sir Purushottamdas, for his part, was willing to give up the idea of a city state in favour of a composite bilingual province of Marathi-speakers and Gujarati-speakers.[32]

The meeting was civil, but inconclusive. The matter of Bombay was referred to the members of the States Reorganization Commission, as the hottest of the many hot potatoes it became their misfortune to handle.

V

The members of the States Reorganization Commission (SRC) were a jurist, S. Fazl Ali; a historian and civil servant, K. M. Pannikar; and a social worker, H. N. Kunzru. Notably, none had any formal ties, past or present, with the Congress. In October 1955, after eighteen months of intensive work, the three submitted their report. They first carefully outlined the arguments for and against linguistic states and urged a "balanced approach" which recognized "linguistic homogeneity as an important factor conducive to administrative convenience and efficiency" yet not "as an exclusive and binding principle, over-riding all other considerations." Among these other considerations were, of course, the unity and security of India as a whole.[33]

Next, in nineteen chapters, the report outlined their specific proposals for reorganization. With respect to the southern states, it seemed easy enough to redistribute areas according to the major language zones: Telugu, Kannada, Tamil, and Malayalam. Districts and *taluks* were reallocated with regard to which linguistic group was in the majority. Four compact states would replace the melange of territories deriving from the British period.

With regard to north India, the SRC likewise sought to divide the huge Hindi-speaking belt into four states: Bihar, Uttar Pradesh, Madhya Pradesh, and Rajasthan. In the east, the existing provinces would stay as they were, with minor adjustments. The SRC rejected the demand for tribal states to be carved out of Bihar and Assam.

The SRC did not agree to the creation of a Sikh state. And it refused to allocate Madras city to Andhra. However, its most controversial recommendation was not to permit the creation of a United Maharashtra. As a sop, the commission proposed a separate state of Vidarbha, comprising the Marathi-speaking districts of the interior. But Bombay state would stay as it was, a bilingual province of Gujarati-speakers and Marathi-speakers. The commissioners respected the arguments of the Samyukta Maharashtra movement, they said, but they could "not lightly brush aside the fears of the other communities."

VI

The SRC's recommendation that Bombay be the capital of a bilingual state was discussed in Parliament on 15 November 1955. The ambitious member of Parliament from Bombay, S. K. Patil, thought the commission should have gone further. He thought the government should create a city state of Bombay, no doubt hoping that it might come to be managed by himself. The prospective city state, he argued, had a "cosmopolitan population in every respect"; it had been "built upon the labour of everybody." If left to govern itself, Bombay would "be a miniature India run on international standards . . . [a] melting pot which will evolve a glorious new civilisation. . . . And it is an extraordinary coincidence that the population of the city should be exactly one per cent of the population of the whole country. This one per cent drawn from all parts of the country will set the pace for other states in the practice of secularism and mutual understanding."

Patil, like the SRC itself, asked the Maharashtrians to give up their claim to Bombay in the spirit of compromise. But it soon became clear that he did not speak for his fellow Maharashtrians. Speaking immediately after Patil in the Lok Sabha was the Congress member from the city of Pune, N. V. Gadgil. Gadgil insisted that while he was in favour of compromise, "there is a limit. That limit is, nobody can compromise one's self-respect, no woman can compromise her chastity and no country its freedom." Everywhere the principle of language had been recognized, except in this one case. The report of the commission had caused great pain throughout the Marathi-speaking world. The reports of protest meetings should make it clear "that anything short of Samyukta Maharashtra with the city of Bombay as capital will not be acceptable." If these sentiments went unheeded, Gadgil warned, then the future of Bombay would be decided on the streets of Bombay.

The SRC urged the Maharashtrians to accept the loss of Bombay in the name of national unity. Gadgil protested against this attempt at blackmail. The last 150 years, he said, had seen Maharashtrians contributing selflessly to the growth of national feeling. Marathi-speakers founded the first Indian schools and universities, and helped found the Indian National Congress. The Maharattas were "the pioneers of violent action" against the British. Later, in the early twentieth century, when the Congress party languished, "who was it that brought in new life? Who propounded the new tenets and new philosophy? It was Lokmanya Tilak. In the Home Rule movement he led and in the 1920 movement we were behind none and ahead of many provinces. . . . I will merely quote the certificate given to us by no less a person than Mahatma Gandhi that Maharashtra is the beehive of [national] workers." Even now, in independent India, it was a Maharashtrian, Vinoba Bhave, who was "carrying the flag of Gandhian philosophy and spreading his message from place to place."

In the matter of Bombay, the Maharashtrians were being lectured on the need to "work for the unity and safety and good of the country." But, Gadgil said bitterly, all these years "we have done nothing else." Gadgil's was a moving peroration—and the last line was the best: "To ask us to serve the nation is to ask *chandan* [sandalwood] to be fragrant."[34]

The matter now shifted, as Gadgil had predicted, from the chamber to the streets. These, as one weekly in Bombay warned, were "seething with an unrest that may possibly erupt into something terrifyingly coercive, making ordered life impossible for some time to come."[35] The discontent was being stoked by politicians on both the left and the right. The communist leader S. A. Dange had thrown his weight behind Samyukta Maharashtra; so had the leading low-caste politician, B. R. Ambedkar. With them were the Jana Sangh, and the socialists, who were perhaps the most active of all. Many dissident congressmen had also joined, making this a comprehensively representative coalition of angry and disillusioned Maharashtrians.

This capacious inclusiveness was reflected in an amended name: Samyukta Maharashtra Parishad had become Samyukta Maharashtra Samiti. The word "Parishad" is best translated as organization, implying the central role of officers; "Samiti," or society, connotes a more cooperative and participatory endeavour. [36]

In the early hours of 16 January, the Bombay police, fearing trouble, swooped down on the leaders and activists of the newly constituted All-Party Action Committee for Samyukta Maharashtra. They made nearly 400 arrests in all. This prompted a call for a general strike on 18 January. That day, shops and factories were closed, and buses and trains did not run. Processions went through the streets, burning effigies of Nehru and of the Gujarati-speaking chief minister of Bombay state, Morarji Desai. When a European journalist stopped to take a photograph of Nehru's portrait, smashed and trampled on in the street, "tremendous cheers rose from the balconies and the roofs. 'Take it, take it and show the world what we think of Nehru,' the people shouted."[37]

In the afternoon of 16 January the first clashes between the police and protesters was reported. Mobs were on the rampage, looting shops and offices. For nearly a week the city was brought to a complete standstill. Fifteen thousand policemen were called out to battle the rioters. When the smoke lifted, more than a dozen people were dead, and property worth billions of rupees had been destroyed. It had been the worst riot in living memory.[38]

Jawaharlal Nehru was deeply shaken by the events in Bombay. The linguistic question, he wrote to a colleague in the cabinet, "is more serious than even the situation created by the Partition and we have to give a positive lead."[39] Meeting in Amritsar in the third week of January, the All India Congress Committee deplored the violence by which "Bombay and India were disgraced and dishonoured." Under Nehru's direction, the party urged its members to discourage forces of "disruption, separatism and provincialism," and instead work for "the integration of all parts of this great country." The Congress chief ministers of Bihar and West Bengal issued a joint statement proposing that their two states be merged into one. This union, they hoped, would quell "separatist tendencies," aid economic progress, and above all be "a significant example of that positive approach to the problem of Indian unity" that the party bosses had called for.[40]

Among Nehru's allies were the home minister, G. B. Pant; and the chief minister of Bombay state, Morarji Desai. The intention of the protesters, said Desai, was to "overturn Government practically and to take possession of the City by force. It was also their purpose in overaweing the non-Maharashtrian elements in the City into submission and into agreeing that Bombay City should go to Maharashtra."

This interpretation was vigorously contested by N. V. Gadgil. He believed the administration had overreacted. Gadgil wrote to both Nehru and Pant that the firing and the lathi charges by the police had been "on a scale which will make even the ex-British officials in England blush." In 1919, the British had described a peaceful meeting in Amritsar's Jallianawala Bagh as a "rebellion against the Government," to justify the slaughter by General Dyer. In the same way, Morarji Desai had now exaggerated the protests in Bombay to "justify police atrocities." When "the choice was between Morarji and Maharashtra," wrote Gadgil bitterly, Delhi had chosen Morarji on the grounds that "one who shoots is a good administrator." But the costs to the party were huge: "in Bombay indiscriminate firing by the police and other atrocities have resulted in complete alienation of Maharashtrian people from the Congress and the Government of India."[41]

Meanwhile, resentment smouldered. The slogan on (almost) every Maharashtrian's lips was: *lathi goli khayenge, phir bhi Bambai layenge* ("We will face sticks and bullets, but get our Bombay in the end").[42] On

26 January, Republic Day, black flags were flown in several working-class areas of Bombay. When Jawaharlal Nehru planned a visit to Bombay in February, the Samyukta Maharashtra people organized a petition signed by 100,000 children, to be presented to the prime minister with the slogan *Chacha Nehru, Mumbai dya* ("Uncle Nehru, hand over Bombay"). Nehru came, but amid tight security; he did not meet the press, let alone the children.[43]

In June 1956 the annual session of the Congress was to be held in Bombay. Nehru was met with black flags at the airport, and all along the route into town. The atmosphere outside the meeting hall was tense. On the second day of the session, a crowd threw stones at the members. Several were hurt, prompting a volley of tear-gas shells by the police.

Nehru's problems were compounded by the now open disaffection among some Maharashtra congressmen. The finance minister, C. D. Deshmukh, who was also the member of Parliament for the coastal district of Kulaba, resigned in protest against the city's not being allotted to Maharashtra. Other resignations followed.

Through the summer of 1956, both sides waited anxiously for the Centre's decision on Bombay. Although the cabinet had accepted the other recommendations of the SRC, it was rumoured that both Nehru and the home minister, G. B. Pant, were inclined to make Bombay city a separate Union Territory. In the prevailing climate this was deemed unfeasible. On 1 November the new states based on language came into being. Joining them was a bilingual state of Bombay. The only concession to the protesters was the replacement of Morarji Desai as chief minister by a forty-one-year-old Maratha, Y. B. Chavan.[44]

VII

The creation of linguistic states was, among other things, a victory of the popular will. Jawaharlal Nehru did not want it, but Potti Sriramulu did. Sriramulu's fast lasted fifty-eight days, and for the first fifty-five days the prime minister ignored it completely. During this time, according to one journalist, he criss-crossed India, delivering 132 speeches, all on topics other than language.[45] But once Nehru conceded Andhra, and set up the States Reorganization Commission, it was inevitable that the country as a whole would be reorganized on the basis of language.

The movements for linguistic states revealed an extraordinary depth of popular feeling. For Kannadigas and Andhras, for Oriyas and

Maharashtrians, language proved a more powerful marker of identity than caste or religion. This was manifest in their struggles, and in their behaviour when the struggle was won.

One sign of this was official patronage of the arts. Thus great effort, and cash, went into funding books, plays, and films written or performed in the official language of the state. Much rubbish was funded as a result, but also much work of worth. In particular, the regional literatures have flourished since linguistic reorganization.

Another manifestation was architecture. To build a new capital, or at least a new legislative assembly, became a sine qua non of the new states. In Orissa, for example, two architects were commissioned to design and plan a wide range of government buildings. These, the architects were told, had to "represent Orissan culture and workmanship." The final product made abundant use of indigenous motifs: columns, arches, and sculptured images of gods. The architecture of new Bhubaneshwar, writes its historian, "is an architecture which has risen from the native soil, sacred and pure."[46]

A more spectacular exhibition of provincial pride was the new assembly-cum-secretariat of the state of Mysore. This was built opposite the Bangalore high court, a fine columned building in red which remains perhaps the city's prettiest structure. However, the chief minister of Mysore, K. Hanumanthaiya, saw the high court as a colonial execrescence. He first sought permission to demolish it; when this was denied, he resolved that the new Vidhan Souda would dwarf and tame it. The new structure had to convey an "idea of power and dignity, the style being Indian, particularly of Mysore and not purely Western."

The end product drew eclectically from the architecture of the great kingdoms of the Carnatic plateau. Hanumanthaiya gave very specific instructions to the builders, asking them to copy pillars from a particular room in the Mysore palace, or doors from a particular old temple. The building as it came up was, as it were, a mighty mishmash. Yet it has served its central purpose, which was to stand, "measure for measure, in triumph over the colonial Attara Kacheri [the high court]," and thus to "successfully function as a distilled essence of Kannada pride."[47]

When it began, the movement for linguistic states generated deep apprehensions among the nationalist elite. They feared it would lead to the Balkanization of India, to the creation of many more Pakistans. "Any attempt at redrawing the map of India on the linguistic basis," wrote the *Times of India* in early February 1952, "would only give the long awaited opportunity to the reactionary forces to come into the open and assert themselves. That will lay an axe at the very root of India's integrity."[48]

In retrospect, however, linguistic reorganization seems rather to have consolidated the unity of India. True, the artifacts that have resulted, such as Bangalore's Vidhan Souda, are not to everybody's taste. And there have been some serious conflicts between states over the sharing of river waters. However, on the whole the creation of linguistic states has acted as a largely constructive channel for provincial pride. It has proved quite feasible to be peaceably Kannadiga—or Tamil, or Oriya—as well as contentedly Indian.

An early illustration was the assembly elections in Andhra in 1955. Three years earlier, the Congress had done disastrously in the region. The party was suspect because of its prevarication on the question of statehood. By contrast, the communists had successfully ridden the bandwagon for "Vishal (greater) Andhra." But in 1955, with Andhra Pradesh firmly established, the Congress won in a landslide. Its main rivals, the communists, were comprehensively routed. Now, wrote one relieved commentator, "Andhra Desa will no longer be suspect as the potential Yenan of India."[49]

The Andhras would not secede from India, but they did redefine what it means to be Indian. Or at least one Andhra did. Potti Sriramulu is a forgotten man today. This is a pity, for he had a more-than-minor impact on the history, as well as the geography, of his country. His fast and its aftermath sparked a redrawing of the map of India according to linguistic lines. If Jawharlal Nehru was the "maker" of modern India, then perhaps Potti Sriramulu should be called its Mercator.

10

THE CONQUEST *of* NATURE

[The Indian people] have to choose whether they will be educated
or remain ignorant; whether they will come into closer contact
with the outer world and become responsive to its influences, or
remain secluded and indifferent; whether they will be organized
or disunited, bold or timid, enterprising or passive; an industrial
or an agricultural nation, rich or poor; strong and respected or
weak and dominated by forward nations. Action, not sentiment,
will be the determining factor.

The engineer M. VISVESWARAYA, writing in 1920

The Indian commitment to the semantics of socialism is at least as
deep as ours to the semantics of free enterprise. . . . Even the most
intransigent Indian capitalist may observe on occasion that he is
really a socialist at heart.

The economist J. K. GALBRAITH, writing in 1958

I

MAHATMA GANDHI liked to say that "India lives in her villages." At independence, this was overwhelmingly a country
of cultivators and labourers. Nearly three-fourths of the
workforce was in agriculture, a sector which also contributed close to
60% of the gross domestic product. There was a small but growing industrial sector, which accounted for about 12% of the workforce and
25% of the nation's income.

The peasant was the backbone of the Indian nation, and of the Indian economy. There existed enormous variations in agricultural practices across the subcontinent. There was, for instance, a broad division
between the wheat regions of the north and west, where women generally did not participate in cultivation; and the rice regions of the south
and east, where women's work was critical to the raising of seedlings.
Large parts of peninsular India grew neither rice nor wheat: here, the
chief cereals were an array of drought-resistant millets. Besides grain,

peasants grew a wide range of fruit crops, as well as market-oriented produce such as cotton and sugar cane.

These variations notwithstanding, everywhere in India agriculture was largely empirical, based on knowledge and traditions passed down over the generations, rather than on ideas from books. Everywhere, it was chiefly based on local inputs. The water, the fuel, the fodder, the fertilizer—these were all gathered in the vicinity of the village. The land was tilled with a plough pulled by a pair of bullocks. The homes were built of wood and thatch brought by hand from the nearby forests.

Everywhere, those who worked on the land lived side by side with those who didn't. The agriculturists who made up perhaps two-thirds of the rural population depended crucially on the service and artisanal castes: blacksmiths, barbers, scavengers, and the like. In many parts there were vibrant communities of weavers. In some parts, there were large populations of nomadic pastoralists.

On the social side, too, there were similarities in the way life was lived across the subcontinent. Levels of literacy were very low. Caste feelings were very strong, with villages divided into half a dozen or more endogamous jatis. And religious sentiments ran deep.

Rural India was pervaded by an air of timelessness. Peasants, shepherds, carpenters, and weavers all lived and worked as their forefathers had done. As a survey in the 1940s put it, "there is the same plainness of life, the same wrestling with uncertainties of climate (except in favoured areas), the same love of simple games, sport and songs, the same neighbourly helpfulness, and the same financial indebtedness."[1]

To the Indian nationalist, however, continuity was merely a euphemism for stagnation. Agricultural productivity was low; hence, so were the levels of nutrition and health. About the only thing that was rising was population growth. From the late nineteenth century, as medical services expanded, the death rate rapidly fell. And because birth rates remained constant, there was a steady rise in population. Between 1881 and 1941 the population of British India rose from 257 million to 389 million. At the same time, the per capita availability of food grains declined from an already low level of 200 kilograms per person per year to only 150.

Almost from the time the Congress was founded in 1885, Indian nationalists had charged the British with exploitation of the peasantry. They resolved that when power came to them, agrarian reform would be at the top of their agenda. Three programmes seemed critical. The first was the abolition of land revenue. The second was an extensive expansion of irrigation, both to augment productivity and to reduce dependence on the monsoon. The third was the reform of the system of land tenure. Particularly in north and east India, the British had encouraged a system of absentee landlordism. In many other districts too, those who tilled the land usually did not own it.

While tenants did not have security of tenure, agricultural labourers had no land to till in the first place. Inequalities in the agrarian economy could be very sharp indeed. The forms of exploitation were manifold and highly innovative. Thus, apart from the land tax, zamindars in the United Provinces levied an array of additional taxes on their peasants, such as *motorana* (to pay for the zamindar's new car) and *hathiana* (to pay for his elephants).[2] The landlord was apt to treat his animals and his vehicles far better than he treated his labourers. Two weeks before independence, a progressive weekly from Madras ran a story about distress in rural Malabar. This profiled a large landlord who owned seven elephants, for which he needed some 25,000 kilograms of paddy. His own tenants, meanwhile, were given three days' rations for the whole week.[3]

The socialist elements in the Indian National Congress pushed to commit it to thoroughgoing land reform, such as the abolition of large holdings, the promotion of the security of tenants, and the redistribution of surplus land. They also advocated an expansion of credit, to overcome the widespread problem of rural indebtedness.[4]

But, as the nationalists also recognized, agrarian reform had to be accompanied by a spurt in industrial growth. The nation needed more factories to absorb the surplus of underemployed labourers in the countryside. It also needed factories to prove to itself that it was modern. To enter the comity of nations, India had to be educated, united, outward-looking, and above all industrialized.

In colonial times, there had been a sharp divide between factories owned by British firms and those owned by Indians. Jute, for instance, was largely in the hands of the foreigner; cotton textiles were in the hands of the native. The Raj was frequently (and for the most part, justly) accused of deliberately discouraging Indian enterprise, and of distorting the tariff and trade structure to favour British firms. While some Indian capitalists were studiously non-political, others had been vigorous supporters of the Congress. They naturally hoped that when freedom came, the biases would be reversed, placing foreign capitalists at a disadvantage.[5]

If India had to be industrialized, which model should it follow? To the leaders of the national movement, "imperialism" and "capitalism" were both dirty words. As John Kenneth Galbraith pointed out, "until recent times a good deal of capitalist enterprise in India was an extension of the arm of the imperial power—indeed, in part its confessed *raison d'être*. As a result, free enterprise in Asia bears the added stigmata of colonialism, and this is a formidable burden."[6]

What then were the alternatives? Some nationalists wrote admiringly of the Soviet Union, and of "the extraordinary use they have made of modern scientific knowledge in solving their problems of poverty and want"—thus passing in just two decades "from a community of half-starved peasants to well-fed and well-clad industrial workers." This had been accomplished by "eliminating the profit motive from her industries which belong to and are being developed in the interest of the nation"; by feats of engineering that had made rivers into "mighty sources of electric power"; and by a system of planning by disinterested experts which had increased production ninefold and where "unemployment and anarchy of production are unknown."[7]

Another much admired model was Japan. Visting that country during the First World War, the prominent congressman Lala Lajpat Rai marvelled at the transformation it had undergone: moving from (agrarian) primitivism to (industrial) civilization in only fifty years. Japan, he found, had built its factories and banks by schooling its workers and keeping out foreign competition. The role of the state was crucial—thus "Japan owes its present industrial prosperity to the foresight, sagacity and patriotism of her Government." Once as backward as India, Japan had "grown into a teacher of the Orient and a supplier of all the necessaries and luxuries of life which the latter used to get from the Occident."[8]

II

In 1938, the Congress set up a National Planning Committee (NPC), charged with prescribing a policy for economic development in an India which was soon to be free. Chaired by Jawaharlal Nehru, the committee had some thirty members in all, divided almost equally between the worlds of science, industry, and politics. Subcommittees were allotted specific subjects such as agriculture, industry, power and fuel, finance, social services, and "women's role in planned economy." The NPC outlined "national self-sufficiency" and the doubling of living standards in ten years as the main goals. Planning itself was defined as "the technical co-ordination, by disinterested experts, of consumption, production, investment, trade, and income distribution, in accordance with social objectives set by bodies representative of the nation."[9]

From Japan and Russia, the NPC took the lesson that countries that industrialized late had to depend crucially on state intervention. This applied with even more force to India, whose economy had been distorted by two centuries of colonial rule. As one NPC report put it, planned development upheld the principle of "service before profit." There were large areas of the economy where the private sector could not be trusted, where the aims of planning could be realized only "if the matter is handled as a collective Public Enterprise."[10]

Notably, the private sector concurred. In 1944, a group of leading industrialists issued what they called "A Plan of Economic Development for India" (more commonly known as the "Bombay Plan"). This conceded that "the existing economic organization, based on private enterprise and ownership, has failed to bring about a satisfactory distribution of the national income." Only the state could help "diminish inequalities of income." The state was also necessary for augmenting production. Energy, infrastructure, and transportation were sectors where the Indian capitalists themselves felt the need for a government monopoly. In the early stages of industrialization, they argued, it was necessary that "the State should exercise in the interests of the community a considerable measure of intervention and control." Indeed, "an *enlargement* of the positive as well as preventative functions of the State is *essential* to any large-scale economic planning."[11]

Now largely forgotten, the Bombay Plan gives the lie to the claim that Jawaharlal Nehru imposed a model of centralized economic development on an unwilling capitalist class. One wonders what free-market pundits would make of it now. They would probably see it as a dirigiste tract, unworthy of capitalism and capitalists. In truth, it should be seen simply as expressing the zeitgeist, the spirit of the times.[12]

That spirit was all in favour of centralized planning, of the state's occupying what was called the "commanding heights" of the economy. Thus the constitution of India directed the government to ensure that "the ownership and control of the material resources of the community are so distributed as best to subserve the common good" and that "the operation of the economic system does not result in the concentration of wealth and means of production to the common predicament." Within a month after the constitution was adopted, the government set up a Planning Commission to carry out these "directive principles." Chaired by

Nehru, the commission included high cabinet ministers as well as experienced members of the Indian civil service.

In the summer of 1951, the Planning Commission issued a draft of the first five-year plan. This focused on agriculture, the sector hardest hit by partition. Besides increasing food production, the other major emphases of the plan were the development of transportation and communications, and the provision of social services. Introducing the proposals in Parliament, Jawaharlal Nehru praised the plan as the first of its kind to "bring the whole of India—agricultural, industrial, social and economic—into one framework of thinking." The work of the commission, he said, had "made the whole country 'planning conscious.'"[13]

The expectations of the Planning Commission ran high. As a columnist wrote, "one drawback of democracy is that it works slower than other political systems. But the people of India will not tolerate undue delay in their economic advancement."[14] After the first general elections, the urgency intensified. Critics from left and right lambasted the first five-year plan as lacking in vision and ambition. True, the production of food grain increased substantially, but output in other sectors failed to reach the targets.[15]

When he introduced the first five-year plan, Nehru had said that "it was obvious to me that we have to industrialise India, and as rapidly as possible." This objective was given pride of place in the second five-year plan. Its drafting was the handiwork of Prasanta Chandra Mahalanobis, a Cambridge-trained physicist and statistician steeped in Sanskrit philosophy and Bengali literature—in sum, "an awesome polyglot, the kind of man for whom Nehru was guaranteed to fall."[16]

Mahalanobis was, among other things, the man who brought modern statistics to India. In 1931 he set up the Indian Statistical Institute (ISI) in Calcutta. Within a decade, he had made the ISI a world-class centre of training and research. He was also a pioneer of interdisciplinary research, innovatively applying his statistical techniques to anthropology, agronomy, and meteorology.

In February 1949, Mahalanobis was appointed honorary statistical adviser to the Union Cabinet. The next year he helped establish the National Sample Survey (NSS); and the year following, the Central Statistical Organization (CSO). These were set up to collect reliable data on changing living standards in India—on wages, employment, consumption, and the like. The NSS and the CSO are two reasons why India has a set of official statistics more reliable than those found anywhere else in the non-western world.[17]

Such are the uncontentious aspects of Mahalanobis's legacy. Perhaps more important, but certainly more controversial, are his contributions to the theory and practice of planning. In 1954, Nehru committed his party, and by extension his country, to the creation of a "socialistic pattern of society." The same year, the ISI was asked by the government to study the problem of unemployment. Mahalanobis wrote a note on the subject, which seems to have impressed Nehru enough for him to assign the ISI the responsibility for drafting the second five-year plan.

Mahalanobis took the task very seriously indeed. In the late summer of 1954, he set off for a long tour of Europe and North America. He had, he confessed, an "inferiority complex about economic matters." This trip abroad was thus educational—to improve his own knowledge about the subject—but also frankly propagandist. By cultivating foreign economists, he hoped to bring their Indian counterparts around to his own point of view. As he told a friend, "at the back of everything is one single aim in my own mind—what effective help can we secure in making our own plans and in implementing them."[18]

Mahalanobis first went to the United States, where he collected information on input-output coefficients, maintained in a deck of 40,000 Hollerith punched cards. He talked to the man who had done the work (Wassily Leontief, a future Nobel laureate), before crossing the Atlantic to meet the dons of Cambridge. "The most brilliant" of these was Joan Robinson, then just back from a trip to China (where she was "much impressed by the progress they are making"). She thought that the export-import sector in India needed more government control. Mahalanobis agreed, and in turn asked Robinson to visit India as a guest of the ISI. This visit, he told her, "might be of very great help to us because her support may carry conviction that our approach to development planning is not foolish. She smiled and said—'Yes, I think I would be able to knock some sense into the heads of the economists in your country.'"

Mahalanobis now crossed the Channel, to converse with the French Marxists. Then it was time to shift to the other side of the Iron Curtain. He reached Moscow via Prague, and was at once impressed by the "amazing" pace of construction: buildings far bigger, and built much faster, than any he had ever seen. He had long talks with Soviet academicians, who said that if India wanted "to do any serious planning we must have the active help of, not scores, but hundreds of technologists and scientists and engineers." Mahalanobis agreed, and invited them to visit his country, so urgently in need of "specialists and experts in the economics of planning."[19]

These travels and talks finally bore fruit in a long paper presented to the Planning Commission in March 1954. Here Mahalanobis outlined eight objectives for the second five-year plan. The first objective was "to attain a rapid growth of the national economy by increasing the scope and importance of the public sector and in this way to advance to a socialistic pattern of society"; the second, "to develop basic heavy industies for the manufacture of producer goods to strengthen the foundation of economic independence." Other and (we may assume) lesser objectives included the production of consumer goods by both the factory and the household sector; the increasing of agricultural productivity; and the provision of better housing, health, and education facilities.

The emphasis on capital goods was justified in two principal ways. First, it would safeguard this former colony's economic, and hence political, independence. Second, it would help solve the pressing problem of unemployment. "Unemployment is chronic because of [the unavailability of] capital goods," argued Mahalanobis; it occurs "only when means of production become idle." The quickest way to create jobs was to build dams and factories.[20]

Mahalanobis's draft plan was submitted to a panel of expert economists. With one exception, all endorsed the emphasis on capital goods and the role of the public sector. To be sure, there were a number of caveats. Some economists urged a greater complementarity of agricultural and industrial production; others worried about where the funds for the plan would come from. Increased taxes would not by themselves suffice, and deficit financing might lead to high inflation. But on the whole, the leading economists of India were behind what was already being called "the Mahalanobis Model of Planning."[21]

This model was, among other things, a evocation of the old nationalist model of swadeshi, or self-reliance. Once, Gandhian protesters had burned foreign cloth to encourage indigenous textiles; now, Nehruvian technocrats would make their own steel and machine tools rather than buy them from outside. As the second plan argued, underdevelopment was "essentially a consequence of insufficient technological progress."[22] Self-reliance, from this perspective, became *the* index of development and progress. From soap to steel and cashews to cars, Indians would meet their material requirements by using Indian land, Indian labour, Indian materials, and above all Indian technology.

Table 2 compares the sectoral outlays for the first and second five-year plans. In proportional terms, power, transportation and communi-

TABLE 2: SECTORAL OUTLAYS IN THE FIRST TWO PLANS

SECTOR	OUTLAY IN FIRST PLAN		OUTLAY IN SECOND PLAN	
	Total*	%	Total*	%
Agriculture and Community Development	372	16	530	11
Irrigation	395	17	420	9
Power	266	11	445	10
Industries and Minerals	179	7	1,075	24
Transportation and Communications	556	24	1,300	28
Social Services, Housing, etc.	547	25	830	18

*In crores of rupees (1 crore = 10 million)

Source: Compiled from A. H. Hanson, *The Process of Planning: A Study of India's Five Year Plans, 1950–1964* (London: Oxford University Press, 1966), table 7, p. 134.

cations, and social services retained broadly the same importance. The decisive shift was from agriculture to industry; this was compounded by a decline in the importance of irrigation.

Although heavy industry would be owned by the state, there was still plenty of room for private enterprise, for in "an expanding economy the private sector would have an assured market." The main contribution of private enterprise would come in the form of consumer goods, to be produced by large as well as small units.[23]

A government resolution of 1956 classified new industries into three categories. Class I would be the "exclusive responsibility" of the state; these included atomic energy, defence-related industries, aircraft, iron and steel, electricity generation and transmission, heavy electricals, telephones, and coal and other key minerals. Class II would have both the public and the private sector as participants; it included the lesser minerals, chemicals, pharmaceuticals, fertilizers, pulp and paper, and road transport. Class III consisted of all the remaining industries, to be undertaken "ordinarily through the initiative and enterprise of the private sector."[24]

Would the Mahalanobis model succeed? Many Indians thought so, and most Indians certainly hoped so—as did their sympathizers worldwide. Representative here are the views of J. B. S. Haldane, the great

British biologist, who was then planning to move to India and join the ISI. When shown the draft plan by Mahalanobis, Haldane commented:

> Even if one is pessimistic, and allows a 15 per cent chance of failure through interference by the United States (via Pakistan or otherwise), a 10 per cent chance of interference by the Soviet Union and China, a 20 per cent chance of interference with civil service traditionalism and political obstruction, and a 5 per cent chance of interference by Hindu traditionalism, that leaves a 50 per cent chance for a success which will alter the whole history of the world for the better.[25]

III

If Mahalanobis was the chief technician of Indian planning, then Nehru was its chief missionary. The prime minister believed that in the Indian context, planning was much more than rational economics. It was good politics as well. While the five-year plan was based on the work of economists and statisticians, to realize its goal the "people must have the sensation of partnership in a mighty enterprise, of being fellow-travellers towards the next goal that they and we have set before us." Popular participation was the only way to make "this Plan, which is enshrined in cold print, something living, vital and dynamic, which captures the imagination of our people."[26]

Planning was thus a "mighty co-operative effort of all the people of India." Nehru hoped that the new projects would heal the schisms of caste, religion, community, and region. Introducing the first plan to his chief ministers, he wrote that "the more we think of this balanced picture of the whole of India and of its many-sided activities, which are so interrelated with one another, the less we are likely to go astray in the crooked paths of provincialism, communalism, casteism and all other disruptive and disintegrating tendencies." Introducing the second plan, he called it a "brave effort to fashion our future," which will "require all the strength and energy that we possess." He believed that "ultimately this is the only way to deal with the separatism, provincialism and sectarianism that we have to combat."[27]

On the economic side, Nehru identified two activities as providing the "essential bases" for planning: the production of power and the production of steel.[28] At independence, India had only two steel plants, both privately owned, which produced just over 1 million tons a year. This was inadequate for an expanding economy, especially one that had committed itself to building heavy industry.

The private sector was barred from starting new enterprises in steel, which, along with coal, shipbuilding, atomic energy, and aircraft production, was deemed too important to be subject to the profit motive. The forest belt that runs across central India was rich in iron ore and coal and also had plenty of rivers. At once, a lively competition began between the states in this belt, each seeking to have the first public sector steel plant within its borders. This was paralleled by a competition between the industrialized countries of the West, each of which wanted the contract to build the first plant.[29]

The second plan had set a target of 6 million tons of steel. The output was needed to provide inputs to other planned industries. But it was also a way of promoting forced savings. As one economist famously put it, "you can't eat steel." While the second plan was being finalized, the Indian government signed three separate agreements for the construction of steel plants. The Germans would build one in Rourkela in Orissa; the Russians one in Bhilai in Madhya Pradesh; the British one in Durgapur in West Bengal. The Americans, much to their sorrow, had lost out. That the war-ravaged countries of Europe had grabbed two contracts was bad enough; that their hated cold war rival had taken the third was worse. Years later, an American friend remembered how the decision that Bhilai was going to the Russians was communicated over the radio in tones of palpable sadness by the fabled broadcaster Ed Murrow.[30]

The Russians, of course, were delighted. Nikita Khrushchev visited Bhilai and called it the "Magnitogorsk of India." *Pravda* ran lavish photo features hailing Bhilai as a symbol of Indo-Soviet cooperation.[31] The Indians were more enthusiastic still. A Bengali chemist who worked in Bhilai recalled that his Russian boss, over the years, became an intimate friend as well. When the time came for the foreign expert to leave, the Indian could not contain his tears. The Russian was stoic, but his wife had sympathetic drops tricking from her eyes. For the Bengali, those tears "were nothing to me but the drops of the holy water of the Volga, which pervasively mingled with the stream of our Ganges, and inundated our fraternity and imperishable friendship."

In Bhilai, Russian and Indian worked shoulder to shoulder, clearing the land, building the roads and houses, erecting the plant. Those who were part of this effort remembered it with warm affection. It was, recalled one participant, "a frenzy without panic, a tempo with a plan.

The construction team glowed with pride and satisfaction at the new-born plant they had brought to life, the operation team was anxiously eager to nurture it to its full stature. . . . Each of us were helping build the future—a future one could almost see, touch, and feel." Finally, in February 1959, under the benign eyes of the president of India, the first molten iron came out of a blast furnace in Bhilai. All around, there were tears of joy and rejoicing. Those who were there long remembered these as "the most exciting moments of [their] life."[32]

The Indian steel industry was described by a senior official as "at once a school of technique and the mainspring of other industrial activities."[33] In fact it was more. The steel factory was a refutation of the belief that Indians were non-productive and prescientific—in a word, backward.

IV

In the economic modernization of India, large dams occupied a rather special place. They would, on the one hand, emancipate agriculture from the tyranny of the monsoon; and, on the other, provide the electric power to run the new industries mandated by the five-year plans. Jawaharlal Nehru was enchanted by dams, which he called "the temples of modern India." His fascination was shared by millions of his countrymen, who came to venerate these towering new monuments built in mud and concrete.

Indian intellectuals greatly admired the Tennessee Valley Authority, the integrated project that was a cornerstone of Franklin Roosevelt's New Deal. But they also admired the massive multi-purpose projects undertaken in the Soviet Union. In the 1940s, anticipating independence, Indian scientists and engineers made trips to America and Russia to acquaint themselves first-hand with how dams were built. They were deeply impressed by what they saw.[34] On either side of the Iron Curtain, these projects represented "the triumph of science, technology, foresight and centralized government over politics, petty local authorities and powers, ignorance, superstition, and backwardness." They represented, indeed, "the salvation of the nation through rationality and strength."[35]

Like North America and Russia, the subcontinent had numerous large rivers. Damming and taming these rivers would kill three birds with one stone: generate electricity, provide water for irrigation, and prevent flooding. After a particularly deadly bout of flooding on the Godavari in the monsoon of 1953, a leading engineer wrote to a leading politician that this was a river

with enormous potential for good. The destruction caused by floods
of this year has, however, demonstrated that if these floodwaters are
not harnessed for beneficial use, they will constitute a potential threat
to the well-being of the people. Properly conserved, these floodwaters
will satisfy all the needs of the Godavari basin and leave ample reserves, which integrated with the Krishna waters will enable irrigation and power benefits to be extended right down to Madras and
further south. . . . No effort should therefore be spared in harnessing
of the Godavari waters, in optimum integration with the Krishna,
nor extraneous reasons permitted to delay or jeopardise their con-
summation.[36]

Here was a proselytizing technocrat, speaking to the converted. For
while the Godavari was still undammed, most of the other major rivers
had already come under the hand of man. Among the massive dam projects under way were those on the Mahanadi, Rihand, Tungabhadra,
Damodar, and Sutlej rivers.

In the mid-1950s, the political scientist Henry Hart wrote a lyrical
account of the transformation of "new India's" rivers. For Hart, these
projects were "the greatest of the monuments of free India"; to them
"men and women come, in a pilgrimage growing season by season, to
see for themselves the dams and canals and power stations." In Hart's
book, there is a particularly fine description of the construction of the
Tungabhadra dam. When finished, the dam would embody 32 million
cubic feet of masonry, these having been laid at the rate of 40,000 cubic
feet a day, every day for five years. The sheer scale could be conveyed
only by analogy. "Imagine the masonry in Tungabhadra Dam," wrote
Hart, "being laid as a highway, 20 feet wide, 6 inches thick. It would extend from Lucknow to Calcutta, or from Bombay to Madras."[37]

Without question, the most prestigious of all these schemes was the
Bhakra-Nangal project in northern India. Again, its scale is best expressed
in numbers. At 680 feet, the Bhakra dam was the second highest in the
world; only the Grand Coulee Dam, on the Colorado River, was higher.
The concrete and masonry that would finally go into it were estimated at
500 million cubic feet, "more than twice the cubic contents of the seven
great pyramids of Egypt." The project would generate nearly 1 million
kilowatts of electricity annually, while the water from the reservoir would
irrigate 7.4 million acres of land. The water for irrigation would be carried
in canals, for whose excavation 30 million cubic yards of mud and stone
had to be removed.[38]

This project was a form of compensation for the refugee farmers from West Punjab, a substitute for the "canal colonies" they had left behind on the other side of the border. These peasants, predominantly Sikh, had "a martyr-like yearning to re-create within their own lifetimes the prosperity of which they have been cruelly deprived." Bhakra-Nangal gave them "the field and the resources from which they can rebuild and resettle themselves." In fact, it gave them more—for in addition to the water there was power, from which the Punjabis could, if they chose, for the first time build an industrial future for themselves.

The Bhakra-Nangal project was described in minute detail in a special number of the *Indian Journal of Power and River Valley Development*. The issue opened with a set of four very revealing photographs. The first showed the densely wooded site before work began; it had the caption, "River Sutlej at Bhakra in its primeval splendour—the site as it was." The second showed crane-like structures in the water and a low bridge slung across the gorge: this was "Exploratory drilling in riverbed with drills mounted on pontoons—the first invasion." The third photo, apparently taken in the dry season, showed hillsides by now quite bare, with trucks and bulldozers on the riverbed: "Concreting of the Dam begins—man lays the foundation for changing nature." In the last photo, the dam had begun to rise, aided by machines of a shape and size never before seen in India: "Excavation with heavy machines in progress in pit-area—the struggle with nature."[39]

The men and women who worked at Bhakra were all Indian, with one exception. This was an American, Harvey Slocum. Slocum had little formal education; starting out as a labourer in a steel mill, he had risen to the position of construction superintendent on the Grand Coulee dam. Slocum joined the Bhakra team as chief engineer in 1952, and imprinted on it his own distinctive style of working. Officers and workers of all levels were ordered to dress uniformly. Slocum himself was at the site at 8 a.m. sharp, staying there until late evening. A stern disciplinarian, he could not abide the sloth and inefficiency that were rampant around him. Once, when the telephone system broke down, he wrote to inform the prime minister that "only God, not Slocum, could build the Bhakra Dam on schedule."[40]

In the first week of July 1954, Nehru visited Bhakra to formally initiate the project. As he flicked on the switch of the powerhouse, Dakotas of the Indian air force dipped their wings overhead. Next he opened the sluice gates of the dam. Seeing the water coming toward them, the villagers downstream set off hundreds of home-made firecrackers. As one eyewitness wrote, "for 150 miles the boisterous celebration spread like a chain reaction along the great canal and the branches and distributaries to the edges of the Rajasthan Desert, long before the water got there."[41]

V

In the push to industrialize India, a key role had to be played by technology and technologists. From his days as a student at Cambridge, Jawaharlal Nehru had been fascinated by modern science. "Science is the spirit of the age and the dominating factor of the modern world," he wrote. Nehru wanted what he called "the scientific temper" to inform all spheres of human activity, including politics. More specifically, in an underdeveloped country like India, science must be made the handmaiden of economic progress, with scientists devoting their work to augmenting productivity and ending poverty.[42]

At the time of Indian independence only 0.1% of the gross national product (GNP) was spent on scientific research. Within a decade the figure had jumped to 0.5%; later, it was to exceed 1%. Under Nehru's active direction, a chain of new research laboratories were set up. These, following the French model, were established independently, outside the existing universities. Within the ambit of the Council for Scientific and Industrial Research were some two dozen individual institutes. There was a strong utilitarian agenda at work, with scientists in these laboratories encouraged to develop new products for Indians rather than publish academic papers in foreign journals.[43]

An Indian scientist whom Nehru supported early and consistently was the brilliant Cambridge-educated physicist Homi Bhabha. Bhabha founded and directed two major scientific institutions. The first was the Tata Institute of Fundamental Research in Bombay, which, as its name implies, was aimed mostly at basic research. It had world-class departments of physics and mathematics, and also, in time, housed India's first mainframe computer. The second was the Atomic Energy Commission, mandated to build and run India's nuclear power plants. This was handsomely funded by the government, with an annual budget, in 1964, of about 100 million rupees.[44]

Many new engineering schools were also started. These included the flagship Indian Institutes of Technology (IITs), five of which were inaugurated between 1954 and 1964. Like the new laboratories, the new colleges were intended to augment indigenous technical capability. Both Nehru and Bhabha were determined to lessen India's dependence on the

West for scientific materials and know-how. They believed that "if an item of equipment was imported from abroad, all one got was that particular instrument. But if one built it oneself, an all-important lesson in expertise was learnt as well."[45]

VI

The industrial bias of Indian planning was tempered by a range of programmes promoting agrarian uplift. On the morning of 2 October 1952 (Mahatma Gandhi's birthday), the president of India inaugurated, with a broadcast over the radio, a nationwide Community Development Programme. Fifty-five projects were launched across India that day, funded jointly by the governments of India and the United States. Among the schemes to be promoted by Community Development were roads and wells, cattle welfare, and improved methods of cultivation.

The projects were launched by ministers, chief ministers, and commissioners. These dignitaries helped remove earth for building roads, and laid foundation stones for schools and hospitals. In Alipur village, twelve miles outside Delhi on the road to Karnal, Jawaharlal Nehru dug into the earth to help prepare a road. "With verve and vigour he plunged into the work, having taken his jacket off." His companion, the American ambassador, also carried some baskets of earth. Not everyone was as agile as these two. When a well-dressed official attempted to imitate the prime minister, the villagers shouted "Sar par! sar par!"—meaning, carry the baskets on your head, you fool, not with your hands. Speaking to the villagers, Nehru said that Community Development would bring about a rural revolution by peaceful means, not, as in other places, by the breaking of heads.[46]

How did these schemes work in practice? Two years after they began, the anthropologist S. C. Dube studied a Community Development project in western Uttar Pradesh. He looked at it from the viewpoint of the "village-level worker" (VLW), the government functionary mandated with taking new ideas to the peasants.

By Dube's account, these "agents of change" certainly had energy and enterprise. They got up at the crack of dawn and worked all day. Among their duties was demonstrating to the villagers the merits of new seeds and chemical fertilizers. These were tried on sample plots, the peasants looking on as the VLW explained scientific methods of dibbling. Different crops were tried, and also different combinations of fertilizers. The VLW also offered the villagers free angrezi khad ("English manure") for use on their fields.

It appears that the peasants of Uttar Pradesh were somewhat ambivalent about the new techniques. Here is a conversation between the VLW (Q) and a farmer known by his initials (M.S.):

Q. What do you think of the new seed?

M. S. What can I think? If the government thinks it is good, it must be good.

Q. Do you think it is better than the local variety?

M. S. Yes. It resists disease much better. It can stand frost and rain, and there is more demand for it in the market.

Q. What about yield?

M. S. I cannot say. Some people say it is more, others say it is not.

Q. Some people say it is not as good in taste.

A. They are right. It is not half as good. If the *roti* [bread] is served hot it is more or less the same, but if we keep it for an hour or so it gets as tough as hide. No, it is not as good in taste. People say that we all get very weak if we eat this wheat.

Q. What is your experience?

M. S. Many more people suffer from digestive disorders these days. Our children have cough and cold. Perhaps it is because of the new seed and sugarcane. It may be that the air has been spoilt by the wars.

Q. And what about the new fertilizer?

M. S. They increase the yield; there is no doubt about it. But they probably destroy the vitality of the land and also of the grain.[47]

Indian peasants had mixed feelings about the new seeds and fertilizers. But they wholeheartedly welcomed fresh supplies of water. At the same time as S. C. Dube was studying Community Development in Uttar Pradesh, the British anthropologist Scarlett Epstein was living in Wangala, a village in southern Mysore that had recently received canal irrigation. Until the water came, this had been like any other hamlet in the interior Deccan, growing millet for its own consumption. With irrigation came new crops such as paddy (rice) and sugar cane. These were sold outside the village for a handsome return. Paddy gave a profit after expenses of 136 rupees per acre; sugar cane as much as 980 rupees per acre. These changes in local economics fostered changes in lifestyle as well. Before the canals arrived, the residents of Wangala wore scruffy clothes and rarely ventured outside the village. But "Wangala men now wear shirts and a number also wear dhotis; their wives wear colourful saris bought with money and they all spend lavishly on weddings. Wangala men pay frequent visits to Mandya [town] where they visit coffee shops and toddy shops; rice has replaced ragi as their staple diet."

These and other changes were made possible only by the extension of irrigation. As Epstein found, the coming of canal water was the turning point in the history of the village. Events of note, such as weddings, deaths, and murders, were dated by whether they happened before or after irrigation.[48]

VII

Guaranteed irrigation and chemical fertilizers increased agricultural productivity. But they could not solve a fundamental problem of rural India; inequality in access to land. Therefore, landless peasants were encouraged to settle in areas not previously under the plough. In the first decade of independence, close to 500,000 hectares of land were settled, principally malarial forests in the northern Terai, the central Indian hills, and the Western Ghats. Previously, these areas had been inhabited only by tribes genetically resistant to malaria. With the invention of DDT, it became possible for the state to clear the forests. These lands were naturally fertile; rich in calcium and potassium and organic matter (if poor in phosphates). In any case, there was no shortage of peasants who wanted them.[49]

A second way of tackling landlessness was to persuade large landholders to voluntarily give up some of what they possessed. This was a method pioneered by a disciple of Gandhi, Vinoba Bhave. In 1951, Bhave undertook a walking tour through the then communist-dominated areas of Telengana. In Pochempelli village, he persuaded a zamindar, Ramchandra Reddi, to donate 100 acres of land. This encouraged Bhave to make this a countrywide campaign, known as the Bhoodan movement. Bhave trudged through the Indian heartland, giving speeches wherever he went. He walked perhaps 50,000 miles, obtaining more than 4 million acres. At first his mission was reckoned a success: like Community Development, it was a noble Gandhian alternative to violent revolution. But later assessments were less charitable. Bhave was certainly saintly, but like some other saints, he preferred the grand gesture over humdrum detail. Critics pointed out that most of the land donated to Bhave had never been distributed to the landless; over the years, it had slowly returned to the original owners. Besides, much of the land that stayed under Bhoodan was rocky and

sandy, unfit for cultivation. In few places were the intended benefi-
caries organized to work the land they had been gifted. On balance,
the Bhoodan movement must be reckoned a failure, albeit a spectacular one.[50]

A third way of ending landlessness was to use the arm of the state.
Land reform legislation had long been on the agenda of the Congress.
After independence, the different states passed legislation abolishing the
zamindari system, which, under the British, had bestowed effective
rights of ownership on absentee landlords. The abolition of zamindari
freed large areas of land for redistribution, while also freeing tenants
from taxes and rents previously exacted from them.

After the end of zamindari, the state vested rights of ownership in
the tenants. These, typically, came from the intermediate castes. Left
unaffected were those at the bottom of the heap, such as low-caste
labourers and sharecroppers. Their well-being would have required a
second stage of land reforms, in which ceilings would be placed on holdings, and excess holdings handed over to the landless. This was a task
that the government was unable or unwilling to undertake.[51]

Even after a decade of planning, access to land remained very unequal, as Table 3 indicates:

TABLE 3: ACCESS TO LAND IN INDIA, 1953–1960

SIZE CLASS (IN HECTARES)	PERCENTAGE OF HOLDINGS		PERCENTAGE OF AREA OPERATED BY	
	1953–1954	1959–1960	1953–1954	1959–1960
less than 1	56.15	40.70	5.58	6.71
1 to 2	15.08	22.26	10.02	12.17
2 to 4	14.19	18.85	18.56	19.95
4 to 10	10.36	13.45	29.22	30.47
more than 10	4.22	4.74	36.62	30.70

Source: Nripen Bandyopadhyaya, "The Story of Land Reforms in Indian Planning," in Amiya Kumar Bagchi, editor, *Economy, Society and Polity: Essays in the Political Economy of Indian Planning in Honour of
Professor Bhabatosh Datta* (Calcutta: Oxford University Press, 1988).

If we define those who own less than four hectares as "small and
marginal" farmers, and those who own more than four hectares as "medium and large farmers," then this table can be compressed into another
one (Table 4).

TABLE 4: CHANGES IN LAND INEQUALITY IN INDIA, 1953–1960				
CLASS OF FARMERS	PERCENTAGE OF HOLDINGS		PERCENTAGE OF AREA OPERATED BY	
	1953–1954	1959–1960	1953–1954	1959–1960
Small and Marginal	85.42	81.81	34.16	38.83
Medium and Large	14.58	18.19	65.84	61.17

Table 4 reveals a slight diminution in inequality, with a 3.6% drop in the number of "small and marginal" farmers and a 4.6% increase in the land held by them. The operative word is "slight"—so slight as to be almost imperceptible, and, in a democracy committed to a "socialistic pattern of society," simply unacceptable.

VIII

The Nehru-Mahalanobis model emphasized heavy industrialization, state control and ultimately a subsidiary role for the private sector. Behind it was a wide consensus—and not merely in India. That in a complex modern economy the state must occupy the "commanding heights" was a belief then shared by governments and ideologues all over the world.

In the United States, purposive government intervention had brought the country out of the Great Depression. In Britain, Keynesian economics was being energetically applied by the Labour government that came to power in 1945. An appreciation of the state as a positive agent in economic change was also heightened by the recent achievements of the Soviet Union. At the time of the First World War Russia was a backward peasant nation; by the time of the Second World War it was a mighty industrial power. Particularly impressive were its military victories against Germany, which had a far longer history of technological and industrial development. For the western democracies, the feats of the Soviets underlined the importance of state direction of economic development.[52]

To be sure, there were dissenters. In the West there was Friedrich Hayek, who advocated a retreat of the state from economic activity. His ideas, however, were treated with benign—and sometimes not-so-benign—contempt. (He could not even get a position in the department of economics in the University of Chicago, being placed instead in the Committee on Social Thought.) And in India there was B. R. Shenoy, the sole economist in the panel of experts who disagreed with the basic approach of the second five-year plan. As one commentator wrote, Shenoy "appeared to be committed to laissez-faire methods in so doctrinaire a manner that no one, outside certain business circles, took much note of his criticisms."[53]

In truth, Shenoy's arguments went beyond a mere belief in laissez-faire. While he opposed the "general extension of nationalisation on principle," his main criticism of the plan was that it was overambitious. It had, he thought, seriously overestimated the rate of savings in the Indian economy. The shortfall in funds would have to be made up by deficit financing, contributing to greater inflation.[54]

Another dissenter was the economist Milton Friedman of Chicago. Visiting India in 1955 at the invitation of the government, he wrote a memorandum setting out his objections to the Mahalanobis model. He thought it too mathematical: it was obsessed with capital-output ratios, rather than with the development of human capital. He deplored the emphasis in industrial policy on two extremes—large factories that used too little labour and cottage industries that used too much. As he saw it, the "basic requisites" of economic policy in a developing country were "a steady and moderately expansionary monetary framework, greatly widened opportunities for education and training, improved facilities for transportation and communication to promote the mobility not only of goods but even more important of people, and an environment that gives maximum scope to the initiatives and energy of farmers, businessmen, and traders."[55]

Independently of Friedman, a young Indian economist had taken up one aspect of this critique—the neglect of education. The constitution mandated free and compulsory schooling for children up to the age of fourteen. But the sums allocated for this by the second plan, wrote B. V. Krishnamurti, were "absurdly low." He called for a "substantial increase" in the allotment for education, with the budget being balanced by an "appropriate curtailment in the outlay on heavy industries." Attention to detail was also crucial—the enhancement of the social prestige of schoolteachers, higher salaries for them, better buildings and playgrounds for the children. As Krishnamurti argued:

> A concerted effort on these lines to educate the mass of the population, specially in the rural areas, would undoubtedly have far-reaching benefits of a cumulatively expansionist character. This would greatly lighten the task of the Government in bringing about rapid economic

development. For in a reasonable time, one could expect that the ignorance and inertia of the people would crumble and an urge to improve
one's material conditions by utilising the available opportunities
would develop. If this were to happen, the employment problem would
take care of itself. The people of the country would begin to move
along the lines of those in the advanced democratic countries such as
Great Britain and Switzerland.[56]

If B. V. Krishnamurti had been a professor at the centre of power,
Delhi, rather than a lowly lecturer in Bombay, he might have gotten a
hearing. In Friedman's case, his high position and prestige was offset by
foreign economists of equal distinction with opposed views. He was to
them what B. R. Shenoy was to the Indian economists—a lone free-
marketeer drowned out by a chorus of social democrats and leftists.[57]

A different critique came from the Marxists. They thought that the
Mahalanobis model gave the market not too little importance, but too
much. The second plan, they felt, should have mandated a thoroughgoing process of nationalization, whereby the state would not merely start
new industries, but take under its wing the private firms already in operation. They wanted the working class to be involved with planning, on
the model of the "people's democracies" of eastern Europe.[58]

Then there were the Gandhians, who provided a precocious ecological critique of modern development. In the vanguard of this "early environmentalism" were two of the Mahatma's closest disciples, J. C.
Kumarappa and Mira Behn (Madeleine Slade). Through the 1950s, they
pungently dissented from the conventional wisdom on agricultural policy. They argued that small irrigation systems were more efficacious than
large dams; that organic manure was a cheap and sustainable method of
increasing soil fertility (compared with chemicals that damaged the earth
and incurred foreign debt); that forests should be managed from the
point of view of water conservation rather than revenue maximization
(by protecting natural multi-species forests rather than the monocultural
stands favoured by the state). These specific criticisms were part of a
wider understanding of the world of nature. Mira Behn wrote in 1949:

The tragedy today is that educated and moneyed classes are altogether
out of touch with the vital fundamentals of existence—our Mother
Earth, and the animal and vegetable population which she sustains.
This world of Nature's planning is ruthlessly plundered, despoiled
and disorganized by man whenever he gets the chance. By his science

and machinery he may get huge returns for a time, but ultimately will come desolation. We have got to study Nature's balance, and develop our lives within her laws, if we are to survive as a physically healthy and morally decent species.[59]

One modern technology the Gandhians had deep reservations about was the large dam. They thought large dams costly and destructive of nature. As Indians were soon to find out, dams were destructive of human community as well. By the early 1950s, reports began appearing about the suffering of people displaced by dams. In the summer of 1952, when the Hirakud authorities issued eviction notices to the residents of the 150 villages that the project would submerge, they met with stiff resistance. A reporter on the spot concluded that "the prosperity of Hirakud will be built on the sacrifice of such people who are now being destituted (sic) by the Government of Orissa without compensation and rehabilitation." Three years later, a similar tale surfaced of villagers in Himachal Pradesh, who had to make way for the reservoir of the Bhakra dam. A full year had passed since Nehru had inaugurated the powerhouse; yet "complacency and indifference seem to be guiding the counsels of the Bhakra Control Board, particularly the Rehabilitation Committee." Even "the basic question of compensation, and the where, why and how of it remains to be decided to the satisfaction of the people concerned."[60]

IX

The free-market critique; the human capital critique; the ecological critique—these make fascinating reading today. But at the time these notes of dissent were scattered, and they were politically weak. There was then an overwhelming consensus in favour of a heavy-industry-oriented, state-supported model of development. This was a consensus among intellectuals; no fewer than twenty-three of the twenty-four expert economists asked to comment on the Mahalanobis plan agreed with it in principle.[61]

This consensus was shared by large sections of the ruling class as well. In their "Bombay Plan," the leading industrialists had asked for an "enlargement of the positive functions of the State." They approvingly quoted the Cambridge economist A. C. Pigou's view that freedom and planning were entirely compatible. Indeed, these big businessmen went so far as to state that "the distinction between capitalism and socialism has lost much of its significance from a practical standpoint. In many respects there is now a large ground common to both and the gulf between the two is being steadily narrowed further as each shows signs of modifying itself in the direction of the other. In our view, no economic organization can function effectively or possess lasting qualities unless it accepts as its basis a judicious combination of the principles associated with each school of thought."[62]

For a final word on the romance and enchantment of planning in India, we turn to an anonymous journalist covering one of its showpiece projects. This was Bokaro, site of both a thermal power project and a large reservoir. Visiting the place in September 1949, the journalist reported that "Bokaro stood in the midst of barren, rocky land, overlooking the confluence of two sandy rivers. The only habitation there was the office of the Executive Engineer manned by half-a-dozen persons, without any living or other facilities. One could reach Bokaro only by jeep and we had to carry our own food."

Three and a half years later, the journalist went back to Bokaro, to see the prime minister inaugurate the power plant and the dam. "What a different sight met my eyes," he exulted. Approaching the Bokaro valley on a "first-class tarmac road," he saw "the three sturdy stacks of the Power Station against the grey background of the hills." What had been "a dry river bed in 1949 has been turned into a fair-sized lake" with a concrete barrage thrown across it. For those who worked in the dam and the plant, there was now "a modern residential area with tarred roads, electric lighting, a high school, hospital, filtered water supply and all the amenities one expects in the present day."[63]

"Whenever I see these great engineering works," wrote Jawaharlal Nehru, "I feel excited and exhilarated. They are visible symbols of building up the new India and of providing life and sustenance to our people."[64] It appears that the excitement and exhilaration were felt by plenty of other Indians as well.

11

THE LAW *and the* PROPHETS

Some of these progressive movements have a great fascination for Nehru. He always likes to be looked upon as a modern; he wants to be a Picasso hung up in the Royal Academy, looking upon the classical forms around him with a supercilious air.

The columnist D. F. KARAKA, writing in 1953

It is a settled fact that every country and every nation has its own character. It is in-born and instinct with it. It cannot be changed. Shakespeare and Kalidas are both great poets and dramatists. . . . India . . . could not produce a Shakespeare and similarly England a Kalidas. I ask the sponsors of the reform, with all force and self confidence, where is the necessity of *Europeanisation of Hindu* Law? . . . In codifying it there is danger of hurting seriously the susceptibilities and devotional feelings of millions of people.

A Hindu lawyer, writing in 1954

I

THE FRENCH WRITER André Malraux once asked Jawaharlal Nehru what had been his "greatest difficulty since Independence." Nehru replied: "Creating a just state by just means." Then he added: "Perhaps, too, creating a secular State in a religious country."[1]

Secularism was, indeed, an idea that underlay the very foundations of free India. The Indian national movement refused to define itself in religious terms. Gandhi insisted that the multiple faiths of India could and must coexist peaceably in a free nation. This was a belief shared by Gandhi's most prominent follower, Nehru; and by his acknowledged mentor, Gopal Krishna Gokhale.

Congress nationalism suffered a body blow at independence. Freedom came, not, as Gandhi and his colleagues had hoped, to one nation, but to two. Secularism now faced a fresh set of challenges. One pertained to the domain of personal laws. In colonial times, the whole of India had come under a common criminal code, drafted in the 1830s by the historian Thomas Babington Macaulay. But there was no attempt to replace the personal laws of various sects and religions with a common penal code. Here, as the British saw it, the colonial state's role was restricted to adjudicating between different interpretations of religious law.

After independence, among those favouring a common civil code were the prime minister, Jawaharlal Nehru; and the law minister, Dr. B. R. Ambedkar. Both were of a modernist cast of mind, and both were trained in the western legal tradition. For both, the reform of personal laws became an acid test of India's commitment to secularism and modernization.

II

Article 44 of the constitution of India reads: "The State shall endeavour to secure for the citizens a uniform civil code throughout the territory of India."

When this article was discussed in the Constituent Assembly, it provoked much agitation, particularly among Muslim members. During the two centuries of their rule, the British interfered little with personal laws; why could not the successor state follow their example? One member pointed out that "as far as the Mussalmans are concerned, their laws of accession, inheritance, marriage and divorce are *completely dependent* upon their religion." A second felt that "the power that has been given to the State to make the Civil Code uniform is in advance of the time." A third believed that the clause contravened another clause in the Constitution: the freedom to propagate and practice one's religion.[2]

These arguments were forcefully rebutted by B. R. Ambedkar. As he saw it, "if personal laws are to be saved, . . . in social matters we will come to a standstill." In traditional societies, religion presumed to hold a "vast, expansive jurisdiction so as to cover the whole of life." But in a modern democracy this license had to be curtailed, if only "in order to reform our social system, which is so full of inequities, so full of inequalities, discriminations and other things, which conflict with our fundamental rights." To assuage the apprehensions, Ambedkar said that the state might choose to apply a uniform civil code by consent, that is, only to those who chose voluntarily to submit to it.[3]

As it happened, during the last years of their rule, the British had belatedly initiated the framing of a uniform code for Hindus. This sought to reconcile the prescriptions of the two principal schools of law—the Mitakshara and the Dayabhaga—and their numerous local variations. A committee was set up in 1941, chaired by Sir B. N. Rau, who was also to play a crucial role in drafting the Indian constitution. The Rau Committee toured India, soliciting a wide spectrum of Hindu opinion on the changes the members proposed. Their progress was interrupted during the war, but by 1946 they had prepared a draft of a personal law code to be applied to all Hindus.[4]

The Hindus were singled out in part because they were the largest community, and in part because there was a vigorous reform movement among them. Mahatma Gandhi, in particular, had challenged the discriminations of caste and gender, by seeking the abolition of untouchability and by bringing women into public life. Although there remained an influential orthodox section, modernist Hindus had campaigned strongly for laws that would make caste irrelevant and enhance the rights of women.

In 1948, the Constituent Assembly formed a Select Committee to review the draft of a new Hindu code. It was chaired by B. R. Ambedkar, as law minister. The code drafted by the Rau Committee was revised by Ambedkar himself, and then subjected to several close readings of the Select Committee.

Despite its name, the Hindu Code Bill was to apply to Sikhs, Buddhists, and Jains apart from all castes and sects of Hindus. Introducing the new bill, Ambedkar told the assembly that its aim was to "codify the rules of Hindu Law which are scattered in innumerable decisions of the High Courts and of the Privy Council, [and] which form a bewildering motley to the common man and give rise to constant litigation." The codification had a dual purpose: first, to elevate the rights and status of Hindu women; second, to do away with the disparities and divisions of caste. Among the notable features of the proposed legislation were these:

1. Awarding to the widow and daughter *the same share as the son* in the property of a man dying intestate (which in the past had gone only to his male heirs). Likewise, a Hindu woman's estate, previously limited, was now made absolute, to be disposed of as she wished.
2. Granting maintenance to the wife who chose to live separately from the husband if he had a "loathsome disease," was cruel to her, took a concubine, etc.

3. Dispensing with the rules of caste and sub-caste in sanctifying a marriage. All marriages between Hindus would have the same sacramental as well as legal status, *regardless* of the castes to which the spouses belonged. An inter-caste marriage could now be solemnized in accordance with the customs and rites of *either* party.
4. Allowing either partner to file for and obtain a divorce on certain grounds, such as cruelty, infidelity, incurable diseases, etc.
5. Making monogamy *mandatory*.
6. Allowing for the adoption of children belonging to a different caste.

These changes went very far in the direction of gender equity. Much later, feminist scholars were to argue that the changes did not go far enough—that they exempted agricultural property, for example, or that the advantages conferred on female heirs by the new laws were greater in the case of self-acquired property as compared with inherited property.[5] But from the viewpoint of Hindu orthodoxy the changes had already gone far enough. They constituted radical departures from the main body of Hindu law, where the son had a much larger claim than the wife and daughter on his father's property, where marriage was considered a sacrament and hence indissoluble, where a man was allowed to take more than one wife, and where marriage was governed strictly by the rules of caste.

In arguing for these changes, Ambedkar was at times rather defensive. Thus he argued that the shastras, the Hindu holy texts, did not give the husband "an unfettered, unqualified right to polygamy." The "right to marry a second time has been considerably limited by the [ancient lawmaker] Kautilya." Again, the customary law of the various low castes, or *shudras*, had always allowed divorce. As for the woman's right to property, some schools allowed her a one-fourth share in her father's property; all Ambedkar had done was to "raise [the daughter] up in the share of heirs," by making her share full and equal to that of the son.[6]

Ambedkar was here putting the best possible, or most liberal, "spin" on Hindu texts and traditions. But alternative intepretations were possible, and certainly more plausible. Not surprisingly, Ambedkar's proposals provoked "loud denunciations" from the orthodox, who viewed them as "a complete abrogation of the Hindu customs and traditions," an unacceptable interference with the rules of caste and the traditional relations between the sexes.[7]

A doughty opponent of the bill was the Constituent Assembly's president, Rajendra Prasad. In June 1948, shortly after the Select Committee had been set up, Rajendra Prasad warned the prime minister that to introduce "basic changes" in personal law was to impose the "progressive ideas" of a "microscopic minority" on the Hindu community as a whole. Nehru answered that the cabinet had declared itself in favour of the bill, and that "personally, I am entirely in favour of the general principles embodied in it." To scrap the bill now would be to give rise to a suspicion that the Congress was "a reactionary and a very conservative body"; nor would it go down well "in the mind of foreigners outside India." Prasad shot back that the opinions of the "vast bulk of [the] Hindu public" were more important than the views of foreigners.[8]

Within the Constituent Assembly there were other opponents as well. They stalled and thwarted the proceedings, until Nehru, in high dudgeon, told them that to him the passing of the bill had become a matter of prestige. Prasad, in response, drafted a letter warning the prime minister that this would be "unjust and undemocratic," as this "fundamental and controversial legislation" had never been considered by the Indian electorate. Fortunately for him, Prasad consulted Vallabhbhai Patel before sending Nehru the letter. The timing is crucial here, for it was now December 1949, and soon the Congress would choose the first president of India, from a short list that comprised Rajendra Prasad and C. Rajagopalachari. With this in view, Patel told Prasad not to send the prime minister his criticisms of the Hindu Code, lest it "prejudice your position within the party."[9]

So Prasad kept quiet (and was duly elected the first president of the Republic of India). But outside the Council House the cries grew louder. Already, in March 1949, an All India Anti-Hindu-Code Committee had been formed. Its members held that the Constituent Assembly had "no right to interfere with the personal laws of Hindus which are based on Dharma Shastras." Sixty male members of the Delhi bar issued a statement objecting to the codification of Hindu law, on the grounds that "the mass of the Hindus believe in the Divine Origin of their personal laws."

The Anti-Hindu-Code Committee was supported by conservative lawyers as well as by conservative clerics. The influential shankaracharya of Dwarka issued an "encyclical" against the proposed code. Religion, he said, "is the noblest light, inspiration and support of men, and the State's highest duty is to protect it."

The Anti-Hindu-Code Bill Committee held hundreds of meetings throughout India, where sundry swamis denounced the proposed legislation. The participants in this movement presented themselves as religious warriors (*dharmaveer*) fighting a religious war (*dharmayudh*). The Rashtriya Swayamsewak Sangh (RSS) threw its weight behind the agitation. On 11 December 1949, the RSS organized a public meeting at the Ram Lila grounds in Delhi, where speaker after speaker condemned the bill. One called it "an Atom Bomb on Hindu society." Another likened it to the draconian Rowlatt Act introduced by the colonial state; just as the protests against that act led to the downfall of the British, he said, the struggle against this bill would signal the downfall of Nehru's government. The next day a group of RSS workers marched on the assembly buildings, shouting, "Down with Hindu Code Bill" and "May Pandit Nehru Perish." The protesters burned effigies of the prime minister and Dr. Ambedkar, and then vandalized the car of Sheikh Abdullah.

The leader of the movement against the new bill was Swami Karpatriji-Maharaj. We know little of his antecedents, except that he was from north India and appeared to be knowledgeable about Sanskrit. His opposition to the bill was coloured and deepened by the fact that it was being piloted by Ambedkar. He made pointed references to the law minister's caste, suggesting that a former untouchable had no business meddling in matters normally the preserve of the Brahman.

In speeches in Delhi and elsewhere, Swami Karpatri challenged Ambedkar to a public debate on his interpretations of the shastras. To the law minister's claim that the shastras did not really favour polygamy, Swami Karpatri quoted Yagnavalkya: "If the wife is a habitual drunkard, a confirmed invalid, a cunning, a barren or a spendthrift woman, if she is bitter-tongued, if she has got only daughters and no son, if she hates her husband, [then] the husband can marry a second wife even while the first is living." The swami supplied the precise citation for this injunction: the third verse of the third chapter of the third section of Yagnavalkya's smriti on marriage. He did not, however, tell us whether the injunction also allowed the wife to take another husband if the existing one was a drunkard, bitter-tongued, a spendthrift, etc.

For Swami Karpatri, divorce was prohibited in the Hindu tradition, while "to allow adoption of a boy of any caste is to defy the Shastras and to defy property." Even by the most liberal interpretations, the woman's inheritance was limited to one-eight, not one-half as Ambedkar sought to make it. The bill was altogether in violation of the Hindu scriptures. It had already evoked "terrible opposition," and the government could push it through only at its peril. The swami issued a dire warning: "As is clearly laid down in the Dharmashastras, to forcibly defy the laws of God and Dharma very often means great harm to the Government and the country and both bitterly rue the obstinate folly."[10]

III

In December 1949, having agreed upon a constitution, the Constituent Assembly made way for a Provisional Parliament, which was to be in place until the first general elections. Through 1950 and 1951, Nehru and Ambedkar made several attempts to get the Hindu Code Bill passed into law. But the opposition was considerable, both within Parliament and outside it. To quote J. D. M. Derrett, "every argument that could be mustered against the project was garnered, including many that cancelled each other out." The "offer of divorce to all oppressed spouses became the chief target of attack, and the cry that religion was in danger was raised by many whose real objection to the Bill was that daughters were to have equal shares with sons."[11]

In the Provisional Parliament, orthodox members claimed that the Hindu laws had stayed unchanged from time immemorial. "The rules of conduct and duties of men in our country are determined by the Vedas," said Ramnarayan Singh. Despite the challenges down the ages—posed by Buddhism, Islam, and Christianity—"the Vedic religion did not perish . . . [the] Vedic religion is still there." But now, "we have Pandit Nehru's administration whose representative Dr. Ambedkar wants to abrogate with a single stroke all those rules which have existed since the beginning of the world."

Some parliamentarians argued that the government should frame and have passed an Indian code rather than a specifically Hindu one. "I do not believe that only Hindu women are oppressed," said Indra Vidyavachaspati. By passing the bill in its present form, the state would "give encouragement to . . . [the] evil of communalism." If it was not made applicable to all sections of the populations, insisted Vidyavachaspati, then "the feeling of communalism will arise and what should have been a boon will turn into a curse."

Other members were happy enough with the bill as it was. "While I admire those who want to have one Civil Code for the whole of India," said Thakur Das Bhargava, "I do not think that it would be a practical proposition to have one Civil Code for Muslims, Christians, Jews, etc." Muslim members had already expressed their opposition to any tampering with their personal code, which they believed to be the revealed word of Allah himself. To ask at this stage for a uniform code was seen as a stalling tactic, diverting attention from the reform so urgently required within the majority community. As Dr. Ambedkar put it, "those who until yesterday were the greatest opponents of this Code and the greatest champions of the archaic Hindu Law as it exists to-day," now claimed that they were "prepared for an All-India Civil Code." This was because they hoped that while it had already taken "four or five years to draft the Hindu Code [it] will probably take ten years to draft a Civil Code."

Ambedkar knew that while there were enough influential Hindus—such as Jawaharlal Nehru—who were behind progressive legislation, among the Muslims the liberal contingent was nowhere near as strong. The government, he said, could not be so "foolish" as "not to realise the sentiments of different communities in this country." That was why the code at present dealt only with the Hindus.[12]

Of course, not all Hindus were liberal either. The reservations of the orthodox, as expressed in Parliament, were carried forward in the streets by the followers of the Rashtriya Swayamsewak Sangh (RSS). They brought volunteers into New Delhi, to shout slogans against the Hindu Code Bill and risk arrest. Among their larger aims were the dismemberment of Pakistan and the unseating of Jawaharlal Nehru—as they shouted, *Pakistan tod do*, and *Nehru Hakumat Chhod Do*.

The main speaker at these shows organized by RSS was usually Swami Karpatri. Addressing a meeting on 16 September 1951, the swami challenged the prime minister to a debate on the proposed bill. "If Pandit Nehru and his colleagues succeed in establishing that even one section of the proposed Hindu Code is in accordance with the Shastras," said Karpatri, "I shall accept the entire Hindu Code." The next day, in pursuance of this challenge, the swami and his followers marched on Parliament. The police prevented them from entering. In the ensuing scuffle, reported a Hindu weekly, "police pushed them back [and] Swamiji's Danda [stick] was broken, which is like the sacred thread, [the] religious emblem of the sannyasis."[13]

Coincidentally, just two days before Swami Karpatriji's march, the president had written the prime minister a long letter of protest against the bill. As in 1948 and 1949, now too Rajendra Prasad felt that the present Parliament, based like its predecessor on a restricted franchise, was "not competent to enact a measure of such a fundamental nature." The bill, he argued, was "highly discriminatory," for it applied to only one community, the Hindus. Either the same laws governing marriage and property should be applied to all Indians, or else the existing customary laws of the different communities should be left untouched. Prasad wrote ominously that "he proposed to watch the progress of the measure in Parliament from day to day." If the bill was still passed, he would insist on his "right to examine it on its merits . . . before giving assent to it."[14]

Nehru wrote back saying that in his view there was "a very widespread expression of opinion in the country in favour of the Bill." But the president's opposition worried him, for it presaged a possible standoff between the government and the head of state. He showed Prasad's letter to several experts on the constitution. They assured him that the president was bound to act with "the aid and advice of the Council of Ministers and cannot act independently of that advice." As they saw it, the position of the president of India was even weaker than that of the British monarch.[15]

Despite this advice, Nehru chose not to challenge the president. In any case, the progress of the bill in the Provisional Parliament had been painfully slow. An immense number of objections and amendments had been put forward. It took the better part of a year to have a mere four clauses passed. In the end "the session ended, the Bill was virtually talked out, and it lapsed."[16]

The man who was most hurt by this failure was the law minister. Dr. Ambedkar had staked his reputation on the bill, meeting criticisms and calumnies with equal resolution. That Nehru had finally chosen to give in to the opposition pained him deeply. In October 1951 he resigned from the Union cabinet. He intended to announce his decision in the House, but when the deputy speaker asked for a copy of his speech beforehand, he walked out in a huff, and released it to the press instead.

Ambedkar gave several reasons for his decision to resign. He had been in poor health, for one. For another, the prime minister had failed to repose adequate trust in him. Despite having a PhD in economics (from the London School of Economics), he had been left out of discussions on planning and development. A third reason was his growing reservations about the government's foreign policy, particularly with regard to Kashmir. A fourth reason was that the condition of his fellow Scheduled Castes continued to be wretched. Despite the coming of political independence, and a constitution protecting their rights, they faced the "same old tyranny, the same old oppression, the same old discrimination."

Ambedkar came in the end to the issue that had finally provoked him to resign. He had, he said, set his mind on having the Hindu Code Bill passed before the end of the Parliament. He had tried hard to

convince the prime minister about the urgency of the matter. But
Nehru did not give him the kind of support he had hoped for. Facing
opposition within his party, the prime minister, complained Ambedkar, had not "the earnestness and determination" required to overcome it.[17]

                                  IV

In the first months of 1952 India held its first general elections. Over
them, the recent debates on the Hindu Code Bill were to cast a shadow.
Feeling let down by the Congress, Dr. Ambedkar had founded his own
Scheduled Caste Federation in opposition to it. As for the prime minister, in his own constituency of Allahabad he was opposed by a leader of
the now notorious Anti-Hindu-Code-Bill Committee.

This was Prabhu Dutt Brahmachari. He was an ascetic and celibate,
and to signal this he wore saffron. Brahmachari's candidacy was supported by the Jana Sangh, the Hindu Mahasabha, and the Ram Rajya
Parishad. His campaign had a one-point agenda—no tampering with
Hindu tradition. He printed pamphlets detailing the prime minister's attempts to interfere with that tradition, and challenging Nehru to an
open debate on the subject.[18]

Nehru sensibly refused. He won his own seat with a large margin,
and the Congress got a comfortable majority overall. Nehru saw this,
in part, as a mandate for his campaign against communalism. Soon after the Parliament was convened he resurrected the Hindu Code Bill.

Keeping the earlier protests in mind, the bill was now broken up into
several parts. There were separate bills dealing with Hindu marriage
and divorce, Hindu minority and guardianship, Hindu succession, and
Hindu adoptions and maintenance. These component parts retained the
rationale and driving force of the original unified bill. The main thrust
was to make caste irrelevant to Hindus with regard to marriage and
adoption; to outlaw polygamy; to allow divorce and dissolution of marriage on certain specified grounds; and to greatly increase the woman's
share of her husband's and her father's property.[19]

The prime minister was in the vanguard of the movement in favour of
the Bill. He told Parliament that "real progress of the country means progress not only on the political plane, not only on the economic plane, but
also on the social plane." The British had allied themselves with "the most
conservative sections of the community they could find." The conjoining
of tradition and colonialism meant that "our laws, our customs fall heavily

on the womenfolk." Thus "different standards of morality are applied to men and women." Men were allowed more than one wife, but when a woman wished for a divorce she was challenged by men, only "because men happen to be in a dominant position. I hope they will not continue in that dominant position for all time."

Hindu customs and laws were hypocritical as well as unjust. Women were urged to model themselves on mythic figures of devotion and fidelity but, said Nehru, "I do not seem to remember men being reminded in the same manner of Ramachandra and Satyavan, and urged to behave like them. It is only the women who have to behave like Sita and Savitri; the men may behave as they like."[20]

Nehru worked hard to convince his colleagues of the importance of these measures. He wrote to one of his senior ministers, a Brahman who tended toward orthodoxy, that "we have to remember that in the acknowledged social code and practice of India, as it has existed thus far, there was no lack of moral delinquency as well as extreme unhappiness. There were two codes, one for the man and the other for the woman. The woman got the worst of it always." To a young first-time member of Parliament, Nehru wrote that "we should concentrate on the passage through Parliament of the Marriage and Divorce Bills and the Succession Bill. These are the really important ones. The Bills dealing with adoption and guardianship, etc. are relatively unimportant."[21]

By now, the Anti-Hindu-Code-Bill Committee had lost its momentum. After the elections of 1952, the names of Swami Karpatri and Prabhu Dutt Brahmachari do not appear in the newspapers or police records. There were no longer any protests on the streets, but there were still criticisms aplenty in Parliament. The orthodox members of Parliament saw the new bills as designed to destroy Hindu culture. For them, the laws of Manu and Yagnavalkya were immutable and unchangeable, as relevant in AD 1950 as in 950 BC.[22]

But there was also an opposition that was less vulgar and more considered, representing what we might call Hindu conservatism, rather than Hindu reaction. Consider the views of the distinguished historian Radha Kumud Mookerji. He felt that the new proposals, particularly the provisions allowing divorce, were

> against the very spirit of Hindu civilization. . . . The Bill is inspired by the western view of life which attaches more value to the romance of marital relations and married life than to parenthood in which marriage attains its fruition. The Hindu system conceives of parenthood

as something that is permanent, unchangeable, and inviolable. . . . The
Bill seeks to change popular psychology as to the sanctity of marriage
and family and loosen the ties of family as the very foundations of
society. It thinks more of husband and wife than the father and
mother in whom they are to be permanently merged to protect the
child and the future of the race.[23]

This argument did not go uncontested. A woman member felt that
"the effect of a broken home is less injurious than that of a disharmoni-
ous home. Children are of a very receptive mind and the scenes that they
may see of neglect and quarrel between the parents . . . are bound to
leave their mark." If "the home has lost peace," remarked another member, there was no point "forcing them [husband and wife] to live together"; it was better to allow "separation in a respectable fashion."[24]

In the Lok Sabha, the opposition to the reforms was led by the brilliant Hindu Mahasabha lawyer, N. C. Chatterjee. If this was indeed a
secular state, argued Chatterjee, what was the need for a "Hindu" Marriage and Divorce Act? Why not make the same law apply for all
citizens? Thus, if the government honestly believed in the virtues of monogamy, that "this is a blessing and polygamy is a curse, then why not
rescue our Muslim sisters from that curse and from that plight?" "You
have not the courage," Chatterjee told the law minister, "to be logical
and to be consistent."[25]

The socialist J. B. Kripalani likewise felt that by prescribing monogamy only for the Hindus, the government was being hypocritical. "You
must bring it also for the Muslim community," said Kripalani. "Take it
from me that the Muslim community is prepared to have it but you are
not brave enough to do it." But his own wife, the Congress member of
Parliament Sucheta Kripalani, thought that the Muslims were not ready
yet. For "we know the recent past history of our country. We know
what trouble we have had over our minority problem. That is why I
think the Government today is not prepared to bring one Uniform Civil
Code. But I hope the day will soon come in the future when we shall be
able to have one uniform Civil Code."[26]

The elections of 1952 had sent to Parliament an array of articulate
and confident congresswomen. These, naturally, saw the opposition to
the legislation as the work of reactionaries. Subhadra Joshi, speaking in
Hindi, launched a broadside against the custom of arranged marriages,
which virtually sold women into *sharm ki zindagi*, a life of shame and
degradation. Shivrajvati Nehru noted that while male politicians talked

grandly of economic and political reform, they were not willing to make a single change in the sphere of social life and custom. In Hindu society the man was free and sovereign (*purn swatantra*); but the woman was bonded—to him. Even now, the husband was prone to treat this wife as a pair of slippers on his feet, to be discarded at will.[27]

In support of the reforms were several Scheduled Caste members, who knew better than anyone else how Hindu "custom" masked a multitude of sins. One said that if the orthodox had their way, they would

> start amending the Constitution so as to do away with all the mischief done by this Congress Government, and certain new fundamental rights will be added. The first of them will be that all Hindu women will have the wonderful and glorious right of burning themselves on the funeral pyres of their husbands. The second fundamental right would be that the cow will be declared a divine being, . . . and all Indians, including Muslims, Christians and so on will be compelled to worship the cow.[28]

The Communists, for their part, thought the new laws were not radical enough. In the Lok Sabha, B. C. Das called them "a mild, moderate attempt at social reform with all the hesitancy and timidity characteristic of all social measures sponsored by this Government." Still, those who opposed this "moderate measure" had "17th century minds." In the Rajya Sabha, Bhupesh Gupta noted the delay in introducing the legislation; this was caused by the fact that "the Congress Party . . . functions on many occasions like a Rip Van Winkle."[29]

Finally, one must take account of those Muslim members who were effusive in their thanks to government. One, speaking in Hindustani, praised it for keeping their laws intact and not allowing the slightest change. Another thanked the government "for showing their great consideration to the views and the feelings of the Muslim community, and for having exempted them from the operations of this [Marriage] Bill, because there is the personal law for them, based on, and part of their religion, and they hold religion as the most sacred and valuable thing in their life."[30]

V

After a bruising battle extending over nearly ten years, B. R. Ambedkar's Hindu Code Bill was passed into law: not, as he had hoped, all at once, but in several instalments: the Hindu Marriage Act of 1955; and the Hindu Succession, Minority and Guardianship, and Adoptions and Maintenance Acts of 1956.

These acts were piloted through Parliament by the new law minister, H. V. Pataskar. He lacked the stature, and the scholarship, of his predecessor. Once, when he suggested that the Hindu sacramental marriage permitted divorce, N. C. Chatterjee remarked that there was no basis for that statement, adding, "If Shri Pataskar had sat for a Hindu Law examination in any University he would have been ploughed and he would have got zero."[31]

This was probably accurate, but also irrelevant. For, as one dissenter recognized, the new bills constituted a "direct attack on the Hindu *shastras* and Hindu customs."[32] The right of a woman to choose her partner or to inherit property were "un-Hindu" but not undemocratic, since the men had those rights all along. As Pataskar observed, the new laws were based on the constitutional recognition of "the dignity of person, irrespective of any distinction of sex."[33] Another congressman put it more eloquently. Women must have the right to choose (and discard) their husbands, he said, because

> We [Indians] were fighting for freedom. After liberating our country, our motherland, it is our responsibility to liberate our mothers, our sisters, and our wives. That will be the greatest culmination of the freedom that we have attained.[34]

Toward that end the new laws were indeed a notable contribution. Sixty million Hindu women came under their purview. And the changes were significant in moral as well as numerical terms. As the leading American expert on Indian law has written, this was a "wholesale and drastic reform" which "entirely supplants the *shastra* as the source of Hindu law." The leading British scholar of the subject goes further: "for width of scope and boldness of innovation," he says, the series of acts considered here "can be compared only with the *Code Napoléon.*"[35]

The radical changes in the Hindu laws pertaining to marriage and property were principally the work of two men: Jawaharlal Nehru and B. R. Ambedkar. Sadly, in the last, crucial stages of the struggle Ambedkar was a bystander. Having lost the direct elections to Parliament in 1952, he then entered the Upper House. There he sat, silent, while the bills were discussed and passed between 1954 and 1956.[36] He was already a very sick man, with diabetes and complications thereof. In

December 1956 he died. His sometime colleague Jawaharlal Nehru spoke in tribute in Parliament. Ambedkar, said the prime minister, would be remembered above all "as a symbol of the revolt against all the oppressive features of Hindu society." But he "will be remembered also for the great interest he took and the trouble he took over the question of Hindu law reform. I am happy that he saw that reform in a very large measure carried out, perhaps not in the form of that monumental tome that he had himself drafted, but in separate bits."[37]

This was a generous tribute, especially when we consider the bitterness that lay behind Ambedkar's resignation in 1951. Then, Ambedkar thought that Nehru was too weak to fight the opposition within and outside his party. From his point of view the prime minister was going too slowly, but, of course, from the point of view of the orthodox Hindu he was going too fast. In 1949 and 1950, when the bill was first introduced, Nehru was not even in effective control of the Congress. It was only after Vallabhbhai Patel's death that he really took charge, overcoming the conservatives in the Congress and leading his party to a convincing victory in the general elections. With the party, and country, now behind him, he was prepared to introduce, and get passed, the legislation once proposed by Ambedkar.[38]

Nehru was determined to effect changes in the laws of his fellow Hindus, yet prepared to wait before dealing likewise with the Muslims. The aftermath of partition had made the Muslims who were left behind in India vulnerable and confused. At this stage, to tamper with what they considered hallowed tradition—the word of God—would make them even less secure. Thus, when he was asked in Parliament why he had not immediately brought in a uniform civil code, Nehru answered that while such a code had his "extreme sympathy," he did not think that "at the present moment the time is ripe in India for me to try to push it through. I want to prepare the ground for it and this kind of thing is one method of preparing the ground."[39]

Others viewed this caution more cynically. As Dr. Shyama Prasad Mookerjee pointed out in the Provisional Parliament, "it is nobody's case that monogamy is good for Hindus alone or for Buddhists alone or for Sikhs alone." Why not then have a separate bill prescribing monogamy for all citizens? Having asked the question, Dr. Mookerjee supplied this answer: "I am not going to tread on this question because I know the weaknesses of the promoters of the Bill. They dare not touch the Muslim minority. There will be so much opposition coming from throughout India that Government will not dare to proceed with it. But of course you can proceed with the Hindu community in any way you like and whatever the consequences may be."

At this point C. Rajagopalachari interjected: "Because we are the community."[40] "We" meant the Congress, particularly its reformist wing, represented by Nehru and rather ably by Rajagopalachari as well. One can appreciate their hesitancy in taking on people of faiths other than their own. For it had taken them the better part of ten years to "proceed with the Hindu community in any way" they liked—that is, in a way that would help bring their personal laws somewhat in line with modern notions of gender justice.[41]

12

SECURING KASHMIR

> Do we believe in a national state which includes people of all
> religions and shades of opinion and is essentially secular . . . , or
> do we believe in the religious, theocratic conception of a state
> which considers people of other faiths as something beyond the
> pale? This is an odd question to ask, for the idea of a religious or
> theocratic state was given up by the world some centuries ago and
> has no place in the mind of the modern man. And yet the question
> has to be put in India today, for many of us have tried to jump
> back to a past age.
>
> JAWAHARLAL NEHRU

I

THE REFORM of personal laws was one test of Indian secularism. Another, and greater, test was with regard to the future of
Kashmir. Could a Muslim-majority state exist, without undue
fuss or friction, in a Hindu-majority but ostensibly "secular" India?

As we have seen in Chapter Four, by 1949 Sheikh Abdullah was in
firm control of the administration of Jammu and Kashmir. But the status of the territory was still disputed. The United Nations had called for
a plebiscite, and was trying to get India and Pakistan to meet the conditions for holding it.

In February 1950, the Security Council asked both countries to
withdraw their armies from the state. As before, both sides stalled. India asked for the Pakistanis to take their troops out first, while Pakistan
demanded that the National Conference government be removed from
office. India had begun regretting having taken the matter to the United
Nations in the first place. By 1950 it was quite prepared to hold on to its
part of the state, and let Pakistan take the hindmost. The Indian constitution, which went into effect in January 1950, treated Kashmir as part
of the Indian Union. However, it guaranteed the state a certain autonomy; thus Article 370 specified that the president would consult the
state government with regard to subjects other than defence, foreign affairs, and communications.[1]

As for Pakistan, politicians there held that their claim needed no certification from a popular vote. In September 1950, a former prime minister insisted that "the liberation of Kashmir is a cardinal belief of every Pakistani. . . . Pakistan would remain incomplete until the whole of Kashmir has been liberated." Two weeks later, a serving prime minister observed that "for Pakistan, Kashmir is a vital necessity; for India it is an imperialistic adventure."[2]

On each side of the border, the position of the government was echoed and amplified by the press. In the summer of 1950, the British broadcaster Lionel Fielden visited the subcontinent. As a former head of All India Radio, Fielden had many friends in both India and Pakistan. Visiting them and speaking also to their friends, he found that on either side of the international boundary, "the visitor is assailed by arguments and harangues to prove that the other country is not only wrong but diabolically wrong, and mischievously to boot." He observed that "the tone of the Indian Press tends to be a little patronizing, sweetly reasonable but nevertheless obstinate, and rather consciously self-righteous." On the other hand, "the tone of the Pakistan Press and Pakistan leaders tends to be resentful, arrogant and sometimes aggressive." Pakistani hostility was compounded by the fear that powerful forces in India wanted to reconquer or reabsorb their land in a united "Akhand Bharat."

Fielden summarized the two points of view: "In clinging to Kashmir, India wants to weaken Partition; in claiming it, Pakistan wants to make Partition safe." On the issue of Kashmir both sides were absolutely rigid. Thus, "to fight to the last ditch for [Kashmir] is the slogan of all Pakistanis; not to give way on it is rapidly becoming the fixed idea in India."

Fielden ended his analysis with a warning. In the long run, he pointed out, "the most important thing" about the Kashmir conflict was "the expense in armaments in which both countries are getting involved. This means that social services in both countries are crippled, and since both countries, apart from their refugees, have millions of the poorest people in the world, it is easy to see how this can lead to disaster."[3]

The United Nations had tried and failed to solve the dispute. Could another third party succeed? In January 1951, at a meeting at 10 Downing Street, the Australian prime minister, Sir Robert Menzies, suggested that a plebiscite be held under Commonwealth auspices. The British prime minister, Clement Atlee, appeared to favour the idea. But Nehru said that any settlement must have the concurrence of the state government of Sheikh Abdullah. The Pakistani prime minister dismissed that government as "puppets appointed by Nehru [whom] he could change any time."

In reply, Nehru noted that "the Pakistan press was full of this religious appeal and calls for Jehad. If this was the kind of thing that was going to take place during a plebiscite, then there would be no plebiscite but civil upheaval, not only in Kashmir, but elsewhere in India and Pakistan."[4]

II

In 1950, the maps of the government of India claimed the entire state of Jammu and Kashmir as part of its territory. New Delhi's claim to the whole rested on the fact that in October 1947 Maharaja Hari Singh had signed a document acceding to India. Meanwhile, its claim to the part actually held by it rested on the secularist sentiments of Sheikh Mohammed Abdullah.

Abdullah was against Pakistan, but was he for India? That was a question to which the man himself would not give a straight answer. His vacillation is captured in a series of frustrated letters written by Nehru to his sister Vijayalakshmi Pandit:

(10 May 1950): I am sorry to say that Sheikh Abdullah is behaving in a most irresponsible manner. The most difficult thing in life is what to do with one's friends.

(18 July 1950): Meanwhile, Sheikh Abdullah has been behaving very badly in Kashmir in regard to domestic affairs and he appears to be bent on securing a conflict with us. He has gone to wrong hands there and is being misled.

(10 August 1950): Sheikh Abdullah has come round a little and is in a more amenable frame of mind. I wonder how long this will last, because there are too many forces at play in Kashmir, which pull him in different directions.[5]

The note of skepticism in this last letter was warranted, for very soon Abdullah had once more begun behaving in a "most irresponsible manner"; that is, he had begun thinking of ways to detach Kashmir from India. On 29 September 1950, he met the American ambassador, Loy Henderson. In discussing the future of Kashmir, Abdullah told Henderson that

in his opinion it should be independent; that overwhelming majority of the population desired their independence; that he had reason to believe that some Azad Kashmir leaders desired independence and would be willing to cooperate with leaders of National Conference if there was reasonable chance such cooperation would result in independence. Kashmir people could not understand why UN consistently ignored independence as possible solution for Kashmir. Kashmir people had language and cultural background of their own. The Hindus by custom and tradition widely different from Hindus in India, and the background of Muslims quite different from Muslims in Pakistan. Fact was that population of Kashmir homogeneous in spite of presence of Hindu minority.[6]

Abdullah went on to ask the ambassador whether the United States would support an independent Kashmir. Unfortunately, the published records of the State Department do not tell us what answer he got. Did the United States ever seriously contemplate propping up Kashmir as a client state, given that its location could be of immense value in the struggle against communism?

We still can't tell, and it seems that at the time, Abdullah couldn't tell either. He now went back to the Indian government, negotiating with it the terms of Kashmir's autonomy. The state, it was decided, would have its own constituent assembly, to finalize the terms by which it would associate with India. In January 1951, Abdullah wrote to the minister of states that, as he understood it, the Jammu and Kashmir constituent assembly would discuss "the question of accession of the State, the question of retention or abolition of the Ruler as the Constitutional Head of the State and the question of framing a Constitution for the State including the question of defining the sphere of Union jurisdiction over the State." He added that the assembly would "take decisions on all issues specified above," decisions the government of India must treat as "binding on all concerned." This suggested that even Kashmir's accession to India was not final. As the alarmed minister of states noted in the margin of the letter, the sheikh's interpretation was "perhaps going beyond what we said."[7]

The sheikh, as ever, presumed to speak for the state of Jammu and Kashmir as a whole. In truth, while he was still revered in the Valley, he was becoming quite unpopular among the Hindus of the Jammu region, who were eager to quickly merge their part of the state with the Indian Union. In 1949, a Praja Parishad (People's party) was formed to represent the interests of the Jammu Hindus. It was led by a seventy-year-old veteran, Prem Nath Dogra. Characteristically, the sheikh dismissed the opposition in Jammu as "reactionaries."[8]

In October 1951 elections were held for the Kashmir constituent assembly. The Praja Parishad had decided to run, but, early on, the nomination papers of several of its candidates were found to be invalid. In protest it decided to boycott the elections. All seventy-five seats were won by Abdullah's National Conference. All but three of the National Conference candidates won unopposed.[9]

Sheikh Abdullah's opening speech in the constituent assembly lasted a full ninety minutes. Reading from a printed English text, the sheikh discussed, one by one, the options before the people of Kashmir. The first was to join Pakistan, a "landlord-ridden" and "feudal" theocracy. The second was to join India, with which the state had a "kinship of ideals," and whose government had "never tried to interfere in our internal autonomy." Admittedly, "certain tendencies have been asserting themselves in India which may in the future convert it into a religious State wherein the interests of the Muslims will be jeopardized." On the other hand, "the continued accession of Kashmir to India" would promote harmony between Hindus and Muslims, and marginalize the communalists. "Gandhiji was not wrong," argued the sheikh, "when he uttered words before his death which [I] paraphrase, 'I lift up mine eyes unto the hills, from whence cometh my help.'"

Abdullah came, finally, to "the alternative of making ourselves an Eastern Switzerland, of keeping aloof from both States, but having friendly relations with them." This was an attractive option, but it did not seem practical. How would a small, landlocked country safeguard its sovereignty? As the sheikh reminded his audience, Kashmir had once been "independent" of both India and Pakistan, between 15 August and 22 October 1947. Then, its independence was destroyed by the tribal invasion. What was the guarantee that a sovereign Kashmir "may not be victims of a similar aggression?"[10]

Thus, the sheikh rejected the option of independence as impractical, and the option of joining Pakistan as immoral. Kashmir would join India, but on terms of its own choosing. Among these terms were the retention of the state flag and the designation of the head of government as prime minister. Neither was acceptable to the Praja Parishad of Jammu. Asking for the complete integration of Kashmir into India, it had adopted the slogan *Ek vidhan, ek pradhan, ek nishan* ("One constitution, one head of state, one flag").

In January 1952, shortly before Abdullah was due to speak in Jammu town, Hindu students protested against the National Conference flag being flown alongside the Indian tricolour. They were arrested, and later expelled from their college. This sparked sympathy protests, culminating in a march on the Secretariat, where demonstrators entered the offices, broke furniture, and burned records. The police cracked down hard, imposing a seventy-two-hour curfew and arresting hundreds of Parishad members. Also jailed was their aged leader, Prem Nath Dogra, although he himself had not participated in the protests.

The government in Delhi, fearful of a countrywide Hindu backlash, persuaded the Kashmir government to release the Parishad leaders. Abdullah agreed, if reluctantly. On 10 April he made a speech, saying that his party would accept the Indian constitution "in its entirety once we are satisfied that the grave of communalism has been finally dug." He added darkly, "Of that we are not sure yet." The sheikh said that the Kashmiris "fear what will happen to them and their position if, for instance, something happens to Pandit Nehru."[11]

Both the timing and the venue of Abdullah's speech were significant. It was made in Ranbirsingpura, a town only four miles from the border with Pakistan. And India had just come through a general election that appeared to vindicate Jawaharlal Nehru and his policies. The speech was widely reported, and caused considerable alarm. Why did the man who had often issued chits complimenting India on its secularism suddenly turn so sceptical?

The sheikh's change of mind coincided with a visit to Kashmir by the British journalist Ian Stephens. Stephens, who had been editor of the Calcutta *Statesman* during the troubles of 1946–1947, was known to be a strong supporter of Pakistan. He thought that the Kashmir Valley, with its majority Muslim population, properly belonged to that country. Still, he was sensitive to the problems of its leader. He had long talks with Abdullah, whom he saw as "a man of pluck and enlightenment, standing for principles good in their way; a victim, like so many of us, of the unique scope and speed and confusion of the changes in 1947, and now holding a perhaps uniquely lonely and perplexing post." Abdullah's regime was upheld by "Indian bayonets, which meant mainly Hindu bayonets." Admittedly, "in many ways it was a good regime: energetic, full of ideas, staunchly non-communal, very go-ahead in agrarian reform." But, concluded Stephens, "to the eye of history it might prove an unnatural one."[12]

III

Once, Abdullah had been Nehru's man in Kashmir. By the summer of 1952, however, it was more that Nehru was Abdullah's man in India. The sheikh had made known his opinion that only the prime minister stood between India and the ultimate victory of Hindu communalism.

Meanwhile, discussions continued about the precise status of Kashmir vis-à-vis the Indian Union. In July, the sheikh met Nehru in Delhi and also had a round of meetings with other ministers. They hammered out a compromise known as the "Delhi Agreement," whereby Kashmiris would become full citizens of India, in exchange for an autonomy far greater than that enjoyed by other states of the Indian Union. Thus the new state flag (devised by the national conference) would for "historical and other reasons" be flown alongside the national flag. Delhi could not send in forces to quell "internal disturbances" without the consent of Srinagar. Although with regard to other states residuary powers were vested with the Centre, in the case of Kashmir these would remain with the state. Crucially, people from outside the state were prohibited from buying land or property within it. This measure was aimed at forestalling attempts to change the demographic profile of the Valley through large-scale immigration.[13]

These were major concessions, but the sheikh pressed for greater powers still. In a truculent speech in the Jammu and Kashmir constituent assembly he said that only the state could decide what powers to give away to the Indian Union, or what jurisdiction the Indian Supreme Court would have in Kashmir. Then he told Yuvraj Karan Singh, the formal head of state, that if Singh did not fall into line he would go the way of his father, Hari Singh. The young prince, said the sheikh, must "break up with the reactionary elements" and instead identify with the "happiness and sorrow of the common man." For "if he is under the delusion that he can retain his office with the help of his few supporters, he is mistaken."[14]

The "reactionary elements" referred to by the sheikh were the Hindus of Jammu. They had resumed their agitation, with an amended if equally catchy slogan: *Ek desh mein do vidhan, do pradhan, do nishan/ nahin chalenge, nahin chalenge* ("Two constitutions, two heads of state, two flags—these in one state we shall not allow, not allow"). Processions and marches, as well as clashes with the police, became frequent. Once more, the jails of Jammu began to be filled with the volunteers of the Praja Parishad.

The Hindus of Jammu retained a deep attachment to the ruling family, and to Maharaja Hari Singh in particular. They resented his being deposed, and were displeased with his son for being "disloyal" by agreeing to replace him. But their apprehension was also economic—that the land reforms recently undertaken in the Kashmir Valley would be reproduced in Jammu. In the Valley, zamindars had been dispossessed of land in excess of the limit. Since this was fixed at twenty-two acres per family, their losses were substantial. The land seized by the state had been vested chiefly in the hands of the middle peasantry. The agricultural proletariat had not benefited to quite the same extent. Still, the land reforms had gone farther and been more successful here than anywhere else in India.[15]

As it happened, the large landlords in the Valley were almost all Hindu. This gave an unfortunate religious tinge to what was essentially a project of socialist redistribution. That was perhaps inevitable; despite the sincerity of the Sheikh's professed secularism, it could not nullify the legacies of history. Once, the state was controlled by the Dogras of Jammu, who happened to be Hindu; now, it was controlled by the National Conference, which was based in the Valley, and whose leader and most of whose members were Muslim.[16]

IV

Through the years 1950–1952, as the rest of India became acquainted with its new constitution and had its first elections, Jammu and Kashmir were beset by uncertainty on two fronts. There were the unsettled relations between the state and the Indian Union, and there was the growing conflict between the Muslim-majority Kashmir Valley and the Hindu-dominated Jammu region. Here was a situation made to order for a politician in search of a cause. And it found one.

This was Dr. Shyama Prasad Mookerjee, who was to make the struggle of the Dogras of Jammu his own. Dr. Mookerjee had left Jawaharlal Nehru's cabinet to become the founder and president of the Bharatiya Jana Sangh. His new party had fared poorly in the general elections of 1952—only three of its members were elected to Parliament. The troubles in Kashmir came at an opportune time for Dr. Mookerjee and the Jana Sangh. Here was a chance to uplift the dispirited cadres, to forget the disappointment of the elections, and reinvent the party for the national stage.

Mookerjee began his charge in Parliament, with a series of blistering attacks on the government. "Who made Sheikh Abdullah the King of Kings in Kashmir?" he asked, sarcastically. The sheikh had apparently said that the Kashmiris would treat the provincial flag and the national flag "equally"; this, Mookerjee said, showed a "divided loyalty" unacceptable in a sovereign country. Even if the Valley wanted a limited accession, Jammu and the Buddhist region of Ladakh must be allowed to integrate fully if they so chose. But a better solution still would be to make the whole state a part of India, with no special concessions. This would give it the same standing as all the other princely states, which—despite earlier promises made to them about autonomy—had finally to agree to being subject to the provisions of the constitution in toto. Abdullah himself had been a member of the Indian Constituent Assembly, yet "he is asking for special treatment. Did he not agree to accept this Constitution in relation to the rest of India, including 497 States? If it is good enough for all of them, why should it not be good enough for him in Kashmir?"[17]

In the autumn of 1952, Mookerjee visited Jammu and made several speeches in support of the Praja Parishad movement. Its demands, he said, were "just and patriotic." He promised to "secure" the constitution of India for it. He then went to Srinagar, where he had a contentious meeting with Sheikh Abdullah.[18]

The support of a national party and a national leader had given much encouragement to the Dogras. In November 1952, the state government moved to Jammu for the winter. As head of state, Karan Singh arrived first. Years later, he recalled the "derisive and hostile slogans" and the black flags with which he was received by the Praja Parishad. Although "the National Conference had tried to lay on some kind of reception it was swamped by the deep hostility of the Dogra masses." Writing to the government of India, he noted that "an overwhelming majority of the Jammu province seem to me to be emphatically in sympathy with the agitation. . . . I do not think it will be a correct appraisal to dismiss the whole affair as merely the creation of a reactionary clique."[19]

That, of course, is what Sheikh Abdullah was disposed to do. Through the winter of 1952–1953 the Praja Parishad and the state government remained locked in conflict. Protesters would remove the state flag from government buildings, and put the Indian flag in its stead. They would be arrested, but others would soon arrive to replace them. The movement got a tremendous fillip when a Parishad member, Mcla

Ram, was shot by the police near the Pakistan border. In Jammu, at least, Abdullah's reputation was in tatters. He had made his name representing the people against an autocratic monarch. Now he had become a repressive ruler himself.[20]

In January, Mookerjee wrote a long letter to Jawaharlal Nehru in support of the Parishad and its "highly patriotic and emotional" struggle to "merge completely with India." He added a gratuitous challenge with regard to the "recovery" of the part of the erstwhile undivided State now in the possession of Pakistan. How was India "going to get this [territory] back?" asked Mookerjee. "You have always evaded this question. The time has come when we should know what exactly you propose to do about this matter. It will be nothing short of national disgrace and humiliation if we fail to regain this lost portion of our own territory."

Nehru ignored the taunt. As for the Praja Parishad, he thought that it was "trying to decide a very difficult and complicated constitutional question by methods of war." Abdullah (to whom Mookerjee had written separately) was more blunt: as he saw it, "the Praja Parishad is determined to force a solution of the entire Kashmir issue on communal lines."

Mookerjee asked Nehru and Abdullah to release the Praja Parishad leaders and convene a conference to discuss the future of Kashmir. Mookerjee again challenged Nehru to go to war with Pakistan. "You have always evaded this question," he insisted. "Please do not sidetrack the issue and let the public of India know how and when, if at all, we are going to get back this portion of our cherished territory."[21]

Eventually, the exchange ran aground on a matter of pride. Nehru thought the Parishad should first call off the movement, before the government would talk to it; Mookerjee wanted the government to offer talks, in response to which the movement would call off the struggle. When the government refused to bend, Mookerjee decided to take the matter to the streets of Delhi. Beginning in the first week of March, Jana Sangh volunteers, risking arrest, supported the demands of the Praja Parishad. The protesters would collect outside a police station and shout slogans against the government and against the prime minister, thereby violating Section 188 of the Indian Penal Code.

The satyagraha was coordinated by Mookerjee from his office in Parliament House. Participating were members of what the police called "Hindu communal parties": the Jana Sangh, the Hindu Mahasabha, and the Ram Rajya Parishad. By the end of April 1953, 1,300 people had been arrested. Intelligence reports suggest that they came from all parts of India and were overwhelmingly upper-caste: Brahmans, Thakurs, and Banias.[22]

It was now summer, tourist season in the Valley. Among the first visitors to arrive, in late April, was the American politician Adlai Stevenson. He had come to Kashmir to sail on Lake Dal and see the snows, and also to meet Sheikh Abdullah. They met twice, for two hours or more each time. The content of these conversations were not revealed by either side, but some Indians assumed that it was all about independence. A journal in Bombay otherwise known to be sympathetic to the United States claimed that Stevenson had assured Abdullah of much more than moral support. A loan of $15 million dollars would be on hand once Kashmir became independent; besides, the United States would ensure that "the Valley would have a permanent population of at least 5,000 American families, that every houseboat and hotel would be filled to capacity, that Americans would buy up all the art and craft output of the dexterous Kashmiri artisans, that within three years every village in Kashmir would be electrified and so on and so forth."[23]

Stevenson later denied that he had encouraged Abdullah. When the sheikh offered the "casual suggestion that independent status might be an alternative solution," Stevenson stayed silent; he did not, he claimed, give "even unconscious encouragement regarding independence, which did not seem to me realistic. . . . I was listening, not talking."[24]

So the sheikh was once more contemplating independence. But independence for what? Not, most likely, the whole of the state of Jammu and Kashmir. One part (the north) was in Pakistani hands; another part (Jammu) was in the grip of a prolonged agitation. Abdullah's own papers are closed to scholars, and he is silent on the subject in his memoirs. But we can plausibly speculate that it must have been the Valley, and the Valley alone, for which he was seeking independence. Here he was in control, with the population largely behind him; and it was here that the tourists would come to nurture his dreams of an "Eastern Switzerland."[25]

V

Not long after Stevenson, another politician came seeking to fish in troubled waters. On 8 May, Dr. Shyama Prasad Mookerjee boarded a train to Jammu, en route to Srinagar. He had planned to take his satyagraha deep into enemy territory. Anticipating trouble, the state government issued an order prohibiting him from entering. Mookerjee disregarded it and crossed the border on the morning of 11 May. The police asked him to go back, and when he refused, they arrested him and took him to Srinagar jail.

Before the Praja Parishad movement, Mookerjee had been a lifelong constitutionalist. A Bengali *bhadralok* of the old school, he was comfortable in a suit and tie, sipping a glass of whisky. During the entire nationalist movement, he never resorted to satyagraha or spent a single night in jail. Indeed, he had long held, in the words of his biographer, that "legislatures were the only forum for giving vent to diverse viewpoints on Government policies." That belief sat oddly with Mookerjee's support for the protests of the Praja Parishad. And now he was sanctioning and leading a street protest himself.

Why did Mookerjee resort to methods with which he was unfamiliar? He told his follower (and future biographer) Balraj Madhok that he was convinced that this was the only language the prime minister understood. "As a man who had been [an] agitator all his life, Pandit Nehru, he felt, had developed a complex for agitational methods. He would bow before force and agitation but not before right or reason unless backed by might."[26]

Now, in Srinagar jail, while the charges against him were being drawn up, Mookerjee spent his time reading Hindu philosophy and writing to his friends and relatives.[27] In early June he fell ill. Pain in the legs was accompanied by fever. The doctors diagnosed this as pleurisy, but then on 22 June he had a heart attack, and he died the next day.[28]

On 24 June, an Indian air force plane flew Mookerjee's body back to his home, Calcutta. Sheikh Abdullah had laid a shawl on the body while his deputy, Bakshi Ghulam Mohammed, helped load the stretcher onto the plane. In Calcutta, huge crowds lined the thirteen-mile route from Dum Dum airport to the family home in Bhowanipur. Nehru wrote to a friend in Madras that "we are having a great deal of trouble as a result of Dr. Mookerjee's death. The atmosphere in Delhi is bad. It is worse in Calcutta."[29]

And it was worse still in Jammu. When the news reached the town, an angry mob attacked and looted a government arts emporium, and set fire to government offices.[30] In Delhi, meanwhile, a crowd gathered at Ajmeri Gate, wearing black badges, waving black flags, and shouting, *Khoon ka Badla Khoon se lainge* ("Blood will be avenged by blood"). The anger persisted for days. On 5 July a portion of Dr. Mookerjee's ashes arrived in the capital; these were carried in a huge procession, formed by the Jana Sangh, through the old city, with the marchers shouting slogans of revenge and insisting, *Kashmir hamara hai* ("Kashmir shall be ours").[31]

In late June, posters were put up in some parts of Delhi, warning Sheikh Abdullah that he would be killed if he came to the capital. These threats could not be taken lightly because it was in a similarly charged atmosphere that Mahatma Gandhi had been killed. Now, again, it appeared that "in Delhi the entire middle class is in the hands of the [Hindu] communalists." It was feared that not just the sheikh, but also "Mr Nehru may meet the [same] fate as that of Gandhiji due to the intense propaganda of the communalists." The police were instructed to look out for "any propaganda of a serious nature, or any plans, or designs these groups of parties may have against the Prime Minister."[32]

VI

The popular movement led by Dr. Mookerjee planted thoughts of independence in Sheikh Abdullah's head; and the outcry following Mookerjee's death seems to have confirmed them. Sensing this, Nehru wrote two long, emotional letters recalling their old friendship and India's ties to Kashmir. He asked Abdullah to come to Delhi and meet him. The sheikh did not oblige. Then Nehru sent Maulana Abul Kalam Azad (the most senior member of the cabinet) to Srinagar, but that did not help either. The sheikh now seemed convinced of two things; that he had the support of the United States, and that "even Nehru could not subdue [Hindu] communal forces in India." On 10 July, he addressed party workers at Mujahid Manzil, the headquarters of the National Conference in Srinagar. After outlining Kashmir's, and his, grievances against the government of India, he said that "a time will, therefore, come when I will bid them good-bye."[33]

The sheikh's turnabout greatly alarmed the prime minister. Writing to a colleague, Nehru said that the developments in Kashmir were particularly unfortunate, because "anything that happens there has larger and wider consequences." The "problem of Kashmir [was] symbolic of many things, including our secular policy in India."[34]

By now the government of Kashmir was divided within itself; its members (as Nehru observed) likely "to pull in different directions and proclaim entirely different policies." This was in good part the work of the government of India's Intelligence Bureau. Officers of the bureau had been working within the National Conference, dividing the leadership and confusing the ranks. Some leaders, such as G. M. Sadiq, were left-wing and anti-American; they disapproved of the sheikh's talks with Stevenson. Others, like Bakshi Ghulam Mohammed, had ambitions of ruling Kashmir themselves.[35]

There was now an open rift within the National Conference, between the pro-India and pro-independence groups. The latter were led by the sheikh's close associate Mirza Afzal Beg. The former were in close touch with the *sadr-i-riyasat*, Karan Singh. It was rumoured that Sheikh Abdullah would declare independence on 21 August—the day of the great Eid festival—and that he would then seek the protection of the United Nations against "Indian aggression."[36] Two weeks before that date, Abdullah dismissed a member of his cabinet. This gave the others in the pro-India faction an excuse to move against him. Led by Bakshi Ghulam Mohammed, they wrote the sheikh a letter accusing him of encouraging sectarianism and corruption. A copy of the letter was also sent to Karan Singh. He, in turn, dismissed Abdullah and invited Bakshi Ghulam Mohammed to form a government in Abdullah's place.

Abdullah was dismissed in the early hours of the morning. When he was woken up and handed the letter of dismissal, the sheikh flew into a rage. "Who is the Sadr-i-Riyasat to dismiss me?" he shouted. "I made that chit of a boy Sadr-i-Riyasat." The police then told him that he had not just been dismissed, but also placed under arrest. He was given two hours to say his prayers and pack his belongings, before being taken off to jail.

Why was Abdullah humiliated? Did he have to be dismissed in the dead of night, and did he then have to be placed under detention? Karan Singh later recalled that this was done because "Bakshi Ghulam Mohammed made it quite clear that he could not undertake to run the Government if the Sheikh and Beg were left free to propagate their views." In other words, the sheikh was safe and quiet in jail, but as a free man, put out of office, he would quickly mobilize popular sentiment in his favour.[37]

Then, and later, it was widely believed that the arrest of Abdullah was the idea of Rafi Ahmad Kidwai. Kidwai was a left-leaning member of the cabinet, and a close friend of Nehru's. In Delhi it was thought that he wanted to humiliate the sheikh because Abdullah was currying favour with the Americans. In Kashmir, however, it was held that this was a plain, if misguided, act of revenge. In 1947, Kidwai's brother had been murdered in the hill station of Mussoorie, by a Kashmiri. Deposing the sheikh was a way of settling accounts.[38]

Did Jawaharlal Nehru himself approve the arrest of his friend Sheikh Abdullah? Nehru's biographer thinks that he did not know beforehand, but his chief of intelligence suggests that he did. One thing is clear, however: once the deed was done, Nehru did nothing to countermand it.[39]

Like his predecessor, the new prime minister of Kashmir was a larger-than-life figure. He was known commonly as "the Bakshi," much as his predecessor was known as "the Sheikh." Ghulam Mohammed was born in 1907 in modest circumstances and began his political career by organizing a union of carriage drivers in Srinagar. That, and four terms in Hari Singh's jails, gave him sterling nationalist credentials. However, by temperament and orientation he was quite different from the sheikh. One was a man of ideas and idealism, the other a man of action and organization. When the raiders attacked in October 1947, it was Abdullah who gave the rousing speeches, while the Bakshi placed volunteers in position and watched out for potential fifth columnists. After 1947, while Abdullah dealt with Nehru and Delhi, it was the Bakshi who "kept the structure of the State intact, at a time when the whole Government had collapsed and was non-existent." As two Kashmiri academics wrote in 1950, "being a strict disciplanarian himself, he can brook no indiscipline and dilly-dallying tactics. He is no lover of formal government routine and red-tapeism. He believes in quick but right action." The conclusion in India at the time was inescapable: "In fact, Bakshi is to Abdullah what Sardar [Patel] is to Nehru."[40]

The analogy, though attractive, was inexact, because Patel did not covet his boss's job but the Bakshi, having got such a job, intended to keep it. This required, as he well understood, keeping Delhi on his side. Ten days after he had assumed power, he visited Jammu, where he spoke to a large crowd, assuring them that "the ties between Kashmir and India are irrevocable. No power on earth can separate the two." Next, speaking in Srinagar to a meeting of National Conference workers, the Bakshi argued that "Sheikh Abdullah played directly into the hands of foreign invaders by entertaining the idea of an independent Kashmir." That, he said, was "a dangerous game, pregnant with disastrous consequences for Kashmir, India, and Pakistan." Since Kashmir lacked the resources to defend itself, independence was a "crack-brained idea," calculated only to make the state a centre of the superpowers' intrigue. It was an idea "which can devastate the people."[41]

As prime minister, Bakshi Ghulam Mohammed adopted a populist style, holding a *darbar* every Friday at which he heard the grievances of the public. An early move was to raise the procurement price of paddy.

Next, he made school education free, approved new engineering and medical colleges, and abolished customs barriers between Jammu and Kashmir and the rest of India.

In October 1954, the All India Newspaper Editors Conference was held in Srinagar. The state government put the guests up in the best hotels and gave parties at which the finest Kashmiri delicacies were served. A grateful editor wrote that the new regime had been in place for only a year, "yet it can be safely said that the Bakshi Government has, in some fields, brought in more reforms than did Sheikh Abdullah's in its six years of existence." After the public and the press, it was the turn of the president. In October 1955, Dr. Rajendra Prasad arrived in Srinagar amid "carefully whipped up mass enthusiasm"—crowds lining the road from the airport, a procession of boats on the Jhelum. The president had come to inaugurate a hydroelectric project, one of several development schemes started under the new dispensation.[42]

All this time, Sheikh Abdullah was cooling his heels in detention. He was first housed in an old palace in Udhampur, in the plains, before being shifted to a cooler bungalow in the mountains, at Kot. He was raising poultry and was reported to have become "very anti-Indian."[43]

Within and outside Kashmir the Bakshi was viewed as something of a usurper. Relevant here are the contents of two secret police reports on Friday prayers in Delhi's Jama Masjid. On 2 October 1953, the prayers were attended by two members of Parliament from Kashmir. When they were asked by a Muslim cleric to organize a meeting on the situation in Kashmir, the members answered that the time was not right because they were working behind the scenes for the release of Sheikh Abdullah. They also said that "all Kashmiris would remain with India and die for it," but if the sheikh continued to be held in jail, the state might then, in anger, "go to Pakistan for which the responsibility would not be theirs."

Three months later, Bakshi Ghulam Mohammed himself attended prayers in the Jama Masjid. This was a way of claiming legitimacy, because the mosque, built by Shah Jehan in the seventeenth century, was the subcontinent's grandest and most revered. The keepers of the shrine, sensible of the Bakshi's proximity to the ruler of Delhi, received him respectfully enough. But, as a police report noted, "the Muslims who had congregated there, including some Kashmiris, were talking against Bakshi Ghulam Mohammed in whispering tones. They said that he had become the Prime Minister of Kashmir after putting his 'guru'—Sheikh Abdullah—behind bars."[44]

VII

In the 1950s, as in the 1940s, the Valley of Kashmir was troubled and unsettled. Behind the troubles of the 1940s lay the indecision of the maharaja—who refused to accede to either Pakistan or India while there was still time—and the greed and fervour of the tribal raiders who invaded the state. Behind the troubles of the 1950s were the ambitions of Sheikh Abdullah and S. P. Mookerjee. Neither was willing to play within the rules of constitutional democracy. Both raised the political stakes and both, tragically, paid for it.

The developments in Kashmir were worrisome not just to Indians. The British general who had been in charge of the Indian army in 1947 thought that they might very well "result in a worsening of Indo-Pak relations." In the defence of Kashmir he had come to know both Sheikh Abdullah and the Bakshi very well. Abdullah though "never a great man," was nonetheless "sincere, in my opinion, in his love for his own country." On the other hand, the Bakshi was "quite insincere"; he was "an individual without calibre."[45]

In fact, the Bakshi did have a certain talent for organization, and for feathering his nest. He used his closeness to Delhi to get a steady flow of Central funds into his state. These were used to pay for dams, roads, hospitals, tunnels, and hotels. Many new buildings went up in Srinagar, including a new secretariat, a new sports stadium, and a new tourist complex. However, in the development projects undertaken by the Bakshi's government there was always "a percentage for family and friends." His regime soon became known as the BBC, or the Bakshi Brothers Corporation.[46]

The developments of 1952–1953 had raised sharp questions about India's moral claim to the Valley. Six years had elapsed since the invasion of 1947—enough time for the world to forget it, and to remember only that the Valley was Muslim and so was Pakistan. Besides, the Kashmiri leader who had so long been paraded as India's own had now been put into jail by the Indian government.

Could things have turned out otherwise? Perhaps, if Sheikh Abdullah and Shyama Prasad Mookerjee had acted with responsibility and restraint. And perhaps, if Jawaharlal Nehru and the Indian government had listened to an obscure journalist of English extraction then editing a low-circulation liberal weekly in Bangalore. In 1952–1953, while Dr. Mookerjee was demanding that Nehru should invade Pakistan and thus "reclaim" northern Kashmir, Philip Spratt was proposing a radically different solution. India, he said, must abandon its claims to the Valley, and allow the sheikh his dream of independence. It should withdraw its armies and write off its loans to the government of Jammu and Kashmir. "Let Kashmir go ahead, alone and adventurously, in her explorations of a secular state," he wrote. "We shall watch the act of faith with due sympathy but at a safe distance, our honour, our resources and our future free from the enervating entanglements which write a lie in our soul."

Spratt's solution was tinged with morality, but more so with economy and prudence. Indian policy, he argued, was based on "a mistaken belief in the one nation theory and greed to own the beautiful and strategic valley of Srinagar." The costs of this policy, present and future, were incalculable. Rather than give Kashmir special privileges and create resentment elsewhere in India, it was best to let the state go. As things stood, however, Kashmir

> was in the grip of two armies glaring at each other in a state of armed neutrality. It may suit a handful of people to see the indefinite continuance of this ghastly situation. But the Indian taxpayer is paying through the nose for the precarious privilege of claiming Kashmir as part of India on the basis of all the giving on India's side and all the taking on Kashmir's side.[47]

That material interests should supersede ideological ones was an argument which came easily to a former Marxist such as Spratt. It was not, however, an argument likely to win many adherents in the India of the 1950s.

Dividing up British India: Lord Mountbatten *(centre)*, Jawaharlal Nehru *(far left)*, and Mohammad Ali Jinnah *(right)*, discussing the terms of independence and partition, New Delhi, May 1947. *(The Hindu)*

Jawaharlal Nehru in conversation with Lord and Lady Mountbatten, New Delhi, circa November–December 1947. *(Nehru Memorial Museum and Library)*

A group of unknown Indians marching to join Gandhi's funeral procession, New Delhi, 31 January 1948. *(Henri Cartier-Bresson/Magnum)*

Vallabhbhai Patel (1875–1950), the "Iron Man of India," the integrator of the princely states, and a key player in the framing of the Indian Constitution. *(Nehru Memorial Museum and Library)*

The lawyer-economist B. R. Ambedkar (1892–1956), inspirational leader of the low castes and the chairman of the Drafting Committee of the Indian Constitution. *(The Hindu)*

FACING PAGE, TOP: A tent city of partition refugees from East Punjab, Kingsway Camp, Delhi, circa 1948. *(Press Information Bureau)*

FACING PAGE, BOTTOM: A street protest by Bengali refugees in Calcutta, circa 1950. *(Ananda Bazar Patrika)*

Potti Sriramulu (1901–1952), whose death by fasting led to
the creation of the state of Andhra Pradesh and, ultimately, to the redrawing
of the map of India on linguistic lines. *(The Hindu)*

Master Tara Singh (1885–1967), preacher, agitator, institution builder, and institution breaker, whose long struggle for a Sikh province came to fruition only after his death, photographed in Simla, circa 1946. *(The Hindu)*

The controversy over the reform of Hindu personal laws, circa 1949–1950, as captured by the doyen of Indian cartoonists, R. K. Laxman. *(R. K. Laxman)*

M. S. Golwalkar (1906–1973), chief organizer of the Rashtriya Swayamsevak Sangh, mentor and teacher to generations of extremists who have carried forward his struggle for a Hindu nation. *(Ananda Bazar Patrika)*

Jawaharlal Nehru and the Kashmiri leader Sheikh Mohammed Abdullah in days when they were still friends, in Srinagar, circa 1949. *(Nehru Memorial Museum and Library)*

Jawaharlal Nehru addressing a public meeting in Srinagar, 1952. Sheikh Abdullah, who is seated immediately to the right, was to be jailed by Nehru's government a year later. *(Press Information Bureau)*

A group of mostly Muslim women queueing up to vote in the first general elections in the old city of Delhi, February 1952. *(Press Information Bureau)*

FACING PAGE: An election poster issued by the Congress Party in 1952, featuring its president and chief campaigner, Jawaharlal Nehru. The poster was issued in several sizes, colours, and languages—altogether 750,000 copies were printed and distributed. *(Author's collection)*

for a
stable
secular
progressive
state

VOTE
CONGRESS

This Poster (No. 1) issued by the Central Publicity Board became the most popular election poster throughout India and was eagerly sought after by millions. Printed in three colours in sizes 30″×40″, 20″×30″ and 15″×20″, about 7½ lakhs copies were consumed.

One side of non-alignment: Jawaharlal Nehru greeting the Soviet leaders
Nikolai Bulganin and Nikita Khrushchev at Delhi airport, 1955. *(Author's collection)*

Hindi-Chini bhai bhai: Nehru and Chinese Premier Chou En-lai in days
when they were still friends if not brothers, New Delhi, 1956.
(Nehru Memorial Museum and Library)

Jawaharlal Nehru with the scholar-statesman Chakravarti Rajagopalachari, New Delhi, circa 1959. Once a stalwart Congressman, "Rajaji" at age eighty founded and led the Swatantra party to oppose the policies of Nehru and the Congress. *(Author's collection)*

Nehru with the legendary beauty Maharani Gayatri Devi of Jaipur, New Delhi, circa 1955. Gayatri Devi was later to join Rajaji's Swatantra party and, still later, to be jailed by Indira Gandhi. *(Nehru Memorial Museum and Library)*

Angami Zapu Phizo, the unforgiving, unyielding leader of the Naga movement for freedom from Indian rule.
(Ananda Bazar Patrika)

Martyrs memorial in Phizo's home village, Khonoma.
(Ananda Bazar Patrika)

THESE MEN AND WOMEN OF KHONOMA GAVE THEIR LIVES FOR THE VISION OF A FREE NAGA NATION WE REMEMBER AND SALUTE THEM AND STILL HOLD FAST TO THEIR VISION

1956 – 1992

1. PELESATO CHASE
2. PERHIZO "
3. NIVISIE "
4. NIJULHU "
5. DOLHUCHA "
6. ARUNO "
7. VILAU DOLIE
8. NITO "
9. VISOLENO "
10. KIYAWHESIE "
11. MEGOVOR MERU
12. MHIASILIE "
13. KHRIETO SAVINO
14. RUDO-U "
15. LAVITO TERHUJA
16. KRUHELIE "
17. AHUNO "
18. NILELIE KHATE
19. KONIU "
20. VIVOLHUTO THO-U
21. MIAVIU KENIAU
22. DIALHUU "
23. KHRIEVOTSO "
24. LOKHRIETO IRALU
25. JUNO PFULISE
26. JALHULIE KOTSU
27. ULAU "
28. NILHUTUU "
29. THINOKHRIELIE "
30. THAVI CHASIE
31. NGUNYUNO PUNYU
32. CHABIZO SEYIE
33. RUYAHULIE "
34. MENEHENO "
35. HIEPIA VUPRU
36. NURHIU "
37. TISO-U JHUNYU
38. ZAPUNILIE SECHU
39. UVITO RATSA
40. DIEZELHUBIU MOR
41. THEKRUKIETO VIYIE
42. ZAKIESOLIE VAKHA
43. ROKOLALIE "
44. THIYIECHA "
45. RIATO "
46. NIPIELIE CHUCHA

13

TRIBAL TROUBLE

[T]hese tribes . . . not only defend themselves with obstinate
resolution, but attack their enemies with the most daring
courage. . . . [T]hey possess fortitude of mind superior to the
sense of danger or the fear of death.

A British official on the Nagas, c. 1840

I

THROUGH THE 1950S, while the government of India was seeking to maintain its hold on the Valley of Kashmir, its authority
and legitimacy were also being challenged at the other end of the
Himalaya. This was New Delhi's "Naga problem," much less known
than its Kashmir problem, even though it was as old—even older, in fact—
and as intractable.

The Nagas were a group of tribes living in the eastern Himalaya,
along the Burma border. Secure in their mountain fastness, they had
been cut off from social and political developments in the rest of India.
The British administered the area lightly, keeping out plainsmen and not
tampering with tribal laws or practices, except one—headhunting. However, American Baptists had been active since the mid-nineteenth century, converting several tribes to Christianity.

At this time, the Naga Hills formed part of Assam, a province
very diverse even by Indian standards, sharing borders with China,
Burma, and East Pakistan; divided into upland and lowland regions;
and inhabited by hundreds of different communities. In the plains
lived Assamese-speaking Hindus, connected by culture and faith to
the greater Indian heartland. Among the important groups of tribes
were the Mizos, the Khasis, the Garos, and the Jaintias, who took
their names from (or gave their names to) the mountain ranges where
they lived. Also in the region were two princely states—Tripura and
Manipur—whose populations were likewise mixed, part Hindu and
part tribal.

Among the tribes of north-east India the Nagas were perhaps the most autonomous. Their territory was on the Indo-Burmese border—indeed, there were almost as many Nagas in Burma as in India. Some Nagas had contact with Hindu villages in Assam, to whom they sold rice in exchange for salt. Yet the Nagas had been totally outside the fold of the Congress-led national movement. There had been no satyagraha here, no civil disobedience—in fact, not one Gandhian leader in a white cap had ever visited these hills. Some tribes had fiercely fought the British, but over time they and the Raj had achieved mutual respect. For their part, the British affected a certain paternalism, wishing to "protect" their wards from the corrosive corruptions of the modern world.

The Naga question really dates to 1946, the year the fate of British India was being decided in two centres of imperial power: New Delhi and Simla. As elections were held across India, as the cabinet mission came and went, as the viceroy went into conclave with leaders of the Congress and the Muslim League, in their own obscure corner of the subcontinent some Nagas began to worry about their future. In January 1946, a group who were "educated Christians and spoke expressive English" formed the Naga National Council (NNC). This had the classic trappings of a nationalist movement, in embryo: led by middle-class intellectuals, their ideas promoted in a journal of their own, *The Naga Nation*, 250 copies of which were mimeographed and distributed through the Naga country.[1]

The NNC stood for the unity of all Nagas, and for their "self-determination," a term which, here as elsewhere, was amenable to multiple and sometimes mutually contradictory meanings. The Angami Nagas, with their honourable martial tradition and record of fighting all outsiders (the British included), thought it should mean a fully independent state: "a government of the Nagas, for the Nagas, by the Nagas." On the other hand, the Aos, who were more moderate, thought they could live with dignity as part of India, so long as their land and customs were protected, and they had the autonomy to frame and enforce their own laws.

The early meetings of the NNC witnessed a vigorous debate between these two factions, which spilled over into the pages of *Naga Nation*. A young Angami wrote that "the Nagas are a nation because we feel ourselves to be a nation. But, if we are a Nation, why do we not elect our own sovereignty? We want to be free. We want to live our own lives. . . . We do not want other people to live with us." An Ao doctor answered that the Nagas lacked the finances, the personnel, and the infrastructure to become a nation. "At present," he wrote, "it seems to me, the idea of independence is too far off for us Nagas. How can we run an independent Government now?"

Meanwhile, the moderate wing had begun negotiations with the Congress leadership. In July 1946, the NNC's general secretary, T. Sakhrie, wrote to Jawaharlal Nehru, and in reply got an assurance that the Nagas would have full autonomy, but within the Indian Union. They could have their own judicial system, said Nehru, to save them from being "swamped by people from other parts of the country who might go there to exploit them to their own advantage." Sakhrie now declared that the Nagas would continue their connection with India, "but as a distinctive community. . . . We must also develop according to our own genius and taste. We shall enjoy home rule in our country but on broader issues be connected with India."[2]

The radicals, however, still held out for complete independence. In this they were helped by some British officials, who were loath to have these tribes come under Hindu influence. One officer recommended that the tribal areas of the north-east be constituted as a Crown Colony, ruled directly from London, and not linked in any way to what would soon be the independent nation of India.[3] Other officials advised their wards to strike out for independence, as the state of India would soon break up anyway. The superindent of the Lushai Hills (later the Mizo Hills) wrote in March 1947:

> My advice to the Lushais, since the very beginning of Lushai politics
> at the end of the War, has been until very recently not to trouble them-
> selves yet about the problem of their future relationship to the rest of
> India: nobody can possibly foretell what India will be like even two
> years from now, or even whether there will be an India in the unitary
> political sense. I would not encourage my small daughter to commit
> herself to vows of lifelong spinsterhood; but I would regard it as an
> even worse crime to betroth her in infancy to a boy who was himself
> still undeveloped.[4]

In June 1947, a delegation of the NNC met the governor of Assam, Sir Akbar Hydari, to discuss the terms by which the Nagas could join India. The two sides agreed that tribal land would not be transferred to outsiders, that Naga religious practices would not be touched, and that the NNC would have a say in staffing government offices. Next, a delegation went to Delhi, where they met Nehru, who once more told them that they could have autonomy but not independence. They also called on Mahatma Gandhi, in a meeting of which many versions have circulated down the years. In one version, Gandhi told the Nagas that they could declare their independence if they wished; that no one could compel them to join India; and that if New Delhi sent in the army, Gandhi himself would come to the Naga Hills to resist it. He apparently said, "I will ask them to shoot me first before one Naga is shot."[5] The version printed in *The Collected Works of Mahatma Gandhi* is less dramatic; here, Gandhi is reported as saying, "Personally, I believe you all belong to me, to India. But if you say you don't, no one can force you." The Mahatma also advised his visitors that a better proof of independence was economic self-reliance; they should grow their own food and spin their own cloth. "Learn all the handicrafts," said the Mahatma. "That's the way to peaceful independence. If you use rifles and guns and tanks, it is a foolish thing."[6]

The most vocal spokesmen for independence were the Angamis from the village of Khonoma, which had fought the British army to a standstill in 1879–1880 and whose residents were "known and feared" across the Naga Hills.[7] A faction calling itself the People's Independence League was putting up posters calling for complete independence, in terms borrowed (with acknowledgement) from American freedom fighters: "It is my living sentiment, and by the blessing of God it shall be my dying sentiment—Independence now and Independence forever" (John Adams). "This nation, under God, shall have a new birth of freedom" (Abraham Lincoln). "Give me liberty, or give me death!" (Patrick Henry).[8]

Meanwhile, the British Raj departed from New Delhi, and the new Indian state began to consolidate itself. The secretary to the governor of Assam told the Nagas that they were too few to successfully rebel against a nation of 300 million. Writing in *Naga Nation*, he related the story of the dog with a bone in his mouth who looked into the water to see a dog with a bigger bone staring back at him; he chased after the mirage, dropping and losing what he had. Concluded the official: "Why lose the bone of 'autonomy' to try to get the bone of 'independence' which it is not possible to get?"

The parable did not go down well with the educated Nagas. "Bones, bones," remarked one angry member of the NNC. "Does he think that we are dogs?" However, the same warning was issued in more palatable form by Charles Pawsey, the departing deputy commissioner—an official whom the Nagas loved and admired. Also writing in *Naga*

Nation, Pawsey emphasized that autonomy within the Indian Union was the more prudent course to follow. "Independence will mean: tribal warfare, no hospitals, no schools, no salt, no trade with the plains and general unhappiness."[9]

II

As the Naga intelligentsia was struggling to define its "independence," the Constituent Assembly of India was meeting in New Delhi. Among the topics for discussion was the place of tribals in a free and democratic India. On 30 July 1947, Jaipal Singh informed the assembly that "some very unhappy developments" were brewing in the Naga Hills. Jaipal had been receiving "a telegram per day," the "latest telegram becoming more confounded than the previous one. Each one seems to go one step further into the wilderness." As he saw it, the Nagas had been "misguided" into the belief that their status was similar to that of the princes, and that like the princes they could reclaim their sovereignty once the British left. When the Naga delegates had come to Delhi to meet Nehru and Gandhi, they had also met Jaipal, who apprised them of the "blunt fact" that "the Naga Hills have always been part of India. Therefore, there is no question of secession."[10]

Jaipal Singh was of course a tribal himself, one of several million whose homes were in the hilly and forested belt that ran across the heart of peninsular India. Known as Adivasis (original inhabitants), the central Indian tribals were somewhat different from those who lived in the north-east. Like them, they were chiefly subsistence agriculturists, who depended heavily on the forests for sustenance. Like them, they had no caste system organized in clans; like them, they manifest far less gender inequality than in supposedly more "advanced" parts of the country. However, unlike the Nagas and their neighbours, the tribes of central India had long-standing relations with Hindu peasant society. They exchanged goods and services, sometimes worshipped the same Gods, and had historically been part of the same kingdoms.

These relations had not been uncontentious. With British rule, the areas inhabited by tribes had been opened up to commercialization and colonization. The forests they lived in suddenly acquired a market value; so did the rivers that ran through these forests and the minerals that lay underneath. Some parts remained untouched, but elsewhere the tribals were deprived of access to forests, were dispossessed of their lands, and became indebted to moneylenders. The "outsider" was increasingly seen as someone who was seeking to usurp the resources of the Adivasis. In the Chotanagpur plateau, for example, the non-tribal was known as *diku,* a term that evoked fear as well as resentment.[11]

The Constituent Assembly recognized this vulnerability, and spent days debating what to do. Ultimately, it decided to designate some 400 communities as "scheduled tribes." These constituted about 7% of the population, and had seats reserved for them in the legislature as well as in government departments. Schedule V of the Constitution pertained to the tribes that lived in central India: it allowed for the creation of Tribal Advisory Councils and for curbs on moneylending and on the sale of tribal land to outsiders. Schedule VI pertained to the tribes of the northeast: it went farther in the direction of local autonomy, constituting District and Regional Councils; protecting local rights in land, forests, and waterways; and instructing state governments to share mining revenues with the local council, a concession not granted anywhere else in India.

Jaipal Singh thought that these provisions would have real teeth only if the tribals could forge a separate state within the Indian Union. He called this putative state "Jharkhand"; in his vision it would incorporate his own Chotanagpur plateau, then in Bihar, along with contiguous tribal areas located in the provinces of Bengal and Orissa. The proposed state would cover an area of 48,000 square miles and have a population of 12 million.[12] The idea caught the imagination of the youth of Chotanagpur. Thus in May 1947, the Adibasi Sabha of Jamshedpur wrote to Nehru, Gandhi, and the Constituent Assembly urging the creation of a Jharkhand state out of Bihar. "We want Jharkhand Province to preserve and develop Adibasi Culture and Language," said their memorandum, "to make our customary law supreme, to make our lands inalienable, and above all to save ourselves from continuous exploitation."[13]

In February 1948, Jaipal Singh delivered the presidential address to the All India Adivasi Mahasabha, an organization that he had led since its inception a decade previously. He spoke here of how, after independence, "Bihari imperialism" had replaced "British imperialism" as the greatest problem for the Adivasi. He identified land as the most crucial question, and urged the speedy creation of a Jharkhand state. Notably, he simultaneously underlined his commitment to the Indian Union by speaking with feeling about the "tragic assassination of Gandhiji," and by presenting a slogan that combined local pride with a wider Indian patriotism: *Jai Jharkhand! Jai Adibasi! Jai Hind!*[14]

The Adibasi Mahasabha was now renamed the Jharkhand party; and after several years of steady campaigning, it fought under that name in the first general elections of 1952. With its symbol of a fighting cock, the party met with a success beyond its own imaginings, winning three seats in Parliament and thirty-three in the state assembly. These victories all came in the tribal regions of Bihar, where it trounced the ruling Congress party. At the polls at any rate, the case for Jharkhand had been proved.

III

Jaipal Singh and his Jharkhand party offered one prospective path for the tribals; autonomy within the Indian Union, safeguarded by laws protecting their land and customs, and by the creation of a province in regions where the tribals were in a majority. The Naga radicals offered another—an independent, sovereign state carved out of India and distinct from it. Among the Nagas, this view was upheld most insistently by the Angamis, and among them by a resident of Khonoma village, yet another remarkable maker of Indian history who is still to find a biographer.

This was Angami Zapu Phizo, with whose name the Naga cause was to be identified for close to half a century. Phizo was born in 1913. He was fair and slightly built, with his face horribly twisted by a paralytic attack that he suffered when he was young. Educated by the Baptists, and a poet of sorts—among his compositions was a "Naga National Anthem"—he sold insurance for a living before migrating to Burma. He was working on the docks in Rangoon when the Japanese invaded Burma, and he joined them on their march to India, apparently in return for a promise of Naga independence should Japan succeed in winning its war against the British.[15]

After the war, Phizo returned to India. He joined the NNC and quickly made his mark with his impassioned appeals for sovereignty, which were often couched in a Christian idiom. He was part of the NNC delegation that met Mahatma Gandhi in New Delhi in July 1947. Three years later he was elected president of the NNC, and committed the Nagas to "full independence." He quelled the doubters and naysayers, who wanted an accomodation with India. Many young Nagas were willing to go all the way with Phizo. Travelling in the area in December 1950, the Quaker Horace Alexander met two members of NNC whose "minds are obsessed with the word 'independence,' and I do not believe that any amount of argument or appeals to the [Indian] constitution, still less any threat, will shake them out of it."[16]

Phizo was a man of great energy and motivational powers. Through 1951 he and his men toured the Naga Hills, obtaining thumb impressions and signatures to a document affirming support for an independent Naga state. Later, it was claimed that the bundle of impressions weighed eighty pounds, and that this was a comprehensive plebiscite revealing that "99.99% had voted in favour of the Naga independence."[17] These figures call to mind similar exercises in totalitarian states, where, for example, 99.99% of the Russian people are said to have endorsed Stalin as their supreme leader. Still, there is no doubt that Phizo himself wanted independence, and so did many of his followers.

By now India itself had been independent for four years. The British officers had been replaced by Indian ones, but otherwise the new state had not had much impact on the Naga Hills. Busy with healing the wounds of partition, with settling refugees and integrating princely states and drafting a constitution, the political elite in New Delhi had not given these tribes much thought. However, in the last week of 1951 the prime minister was in the Assam town of Tezpur, campaigning for his party in the general election. Phizo came with three compatriots to meet him. When Phizo said that the Nagas wanted independence, Nehru called it an "absurd" demand, which attempted "to reverse the wheels of history." He told them that "the Nagas were as free as any Indian," and under the constitution they had "a very large degree of autonomy in managing their own affairs." He invited Phizo and the others to "submit proposals for the extension of cultural, administrative and financial autonomy in their land." Their suggestions would be considered sympathetically, and if necessary the constitution could also be changed. But independence for the Nagas was out of the question.[18]

The NNC's response was to boycott the general elections. After the elected Congress government was in place, Phizo sought another meeting with the prime minister in New Delhi. In the second week of February 1952, he and two other NNC leaders met there with Nehru. The prime minister once more told them that while independence was not an option, the Nagas could be granted greater autonomy. But Phizo remained adamant. At a press conference, he said, "we will continue our struggle for independence, and one day we shall meet [Nehru] again for a friendly settlement" (as representatives of a separate nation). The free state he had in mind would bring together 200,000 Nagas in India; another 200,000 in what he called "no-man's" land; and 400,000 who were then citizens of Burma.[19]

Afterwards, the Jharkhand leader Jaipal Singh hosted a lunch for Phizo and his group. A journalist who was present described Phizo as a "short, slim man with [a] Mongolian look, with spectacles that hide the fires of dedicated eyes." This journalist also heard Jaipal say that while he sympathized with the Naga cause, he "abhorred any further fragmentation of India in the form of a new Pakistan." Jaipal advised Phizo not to ask for a separate, sovereign state, but to fight for a tribal province in the north-east, a counterpart to the Jharkhand he himself was struggling for. His guest answered that "Nagas are Mongoloid and thus they have no racial affinity with the people of India." Phizo said he hoped to unite the Nagas on this side with the Nagas on the Burmese side to form a country of their own. But, as the journalist observed, "according to the official view in Delhi, such a State cannot be viable, and as those haunting hills form a strategic frontier between nations, it would be dangerous to let the Nagas let loose."[20]

IV

In October 1952, Prime Minister Nehru spent a week touring the North-East Frontier Agency (NEFA). He already had some acquaintance with the tribes of the peninsula, whose artistic traditions and zest for life he greatly admired. That past June, addressing a conference of social workers in New Delhi, Nehru had condemned those who wished to make tribals "second-rate copies of themselves." He thought the civilized world had much to learn from the Adivasis, who were "an extremely disciplined people, often a great deal more democratic than most others in India. Above all they are a people who sing and dance and try to enjoy life, not people who sit in stock exchanges, shout at one another and think themselves civilized."[21]

Nehru's first extended exposure to the north-east renewed this appreciation of the tribals. As he wrote to a friend in government, his visit had been "most exhilarating." He wished these areas "were much better known by our people elsewhere in India. We could profit much by that contact." Nehru found himself "astonished at the artistry of these so-called tribal people," by their "most lovely handloom weaving." However, there was a danger that this industry would come into competition with uglier but cheaper goods made by factories in the plains. Nehru came back with "a most powerful impression that we should do everything to help these tribal folk in this matter."[22]

The prime minister wrote a long report on his trip, which he sent to all chief ministers. There was, he noted, a movement for "merging . . . the tribal people into the Assamese." Nehru thought that the effort rather should be "on retaining their individual culture," on making the tribals feel "that they have perfect freedom to live their own lives and to develop according to their wishes and genius. India to them should signify not only a protecting force but a liberating one."

The territory Nehru had traversed, NEFA, adjoined the Naga district and indeed had many Nagas within it. While dismissing the demand for an independent Naga nation as "rather absurd," Nehru "had the feeling that the situation in the Naga Hills would have been much better if it had been handled a little more competently by the local officers and if some officers who were notoriously unpopular had not been kept there. Also, any attempt to impose new ways and customs on the Nagas merely irritates and creates trouble."[23]

Even as Nehru was urging the officials to behave more sympathetically toward the Nagas, the NNC was issuing him an ultimatum. This was carried in a letter dispatched to New Delhi on 24 October, while the prime minister was still in NEFA. In the letter, Phizo and his men insisted that "there is not a single thing that the Indians and the Nagas share in common. . . . The moment we see Indians, a gloomy feeling of darkness creeps into our mind."[24]

Six months later, Nehru visited the Naga capital, Kohima, in the company of the Burmese prime minister, U Nu. When a Naga delegation wished to meet Nehru to present a memorandum, local officials refused to allow them an audience. Word spread of the rebuff, so that when the prime minister and his Burmese guest turned up to address a public meeting in their honour, they saw their audience walking out as they arrived. In one account the Nagas bared their bottoms as they went. In another, Nehru's daughter, Indira Gandhi, said, into a live microphone, "*Papa, wo jaa rahe hain*" ("Father, these guys are all leaving"); to which he answered, wearily, "*Haan beti, main dekh raha hoon*" ("Yes, child, I can see them go").[25]

This walkout, it was said later, hardened Nehru against the Nagas. In truth, Phizo and the NNC had set their minds on independence anyway. They were already collecting arms and organizing "home guards" in the villages. The state, for its part, was moving platoons of the paramilitary Assam Rifles into the district.

By the summer of 1953 the top NNC leadership had gone underground. Searching for them, the police raided Angami strongholds, further alienating the villagers. Apart from local knowledge and local support, the rebels had one great advantage—the terrain. It was indescribably beautiful: "the scenery was the loveliest I have seen," remarked one British visitor, "range upon range of forested hills which change their grouping continually as we climb and climb. The tops rise out of the mist like islands in a white sea."[26] It was also perfectly suited for guerrilla warfare: as a veteran of the Japanese campaign observed, this was "a country where a platoon well dug in can hold up a division, and a company can hold up an Army Corps."[27]

This was a war conducted completely out of sight of the wider world. No journalists or other outsiders were allowed into the district. Reconstructing its history is a difficult task that necessarily involves relying mostly on narratives gathered later by reporters and scholars. From these it appears that 1954 was when the situation turned decidedly for the worse. In the spring of that year, an army officer riding a motorcycle in Kohima accidentally knocked down a passer-by. A crowd collected in protest, whereupon the police fired in panic, killing a respected judge who was also an NNC member.

This incident created great resentment among the Nagas: it "increased the depth of their hatred of the 'unwanted Indians' and precipitated the revolt." The extremists gained control of the NNC; petitions and demonstrations were abandoned, and preparations were made for an armed uprising. The rebels began transporting weapons to a safe haven in the Tuensang area. In June 1954 the Assam Rifles attacked a village believed to be sympathetic to the guerrillas. In September some rebels declared a "Federal Government of Nagaland."

By now killings and counter-killings were occuring with regularity. There were villages loyal to the government which were targeted by the rebels, and villages sympathetic to the freedom struggle which were attacked by the authorities. A division of the Indian army was called in to quell the revolt, to add to the thirty-five battalions of the Assam Rifles that were already in action. In March 1955 a bitter battle broke out in Tuensang; when the firing ended and the smoke cleared, sixty houses and several granaries were found to have been burned down.[28]

Despite the civil war, some channels of communication were still open. In September 1955, Phizo himself went with two colleagues to meet the Assam chief minister. No details of the meeting are available; after it was over Phizo returned to the jungle. However, one of his key aides, T. Sakhrie, had come around to the view that the Nagas could not ever hope to defeat the Indian army. Having made their point, the NNC should lay down their weapons, and seek an honourable settlement with the government in New Delhi.

Phizo, on the other hand, had pledged himself to a "war that would not admit of truces, retreats or compromises." The suggestion that he negotiate offended him greatly, not least because Sakhrie was, like him, an Angami from Khonoma, indeed from the same *khel* or clan of Merhuma. "Phizo was absolutely furious with Sakhrie's softening posture," which came when many young men were flocking to the rebel cause, with the guerrilla army at an all-time high of 15,000 members. But Sakhrie was convinced that they still stood no chance against the mighty Indian nation. He began touring the villages, preaching against Phizo's extremism, and warning that violence would only beget more violence.[29]

In January 1956 T. Sakhrie was dragged out of bed, taken to the jungle, tortured, and then killed. It was widely believed that Phizo had ordered the murder, although he denied it. Anyhow, the message had gone home—this is how betrayers of the cause would be treated. In March a fresh announcement of a "Federal Government of Nagaland" was made. A national flag was designed, and commanders were appointed for the different regions of the designated homeland. Then, in July, there occurred a killing that hurt India's image as much as Sakhrie's murder had hurt the NNC. A group of soldiers, having just beaten off a rebel ambush, were returning to Kohima. The town was under curfew; no one was supposed to be out on the streets. But a solitary old man was; seeing him, the soldiers ordered him off the road. When the man protested, the jawans beat him with rifle butts and finally pushed him off a cliff.

The man that the soldiers had so callously killed was a doctor named T. Haralu. He was, in fact, the first allopathic practitioner in the Naga Hills and, as such, known and revered in and around Kohima. His killing dissipated any propoganda advantage the Indians might have received from Sakhrie's murder. For if that death had "intensified defections from [the NNC] to New Delhi, exactly the reverse happened by the killing of Dr. Haralu."[30]

Meanwhile, the army's presence had considerably increased. The newly named Naga Hills Force consisted of one regiment of mountain artillery, seventeen battalions of infantry, and fifty platoons of Assam Rifles. The rebels also had their own military structure—headed by a commander-in-chief (a brilliant strategist named Kaito), with four commanders under him, their troops grouped into battalions and companies. The Nagas were equipped with British and Japanese rifles, and with Sten guns and machine guns, all part of the debris left behind after the Second World War. The rebels also used locally made muzzle-loaders and, in hand-to-hand combat, the traditional Naga sword, or *dao*.

To add to the regular Naga forces there were highly effective bands of irregulars, divided into "volunteer parties," "courier parties," and "women's volunteer organizations." The last-named were nurses who could, when called on, fight very well indeed. And there was also the silent support of the ordinary villager. As part of its counter-insurgency operations, the Indian army brought isolated hamlets together in "grouped villages"; the residents had to sleep here at night, going out in the morning to work in the fields. Intended to break the chain of information from peasant to rebel, this strategy merely increased the Army's unpopularity among the Nagas.[31]

By the middle of 1956, a full-scale war was on in the Naga Hills. In a statement to Parliament in the last week of July, the home minister, Govind Ballabh Pant, admitted that the Indian army had lost sixty-eight men, while killing 370 "hostiles." Pant accused Phizo of murdering Sakhrie—whom he called the "leader of the sensible and patriotic group"—and of "leading them [the Nagas] to disaster." The talk of Naga independence he dismissed as "mere moonshine." Pant expressed the hope "that good sense will prevail on the Nagas and they will realize that we all belong to India."[32]

The Indian (and international) press was not covering the conflict, but we can get a sense of its scale from letters written by a Naga doctor to the last British deputy commmmissioner of the Naga Hills, Charles Pawsey. A letter of June 1956 describes a tour in the interior where "every night we looked up and saw villages burning in the hills—set alight by either the rebels or the army, no one knows." As for the rebel leader,

> Phizo is being absolutely horrible to any Naga Government servant he catches, and even more so to any Naga who was on his council and has left him, as many have, because of his extreme methods. . . . Many dobashis [headmen] have vanished and no one knows whether they are in hiding or Phizo's got them. Of course, their position is very difficult, for if they go about Government business Phizo gets them, and if they don't, the Government gets them.

Two months later, the Naga doctor wrote to Pawsey:

> As I see it, 0.5% of the Nagas are with Phizo; 1% are more moderate, and want to break away from Assam and come under Delhi, and

98.5% just want to be left alone. . . . Of course the way the army has
behaved and is behaving means that now voluntary co-operation between the Nagas and any Government is beyond hope.

The methods of the army, he added, were such that they "will affect
Naga/Indian relations for the next 50–100 years."[33]

In August 1956 there was an extended debate in the Lok Sabha on
the situation in the Naga Hills. A Meitei member from Manipur recounted a recent visit to the region, when the convoy of vehicles he was
travelling in was attacked by the rebels. On the basis of his enquiries, it
appeared that "it is very difficult to bring them round to our way of
thinking and ways of life; more especially, Phizo is a hard nut to crack."
The Meitei member agreed that the Nagas could not "have separate independence," yet thought that they should immediately be granted a separate state within the Indian Union.

The next speaker was the socialist Rishang Keishing, who fiercely
attacked the army for burning villages and killing innocent people.
(Keishing was himself a Thangkul Naga from Manipur). "The Army
men have shown an utter disregard for the sentiments of the local Nagas, for, they have tried to terrify them by carrying the naked corpses of
the Nagas killed by them." When Phizo had met Nehru in 1951 and
1952, said Keishing, "the parties did not try to understand each other's
mind and the atmosphere was soon vitiated and tempers lost." He
wished "that the Prime Minister had displayed here the same amount of
patience and psychological insight for which he is famous in the field of
international diplomacy." In the years since, brutal methods had been
used by both sides. "Who can boast of an untarnished record?" asked
Keishing. "Who can dare fling the first stone and assert that they are not
sinners? I ask this of the hostile Nagas as well as of the Government."
He recommended "an immediate declaration of general amnesty," the
sending of an all-party delegation of parliamentarians to the disturbed
region, and a meeting between the government and the NNC. He also
appealed to Phizo's men to agree to a truce, "because the continuation
of hostilities means the ruins of innocent citizens."

The prime minister, in reply, admitted that there had been some
killings—including that of Dr. Haralu, "which has distressed us
exceedingly"—but claimed "that by far the greater part of the burning
is done by the Naga hostiles." He argued that the government was seeking the cooperation of the Nagas and that, as he had several times told
Phizo, New Delhi was always willing to consider suggestions to improve

the working of the Sixth Schedule, which allowed tribal areas great autonomy in the management of their land and resources. He did not, however, think the time ripe for sending a delegation of parliamentarians to the Naga Hills. And he insisted that "it is no good talking to me about independence [for the Nagas]. . . . I consider it fantastic for that little corner between China and Burma and India—a part of it is in Burma—to be called an independent State."[34]

In December 1956, a publication put out by the Indian High Commission in London reported the "success" of army operations in the Naga Hills. It claimed that the military had broken the back of the rebels, and was now "engaged in mopping-up operations." The claim appears to have been swallowed whole, for weeks later the *Manchester Guardian* ran an item with the headline "Naga Rebellion Virtually Over." The Indian government, it said, was taking steps "to arrive at some understanding with the Naga moderates, whose ranks are swelling steadily." There was, however, no evidence of any independent confirmation of this new dawn said to be emerging.[35]

V

Through the 1950s the Jharkhand movement carried on its campaign for a province within India run for and by Adivasis. When the States Reorganization Commission visited the area in January 1955, its members were met everywhere by demonstrators shouting the slogan *Jharkhand alag prant!* ("Jharkhand must be a separate state"). As one participant in the protests recalled, the "Jharkhand demand was writ large on every Adivasi face."[36]

Across the country, in Manipur, a struggle was afoot to have that former chiefdom declared a full-fledged state of the Indian Union. In 1949, a popular movement had forced the maharaja to convene an assembly elected on the basis of universal adult franchise. But the assembly was dissolved when Manipur merged with India. The territory was now designated a "Part C" state; this term meant that it had no popularly elected body and was ruled by a chief commissioner responsible directly to Delhi.

Manipur covered an area of 8,600 square miles. There were only 700 square miles of valley, inhabited by 380,000 Meiteis owing allegiance to the Vaishnava traditions of Hinduism. The larger, hilly section was home to 180,000 Naga and Kuki tribals. It was one such tribal, the aforementioned Rishang Keishing, who in 1954 began a movement for

representative government in Manipur. Keishing and his fellow socialists daily picketed the office of the chief commissioner in Imphal. Thousands of satyagrahis were arrested, many of them women. But the
government would not yield. Speaking in Parliament, the home minister said that the time was not ripe for the creation of legislative assemblies in Part C states such as Manipur and Tripura. "These States," he
said, "are strategically situated on the borders of India. The people are
still comparatively politically backward and the administrative machinery in these States is still weak."[37]

One does not know whether the Naga National Council took cogni-
zance of the struggles for Jharkhand and Manipur, or of New Delhi's reluctance to give in. In any case, Phizo and his men were holding out for
something much more ambitious—not just a province within India, but a
nation outside it. The demand might have been "absurd," yet it inspired
numerous Nagas to abandon their villages and join the guerrillas.

At this time, the mid-1950s, there were roughly 200,000 Nagas in
the district that bore their name. There were a like number in the adjoining districts of NEFA, with another 80,000 in Manipur. Half a million Nagas in all, with perhaps 10,000 of them in the struggle full-time.
However, weakness in numbers was amply compensated for by strength
of will. A small community of rebels had forced the Indian state to send
in large military contingents to suppress it.

Few Indians outside the north-east, and virtually no foreigners,
knew of the Naga conflict at the time. Yet the conflict had serious implications for the unity of the nation, for the survival of its democracy, and
for the legitimacy of its government. Nowhere else in the country, not
even in Kashmir, had the army been sent in to quell a rebellion by people
who were formally citizens of the Indian state.

In its first decade, this state had faced problems aplenty—among
them oppositional movements based on class, religion, language, and
region. These had been handled by reason and dialogue or, very rarely,
by the use of regular police. The conflict in the Naga Hills, on the other
hand, would not admit of such resolution. There was a fundamental in-
commensurability between what the NNC was demanding and what the
government of India was willing to give. This was an argument which, it
seemed, could be ended only by one party's prevailing, militarily, over
the other.

Jawaharlal Nehru keenly understood the uniqueness of the Naga situation. Writing to his cabinet in March 1955, he alerted it to "the rather
difficult problem in our tribal areas of the North East . . . [where] we

have not succeeded in winning the people of these areas. In fact, they have been drifting away. In the Naga Hills district, they have non-cooperated for the last three and a half years and done so with great discipline and success."[38]

A year later, Nehru wrote to the chief minister of Assam that while the army would be deployed so long as the rebels had arms and were willing to use them, "there is something much more to it than merely the military approach." Although "there can be no doubt that an armed revolt has to be met by force," said Nehru, "our whole past and present outlook is based on force by itself being no remedy. We have repeated this in regard to the greater problems of the world. Much more must we remember this when dealing with our own countrymen who have to be won over and not merely suppressed."[39]

Hidden away from the eyes of the world, unknown even to most Indians, the Naga rebellion was withal a serious headache for the government of India. Otherwise, Nehru's regime seemed secure and stable. It had been democratically elected, with a comfortable majority, and its foreign and domestic policies rested on a wide national consensus. Soon, however, other challenges were to arise, not in the periphery but in regions considered to be solidly part of India.

PART III

SHAKING *the* CENTRE

14

THE SOUTHERN CHALLENGE

Jawaharlal derives strength from the people. He likes vast crowds.
Personal popularity leads him to believe that the people are
satisfied with his administration: this conclusion, however, is not
always justified.

The socialist NARENDRA DEVA, writing in 1949

As the years rolled by, the very foundations on which Nehru's
prestige and reputation rested began to weigh him down. At one
time, he had a solution to every difficulty; today, he faces a
difficulty in every solution.

The cartoonist R. K. LAXMAN, writing in 1959

I

THE YEARS 1757 AND 1857 are much memorialized in Indian history. In 1757, the East India Company defeated the ruler of Bengal in the battle of Plassey, gaining the British their first bridgehead on the subcontinent. In 1857, the British faced, and eventually overcame, the massive popular uprising known to some as the Sepoy Mutiny and to others as the First War of Indian Independence.

Like 1757 and 1857, 1957 was also a year of momentous importance in the history of modern India. For it was in 1952 that India held its second general elections. After the Second World War, dozens of African and Asian nations won freedom from their European colonizers. At their inception, or very soon afterwards, most of these new nations became autocracies ruled by communists, the military, or unaffiliated dictators. India was one of the very few exceptions and, because of its size and social complexity, the really remarkable one. Before and after the great gamble of 1952 a series of provincial elections were held, and the verdict of the ballot was honoured. Still, for India to certifiably join the league of democracies there had to be a second general election to follow the first. This was held over a period of three weeks in the spring of 1957.

As it happened, Sukumar Sen still served as chief election commissioner. The continuity was important, so that the man who had designed the systems could test afresh how they worked. The evidence suggests that they worked quite well; thus this general election cost the exchequer 45 million rupees less than the previous one. The prudent Sen had safely stored the 3.5 million ballot boxes used the first time around; now only 500,000 new ones had to be made.

Before the election, the Ministry of Information and Broadcasting distributed a film called *It Is Your Vote*. Dubbed in thirteen languages, the film—which took "scrupulous care . . . to avoid any matter which might be construed as propaganda in favour of any political party"—was shown in 74,000 movie theatres around the country. Among the viewers were many women who, the chief election commissioner noted, "have come to value their franchise greatly." Ninety-four per cent of adult women were now registered as voters.

In all, 193 million Indians were registered to vote, and slightly less than half actually did. The ballots they marked collectively consumed 197 tons of paper. Keeping them in line were 273,762 policemen, aided by 168,281 village chowkidars (watchmen).

The Election Commission had recommended that liquor stands be kept shut on the days of voting, so that "no alcoholic beverages might be available to the rowdy elements in the locality." But there was plenty of colour nonetheless. A candidate in New Delhi insisted on filing his nomination in the name of "Lord Jesus Christ"; a man in Madras refused to vote for anyone other than "Shri Sukumar Sen, Election Commissioner." In Orissa a dwarf, only two and a half feet tall, carried a stool with him to the voting booth. Everywhere, ballot boxes were found to contain much else besides ballot papers; abusive notes addressed to candidates in one place, photographs of film actors in another. Some boxes were even found to have cash and change, which "of course, [was] credited to the Treasury."[1]

II

As in 1952, this general election was in essence a referendum on the prime minister and his party. Nehru was, again, the chief thinker, propagandist, and vote-getter for the Congress. Helping him behind the scenes was his only child, Indira Gandhi. She was estranged from her husband, Feroze; and she and her two sons stayed with her widowed father in his spacious official residence, Teen Murti House.[2] Mrs. Gandhi was often the last person the prime minister saw in the evening and the first he saw in the morning. Serving as his official hostess, she met and mixed with the high of this land and of many others. Her health, previously frail, had noticeably improved. Contemporary photographs show that her once sickly frame had filled out; the improvement was apparent not just in her looks but in her manner as well. One biographer has linked this improvement to new drugs, such as penicillin, which cured the traces of tuberculosis she was thought to suffer from.[3]

What we know of Mrs. Gandhi's medical condition is based on reasonable speculation. However, there is also hard evidence that between the first and second general elections she became more of a person in her own right. In March 1955 she was appointed to the Congress Working Committee to "represent the interests of women." Following this appointment she began touring the country speaking to women about their rights and responsibilities. Her interests were not restricted to her own gender; she presided over meetings held in Bombay to hasten the liberation of Goa from Portuguese rule.

To those who knew her in her pre-political days, Indira Gandhi sometimes affected a disdain for her new role. "*Mera sara samay kumaitiyon thatha dusron kamon mein lag jata hai,*" she complained to a friend: "All my time now goes in committees and suchlike."[4] But other evidence suggests that she rather liked it. The man who knew her best of all wrote about her energetic participation in the election campaign of 1957:

> When voting finished today, large numbers of our Congress workers turned up at Anand Bhawan, including many women. Indu has specially shaken up the women, and even Muslim women came out. Indu has indeed grown and matured very greatly during the last year, and especially during these elections. She worked with effect all over India, but her special field was Allahabad City and District which she organized like a general preparing for battle. She is quite a heroine in Allahabad now and particularly with the women.[5]

III

In 1952, the most powerful ideological challenges to Nehru and his Congress party had come from the Jana Sangh on the right and from the Socialists on the left. Both those parties were now in disarray, caused in part by the departure of their charismatic leaders. S. P. Mookerjee was dead; and Jayaprakash Narayan had abandoned politics for social service. Across northern India the Congress was virtually unchallenged. It won 195 seats in the north (out of 226 it ran for), and this dominance contributed handsomely to its overall tally of 371 seats, which gave it a comfortable majority in Parliament.[6]

Its overall triumph notwithstanding, there were worrying signs for a party that had led the struggle for freedom and had since guided the Indian state. Outside the Indo-Gangetic plain, a variety of challenges were taking shape. In Orissa the Congress was opposed by the Ganatantra Parishad—a group of local landlords—which, with the left parties, reduced it to a tally of seven seats out of twenty. In Bombay province, once the heartland of Indian nationalism, the Congress won thirty-eight seats out of a total of sixty-six. Most of the others went to the Samyukta Maharashtra Samiti or the Mahagujarat Parishad, each of which was fighting for a separate state. (In what was effectively a plebiscite on the creation of a Marathi-speaking state with Bombay as its capital, the Samyukta Maharashtra Samiti garnered 5.5 million votes to the Congress's 5.3 million.) These losses were reproduced in the local elections which followed, with the Samiti capturing the municipalities of the great historic cities of Poona and Bombay.

A regional challenge was also brewing in the south. This took the shape of the Dravida Munnetra Kazhagam (DMK), a party which grew out of the Dravidian movement started by E. V. Ramaswami. Known as Periyar ("great man"), Ramaswami was a fervent opponent of the northern domination of Indian politics, culture, and religion. He wished to create a separate nation in south India, to be called "Dravida Nadu." The DMK was started by a group of his former followers, who sought to use parliamentary politics to articulate their secessionist demands. The elections of 1957 were the first they took part in. Although they won only a few seats—mostly in the assemblies—their gradual successes were worrying, since the party stood not merely for a new province based on ethnicity or language, but for a separate nation state altogether.[7]

It was, however, in the southernmost state that the Congress's claim to represent all of India was most seriously undermined. The state was Kerala, where a resurgent Communist Party of India (CPI) had emerged as a strong popular alternative to the ruling party. In the parliamentary elections the CPI won nine seats out of the eighteen it fought for (the Congress won only six). In the assembly elections, which were held at the same time, the CPI won sixty seats out of 126, the support of five Independents ensuring it a slim majority.

The victory of the CPI in the Kerala assembly elections was a spectacular affirmation of the possibilities of a path once dismissed by Lenin as "parliamentary cretinism." A town in Italy had recently elected a Red mayor, but here was something qualitatively new: a first chance for communists to govern a full-fledged province of a very large country. With the cold war threatening to turn hot, what happened in Kerala was of world-wide interest. But it also posed sharp questions for the future of Indian federalism. There had, in the past, been a few provincial ministries led by opposition parties or Congress dissidents. What New Delhi now faced was a different matter altogether: a state ruled by a party which had been underground till the day before yesterday, which still professed a theoretical allegiance to armed revolution, and whose leaders and members were known to have sometimes taken their orders from Moscow.

IV

Situated on the south-western tip of India, Kerala is a very beautiful state, with a long coastline and high mountains. The monsoon is both early and abundant, and the vegetation is gorgeously diverse; no part of India is greener. And no part is as culturally diverse. Hindus constitute about 60% of the population; Muslims and Christians, the remaining 40%. Crucially, these minority communities have a very long history indeed. The "Syrian" Christians of Kerala claim to have been converted by Saint Thomas in the first century of the Christian era. More recently, Protestant and Catholic missionaries had also enjoyed conspicuous success. The first Muslims were a product of trade with the Arabs, and go back to at least the eighth century after Christ. These are the oldest communities of Christians and Muslims in the subcontinent. Like the Hindus of Kerala they spoke the local tongue, Malayalam. However, their relative abundance in the population lent the state a certain distinctiveness, as Table 5 indicates.

TABLE 5: RELIGIOUS COMPOSITION OF KERALA COMPARED WITH INDIA AS A WHOLE

	PERCENTAGE OF TOTAL POPULATION		
	Hindus	Christians	Muslims
Kerala	60. 83	21. 22	17. 91
India	83. 51	2. 44	10. 69

Source: K. G. Krishna Murthy and G. Lakshmana Rao, *Political Preferences in Kerala* (New Delhi: Radha Krishna, 1968), p. 10.

From the late nineteenth century, Kerala had been in a state of social ferment. These changes were being directed by four kinds of actors. First, there were the missionaries who, because of the Christian influence, found it easier to work here than in other parts of British India. Their churches promoted modern education through a vast, interconnected network of schools and colleges. Second, there were the successive maharajas of Cochin and (especially) Travancore, more progressive than most of their counterparts, and challenged by the missionaries to open decent schools of their own. Third, there were energetic caste associations, such as the Nair Service Society, which represented the dominant landed caste; and the Sree Narayana Dharma Paripalana (SNDP), named for Narayana Guru, the legendary leader of the Ezhavas, a caste of palm alcohol makers, called toddy tappers, ranked low in the traditional hierarchy. These too ran their own educational institutions, as well as societies devoted to welfare and charity. Finally, there were the political parties, which included the Congress, of course, and also the CPI.[8]

The Kerala unit of the CPI was strongly rooted in the local soil. Its most influential leaders had started life in the Congress, then graduated leftwards. They started peasant unions to demand security for tenants, and labour unions to demand better wages and working conditions for the landless. They established "reading rooms" where intellectuals communicated radical ideas to their less privileged audiences. Theatre and dance were also pressed into the service of left-wing propaganda. Through the late 1930s and beyond, the communists made steady gains, their ideas and manifest idealism appealing to a divided society further hit by the Depression and the war.

In a country generally riven by inequality, Kerala still stood out for the oppressiveness of its caste system. Here, the lowest of the low were not merely untouchable but "unseeable." When a Namboodiri Brahman approached, a Paraiya labourer had to cry out in advance, lest the sight of him pollute his superior. Yet the combined efforts of the missionaries, the princes, the caste societies, and the communists had undermined traditional structures of authority. In just half a century, between 1900 and 1950, defiance had replaced deference as the idiom of social exchange in the Kerala countryside.[9]

When, after 1947, universal suffrage came to the state, the communists were in a very good position to exploit it. But instead they went underground, following orders from Moscow. The CPI resurfaced in time for the elections of 1952, and made a decent showing. Through the

1950s it worked steadily at expanding its influence. In February 1956, less than a year before the Indian general election, the Communist party of the Soviet Union had its Twentieth Congress. Here Khrushchev famously denounced Stalin, and in passing also endorsed the possibility of a peaceful transition to socialism. In his words, "The winning of a stable parliamentary majority backed by a mass revolutionary movement of the proletariat and of all the working people could create for the working class of a number of capitalist and former colonial countries the conditions needed to secure fundamental social changes."[10]

There would of course be no elections in the Soviet Union, but Big Brother now did not mind, indeed perhaps approved of, participation in elections by comrades elsewhere. (This shift was caused in part by imperatives of foreign policy—competing with another superpower for allies, the Russians had to cultivate former colonial regimes that were often unsympathetic to revolutionary communism.) The CPI in Kerala could now throw itself more energetically into its campaign. The party manifesto declared that it wished only to make this a "democratic and prosperous state," by starting new industries, increasing food production, raising wages of workers in factories and farms, nationalizing plantations, building houses, and streamlining schools. The party of protest sought to become a party of governance—a transition which, it told the voter, its stewardship of local bodies had prepared it for. As the manifesto declared,

> the people also know that the administration of many municipalities and of the Malabar District Board under the leadership of the Communist Party is better than before, and that both the panchayats [village councils] which won awards from Prime Minister Nehru for good administration are under the leadership of the Communist Party. These experiences have made it clear that the Communist Party is capable not only of uniting the people for conducting agitation, but that it can also take over and run the administration succesfully.[11]

V

The newly elected communist chief minister of Kerala was E. M. S. Namboodiripad, known as EMS to foe and friend alike. He was a small, man barely five feet tall, who had a deep commitment to his creed, allied with a fierce intelligence. He had been born into a Brahman family and had donated his ancestral home to the party. He read widely and wrote prodigiously—among his many works was an authoritative history of Kerala. Like Sheikh Abdullah, Master Tara Singh, and A. Z. Phizo, EMS was, in this huge country, considered merely a "provincial" leader. Yet he remains a figure of considerable historical interest, both because of the size of his province and the distinctiveness of his politics.[12]

Virtually the first act of the new government was to commute the sentences of prisoners on death row. Next, cases against those involved in labour disputes or other such "political struggles" were withdrawn. More substantive measures were to follow, such as the opening of thousands of "fair price" shops, to aid the distribution of food to the needy in a food-deficient state.[13]

The communist ministers made an impression with their efficiency, in stark contrast with the sloth of their Congress counterparts. A liberal monthly praised EMS for his "enviable record of public service," and for choosing as his colleagues "people with the sovereign quality of throwing their minds into joint stock in the hour of deliberation. They will not be simple feeders at the public trough."[14] They weren't; thus an otherwise congenitally anti-communist weekly was deeply impressed when the irrigation minister, V. R. Krishna Iyer, responded immediately to a call from a remote hamlet where a bund had been breached. The minister "at once cut through his tour programme, and personally visited the place. He issued orders on the spot for immediate repairs, and personally supervised the carrying out of the job." Further, he promised an enquiry into the conduct of those officials whose negligence had endangered the paddy crop.[15]

By taking office, the communists had pledged to work within the framework of the Indian constitution; by accepting federal funds, they pledged to abide by the recommendations of the Planning Commmission. But there was plenty they could still do within these constraints. For one, they could reform the archaic, inefficient, and grossly inequitable system of landholding. Here they had the approval not just of the Planning Commission and the constitution, but of successive policy documents of the Congress party itself. These stated a commitment to land reform—a commitment that, as Ronald Herring has noted, "did not become operative under any Congress regime but was closely approximated by the reforms of the Communist Party of India in Kerala."[16]

The aims of the Agrarian Relations Bill introduced by EMS's government were modest: not the socialization or collectivization of land, not even the bestowing of land titles on the landless, but merely the providing of stable tenure to the mass of peasants who cultivated small holdings owned by absentee landlords. The bill sought to curb the wide powers of eviction previously enjoyed by landlords; to reduce rates of rent and waive arrears; and to fix a ceiling on ownership, and redistribute the surplus land thus obtained. These were important measures, helping hundreds of thousands of poor peasants, but still somewhat short of what the communist catechism prescribed. The contradiction was resolved by recourse to the "stages" theory of classical Marxism. It was argued that rural India was still "semi-feudal." All non-feudal classes were to be rallied around the proposed reforms, which, when in place, would unleash agrarian capitalism, the next, necessary stop on the high road to socialism.[17]

The standard history of Kerala communism is subtitled "A Study in Political Adaptation" (that is, to bourgeois democracy). Reformism in agriculture was one manifestation of this; a second, which must surely have confused the cadres more, was the encouragement of private enterprise. The party's manifesto had threatened to nationalize plantations, many of them foreign-owned. After the elections this idea was quietly abandoned. Then, within its first few months in office the Kerala government invited India's largest capitalist house, the Birlas, to set up a rayon factory in Mavoor. The entrepreneurs were assured of subsidized supplies of bamboo—to be handed over to the Birlas at 1 rupee per ton, when the prevailing market price was perhaps 1,000 rupees. This project constituted, on the capitalist's side, a breaking of ranks, for the Indian industrial class detested the communists. Their hope was that the central government would be likewise disturbed by the "red menace," that "Home Minister [Govind Ballabh] Pant and his New Delhi group [of Congressmen] comes down on the Kerala Communists with a heavy hand and knocks them out of office."[18] The pragmatic Birlas, however, were responding to the fact that the CPI controlled trade unions in important industrial centres outside Kerala. To start a plant here was to buy peace here—as well as elsewhere. As one columnist commented, it was hard to believe that the clan's patriarch, Ghanshyamdas Birla, had succumbed to the "superlative charm of Chief Minister Namboodiripad"; it was more likely that he was "getting ready for a Communist triumph in Bengal, where his interests are concentrated."[19]

In office, as in opposition, the communists attracted a wide range of interested comment, ranging from the warmly approbatory to the viciously hostile. There were those who wrote of an emerging new dawn, in terms reminiscent of the opening pages of George Orwell's *Homage to Catalonia*, with its sincere salute to the soul of man under socialism.

On the first anniversary of the assumption of office by EMS's government, a journalist went to a tea shop where

> the central figure was the boy serving tea. Most of the discussions were based on rumours. But the boy was always sure of his facts as retailed by "Janayugam," the Communist daily. It was a delight to watch this lad of sixteen arguing with a school-teacher on the wrong side of forty, a NGO (non-gazetted officer) in his twenties and the others in the presence of his boss, the tea-shop owner, and at the same time performing his own duties uninterrupted by the discussion. This can happen only in Kerala.[20]

On the other side, there was talk of "red terror," and a Kerala newspaper wrote in apocalyptic mode of a class war to the finish, with the state taking the side of the lower orders:

> If there is a conflict arising between labourers and company managements woe betide the company managements, the police will side with the labour.
>
> If a jenmi (landlord) is so ill-advised as to pick a quarrel with his agricultural labourers, woe unto the jenmi. The police will know what to do. . . .
>
> If a howling mass besiege a college or a bishop's palace, it will be termed as a popular, peaceful and constitutional agitation of aggrieved students.[21]

VI

In the winter of 1957–1958, the Hungarian writer George Mikes travelled through India. As a refugee from communism—now settled comfortably in London—he found "the Kerala affair" most intriguing. "What is a democratic Central Government to do with a Communist state?" he asked. "What would the American administration do if California or Wisconsin suddenly—and I admit, somewhat unexpectedly—turned Communist? And again, how is a Communist government itself to behave with democratic overlords sitting on its neck?"[22]

One cannot say how an American president would have behaved in a similar situation—would he have sent in the Marines?—but in India the prime minister of the day was inclined to wait and watch. This was because the land reforms proposed by EMS's government were merely

those promised by Congress governments, and because the personal integrity of the ministers in Kerala was not absent in the best congressmen, such as Jawaharlal Nehru himself.

More controversial by far were the educational initiatives of the Kerala government. In the summer of 1957 it introduced an education bill
aimed at correcting the abuses in privately owned schools and colleges.
These were the norm in Kerala, with schools managed by the church,
the Nair Service Society, and the SNDP. The bill sought to enhance the
status of teachers by checking the powers of management to hire and
fire at will, by setting norms for recruitment, and by prescribing salaries
and humane working conditions. It also gave the state the power to take
over schools that did not abide by the bill's provisions.[23]

The opposition to the bill was led by the church, whose own
powers—moral as well as material—depended crucially on its control of
educational institutions. The clergy were deeply anti-communist, a sentiment they managed to instill in their flock. In the elections of 1957, for
example, the CPI had won only three out of eighteen seats in Kottayam
District, the Syrian Christian heartland.[24]

As it happened, the minister of education, Joseph Mundaserry, had
spent decades teaching in a Catholic college in Trichur. He knew the
corruptions of the system, and his bill was in some respects a brave attempt to correct them. However, his government sought to do more than
modernize the management; it wanted also to introduce changes in the
curriculum. New textbooks were prepared, which sought, not always
subtly, to present history through a communist lens. The lens used by
Christian pedagogues was made in a very different factory. Consider
these alternative versions of the Russian Revolution, in circulation in the
schools of Kerala in these years:

(New version): A republican Government was established under
George Lavoff, a member of the Royal Family. It failed to secure popular support and proved incapable of ending the war or of effecting
social and economic reforms. At this time, Lenin arrived in Russia
and this gave impetus to the Russian people. A new Government
with Lenin as President was evolved. First, Lenin made the Treaty of
Brest-Litovsk with Germany. Then land and other capital goods
were nationalised. All agricultural land was taken away from the
landlords and divided among the peasants. All factories became the
property of the State. The privileges of the clergy and the nobility
were abolished. Mines, railways and banks were taken over by the

Government. And thus to the astonishment of all, a new world, based upon Socialism, took shape in Russia and the dreams of Karl Marx were realized in this way.

(Old version): Lenin established a Workers' Government. But the first election showed that the Bolsheviks had no majority. However, to maintain themselves in power, they dissolved the Duma on the ground that it was reactionary. Local Soviets who did not support the Bolsheviks were also disbanded. Private schools were forbidden and education was taken over by the State. Voting right was denied to the nobility and the clergy. Communism encourages violence, and does not believe in an omnipotent God. The Communists forget that man has a soul. It is a one-party Government that prevails in Communist Russia. There is neither freedom of opinion nor of religion. Many other defects in the System may also strike the eye of an observant critic.[25]

Here were two alternative visions of the kind of society Kerala should become, masquerading as two alternative readings of the Russian Revolution. One can see how the Christian version would enrage the communists, and vice versa. Anyhow, the dispute over the textbooks added fuel to the fire. By this time, the Christians opposing the bill had been joined by the Nairs, the other community that loomed large in the economic life of Kerala. Whereas the Christians had always supported the Congress, the Nairs were split down the middle; about half of them had voted for the CPI, the other half against it. However, since the Nair Service Society also ran schools and colleges, the new bill helped tilt it against the communists, and into a somewhat opportunistic alliance with the Christians.[26]

More opportunistic still was the local Congress party. Defeated in the elections, its leaders saw in the resentment against the education bill a chance to regain power. They proposed an anti-communist "Popular Front," an idea attractive to "the reactionary Catholic Church, landlords, planters and the other disgruntled elements," but a seeming betrayal of the socialistic philosophy of its leaders at the Centre.[27] Through the latter part of 1958 there were a series of strikes and protest marches in Kerala. In one incident in Trichur the police fired on a crowd of congressmen, killing six.[28]

Feeling besieged, E. M. S. Namboodiripad was compelled to state his case in the pages of the country's most popular English-language weekly. His "opponents were scandalised," he said, because his government sought sometimes to act against the landlords, even if it did so strictly within the framework of the constitution. A Congress leader answered back, writing in the same columns about the growing "lawlessness and insecurity in Kerala," caused by the tendency of communists to raise themselves above the law while acting vindictively against those who did not agree with them.[29]

After the Supreme Court rejected an appeal in February 1959, the Kerala Education Bill received the assent of the president of India. In the same month Mrs. Indira Gandhi was elected the president of the Indian National Congress. She was the first woman to hold the post in twenty-six years. Asked whether her domestic duties would suffer, Mrs. Gandhi answered with asperity: "My household work takes ten minutes only."[30]

At this time, the Congress was "speaking with three voices: the members in Kerala active in violent agitation, the central leadership permitting such activity without approving of it, and Nehru disapproving of it but taking no action to curb it."[31] Meanwhile, the agitation intensified with the entry of the Nair doyen, Mannath Padmanabhan, a founder of the Nair Service Society, long active in its schools and colleges. Mannath was an austere man who wore a dhoti and spoke only Malayalam. It was said that he had turned against the communists when they refused permission for him to start an engineering college in Palghat. Now he intended to dispatch "these Communists, bag and baggage, not merely from Kerala, but from India and driv[e] them to their fatherland—Russia." When an interviewer asked whether his age was not against him (he was eighty), Mannath reminded him of Bhishma Pitamah, the octogenarian warrior who had led the Pandavas into their own *dharma yuddh,* or holy war.[32]

The clash in Kerala is perhaps best understood in terms of W. H. Morris-Jones's characterization of the three "idioms" of Indian politics. The first idiom was the "modern," based on universal ideas of freedom and justice, and expressed in Parliament, the law courts, and the English-language press. The second was the "traditional," which emphasized primordial loyalties, the interests of one's caste or religion. The third was the "saintly," which Morris-Jones saw as operating "at the margin" of Indian politics—as in the social work of Vinoba Bhave.

In its first phase, the education bill, like so much else in modern India, involved simply a clash between the modern and traditional idioms. Mannath, however, brought the third idiom into direct engagement with the other two—just as, long before, and to even more spectacular effect, Mahatma Gandhi had done. The people of Kerala followed Mannath in part for the same reasons that the people of India had followed

Gandhi: his personal integrity was unimpeachable, and he had never sought or held political office.[33]

Mannath's arrival gave a huge boost to the movement, which soon included, in the patriarch's words, "everyone in Kerala who is not a Communist." On 1 May 1959, a conference of community organizations met at Changanacheri to form a Vimochana Samara Samithi, or Liberation Committee, under Mannath's leadership. Over the next month, its members carried their message into schools and colleges; into churches and temples; into the homes of fisherfolk, peasants, merchants, and workers.

By early June, thousands of volunteers were ready to face arrest. Now commenced a series of hartals, or shutdown strikes, leading to the closure of schools, hospitals, public offices, and factories. Large processions were taken out, often headed by Mannath, who—belying his saintly pretensions—allowed himself to be carried on a white horse with a silk umbrella held over him. Nair youths with swords walked menacingly in front of him.

The communists "replied with organized brutality." By one estimate there were 248 lathi charges by the police; also, many bullets were fired, leaving at least twenty people dead and many more wounded, children and women among them. Each lathi charge served to further swell the ranks of the protesters. Some 150,000 protesters were jailed; one-fourth of these were women.[34]

VII

It is hard to say who found the situation more distasteful—E. M. S. Namboodiripad, as the head of a "people's government" that was now ordering daily lathi charges and incarcerating thousands of ordinary folk; or Jawaharlal Nehru, the constitutional democrat who watched as his party took to the streets to dislodge a lawfully elected government. In Nehru's case the agony was compounded by the fact that he largely approved of the agrarian and educational policies of the Kerala government.[35]

Buoyed by the success of the agitation, congressmen in Kerala were pressing for the Centre to invoke Article 356 of the constitution, whereby the president could dismiss a state government on account of a breakdown in law and order. The article had been used four times in the past, usually to call midterm elections when a ruling party had lost its majority as a result of a split or defections.

To see the situation for himself, Nehru visited Kerala in the last week of June 1959. He was alarmed at the "thick walls of group hatred"; the two sides, he thought, were almost like two hostile countries at war.[36] But he remained reluctant to ask the president to dismiss EMS's government. His hesitancy was not shared by his daughter Indira Gandhi, who thought the action was long overdue. "When Kerala is virtually on fire," said Mrs. Gandhi in a speech in Delhi, "it becomes the Centre's duty to go to the aid of the people; the misrule of the Communist rulers of the State has created a situation which is unparalleled in the history of our country. *Such a situation does not brook legal quibbling.*"[37]

Mannath and his warriors were now preparing for a final showdown. The Muslim League had joined the struggle, lending it more legitimacy still. Through the month of July there were daily marches, with the protesters provoking the police into violence. In one gruesome incident, the police entered a fishing hamlet and fired on bystanders, killing a pregnant woman and two others near her.[38]

The Vimochana Samara Sathi had declared 9 August "Zero Day," when 50,000 volunteers, representing all classes and communities, would descend on Trivandrum to paralyse the administration. On 26 July, groups started marching on the capital from all parts of the state, gathering momentum and men along the way. "The hour was approaching when the Communists must choose between massacre and defeat."[39] A letter from the state governor, pleading with the Centre to intervene, strengthened the hands of the Congress president, Indira Gandhi. The prime minister, her father, finally succumbed, writing to Namboodiripad on 30 July that an order of dismissal was on the way, since "it is no longer possible to allow matters to deteriorate, leading to continuing conflicts and human suffering. We have felt that, even from the point of view of your government, it is better for Central intervention to take place now."[40]

Six months later Kerala went to the polls again. The Congress, allied with the Socialists and the Muslim League, asked the voters to choose between "Democracy and Communism." Nehru led a band of stalwarts in a campaign that featured posters of "Flory Mata," the pregnant fisherwoman shot by the police during the "liberation struggle." A record 84% of the electorate turned out to vote. In a House of 127 the communists won only twenty-six seats. The Congress won sixty, and its allies won thirty-one.[41] The results appeared to vindicate the dismissal of Namboodiripad's government. But, as Sarvepalli Gopal points out, that decision had "tarnished Nehru's reputation for ethical behaviour in politics and, from a long-term view, weakened his position."[42]

VIII

In the early years of independence, the Congress had faced challenges from two kinds of extremism. The communists, claiming that this was a false freedom, had launched a bloody revolution against the nascent Indian state. On the other side, the RSS was mobilizing the forces of reaction in an attempt to create a Hindu Pakistan. The Centre had held, and the Congress had successfully tamed these threats, by drafting a democratic constitution, winning a democratic election, and putting in place the rudiments of a modern pluralist state.

Now, a decade later, the Congress was once more under attack from the edges of the political spectrum. The left's challenge this time was democratic, and hence potentially more dangerous. For if EMS's government was to successfully bring about social reform, by redistributing land to the poor and creating schools for all, it might create a domino effect: that is, the victory of non-Congress parties in other states of the Indian Union.

As it happened, there was also a new challenge from the right. This came from C. Rajagopalachari, "Rajaji," the veteran Congressman who had previously served as governor of Bengal, governor general of India, and home minister of the Indian Union. In 1952 the Congress asked Rajaji to take over as chief minister of Madras province. He stayed in that post until April 1954, when his party indicated that it wanted the powerful backward-caste leader K. Kamaraj to replace him. Now Rajaji settled down in a small house to spend his days, he said, reading and writing. (He was an accomplished short-story writer in his native Tamil, and had also written masterful versions of the *Ramayana* and the *Mahabharata*.)

However, philosophy and literature proved an inadequate substitute for public affairs. Thus Rajaji was moved to comment from time to time on the nuclear arms race between the Soviet Union and the United States, regarding which he took a line not dissimilar to Nehru's. Then, when the second five-year plan committed the government of India to a socialist model of economics, he began commenting on domestic affairs too. Here, however, he came to be increasingly at odds with the prime minister.

The differences were in part political. Rajaji felt that the Congress had become complacent in the absence of a strong opposition. In October 1956 he made public his belief that there should be an opposition group *within* the Congress. Without such a group, he feared, the party

"would simply degenerate into a hunting ground for every kind of ambition and self-seeking."[43] The proposal was rejected, so Rajaji turned to
promoting an opposition outside the Congress instead. In May 1958, he
published an article with the suggestive title "Wanted: Independent
Thinking." This argued that "probably the main cause for the collapse
of independent thinking" in India was "the long reign of popular favourites without any significant opposition." However, a healthy democracy
required "an Opposition that thinks differently and does not just want
more of the same, a group of vigorously thinking citizens which aims at
the general welfare, and not one that in order to get more votes from the
so-called have-nots, offers more to them than the party in power has
given, an Opposition that appeals to reason."[44]

The differences between Nehru and Rajaji were also economic. Rajaji worried that the second five-year plan would lead to an excessive centralization of state power. He was disturbed by the large increases in
taxation, which were conceived in the interests of the public sector but
which might serve only to "discourage and deject citizens and wither the
private sector." In his view, the plan must "be conceived as a supplement
to rather than a substitute for the market economy."[45]

In May 1959, and touching eighty, Rajaji launched a new political
party, the Swatantra party. It focused its criticism on the "personality
cult" around the prime minister, and on the economic policies of the
ruling Congress. Its founding statement asked for a "proper decentralized distribution of industry" through the nurturing of "competitive enterprise"; and, in agriculture, for the encouragement of the "self-employed
peasant proprietor who stands for initiative and freedom." It rejected
the "techniques of so-called socialism" and the "bringing into being of
'Statism.' "[46]

A democracy run by a single party automatically becomes a tyranny; such was Rajaji's rationale for starting Swatantra. For "the Congress Party has so far run without a true Opposition. It has run with
accelerators and no brakes."[47] This party started by an octogenarian
quickly gathered momentum. Those who joined included captains of
industry, naturally, but also peasant leaders worried by Congress's
threat to promote "co-operative farming." Although conventionally described as "Conservative," the party was in fact a curious amalgam of
free-market liberals and agrarian leaders seeking an alternative to the
Congress.[48]

Congress cheerleaders dismissed Swatantra as a party of "right reaction." The prime minister himself affected an airy disdain. When asked

at a press conference about Rajaji's new party, he merely joked: "He likes the Old Testament. I like the New Testament."[49]

IX

The challenges posed by the CPI on the left and the Swatantra Party on the right were compounded by serious accusations of financial malfeasance against the government in New Delhi. In September 1957, questions were raised in Parliament about the propriety of large investments made by the state-owned Life Insurance Corporation of India (LIC) in a private firm in Kanpur owned by an industrialist, Haridas Mundhra. When the finance minister, T. T. Krishnamachari, gave an equivocal reply, dissident congressmen in Parliament began to ask sharper questions. Prominent in the debate was the prime minister's estranged son-in-law, Feroze Gandhi. He claimed that the shares in Mundhra's firm had been bought to boost their price well above their true market value. He wondered how "the Life Insurance Corporation became a willing party to this questionable transaction with the mystery man of India's business underworld." There was, Feroze Gandhi concluded, "a conspiracy to beguile the [state-owned] Corporation of its funds."[50]

Bowing to the criticism, the government announced a commission of inquiry into the affair. As it turned out, there were two separate, successive enquiries, each headed by an eminent judge. Their findings were not complimentary to the Congress government. The LIC had a publicly stated "blue chips" policy, which committed it to investing money only in firms of high reputation and sound management. Mundhra's companies were neither; yet, the LIC had seen fit to make its largest investment in their stock. The officials quizzed by the judges could not satisfactorily explain their decision; nor could their minister.

The proceedings of these commissions were held in Delhi and Bombay, and kept open to the public. They attracted great attention, most of it critical. People flocked to the hearings, to see the minister and his officials fumble under questioning, or contradict one another. The final reports of the judges were damning, and exacted a price: both the minister and his secretary were forced to resign.[51]

The judicial probe into the LIC's investment, wrote the *Hindustan Times*, "had the effect of an overall political shake-up, the like of which has not been experienced since Independence." What "looked like a molehill when the issue was first ventilated in Parliament" had "assumed the proportion of a mountain."[52] Known to begin with as the "Mundra affair," it was soon renamed the "Mundhra scandal." Until it erupted, the ministers of Nehru's government were widely held to be fond of power, yet above financial impropriety. A halo of Gandhian austerity still hung around them. The Mundhra affair made the first serious dent in this image. It was a dent as deep, and as damaging, as those made by political parties on the left or right.

15

THE EXPERIENCE *of* DEFEAT

A divided India augurs ill not only for the Indian people but also
for all Asia and world peace.

AUNG SAN OF BURMA, speaking in June 1947

I

ON THE LAST DAY of March 1959, the Dalai Lama crossed
the McMahon Line into the territory of the Republic of India.
For years the Tibetan god-king had sat uncomfortably on his
throne in the Potala Palace in Lhasa, while the Chinese tightened their
hold on his country. One contemporary source claimed that there were
500,000 Chinese troops in Tibet. In their wake had come perhaps ten
times as many Han settlers.[1]

This figure was certainly an overestimate. Even so, there were far
too many Chinese for the Tibetans' liking. In 1958, the Khampas of
eastern Tibet began an armed uprising against the occupiers. After
some initial successes, the revolt was put down by the Chinese. The reprisals that followed threatened to touch the Dalai Lama himself.
When New Delhi agreed to grant him political asylum, he fled Lhasa under cover of darkness, with a small group of carefully chosen
escorts.

The Dalai Lama spent his first night on Indian soil at the Buddhist
monastery at Tawang. Then he made his way down to the plains, to the
Assam town of Tezpur, where Indian officials "debriefed" him. Three
weeks later he was taken to New Delhi to meet the prime minister.

The conversation began with the Dalai Lama telling Nehru about
the Khampa rebellion. The fighting was bitter, and there were heavy
losses on both sides. Across Tibet, there was deep resentment against
the anti-religious propaganda of the communists. When the Chinese
invited the Dalai Lama to Peking to attend a "cultural function," his
advisers warned him that this was a plot to capture and confine him.

When he refused to come, the Chinese used threats. So he decided to leave for India.

The Dalai Lama told Nehru that any reforms in Tibet should be undertaken by the Tibetans in keeping with their religion and traditions. The Chinese way would leave them "a people without their souls." His own hope now was to bring about Tibet's independence, with India's help. His old tutor Heinrich Harrer (author of the classic *Seven Years in Tibet*) was also encouraging him to canvass support in the West.

In reply, Nehru told his visitor that India could not start a war with China for Tibet's freedom. Indeed, "the whole world cannot bring freedom to Tibet unless the whole fabric of the Chinese state is destroyed." Were he to go to the West, Nehru told the Dalai Lama, he would "look like a piece of merchandise." The Americans or Europeans had no real sympathy with his people or his cause: "all they want is to exploit Tibet in their cold war with the Soviet Union."

An "independence or nothing" attitude, Nehru felt, would get the Tibetans nowhere. They must keep the door open for a negotiated settlement with the Chinese. India could help, but only after it had mended its own broken fences with Peking. As Nehru put it, "at the moment our relations with China are bad. We have to recover the lost ground. By threats to China or condemnation of China we do not recover such ground."[2]

II

By the time of the Dalai Lama's flight, India's relations with China were very bad indeed. In the summer of 1957, the Ladakhi lama and parliamentarian Kushak Bakula visited Tibet and noticed much evidence of road building toward Sinkiang. Then, in July 1958, an official magazine, *China Pictorial,* published in Peking, printed a map that showed large parts of the North-East Frontier Agency (NEFA) and Ladakh as Chinese territory. On 21 August, a counsellor in the Chinese embassy was called in to the Foreign Office, where a deputy secretary handed over a note of protest about the map. The correspondence grew more elevated, and the stakes grew higher.[3] On 18 October, the foreign secretary wrote to the Chinese ambassador protesting against the section of the Sinkiang-Tibet highway that passed "across the eastern part of the Ladakh region of the Jammu and Kashmir State, which is part of India."[4] And by the end of 1958, the prime ministers of the two nations—Jawaharlal Nehru

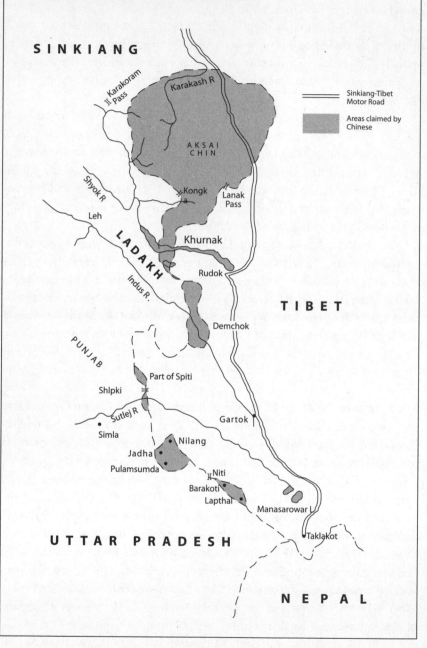

India – China Boundary Dispute: Western and Middle Sectors

SINKIANG

Karakoram Pass

Karakash R

AKSAI CHIN

Shyok R

Kongka

Lanak Pass

Leh

LADAKH

Khurnak

Indus R.

Rudok

TIBET

Demchok

PUNJAB

Part of Spiti

Shlpki

Sutlej R

Gartok

Simla

Nilang

Jadha

Pulamsumda

Niti

Barakoti

Lapthal

Manasarowar L

UTTAR PRADESH

Taklakot

NEPAL

Sinkiang-Tibet Motor Road

Areas claimed by Chinese

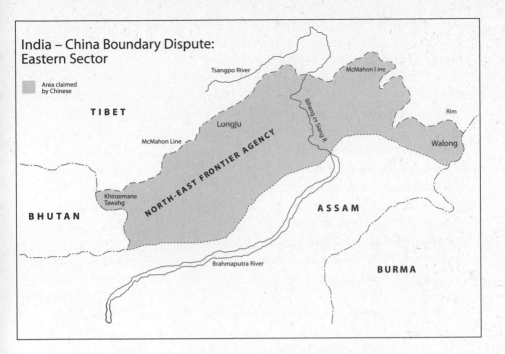

and Chou En-lai—were writing letters to each other, in an exchange that was to carry on for the next few years, marked at first by pain and bewilderment and in the end by anger and resentment.

The letters between Nehru and Chou remain a key to understanding the border dispute. They may have been drafted by officials, but we can be sure that they were carefully checked by their signatories for tone as well as content. These were two politicians deeply interested in history. Each was imbued with—one might say carried by—a sense of mission, by a desire to take his long-subjugated country to the first rank in the modern world.

In the hierarchy of contemporary Chinese nationalism, Chou En-lai occupied second place to Mao. In most matters he, like some eight hundred million others, deferred to the will, not to say whim, of the Great Helmsman. But when it came to foreign policy, Chou was given a free hand. Among the top Chinese leaders, only he had lived and studied in the West. Having come of age, intellectually, in Paris, Chou spoke French fluently, and also some English. He affected a cosmopolitan manner; when asked what had been the impact of the French Revolution, he answered: "It is too early to tell."

As Stuart Schram writes, by the time of the Bandung Conference of 1955, Chou had made his mark as "an urbane and skilful diplomat," who appeared "side by side with Nehru as one of the two principal representatives of the non-European world, divided by ideology, but united by the fact that they were Asian."[5]

In 1955 Chou and Nehru might have been divided only by political ideology. By 1958, they were divided also by national interest. In December 1958, the Indian prime minister wrote the first of a long series of letters to Chou. Nehru began by expressing admiration for China's economic progress before turning, gingerly and gently, to the question of the border. He recalled that when they met in 1956, Chou had thought that the McMahon Line was a legacy of British imperialism but, "because of the friendly relations" between China and India, had indicated that the Chinese government would, after consulting with the local Tibetan authorities, give it recognition. Chou had then confirmed Nehru's impression that "there was no major boundary dispute between China and India." But now came this map in *China Pictorial*, whose border "went right across Indian territory."

A month later Chou replied, stating that "historically no treaty or agreement on the Sino-Indian boundary has ever been concluded." The McMahon Line was "a product of the British policy of aggression against the Tibet Region of China" and "it cannot be considered legal." The Indians had protested about a road in an area which, in Chou's opinion, "has always been under Chinese jurisdiction." "All this shows that [contrary to Nehru's claim] border disputes do exist between China and India." That was the context in which the map in *China Pictorial* should be viewed. Chou suggested that both sides temporarily maintain the status quo, pending a final "friendly settlement" of the border question.

On 22 March 1959 Nehru wrote back. He was "somewhat surprised" to hear that the frontier between India and the "Tibet Region of China" was not accepted by Peking, for it reflected several specific agreements. These included some between Kashmir and Lhasa in 1842 and, in the east, the McMahon Line, agreed on in 1913–1914. Besides, there were clear natural features—watersheds and mountain tops—that defined the borders between the two countries. There might be gaps here and there, but, said Nehru, for "much the larger part of our boundary with China, there is sufficient authority based on geography, tradition as well as treaties for the boundary as shown in our published maps." The letter ended with the hope that "an early understanding in this matter will be reached."

Before Chou, could reply, the Dalai Lama fled to India. This greatly complicated matters, as the Chinese were deeply resentful of the welcome given to him by large sections of the Indian public. For this they blamed New Delhi. Had not the granting of an audience by Nehru himself given an unfortunate legitimacy to the Tibetan leader? Peking's position was that the Tibetan revolt, far from being a popular uprising, was the product of "fugitive upper class reactionaries" aided by the "American imperialists" and the "Chiang Kai-shek clique." Some of the Chinese media went so far as to claim that the Indian town of Kalimpong was the "commanding centre of the revolt," that the government in Delhi was being influenced by "imperialist propaganda and intrigues," and that Sino-Indian friendship was "being destroyed from the Indian side."[6]

There was some propaganda by Tibetan refugees in Kalimpong, but its importance was greatly exaggerated by the Chinese. In fact, much louder protests had emanated from Indian sources, in particular the politician turned social worker Jayaprakash Narayan. "JP" was a fervent advocate of Tibetan independence, a cause also supported by other, less disinterested elements in Indian politics, such as the Jana Sangh, which wanted New Delhi to openly ally with the United States in the cold war and seek its assistance in "liberating" Tibet.[7] But, as the foreign secretary assured the Chinese ambassador a month after the Dalai Lama's flight into exile, "India has had and has no desire to interfere in internal happenings in Tibet." The Dalai Lama "will be accorded respectful treatment in India, but he is not expected to carry out any political activities from this country." This was the government's position, from which some Indians would naturally dissent. For, as the foreign secretary pointed out, "there is by law and Constitution complete freedom of expression of opinion in Parliament and the press and elsewhere in India. Opinions are often expressed in severe criticism of the Government of India's policies."

This was not a nuance Peking could easily understand, because in China, at least in public, there could be no criticism of the government's policies. The difference between these two political systems—call them totalitarianism and democracy—was most strikingly reflected in an exchange about an incident that took place in Bombay on 20 April. According to the Chinese version—communicated to New Delhi by Peking in a letter dated 27 April—a group of protesters displayed slogans and made speeches which branded China's putting down of the rebellion in her own territory, the Tibetan Region, as [an] imperialist action and made all sorts of slanders. What is more serious is that they pasted up a portrait of Mao Tse-Tung, Chairman of the People's Republic of China, on the wall of the Chinese Consulate-General and carried out wanton insult by throwing tomatoes and rotten eggs at it. While these ruffians were insulting the portrait, the Indian policemen stood by without interfering with them, and pulled off the encircling spectators for the correspondents to take photographs.

This incident in Bombay constituted, in Peking's view, "a huge insult to the head of state of the People's Republic of China and the respected and beloved leader of the Chinese people." It was an insult that "the masses of the six hundred and fifty million Chinese people absolutely cannot tolerate." If the matter was "not reasonably settled," said the complaint, if "the reply from the Indian Government is not satisfactory," the "Chinese side will never come to a stop without a satisfactory settlement of the matter, that is to say, never stop even for one hundred years."

In reply, the Indian government "deeply regret[ted] that discourtesy was shown to a picture of Chairman Mao Tse-tung, the respected head of a State with which India has ties of friendship." But India denied that the policemen on duty had in any way aided the protesters; to the contrary, they "stood in front of the picture [of Mao] to save it from further desecration." The behaviour of the protesters was "deplorable," the reply went on, but

the Chinese Government are no doubt aware that under the law in India processions cannot be banned so long as they are peaceful. . . . Not unoften they are held even near the Parliament House and the processionists indulge in all manner of slogans against high personages in India. Incidents have occurred in the past when portraits of Mahatma Gandhi and the Prime Minister were taken out by irresponsible persons and treated in an insulting manner. Under the law and Constitution of India a great deal of latitude is allowed to the people so long as they do not indulge in actual violence.

III

In the first week of September 1959, the government of India released a White Paper containing five years of correspondence with its Chinese counterpart. The exchanges included trifling disputes, occasioned by the straying by armed patrols into territory claimed by the other side; larger questions about the status of the border in the west and the east; and disagreements about the meaning of the rebellion in Tibet.

For some time now the opposition members of Parliament, led by the effervescent young Jana Sangh leader Atal Behari Vajpayee, had been demanding that the government place before Parliament its correspondence with the Chinese. The release of the White Paper was hastened by a series of border incidents in August. Chinese and Indian patrols had clashed at several places in the North-East Frontier Agency (NEFA). One Indian post, at Longju, came under sharp fire from the Chinese and was ultimately overwhelmed.

Unfortunately for the government, the appearance of the White Paper coincided with a bitter dispute beween the defence minister and his chief of army staff. The minister was Nehru's old friend V. K. Krishna Menon, who had been placed in that post in 1957 as a compensation for being drawn away from diplomatic duties. The appointment was at first welcomed within the army. Previous incumbents had been lacklustre; this one was anything but, and was close to the prime minister besides. But just as he seemed well settled in his new job, Menon got into a fight with his chief of staff, General K. S. Thimayya ("Timmy"), a man just as forceful as he was.

The son of a coffee planter in Coorg, Thimayya stood six feet three inches in his socks and had an impressive personality and an even more impressive military record. As a young officer in Allahabad, he met an elderly gentleman in a cinema, who asked him: "How does it feel to be an Indian wearing a British army uniform?" Timmy answered with one word: "Hot." The old man was Motilal Nehru, father of Jawaharlal and himself a celebrated nationalist. Later, when they had become friends, Thimayya asked whether he should resign his commission and join the nationalist movement. Motilal advised him to stay in uniform, saying that after freedom came India would need officers like him.[8]

Thimayya fought with distinction in the Second World War before serving with honour in the first troubled year of Indian freedom. During partition, he oversaw the movement of refugees in the Punjab, and was then sent to Kashmir, where his troops cleared the Valley of the raiders. Later, he headed a United Nations truce team in Korea, where he supervised the disposition of 22,000 communist prisoners of war. His leadership was widely praised on both sides of the ideological divide, by the Chinese as well as the Americans.

Timmy was the closest the pacifist Indians had yet come to having an authentic military hero.[9] However, he did not see eye to eye with his defence minister. Thimayya thought that his troops should be better prepared for a possible engagement with China. But Krishna Menon insisted that the real threat came from Pakistan, and so the bulk of India's troops were deployed along the Pakistani border. Thimayya was also concerned about the age of the arms his troops currently carried. These included the .303 Enfield rifle, which had orginally been used in the First World War. When the general suggested to the minister that India should manufacture the Belgian FN 4 automatic rifle under license, "Krishna Menon said angrily that he was not going to have NATO arms in the country."[10]

In the last week of August 1959 Thimayya and Menon fell out over Menon's decision to appoint to the rank of lieutenant general an officer named B. M. Kaul, passing over twelve officers senior to him. Kaul had a flair for publicity—he liked to act in plays, for example. He had supervised the construction of a new housing colony, which impressed the defence minister as an example of how men in uniform could contribute to the public good. In addition, Kaul was also known to Jawaharlal Nehru, a fact the general liked to advertise.[11]

Kaul was not without virtues. A close colleague described him as "a live-wire—quick-thinking, forceful, and venturesome." However, he "could also be subjective, capricious and emotional."[12] Thimayya was concerned that Kaul had little combat experience, having spent much of his career in the Army Service Corps, a background that did not really qualify him for a key post at army headquarters. Kaul's promotion, when added to the other insults from the minister, provoked General Thimayya into offering his resignation. On 31 August 1959, he wrote to the prime minister to say how "impossible it was for me and the other two Chiefs of Staff to carry out our responsibilities under the present Defence Minister." He said the circumstances did not permit him to continue in his post.[13]

The resignation of the army chief leaked into the public arena. The matter was discussed in Parliament, and in the press as well. Those who were not on Thimayya's side were the communists, such as E. M. S. Namboodiripad, who said that Thimayya should be court-martialled; and the crypto-communists, such as the Bombay weekly *Blitz*, which claimed that Thimayya had unwittingly become a tool of the "American lobby." Those who sided with him against the defence minister included *Blitz*'s great (and undeniably pro-American) rival, the weekly *Current*, as well as large sections of the non-ideological press. The normally pro-government *Hindustan Times* said that "Krishna Menon Must Go" instead of Thimayya. It accused the minister of reducing the armed forces to a "state of near-demoralization" by trying to create, at the highest level, a cell of officers who would be personally loyal to him.[14]

Some people hoped that the outcry over Thimayya's resignation would also force Krishna Menon to hand in his papers. Writing to the general, a leading lawyer called the minister an "evil genius in Indian politics," adding, "If as a result of your action, Menon is compelled to retire, India will heave a sigh of relief, and you will be earning the whole-hearted gratitude of the nation." Then Nehru called Thimayya into his office, and over two long sessions persuaded him to withdraw his resignation. He assured the army chief that he would be consulted in all important decisions regarding promotions. An old colleague of Timmy's, a major general now retired to the hill town of Dehradun, wrote to his friend saying he should have stuck to his guns, for "the solution found is useless as now no one has been sacked or got rid off. The honeymoon cannot last long as you will soon find out."[15]

The release of the White Paper on China, coming at the same time as the drama of the general's resignation, intensified the feelings against the defence minister. Even members of Parliament had not known the extent of China's claim on Indian territory. That Chinese posts had been established and a motor road built through what, at least on maps, was "India," was seen as an unconscionable lapse on the part of those charged with guarding the borders. Opposition politicians, naturally, seized on China's "cartographic war against India." As a socialist member of Parliament put it, New Delhi might still believe in "Hindi-Chini Bhai Bhai," but Peking followed Lenin's dictum that "promises, like piecrusts, are meant to be broken."[16]

Perhaps the prime minister should have been held accountable, but for the moment fingers were pointed at his pet, Krishna Menon. If the country was "woefully unprepared to meet Chinese aggression," said one journal, the fault must lie with the person "at the helm of India's Defence Forces," the defence minister. Even congressmen were now calling for Menon's head. The home minister, Govind Ballabh Pant, a veteran of the struggle for freedom and a long-time comrade of Nehru's, advised the prime minister to change Menon's portfolio—to keep him in the cabinet, but allot him something other than defence.[17] The respected journalist B. Shiva Rao, now a member of Parliament, wrote to Nehru that he was "greatly disturbed by your insistence on keeping Krishna

Menon in the Cabinet. We are facing a grave danger from a Communist Power. As you are aware, there are widespread apprehensions about his having pro-Communist sympathies." It was "not easy for me to write this letter," said Shiva Rao, and "I know it will be a very difficult decision for you to make." However, "this is an emergency whose end no one can predict."[18]

Nehru, however, stuck to his guns—and to Krishna Menon. Meanwhile, the "diplomatic" exchanges with China continued. On 8 September 1959, Chou En-lai finally replied to Nehru's letter of 22 March, which had set out India's position. Chou expressed surprise that India wanted the Chinese to "give formal recognition to the situation created by the application of the British policy of aggression against China's Tibet region." The "Chinese Government absolutely does not recognise the so-called McMahon Line." It insisted that "the entire Sino-Indian boundary has not been delimited," and called for a fresh settlement, "fair and reasonable to both sides." The letter ended with a reference to the increasing tension caused by the rebellion in Tibet, after which Indian troops had started "shielding armed Tibetan bandits" and began "pressing forward steadily across the eastern section of the Sino-Indian boundary."

Nehru replied almost at once, saying that the Indians "deeply resent this allegation" that "the independent Government of India are seeking to reap a benefit" from British imperialism. He pointed out that between 1914 and 1947 no Chinese government had objected to the McMahon Line. He rejected the charge that India was shielding armed Tibetans. And he expressed "great shock" at the tone of Chou's letter, reminding him that India was one of the first countries to recognize the People's Republic and had consistently sought to befriend it.[19]

By this time, the India-China conversation was composed of bullets as well as letters. In late August 1959, there was a clash of arms at Longju, along the McMahon Line in the eastern sector. Then in late October 1959 an Indian patrol in the Kongka Pass area of Ladakh was attacked by a Chinese detachment. Nine Indian soldiers were killed, and as many captured. The Chinese maintained that the Indians had come deliberately into their territory; the Indians answered that they were merely patrolling what was their own side of the border.

These clashes prompted New Delhi to review its frontier policy. Remarkably, till this time responsibility for the border with China had rested not with the army but with the Intelligence Bureau. Such posts as existed were manned by paramilitary detachments: the Assam Rifles in the east and the Central Reserve Police in the west. Regular military forces were massed along the border with Pakistan, which was considered India's main and perhaps sole military threat. But after the incidents at Longju and Kongka Pass, the Fourth Division was pulled out of Punjab and sent to NEFA. This was a considerable change; trained for tank warfare in the plains, the Fourth would now have to operate in a very different terrain.

Through this new "forward policy," the Indian government aimed to inhabit no-man's-land, by situating a series of small posts along or close to the border. The operation was much touted in Delhi, where maps sprang up in Defence Ministry offices with little blue pins marking where these posts had been located. Not to be found on these maps were the simultaneous attempts by the Chinese to fill in the blanks, working from their side of what was now a deeply contested border.[20]

IV

By 1959, at least, it was clear that the Indian and Chinese positions were irreconcilable. The Indians insisted that the border was, for the most part, recognized and ensured by treaty and tradition; the Chinese argued that it had never really been delimited. The claims of both governments rested in part on the legacy of imperialism; British imperialism (for India), and Chinese imperialism (over Tibet) for China. In this sense, both claimed sovereignty over territory acquired by less than legitimate means.

In retrospect, it appears that the Indians underestimated China's resentment of "western imperialism." In the first half of the twentieth century, when China was weak, it had been subjected to all sorts of indignities by the European powers. The McMahon Line was one of them. Now that, under the communists, China was strong, it was determined to undo the injustices of the past. Visiting Peking in November 1959, the Indian lawyer Danial Latifi was told by his Chinese colleagues that "the McMahon Line had no juridical basis." Public opinion in China appeared "to have worked itself up to a considerable pitch" on the border issue. Reporting his conversations to Jawaharlal Nehru, Latifi tellingly observed, "As you know, probably too well, it is difficult *in any country* to make concessions once the public has been told it [the territory under dispute] forms part of the national homeland."[21]

It is also easy in retrospect to see that after the failure of the Tibetan revolt, the government of India should have done either or both of the following things: (1) strengthened its defences along the Chinese border, importing arms from the West if need be; (2) worked seriously for a new settlement of the border with China. But the non-alignment of Nehru precluded the former, and the force of public opinion precluded the latter. In October 1959, the *Times of India* complained that the prime minister had shown "an over-scrupulous regard for Chinese susceptibilities and comparative indifference towards the anger and dismay with which the Indian people have reacted."[22] Another newspaper observed that Nehru was "standing alone against the rising tide of national resentment against China."[23]

As Steven Hoffman has suggested, the policy of releasing White Papers limited Nehru's options. Had the border dispute remained private, the prime minister could have used the quieter back channels of diplomatic compromise. But with the matter out in the open, sparking much angry comment, he could only "adopt those policies that could conceivably meet with approval from an emotionally aroused parliament and press." The White Paper policy precluded the spirit of give and take, and instead fanned patriotic sentiment. The incident at Kongka Pass, in particular, had led to furious calls for revenge from India's political class.[24]

After the border clashes of September and October 1959, Chou Enlai wrote suggesting that both sides withdraw 20 kilometres behind the McMahon Line in the east, and behind the line of actual control in the west. Nehru, in reply, dismissed the suggestion as merely a way of legitimizing Chinese encroachments in the western sector, of keeping "your forcible possession intact." The "cause of the recent troubles," he insisted, "is action taken from your side of the border." Chou now pointed out that despite its belief that the McMahon Line was illegal, China had adhered to a policy of "absolutely not allowing its armed personnel to cross this line [while] waiting for a friendly settlement of the boundary question." Thus

> the Chinese Government has not up to now made any demand in regard to the area south of the so-called McMahon line as a precondition or interim measure, and what I find difficult to understand is why the Indian Government should demand that the Chinese side withdraw one-sidedly from its western frontier area.

This was an intriguing suggestion, which, stripped of its diplomatic code, read: You keep your (possibly fraudulently acquired) territory in the east, while we shall keep our (possibly fraudulently acquired) territory in the west.[25]

Writing in the *Economic Weekly* in January 1960, the sinologist Owen Lattimore acutely summed up the Indian dilemma. Since the boundary with China was evidently a legacy of British imperialism, the "cession of a large part of the disputed territory . . . would not involve Indian national pride had it not been for the way the Chinese have been trying to draw the frontier by force, without negotiation." For "what Mr. Nehru might concede by reasonable negotiations between equals he would never concede by abject surrender."[26]

In the same issue of this journal, a contributor calling himself "Pragmatist" urged a strong programme of defence preparedness. The leadership in Peking, he wrote acidly, "may not think any better of the armed forces of India than Stalin did of those of the Vatican." The Chinese army was five times the strength of its Indian counterpart, and equipped with the latest Soviet arms. Indian strategic thinking, for so long preoccupied with Pakistan, must now seriously consider the Chinese threat, for the friendship between the two countries had "definitely come to an end." Now, the "first priority in our defence planning" must be "keeping Chinese armies on the northern side of the border." India should train mountain warfare units, and equip them with light, mobile equipment. Waiting in support must be a force of helicopters and fighter-bombers. And "the important thing," said "Pragmatist," is to "build up during the next two or four years, a strong enough force which will be able to resist successfully any blitzkrieg across our Himalayan borders."[27]

The political opposition, however, was not willing to wait that long. "The nation's self-interests and honour," thundered the president of the Jana Sangh in the last week of January 1960, "demand early and effective action to free the Indian soil from Chinese aggression." The government in power had "kept the people and Parliament entirely ignorant in respect of the fact of aggression itself"; and now "it continues to look on helplessly even as the enemy goes on progressively consolidating its position in the occupied areas."[28]

Suspicion of the Chinese, however, was by no means restricted to parties on the right. In February 1960, the president, Rajendra Prasad, commented on the "resentment and anger" among students in his native Bihar. These young people, he reported, wanted India to vacate "the Chinese aggression" from "every inch of our territory." They "will not tolerate any wrong or weak step by the government."[29]

With positions hardening, New Delhi invited Chou En-lai for a meeting on the border question. The meeting was scheduled for late April, and in the weeks leading up to it there were many attempts to frustrate it. On 9 March the Dalai Lama appealed to the world "not to forget the fight of Tibet, a small but independent country occupied by force and by a fanatic and expansionist power." Three days later a senior leader of Jana Sangh urged the prime minister to "not compromise the sentiments of hundreds of millions of his countrymen" and "to take all necessary steps against further encroachment by the Chinese." Less expected was a statement of the Himalayan Study Group of the Congress Parliamentary Party, which urged the prime minister to take a "firm stand on the border issue."[30]

In the first week of April, the leaders of the non-communist opposition sent a note to the prime minister reminding him of the "popular feeling" with regard to China. They asked for assurance that in his talks with Chou En-lai "nothing will be done which may be construed as a surrender of any part of Indian territory."[31] Hemmed in on all sides, the prime minister now sought support from the Gandhian sage Vinoba Bhave, who was on a walking tour through the Punjab countryside. Nehru spent an hour closeted with Bhave in his village camp; although neither divulged the contents of their talks, these became fairly clear in later speeches by the sage. On 5 April, Bhave addressed a meeting at Kurukshetra—the site, in mythical times, of a great war between the Pandavas and the Kauravas. On this battlefield he offered a prayer for the success of the talks between Nehru and Chou. "Distrust belonged to the dying political age," said the Gandhian: "the new age was building itself around trust and goodwill." The conversations with the Chinese visitor, Bhave hoped, would be free of anger, bitterness, and suspicion.

It was not a message that went down well or widely. Five days before Chou En-lai was to come, the Jana Sangh held a large demonstration outside the prime minister's residence. Protesters held up posters reminding Nehru not to forget the martyrs of Ladakh and not to surrender Indian territory. The next day, the non-communist opposition held a mammoth public meeting in Delhi, warning the prime minister that if he struck a deal with the Chinese his "only allies would be the Communists and crypto-Communists." In this atmosphere, the respected editor Frank Moraes thought the talks were doomed to failure. The gulf between the two countries was "unbridgeable," he wrote, adding, "If Mr. Chou insists on maintaining all the old postures, all that Mr. Nehru can tell him politely is to go back to Peking and think again."

Nehru, however, insisted that the Chinese Prime Minister "would be accorded a courteous welcome befitting the best traditions of this country." Chou was then on a visit to Burma; an Indian viscount went to pick him up and fly him to Delhi. When he came in 1956, he had been given a stirring public reception; this time—despite Nehru's hopes—he arrived "amidst unprecedented security arrangements," travelling from the airport in a closed car. The Hindu Mahasabha organized a "black flag" demonstration against Chou, and his visit was also opposed by the more mainstream parties. Two jokes doing the rounds expressed the mood in New Delhi. One was that "Hindi-Chini Bhai Bhai" had become "Hindi Chini Bye Bye"; the other asked why Krishna Menon was not in the Indian delegation for the talks, and answered: "Because he is in Mr. Chou En-lai's party."[32]

Chou En-lai spent a week in New Delhi, meeting Nehru every day, with and without aides. A photograph appearing in *Indian Express* after the second day of talks suggested that they were not going well. It showed Chou making a toast to Sino-Indian friendship, by clinking his glass with Indira Gandhi's. Mrs. Gandhi was stylishly dressed, in a sari, but was looking quizzically across at her father. On the other side of the table stood Nehru, capless, drinking deeply and glumly from a wine glass, and avoiding Chou En-lai's gaze. The only Indian showing any interest at all was the vice president, S. Radhakrishnan, seen reaching across to clink his glass with Chou's.

Chou En-lai and Nehru spent nearly twenty hours in conversation. The transcripts of their talks are still officially secret, but copies kept by a vigilant (or rule-breaking) official have been consulted by this writer. These highlight, vividly, the hurt and hostility that pervaded the discussion. Nehru began by recalling all that India had done for China, such as introducing its leaders to the Asia-Africa conference at Bandung, and pressing its case in the United Nations. In light of these good turns, the Chinese "infringement" of India's frontiers "came as a great shock." Chou answered with a complaint of his own: that in view of the friendship, ancient and modern, between India and China, "the activities of Dalai Lama and his followers have far exceeded the limits of political asylum."

For two days Nehru and Chou traded charges and countercharges. If Nehru insisted that the Himalaya had long been considered India's natural as well as its cultural frontier, then Chou dismissed the McMahon Line as a pernicious legacy of imperialism. Both prime ministers showed an excellent grasp of detail, each defending his case with impressive exactitude, each mentioning specific villages, valleys, hilltops, rivers, posts, and treaties to make or advance his country's claims. Finally, Chou suggested that they try to "seek a solution" rather than "repeat arguments." A suitable settlement, in his view, would be that "neither side should put forward claims to an area which is no longer under its administrative control." Some hours later he became more explicit, saying:

> In the eastern sector, we acknowledge that what India considers its border has been reached by India's actual administration. But, similarly, we think that India should accept that China's administrative personnel has reached the line which it considers to be her border in the western sector.

Again, suitably decoded, this meant: Your case is stronger in the west, but our needs are greater there. And while our case is stronger in the east, perhaps more of your interests are at stake there. Please keep Tawang and its environs, Chou was saying, for all we want is Aksai Chin and the road linking Sinkiang to Tibet.

Chou advocated retaining and recognizing the status quo, but as Nehru pointed out in reply, the term "status quo" was itself disputed. "The question is what is status quo?" he asked. For "the status quo of today is different from the status quo of one or two years ago. To maintain today's status quo would be very unfair if it is different from a previous status quo." The solution suggested by Chou would justify gains that, in Nehru's (and India's) view, China had made illegally and by stealth. [33]

Chou En-lai also met the home minister, G. B. Pant; and the vice president, Dr. S. Radhakrishnan—both of whom complained, more in sorrow than in anger, about China's lack of appreciation for all India had done to gain its commmunist government legitimacy in the eyes of the world. Chou was more combatively challenged by the brilliant and opinionated finance minister, Morarji Desai. When the Chinese leader asked how the Indians could have allowed their soil to be used by Tibetan dissidents, Desai answered that "in our country everybody holds conventions; the Algerians do so and so do the Indians sometimes [against their Government]." Then he cleverly (perhaps wickedly) added, "The Chinese Prime Minister is aware that Lenin sought asylum in the U[nited] K[ingdom] but nobody restricted his political activities. We in India do not encourage anyone to conspire against China but we cannot prevent people from expressing their opinions. Freedom of speech is the basis of our democracy."[34]

Reporting to the Indian Parliament on his talks with Chou En-lai, Nehru drily noted that "the significant sentence in the [joint] communique is that in spite of all these efforts no solution was found." An apt epitaph to Chou's visit was also provided by Frank Moraes: "Like Charles II the Sino-Indian talks seem a long time dying." They did indeed. The failed meeting was followed by talks between lesser officials, held in Peking in June–July 1960; in New Delhi in August–October; and finally in the Burmese capital, Rangoon, in November–December. Each side put forward masses of notes, maps, documents, and letters to buttress its arguments. A contemporary commentary on this mountain of evidence remarks that "it is quite evident that as far as consistency is concerned—and the length of time the claims have been advanced—the advantage lies with the Government of India." No official Chinese maps showed Aksai Chin as part of China before the 1920s, and a Sinkiang map of the 1930s showed the Kunlun Shan rather than the Karakoram to have been the customary boundary—as India had claimed all along. At least in the western sector (where the Chinese incursions had taken place) India seemed to have the stronger case. "The Indian Government was both thorough and careful in presenting its case," whereas the Chinese presentation was marked by a "maze of internal inconsistencies, quotations out of context, and even blatant and easily discernible falsehoods."[35]

Even if New Delhi had the better of this argument overall, the Indian and Chinese positions remained incompatible. Any evidence emanating from western sources—even unaffiliated travellers and itinerant Jesuit priests—was dismissed as tainted by "imperialism." The Chinese would, up to a point, present counter-evidence, but in the end they would back off, saying that the border had not been delimited between the two countries as sovereign nations, that India could not claim the (ill-gotten) legacy of British India, and that the People's Republic of China did not stand by any treaties negotiated by anyone presuming to represent Tibet or China before the year of the revolution, 1949.[36]

It is noteworthy that the Chinese wished to maintain their gains in the western sector, where their historical position was weak. In exchange, they were willing to forfeit their much stronger claims in the east. This was clearly because of their need to have speedy access to Tibet. In October 1960, after his own summit with Nehru had failed and the officials' meetings were going nowhere, Chou En-lai vented his frustration in this regard to the American journalist Edgar Snow. Chou claimed that the boundary dispute "came to the fore" only after "the Dalai Lama had run away and democratic reforms were started in Tibet." He accused India of wanting to "turn China's Tibet region into a 'buffer zone.'" "They don't want Tibet to become a Socialist Tibet, as had other places in China," he complained. And then he drew this somewhat far-fetched conclusion: "The Indian side . . . is using the Sino-Indian boundary question as a card against progressive forces at home and as capital for obtaining 'foreign aid.'"[37]

V

The territorial map of India was being challenged from the outside by the Chinese—and also from within, by various linguistic groups that wanted it redrawn, having been left dissatisfied by the recommendations of the States Reorganization Commission of 1956. The Maharashtrians continued to press the Centre to give them the city of Bombay. Their case was artfully presented by the dynamic young chief minister, Y. B. Chavan, who argued that in this way the Congress could make up the losses of the 1957 election, when the Samyukta Maharashtra Samiti had won a number of its seats. Eventually, on 1 May 1960, the states of Gujarat and Maharashtra came into being, with Bombay alloted to the latter.

The creation of Maharashtra quelled resentment in the west of India, while giving a boost to unfulfilled expectations in the north. For the Punjabis were the one major language group that still had no state of its own. Their demand had not been granted, on the grounds that here language was dangerously allied with religion: that what was presented as "Punjabi Suba" was in fact a "Sikh Suba," a pretext for what could even become a separate nation of the Sikhs. But through 1960 and 1961 the indefatigable Master Tara Singh initiated a series of agitations for a Punjabi-speaking state. With him was another Sikh holy man, Sant Fateh Singh ("the Sant"), a deputy who would later become a rival of the master. Led by these two men, the Akali Dal volunteers began to provoke unrest in groups. Meanwhile, Tara Singh and the Sant would go on periodic fasts; each was announced as being "unto death," but each was called off in advance of that supreme sacrifice.[38]

Against the Akalis, Nehru stood firm; the Congress chief minister of Punjab, Pratap Singh Kairon, firmer still. Kairon came down hard on the Akali agitation, putting thousands of protesters in jail. He had been educated in America and was a man of drive and ambition, characteristics somewhat lacking in the other chief ministers of the day. Nehru thought these also translated into popular appeal. As he wrote to a friend, "Sardar Pratap Kairon's strength in the Punjab is that he represents, and is largely trusted by, the rural people. Those who criticize him are usually city people, whether Sikh or Hindu. During the recent fast of Master Tara Singh, it is extraordinary how the rural areas were not affected by it. They were busy with the Panchayat elections and other activities."[39]

Kairon was the uncrowned king of Punjab for the eight years he was in power. He had dash and vision; he started an agricultural university, pioneered the tube well revolution, and persuaded peasants to diversify into such remunerative areas as poultry farming. He drew out the Punjabi women, persuading them to study, work, and even—given their athleticism—participate in competitive sports. He mingled easily with the common folk; anyone could walk into his office at any time. On the other side, his methods of justice were rough and ready. Thus he instructed his police to fine rather than imprison a peasant protester, who didn't mind becoming a martyr in the off season, but "can't bear losing his earnings." But a townsman who broke the law must be jailed, "for he can't stand separation from the sweet lubricants of family."[40]

As it happened, these were lubricants that Kairon could not be easily separated from himself. His two sons ran amok during his chief ministership, building huge business empires with the help of the state machinery, flouting property laws and zoning clauses. The chief minister was accused of "gross abuse of office to promote the business interests of his sons who have minted crores of rupees in the last few years." Civil servants were instructed to turn a blind eye to these transgressions. Sharp questions were asked in Parliament. Several Congress leaders, among them Indira Gandhi, urged the prime minister to replace Kairon. But Nehru stood by his man, expressing admiration for Kairon's drive and his stalwart stand against Punjabi Suba. However, he did agree to establish a commission, headed by a Supreme Court judge, to enquire into the allegations against Kairon.[41]

As A. G. Noorani has written, "in very many ways Sardar Pratap Singh Kairon [of Punjab] and Bakshi Ghulam Mohammed [of Kashmir] were alike." Both men "were blunt in speech, direct in approach, impatient with bureaucratic delays and disdainful of the proprieties of public life. Each did a hatchet man's job." And "both enjoyed the patronage of Prime Minister Nehru."[42]

There was bad publicity for the prime minister in one border state, the Punjab, caused by the Akali agitation and the malfeasance of the state administration. And there was worse publicity in another border area, the Naga Hills, caused by the dramatic appearance in London of the rebel leader A. N. Phizo. Sometime in 1956 Phizo had crossed into Burma and then into East Pakistan, from where he continued to direct the Naga resistance movement. After three years of long-distance generalship, he decided that his cause needed the backing of the western world. Travelling with a forged El Salvadoran passport, he reached Switzerland, where he made contact with Reverend Michael Scott, a radical Anglican priest who had previously worked with the anti-apartheid movement in South Africa. With Scott's help he reached the United Kingdom.[43]

In London, Phizo called a series of press conferences, where, with Michael Scott at his side, he accused the Indian army of committing genocide against the Naga people. Also with Scott's help, he printed a pamphlet in which he spoke of how "our age-old freedom has been and is being systematically destroyed by the Indian Army. . . . They have tried to subjugate our nation and to annihilate it." The army's campaign was described as "a plan of racial extermination in the worst manner of the European fascists." Indian troops, Phizo claimed, were "shooting Christian pastors and church leaders, burning men and women alive, burning churches." His pamphlet called for an end to the "slaughter," and demanded a recognition by the government of India of "the sovereign and independent state of Nagaland." Phizo said that an independent Nagaland would "wish to remain within the fold of the Christian nations, and the Commonwealth. . . . [T]iny Nagaland is happy to be a follower of Jesus Christ, whom we have come to believe in as our Saviour."[44]

Phizo was simultaneously appealing to the British love of the underdog, to memories of the recent war against fascism (with the Nagas placed in the role of the Jews, and the Indian government as the Nazis), and to the Christian sentiments of his audience. The rhetoric was somewhat artless, and yet surprisingly successful. His cause was taken up by David Astor, the liberal owner of the newspaper *The Observer*, who had played a stellar role in the fight against the Nazis. Phizo's charges were given wide play by this newspaper, and by several other periodicals.[45]

Always sensitive to the opinions of the British press, the government of India answered with a propogandist tract of its own. This said that although the prime minister had assured the Nagas of "maximum autonomy," under Phizo's leadership "the Naga movement began to assume a violent character." The violence and the suffering of civilians were not denied, but the blame for these was placed on the insurgents. The government's stand remained that "they are prepared to concede the largest possible autonomy to the Nagas in their internal affairs in addition to all the privileges of Indian citizenship, such as representation in Parliament, but they could not agree to an independent state for them."

This was reasonably put, but the effect was spoilt by an appendix that cast Phizo as a villain motivated merely by frustration and failure. "Phizo's mental attitude," said the government of India, "has been conditioned by a series of frustrations and set backs. He failed in the Matriculation examination. His attempts to establish himself first in motor-parts business and then as an insurance man did not meet with success. He was attacked by paralysis, which disfigured his face and as a result he acquired a strong complex. . . . He has been known to have been suffering from a strong feeling of guilt for having misled his co-tribesmen into a path of hostility and violence, resulting in many deaths and reducing many of them to a state of misery."[46]

As it happened, between the government of India and the leader of the Naga National Council (NNC) stood a number of "moderate" Nagas. These had banded together in a Naga Peoples' Convention, which, from 1957 on, had begun seeking a peaceful settlement to the problem. The Aos were prominent among these peacemakers, but there were also representatives of other tribes. On 30 July 1960, the Naga Peoples' Convention presented a memorandum to the prime minister demanding a separate state of Nagaland within the Indian Union. This would have its own governor, chief minister, council of ministers, and legislative assembly. Moreover, the Parliament of the Indian Union would not have the power to interfere with Naga religion, social practices, or customary law.[47]

The demand for a Naga state within India was resisted by the Assamese elite, loath to let go of any part of their province. But with the Naga question now successfully internationalized, Nehru thought it prudent to make the concession. In the first week of August 1960, he announced in Parliament that a state of Nagaland was to be carved out of Assam. The decision to create this, the smallest state of the Union, gave rise to a series of responses that were interesting, varied, and yet utterly predictable. The right-wing Jana Sangh saw the creation of Nagaland as "an act fraught with explosive possibilities"; it was a concession to terror, "tantamount to putting a premium on violence and rebellion," a wanton encouragement to "regionalism and parochialism" that would endanger "the unity and integrity of the country." Some other tribes in Assam, the Khasis, the Garos, and the Jaintias, resolved to fight for a state of their own, to be called "Eastern Frontier."[48]

Also predictable was the response of Phizo's men. Some Naga intellectuals thought that statehood within India was "not only all they can hope to get but all they need to protect their social and political identity." But how was one to convince the ordinary villager of this? As one newspaper noted, the "armed rebels can emerge from the jungle any night with arguments that the statehood party are Quislings, and with bullet or bayonet correct any who disagree."[49]

VI

After a decade when it had seemed confidently in control, Jawaharlal Nehru's government suddenly looked very shaky indeed. There was dissent in the south, in Kerala and Tamil Nadu; and in the border zone, in Punjab and the Naga Hills. Meanwhile a report by the Ford Foundation warned of the "stark threat" of an "ominous crisis" in the agricultural sector. Unless food production was tripled in the next decade, it claimed, there would be mass starvation and famine in India.[50]

More worrying, at least to Nehru, was the resurgence of communal conflict after a decade of comparative social peace. In June 1960, virulent anti-Bengali riots broke out in Assam. The victims were post-partition refugees from East Bengal, who were accused of taking away jobs from the Assamese and not speaking their language. Thousands of homes were destroyed, and many Bengalis were killed. Others fled across the border into refugee camps in West Bengal. The home minister, Lal Bahadur Shastri, flew to Assam to forge an uneasy peace, which endorsed Assamese as the official state language while permitting the use of Bengali in the district where the migrants were in a majority.[51]

Then, in January 1961, a religious riot broke out in the central Indian city of Jabalpur. A Hindu girl had committed suicide, allegedly because she had been assaulted by two Muslim men. The claim was given lurid publicity by a local Jana Sangh newspaper, whereupon Hindu students went on a rampage through the town, attacking Muslim homes and burning shops. In retaliation a Muslim group torched a Hindu neighbourhood. The rioting continued for days, spreading also to the countryside. It was the most serious such incident since partition, its main sufferers being poor Muslims, mostly weavers and bidi workers.[52]

The troubles on the border with China, and the intensification of social conflict within the country, gave rise to fresh concerns about the future of democratic India. In 1960 an American scholar published an impressively learned book with a simple title—*India*—but a portentous subtitle: *The Most Dangerous Decades*. The chapter and section titles were also revealing—"Will the Union Survive?" was one, and "Totalitarian Equilibrium?" another. The writer was disturbed by the divisions of caste, region, religion, and language, and by the rise of Indian communism. There were, he felt, "seemingly irrestible compulsions of totalitarian experiments of one sort or another in the nature of the Indian Union."[53]

The following year, 1961, the writer Aldous Huxley visited India after an absence of thirty-five years. He was overwhelmed by what he found: "the prospect of overpopulation, underemployment, growing unrest." "India is almost infinitely depressing," he wrote to a friend, "for there seems to be no solution to its problems in any way that any of us [in the West] regard as acceptable." Writing to his brother Julian, Huxley said that "when Nehru goes, the government will become a military dictatorship—as in so many of the newly independent states, for the army seems to be the only highly organized centre of power."[54]

The verdict of the British intellectual was echoed by the workaday journalist. Visiting India soon after Huxley, a reporter for the London *Daily Mail* thought that "until now Nehru alone has been the unifying, cohesive force behind India's Government and foreign policy." But after Nehru was gone, "the powers of caste and religion, of Rightism and Leftism . . . could eventually split this country from top to bottom and plunge it back 100 years."[55]

VII

Through 1960 and 1961, as some Indians rioted and others protested, their government continued its correspondence with China. No longer were these exchanges statesmanlike, or conducted by statesmen; rather, they consisted of notes by anonymous functionaries accusing each other of transgressions of one kind or another. A note from China listed fifteen violations of Chinese airspace by Indian aircraft; a note from India listed various incidents of ill-treatment of Indian citizens in Tibet.[56]

The exchanges, published in successive White Papers brought out by the government of India, led to a renewed call for Krishna Menon's head. Leading the charge was J. B. Kripalani, the socialist member of Parliament from Sitamarhi in Bihar. Scholar, teacher, khadi worker, and rebel, Kripalani was an authentic hero of the Indian struggle for freedom. His moral authority derived, in part, from the fact that he had come close to Gandhi while aiding him in the Champaran satyagraha of 1917, years before Nehru himself made the acquaintance of the Mahatma. Kripalani had also been president of the Congress and, of course, spent many years in jail for his cause.

On 11 April 1961, Kripalani delivered what was described at the time as "perhaps the greatest speech that has been made on the floor of that House since Independence." This was a blistering attack on the defence minister. Under Krishna Menon's stewardship, said Kripalani, "we have lost 12,000 square miles of our territory without striking a single blow." Army promotions, he claimed, were not based on merit but were made "according to the whims and fancies of the Defence Minister or what will suit his political and ideological purposes." Menon had "created cliques [and] lowered the morale of our Forces." In a stinging indictment, Kripalani charged the minister with "wasting the money of this poor and starving nation," with "the neglect of the defence of the country," and with "having lent his support to the totalitarian and dictatorial regimes against the will of the people for freedom."

Kripalani ended his speech with an appeal to the conscience of the members of the ruling party. Recalling how, in 1940, the Conservative members of the British Parliament had compelled their prime minister to resign, he appealed to those "Congressmen who were not afraid of the British bullets and bayonets to place the good of the nation above the good of the party." With this parting shot Kripalani sat down, to vigorous applause from the opposition benches.[57]

Through the second half of 1961, the Indian Parliament witnessed a series of bitter debates about the dispute with China. The prime minister himself was harried and hurt by a group of terriers at his heels. Three in particular nipped hard: Atal Behari Vajpayee of the Jana Sangh, Hem Barua of the Praja Socialist party, and N. G. Ranga of the Swatantra party. Nehru was accused of turning a blind eye to a Chinese "occupation" of Indian territory and of placing himself magisterially above the fray. "In regard to border disputes," said one member, "the Prime Minister has a tendency to act like an umpire in a cricket match rather than as one whose interests are involved." The criticisms had a personal, polemical, edge, because Nehru also served as the foreign minister, and the policy of friendship with China was known to be his particular project. Unaccustomed to such hostility, the prime minister became increasingly irritable, on one occasion going so far as to refer to his critics as "childish and infantile."[58]

By now, there were elements in his own party who had made known their view that the prime minister should take a stronger line on China. When an opposition member taunted Nehru with regard to his remark that Aksai Chin was barren land, with no grass growing on it, a Congress member added this telling supplement: "No hair grows on my head. Does it mean that the head has no value?" This was widely viewed as a dig at Nehru, who was completely bald himself.[59]

VIII

In the third week of December 1961, a detachment of the Indian army moved up to the borders of the Portuguese colony of Goa. For a decade, New Delhi had sought, by persuasion and non-violence, to persuade Portugal to give up that territory. With those measures failing, Nehru's government decided to "liberate" Goa by force.

On the morning of 18 December, Indian troops entered Goa from three directions: Savantvadi in the north, Karwar in the south, and Belgaum in the east. Meanwhile, airplanes dropped leaflets exhorting the Goans to "be calm and brave" and to "rejoice in your freedom and strengthen it." By that evening, the capital, Panjim, had been encircled. The troops were helped by the locals, who pointed out where the Portuguese had laid mines. The colonists fired a few shots before withdrawing. In the smaller enclaves of Daman and Diu the resistance was somewhat stiffer. In all, some fifteen Indian soldiers, and perhaps twice as many Portuguese, lost their lives. Thirty-six hours after the invasion began, the Portuguese governor general signed an unconditional document of surrender.[60]

The western press had a field day with this display of "Indian hypocrisy." Subjected for so long to lectures by Nehru and Krishna Menon, they now hit back by attacking the use of force by a nation that professed "non-violence." The action was also represented as a breach of international law; and, more absurdly, as a threat to Christians and Christianity in Goa.[61] In fact, 61% of Goa was Hindu; and prominent Goan Christians, such as the journalist Frank Moraes and the archbishop, Cardinal Gracias, had an honoured place in Indian public life.

There had long been an indigenous freedom movement within Goa, and many, perhaps most, Goans welcomed the Indian action. In any case, the Goans were now at liberty to choose their own leaders, a choice always denied them by the Portuguese.

That Goa was legitimately part of India was not in dispute. That India had waited long enough before acting was also evident. Still, the timing of what was called "Operation Vijay" was open to question. Why did it take place in December 1961, rather than December 1960 or December 1962? Nehru perhaps thought he had waited long enough for the Portuguese to leave: fourteen years. And he was under pressure from both left and right; the Jana Sangh and the communists, in a rare show of agreement, were urging him to use the army to liberate the colony. Still, the suspicion lingered that the precise timing of the invasion was determined by the electoral needs of his colleague Krishna Menon. Before the troops went in, the defence minister inspected them on the border. As the *New York Times* wrote, he was here "conducting a double campaign"; one for the war that was about to commence, the other for the general election that had been scheduled for February 1962.[62]

In that election, Krishna Menon would be opposed by his parliamentary bête noire, Acharya Kripalani, who had announced that he would shift from the safe seat of Sitamarhi and take on the defence minister in the constituency he represented, North Bombay. All the opposition parties (the communists excepted) announced that they would support Kripalani. A battle of prestige was brewing; since the prime minister had refused to drop Menon from the cabinet, the opposition now hoped that he would be removed by the voters.

Less than two months after his troops marched into Goa, Menon was in Bombay to fight his corner of the general elections of 1962. Going to bat for him were the powerful Maharashtra chief minister, Y. B. Chavan, and senior members of the Union cabinet. Even Menon's known critics in government, such as Morarji Desai and Jagjivan Ram, were commanded to go out and campaign on his behalf. Speaking on Kripalani's side were such stalwarts as C. Rajagopalachari, as well as many distinguished non-party men—lawyers, intellectuals, and industrialists.

The contest was, among other things, a tribute to the cosmopolitan character of Bombay, with a Malayali and a Sindhi competing for the affections of the people in a state not their own. The constituency was very heterogeneous, with many Marathi-speakers and Gujarati-speakers, and also many Bhaiyyas from Uttar Pradesh, Goans, Sindhis, and Tamilians. These various segments were wooed by both contestants, and the campaign had an intensity commensurate with the stature of the disputants and the importance of their dispute.

In the rich and by now extensive history of Indian elections, perhaps no single contest has been played up as much as this one. The journal *Link*, sympathetic to Menon, called it "the most important election in the history of our democracy." The social worker Jayaprakash Narayan, a friend of Kripalani's, said that in this contest "the future of Indian democracy and our spiritual values are at stake."

The campaign was colourful, replete with evocative posters and savage slogans. The left-wing weekly *Blitz* ran a sharp campaign against a man it chose to refer to as "Cripple-looney." On the other side, Menon was lampooned by versifiers in several languages. One ditty went: *Chini hamla hote hain/ Menon Saab sote hain/Sona hai tho sone do/Kripalani ji to aane do* ("As China advances, Menon sleeps/Let him sleep if he must/But call Kripalani to be with us"). An English verse expressed the same sentiments, if more elegantly: *I do not hold with all these cracks and mockery/At Krishna Menon./It is his virtues I would rather pin on./For instance, consider his skill with crockery:/What could be finer/ Than the loving care with which he handles china?*

The prime minister took the challenge to Menon as a challenge to himself. Nehru inaugurated the Congress campaign in Bombay, and found reason to support his man in other places as well. In Sangli, in Poona, and in Baroda, he said that a defeat for Menon would signal a defeat for his own policies of socialism and non-alignment. His mentor's support helped Menon immeasurably. So did the liberation of Goa, which resonated well with the public of north Bombay, and not just with the Goans among them.

In the event, Kripalani's campaign was undone by Nehru's speeches, the action in Goa, and the strength of the Congress party machinery. He lost by more than 100,000 votes.[63]

IX

In the general elections of 1952 and 1957 the Congress had made much of being the party of the struggle for freedom. In 1962, however, its campaign focused more on what it had done since. Its policies, it said, had increased agricultural and industrial production, enhanced education and life expectancy, and promoted the unity of the country. Never having held power, the opposition could not match these claims with counterclaims of its own.[64] So the Congress retained its majority in Parliament, winning 361 seats out of 494. The communists won twenty-nine seats, while the new opposition party, Swatantra, won eighteen—a respectable number. In the state of Madras there was a challenge from the quasi-secessionist DMK, which won seven seats in Parliament (and fifty in the Legislative Assembly). But on the whole the pre-eminence of the Congress was confirmed, and Jawaharlal Nehru entered his fourth term as prime minister.

The opposition within had been shown its place, but the opposition without remained. Through the spring and summer of 1962 clashes on the border continued. In July, the journal *Seminar* in Delhi ran a symposium on India's defence policy. One contributor insisted that "the People's Republic of China does not pose any military threat to our country." Another contributor was not so sure. This was General Thimayya, now retired, who noted that there were threats from both Pakistan and China. Whereas India was moderately well placed to meet an attack from the former, Thimayya could not "even as a soldier envisage India taking on China in an open conflict on its own. China's present strength in man-power, equipment and aircraft exceeds our resources a hundredfold with the full support of the U.S.S.R., and we could never hope to match China in the foreseeable future. It must be left to the politicians and the diplomats to ensure our security." The "present strength of the army and air forces of India," said the general, "are even below the 'minimum insurance' we can give to our people."[65]

The implications were clear: either the diplomats should seek a treaty with China, or the politicians should canvass for military help from the western bloc. But the rising tide of patriotic sentiment ruled out the first; and the non-alignment of the prime minister, strengthened by the anti Americanism of his defence minister, ruled out the second.

In the third week of July 1962, there were clashes between Indian and Chinese troops in the Galwan valley of Ladakh. Then, in early September, a conflict arose over the Dhola–Thag La ridge, in the valley of the Namka Chu River, about sixty miles west of Tawang. The region was where the borders of India, Tibet, and Bhutan all met; the exact alignment of the McMahon Line was in dispute here. The Indians claimed that the ridge fell south of the McMahon Line; the Chinese argued that it was on their side.[66]

Earlier, in June, a platoon of the Assam Rifles had established a post at Dhola, as part of the continuing forward policy. On 8 September the Chinese put a post of their own at Thag La, which overlooked (and threatened) Dhola. Peking and New Delhi exchanged angry letters. The

Indian commanders were divided as to what to do. Some said that the Chinese must be shifted from Thag La. Others said that this would be too difficult, since the terrain was disadvantageous to the Indians (Thag La was about 2,000 feet above Dhola). Meanwhile, at the site itself, the Chinese troops began using a megaphone to make exhortations in Hindi. *Hindi-Chini bhai-bhai*, they shouted: *Ye zamin hamara hai. Tum vapas jao* ("Indians and Chinese are brothers in arms, but this land is ours, so you will please vacate it").

The stalemate continued for three weeks, with troops of the two nations facing each other across a narrow river, not knowing whether their leaders were making peace or about to go to war. Finally, on 3 October, Lieutenant General Umrao Singh, who had counselled prudence, was replaced as corps commander by B. M. Kaul, who flew in from Delhi to take command in NEFA. Those who recommended caution were overruled. "To all objections Kaul gave sweeping and unrealistic assurances, based on the assumption of Delhi's future logistical support for any gamble he might now take."[67] To dislodge the Chinese from Thag La, he now moved two battalions up from the plains. The troops had light arms and only three days of rations; they had no mortars or rocket launchers, and only promises of supplies to come and catch up with them.

Indian soldiers reached the Namka Chu valley on the afternoon of 9 October, after a march through "mud, mountains and rain." "Exhausted by days of marching over massive heights and appalling weather conditions, [these were] troops badly in need of a breather and the tools for war."[68] That same evening they set up a post in a herder's hut from where they would, when reinforcements arrived, try to uproot the enemy. They were not given the chance. On the morning of 10 September, the Chinese attacked. The jawans fought hard, but they had been drained by the long march up. They were also outnumbered and outgunned, their light arms proving no match for the heavy mortar used by the Chinese.

From 1959, in both Ladakh and NEFA, the Chinese and Indians had played cat and mouse, sending troops to fill up no-man's-land, clashing here and there, while their leaders exchanged letters and occasionally even met. Now the situation escalated to an unprecedented level. The Indian's positioning at Dhola was answered when the Chinese came to Thag La, directly above it; this in turn provoked an attempt by the Indians to shift them. When this failed, Nehru, in Delhi, told the press that the army had been given instructions to try once more to push out the "enemy."

But it was the enemy who acted first. A phony war, which had lasted all of three years, became real on the night of 19–20 October, when the Chinese simultaneously invaded the eastern and the western sectors. The "blitzkrieg" across the Himalaya had come, as "Pragmatist" had predicted it would. And as he feared, the Indians were unprepared. That night, the *New York Times* wrote, a "smouldering situation burst into flame" as "heavy battles broke out in both of the disputed areas. Masses of Chinese troops under the cover of thunderous mortar fire drove the Indians back on each front." Both sides had built up forces on the border, but "independent observers laid the onslaught to the Chinese." The Chinese attacked in waves, armed with medium machine guns backed by heavy mortars. Two Chinese divisions were involved in the invasion, using five times as many troops as the Indians.[69]

The Indians were "taken by surprise" as the Chinese quickly over-ran many positions, crossed the Namkha Chu valley, and made for the monastery in Tawang. Another detachment made for the eastern part of NEFA. Chinese troops moved deeper and deeper into Indian territory. Eight posts were reported to have fallen in Ladakh, and almost twenty in NEFA. Tawang itself had come under the control of the Chinese.[70]

The ease with which the Chinese took Indian positions should not have come as a surprise. Their troops had been on the Tibetan plateau in strength from the mid-1950s, fighting or preparing to fight Khampa rebels. Unlike the Indians, the Chinese were used to battles in the high mountains. Besides, access was much easier from the Tibetan side, where the terrain was relatively flat, conducive to road building and troop movements. The geographical advantage was all to the Chinese. From Assam up to the McMahon Line the climb was very steep, with the hills covered with thick vegetation and the climate often damp and wet. The Indian forward posts were hopelessly ill-equipped: with no proper roads, these posts "lived from air-drop to air-drop," dependent on supplies and on sorties by helicopters for survival.[71]

The Indians' problems were compounded by a lack of leadership. On 18 October General Kaul had developed acute chest pains. He was evacuated to Delhi, and his corps was left leaderless for five days, by which time Tawang had fallen.

On 24 October the Chinese halted their advance, while Chou En-lai wrote to Nehru seeking a way to "stop the border clashes" and "reopen border negotiations." Over the next fortnight they wrote each other two letters apiece, but these got nowhere. Chou said that China and India had a common enemy, "imperialism." The current conflict notwithstanding, he thought it possible for both of them to "restore Sino-Indian relations to the warm and friendly pattern of earlier days and even improve on that pattern." His solution was for each side to withdraw twenty kilometres behind the line of actual control, and disengage.

Nehru's replies displayed his wounds for all to see. "Nothing in my long political career has hurt me more and grieved me more," he said, than "the hostile and unfriendly twist given in India-China relations" in recent years, these culminating in "what is in effect a Chinese invasion of India," in "violent contradiction" of the claim that China wanted to settle the border question by "peaceful means." Peking had made "a deliberate cold-blooded decision" to "enforce their alleged boundary claims by military invasion of India." Chou's offer, he wrote, was aimed at consolidating and keeping the gains of this aggression. The solution Nehru proposed was for Chinese troops to get behind the McMahon Line in the east, and to revert in the west to their position as of 7 November 1959, thus cancelling out three years of steady gains made by establishing posts in territory under dispute.[72]

Meanwhile, a casualty in Delhi had been added to all those suffered on the front. Now that Indian weaknesses had been so comprehensively exposed, V. K. Krishna Menon was finally removed as defence minister. (He was first shifted to the Ministry of Defence Production, then dropped from the cabinet altogether.) Menon's exit was accompanied by a call by Delhi for western arms. On 28 October the American ambassador went to see the prime minister. Nehru "was frail, brittle and seemed small and old. He was obviously desperately tired." They must have military aid from the West, Nehru said.[73] Soon, Britain and America were sending transport planes with arms and ammunition. France and Canada had also agreed to supply weapons.[74]

On 8 November, the prime minister moved a resolution in Parliament deploring that China had "betrayed" the spirit of Panchsheel and India's "uniform gestures of goodwill and friendship" by initiating "a massive invasion." The hurt was palpable that "we in India, who have . . . sought the friendship of China . . . and pleaded their cause in the councils of the world should now ourselves be victims of new imperialism and expansionism by a country which says that it is against all imperialism." China may call itself "communist," said Nehru, but it had revealed itself as "an expansionist, imperious-minded country deliberately invading into a country."

Nehru's speech might be read as a belated acknowledgement of the correctness of Vallabhbhai Patel's warning of 1950: that communism in

China was an extreme expression of nationalism, rather than its nullification. The debate that followed took a full week; 165 members of Parliament spoke, apparently a record.[75]

On the borders, the lull in the fighting was broken by a second Chinese offensive on 15 November. A 500-mile front was attacked in NEFA. There was a bitter fight in Walong, where soldiers from the Dogra and Kumaon regiments, all hardy hill men, fought heroically and almost wrested control of a key ridge from the Chinese.[76] There was also some spirited resistance in Ladakh, where the field commander was not subject to conflicting signals from Delhi. Here the troops stood their ground, and "forced the Chinese to pay dearly for the territory they won."[77]

But across most of NEFA it had been a very poor showing indeed. Here the Indians simply disintegrated, with platoons and even whole regiments retreating in pieces. When the Chinese swept through there was much confusion among the Indian commanders. Where should they make their first, and perhaps last, stand? The option of Tawang was considered and abandoned. One general advocated Bomdi Lal, sixty miles to the south, to which supplies could be easily sent up from the plains. Finally, it was decided to stop the Chinese advance at Se La, only fifteen miles from Tawang.

The decision to make a stand at Se La was Kaul's. When he fell ill, his place had been taken by Lieutenant General Harbaksh Singh, a highly regarded commander with much field experience. But before Singh could adequately reorganize the defences, Kaul had flown back from Delhi to take charge once more.

The Chinese had occupied Tawang on 25 October. When they halted there, the Indians were deceived into inaction. In fact, the Chinese were working on improving the road to Se La. On 14 November, the Indians began a proposed counter-attack, choosing as their target an enemy post near Walong. Meanwhile, battles broke out north of Se La, with the Chinese again having the advantage. The garrison commander, in a panic, ordered withdrawal, and his brigade began retreating toward Bomdi La. There they found that the Chinese had already skirted Se La and cut off the road behind them. Large sections were mowed down in flight, while others abandoned their arms and fled singly or in small groups. Se La was easily taken, and Bomdi La fell soon afterwards.[78]

The fall of Bomdi La led to panic in Assam. An Indian reporter, reaching Tezpur on 20 November, found it a "ghost town." The administration had pulled back to Gauhati, after burning the papers at the Collectorate and the currency notes at the local bank. Before the administration left, "the doors of the mental hospital [were] opened to release the bewildered inmates."[79]

In Delhi and Bombay, young men were lining up to join the army. The recruiting centres were usually sleepy places, open one or two days a week; and 90% of the men who showed up failed the first examination. Now these compounds were "besieged by thousands of would-be recruits." Some were labourers and factory workers; others were unemployed graduates. They all hoped that in this emergency the army would "lower its physical requirements and give them food and lodging and a purpose in life."[80]

It seems unlikely that these men would have made a better showing than those who had already fought and lost. In any case they did not get the chance. Poised to enter the plains of Assam, the Chinese instead announced a unilateral ceasefire on 22 November. In NEFA they pulled back to north of the McMahon Line. In the Ladakh sector they likewise retreated to positions they had held before the present hostilities began.

Why did the Chinese pack up and go home? Some commentators thought they were deterred from coming further by the rallying of all parties, including the communists, around the Indian government. The western powers had pledged support, and were already flying in arms and ammunition.[81] As important as these political considerations were the facts of nature. Winter was setting in, and soon the Himalaya would be snowbound. And by pressing deep into India, the Chinese would make their supply lines longer and more difficult to maintain.

While the end of the war can be thus explained, its origins are harder to understand. There were no White Papers issued from the Chinese side, and China's records are not open—and perhaps never will be. All one can say is that behind such a carefully coordinated attack there must have been several years of preparation. As for its precise timing, speculation which was offered at the time—and which still seems plausible—was that the two superpowers, the Soviet Union and the United States, were preoccupied with the Cuban missile crisis, allowing Peking its little adventure without fear of reprisal.

The border war had underlined Chinese superiority in "arms, communications, strategy, logistics, and planning."[82] According to the Defence Ministry's statistics, 1,383 Indian soldiers had been killed; 3,968 were taken prisoner; and 1,696 were still missing.[83] These losses were small by the standards of modern warfare, yet the war represented a massive defeat in the Indian imagination. Naturally, the search began for scapegoats. Over the years, a series of self-exculpatory memoirs were published by the generals in the field. Each sought to shift the blame away from himself and toward another commander, or toward the politicians who had neglected his warnings and issued orders that were impossible to carry out. Major General D. K. Palit—director general of military operations at the time of the war—notes in his own contribution to the genre that in these memoirs "there are striking inconsistencies; each had his own wicket to defend." He adds, "Hindsight tends to lend rationality to events that in fact are innocent of coherence or logical sequence."[84]

Among the Indian public, the principal sentiment was a sense of betrayal, of being taken for a ride by an unscrupulous neighbour whom they had naively chosen to trust and support. In his letters to Chou En-lai, Nehru expressed these feelings as well as anyone else. But for the deeper origins of the dispute one must turn to his earlier writings, in particular to an interview at which he spoke not as India's leader but as a student of world history. In 1959, Nehru had told Edgar Snow that "the basic reason for the Sino-Indian dispute was that they were both 'new nations,' in that both were newly independent and under *dynamic nationalistic leaderships*, and in a sense were 'meeting' at their frontiers for the first time in history." In the past, "there were buffer zones between the two countries; both sides were *remote* from the borders." Now, however, "they were meeting as *modern nations* on the borders." Hence it "was natural that a certain degree of conflict should be generated before they can stabilize their frontiers."[85]

The conflict between India and China, then, was a clash of national myths, national egos, national insecurities, and—ultimately and inevitably—national armies. In this sense, although the conflict seemed unique (and uniquely disturbing) to Indians, it was very representative. Competing claims to territory have been an all too common source of conflict in the modern world. Nehru said as much to Edgar Snow. However, let us give the last word to an unlikely authority, the beat poet Allen Ginsberg. In March 1962 Ginsberg began a two-year trip around the subcontinent, bumming and slumming in search of nirvana. In August, just as the clashes on the border began to intensify, he made an entry in his diary which set the border conflict in perspective:

The Fights 1962:
U. S. vs Russia in General/China vs Formosa over possession/India vs China over border territory/India vs Pakistan over possession Kashmir—Religious/India vs Portugal over possession Goa/India vs Nagas over Independence/Egypt vs Israel over possession of territory and Religion/

E. Germany vs W. Germany sovereignty/Cuba vs U. S. A.—Ideas/N.Korea vs So. Korea—Sovereignty/Indonesia vs Holland—Territory/France vs Algeria—Territory/Negroes vs whites—U. S./Katanga vs Leopoldville/Russian Stalinists vs Russian Kruschevists/Peru A. P. R. A. vs Peru Military/Argentine Military versus Argentine Bourgeois/Navajo Peyotists vs Navajo Tribal Council—Tribal/W. Irian?/Kurds vs Iraq/Negro vs Whites—So. Africa—Race/U. S. Senegal vs Red Mali—Territory/Ghana vs Togo—Territory/Ruanda Watusi vs Ruanda Bahutu—Tribe power/ Kenya Kadu vs Kenya Kana—Tribe power/Somail vs Aethopia, Kenya, French Somali/Tibet Lamas vs Chinese Tibetan secularists/India vs E. Pak—Aasam Bengal over Border & Tripura/Algeria vs Morocco over Sahara.[86]

16

PEACE *in* OUR TIME

Here we are having a grudging time, both with the weather and
the problems which are arising; Kashmir, in particular, is giving
us a severe headache.

VALLABHBHAI PATEL to G. D. BIRLA, May 1949

I

APART FROM the several thousand Indian soldiers dead or
injured, the casualties of the war with China included the
chief of army staff, General P. N. Thapar (who resigned, citing ill-health); the failed strategic thinker Lieutenant General B. M.
Kaul (who was retired prematurely); and the Defence Minister, V. K.
Krishna Menon (who was dismissed). Another casualty was the reputation of Jawaharlal Nehru. The border war was Nehru's most consequential failure in fifteen years as prime minister. The inability to bring
about radical land reform affected the rural poor; the dismissal of the
Kerala communists angered many people in that state; other sections
likewise had their own grievances against the government. But the failure to protect the nation's territory was a different matter altogether.
The humiliation that resulted was felt, as military defeats invariably are,
by the nation as a whole.

Krishna Menon and the army brass had been sacrificed, yet the
prime minister knew deep down that he was ultimately responsible for
the disaster—in a general sense, as the head of government; and in a
very specific sense, as one who had guided and determined India's attitudes and policies toward China.

Those attitudes and policies now had to be rethought. Nehru could
at last see what Vallabhbhai Patel had sensed long ago: that communism
in China was merely a more bellicose form of nationalism. The border
war provoked in Nehru a reluctant tilt toward the United States, which
came forth with arms while Soviet Russia stayed neutral. A key player in

this shift was the American ambassador in New Delhi, John Kenneth Galbraith. An economics professor at Harvard who was sceptical about the free market, a scholar of art history, a noted bon vivant and wit, Galbraith was, to Indian eyes, a very untypical American indeed. (In fact, he was by birth Canadian.) Things were changing in Washington, where a new young president, John F. Kennedy, was seeking to reverse the American government's image as uncaring at home and arrogant abroad. It was these winds of liberalism that carried Galbraith along to India.

From the time he took charge in April 1961, the ambassador got on famously with Nehru. They discussed art and music and literature; this, on Nehru's part, was a welcome diversion from the daily grind; but on Galbraith's, it was a shrewd softening-up of a mind long prejudiced against his country. In March 1962, the first lady, Jacqueline Kennedy, arrived for a trip through India, where she saw the Taj Mahal and Rajput forts, and had extended conversations with the prime minister.

Nehru was charmed by Mrs. Kennedy's beauty, as he had been by her envoy's brains. But the thaw would not have become a tilt had it not been for the war with China. On 9 November, after the first wave of attacks, Galbraith was called in to meet with the prime minister. He found Nehru "deathly tired and I thought a little beaten." (Earlier in the day, Nehru had made a speech in Parliament that was "a good deal less than Churchillian.") A request was made for arms from America. This came at a cost that could never be measured in money alone, for, as Galbraith wrote to President Kennedy, all his life Nehru had

> sought to avoid being dependent upon the United States and the United Kingdom—most of his personal reluctance to ask (or thank) for aid has been based on this pride. . . . Now nothing is so important to him, more personally than politically, than to maintain the semblance of this independence. His age no longer allows of readjustment. To a point we can, I feel, be generous on this.[1]

By late November the arms began arriving, carried by planes bearing soldiers in uniform. As an American journalist wrote, this meant the "collapse of his [Nehru's] non alignment policy"; to many those dark blue uniforms carried "a special meaning," contained in a single word: "failure."[2] For the American ambassador, however, those uniforms spelled the word "opportunity." This might be the beginning of an entente to contain a communist power potentially more threatening than the Soviet Union itself. As Galbraith wrote to President Kennedy,

> the Chinese are not quarreling with the Soviets over some academic points of doctrine. They are, one must assume, serious about their revolution. The natural area of expansion is in their part of the world. The only Asian country which really stands in their way is India and *pari passu* the only Western country that is assuming responsibility is the United States. It seems obvious to me [that] there should be some understanding between the two countries. We should expect to make use of India's political position, geographical position, political power and manpower or anyhow ask.[3]

II

In response to India's request, President Kennedy sanctioned the supply of a million rounds for machine guns; 40,000 landmines; and 100,000 mortar rounds.[4] This fell far short of the grand alliance that his ambassador was recommending; yet it was far in excess of what other Americans thought New Delhi deserved. A bitter opponent of supplying arms to India was Senator Richard B. Russell of Georgia, the long-serving chairman of the Senate Armed Forces Committee. A crusty old reactionary— doughtily opposed to desegregation and the like—Russell had previously called India an "unreliable friend" and Nehru a "demagogue and a hypocrite." Now he told the Associated Press that he was "against giving India any of our modern weapons for the principal reason that we would be just giving them to the Chinese Communists." The Indians, said the senator, had "put on a disgraceful exhibition in permitting themselves to be driven out of what should have been impregnable strongholds in the border mountains. They seem incapable of fighting and if we supply them with weapons they will just fall into the hands of the Communists." While he was at present opposed to giving "one dime of weapons to India," Russell said he might rethink the matter if India's old rulers, the British, were prepared to "take over the matter of re-organizing and re-training their military forces."[5]

Russell's remarks were widely reported in the United States as well as India. The stormy correspondence that they generated provides a unique prism by which one can view relations between the United States and India. One would expect the two countries to have been allies, if only because both were large and culturally diverse democracies. However, their relationship had been clouded by suspicion—suspicion of India's non-alignment on one side, and of American military aid to Pakistan on the other. It did not help that these were both preachy peoples, whose foreign policy and diplomacy were invariably accompanied by an unctuous self-righteousness. Whereas democratic ideals brought the two countries closer together, pride and patriotism pulled them further apart.

Thus, while Kennedy and Galbraith might have deplored Senator Russell's stand, Russell received much support from across middle America. A correspondent from Wichita, Kansas, thanked the senator for warning that it was "very dangerous for the U. S. to make a doormat of itself to a country whose leaders have shown little interest or support to the U. S. except to take our money and aid and then villify us at every turn." A woman from Loomis, California, agreed that "nothing should be sent to that pro-Communist hypocrite and political actor Nehru and his Communist ministers." A man from Plantation, Florida, thought that the Indians' troubles were "of their own consequences and making"; specifically, they were due to the "Neutralist Policy" which they followed even while "the Communists have swallowed millions of people" the world over. An eighty-five-year-old Democrat from South San Gabriel endorsed Russell's "objection to this country saddling its taxpayers with the upkeep of four hundred million ignorant, starving people of India, whose leaders including Nehru and others are strikingly procommunist and hostile to our form of government. . . . Nehru's so-called neutralism . . . should teach this nation to let India stew in its own superstitious and ignorant juices."

From his compatriots, Senator Russell received dozens of letters of congratulation, but only one of dissent. This was written by a Fulbright scholar based in Madras, who said it was time to undo the American policy of arming Pakistan while denying aid to India. India, said the scholar, was a "popular democracy," whereas Pakistan was a military dictatorship which "exists as a political entity solely on its emotional antagonism to India." Besides, it was not true that the Indian troops had simply fled. They had fought hard in some places; and had they been better armed, they could have held their own. Now, "India is seeing to the recruitment of more troops; I should think that it would be in our best interests to see that they are properly armed."

There were also letters to the senator from Indians, who were naturally angry and hurt. A correspondent from Bombay agreed that Nehru "used foggy thinking with regard to the Chinese intentions," but refused to accept Russell's insinuation that "courage and defiance [were] a monopoly of white skins." The Indian jawan matched the American GI in grit as well as guts, as was manifest in the jawan's heroism in the crucial battles of the two world wars. But this time the "War Machinery was just not good enough (thanks to Mr. Menon). Our boys did without the luxury of air cover, automatic rifles, ear muffs, K-Rations and Bob Hope to cheer them up on the frigid front lines."

Russell's biliousness was answered in kind by the novelist and script-writer K. A. Abbas, one of India's most prominent fellow-travelling intellectuals. Abbas said that although there was a long history of stupid remarks by westerners about India, Russell's interview "takes the cake for unwarranted slander and unmitigated mischief." "But surely, Senator Russell," wrote Abbas, "if you are looking for 'disgraceful exhibitions' of military debacles, you will find ample material nearer home"—in Pearl Harbour, in the early reverses in the Korean War, in the Bay of Pigs. He referred Russell to General Eisenhower's praise for the Indian soldier, who had thwarted Rommel at El Alamein and, in other sectors across Europe and Africa, had fought "to save Senator Russell and his 'free world' from the menace of Hitler."

Senator Russell's remarks brought to the fore the misunderstandings between Indians and Americans as they had been up to 1962 and beyond. Behind these lay different perceptions of foreign policy and national interest, and also a certain incompatibility of cultures. The two peoples ate, drank, sang, dressed, and thought differently. As an admirer in Jacksonville wrote to the Senator: "This Nehru, technically Caucasian, politically nothing of the sort. . . . How can there be a 'meeting of minds' with a man who stands on his head?" The reference was to Jawaharlal Nehru's love of yoga, a form of therapy that was then completely alien to the American way of life.[6]

III

The defeat by China caused the prime minister a certain loss of face in the international arena. It also undermined his position at home. Criticism of his leadership grew more strident. In the summer of 1963, the Congress lost a series of important by-elections, which put into Parliament three opposition stalwarts: Minoo Masani, J. B. Kripalani, and Rammanohar Lohia.

In June 1963 Nehru held a press conference, his first in many months. It lasted ninety minutes and was notable for the anger the prime minister directed at the Chinese. He spoke of the "dark spate of falsehoods emanating from Peking," and of their "high record in vituperation." Explaining the war, and India's defeat, Nehru claimed that "the Chinese are a military-minded nation, always laying stress on military roads and preparedness. . . . Right from the beginning of the present regime there, they have concentrated on the military apparatus being stronger. It is a continuation really of the past civil wars. So, they are normally strong."[7]

Nehru also said that in attacking him personally, the Chinese "have something in common with some of our opposition leaders here." He then added, gratuitously, "As for our opposition leaders, they have the habit of combining with anybody and everybody regardless of principle and a time may come when some of them may for the purpose combine with the Chinese." Soon, the opposition leaders did formally combine among themselves to introduce a "no confidence" motion in Parliament, an act of daring that would have been inconceivable at any time between August 1947 and November 1962. The Congress had the numbers to easily defeat the vote, but the debate lasted four days, during which a series of telling points were made against the prime minister, his party, and his government.[8]

The criticisms in and out of Parliament prompted serious rethinking among the Congress leadership. Fifteen years in power had made the party complacent, somewhat out of touch with reality—as was evidenced in the by-election defeats and the growing strength of regional parties like the Dravida Munnetra Kazhagham (DMK). The chief minister of Madras, K. Kamaraj, was himself most threatened by the DMK; now, to check its rise and stem the rot within, he recommended that senior Congress ministers leave their posts to help rejuvenate the party. Under the "Kamaraj plan," six chief ministers resigned in order to work for the party—these included Bakshi Ghulam Mohammed of Kashmir and Kamaraj himself. Six senior Union ministers also resigned—among them Jagjivan Ram, Morarji Desai and Lal Bahadur Shastri.[9]

The prime minister stayed in his job. But he was noticeably weakened, in body as well as mind. In September 1963, the socialist member of Parliament H. V. Kamath saw Nehru walking in to take his seat: "an old man, looking frail and fatigued, with a marked stoop in his gait, coming down the gangway opposite with slow, faltering steps, and clutching the backrests of benches for support as he descended." Kamath's mind went back to his own early visions of a man he had once venerated: at a Congress session in Madras, where Nehru stood "sprightly, slim and erect"; at his home in Allahabad, where Nehru "jumped two steps at a time, with me emulating him, as I followed him upstairs."[10]

Whereas Indians would not speculate openly about Nehru's death, western observers had no such inhibition. In 1963, the American journalist Wells Hangen published a book—*After Nehru, Who?*—that listed eight possible successors, each of whom was allotted a separate chapter. Five were congressmen: Morarji Desai, V. K. Krishna Menon, Y. B. Chavan, Lal Bahadur Shastri, and S. K. Patil. One was a congresswoman: Indira Gandhi. A seventh candidate was the social worker and sometime socialist revolutionary Jayaprakash Narayan. The last candidate listed was a general—B. M. Kaul.[11]

The question now being asked was not just "After Nehru, who?" but also "After Nehru, what?" Shortly after the publication of Hangen's book, a reporter for the *Sunday Times* of London spent several weeks travelling through India. He met the prime minister, and found that "old Nehru has gone downhill so fast recently." The decay of the man mirrored the decay of his country. In contrast to the "intensity and unfathomable ambition of a wild young China," India was a land of "indescribable poverty" and a "will-less Government." What would happen after Nehru passed on? The reporter thought that the battle would "lie between the Communists and the new generation of political bandits emerging in the States." A third contender was the army; thus far, the generals had stayed aloof from politics, but "would they stand aside while India collapsed into disorder or was swept into Communism?" Such were the prospects for the future; meanwhile, "the free world must grow accustomed to its most populous member being without coherent leadership, swallowing aid and arms without significant effect, a tempting prey to the predatory-minded, an indictment of the free and democratic method of advancement in Afro-Asian eyes, where mature authority is so deeply needed."[12]

Contemporary photographs confirm that Nehru was in physical decline—with sunken shoulders; a tired, even doped, look on his face; an unfamiliar bulge around his waist. In the first week of September 1963, Indira Gandhi wrote to a friend that her father now needed to have weekly readings taken of his blood pressure, weight, and urine. "The strain, physical, mental and emotional is tremendous and he is bound to look tired," wrote Mrs. Gandhi. "The only medicine that can help is rest and relaxation."[13]

Of which, of course, he got none. He still had to undertake the duties of prime minister and foreign minister, and to contribute his mite to the revival of the Congress. As the single recognizable face of party and government, Nehru continued to maintain a punishing schedule, going to the four corners of India to address public meetings, open schools and hospitals, and speak to party workers. In December 1963, for example, he visited Madras, Madurai, Chandigarh, Calcutta, Bihar, and Bombay (twice).[14]

One place where the Prime Minister could have gone, but chose not to go, was Nagaland. A state of that name had finally come into existence on 1 December 1963. In other circumstances Nehru would have been keen to inaugurate it himself. But the journey to Kohima was long and arduous, and perhaps he also remembered the hostile reception he had gotten there in 1953. So the new president of the republic, Sarvepalli Radhakrishnan, did the honours. However, the new chief minister and his fellow ministers were dismissed as "traitors" by the underground, whose writ still ran across large parts of the state.[15]

In January 1964, Nehru crossed the country again, to attend the annual meeting of the Congress, held that year in the capital of Orissa, Bhubaneswar. He collapsed on the stage and had to be helped to his feet and rushed back to Delhi. The diagnosis was that he had suffered a mild stroke on the left side. As one headline put it: "Mr. Nehru's Illness Casts Gloom over Bhubaneshwar Meet."[16]

IV

The war with China had weakened Nehru's position not just in India or the world, but also within the Congress party itself. The locus of decision making had now shifted from the prime minister's home to the Congress parliamentary party. Nehru could no longer get the party to always do his bidding in matters big and small.[17] For instance, he had not welcomed the Kamaraj plan, on the grounds that it would deplete his government of experience and talent.

After his illness, Nehru was able to persuade the party to return Lal Bahadur Shastri to the Cabinet. Shastri was officially called a minister without portfolio, but in fact he functioned as the de facto deputy to the prime minister. The two shared a language, a home state, and a history of being in the same jails at around the same time. Nehru trusted and liked Shastri, whose quiet, understated personality was in such marked contrast to his own.

The first assignment entrusted to Shastri pertained to the state of Jammu and Kashmir. On 27 December 1963, a crisis had been sparked by the theft of a holy relic, a hair of the Prophet Muhammad, from the

Hazratbal Mosque in Srinagar. A week after it vanished, the relic mysteriously reappeared in the mosque. No one knew how it came back, just as no one knew how it had vanished in the first place. And no one knew whether the relic now in place was genuine or a fake.

Through January there were protests and demonstrations in the Valley. The ripples spread through the Muslim world. In distant East Pakistan there were religious riots aimed against the minority Hindu community, hundreds of thousands of whom fled to India. Now there was a danger of retaliatory riots against Muslims in India itself.

In the last week of January, Nehru dispatched Lal Bahadur Shastri to Kashmir. After speaking to officials and consulting local politicians, Shastri decided to hold a special showing, or *deedar*, to certify whether the returned relic was genuine. A panel of senior clerics was formed to view the relic. The clerics did so on 3 February and, to everyone's palpable relief, decided that it was the real one. Calm returned to the Valley. To sustain the peace, the government of India appointed, as chief minister, G. M. Sadiq, a politician known for his left-wing views but also for his integrity.[18]

The Hazratbal incident brought home, once more, the fact that trouble in Kashmir had repercussions in the subcontinent as a whole. The fiasco with China had made Nehru more alert to the need to seek a final resolution of the dispute over Kashmir. India could not afford to have two hostile fronts. Nehru was encouraged in this line of thinking by his old friend Lord Mountbatten. In April 1963, Mountbatten had told Nehru that "if his glory had at one time, brought India credit" in the world, the country, and he, now had a "tarnished image," principally owing to the failure to settle the question of Kashmir. Mountbatten felt that this could be "rectified" by a "heroic gesture by India," such as the "granting of independence to the [Kashmir] valley regardless of the Pakistani attitude."[19]

In fact, through 1962 and 1963 there were several rounds of talks with Pakistan on the issues that divided the two countries. Here, the government of India was represented by the experienced Sardar Swaran Singh, and Pakistan was represented by the young and ambitious Zulfiqar Ali Bhutto. At these talks no one represented Kashmir. But, as the Hazratbal incidents showed, it was not prudent to neglect the feelings of the people at the centre of the dispute. And who better to take their pulse than Sheikh Abdullah? By the end of 1963, Nehru was already thinking of releasing the sheikh, who by this time had been in jail for ten years. The stroke at Bhubaneswar, with its intimations of mortality, made him think further in this regard. Why not release Abdullah and have a last shot at solving the problem of Kashmir before he was gone?

V

Sheikh Abdullah, we may recall, had been arrested by the government of India in August 1953. No charges were brought against him, and in January 1958 he was suddenly released. He made his way to the Valley, where he met with a spectacular reception. He addressed well-attended public meetings in Srinagar, including one at the Hazratbal mosque. This seems to have unnerved his enemies in the administration. Toward the end of April he was arrested once more. This time he was sent to a jail in Jammu and was charged with plotting with Pakistan to break up India. He was accused, among other things, of attempting "to facilitate wrongful annexation of the territories of the State by Pakistan; create communal ill-feeling and disharmony in the state and receive secret aid from Pakistan in the shape of money, bombs, etc."[20]

The charges were, to put it bluntly, trumped up. Although the sheikh contemplated independence, he never wanted to join Pakistan. And although the idea of being the ruler of a free Kashmir appealed to him, he saw as his subjects all the people of the state, regardless of religion. As even his political opponents conceded, he had not a communal bone in his body.

Speaking at his trial, the sheikh said that he stood for a single objective: the right of self-determination for the people of Jammu and Kashmir, who, he insisted, were "not a flock of sheep and goats to be driven by force one way or another." Even so, he repeatedly underlined his commitment to secularism, his admiration for Mahatma Gandhi, and his once strong friendship with Jawaharlal Nehru. He recalled that Nehru himself had conceded that "the people of the state are the final arbiters of their fate," significantly adding, "He does not, I believe, deny this right to us even now."[21]

Two months after the sheikh's first arrest, in 1953, Nehru had written that "the mere fact of his detention is of course a matter which troubles me greatly."[22] The months turned into years, deepening his guilt. One way of sublimating it was to take a close interest in the education of his friend's children (which, by some accounts, he even helped pay for). In July 1955, Nehru was visited by Abdullah's eldest son, Farooq, then studying at a medical college in Jaipur. Farooq told the prime minister that his classmates routinely referred to his father as a "traitor." This prompted Nehru to write to a minister in the Rajasthan state government, asking him to ensure that the boy had "proper living quarters and some friendly companionship," so that he did not develop any "complexes and the like." As Nehru put it, "Some people foolishly imagine that because we have had difference with Sheikh Abdullah, therefore we are not favourably inclined towards his son and his family. This, of course, is not only absurd but is just the reverse of how we feel. Personally, because Sheikh Abdullah is in prison, I feel rather a special responsibility that we should try to help his sons and family."[23]

In 1964 the sheikh had spent much of the last decade in prison. Woken up by the China war, and put on high alert by his own fading health, Nehru decided to put an end to the matter. He spoke to the chief minister of Jammu and Kashmir, and after obtaining his consent, decided to release Sheikh Abdullah. The news was conveyed to the world by Nehru's confidant Lal Bahadur Shastri. Abdullah's detention, said Shastri, had been "a matter of pain to the Government, and particularly to the Prime Minister."[24]

On the morning of 8 April, the sheikh stepped out of Jammu jail, a free man once more. He drove in an open car through the streets of the town, accepting garlands and bouquets. The next day he gave his first public speech. According to a newspaper report, "Sheikh Abdullah said the two pressing problems facing the sub-continent—communal strife and Kashmir—should be solved during Prime Minister Nehru's lifetime. He described Mr. Nehru as the last of the stalwarts who had worked with Gandhiji and said that after him a solution of these problems would become difficult."

Nehru had invited Abdullah to stay with him in New Delhi. The sheikh said he would first go to the Valley, consult his friends and supporters, and go to meet the prime minister after the Eid festival (which fell on 23 April). On 11 April he set off by car to Srinagar, a journey that normally would take a few hours. But the Sheikh did it leisurely, stopping at towns and villages on the way. Wherever he halted, he also spoke. Thousands turned up to see and hear him, trudging miles from their own isolated hamlets. At these gatherings, women outnumbered men.

In his speeches, Abdullah described his state as a bride cherished by two husbands—India and Pakistan—neither of whom "cared to ascertain what the Kashmiris wanted." He said he would meet Jawaharlal Nehru with an open mind, and asked the Indians not to make up their minds beforehand either. As a journalist who interviewed him noted,

the sheikh had "no personal bitterness, no rancour"—rather, he was imbued with "a strong sense of mission," a compelling desire to seek a solution for Kashmir. At one meeting he was asked what he now felt about
Nehru. Abdullah answered that he bore no ill will, for "misunderstandings do occur even among brothers. I shall not forget the love Mr. Nehru
has showered on me in the past. . . . I will meet him as an old friend and
comrade."

On 18 April—a week after he had left Jammu—the sheikh drove in
an open jeep from Anantnag to the Kashmiri capital, Srinagar. The thirty-
mile route was lined by a "near-hysterical crowd" of 500,000 people.
The road was covered with freshly plucked daisies and tulips, and fes-
tooned with arches and bunting. When he finally entered the town, "Srinagar's entire population . . . jammed the labyrinth streets which were
so richly decorated that even the sun did not penetrate the canopy of
Kashmir silks, carpets and shawls."

Meanwhile, in Delhi, the prospect of talks between Nehru and
Abdullah alarmed many members of the ruling Congress party. Senior
cabinet ministers issued statements insisting that the question of Kashmir was "closed"; the state was, and would stay, an integral part of India. More combative still were members of the Jana Sangh. The party's
general secretary, Deen Dayal Upadhyaya, deplored the sheikh's recent
speeches, in which he seemed to have "questioned even the axiomatic
facts of the Kashmir question" (such as its final accession to India). "Instead of stabilizing the political situation of the State," complained
Upadhyaya, "Sheikh Abdullah has tried to unsettle every issue."

The opposition from the Hindu right was predictable. As it happens,
though, the left was also suspicious of Abdullah and his intentions. The
Communist party thought he was in danger of falling into an "imperialist trap," designed to detach Kashmir from India. In the political establishment, it seems, only Nehru's mind remained open. But he was to
receive unexpected support from two Indians who had also worked
with Mahatma Gandhi. One was Jayaprakash Narayan, popularly
known as JP, the former radical socialist who for the past decade had
been a leading light of the Sarvodaya movement. JP was an old friend of
the sheikh; he had also been a vocal advocate of better relations with
Pakistan. In 1962, he had set up an India-Pakistan Conciliation Group,
which, among other things, sought to find an "equitable and honourable" solution to the dispute over Kashmir.[25]

Now, welcoming Sheikh Abdullah's release in a signed article in
the *Hindustan Times*, JP deplored the insinuations against Abdullah by

politicians inside and outside the Congress. These had threatened that he would be put back in jail if he went "too far." "It is remarkable," commented JP acidly, "how the freedom fighters of yesterday begin so easily to imitate the language of the imperialists."

What alarmed politicians in Delhi was the sheikh's talk about ascertaining afresh the wishes of the Kashmiri people. JP thought this eminently reasonable, for the elections in Jammu and Kashmir in 1957 and 1962 were anything but free and fair. In any case, if India was "so sure of the verdict of the people, why are we so opposed to giving them another opportunity to reiterate it?" A satisfactory settlement of the question of Kashmir would greatly improve relations between India and Pakistan. JP hoped that the leaders of India would display "the vision and statesmanship that this historic moment demands." He added, "Happily, the one sane voice in the ruling party is that of the Prime Minister himself."[26]

More unexpected perhaps was the endorsement received by Nehru from C. Rajagopalachari ("Rajaji"), the statesman who had once been an intimate associate of the prime minister but had latterly become a political opponent. As the founder of the Swatantra Party, Rajaji had savaged the prime minister's economic policies. These criticisms sometimes had a sharp personal edge. Now, to the surprise of his followers, he came out strongly in favour of Nehru's initiative in releasing Abdullah. Like JP, he deplored the threats to put the sheikh back in jail, thus to "force him into silence and submission." Fortunately, "the Prime Minister may be ill but he preserves his balance, and has evidently refused to take any foolish step and degrade India."

The freeing of Abdullah, argued Rajaji, should act as a prelude to allowing "the people of Kashmir [to] exercise their human right to rule themselves as well as they can." Indeed, solving the tangle over Kashmir would pave the way for a larger resolution of the dispute between India and Pakistan. Thus, Rajaji wrote of the need to

> try and think fundamentally in the present crisis. Are we to yield to the fanatical emotions of our anti-Pakistan groups? Is there any hope for India or for Pakistan, if we go on hating each other, suspecting each other, borrowing and building up armaments against each other— building our two houses, both of us on the sands of continued foreign aid against a future Kurukshetra? We shall surely ruin ourselves for ever if we go on doing this. . . . We shall be making all hopes of prosperity in the future, a mere mirage if we continue this arms race based on an ancient grudge and the fears and suspicions flowing from it.[27]

VI

In Kashmir, meanwhile, Sheikh Abdullah was talking to his colleagues and associates. He discovered that while he was away in jail, he had come to be associated with the Pakistan party. At his trial, Abdullah had insisted that he never expressed a desire for Kashmir to join Pakistan. India or independence; those were the only two options he had countenanced. But the trial proceedings never reached the common people of the Valley. They knew only that he was being tried for conspiracy against the Indian nation. Would not that make him, by default, a friend of Pakistan?

The common people were strengthened in their beliefs by the propaganda of Bakshi Ghulam Mohammed's government, which had painted the sheikh as an agitator for a plebiscite, and hence anti-Indian. Moreover, the chicanery and corruption of the Bakshi regime had tarnished the image of India among the Kashmiris. Abdullah found that the pro-Pakistani elements were now perhaps in a majority. This did not please him. But, understanding the mood, he worked to gradually win over the people to his point of view. He met the influential priest Maulvi Farooqi, and urged him to support a "realistic" solution, rather than claim that Kashmir should accede to Pakistan in pursuance of the two-nation theory.[28]

On 23 April, two weeks after he was released, Sheikh Abdullah addressed a prayer meeting in Srinagar. A solution to the dispute over Kashmir, he said, must take into account its likely consequences for the 50 million Muslims in India, and the 10 million Hindus in East Pakistan. Three days later, in his last speech before leaving for Delhi, he urged the Kashmiris to maintain communal peace and thus set an example for both India and Pakistan. "No Muslim in Kashmir will ever raise his hand against the minorities," he proclaimed.

On 28 April, the day before Abdullah was due to arrive in Delhi, the Jana Sangh took out a large procession in the capital. The marchers shouted slogans against Abdullah and Nehru, and demanded that the government of India abrogate Article 370 and declare Kashmir an "integral and indivisible" part of India. At a public meeting held the same day, A. B. Vajpayee demanded that the prime minister tell Abdullah that Jammu and Kashmir had "already been integrated with the Indian Union and that there was no scope for discussion on this matter."

On 29 April, Abdullah flew into Palam airport with his principal associates. The party drove on to Teen Murti House, where the prime minister was waiting to receive Abdullah. It was the first time the two

men had seen each other since Nehru's government had locked up the
sheikh in August 1953. Now, as one eyewitness wrote, "the two em-
braced each other warmly. They were meeting after 11 years, but the
way they greeted each other reflected no traces of embarrassment, let
aside bitterness over what happened in the intervening period." The
two posed for the battery of press photographers before going inside.

This was a reconciliation between the leader of the nation and a man
till recently regarded as a traitor. It anticipated, by some thirty years,
the similarly portentous reconciliation between the president of South
Africa and his most famous political prisoner. But F. W. De Klerk did
not go so far as to ask Nelson Mandela to stay with him.

On this visit, Abdullah stayed with Nehru in Teen Murti House for
five days. They met at least once or twice a day, usually without aides.
While the prime minister was otherwise occupied, the sheikh canvassed
a wide spectrum of Indian opinion. He spoke to Congress ministers, to
leaders of the opposition, and to prominent non-political figures such as
Jayaprakash Narayan. He placed a wreath on Gandhi's tomb in Rajghat
and addressed a prayer meeting at Delhi's greatest mosque, the Jama
Masjid.

That Nehru was talking to Abdullah was not to the liking of the
Jana Sangh. Notably, it also caused disquiet among members of Nehru's cabinet, who worried that the question of Kashmir would now be
"reopened." To preempt the possibility, a senior minister told Parliament that the "maintenance of the status quo [in Kashmir] was in the
best interests of the subcontinent." And twenty-seven Congress members of Parliament issued a statement arguing that "you can no more
talk of self-determination in the case of Kashmir than in the case of,
say, Bombay or Bihar."

Within his party, the only senior man who appeared sympathetic to
Nehru's efforts was Lal Bahadur Shastri. There were, however, some opposition politicians who saw the point of speaking seriously with Abdullah. Thus the Swatantra party leader Minoo Masani urgently wired to
Rajaji:

> Understand Nehru and Lalbahadur endeavouring to find solution
> with Sheikh Abdullah but are up against confused thinking within
> Congress Party alongside of Jan Sangh Communist combination stop.
> If you think telegram or letter to Jawaharlal from yourself encourag-
> ing him [to] do the right thing and assuring your personal support
> would help please move in the matter.[29]

Rajaji chose not to write to Nehru, perhaps because he was too proud, or feared a rebuff. But he did write to Lal Bahadur Shastri, urging that Kashmir be given some kind of automonous status. As he saw it, "self-determination for Kashmir is as far as we are concerned a lesser issue than the aim of reducing Indo-Pak jealousy." He thought that "the idea that if we 'let Kashmir go,' we shall be encouraging secessions everywhere is thoroughly baseless." "I hope you and Jawaharlalji," Rajaji wrote to Shastri, "will be guided by Providence and bring this great opportunity to a good result."[30]

Shortly after his release Abdullah had expressed a wish to "pay my respects personally to Rajaji, and have the benefit of his mature advice."[31] Now, after his conversations with Nehru, he set off south to meet Rajaji, the Prime Minister's friend turned rival turned ally. He planned to stop at Wardha en route, to pay his respects to the Gandhian leader Vinoba Bhave. As he jokingly told a journalist, he would discuss "spirituality" with Vinoba and "practical politics" with Rajaji.

On 4 May, Lal Bahadur Shastri wrote to Rajaji urging him "to suggest to Sheikh Saheb not to take any extreme line. . . . Sheikh Saheb has just come out [of jail] and it would be good for him to give further thought to the different aspects of the Kashmir question and come to a judgement after full and mature introspection and deliberation. It will be most unfortunate if things are done in a hurry or precipitated."[32]

This was an airmail letter, but one does not know whether it reached Madras before 5 May, when Abdullah finally met Rajaji. They spoke for three and a half hours, and their meeting received a front-page headline in the *Hindustan Times*: "ABDULLAH, CR, EVOLVE KASHMIR FORMULA: PROPOSAL TO BE DISCUSSED WITH PRIME MINISTER." Rajaji did not say a word to the press, but Abdullah was slightly more forthcoming. Speaking to the wise old man, he said, "had helped clear his mind about what would be the best solution which would remove this cancer from the body politic of India and Pakistan." Pressed for details, the sheikh said these would have to await further talks with the prime minister. He did let on, however, that Rajaji and he had worked out "an honourable solution which would not give a sense of victory either to India or Pakistan and at the same time would ensure a place of honour to the people of Kashmir."

While Abdullah was in Madras, word reached him that President Ayub Khan had invited him to visit Pakistan. On returning to Delhi on 6 May, he went straight to Teen Murti House. He spent ninety minutes with Nehru, apprising him of what was being referred to, somewhat mysteriously, as "the Rajaji formula." The prime minister next directed Abdullah to an informal committee of advisers. This consisted of the foreign secretary, Y. D. Gundevia; the high commissioner to Pakistan, G. Parthasarathi; and the vice chancellor of the Aligarh Muslim University, Badruddin Tyabji.

Over two long days, Abdullah and the prime minister's men discussed the Kashmir issue threadbare. All kinds of alternatives were discussed. These included a plebiscite for the entire undivided state of Jammu and Kashmir as it existed before 1947; the maintenance of the status quo; and a fresh division of the state, such that the Jammu and Ladakh regions would go to India, Azad or nothern Kashmir would go to Pakistan, and a plebiscite would be held in the Valley alone to decide its future. Abdullah told the officials that while they could work out the specifics of the solution, he wanted it to: (1) promote Indo-Pakistani friendship; (2) not weaken the secular ideal of the Indian constitution; (3) not weaken the position of the minorities in either country. He asked them to give him more than one alternative, which he could take with him to Pakistan.

The sheikh's conditions more or less ruled out a plebiscite, whose result, whatever it was, would leave one country dissatisfied and minorities on both sides more vulnerable. What about the Rajaji formula? This, it appears, was for a condominium over Kashmir between India and Pakistan, with defence and external affairs being the joint responsibility of the two governments. (The model here was Andorra, a tiny autonomous enclave whose security was guaranteed by its two large neighbours, France and Spain.) Another possibility was to create a confederation between India, Pakistan, and Kashmir.[33]

The three men advising Nehru had been selected for their ability and knowledge; but it is also noteworthy that they came from three different religious traditions—and that all were officials. Recall that when there was a chance to settle the dispute with China, the jingoism of the politicians compelled Nehru to take positions more hard-line than he otherwise might have taken. Now, in seeking a settlement with Pakistan, Nehru sought to work with his officials, rather than his ministers. The wisdom of this approach was made clear in a letter to Rajaji by the writer and parliamentarian B. Shiva Rao:

> There is a clear attempt both from within the Cabinet and in Parliament to prevent the Prime Minister from coming to terms with Sheikh

Abdullah if it should mean the reopening of the issue of accession. Many of these Ministers have made public statements while the discussions between the two are going on. It's a sign of the diminishing prestige and influence of the P. M. that they can take such liberties.

This was interesting, and the reply was more interesting still. This fleshed out the "Rajaji formula," while putting Nehru's predicament in perspective. Rajaji wrote:

Asking Ayub Khan to give a commitment in advance about Azad Kashmir now will break up the whole scheme. He will and cannot give it. He is in a worse situation than Nehru in regard to public pressures and emotional bondage. . . . Any plan should therefore leave the prizes of war to be left untouched. . . . Probably the best procedure is for Sheikh to concentrate on the valley leaving Jammu as a counterpoise to Azad Kashmir, to be presumed to be integrated to India without question.

This reduced shape of the problem is good enough, if solved as we desire, to bring about an improvement in the Indo-Pakistan relationship. And being of reduced size, would be a fitting subject for UN trusteeship partial or complete.[34]

On the Indian side, the best hope for peace was Jawaharlal Nehru. Sheikh Abdullah appears to have thought that Nehru was also the last hope. On 11 May the sheikh told reporters, "I do not want to plead for Nehru but he is the symbol of India in spite of his weakness. You cannot find another man like him." He added that "after Nehru he did not see anyone else tackling [the problems] with the same breadth of vision."

For his part, Nehru was also quite prepared to vouch for the character of his old comrade and sometime adversary. Speaking to the All India Congress Committee in Bombay on 16 May, the prime minister said that Sheikh Abdullah was wedded to the principles of secularism. Nor did he believe in the two-nation theory. Both Nehru and he hoped that "it would be possible for India, holding on to her principles, to live in peace and friendship with Pakistan and thus incidentally to put an end to the question of Kashmir." "I cannot say if we will succeed in this," said the prime minister, "but it is clear that unless we succeed India will carry the burden of conflict with Pakistan with all that this implies."

VII

On 20 May, Sheikh Abdullah returned to Delhi, to stay at Teen Murti House, and have a final round of talks with Nehru before travelling to Pakistan. At a press conference on 22 May, Nehru declined to disclose the details, saying that he did not want to prejudice the sheikh's mission. But he did indicate that his government was "prepared to have an agreement with Pakistan on the basis of their holding on to that part of Kashmir occupied by them."[35]

Nehru's own papers on this subject are closed to scholars, but a letter by his foreign secretary gives a clue to his thinking at the time. The prime minister had apparently asked legal experts to explore the implications of a confederation between India, Pakistan, and Kashmir, "as a possible solution to our present troubles." Such an arrangement would not imply an "annulment" of partition. India and Pakistan would remain separate sovereign states. Kashmir would be part of the confederation, with its exact status to be determined by dialogue. There might be a customs union of the three units, some form of financial integration, and special provisions for the protection of minorities.[36]

To keep the discussion going, India was prepared to concede Pakistan's hold over Azad Kashmir and Gilgit, the two parts of the state that it had lost in the war of 1947–1948. Would Pakistan in turn concede anything? As Abdullah prepared to depart for Rawalpindi, Minoo Masani wrote to A. K. Brohi, sometime Pakistani high commissioner to India and now a leading lawyer in Karachi, a certified member of the Pakistani establishment who had the ear of President Ayub Khan. "The nature of the response which he [the Sheikh] is able to evoke from President Ayub," Masani said to Brohi, would "have a decisive influence in strengthening or weakening the hands of those who stand for Indo-Pakistan amity here." Nehru's Pakistan initiative was bitterly opposed from within his party and outside it. For the initiative to make progress, for there to be a summit meeting between the prime minister and President Ayub Khan, it was "of the highest moment that Sheikh Abdullah should come back with something on which future talks could be based." Masani urged Brohi to use his influence with Ayub and other leaders, so that their talks with Abdullah "yield fruitful results in the interests of both countries."[37]

Meanwhile, Abdullah proceeded to Pakistan. He hoped to spend two weeks there, beginning with the capital, Rawalpindi; moving on to Azad Kashmir; and ending with East Pakistan, where he intended, among other things, to check on the feelings of the Hindu minority. On 24 May he touched down in Rawalpindi, to a tumultuous reception. He drove in an open car from the airport to the town, the route lined by thousands of cheering Pakistanis. The welcome, said one reporter, "surpassed in intensity and depth that given to Mr. Chou En-Lai in February."[38]

Later, talking to reporters, Abdullah called his visit "a peace mission of an exploratory nature." He appealed to the press to help cultivate friendship between India and Pakistan. "He said he had come to the definite conclusion that the armed forces of both the countries facing each other on the ceasefire line must be disengaged and that the edifice of a happy and prosperous Kashmir could be built only on permanent friendship between India and Pakistan." As in New Delhi, here too he emphasized that any solution to the dispute must not foster a sense of defeat for either India or Pakistan, must not weaken India's secularism or the future of its 60 million Muslims, and must satisfy the aspirations of the Kashmiris themselves.

The next day, 25 May, Sheikh Abdullah met with Ayub Khan for three hours. The sheikh would not touch on the details, saying only that he found in Rawalpindi "the same encouraging response as in Delhi. There is an equal keenness on both sides to come to a real understanding."

Later that day, Abdullah addressed a large public meeting in Rawalpindi. He was "cheered repeatedly as he spoke for two hours bluntly warning both Indians and Pakistanis from committing wrongs which would endanger the lives of the minorities in both countries." The time had come, said Abdullah, for India and Pakistan to bury the hatchet. For if "the present phase of tension, distrust and misunderstanding continued, both countries would suffer and their freedom [would be] imperilled."

On 26 May Abdullah met Ayub Khan again, this time for four hours, and came out beaming. The Pakistani president, he told a crowded news conference, had agreed to a meeting with Prime Minister Nehru in the middle of June. The meeting would take place in Delhi, and Abdullah would also be in the city, available for consultation. "Of all the irritants that cause tension between India and Pakistan," said the sheikh, "Kashmir is the most important. Once this great irritant is removed, the solution of other problems would not present much difficulty."

By this time, however, enchantment with the sheikh was wearing thin among the Pakistani elite. Their representative voice, the newspaper *Dawn*, wrote that Abdullah's statements, "especially his references to India's so-called secularism, have caused a certain amount of disappointment among the public in general and the intelligentsia in particular." *Dawn* thought that the sheikh had been "lured by the outward show of Indian secularism, obviously forgetting the inhuman treatment meted out to 60 million Muslims in the so-called secular state." The newspaper also had a more fundamental complaint, that Abdullah had "taken up the role of an apostle of peace and friendship between Pakistan and India, rather than that of the leader of Kashmir, whose *prime objective should be to seek their freedom from Indian bondage.*"[39]

On 27 May, Abdullah proceeded to Muzaffarabad, a town he had not seen since Kashmir was divided in 1947. He had no idea of how the Kashmiris on this side of the ceasefire line would react to his proposals. Before he could find out, news reached him that, back in New Delhi, Nehru was dead. Abdullah at once "broke into tears and sobbed." In a muffled voice he told the reporters gathered around him, "he is dead, I can't meet him." When asked for more reactions he retired to a room, to be alone with his grief.

Abdullah drove down to Rawalpindi, and got on the first flight to Delhi. When he reached Teen Murti and saw the body of Nehru, "he cried like a child." It took him some time to "compose himself and place the wreath on the body of his old friend and comrade." To this account of a newsman on the spot we must add the witness of a diplomat who accompanied Nehru's body to the cremation. As the fire was burning the body to ashes, buglers sounded the last post: "thus was symbolized the inextricability of India and England in Nehru's life." Then, before the fire finally died down, "Sheikh Abdullah leapt on the platform and, weeping unrestrainedly, threw flowers onto the flames; thus was symbolized the inextricability of the Muslim world in Nehru's life and the pathos of the Kashmir affair."[40]

VIII

The events of April–May 1964 have unfortunately been neglected by scholars, including Nehru's biographers and analysts of the dispute over Kashmir.[41] I have discussed them here because they shed fresh light on this most intractable political problem—this "severe headache," as Vallabhbhai Patel called it; this "cancer [in] the body politic of India and Pakistan" as Sheikh Abdullah described it—and because they provide a peculiarly poignant coda to the life and work of Jawaharlal Nehru.

The question remains—how serious were the three campaigners for peace in April–May 1964? The one who did not reveal his mind at all, at least not in the public domain, was Field Marshal Ayub Khan. We know nothing about what he really thought at the time, whether he was indeed serious about a negotiated settlement on Kashmir, and if so whether he could "sell" an agreement with India to his people. Sheikh Abdullah, on the other hand, was forthcoming with his views, expressing them to the press and in countless public meetings and orations. Some people thought his words were a mask for personal ambition. Writing in the *Economic Weekly*, one commentator claimed that "even a superficial study of his political behaviour convinces that he is embarked on a most ramified plan to win an independent State by skilfully exploiting the hates and the prejudices, conscious and unconscious, and the power political tangles which provide the background to Indo-Pakistan relations."[42]

This seems far too cynical. Abdullah's words, and still more his actions, make manifest his commitment to secularism, and his concern for the minorities in both India and Pakistan. He was ambitious, certainly, but while in 1953 he seems to have fancied himself as the uncrowned king of Kashmir, in 1964 he saw himself rather as an exalted peacemaker, the one man who could bring tranquillity and prosperity to a poor and divided subcontinent.

Regarding Jawaharlal Nehru's motives there should be no doubt at all. He felt guilty about Abdullah's long incarceration; he was worried about the continuing disaffection in Kashmir; and he was sensible of the long-term costs of the dispute to both India and Pakistan. The question was not his motives, then, but his influence. Would his colleagues listen to him? Had he and Ayub Khan, with a little help from Abdullah, actually worked out a settlement, would it have passed muster with the Congress party, or the Indian Parliament?

Possibly not. And even if it did pass, would it have worked in the long run? The legal expert consulted by Nehru's office on the idea of a confederation delicately pointed out that "historically, confederations have been dominated by one member or united under stress."[43] In sheer size India towered above both Pakistan and Kashmir. Would it then behave like a Big Brother? Relevant here is a cartoon by Rajinder Puri that appeared in the *Hindustan Times* the day Abdullah met Ayub Khan. It showed Field Marshal Ayub Khan standing ruminatively, finger on chin, while the sheikh said, expansively gesticulating, "You're afraid Delhi will try to dominate Pindi? My dear chap, when Delhi can't dominate Lucknow or Chandigarh . . ."[44]

Here then were a host of imponderables—Ayub's motives, Abdullah's beliefs, Nehru's strength, the viability of a condominium or a confederation. In the end it was Nehru's strength that gave way—literally. And, as a Pakistani newspaper noted, his death meant "the end of a negotiated settlement of the Kashmir issue." Whoever succeeded Nehru would not have "the stature, courage and political support necessary to go against the highly emotional tide of public opinion in India favouring a status quo in Kashmir."[45]

17

MINDING *the* MINORITIES

The first law of decency is to preserve the liberty of others.

FRIEDRICH SCHILLER

I

ON THE AFTERNOON of 27 May 1964, as the news of Jawaharlal Nehru's death spread through New Delhi, one of the people it reached was an American graduate student named Granville Austin. Austin was writing a thesis on the making of the Indian constitution, and thus had a more than ordinary interest in what Nehru stood for. He made his way to Teen Murti House, there to join an already large crowd of Indian mourners. As Austin wrote in his diary the next day, "all wanted to go in, but they were prepared to wait." The crowd stood, "orderly and not noisy," as diplomats and ministers were ushered in by the prime minister's staff. Among the VIPs was Dr. Syed Mahmud, a freedom fighter who had been with Nehru at Cambridge and in jail. Like the others he was forced to leave his car, and walk up the steeply sloping lawn in front of the prime minister's residence. Austin saw a weeping Mahmud given a helping hand by Jagjivan Ram, the senior congressman and cabinet minister, who was of low-caste origin. This was truly "a scene symbolic of Nehru's India: a Muslim aided by an Untouchable coming to the home of a caste Hindu."[1]

Between them, Muslims and untouchables constituted one-fourth of the population in free India. Before 1947, two leaders had most seriously challenged the Congress's claim to represent all of India. One was a Muslim, M. A. Jinnah, who argued that the party of Gandhi and Nehru represented only the Hindus. The other was a former untouchable, B. R. Ambedkar, who added the devastating rider that the Congress did not even represent all Hindus, but only the upper castes.

These claims were stoutly resisted. Gandhi himself had struggled against untouchability long before Ambedkar had entered politics. And he had given his life in the cause of Hindu-Muslim harmony. For the Mahatma, Swaraj, or freedom, would have meaning only if it came to all Indians, regardless of caste or creed (or gender).

These were commitments Jawaharlal Nehru shared with Gandhi. In other matters, he might have been a somewhat wayward disciple. With his fellow intellectuals he chose to take India down the road of industrial modernization, rather than nurture a village-centred economy (as Gandhi would have wanted). But when it came to preserving the rights of minorities he stood shoulder to shoulder with the Mahatma. His was likewise a nationalism that was composite as well as egalitarian.

Inspired by Gandhi, and guided by Nehru, the Indian constitution abolished untouchability and proclaimed the state neutral in matters of religion. Such was the law; what was the practice? Among all the tests faced by the new state this, perhaps, was the sternest. Since Hindus were in a numerical majority and politically pre-eminent, the idea of India would withstand scrutiny only if they respected the rights and liberties of Indians different from themselves.

II

The idea of Pakistan had as its justification the need for minorities to be free of the fear of Hindu domination. Paradoxically, though, the state of Pakistan was created out of Muslim-majority areas where this problem did not exist in the first place.

After 1947 there were large populations of Muslims scattered all over peninsular India—as they had been before that date. Several million Muslims migrated across the borders to East and West Pakistan; but many more elected to stay behind in India. The creation of Pakistan had made their position deeply vulnerable. This was the view, ironically, of two men who had played critical roles in the making of Pakistan: H. S. Suhrawardy of the Bengali Muslim League and his counterpart in the United Provinces, Chaudhry Khaliquzzaman. On 10 September 1947—less than a month after independence and partition—Suhrawardy wrote to Khaliquzzaman, in horror, saying that "the Muslims in the Indian Union have been left high and dry." The antagonism caused by the formation of Pakistan had been heightened by the flight into India of Hindu and Sikh refugees. Suhrawardy now feared that "there may be a general conflagration which can well destroy the Muslim minority in the Indian Union." As for Khaliquzzaman, he had reached the melancholy conclusion that "the partition of India [had] proved positively injurious to the Muslims of India, and on a long-term basis for Muslims everywhere."

To protect their interests—and their lives—Suhrawardy drafted a "declaration of cooperation and mutual assistance between the two Dominions," committing both to protecting their minorities and to not making provocative statements against each other. Suhrawardy got Gandhi to endorse the declaration, but failed to get Jinnah to consent, despite begging him to do so, "for the sake of the helpless and hapless Muslims of the Indian Union."[2]

As we have seen, the creation of Pakistan provided a fillip to Hindu communalism. The RSS and similar groups could now argue that the Muslims were betrayers who had divided the nation. In the view of the extremist Hindu, these Muslims should either go to Pakistan or face the consequences. The RSS grew in strength immediately after partition—and although the murder of Gandhi in January 1948 slowed its rise, the organization continued to exercise considerable influence in northern and western India.

Truth be told, there were chauvinists within the ruling Congress itself, men who were not completely convinced that Muslims would be loyal to the new nation. Some of these chauvinists were in positions of high authority. The governor of Bihar warned the owners of the great steel mill in Jamshedpur that their Muslim employees would leave for Pakistan and would destroy the machinery before going. There were other such rumours around the town, but the factory owners stayed steadfast, issuing a notice that they had no intention of dismissing their Muslim employees or of promoting communal disunity among the workforce.[3]

The deep insecurity of the Indian Muslim was foregrounded in a survey conducted by an American psychologist in 1950. His Muslim respondents—who were from towns in north and west India—were beset by fear and suspicion. "We are regarded as Pakistani spies," said one. "It is dangerous to live in a Hindu locality because they may abduct and rape our women," said a second. "Hindus charge heavy black market prices for goods they sell to Muslims," said a third.[4]

III

Among those who did not wholly trust the Muslims was Vallabhbhai Patel, home minister of India. Patel remembered that the majority of Muslims had voted for the Muslim League in 1946, even in areas that would not form part of Pakistan. After the two states were created he remained suspicious of those who had stayed behind. In a speech at Lucknow in Uttar Pradesh (UP) in early January 1948, he reminded his audience that "the foundation of the two-nation theory was laid" there. It was the intellectuals of Uttar Pradesh who had claimed that "Muslims were a separate nation." Now, for those who had chosen not to go to Pakistan, it was not enough to give "mere declarations of loyalty to the Indian Union": they "must give *practical proof* of their declarations."[5]

Later that year, the secretary of Patel's Home Ministry wrote to the secretaries of all other departments, drawing their attention

> to one aspect of security which has assumed urgency and importance in the present context of relations with Pakistan. There is growing evidence that a section of Muslims in India is out of sympathy with the Government of India particularly because of its policy regarding Kashmir and Hyderabad, and is actively sympathetic to Pakistan. Such Government servants are likely to be useful channels of information and would be particularly susceptible to the influence of their relatives.
>
> It is probable that among Muslim employees of Government there are some who belong to these categories. It is obvious that they constitute a dangerous element in the fabric of administration; and it is essential that they should not be entrusted with any confidential or secret work or allowed to hold key posts. For this purpose I would request you to prepare lists of Muslim employees in your Ministry and in the offices under your control, whose loyalty to the Dominion of India is suspected or who are likely to constitute a threat to security. These lists should be carefully prepared and scrutinised by the Heads of Departments or other higher authority, and should be used for the specific purposes of excluding persons from holding key posts or handling confidential or secret work.
>
> I need scarcely add that I am sure you will see that there is no witch hunting; and that only genuine cases are included in the lists. Those who are loyal and whose work is satisfactory should of course be given every cause to feel that their claims are no less than those of men belonging to the majority community.[6]

This was an extraordinary letter, which set off, if not a witch-hunt, an energetic attempt to seek out traces of disloyalty among the Muslim employees of the government of India. Consider the Archaeological

Survey of India (ASI), which had numerous Muslim employees, en-trusted with the upkeep of the great buildings of medieval India. When this letter was passed on to him by the education secretary, the ASI's director general wrote to his "circle heads" asking them to furnish lists of Muslim employees: those loyal to the Dominion of India and those "likely to constitute a danger to security." The "circle heads" then commenced secret investigations among their staff members, the re-sults of which were communicated back to headquarters. Half a cen-tury later, their reports make for interesting and in some cases chilling reading.

Several heads wrote back saying that they did not personally distrust any of their employees. However, they were pressured to transfer those likely to be in a vulnerable position. The major of an infantry unit in Bijapur had advised the ASI that the custodian of the Gol Gumbuz was "not considered reliable"; he, apparently, had relatives in Hyderabad, a state that was refusing to join the Indian Union. The custodian was then transferred to the Kanheri caves in Bombay.

The most detailed report came from the superintendent of the Northern Circle, which had its headquarters in Agra and had within its purview the Taj Mahal and Fatehpur Sikri. He listed twenty-eight em-ployees whose relatives had migrated to Pakistan. Of these, he iden-tified five "as persons whose loyalty to the dominion of India may not be above suspicion," who "may constitute a danger to security if they get a favourable opportunity." One was a booking clerk in Agra Fort, with a brother, son, and mother in Hyderabad (Sindh); a second was a watchman at the Taj Mahal with a wife in Karachi. Another watchman at the Taj Mahal had two sons and a daugher in Karachi. The superin-tendent listed seven more employees who "do not seem mischievous by nature, but may prove a useful channel for communicating information under the influence of their relations in Pakistan."

On 20 October, the home secretary sent a follow-up letter, targeting officials who had close relatives in Pakistan. Now that several months had passed since partition, he said, "there was no longer any reason [for] Gov-ernment servants to keep their families in Pakistan. On the contrary, having regard to the strained relations between the two Dominions that would be *prima facie* evidence of disloyalty to the Dominion of India." Employees who had their familes in Pakistan would have to bring them back within a month. The Home Ministry asked for lists of delinquents; it would then decide, case by case, whether "the interests of the country" required disciplinary action against them.

Once more, the home secretary's letter was passed on by the director general of the ASI to all his circle heads. Once more, the most detailed report came from the superintendent of the Agra Circle, who did seem to regard this, with some relish, as a sort of witch-hunt. His ire was reserved particularly for the *khadims*, or hereditary watchmen, of the Taj Mahal, eighteen in all, whose posts had been created by Emperor Shah Jahan in the seventeenth century, and later confirmed by the British. In the eyes of the superintendent they all seemed to be enemy agents, "unwilling to tell the whole truth about themselves." At least six still had families in Pakistan. One *khadim* had stayed too long with his relatives across the border; he had been suspended, and was ordered to "hand over both summer and winter liveries and all other Government articles in his possession." The superintendent wanted to suspend a second *khadim*, whom he suspected of planning to sell his property in Agra before migrating "to Pakistan surreptitiously." This official had also targeted a third man, who "appears to have made efforts though not energetic enough to bring back the members of his family to India."

Agra was in UP, whose Muslims were deeply divided. The Muslims of the Punjab had migrated en masse across the border. From Bombay and the south, many intellectuals had voluntarily migrated to Pakistan, but the working-class Muslims had stayed behind. Pakistan was too far and too alien for them to consider making a new life in a new place. However, the Muslims of Uttar Pradesh spoke Urdu—the official language of Pakistan—and also lived close enough to be able to catch a train and go there. Many went; but many others stayed where they were.

Almost every Muslim family in the UP was divided, and the employees of the ASI were no exception. The superintendent of the Agra Circle, however, had no sympathy for employees with kin in what he considered "enemy" territory. Bring them back, he told his subordinates, or face the consequences. A *khadim* named Shamsuddin had aroused his boss's suspicion by selling his house when his entire family was in Pakistan. In a somewhat pathetic petition dated 8 December 1948, Shamsuddin said that he had "not the least idea of ever going to Pakistan." There were four reasons why he had disposed of his house: (1) to pay back a debt he owed his relatives; (2) "my daughters are to be married, and I have to invest money in this peon's duty of mine"; (3) the refugee tenants who had been allotted his house were misusing it, and it was best to sell the house before the condition deteriorated further; (4) "I have to make arrangements for the last ceremonies of my life as my sons have deserted me."

The superintendent was not convinced, demanding more positive proof of Shamsuddin's loyalty to the Union of India. A note of 13 June 1949 tells us that the *khadim* had travelled to Pakistan and brought back with him his two unmarried daughters, and two grandchildren of a deceased daughter "over whom he could exercise control."[7]

Were the records of the government of India for those years ever to be thrown open, one might find that such loyalty oaths, extracted under pressure by senior officials, were very nearly ubiquitous. One scholar has recently found a statement issued in 1951 by Muslim pastoralists of Kachchh, the semi-arid part of Gujarat state that bordered the Sindh province in Pakistan. This assured the chief commissioner that "we are loyal to the Government of India, and if [the] Pakistan government attacks the Indian government, we will sacrifice our lives for the security of India."[8]

IV

It is not clear whether the prime minister approved of the attempts to ascertain the loyalty of certain select employees of the government of India. But we do know that his view of the Muslim situation was somewhat different from that of his deputy. As he wrote to Patel, he deplored the "constant cry for retaliation and of vicarious punishment of the Muslims of India, because the Pakistanis punish Hindus. That argument does not appeal to me in the slightest. I am sure that this policy of retaliation and vicarious punishment will ruin India as well as Pakistan."[9] Whereas the home minister demanded that the Muslims prove their loyalty, the prime minister placed the onus on the Indian state, which had a constitutional obligation to make all its citizens, especially the Muslims, feel secure.

Nehru expressed these views to Patel,[10] and in a series of letters he wrote to the chief ministers of the different provinces. Three months after partition, he reminded them that "we have a Muslim minority who are so large in numbers that they cannot, even if they want, go anywhere else. That is a basic fact about which there can be no argument. Whatever the provocation from Pakistan and whatever the indignities and horrors inflicted on non-Muslims there, we have got to deal with this minority in a civilized manner. We must give them security and the rights of citizens in a democratic State. If we fail to do so, we shall have a festering sore which will eventually poison the whole body politic and probably destroy it." Later in the same letter, he drew attention to "the paramount importance of preserving the public services from the virus of communal politics."[11]

This was a subject to which Nehru necessarily had to return. One provocation was quarrels about property, for in some places Muslims were being asked by over-energetic officers to give up their homes in favour of Hindu and Sikh refugees. The prime minister used the anniversary of Gandhi's birth to warn against "creating an atmosphere of uncertainty and lack of security in the minds of large numbers of our Muslim fellow-countrymen." That would have "far-reaching consequences not only in India but also in Kashmir. It affects our reputation abroad. A few houses or shops attached or taken possession of do not make very much difference. But, if wrongly done, they do affect our reputation and thus injure us."

The prime minister acknowledged that "Pakistan is pursuing a policy of utter callousness in this matter." However, he insisted that "we cannot copy the methods or the ideals of Pakistan. They have declared themselves openly to be an Islamic State believing in the two-nation theory. We reject the theory and call ourselves a secular State giving full protection to all religions. We have to live up to our ideals and declarations. More especially on this day, Gandhi Jayanti, it is for us to remember what Gandhiji taught us and what he died for."[12]

Nehru had made communal organizations his principal target during the election campaign of 1951–1952. That election was fought and won on the principle of not making India a "Hindu Pakistan." However, Nehru continued to worry about the rights of Indians whose culture and faith set them apart from the majority. A particular concern was the very low proportion of Muslims in positions of authority. There were hardly any Muslim officers left in the Defence Services, and not very many in the Secretariat. This situation, he sensed, was the consequence of a failure in creating a proper "sense of partnership in every group and individual in the country, a sense of being a full sharer in the benefits and opportunities that are offered." If India was to be "a secular, stable and strong state," he told his chief ministers, then "our first consideration must be to give *absolute fair play* to our minorities, and thus to make them feel *completely at home* in India."[13]

V

The acknowledged political leader of the Muslims left behind in the Indian Union was Maulana Abul Kalam Azad. Unlike his great rival Mohammed Ali Jinnah, Azad believed that non-Hindus could live with peace and honour in a united India. In Nehru's characteristically eloquent formulation, Maulana Azad was "a peculiar and very special representative in a high degree of that great composite culture which has gradually grown in India." He embodied that "synthesis of various cultures which have come one after another to India, rivers that have flowed in and lost themselves in the ocean of Indian life."[14]

Azad was deeply wounded by partition. Seeing it as the failure of his life's mission, he retreated from party politics. (In any case his orientation was always more that of the scholar than of the mass leader.) He served as education minister in the Union cabinet, and in that capacity helped promote new academies for nurturing Indian literature, dance, music, and art. His age and temperament, however, confined him, for the most part, to Delhi.

A younger congressman who sought a more active political role was Saif Tyabji, scion of a famous nationalist family. Grandson of an early president of the Congress, and himself an engineer educated at Cambridge, Tyabji was well placed to be a modernist bridge between the Congress and the Muslim masses. In 1955 he wrote a series of essays in the influential Urdu newspaper *Inqilab*; these were later translated into English and published under the title *The Future of Muslims in India*. In the elections of 1952, Muslims had voted in large numbers for the Congress, a party which, under Nehru's leadership, they felt they could trust more than its rivals.[15] Tyabji, however, felt that the Muslims should do more than vote for India's dominant party—they should join it, and influence its policies.

Saif Tyabji pointed out that the Congress was a democratic institution, with its national council made up of elected representatives sent from the states, these in turn chosen from district and *taluk* committees. All it cost to become a member of the Congress was a subscription fee of four annas (a quarter of a rupee). Spread out across India, the Muslims could enrol in numbers in all the districts, and thus influence the selection of Congress leaders at the higher levels of the organization. Such was Tyabji's political strategy, but he also urged his co-religionists to engage more fully in the cultural life of the country. As a "patriotic Indian," he wished that the "new Indian Culture" that was arising would "be as rich and varied and vigorous as possible, and this can only be so if it draws its nourishment from all possible sources." Like other Indians, Muslims had to "take an active part in its formation." But "if the Muslims sit back with folded arms, we can rest assured that the new

Indian Culture will have little to do with the achievements in this country between the 11th century and the coming of the British. By this all Indians will suffer, but the responsibility for the loss will lie heavily on those Indians who are Muslims."

Among Tyabji's other suggestions was that Muslims ask for technical and commercial education, rather than merely study the humanities and join the ranks of the educated unemployed. Even as regarded humanistic learning, he deplored the attempts to "keep our Islamic culture . . . in a state of fossilized purity." Rather than mourn the decline of their language, Urdu, the Muslims should recognize that Hindi in the Devanagari script was here to stay. Urdu would be made more contemporary by making its literature available in Devanagari, and by suggesting appropriate words and idioms to enrich the new, emerging modern Hindi.[16]

Whereas Maulana Azad and Saif Tyabji, for example, sought to make Muslims into congressmen, there were others who argued that the community could better represent itself through its own organizations. In October 1953, a group of intellectuals and professionals met in Aligarh, to discuss founding a political party that would "protect the minority rights of Muslims, and to enable them to lead an honourable life in this country." Among their concerns were the low proportion of Muslims in the legislatures, and in the higher civil service.[17] Presiding over this convention was a former mayor of Calcutta, who claimed that if present trends continued, the future held only "economic paralysis, cultural death or disintegration and political helotage for Muslims."[18] Six months later, in a speech at the Jama Masjid in Delhi, the secretary of the UP Jamiat attacked the government of India as anti-democratic and pro-Hindu. "It is high time," he said, "for Muslims of India to unite and organise themselves under one leadership to face the eventualities in future."[19]

Meanwhile, in southern India specific steps were being taken in this regard. In September 1951 the Indian Union Muslim League (IUML) came into being in Madras, both its name and its charter distinguishing it from the pre-partition party some might think it resembled. It sought to "secure, protect, and maintain" the religious, cultural, economic, and other "legitimate rights and interests of the Muslims and other minorities," but also pledged itself to uphold and defend "the independence, freedom and honour" of the Indian Union.[20] Several years later, a party was formed in Hyderabad to represent the city's Muslims—the Majlis Ittihad-ul-Musilmin. The Majlis put up several candidates in the elections of 1957, but won only a single assembly seat. The IUML was more successful in its own bastion, Kerala, where it won ten seats in the midterm elections of 1960.[21]

VI

Writing in 1957, W. C. Smith observed that in the history of Islam, Indian Muslims were unique, in that they were very numerous and yet did not live in a state of their own. Unlike the Muslims of Iran, Iraq, Pakistan, or Turkey, they shared their citizenship in the new Indian republic "with an immense number of other people. They constitute the only sizable body of Muslims in the world of which this is, or ever has been true."[22]

The Muslims of India were a large minority, as well as a vulnerable one. They were under threat from Hindu communalism and from the provocation of Pakistan. The Pakistani leaders tended to deride Indian secularism, and "to presume and encourage a disloyalty of Indian Muslims to their state." Muslims were hostages to India-Pakistan relations in general, and to Pakistan's treatment of its own minorities in particular. Thus "each new Hindu discontent fleeing from East Pakistan, and each new border incident or exacerbation of canal-water dispute or refugee-property question, [has] had repercussions on Muslim life within India."[23]

Another problem, also linked to partition, was the lack of a credible middle class. At or shortly after partition, large numbers of Muslim civil servants, lawyers, scholars, doctors, and entrepreneurs migrated to the new Islamic state, there to carve out careers unimpeded by competition from Hindus. The Muslims who remained in India were the working poor—the peasants, labourers, and artisans who were now seriously in want of an enlightened and liberal leadership. As a perceptive British official wrote, it was "one of the curses of Partition" in Bengal that the Muslim officers had all opted for Pakistan, so that "the Muslim minorities in West Bengal will be without representation in the services or anywhere else where they could look for help or protection."[24] A partial exception was Kashmir, where under Sheikh Abdullah's regime between 1947 and 1953 Muslims were encouraged to own land, take to the professions, and above all educate themselves. Among the more far-sighted reforms was the creation of schools and colleges for girls, with the Women's College in Srinagar justly winning a countrywide reputation for excellence.[25] Elsewhere, Muslims continued to labour in menial jobs while being under-represented in education, the professions, the legislatures, and the administration.[26]

On the other side, there was the effort of the Indian political leadership to create a secular state, and to instil a feeling of belonging among minorities. Nehru was the key figure here, but he was aided by other congressmen brought up in the school of Gandhi. When street clashes threatened to escalate into a riot in Ahmedabad in 1956, the chief minister, Morarji Desai, went on an indefinite fast to restore peace.[27] Such acts were prompted in part by genuine belief, and in part by diplomatic exigencies—the need to put one's best foot forward while making the case for Kashmir. Attacks on Muslims would make India's claim for the Valley more fragile.[28] Still, it was "no small matter that the Hindu leaders of the nation, in the name of secularism and humanity, restrained the natural and potentially ferocious impetus of the Hindu majority to wreak vengeance on the Muslim group."[29]

Some observers, immediately after partition, had feared a conflagration that would destroy the Muslim minority in India. Instead, as Mushirul Hasan has noted, "the communal temperature in the 1950s remained relatively low. There was a lull after a violent storm, a clear and downward trend in communal incidents."[30] There was suspicion; there was tension; there were sporadic incidents of violence—but there were no riots of the scale witnessed during the 1920s, 1930s, or 1940s. The conflicts of the 1950s were rooted in language, ethnicity, class, and caste, rather than in religion.

The lull was broken by the Jabalpur riots of early 1961, in which some fifty Indians, mostly Muslims, lost their lives. But this was a minor affray in comparison with what happened in the winter of 1963–1964. Then, the theft of the Prophet's hair from the Hazratbal mosque in Srinagar prompted a series of attacks on Hindus in distant East Pakistan. Thousands of refugees fled into India, their stories leading to a rise in the communal temperature and to retributory violence against Muslims. In and around Calcutta 400 people died in religious rioting, 300 of them Muslims. Some of the violence was motivated by speculators seizing the chance to obliterate squatter colonies and develop them for sale. There was also serious rioting in the steel towns of Jamshedpur and Rourkela, in which perhaps as many as 1,000 people died, most of them Muslims.[31]

By this time partition was almost two decades in the past, yet its residue remained. As a Muslim leader in Madras bitterly remarked, the violence of 1963–1964 reinforced the "fear that anything happening in

Pakistan will have its repercussions on Muslims in India, particularly when exaggerated reports appear in the Indian Press, and people and parties inimical to Muslims are ready to seize the opportunity."[32]

VII

Like the Muslims, the untouchables were spread all across India. Like them, they were poor, stigmatized, and often at the receiving end of upper-caste violence. The untouchables worked in the villages, in the lowliest professions, as farm servants, agricultural labourers, cobblers, and scavengers. According to Hindu orthodoxy their touch would defile the upper castes, and in some regions their very sight too. They were denied access to land, and to water sources; even their homes were set apart from the main village.

Under British rule, opportunities had arisen for some untouchables to escape the tyranny of the village. These gained employment in the army, or worked in factories and urban settlements. Here too they were usually assigned the most menial as well as the most degrading jobs—scavenging, for example.

Gandhi had redesignated the untouchables as Harijans, "children of God." The constitution of India abolished untouchability, and listed the erstwhile untouchable communities in a separate schedule—hence their new collective name, Scheduled Castes. However, village ethnographics of the 1950s confirmed that the practice of untouchability continued as before. The Scheduled Castes still owned little or no land, and were still subject to social and in some cases sexual abuse. But these ethnographies also revealed that at the bottom things were changing, albeit slowly. In some areas the low castes were refusing to perform tasks that they considered defiling. No longer would they carry loads free, or submissively allow upper-caste males to violate their women. More daringly, they were beginning to ask for higher wages and for land to cultivate, sometimes under the aegis of communist activists.[33]

In the cities, lower-caste assertiveness took a more organized form. Under the encouragement of the Communist Party of India (CPI), the municipal sweepers of Delhi—who belonged to the Balmiki caste—formed a union of their own. In October 1953 this union presented a charter of eleven demands to the Municipal Corporation, focusing on better pay and work conditions. The sweepers held processions and public meetings, and marched to the town hall in a show of strength. There were also a series of fasts, and at least one major confrontation with the police. The historian of these protests notes that they were "not just about wages, but also about dignity and the value of the labour of the Balmikis."[34]

VIII

The burgeoning genre of autobiographies of untouchables also shows that the 1950s were a time of flux. Caste prejudice and caste discrimination were rampant, but no longer were they accepted so willingly. There was an incipient stirring, manifested in social protest and aided by the new avenues of social mobility.[35]

The first such avenue was education. After independence there was a great expansion of school and college education. By law, a certain portion of the places in educational institutions were reserved for the Scheduled Castes. By policy, various state governments endowed scholarships for children from disadvantaged homes. When they could, these families took advantage of the opportunity, and so an entire generation of first-generation learners came into being. According to one estimate, while the school population doubled in the first decade of independence, the number of former untouchables in schools swelled eightfold or tenfold. There were also many more Scheduled Caste students at universities than ever before.[36]

A second avenue was government employment. By law, 15% of all jobs in state and state-aided institutions were reserved for the Scheduled Castes. Again, there was a massive expansion after 1947, with new positions available in the Secretariat and in government-run schools, hospitals, factories, and infrastructure projects. Although exact figures are hard to obtain, it is likely that several million jobs were created for Scheduled Castes in the state sector in the first two decades after independence. These were permanent positions, to be retained until retirement, and with pension and health benefits. In theory, such reserved positions existed at all levels of government; in practice, those at the lower levels tended to be filled first and fastest. As late as 1966, while only 1.77% of senior administrative posts were occupied by Indians of low-caste origin, 8.86% of clerical jobs were, and as many as 17.94% of posts of peons and attendants.[37]

There was also reservation in Parliament and in state assemblies, where 15% of all seats were filled by Scheduled Caste candidates. Besides, universal franchise meant that they could influence the outcome of elections in the "unreserved" category as well. In many places, Scheduled Castes were quick to seize the opportunities the vote presented to them.

As one low-caste politician in Agra observed, his constituents "may not understand the intricacies of politics," but they did "understand the power of the vote and want to use it."[38] And they understood it in all contexts—national, provincial, and local. By the early 1950s, cases were reported of Scheduled Castes forging alliances to prevent upper-caste landlords from winning elections to village panchayats (councils).[39] The vote was soon perceived as a bargaining tool; for instance, in a UP village, the shoemakers told an upper-caste candidate that they would support him if he agreed to shift the yard for the disposal of dead animals from their compound to a site outside the village.[40]

For a fair number of Scheduled Castes, affirmative action did bring genuine benefits. Now, children of farm labourers could (and did) become members of Parliament. Those who joined the government as lowly "Class IV" employees could see their children become members of the elite Indian Administrative Service. But affirmative action also brought a new kind of stigma. Intended to end caste discrimination, it fixed the beneficiaries ever more firmly in their own, original caste. Suspicion and resentment arose among the upper castes; and there was sometimes a tendency, among the beneficiaries, to look down on, or even forget, their fellows. As one scholar somewhat cynically wrote, reservation had created "a mass of self-engrossed people who are quickly and easily satisfied with the small gains they can win for themselves."[41]

A final avenue of mobility was economic development in general. Industrialization and urbanization meant new opportunities away from the village, even if—as in the state sector—the Scheduled Castes came to occupy only the less skilled and less lucrative positions. Living away from home helped expand the mind, as in the case of a farm labourer from UP who became a factory worker in Bombay and learned to love the city's museums, especially its collections of Gandhara art.[42] And sometimes there were economic gains to be made. Consider the Jatavs of Agra, a caste of cobblers and shoemakers whose world changed with the growth of a market for their products in the Middle East and the Soviet Union. The Jatavs became an "urban yeomanry," now able to build and own their own houses. While many continued as self-employed shoemakers, some Jatavs were able to start factories of their own, where the wages paid to their workers were considerably higher than what they themselves had once hoped to earn. In 1960 a master craftsman took home about 250 rupees a month, a factory worker about 100—and even the lesser figure was many times what an unskilled labourer earned. Although the distribution of gains was by no means even, the market had helped enhance the Jatavs' economic as well as social status. The situation c. 1960 was "a far cry from the pre-1900 days, when most Jatavs were little more than labourers and city servants."[43]

IX

Like the Muslims, the Scheduled Castes formed an important constituency for the Congress. They too tended to trust the party of Mahatma Gandhi more than they trusted its rivals. In the elections of 1957, for example, the Congress won sixty-four of the seventy-six seats reserved for Scheduled Castes in Parliament, and as many as 361 of the 469 seats reserved for them in the legislative assemblies.

When the seats reserved for Scheduled Tribe members were added, nearly one in four members of Parliament came from a "disprivileged" background. Yet the ministers in Jawaharlal Nehru's cabinet were overwhelmingly upper-caste. This worried Nehru: "one of my greatest difficulties," he told a senior colleague, "is to find suitable non-Brahmins." Nehru asked the colleague to suggest candidates, but then found one himself: Mrs. Chandrasekhar from Madras, an educated Scheduled Caste whom he inducted as deputy minister.[44]

The ranking Scheduled Caste minister in the Indian cabinet was Jagjivan Ram from Bihar. He was born into a Chamar (cobbler) home, and he became the first such boy from his village to go to high school and from there, to the Banaras Hindu University. On graduation he joined the Gandhian movement. His steady work was rewarded after 1947 by a series of cabinet appointments. Among the ministries he ran were labour, communications, mines, and railways. Jagjivan Ram had a reputation as a first-class administrator, although he did not live the squeaky-clean life his Gandhian background perhaps demanded of him.[45]

The most charismatic Scheduled Caste leader, however, remained outside the Congress. This was B. R. Ambedkar, who had joined Nehru's cabinet as an independent and had left the government in 1951 to restart his Scheduled Caste Federation. His party fared disastrously in the elections of 1952, although Ambedkar himself was later elected to the Upper House. By now this long-time foe of Hinduism was seeking a way to leave the ancestral fold. He had contemplated converting to Sikhism, then to Islam, then to Christianity. He finally settled on Buddhism, a faith of Indian origin that seemed best suited to his own rationalist and egalitarian temperament.

After he left the cabinet, Ambedkar immersed himself in literature about the Buddha. He became a member of the Mahabodhi Society, and travelled through the Buddhist countries of South-east Asia. At a public meeting in Bombay in May 1956, Ambedkar announced that he would convert to Buddhism before the end of the year. His mammoth study, *The Buddha and His Dhamma*, was already in press. Ambedkar considered having the conversion ceremony in Bombay—where the publicity would be immense—or in the ancient Buddhist site of Sarnath. He eventually chose Nagpur, a city in the centre of India where he had a large and de-voted following. Many joined him in embracing Buddhism, in a colourful and well-attended ceremony that took place on 15 October 1956. Six weeks later Ambedkar died suddenly. He was cremated in Bombay, with an icon of the Buddha placed under his head. A million people partici-pated in the funeral procession.[46]

Shortly before he died Ambedkar had decided to start a new party, called the Republican Party of India. This formally came into being in 1957. Its leaders and members were, like Ambedkar himself, from the Mahar caste. It was also mostly Mahars who had followed their leader into Buddhism. Ambedkar was a revered figure among the Mahars of the Nagpur area. In his lifetime they celebrated his birthday with gusto, orga-nizing processions in which his photograph was held aloft. When he came to town to speak, the factory workers would crowd in to hear him; even the "women went to these parades as to a wedding." Under his inspiration the Mahars began troupes that performed plays parodying Hindu ritual and the behaviour of the upper castes. They also sang songs in his honour: "From the moment that the glance of Bhim[rao Ambedkar] fell upon the poor," began one song, "From that day our strength grew."[47]

But it was not merely in Mahar strongholds that Ambedkar was re-spected. All across northern India, he was admired for his scholarship—he had doctoral degrees from Columbia and London universities—and for his political achievements, notably his drafting of the constitution of India. For Scheduled Castes who had some learning themselves—those who had been to high school or travelled outside their village—Ambedkar was both exemplar and icon, a man who had breached the upper-caste citadel and encouraged his fellows to do likewise.

Ambedkar's slogan for his followers was "Educate, agitate, orga-nize." He set up a People's Education Society that ran schools and at least two good colleges. Scheduled Castes who went to these or other schools came invariably to regard Ambedkar as their mentor. Among the

Scheduled Caste intelligentsia, books or pamphlets by Ambedkar became required reading, lovingly passed on from hand to hand.[48] Thus the son of a dock worker, sent by government scholarship to Siddharth College in Bombay, began contributing to magazines and participating in debates—where "the topic of all these writings and speeches was always Babasaheb [Ambedkar] and his Dalit movement."[49]

The presence of B. R. Ambedkar underlines a profound difference between the Scheduled Castes and the other minority with whom I have here compared them. For the Muslims had no seats reserved for them in the Secretariat or in Parliament. Nor, in independent India, did they have a leader of Ambedkar's stature to inspire and move them while he was alive or after he was gone.

X

In March 1949, a group of Scheduled Castes from the villages around Delhi walked to Mahatma Gandhi's memorial in the city. They had been thrown out of their homes by Jat landowners, who were angered that these previously bonded servants had the effrontery to take part in local elections and graze their cattle in the village commons. In the heart of the capital, these outcastes began a hunger strike. By sitting on a memorial to the father of the nation, and by using the methods of protest developed by him, they attracted wide attention, including solicitous visits by prominent Gandhians and cabinet ministers.[50]

We turn next to a case from urban India: a newly elected Scheduled Caste member of Parliament who applied to join the bar association in his hometown, Sitapur. His application was kept pending for four months, after which he was told that he could join but could not use the washroom, and he could be served only by a Muslim attendant. The legislator brought the matter to the attention of the prime minister, who intervened to have him admitted without any conditions.[51]

Elsewhere, Scheduled Castes who asserted themselves were not so fortunate. The sociologist N. D. Kamble collected hundreds of examples of "atrocities" committed against Scheduled Castes in independent India. Here are a few choice—if that is the word—instances from Kamble's research:

April 1951: A labour camp in Matunga, Bombay.
A group of factory workers stage a play on Ambedkar's birthday.

Upper-caste young men break up the performance, assault the actors, and damage the stage.

June 1951: A village in Himachal Pradesh.
A conference of Scheduled Castes (SCs) is attacked by Rajput land-lords. The SCs are beaten up with sticks: their leaders are tied up with ropes and confined to a cattle pound.

July 1951: A rural school in the Jalgaon district of Bombay state.
A Brahman teacher abuses Ambedkar for introducing the Hindu Code Bill in Parliament. A SC boy protests, whereupon he is beaten and re-moved from the school.

June 1952: A village in the Madurai district of Madras state.
A SC youth asks for tea in a glass at a local shop. Tradition entitles him only to a disposable coconut shell. When he persists, he is kicked and hit on the head by caste Hindus.

June 1957: A village in the Parbani district of Madhya Bharat.
Newly converted Buddhists refuse to flay carcasses of dead cattle. They are boycotted by the Hindu landlords, denied other work, and threatened with physical reprisals.

May 1959: A village in the Ahmednagar district of Bombay state.
A Buddhist marriage party is not allowed to enter the hamlet through the village gates. When members of the wedding party persist, caste Hindus attack them with stones and swords.

October 1960: A village in the Aurangabad District of Maharashtra.
Caste Hindus enter the SC hamlet and break a statue of the Buddha into tiny pieces.[52]

What these cases—and the many more like them—reveal is a system that was undergoing profound churning. All across India, the winds of democratic politics had made the Scheduled Castes more ready to ask for their rights. Aided by reservation in schools, offices, factories, and legislatures; inspired by the example of their leader, B. R. Ambedkar; and encouraged by the constitutional provisions in favour of social equality, many among them were inclined to abandon the old idiom of deference in favour of the more rocky path of defiance. This in turn pro-voked a sometimes nasty reaction from those who persisted in thinking of themselves as social superiors.

XI

In the winter of 1925–1926, the writer Aldous Huxley went on a long
trip through British India. He attended the Kanpur session of the Indian
National Congress, and heard speeches asking for freedom. Huxley had
some sympathy with these aspirations, yet worried that they represented
only the interests of the upper-caste Hindus. He wrote in a book about
his travels:

> That the lower-caste masses would suffer, at the beginning, in any
> case, from a return to Indian autonomy seems almost indubitable.
> Where the superiority of the upper castes to the lower is a matter of
> religious dogma, you can hardly expect the governing few to be par-
> ticularly careful about the rights of the many. It is even something of a
> heresy [for them] to have rights.[53]

Two decades later India became independent, and the constitution
bestowed rights of equality on all citizens, regardless of caste, creed,
age, or gender. The lower castes were in fact granted special rights, special access to schools and jobs, in compensation for the discrimination
they had suffered down the centuries. But, as a Scheduled Caste member
of the Constituent Assembly pointed out, state law was one thing and
social practice quite another. The prejudices of caste had been opposed
by reformers from Gautama Buddha to Mahatma Gandhi, yet they had
all "found it very difficult to get rid of this ghost of untouchability."
Laws had been enacted removing discrimination against untouchables—
with regard to entering temples, for example. "What is the effect of
these laws?" asked the member. He then supplied this answer:

> Not an inch of untouchability has been removed by these laws. . . . If
> at all the ghost of untouchability or the stigma of untouchability from
> India should go the minds of these crores and crores of Hindu folks
> should be changed and unless their hearts are changed, I do not hope,
> Sir, that untouchability will be removed. It is now up to the Hindu
> society not to observe untouchability in any shape or form.[54]

There was pessimism about the position of untouchables in free India, and pessimism also about the future of that other large and insecure
minority, the Muslims. Travelling through India and Pakistan in 1951,
the Aga Khan—the influential leader of the Ismaili sect—found "a hor-

rible fear" among Muslims on both sides of the border, but especially in India. He wrote to Jawaharlal Nehru of "the fear amongst Muslims which I myself share to a great extent." This was that "five or ten years hence there may be a [Hindu] Mahasabha Government who openly make the union of what is now Pakistan—both East and West—with Bharat [India] the main purpose of foreign policy and high politics." The Muslim leader thought that a Hindu chauvinist party, once in power, would use atomic explosives to divert the rivers flowing through Kashmir into Pakistan, thus bringing that state down to its knees. He drew a parallel with the situation in the Arab world, where—so he claimed—Sudan was preparing to stop the flow of the Nile into Egypt. In the Aga Khan's view, Hindu India was to Muslim Pakistan as Christian Sudan was to Muslim Egypt. As he put it, "I have felt that this atmosphere of doom prevails amongst Muslims on account of this very water question. . . . [It] is a replica of the similar fear in Egypt."[55]

This letter is notable for at least three reasons. First, it is an early illustration of the now widespread fear that Muslims were being persecuted worldwide. Second, it equates the interests of Indian Muslims with the welfare of Pakistan. Third, and perhaps most tellingly, it predicts that the Republic of India would become a Hindu state within ten years.

The Aga Khan and Aldous Huxley were right and wrong in their skepticism—right with regard to the continuing social prejudice, wrong with regard to the intentions of the top political leadership. For the "governing few" were in fact very careful of the rights of the many. Writing in 1959—more than a decade after independence—an Indian editor who was bitterly opposed to Jawaharlal Nehru was constrained to recognize Nehru's two greatest achievements: the creation of a secular state and the granting of equal rights to untouchables. Recalling the "reactionary forces which came into play after partition," the editor remarked that "had Nehru shown the slightest weakness, these forces would have turned this country into a Hindu State in which the minorities . . . could not have lived with any measure of safety or security." It was also to Nehru's "everlasting credit" that he insisted that untouchables be granted full rights, so that "in public life and in all government action, the equality of man would be scrupulously maintained in the secular state of India."[56]

To be sure, there remained a gap between public policy and popular practice. Laws promoting secularism and social equality were in force, but most Muslims and most Scheduled Castes remained poor and mar-

ginalized. The threat of violence was never far away. Still, given the
bloody birth of the nation, and the continuing provocation from Pakistan, it was no small matter that the Indian government refused to
merge faith with state. And given the resilience of social institutions in
general, and the ancient and sanctified history of this one in particular,
it was remarkable that the caste system changed as much as it did. The
progress made in abolishing untouchability or in ensuring equal rights
for all citizens was uneven, and—by the standards of understandably
impatient reformers—very slow. Yet more progress had probably been
made in the first seventeen years of Indian independence than in the previous 1,700 put together.

PART IV

THE RISE *of* POPULISM

18

WAR *and* SUCCESSION

There is no question of Nehru's attempting to create a dynasty of
his own; it would be inconsistent with his character and career.

The columnist FRANK MORAES, writing in 1960

I

JAWAHARLAL NEHRU DIED on the morning of 27 May 1964. The
news was conveyed to the world in the 2 p.m. bulletin of All India
Radio. Two hours later, the home minister, Gulzarilal Nanda, was
sworn in as acting prime minister. Almost immediately, the search began for a more permanent successor.

The central figure in the choice of a new prime minister was the Congress president, K. Kamaraj. He was born in 1903, in a low-caste family
in the Tamil country, and dropped out of school to join the national
movement. He spent nearly eight years in jail: this spread out over two
decades and six prison sentences. His status among the people was consolidated by his lifestyle—he lived austerely and never married. He
climbed steadily up the party hierarchy, and served as president of the
Tamil Nadu Congress as well as chief minister of Madras before heading the party at the national level.[1]

Kamaraj was a thickset man with a white moustache—according
to one journalist, he looked "like a cross between Sonny Liston and
the Walrus." Like the boxer (but unlike the Lewis Carroll character)
he was a man of few words. Journalists joked that his answer to all
questions put by them was one word in Tamil: *Parkalam* ("we shall see").
His reticence served him well, never better than after Nehru's death,
when he had to listen to what his party men wanted to say. From 28
May, Kamaraj began consulting with chief ministers and party bosses
(the "Syndicate," as they were called) on the best person to succeed
Nehru. An early name to consider was Morarji Desai, the outstanding administrator from Gujarat, who had made it clear that he wanted
the job.

In four days Kamaraj met a dozen chief ministers and as many as 200 members of Parliament. From these conversations it became clear that Desai would be a controversial choice: his style was too abrasive. The person most members seemed to prefer was Lal Bahadur Shastri, also a fine administrator, but one who was more accessible, and was from the Hindi heartland besides. Moreover, Nehru, in his last days, had come increasingly to rely on Shastri. These factors all weighed heavily with Kamaraj, who was concerned that the succession should signal continuity.

Desai was persuaded to withdraw his candidacy. On 31 May the Congress Working Committee approved the choice of Lal Bahadur Shastri. The next day the name was ratified by the Congress Parliamentary party, and the day following Shastri was sworn in as prime minister. Very soon the new incumbent was asserting his authority. Desai was dropped from the cabinet because he insisted on the number two position. There was a clamour to include Nehru's daughter, Indira Gandhi: Shastri complied, yet gave her an insignificant portfolio: information and broadcasting. Mrs. Gandhi, in turn, forestalled any move by Shastri to move into Teen Murti House (where Nehru had lived as prime minister) by proposing that it be made into a memorial to her father.[2]

Announcing the choice of Shastri to the press, Kamaraj had said that the undisputed rule of a great man would now be replaced by a form of collective leadership. Shastri had other ideas. An early innovation was the creation of a separate prime minister's secretariat, where carefully chosen officials would prepare papers on matters of policy. This was to fill in the gaps in the prime minister's learning—gaps larger by far than was the case with Nehru—and also to provide him with an independent, non-partisan source of advice, freeing him of excessive dependence on the cabinet.[3]

Not long before Nehru's death, the United Kingdom had its own drama, with the Conservatives deeply split on the choice of Harold Macmillan's successor. The traditionally anti-Tory paper *The Guardian* gleefully remarked that the "new Prime Minister of India, in spite of all forebodings, has been named with more dispatch, and much more dignity, than was the new Prime Minister of Britain."[4] The paper's New Delhi correspondent met Nehru's successor, whom he found "rock-sure of himself," a "very strong man indeed," who spoke in short, sharp sentences—"no words wasted."[5]

Old colonial hands were less optimistic. Nehru's death, wrote one ICS man to another, had made India's future fraught with uncertainty:

"I can't imagine S[h]astri has the stature to hold things together, and all the trouble-makers from Kashmir to Comorin will work to fish in troubled waters, to say nothing of China and Pakistan. Cyprus on a big scale? What revolting times we live in!"[6]

II

With his death, Nehru's initiative for Kashmir also died. However, on the other side of the country, moves were afoot to resolve the dispute between the Naga rebels and the government of India. Pained by a decade of bloodshed, the Baptist Church of Nagaland had formed a "peace mission" consisting of individuals trusted both by the underground and by the government of India. The three members agreed on were the chief minister of Assam, B. P. Chaliha; the widely respected Sarvodaya leader Jayaprakash Narayan; and the Anglican priest Michael Scott, who had helped secure refuge in London for the Naga leader A. Z. Phizo.

Through the summer of 1964, this peace mission travelled through the territory, meeting members of the state government and of the "Federal Republic of Nagaland." A ceasefire agreement was signed by both sides; it went into effect on 6 September, signalled by the pealing of church bells. Two weeks later the first round of talks began between the government of India and the rebels.[7]

From Kohima, Jayaprakash Narayan wrote to a friend that while the situation was still unpredictable, "the strongest desire of almost every Naga at the present time seems to be for a lasting peace. The Naga people are dreading nothing more than the resumption of hostilities." Then he added, less optimistically, "However, it has to be said that as far as the talks between the Government of India and the underground leaders are concerned, very little progress so far has been made."[8]

The printed records of the talks between the government and the rebels do reveal a fundamental incompatibility of positions. The NNC leader, Isak Swu, began by saying that "today we are here as two nations—Nagas and Indians, side by side." The foreign secretary, Y. D. Gundevia, answered that "we are not living as two nations side by side. History tells us that Nagaland was a part and parcel of India." Between these two opposed positions, B. P. Chaliha and Jayaprakash Narayan tried valiantly to find a meeting ground. Chaliha praised the Nagas as "a people of rare and high qualities" and hoped that "both parties will find a way to remove the gulf" between them. Narayan argued that "compromise is possible because we think that both sides have part of the truth. If one were 100% right, or 100% wrong, there could be no question of compromise."[9]

The demand for Naga independence challenged the idea of India. Another, somewhat different challenge was presented when China tested a nuclear device in October 1964. Immediately, there were calls for India to develop an atom bomb of its own. On 24 October, the director of the Atomic Energy Commission, Dr. Homi J. Bhabha, gave a talk on All India Radio about the nuclear question. He spoke of a need for universal nuclear disarmanent, yet hinted that, pending this eventuality, India might develop a nuclear deterrent of its own. There was no means of successfully stopping a nuclear thrust in mid-flight, said Dr. Bhabha, adding, "The only defence against such an attack appears to be a capability and threat of retaliation." Further, "atomic weapons give a State possessing them in adequate numbers a deterrent power against attack from a much stronger State." Later in his talk, Dr. Bhabha examined the cost of constructing an atomic stockpile. By his calculations, fifty bombs would cost about 100 million rupees, an expenditure that was "small compared with the military budgets of many countries."[10]

The scientist's talk was grist to the mill of those politicians—mostly from the Jana Sangh—who had long advocated that India test its own atom bombs. The member of Parliament from Dewas, Hukum Chandra Kachwai, moved a resolution in the Lok Sabha to this effect. In an eloquent speech, he identified China as India's main *dushman* (enemy) and said, "Whatever weapons the enemy possesses, we must possess them too." Invoking memories of the war of 1962, he said that the nation should not rest until it had reclaimed every inch of land lost to or stolen by China. The possession of an atomic stockpile would, he argued, also increase India's prestige in the world.

A lively debate ensued, with some members endorsing Kachwai and others opposing him because of India's reputation as a force for peace. The prime minister then claimed that the promoters of the bomb had misread Dr. Bhabha's intentions. Bhabha was calling for disarmanent, and the production costs referred to the United States, whose developed atomic infrastructure made the additional bombs possible at little expense. In India, the costs would be prohibitive, said Shastri; in any case, to manufacture these deadly weapons would be to depart from the tradition of Gandhi and Nehru. Notably, the prime minister spoke not in narrow nationalistic terms but from the perspective of the human race. These bombs, he said, were a threat to the survival of the world, an affront to humanity (*manushyata*) as a whole.

Shastri's speech was somewhat defensive, and certainly less stirring than that of the chief speaker on the other side. But the large Congress majority in the House ensured that the resolution asking India to take the nuclear route was comfortably defeated.[11]

III

India's Republic Day, 26 January, is celebrated annually in New Delhi by a government-sponsored march down Rajpath (formerly Kingsway), with gaily decorated floats representing the different states competing for attention with tanks and mounted submarines. In 1965, Republic Day was to be more than a symbolic show of national pride—it would also be an affirmation of national unity. In 1949, the Constituent Assembly had chosen Hindi as the official language of the Union of India. The constitution, which ratified this, went into effect on 26 January 1950. However, there would be a fifteen-year grace period when English was to be used along with Hindi in communication between the Centre and the states. Now, this period was ending; henceforth, only Hindi would prevail.

Southern politicians had long been worried about the change. In 1956, the Academy of Tamil Culture passed a resolution urging that "English should continue to be the official language of the Union and the language for communication between the Union and the State Governments and between one State Government and another." The signatories included C. N. Annadurai, E. V. Ramaswami "Periyar," and C. Rajagopalachari. The campaign was organized chiefly by the Dravida Munnetra Kazhagam (DMK), which held many protest meetings against the imposition of Hindi.[12]

In the aftermath of the war with China the DMK had dropped its secessionism. It no longer wanted a separate country; but it did want to protect the culture and language of the Tamil people. The DMK's acknowledged leader was C. N. Annadurai, known as Anna ("elder brother"). He was a brilliant orator who had done much to build his party into a credible force in the state. In Anna's opinion Hindi was merely a regional language like any other. It had no "special merit"; in fact, it was less developed than other Indian tongues, less suited to a time of rapid advances in science and technology. To the argument that more Indians spoke Hindi than any other language, Anna sarcastically answered, "If we had to accept the principle of numerical superiority while selecting our national bird, the choice would have fallen not on the peacock but on the common crow."[13]

Jawaharlal Nehru had been sensitive to the sentiments of the south, sentiments shared by the east and north-east. In 1963, he piloted an Official Languages Act, which provided that from 1965 English "may" still be used along with Hindi in official communication. That caveat proved problematic; for while Nehru explained that "may" meant "shall," other congressmen thought it actually meant "may not."[14]

As 26 January 1965 approached, the opponents of Hindi geared up for action. Ten days before Republic Day, Annadurai wrote to Shastri, saying that his party would observe the day of the changeover as a "day of mourning."But, interestingly, he added a request to postpone the day of imposition by a week. Then the DMK could enthusiastically join the rest of the nation in celebrating Republic Day.

Shastri and his government stood by the decision to make Hindi official on 26 January. In response, the DMK began a statewide campaign of protest. In numerous villages the Hindi demoness was burned in effigy. Hindi books and the relevant pages of the constitution were also burned. In railroad stations and post offices, Hindi signs were removed or blackened over. In towns across the state, there were fierce and sometimes deadly battles between the police and angry students.[15]

The protests were usually collective: strikes and processions; bandhs, hartals, and dharnas. Headlines in the newspaper *The Hindu* tell part of the story:

TOTAL HARTAL IN COIMBATORE

ADVOCATES ABSTAIN FROM WORK

STUDENTS FAST IN BATCHES

PEACEFUL STRIKE IN MADURAI

LATHI-CHARGE IN VILLUPURAM

TEAR-GAS USED IN UTHAMAPALYAM

One form of protest was individual, and disturbingly so: the taking of one's life. On Republic Day, two men set themselves on fire in Madras. One left a letter saying he wanted to sacrifice himself at the altar of Tamil. Three days later, a twenty-year-old man in Tiruchi killed himself by swallowing insecticide. He too left a note saying that his suicide was in the cause of Tamil. These "martydoms" set off dozens more strikes and boycotts.

There is a vivid account of the revolt by a police officer sent to quell it. When a party of constables entered the town of Tiruppur, they found that the rioting was over but crowds still hung around curious or sullen. Police lorries and jeeps lay burnt and smouldering on the streets and in the taluk office compound. The police station was . . . a shambles, a spare transmitter overturned, all the glass broken and the verandah fence torn down. Injured constables were resting inside and the Inspector was on his back with a stomach injury. Dead bodies of rioters were strewn about, one on the station steps, another on a street behind. A third, shot clean through the navel, lay on a river bank close by, an abusive crowd behind it still being held at bay by a rifle party.

The "real mistake," writes this officer, was "the failure to appreciate the depth of feeling" evoked by the imposition of Hindi. What some people in New Delhi saw as "an exhibition of mere parochial fanaticism" was in fact "a local nationalist movement."[16]

The intensity of the anti-Hindi protests alarmed the central government. Soon it became clear that the ruling Congress party was split down the middle. On the last day of January, a group of prominent congressmen met in Bangalore to issue an appeal to "the Hindi-loving people not to try to force Hindi on the people of non-Hindi areas." The hasty imposition of Hindi, they said, would imperil the unity of the country.

The signatories to this appeal included S. Nijalingappa (chief minister of Mysore), Atulya Ghosh (the boss of the Bengal Congress), Sanjiva Reddy (a senior Union minister), and K. Kamaraj (the Congress president). On the same day, they were answered by the high-ranking Congress leader Morarji Desai. Speaking to the press in Tirupati, Desai claimed that by learning Hindi the Tamil people would actually increase their influence in India as a whole. The Congress leaders in Madras, he said, should "convince the people of their mistake [in opposing Hindi] and get them around." Desai regretted that Hindi had not been made official in the 1950s, before the protests against it had crystallized. Only Hindi could be the linking language in India; the alternative, English, "is not our language." "No regional sentiments," insisted Desai, "should come in the way of this move of the Government to forge the integration of the country further."[17]

The prime minister, Lal Bahadur Shastri, was now in the hot seat. His heart was with the Hindi zealots; his head, however, urged him to listen to other voices. On 11 February, the resignation of two Union ministers from Madras forced his hand. The same evening the prime minister went on All India Radio to convey his "deep sense of distress and shock" at the "tragic events." To remove any "misapprehension" and "misunderstanding," he said he would fully honour Nehru's assurance that English would be used as long as the people wanted. Then he made four assurances of his own:

> First, every State will have complete and unfettered freedom to continue to transact its own business in the language of its own choice, which may be the regional language or English.
>
> Secondly, communications from one State to another will either be in English or will be accompanied by an authentic English translation.
>
> Thirdly, the non-Hindi States will be free to correspond with the Central Government in English and no change will be made in this arrangement without the consent of the non-Hindi States.
>
> Fourthly, in the transaction of business at the Central level English will continue to be used.

Later, Shastri added a crucial fifth assurance—that the All India Civil Services examination would continue to be conducted in English rather than (as the *Hindiwallahs* wanted) in Hindi alone.[18]

A week after the prime minister spoke on the radio, there was a long, heated discussion in Parliament on the riots in the Tamil country. Proponents of Hindi insisted that those who opposed the language were against the constitution and in effect anti-national; they also claimed that by giving in to violence the government would encourage more outbreaks of violence. Tamil members answered that they had "already sacrificed enough for the Hindi demon." They were supported by two members from Bengal—Hiren Mukherjee from the left, who accused the Hindi zealots of a "contemptuous disregard" for those who did not speak their language; and N. C. Chatterjee from the right, who pointed out that "the greatest integrating force today is the juridical and the legal unity of India," which was enabled by the fact that the Supreme Court and the high courts functioned in English. The Anglo-Indian member, Frank Anthony, deplored the "increasing intolerance, increasing obscurantism, increasing chauvinism of those who purport to speak on behalf of Hindi." J. B. Kripalani, speaking in a lighter vein, thought that the Hindi chauvinists had no hope at all. Even Indian babies, he noted, now "do not say: Amma or Appa, but mummy and papa. We talk to our dogs also in English." Kripalani remarked, "Mr. Anthony is very unnecessarily excited about the fate of his mother tongue. In England it [English] may disappear, [but] in India it will not disappear."[19]

The parallels with the language question of the 1950s are striking. Then, too, a popular social movement led the prime minister to reconsider both the stated official position and his own preferences. Nehru opposed linguistic states; Shastri believed Hindi should be the sole official language of the Indian Union. But when protest spilled out into the streets, and when protesters were willing to offer their lives—Potti Sriramulu in 1953, a dozen young Tamil men in 1965—the prime minister was forced to reconsider. In each case the rank and file of Congress seemed to side with the opposition rather than with their own government. As with Nehru, Shastri's change of heart was occasioned as much by considerations of preserving party unity as by the unity of the nation itself.

IV

From south India, let us move back to that old trouble spot in the north, Kashmir. In March 1965, Sheikh Abdullah set out on a pilgrimage to Mecca. He took the long route, via London, where one of his sons was based. The sheikh had been told by Shastri, via Sudhir Ghosh—a Rajya Sabha member of Parliament and a one-time associate of Mahatma Gandhi—that the best he could hope for was an autonomous Valley within the Indian Union. Ghosh thought the "lion of Kashmir" was coming around to the idea, if slowly. He wrote to the Quaker Horace Alexander, an old friend of India, to keep a watch on Abdullah in London; the solution being charted for Kashmir would "be ruined if, under pressure from over-zealous British newspaper men, Sheikh Abdullah makes a few unwise statements in London. . . . A few wrong remarks will give those elements in the Congress Party who are anxious to push their knives into Sheikh the necessary handle to upset the possibility of any settlement."[20]

Abdullah seems not to have said anything indiscreet in the United Kingdom. He proceeded to Mecca and stopped in Algiers on his way home. There he did something far worse than speak carelessly to a British journalist; he met with the Chinese prime minister, Chou En-lai, who also happened to be in the Algerian capital. The content of their conversations was not disclosed; but it was enough that he had supped with the enemy. It was assumed that—as in 1953, when he met with Adlai Stevenson—Sheikh Abdullah had discussed the possibility of an independent Kashmir. In 1953 it took four months for the sheikh to be jailed. Now, he was placed under arrest as he got off the plane at Palam airport in New Delhi. He was taken to a government bungalow in the capital and, a little later, transported across the country to the southern hill town of Kodaikanal. Here he was given a charming cottage, with fine views of hills not nearly as grand as those in Kashmir, but forbidden to travel outside municipal limits or meet visitors without official permission.

The news of Abdullah's arrest was greeted by loud cheers in both houses of Parliament. He was seen as having betrayed India not just by talking to a Chinese leader, but by doing so while the other foe, Pakistan, was nibbling away at the borders. For while Abdullah was on pilgrimage a conflict broke out over the Rann of Kachchh, a salt marsh claimed by both Pakistan and India. In the first week of April, troops exchanged fire in the Rann. The Pakistanis used their American tanks to shell enemy positions—successfully, for the Indians had to withdraw some forty miles to dry land. Angry telegrams were exchanged before the two sides agreed to international arbitration under British auspices.[21]

One person dismayed by the rise of jingoism was the Quaker Horace Alexander. He wrote to Indira Gandhi and received a reply putting the inflamed sentiments in perspective. "What Sheikh Sahib does not realize," said Mrs. Gandhi, "is that with the Chinese invasion and the latest moves in and by Pakistan, the position of Kashmir has completely changed." The frontiers of the state touched China and the Soviet Union as well as India and Pakistan. And "in the present world situation, an independent Kashmir would become a hot-bed of intrigue and, apart from the countries mentioned above, would also attract espionage and other activies from the USA and UK."[22]

Abdullah's arrest and the clash in Kachchh had put an idea into the head of the Pakistani president, Ayub Khan. This was to foment an insurrection in the Indian part of Kashmir, leading either to a war, ending with the state being annexed to Pakistan, or to international arbitration, with the same result. In the late summer of 1965, the Pakistani army began planning "Operation Gibraltar," named for a famous Moorish military victory in medieval Spain. Kashmiri militants were trained in the use of small arms, with their units named after legendary warriors of the Islamic past—Suleyman, Salahuddin, and so on.[23]

In the first week of August, groups of irregulars crossed the ceasefire line into Kashmir. They proceeded to blow up bridges and firebomb government installations. The intention was to create confusion, and also to create unrest. Radio Pakistan announced that a popular uprising had broken out in the Valley. In fact, the local population was mostly apathetic—some intruders were even handed over to the police.[24]

When the hoped-for rebellion did not materialize, Pakistan turned to its reserve plan, codenamed "Operation Grand Slam." Troops crossed the ceasefire line in the Jammu sector and, using heavy artillery and mortar, made swift progress. The Indians fought back and, in the Uri sector, succeeded in capturing the Haji Pir pass, a strategic point from which they could look out for infiltrators.[25]

On 1 September the Pakistani army began a major offensive in Chhamb. An infantry division with two regiments of American Patton tanks crossed the border. Catching the Indians by surprise, they occupied thirty square miles within twenty-four hours. Their aim was to capture the bridge at Akhnoor and thus to sever links between Jammu and Kashmir and the state of Punjab. The defenders now called in their air force, with some thirty aircraft raining down bombs on the enemy. The Indian Vampires were answered by Pakistani Sabre jets.

By 5 September the Indian position was getting desperate, with the Pakistanis pressing hard on Akhnoor. To relieve the pressure, New Delhi ordered the army to open a new front. On the morning of 6 September, several tank regiments, supported by infantry, crossed the international border that divided the Punjab. They were heading straight for Pakistan's first city, Lahore. Pakistani troops and tanks were hastily redeployed from the Kashmir operation. Now commenced perhaps the most bitter tank battle anywhere since the end of the Second World War. The two sides fought each other inch for inch, sometimes in barren soil, at other times in the middle of sugar cane fields. The Indians routed the Pakistanis around Asal Uttar but then, attempting to recapture Khem Karan, were mauled in turn. The Indian commander, a veteran of World War II, said that he had "never seen so many tanks destroyed, lying there in the battlefield like abandoned toys."[26]

Overhead, the airplanes screamed en route to attack the enemy's bases. A large tonnage of bombs was dropped by both sides, but—as an Indian chronicler later wrote—"luckily or unluckily some of the bombs failed to explode—they were old and had been supplied to the contending parties mostly by the same source."[27]

As the battles raged, the Chinese weighed in with words in support of the Pakistanis. On 4 September, Marshal Chen Yi, visiting Karachi, condemned "Indian imperialism for violating the Cease-Fire Line," and endorsed "the just actions taken by the Government of Pakistan to repel India's armed provocations." Three days later Peking issued a statement claiming that India was "still entrenched" in large sections of Chinese territory. The next day Chou En-lai stated that "India's acts of aggression pose a threat to peace in this part of Asia."[28]

In New Delhi, a surge of patriotism had come over the population. At the daily press briefing, newsmen would ask the government spokesman: "Has Lahore airport fallen?" "Is the radio station under our control?" Lahore never fell, although why this was so remained a matter of dispute. The Indians argued that capturing the city was never on the agenda—why get into a house-to-house operation with a hostile population? The Pakistanis claimed that the Indian chief of army staff had bragged that he would have his evening drink at the Lahore Gymkhana—but the brave defenders of the city never allowed him to.[29]

The escalation of hostilities alarmed the superpowers, and on 6 September the United Nations Security Council met to discuss the matter. The UN secretary general, U Thant, flew to the subcontinent, and after meeting leaders in both capitals got them to agree to a ceasefire. The decision was made easier by the fact that in the Punjab the two sides had fought themselves to a stalemate. On 22 September, hostilities were finally called off.

The battles took place principally in two sectors in the north-west—Kashmir and the Punjab. There were some exchanges in Sindh, but the eastern border—dividing the two halves of Bengal—stayed quiet. As is common in such cases, both sides claimed victory, exaggerating the enemy's losses and underestimating their own. In truth, the war must be declared a draw. According to a reasonably independent authority, the Pakistanis lost 3,000 to 5,000 men and about 250 tanks and fifty aircraft, whereas the casualties on the Indian side were 4,000 to 6,000 men, about 300 tanks, and fifty aircraft. With their much larger population, and bigger army, the Indians were better able to absorb these losses.[30]

For the western public, the magazine *Reader's Digest* provided this colourful summary of the faraway war:

> The blood of Pakistani and Indian soldiers stained the wheat-lands of the Punjab and the stony ridges of Kashmir; vultures hung over corpses on the Grand Trunk Road, the immortal highway of Kipling's *Kim*; and refugees huddled against tilting bullock carts, hesitant to start the journey home.[31]

V

Before the war Shastri and Ayub Khan had met once, at Karachi in October 1964, when the Indian leader stopped there on his way home from Cairo. There is a photograph of the two together, the army man dressed in a suit, towering over the little Gandhian in his dhoti. Ayub was entirely unimpressed by the Indian, telling an aide, "So this is the man who has succeeded Nehru!"[32]

There is little question that the Pakistani leadership seriously underestimated the Indian will to fight. Operation Gibraltar was conceived in the "euphoric aftermath" of the conflict at Kachchh, which had "shown the Indians in a poor light."[33] In the first week of June 1965, the newspaper *Dawn* carried an essay written under a pseudonym by a high official, who analysed Indian troop deployment before recommending that Pakistani strategy should "obviously be to go for a knock-out in the Mohamed Ali Clay style."[34] An army directive confidently stated that "as a general rule Hindu morale would not stand more than a couple of hard blows delivered at the right time and place."[35]

There was, indeed, an unmistakably religious idiom associated with an operation initiated by Pakistani Muslims on behalf of their brethren in Kashmir. Memories of wars fought and won ten centuries ago were invoked. The radicals in Pakistan believed that the Kafir would be vanquished by the combination of Islamic fervour and American arms.[36] The hope was that after the Kashmiris had risen, their brothers would cut off enemy communications and "start the long expected tank promenade down the Grand Trunk Road to Delhi," forcing a humiliating surrender.[37] The song on the lips of the warriors was: *Hus ke liya hai Pakistan, ladh ke lenge Hindustan* ("We achieved Pakistan laughing; we will take India fighting").

As it happened, the attack united the Indians. Many Kashmiris stood with the army against the invaders. A Muslim soldier from Kerala won India's highest military honour, the Param Vir Chakra. Another Muslim from Rajasthan—named, ironically, Ayub Khan—knocked out a couple of Pakistani tanks. All across India, Muslim intellectuals and divines issued statements condemning Pakistan and expressing their desire to sacrifice their lives for the motherland.[38]

Ayub and his countrymen were encouraged by the debacle inflicted by China in 1962. But that was in the wet and slippery Himalaya, whereas this was terrain the Indians knew much better. The Indian army commanders in 1965 had won their spurs fighting tank battles on flat land during the Second World War. Besides, in the years since 1962 they had been provided with more (and better) equipment. The new defence minister, Y. B. Chavan, had gone on a shopping spree in 1964, visiting western capitals and the Soviet bloc to buy the tanks, planes, rifles, and submarines that his forces required.[39]

Also, this defence minister was more respected by his troops than his counterpart in 1962. Chavan was no Krishna Menon; and, when it came to the conduct of war, Shastri was no Nehru either. He certainly preferred peace; he wrote to a friend after the conflict in Kachchh that in his view the problems between India and Pakistan should be settled amicably, step by step. He hoped that "our fights and disputes do not take a form that makes battle inevitable."[40] But when war came he was decisive, swift to take the advice of his commanders and order the strike across the Punjab border. (In a comparable situation, in 1962, Nehru had refused to call in the air force to relieve the pressure.) And when the conflict ended, he was happy to be photographed—dhoti and all—atop a captured Patton tank, a gesture that would not have come easily to his predecessor.

However, in one respect Shastri was indeed like Nehru—the refusal to mix matters of state with matters of faith. Days after the ceasefire, with patriotic feelings running high, Shastri spoke at a public meeting at the Ram Lila grounds in Delhi. Here he took issue with a report by the BBC, which had claimed that "since India's Prime Minister Lal Bahadur Shastri is a Hindu, he is ready for war with Pakistan." Shastri said that while he was a Hindu, "Mir Mushtaq who is presiding over this meeting is a Muslim. Mr. Frank Anthony who has addressed you is a Christian. There are also Sikhs and Parsis here. The unique thing about our country is that we have Hindus, Muslims, Christians, Sikhs, Parsis and people of all other religions. We have temples and mosques, gurdwaras and churches. But we do not bring this all into politics. . . . This is the difference between India and Pakistan. Whereas Pakistan proclaims herself to be an Islamic State and uses religion as a political factor, we Indians have the freedom to follow whatever religion we may choose [and] worship in any way we please. So far as politics is concerned, each of us is as much an Indian as the other."[41]

VI

During the war with Pakistan, the prime minister coined the slogan *Jai Jawan Jai Kisan*. To salute the ordinary soldier (*jawan*) in a nation given birth by Gandhian pacifism was distinctive, and so was the invocation of the humble farmer, or *kisan*, in a nation taught to admire blast furnaces and high hydroelectric dams.

In fact, one of Shastri's first acts as prime minister was to increase budget allocations to agriculture. He was deeply concerned about the shortfalls in food production in recent years. The rate of increase of food grain had just about kept pace with the growth of population. If the rains failed, panic set in, with merchants hoarding grain and the state desperate to move stocks from surplus to deficit areas. There had been a drought in 1964, and another in 1965. Seeking a long-term solution, Shastri appointed C. Subramaniam to head the Food and Agriculture Ministry. Subramaniam was born in 1910 into a family of farmers; he had degrees in science and the law, and had practiced law before joining the struggle for freedom. He had been a member of the Constituent Assembly, and was a widely admired minister in Madras before he joined the Union cabinet. Subramaniam was known to be intelligent and a go-getter; that was why Nehru had put him in charge of the prestigious Steel and Mines Ministry. To shift him from Steel to Agriculture signalled a major change indeed.[42]

Subramaniam took up his new job with vigour. He focused on the reorganization of agricultural science, improving the pay and working conditions of scientists and protecting them from bureaucratic interference. The Indian Council for Agricultural Research (ICAR), previously a somewhat somnolent body, acquired a new life and identity. Besides reviving the ICAR, Subramaniam also encouraged the states to set up agricultural universities whose research focused on regional crops. He began experimental farms, and set up a Seed Corporation of India to produce, in bulk, the high-quality seeds that would be needed for the proposed programmes of agricultural intensification.

Two of Subramaniam's key aides were, like him, from the Tamil country. One was the able secretary of agriculture, B. Sivaraman; the other was the scientist M. S. Swaminathan, who was directing the research teams adapting Mexican wheat to Indian conditions. It was around this crop that the new strategy revolved. Notably, although wheat is grown principally in the north of the country, these three architects of India's agricultural policy were all from the (very deep) south.[43]

Meanwhile, Subramaniam prevailed on the United States to provide food aid till such time as the Indians were able to augment their own production. He met with and impressed the American president, Lyndon Johnson, and developed a close partnership with the secretary of agriculture, Orville Freeman. In December 1965 Subramaniam and Freeman signed an agreement in Rome, whereby India committed itself to a substantial increase in investment in agriculture, to a reform of the rural credit system, and to an expansion of fertilizer production and consumption. In return, the Americans provided a series of soft loans and agreed to keep wheat supplies going to tide India over its shortages.[44]

While Subramaniam was signing what was informally called the "treaty of Rome," the prime minister was preparing to go to Moscow to sign a treaty of his own. This was with his Pakistani counterpart, Ayub Khan. After the war had ended, the Soviet Union offered help in working out a peace settlement. In the first week of January 1966, Shastri and Ayub Khan met in Tashkent, with the prime minister of the Soviet Union, Aleksey Kosygin, as the chief mediator. After a week of hard bargaining each side agreed to give up what it most prized—international arbitration of the Kashmir dispute for Pakistan; the retention of key posts captured during the war (such as the Haji Pir Pass) for India. The "Tashkent agreement" mandated the withdrawal of forces to the positions they held before 5 August 1965, the orderly transfer of prisoners of war, the resumption of diplomatic relations, and the disavowal of force to settle future disputes.[45]

The agreement was signed on the afternoon of 10 January 1966. That night Shastri died in his sleep, of a cardiac arrest. On 11 January his body was flown to New Delhi on a Soviet aircraft. The next morning the body was placed on a gun carriage, and taken in procession to the banks of the Jamuna, to be cremated not far from where Gandhi and Nehru had been. *Life* magazine made the event a cover story—as it had done with the death of Shastri's predecessor twenty months before. There were vivid pictures of the crowd numbering 1 million people who had come to honour a man "with whom many [Indians] felt a closer affinity than with Nehru." What Shastri gave India, said *Life*, "was mainly a mood—a new steeliness and sense of national unity." The Chinese war had brought the country to a state of near collapse, but this time, when war came, "everything worked—the trains ran, the army held fast, there was no communal rioting. The old moral pretentiousness, the disillusion and drift, the fear and dismay were gone."[46]

This was a handsome tribute, but more notable perhaps were the compliments paid by those predisposed by ties of kin to see Shastri as an interloper. In the first months of the new prime minister's tenure, Indira Gandhi had complained that he was departing from her father's legacy. Within a year she was constrained to admit that "Mr. Shastri is, I think, feeling stronger now and surer of himself."[47] Then there was

Vijayalakshmi Pandit, who was even more fanatically devoted to her brother's memory. In July 1964 she thought that the morale of the government of India was at "an unbelievably low level"—and "there is now no Jawaharlal Nehru to stand up and restore confidence in the minds of the people." On Shastri's death, however, she felt "very sad," for "he had begun to grow and we all thought he would put India on the right road."[48] The condescension was characteristic, but when we consider who was writing this and when, it must be considered high praise.

Lal Bahadur Shastri may perhaps be seen as being in relation to Jawaharlal Nehru as Harry Truman was to Franklin Delano Roosevelt. Nehru and Roosevelt both came from upper-class backgrounds, enjoyed long periods in power, undertook fundamental changes in their society and nation, and were greatly venerated for doing so. Shastri, like Truman, was a small-town boy of modest background, whose lack of charisma concealed a firm will and independence of mind. Like Truman's, his background had endowed him with a keen practical sense, in contrast to the more consciously intellectual—not to say ideological—style of his predecessor. But the comparison breaks down with regard to length of service. Whereas Truman had a full seven years as president of the United States, Shastri died less than two years after being sworn in as prime minister of India.

VII

On Shastri's death, Gulzarilal Nanda was once more sworn in as interim prime minister, and once more Kamaraj went in search of a permanent successor. Once more, Morarji Desai threw his hat into the ring. Once more, Kamaraj rejected him in favour of a more widely acceptable candidate.

The person whom the Congress president had in mind to succeed Shastri was Indira Gandhi. She was young—having just turned forty-eight—attractive, known to world leaders, and the daughter of the best-loved of Indians. To soothe a nation struck by two quick losses, she seemed the most obvious choice. True, she had little administrative experience, but this time the Congress "Syndicate" would ensure that hers would be a properly "collective" leadership.

The chief ministers consulted by Kamaraj quickly endorsed Indira Gandhi's name. So far, so good—except that Morarji Desai decided he would contest for the leadership. So New Delhi now "became the cockpit of concerted canvassing, large-scale lobbying, and hectic horse-trading."

Mrs. Gandhi and Morarji Desai met with major leaders, while their seconds stalked the rank and file.[49]

In terms of experience as well as ability Desai should have been the favourite. Jawaharlal Nehru had once written that there "were very few people whom I respect so much for their rectitude, ability, efficiency and fairness as Morarji Desai."[50] It is doubtful whether he would have written about his own daughter in quite that fashion—certainly, he had no hope that Indira Gandhi would ever succeed him as prime minister. However, the words I have quoted are from a private letter; neither Desai nor his supporters were privy to it. Even if they were, it is unlikely that it would have helped. With Kamaraj and the Syndicate solidly backing Mrs. Gandhi, and other congressmen having their own doubts as regards Desai, Nehru's daughter commanded majority support in the Congress Parliamentary party. When that body voted to choose a prime minister on 19 January, she won by 355 votes to 169. Kamaraj had "lined up the State satraps behind Mrs. Gandhi," wrote one Delhi journal somewhat cynically, because "the State leaders would accept only an innocuous person for Prime Minister at the Centre."[51]

VIII

Indira Gandhi was the second woman elected to lead a free nation (Sirimavo Bandarnaike of Ceylon being the first), and the second member of her own family to become prime minister of India. Her first months in office were, if anything, as troubled as her father's. Nothing much happened in February, but in March a major revolt broke out in the Mizo Hills. A tribal district bordering East Pakistan, these jagged hills had a population of only 300,000. But, as in Nagaland, among them were some motivated young men determined to carve out a homeland of their own.

The origins of the Mizo conflict go back to a famine in 1959, when a great flowering of bamboo led to an explosion in the population of rats. These devoured the grain in the fields and in village warehouses, causing a scarcity of food for humans. A Mizo National Famine Front was formed, which found the state's response wanting. The organization then dropped the word "Famine," becoming the Mizo National Front (MNF). It asked first for a separate state within the Indian Union and then for a separate country itself.

The leader of the MNF was a one-time accountant named Laldenga. Deeply affected by the famine, he sought succour in books—the detective stories of Peter Cheyney to begin with—graduating in time to the works of Winston Churchill and primers on guerrilla warfare. In the winter of 1963–1964, Laldenga made contact with the military government of East Pakistan, which promised him guns and money, and a base from which to mount attacks. The arms so obtained were stored in forests along the border.[52]

After years of patient planning, during which he recruited many young Mizos and trained them in the use of modern weaponry, Laldenga launched an uprising on the last day of February 1966. Groups of MNF soldiers attacked government offices and installations, looted banks, and disrupted communications. Roads were blocked to prevent the army from moving troops into the area. In early March the MNF announced that the territory had seceded from the Indian Union and was now an independent republic.[53]

The MNF captured one main town, Lungleh, and pressed hard on the district capital, Aizawl. The Indian response was to call in the army and the air force. Lungleh was strafed to force the rebels out; this was the first time air power had been used by the Indian state against its own citizens. As in Nagaland, the rebels took refuge in the jungles, visiting the villages by night. After a fortnight of fierce fighting, a Welsh missionary working in the area managed to smuggle out this report to a friend in England:

> On Saturday morning we packed as many of our things as we could into trunks . . . and packed [a bag] to carry to go to Durlang through the jungle. . . . Five minutes before we were due to start an aeroplane came overhead machine gunning. . . . They were not firing at random, but trying to aim at the rebels' position as it were. . . . We were there all day and the men were digging a trench, and we sheltered in it every time the jets came over firing. Pakhlira saw his house go up in flames. We prepared a meal of rice in a small house, but decided that it wasn't safe to sleep there and we all slept out in a terrace in the jungle where there was a sheltering bank. Not much sleep. We rose in the night and saw the whole Dawrupi go into flames from the furthest end to the Republic Road. They say that it was an effort by Laldenga's followers to burn the Assam Rifles out of the town.

The letter vividly captured the fear of the ordinary Mizo, caught in the crossfire between the insurgents and the state. It went on to speak, in a more reflective vein, of how the conflict will be a very serious setback for the country. . . . The government had to send in an army such as this so as to put a stop to this thing from the beginning in case it turns out to be like the country of the Nagas. We can only hope that the rebels will surrender so that things can get back to normal as soon as possible, but education will be in a complete mess for some time. The Matric[ulation] Exam is supposed to start next week. A very great responsibility rests on the shoulders of men like Laldenga and Sakhlawliana for reducing the country to this sad condition.[54]

Far from surrendering, the rebels fought on, and the conflict continued for the rest of the year, and on into the next. Meanwhile, in Nagaland the peace mission had collapsed. In the last week of February 1966, Jayaprakash Narayan (JP) resigned from the peace mission, saying that he had lost the confidence of the Nagas. JP had told the underground that in the aftermath of the Indo-Pakistan war it should drop its demand for independence, and settle for autonomy within the Indian Union. In the federal system, foreign affairs and defence were in the hands of the Centre, but the issues that most mattered—education, health, economic development, culture—were in the control of the states. So JP advised Phizo's men to shed their arms and run for election, in order to take over the administration by peaceful means.[55]

At the same time as JP became disenchanted with the rebels, Michael Scott had forfeited the confidence of the Indian government. It accused him of seeking to "internationalize" the Naga issue by approaching the United Nations. Scott had suggested that likely models for Nagaland were Bhutan and Sikkim—nominally independent countries, each with its own flag, currency, and ruler, but militarily subordinated to India. In May 1966, New Delhi asked Scott to leave the country, making it clear that he was not supposed to return.[56]

There was no question that Michael Scott was deeply committed to the Naga cause. Between 1962 and 1966 he must have visited India a dozen times on Phizo's behalf. But he could not see that political independence for the Nagas was unacceptable to the Indian government. The government was prepared to grant Phizo amnesty, safe passage into Nagaland, and even the chief ministership of the state if he so desired. But the old rebel doggedly held out for more, and Scott supported him. Another Englishman with long experience of India, the journalist Guy Wint, was moved to comment that "the main obstacle to peace [in the Naga Hills] lies in the fanaticism of such people as Michael Scott and

David Astor; both of whom allow themselves to be used by Phizo. Neither has any conception of what is at stake in accepting the Naga claim for complete secession."[57]

The breakdown of the peace talks was signalled by a wave of attacks on civilian targets. On 20 April a bomb went off in a train in upper Assam, killing fifty-five passengers. Three days later another explosion on a train claimed forty lives. The Naga radicals were now making contact with Peking, whose help they sought in renewing their struggle.[58]

Tribes were restless on the borders, and in parts of the heartland as well. Food shortages in the district of Bastar, in central India, had sparked a popular movement led by the deposed maharaja, Pravir Chandra Bhanj Deo. Pravir Chandra and his followers claimed that prosperity would return only when he, the rightful heir, was returned to the throne. The maharaja was traditionally regarded as quasi-divine, as the key intermediary between the people and their gods. A man whose eccentricity bordered on lunacy—this was the reason the government had replaced him with his brother—Pravir Chandra was nonetheless revered by his people. There were a series of protests asking for his restoration; and then, on 25 March, several thousand people marched on the old capital, Jagdalpur. A battle broke out between the tribals, using bows and arrows; and the police, using tear gas and bullets. When the smoke cleared about forty people were found dead: one policeman and the rest tribals. Among those killed was Pravir Chandra himself. This was, to quote the chief minister of Madhya Pradesh—writing to the home minister in New Delhi—a "tragic incident," "shocking and regrettable."[59]

From these rebellions the new prime minister turned with relief to the creation of a separate state for the Sikhs. In the war against Pakistan, many Sikh commanders as well as jawans had distinguished themselves. So had the ordinary Punjabi. Farmers opened stands on the roadside to feed troops with the choicest delicacies. Others offered their homes; some people nursed the wounded. As the general in command remembered, "the whole province was electrified to a man. There were no reservations in offering help for the cause."[60]

Their bravery in the war impelled the government of India to concede a long-standing demand of the Sikhs. In March 1966, a committee of members of Parliament recommended a division of the existing state into three parts, with the hill districts going to Himachal Pradesh and the eastern, Hindu-majority areas coming to constitute a new state, "Haryana." What these deletions left behind was a Punjab that, finally, was both Punjabi-speaking as well as dominated by Sikhs.[61]

IX

In the middle of March the prime minister left for her first foreign tour. She stopped at Paris and London, but her main destination was the United States, a country whose goodwill and grain were greatly desired by India. For it would be some time before the new agricultural strategy would take effect. C. Subramaniam had ploughed up the lawns of his bungalow in Delhi to plant a new high-yielding variety of wheat, one of a series of experiments to test these new seeds for local conditions. Meanwhile, American farmers had perforce to help in feeding Indian mouths.[62]

"New Indian Leader Comes Begging," was how one Alabama paper headlined its story on Mrs. Gandhi's visit. She made a more positive impression along the East Coast, handling the press well and impressing the public with the elegance of her dress and the dignity of her manner. Lyndon Johnson seems also to have warmed to her.[63] But after her return, Johnson chose to keep supplicants on a tight leash. Whereas the Indians had asked for an annual commitment of food aid, he released ships month by month. The American ambassador in New Delhi privately described Johnson's practice as a "cruel performance. The Indians must conform; they must be made to fawn; their pride must be cracked." Despairing of the Indians' ever getting their act together, at one stage Johnson suggested sending 1,000 extension workers to teach them how to farm. His ambassador found the thought "appalling"; not only would these Americans know nothing about agriculture in Asia, but they would bring with them "950 wives, 2,500 children, 3,000 air-conditioners, 1,000 jeeps, 1,000 electric refrigerators (many of which won't work), 800 or 900 dogs and 2,000 or 3,000 cats."[64]

In both 1965 and 1966 India imported 15 million tons of American wheat under the PL-480 scheme, to feed 40 million people. A memorandum prepared at the U.S. Department of Agriculture stated baldly that "India was destitute." When the rains failed again in 1966 the prospect for India was "one more drought, one more year of acute dependence on PL-480 imports, one more year of exposure to the world as paupers."[65]

Some people in the Washington establishment thought the Indians hypocritical, asking for aid with one hand while attacking American foreign policy with the other. New Delhi's criticisms of the Vietnam War rankled deeply. Lyndon Johnson was not pleased when the Indian president, S. Radhakrishnan, sent a message urging that "the United States unilaterally and without any commitments cease bombing North Vietnam," adding that when this happened, "the rest of the world would, through the force of world opinion, bring about negotiations."[66]

X

The purchase of arms and grain from abroad, along with the import of machinery and materials for industrial development, caused a dangerous dip in India's foreign exchange reserves, which were down to $625 million in March 1966. To counter this, the government decided to devalue the rupee in June. Earlier pegged at 4.76 rupees to $1 (U.S.), the exchange rate now became 7.50 rupees to $1.[67]

The World Bank and the International Monetary Fund had both recommended devaluation, though its extent exceeded even their expectations. However, the action was greeted by a storm of protest on the left. The communist member of Parliament Hiren Mukherjee claimed that devaluation had been forced on India "by the cloak and dagger aid givers of America." A communist trade union called it "a shameful act of national betrayal."

Large sections of Indira Gandhi's own party were opposed to devaluation. Kamaraj, for one, saw it as undermining the policy of national self-reliance. But the action was supported by the free-market Swatantra party, whose main spokesman in Parliament, Minoo Masani, said that "if devaluation constituted a first step in a policy of economic realism in place of the doctrinaire policies pursued by the Congress Government, it would have some desirable results in boosting the exports and promoting the inflow of foreign capital."

Writing to a friend, the prime minister said that the devaluation was a "most difficult and painful decision," made only "when various other palliatives which had been tried for the last two years did not produce satisfactory results."[68] The liberal Delhi journal *Thought* went further— this, it said, was "the hardest decision the Government of India has taken since this country became independent." The editors hoped that it would lead to a redirection of economic policy, toward producing goods for export and strengthening India's trading position. Devaluation, said *Thought*, should "logically mean the end of giganticism in our efforts to develop the nation's economy."[69]

In the end, though, devaluation was not accompanied by a liberalization of the trade regime. Controls on the inflow of capital remained in place, and there was no push to increase exports. It appears that the criticism from within and outside her party inhibited Mrs. Gandhi from promoting more thoroughgoing reform. The support from Swatantra would not have helped either—if anything, it would have tended to push Nehru's daughter back toward the left.

XI

Through 1966, one place that had stayed unusually quiet was the Valley of Kashmir. The war of 1965 had put secessionists on the back foot. The chief minister, G. M. Sadiq, was providing an efficient and clean administration, conspicuously so in comparison with Bakshi Ghulam Mohammed's. The tourist trade was doing well, as was the market for Kashmiri handicrafts.

In the late summer of 1966, Jayaprakash Narayan wrote Mrs. Gandhi a remarkable letter seeking a permanent solution to a problem that had "plagued this country for 19 years." "Kashmir has distorted India's image for the world as nothing else has done," said JP. Even now, while peace reigned on the surface, beneath there was "deep and wide-spread discontent among the people." The only way to end this was to release Sheikh Abdullah after promising "full internal autonomy, i.e., a return to the original terms of the accession." A settlement with Abdullah, JP believed, "may give us the only chance we may have of solving the Kashmir problem." For "the Sheikh is the only Kashmiri leader who could swing Muslim opinion in the valley towards his side."

His talks with Chou En-lai led to Sheikh Abdullah being dubbed a "traitor," but in JP's view that act, though indiscreet, was certainly not treasonable. In any case, the sheikh had come back to India to answer his detractors. JP's associate, Narayan Desai, met the sheikh in Kodaikanal, and found him amenable to the idea of full autonomy. In the aftermath of the recent war with Pakistan, Abdullah saw quite clearly that an independent Kashmir was out of the question. So Narayan now suggested that the government release Abdullah and permit him to contest the 1967 general elections, to assure the Kashmiris that "they would be rid of the overbearing Indian police and enjoy full freedom to order their lives as they liked." If the sheikh fought and won the elections, if "it could be shown that they [the Kashmiris] had taken that decision freely at an election run by their own genuine leaders, . . . Pakistan will have no ground left to interfere in their affairs."

To "hold a general election in Kashmir with Sheikh Abdullah in prison," remarked Narayan, "is like the British ordering an election in India while Jawaharlal Nehru was in prison. No fair-minded person would call it a fair election." This was a point that should have counted with Mrs. Gandhi, but in case it didn't, JP offered the following melancholy prediction:

> If we miss the chance of using the next general election to win the consent of the [Kashmiri] people to their place within the Union, I cannot see what other device will be left to India to settle the problem. To think that we will eventually wear down the people and force them to accept at least passively the Union is to delude ourselves. That might conceivably have happened had Kashmir not been geographically located where it is. In its present location, and with seething discontent among the people, it would never be left in peace by Pakistan.[70]

The prime minister wrote a brief note in return, thanking JP "for sharing your views on Kashmir and Sheikh Sahib."[71] But no action was taken on his letter, and Sheikh Abdullah remained in confinement. However, in October 1966 the prime minister visited the Kashmir Valley for the first time since assuming office. At the sports stadium in Srinagar, she spoke of her "special love" for Kashmir and Kashmiris. A large crowd turned out to hear her; in fact, wherever Mrs. Gandhi went in the Valley, the people lined up along the roads to see her.[72]

XII

For now, Kashmir appeared quiet—and its people quiescent. But in the south, in Andhra Pradesh, an agitation was gathering ground. The protest was led by students, who demanded that a proposal by the Planning Commission for a steel plant in Vishakhapatnam (Vizag) be implemented forthwith. The plant had been approved several years ago, but the fiscal crisis of the government had led to its being put on the shelf.

The decision to delay the Vizag steel plant caused an outcry in the Andhra country. For the young, a massive state-run factory still carried enchantment—it offered the hope of productive employment. Protesters blockaded roads, stopped trains, and attacked shops and offices. The movement spread through the state—"The entire student community of Guntur seems to be on the streets," said one report. The police were called out in several cities, and in Vizag itself the navy stood guard over key installations. A railroad station was set ablaze in one place; a crowd was fired on by the police in another. Students damaged the lighthouse in Vizag and forced the radio station to go off the air. All trains running through the state were cancelled.[73]

Meanwhile, to the north, a famine loomed in Bihar. The tribal areas were worst hit; in the Munger district, the Adivasis were reduced to eating roots. There were acute shortages of water and fodder. The poor had looted grain here and there; the upper classes in the countryside now lived in fear of a more generalized rebellion.[74]

To striking students and starving peasants were added some more curious dissidents—Hindu holy men, or sadhus. Hindu orthodoxy had long called for an end to the killing of the sacred cow; now, with the help of the Jana Sangh, the call had been converted into a social movement.

On 6 November, a huge procession went through the streets of the capital. Among the 100,000 marchers were many sadhus, brandishing tridents and spears. The march culminated in a public meeting outside Parliament, where the first speaker was Swami Karpatri (of Anti-Hindu Code Bill fame). The crowd was further warmed up by Swami Rameshwaranand, a Jana Sangh member of Parliament who had recently been suspended from the Lok Sabha for unruly behaviour. He asked the sadhus to *gherao* (surround) Parliament. The "excited crowd made a beeline for Parliament, shouting 'Swami Rameshwaranand ki jai.'" At this point the Jana Sangh leader Atal Behari Vajpayee appealed to the swami to withdraw his call. It was too late. As the sadhus surged toward Parliament's gates, they were turned back by mounted police. A ding-dong battle ensued, with tear gas and rubber bullets on the one side, sticks and stones on the other. As thick columns of smoke rose over the houses of Parliament, the crowd retreated, venting its anger on what lay in its way. The guardroom of All India Radio was gutted, and the house of the Congress president (K. Kamaraj) was set on fire. Also destroyed were an estimated 250 cars, 100 scooters, and 10 buses. By the evening the army was patrolling the streets, for the first time since the dark days of 1947.

An agitation led by holy men, commented one journal acidly, had resulted in an "orgy of violence, vandalism and hooliganism." A. B. Vajpayee issued a statement deploring the fact that "the undesirable elements, who resorted to violent activities in the demonstration against cow-slaughter, had done a great harm to the pious cause."[75]

XIII

There was a line of thinking, widely prevalent in the West, which held that only the personality and example of Jawaharlal Nehru had kept India united and democratic. The quick changes of guard since his death, the successive droughts, the countless small rebellions, and the war with Pakistan—these, taken together, seemed to confirm these fears. In December 1965, the *Sydney Morning Herald* worried about the future of democracy in India. Its editors saw a "sweeping upsurge of nationalistic spirit" in India, a spirit that was "in danger of turning into chauvinism, with increasing bitterness towards the Western powers." This intolerance seemed also to be directed inward: "what many foreign observers are finding particularly perturbing is that free expression of liberal views by Indians seems to be in danger."[76]

The same year, 1965, the writer Ronald Segal published a large book called *The Crisis of India*. On a study tour of the country he found India on "the economic precipice," with the "ground . . . crumbling beneath her." Meanwhile, "her international stock was low and falling." With poverty, scarcity, regional conflicts, and corruption all rampant, India reminded Segal at times of Weimar Germany, at other times of Kuomintang China. He had little hope that democracy could survive. Among the "authoritarian alternatives" were "Communism on the left" and "militant communalism on the right," one or other of which was likely to succeed before many years had passed.[77]

Also despairing of the country's future was Reverend Michael Scott. A friend who met him in May 1966 found him

> very depressed, not about his failure in regard to the Naga settlement, but about India in general. His view is that the older and abler generation is now dying off and being replaced by little, corrupt and wholly inefficient men. He has a strong feeling that sooner or later India is going to disintegrate and that the whole thing may sink into a Vietnam-type morass into which Britain and America may be drawn.[78]

When the monsoon failed again in 1966, the predictions were of mass starvation rather than of the break-up of India or the abrogation of democracy. To many western environmentalists, India seemed to provide striking proof of Malthus's prophecy that human population growth would one day outstrip the food supply. The respected biologist Paul Ehrlich of Stanford wrote that while he had "understood the population explosion intellectually for a long time," he "came to understand it emotionally one stinking hot night in Delhi a couple of years ago." As his taxi crawled through the streets, he saw around him "people eating, people washing, people sleeping. People visiting, people arguing and screaming. People thrusting their hands through the taxi window, begging. People defecating and urinating. People clinging to buses. People herding animals. People. People. People."[79]

The same year Ehrlich was writing this, two other American biologists were finishing a book in which they argued that "today, India is the first of the hungry nations to stand at the brink of famine and disaster." Tomorrow, "the famines will come," and "riding alongside will surely be riots and other civil tensions which the central government wil be too weak to control." The year 1975 was the time by which "civil disorder, anarchy, military dictatorships, runaway inflation, transportation breakdowns and chaotic unrest will be the order of the day."[80]

In truth, even some knowledgeable Indian observers had begun to fear for the future of their country. In the first week of November 1966, a traditionally pro-Congress paper published a leading article entitled "The Grimmest Situation in 19 Years." The student strikes and the food shortages were attributed to a "virtual breakdown of authority." The article predicted that "the wave of violence will grow in intensity," with "many other parts of the country being turned into Bihars." "The future of the country is dark for many reasons," said the *Hindustan Times*, "all of them directly attributable to 19 years of Congress rule."[81]

19

LEFTWARD TURNS

Never, never underestimate a politician's need to survive. . . .
I will not make the mistake of underestimating the political
instinct of a Kashmiri, who is, additionally, Jawaharlal Nehru's
daughter.

Anonymous Indian columnist, writing in May 1966

I

THE GENERAL ELECTIONS scheduled for early 1967 would be
the fourth since independence, and the first since Jawaharlal
Nehru's death. In the last weeks of 1966, an American magazine
sent a reporter to assess the lay of the land. He was struck by "the bizarre
range of India's seething problems of religious fanaticism, language barriers, regional feuds." Adding to the unrest were food shortages, inflation, and "a continuing population explosion [which] impedes almost all
progress." Varied forms of violence had "raised speculation that the elections [of 1967] may not be held." The reporter thought it possible that
"the breakdown of law and order will be so complete that the Army will
take power, as happened in neighbouring Pakistan and Burma." And
there was a more dismal prospect still—that the "collapse of the present
regime [in India] would add a grim new element to the job the U.S. has
taken on in Vietnam—the effort to assure political stability and economic
strength in Asia."[1]

To the average western visitor, India was—and remains—a strange,
even overwhelming, place. This particular journalist was on his first—
and so far as one can tell, his last—visit. But as it happened, his prognosis was endorsed by a reporter who doubtless knew India much better,
having already lived here for six years at the time.

This was Neville Maxwell of the London *Times*, who in the first
weeks of 1967 wrote a series of articles entitled "India's Disintegrating
Democracy." As Maxwell saw it, "famine is threatening, the administration is strained and universally believed to be corrupt, the govern-

ment and the governing party have lost public confidence and belief in themselves as well." These various crises had created an *"emotional readiness* for *the rejection of Parliamentary democracy."* The "politically sophisticated Indians" to whom Maxwell spoke expressed "a deep sense of defeat, an alarmed awareness that the future is not only dark but profoundly uncertain."

Maxwell's own view was that "the crisis is upon India"—he could discern "the already fraying fabric of the nation itself," with the states "already beginning to act like sub-nations." His conclusion was unequivocal: that while Indians would soon vote in "the fourth—and *surely last*—general election," "the great experiment of developing India within a democratic framework has failed."

The imminent collapse of democracy in India, thought Maxwell, would provoke a frantic search for "an alternative antidote for the society's troubles." As he saw it, "in India, as present trends continue, within the ever-closing vice of food and population, maintenance of an ordered structure of society is going to slip out of reach of an ordered structure of civil government and the army will be *the only alternative source* of authority and order. That it will be drawn into a civil role seems inevitable, the only doubt is how?"

Maxwell thought that "a mounting tide of public disorder, fed perhaps by pockets of famine," would lead to calls for strengthening the office of the president, who would be asked "to assert a stabilizing authority over the centre and the country." Backing him would be the army, which would come to exercise "more and more civil authority." In this scenario, the president would become "either the actual source of political authority, or a figure-head for a group composed possibly of army officers and a few politicians."[2]

II

There are some fine ethnographic accounts of the elections of 1967, field studies of different constituencies by scholars familiar with their culture and social composition. These show that elections were no longer a top dressing on inhospitable soil; they had been fully internalized, made part of Indian life. An election was a festival with its own unique set of rituals, enacted every five years. The energy and intensity of this particular iteration were manifest in the large turnout at rallies and leaders' speeches, and in the colourful posters and slogans used to glorify one's party or debunk its opponents. The rivalries were intense, at the state as well as the national levels. Opposing the ruling Congress were parties to its left, such as the various communist and socialist fragments; and parties to the right, such as Jana Sangh and Swatantra. In some states the competition came from regional groupings such as the Akali Dal in the Punjab and the DMK in Madras.

As these ethnographies revealed, twenty years of economic development had deepened and complicated the process of political competition. Often, rival candidates had cut their teeth running schools, colleges, and cooperatives before entering a legislative or parliamentary election. Those institutions were vehicles of prestige and patronage, their control valuable in itself and a means of mobilizing support among voters.[3]

The elections of 1967 are the first I myself have any memories of. What I remember best was this slogan, shouted with vigour along the streets of the small sub-Himalayan town where I lived: *Jana Sangh ko vote do, bidi peena chhod do/Bidi mein tambaku hai, Kangresswala daku hai.*

The congressman was a thief, and the cheroot contained that dangerous substance, tobacco: by rejecting both and embracing the Jana Sangh— the leading opposition party in town—the voter would purify himself as well as the government. Such was the slogan's message, which apparently resonated with many citizens. That was the finding of a survey of voters in thirteen states, conducted just before the election by the country's pioneer pollster, E. P. W. da Costa of the Indian Institute of Public Opinion. This survey concluded that the Congress had "lost a great deal of its charisma"; it approached the elections "for the first time, as a political loser not as a guaranteed victor."

The survey suggested that while the Congress would retain power in the Centre, its vote share would drop by two to three percentage points, it would lose perhaps fifty seats in the Lok Sabha, and it would lose even more heavily in the states. According to da Costa, non-Congress governments would be formed in the states of Kerala, Madhya Pradesh, and Rajasthan, and perhaps also in Orissa, West Bengal, Bihar, Uttar Pradesh, and Punjab.

Why had support for the Congress declined? The survey found that the minorities, once a loyal constituency, were disenchanted with the party, as were large sections of the young and the less educated. By contrast, the opposition was more united than before. In most states, non-Congress parties had made seat adjustments—which meant that the Congress could no longer easily benefit from a three-way or four-way division of the vote.

TABLE 6: PERFORMANCE OF THE CONGRESS IN INDIAN ELECTIONS,
1952–1967: VOTES AND SEATS AS A PERCENTAGE OF THE TOTAL

YEAR	LOK SABHA		STATE ASSEMBLIES	
	Votes Won	Seats Won	Votes Won	Seats Won
1952	45	74.4	42	68.4
1957	47.8	75.1	45.5	65.1
1962	44.5	72.8	44	60.7
1967	40.7	54.5	40	48.5

As da Costa saw it, this fourth general election would usher in a "second Non-Violent Revolution in India's recent history." The first was begun by Mahatma Gandhi in 1919, and culminated in Indian independence in 1947. Since then, the Congress had held power in the Centre as well as all the states, except for a very brief spell in Kerala. Now, these elections would signal "the disintegration of the monolithic exercise of power by the Congress party." Da Costa's conclusion is worth quoting: "To the candidates this is, perhaps, a struggle for power; to the political scientist it is, as nearly half a century ago, the beginning of a break with the past. It is by no means yet a revolt; but it may in time be a revolution."[4]

Pollsters are notorious for being wrong—in India perhaps even more than elsewhere. But when the results came in, da Costa must have felt vindicated. In the Lok Sabha the Congress's seats had dropped from 361 to 283, and its losses in the state assemblies were even greater. The party's decline is summed up in Table 6.

III

The most humiliating defeat suffered by the Congress was in the southern state of Madras. Here, the Dravida Munnetra Kazhagam swept the election, winning 138 seats out of a total of 234 in the assembly. The Congress won a mere fifty. The DMK leader C. N. Annadurai was sworn in as chief minister.

Madras had long been a Congress stronghold; many national leaders, past and present, came from this state. Now, even the venerable K. Kamaraj was washed away in the landslide. He lost in his hometown, Virudunagar, to a twenty-eight-year-old student activist, P. Srinivasan.

When the news reached Madras, jubilant members of DMK found a namesake of the victor, placed him on a horse, and paraded him through the city. Of the Congress president's defeat, a respected weekly wrote that "in terms of political prestige, here and abroad, it was beyond any doubt, the worst blow ever suffered by Mr. Kamaraj's party, before or after independence."[5]

The Congress had a fairly good record in the state; its administration was known to be clean and efficent. Some commentators thought that the DMK rode to victory on the back of the anti-Hindi agitation of 1965. However, the anti-Hindi struggle itself was made possible by patient organizational work over the past decade. The DMK had fanned out into the towns and villages, creating local clubs and party branches. Crucial here were its links with the hugely popular Tamil film industry. One of the DMK's leaders, M. Karunanidhi, was a successful scriptwriter. More important, the DMK had the support—moral as well as material—of the great popular film hero M. G. Ramachandran (MGR).

MGR was originally from Kerala, but had been born to a family of plantation labourers in Sri Lanka. He had a fanatical following in the Tamil countryside. In his films he vanquished the forces of evil, variously represented as policemen, landlords, foreigners, and the state. His movies played to packed houses, and people came back to see them over and over again. Many of his most devoted fans were women.

All across Madras, MGR *manrams* (fan clubs) had been formed. Their members discussed his films and also his politics. For MGR was a long-time supporter of the DMK. He gave money to the party, and was always at hand to speak at its rallies and conferences.

A month before the elections of 1967, MGR was shot and wounded by a rival film star, M. R. Radha (the two, apparently, had fallen out over what men in general, and Indian film stars in particular, usually fall out over). Photographs of the wounded hero were abundantly used in the election campaign. MGR himself decided to run—he won easily, and his party did the same.[6]

In power, the DMK practised what one scholar has called "assertive and paternalist populism." Whereas the Congress brought large industrial projects to the state, the DMK focused on schemes that might win it immediate support. Thus it increased the percentage of government jobs reserved for the backward castes who were its own chief source of support. Greater control was exercised over the trade in cereals, and food subsidies were granted to the urban poor. Meanwhile, to foster regional pride, the government organized an international conference on

Tamil culture and language; scholars from twenty countries participated, and the chief minister expressed the hope that Tamil would become the link language for the whole of India.[7]

IV

The Congress also lost in Kerala, to an alliance of left parties. In 1963
the Communist Party of India (CPI) had split into two fractions, the
newer one called the Communist Party of India (Marxist), or CPM. The
CPM had the more dynamic leaders, including E. M. S. Namboodiripad. Now, the CPM won fifty-two of the 133 seats in the state assembly; the Congress won thirty: and the CPI won nineteen. The communists
came together to form the government, with EMS being sworn in for his
second term as chief minister.

The Congress had previous experience of losing in Kerala. But now,
to its distress, it also lost power in West Bengal, where it had held undisputed sway since 1947. The winners in West Bengal were the United
Front–Left Front (UF-LF) alliance; its main members were the Bangla
Congress (as its name suggests, a breakaway from the mother party),
and the CPM. In the assembly elections, the Congress won 127 seats out
of 280. The CPM won forty-three and the Bangla Congress won thirty-
four; so, joined by an assortment of left groups and independents, these
two could just about muster a majority.

The Bangla Congress leader, Ajoy Mukherjee, became chief minister. The deputy chief minister was Jyoti Basu, an urbane, London-
educated lawyer who had long been the civilized face of Bengali
communism. Basu and some others thought that their party could shape
the government's policies from within. Other members of the CPM, notably its chief organizer, Promode Dasgputa, thought that the party
should never have joined the government at all.[8]

Whole books have been written on doctrinal disputes within the Indian communist movement. Here, we need know only that the CPI split
in 1963 because of two differences: one external to the country, the
other internal to it. The two issues were connected. The parent party,
the CPI, was tied to the apron strings of the Communist party of the Soviet Union, and in consequence had forsworn armed revolution, if only
because the Soviet Union wanted good relations with the government
of India. The breakaway CPM believed in fraternal relations with the
Communist parties of both the Soviet Union and China. It saw the Indian state as run by a bourgeois-landlord alliance and parliamentary

democracy as mostly a sham, to be used when it suited one's purposes, and to be discarded when it didn't.[9]

The decision of the CPM to join the government was preceded by a bitter debate, with Jyoti Basu speaking in favour and Promode Dasgupta against. Ultimately the party joined, creating a great sense of expectation among the rank and file. An early gesture was to rename Harrington Road after a hero of the world communist movement, so that at the height of the Vietnam War the address of the United States consulate was 7, Ho Chi Minh Sarani, Calcutta.

That was easy enough; but thereafter the decisions became harder. In the spring of 1967 a land dispute broke out in Naxalbari, in the Darjeeling district, where India bordered Nepal on the west and Pakistan on the east, with Tibet and the semi-independent kingdoms of Bhutan and Sikkim not far away. The economy in these Himalayan foothills was dominated by tea plantations, many run by British-owned companies. There was a history of land scarcity, and of conflicts over land—with plantation workers seeking plots of their own and indigenous sharecroppers seeking relief from usurious landlords.

In the Naxalbari area, the rural poor were mobilized by a Krishak Samiti (Peasants' Organization) owing allegiance to the CPM. Its leader was a middle-class radical, Kanu Sanyal, whose rejection of his social milieu in favour of work in the villages had won him a considerable following. From late March 1967, the Krishak Samiti organized a series of demonstrations against landlords who had evicted tenants or hoarded grain, or both. These protests became more militant, leading to skirmishes with the police, which turned violent. A constable was killed; in retaliation, the police fired on a crowd. The peasant leaders decided to take to arms, and soon landlords were being beheaded.

The protests had their roots in the deeply inequitable agrarian structure of northern Bengal. But they might not have taken the form they did had the CPM not joined the government. Some activists, and perhaps many peasants, felt that with their party in power, they were at liberty to set right the feudal structure on their own. To their surprise, the party reacted by taking the side of the forces of law and order. By the late summer of 1967 an estimated 1,500 policemen were on duty in Naxalbari. Kanu Sanyal and his fellow leaders were in jail, while other rebels had taken refuge in the jungle.[10]

Naxalbari quickly came to enjoy an iconic status among Indian revolutionaries. The village gave its name to the region and, in time, to anyone anywhere who was prepared to use arms against the Indian state on behalf of the oppressed and disinherited. "Naxalite" became shorthand for "revolutionary," a term evoking romance and enchantment at one end of the political spectrum, and distaste and derision at the other.[11]

Among those who approved of the Naxalites were the leaders of the People's Republic of China. In the last week of June 1967, Radio Peking announced:

> A phase of peasants' armed struggle led by the revolutionaries of the Indian Communist Party has been set up in the countryside in Darjeeling District of West Bengal State in India. This is the front paw of the revolutionary armed struggle launched by the Indian people under the guidance of Mao Tse-tung's teachings. This represents the general orientation of the Indian revolution at the present time. The people of India, China and the rest of the world hail the emergence of this revolutionary armed struggle.[12]

While the first sparks of revolution were being struck in Naxalbari, another group of Maoists were preparing for action in Andhra Pradesh. The Andhra Naxalites were active in two regions: Telengana, where there had been a major communist insurgency in 1946–1949; and the Srikakulam district, bordering Orissa. In both regions the disputes were over land and forests. In both the main agents of exploitation were the state and landlords, and the main victims were peasants and (especially) tribals. And in both, communist mobilization focused on free access to forest produce, better wages for labourers, and the redistribution of land.

In Srikakulam the struggle was led by a schoolteacher, Vempatapu Satyanarayana. He led the tribals in a series of labour strikes, and in seizing grain from the fields of rich farmers and redistributing it to the needy. By the end of 1967 the landlords had sought the help of the police, who came in and arrested hundreds of protesters. Satyanarayana and his men now decided to take to arms. The houses of landlords and moneylenders were raided, and their records and papers burned. The state's response was to send in more police; by early 1969, there were as many as nine platoons of Special Armed Police operating in the district.

The struggle in Telengana was led by Tarimala Nagi Reddy. He was a veteran of the communist movement, who had spent years organizing peasants and had also served several terms in the state legislature. Now, he proclaimed the futility of the parliamentary path; resigning from the assembly as well as from the CPM, he went once more to the villages.

He linked up with grass-roots workers in mobilizing peasants to ask for higher wages and for an end to corruption among state officials. Young militants were trained in the use of arms. The district was divided into zones; to each zone were assigned several *dalams*, or groups of dedicated revolutionaries.[13]

In West Bengal, the coalition government had fallen apart in less than a year. President's Rule was imposed before new elections in early 1969, in which the CPM substantially increased its tally. It won eighty seats, becoming by far the biggest partner in a fresh alliance with the Bangla Congress and others. Ajoy Mukherjee once more became chief minister; the CPM preferred to keep the home portfolio and generally play Big Brother.

These were years of great turmoil in the state, as indicated by the titles of books written about the period, for example *The Agony of West Bengal* and *West Bengal: The Disinherited State*. One axis of conflict was between the Centre and the state. The government of India was worried about law and order; the ruling Congress was peeved about its own loss of power in West Bengal. The governor became an important player, communicating the concerns of the Centre (and, less justifiably, those of the Congress) to the local politicians. The assembly was disrupted regularly; on one occasion, the governor was physically prevented from delivering his customary opening address and had to flee the premises under police escort.[14]

A second axis of conflict was between the two main parties in the state government. Whereas Ajoy Mukherjee and his Bangla Congress tried (though weakly) to keep the machinery of state in place, the CPM was not above stoking street protest and even violence to further its aims. In factories in and around Calcutta, workers took to the practice of gherao—surrounding their managers to demand better wages and working conditions. Previously, the management had been able to call in the police; the new government, however, insisted that any such stoppage of work had to be referred first to the labour minister (a CPM man). This was an invitation to strike: according to one estimate, there were more than 1,200 gheraos in the first six months of the first UF-LF government.[15]

These stoppages created a ripple in the British press, in part because many of the great Calcutta firms were British-owned, and in part because this had once been the capital of the Raj. "West Bengal Expects More Lawlessness" ran one headline; "Riot Stops Opening of West Bengal Assembly" ran another. The response of many factory owners, Indian as well as European, was to shut down their units. Others shifted

their business elsewhere, in a process of capital flight that displaced Calcutta as the leading centre of Indian industry.[16]

Apart from capitalists worried about their profits, the prevailing
lawlessness also disturbed the chief minister of West Bengal. He saw it
as the handiwork of the CPM, whose ministerial portfolios included
land and labour, where the trouble raged, and home, where it could be
controlled but wasn't. So in protest against the protests, the old Gandhian
Ajoy Mukerjee decided to organize a satyagraha of his own. He toured
the districts delivering speeches, railing against the CPM for promoting
social discord. Then, on 1 December, he began a seventy-two-hour fast
in a very public place—Curzon Park in south Calcutta. In the rich history of Indian satyagrahas, this must surely be the most bizarre: a chief
minister fasting to protest against his own government's failure to keep
the peace.[17]

A third conflict was between the CPM and the Naxalites. The latter
had now formed a new party, called the Communist Party of India
(Marxist-Leninist), or CPI (ML). In district after district, cadres left the
parent party to join the new one, just as in 1963–1964 they had left the
CPI to join the CPM. The rivalry between the CPI and the CPI (ML) was
intense and often violent. The leader of the CPI (ML), Charu Mazumdar,
urged the elimination of landlords, who were "class enemies," as well as
the elimination of CPM cadres, who were "right deviationists." On its
part, the CPM raised a private army (euphemistically called a "volunteer
force") to further its version of the "people's democratic revolution."[18]

As in British times, the reports of the Intelligence Bureau (IB) best
capture the contours of political unrest. One IB report listed 137 "major
cases of lawlessness in West Bengal" over a period of only six weeks, between 19 March and 4 May 1970. These were classified under different
headings. Several incidents pitted two parties against each other: "CPM
vs. CPI, CPM vs. Congress, CPM vs. CPML." Sometimes ire was directed
against the state: "CPM vs. Police Party," for example, or "Extremists vs.
Constables," the latter referring to an attack on a police station in Malda
district, where Naxalites speared a constable to death and looted the ar-
moury. There was a case listed as "Extremist Students vs. Vice Chancellor," referring to an incident at Jadavpur University in Calcutta, where
radical students held the vice chancellor captive for several hours, before
damaging the furniture and scribbling Maoist slogans on the walls in his
office.[19]

In the villages, Naxalites had hoped to intensify unrest by beheading
landlords; they thought that the same effect could be achieved in the city

by random attacks on policemen. Kipling had once called Calcutta the "City of Dreadful Night"; now the citizens lived in dread by day as well. The shops began closing in the early afternoon, and by dusk the streets were deserted.[20] "Not a day passes in this turbulent and tortured city," wrote one reporter, "without a few bombs being hurled at police pickets and patrols." The police, meanwhile, raided houses and college hostels in search of the extremists. In one raid they seized explosives sufficient to make 3,000 bombs.[21]

V

Tamil pride was resurgent in the south, class warfare was on the rise in the east, and the Congress consensus was crumbling elsewhere as well. In the state of Orissa, the Congress had been routed by a partnership between Swatantra and the party of the local landed elite. The election campaign of this partnership had targeted two leading congressmen, Biju Patnaik and Biren Mitra, accusing them of corruption and an opulent lifestyle. Allegedly, while in power in the state, Patnaik and Mitra had taken bribes from businessmen and had awarded lucrative government contracts to their own friends and relatives.[22] A popular slogan—a local variant, so to say, of the one shouted in distant Dehradun—was *Biju Biren kauthi/Mada botal jauthi* ("Where there are liquour bottles, there you will find Biju and Biren"). On coming to power, the Swatantra–Jana Congress alliance immediately set up a commission to enquire into the corruption of the previous government.[23]

Challenged by parties of the left and right, the Congress also found itself bleeding internally. In most states in northern India it had won slender majorities. These became prey to intrigue, with the formation of factions by ambitious leaders seeking to become chief minister. In the states of Uttar Pradesh, Madhya Pradesh, Haryana, and Bihar, Congress governments were formed, only to fall when a group of disgruntled defectors moved across to the other side. In a political lexicon already rich in abbreviations, Samyukta Vidhayak Dal (SVD)—or the United Legislators party—was, as the name suggests, a ragtag and bobtail outfit, a coalition of legislators left, right, and centre, united only by a desire to grab power.

The SVD governments were made up of the Jana Sangh, socialists, Swatantra, local parties and defectors from the Congress—the defectors often being the element that made a numerical majority possible. At one level, the SVD phenomena signalled the rise of the backward castes, who had benefited from land legislation but had been denied the fruits of political power. In the north, these castes included the Jats in Haryana and Uttar Pradesh, the Kurmis and Koeris in Bihar, the Lodhs in Madhya Pradesh, and the Yadavs in all these states. In the south, they included the Marathas in Maharashtra, the Vokkaligas in Mysore, the Vellalas in Madras, and the Reddys and Kammas in Andhra Pradesh. These castes occupied an intermediate position in the social hierarchy, below the Brahmans but above the untouchables. In many areas they were the "dominant caste," numerically significant and well organized. What they lacked was access to state power. The DMK was chiefly supported by the backward castes, as were the socialists, who had increased their share of votes in the north. Notably, many of the defectors from the Congress also came from this stratum.

At another level, the SVD governments were simply a product of personal ambition. Consider the state of Madhya Pradesh. Here, the Congress's troubles started before the election, when the *Rajmata* (queen mother) of Gwalior left the party because she had not been consulted in the choice of candidates. With her son Madhavrao she campaigned energetically against the Congress. According to a report by the Intelligence Bureau, the Rajmata spent 3 million rupees in the election. Although the Congress came back to power, in the Gwalior region the party was wiped out. Now—again according to the report—the Rajmata was planning to spend more money "to subvert the loyalties of some Congress legislators . . . [and] bring about the downfall of the new Congress Ministry."[24]

The chief minister, a canny operator named D. P. Mishra, was quite prepared for this. He was wooing defectors from other parties himself—as he wrote to the Congress president, he had "to open the door for all who wish to join the Party."[25] Eventually, though, the rajmata was successful, when a prominent defector from Congress, Govind Narain Singh, got twenty-eight others to leave the party with him. Before the crucial vote in the House, Singh kept his flock sequestered at his own home, watching over them with a rifle, lest they be kidnapped or seduced away.

Not sure how long it would last, the SVD government had to make every day, or every order, count. Ministers specified a fee for approving or stopping transfers of officials. Thus "orders, particularly transfer orders, were issued and cancelled with bewildering rapidity." Characteristically, the Jana Sangh wanted the education portfolio, so that it "could build up a permanent following through the primary schools." It eventually got the home portfolio. There, it maintained communal peace by keeping its followers in check, yet took great care "to see that no key post in any department went to a Muslim."[26]

Despite the defections and the corruption they engendered, what transpired after the elections of 1967 was indeed what E. P. W. da Costa had called it—India's second non-violent revolution. One could now take a train from New Delhi to Calcutta, a journey of 1,000 miles through the heartland, and not pass through a single state ruled by the Congress.

VI

The late 1960s brought fresh assertions of regionalist sentiment. Parts of the old Hyderabad state, merged with Andhra Pradesh in 1956, now wanted to leave it. The movement was led by students of the Osmania University, who complained that Andhra was run for the benefit of the coastal elite. The new state they demanded, to be named Telengana, would centre on the neglected inland districts. It would have Hyderabad as its capital. Strikes and processions were called, trains were stopped, and accusations of "colonization by Andhras" and "police *zulm*" (terror) were made.[27]

Across the country, a new state had in fact been created out of the tribal districs of Assam. The movement here had a long history. An Eastern Indian Tribal Union was formed in 1955 to represent the inhabitants of the Khasi, Jaintia, and Garo Hills. Five years later it was renamed the All Party Hill Leaders Conference (APHLC). In the elections of 1967, the Congress was routed in the hills by the APHLC. This experience, along with the fear of an insurgency like the Naga and Mizo movements, prompted the Centre to create a new province in December 1969. The state was called Meghalaya, "abode of the clouds."[28]

In Punjab, meanwhile, an existing state was in search of a capital of its own. After the state's division in 1966, Chandigarh served as the capital of both Punjab and Haryana. The Sikhs believed, with reason, that the city should be reserved for them—indeed, the Centre had indicated that it would be. Now, the Punjabis were urging the government to fulfil its promise. Through 1968 and 1969, there were popular demonstrations; and in October 1969, the veteran freedom fighter Darshan Singh Pherumal died after a fast intended to make New Delhi hand over Chandigarh. The prime minister issued an anodyne note of sympathy: she hoped that Pherumal's death would "move the people of Punjab and of Haryana towards bringing their hearts and minds together in an act of great reconciliation."[29]

The Sikhs wanted Chandigarh exclusively for themselves; so, with regard to Bombay, did some Maharashtrians. Bombay had a new political party, named the Shiv Sena after the medieval Maratha warrior Shivaji. In some ways this was a continuation of the old Samyukta Maharashtra Samiti—albeit in a more extreme form. Instead of "Bombay for Maharashtra" the call now was "Bombay for Maharashtrians." The Shiv Sena was the handiwork of a cartoonist, Bal Thackeray. His main target was south Indians, who he claimed were taking away jobs from the natives. Thackeray lampooned dhoti-clad "Madrasis" in his writings and drawings; his followers attacked Udupi restaurants and the homes of Tamil-speakers and Telugu-speakers. Another target was the communists, whose control of the city's textile unions the Shiv Sena sought to undermine by making deals with the management.

Bombay was India's *urbs prima*; its financial and industrial capital, and the centre of its entertainment industry. In this most cosmopolitan of cities, a nativist agenda proved surprisingly successful, being especially attractive to the educated unemployed. In 1968, the Sena won forty-two seats in the Bombay municipal elections, coming in second only to the Congress.[30]

These calls for greater autonomy in the heartland were accompanied by stirrings in the periphery among groups and leaders who had never been entirely reconciled to being part of India in the first place. In March 1968 Sheikh Abdullah was freed from house arrest in Kodaikanal, and allowed to return to his Valley. This was a year after the elections of 1967, which, in Kashmir at any rate, had not really been free and fair. In twenty-two of seventy-five constituencies, the Congress candidate was returned unopposed, when his rivals' nomination papers were rejected.[31] Indira Gandhi's advisers now prevailed on her to free Abdullah. According to their information, the sheikh was "gradually adapting himself" to the fact that the accession of Kashmir to India was irrevocable.[32]

As in 1964, the "lion of Kashmir" returned home to a hero's welcome, driving in an open jeep into the Valley, accepting garlands from admirers who had lined the roads to greet him—it was estimated that 500,000 people had turned out. As ever, his statements were amenable to multiple interpretations. At one place he said that he would discuss "all possibilities" with the Indian government; at another place he said that he would never compromise on the Kashmiris' "right to self-determination."

To a British newspaper he offered a three-way resolution: Jammu to go to India and Azad Kashmir to Pakistan, with the Valley—the real bone of contention—to be put under UN trusteeship for five years, after which it would vote on whether to join India or Pakistan, or be independent. Although equivocal on politics, the sheikh was, just as characteristically, direct in his defence of secularism. When a dispute between students threatened to escalate into a riot between Hindus and Muslims, Abdullah pacified the students, then walked the streets of the old city urging everyone to calm down. He made his associates take a pledge that they were "prepared to shed their blood to protect the life, honour and property of the minorities in Kashmir."[33]

Meanwhile, the rebels in Nagaland were also seeking a new resolution. With Phizo in London, the movement was passing into the hands of younger radicals, such as Isak Swu and T. Muivah. Whereas Phizo had opposed seeking help from communist China—owing to its hostility to the Christian faith—these men had no such inhibitions. Reports came that 1,000 Nagas had crossed into Yunan via Burma, there to receive Chinese machine guns, mortars, and rocket launchers, as well as instructions on how to use them. In Nagaland, there were sharp clashes between the Indian army and the rebels.[34]

Endorsing the move toward Peking was the long-time supporter of the Naga cause, David Astor of the *Observer*. He predicted that Nagaland would follow the course set by Ireland—where a colonial government had reluctantly granted independence to the southern part of the island. Since the Nagas were as stubborn as the Irish, Astor thought that they "can now use the leverage of Chinese support . . . to survive successfully." He hoped that "friendly British voices would point out to Delhi the relevance of the lesson we had to learn when similarly challenged by the Irish."[35] The advice rested on a serious, not to say tragic, underestimation of the powers of the Indian state.

VII

Disturbingly, the late 1960s also brought a rise in violence between Hindus and Muslims. According to figures released by the National Integration Council, there were 132 incidents of communal violence in 1966, 220 in 1967, and 346 in 1968 (the upward trend continued through 1969 and 1970). These conflicts often had their origins in petty disputes, such as the playing of music before a mosque, or the killing of a cow near a temple. Sometimes, attacks on women or fights over property started the trouble. The states of Bihar and Uttar Pradesh had the highest number of incidents.[36]

One reason for this spurt in violence was the weakness of state governments. Particularly culpable were the SVD regimes, which vacillated in using force to quell riots or rioters. Another reason was that, in the aftermath of the war of 1965, feelings against Pakistan ran high. These could easily be turned against Indian Muslims, who were seen (unfairly) as fifth columnists working on behalf of the enemy. Hindus inspired by Jana Sangh were particularly prone to taunting Muslims in this way. Now, when a dispute broke out, to the old religious slogans—*Har Har Mahadev* and *Allah O Akbar*—the Hindus added a new one: *Pakistan ya Kabristan* ("Go to Pakistan, or else we will send you to your grave").[37]

One of the worst riots took place in Ahmedabad, the Gujarati city that had once been Mahatma Gandhi's home. Ironically, this riot took place on the eve of the hundredth anniversary of Gandhi's birth, and was thus a source of embarrassment to the government, which had planned a lavish celebration, with dignitaries coming in from all over the world. On 12 September 1969, a procession commemorating a Muslim saint encountered a group of sadhus walking back to their temple with cows. Hot words were exchanged, whereupon Muslim youths entered the temple and smashed a few idols. A Muslim delegation, led by a respected lawyer, went immmediately to apologize, but the priests were not to be pacified. As word spread of the desecration, crowds of Hindus began collecting, looking for targets to attack. Korans were burned in one place; Muslim shops were attacked in another. With the Muslims fighting back, the trouble spread through the city and eventually to towns near Ahmedabad. As the police looked mutely on, gangs battled each other in the narrow streets of the old city. After a week of fighting, the army was called in to restore peace. More than 1,000 people had died, and 30,000 were homeless. A majority of both the dead and the homeless were Muslim.[38]

There was a serious riot in Ranchi, in Bihar, in the summer of 1967, and a bad one in Jalgaon, in Maharashtra, three years later. In between, numerous other towns in north and west India experienced intercommunal violence. The writer Khushwant Singh noted that the Indian adolescent was now learning the geography of his country through the history of murder. Aligarh, Ranchi, and Ahmedabad were no longer centres of learning or culture or industry, but places where Indians butchered one another in the name of religion. As Singh pointed out, in these riots "nine out of ten killed are Muslims. Nine out of ten homes and business establishments destroyed are Muslim homes or enterprises." The majority of those made homeless and arrested by the police were also Muslim. "Is it any great wonder," asked Singh, "that an Indian Muslim no longer feels secure in secular India? He feels discriminated against. He feels a second-class citizen."[39]

In 1967–1968, when the communal temperature began to rise, India had a Muslim president (Dr. Zakir Hussain) as well as a Muslim chief justice of the Supreme Court (M. Hidayatullah). However, as a journal in Delhi pointed out, they were by no means representative of "the position of Muslims in the totality of Indian life." Muslims were seriously underrepresented in professions like engineering and medicine, and in industry, trade, and the armed forces. This situation was in part because of the flight of the Muslim upper class to Pakistan, yet subtle social prejudice also contributed to it. The Muslims had long stood solidly behind the Congress; but in the elections of 1967 they voted in large numbers for other parties, to show their disillusionment. The Muslims' predicament was a product of bigotry and communal politics on the Hindu side, and of an obscurantist leadership on their own.[40]

VIII

To the historian, the late 1960s are reminscent of the late 1940s, likewise a time of crisis and conflict; of resentment along lines of class, religion, ethnicity, and region; of a Centre that seemed barely to hold. I wonder if these parallels occurred to the Indians who lived through those times—to people in authority in particular, and to the prime minister most of all.

The resonances were not merely national or sociological, but also familial. With the Raj in its death throes, Jawaharlal Nehru became prime minister of an interim government in 1946; the next year, when India became independent, the post became more substantial. Indira Gandhi was unexpectedly thrust into office in 1966; the next year, the job was confirmed formally, when she led her party to victory in an election. Like Nehru, she was in control in Delhi; like him, she could not be certain how far her government's writ ran beyond it. He and she both had to contend with communist insurrection and communal conflict; he was additionally faced with the problem of the princely states, she with the problem of a dozen anti-Congress state governments.

Here the parallels end. Seeking to unite a divided India, Nehru articulated an ideology that rested on four main pillars. First, there was democracy, the freedom to choose one's friends and speak one's mind (and in the language of one's choice)—above all, the freedom to choose one's leaders through regular elections based on universal adult franchise. Second, there was secularism, the neutrality of the state in matters of religion, and its commitment to maintaining social peace. Third, there was socialism, the attempt to augment productivity while ensuring a more egalitarian distribution of income (and of social opportunity). Fourth, there was non-alignment, the placement of India beyond and above the rivalries of the great powers. Among the less compelling, but not necessarily less significant, elements of this worldview were the conscious cultivation of a multiparty system (notably through debate in Parliament) and respect for the autonomy of the judiciary and the executive.

Although re-articulated in the context of a newly independent India, these beliefs had been developing over a period of more than twenty years. Nehru was a well-read and widely travelled man. Through his travels and his reading, he arrived at a synthesis of socialism and liberalism that he thought appropriate to his country. In other words, the political beliefs he came to profess—and invited the people of India to share—were his own.

With Indira Gandhi one cannot be so sure. She was neither well-read nor widely travelled. She was unquestionably a patriot; growing up in the freedom movement, and with its leaders, she was deeply committed to upholding India's interests in the world. How she thought these could best be upheld was less certain. In all the years she had been in politics her core beliefs had not been revealed to her party or to the public. They did not know what she really thought of the market economy, the cold war, the relations between religions, or the institutions and processes of democracy. The many volumes of Nehru's *Selected Works* are suffused with his writings on these subjects—subjects on which Mrs. Gandhi, before 1967, spoke scarcely a word.

The prime minister was, so to say, non-ideological—an attribute not shared by her advisers. The chief among these was her principal secretary, P. N. Haksar. He had been educated at the London School of Economics (LSE) and was called to the bar in the United Kingdom, before returning to practice law in Allahabad. At independence he joined the foreign service, and became India's ambassador to Austria and its first high commissioner to Nigeria. In 1967, he was deputy high commissioner in London, when Mrs. Gandhi asked him to join her Secretariat. Haksar and she shared a hometown, a common ancestry—both were Kashmiri Pandits—and many common friends.

Haksar was a kind of polymath: a student of mathematics, he was also keenly interested in history, particularly diplomatic and military history. Among his other interests were anthropology—he had attended Bronislaw Malinowski's seminar at the LSE—and food (he was a superb cook). Haksar tended to overpower his friends and colleagues with the range of his knowledge and the vigour of his opinions. However, in his case intellectual force was not necessarily matched by intellectual subtlety. His political views were those of the left wing of the British Labour Party, c. 1945: pro-state and anti-market in economic affairs, pro-Soviet and anti-American in foreign policy. He was also, it must be added, a man of unshakeable integrity.[41]

This book owes a great deal to P. N. Haksar, whose papers, all 500 files of them, provide a privileged window into the history of the times. But the prime minister of the day owed him even more. For, as Katherine Frank writes, "Indira trusted Haksar's intelligence and judgement implicitly and completely. From 1967 to 1973, he was probably the most influential and powerful person in the government."[42] Haksar shared his influence and power with the career diplomat T. N. Kaul, the politician turned diplomat D. P. Dhar, the economist turned mandarin P. N. Dhar, and the policeman turned security analyst R. N. Kao. Collectively they were known (behind their backs) as the "Panch Pandava," after the five heroic brothers of the *Mahabharata*. Coincidentally, all were Kashmiri Brahmans. There was also an outer group of advisers, who were likewise officials or intellectuals rather than politicians per se.

This was not accidental. Even more so than Lal Bahadur Shastri, Mrs. Gandhi needed to assert her independence of the Congress "Syndicate" that had chosen her. Socially, she shared little with the party bosses—her own friends came from a more rarefied mileu. Also, she could not be certain when the bosses might try to unseat her. Thus she came to rely on the advice of the mandarins around her. They had no political ambitions for themselves, but they did have political views, to which, in time and for her own reasons, she came to subscribe.

IX

After the elections of 1967, Morarji Desai once more made clear his desire to become prime minister. A compromise was worked so that he would serve as finance minister and deputy prime minister—the latter a post that no one had held since the death of Vallabhbhai Patel.

Hemmed in by the Syndicate, and threatened by Desai, the prime minister now sought to mark out her own identity by presenting herself as a socialist. This was done at the advice of P. N. Haksar. In a note he prepared for her in January 1968, he advised her to clip Desai's wings, perhaps by appointing one or two additional "deputy" prime ministers. While choosing ministers loyal to her, the prime minister also had to develop "wider progressive alliances under [her] more effective personal lead." For this, she needed to "project more assertively [her] own ideological image directly to the people over the heads of [her] colleagues and partymen."[43]

Indira Gandhi had rarely invoked the word "socialist" before 1967, although it was one of the four pillars of her father's political philosophy. Notably, it was the pillar that was propped up most enthusiastically by her mandarins. In part, the appeal was negative, stemming from a Brahmanic distaste for business and businessmen. But there was also a positive identification with the idea of socialism. A greater role for the state in the economy, they believed, was necessary for ensuring social equity as well as promoting national integration. The public sector, wrote one mandarin, was "a macrocosm of a united India." In the private sector, Punjabis employed Punjabis, Marwaris trusted only Marwaris; but in the Indian railroads and the great steel factories Tamils worked alongside Biharis, Hindus with Muslims, Brahmans with Harijans. Whether or not socialism was economically feasible, it was a "social necessity." "Socialism and a large public sector . . . are effective weapons for forging a united and integrated India."[44]

There was a strong moral core to the socialism of P. N. Haksar and his colleagues. For the prime minister, however, the appeal was pragmatic; this was a means of distinguishing herself from the old guard in the Congress. In May 1967 she presented a ten-point programme of reform to the party: it included the "social control" of banking, the abolition of the privy purses of princes, and guaranteed minimum wages for rural and industrial labour. The Syndicate was unenthusiastic, but the programme appealed to the younger generation, who saw the party's recent reverses as a consequence of the promises unfulfilled over the years.[45]

In speeches after her re-election Mrs. Gandhi identified explicitly with the poor and vulnerable. Speaking to the Lok Sabha in February 1968, she stressed the problems of landless labour; expressed her "concern for all the minorities of India"; and defended the public sector from the criticism that it was not making a profit (her answer was that it did not need to be profitable, since it was building a base for economic development). Speaking to the Rajya Sabha in August, she asked for a "New Deal for the Down-trodden," in particular, the Scheduled Castes and Scheduled Tribes, pledging her "unceasing attention and effort to this cause." A few days later, in her Independence Day address from the ramparts of the Red Fort, she singled out "industralists and businessmen" who had the nerve to talk about undisciplined workers while continuing to "make big profits and draw fat salaries."[46]

These views resonated with the so-called "Young Turks" in the Congress, who had started a socialist faction within the party. They used the pulpit of Parliament to ask embarrassing questions of the more conservative ministers. One Young Turk, Chandra Shekhar, raised charges of corruption against Morarji Desai's son, Kanti. He also insinuated that the finance minister had issued licenses out of turn to a large industrial house. It was believed that he was speaking as a proxy for the prime minister—at any rate, she refused to censure him.[47]

Through 1968 and 1969, one biographer writes, Mrs. Gandhi was a "frustrated leader. She was not strong enough to defy the [Congress] organization and not rash enough to quit."[48] Her chance came in the summer of 1969, when Dr. Zakir Hussain died halfway through his term as president of the republic. The Syndicate wished to replace him with one of its own: N. Sanjiva Reddy, a former speaker of Lok Sabha and chief minister of Andhra Pradesh. Mrs. Gandhi, however, preferred the vice president, V. V. Giri, a labour leader with whom her own relations were very good.

In July 1969, the All India Congress Committee (AICC) met in Bangalore. Before leaving for this meeting, the prime minister was apparently told by P. N. Haksar that "the best way to vanquish the Syndicate would be to convert the struggle for personal power into an ideological one."[49] In Bangalore, Mrs. Gandhi openly showed that she was on the side of the Young Turks by proposing the immediate nationalization of the major banks. She also opposed Sanjiva Reddy's candidacy for president, but she was overruled by a majority of the Working Committee.

On returning to Delhi, Mrs. Gandhi divested Morarji Desai of the finance portfolio. He was a known opponent of bank nationalization, once telling Parliament that it would "severely strain the administrative resources of the Government while leaving the basic issues untouched." The state takeover of banks, Desai believed, would reduce the resources available for economic development and increase bureaucracy and red tape.[50]

After relieving Desai of the Finance Ministry, Mrs. Gandhi issued an ordinance announcing that the state had taken over fourteen privately owned banks. Explaining the action over All India Radio, she said that India was "an ancient country but a young democracy, which has to remain ever vigilant to prevent the domination of the few over the social, economic or political systems." This mandated that "major banks should be not only socially controlled but publicly owned," so that they could give credit not just to big business but to "millions of farmers, artisans, and other self-employed persons."[51]

In a statement to the press, the prime minister claimed that there was "a great feeling in the country" regarding the nationalization: 95% of the people supported it, and only big newspapers representing commercial interests opposed it. However, a small, independently owned weekly suggested that this might be an individual quest masquerading as an ideological battle. Mrs. Gandhi had "chosen to adopt a radical stance suddenly as a tactic in the personal strife for dominance within the Congress party," said *Thought*: she now wished to "project herself as a national figure who needs the Congress less than it needs her."[52]

The nationalization of the banks was challenged in the Supreme Court; the challenge was upheld, but the judgement was immediately nullified by a new ordinance brought in by the government, signed this time by the president. In the first six months of state control there was an enormous expansion in the banking sector—as many as 1,100 new branches were opened, a large proportion of them in remote rural areas that had never before been serviced by formal credit.[53]

X

Attention now shifted to the election of a new president, in which all members of Parliament and the state assemblies would vote. The official Congress candidate was Sanjiva Reddy. V. V. Giri had decided to run as an independent. The opposition had put up C. D. Deshmukh, a former civil servant and cabinet minister. In violation of party practice and party discipline, the prime minister decided to support V. V. Giri. This decision was not made public, but it was conveyed to her followers, who went around asking the younger Congress members to vote for Giri. The Congress president, S. Nijalingappa, now pressed the prime minister to issue a public declaration of support for Reddy. When she wouldn't, he spoke to the leaders of Jana Sangh and Swatantra, asking them to shift their own allegiance from Subba Rao to Reddy. This move was seized on by Mrs. Gandhi's camp, which accused Nijalingappa of fraternizing with the enemy and "requisitioned" a meeting of the AICC to discuss the matter. The request was refused.

Four days before the presidential elections—due on 20 August 1969—Mrs Gandhi finally spoke. She asked for a "vote of conscience." This was a call to congressmen to defy their organization and vote for the rival candidate. They did, and in fairly large numbers. Many of the older party men voted for Reddy, but in the end Giri won, on the second count. Now commenced a bitter exchange of letters between the Congress party's president and the prime minister. Finally, on 12 November, Mrs. Gandhi was expelled from the Congress for "indiscipline." By this time many members of Parliament had thrown in their lot with her. In December, rival Congress sessions were held: the parent body met in Ahmedabad and its new challenger in Bombay. These parties were becoming known as Congress (O) and Congress (R). The letters stood, in one version, for "Organization" and "Requisitionist"; in another version, they stood for "Old" and "Reform."[54]

In expelling Mrs. Gandhi from the Congress, Nijalingappa accused her of fostering a cult of personality, of promoting herself above party and nation. The history of the twentieth century, he pointed out,

> is replete with instances of the tragedy that overtakes democracy when a leader who has risen to power on the crest of a popular wave or with the support of a democratic organisation becomes a victim of political narcissism and is egged on by a coterie of unscrupulous sycophants who use corruption and terror to silence opposition and attempt to make public opinion an echo of authority. The Congress as an organisation dedicated to democracy and socialism has to combat such trends.[55]

Nijalingappa was a lifelong congressman, a man from peasant stock who had joined the freedom movement as a very young man. He built up the party in Mysore, later serving three terms as the state's chief minister.[56] About his commitment to the party and to democracy there could be no question. But "socialism" was another matter. The nationalization of the banks had strengthened his rival's claim to that label, while Nijalingappa's wooing of the Jana Sangh and Swatantra had weakened his own. This contrast was assiduously developed in speeches and letters that bore Mrs. Gandhi's name but were actually the handiwork of P. N. Haskar and his colleagues. Here, the prime minister was presented as standing for socialism in economics and secularism in matters of religion, as being pro-poor and for the development of the nation as a whole. The party president, on the other hand, was said to be promoting capitalism in economics and communalism in religion.[57]

The presentation was markedly successful. Of the 705 members of the AICC, 446 attended the Congress (R) session; of the 429 Congress members of Parliament (in both houses), 310 joined the prime minister's camp. Two hundred and twenty were from the Lok Sabha, leaving the Congress (R) some forty-five seats short of a majority. To make up the numbers it turned to independents and to the Communist Party of India. The CPI was delighted to join up, seeing in Mrs. Gandhi's left turn an opportunity for expanding its own influence. In August 1969, writing about the battle within the Congress, an influential journalist close to the CPI said that "the Syndicate pretentions have been torn to pieces." "A tide has come in the affairs of the nation," he wrote,

> and there is little doubt that Smt Indira Gandhi is taking it at the flood. . . . The tide is symbolised by the enthusiastic crowds from different walks of life that have been flocking to the Prime Minister's House everyday. This is no ordinary craving for *darshan* of a beautiful face; they represent a new assertion of the power of the *demos*.

The journalist then looked forward to the "implementation of a radical economic agenda and [a] firm stand against communalism."[58]

In a comparable situation, in 1950–1952, Jawaharlal Nehru had bided his time. Faced with the conservative challenge of Tandon and company, he had worked to get his way with the party rather than divide it in two. But now, as one knowledgeable observer remarked, Mrs. Gandhi had "displayed a militancy foreign to Congress tradition." In contrast to the incremental approach of Nehru and Shastri, she "represented something ruthless and new. She had astonished people with her flair for cold assessment, shrewd timing, and the telling theatrical gesture; above all, with her capacity for a fight to the finish, even to bringing the eighty-four-year-old party of liberation to rupture."[59]

XI

With the banks nationalized, Mrs. Gandhi now turned to the abolition of the privileges of the princes. When their states merged with the Indian Union, the princes were given a constitutional guarantee that they could retain their titles, jewels, and palaces; would be paid an annual privy purse in proportion to the size of their states; and would be exempt from central taxes and import duties. With so many Indians so poor, it was felt that these privileges were "out of place and out of time"—these are the words of P. N. Haksar, but they were widely endorsed within and outside his circle.[60]

As early as July 1967, the AICC passed a resolution asking for an end to titles and privy purses. The Home Ministry prepared a detailed note, recommending action through legislation rather than executive action. The home minister, Y. B. Chavan, was asked to begin negotiations with the princes, represented in these talks by the Maharaja of Dhrangadhra. It was hoped that the princes would be amenable to the change; if not, a constitutional amendment would have to be passed.[61]

Chavan and the maharaja had several long meetings in 1968, but no compromise could be reached. In any case the power struggle within the Congress ruled out hasty action. There were many members of Parliament who were either princes or under the control of princes; and these members' votes were needed to see Mrs. Gandhi's candidate for president through. After Giri's election the government and the princes continued to talk, each side proving as obdurate as the other. At this stage, in December 1969, the Jam Saheb of Nawanagar sent New Delhi an intriguing proposal. He criticized both parties: the princes for adopting "a most adamantly uncompromising stand," the government for "going back on their [constitutional] commitments and assurances." The Jam Saheb suggested, as a way out of the impasse, that the government abolish the princes' privileges, but pay them twenty years' worth of privy purses: 25% in cash, 25% in bonds to be redeemed after twenty years, and 50% to a public charitable trust headed by the ruler. The aims of this trust would be the promotion of sport, the education of backward classes, and above all the protection of "our fast disappearing wild life."[62]

The Jam Saheb thought that this scheme "would befit the dignity of the Nation." Mrs. Gandhi passed it on to the home minister, noting that it was "animated by a constructive purpose." But nothing came of it. On 18 May 1970—the last day of the summer session of Parliament—Y. B. Chavan introduced a bill calling for a constitutional amendment annulling the privileges of the princes. The bill was taken up in the next session, and Mrs. Gandhi described it as an "important step in the further democratisation of our society."

The Lok Sabha adopted the bill by the necessary two-thirds margin—336 for, 155 against. However, in the Rajya Sabha the motion failed by a single vote. The prime minister had apparently anticipated this adverse vote in the Upper House, for soon afterwards a presidential order was issued derecognizing the princes.

Four days later, on 11 September 1970, a group of maharajas appealed to the Supreme Court against the order. The case was heard by a full bench, headed by the chief justice. On 11 December the bench ruled that the order was arbitrary and against the spirit of the constitution. Some legal scholars viewed the judgement as a victory for democracy, whereas left-wing radicals saw it as consistent with the "tendency of the Supreme Court to protect the vested interests."

With regard to bank nationalization, too, the court had put a spanner in the works. This additional challenge to her authority prompted the prime minster to dissolve Parliament and call for a mandate from the people. The House still had a year to run. Explaining the decision over All India Radio, Mrs. Gandhi said that while her government had sought to "ensure a better life to the vast majority of our people and satisfy their aspiration for a just social order . . . reactionary forces have not hesitated to obstruct [this] in every possible way."[63]

XII

On one front, at least, there was good news for Mrs. Gandhi's government— the new agricultural strategy had begun paying dividends. In 1967 there was a severe drought, which particularly affected the state of Bihar; but the next year saw a bumper crop of food grains, 95 million tons in all. Much of this increase was accounted for by Punjab and Haryana, whose farmers had planted the new dwarf varieties of wheat developed by Indian scientists from Mexican models. However, the new varieties of rice had also done quite well, as had cotton and peanuts.

C. Subramaniam's strategy had been to identify districts where irrigation was available and farming communities most likely to take to the new seeds, and the heavy doses of fertilizers that went with them. The results were sensational. Between 1963 and 1967, before the new methods had been tried, the annual production of wheat in India was between 9 million tons and 11 million tons. Between 1967 and 1970 it ranged from 16 million to 20 million tons. The corresponding figures for rice ranged from 30 million and 37 million tons for the earlier period, and between 37 million and 42 million tons for the latter.[64]

These figures masked enormous variations by region. There remained large areas where agriculture depended on rain, and where only one crop could be grown per year. Still, there was a feeling that endemic scarcity was a thing of the past. Modern science was laying the ghost of Malthus. In August 1969, a British journalist who was an old India hand wrote that "for the first time in all the years I have been visiting the country, there is a coherence in the economic picture, for the first time an absence of feeling that the economy rested almost wholly on the simple success or failure of the monsoon."[65]

The food problem was solved, but India might still fall apart—simply because, as Neville Maxwell and others had claimed, it was too diverse. In an editorial marking twenty years of India's existence as a republic, the *New York Times* called it a "remarkable achievement," then went on to say that "both Union and democracy are under increasing strain these days, with the future of both in doubt."[66] However, most Indians were by now comfortable with diversity. They could see what bound the varied religions, races, and regions: a shared political history (from the national movement onward), a pluralistic constitution, and a tradition of regular elections. Nor did they think the challenges of states a threat to national unity. As one commentator wrote—in rebuttal of doomsayers like Maxwell—"a strong Centre is not necessarily conducive to democracy." Federalism and rule by regional parties could help sustain democracy in India, in contrast to, say, Indonesia and Ghana, where the efforts of Sukarno and Nkrumah to impose a strong centre had led to dictatorship.[67]

Among thinking Indians, then, there was little fear that the events of the late 1960s would presage the break-up of the country or the replacement of elected politicians by soldiers in uniform. Army rule was out of the question, but there was still the prospect of an armed communist movement engulfing large parts of the country. The green revolution could turn red, for agricultural prosperity had also created social polarities. And the location of Naxalbari was significant: a thin strip of India, wedged between East Pakistan and Nepal, that was not far from China and provided the only access to the states of the north-east. This was an "ideal operational field" for beginning a revolution, escaping into Pakistan or Nepal when one wished, and getting arms from China if one wanted. So the worry grew in New Delhi that these pro-Peking communists would "fan out from Naxalbari to link up with their cells in Bengal, till they come right into the heart of Calcutta. Behind them will be the Chinese army menacing the Himalayan border."[68]

On the other side, there were some who looked forward to the revolution in the making. These included the Naxalites, of course, but also western fellow travellers. In the winter of 1968–1969, the Marxist anthropologist Kathleen Gough—originally American but then teaching in Canada—wrote an article which saw, as "the most hopeful way forward for India," a "revolutionary movement that would root itself in the countryside" where the bulk of the poor were located. Taking heart from the progress, here and there, of the Naxalites and their ideology, Gough said that "parliamentarism seems doomed to failure, and the rebel Communists' path the only hopeful alternative."[69]

Gough was not alone in seeing revolutionary communism as India's main hope, perhaps its only hope. That same winter, a young Swedish couple animated by the spirit of 1968 travelled through the Indian countryside. They covered the land from tip to toe, from the parched fields of eastern Uttar Pradesh to the rich rice paddies of the southern Cauvery delta. They saw a new critical awareness among the oppressed, manifest in "growing antagonisms in Indian society." Caste conflict was turning into class conflict (as Marxist theory said, and hoped, it would). Among the intellectuals, they saw a (to them welcome) skepticism about parliamentary democracy. As one left-wing student leader remarked, "we must not let ourselves be fooled by the hocus-pocus of elections every fifth year."

These changes, the Swedish sociologists predicted, "will have widespread consequences for India's future." Blood was being spilt (as Marxist theory said it must). "The antagonisms are sometimes so violent that they are hard to imagine." Fortunately, "the new revolutionary movement . . . was growing in India today." The authors were sure that "only when these millions of poor people take their future in their own hands will India's poverty and oppression be brought to an end." They left their readers with this hope: "Perhaps Naxalbari does stand for the Indian revolution."[70]

20

THE ELIXIR *of* VICTORY

Gungi gudiya [dumb doll].
RAMMANOHAR LOHIA
on Indira Gandhi, c. 1967

I

IN NOVEMBER 1969, *Thought*, a weekly published in Delhi, commented that "the Congress seems to have written itself off as a nationally cohesive force." The once mighty party was now split into disputatious parts. When the next general elections came, said *Thought*, "Congressmen will be fighting Congressmen to the obvious advantage of regional or sectarian groups." Consequently, "Mrs. Gandhi's party may not secure more than one-third of the seats in Parliament. The chances of the other group seem to be even slimmer."[1]

A year later the prime minister called for elections, fourteen months ahead of schedule. Her party—which called itself the Congress (R)—wanted a popular mandate to implement its progressive reforms, now held up by the "reactionary" forces in Parliament. Its manifesto offered a "genuine radical programme of economic and social development," upholding the interests of the small farmer and the landless labourer, and of the small entrepreneur against the big capitalist. It stood for the betterment of the lower castes, and for protection of the minorities. Particular mention was made of the Urdu language, which "shall be given its due place which has been denied to it so far." It promised a "strong and stable Government," and asked for support in the fight against the "dark and evil forces of Right reaction," which were "intent upon destroying the very base of our democratic and socialist objectives."[2]

The position in which Indira Gandhi found herself in 1971 was in many ways reminiscent of her father's in 1952. Like Nehru then, Mrs. Gandhi went into the election having fought a bruising battle with her own party. Like him, she offered to the people a fresh, progressive-sounding mandate. And, like him, she was her party's chief campaigner and spokesperson, the embodiment of what it said it stood for.

In calling for elections, the prime minister had astutely dissociated the general elections from elections to the various state assemblies. In the past they had always been combined, and as a result parochial considerations of caste and ethnicity got mixed up with wider national questions. In 1967 this proved to be detrimental to the Congress. This time, Mrs. Gandhi made sure to separate the two, by calling a general election in which she could place a properly national agenda before the electorate.

The opposition, meanwhile, was seeking to build a united front against the ruling party. Urging it on was C. Rajagopalachari—"Rajaji"—now past ninety years of age. A common leader could not be agreed on; so, said Rajaji, the fight had to be conducted "on the pattern of guerrilla warfare. Indira's candidates . . . must be opposed everywhere on the single ground that we oppose the conspiracy to tear up the Constitution and to extinguish the people's liberties and put all power in the hands of the State."[3]

The opposition constructed a "grand alliance," bringing together Jana Sangh, Swatantra, Congress (O), the socialists, and regional groupings. The idea was to limit the number of multi-cornered contests. A copywriter came up with the slogan *Indira Hatao* ("Remove Indira"). This prompted a rejoinder, from the lips of the prime minister herself: *Wo kehte hain Indira Hatao, hum kehte hain Garibi Hatao* ("They ask for the removal of Indira, whereas we want an end to poverty itself ").

Whether it was coined by the prime minister or one of her now forgotten minions, *Garibi Hatao* was inspired. It allowed the Congress (R) to take the moral high ground, representing itself as the party of progress, against a reactionary alliance. Personalizing the election was to backfire, hurting the opposition. Its agenda was portrayed as negative, in contrast to the forward-looking programme of the ruling party.

Mrs. Gandhi worked tirelessly to garner votes for her party. Between the dissolution of Parliament, in the last week of December 1970, and the elections, held ten weeks later, she travelled 36,000 miles. She addressed 300 meetings, and was heard or seen by an estimated 20 million people. These figures were recounted, with relish, in a letter written by Mrs. Gandhi to an American friend. She clearly enjoyed the experience; as she remarked, "it was wonderful to see the light in their [the people's] eyes."[4]

The prime minister's speeches repeatedly stressed the contrast, perceived and real, between the party she had left behind and the party she had founded. The "Old" Congress was in thrall to "conservative elements" and "vested interests," whereas the "New" Congress was committed to the poor. Did not the nationalization of banks and the abolition of the privy purses show as much? The message sounded a strong chord. One somewhat cynical journalist wrote:

> The man lying in a gutter prizes nothing more than the notion pumped into him that he is superior to the sanitary inspector. That the rich had been humbled looked like the assurance that the poor would be honoured. The instant "poverty-removal" slogan was an economic absurdity. Psychologically and politically, for that reason, it was however a decisive asset in a community at war with reason and rationality.[5]

Her travels within India had made the prime minister far better known than she had been in 1967. In asking for votes, she exploited her "charming personality," her "father's historical role," and above all that stirring slogan *Garibi Hatao*. The landless and low castes voted en masse for the Congress (R), as did the Muslims, who had been lukewarm the last time around. The new party's organizational weakness was remedied by its young volunteers, who went around the countryside amplifying their leader's words. The huge turnout on election day suggested that "the people had been fired with a new hope of redemption."[6]

In 1952, it had been said that a lamppost could win if it ran on the Congress ticket. But Mrs. Gandhi's victory was even more spectacular than her father's. The Congress (R) won 352 out of 518 seats; the next highest tally was that of the CPM, which won twenty-five. Both victor and vanquished agreed that this result was chiefly the work of one person. As the writer Khushwant Singh commented, "Indira Gandhi has successfully magnified her figure as the one and only leader of national dimensions." Then he added, ominously, "However, if power is voluntarily surrendered by a predominant section of the people to one person and at the same time opposition is reduced to insignificance, the temptation to ride roughshod over legitimate criticism can become irresistible. The danger of Indira Gandhi being given unbridled power shall always be present."[7]

Among the consequences of the election of 1971 was a change in the name of the ruling party. The Congress (R) now became known as Congress (I), for "Indira"; later, even the (I) was dropped. By its margin of victory, Indira's Congress was confirmed as the real Congress, requiring no qualifying suffix.

Her success at the polls emboldened Mrs. Gandhi to act decisively against the princes. Through 1971, the two sides tried and failed to find a settlement. The princes were willing to forgo their privy purses, but hoped at least to save their titles. But with her overwhelming majority in Parliament, the prime minister had no need to compromise. On 2 December she introduced a bill to amend the constitution and abolish all princely privileges. It was passed in the Lok Sabha by 381 votes to six, and in the Rajya Sabha by 167 votes to seven. In her own speech, the prime minister invited "the princes to join the élite of the modern age, the élite which earns respect by its talent, energy and contribution to human progress, all of which can only be done when we work together as equals without regarding anybody as of special status."[8]

II

The statistics of the fifth general election were printed in loving detail in the report of the chief election commissioner (CEC). The size of the electorate was 275 million, 100 million more than it had been in 1952. No Indian had needed to walk more than two kilometres to vote. There were now as many as 342,944 voting stations, up 100,000 from 1962. Each station was supplied with forty-three separate items, such as ballot papers, boxes, indelible ink, and sealing wax. About 282 million ballot papers were printed, 7 million more than the number of eligible voters (to allow for accidents and errors). And 1,769,802 Indians were on duty at the polls; for the most part, these were officials of the state and central governments.

The CEC then turned, with less pleasure, to electoral malpractice. A study of the elections of 1967 had found 375 cases of electoral violence of all kinds; of these, ninety-eight were in Bihar.[9] In 1971, the Election Commission reported sixty-six instances of "booth-capturing": ballot boxes were seized by force and stuffed with ballots in favour of one's candidate. In Anantnag in the Kashmir Valley, a woman took away a ballot box under her burka and then returned it, now heavier by several hundred ballots. Again, the most violations were in Bihar—this state accounted for fifty-two of the sixty-six booths captured, by hooligans hired by leaders of caste factions. The CEC believed this was "perhaps the most caste-ridden State in the whole [of] India and this bane of excessive casteism vitiates in no mean degree the political atmosphere."

These disfigurements notwithstanding, the holding of its fifth general election was something on which the country could congratulate itself. So wrote the CEC, in a preface whose lyricism sat oddly with the hard-nosed numerical analysis that followed. In between the last elections and this one, "India was in the middle of the deepest and darkest woods and was groping for a way out." Factionalism was rife; SVD governments came and went, and the president of the republic died, making "the already dark political situation . . . darker." Then the mighty Congress party split; this, in the CEC's view, was comparable only to "the Great Schism in the Whig Party in Great Britain in the year 1796." In this "state of tension, stress, confusion and flux, the prophets of doom, both inside and outside the country, started expressing serious misgivings and doubts as to the very survival of democracy in this Great Land."

These doomsayers, said the CEC, had not reckoned with "The Supreme Dispenser of India's Destiny" (*Bharata Bhagya Vidhata*), which from "ancient times" had thwarted "adverse and hostile circumstances" by blowing "into the soul of India that elixir-giving inspiration which imparted rejuvenated vigour to her vital, moral and spiritual forces." Others might have disagreed, seeing this election not as a victory for Indian spiritualism but as a vindication of a very modern political form, electoral democracy.[10]

III

Three months before India held its fifth general elections, Pakistan had held its first elections based on adult franchise. The poll had been called by General Yahya Khan, Ayub Khan's successor as president and chief martial law administrator.

Two parties dominated the campaign: Zulfiqar Bhutto's Pakistan People's Party (PPP), in West Pakistan; and Sheikh Mujibur Rahman's National Awami League, in East Pakistan. Bhutto was the son of a large landowner and had been educated at Oxford and Berkeley, but he sought to declass himself, at least rhetorically, by promising every Pakistani *roti, kapda, aur makaan* ("food, clothing, and a roof over your head"). Mujib's campaign was based on East Pakistan's sense of victimhood, its anger at the suppression of the Bengali language and the exploitation of its rich natural resources by the military rulers of the western half of the country.[11]

Yahya Khan appears to have called for elections in the hope that Bhutto's PPP would win, and allow him to continue as president. The election was held in the third week of December 1970. The PPP won eighty-eight out of the 144 seats in West Pakistan; the Awami League swept the more populous East, winning 167 of its 169 seats. These results surprised Mujibur Rahman and shocked Yahya Khan. The president had intended that the newly elected assembly would frame a democratic constitution; the worry now was that the Awami League, with its majority, would insist on a federation in which the eastern wing would manage its own affairs, leaving only defence and foreign policy to the central government. Mujib had already indicated that he would like the East to have control over the foreign exchange its products generated, and perhaps issue its own currency as well.

Yahya's reservations were reinforced by the ambitions of Bhutto. The relationship between Pakistan's two wings had always been colonial, with the West dominating the East militarily, economically, and even culturally. For both general and patrician, the prospect of having a Bengali decide their destiny was too horrible to contemplate. The Bengali Muslim was regarded by his West Pakistani counterpart as effete and feminine, and too easily corrupted by proximity to Hindus (over 10 million of whom still lived in their midst). Among these Hindus were many professionals—lawyers, doctors, university professors. The fear of the West Pakistan elite was that if Mujib's Awami League came to form the government, "the constitution to be adopted by them will have Hindu iron hand in it."[12]

On the other side, the East Pakistan Muslims looked upon their West Pakistan counterparts as "the ruling classes, as foreign ruling classes and as predatory foreign ruling classes." They resented the rulers' dismissal of their language, Bengali; they complained that their agricultural wealth was being drained away to feed the western sector; and they noted that Bengalis were very poorly represented in the upper echelons of the Pakistani bureaucracy, judiciary, and, not least, army. The feeling of being discriminated against had been growing over the years. By the time of the elections of 1970, "the politically-minded" East Bengali had become "allergic to a central authority located a thousand miles away."[13]

In January 1971 Yahya Khan and Bhutto travelled separately to the capital of East Pakistan, Dacca. They held talks with Mujib, but found him firm on the question of a federal constitution. The president then postponed the convening of the national assembly. The Awami League answered by calling an indefinite general strike. Throughout East Pakistan shops, offices, and even railroads and airports closed. Clashes between the police and demonstrators became a daily occurrence.

The military decided to quell these protests by force. Troop reinforcements were flown in or sent by ship to the principal eastern port, Chittagong. On the night of 25–26 March, the army began a major attack on the Dacca University, whose students were among the Awami League's strongest supporters. A parade of tanks rolled onto the campus, firing on the dormitories. Students were rounded up, shot, and pushed into graves hastily dug and bulldozed over by tanks. There were troop detachments at work in other parts of the city, targeting Bengali newspaper offices and homes of local politicians. That same night, Mujibur Rahman was arrested at his home and flown to a secret location in West Pakistan.[14]

The Pakistani army fanned out into the countryside, seeking to stamp out any sign of rebellion. East Bengali troops mutinied in several places, including Chittagong, where one major captured a radio station and announced the establishment of the "Independent People's Republic of Bangladesh."[15] To combat the guerrillas the army raised bands of local loyalists, called Razakars, who put the claims of religion—and hence of a united Pakistan—above those of language. Villages and small towns, and even a few airports, fell into rebel hands, then were recaptured. The reprisals grew more brutal. An American consular official reported, "Army officials and soldiers give every sign of believing that they are now embarked on a Jehad against Hindu-corrupted Bengalis."[16]

One soldier later wrote a vivid recollection of the counter-insurgency, the "reassertion of state power," and the capture of those "places [which] had been occupied by anti-state elements." As he remembered, "there was more resistance offered by the terrain than by the miscreants. Extensive damage to land communications and free intermingling of hostiles with the general populace made progress tedious."[17]

After the first swoop, foreign correspondents were asked to leave East Pakistan, but later in the summer some were allowed to return. A German journalist saw signs of the civil war everywhere, in bazaars burned in the cities and homesteads razed in the villages. There was "a ghostly emptiness in settlements once bubbling with life and energy." An American reporter found Dacca "a city under the occupation of a military force that rules by strength, intimidation and terror." The army was harassing the Hindu minority in particular; the authorities were "demolishing Hindu temples, regardless of whether there are any Hindus to use them." A World Bank team visiting East Pakistan found a "general destruction of property in cities, towns, and villages," leading to an "all-pervasive fear" among the population.[18]

The army action in Dacca sparked a panic flight out of the city. The repression in the hinterland magnified this flight, directing it across the border into India. By the end of April 1971 there were 500,000 refugees from East Pakistan in India; by the end of May, 3.5 million; by the end of August, more than 8 million. Most (though by no means all) were Hindus.[19] Refugee camps were strung out along the border, in the states of West Bengal, Tripura, and Meghalaya. To distribute the burden, camps were also opened in Madhya Pradesh and Orissa. The refugees were housed in huts made of bamboo and polyethylene; the luckier ones were in the verandas of schools and colleges. The food came from Indian warehouses—not as bare as they would have been before the green revolution—and from supplies provided by western aid agencies.[20]

From the beginning, the Indian government had followed an "open door" policy; anyone who came was allowed in. Significantly, the Centre, not the states had responsibility for the camps. In fact, from the beginning of the conflict New Delhi had taken a very keen interest in the future of what was already being referred to in secret official communications as the "struggle for Bangladesh." On the other side, Islamabad spoke darkly of "an Indo-Zionist plot against Islamic Pakistan."[21] This was an exaggeration; the origins of the problem were internal to Pakistan, and Israel was not in the picture at all. Still, once the dispute presented itself, the Indians were not above stoking it for their own ends.

A key player here was the Research and Analysis Wing (RAW), an intelligence agency set up in 1968 on the model of the CIA. Its purpose was to pursue Indian interests worldwide; its activities were screened from parliamentary enquiry; and it reported directly to the prime minister's office. The head of RAW was (perhaps inevitably) a Kashmiri Brahman, R. N. Kao; its officers came from the police and, on occasion, the army. No sooner had the Pakistani elections been called than RAW was kept busy writing reports. A memorandum of January 1971 presented a somewhat alarmist picture of Pakistan's armed strength: listing numbers of troops, tanks, aircraft, and ships, it claimed that Pakistan had "achieved a good state of military preparedness for any confrontation with India." It thought the "potential threat" of an attack on India "quite real, particularly in view of the Sino-Pakistan collusion." Besides, the constitutional crisis might encourage the generals to undertake a diversionary adventure, and to begin, as in 1965, with an "infiltration campaign in Jammu and Kashmir."[22]

Whether Yahya Khan had any such plans in January 1971 only the Pakistani archives can reveal. The archives on this side tell us that India had certain designs of its own, aimed naturally at Pakistan. Thinking through these designs were P. N. Haksar and his colleague D. P. Dhar, who was then the Indian ambassador to the Soviet Union. In April 1971 Dhar wrote to Haksar expressing pleasure that India was winning the propaganda war with Pakistan—chiefly by providing succour to the victims of its repression. Some analysts wanted quick military action, but, advised Dhar, instead of "policies and programmes of impetuosity," what India had to plan for

> is not an immediate defeat of the highly trained [army] of West Pakistan; we have to create the whole of East Bengal into a bottomless ditch which will suck the strength and resources of West Pakistan. Let us think in terms of a year or two, not in terms of a week or two.[23]

IV

By the summer of 1971, along with the hundreds of camps for refugees, India was also hosting training camps for Bengali guerrillas. Known as the "Mukti Bahini," these fighters numbered some 20,000 in all: regular officers and soldiers of the once united Pakistani army, plus younger volunteers learning how to use light arms. The instruction was at first in the hands of the paramilitary Border Security Force, but by the autumn the Indian army had assumed direct charge. From their bases in India, the guerrillas would venture into East Pakistan, to attack army camps and disrupt communications.[24]

In April 1971, the Chinese prime minister, Chou En-lai, wrote to the president of Pakistan deploring the "gross interference" by India in the "internal problems" of Pakistan. He dismissed the resistance as "a handful of persons who want to sabotage the unification of Pakistan." He assured Yahya Khan that "should the Indian expansionists dare to launch aggression against Pakistan, the Chinese Government and people will, as always, support the Pakistan Government and people in their just struggle to safeguard state sovereignty and national independence."[25]

Chou's letter was printed in the Pakistani press, and must certainly have been read across the border as well. Meanwhile, New Delhi dispatched senior cabinet ministers to countries in Europe and Africa, to speak there of the unfolding tragedy and India's efforts to manage it. The prime minister wrote to world leaders urging them to rein in the Pakistani army. In the first week of July 1971, Dr. Henry Kissinger—at the time national security adviser to President Nixon—met Mrs. Gandhi in New Delhi, where he was acquainted for the first time with "the intensity of feelings on the East Bengal issue." The influx of refugees had placed a great burden on India—"we were holding things together by sheer will-power," said the prime minister. The crisis could be resolved only when "a settlement which satisfied the people of East Bengal was reached with their true leaders." America was asked to press such a settlement on the military rulers of West Pakistan.[26]

From New Delhi, Kissinger proceeded to Islamabad, and from there—in secret—to the Chinese capital, Peking. Pakistan had brokered this breaking of the ice between two countries long hostile to each other. Their help with China was another reason for the United States to stand solidly behind the generals in Islamabad. Thus Kissinger had carried a letter from Nixon to Mrs. Gandhi, asking her to help in the peaceful return of the refugees and the maintenance of Pakistan as a united entity. In a combative reply, the prime minister lamented the fact that arms supplied by the Americans to Pakistan, directed in 1965 against India, were now "being used against their own people, whose only fault appears to be that they took seriously President Yahya Khan's promises to restore democracy." The president had asked for UN observers to supervise refugee repatriation; but, asked Mrs. Gandhi, "would the League of Nations observers have succeeded in persuading the refugees who fled from Hitler's tyranny to return even whilst the pogroms against the Jews and political opponents of Nazism continued unabated?"[27]

Recently declassified documents indicate a distinct difference of perspective between President Nixon and his chief adviser. The historian in Kissinger could foresee that "there will some day be an independent Bangla Desh." He also sensed—as he told the Indian ambassador to Washington—that while "India was a potential world power, Pakistan would always be a regional power."

Nixon, however, placed his hopes in a military solution to the problem of East Bengal. He had a deep dislike of one country—"the Indians are no goddamn good," he told Kissinger—and a sentimental attachment to the leader of the other. In the president's opinion, Yahya Khan was "a decent and reasonable man" whose loyalty to the United States had to be rewarded by supporting his suppression of the revolt in East Bengal. When, in April 1971, Kissinger prepared a note suggesting that the future for East Pakistan was "greater autonomy and, perhaps, eventual independence," the president scribbled on it: "Don't squeeze Yahya at this time."

As Kissinger somewhat despairingly told a colleague, "the President has a special feeling for President Yahya. One cannot make policy on that basis, but it is a fact of life." Nixon expressed his prejudices forcefully: speaking to his staff in August 1971, he said that while the Pakistanis were "straightforward" if "sometimes extremely stupid," the "Indians are more devious, sometimes so smart that we fall for their line." The president insisted that the United States "must not—cannot—allow India to use the refugees as a pretext for breaking up Pakistan."[28]

As India drew apart from one superpower, it was coming closer to the other.[29] Moscow concurred with New Delhi's assessment that the "twains of East and West Pakistan are not likely to meet again." The Soviet Union and India were now contemplating closer economic cooperation, through a greater flow of raw materials and finished goods between the two countries. As an inducement, the Soviet Union offered to sell the Indian air force a number of its TU-22 bombers. Recommending the proposal, the Indian ambassador, D. P. Dhar, admitted that while these were inferior to western models, to buy the planes from a NATO country would involve conditions that were both "politically unacceptable and financially prohibitive."[30]

In June 1971, the Indian foreign minister, Sardar Swaran Singh, was due to visit Moscow. On the eve of his arrival, the Soviet foreign minister approached D. P. Dhar with the suggestion that the Soviet Union and India sign a treaty of friendship, which would "act as a strong deterrent to force Pakistan and China to abandon any idea of military adventure." Dhar was told that "India need not be worried about Pakistan, but should take into account the unpredictable enemy from the North" (namely, China).[31] Later, when the two foreign ministers met, their common suspicion of China was high on the agenda. Swaran Singh remarked that China was the only country to give "all out, full and unequivocal support" to the Pakistani military regime. Gromyko answered that "the Chinese are always against whatever the USSR stands for. Any cause which we support invites their opposition and anything which we consider unworthy of our support secures their support. I cannot think of any particular exception to this general rule."[32]

India's hostility to China dated back to the border conflict of 1959–1962. The Soviet Union's hostility was more recent, a product of rivalry for leadership of the world communist movement. Mao Zedong had

spoken sneeringly of "Russian revisionism"; the armies of the two sides
had clashed on the Uri River in 1969. India and the Soviet Union did not
touch one another at any point, but each had a very long border with
China. A closer alliance was in the interest of both. The secret documents quoted above, however, reveal that, contrary to the received wisdom, the alliance was first suggested not by the poor underdeveloped
country but by the superpower.

After meeting Gromyko, Swaran Singh discussed a possible treaty
with the chairman of the Presidium of the Soviet Union, Aleksey Kosygin. Drafts were exchanged before a final document was signed in New
Delhi on 9 August 1971, by the foreign ministers of the two sides. For
the most part, the "Treaty of Peace, Friendship and Cooperation between the Republic of India and the Union of Soviet Socialist Republics" was boilerplate: declarations of undying friendship between the
"High Contracting Parties." The crux lay in a single sentence of Article IX:

> In the event of either Party being subjected to an attack or a threat
> thereof, the High Contracting Parties shall immediately enter into
> mutual consultations in order to remove such threat and to take ap-
> propriate effective measures to ensure peace and the security of their
> countries.[33]

By the late summer of 1971, the axes of alliance on the subcontinent
were quite clear: on the one side, there was (West) Pakistan with China
and the United States; on the other, (East) Pakistan with India and the
Soviet Union.

V

In the last week of September 1971 Indira Gandhi travelled to the Soviet
Union. The next month she visited a series of western cities, ending in
the capital of the Free World. Everywhere, she spoke of the worsening
crisis in East Pakistan. As she told the National Press Club in Washington, this was "not a civil war, in the ordinary sense of the word; it is a
genocidal punishment of civilians for having voted democratically."
"The suppression of democracy is the original cause of all the trouble in
Pakistan," she said, adding, "If democracy is good for you, it is good for
us in India, and it is good for the people of East Bengal."[34]

On her visit in November, Mrs. Gandhi had two meetings with President Nixon. Kissinger had the impression that this was "a classic dialogue of the deaf." Nixon said that the United States would not be a party to the overthrow of Yahya Khan, and warned India that "the consequences of military action were incalculably dangerous." Mrs. Gandhi answered that it was the Pakistanis who spoke of waging a "holy war." She also pointed out that while the West Pakistanis had "dealt with the Bengali people in a treacherous and deceitful way and . . . always relegated them to an inferior role," India, "on the other hand, has always reflected a degree of forbearance toward its own separatist elements."[35]

While Mrs. Gandhi was away, the conflict had intensified. From the end of October, the shelling along the border became more fierce, encouraged by the Indian army, which saw the exchanges as a cover for insurgents to creep in and out. By the third week of November, heavy artillery was being used. In a battle on 21 November the Pakistanis were said to have lost as many as thirteen tanks.[36] Reporting this to Nixon, Yahya Khan complained that India had "chosen the path of unabashed and unprovoked aggression." Twelve Indian divisions were massed near East Pakistan, seeking to turn "localized attacks to open and large scale warfare."[37]

At this time in their history, the armies of the two sides were grossly mismatched. In the past decade, the Indian armed forces had augmented their equipment, modernized their organization, and laid the foundations of an indigenous weapons industry. Indian intelligence had exaggerated Pakistan's strength; a study by the International Institute of Strategic Studies found that India in fact had twice as many tanks and artillery guns as its neighbour. Further, the morale of the Pakistan army had been deeply affected by the civil war, by the defection of Bengali officers, and by having to fight people presumed to be one's own.[38]

As it happened, the weaker side sought to seize the initiative. On the afternoon of 3 December, Pakistani bombers attacked airfields all along the western border. Simultaneously, seven regiments of artillery attacked positions in Kashmir.

The Indians retaliated with a series of air strikes. In Kashmir and Punjab they answered back on the ground while, in the seas beyond, the navy saw action for the first time, moving toward Karachi. The eruption of conflict in the west provided a perfect excuse for India to move its troops and tanks across the border into East Pakistan, turning a shadowy struggle into an open one.[39]

Yahya Khan's decision to attack India from the west seemed, at first and subsequently, somewhat surprising; a military historian has even described it as "barely credible."[40] Perhaps the Pakistanis hoped to effect quick strikes, calling for intervention by the UN or the United States before the conflict got out of hand. Some generals in Islamabad also believed that succour would come from the Chinese. Thus, on 5 December, the commander of the Pakistani troops in East Pakistan, Lieutenant General A. A. K. Niazi, received a message from army headquarters informing him that there was "every hope of Chinese activities very soon."[41]

Such help might not have come anyway, but in December it was made impossible by the snows that covered the Himalaya. This, indeed, was the perfect season for the Indians to effect their march on Dacca. Three months earlier the rains from the monsoon would have made the ground soft underfoot; three months later the Chinese would have had the option of crossing into the "trijunction" with India and East Pakistan. The weather was in favour of the Indians, as was the support of the local population; this was to add to an overwhelming superiority in numbers.

The Indian army moved toward Dacca from four directions. The delta was criss-crossed by rivers, but the Mukti Bahini knew where best to build bridges, and which town housed what kind of enemy contingent. The Bahini were in turn helped by their civilian comrades; as the Pakistani commander was to later recall, "the Indian Army knew of all our battle positions, down to the last bunker, through the locals."[42] Their path thus smoothed, the Indians made swift progress. Communications were snapped between Dacca and the other main city, Chittagong. Vital railheads were captured, immobilizing the defenders.[43]

On 6 December the government of India officially revealed an intention it had long nurtured—to support and facilitate the formation of a new nation state to replace the old East Pakistan. On this day, it formally recognized the Provisional Government of the People's Republic of Bangladesh. In Mujibur Rahman's absence, Syed Nazrul Islam served as acting president of the new state, with a full cabinet. These men were to the Indians as De Gaulle's Free French forces had been to the Allies: waiting, not very patiently, while Big Brother recaptured their beloved city and handed it over to them. A week after the war began, the Indian troops were within striking distance of Dacca. Artillery fire rained down on the city, with troops advancing from the north, south, and east. A temporary hiccup was provided by an aircraft carrier of the American Seventh Fleet, which moved into the Bay of Bengal, by way—to quote Henry Kissinger—of "registering our position."[44]

The threat was idle. Tied down in Vietnam, the Americans could scarcely jump into another war, which might—given the Indo-Soviet Treaty—get horribly out of hand. As the collapse of Dacca became imminent, an argument broke out between East Pakistan's civilian governor, who wanted to surrender, and the general in command of the besieged troops, who wanted to fight on. On 9 December, the governor wired Islamabad asking the government to sue for an "immediate cease-fire and political settlement." Otherwise, "once Indian troops are free from East Wing in a few days even West Wing will be in jeopardy." He considered the "sacrifice of West Pakistan meaningless," noting that "General Niazi does not agree as he considers that his orders are to fight to the last and it would amount to giving up Dhaka [Dacca]."[45]

The governor's views were independently confirmed by Pakistan's two main allies, China and the United States. On 10 December, Kissinger met with Ambassador Huang Hua in Washington. The Chinese diplomat bitterly remarked that the creation of Bangladesh would create a "new edition of Manchukuo," an Indian puppet regime on the model of the one the Japanese had once run in China. Kissinger replied that "it is our judgement, with great sorrow, that the Pakistan army in two weeks will disintegrate in the West as it has disintegrated in the East." "We are looking for a way to protect what is left with Pakistan," he said, adding by way of consolation, "We will not recognize Bangla Desh. We will not negotiate with Bangla Desh."[46]

On the night of 13 December, the Indians bombed the house of the governor in Dacca. The same night Niazi received a message from Yahya Khan advising him to lay down arms, as "further resistance is not humanly possible." The general waited a full day before deciding that he had no choice but to obey. On the morning of 15 December he met the American consul general, who agreed to convey a message to New Delhi. The next day, 16 December, Lieutenant General J. S. Aurora of the Indian army's Eastern Command flew into Dacca to accept a signed instrument of surrender.[47] That same evening, the prime minister made an announcement in the Lok Sabha that "Dacca is now the free capital of a free country." "Long live Indira Gandhi," shouted the Congress members, and even an opposition member was heard to say that "the name of the Prime Minister will go down in history as the golden sword of liberation of Bangla Desh."[48] From Parliament Mrs. Gandhi went to the studios of All India Radio, to announce a unilateral ceasefire on the western front. Twenty-four hours later, General Yahya Khan spoke over the radio, saying that he had instructed his troops to cease fire as well.[49]

The war had lasted a little less than two weeks. The Indians claimed to have lost forty-two aircraft compared with Pakistan's eighty-six; and eighty-one tanks compared with their 226.[50] The largest disparity was in the number of prisoners. In the western sector, each side took a few thousand POWs, but in the east the Indians now had to take charge of about 90,000 Pakistani soldiers.

President Richard Nixon was less than pleased with the outcome of the war. "The Indians are bastards anyway," he told Henry Kissinger. "Pakistan thing makes your heart sick," he said; "For them to be done so by the Indians and after we had warned the bitch." Nixon wondered whether, when Mrs. Gandhi had visited Washington in November, he had not been "too easy on the goddamn woman"—it seems to have been a mistake to have "really slobbered over the old witch." By this time, even Kissinger had been turned off the Indians. He was cross with himself for having underestimated their military strength—"The Indians are such poor pilots they can't even get off the ground," he had claimed in October. His hope now was that "the liberals are going to look like jerks because the Indian occupation of East Pakistan is going to make the Pakistani one look like child's play."[51]

As for the American press, *Time* magazine even-handedly blamed both sides; Yahya's "murderous rampage against rebellious Bengalis," along with Indira Gandhi's launching of "full-scale warfare," had "brought more suffering to the subcontinent." However, the influential columnist James (Scotty) Reston of the *New York Times* took a more partisan line, writing a brooding, almost conspiratial piece in which he saw the Soviet Union as the real beneficiary of "this squalid tragedy." Its new ally, India, would "provide access to Moscow's rising naval power to the Indian Ocean, and a base of political and military operations on China's southern flank." "The Soviet Union now has the possibility of bases in India," claimed Reston. He thought that India's experiment with democracy was in peril, and he wondered whether "India will be able to encourage independence for one faction in Pakistan without encouraging independence for other factions in India itself, including the powerful Communist faction in the Indian state of Kerala."[52]

VI

The victory over Pakistan unleashed a huge wave of patriotic sentiment. One periodical hailed it as "India's first military victory in centuries,"[53] meaning here not India the nation, but India the land mass and civilization. In the first half of the second millennium, a succession of foreign armies had come in through the north-west passage to plunder and conquer. Later rulers were Christian rather than Muslim, and came by sea rather than over land. Most recently, there had been a crushing defeat at the hands of the Chinese. For so long used to humiliation and defeat, Indians could at last savour the sweet smell of military success.

On the other side of the border the view was all too different. After the news came that their troops had surrendered, an Urdu newspaper in Lahore wrote that "today the entire nation weeps tears of blood. . . . Today the Indian Army has entered Dacca. Today for the first time in 1,000 years Hindus have won a victory over Muslims. . . . Today we are prostrate with dejection." Within days, however, the Urdu press was seeking consolation from the lessons of history. While the defeat was certainly "a breach in the fortress of Islam," even the great Muhammad of Ghori had lost his first war in the subcontinent. And as another newspaper in Lahore reminded its readers, Ghori had come back "with renewed determination to unfurl the banner of Islam over the Kafir land of India."[54]

In India, credit for the victory was shared by countless mostly unnamed soldiers and a single specific politician—the prime minister. Mrs. Gandhi was admired for standing up to the bullying of the United States, and for so coolly planning the dismemberment of the enemy. The men of her party went overboard in their salutations, and even opposition politicians were now speaking of her as Durga, the all-conquering goddess of Hindu mythology. The intellectual and professional classes, usually so sceptical about politics and politicians, were also generous in their praise.

Representative of this mood of all-round admiration was a symposium on the liberation of Bangladesh organized by the Gandhi Peace Foundation in New Delhi. This began with the editor of the *Times of India*, Girilal Jain, saying that "India's self-esteem and image in the world have improved considerably as a result of the revival of the fortunes of the Congress party under Mrs. Indira Gandhi's leadership." It continued with K. R. Malkani of the RSS describing 1971 as "a watershed in the political evolution of India." With the events of that year, "the old image of peace is being replaced by the new one of power. The old image only elicited patronizing smiles; the new image commands attention, and respect." Then the diplomat G. L. Mehta claimed that "the people have a new sense of self-confidence and not an unreasonable pride over its newly won prestige in the world." The left-wing journalist Romesh Thapar concurred: the "success of the Bangla Desh policy," he remarked, had given "the thinking Indian a sense of achievement and power." The left-wing jurist V. R. Krishna Iyer saw in the recent events a progressive maturation of Indian leadership: "What in Gandhian days was a vague creed was spelt out in Nehru's time as an activist social philosophy, and became, under Mrs Gandhi's leadership, a concrete and dynamic program of governmental action."[55]

Away from India, Mrs. Gandhi's calm in the crisis was also admired by a woman who had seen some history in her time, the philosopher Hannah Arendt. In early November, Arendt met the prime minister at the home of a friend in New York. A month later, with Indian troops advancing on Dacca, she wrote to the novelist Mary McCarthy about seeing Mrs. Gandhi:

> very good-looking, almost beautiful, very charming, flirting with every man in the room, without chichi, and entirely calm—she must have known already that she was going to make war and probably enjoyed it even in a perverse way. The toughness of these women once they have got what they want is really something![56]

VII

The prime minister, and her party, naturally sought to make political capital of what the soldiers had accomplished. In March 1972, elections were called in thirteen states, of which some had opposition governments and others had uneasy coalitions led by Congress. In all thirteen, the Congress won comfortably; these included such crucial states as Bihar, Madhya Pradesh, and Maharashtra. As the Jana Sangh leader Atal Behari Vajpayee ruefully remarked, the opposition had put up 2,700 candidates, but the ruling party had in effect run the same person in all the constituencies—Indira Gandhi.[57]

However, in at least one state the presence and example of the prime minister were not enough. This was West Bengal, where the Congress won by a mixture of terror, intimidation, and fraud. Gangs of hooligans stuffed ballot boxes as the police watched idly. There was "mass scale rigging" in Calcutta; as one activist recalled, goondas paid by the Congress told voters assembled outside polling stations that they might as well go home, since the goondas had already cast all the registered votes.[58] Now in alliance with the CPI, the Congress won 251 of the 280 seats in the assembly, ending five years of political instability and bringing the state within the ambit of New Delhi.

Her domestic rule secured, the prime minister turned her attention to a settlement with Pakistan. Yahya Khan had resigned, and Z. A. Bhutto stepped in to take his place. Bhutto told the former British prime minister, Sir Alec Douglas-Home, that he was eager to have "an entirely new relationship with India," beginning with a summit meeting with Mrs. Gandhi. The message was passed on, with the tip that in view of Pakistan's wounded pride, the invitation should come from India.[59]

The Indians were at first apprehensive, given Bhutto's unpredictability and history of animosity against India. Confidants of the Pakistani president rushed to assure them of his good intentions. The economist Mahbub ul Haq told an Indian counterpart that Bhutto was now "in a very chastened and realistic mood."[60] The journalist Mazhar Ali Khan, editor of *Dawn*, told his fellow ex-communist, the Indian Sajjad Zaheer, that Bhutto was honestly trying to forget the past. New Delhi should work to strengthen his hand; otherwise, the army and the religious right would gang up to remove him, an outcome that would be disastrous for both India and Pakistan.[61]

Zaheer and Khan had worked together before partition, as activists in the Student Federation of India. Now, encouraged by a former fellow traveller, P. N. Haksar, they met in London in the third week of March 1972, to discuss the terms of a possible agreement between their two national leaders. Khan's suggestions included a return of all Pakistani POWs, and Pakistan's recognition of Bangladesh; also, troops would withdraw to positions held before the conflict, and there would be a joint declaration of peace. Coming finally to Kashmir, Khan said that the dispute should "not be mentioned at all in the declaration as this will open a Pandora's box." Zaheer answered, "India must get an assurance that there will be no more attack, infiltration, subversion, anti-India propaganda in Kashmir by Pak[istan]." Khan agreed but said that this "should be demanded by India *in practice*. He said we should realise that no Government in Pak[istan] can survive if it renounces, outright, its support to Kashmiris' right of self-determination."[62]

Khan reported on these talks directly to Bhutto; Zaheer conveyed them via P. N. Haksar to Mrs. Gandhi. The Pakistani president was invited for a summit to be held in the old imperial summer capital of Simla, in the last week of June 1972. He came accompanied by his daughter Benazir and a fairly large staff. First the officials met, and then their leaders. The Indians wanted a comprehensive treaty to settle all outstanding problems (including Kashmir); the Pakistanis preferred a piecemeal approach. At a private meeting Bhutto told Mrs. Gandhi that he could not go back to his people "empty-handed." The Pakistanis bargained hard. The Indians wanted a "no-war pact"; they had to settle for a mutual "renunciation of force." The Indians asked for a "treaty"; what they finally got was an "agreement." India said that they could wait for a more propitious moment to solve the dispute over Kashmir, but asked for an agreement that the "line of control shall be respected by both sides." Bhutto successfully pressed a qualification: "Without prejudice to the recognised position of either side."[63]

One of Mrs. Gandhi's advisers, D. P. Dhar, wanted her to insist on "the settlement of the Kashmiri issue as an integral and irreducible content of a settlement with Pakistan," and to make this a preconditon for the repatriation of POWs.[64] Dhar was a 100% Kashmiri, born and raised in the Valley. The prime minister, Kashmiri by distant origin only, felt less strongly on the subject; she was also more conscious of world opinion, and (as Mazhar Ali Khan had warned) mindful of Bhutto's precarious position within Pakistan. The agreement they finally signed—shortly after noon on 3 July—spoke only of maintaining the line of control. However, at the insistence of the Indians, a clause was added stating that the two countries would settle all their differences "by peaceful means through bilateral negotiations or by any other peaceful means mutually agreed upon"—this, in theory, would rule out either third-party mediation or the instigation of violence in Kashmir.[65] However, Bhutto had apparently assured Mrs. Gandhi that, once his position was more secure, he would persuade his people to accept conversion of the line of control into the international border.

The ink had hardly dried on the Simla Agreement when Bhutto reneged on this (admittedly informal) promise. On 14 July he spoke for three hours in the National Assembly of Pakistan, his text covering sixty-nine pages of closely printed foolscap paper. He talked of how he had fought "for the concept of one Pakistan from the age of 15." He blamed Mujib, Yahya, and everyone but himself for the "unfortunate and tragic separation of East Pakistan." Then he came to the topic that still divided Pakistan and India—the future of Jammu and Kashmir. As the victor in war, said Bhutto, "India had all the cards in her hands"—yet he had still reached an equal agreement from an unequal beginning. The Simla accord was a success, he argued, because Pakistan would get back its POWs and land held by Indian forces, and because it did "not compromise on the right of self-determination of the people of Jammu and Kashmir." He offered the "solemn commitment of the people of Pakistan, that if tomorrow the people of Kashmir start a freedom movement, if tomorrow Sheikh Abdullah or Maulvi Farooqi or others start a people's movement, we will be with them."[66]

The Indians complained that Bhutto had gone back on his word.[67] They should perhaps have thought of how they had themselves felt in the last days of 1962. The Chinese had then inflicted a humiliation on India, felt nationally by leaders and citizens of all shades and stripes. That is also how the Pakistanis felt, in 1972, having suffered a comparable defeat at the hands of the Indians. In truth, they felt even worse, for while the Chinese had merely seized some (mostly useless) territory from India, the Indians had, by assisting in the creation of Bangladesh, blown a hole in the founding ideology of the Pakistani nation. To this there could be only one effective answer—to assist in the separation of Kashmir from India, and thus to blow a hole in the founding idea of Indian secularism.

21

THE RIVALS

Indira is India, India is Indira.
D. K. BAROOAH,
Congress president, c. 1974

I

ON 15 AUGUST 1972, India celebrated the twenty-fifth anniversary of its independence. Parliament held a special midnight session at which the prime minister spoke, recalling the struggle for freedom from the rebellion of 1857 to the present, and noting the landmarks along the way. India's quest, said Mrs. Gandhi, "has been friendship with all, submission to none."[1] The next morning she addressed the nation from the ramparts of the Red Fort. "India is stronger today than it was twenty-five years ago," said the prime minister. "Our democracy has found roots, our thinking is clear, our goals are determined, our paths are planned to achieve the goals and our unity is more solid today than ever before." "Nations march ahead," Mrs. Gandhi said, "not by looking at others but with self-confidence, determination and unity."[2]

It is noteworthy that Mrs. Gandhi's speech did not touch on economics. Since independence, the Indian economy had grown at a rate of 3% to 4% a year. The output of the factory sector increased by about 250%, the rise being more marked in heavy industry than in consumer goods. A new class of entrepreneurs had sprung up, whose units were situated away from the old centres of industry. The state augmented infrastructural facilities: fifty-six kilowatt-hours of power were generated in 1971 (compared with 6.6 in 1950); the extent of paved roads more than doubled; and the freight carried by the railroads almost tripled.[3]

These developments helped rural as well as urban producers. Where irrigation was available—through dams or tube wells—farmers increased their production of cereals and crops such as cotton, chillies, and vegetables. Previously isolated villages were now integrated with the outside world. Roads took out crops and brought in commodities; they also transported villagers to the city and back, exposing them to new ideas. Within the village, there was a gradual spread of artefacts such as the bicycle, the telephone, and above all the school.[4]

These aggregate improvements masked significant regional variations. The green revolution had touched less than one-tenth of the districts in rural India. Most farming areas still depended on rain. Thus, despite the rise in industrial and agricultural production, there was still widespread destitution in the countryside. The year before the prime minister's anniversary speech, two economists in Pune, V. M. Dandekar and Nilakantha Rath, published a large study entitled, simply, *Poverty in India*. Drawing on countrywide surveys, they concluded that 40% of the rural population and 50% of the urban population did not have even a "minimum level of living"—defined as a per capita annual expenditure of 324 rupees in the villages and 489 rupees in the cities. The incidence of poverty had increased over the decade. At the beginning of the 1960s, 33% of the rural and 49% of the urban population lived below this poverty line. In or around 1970, Dandekar and Rath estimated, 223 million Indians were poor, out of a total population of about 530 million.

Other economists made other estimates: some thought that the percentage of the really poor was even higher than this; others said it was slightly lower. But although the economists disputed exactly how many poor people there were in India, all agreed that there were too many—by the most conservative reckoning, closer to 200 million than 100 million. These studies found that the poor in rural India spent roughly 80% of their income on food and 10% on fuel, leaving only 10% for clothing and other items.[5]

Another failure was education. There had been an enormous growth in the number of colleges offering instruction in the sciences and the humanities. An even greater expansion was in professional courses, such as engineering and medicine. But basic education had done poorly. There were more illiterates in 1972 than there had been in 1947. While thousands of new schools opened, there had been scarcely any attempt to bring literacy to the millions of adults who could not read or write. And even among those who entered school, only a small proportion graduated; the dropout rates were alarmingly high, especially among girls and children of low castes.[6]

A few months after Mrs. Gandhi's address at the Red Fort, the economist Jagdish Bhagwati spoke to a rather more select audience in the southern city of Hyderabad. Independent India presented itself as a mixed economy, partaking of both socialism and capitalism. But, argued Bhagwati, it had failed on both counts. It had grown too slowly to qualify as a "capitalist" economy; and by its failure to eradicate illiteracy or reduce inequalities, it had forfeited any claims to being "socialist."[7]

II

The prime minister claimed that democracy had put down roots in India. In some crucial ways it certainly had. Five general elections had been successfully conducted, plus close to 100 elections in states as large as France or Germany. In addition to free elections there was also a free movement of people and ideas, the latter expressed vigorously in a very free press.

In other respects, the democratic foundations of the nation were not so secure. The All India Congress Committee had once elected representatives from the states, these in turn sent up by Congress bodies at the *taluk* and district levels. More significantly, the chief ministers of states ruled by Congress were chosen by the local legislators alone. However, after the Congress split in 1969, Mrs. Gandhi was able to place her own candidates in key positions. This centralizing process was confirmed after her spectacular victory in the elections of 1971. Later in the year, she dismissed, in quick succession, the chief ministers of Rajasthan and Andhra Pradesh, replacing them with her own favourites. As one journal remarked, it mattered little who would be the new man in Andhra: "he that ascends the gaddi [seat of power] will have to look for his survival to the lady in Delhi rather than to the Legislators in Hyderabad or the Constituents in Andhra at large."[8]

After the elections of 1971, the prime minister's second son, Sanjay, became more visible in public life. He had been expelled from his first Indian school, graduated with difficulty from the second, briefly worked as an apprentice with Rolls-Royce in the United Kingdom, and then returned home to start a car factory of his own. While he looked for land for that project, he took his first steps in politics. In May 1971 he was sent by his mother to inaugurate the Congress campaign in the Delhi municipal elections. The next month he gave an interview to a widely read weekly; he struck his questioner as not "particularly keen on discussion or prolonged dialogue. He seems to be keen on results." Sanjay also offered the opinion that "the Indian youth are lily-livered. They have no guts. In their thinking they are dovetailed to the mental framework of their parents."[9]

The prime minister's first son, Rajiv, was a trained pilot working for Indian Airlines. Mrs. Gandhi worried greatly about Sanjay, writing to a colleague in February 1971 that "Rajiv has a job but Sanjay doesn't and is also involved in an expensive venture. He is so much like I was at that age—rough edges and all—that my heart aches for the suffering he may have to bear."[10] As it happened, Sanjay's factory project was cleared with undue haste. Eighteen applications were received for a license to make small cars; only that of the prime minister's son was approved, despite his having no past experience in this regard. The Congress chief minister of Haryana, Bansi Lal, gave Sanjay's Maruti car company 300 acres of land at a bargain price.[11]

Sharp questions were asked by opposition members of Parliament. These Mrs. Gandhi dismissed, but then her closest adviser, P. N. Haksar, expressed his own reservations. According to one report, he "advised the Prime Minister to dump [her son's] Maruti [car] project and extricate herself from her son Sanjay's doings."[12] The advice was disregarded: Sanjay came to be seen more and more at his mother's side, while Haksar's own influence within the secretariat declined.

By 1972, the Congress was subject to creeping nepotism, and to galloping corruption. In June 1971, P. N. Haksar drew the prime minister's attention to the "deeply entrenched and institutionalized corruption" in Congress-ruled Rajasthan.[13] Ministers were in collusion with civil servants, taking cuts on government projects. In the central government too, such practices were growing. One Union minister from Assam had acquired a great deal of property by dubious means; another, from Madhya Pradesh, was working hand in glove with a French arms dealer, promising contracts in exchange for commissions.[14]

III

Socially, one indicator of India's distinction was that it had a woman prime minister. What, however, of Indian women in general? While Mrs. Gandhi was winning elections and a war, the Indian Council of Social Science Research (ICSSR) had commissioned seventy-five separate studies on the status of women, with regard to the law, the economy, employment, education, health, and so forth.[15] The results were not altogether encouraging. In many ways, the modernization promoted since independence had increased the gender divide. For instance, it was chiefly men who had taken advantage of the improvement in health facilities. This aggravated the sex ratio, which, in 1971, was 931 women to 1,000 men. The proportion of women in the industrial labour force had declined, from 31.53% in 1961 to 17.35% in 1971. Factories had once recruited couples, but technical improvements had rendered redundant unskilled jobs previously taken by women.

The vast majority of women laboured in the countryside. Among families of peasant cultivators there were fifty women workers to every 100 male workers; among families that owned no land there were as many as seventy-eight women to every 100 men. The most hazardous operations were often the preserve of women, such as the transplantation of rice, which left them vulnerable to intestinal and parasitical infections. To these hazards were added the burdens of child rearing and gathering fuel and fodder, tasks performed by women and little girls alone.[16]

The literacy rate was dismal in general and disastrous for women: 39.5% of males could read and write in 1971, but only 18.4% of females. Only 4% of women in rural Bihar were literate. The poverty in states like Bihar and Orissa had led to the mass migration of males in search of work, placing even greater burdens on the women.

The ICSSR reported that "what is possible for women in theory, is seldom within their reach in fact." Their studies indicated "that society has failed to frame new norms and institutions to enable women to fulfil the multiple roles expected of them in India today. The majority do not enjoy the rights and the opportunities guaranteed by the Constitution. Increasing dowry and other phenomena, which lower woman's status further, indicate a regression from the norms developed during the Freedom Movement."

Social reform had an impact only in the cities, among high-caste families who spoke English or knew some English and who educated their girls and sent them to professional colleges. Among this select section, there was an increase in the number of women doctors, professors, civil servants, and scientists. On the other hand, many lower-class and farming communities had changed from offering a bride price to demanding a dowry—a clear indication of the declining status of their women. Rapid urbanization and male migration had also led to an increased traffic in sex workers.

A heartening sign was an increase in the percentage of eligible women voting in elections: from 46.6% in 1962 to 55.4% in 1967 and

59.1% in 1971. In the early 1970s there were also signs of an incipient feminist movement, with the first organizations being formed to protect the rights of women workers and labourers, and to protest against rising prices.[17]

As with low castes, there were two ways to look at the question. From one perspective women were still grievously exploited; from another, there had indeed been progress, given the very low baseline at independence and the cumulative history of women's oppression, legitimized by tradition. Thus, while the literacy rate remained shockingly low, the development since 1947 had "been phenomenal," as Table 7 indicates.

The most visible gains were in India's southernmost state, Kerala. Here, the sex ratio was 1,019 women to 1,000 men; this was the only state that had more women than men. It ranked first in female life expectancy (60.7 years), in women's literacy (over 60%, compared with a national average of less than 20%), in expenditure on health care per capita, and in the proportion of births attended by trained midwives. Kerala also had the lowest infant mortality rate for girls: 48.5 per 1,000 births.[18]

Kerala was exceptional not merely regarding women. Here, men too were better educated and had access to better health facilities. The statistics represented a more substantive social equality. There had been a remarkable assertion of the lower castes—untouchability had been more or less extinguished—as well of the lower classes: the trade union movement was most highly developed in this state.

Why was Kerala so different? As explained in Chapter Fourteen, it had a history of progressive maharajas and missionaries, and of major social movements involving both caste and class. These reforming traditions were picked up by the first communist ministry in 1957–1959 and were renewed in the early 1970s, when the state was ruled by an alliance of the CPI and Congress, with a communist, C. Achuta Menon, as chief minister. This government transferred large amounts of land from

TABLE 7: EDUCATION BY GENDER IN INDIA

GIRLS PER 100 BOYS ENROLLED, YEAR	PRIMARY SCHOOL	MIDDLE SCHOOL	HIGH SCHOOL	UNIVERSITY
1947	36	22	14	19
1971	62	43	36	31

absentee owners to tenant farmers, and passed a new Agricultural Workers Act to improve the wages and living conditions of the landless. Although these reforms fell short of what was demanded by radical intellectuals, they were much in advance of what was on offer elsewhere, furthering Kerala's reputation as, if not the most egalitarian, certainly the least unjust state in India.[19]

IV

In March 1973 the government appointed a new chief justice of the Supreme Court. In the past, when a chief justice retired the most senior member of the bench took his place. This time, Justice A. N. Ray was chosen although three colleagues were senior to him. The appointment was politically motivated, a manifestation of the government's increasing desire to control the judiciary. The law minister, H. R. Gokhale, had—in Parliament—spoken with contempt of the court's recourse to "the now archaic and long-past dead theories of Blackstone who regarded property as a natural right." This attitude, he warned, stood in the way of the government's commitment to restructure "the entire socio-economic fabric of our country . . . [through] greater and greater State intervention."[20]

In recent years the Supreme Court had been critical of attempts to disturb the basic structure of the Indian constitution. In both the bank nationalization and privy purse cases, the court had passed judgements unfavourable to the government, forcing it to use the power of Parliament to amend the constitution. Meanwhile, in a public lecture in Bombay, Justice K. S. Hegde had expressed concern that the "political exigencies and self-interest of individual leaders . . . [had] perverted the working of the administrative machinery." He thought that "the Centre has encroached on the powers reserved to the States, by recourse to extra-Constitutional methods." And he commented on the growing corruption, on "too much hankering after pelf and patronage."[21]

In the first weeks of 1973 the Supreme Court heard a petition challenging a new law that gave Parliament greater power to amend the constitution. A full bench heard the case, with six judges voting to restrict Parliament's power and seven upholding it. Among those voting on the government's side was Justice A. N. Ray; among those on the other side, Justice Hegde. Ray's appointment as chief justice was linked to this particular case, as well as to a more general view, held most strongly by

P. N. Haksar, that judges as well as civil servants should be "committed" to the policies and philosophy of the government in power.

Among the critics of the appointment of A. N. Ray was the Sarvodaya leader Jayaprakash Narayan. He wrote to the prime minister asking whether such an out-of-turn promotion was intended to make the Supreme Court "a creature of the Government of the day." She answered that Narayan's "dismal conclusion" was "unwarranted," adding that a mechanical adherence to the "seniority principle had led to an unduly high turnover of chief justices."[22] Another critic was the constitutional expert A. G. Noorani, who in a thoughtful essay deplored the politicization of judges—many of whom had begun speaking on matters well outside their purview—and of the judiciary, as manifested in the elevation of A. N. Ray and other professedly "progressive" judges. Noorani worried that neither the press nor the bar was sufficiently alert to threats to judicial independence. Unless these challenges were met, he warned, "we might as well resign ourselves to the loss of individual liberty in India."[23]

In fact, even before the new chief justice was chosen, many key jobs in government had been assigned to bureaucrats who shared the socialist ideology of Mrs. Gandhi and her advisers.[24] By 1973, this ideology had extended out into ever newer areas. There was now a Monopoly and Restrictive Trade Practices Commission, which sought to curb the growth of big business houses and instead encourage small-scale enterprise. There was a continuing expansion of the public sector, and further nationalization of private industry. Coal and oil were now under government ownership. The oil crisis of April 1973 hit India nevertheless; when it came, the prime minister—spectacularly and with much publicity—rode from her home to Parliament in a horse-drawn buggy.

Halfway into her third term in office, Indira Gandhi appeared to be in control, so much so that she had even begun negotiations with Sheikh Abdullah. The situation in the bitterly contested Kashmir Valley had been altered by India's emphatic victory in the war of December 1971. Now, it was reported, there was a "measure of disllusionment" in the secessionist camp. Even radicals in the Valley were talking of a settlement within the framework of the Indian constitution.[25]

In his own recent statements, Sheikh Abdullah had left it unclear what he meant by "self-determination": was it autonomy, or was it independence? Through 1971 he was living in Delhi. Here he saw, firsthand, Mrs. Gandhi's emergence as a national leader. The war made him less confused; it now appeared that independence for his people was out of the question. In June 1972 he met the prime minister. The content of the talks was kept secret, but shortly afterwards he was allowed back into Kashmir. As ever, he was greeted by large and mostly cheering crowds. But there were also some dissenters holding up placards saying "No Bargaining on Kashmir" and "We Want Plebiscite."[26]

In 1964, by sending Abdullah to meet Ayub Khan, Jawaharlal Nehru had apparently accepted that Pakistan was a party to the dispute over Kashmir. Now, after the dismemberment of Pakistan, Mrs. Gandhi made it clear that this was no longer the case. After his return to the Valley, Abdullah told his people that they should not look to Islamabad for help; instead, they should work out an honourable accommodation with New Delhi. In September, while speaking at a function to mark his sixty-seventh birthday, the sheikh went so far as to say, "I am an Indian and India is my homeland."[27]

Abdullah hoped now to return as chief minister, and from that position to work for greater autonomy for the state. He wanted the government to hold midterm elections, which he was confident his National Conference would win. However, this idea was resisted by the state Congress leaders, who would not give up their offices so easily.

Through 1972 and 1973, there were many rounds of talks between Mirza Afzal Beg, representing the sheikh, and G. Parthasarathi, representing the prime minister. They discussed how Abdullah could be reinstated without hurting either Kashmiri sentiments or Congress ambitions.[28]

At the other end of the Himalaya, there were signs that more Nagas, too, were thinking of living within India. From the creation of their state in 1963, it had been ruled by a faction at ease with the Indian constitution. There remained insurgents in the jungle, and there were occasional attacks on army convoys and mainstream politicians. But there were signs of normality as well. For example, in November 1972 the evangelist Billy Graham came to preach in Kohima, and 25,000 Nagas came to hear him, being bussed in from all parts of the state. Graham gave three sermons in three days, praising the beauty of the hills, deploring the ramshackle condition of the local churches, and asking the Nagas to "commit everything to God." A year later, India's leading soccer club, Mohun Bagan, played a series of exhibition matches in Kohima. In the first match, "amidst great excitement and shouts from a jubilant crowd of about fifteen thousand," a Kohima team beat the visitors by one goal. The next day, India's honour was restored, when Mohun Bagan won the return match by five goals to zero.

On 1 December 1973, Indira Gandhi visited Kohima to mark the tenth anniversary of Nagaland's becoming a full-fledged state of the Indian Union. In her speech—heard by an estimated 15,000 people—she urged the underground to "come out and shoulder the responsibilities of building up Nagaland." Several hundred rebels had already surrendered, and more came aboveground before the state elections of February 1974. For good or ill, the Nagas were getting a taste of Indian democracy. Thus, when the elections were held, the streets were overrun by young men yelling, " 'Vote for . . .' at full blast," because "a plate of rice and meat, and a sip of wine and a few currency [notes] are all that is needed to set a canvaser (sic) go ashouting for any prospective candidate." Meanwhile,

> promises, particularly from ministers, are flowing generously. A club, dispensary, a school building for long neglected schools, a road where no road was . . . are promised even though for the past ten years there had been nothing done for them.[29]

These elections brought a coalition government to power. It included several former rebels, who said they wanted to work for "a final, negotiated settlement," to be brought about by "faith, not guns." A journal in Delhi wrote hopefully that "by and large the Nagas have been reconciled and if the Government of India diverts more funds for education, employment and economic development, the 'hard core' will crack in the course of time, and there will be peace which is so urgently and vitally required in this border state."[30]

V

In its career as an independent nation, India had faced numerous conflicts—over land, language, region, and religion. Of these, the troubles in Kashmir and Nagaland had perhaps been the most serious. Ever since 1947, there had been charismatic leaders in both places, seeking a free state of their own. Their message had resonated widely among the people. Were they given the option, a majority of the inhabitants of the Naga Hills as well as the Kashmir Valley might very well have chosen independence rather than statehood within India.

In 1973–1974, however, Sheikh Abdullah was preparing to rejoin the system in Kashmir, and many rebel Nagas had come aboveground and taken part in elections. The once turbulent extremities were quiet.

As if to compensate, there was now trouble in the heartland, in parts of the country that, for reasons of history, politics, tradition, and language, had long considered themselves integral parts of the Republic of India.

The trouble began in Gujarat, the land of Gandhi, the father of the nation. The state was run by a Congress regime notorious for corruption; the chief minister, Chimanbhai Patel, was popularly known as Chiman *chor* ("thief"). In January 1974 students led a movement demanding the dismissal of the state government. It called itself Nav Nirman, "the movement for regeneration." The protests turned violent, with busses and government offices being burned. Chiman *chor* was compelled to resign, and Gujarat came under "President's Rule."[31]

The events in Gujarat inspired students in Bihar to struggle against misgovernment in their own state. Bihar had experienced a great deal of political instability, with many defections and governments made and unmade. A Congress regime came to power in 1972, but within it corruption was rife. There was deep discontent in the countryside, where land was very unequally held, and in the cities, where there had been a steep rise in the prices of essential commodities. Leftist groups, led by the Communist Party of India (CPI), had formed a front with simple aims and a complicated name—Bihar Rajya Mahangai Abhaab Pesha Kar Virodhi Mazdur Swa Karamchari Sangharsha Samiti (Bihar State Struggle Committee of Workers and Employees Against Price Rise and Professional Tax). Through the last week of 1973, the front organized a series of mass demonstrations, at which the call was heard, *Pura rashan pura kam, nahin to hoga chakka jam*—"Give us work and give us food, or else we will bring life to a standstill," which is exactly what they did.

These protests by the left set off a rivalry with the Akhil Bharatiya Vidyarthi Parishad (ABVP), the student union linked to the Jana Sangh. The ABVP and other, non-communist student groups came together in a united front of their own, the Chatra Sangharsh Samiti (CSS). This grew rapidly and soon had branches in most towns of the state. Campus life was in turmoil, and classroom instruction came to an abrupt halt.

On 18 March 1974, the CSS marched on the state assembly in Patna. When the police pushed them back, the retreating mob set fire to government buildings, a warehouse of the Food Corporation of India, and two newspaper offices. The police clashed with protestors in several parts of the city; several students were badly hurt, and at least three died. The news of the trouble spread, provoking clashes between students and the police across the state.[32]

After the incidents of 18 March the students asked Jayaprakash (JP) Narayan to step in and lead their movement. JP was now seventy-one, a veteran of movements militant as well as peaceful, the upholder or instigator of a hundred mostly worthy causes. In recent years he had worked for reconciliation in Nagaland and Kashmir, sought to understand the Naxalities, and persuaded the notorious bandits of the Chambal Valley to lay down their arms. The call from the students was one he found impossible to refuse. Long ago, he had started out as a student radical himself. That was in the American state of Wisconsin, and the call now was from his own native state of Bihar.

In Jawaharlal Nehru's lifetime, Narayan and Nehru had many exchanges. The older man tried to get JP to join his cabinet, but JP preferred to stay outside. From there he chastised and scolded Nehru, but he was nevertheless devoted to him, and was devastated by his death. Through their friendship, JP knew Nehru's daughter, too. He was one of the first to congratulate Mrs. Gandhi when she became prime minister, and in the years following, he frequently offered her (unsolicited) advice. He applauded her leadership during the war over Bangladesh, but was less approving of her conduct during the presidential election and (as we have seen) with regard to the supersession of the judges of the Supreme Court.[33]

When the Chatra Sangharsh Samiti asked JP to lead their movement, he agreed, on two conditions—that it should be scrupulously non-violent, and that it should not be restricted to Bihar. On 19 March, immediately after the clashes in Patna, Narayan said he could no longer "remain a silent spectator to misgovernment, corruption and the rest, whether in Patna, Delhi or elsewhere." "It is not for this that I had fought for freedom," he continued. He had now "decided to fight corruption and misgovernment and blackmarketing, profiteering and hoarding, to fight for the overhaul of the educational system, and for a real people's democracy."[34]

Narayan was a figure of great moral authority, a hero of the struggle for freedom who, unlike many others, had not been sullied by the loaves and fishes of office. He gave the struggle in Bihar a great boost, and also changed its name; what was till then the "Bihar movement" now became the "JP movement." He asked students to boycott classes, to leave their studies for a year and work at raising the consciousness of the people. All across Bihar there were clashes between students seeking to shut down schools and colleges and policemen called in by the authorities to keep them open. In the towns, at least, the support for the struggle was

widespread. In Gaya, for example, the courts and offices were closed as
a consequence of "housewives of respectable families of the town who
were rarely seen out of [purdah] sitting on [strikes] with small boys."
The authorities tried to clear the streets, but this provoked violence,
with students raining bottles and sticks on the police and being answered by bullets. When the smoke cleared three people were found
dead, and twenty grievously injured.[35]

The Gaya incident took place in the middle of April 1974. The call
was now renewed for the dissolution of the state assembly, and for the
imposition of President's Rule following the example of Gujarat. On 5
June, Narayan led a massive procession through the streets of Patna.
The march culminated in a meeting at the Gandhi Maidan, where JP
called for a "total revolution" to redeem the unfulfilled promises of the
freedom movement. India had been free for twenty-seven years, said JP,
yet "hunger, soaring prices and corruption stalk everywhere. The people
are being crushed under all sorts of injustice." Addressing himself to the
students in the crowd, he warned that the road ahead would be rocky:

> You will have to make sacrifices, undergo sufferings, face lathis and
> bullets, fill up jails. Properties will be attached.

Yet, he was convinced, in the end the struggle would be worthwhile:

> Gandhiji spoke of Swaraj [freedom] in one year. I speak today of real
> people's government in one year. In one year the right form of edu-
> cation will emerge. Give one year to build a new country, a new
> Bihar.[36]

It was at this meeting that JP spoke of "total revolution" for the first
time. The term, the struggle, and the chosen agents all recall the activities a decade previously of the chairman of the Chinese Communist
party. In the late evening of his life, Mao had called on the youth—in his
case, the Red Guards—to rid society of its accumulated corruptions, to
stamp out revisionists and capitalist-roaders who stood in the way of the
creation of the perfect society. Robert Jay Lifton has suggested that the
Cultural Revolution was impelled by Mao's frustration at the gap between expectations and reality, by his impatient desire to transform
China before he himself left this earth. I find this argument persuasive,
not least because it also helps explain the events in Bihar and India in
1974—the sudden turn toward radical politics by a man who, for many

years past, had disavowed politics altogether. Through the 1950s and 1960s JP had been a social worker, a reconciler, a bridge builder. Now, like Mao, he turned to the students, to what he called *yuvashakti* ("youth power"), to bring about the total revolution he had dreamed of in his own younger days.[37]

In between the incident at Gaya and JP's speech at Patna, the country was paralysed by a railroad strike, led by the socialist George Fernandes. The strike lasted three weeks, bringing the movement of people and goods to a halt. As many as 1 million railroad workers participated. The Western Railways, which serviced the country's industrial hub, was worst hit. There were militant demonstrations in many towns and cities—in several places, the army was called out to maintain peace.[38]

While the strike was on, India exploded a nuclear device. For several years, scientists had been pressing the government to conduct an atomic test. When the prime minister finally agreed, in May 1974, it was because the test helped divert attention from the challenges posed by the railroad workers and by the students in Bihar. Among certain people the blast evoked a surge of patriotic pride. There was, a reporter wrote, an "unmistakable air of excitement in Delhi" when the news of the explosion came through. Members of Parliament gathered in the central hall of the parliament building to congratulate one another—for them, "the railway strike and the country's numerous economic problems had suddenly disappeared from view."[39]

Others were less impressed, pointing out that membership in the nuclear club could not change the fact that India ranked 102nd among the nations of the world in per capita income. The test was also deplored in Pakistan, as a setback to the normalization of relations between the two countries.[40]

Following the nuclear test, Mrs. Gandhi and Jayaprakash Narayan exchanged a series of letters, beginning on a civil note but ending in acrimony. On 22 May the prime minister wrote to JP expressing concern about his ill-health, and hoping that, in view of the long friendship between the two families, their political disagreements could be expressed "without personal bitterness or questioning of each other's motives." Narayan answered that Mrs. Gandhi was being disingenuous, for in a recent speech in Bhubaneswar she had alluded to JP's associating with the rich and "living in the posh guest-houses of big businessmen." Those remarks, he said, had "hurt and angered me." He added that her recent comments seemed "not only to misunderstand me profoundly but also to miss—and to do so at the risk of tragic consequences—the meaning of the upsurge that is welling up from below."

Mrs. Gandhi replied immediately, clarifying that in those remarks about the corruption of Sarvodaya leaders, "I did not take your name or make any references personally derogatory to you. I cannot help if some newspapers added their own intepretation." (This *was* disingenuous—the interpretation made by the newspapers was the only one possible in the circumstances.) She suggested that even if he was incorruptible, perhaps his associates were not. That was why some of his ideas "which appear rather utopian to me could perhaps work if the whole population consisted of Jayaprakashs." Mrs. Gandhi also challenged his claim to be the nation's moral conscience: "May I also, in all humility, put to you that it is possible that others, who may not be your followers, are equally concerned about the country, about the people's welfare, and about the need to cleanse public life of weakness and corruption."

The exchange was concluded by JP six weeks after it began. He had hoped, he said, that she would have the grace to clarify *publicly* that in making those remarks in Bhubaneswar she was not casting aspersions on his probity or character. That she would not do this hurt him; as he put it, "I am only a private citizen but I do have my self-respect." What seemed clear was that "misunderstanding is growing and not lessening by correspondence between us."[41]

It was time to return to the movement. In August JP toured the Bihar countryside, to a rapturous reception. "JP is driven in procession . . . [and] cheering onlookers line the roads," wrote the journalist Ajit Bhattacharjea in his diary: "Arches every hundred yards or so. The cars inch[es] through the crowd to the podium—JP helped up the steps pausing at every one." After his tour, Narayan called for a conference of all opposition parties—except the CPI—to "channel the enthusiasm among the people into the nation-wide people's movement." The struggle in Bihar, wrote JP, had "acquired an all-India importance and the country's fate has come to be bound up with its success and failure." He appealed to trade unions, peasant organizations, and professional bodies to come aboard.[42]

At least one opposition party was already present in the JP movement—the Jana Sangh. Its student wing, the ABVP, had been there from the beginning, and older activists were now moving into key roles. A Gandhian associate of JP's wrote to him in alarm that "the leadership of the movement, at least at local levels, is passing into the hands of the Jana Sangh." He also worried that "the common man has yet to be educated into the ways and values of our movement, whose appeal to him continues to be more negative than constructive."[43]

A more detailed critique of JP's movement was offered by R. K. Patil, a former ICS officer who had later become an admired social worker in rural Maharashtra. At JP's invitation, Patil spent two weeks in Bihar, travelling through the state and talking to a wide cross section of people. In a long (and remarkable) letter he wrote to Narayan—dated 4 October 1974—he conceded that "there can be no doubt about the tremendous popular enthusiasm generated by the movement." He saw "unprecedented crowds attending your meetings in pin drop silence." However, when they were on their own these crowds were less disciplined, as in the attacks on the state assembly and the forcible prevention of the governor of Bihar from delivering his annual address.

Patil wondered whether the modes of protest being adopted in Bihar conformed strictly to Gandhian standards. But he went further, asking: "What is the scope for Satyagraha and direct action in a formal democracy like ours?" By demanding the dismissal of a duly elected assembly, Patil argued, "the Bihar agitation is both unconstitutional and undemocratic." True, the electoral process had to be reformed—made more transparent and purged of the influence of power and money. Yet once an election was held, its verdict had to be honoured, for "there is no other way of ascertaining the general opinion of the people in a Nation-State, except through free and fair elections."

Patil wrote, in conclusion, that he was "well aware of the patent drawbacks of the Government presided over by Indira Gandhi." But he still wasn't certain that it was "wise to substitute for the law of 'Government by Discussion,' the law of 'Government by Public Street Opinion.'" "Today you are a force for good," wrote Patil to JP, "but History records that the crowds can produce a Robespierre also. Hence perhaps my instinctive aversion to the Bihar type agitation."[44]

On 1 November 1974 Mrs. Gandhi and JP had a long meeting in New Delhi. The prime minister agreed to dismiss the Bihar ministry, on condition that the movement drop its demand for the dissolution of other state assemblies. The compromise was rejected. The meeting was acrimonious, although it ended on a poignant note, with JP handing over the letters written by Mrs. Gandhi's mother, Kamala Nehru, to Narayan's recently deceased wife, Prabhavati.[45]

Three days later, Narayan was manhandled by the police while on his way to a public meeting in Patna. As he was warding off a baton, he stumbled to the ground. The picture was splashed across the newspapers the next day. He was an old man as well as a sick man (he had diabetes), and although the injuries were slight the indignity provoked much outrage. The Bihar administration was compared to its colonial predecessor—as one journal wrote, somewhat hyperbolically, "JP was, for the first time in free India, a victim of police repression."[46]

VI

In September 1974, the Republic of India acquired a chunk of territory that previously constituted the quasi-independent state of Sikkim. While Sikkim had its own flag and currency, and was ruled by its hereditary monarch—known as the Chogyal—it was economically and militarily dependent on New Delhi. In 1973 some citizens of the kingdom had begun asking for a representative assembly. The Chogyal asked the government of India for help in taming the rebellion. Instead, New Delhi stoked it further. When an assembly was proposed and elections were held, the pro-India party won all but one seat. The Chogyal was forced to abdicate, and the Indian constitution was amended to make Sikkim an "associate state," with representation in Parliament.[47]

Sikkim was a very beautiful state, and also shared a border with China. At another time, the prime minister would have drawn comfort from this augmentation of the nation's territory. But the annexation of Sikkim provided Mrs. Gandhi only a temporary diversion from her battle with Jayaprakash Narayan. By the end of 1974, the Bihar movement was poised to become a truly national one. Letters of support for JP were streaming in from all over the country. A communication from an advocate in Andhra Pradesh saluted JP for "breaking new ground at an age where people retire," and professed "admiration and respect at the movement you are directing."[48] Prominent politicians would visit Bihar and promise to take the ideas of the struggle back to their own states. In the last week of November, JP convened a meeting of opposition parties in New Delhi, where he expressed the view that the lesson of Bihar was a need for "radical changes all round, on institutional as well as moral planes, involving drastic changes in Government policies in the centre as well as in the States."[49]

It is tempting to see the JP movement as a nationwide reprise of the popular struggle against the communist government in Kerala in 1958–1959. The parallels are uncanny. On the one side was a legally elected government suspected of wanting to subvert the constitution. On the other side was a mass movement drawing in opposition parties and many non-political or apolitical bodies. Like Mannath Padmanabhan, JP was a leader of unquestioned probity, a saint who had been called on to save politics from the politicians. His behaviour was, or was perceived to be, in sharp contrast to that of his principal adversary—for, like E. M. S. Namboodiripad in 1958–1959, Mrs. Gandhi had no desire to accede to her opponents' demand and voluntary relinquish power.

This was a political rivalry, but also a personal one. As a veteran of the struggle for freedom, and as a comrade of her father's, Jayaprakash Narayan would regard Mrs. Gandhi as something of an upstart. For her part, having recently won an election and a war, the prime minister saw JP as a political naif, who would be better off if he had stuck to social work.

By the end of 1974, the polarization was nearly complete. There were many Indians who were not members of the right-wing Jana Sangh party, and yet thought the Congress too corrupt and Mrs. Gandhi too insensitive to criticism. Some went so far as to hail JP's movement as a "second freedom struggle," completing the business left unfinished by the first. There were many other Indians, not necessarily members of the Congress, yet pained by JP's making common cause with the Jana Sangh; they saw his movement as undermining the institutions of representative democracy. The first kind of Indian criticized Indira Gandhi, with much force; the second kind criticized JP, albeit with less enthusiasm.[50]

In the first week of January 1975, a key aide of the prime minister was assassinated in JP's home state, Bihar. This was L. N. Mishra, who had held various cabinet appointments under Mrs. Gandhi and, more crucially, was a major fund-raiser for the Congress party. A politician wholly free of ideology, Mishra had collected large sums of money from the Soviet Union and the Indian business class. It was not clear who murdered him—a personal rival, or a trade unionist bitter about Mishra's role in the suppression of the railroad strike of 1974. The prime minister blamed the assassination on the "cult of violence" allegedly promoted by Jayaprakash Narayan and his movement.[51]

Mishra's death did not impede JP's plans to march on Parliament in the spring, when the weather would be more hospitable to protesters from across the country. Through January and February JP travelled across India to drum up support.[52] In his speeches JP urged the people to remain non-violent: any untoward incidents, he said, would prompt the prime minister to assume dictatorial powers. At several places he claimed that Mrs. Gandhi was looking for an excuse to arrest him.

That, he predicted, would only make the movement more widespread, as in 1942, when the jailing of Mahatma Gandhi had led to an intensification of the "Quit India" movement.

JP implicitly compared himself to Gandhi; more explicitly, he compared the Congress regime to the colonial state. These were comparisons the prime minister naturally rejected. In an interview she gave to a Japanese paper, she said that while she was not certain what the JP movement was for, "it is clear what it is against. It is against my party, it is against me personally and all that I have stood for and stand for today."

In fact, there were by now some members of Mrs. Gandhi's party who had sympathy for the other side. Among them were the erstwhile "Young Turks," Chandra Shekhar and Mohan Dharia. Shekhar and Dharia called for a national dialogue on rising prices, corruption, and unemployment—issues, they said, that were conspicuous in the Congress's own manifesto of 1971.

Another man caught betwixt and between was Sheikh Mohammed Abdullah. The government and he had finally come to an agreement, by which the Congress Legislature party of Jammu and Kashmir would elect him as its leader, and hence also as its chief minister. Two days before his installation, he went to the Gandhi Peace Foundation in Delhi to seek the blessing of his old friend and supporter, Jayaprakash Narayan. The newspapers carried a photograph of the two in a bear hug, the Kashmiri towering above the Gandhian.

JP told the press that he welcomed the sheikh's return to Kashmir; the state, he said, needed the sheikh at its helm. But his friends in the Jana Sangh attacked the accord that brought the "lion of Kashmir" back to power. The party president, L. K. Advani, claimed that Abdullah still "wanted to use the instrument of power to pursue his ambition of an independent Kashmir." Others saw the matter very differently. After the sheikh was sworn in as chief minister on 25 February, the *Indian Express* called it an "epochal event in the history of free India." Abdullah's return to his old post, twenty-three years after he had been forced to leave it, was "a tribute to the resilience and maturity of Indian democracy, for it is only in a true democratic set-up that even the most serious differences can be harmonised and reconciliations effected within the framework of common loyalty to the country."

The Kashmir chapter seemed, finally, closed. Jayaprakash Narayan was delighted that Sheikh Abdullah had rejoined the mainstream. On this, and perhaps this alone, he and Mrs. Gandhi saw eye to eye. For on the same day that Abdullah was taking the oath in Jammu, JP called for a "national stir" to oust the "corrupt Congress leaders from power." The Jana Sangh joined him here even as it opposed him on Kashmir—such were the contradictions of Indian politics.

On 2 March, four days before the planned march on Parliament, Mrs. Gandhi dropped Mohan Dharia from her council of ministers. His mistake had been to ask her to resume talks with Narayan. JP's response was to ask senior ministers such as Y. B. Chavan and Jagjivan Ram to resign in protest, and thus to "save their party from destruction" and restore its "traditional values."

On 3 March, Delhi's inspector general of police convened a meeting on how to handle the coming influx of protesters. As many as 15,000 policemen would be on duty. To limit the number of marchers, the administration forbade the entry of trucks and buses from neighbouring states.

Despite the ban on buses, people began streaming into the capital. They were housed in a tent camp outside the Red Fort, now named Jayaprakash Nagar. On the morning of 6 March, they began walking toward the venue of the public meeting, the Boat Club lawns, adjacent to the Houses of Parliament. Leading them, in an open jeep, was Jayaprakash Narayan. JP was cheered by the crowds assembled along the way, who offered garlands and showered him with petals. The slogans on display were chiefly addressed to his rival. One read: "Vacate the Throne, the People Are Coming." A Hindi variation of this English message read: *Janata ka dil bol raha hai, Indira ka singhasan dol raha hai* ("The heart of the people is singing; Indira's regime is sinking"). Behind JP came jeeps bearing leaders of the opposition parties. All together, it was one of the largest processions ever seen in Delhi, with an estimated 750,000 participants. There were representatives from all over India, but the largest contingents by far came from the states of Uttar Pradesh and Bihar.

At the Boat Club lawns, JP spoke in an "emotion-charged voice." He compared the day's events to Gandhi's historic "Salt March," and asked the crowd to be prepared for a long struggle. After the meeting, he led a delegation to Parliament, where he presented the Speaker with a list of the movement's demands. These included the dissolution of the Bihar assembly, electoral reforms, and the setting up of tribunals to investigate allegations that the Congress was engaging in rampant corruption.

Mrs. Gandhi answered JP two days later, in a speech at the steel town of Rourkela. She said that the agitators were bent on destroying the fabric of Indian democracy. Without mentioning her antagonist by name, she claimed that his movement was nourished by foreign donations. On 18 March, JP led a procession in Patna to mark the first anniversary of the movement. There was much singing, dancing, and throwing colour, this also being the day of the Holi festival. In his speech, Narayan urged the formation of a single opposition party, or, at the very least, of a common front to fight the Congress in all future elections.

JP's movement was strongly rooted in the northern states. He had supporters in the west, particularly in Gujarat, but the south was territory so far mostly untouched. So he now began a long tour of the states south of the Vindhyas, drawing decent but by no means huge crowds. In Tamil Nadu, people warmly recalled that he had been against the imposition of Hindi.[53]

VII

While the JP movement was gaining ground, the prime minister was facing another kind of challenge, posed not by passionate sloganeering in the streets but in the cold language of the law. The scene here was the Allahabad high court, which was hearing a petition filed by Raj Narain, the socialist who had lost to Mrs. Gandhi in the Rae Bareilly parliamentary election of 1971. The petition alleged that the prime minister had won through corrupt practices, in particular by spending more money than was allowed, and by using in her campaign the official machinery and officials in government service. Through 1973 and 1974 the case dragged on, with arguments and counter-aguments being presented before the judge, Justice Jag Mohan Lal Sinha.[54]

On 19 March 1975, Indira Gandhi became the first Indian prime minister to testify in court. She was in the witness box for five hours, answering questions about her election. The prime minister had left her son Sanjay behind in Delhi. With her instead was her elder son, Rajiv, who, while his mother spoke in court, "took his Italian wife, Sonia, to see the ancestral home of the Nehrus."[55]

In April, Morarji Desai—who had been a rival of Mrs. Gandhi even longer than JP—began a fast in Gujarat in protest against the continuation of President's Rule. New Delhi backed down, ordering elections for June. The opposition parties began the process of forming a common front to fight the Congress.

As Gujarat went to the polls, in the second week of June, L. K. Advani said that the campaign had "accelerated the polarisation of political parties and the Jana Sangh would try to further this process." He looked forward to his party's increasing its strength "manifold."[56]

While the votes were being counted, attention shifted to the high court in Allahabad. On the morning of 12 June, in Room 15 of a court in which Mrs. Gandhi's father and grandfather had both practised, Justice Sinha read out his decision in the case brought before him three years previously by Raj Narain. He acquitted the prime minister on twelve of fourteen counts. The counts he found her guilty of were, first, that the government of Uttar Pradesh had constructed high rostra to allow her to address her election meetings "from a dominating position"; and second, that her election agent, Yashpal Kapoor, was still in government employment at the time the campaign began. By this judgement, her election to Parliament was rendered null and void. However, Sinha allowed Mrs. Gandhi a stay of twenty days on his order, to make possible an appeal in the Supreme Court.[57]

This day—12 June—was a very bad one for Mrs. Gandhi. Early in the morning she was told that her long-time associate D. P. Dhar had died during the night. A little later came the news from Gujarat, which was also grim—the "Janata Front" was heading for a majority in the state elections. Then, finally, came this last and most telling blow, from her own hometown, Allahabad.

The judgement provoked immoderate interest in the intentions of the judge. Justice Sinha had been educated in Aligarh and had practised at the bar in Bareilly for fourteen years before becoming a district judge. He had been appointed to the high court in 1970. Some people claimed that his judgement was biased by the fact that he and JP came from the same Kayasth caste. Others believed that in the days before the judgement the prime minister's men had offered him a seat on the Supreme Court if he would rule in Mrs. Gandhi's favour.[58]

Mrs. Gandhi's election had been overturned on a quite minor charge, yet Justice Sinha's verdict also concentrated the popular mind on the more serious accusations made against her by JP's movement. The day after the judgement, opposition politicians began a dharna outside Rashtrapati Bhavan, demanding that the president dismiss the "corrupt" prime minister. In Patna, JP issued a statement, saying that it would be "shameful and cynical" were Mrs. Gandhi to listen to the "yes-men" around her and stay on in office. He also noted that the election results in Gujarat suggested that the "Indira wave" and "Indira magic" were matters of the past.

On the other side, the yes-men were very busy. On 13 June, the Congress chief minister of Haryana, Bansi Lal, began ferrying supporters into Delhi, to publicly proclaim their loyalty to Mrs. Gandhi. The streets outside the prime minister's house were choked with her admirers. They shouted slogans in her favour and burned effigies of Justice Sinha. Mrs. Gandhi came out to address them, saying that foreign powers were conspiring with her domestic opponents to get rid of her. Her adversaries, she claimed, had "lots of money at their disposal."

Every day, a fresh round of supporters would assemble outside Mrs. Gandhi's house; every day, she would come out and speak to them. Some Congress members privately deplored these populist demonstrations. Others publicly encouraged them. Addressing a Congress rally in Delhi, the party president, Dev Kanta Barooah, said that "laws are made by people and the leader of the people is Mrs Gandhi." Judges and lawyers— including the eminent lawyer-turned-judge M. C. Chagla, once a member of Mrs. Gandhi's own cabinet—thought the prime minister was morally bound to resign, at least until her appeal was heard and disposed of. On the other side, 516 members of Parliament from the Congress party signed a resolution urging her to stay on. Ten thousand Congress members from Karnataka signed a similar appeal, in blood. In the middle of the debate a voice spoke from across the border—Zulfiqar Ali Bhutto worried that Mrs. Gandhi would find a way out of her difficulties through "an adventurist course against Pakistan."

On 20 June, Mrs. Gandhi addressed a huge rally on the Boat Club lawns. A million people were said to have attended, even more than those who had heard JP at the same place three months previously. The prime minister claimed that the opposition was bent on liquidating her physically. Speaking after her, D. K. Barooah read a couplet he had composed for the occasion:

> *Indira tere subah ki jai, tere sham ki jai,*
> *Tere kam hi jai tere naam ki jai*

Or, in less expressive English: "Indira, we salute your morning and your evening too/We celebrate your name and your great work too."

Two days later, the opposition answered with a rally of its own. Despite heavy rain, hundreds of thousands came. JP was the featured speaker, but his flight from Calcutta was cancelled at the last minute ("mechanical trouble," said Indian Airlines). Representatives of the main opposition parties spoke, and Morarji Desai called for a "Do or Die" movement to get rid of the Indira Gandhi regime.

On 23 June, the Supreme Court began hearing Mrs. Gandhi's petition. The next day, Justice V. R. Krishna Iyer issued a conditional stay of
the high court's judgement: the prime minister could attend Parliament,
he said, but could not vote there until her appeal was fully heard and
pronounced on. The *Indian Express* thought this meant that Mrs. Gandhi "must resign forthwith in the nation's and her interests."

By now, at least some senior congressmen thought that resignation
would also be in the party's interests. If Indira Gandhi couldn't vote in
Parliament, she could scarcely lead her government to any purpose. She
was advised to step down temporarily and let one of her colleagues in
the cabinet—the uncontroversial Swaran Singh, perhaps—keep the seat
warm until the Supreme Court upheld her appeal (as her lawyers were
confident it would), allowing her to return as prime minister.

Urging Mrs. Gandhi not to resign were her son Sanjay and the chief
minister of West Bengal, Siddhartha Shankar Ray, a well-trained barris-
ter who had come from Calcutta to be at hand. Their advice was readily
accepted. As Mrs. Gandhi later said to a biographer, "what else could I
have done except stay? You know the state the country was in. What
would have happened if there had been nobody to lead it? I was the only
person who could, you know."[59]

Once the decision was made, it was executed with remarkable swift-
ness. On 25 June, S. S. Ray helped draft an ordinance declaring a state
of internal emergency, which the pliant president, Fakhruddin Ali Ahmad, signed as soon as it was put in front of him. That night, the power
supply to all of Delhi's newspaper offices was switched off, so there were
no editions on 26 June. The police swooped down on the opposition
leaders, taking JP, Morarji Desai, and many others off to jail. The next
day, the public in Delhi, and in India as a whole, heard on the state-
controlled radio that an emergency had been declared, and that all civil
liberties were suspended.

At the time, and later, it was thought that this reaction far exceeded the original provocation. Justice Sinha had indicted Mrs. Gandhi for two trifling offences. The Supreme Court was less likely to
construe the height of a rostrum as an "election malpractice." As for
the second charge, Yashpal Kapoor had resigned from government service before joining the campaign, although there was some dispute
about the date on which his resignation was accepted. Most lawyers
believed that the Supreme Court would reverse the judgement of the
Allahabad high court. Yet, as one respected jurist in Delhi put it, the

prime minister forsook "the advantages of the ordinary judicial remedy of appeal and resorted instead to the extraordinary, undemocratic and unconstitutional measures of Emergency."[60]

Just four months before the emergency was declared, the *Indian Express* had paid tribute "to the resilience and maturity of Indian democracy," noting that it allowed "even the most serious differences [to] be harmonised and reconciliations effected." The paper now had to eat its words. Indian democracy, c. 1975, could reconcile the Valley of Kashmir with the Union of India, but not Indira Gandhi with Jayaprakash Narayan.

22

AUTUMN *of the* MATRIARCH

Future generations will not remember us by how many elections
we had, but by the progress we made.

SANJAY GANDHI, speaking in December 1976

I

AT 6 A.M. ON 26 JUNE 1975, a meeting of the Indian cabinet
was convened. The ministers, unthinking and bleary-eyed,
were informed of the emergency, in effect since midnight. Their
formal consent was obtained before Mrs. Gandhi proceeded to the studios of All India Radio (AIR) to convey the news to an equally unsuspect-
ing nation. "The President has proclaimed Emergency," she announced.
"There is nothing to panic about." This, she said, was a necessary response
to "the deep and widespread conspiracy which has been brewing ever
since I began to introduce certain progressive measures of benefit to the
common man and woman of India." "Forces of disintegration" and "communal passions" were threatening the unity of India. "This is not a personal matter," she claimed. "It is not important whether I remain Prime
Minister or not." Still, she hoped that conditions would "speedily improve
to enable us to dispense with this Proclamation as soon as possible."[1]

The disclaimers betray a certain defensiveness. For the fact was that the
emergency had come on the heels of the Supreme Court order forbidding
her from voting in Parliament. When the emergency was declared, the
prime minister's closest friend, the designer Pupul Jayakar, was away in the
United States. On 27 June Mrs. Gandhi sent her a long note, explaining
that the action was taken in response to the "increasing violence" caused by
a "campaign of hate and calumny." The number of arrests, Mrs. Gandhi
claimed, was only 900, and most detainees were kept not in jail but "comfortably, in houses." The "general public reaction" was "good," and there
was "tranquility all over the country." The emergency, the prime minister
told her friend, was "intended to enable a return to normal democratic
functioning."[2]

Across India, people were being picked up and put into jails. They included leaders and legislators of parties other than the Congress, student activists, trade unionists—indeed, anyone with the slightest connection to the Jana Sangh, the Congress (O), the socialists, or other groups opposed to the ruling party. Some of the detainees, like Jayaprakash Narayan and Morarji Desai, were placed in government rest houses in the state of Haryana, not far from Delhi. However, the majority were sent to already overcrowded jails. And Mrs. Gandhi's arithmetic was soon shown to be wildly off the mark. Thousands were arrested under the Maintenance of Internal Security Act (MISA), known by its victims as the Maintenance of Indira and Sanjay Act. And there were other legal instruments at hand. The rajmatas of Gwalior and Jaipur, old political opponents of Mrs. Gandhi, were jailed under an act supposedly meant for black marketeers and smugglers.[3]

In the first few months of the emergency, the prime minister gave a flurry of interviews defending its proclamation. In these too she displayed a deep defensiveness. "It is wholly wrong to say that I resorted to Emergency to keep myself in office," she told the *Sunday Times* of London. "The extra-constitutional challenge [of the JP movement] was constitutionally met." The emergency was "declared to save the country from disruption and collapse"; it had "enabled us to put through the new economic programme" and led to "a new sense of national confidence." "What has been done," she told the *Saturday Review* of New York, "is not an abrogation of democracy but an effort to safeguard it." In these interviews she attacked the western press for "India-baiting," for picking on her country in preference to more visibly authoritarian nations such as Pakistan and China.[4]

In her interviews and broadcasts, the prime minister spoke of a need for a "new spirit of discipline and morale." The government's copywriters were put to work, coining slogans such as "Discipline Makes the Nation Great"; "Talk Less, Work More"; "Be Indian, Buy Indian"; and "Efficiency Is Our Watchword." Other exhortations were less impersonal, such as "She Stood Between Order and Chaos" and "Courage and Clarity of Vision, Thy Name Is Indira Gandhi." Rendered in Hindi as well as English, these slogans were painted on the sides of buses, across bridges, and on huge billboards placed in front of government offices.

These were the signs of a creeping dictatorship. Like military men who seize power in a coup, Mrs. Gandhi claimed to have acted to save the country from itself. And, like them, she went on to say that while she had denied her people freedom, she would give them bread in exchange. Within a week of the emergency she was offering a "Twenty Point Programme for Economic Progress." This promised a reduction in prices of essential commodities, the speedy implementation of land reforms, higher wages for workers, lower taxes for the middle class, and the abolition of indebtedness and of bonded labour.[5]

Women dictators are rare—in the twentieth century Mrs. Gandhi may have been the only one. However, as a woman autocrat, she could use images and symbols denied to her male counterparts. On 11 November, four and a half months into the emergency, the prime minister came to the microphone to "meet" and "have a heart to heart talk" with her countrymen. She spoke for over an hour, on the need for discipline, on her economic programme, on the glories of ancient India and the duties of its modern citizens. "Our opponents" wanted to "paralyze the work of the Central Government," said the prime minister, and thus

> we found ourselves in a serious situation. And we took certain steps. But many of the friends in the country were rather puzzled as to what has Indiraji done? What will happen to the country now? But we felt that the country has developed a disease and, if it is to be cured soon, it has to be given a dose of medicine even if it [is] a bitter dose. However dear a child may be, if the doctor has prescribed bitter pills for him, they have to be adminstered for his cure. . . . So we gave this bitter medicine to the nation.
>
> . . . Now, when a child suffers, the mother suffers too. Thus we were not very pleased to take this step. . . . But we saw that it worked just as the dose of the doctor worked.[6]

II

On 15 August 1975, the *Times* of London carried a full-page advertisement by the "Free JP Campaign." The ad had been paid for by individuals, the first person to contribute being Bishop Trevor Huddleston, the last, Dame Peggy Ashcroft. The other signatories included such long-standing friends of India as the socialist Fenner Brockway, the economist E. F. Schumacher, and the political scientist W. H. Morris-Jones, as well as celebrities with no specific connection to India, such as the actress Glenda Jackson, the historian A. J. P. Taylor, and the critic Kenneth Tynan. On the page were printed photographs of Mahatma Gandhi and Jayaprakash Narayan. Aside from the long list of names, the text featured a testament to JP's character and patriotism from the Mahatma himself.

"Today is India's Independence Day," said the ad. "Don't Let the Light Go Out on India's Democracy." The signatories called on Mrs. Gandhi to release all political prisoners, especially Jayaprakash Narayan. The singling out of one person was not just in deference to his leadership of the oppositional movement in India. The prime movers of the "Free JP Campaign" had known him from long before he began his "total revolution." The left-wing Labourites, such as Brockway, had known him from the 1930s, as a hero of the independence movement. The environmentalists, such as E. F. Schumacher, had known him in the 1950s, as a like-minded votary of decentralized development. The political scientists had known him before and after independence, as an ever-present, always influential exemplar of what Morris-Jones had once called the "saintly idiom" in Indian politics.

These foreign friends of India's freedom were old enough to have seen how close Jawaharlal Nehru and Jayaprakash Narayan had once been. They were appalled that Nehru's daughter had jailed JP, and hoped that an appeal to history would take him out of prison. So did that great group of pacifists, the Quakers, who did not sign the advertisement in the *Times*, but tried the back channels of reconciliation. The Quakers had a long and honourable connection with India. Quakers such as Agatha Harrison and Horace Alexander had been intermediaries between British colonialists and Indian nationalists. More recently, they had worked with JP in attempting a reconciliation between India and Pakistan and between the Naga rebels and the government in New Delhi.

In August, a month after the emergency was declared, the sociologist Joe Elder was sent by his fellow Quakers on a fact-finding mission to India. He met many people: JP's followers, congressmen, and the prime minister. He found himself "decreasingly prone to condemn one side or the other." JP had erred in starting a mass movement without an organization of disciplined, non-violent volunteers. His ideas had "struck many as naive, untested, or unconvincing." His movement's credibility was weakened by the presence within it of extremists of the left and right. On the other hand, the prime minister had clearly overreacted in imposing the emergency. This had created fear in the minds of the people, and undermined the democratic process and democratic institutions.[7]

As Elder's account suggests, the emergency was a script created jointly by JP and Mrs. Gandhi. Both had shown too little faith in representative

institutions: JP by asking for the premature dismissal of elected governments, Mrs. Gandhi by jailing legally elected members of Parliament
and legislative assemblies. Neither properly appreciated the role of the
state in a modern democracy. JP wished simply for the state to disappear,
for the police and army to "disobey immoral orders." On the other
hand, Mrs. Gandhi sought to make the state's functionaries ultimately
dependent on the will of a single person at the helm.

The clash was poignant because the adversaries had once been
friends, bound by ties of history and tradition and by intimate personal
relationships streching across generations. One does not know how
Mrs. Gandhi felt about jailing JP. We do know that her staff had deeply
ambivalent feelings. The prime minister's information adviser, H. Y.
Sharada Prasad, was a patriot and had been a freedom fighter himself.
He had been jailed in 1942, in the same "Quit India" campaign that
first made JP a national figure. Unlike Joe Elder, he could not bring himself to admit that the prime minister had overreacted. Yet, as he wrote to
a friend, he grieved that a man like JP, "at a moment of crucial ethical
importance, decide[d] that RSS and CPM are more acceptable than the
Congress. This is an excursion in reasoning that I have not been able to
understand, much less excuse. I can only console myself with the thought
that he would not have been so desperate if [his wife] Prabhavatiji had
been alive."[8]

Also unhappy about JP's incarceration was the economist P. N.
Dhar, who had succeeded P. N. Haksar as the prime minister's principal
secretary. He sent several emissaries to JP, to see whether a conciliation
could be effected, with prisoners released and the emergency lifted, in
time for the next parliamentary elections, due in early 1976. The emissaries found JP willing to negotiate. A flood in Bihar had made him impatient to go and work among the victims. Talk that his irresponsibility
had caused the emergency had reached his ears. He said he had no desire
to revive the popular movement, but when elections were called would
ask for a combined front to oppose the Congress and canvass for its
candidates.[9]

JP was eager for his old friend Sheikh Abdullah, now also a part of
the Indian establishment as chief minister of Jammu and Kashmir, to be
the mediator between him and Mrs. Gandhi. He had read a report quoting the sheikh as being in favour of "conciliation at All-India level," and
as saying that the prime minister was "more than keen to end the emergency." JP now wrote to Abdullah offering "full cooperation" in any
move he might make to resolve the differences between the opposition

and the government. That said, the letter betrayed signs of wounds still not healed, as in JP's reference to himself being portrayed as "the villain of the piece, the arch-conspirator, the culprit number one," and in his concluding challenge that "the first test" of the prime minister's keenness to end the emergency "will be whether this letter is allowed to be delivered to you and whether you are permitted to see me."[10]

The prime minister failed the test. The letter was not passed on to the sheikh, and the moves to effect a reconciliation died with it. However, in November 1975 JP's health took a turn for the worse. With his kidneys failing, he was taken to a hospital in Chandigarh; and when the doctors there proved unequal to the task, he was released on parole and shifted to the Jaslok Hospital in Bombay, to be placed under the care of the nephrologist M. K. Mani. The government's action was hastened by the realization that all hell might break loose if JP were to die in jail.[11]

Although JP lay in bed in Bombay, chained to a dialysis machine, there was no general parole of political prisoners. An estimated 36,000 people were in jail under MISA, detained without trial. These were rather ecumenically spread across the states of India: 1,078 from Andhra Pradesh; 2,360 from Bihar; and so on down the letters of the alphabet, until one reached 7,049 from Uttar Pradesh and 5,320 from West Bengal.[12]

These victims of political vengeance were housed, fed, and clothed like common criminals—in fact, they had to share their cells with such criminals (prompting the witticism that Mrs. Gandhi's much vaunted socialism was at least practiced in the jails). Older prisoners looked nostalgically back to the days of the Raj, when the jails had been cleaner and the jailors altogether more humane. It seemed that women prisoners were singled out for special treatment. The rajmatas of Gwalior and Jaipur were now living in conditions of unaccustomed austerity and filth. The socialist Mrinal Gore, more used to the simple life, was asked to share a toilet with the woman in the adjoining cell—who happened to be a leper. In the cell opposite was a woman lunatic who wore no clothes and shrieked day and night.[13]

III

Writing to a friend in January 1963, Indira Gandhi complained that democracy "not only throws up the mediocre person but gives strength to the most vocal howsoever they may lack knowledge and understanding."[14] Three years later, when she had just become prime minister, Mrs. Gandhi told a visiting journalist that "the Congress has become moribund," adding, "Sometimes I feel that even the parliamentary system has become moribund." Besides, the "inertia of our civil service is incredible"; "we have a system of dead wood replacing dead wood." "Sometimes I wish," said the newly elected prime minister of the world's most populous democracy, that "we had a real revolution—like France or Russia—at the time of independence."[15]

The impatience with democratic procedure had been manifested early, for instance, in the packing of the civil service, the judiciary, and the Congress party with individuals committed to the prime minister. But the process was taken much further with the emergency. Now, with opposition members of Parliament locked away, several constitutional amendments were passed to prolong Mrs. Gandhi's rule. The Thirty-Eighth Amendment, passed on 22 July 1975, barred judicial review of the emergency. The Thirty-Ninth Amendment, introduced two weeks later, stated that the election of the prime minister could be challenged not by the Supreme Court, but only by a body constituted by Parliament. This came just in time to help Mrs. Gandhi in her petition to the Supreme Court; the court now held that there was no case to try, since the new amendment retroactively rendered her actions during the elections of 1971 outside the purview of the law.[16]

Some months later, the Supreme Court did the prime minister a greater favour still. Lawyers representing the thousands jailed under MISA argued that the right of habeas corpus could not be taken away by the state. Judgements in the lower courts seemed to favour this view, but when the case reached the Supreme Court it held that detentions without trial were legal under the new dispensation. Of the five-member bench only one member dissented: this was Justice H. R. Khanna, who pointed out that "detention without trial is an anathema to all those who love personal liberty."[17]

It was suggested that the judgement was influenced by extra-legal considerations—by the hope of three of the judges that they might one day become chief justice, and by the fear inspired by the punitive transfers of officials that had commenced with the emergency. In a despairing editorial headed "Fading Hopes in India," the New York Times remarked that "the submission of an independent judiciary to an absolutist government is virtually the last step in the destruction of a democratic society."[18]

In fact, there were other steps still to be taken. These included the Forty-Second Amendment, a twenty-page document giving unprecedented powers to Parliament. It could now extend its own term—as it immediately did. The amendment gave laws passed by the legislature further immunity from judicial scrutiny, and further strengthened the powers of the Centre over the states. All in all, the Forty-Second Amendment allowed Parliament "unfettered power to preserve or destroy the Constitution."[19]

In January 1976, the term of the DMK government ended. Rather than call elections, the Centre ordered a period of President's Rule. Two months later the same medicine was applied to Gujarat, where the Janata Front had lost its majority owing to defections.

Indira Gandhi and the Congress were now supreme all over the land. When the art historians Mildred Archer and W. G. Archer went to meet Mrs. Gandhi in March 1976, the prime minister expressed satisfaction with the progress of the emergency. The new regime, she told them, "had made the State Ministers shake in their shoes." This was "long over-due and was excellent," for "too much devolution [was] fatal to India." "I have to keep India together," insisted Mrs Gandhi. "That is an absolute must."[20]

IV

Among the victims of the emergency was freedom of the press. Within its first week, the government had instituted a system of "pre-censorship" whereby editors had to submit, for scrutiny and approval, material deemed to be critical of the government or its functionaries. Guidelines were issued on what did and did not constitute "news." There could be no reports on processions, strikes, political opposition, or conditions in the jails. Reports of open dissidence were naturally forbidden, but even stories mildly critical of the administration were not permitted.[21] As a newspaper in the Punjab was to recall, items "killed" by the censor included

> reports about the closure of shops in Chandigarh's Bajwara market to protest against the arrest of shopkeepers, the six-year absence of a health officer and observations about the town's sanitation, especially the open drains; . . . three letters to the editor about pay anomalies and inadequate salary scales of college lecturers in Himachal Pradesh; an unsatisfactory bus service; a Chandigarh report about the rise in the price of tomatoes; the death of two persons while patrolling the rail tracks near Amritsar; and a brief item about black-marketing in essential drugs.[22]

The space had to be filled; and it was, by the words of the prime minister or by stories in praise of her government. (Editors who tried to print the liberty-loving essays of Tagore, Gandhi, and Nehru instead were quickly brought to book.) "Our newspapers, of course, give world news all right," wrote a reader in Simla to an English friend, "but hardly any other news pertaining to the country itself, except the speeches of the P.M. . . . I have decided to forgo the pleasures of reading a newspaper."[23] This disgust was shared by the journalists themselves. As a reporter for the Bombay weekly *Blitz* told his own English friend: "My paper is a supporter of the Emergency. But if we only sing the praises of the Government, what will our readers think of us?"[24]

Jokes tinged with satire were especially forbidden. The Tamil humorist Cho Ramaswamy failed to smuggle in a cartoon that showed the prime minister and her son talking, with the legend: "A national debate on the Constitutional Amendments." When a reader asked, "Who is Indira Gandhi," Cho answered, "She is the granddaughter of Motilal Nehru, the daughter of Jawaharlal Nehru, and the mother of Sanjay Gandhi." This, too, was cut. The censors were vigilant, but occasionally a joke or two escaped their eye. Thus V. Balasubramaniam was able to print an article in the *Eastern Economist*, "Livestock Problems in India," which began: "There are at present 580 million sheep in the country." And an anonymous democrat was able to place an ad in the *Times of India* announcing the "death of D. E. M. O'Cracy, mourned by his wife T. Ruth, his son L. I. Bertie, and his daughters Faith, Hope, and Justice."[25]

As the emergency proceeded, the government tightened its hold over the dissemination of information. The independent news agencies—United News of India (UNI) and Press Trust of India (PTI)—were amalgamated with two lesser agencies into a single state-controlled news service called Samachar. The Press Council, an autonomous watchdog body, was abolished. A law granting immunity to journalists covering Parliament was repealed. And as many as 253 journalists were placed under arrest. These included Kuldip Nayar of the *Indian Express*, K. R. Sunder Rajan of the *Times of India*, and K. R. Malkani of the *Motherland*.[26]

Some freedom-loving journalists resisted, but the owners of newspapers were mostly compliant, fearing that the government might shut down their presses or seize their property. They not only feared the stick but were happy to bite at the carrot. The latter took the shape of government announcements paid for by the Directorate of Audio-Visual Publicity

(DAVP). While "liberally granting advertisements to so-called 'friendly' periodicals," the DAVP withdrew its favours from those deemed critical of the government. More than one newspaper, and editor, and owner, was happy to change its tune in response to the inducements on offer.[27]

Among the major newspapers that willingly complied with the new regulations were the *Hindu*, the *Times of India*, and especially the *Hindustan Times*. The editor of the *Hindustan Times*, the hugely respected B. G. Verghese, was dismissed by its owner, the industrialist K. K. Birla, merely to please Mrs. Gandhi. (Birla was a devoted acolyte of the prime minister—after the decision by the Allahabad high court of 12 June, he had taken a delegation of 500 businessmen to plead with her to stay on in office.)[28] Among the newspapers that struggled nobly to maintain their independence were the *Indian Express* and *The Statesman*. Both refused to toe the government line, resisting threats and blandishments alike. When their power was cut, they got the courts to restore it. When their own stories were censored, they chose to leave white space rather than fill the pages with propaganda. And they artfully reproduced, without comment, reports on the Indian situation in the foreign press, under such neutral headings as "News Digest" or "What Our Contemporaries Say."[29]

The mass-circulation newspapers were hardest hit, but the government did not spare the high-quality, slow-selling journals of opinion either. Two esteemed journals in Delhi, the weekly *Mainstream* and the monthly *Seminar*, closed rather than submit to the censor's scrutiny. The weekly *Himmat*, in Bombay, fought the censor doggedly, but finally shut down when asked to pay a prohibitively high deposit as a guarantee of good behaviour. This was a fine imposed for a piece that quoted, among other people, the Mahatma. Literary magazines also closed down, finding it impossible to live with the curbs on their independence.

In some ways the government feared the little magazines even more. Their owners could not be bought, so they had to be coerced or bankrupted instead. Among the targets was *Opinion*, a four-page newsletter brought out in Bombay by the former ICS officer A. D. Gorwala. A man of legendary integrity, Gorwala focused on attacks against the individual by the agencies of the state. He had also fought a long battle against corruption. A year into the emergency, *Opinion* was ordered to shut down, but Gorwala was able to print one last issue, in which he observed that

the current Indira regime, founded on June 26, 1975, was born through lies, nurtured by lies, and flourishes by lies. The essential ingredient of its being is the lie. Consequently, to have a truth-loving, straight-thinking journal examine it week after week and point out its falsehoods becomes intolerable to it.[30]

V

The day after the emergency was declared, a British reporter found the streets of Delhi "uncannily normal." The city's "jingling flotilla" of cyclists set off for work in the morning. "No angry crowds gathered. Shops and factories opened as usual. Beggars begged. The sleek race horses of the rich had their daily exercise."[31] As the journalist Inder Malhotra wrote, "in its initial months at least, the Emergency restored to India a kind of calm it had not known for years."[32]

The calm was in sharp contrast to the strife-filled decade that preceded it: one reason why the emergency was widely welcomed by the middle class. The crime rate had come down, and the trains ran on time. A good monsoon in 1975 meant that prices also fell. A visiting American journalist was told by an official in Delhi that only foreigners cared for such things as the freedom of expression. "We are tired of being the workshop of failed democracy," said the official. "The time has come to exchange some of our vaunted individual rights for some economic development."

The journalist found that the business community were especially pleased with the emergency. A hotel owner in Delhi told him that life now was "just wonderful. We used to have terrible problems with the unions. Now when they give us any troubles, the Government just put them in jail." In Bombay, the journalist met J. R. D. Tata, arguably India's most respected industrialist. Tata too felt that "things had gone too far. You can't imagine what we've been through here—strikes, boycotts, demonstrations. Why, there were days I couldn't walk out of my office into the street. The parliamentary system is not suited to our needs."[33]

One fact is conclusive proof of the acquiescence of the middle class—that hardly any officials resigned in protest against the emergency. In the days of British rule, Gandhi's call to "non-cooperate" with the rulers led to thousands of resignations of teachers, lawyers, judges, and even ICS officers. Now, the abrogation of democracy was protested by only a few of the people employed by the government. These included Fali Nariman, who resigned as additional solicitor general; M. L. Dantwala, who declined to continue as an adviser to the Reserve Bank; and Bagaram Tulpule, who left his high position in a public-sector undertaking.

However, some resistance was offered in the Indian Parliament. On 23 July the House met to ratify the emergency. The Congress had a majority, and thirty-four members of Parliament were in jail. The opposition members at liberty to attend made speeches of protest before walking out. The CPM member A. K. Gopalan said the arrests had reduced Parliament to a "farce and an object of contempt." A Jana Sangh member accused Mrs. Gandhi of betraying the motherland for "the sake of personal ends."[34]

The opposition members later boycotted the House (or were jailed), but an independent member who continued to attend was P. G. Mavalankar of Ahmedabad, a political scientist by vocation and the son of the first Speaker of the Lok Sabha. His lineage made it difficult for the government to arrest him. So he stayed and, when given the chance, quoted the holy trinity of Indian nationalism—Tagore, Gandhi, and Nehru—on the merits and virtues of liberty and freedom. Their views were contrasted with the "draconian" MISA, used to further "the political purpose of a vindictive government," an act which was "the most obnoxious piece of legislation ever enacted in the recent history of India."[35]

There was also resistance in the streets. On 14 November 1975—the birthday of Jawaharlal Nehru—a group styling itself the Lok Sangharsh Samiti (People's Struggle Committee) began a satyagraha in Bombay. Every day, protesters would stand at a busy intersection and shout slogans like "Down with Dictatorship" and "JP Zindabad." In a month 1,359 arrests were made—these included 146 women. The protests spread to other states, where bus stops, railroad stations, and government offices became places where slogans were shouted and demonstrators courted arrest. One report claimed that in the first three months of the satyagraha as many as 80,000 people had been put behind bars.[36]

On 15 August 1976 (Independence Day) another satyagraha began in Ahmedabad. It was led by Manibhen Patel, daughter of India's first home minister, Vallabhbhai Patel. Displaying slogans such as "Remove Emergency" and "Release Political Prisoners," fifty marchers proceeded on the road to Dandi, the same route that Gandhi had taken to break the colonial salt laws forty-six years before. Manibhen Patel was arrested a mile down the road, but the next day a judge ordered her release. She continued the march to the sea, accompanied by a few policemen in plain clothes.[37]

One of those arrested in the satyagraha at Bombay was the distinguished Marathi writer Durga Bhagwat. Other members of her fraternity protested in ways more congenial to their profession. A group of

Kannada writers printed and circulated, in samizdat form, poems satirizing the emergency and its prime mover. Consider these stanzas from G. S. Shivarudrappa's poem "In This Country":

> In this country
> Hero worship, family pride
> Should all go.
> But
> Concessions to my family deity
> Should stay untouched.
> In this country
> Everybody should shut their mouth
> And remain quiet.
> But
> They better keep their ears open
> For my words.[38]

Other writers expressed their dissent in other ways. The Bengali essayist Annada Sankar Ray announced that he would "stop writing altogether in a fit of non-cooperative pique." He refused to "put pen to paper so long as the state of Emergency continues." The cartoonist K. Shankar Pillai, who had once compared the loquacious Nehru to Niagara Falls (and been cheered by his victim for it), now closed down his magazine before the state could close it. "Dicatorships cannot afford laughter," he remarked mournfully. "In all the years of Hitler, there never was a good comedy, not a good cartoon, not a parody, or a spoof." The Hindi novelist Phanishwaranath Renu returned the Padma Shri bestowed upon him by the government of India; this action recalled Tagore's disavowal of his knighthood after the massacre at Jallianwala Bagh. And the Kannada polymath Shivarama Karanth gave back an even higher honour, the Padma Bhushan. In the 1920s, he had entered the freedom movement under the inspiration of Gandhi; now, after fifty years of striving to uphold its values, Karanth felt "impelled to protest against such indignities done to the people of India."[39]

Finally, some resistance was carried on underground. The key figure here was George Fernandes, the firebrand socialist who had led the railroad strike of 1974. When the emergency was declared Fernandes was in the town of Gopalpur-on-Sea in Orissa. He lay low for a few weeks, grew a beard, and disguised himself as a Sikh. Then he travelled from town to town, meeting comrades and planning to sabotage state installations. Dynamite was collected and stored, and young men were trained in blowing up bridges and railroad tracks. From his ever-shifting hiding places, Fernandes sent out letters attacking "the dictator," "that woman," and "the Nehru dynasty" and urging the people to rise up against the regime.

No dynamite was actually used, yet the government of India was obviously angry that it could not capture Fernandes. His brother Lawrence was taken from his home in Bangalore and brutally beaten and tortured. His friend, the actress Snehalata Reddy, was also imprisoned. She was held in a damp cell and denied proper food, so that her asthma was seriously aggravated—released on parole, she died a few weeks later. George Fernandes's wife and child fled the country, fearing persecution if they stayed. Fernandes himself was finally arrested in Calcutta on 10 June 1976, nearly a year into the emergency.[40]

In the summer of 1976, one of the few opponents of the regime still at large was the nonagenarian J. B. Kripalani. He complained that he had been left out while all his friends were given the privilege of imprisonment. Then he recalled a Sindhi proverb: "When a witch goes through a street destroying everything, she leaves one house untouched."[41] On 2 October 1975, Gandhi's birthday, Kripalani led a prayer meeting at the Mahatma's memorial in New Delhi—speeches were made, and several people were arrested, but he was not. It was not so much his age as his stature that kept him at large. Not Shivarama Karanth, not Morarji Desai, not even JP had patriotic credentials as good as Kripalani's. He had joined the Mahatma in the Champaran satyagraha of 1917, several years before Jawaharlal Nehru became part of the movement. Kripalani had been president of the Congress when freedom came three decades later. Three different states had sent him as their representative to the Indian Parliament. In sum, his curriculum vitae was such that even the prime minister would have been embarrassed to arrest him for activities deemed a threat to the "unity and stability" of the country.

In April 1976 Kripalani dared the government to print the names of those it had put in jail. Then he fell seriously ill. He was taken to a hospital, where all manner of tubes and wires were put into him. When a friend came visiting, Kripalani had a fresh complaint: "I have no Constitution—all that is left are Amendments."[42]

VI

The emergency revived the debate as to whether India could, should, or ever would be reliably democratic. In October 1975, a reporter from *Time* visited the country, and was much impressed by what he saw. He

thought that freedom of the press and the like were "of no great interest
to the majority of India's 600 million people," who were "more concerned" with the rate of inflation (down 31% in the past year). "The
Prime Minister," he wrote, "has won widespread support for seizing a
rare opportunity to ram through a score of social reforms. These days
India is engrossed in a frenzied campaign to encourage discipline, punc-
tuality, cleanliness, courtesy."[43]

So at least someone was taking the slogans seriously. Whereas the
reporter for *Time* thought that democracy was unsuited to India, the
Sydney Morning Herald despaired that it had died out in a country
which had been "the main hope of democracy in Asia, indeed in the
developing world." If India had "relapsed into traditional Asian autocracy," said the *Herald*, the blame must be shared between "Empress Indira" and her father, who had foisted "heavy industrialization
and nationalised bureaucracies upon the Indian entrepreneur, Soviet
style, in the name of 'socialism.' To make his 'socialism' work his
daughter has merely added the complementary Soviet style political
dictatorship."[44]

The question of India and democracy was, as one might expect,
most vigorously discussed in the British press. The political class in the
United Kingdom was divided; while some members of Parliament signed
the "Free JP" appeal, Mrs. Gandhi's regime was endorsed by, among
others, Michael Foot (on the grounds that Nehru's daughter could do no
wrong), and Jennie Lee and Margaret Thatcher, both of whom visited
India and concluded that the emergency was, on balance, beneficial to
its people. After travelling to India and speaking to Congress leaders, a
member of Parliament named Eldon Griffith wrote to the *Times* that the
regime was "far less oppressive" than this paper had reported it to be.
He also suggested that the Westminster model was unsuited to non-
western contexts. In a spirited rejoinder, W. H. Morris-Jones observed
that such denigration was "a sport in which high imperial Tory and revolutionary Marxist could find common enjoyment." As Morris-Jones
pointed out, a "growing number of Indians had begun to make the habit
of liberal democracy indigenous." Five elections had been successfully
conducted, and a free press and autonomous institutions had been developed, before the emergency brought "massive damage" to "a way of
political life which in two decades had already converted into citizens so
many who had been subjects beyond the political pale."[45]

What was the prospect for the future? In an assessment on the first
anniversary of the emergency, the *Observer* claimed to see a stirring

beneath the calm. A bad monsoon could shatter the fragile economy, leading to inflation, and "igniting the mass discontent that smoulders beneath the surface. The resulting explosion might well produce a political crisis more serious than that of June 1975." Among the possible outcomes, according to the *Observer*, one could discount a return to democracy, because "the most likely successor to Congress remains the Army."[46]

VII

The *Observer* made the mistake of focusing on institutions rather than individuals. For, within India, what was being witnessed was not the army rising behind the facade of Congress's rule, but the prime minister's second son emerging as her most likely successor.

It was Sanjay Gandhi who had warned his mother against resigning and had most strongly endorsed the emergency. In its first months he raised his public profile. He was often to be seen at Mrs. Gandhi's side, and was even advising her on cabinet appointments. When the liberal I. K. Gujral was seen as being too soft on the press, he was replaced as minister of Information and Broadcasting (I&B) by the more hard-line V. C. Shukla. When the experienced Swaran Singh (once a senior member of Nehru's cabinet) was less than enthusiastic about the emergency, he was replaced as defence minister by Sanjay's friend Bansi Lal.[47]

Six weeks into the emergency, Sanjay Gandhi gave a long interview to a magazine, *Surge*, published in Delhi. He spoke of his personal life—he didn't drink or smoke—and of his relationship with his mother. ("Yes, she obviously listens to my views," he said in answer to one question. "She listened to them even when I was five years old.") He spoke of his work—he claimed to spend twelve to fourteen hours a day at his Maruti factory—and of the car he would soon produce, which would "out corner either the Fiat or the Ambassador" (the two cars that dominated the Indian market). He expressed himself in favour of free enterprise—"the quickest way to grow"—and thought that the government should remove all controls on where, how, and in what manner industries were established. Asked about his idea of democracy, he said that it "doesn't mean the freedom to destroy everything there is in a country. Democracy means the freedom to build a country." Asked about the Congress, he said it should become a "cadre-based party." When the interviewer pointed out that both the Jana Sangh and the communists were based on cadres, Sanjay dismissed the first as "a favour based party." As for the latter, he commented that "if you take all the people in the Communist Party, the big wigs—even the not-so-big wigs—I don't think you will find a richer or more corrupt people anywhere."[48]

Surge was a new magazine, and the interview was a scoop. The editor quickly sold the story to the agencies, which in turn passed it on to Indian and foreign newspapers. These chose to highlight Sanjay Gandhi's views on free enterprise—at odds with his mother's professed socialism—and his characterization of her loyal allies, the communists, as "corrupt." When these excerpts were published, the prime minister sent a panic-striken note to her secretary, P. N. Dhar. Sanjay's comments were "exceedingly stupid," she wrote. They would "not only grievously hurt those who have helped us" but create "serious problems with the entire Socialist Bloc." Dhar was able to contain the damage—no more snippets appeared in the press, and *Surge* was prevented from printing the interview. Sanjay himself was persuaded to issue a statement to the effect that leaders in the Jana Sangh and Swatantra parties were even more "corrupt," and that the CPI must be saluted for its support of "progressive policies, specially those affecting the poor people."[49]

Sanjay was not deterred from giving more interviews, though. When the *Illustrated Weekly of India* asked him about curbs on the press, he answered that the papers "constantly told blatant, malicious lies. Censorship was the only way to put an end to this." Asked to provide a balance sheet of the emergency, he said that "the greatest gain is a sense of discipline and the speeding up of work." And "what has the country lost? Smuggling, blackmarketing, hoarding, bus burning and the habit of coming late to work."[50]

The editor of the *Weekly*, Khushwant Singh, emerged as the chief cheerleader and trumpeter of the rising son. Sanjay was called "The Man Who Gets Things Done" and chosen as the "Indian of the Year." The *Weekly* ran lavish features on Sanjay and his young wife, Maneka, pages and pages of photographs accompanying an invariably fawning text. (Samples: "He has determination, a sense of justice, a spirit of adventure and a total lack of fear." "Sanjay Gandhi has added a new dimension to political leadership: he has no truck with shady characters or sycophants; he is a teetotaller, he lives a simple life, . . . his words are not hot air but charged with action.")[51]

Less surprising, perhaps, was the attention paid to the prime minister's son by All India Radio (AIR) and the state-run television channel, Doordarshan. In a single year, 192 news items were broadcast about

Sanjay Gandhi by the Delhi station of AIR, and 265 by Doordarshan. When Sanjay made a twenty-four-hour trip to Andhra Pradesh, the Films Division shot a full-length documentary called *A Day to Remember*, with commentary in three languages.[52]

The surest sign of Sanjay Gandhi's growing importance in Indian politics was the deference shown by cabinet ministers and chief ministers. Before deciding on which admiral to promote, the defence minister, Bansi Lal, took the two candidates to be questioned by Sanjay. When the young man visited Rajasthan, the state's chief minister came to the airport to receive him; on his drive into Jaipur city, Sanjay inspected 501 arches erected in his honour. A similar show was organized when he visited Uttar Pradesh; at Lucknow airport, when Sanjay slid on the tarmac and lost his slipper, it was picked up and reverentially handed back by the chief minister himself.[53]

VIII

The prime minister had once chastised the Indian princes for promoting birth over talent. Now she had succumbed to that temptation herself. The elevation of her son followed a notably feudal route. Just as an heir apparent is given a title at a early age—duke of this or prince of that—Sanjay was given charge of the Congress's youth wing. (He was in theory merely a member of the Executive Council, but in practice the Youth Congress's president took her orders from him.) And just as the sons of Mughal emperors were once given a *suba* (province) to run before taking over the kingdom itself, Sanjay was asked to look after affairs in India's capital city. Within a few months of the emergency, the word had gone around: "the P. M. herself wanted all matters pertaining to Delhi to be handled by her son."[54]

By now, Sanjay Gandhi had formulated a five-point programme to complement his mother's twenty-point programme. His five points were family planning, afforestation, abolition of dowry, eradication of illiteracy, and slum clearance. Of these the focus was on the first, nationally; and on the fifth, with regard to Delhi. The capital was dotted with slums that had formed spontaneously to house the migrants who did the low-paying jobs in residential neighbourhoods and government offices. Here lived sweepers, rickshaw pullers, domestic servants, office boys, and their families. There were almost 100 such settlements in the city, housing close to 500,000 people.[55]

Sanjay Gandhi wanted these slums demolished, and their inhabitants settled in farmland across the Yamuna River. Here, his ideas coincided with those of Jagmohan, the ambitious vice chairman of the Delhi Development Authority (DDA). Jagmohan's hero was Baron Haussmann; he hoped to do for Delhi what Haussmann had done for Paris. By clearing the slums and building boulevards, the baron had transformed the French capital from "an ugly and despicable town" to a "seat of vigorous and vibrant culture." Actually, Jagmohan's admiration for autocratic methods was catholic. He praised what the Chinese communists had accomplished in Shanghai, for example, as a "result of firm national policy and commitment," when "in India, on the other hand, we are still in a state of drift." Jagmohan once lamented that he was

> No Haussmann reborn
> No Lutyens with a chance
> Nor Corbusier with Nehru's arms
> I am a little fellow
> An orphan of these streets

Still,

> With all the millstones
> Around my neck
> I stand erect
> Restless and keen
> Willing to fight
> Willing to dream.[56]

This was written in 1974, before the emergency. A year later Sanjay Gandhi arrived, to remove the millstones from Jagmohan's neck. The town planner had long been disturbed by slums, signs of a "sick and soulless city." Impatient to clean and clear them, he had been impeded by the messiness of democratic procedure—the need to obtain consent, to provide proper resettlement, to deal with political activists purporting to represent the people.

Jagmohan was an important member of a coterie that had sprung up around Sanjay Gandhi. Others included Naveen Chawla, who was secretary to the lieutenant governor, and the senior police officer P. S. Bhinder. Among the women who worked with Sanjay were the president of the Youth Congress, Ambika Soni, and a socialite and social worker, Ruksana Sultana, who was seen as his unofficial representative to the slum dwellers. Every morning the group met in Sanjay's office, to take orders and provide reports. Also in attendance was the prime minister's stenographer, R. K. Dhawan, who provided the link between this coterie and the doings of the government of India. Preceptor to all of them was Dhirendra Brahmachari, a long-haired swami who first entered the Gandhi home as Indira's yoga teacher and stayed on to become a favourite of her son. Dressed and trained as a Hindu holy man, Brahmachari was nevertheless modern enough to own and run a gun factory in Kashmir.

The names of this coterie became known in the city, their doings discussed in whispers. It was said that the surest way to have the government act in your favour was to speak to (and please) one of them. Businessmen seeking licenses or tax exemptions rushed to them; so did members of Parliament hoping for a cabinet appointment. Contrasts were drawn between Sanjay's brash "Punjabi mafia" and his mother's sophisticated, once powerful Kashmiri lobby. However, the differences were a matter not so much of style as of intent. Whereas the Kashmiris were "committed" to their shared socialist ideology as much as to their leader, Sanjay's gang was committed only to Sanjay himself.[57]

The exception to this general rule was Jagmohan. He had already identified the tidying up of Delhi as his life's mission—and was delighted to find it endorsed by the prime minister's son. Now, Sanjay's support and the emergency's cover gave legitimacy to Jagmohan's preference for coercion over persuasion. The bulldozers could move into the slums, unseen even by the probing eye of the press. In the fifteen years preceding the emergency, the DDA had moved only 60,000 families; in the fifteen months since, the number more than doubled.[58]

Jagmohan's operations focused on the old city, where Mughal monuments and mosques nested cheek-by-jowl with damp houses on dark streets. On the morning of 13 April 1976, a bulldozer moved into the Turkman Gate area, behind Asaf Ali Road, the street that divides Old Delhi from New. In two days it had demolished a slum of recent origin, housing forty families. Then it moved toward a set of pukka houses of uncertain antiquity. The residents contacted their member of Parliament, a congresswoman and associate of Mrs. Gandhi named Subhadra Joshi. Mrs. Joshi in turn contacted the officials of the DDA; Jagmohan himself was appealed to.

The negotiations stalled the operations temporarily, but in a couple of days they had resumed. Three bulldozers were at work, acting, the drivers said, on Jagmohan's orders. They had demolished more than 100 houses when, in desperation, a group of women and children squatted on the road and defied the bulldozers to run over them. When they refused to move, the DDA called for the police. In sympathy with the protesters, shops in the vicinity began to close.

The police tried using sticks to shift the squatters; when these failed, they tried tear gas. Retaliation took the form of stones. The fighting escalated, and spread into the narrow lanes. The numbers of the mob grew; the police progressed from using tear gas to using bullets. It took the better part of a day before order was restored. Estimates of the number who died in the fighting range from ten to 200. Curfew was imposed in the Old City; a full month passed before it was lifted.[59]

The offices of India's leading newspapers are on Bahadur Shah Zafar Marg, less than a mile away from Turkman Gate. Yet under the conditions of the emergency none of them could write about the incident. However, the underground picked it up and played it up. The news reached Sheikh Abdullah, who was "terribly distressed" by the shootings. He complained to the prime minister, who agreed that he could visit the area. Accompanied by a leading congressman, Abdullah toured the Old City, speaking to people about their recent experiences.[60] There he learned that aside from the natural reluctance to leave their houses, the protesters had been hurt by being subject to the first of Sanjay Gandhi's five points—family planning. In June 1976, the underground newspaper *Satya Samachar* reported that the sheikh had told a group of Congress members of Parliament that

> the whole trouble began when young, old and even invalid people were dragged off to the sterilization camps. Nobody has any quarrel with the economic policies of the Prime Minister, but the way in which they are being implemented, I am sure, will lead to an explosion.[61]

IX

In fairness, Sanjay Gandhi was not the only person concerned about India's large and still growing population. The Malthusian spectre had long haunted India, as the pages of this book should have made clear already. Western journalists feared large-scale famine; western biologists had written India off altogether. Many Indians also worried that a rising population would negate the other achievements of their nation. Between 1857 and 1947, the gross national product (GNP) stagnated; there were periods in which it even declined. After independence, GNP grew at 3% per annum. However, with the high increase in human numbers, per capita income grew at only 1% a year.

The debates over the size of India's population dated from the earliest days of independence. Social workers had set up a Family Planning Association of India in 1949. The Planning Commission had spoken of the importance of family planning since its inception in 1950–1951. However, culture and economics worked in favour of large families. The biases in educational development meant that girls were still valued more as child bearers than as wage earners. The continuing dependence on agriculture placed a premium on children. Indian Muslims and Catholics were enjoined by their clergy to abjure family planning. And Hindu couples greatly preferred sons to daughters, trying and trying again until they had a son.

In 1901, the population of India was about 240 million; by 1971 it had reached nearly 550 million. In this period, the birth rate had fallen slightly, from nearly fifty births per 1,000 Indians to about forty. However, the decline in the death rate had been far steeper, from forty-two per 1,000 at the turn of the century to fifteen by the 1970s. Advances in medical care and more nutritious food allowed all Indians, including infants previously at risk of early death, to live longer. And since the birth rate and average family size did not decline at a comparable rate, the population continued to rise.[62]

It is difficult to precisely date Sanjay Gandhi's own interest in family planning. His interview with *Surge* in August 1975 does not mention the subject at all. Yet a year later, the *Illustrated Weekly of India* mentioned that "Sanjay has given a big impetus to the Family Planning Programme throughout the country." He claimed that if his programme was implemented, "50 per cent of our problems will be solved." He expressed himself in favour of compulsory sterilization, for which facilities should be provided "right down to the village level."[63]

Of Sanjay Gandhi's five points, his biographer writes, the other four were humdrum, unglamorous, "hardly the stuff to build charismatic leadership credentials on." But "family planning was . . . a herculean project, the solving of which, everyone acknowledged, was vital if the nation hoped to survive, let alone prosper." And so, "family planning became the lynchpin of Sanjay Gandhi's Emergency activities."[64]

In his tours around India, Sanjay Gandhi stimulated competition between the states of the Indian Union. Sanjay would tell one chief minister about what another had claimed to have done—"60,000 operations in two weeks"—and encourage him to exceed it. These targets were announced to district officials, who were rewarded if they met or exceeded them, and transferred otherwise. The process led to widespread coercion. Lower government officials had to submit to the surgeon's knife before arrears of pay were cleared. Truck drivers would not have their licenses renewed if they did not produce a sterilization certificate. Slum dwellers would not be allotted a plot for resettlement unless they did likewise.[65]

The hand of the state fell heavily on the towns, but villagers were not spared. An anthropologist doing fieldwork in Maharashtra's Satara district reported that the emergency had little impact in its first year. A few homes were built for the landless under the twenty-point programme; a few slogans were painted denouncing the dictatorship. Then, in September 1976—shortly after Sanjay Gandhi's visit to the state—a campaign for compulsory sterilization began in the villages. Local officials prepared lists of "eligible men," those who already had three or more children. Police vans would come and take them off to the nearest health centre. Some men fled into the hills to escape. Those who had undergone a vasectomy were too embarrassed to talk about it.[66]

As with slum demolition, there was resistance. In September 1976, an underground newspaper reported a "wave of protests" against family planning in Delhi and Uttar Pradesh. There were clashes between health officials and shopkeepers who refused to be sterilized. Resistance was reported from many towns in Uttar Pradesh—Sultanpur, Kanpur, Bareilly. There was great resentment among schoolteachers, who had been asked to conduct house-to-house surveys in pursuance of the sterilization campaign. As many as 150 teachers were arrested for defying orders.

The worst incident—the Turkman Gate of family planning, so to speak—took place in the town of Muzaffarnagar, seventy miles northwest of Delhi. The district magistrate here was notorious for his zeal and his communalism—under his orders, the chiefly Hindu police had gone with particular relish after Muslim artisans and labourers. On 18 October, a scuffle broke out between officials promoting sterilization and their potential victims. Releasing pent-up anger, a mob torched the health clinics and threw bottles and stones. The police were called in and resorted very quickly to shooting; more than fifty people died. A delegation of opposition members of Parliament rushed to the town, but they were prohibited from speaking to the residents. However, reports leaked into the foreign press, and the prime minister was forced to admit in Parliament that there had been an "incident" in Muzaffarnagar.[67]

An incidental victim of Sanjay Gandhi's drive for family planning was the great popular singer Kishore Kumar. Other film stars and musicians agreed to perform in a programme to raise money for sterilization, but Kishore refused. As a consequence, his songs were banned from Vividh Bharati, the AIR channel that exclusively broadcast film music. The Film Censor Board was instructed to hold up the release of movies in which Kishore acted or sang. Sanjay's men also warned record companies against selling Kishore's songs. It was an act of petty vindictiveness in keeping with the times.[68]

XI

That the prime minister chose, at a time of crucial political importance, to rely on Sanjay Gandhi rather than P. N. Haksar and company—this was an excursion in reasoning which even her close friends found difficult to understand. Various theories were offered: that she felt guilty, as a working mother and single parent; that she was paranoid about assassination and hence could trust only her family; that Sanjay knew her darkest secrets and hence had a hold over her; that she was grateful for his support when the emergency was declared. Such speculation may appeal to the biographer, but to the historian it is nearly useless. What matters is not intent but consequences—not why Mrs. Gandhi chose to rely so much on her younger son but on what this choice meant for India and Indians.

It is tempting to view Mrs. Gandhi's political career as being divided into two phases, with the emergency and Sanjay Gandhi providing the dividing line. Before Sanjay, it might be said, she won elections, created Bangladesh, reformed the Congress party, and made bold attempts to reorganize the economy. Under Sanjay's malign influence she turned her back on these larger social goals and became obsessed with the preservation of herself and her family.[69]

However, when one views the prime minister's career as a whole, Sanjay and the emergency can be said to mark not a radical departure from past practice, but a deepening of it. From the time of the split within the Congress Mrs. Gandhi had worked to place loyal individuals in positions of authority, and to make public institutions an instrument of her will. Institutions such as the bureaucracy, the judiciary, the presidency, and the Congress party had been eroded well before the emergency. Sanjay's arrival took the process further—some would argue much further—and also vulgarized and corrupted it, and made it more violent. But the process itself antedated Sanjay's entry into Indian politics.

By June 1975, Mrs. Gandhi had been prime minister of India for a little less than a decade. When one compares her time in office with that of her father, one is struck by a striking paradox—Nehru's halting yet honest attempts to promote a democratic ethos in a hierarchical society were undone by his own daughter, and in decisive and dramatic ways. The grievously mistaken dismissal of the Communist government in Kerala aside, Nehru took seriously the idea of an opposition. But Mrs. Gandhi paid other political parties scant respect. She attended Parliament less regularly than Nehru and spoke much less when she did attend. Nehru developed abiding friendships with politicians of other parties—something quite inconceivable in the case of Mrs. Gandhi. Then there was a contrast in how they treated their own party. In Nehru's time the Congress was a decentralized and largely democratic organization. Even had he been so inclined, he would not have been able to impose a chief minister against the will of a state's own politicians.

The contrast is reinforced when one considers the other, non-political aspects of democratic life in India. Nehru respected the freedom of the press, and allowed it to flourish. He respected the autonomy of the bureaucracy and the judiciary: there are no known cases of his having intervened to favour or disfavour a particular official.

At least from the time of the split with the Congress in 1969, Mrs. Gandhi had begun to depart from the political traditions of India's founding prime minister. The departures became more marked over the years, but they became fully visible only with the enactment of the emergency, and the repression that followed. For partisan reasons of their own, opposition politicians could not draw a contrast between the first and third prime ministers of India. Because they had once opposed Nehru, and because the Congress was now led by his daughter, they could scarcely praise one and diminish the other.

But western writers were under no such constraints, and those who knew both leaders could see quite clearly how Indira Gandhi had departed from Jawaharlal Nehru. A year into the emergency, two British friends of Nehru made the contrast the focus of their criticisms of the regime. Writing in the *Times*, Fenner Brockway deplored the conversion of "the world's greatest democracy" into a "repressive dictatorship."

Himself "a son of India," Brockway appealed to Mrs. Gandhi "in memory of the principles of her distinguished father, to end these denials of freedom and liberty."[70] Writing in the *Spectator*, John Grigg recalled Nehru's commitment to free elections and a free press. India's first prime minister was "a true patriot because he was a true democrat. . . . During his long premiership he made many mistakes but on the vital libertarian issue he never broke faith with the Indian people." But now, Grigg noted sadly, "Nehru's tryst with destiny seems to have been turned into a tryst with despotism—and by his own daughter." Mrs. Gandhi "should have been the proudest upholder of India's democratic experiment, which was proving to the whole world that people did not have to be rich or educated to enjoy civil liberties." Yet by her actions she had "spuriously confirmed" the view of "old fashioned imperialists" that "only authoritarian methods can work in a country like India." Grigg asked the prime minister to free herself from her son's influence and return to the values of her father's generation. Indeed, he implored her—"at whatever cost in power, 'face,' and mother-love—to restore the freedoms she has taken away." To do so, he wrote, "would be the hardest act of her career but it would also be the bravest and best."[71]

Other British friends wrote privately to Mrs. Gandhi, urging her to end the emergency. One of these was the Quaker Horace Alexander, who had once mediated between Mahatma Gandhi and the British Raj, and also first introduced the current prime minister to the delights of birdwatching in the Indian countryside.[72] There was also impersonal, public criticism, offered in the *Times* by the widely respected columnist Bernard Levin. In October 1976 Levin wrote two long articles about the recent attacks on democracy in India. Speaking of the suspension of habeas corpus, and of the curbs on the press, he warned that Mrs. Gandhi was turning her country into a "tin pot dictatorship." In the first week of January 1977, he wrote two more essays, criticizing the constitutional amendments passed to emasculate the presidency and the judiciary. These "tyrannous provisions" were "entirely unnecessary except to one who wants total power and the ability to use it without check." These latest changes, said Levin, had confirmed the "transformation of India into a fully authoritarian regime under its seedy dictator, Mrs. Indira Gandhi."[73]

On 18 January 1977, the prime minister announced that Parliament was to be dissolved and elections were to be held. This came as a surprise to her political opponents, who were let out of their cells even as the announcement was being made on All India Radio. And, from all accounts, it came as a shock to her son Sanjay, who also had not been informed beforehand. The term of the present Parliament could have been extended, year after year. The underground resistance had been tamed. And yet Mrs. Gandhi decided, suddenly and without consulting anyone, to return India to democracy.

There was much speculation about why the prime minister had turned her back on emergency rule. In the coffee houses of Delhi, the gossip was that her intelligence chief had assured her that the Congress would be re-elected with a comfortable majority. Some people felt that her decision was a consequence of competitive one-upmanship. Bhutto had just announced elections in his usually autocratic Pakistan; could Mrs. Gandhi delay elections in her unnaturally autocratic India? Her secretary, writing long after the event, offered a third explanation. The emergency, he noted, had cut Mrs. Gandhi off from the public contact that previously nourished her. "She was nostalgic about the way people reacted to her in the 1971 campaign and she longed to hear again the applause of the multitudes."[74]

Perhaps all these factors contributed. So did the criticism from western observers and (especially) friends. Aside from those already quoted, the emergency was sharply condemned by Willy Brandt and the Socialist International ("all socialists must now feel a great sense of personal tragedy at what is happening in India"); by the World Council of Churches in Geneva ("a very serious abridgement of human rights"); and by the leading American trade union organization, the AFL-CIO ("India has become a police state in which democracy has been smothered").[75]

What, finally, persuaded Mrs. Gandhi to end the emergency? One cannot say for certain, but it does seem that she was stung by the comments of those foreign observers who were impossible to dismiss as enemies of India. Fenner Brockway and John Grigg were not Richard Nixon and the CIA. Nor were they sceptics who had sneered at India or hoped that its democracy would fail. Rather, they were very old friends of India's freedom. While the Raj lasted they had pressed the British to leave, and after independence they had saluted the installation of a democratic regime. We do not know whether Mrs. Gandhi read their essays or the articles by Bernard Levin. Yet it is more likely than not that she did. These writings might have been placed before her without comment by a member of her own staff, or of her intimate circle, himself less than pleased with the emergency. It is a striking coincidence that the elections were called two weeks after Levin's second series in the

Times—just long enough for them to be air-mailed to India, seen by someone in her office, clipped, and passed on to her.

We may never know for sure, one reason being that Mrs. Gandhi's papers remain closed. Still, it is appropriate to end this chapter with a fragment underlining how much the dictatorship imposed by India's third prime minister was at odds with the democratic legacy of her father, India's first prime minister. Visting New Delhi during the emergency, A. M. Rosenthal of the *New York Times*—who had once served as its correspondent in India—concluded that had Jawaharlal Nehru lived while Indira Gandhi reigned, the two would have been political opponents, rather than allies. An Indian friend of Rosenthal's captured that imagined scenario: "Indira is in the Prime Minister's house, and Jawaharlal is back to writing letters to her from jail again."[76]

The allusion was to a series of letters written to Indira Gandhi by Nehru in the early 1930s, while he was in a British jail. These presented his thirteen-year-old daughter with a panoramic sweep of world history. Starting with the Greeks and ending with the Indian struggle for freedom, the story as told by the father unfolded the (often interrupted) progress of the human animal toward greater sociability and freedom. The later letters explored how "democracy, which was for a century and more the ideal and inspiration of countless people, and which can count its martyrs by the thousands," was now "losing ground everywhere." The last letter, sent to Indira on 9 August 1933—three years after the first—ended with the stirring paean to freedom contained in Rabindranath Tagore's great poem "Gitanjali."

When they were published in book form, the letters sold briskly, and in time the author was persuaded by his publisher to bring out an expanded edition. A specially writen postscript, dated 14 November 1938, outlined the major political developments of the latter part of the decade. "The growth of fascism during the last five years and its attack on every democratic principle and conception of freedom and civilization," Jawaharlal wrote to Indira, "have made the defence of democracy the vital question today." Unfortunately, "democracy and freedom are in grave peril today, and the peril is all the greater because their so-called friends stab them in the back."[77]

23

LIFE WITHOUT *the* CONGRESS

All my father's works have been written in prison. I recommend prison life not only for aspiring writers but for aspiring politicians too.

INDIRA GANDHI, speaking in 1962

I

IN JANUARY 1977, while announcing fresh elections, the prime minister recalled that "some eighteen months ago, our beloved country was on the brink of disaster." The emergency had been imposed "because the nation was far from normal." Now that it "is being nursed back to health," elections were permissible.

Even as Mrs. Gandhi spoke over the radio, her opponents were being released from jails across the country. The next day, 19 January, the leaders of four parties met at the residence of Morarji Desai in New Delhi. These parties were the Jana Sangh, the Bharatiya Lok Dal (a party principally of farmers, led by Charan Singh), the Socialist party, and Morarji's own Congress (O). The following day, Desai told the press that they had decided to campaign in the elections under a common symbol and a common name. On 23 January, the Janata (People's) party was formally announced at a news conference in the presence of Jayaprakash Narayan.[1]

Ten days after the formation of the Janata party, Jagjivan Ram announced that he was leaving the Union government. Ram—known as Babuji—was a lifelong congressman; a prominent minister in Nehru's and Indira Gandhi's cabinets; and, most crucially, the acknowledged leader of the Scheduled (formerly untouchable) Castes, who made up about 15% of the electorate. It was Ram who had moved the resolution endorsing the emergency in the Lok Sabha. His resignation came as a shock to the Congress and was taken as a harbinger of things to come, because Babuji was renowned for his political acumen; that he chose to leave the Congress was widely considered a sign that this ship was, if not yet sinking, leaking heavily. In resigning from his old party, Ram formed a new one, called the Congress for Democracy (CFD). The CFD, he said, would seek seats with the Janata party so that the Congress could not gain from a splitting of the opposition vote.

The elections had been scheduled for the third week of March. The opposition campaign kicked off with a mass rally at the Ramlila Grounds in New Delhi on Sunday, 6 March. In a desperate measure to reduce the size of the crowd, the government chose to show a popular romantic film, *Bobby*, on television at the same time as the rally was being held. In 1977 there was only one television channel, run by the state, and in normal circumstances half of Delhi's adult population would have been huddled around the screen. But, as one pro-Janata paper gleefully reported, on this day Babuji won over *Bobby*. A million people heard JP and Jagjivan Ram speak, along with the leaders of the other opposition parties, all now pledged to a common fight against Indira Gandhi and the Congress.[2]

In India's commercial capital, Bombay, 6 March saw the city's most popular weekly reach the stands with interviews of Indira Gandhi and Jayaprakash Narayan, a veritable double scoop. The prime minister told the interviewer that the Janata men "are only united against me, but not on any positive programme." The new name could not hide the "same old aim, which is to get rid of Indira Gandhi." In his interview, JP claimed that "the Janata Party is no greater hotchpotch than the Congress," which had within it "all types of vested interests and it is seething with internal differences." Asked for a message to the weekly's readers, Narayan said they should vote without fear, and remember that "if you vote for the Opposition you will vote for Freedom. If you vote for the Congress you will vote for Dictatorship."[3]

The protagonists of the conflicts of 1973–1975 were also the chief campaigners in the elections of 1977. Despite his age and indifferent health, JP hit the road. Between 21 February and 5 March he spoke at Patna, Calcutta, Bombay, Chandigarh, Hyderabad, Indore, Pune, and Ratlam—pausing only to spend time with his dialysis machine. Everywhere, he warned the audience that "this is the last free election if the Congress is voted back to power"; then, "nineteen months of tyranny shall become nineteen years of terror."[4] In her speeches, Mrs. Gandhi denied that her party was the monopoly of one family. In any case, "few families in the world" had a comparable record of service and sacrifice. She admitted that there had been some excesses during the emergency, yet defended the regime as necessary at the time. "We don't care who criticises us," she insisted. "We have to proceed on the right path guided by sound policies, programmes and principles."[5]

At least in northern India, the elections were seen as a referendum on those policies and programmes, and on one programme in particular: compulsory sterilization. There was, one journalist reported, a "burning hatred against forced vasectomies"; this "extremely emotive and explosive issue" had "become the focus of all pent-up frustrations and resentment." Voters told Congress candidates to show their own sterilization certificates; when they couldn't, they were simply asked to leave. Opposition election slogans also harped on the issue; these dismissed the Congress as a *sarkari khasi kendra*, the official castration centre, and warned that to re-elect the party would be to bring back forcible sterilization. Other slogans targeted the programme's chief promoter: *Gandhi Nehru ke desh main kaun hai ye Sanjay Gandhi?* said one: "In the land of Gandhi and Nehru, who is this impostor Sanjay Gandhi?" Particularly active in the election campaign were schoolteachers and minor officials, those whose promotions had been stopped or who were punitively transferred for not having met their assigned quotas of males to be sterilized.[6]

On the night of 20 March 1977, the election results were posted outside newspaper offices in Delhi as they came in. The next day's papers reported that the crowds "were partisan and loudly pro-Janata," cheering as "the kingpins of the Congress Party tumbled one after another." When news of Mrs. Gandhi's defeat for her previously safe seat of Rae Bareilly was announced, "the people in high spirits thronging the streets began shouting slogans and bursting crackers." The news of Sanjay Gandhi's defeat was followed by even louder cheers and more prolonged celebrations. Mrs. Gandhi had lost to her old foe and litigant, Raj Narain; in the adjoining constituency of Amethi, Sanjay had been defeated by an obscure student leader.[7]

The defeat of mother and son was part of a wider wash-out of the Congress in Uttar Pradesh. It lost all eighty-five seats in the state, and all fifty-four seats in neighbouring Bihar, to the Janata-CFD alliance. In Rajasthan the Congress won one seat out of twenty-five; in Madhya Pradesh, one out of forty. These losses were somewhat offset by a robust performance in southern India, where the emergency had rested lightly. In Andhra Pradesh the Congress won forty-one seats out of forty-two; in Karnataka, twenty-six out of twenty-eight; in Kerala, eleven out of twenty; in Tamil Nadu, fourteen out of thirty-nine. The Janata surge had scarcely dented the south; still, given the higher population densities and seat shares of the northern states, in the aggregate the Congress fell far short of a majority. It won 153 seats in a house of 540, down more than 200 from the elections of 1971. On the other side, as many as 298 Janata and CFD candidates were successful.[8]

The elections had revealed a regional divide, and also a divide by caste and religious affiliation. Two groups in particular, long considered to be loyal voters for the ruling party, had this time deserted the Congress. One was the Scheduled Castes, many of whom were swayed by the defection of Jagjivan Ram into voting for Janata. The other was the Muslims, who had suffered grievously at the hands of Sanjay's pet programmes. When elections were called, the influential imam of Delhi's greatest mosque, the Jama Masjid, asked Muslims to vote against the Congress. This they mostly did, contributing in good measure to the party's disastrous showing in northern India.[9]

Sober commentators spoke of a "Janata wave"; less sober ones, of a "revolution." For the first time in the nation's thirty-year history, a party other than the Congress would govern at the Centre. No Indian alive in 1977 knew what it was like not to have the Congress as the country's dominant and ruling political party. Few knew what it was like not to have Nehru or Indira Gandhi as the dominant and ruling political figure.

The results of the elections delighted many, angered some, and surprised all. In a letter to a friend, Mrs. Gandhi attributed her defeat to malign forces. "People have always thought that I was imagining things and overreacting," she wrote, "but there has been a deep conspiracy and it was bound to overtake us."[10] An editor who had been among her most steadfast supporters took the long and more hopeful view. Like Winston Churchill, Indira Gandhi had led her nation to victory in war; like him, she had been cheered for it; and like him, again, she had been thrown out of power by an ungrateful people. There was consolation here for Mrs. Gandhi, as well as a lesson for those who had replaced her. Thus the Janata-CFD regime "will soon learn that promises are like lollipops, but performance is like a dose of bitter medicine. And the people are as mercurial as quicksilver. The cheering crowds of yesterday may turn into a jeering mob tomorrow."[11]

II

Unlike the Congress, the Janata party had not campaigned under a single leader. After the election results were in, a controversy arose as to who should be chosen prime minister. The supporters of Charan Singh felt that the sweep in northern India made him the logical choice. Jagjivan

Ram's men argued that since his defection had been decisive, he should be considered. Then there was Morarji Desai, who had almost become prime minister in 1964 and again in 1967.

During the last week of March there was hectic canvassing on behalf of the three candidates. Finally, it was decided that the "grand old men" behind Janata—Jayaprakash Narayan and J. B. Kripalani—would make the choice. They settled on Desai, who had unparalleled administrative experience as well as a spotless personal record. Jagjivan Ram was offered the prestigious Defense Ministry, Charan Singh the powerful Home Ministry. Finance went to the former civil servant H. M. Patel, and External Affairs to the Jana Sangh leader Atal Behari Vajpayee.

What would be the policies of the new government? That was hard to predict, since within both party and cabinet there was a mishmash of ideologies: "some baiting Nehru, others praising him, some talking about the commanding heights of the public sector, and others brashly championing the Japanese and American models, some asserting the need for heavy industries, other clamouring for a 'return to the villages.' "[12] The importance of Charan Singh signalled an anti-urban bias; indeed, the Planning Commission was now dominated by economists who specialized in agriculture rather than industry. The importance of the socialists signalled a hard time for foreign capital; indeed, the minister of industries, the fiery trade union leader George Fernandes, announced that the American multinationals Coca-Cola and IBM would both be made to quit India (as in due course they were).

Among the more pragmatic ministers was Madhu Dandavate, who was put in charge of the railroads. This branch of government serviced more Indians than any other, and none too well. Dandavate too was a socialist, but his socialism eschewed rhetoric against the rich in favour of policies for the poor. As he put it, "what I want to do is not degrade the first class but elevate the second class." Dandavate initiated the computerization of train reservations, which reduced corruption among booking clerks and uncertainty among customers. He set in motion the repair or replacement of 5,000 kilometres of worn-out tracks. But his most far-reaching measure was to place two inches of foam on the hard wooden berths that passed for second-class "sleepers," thus making them more comfortable and closer to the standard prevailing in the first-class section of trains. Introduced at first on the major routes, this change was in time effected on all trains, helping hundreds of millions of travellers.[13]

In the government's early months, observers waited eagerly for a shift in foreign policy. The day after the election results were announced, the *New York Times* wrote that whereas the attitude of the Congress toward the West had "varied from a self-righteous edginess" to "a chilliness bordering on hostility," "all indications" from the Janata alliance were that "a friendly attitude can be expected towards the United States, with a noticeable cooling of feelings for the Soviet Union." American strategists were salivating at the prospect of a alliance between China, India, and the United States against the Soviet Union. The Janata victory, they thought, represented "something of a windfall for Washington."[14]

The mistake being made here was to equate one family with the nation as a whole. Washington believed it was only the personal choices of Jawaharlal Nehru and his daughter that explained the alliance with the Soviet Union. In truth, this also had to do with a more general scepticism about American intentions, caused both by its support of Pakistan and by the Indian intellectuals' distaste for unbridled capitalism. Besides, the threat from China meant that New Delhi could scarcely turn its back on Moscow.

The Janata leaders wanted, not to reject the Soviet Union for the United States, but to move toward a principled equidistance from the superpowers. As the influential editor (and biographer of JP) Ajit Bhattacharjea remarked, the challenge for the new regime was "to correct the tilt non-alignment had acquired over the years towards the Soviet Union without, if possible, antagonising Moscow."[15] Thus in October 1977 Morarji Desai and A. B. Vajpayee together visited the Soviet Union, to underline that the relationship between the two countries was much more than a familial matter.

At the same time, overtures were also made to the other side. The jurist Nani Palkhivala, known for his pro-western and free-market leanings, was sent as ambassador to Washington. In reciprocation, Jimmy Carter came to India in January 1978, the first American president to do so since Eisenhower. In a moving address to the Indian Parliament, he spoke of the "commonality of our fundamental values" and of how both countries had recently passed through "grave crises" (Watergate and the emergency) yet had come through with their commitment to democracy intact. Then, in a spontaneous coda to his prepared text, he spoke of the debt owed by Martin Luther King's civil rights movement to the ideas of Mahatma Gandhi.[16]

The Janata government also sought to mend fences with India's neighbours. In November 1977, India and Bangladesh signed an agreement for sharing the Ganges (Ganga) waters, which gave the former 20,500 cubic feet of water during the lean season, and the latter 34,500 cubic feet. The accord was signed over the protests of the state government of West Bengal, which claimed that Calcutta's port would silt up if denied adequate water.[17] In February 1978, External Affairs Minister Vajpayee visited Pakistan, where he charmed his hosts, the dictator General Zia-ul-Haq included, who had assumed that a man reared in the Jana Sangh would exhibit a fanatical hatred of Muslims.[18] A year later, Vajpayee visited China, the highest-ranking Indian to do so since the border war of 1962. On this occasion, however, the trip was marred by the Chinese attack on Vietnam, undertaken in arrogant disregard of India's long friendship with the country being invaded.

On economic and foreign policy the Janata government was less than unified. The clearest consensus was on the new regime's treatment of the former prime minister. The Janata leaders were determined to make Mrs. Gandhi pay for having imposed the emergency. As many as eight commissions of enquiry were appointed, each headed by a retired judge. Several dealt with the corruption of Congress chief ministers; one with the treatment of JP in jail; and one, absurdly, with the possible maltreatment in a government hospital, in 1967, of the socialist leader (and founder of "anti-Congressism") Rammanohar Lohia. There was also a commission set up to enquire into the affairs of Sanjay Gandhi's Maruti company.

The enquiry with the widest ambit was the Shah Commission, set up to punish those guilty of the excesses of the emergency. It was headed by a former chief justice of the Supreme Court, J. C. Shah. It met in a courtroom of Patiala House, in central Delhi, where the white-haired justice sat on a raised platform, flanked by two assistants. Below him, at a table with a microphone, sat the witness of the day, his testimony heard by a crowd composed mostly of journalists.[19]

In its first few months the Shah Commission examined scores of witnesses: bureaucrats, police officers, municipal officials, members of Mrs. Gandhi's cabinet. But Mrs. Gandhi herself refused to testify. Three times she was called to the witness box; three times she came, and chose not to answer questions, claiming to be bound by the cabinet's oath of secrecy. A journal victimized during the emergency saw this as "an outrageous attempt to make a mockery of the proceedings of the Commission."[20] A journalist more sympathetic to the other side commented that the

> Shah Commission was supposed to be a sort of Nuremberg Trial. Instead it has become a tamasha in which the heroine (or vamp) is constantly absent, and minor villains or comedians hold the stage. It is even losing its publicity value, as people have got bored with the commentaries on T. V. and radio and switch it off, just as the name of the Shah Commission is mentioned.[21]

III

The change of government at the Centre presaged changes of regime in the provinces as well. Following Mrs. Gandhi's lead in 1971, Janata dismissed state governments across northern India, claiming that the results of the general election showed that these had "lost the confidence of the people." In new elections held for the state assemblies, Janata won easily in Uttar Pradesh, Madhya Pradesh, Rajasthan, and Bihar.

In other states too changes were afoot. In West Bengal, a coalition of left parties came to power with a considerable majority. The CPM itself won 178 seats out of 294; its allies won a further fifty-two. In 1967 and 1969, the CPM had shared power in Bengal with non-communist parties, in unstable coalitions easily undone by Machiavellian governors sent from New Delhi. Now they faced no such problem, and could set about effecting reform within the bourgeois system.[22]

The new chief minister was Jyoti Basu, the Middle Temple lawyer who had been number two in the United Front–Left Front governments of the 1960s. Others in his cabinet were less genteel, coming from a background of work with farmers and labourers. Their top priority was agrarian reform. This focused on legalizing the rights of the *bargadars* (sharecroppers), who cultivated most of the land in rural Bengal. The new government's "Operation Barga" set about recording their rights, and increasing the share of the crop they could keep. Previously, the landlord would take half or more of the crop from the tenant; after the reforms, the landlord's share was reduced to 25%, with 75% being retained by the *bargadar*. More than 1 million poor peasants benefited from the reforms.

Meanwhile, the Left Front also held elections for village panchayats. *Panchayati raj*—local self-government—was a stated policy of the government, mandated by the constitution, but it had been honoured mostly in the breach. The panchayat elections of 1977 in West Bengal were the first conducted with such seriousness and on such a wide scale. As many as 55,000 seats were involved, and Left Front candidates won two-thirds of them. Notably, most of those elected on the communist ticket were not sharecroppers but small landholders, teachers, and social workers, members of what classical Marxism would call the petite bourgeoisie. But they were nonetheless party members or sympathizers. Along with Operation Barga, the panchayat elections helped strengthen the hold of the Left Front on the Bengal countryside.[23]

There was also a change of regime in Tamil Nadu. Here, the DMK had ruled for a decade, before being dismissed on spurious grounds during the emergency. In the elections now held, its main rival was the All India Anna Dravida Munnetra Kazhagam party, or AIADMK, which had broken away from the parent party and was led by and completely identified with the film star M. G. Ramachandran (MGR). Even the superior organizational machine of the DMK proved no match for MGR's charisma and appeal. The AIADMK won 130 seats to the DMK's forty-eight. MGR quickly made it clear that the old slogans of "Northern-Hindi imperialism" were now out of date; he wanted, he said, good relations with the Centre. In Tamil Nadu, the government instituted populist schemes in keeping with the chief minister's image, on the silver screen, of being a friend to the poor and needy. Among them was a "midday meal" provided at state schools, in the hope that this would induce girls to come to classes and stay there.[24]

In the east, communists were becoming reconciled to bourgeois democracy; in the south, erstwhile secessionists were making their peace with the Indian nation state. And there were also hopeful developments in regions and among peoples traditionally more truculent. In the summer of 1977, Morarji Desai met the Naga leader A. Z. Phizo in London; although no settlement was reached, the fact that the two had met, and in a foreign country, was seen as a significant concession by the Indian government. Later in the year, assembly elections were held in Nagaland. The eighty-two-year-old Desai went out to campaign, braving the risks of landing in mist-covered valleys. His visit, commented one newspaper, was "testimony to the importance" he attached to the elections, which New Delhi hoped would "end once and for all the sectional claims of Mr. Phizo and his followers."[25]

There were also elections at the other and equally troublesome end of the Indian Himalaya. Before the emergency, Sheikh Abdullah had come to power in Kashmir at the head of a Congress regime, as part of an accord he had signed with Mrs. Gandhi. Morarji Desai was keen that elections be held, to test the legitimacy of a piece of paper signed by two individuals. The assembly was dissolved, and the sheikh re-established his National Conference (NC). The revival of the party aroused great enthusiasm; as one Kashmiri recalled, "the entire valley was red with N. C. flags. Every house and every market stood decorated with buntings."[26] The NC won forty-six of seventy-five seats, though its majority was somewhat distorted by the fact that whereas the sheikh's men had swept the Muslim-dominated Kashmir Valley, in the Hindu-majority Jammu region it won only seven of thirty-two seats. That said, this was still the first "truly fair and free" election in the state since independence, "proving to the people of Kashmir that they too have the same fundamental rights which the people in the rest of the country enjoy and exercise."[27]

IV

In the winter of 1978–1979, the Swiss economist Gilbert Etienne travelled through the Indian countryside, visiting villages he had studied fifteen years earlier. He found a marked contrast between, on the one hand, "dynamic" areas such as western Uttar Pradesh and the Kaveri delta of Tamil Nadu and, on the other, "slow or no growth" areas such as eastern Uttar Pradesh and Orissa. What seemed crucial to rural prosperity was water management. Where irrigation facilities had been extended, productivity had risen, and incomes and lifestyles with it. Apart from water, a crucial input was chemical fertilizers: their use had increased fourfold in the green revolution districts.

The gains from agricultural growth, Etienne discovered, had accrued chiefly to the rising "backward" castes—such as the Jats in Uttar Pradesh, the Kurmis and Yadavs in Bihar, the Marathas in Maharashtra, and the Vellalas in Tamil Nadu. The upper or forward castes, who once owned much land, had relocated to the cities. It was their space that these backward castes sought to fill. However, the position of those below them remained lamentable. The Scheduled Castes, who were at the bottom of the ritual hierarchy, had gained little from such rural development as had taken place in the 1960s and 1970s. The Musahars of Bihar were representative. Etienne found that "their children were malnourished and the caste generated an air of acute misery."[28]

Etienne reported that "one of the most dynamic schemes" in rural India sought to increase the production of milk by producers' cooperatives. This scheme had its origins in a project started in the 1940s in the village of Anand, in central Gujarat. In the 1950s, the cooperatives came to cover the whole of the Kaira district, where Anand was situated. The milk they produced went to the city of Bombay, five hours away by express train. The success of this scheme (known as AMUL, with the first letter standing for the village where it began) prompted a countrywide extension in the 1970s. At the beginning of the decade, there were 1,000 cooperatives involving 240,000 farmers and producing 176 million litres of milk each year; by its end, 9,000 cooperatives with 1 million members all told were producing and selling nearly 500 million litres of milk annually.

These figures led some enthusiasts to speak of a "white revolution" that had complemented the green one. In truth, as in that other revolution, the gains from this one were very unevenly distributed. The scheme worked well in Tamil Nadu, a state with good rail and road facilities and a large urban population. In states with poorer infrastructure the results were disappointing. And everywhere, it was the middle-class and rich farmers who had gained most; that is, those who had access to more fodder (in the form of crop residues from their lands), more space to keep cows and buffalo, and better access to credit.[29]

The commercialization of agriculture and milk production had benefited a significant section of farmers in rural India. Crucially, economic gains had converted themselves into political ambition. In the 1960s, it was these rising rural castes who came to dominate the state governments in northern India. By the 1970s, they had made their presence felt in national politics. In the Janata dispensation the force of rural assertion was "dramatically represented in the personality and ideology of Charan Singh." But it ran deeper. After the Lok Sabha elections of 1977, 36% of all members of Parliament came from farming backgrounds, compared with 22% in 1952. Their impact was felt in the rural orientation of the government's economic policies, and in the ever-higher procurement price paid by the state for wheat and rice.[30]

V

Some commentators interpreted this rising rural power in terms of class. They saw "urban-rural struggles" and a sharpening of the conflict between factory owners and farmers. The terms of trade between industry and agriculture, once so heavily weighted in favour of the former, were now tilting toward the latter.[31] But this was also, and perhaps more significantly, a conflict that ran along the lines of caste.

In fact, when the situation was viewed in terms of caste rather than class, one could identify two distinct axes of conflict. The first was in politics and administration, where the "backwards" sought to contest the previous pre-eminence of the "forward castes" such as Brahmans, Rajputs, Kayasths, and Banias, who had historically monopolized literacy, scholarship, commerce, and political power.

The national movement had been dominated by the forward castes, so when independence came the governments at the Centre and in the states were also dominated by them. Slowly, the pressures of representative democracy advanced the claims of those lower in status but more numerous. More chief ministers in the states came now from the backward castes. So did an increasing number of cabinet ministers at the Centre. One citadel remained unconquered—the prime ministership. Like Nehru and Indira, Morarji Desai was from the highest-ranked Brahman caste. (Although not a Brahman, Lal Bahadur Shastri was a Kayasth, from an elite caste of scribes.)

In south India, a system of affirmative action, first instituted under colonial rule, had restricted the proportion of state jobs that the "forwards" could fill. Now the Janata regime sought to extend this system to its own strongholds in the north. In Bihar, a commission set up in the early 1970s had recommended that 26% of all positions in the administration be reserved for the backward castes. The report had been buried during the emergency. After the victory of the Janata party in Bihar in 1977, the new chief minister, Karpoori Thakur, dug up the report and decided to implement it.

Thakur's decision led to a storm of protest from the forward castes. Rajput and Bhumihar students burned buses and trains and vandalized government buildings. The leaders of backward castes were unyielding. Their resolve was strengthened by their strong representation in the state legislature, where nearly 40% of the members came from castes that would benefit from the extension of reservation. As one politician put it, "our movement is not only for reservation, it is for capturing political power in north India and in Delhi." Indeed, under pressure from the backward castes' lobby within Janata, Morarji Desai had appointed a commission to examine whether reservation should also be extended to jobs in the central government. As mandated by the constitution, 15% of these jobs went to Scheduled Castes and 7.5% to Scheduled Tribes; now the backwards wanted a share as well. The commission that would look into this matter was headed by a politician from Bihar, B. P. Mandal.[32]

Beyond the backward-forward divide, Bihar had become a metaphor for all that was wrong in India. Leading articles complained about the "deteriorating law and order in the districts," the corruption and inefficiency of government officials, and the instability of the state's politics (as many as nine chief ministers had been sworn in since 1967), all of which made Bihar "a pitifully poor state." Its present condition was contrasted with the halcyon days of yore, when Bihar had produced the Buddha, Emperor Ashoka, and the great Mauryan Empire. Now, alas, "the only time Bihar ever manages to hit the headlines is either when it is devastated by floods and famine or, when nature takes a respite, there are reports about coalmine tragedies, atrocities on Harijans, and corruption."[33]

VI

Those atrocities were a consequence of the sharpening of a second kind of caste conflict—that between the backwards on the one side and the Scheduled Castes, or Harijans, on the other. This conflict too had a material basis; it was the former who mostly owned the land, and the latter who mostly laboured on it. Beyond disputes about wages and working conditions, this was also a dispute about dignity. The backwards slipped easily into the shoes of the forwards whose land they had gained. Like them, they treated the Harijans with disdain and often violated their women. Once, the lowest castes had no option but to suffer in silence. However, the expansion of education and the spaces opened up by political representation meant that the younger Harijans were "no longer ready to put up with contempt, abuse, beating and other forms of insult which were accepted by earlier generations as a matter of course."[34]

There had been a dramatic increase in the number of attacks on Harijans since the new government assumed power in New Delhi. In the ten years that Mrs. Gandhi was in power the number of reported incidents was 40,000. Between April 1977, when Janata assumed office, and September 1978, 17,775 cases of "atrocities against Harijans" were reported. It was estimated that two-thirds of these incidents were in the north, in states where Janata regimes were in power.[35]

The most serious conflict, however, took place in Marathwada, the arid interior districts of Maharashtra that had once formed part of the Nizam's Dominions. Here, the Scheduled Castes were deeply influenced by the example of Dr. B. R. Ambedkar. Many had converted to Buddhism, and many others had chosen to replace Gandhi's name for them—Harijan, meaning "children of God"—with the more assertive Dalit, meaning "oppressed." A group of writers and poets calling themselves the Dalit Panthers demanded that the university in the region's main town of Aurangabad be named after their great leader. On 27 July 1978 this request was finally granted, when the state government passed a resolution to rename Marathwada University as Dr. Babasaheb Ambedkar University.

The renaming was bitterly opposed by the dominant Maratha caste. Students declared a bandh in the region's towns, closing schools, colleges, shops, and offices. Then they spread into the villages, attacking and sometimes burning Dalit hamlets. An estimated 5,000 people, almost all low-caste, were made homeless. The order to rename the university was withdrawn.[36]

Three months before the riots at Marathwada, there had been a violent clash between Dalits and upper castes in the town of Agra in Uttar Pradesh. Once again, public admiration of Dr. Ambedkar set off the trouble. Agra had a strong community of Jatavs, cobblers who had made money in the shoe trade. On 14 April 1978, Ambedkar's birthday, they took out a procession, led by an elephant bearing a garlanded portrait of their hero. That a vehicle traditionally associated with Hindu kings was being used by Dalits was too much for the upper castes to abide. The procession was attacked; in retaliation, the Jatavs stormed into shops owned by the upper castes. Two weeks of sporadic fighting ensued; finally, the army was called in to restore order.[37]

VII

Of the 10,000 or more episodes of caste violence reported in the first year of Janata rule, one was to have an impact far beyond its place of origin. This was the incident at Belchi, a village in Bihar where, on 27 May 1977, nine Harijans were burned to death by an upper-caste mob. Y. B. Chavan, leader of the opposition in Parliament, announced that he would go there to conduct an enquiry. When Chavan failed to honour his promise, his party colleague and erstwhile prime minister chose to go instead.

In the months between her defeat in the elections and her visit to Belchi Mrs. Gandhi had been very depressed. She and Sanjay both contemplated retiring from politics and perhaps settling in a cottage in the Himalaya. But the killings in Bihar impelled her to take action. Her political instincts told her that this might be the start of a possible comeback. So, while Chavan prevaricated, Mrs. Gandhi flew to Patna and proceeded to Belchi. The roads had been washed away in the rains; she had to exchange her car for a jeep, then exchange the jeep for a tractor, then—when the mud got too deep—exchange the tractor for an elephant. It was by elephant that the former prime minister reached Belchi to console the families of those killed in the violence.[38]

This dramatic gesture brought Indira Gandhi back to the centre of the political stage. As one of her opponents later recalled, her visit to Belchi "served several purposes. It helped damn the Janata Government as being indifferent to the fate of the poor and the Harijans. The ride refurbished Indira Gandhi's image as a friend of the poor and the lowly. It also showed to average Congressmen and women that Indira Gandhi was a woman of action and she alone could be trusted to lead the fight back to power."[39]

The visit to Belchi was her own idea, but Mrs. Gandhi's rehabilitation was also helped by a less inspired initiative of the government in power. In the first week of October 1977, the home minister, Charan Singh, decided that he must arrest the former prime minister. Acting on his instructions, the Central Bureau of Intelligence prepared a charge sheet accusing her of corruption. Armed with this piece of paper, the police went to Mrs. Gandhi's house and took her into custody. Their plan was to drive her to a rest house in the neighbouring state of Haryana. On the way, they were forced to stop at a railroad crossing. Mrs. Gandhi got out and sat down on a culvert. Her lawyers, meanwhile, told the police the warrant did not permit them to take their client out of Delhi. An argument ensued, conducted in the presence of many interested bystanders. Eventually the police conceded the point, and the party drove back to the capital.

Mrs. Gandhi was kept overnight by the police, but when they produced her before a magistrate the next morning, he threw out the charge sheet as insubstantial. The bungled arrest redounded badly on the Janata government, and helped redeem the reputation of its hated opponent. She began making combative speeches against the new regime, citing the increase in crime and inflation (running at double-digit levels), and the profiteering of hoarders and black marketeers. The deposed prime minister, commented the *New York Times* in the last week of October, "has been speaking more and more boldly lately, trying to assume once more the posture of a national leader."[40]

Mrs. Gandhi's resurgence alarmed Janata, as well as many leaders in her own party. Some Congress ministers had already testified against her before the Shah Commission. In January 1978 the Congress formally split into two factions, those who stayed with Mrs. Gandhi forming the Congress (Indira). The next month this party easily won state elections in Andhra Pradesh and Karnataka. The former prime minister had been the chief campaigner; as the results showed, at least in the south her image as a saviour of the poor, the tribals, the Scheduled Castes, and women was intact.[41]

Mrs. Gandhi now began looking around for a safe seat, in order to re-enter Parliament. Eventually she chose a constituency named Chikmaglur, in the coffee belt of Karnataka. The state's chief minister, Devaraj Urs, had a reputation for high efficiency; among his achievements was bestowing ownership rights on hundreds of thousands of tenant cultivators. The work of Urs and her own largely unimpaired standing in south India persuaded Mrs. Gandhi to seek election at the other end of the country from her native Uttar Pradesh.[42]

Running against her was a former (and much respected) chief minister of Karnataka, Veerendra Patil. Leading Patil's campaign was Mrs. Gandhi's adversary during the emergency period, George Fernandes, now minister for industries in the Janata government. "I will not stir out of the constituency till the polling is over," declared Fernandes to a reporter. "We must defeat her." Mrs. Gandhi took the challenge seriously; as the same reporter noted, she "smiles graciously at the women and children, accepts garlands at hundreds of roadside meetings, makes detours to visit numerous places of worship, calls on saints of all denominations."[43]

In the event, Mrs. Gandhi won easily. No sooner had she re-entered the Lok Sabha than she had to face a "privilege motion" against her. A Parliamentary committee, stacked with Janata members, reported that in 1974, when she was prime minister, Mrs. Gandhi had obstructed an enquiry into Sanjay's Maruti factory, and deliberately misled Parliament while doing so. Her punishment was left to the "wisdom of the House." The Janata majority decided that she must be sent to jail for a week. The spell in prison, the election commissioner ruled, meant that she would have to resign her seat. One more by-election was called in Chikmaglur, which Mrs. Gandhi contested, and won.[44]

VIII

Janata's attempts to humiliate the former prime minister were seriously misjudged. The stoicism with which Mrs. Gandhi bore her sufferings was much admired, and the two brief arrests gave her a halo of martyrdom. Admittedly, the men now in power had been victimized during the emergency. But that they chose to focus on taking revenge against an individual, when they should really have been running a government, bespoke a certain smallness of mind.

Behind the attempts to arrest Mrs. Gandhi lay personal rivalries within the Janata camp. The home minister, Charan Singh, was not reconciled to being number two in the cabinet. His move against Mrs. Gandhi was an attempt to steal the thunder from Morarji Desai. He opened another front in the same battle when he wrote to the prime minister complaining about the growing influence of Desai's son Kanti. Kanti Desai lived with his father, and handled his appointments. Unflattering comparisons were made to the role once played by Sanjay Gandhi.

Through the first half of 1978, Charan Singh and Morarji Desai exchanged a series of angry letters. Eventually, in June 1978, Desai was compelled to dismiss Singh from the cabinet, along with Singh's chief lieutenant, Raj Narain. Others within Janata tried to broker a peace, but to no avail. In December, Singh emerged from months of seclusion to organize a huge farmers' rally in the capital. About 200,000 peasants, mostly from northern India, and many from Charan Singh's own Jat caste, came to Delhi in their tractors and trucks to hear their leader speak.

This show of strength forced Desai to recall Charan Singh to the cabinet. In February 1979 Singh was appointed finance minister. He was now also one of two deputy prime ministers, the other being Jagjivan Ram. Singh's first budget offered sops to farmers, such as an increased subsidy for fertilizers and irrigation. But the patch-up proved short-lived. One important constituent of Janata, the socialists, mostly sided with Singh; another, the Jana Sangh, decided to back Desai. Deepening the rift was the question of "dual membership," the growing feeling that the Jana Sangh members of the Janata party owed their primary allegiance to the Rashtriya Swayamsevak Sangh (RSS). In March 1977, Atal Behari Vajpayee had proclaimed that his old party was "dead and buried." But the feeling persisted that the RSS directed the actions of Janata members and ministers who had a Jana Sangh background. They were asked to disavow their ties with the RSS, but they refused, on the grounds that it was merely a "cultural" body.

In the third week of July 1979, the socialists chose to sit in a separate group in Parliament. This led to a split in Janata, a loss of the majority for Morarji Desai's government, and Desai's own resignation. In his bid to put together a new majority, Desai wooed one Congress faction while Jagjivan Ram wooed another. The third leader in the fray, Charan Singh, now formed an opportunistic alliance with Indira Gandhi. With the help of a letter of support from the Congress party, Charan Singh was able to convince the president that he had a majority in the House. He was sworn in just in time to deliver the prime minister's annual Independence Day speech from the Red Fort, the first farmer to do so.[45]

As the disintegration of the Janata party proceeded, Jayaprakash Narayan wrote despairing letters to his protégés. In October 1979, JP died, a broken man. The liberal editor A. D. Gorwala paid tribute to Narayan as "the great moral force of the country, the touchstone of right and wrong." His "last great effort," Gorwala wrote, was the formation and victory of the Janata Party, whose "narrow, stupid partisan men . . . absorbed in their own self-interest and self-importance, failed him badly."[46] Those self-absorbed men—Morarji Desai, Charan Singh, Jagjivan Ram—all came to JP's funeral in Patna, as, more strikingly, did Sanjay Gandhi and his mother. "Poor old J. P.!" wrote Mrs. Gandhi to a friend afterwards. "What a confused mind he had leading to such a frustrated life!" She attributed his twists and turns to "Gandhian hypocrisy," to the vow of celibacy extracted from him when he married the Mahatma's disciple Prabhavati. "That and jealousy of my father probably conditioned the rest of his life," she remarked, adding, "It is nonsense to say that he did not want office. One part of him did, very much so. He was torn between that and the desire to be regarded as a martyr and a saint."[47]

There is a certain spitefulness in this assessment, and also a certain loftiness of tone. Mrs. Gandhi was having the last laugh, not just on her old friend-turned-rival JP, but also on the party he had created. In July, when Morarji Desai had resigned and his successor was being chosen, the journal *Himmat* presciently remarked, "Mrs Gandhi is the only one who would like to have a mid-term poll—and would gain from it in the present climate. It is in her interest to have Mr Charan Singh installed as Prime Minister but only for two to three months."[48]

Charan Singh was sworn in as prime minister in the last week of July 1979; a month later the Congress (I) informed the president that it was withdrawing support. It took the president a month more to explore and reject the alternatives. When he decided that a midterm poll was the only solution, the Election Commission still needed time to prepare for it. So Charan Singh stayed on as prime minister until the end of the year, two months more than *Himmat* had given him.

IX

The Janata party came to power amid a wave of hyperbole, with talk of a second freedom from authoritarian rule and a resounding restoration of democracy. Almost from its first weeks in office, the party seemed determined to squander this goodwill. It was soon noticed that in both the Centre and the states, Janata ministers were grabbing the best government bungalows, raiding the Public Works Department for air conditioners and carpets, organizing lavish parties and weddings for their relatives, running up huge telephone and electricity bills, and travelling abroad at the slightest pretext (or no pretext at all).[49] Even traditionally anti-Congress journals were writing about the "death of idealism" within Janata, saying that it had quickly become a "political party of the traditional type," its members "interested more and more in positions and perquisites and less and less in affecting society." People were saying that while it had taken the Congress thirty years to abandon its principles, Janata had lost them within a year of its formation.[50]

Looking back on the three years of the Janata regime, one analyst remembered it as "a chronicle of confused and complex party squabbles, intra-party rivalries, shifting alliances, defections, charges and counter-charges of incompetence and the corruption and humiliation of persons who had come to power after the defeat of Mrs. Gandhi."[51] Most Indians who lived through those years would make the same assessment, if more succinctly; the Janata party, they would say, was merely a bunch of jokers. It takes a distinguished foreign observer to remind us that, beyond the fighting and squabbling, the Janata government made a notable contribution to Indian democracy. This, in the words of Granville Austin, was its "remarkable success in repairing the Constitution from the Emergency's depredations, in reviving open parliamentary practice through its consultative style when repairing the Constitution, and in restoring the judiciary's independence."[52]

The initiative here was taken by Morarji Desai. In an interview on the eve of the elections of 1977, he remarked that during the emergency, democracy itself had been "vasectomised." If his party won, it would "work for the removal of fear which has enveloped the people." Then it would undertake "to rectify the Constitution." Morarji was clear that "we will have to ensure that Emergency like this can never be imposed. No Government should be able to do so."[53]

After Janata's victory, the job of repairing the constitution was supervised by the hard-working law minister Shanti Bhushan. The most important amendment to be overturned was the Forty-Second. To re-place its "defiling" provisions, two new amendments were drafted, which restored the five-year term of Parliament and state assemblies, re-stored the right of the Supreme Court to adjudicate on any election (that of the prime minister included), limited the period of President's Rule in the states, mandated the publication of parliamentary and legislative proceedings, and made the promulgation of an emergency much more difficult. Any such act had now to be approved by a two-thirds majority in Parliament, had to be renewed every six months after a new vote on it, and had to be in response to an "armed rebellion" (rather than a mere "internal disturbance," as was previously the case). These changes were intended to curb the arbitary powers of the executive and to restore the rights of the courts: in effect, to restore the Constitution to what it was before Mrs. Gandhi's emergency-era amendments.

The drafting of these amendments took time because of the demands of legal precision and the need to ensure the kind of cross-party sup-port that would make their passage in both houses of Parliament possi-ble. As these restorations were being debated, the press was reporting avidly on the Shah Commission, while a succession of books and mem-oirs documenting the excesses of the emergency were being published. In this climate of opinion, even the Congress was in no mood to defend the changes in the constitution that its leaders had wrought. That damage was now undone by the freshly drafted Forty-Fourth Amendment. When this was passed by a large majority on 7 December 1978, among those voting for it were those two old enemies: Morarji Desai and Indira Gandhi.[54]

X

Although it failed to last a full term, the victory of the Janata party was a watershed in Indian politics. For the first time since independence, a party other than the Congress came to govern at the Centre. In the states too the landscape of politics became more variegated, with the victory of the communists in West Bengal and that of the AIADMK in Tamil Nadu.

The Indian political system was being decentred, and not just in terms of parties. The late 1970s also witnessed the flowering of numer-ous "new" social movements. In 1978 there was a major conference of "socialist-feminists" in Bombay, which focused on the increasing viola-tions of women's rights. There were campaigns against dowry and rape, against alcoholism among men and the sexual abuse it frequently resulted in, and for better working conditions for women labouring in factories and household units. This new wave of feminism was widespread as well as wide-ranging, with groups active in many states, mobilizing support through public rallies, street plays, poster campaigns, and house-to-house canvassing.[55]

The late 1970s also saw a vigorous environmental movement. Peasants struggled in defence of their forest rights; tribals protested against their displacement by large industrial projects; and artisanal fisherfolk opposed trawlers that were depleting the fish stock of the ocean. In these protests two things stood out: the leading role of women, who themselves bore the brunt of ecological degradation; and the fact that in India (unlike the West, where the concern for nature was couched in aesthetic terms and voiced by the middle class), this was an "environmentalism of the poor," supported by rural communities for whom access to the gifts of nature was linked to their survival.[56]

Both the feminist movement and the environmental movement had actually started in the early 1970s. Their progress was interrupted by the emergency, but when that ended, they were resumed, with renewed vigour. The same was true of the civil rights movement. This had its origins in the treatment of Naxalite activists incarcerated in the Calcutta jail. When these prisoners began a *bidi-chitti andolan*, a struggle for access to cigarettes and letters (denied to them by their jailers), a retired engineer named Kapil Bhattacharya decided to form an Association for the Protection of Democratic Rights. The emergency inspired the formation of other such groups, based in Delhi, Bombay, Hyderabad, and elsewhere. Some focused on denial of "civil liberties," the violation by the state of the basic human rights of its citizens. Others worked with a broader concept of "democratic rights," which took the right to life and liberty guaranteed by the Constitution as also meaning the right to better wages and working conditions, and to gainful employment itself. The first kind of group took up jail reform and the abuse of power by state authorities (and the police in particular); the second kind also looked at the impact of state policies on the lives and livelihoods of the disprivileged, particularly the low castes and tribals. These groups produced dozens of reports on violations of civil liberties and democratic rights by the state, drawing on field investigations, often in remote parts of the country, conducted by public-spirited intellectuals based in the cities.[57]

These movements were described as "new" because they took up issues neglected by the old, class-based social movements of peasants and workers. However, during the late 1970s those older movements also expressed themselves in new forms. Thus the trade union movement, which had historically focused on the factory sector, now began working among miners and labourers in household and cottage industries. Among the more notable initiatives was the Chattisgarh Mineworkers Shramik Sangh (CMSS), whose leader, Shankar Guha Niyogi, sought to blend the ideas of Gandhi and Marx. The mines where the CMSS was active serviced the great public-sector steel industry at Bhilai. Working with miners of a chiefly tribal background, Niyogi campaigned for equal pay for women workers and against alcohol abuse by men, set up schools for children, and struggled to make the mine owners pay as much attention to health and safety as to a decent living wage.[58]

Accompanying and complementing these movements was a new kind of Indian press. The end of the emergency unleashed the energies of journalists as only the struggle for national independence had done before it. Censorship was dead; there were now no limits to what reporters and editors could write about, or to the length of their stories. It also helped that the first offset presses arrived in India in the 1970s. Type no longer had to be laboriously set in hot metal; journals no longer had to be printed only in the bigger towns and cities.

The historian Robin Jeffrey has authoritatively traced India's "newspaper revolution," which began in 1977 and has gathered pace ever since. Among the components of this revolution we may single out five. Two were enabled by new technology: the simultaneous printing of multiple editions of the same paper in towns far distant from one other; and the enhancement of print quality and, especially, of the production of pictures and other visual material. Other innovations were a product of changes in society and politics. The end of censorship facilitated the rise of investigative journalism, such as hard-hitting stories on crime and political corruption. The spread of education and the expansion of the middle class gave an enormous fillip to Indian-language journalism. A National Readership Survey, conducted in 1979, and restricted to the towns and cities, estimated that as many as 48 million urban Indians regularly read a periodical of some kind. The quickest increase was in the smaller towns and among Indian languages. In 1979, for the first time, those who read newspapers in Hindi (a language spoken by 40% of Indians) numbered more than those who read them in English (a language spoken by only 3% of Indians). The new journalism substituted colloquial, demotic prose for the stiff, formal style once preferred by editors and reporters. Idioms and phrases derived from classical Sanskrit, once obligatory, were now abandoned in favour of the rhythms and cadences of everyday speech.[59]

Two somewhat contradictory trends were visible in India during the late 1970s. On the one hand, there was an increasing fragmentation of the polity, as manifested in the rapid turn-over of governments. With fewer and fewer exceptions, politicians and parties had abandoned ideology for expediency, and principle for profit. On the other hand, there were new forms of social assertion among historically subordinated groups such as low castes, women, and unorganized workers. There was now, for the first time, an active civil liberties movement. The press, which during the emergency had mostly knuckled under without a fight, had become livelier than ever before.

From the more formal, purely political side, it appeared that Indian democracy was being corroded and degraded. If one took a more "social" view, however, it seemed that Indian democracy was, in fact, being deepened and enriched.

24

DEMOCRACY *in* DISARRAY

> Not every individual or party is always disposed to use our
> democratic framework to further constructive purposes. It seems
> that the exercise of the democratic right sometimes takes the form
> of freedom even to destroy.
>
> INDIRA GANDHI to Jayaprakash Narayan, May 1968

I

WRITING SHORTLY after the elections of 1977, the *Guardian*'s correspondent in India thought that the return to democracy might be short-lived. "Democracy can only survive if there is economic progress and reform," he remarked. "Already, the new [Janata] Government faces an economic crisis; inflation rampant again, an explosion of wage demands, and a wave of strikes. If it is overwhelmed by protest, the cycle of repression could start all over again."[1]

Altogether more optimistic was the old India hand Horace Alexander, now eighty-seven, and living in retirement in a Quaker home in Pennsylvania. In a letter published in the *New York Times*, Alexander said "the astonishing Indian elections" showed that "the common people of India have political courage," derived from Gandhi and the heritage of the freedom movement. In a letter to a fellow Quaker, he likewise called the elections "a triumph for the common people of India," adding, "Let none ever say that 'democratic liberty' is a bourgeois conception, which is only meaningful to a small number of left-wing intellectuals."[2]

The indefatigable Alexander also wrote to Mrs. Gandhi. During the emergency he had peppered her with anxious letters about the fate of freedom and of the men she had detained. Now he remembered his old friend Jawaharlal Nehru wishing for a spell away from politics, to read and simply relax. He wondered whether Nehru's daughter, out of power, would "spend some time enjoying birds, up in the Himalaya, or in Kashmir." There was some chit-chat about art and literature, and then the letter concluded: "We shall try to keep up with the news from India, and perhaps in five years from now, you will be in office once again with the biggest majority ever. Such is democracy!"[3]

Actually, it took less than three years for Mrs. Gandhi to return to power. Her Congress party won 353 seats in the elections of 1980, one more than in the "Garibi Hatao" campaign of 1971. It did very well in the south, as before, and in the north it benefited hugely from a division of the vote between the two rival Janata factions, here campaigning as separate parties. In the key state of Uttar Pradesh, for example, the Congress obtained 36% of the popular vote, yet won 60% of the parliamentary seats. One Janata faction got 22.6% of the vote, the other 29%; between them, they won thirty-two seats in the state to the Congress's fifty.[4]

The elections of 1980, notes the editor Prabhas Joshi, marked the "end of ideology" in Indian politics. Previous elections were fought and won on the concepts of democracy, socialism, secularism, and nonalignment. In 1980, however, Mrs. Gandhi spoke not of the abolition of poverty but of her ability to rule. Janata could not hold together a government, she told the voters, whereas she could and had done so. Its bickering apart, other factors also went against Janata. There were shortages of basic consumer goods, these attributed naturally to the party in power. As one election slogan went: *Janata ho gayi fail/Kha gayi chini aur mitti ka tel* ("The Janata party has failed/Eaten up sugar and kerosene on the way").[5]

The Janata party had thoroughly discredited itself. As a reporter covering the elections found, although Indira's Gandhi had a "tarnished image," her opponents were "all tarnish and no image."[6] Meanwhile, the rash of attacks on Scheduled Castes turned this very numerous voting segment back toward the Congress. Sanjay Gandhi had apologized to the Muslims for the excesses of the emergency; sections of this voting bloc returned to the fold as well.[7]

In most of India the elections were moderately free. In parts of Bihar and Uttar Pradesh, however, where roads were poor and telephone lines non-existent, the Election Commission was unable to monitor or check the seizing of booths by armed gangs. Here, there was a "free enterprise militia" operating, so that "adult franchise" had been "replaced by vicarious franchise," where the candidate with the most guns at his command could "perform the function of 'mass voting' on behalf of the electorate."[8]

II

Not long after Mrs. Gandhi returned to power, a political scientist whose sympathies were with Congress advised her to remake the party as "the palpably real institution that the Congress was under Nehru." It was "essential that a sharing of power replace its personalisation, that a leadership drawing its power from the grassroots rather than above should be allowed to emerge." Mrs. Gandhi's "restored charisma" could then be used "in the service of shoring-up and reinforcing the institutions of an open polity before it dissipates again as in the past."[9]

These sentiments were at once noble and naive. For it was not just the Congress party that Mrs. Gandhi believed she embodied, but the Indian nation itself. In May 1980 she told a visiting journalist that "for many long years I have been the target of attack [from] individuals, groups and parties," either "Hindu and Muslim fanatics" or "old feudal interests" or people "sympathetic to foreign ideologies." Whereas she stood "for India's unfettered independence of action, self-reliance and economic strength," those "who are against self-reliance, or secularism or socialism find some reason or other to malign me."[10]

"Paranoia" may be the most appropriate word here. In this frame of mind Indira Gandhi was not ready to seriously share power, unless it was with her son Sanjay, who was now both a member of Parliament and the general secretary of the Congress party. Indeed, as one journal in Delhi remarked, Sanjay was once more "the most vital factor in Indian politics." When Mrs. Gandhi dismissed nine state governments after the elections of 1980, it was Sanjay who alloted the Congress tickets for the assembly seats, Sanjay who decided who would be chief minister when and if Congress won. The newly appointed chief minister of Uttar Pradesh, Vishwanath Pratap Singh, spoke for many when he told the press, "Sanjay is a leader in his own right and he is my leader too."[11]

Mrs. Gandhi was now sixty-three, and thoughts of the succession were not far from her mind. However, on 23 June 1980 Sanjay was killed while flying a single-engine plane for fun, as he was wont to do. He did three loops in the air and tried a fourth but then lost control. The plane crashed 500 yards from the home he shared with his mother. Both Sanjay and his co-pilot died instantly.[12]

Mrs. Gandhi returned to work four days later. She was desperately lonely. One reporter remarked on her "total and inviolable aloofness."[13] By the end of August she had persuaded her elder son to fill the breach. Until this time Rajiv Gandhi had shown little interest in politics. He was a family man, devoted to his Italian wife, Sonia, and to their two little children. He worked as a pilot with the sole domestic carrier, Indian Airlines. He flew Avros to Lucknow and Jaipur, and his main professional ambition was to be allowed to pilot Boeings between Delhi and Bombay.

Now, however, there was increasing pressure on him to enter politics, most of it coming from the prime minister herself. Speaking to an interviewer in August 1980, Rajiv Gandhi said that there was "no question of my stepping into [Sanjay's] shoes." Asked whether he would take up a party post or run for office, Rajiv answered that he "would prefer not to." He added that his wife, Sonia, was "dead against the idea of my getting into politics."[14]

Nine months later Rajiv Gandhi was elected a member of Parliament from his brother's old constituency, Amethi. When asked why he had changed his mind, Rajiv answered, "The way I look at it is that Mummy has to be helped somehow." His entry into politics, wrote one very sympathetic journalist, "surreptitious though it is, may be Mrs. Gandhi's concept of giving India stability in leadership and continuity in government." With the "lack of leadership of any kind on the horizon," being a member of the Nehru family gave him a "high identification quotient" and "a head-start."[15]

Recognizing the signs—or bowing to the inevitable—Congress members and ministers all across the country lined up to salaam Rajiv. He was asked to lay foundation stones for medical colleges, open electric lines to Harijan colonies, and give speeches to Congress clubs on Nehru's birthday.[16]

As Rajiv Gandhi took his first steps in Indian politics, his mother was at work on the world stage, rebuilding bridges torn down during the emergency. Mrs. Gandhi was deeply concerned about the battering her image had taken in the West. Now that she had been returned to power by the ballot box, she was determined to repair the damage. For a full eight months in 1982, the United Kingdom hosted a Festival of India, featuring exhibitions of Indian art at the Victoria and Albert Museum, concerts by Ravi Shankar and M. S. Subbulakshmi at the Royal Festival Hall, and much else. The performances ran the gamut from high and classical to earthy and folk. Thus a high school in Worcestershire was turned into a "miniature Rajasthan," with dancers and storytellers from that state camping for a week, their performances repaid in kind by the school's putting on a performance of Kipling's *Jungle Book*.

The festival was promoted and partly funded by the government of India. The prime minister visited the United Kingdom at its beginning and end, emerging as the "star of the show." During the emergency, sections of the British press had portrayed her as an ogress; now, commented one columnist, "she must welcome the somewhat more flattering attention she is receiving." At one function, where she and the British prime minister were the chief guests, Mrs. Gandhi said that "India was committed to democracy and socialism," adding that "in respect of the latter we differ from Mrs. Thatcher." Meeting a group of newspaper editors, she tartly remarked, "I hope you will give up calling me Empress of India now."

The Festival of India was deemed a great success by its organizers; encores were to follow in the United States, the Soviet Union, and France. The last word on the tamasha might rest with the cartoonist R. K. Laxman, who portrayed two half-naked men on an Indian street, one reading a newspaper and saying to the other: "But for such a festival we wouldn't know how great we and our achievements are!"[17]

III

Cartoonists are professionally obliged to mock the mighty, but in Laxman's case his comments might also have had something to do with the fact that he lived in Bombay, a city where the extremes of wealth and poverty were more striking than anywhere else in India. As it happened, the festival in London coincided with an indefinite strike by the textile workers of Bombay. They were led by Datta Samant, a medical doctor whose political ideology was uncertain, but whose charisma was vast enough to allow him to supplant the socialists and communists who had hitherto led the city's trade unions.

Datta Samant's career in Bombay began with a factory called Empire Dyeing, where he was able to get the workers a salary increase of 200 rupees a month. His success encouraged him to move into other factories; soon, most of the workers in Bombay's vast textile industry were loyal to him. Their wages had grown incrementally over the years; inadequately protected against inflation, they sought an overhaul of the salary structure. Samant asked that the minimum wage be increased from 670 to 940 rupees a month; when the demand was rejected out of hand, he called for a strike. Beginning on 18 January 1982, the strike was to last almost two years. More than 200,000 workers participated, and more than 22 million man-days of work were lost.

This was a genuine mass movement, whose ripples were felt throughout the city and beyond. Thousands of workers risked arrest; others clashed with strike breakers. The truculent mood affected other sectors of the city's labour force. Underpaid policemen sought to form a union of their own; their protests spilled out into the streets. Eventually, the policemen had to be disarmed and jailed by the paramilitary Border Security Force.[18]

In the countryside too there were stirrings along class lines. Naxalite activists, arrested during the emergency but released afterwards, were making their presence felt in the tribal areas of Andhra Pradesh, among communities oppressed by the state's forest department and by Hindu moneylenders. Other Naxalite groups were at work in the plains of central Bihar, organizing Harijan labourers against their upper-caste landlords. Some sympathizers, such as the Swedish writer Jan Myrdal, saw in these stirrings the possibility, and hope, that the Chinese revolution might one day have an Indian counterpart.[19]

In the early 1980s there was mobilization on the lines of ethnicity as well. The movement for a tribal state of Jharkhand had taken more militant forms. By official figures, 30 billion rupees had been spent on "tribal development" in the Chotanagpur plateau. Where this money had gone it was hard to say, for the people still lived in "a primeval darkness" without schools, hospitals, roads, or electricity, and with their lands seized by outsiders and their forests closed to them by the state. "The Jharkhand demand is set against such a background," reported the writer Mahasveta Devi. "Tales of woe and exploitation on the one hand; the pulse of resistance on the other."[20]

The protests in Jharkhand were led by Shibu Soren, a young man with long black locks who quickly became a folk hero. He organized the forcible harvest of paddy in lands "stolen" from the Adivasis by *dikus* (outsiders), as well as the invasion of forest lands that the Adivasis claimed as their own. In September 1980, the police fired on a crowd of protesting tribals at Gua, killing at least fifteen people. The incident intensified the demand for Jharkhand.[21]

There were also demands, if not as actively expressed as in Jharkhand, for a state called Chattisgarh, to be carved out of the tribal areas of Madhya Pradesh, and for a state called Uttarakhand, constituting the Himalayan districts of Uttar Pradesh. These too were regions rich in timber, water, and minerals—resources increasingly exploited by and for the benefit of the larger national economy, dispossessing the local inhabitants in the process.[22]

The 1980s also saw a renewal of Naga militancy. During the emergency, the government of India was able to persuade many members of Phizo's Naga National Council (NNC) to lay down their arms and come aboveground. Some people in the administration hoped that this "Shillong

Accord" (named for the town where it was signed) would signal the end of the rebellion. However, the accord was seen as a sell-out by Naga radicals like T. Muivah. Muivah was a Thangkul Naga who, in the 1960s, had been one of the first to seek the help of China. He had stayed four years in Yunnan, being trained by the People's Liberation Army. Deeply impressed by the Cultural Revolution, he sought to blend its ideals with the faith he was born into, thus combining evangelical Christianity with revolutionary socialism.

In 1980, Muivah and Isak Swu set up the National Socialist Council of Nagaland (NSCN). By now Chinese aid had dried up, so Muivah instead forged links with other insurgent groups in India's north-east and in Burma. A journalist who met him in his jungle hideout reported Muivah's view that "the only hope the Nagas had to achieve their independence would be if India itself broke up." The Naga leader had contacts among Sikh militants and Kashmiri separatists, and "he fervently hoped a similar movement would emerge among the Tamils of southern India— which would indeed plunge the country into the anarchy he desired."[23]

Muivah's strongest following was among his fellow Thangkuls, who lived in the upland areas of Manipur. Were an independent Naga nation ever formed, these hills would be part of it; but as things stood the Thangkuls were less than happy to be ruled by the Meitei Hindus, who were Manipur's dominant community. Worried by the birth of the NSCN, the Indian government increased troop deployment in the Ukhrul district of Manipur. On 19 February 1982, the insurgents ambushed a convoy on the Imphal-Ukhrul road, killing twenty-two soldiers of the Sikh Regiment, some officers among them. The army's answer was to go on a rampage, searching every village in the district, abusing the men, and attacking the women. A civil liberties team visited the area, recording the testimony of the victims. The team found that "even though only a few people supported the underground they were all suspects in the eyes of the army."[24]

IV

There were movements for separate or new states within or outside the Indian Union, and movements for greater autonomy within existing states. In the old Congress stronghold of Andhra Pradesh, there was growing resentment at the Centre's tendency to "impose" chief ministers. Between 1978 and 1982 Mrs. Gandhi changed the state's chief minister no fewer than four times. In February 1982, the new incumbent, T. Anjaiah, went to the Hyderabad airport to welcome Rajiv Gandhi, accompanied by a large group of supporters with garlands. Rajiv chastised the chief minister for bringing a crowd, and in such strong words that there were tears in Anjaiah's eyes.[25]

The humiliation was felt personally and collectively, with the Telugu media portraying it as an insult to the pride of the Andhras. Among those provoked into action was the great film actor N. T. Rama Rao (known as NTR), who was to Telugu cinema what M. G. Ramachandran had been to its Tamil counterpart—an acknowledged hero and superstar. By one reckoning Rao had acted in 150 movies; by another, 300. (A third source chose to be very precise, putting the number at 292.)

Unlike MGR, NTR had no political past. Nor did his films usually carry a social message (they were mostly based on mythological themes). Now, on the eve of his sixtieth birthday, he formed a new regional party, Telugu Desam, which stood for "the honour and self-respect of the 60 million Telugu speaking people." No longer, he said, would the great state of Andhra Pradesh be treated as a "branch office" of the Congress party.[26]

The new party was formed in March 1982; elections to the state assembly were due at the end of the year. In preparation, NTR toured the districts of the state, speaking out against the "corrupt" administration of the Congress. He travelled in a van remodelled to look like a chariot. At public meetings he would emerge dramatically from the vehicle, atop a platform raised with the help of a generator. He usually wore saffron, the colour of renunciation, indicating that he had given up his film career to serve the people. He was the mythological hero made real, come to rid the world of greed and corruption and bring justice for all. Women flocked to his meetings—he, in turn, offered them universities of their own and the preferential allotment of jobs in the state sector.[27]

While the national press was sceptical about NTR's chances, the major Telugu daily *Eenadu* threw its considerable weight behind him. Its confidence was rewarded when the Telugu Desam won a two-thirds majority in the assembly. In the second week of January 1983, Rama Rao was sworn in as chief minister at the Fateh Maidan in Hyderabad, with 200,000 cheering Andhras crowded into the grounds.[28]

One of NTR's first acts on assuming power was to instruct his food department to sell rice at two rupees a kilogram, to fulfil a promise made before the election. In general he acted as if he was the party as well as the government, in this respect imitating his friend MGR as well as his rival Indira Gandhi. "If the Prime Minister thinks that she is India," commented one socialist, then "NTR behaves as if he is the sole representative of six and half crores of Telugu people. Telugu Desam MLAs have no voice in shaping the policies and programmes of the Government. NTR runs the show both as Chief Minister and also as the President of his party."[29] Again like Mrs. Gandhi, NTR was partial to his own family, as when he allowed a film studio to be built by his son on unauthorized land.[30]

V

Another, more serious, movement for autonomy was taking shape in the state of Assam. One says "more serious" because it resulted from a groundswell of opinion rather than from individual charisma, and because this state was located not in the Indian heartland but in a long-troubled extremity.

Assam shared borders with West Bengal and several states of the north-east, as well as with the countries of Bangladesh and Bhutan. Assamese was the state language, but Bengali was also widely spoken. There was a long history of hostility between the speakers of the two languages. Bengalis had dominated the middle and lower rungs of the colonial administration. As officials, teachers, and magistrates, they exercised great authority and power over the local Assamese, treating them with condescension and even contempt. Beginning in the late nineteenth century, land-hungry Bengali peasants had begun to move into the forests and lowlands of Assam. After independence, this migration continued, accelerating whenever political instability or an economic crisis affected East Bengal or, as it later became, Bangladesh. In the 1970s, for example, the number of registered voters in Assam jumped from 6.2 million to almost 9 million, the increase accounted for chiefly by immigrants from Bangladesh.[31]

The Assamese feared cultural subordination at the hands of the Bengali middle class, and demographic conquest at the hands of the Bengali peasantry. There were episodic riots in the 1950s and 1960s, aimed at driving the immigrants back to where they came from. However, it was only from the late 1970s that these sentiments were transmuted into a widespread social movement.[32]

The key organization in this transformation was the All Assam Students Union (AASU). Its network extended throughout the state; all student unions in schools and colleges were affiliated with it. Beginning in 1979 and continuing over the next five years, the AASU led hundreds of strikes and processions, intended to press the central government to clear Assam of the infiltrators.

Assamese nationalists had based their arguments on culture and demography. AASU added a third leg to the stool: economics. The economy of Assam was manifestly dominated by outsiders. The rich tea gardens of the state were mostly owned by firms based in London or Calcutta. Assam had India's most productive oilfields, yet the oil was pumped up by public-sector firms that employed few locals (and none at the top level of management). Worse, the oil was then sent to refineries located in other states. Local trade and commerce were controlled by Marwaris from Rajasthan. All in all, Assam was an "internal colony," supplying cheap raw materials for metropolitan India to process and profit from.

The larger demand of the Assam movement was for a new economic policy, so that the state's residents could obtain income and employment from the best use of its natural resources. A more immediate demand, however, was for the deletion of immigrants from the list of voters, preparatory to their deportation from the state. This led to an unfortunate but perhaps inevitable polarization on communal lines, because many of the more recent immigrants were, in fact, Muslims. The Congress party, then ruling in the Centre and long dominant in the state, was accused of protecting the immigrants as a captive voting bloc. Also hastening the polarization was the formation of an All Assam Minorities Students Union (AAMSU).[33]

Visiting Assam in the summer of 1980, a journalist from Delhi found that the "movement had undoubtedly acquired gigantic proportions." No longer was it confined to the literate or articulate. The Assamese people as a whole felt "increasingly frustrated, driven to the wall. Aside from the anti-foreigner sentiment, the movement has developed other dangerous strains—anti-Bengali, anti-Left, anti-Muslim, anti-non-Assamese, and slowly but discernibly, even anti-Indian."[34] Bengalis were being attacked, and their homes burned. But the central government was also targeted. Railroad tracks were uprooted by individual saboteurs, and AASU stopped the export of plywood and jute from the state. AASU was even successful in blocking the flow of oil, forcing the government to declare the pipeline and the land extending up to half a kilometre on either side a "protected area." Ultimately, the army had to be called in to get oil supplies from Assam to a refinery in distant Bihar.[35]

In the last week of July 1980, the prime minister warned the AASU leaders that their actions could lead to retribution. "Suppose other states refused to supply Assam with steel?" she asked. "How would the Assamese develop their industry?" Indian federalism was based on interdependence:

"it was only in the shadow of a bigger unit that each unit can survive; otherwise outside pressures will be too great to bear."[36]

Even as this warning was issued, however, the central government had begun negotiations with the AASU leaders. The talks were to continue for the next three years, on and off; and whenever they broke down, strikes and protests would start again. Officially, the negotiators were AASU on the one side and the Home Ministry on the other. But numerous interlocutors were also used, among them the Gandhi Peace Foundation and the Manipur chief minister, R. K. Dorendra Singh. The real bone of contention was the cut-off date beyond which immigration could be considered "illegal." The AASU wanted all migrants who came in after 1951 to be crossed off the list of voters and deported. The government of India thought this struck at the federal principle, violating the freedom of citizens to move from one part of the country to another. It was prepared, however, to recognize 1971 as the cut-off date, for in 1971 the happenings in East Pakistan had provoked an unprecedented migration across the borders that could be considered "unnatural."

By one account, representatives of the government and the AASU met on 114 days in the calendar years 1980, 1981, and 1982. Various compromises were discussed: one, suggested by the Gandhi Peace Foundation, was that those who entered Assam between 1951 and 1961 be conferred rights of residence and voting (in effect, citizenship), those who came between 1961 and 1971 be dispersed to other states of India, and those who came after 25 March 1971 (the date on which Bangladesh declared itself a sovereign state) be deported.[37]

But the situation proved intractable. The conflict resumed, taking uglier forms. In one gruesome incident in February 1983, hundreds of Bengali Muslims were slaughtered by a mob of Assamese Hindus and tribals. Thus was fulfilled the grim prediction of the journalist Devdutt, who, writing when the talks between the movement and the government were in their early stages, noted that if no resolution was found, "like the turbulent Brahmaputra coursing along 450 miles in Assam, the seething discontent and disaffection will also wreak havoc."[38]

VI

Contemporaneous with the Assam movement, there was a still more serious agitation for greater autonomy in the state of Punjab. I say "still more serious" because Punjab bordered Pakistan, a country with which India had fought three wars. Besides, the majority community of the state was not Hindu but Sikh. To the primordial attachments of language and region was thus added the potentially deadly element of religion.

As in Assam, the Punjab "agitation" or "movement" or "crisis" (to give it three of its many names) had causes both distant and proximate. A section of the Sikh intelligentsia hoped for a renewal, in some shape or form, of the Sikh state ruled by Maharaja Ranjit Singh in the first half of the nineteenth century. Others looked only as far back as partition, and the tragedies and losses suffered by the community then. It had taken twenty years of almost ceaseless struggle to compel New Delhi to constitute a Sikh-majority province within India. However, even after the new Punjab was formed in 1966, the major Sikh political party, the Akali Dal, was unable to authoritatively rule the state. It rankled deeply that in 1967 and 1969, the Akalis had to form unstable coalitions with "Hindu" parties such as the Jana Sangh, whereas in 1971 the rival Congress was able to come to power in the Punjab on its own.[39]

In October 1973 the Working Committee of the Akali Dal passed the Anandpur Sahib Resolution. This asked the government of India to hand over Chandigarh to Punjab (it shared the city with Haryana); to also hand over Punjabi-speaking areas then with other states; and to increase the proportion of Sikhs in the army. Asking for a recasting of the Indian constitution on "real federal principles," it said that "in this new Punjab and in other States the Centre's interference would be restricted to defence, foreign relations, currency, and general administration; all other departments would be in the jurisdiction of Punjab (and other states) which would be fully entitled to frame [their] own laws on these subjects."

By one reading, the Anandpur Sahib Resolution merely sought to make real the promise of states' autonomy hinted at by the constitution. But the resolution was also amenable to more dangerous interpretations. The preamble spoke of the Akali Dal as "the very embodiment of the hopes and aspirations of the Sikh *Nation*." The "political goal of the Panth [community]" was defined as "the pre-eminence of the Khalsa [or Sikh brotherhood]," with the "fundamental policy" of the Akali Dal being the "realization of this birth-right of the Khalsa through creation of congenial environment and a political set-up."[40]

The year 1973 was not perhaps the best time to make these demands, with Mrs. Gandhi riding high on the wave of a war recently won, and the Centre more powerful than ever before. Its powers were increased still further with the emergency, when thousands of Akalis were put in jail. But in 1977 the emergency was lifted, elections were held, and the Congress party was comprehensively trounced. With the Akalis now in power in the Punjab, the demands of the Anandpur Sahib Resolution were revived, and new ones added. Among the losses at partition were two of the five rivers that gave the state its name; if that was not bad enough, the Indian Punjab had to share the remaining three with the states of Haryana and Rajasthan. The Akalis claimed a greater share of these waters; to this economic demand was coupled a cultural one, the designation of Amritsar, home to the holiest Sikh shrine, the Golden Temple, as a "Holy City."[41]

In April 1978 there was a mass convention at Amritsar of a religious sect, the Nirankaris. They thought of themselves as Sikhs, but since they believed in a living guru, they were regarded as heretics by the faithful. With the Akalis in power, some priests professed shame that the Holy City was being profaned. Leading the opposition to the Nirankaris' meeting was a hitherto obscure preacher, Jarnail Singh Bhindranwale. He was born into a family of Jat Sikhs, and had left his wife and children to become head of a seminary called the Damdami Taksal. He was an impressive presence: over six feet tall, slim and athletic, with probing eyes, and dressed in a long blue robe. He was also an effective and even inspiring preacher, with a deep knowledge of the Sikh scriptures. He claimed that Sikhs "were slaves in independent India," discriminated against by the Hindus. Bhindranwale wanted the Sikhs to purify themselves and return to the fundamentals of their faith. He spoke scathingly of the corrupt and effete Hindu, but mocked even more the modernized Sikh, who had so far forgotten himself as to cut his hair and consume tobacco and alcohol.[42]

By some accounts, Bhindranwale was built up by Sanjay Gandhi and the Union home minister Zail Singh (himself a former chief minister of Punjab) as a counter to the Akalis. Writing in September 1982, the journalist Ayesha Kagal remarked that Bhindranwale "was originally a product nurtured and marketed by the Centre to cut into the Akali Dal's sphere of influence."[43] The keyword here is "originally." Whoever it was that first promoted him, Bhindranwale quickly demonstrated his own independent charisma and influence. To him were attracted many Jats of a peasant background who had seen the gains of the green revolution being cornered by the large landowners. Other followers came from the lower Sikh castes of artisans and labourers; they saw in the process of purification their own social advancement. Bhindranwale also benefited from the general increase of religiosity, which, in the Punjab as in some other places, followed rapid and unexpected economic development.[44]

To return, however, to the Nirankari convention at Amritsar in April 1978: while it was on, Bhindranwale preached an angry sermon from the precints of the Golden Temple. Moved by his words, a crowd of Sikhs descended on the place where the heretics were meeting. The Nirankaris fought back; in the battle that ensued, fifteen people died.

Sikh pride took another blow in 1980, when the Akalis were dismissed and the Congress returned to power in Punjab. In June of that year, a group of students met at the Golden Temple and proclaimed an independent Sikh republic. The republic had a name, Khalistan; and a president, Jagjit Singh Chauhan, a Sikh politician based in London. It was mostly Sikh émigrés who were behind this move; the pronouncement was made simultaneously in the United Kingdom, the United States, Canada, and France.[45]

The government in Delhi was not worried unduly by these elements at the fringe. Its attention was focused on the Akalis, who, out of power, had chosen the path of confrontation. Their new leader, Sant Harcharan Singh Longowal, lodged himself in the Golden Temple, from where he would announce street protests on a variety of themes, such as the handing over of Chandigarh or the greater allocation of canal water. Bhindranwale was operating from another part of the temple. He had acquired a group of devoted, gun-toting followers who acted as his acolytes and bodyguards and, on occasion, as unpaid killers.

Through the early 1980s, the politics of agitation coexisted uneasily with the politics of assassination. In April 1980 the Nirankari leader Baba Gurcharan Singh was shot dead in New Delhi. It was widely believed that Bhindranwale was behind the killing, but no action was taken. Then in September 1981 came the murder of Lala Jagat Narain, an influential editor who had polemicized vigorously against Sikh extremism. This time a warrant went out for Bhindranwale's arrest. The police went to get him from a gurdwara in Haryana. By the time they arrived, he had returned to the safety of his own seminary in the Punjab. The chief minister, Darbara Singh, wanted to go and arrest him but was dissuaded by the home minister, Zail Singh, who was worried about the consequences of such an act. Bhindranwale then sent word that he was willing to be arrested, but only by Sikhs with beards and at a time of his choosing. Amazingly, the Punjab government agreed to these humiliating terms. Two weeks after the murder, he gave himself up outside his seminary, as a crowd of supporters chanted slogans and threw stones at the police. At several other places in the state his followers attacked state property, provoking the police to fire on them. According to one report, a dozen people died in the violence surrrounding Bhindranwale's arrest.[46]

Three weeks later the preacher was released for lack of evidence. Two chroniclers of the Punjab agitation write that "Bhindranwale's release was the turning point in his career. He was now seen as a hero who had challenged and defeated the Indian government." Another says that with the drama of his arrest, "Bhindranwale had transformed himself from a murder suspect [into] a new political force."[47]

Through 1982, there were many rounds of negotiations between the Centre and the Akalis. No agreement was reached, the sticking points being the areas Punjab would give up to Haryana in exchange for Chandigarh, and the sharing of river waters. On 26 January 1983, Republic Day, the Akali legislators in the state assembly resigned, the timing of their action perhaps suggesting an uncertain commitment to the Indian constitution. The challenge of Bhindranwale was forcing them to become more extreme. The Akalis now tended to compare Congress's rule to the bad old days of the Mughals. They began organizing *shaheed jathas* (martyrdom squads) to fight the new tormentors of the Sikhs.[48]

On 22 April 1983, a high-ranking Sikh policeman, A. S. Atwal, was killed as he came out of the Golden Temple after offering prayers. The man who shot him at close range coolly walked in afterwards. Atwal's murder further demoralized the Punjab police force, itself overwhelmingly Sikh. A spate of bank robberies followed. Sections of the Hindu minority began fleeing the state. Those who remained organized themselves under a Hindu *suraksha sangh* (defence force). Centuries of peaceable relations between Hindus and Sikhs were collapsing under the strain.

In interviews with journalists, Bhindranwale described the Sikhs as a "separate *qaum*." The word *qaum* is sometimes taken to mean "community" but can just as easily be translated as "nation." He had not asked for Khalistan, he said, but were it offered to him he would not refuse. The prime minister of India he mocked as a "Panditain," daughter of a Brahman, a remark redolent with the contempt that the Jat Sikh has for those who work with their minds rather than their hands. Asked whether he would meet Mrs. Gandhi, he answered, "No I don't want to, but if she wants to meet me, she can come here."[49]

To his followers, Bhindranwale could be even more blunt. "If the Hindus come in search of you," he told them once, "smash their heads with television antennas." He reminded them of the heroic history of the

Sikhs. When the Mughals had tried to destroy the gurus, "our fathers had fought them with 40 Sikhs against 100,000 assailants." They could do the same now with their new oppressors. There was also a contemporary model at hand—Israel. If the few Jews there could keep the more numerous Arabs at bay, said Bhindranwale, then the Sikhs could and must do the same with the Hindus.[50]

On 5 October 1983, terrorists stopped a bus on the highway, segregated the Hindu passengers, and shot them. The next day President's Rule was imposed in the state. In the last weeks of 1983, Bhindranwale took up residence in the Akal Takht, a building second in importance only to the Golden Temple itself. The latter, standing in the middle of a shimmering blue lake, is venerated by Sikhs as the seat of spiritual authority; the former, an imposing marble building immediately to its north, had historically served as the seat of temporal authority. It was from the Akal Takht that the great gurus issued their *hukumnamas*, edicts that all Sikhs were obliged to follow and honour. It was here that Sikh warriors came to be blessed before starting their guerrilla campaigns against their medieval oppressors.[51] That Bhindranwale chose now to move into the Akal Takht, and that no one had the courage to stop him, were acts steeped in the most dangerously profound symbolism.

VII

The rise of communal violence in the Punjab falsified numerous predictions made about the province and its peoples. In the 1950s it was claimed that the Sikhs would become increasingly "Hinduized," indeed, become a sect of the great pan-Indian faith instead of standing apart as a separate religion. In the 1960s it was argued that having tasted power, the Akali Dal would become "secularized"; its rhetoric and policies would henceforth be directed by economic rather than religious considerations. By the 1970s, conflict had replaced consensus as the dominant motif of Punjab social science, except that the trouble, when it came, was expected to run along the lines of class, with the green revolution turning red.

By the beginning of the next decade, however, the situation of the Sikhs in India was being compared to that of the Tamils in Sri Lanka. In both cases, wrote the political scientist Paul Wallace in 1981, "language, religion and regionalism combined into a potentially explosive context which political elites struggle to contain."[52] Within the next year or two this mixture had been made still more deadly by the addition of a fourth ingredient: armed violence.

Hindu-Sikh conflict was, in the context of Indian history, unprecedented. While it was manifesting itself, other, older and more predictable forms of social conflict were also being played out. Thus the journalist M. J. Akbar, compiling his reports of the 1980s into a single volume, called the book *Riot After Riot*, a title that was melancholy but appropriate.[53]

One axis of this conflict was, naturally, caste. In January–February 1981, the state of Gujarat was convulsed by clashes between forward and backward castes. The issue was the reservation of places in engineering and medical colleges for those of low status. The Harijans in particular were very scantily represented, as students or as professors. Of 737 faculty members in the medical colleges of Gujarat, only twenty-two were Harijan. However, their demands for greater representation were bitterly resisted. The conflict spread well beyond the students. Even the textile workers of Ahmedabad, long united under one banner, were soon divided on caste lines. At least fifty people died in the violence.[54]

A second axis of conflict, even more naturally, was religion. During the Janata regime the communal temperature had begun to rise alarmingly. With politicians allied to it in power in the Centre and in the states, the Rashtriya Swayamsevak Sangh (RSS) grew in strength and influence. In 1979 there was a major riot in the steel town of Jamshedpur; a judicial enquiry ordered by the government concluded that the RSS "had a positive hand in creating a climate which was most propitious for the outbreak of communal disturbances."[55]

After the Janata party was routed in the elections of 1980, its Jana Sangh members broke away to form a party of their own. They called it the Bharatiya Janata Party (BJP); but the new name could not really disguise a very old aim. There was once more a distinct political party to represent and advance the "Hindu" interest. As it happened, the formation of the BJP heralded a wave of religious violence in northern and western India. There were riots between Hindus and Muslims in the Uttar Pradesh towns of Moradabad (August 1980) and Meerut (September–October 1982); in the Bihar town of Biharsharif in April–May 1981; in the Gujarat towns of Vadodara (September 1981), Godhra (October 1981), and Ahmedabad (January 1982); in Hyderabad, capital of Andhra Pradesh, in September 1983; and in the Maharashtra towns of Bhiwandi and Bombay in May–June 1984. In each case the riots ran on for days, with much loss of life and property, and were finally quelled by armed force.[56]

In the numerous studies of these numerous riots one can discern some recurrent themes.[57] A riot was generally set off by a quarrel that was in itself trifling. It could be a dispute over a piece of land, or over street space, claimed by both Hindus and Muslims. It could be provoked by a pig straying into a mosque or a dead cow being found near a temple. Sometimes the cause was a coincidence in time of a Hindu and a Muslim festival—this leading to encounters on the street of large processions of both communities.

In any case, once it began the dispute quickly escalated. The role of rumour was critical here, with the original incident being magnified in each retelling, until a simple clash between two individuals had become a holy war between two simultaneously violated religions. Communal organizations contributed to this escalation, as did party rivalries—local politicians identified with one side or the other. Words gave way to blows, fistfights to sword fights, these in turn to firebombs and bullets. The police either just looked on or took sides. In the states of Bihar and Uttar Pradesh the police invariably favoured the Hindus, encouraging and sometimes even participating in the looting of Muslim homes and shops.

Riots typically took place in towns where the Muslims constituted a significant proportion of the population—between 20% and 30%—and where some of them had lately climbed up the economic ladder, for example as artisans servicing a wider market. Whoever started the quarrel—and there were always claims and counterclaims about this—it was the Muslims and the poor who were the main victims. The Muslims, while numerous enough to fight in their own corner, were in the end outnumbered by two or three to one. The poor lived in the crowded parts of town, in homes built of fragile or inflammable material—a fire, once begun, would quickly engulf the whole neighbourhood. The middle class, on the other hand, lived in spacious residential colonies where it was easier to ensure personal as well as collective security.

In India, caste and communal conflict had usually run in parallel, but in the 1980s they began subtly influencing each other. A critical event here was the decision of an entire village of Harijans in Tamil Nadu to convert to Islam. On 19 February 1981, 1,000 residents of Meenakshipuram became Muslims. They changed not only their religion and personal names, but also the name of their village; henceforth, they said, it would be known as Rehmatnagar.

The incident at Meenakshipuram provoked outrage among the RSS and its affiliated organizations. The cry of "Hinduism in danger" was raised, and the sinister hand of "Gulf money" was seen in the conversions. The Arab countries, it was claimed, were using their petrodollars to proselytize in the subcontinent, and Indian Muslims were their willing accomplices. Islamic preachers were indeed active in the area, but the Harijans were also reacting to continuing oppression by upper-caste landlords, and to the discrimination they faced in entering schools and obtaining government jobs. Their hope was that they could escape social stigma by embracing a faith which believed in the equality of all its believers.[58]

VIII

To the historian, there are uncanny parallels between the early years of Mrs. Gandhi's first period as prime minister and the early years of her second. Both were years of trouble, and more trouble. Between 1966 and 1969 the Congress party and the central government faced serious challenges from within the democratic system—for instance, the victories of the DMK in Madras and the United Front in Bengal—and from without, such as the Mizo rebellion and the Naxalite insurgency. Also, famine loomed large, and there were severe shortages of essential goods.

How Mrs. Gandhi tackled the original crisis we have already seen, our reconstruction helped by the colossal hoard of papers preserved by her principal secretary, P. N. Haksar. But by 1980 Haksar had left her, so there is no paper trail from which we can reconstruct her response to this new crisis, caused by a new wave of ethnic and regional movements and by an intensification of communal conflict.

In 1969 and 1970, the route taken by Mrs. Gandhi was ideological; she reinvented herself as the saviour of the poor, and she forged a new party and new policies to go with it. What path might she have taken now, if she had P. N. Haksar by her side? Or what path might she have taken if Sanjay Gandhi were still alive?

Such speculation is, of course, academic. What we do know is that from late 1982 or thereabouts the prime minister had begun thinking seriously about her re-election. She did not want a defeat like the one in 1977. To avert this possibility, she decided that, in the elections, she would present herself as the saviour of the nation, safeguarding its unity against the divisive forces that threatened it.[59]

The non-Congress parties, meanwhile, were equally aware of the next election, and the need to build a common front. Leading the effort toward unity was N. T. Rama Rao (NTR), who convened a meeting of opposition parties in Vijayawada in May 1983. In attendance was the new chief minister of Jammu and Kashmir, Farooq Abdullah, who had taken his father's job when the sheikh died in 1982.

The prime minister was irritated by NTR's initiative, and by Farooq's participation in it. When elections were held in Jammu and Kashmir state in 1983, she campaigned vigorously for her Congress party. In speeches in the Hindu-dominated Jammu region she portrayed Farooq as a quasi secessionist. The divide between Jammu and the Kashmir Valley had previously been presented as communal, but never before by an Indian prime minister. This was a dangerous strategy, and it didn't work—Farooq and his National Conference were comfortably re-elected.[60]

Meanwhile, the conflict in the Punjab grew to alarming proportions. The attacks on Hindu civilians were more frequent. On 30 April 1984, a senior Sikh police officer, a particular scourge of the terrorists, was killed. Then on 12 May, Ramesh Chander, son of the editor Lala Jagat Narain and inheritor of his mantle, was also murdered. By now Bhindranwale's men had begun fortifying the Golden Temple, supervised by Shubeg Singh, a former major general in the Indian army who had been a hero of the war of 1971 and had trained the Mukti Bahini.

Under Shubeg's guidance, the militants began laying sandbags on turrets, and occupying high buildings and towers around the temple complex. The men on these vantage points were all in radio contact with Shubeg in the Akal Takht. An attack by government troops was clearly anticipated. The defences were prepared in the hope that they might hold out long enough to provoke a general uprising among Sikhs in the villages and a mass march toward the besieged temple. Enough food was stocked to last the defenders a month.

The other side too was preparing for action. On 31 May, Major General R. S. Brar was summoned from Meerut, where he was in charge of an infantry division, and told that he would have to lead the operation to rid the temple of terrorists. Brar was a Jat Sikh, whose ancestral village was only a few miles from Bhindranwale's. And he knew Shubeg Singh well—Singh had been his instructor at the Indian Military Academy at Dehra Dun, and they had worked together in the Bangladesh operations.

Brar was briefed by two lieutenant generals, Sundarji and Dayal. The government, he was told, believed that the situation in the Punjab could no longer be controlled by the civil administration. The Centre's attempts to arrive at a settlement with Akalis had run aground. The Akalis had failed to persuade Bhindranwale to dismantle the fortifications and leave the temple. And they were themselves getting more militant. The Akali leader Sant Longowal had announced that on 3 June he would lead a movement to stop the export of grain from the state. A siege was considered but rejected, because of fear of a rebellion in the countryside. The prime minister had thus decided, "after much reluctance," that the militants had to be flushed out. Brar was asked to plan and lead what was being called Operation Bluestar; it was to be finished in forty-eight hours if possible, with no damage to the Golden Temple, and with minimal loss of life.[61]

Within twenty-four hours of this briefing the army began moving into Amritsar, taking over control of the city from the paramilitary. On 2 June, a young Sikh officer entered the temple, posing as a pilgrim, and spent an hour walking around, carefully noting the preparations made for its defence. Patrols were also sent to study the lookout points occupied by the militants outside, which would have to be cleared before the assault.

On the night of 2 June, the prime minister spoke on All India Radio. She appealed to "all sections of Punjab" not to "shed blood" but to "shed hatred." The call was disingenuous, since the army was already preparing for its assault. On 3 June, Punjab's road, rail, and phone links were cut off. But in Amritsar itself the curfew was lifted, to allow pilgrims to mark the anniversary of the martydom of Guru Arjun Dev.

The next day there was sporadic firing in the temple's perimeter, as the army tried to knock out the towers occupied by the militants. That day and the next, loudspeakers asked pilgrims to leave the temple. The attack itself began on the night of 5 June. Brar's hope was that the peripheral parts of the temple would be seized by midnight, after which a unit would be placed within the Akal Takht and reinforcements would be sent up; the whole place would be cleared by the morning of the next day. His plan grievously underestimated the number of militants, their firepower, their skill, and their resolve. Every window in the Akal Takht had been boarded up, with snipers positioned to fire from cracks within. Other militants with machine guns and grenades were scattered through the complex, using their knowledge of its narrow passages and verandas to make surprise attacks on the advancing troops.

At 2 a.m. on 6 June the troops were considerably behind schedule. Brar writes that "due to intense multi-directional fire of the militants, our forces were unable to get close enough [to the Akal Takht] to achieve any degree of accuracy."[62] Finally, permission had to be obtained from Delhi to use tanks to break the defences. By dawn, several tanks—the estimates range from five to thirteen—had broken through the temple's gates and taken up positions. Through much of the day they rained fire on the Akal Takht. In the evening it was deemed safe to send troops into the building, to capture those defenders who might still remain. They found Shubeg Singh's body in the basement, still clutching his carbine, with a walkie-talkie next to him. Also found in the basement were the bodies of Bhindranwale and a devoted follower, Amrik Singh of the All India Sikh Students' Federation.

The government estimated the number of deaths as four officers, seventy-nine soldiers, and 492 terrorists. Other accounts place the number of deaths much higher: at perhaps 500 or more troops and 3,000 others, including many pilgrims caught in the crossfire.

"Notwithstanding the fact that by converting the House of God into a battlefield, all the principles and precepts of the ten Sikh gurus were thrown overboard," remarks R. S. Brar, "it must be admitted that the tenacity with which the militants held their ground, the stubborn valour with which they fought the battle, and the high degree of confidence displayed by them merits praise and recognition."[63] It is impossible not to sympathize with the writer of these words, whose own job was, without question, the most difficult ever assigned to an Indian army commander in peacetime or in war. The Sikh general to whom both Brar and Shubeg reported during the liberation of Bangladesh had this to say about Operation Bluestar: "The army was used to finish a problem created by the government. This is the kind of action that is going to ruin the army."[64]

IX

The Golden Temple is ten minutes' walk from Jallianawala Bagh, where, in April 1919, a British brigadier ordered his troops to fire on a crowd of unarmed Indians. More than 400 people died, and the incident has a hallowed place in nationalist myth and memory; the collective outrage it provoked was skilfully used by Mahatma Gandhi to launch a country-wide campaign against colonial rule. Operation Bluestar differed in intent—it was directed against armed rebels, rather than a peaceable gathering—but its consequences were not dissimilar. It left a collective wound in the psyche of the Sikhs, and a deep suspicion of the government of India. The regime in Delhi was compared to previous oppressors and desecrators, such as the Mughals, and the eighteenth-century Afghan marauder Ahmad Shah Abdali.[65] A reporter touring the Punjab countryside found a "sullen and alienated community." As one elderly Sikh put it, "Our inner self has been bruised. The base of our faith has been attacked, a whole tradition has been demolished." Now, even those Sikhs who had previously opposed Bhindranwale began to see him in a new light. For, whatever his past errors and crimes, he and his men had died defending the holy shrine from the vandals.[66]

The view from outside the Punjab was quite different. Many people commended Mrs. Gandhi for taking firm (if belated) action against terrorists claimed to be in the pay of Pakistan. The prime minister herself was now prompted to move against elements in other states who were opposed to her. For some time, she had been pressing for the dismissal of Farooq Abdullah's government in Jammu and Kashmir. When the state governor, her own cousin B. K. Nehru, told her it would be unconstitutional, he was replaced by Sanjay Gandhi's former lieutenant, Jagmohan. In July 1984, Jagmohan contrived a split in the ruling National Conference, and declared the leader of the remaining group the new chief minister. Bags of money were sent by the Congress party in Delhi to bribe Kashmiri legislators into deserting their leader. Farooq was not given an opportunity to test his majority on the floor of the House. Indeed, the dismissal order was served on him in the middle of the night, as it had been on his father who, in 1953, had likewise been sent out of office on grounds of dubious legality and still more dubious morality. As B. K. Nehru wrote, the Kashmiris "were convinced now at the second dethronement of their elected leader that India would never permit them to rule themselves."[67]

A month later, a change of regime was effected in Andhra Pradesh. Once more, the governor, a former congressman, played a malevolent role. A section of the Telugu Desam party was induced to break away and, with the support of Congress, form a new government.[68] The dismissals of the chief ministers of Jammu and Kashmir and Andhra were flagrant violations of democratic practice. These were not armed rebels but legally elected governments. One cannot rule out personal vindictiveness—NTR and Farooq, after all, had initiated the efforts to unify the opposition. The prime minister must also have calculated that it would be helpful to have sympathetic regimes in place before the general election. Writing to a friend, she accused the opposition of having "the single-minded objective of removing me"; their "patchwork alliances," she claimed, were based on "regionalism, communalism and casteism."[69] It is tempting to turn the criticism on its head—certainly, many of Mrs. Gandhi's own policies in 1983 and 1984 appear to have been dictated by the single-minded objective of winning the next general elections.

In the aftermath of Operation Bluestar, the prime minister had been warned by intelligence agencies of a possible attempt on her life. She was advised to change the Sikh members of her personal bodyguard. Mrs. Gandhi rejected the suggestion, saying, "Aren't we secular?"[70] On the morning of 31 October, while walking from her home to her office next door, she was shot point-blank by two of her security guards, Satwant Singh and Beant Singh. They were both Sikhs who had recently returned from a visit home and been provoked by the hurt and anger they witnessed to take revenge for Operation Bluestar.

By the time the prime minister was taken to a hospital, she was already dead. By early afternoon the foreign radio stations had put out the news, although All India Radio did not make its own official announcement until 6 p.m. Shortly afterwards her son Rajiv Gandhi was sworn in as prime minister. When his mother was shot he was in Bengal; he rushed back to the capital, where a group of senior cabinet ministers and Congress leaders unanimously decided that he should succeed his mother.

Later that night, some incidents of arson and looting were reported in Delhi. The next morning the body of Mrs. Gandhi was placed in Teen Murti House, where her father had lived as prime minister. All through that day and the next, India's sole television channel, Doordarshan, showed the line of mourners streaming past the body. From time to time, the cameras focused on the crowds outside, who were shouting slogans such as *Indira Gandhi amar rahe* ("Indira Gandhi shall be immortal") and, more ominously, *Khoon ka badla khoon se lenge* ("Blood will be avenged by blood").

The violence that began on the night of 31 October spread and intensified through 1 and 2 November. The first serious episodes occurred in south and central Delhi; later, the violence moved east across the Yamuna River, to the resettlement colonies located there. Everywhere, Sikhs, and Sikhs alone, were the target. Their homes were burned, their shops looted, their shrines and holy books violated and desecrated. As they acted, the mobs also shouted slogans. "Finish off the Sardars," "Kill the *gaddars* [traitors]," and "Teach a lesson to the Sikhs" were some of the slogans people reported hearing.

In Delhi alone, more than 1,000 Sikhs died in the violence. Sikh males between eighteen and fifty years of age were particularly targeted. They were murdered by a variety of methods, often in front of their mothers and wives. Bonfires were made of bodies; in one case, a little boy was burned with his father, the perpetrator saying, *Ye saap ka bachcha hai, isse bhi khatam karo* ("This offpsring of a snake must be finished too").

The mobs were composed of Hindus who lived in and around Delhi: Scheduled Caste sweepers who worked in the city, and Jat farmers and Gujjar pastoralists from villages on the fringes. Often, they were led and directed by Congress politicians: metropolitan councillors, members of Parliament, and even Cabinet ministers. The Congress leaders promised money and liquor to those willing to do the job, in addition to goods stolen on the spot. The police simply looked on, or actively aided the looting and murder.[71]

Rajiv Gandhi's own comment on the riots was: "When a big tree falls, the earth shakes." Without question, the killing of Mrs. Gandhi provoked strong feelings among her many admirers. Sections of the middle class venerated her for her conduct and leadership during the war of 1971; sections of the poor thought her the only Indian politician who empathized with their lot. And Hindus in general were dismayed at the happenings in the Punjab. The Khalistan movement, they believed, was aimed at tearing the country into pieces, and the fact that two Sikhs had killed the prime minister seemed to confirm these fears. Immediately after Mrs. Gandhi's killing, rumours of other actions began to circulate. It was said that trains with dead bodies of Hindus were coming in from the Punjab, and that the capital's water supply had been poisoned by malcontents.

The public mood in Delhi was angry, distorted by happenings real and imagined. That said, Rajiv Gandhi's comment was still deeply insensitive. It was of a piece with the behaviour, overall, of the administration he was now asked to lead. By showing crowds baying for blood in Teen Murti House, state television was making a self-fulfilling prophecy. The indifference of the police was shocking, and the role played by Congress politicians was immoral. But the lapse that perhaps meant more than all the others was the unwillingness to call in the army. There is a large cantonment in Delhi itself, and there were several infantry divisions within a fifty-mile radius of the capital. The army was put on standby, but despite repeated appeals to the prime minister and his home minister, P. V. Narasimha Rao, it was not asked to move into action. Even marches of troops through the city on 1 and 2 November would most likely have quelled the riots—yet the orders never came.

Although the Sikhs in the capital bore the brunt of the violence, there were also attacks on Sikhs in other cities and towns of northern India. More than 200 Sikhs died in incidents in the state of Uttar Pradesh. Twenty Sikhs were killed in Indore, and sixty in the steel town of Bokaro, where the mobs, as in Delhi, were led by local congressmen.

One city where violence was minimal was Calcutta. There were 50,000 Sikhs living in Calcutta, many of them taxi drivers, each one easily identified by his turban and beard. But very few were harmed, and not one died. The chief minister of West Bengal, Jyoti Basu, had ordered the police to maintain peace. The instructions were honoured, with the city's powerful trade unions keeping a vigilant eye. The example of Calcutta showed that prompt action by the administration could forestall communal violence—a lesson, alas, lost on the rest of the country.[72]

X

Mrs. Gandhi's impact on Indian history was definitive—as definitive, indeed, as her father's. Jawaharlal Nehru was prime minister of India for sixteen years and nine months. His daughter served in that post almost as long, in two stretches: from January 1966 to March 1977, and then again from January 1980 to October 1984. These are the two figures of pre-eminent importance in the history of independent India. To compare them is inevitable, and perhaps also necessary.

As a military leader Mrs. Gandhi was immeasurably superior. Her decisiveness at the time of the crisis in Bangladesh was in striking contrast to Nehru's wavering attitude toward the Chinese: now promising undying friendship, now issuing threats with no force to back them. So far as economic policies went, Nehru's stress on the public sector and self-reliance was in keeping with the spirit of the age, whereas in the 1960s, when the time had come to cautiously open up the economy to market forces, Mrs. Gandhi instead further strengthened the hold of the state. Socially, both were genuinely non-parochial, seeking to represent all Indians, regardless of their gender, class, religion, or language.

The advantage rests squarely with Nehru with regard to the processes and procedures of democracy. This point was made, at Mrs. Gandhi's death, by Krishna Raj, the editor of India's leading journal of public affairs, *Economic and Political Weekly*. One point of contrast was how father and daughter treated the party to which both owed lifelong allegiance. When Indira Gandhi took charge in 1966, wrote Krishna Raj, "she found a reasonably well-organised Congress party, with several layers of responsive leadership across the length and breadth of the country." But she then "dismantled the party and she did so with a clear purposiveness. Because she did not trust anyone who would not play a subservient role to her and her family, she got rid of the intermediate leadership and re-built the party as a paper entity, without a democratic structure and with office-bearers personally selected and named by her."

Tragically, not just the Congress party was made an extension of the prime minister's will. So was the government of India. Despite the ignominy of the war with China, when Indira Gandhi came to power in January 1966 "India was a coherent nation, a nation marked by a quiet aura of social stability." There was a set of socio-economic objectives around which it was united. The political class recognized the connection between means and ends. The "faith was still widely shared that the paraphernalia of the state was never intended—at least not consciously intended—to be put to use for advancing private interests." But by the time of Indira Gandhi's death, there had been "a qualitative transformation. India is a divided nation." There were now "deep wounds and deep dissensions." The five-year plans, once acknowledged as "an earnest statement of hopes and aspirations," now "do not mean a thing." Now, the "apparatus of the state is all the time being manipulated for the sake of [the] fractional minority of the population at the top of the social hierarchy." Now, "the government at the centre is corrupt to the core and Indira Gandhi could not be absolved of direct responsibility for this state of affairs."[73]

Some western journalists, meanwhile, saw dark days ahead for India. With Mrs. Gandhi's death, wrote a reporter for the *New York Times*, the country faced a "period of prolonged uncertainty, with the potential for greater domestic instability and new tensions with its neighbours, particularly Pakistan." The New York *Sun* was even more pessimistic; its reporter wrote that the prime minister's assassination "has opened a bleak possibility that India may fly apart, internally, and become increasingly the catalyst for regional and global rivalries." Some officials in Washington were worried that ethnic and religious rivalries would "explode into general violence," that the country would fragment, and that "a desperate leadership in India might look more and more to the Soviet Union for help."[74]

This was not the first epitaph being written for the Union of India; nor, perhaps, would it be the last. Still, it is striking how, like the sycophants in Congress, these western observers appeared to think that Indira was, indeed, India. That this conclusion was reached provided further proof of the late prime minister's success in undermining the institutions that stood between her and the nation.

25

THIS SON ALSO RISES

In India the choice could never be between chaos and stability, but between manageable and unmanageable chaos, between humane and inhuman anarchy, and between tolerable and intolerable disorder.

The sociologist ASHIS NANDY,

writing in 1990

I

EVEN BY THE STANDARDS of Indian politics, 1984 was an especially turbulent year. Operation Bluestar, an unprecedented attack by the state on a place of worship, took place during the first week of June. The assassination of Indira Gandhi, the first major political killing since that of Mahatma Gandhi, took place on the last day of October. Mahatma Gandhi's death had temporarily brought a halt to Hindu-Muslim violence; Indira Gandhi's provoked a wave of violence by Hindus against Sikhs.

A month after Rajiv Gandhi was sworn in as prime minister, the country witnessed a tragedy that claimed as many lives as the anti-Sikh riots. In the early hours of 3 December 1984, white fumes began filling the air in the central Indian city of Bhopal. Citizens asleep in their homes woke up with fits of coughing, vomiting, and a burning sensation in the eyes. In panic they got out of bed and went out into the street, the gas-filled cloud following them. By dawn, "the main thoroughfares of the city were jammed with an unending stream of humanity, plodding its way in search of safer surroundings." Many fell down in the streets, overcome by dizziness and exhaustion. Others found their way, somehow, to the city's few modern hospitals, whose beds were rapidly filled up to capacity.[1]

The deadly gas was methyl isocyanate (MIC), and it came from a pesticide plant owned and run by an American firm, Union Carbide. Stored in underground tanks, it was usually rendered harmless by a scrubber before being released into the atmosphere. However, on this night an unanticipated chemical reaction led to the release of MIC in its toxic state. The effects were devastating. Within hours of the leak, at least 400 people had died of exposure to the gas. The final tally was more than 2,000, making this the worst industrial accident in human history. Most of the victims lived in the slums and shanty towns that ringed the factory. In addition to those who died, 50,000 would suffer, all their lives, from illnesses and injuries caused by exposure to the gas.

In the wake of the tragedy a wave of visitors came to Bhopal, not all of them welcome. There were doctors who came to help, but also lawyers seeking to profit from a class-action suit on behalf of the victims, to be filed in an American court. The CEO of Union Carbide came, was briefly arrested, and then was released on bail and flown back to New York. Ten days after the accident, a team of Indian scientists came to neutralize the MIC that was still being stored in the Union Carbide factory. The project was named Operation Faith, but it inspired only distrust. Fearing another leak, thousands of residents tried to leave Bhopal, with "the city bus terminal and the railway station present[ing] a chaotic scene . . . as fleeing people swarmed them carrying their essential belongings."[2]

Investigations into the leak of 3 December suggested a range of possible causes: that water had gotten into the tank; that the tank had not been properly cleaned; that the MIC was being stored at temperatures higher than recommended.[3] What was clear was that a potentially hazardous industry had no business to be in the city. Before the plant went into production in 1980, the town planner M. N. Buch recommended that Union Carbide choose a safer and less populated location. Indeed, as a report of June 1984 revealed, the plant had a history of gas leaks and burst pipelines—minor accidents, unacknowledged intimations of the major one that was waiting to happen.[4]

II

The accident in Bhopal occurred in the first week of December. At the end of the month, India held its eighth general election. The election was dominated by the murder and memory of Indira Gandhi. The Congress campaign, overseen by the advertising agency Rediffusion, presented Rajiv Gandhi as the logical heir to his mother's legacy, and the party itself as the only bulwark against the forces of secession. "India could be your vote away from unity or separation," said one ad featuring Rajiv. "Will the cast of 1977 ever be united by a common ideology instead of a common greed for power?" said another.[5] The Congress campaign, one commentator wrote, "capitalized on the growing mass insecurities," whereby "Mrs. Gandhi's assassination was equated in the public mind with an assault on the Indian State and that perception was constantly reinforced."[6]

When the results came in, the Congress had swept the election, capturing almost 50% of the popular vote and almost 80% of the seats in Parliament. Under the leadership of a political novice, the Congress won 401 seats, far more than it ever had under Nehru or Indira Gandhi. However, as one of the prime minister's advisers admitted, "the victory was as much his late mother's as his own."[7]

The general elections were won by stoking the fear of secession; but now that he had a strong majority, the prime minister moved swiftly to make peace in the Punjab. The leaders of the Akali Dal were let out of jail, and emissaries were sent to talk to them. Sant Harcharan Singh Longowal seemed as keen as Rajiv Gandhi to put the past behind him. In July 1985 the two leaders signed an accord, agreeing to transfer Chandigarh to Punjab within a specified time, assuring Punjab of a fair share of river waters, and committing the government to a review of relations between Centre and state in general. President's Rule was to be revoked, and elections were to be held in the state.

Following the agreement, Sant Longowal toured the Punjab, speaking at public meetings and preaching in gurdwaras. Everywhere, he asked that the people support the efforts at reconciliation. While he was addressing a congregation in Sangrur, Longowal was shot dead by two young men, who believed he had betrayed the Sikh cause by breaking bread with the rulers in New Delhi. The incident occurred on 20 August; bravely, the government chose to go ahead with assembly elections in late September. Longowal's death created a wave of popular support for his party. The Akali Dal won a significant majority, for the first time in the history of the province. With two-thirds of the adult population voting, the election was interpreted as a victory against extremism.[8]

Meanwhile, at the other end of the country, the government also came to an agreement with the All Assam Students Union. The two sides agreed on cut-off dates for "infiltrators"; those who had arrived after 1 January 1966 but before 25 March 1971 (when the civil war in East Pakistan began) would be allowed to stay but not vote, and those who came later would be identified and deported. Here too President's Rule was ended and elections were announced. A students' union transformed itself into a political party, with AASU members creating the

Asom Gana Parishad (AGP). When elections for the state assembly were held in December 1985, the AGP trounced the once-dominant Congress. The new chief minister, Prafulla Mahanta, was only thirty-two years old: many of his legislators were even younger. As in Punjab, the result was hailed as a vindication of democracy. Senior congressmen in Delhi argued that while their party had lost, the Republic of India had won. "Men who were distributing dynamite earlier were handling poll posters," remarked one Union minister: "From a nationalistic point of view is that victory or defeat?"[9]

In June 1986, the government of India signed a peace agreement with Laldenga, leader of the Mizo National Front (MNF). By its terms, the MNF rebels laid down their arms and were granted an amnesty against prosecution. The government said it would grant full statehood to Mizoram, and Laldenga himself assumed office as chief minister, taking over from the Congress incumbent. The model here was the agreement of 1975 in Kashmir, where Sheikh Abdullah had returned to power in the same fashion.[10]

One journal remarked that Rajiv Gandhi "had brought to the Mizos the goodwill of the nation," as he had previously done for the Sikhs and the Assamese.[11] Although these agreements had actually been envisioned and drafted by officials—such as the veteran diplomat G. Parthasarathi—the credit accrued to the young prime minister, who was seen as standing above party rivalries in the interests of national reconciliation. In all three cases, parties or leaders opposed to the Congress had come to power through peaceful means.

III

That Rajiv Gandhi was an outsider in politics was to his advantage. In the popular mind, "his name was not associated with any controversial issues, he was not aligned to any caucus, and he had not yet created a coterie of his own." His appeal was enhanced by his youth—he was less than forty in 1984—his good looks, and his open manner. Here was a "fine gentleman, thoroughly well-meaning, earnest and honest. . . . [H]is indulgent countrymen stuck the label 'Mr. Clean' on him."[12]

Rajiv's main advisers also came from outside politics. They included Arun Singh and Arun Nehru, two friends from the corporate sector who were made ministers. Like him, they were young and English-speaking. Like him, they were at ease with modern technology. They made manifest their intention to take India directly from the sixteenth century to the twenty-first, from the age of the bullock cart to the age of the personal computer. In some of the media the new recruits attracted derision or amusement, being known as "Rajiv's computer boys." In other media they attracted approbation: Rajiv Gandhi was compared to John F. Kennedy, who had likewise "symbolised youth and the hope of a new generation," assembling a "team of the best and the brightest" to carve out a new future for his land.[13]

In the first year of his term, the prime minister was often on tour, making the acquaintance of parts of the country he had not previously seen. Rajiv Gandhi's "discovery of India" was appreciatively covered in the press, and on television. During the 1980s there had been an enormous growth in the ownership of television sets. With broadcasting still a state monopoly, the government channel, Doordarshan, shot and showed hundreds of hours featuring the young, handsome prime minister: on a houseboat in Kashmir, in a remote tribal hamlet, amid coconut trees in Kerala. Everywhere, he met ordinary Indians and received their petitions, passing these on to the district administration for action.[14]

The first crisis of the new regime was in fact caused by a petition—submitted, however, not to the prime minister but to the Supreme Court of India. The petitioner was an elderly man, Mohammed Ahmed Khan, appealing a lower court's decision that he must pay monthly maintenance to his divorced wife, Shah Bano. Khan contended that he had fulfilled his duties by paying Shah Bano an allowance for three months, the period specified (he claimed) under Islamic law. In rejecting Khan's appeal, the Supreme Court invoked Section 125 of the Criminal Procedure Code, whereby a divorced woman was entitled to claim an allowance from her former husband if he had taken another wife (as Khan had), and if she had not remarried and could not otherwise maintain herself (as was the case with Shah Bano). Section 125, noted the court, "was enacted in order to provide a quick and summary remedy to a class of persons who are unable to maintain itself. What difference would it then make as to what is the religion professed by the neglected wife, child or parent?" In its opinion, the explanations attached to the Criminal Procedure Code showed "unmistakably, that Section 125 overrides the personal law, if there is any conflict between the two."

M. A. Khan had first filed the appeal in 1981; it took four years for the case to come to judgement. Dismissing the appeal on 23 April 1985, the Supreme Court confirmed that Khan would have to continue to pay Shah Bano maintenance as fixed by the high court (at the curious figure of 179.20 rupees per month). Then the judges went beyond the specifics of the case to make some general remarks. They deplored the fact that Article 44 of the constitution, mandating a uniform civil code, "has remained a dead letter." They observed that "a belief seems to have gained ground that it is for the Muslim community to take a lead in the matter of reforms of their personal law. A Common Civil Code will help the cause of national integration by removing disparate loyalties to laws which have conflicting ideologies."[15]

In some circles, these remarks were taken as a gratuitous chastisement of the minority community as a whole. Muslims took exception to the judges' saying that "it is alleged that the 'fatal point in Islam is the degradation of women.' " (In fairness, the judges had also noted that the Hindu lawgiver, Manu, believed that "the woman does not deserve independence.") Muslim clerics criticized the judgement as an attack on Islam. Mosques up and down the country "resounded with the voices of mullahs and maulvis denouncing Shah Bano and the Supreme Court judgement."[16] On the other hand, some Muslim scholars supported the verdict, or at any rate held it to be not inconsistent with scripture, where there existed "ample and respectable Islamic authority" for the proposition that the divorcing husband must provide maintenance until his former wife's death or remarriage.[17]

Three months after the Supreme Court judgement, a member of Parliament, G. M. Banatwala, moved a private member's bill, seeking to exempt Muslims from Section 125. The bill was opposed in the House by the minister of state for home affairs, Arif Mohammed Khan, representing, so to say, the "progressive" Muslim point of view. He defended the court's judgement by quoting Maulana Azad, who was at once the most famous nationalist Muslim and an acknowledged authority on the scriptures. The maulana had written that the "Quran takes occasion to reemphasize that proper consideration should be shown to the divorced woman in every circumstance." This emphasis "was based on the reason that she was comparatively weaker than [the] man and her interests needed to be properly safeguarded." Further, argued Khan, "we should have better practices these days and only if the down-trodden are uplifted, the Islamic tenets can be said to have been followed and justice done."[18]

Arif Mohammed Khan had the support of the prime minister; with the Congress voting against it, the bill was defeated. However, the debate continued outside the House. In her native Indore, the seventy-five-year-old Shah Bano was denounced by conservatives as an infidel; demonstrations were held outside her house: neighbours were asked to ostracize her. On 15 November, Shah Bano succumbed to the pressure, affixing her thumb impression to a statement saying that she disavowed the Supreme Court verdict, that she would donate the maintenance money to charity, and that she opposed any judicial interference in Muslim personal law.[19]

Toward the end of 1985, the Congress party lost a series of by-elections in northern India. Commentators saw a "Shah Bano factor" at work, with rivals of the Congress "whipping up religious fervour" by attacking the Supreme Court in constituencies with large Muslim populations.[20] Reports of the alienation alarmed Rajiv Gandhi, who, within his party and cabinet, began increasingly taking the advice of the conservative Z. A. Ansari rather than the liberal Arif Khan. In a three-hour speech in Parliament, Ansari attacked the Supreme Court verdict as "prejudiced, discriminatory and full of contradictions." The judges, he added maliciously, were "small men who were incompetent to interpret Islamic law."[21]

By now, it was not merely Shah Bano who had succumbed to pressure. The Congress had "accorded recognition to fundamentalists as the sole spokesmen of their community."[22] In February 1986, the government introduced a Muslim Women's Bill in Parliament that sought to overturn the Supreme Court verdict, by taking Muslim personal law out of the purview of the Criminal Procedure Code. The bill placed the burden of supporting the divorced wife on her own relatives; all the husband was obliged to do was provide three months' maintenance. In May, the bill became law, with the Congress issuing a whip to its members to vote for it. Abandoned by his leader, his party, and his government, Arif Mohammed Khan resigned, telling an interviewer that with this new legislation "Indian Muslim women will be the only women to be denied maintenance anywhere in the world."[23]

The controversy over Shah Bano's case was in many ways a reprise of the debates over the reform of Hindu personal laws three decades previously. Then, too, attempts to enhance gender equality had been bitterly resisted by priests claiming to speak for the community as a whole. The claim was tested and found wanting, when Jawaharlal Nehru fought and won the elections of 1952 on, among other things, the issue of the Hindu Code Bill.

Faced with a comparable situation in 1985–1986, Rajiv Gandhi already had the support of 400 members of Parliament. A reform of Muslim personal law to enhance the rights of women was well within reach. So was a gender-sensitive common civil code (as asked for by the Constitution). What was lacking was a prime minister consistently commited to social reform. As a high official in Rajiv Gandhi's government was to recall later, "in the handling of the aftermath of the Shah Bano case the young P[rime] M[inister] was suddenly overwhelmed by the political system." His initiatives in the Punjab and Assam had shown boldness and independence; but here, after first supporting the reformists, he had given way to the conservatives for fear of losing the Muslim vote. And so, "Rajiv Gandhi the statesman started transforming himself into a politician."[24]

IV

Ten months after the Supreme Court handed down its verdict in the Shah Bano case, a judgement by a lower court provoked a controversy more furious still. On 1 February 1986, the district judge of the town of Ayodhya, in Uttar Pradesh, ordered that the locks be opened to permit worship at a small Hindu shrine. Despite its modest size this was a rather special place. It was located inside a large mosque, built as long ago as the sixteenth century by a general of the Mughal emperor Babur (and hence known as the Babri Masjid). Moreover, it was claimed that the site was the birthplace of the Hindu deity Ram, and that before the mosque was built, it had been home to a temple devoted to his worship.

There is no evidence that the hero of the epic *Ramayan* was a historical person. But Hindu sentiment and myth widely held that he was, and that he was born in Ayodhya—indeed, at the very spot where the mosque was later built. The site was known locally as Ram Janmabhoomi, literally, the piece of earth where Ram was born. Through the nineteenth century there were clashes between rival groups claiming possession of the place. The British rulers then effected a compromise, whereby Muslims continued to worship inside the mosque, while Hindus made offerings on a raised platform outside.

India became independent in 1947. Two years later, an official sympathetic to Hindu interests allowed an idol of the child Ram (Ram Lalla) to be placed inside the mosque. This was done under cover of darkness, and devotees were persuaded that it had appeared miraculously, a sign that the displaced deity wanted to reclaim his birthplace. Tension rose again but was lowered by an order allowing the worship of Ram Lalla on a single day in December. For the rest of the year, the idol was kept locked away from worshippers.

For three decades the status quo held, until, in the early 1980s, the Vishwa Hindu Parishad, or VHP (Hindu World Council), began campaigning for the "liberation of the spot where Ram was born." The VHP brought under one banner hundreds of monks from the numerous old temples that dotted Ayodhya. Processions and public meetings were organized, and fiery speeches were made urging Hindus to free their god from "a Muslim jail." A local lawyer then filed a suit seeking public worship of the idol. In response to this appeal, the district judge ruled that the locks be opened, and worship allowed.[25]

The judge's order was widely believed to have been directed from Delhi, from the prime minister's office no less. The local administration seemed to know of the judgement beforehand, for the locks were opened within an hour of the verdict. Remarkably, even the state television channel, Doordarshan, was at hand to capture on camera the precise moment when devotees rushed into the newly opened shrine. There appeared to be a strong connection between the Muslim Women's Bill and the verdict in Ayodhya. It was said that Rajiv Gandhi had the locks opened on the advice of his colleague Arun Nehru, who thought the Congress now needed to compensate the chauvinists on the other side. A left-wing member of Parliament commented sarcastically that while the prime minister presented himself as a thoroughly modern man, striving to take India into the twenty-first century, in fact "he has a mind as primitive as the *mullahs* and the *pandits*."[26] The political analyst Neerja Chowdhury wrote, "Mr. Rajiv Gandhi wants both to run with the hare and hunt with the hounds." If one act was aimed at the "Muslim" vote, this other one seemed to target the far larger "Hindu" vote. Chowdhury warned that "a policy of appeasement of both communities being pursued by the government for electoral gains is a vicious cycle which will become difficult to break."[27]

The opening of the locks emboldened the VHP. It now sought nothing less than the demolition of the mosque, and its replacement with a grand new temple dedicated to Ram. The VHP was working closely with the Rashtriya Swayamsevak Sangh, the older Hindu organization, which had been given a fresh lease of life. The RSS and VHP held meetings across India demanding that the "majority" stand up for their rights. The Muslim Women's Bill was adduced as yet another example showing that the Congress government wanted to placate the minority. Only Hindus, it was alleged, were asked to disown their faith in this mistakenly "secular" state. A new slogan was coined and broadcast:

Garv se kaho hum Hindu hain! ("Say you are a Hindu, and say it with pride.")

This message, as the weekly *India Today* wrote in May 1986, "struck a high-strung emotional chord. Slowly but surely, like a juggernaut gaining angry momentum, a palpable, resurgent, united and increasingly militant movement of Hindu resurgence is sweeping across the land." Here was a movement which was "revanchist" but which had also begun "to smell the political power that comes with unity."[28]

V

It is possible to view the Hindu faith as a river with many branches, tributaries that feed into the mainstream and distributaries that leave it. But perhaps this image is mistaken, for in many respects there is no main river at all. This is a religion that was decentralized like no other. Each district has its own holy shrines; each shrine is run by its own locally revered priest. Sometimes allegiances run by caste as well as region; Madhava Brahmans of, say, the Uttara Kannada district have their own chosen temple, and their own religious preceptor.

The controversy in Ayodhya opened up a possibility of bringing these far-flung traditions together into a unified movement. The Vishwa Hindu Parishad had formed a *dharam sansad* ("faith council") composed of the major *dharmacharyas*, or leaders of Hindu sects. These in turn liaised with the lesser holy men, the thousands of *sants* and sadhus who had modest followings of their own. Beyond the building of a temple to Ram in Ayodhya, these moves toward pan-Hindu unity had rich political possibilities. As one leading priest explained:

> There are dozens of dharmacharyas [in] Hindu society and each has a vote bank of approximately twenty-five lakhs (or 2.5 million). For example, there is Gujarat's sant Sri Murari Bapu, Rajasthan's Sri Ramsukh Dasji Maharaj, U.P.'s sant Sri Devrah Baba, RSS's Sri Deorasji, Ayodhya's Sri Nrittya Gopal Dasji Maharaj, etc. Besides them there are hundreds of dharmacharyas who wield a vote bank of at least one lakh. The Hindu society has about ten lakh strong team[s] of sadhus. If each mobilises a hundred people, the politics of this country would take a new turn and get hinduized.[29]

On the other side, the threats to the old mosque in Ayodhya had mobilized Muslim opinion in its defence. A Babri Masjid Action Committee was formed, which urged the state to ensure that this and other Muslim shrines would not be taken over by radical Hindus. In some sections of the community the mood was truculent. There were calls to allow worship in mosques controlled by the Archaeological Survey of India, and even a call to boycott the Republic Day celebrations if the government did not heed their demands.[30]

The growing Hindu consolidation was helped immeasurably by two contingent events. In September 1987, a young woman named Roop Kunwar committed ritual suicide in a village in Rajasthan, following her husband's death. Although condoned by Hindu tradition, sati had long been banned by law. While Roop Kunwar's act was deplored by the state and, more actively, by feminist groups, it inspired a groundswell of devotion in rural Rajasthan. A temple was erected at the spot where she was burned, attracting thousands of worshippers. Rallies were held hailing Roop Kanwar as an exemplar of Hindu womanhood in her devotion to her husband's memory.[31]

The other and more significant event was the telecast on Doordarshan of a new, spectacular production of the *Ramayan*. Episodes were shown every Sunday morning, beginning in January 1987 and ending in July 1988. There were seventy-eight episodes in all, with the series interrupted by a four-month break.

The *Ramayan* is a capacious epic, a story of love, sacrifice, heroism, and betrayal, with plenty of blood and violence thrown in. It has a rich cast of minor and major characters, and lends itself well to soap-operatic treatment. It was shown at a time when television viewership was rapidly increasing, with 3 million new sets being sold every year.[32] Still, the success of the show exceeded all expectations. There were an estimated 80 million viewers, and "city streets and marketplaces were empty on Sunday mornings. Events advertised for Sundays were careful to mention: 'To be held after Ramayan.' Crowds gathered around every wayside television set." Hotels, hospitals, and factories reported large-scale absenteeism on Sunday mornings.[33]

As much as the numbers of viewers, the intensity of their experience merits attention. Rising early on Sunday mornings, viewers would take a ritual bath and perform their prayers. Before the show began, television sets were garlanded and smeared with sandalwood paste. Notably, the appeal of the serial cut across religious boundaries. Muslims watched it with pleasure and enchantment, and churches rescheduled their services so as to avoid a clash with the viewing of the *Ramayan*.[34] As the anthropologist Philip Lutgendorf wrote, "never before had such a large percentage of South Asia's population been united in a single activity, never before had a single message instantaneously reached so enormous [an] audience."[35]

While Muslims and Christians watched the *Ramayan* as entertainment alone, for many Hindus delight was also mixed with devotion. By accident rather than design, the televised epic was introducing subtle changes in this pluralistic and decentralized religion, long divided up into sects each worshipping different deities and lacking a holy book, a unique and singular god, or a single capital of the faith. Now, in front of their television sets, "for the first time all Hindus across the country and at the same time listened to [and watched] the same thing: the serial in fact introduced a *congregational imperative* into Hinduism."[36]

The *Ramayan* serial had been commissioned by state television independent of the happenings in Ayodhya. But its appeal and influence contributed enormously to the VHP's movement to "liberate" the birthplace of Ram. Hitherto one of many gods worshipped by Hindus, Ram was increasingly being seen, courtesy of the serial on television, as the most important and glamorous of them all.

VI

One of the new prime minister's more daring departures was on the economic front. Rajiv Gandhi appointed as his finance minister V. P. Singh, a low-key politician from Uttar Pradesh with a reputation for integrity. The government's first budget, introduced in March 1985, sought to remove some of the controls and checks in what was one of the most tightly regulated economies in the world. The trade regime was liberalized, with duties reduced on a variety of import items and incentives provided for exporters. The licensing regime was simplified, with crucial sectors such as machine tools, textiles, computers, and drugs deregulated. Curbs on assets of individual companies were partially lifted, and rates of corporate and personal income tax were reduced. These changes, it was argued, would encourage greater production and competitiveness. The Indian economy, said the prime minister in February 1985, had gotten "caught in a vicious circle of creating more and more controls. Controls really lead to all the corruption, to all the delays, and that is what we want to cut out."[37]

Left-wing intellectuals attacked the budget as pandering to the rich. Freeing the trade regime would make India excessively dependent on foreign capital, they argued.[38] However, the new policies were welcomed by the business sector, and by the middle class.[39] The middle class was by now quite numerous. Some estimates put the number as high as 100 million people. There was an expanding market for consumer durables—items such as refrigerators and motor vehicles, previously owned only by the select few. In 1984–1985, the number of scooters and motorcycles sold increased by 25%; the number of cars, by as much as 52%. New trades and businesses were opening all the time. There was a boom in the housing and real estate market, and in restaurants and shopping complexes. The rising middle class, wrote one observer, had "become the most visible sign of a rapidly progressing economy."[40]

The latter half of the 1980s was a good time for Indian business. Industry grew at a healthy rate of 5.5% per year, with the manufacturing sector doing even better, growing at 8.9% per annum. Market capitalization rose from 68 billion rupees in 1980 to 550 billion rupees in 1989.[41] Naturally, some companies grew faster than others. The most spectacular rise was that of Reliance Industries, whose founder, Dhirubhai Ambani, had once been a lowly gas station attendant in Aden. Returning to India, he set himself up in the spice trade before branching out into nylon and rayon exports. Then he turned to manufacturing textiles, before adding petrochemical factories, engineering firms, and advertising agencies to his ever-growing portfolio of interests.

Reliance experienced growth rates unprecedented in Indian industry, and seldom seen anywhere else in the world. Through the 1980s, the company's assets grew at an estimated 60% per year, its sales at more than 30% per year, its profits at almost 50%. Ambani was an innovator, using state-of-the-art technology (usually imported), and raising money from the growing middle class by public issues (something which other Indian family firms were loath to do). Yet his company's rise owed as much to his skilful networking as to his business acumen. He kept politicians and bureaucrats in good humour, giving parties for them and gifting them holidays. As a result, he often knew of impending policy changes—in tariff rates, for example—well ahead of the competition.[42]

Reliance's proximity to men in power was only one sign of a growing nexus between politicians and businessmen. Every large business maintained lobbyists in Delhi, to "stealthily work on politicians and bureaucrats to advance company interests." Nor were these doings confined to the national capital; state ministers and chief ministers were alleged to be handing favours to industrialists in exchange for money. A particularly lucrative source of corruption was transactions in real estate. The law of eminent domain allowed the state to take over farmland in the vicinity of towns at well below market rates, and then hand it over to favoured firms to build factories or offices. Hundreds of millions of rupees changed hand in these deals, some of the money going into the pockets of individual politicians, the rest into their party's treasury, to be used in elections.[43]

Their dealings with big money led to a profound change in the life-style of Indian politicians. Once known for their austerity and simplicity, they now lived in houses that were large and expensively furnished. Driving flashy cars and dining in five-star hotels, these were, indeed, the "new maharajas." The "distance between Gandhi (Mahatma) and Gandhi (Rajiv)," remarked one observer, "is a vast traverse in political ethic. The *dhoti* is out, so is the walking stick, wooden sandals and travelling in third class railway compartments. Gucci shoes, Cartier sunglasses, bullet-proof vests, Mercedes-Benz cars and state helicopters are in. Indian politics no longer smells of sweat, nor is it particularly clean and odourless—it reeks of aftershave."[44]

VII

While industry and the middle class prospered, large parts of India suffered endemic poverty and malnutrition. In the autumn of 1985, a series of deaths from starvation were reported in the tribal districts of Orissa. When the rains failed, and the crops with them, villagers were forced to eat a gruel made of tamarind seed and mango kernel, a mixture that led in many cases to stomach disease. In earlier times the forests had provided food and fruit in times of scarcity; but with rampant deforestation that form of insurance was no longer available. More than 1,000 deaths were reported from the districts of Koraput and Kalahandi alone.[45]

In 1987 there was another and more serious drought. The uplands of Orissa were once more hard-hit; but the semi-arid parts of western India, particularly the states of Gujarat and Rajasthan, were also stricken. In desperation, pastoralists ferried their animals by truck to the rich forests of central India, in search of fodder not available in their own home range. The drought was believed to be the worst of the twentieth century. An estimated 200 million people were affected by it, and their suffering was vividly captured in press photographs of parched and cracked land with carcasses of cattle strewn over it.[46]

The scarcities of 1985 and 1987 underlined the continuing dependence of the economy on the monsoon. Yet even in areas of irrigated agriculture there was discontent. This was stoked by two newly formed farmers' organizations: the Shetkari Sanghatana, active in Maharashtra; and the Bharatiya Kisan Union, based in Haryana and Punjab. The former was led by a one-time civil servant, Sharad Joshi; the latter by a Jat farmer, Mahindra Singh Tikait. According to Joshi, the main axis of conflict was between "India," represented by the city-based, English-speaking middle class; and "Bharat," represented by the villagers. He argued that economic policies had consistently favoured India over Bharat. To reverse this bias, Tikait and he proposed higher prices for farm produce and lower tariffs for electricity for farm use. Both organizations commanded a large base; each could mobilize 50,000 or more farmers to march on the state capital to press their demands.[47]

Although Joshi and Tikait claimed to speak for the rural population as a whole, in truth they represented the middle and rich peasantry, those who used tractors and electrified pumps and had a surplus to sell in the market. The poor were mostly outside their purview. As studies conducted in the 1980s once more confirmed, class strongly overlapped with caste in village India, where the truly disadvantaged continued to be the Harijans or Scheduled Castes (SCs). A survey in Karnataka revealed that nearly 80% of SCs living in the countryside, as well as more than 60% of SCs in towns, were below the official poverty line, with their monthly expenditure less than fifty rupees a month. The picture was much the same in other parts of India.[48]

VIII

In his first year in office, Rajiv Gandhi had worked to resolve a series of ethnic conflicts—in Assam, in Mizoram, in the Punjab. By the end of his second year, however, his regime was confronted with fresh challenges based on claims of ethnicity, added to the ongoing challenges based on religion and class.

As ever, a comprehensive coverage of social conflicts in this (or any other) decade in the history of independent India is beyond reach of a single chapter, book, or scholar. One can only flag some of the more important ones. To begin with, there were conflicts between different groups in the same state. In Bengal, for instance, the Nepali-speaking population of the Darjeeling hills had begun asking for a state of their own. Their leader was a former soldier, Subhash Ghisingh. Among his followers Ghisingh commanded total and unquestioning support; at a word from him they could shut down all the schools and shops in the district. His Gorkha National Liberation Front worked within the democratic process and outside it, sometimes petitioning Union ministers, at other times engaging in pitched battles with the police. Through the latter half of 1986 the clashes were particularly intense. Eventually, the prime minister met with Ghisingh, persuading him to accept an autonomous hill council rather than a state for Nepali-speakers.[49]

Across the border, in Assam, the Bodo tribals were in revolt against the locally dominant Assamese. Their movement, mimicking their adversaries, was led by young men of the All Bodo Students Union (ABSU). Its leaders wanted a separate state to be carved out of Assam; in search of their goal, they blockaded roads, burned bridges, and attacked non-Bodos. When the Assamese radicals retaliated, the clashes turned violent, claiming dozens of lives.[50]

In Tripura, meanwhile, tribal activists had begun a struggle against the Bengalis who had migrated in large numbers to the state after partition. By some definitions the Tripura National Volunteers (TNV) qualified as "terrorists," murdering and kidnapping civilians and ambushing police parties in pursuit of their ends. In 1986 TNV guerrillas killed more than 100 people. In the next year they killed even more. However, in August 1988 the TNV leader Bijoy Hrangkhawl came aboveground to sign an accord with the government. His volunteers laid down their arms, in exchange for more seats for tribals in the local legislature and the provision of rice and cooking oil at subsidized rates in tribal villages.[51]

A second set of conflicts pitted residents of individual states against the Indian Union government. Thus in Punjab, the euphoria generated by the accord between Rajiv Gandhi and Longowal proved to be temporary. The Sant's assassination was a harbinger of things to come, with a new generation of terrorists taking up the struggle for Khalistan. The injuries caused by Operation Bluestar and the anti-Sikh riots in Delhi had brought many new recruits to the cause. So had the failure of the central government to honour its commitment to transfer Chandigarh to Punjab. Militants were once more making their home in the Golden Temple. Statements in favour of Khalistan were being made by priests and, on occasion, by members of the ruling Akali Dal itself.[52]

To tackle the resurgence of terrorism the police force in Punjab was now 34,000 strong. To stiffen its morale a new chief was brought in: a plain-speaking policeman from Bombay, J. F. Ribeiro. Also recruited, a little later, was K. P. S. Gill, a Sikh by extraction who had experience fighting extremism in the north-east. Ribeiro and Gill adopted a carrot-and-stick policy, meeting Sikh peasants in an extensive "mass contact"

programme on the one hand, forming vigilante groups to eliminate terrorists on the other. Police parties fanned out into the countryside,
mounting search operations, firing at men on the run. Dozens of extremists were killed in these searches, but there was also much harass-
ment of ordinary villagers.[53]

But the acts of terror continued. Buses were stopped on the highway
and Hindu passengers were separated from Sikhs and killed. In 1986
there were twice as many killings as there had been in 1984, when Bhindranwale was alive. In panic, many Hindus began fleeing across the border to Haryana.

To get rid of the minorities in the Punjab was indeed one of the terrorists' aims. Another aim was even more sinister: to instil fear in Sikhs
who lived outside the Punjab. To this end, bombs were set off in markets
and bus terminals in Delhi and other towns of northern India. These
were intended to provoke a fresh round of revenge killings against the
Sikhs. Then the Sikhs who survived might come back to the Punjab,
there to form a consolidated, unified, homogeneous community, the better to fight the battle for Khalistan. The model, apparently, was the successful struggle for Pakistan in the 1940s, which had likewise been
helped by creating panic among Muslims living outside the holy land.[54]

In a major operation in May 1988, commandos flushed out some
fifty terrorists holed up in the Golden Temple complex. Unlike Operation Bluestar, this assault took place in daylight so that the adversaries
could be pinpointed more clearly. In any case, these militants were not
as well prepared or as motivated as Bhindranwale's men. They retreated
into the temple's sanctum sanctorum; denied access to food and water,
they surrendered seventy-two hours later.[55]

The revival of terrorism in the Punjab coincided with renewed trouble in another border state, Jammu and Kashmir. In 1984, Mrs. Gandhi
had Sheikh Abdullah's son, Farooq, removed from office; now her son
Rajiv restored the ties that once bound the two families and their respective parties, the Congress and the National Conference. In November 1986 they together formed a caretaker government in the state.
Justifying the alliance, Farooq Abdullah said that "the Congress commands the Centre. In a state like Kashmir, if I want to implement programmes to fight disease and run a government, I have to stay on the
right side of the Centre."[56]

In 1987, elections were held for the Jammu and Kashmir assembly.
Kashmiri politicians seeking autonomy from the Centre—rather than
dependence or subservience—formed an umbrella group, the Muslim

United Front (MUF). The workers of the MUF were harassed by the administration, and the election itself was anything but free and fair. Although the alliance of the National Conference and Congress would probably have won anyway, it increased its margin of victory by rigging the voting in its own favour. Even the Intelligence Bureau conceded that as many as thirteen seats were lost by the MUF owing to "electoral malpractice."[57]

The way the elections of 1987 were conducted led to deep disenchantment among political activists in Kashmir. Despairing of being treated fairly by New Delhi, they began looking to Pakistan for succour. Groups of young men crossed the border, joining training camps run by the Pakistani army. A year later they crossed back, to put into practice what they had learned. In the spring of 1989, the Kashmir Valley was witness to a series of shootings, bomb blasts, and grenade attacks. This lovely Valley was now home to "Kalashnikovs, detonators, Molotov cocktails, gelatine fuses, mortars [and] masked militants." Ninety-seven separate incidents of violence were recorded during the first half of 1989, in which at least fifty-two people were killed and 250 others injured. Kashmir, commented one reporter grimly, "appears to have the makings of another Punjab."[58]

IX

Even as the Indian government was trying—with mixed success—to contain secession at home, it had embarked on an ambitious attempt to end ethnic strife in neighbouring Sri Lanka. That little island—as beguilingly beautiful in its own way as mountainous Kashmir—was caught in a bloody civil war between the Sinhala majority and the Tamil minority. The causes of the conflict were wearyingly familiar, to Indians at any rate: rival claims of language, ethnicity, religion, and territory.

A detailed history of the Sri Lankan conflict would take us too far afield.[59] Suffice it to say that the conflict really began when Sinhala was imposed as the sole "official language." The Tamils asked for parity for their own tongue and, when this was denied, took to the streets in protest. Over the years, non-violent methods were thrown over in favour of armed struggle.

Of the several Tamil resistance organizations, the most influential and powerful was Liberation Tigers of Tamil Eeelam (LTTE). Led by a brutal fighter, Velupillai Prabhakaran, the LTTE had as its aim a separate nation, to be constituted from the north and east of the island, where the Tamils were in a majority. Through the early 1980s, LTTE raided Sri Lankan army camps and committed atrocities on civilians. The Sinhala response was, if anything, even more fierce. This was, in other words, a conflict of almost unspeakable brutality and savagery.

The fighters of LTTE had long used the Indian state of Tamil Nadu as a safe haven. They were actively helped by the state government, with New Delhi turning a blind eye. However, in the summer of 1987, Rajiv Gandhi was asked by the Sri Lankan president, J. R. Jayawardene, to help mediate in the conflict. Under an agreement signed between Colombo and New Delhi, the Indian Peace Keeping Force (IPKF) would be flown to the island. The Sri Lankan army would retreat to the barracks, and the LTTE militants would be persuaded—or forced—to disarm.

In late July 1987, Indian troops began going to Sri Lanka in batches of a few thousand each. (Eventually, as many as 48,000 soldiers of the Indian army would be stationed there.) The presence of the IPKF was unpopular among Sinhala nationalists, who saw it as an infringement of sovereignty, and among the Tamils, who had always thought that India was on their side. When asked to surrender their arms, the LTTE insisted on a series of preconditions, including the release of all Tamil prisoners in government custody and a halt to Sinhala colonization in the east of the island. Until October an uneasy peace held, but this was broken when the IPKF moved against the militants. The LTTE headquarters in Jaffna was stormed and captured, but at an enormous cost. Popular opinion turned decisively against the Indians, who were now seen as an occupying force. The LTTE took to the jungle, from where they would snipe at and harry the Indians. They made particularly effective use of land mines, blowing up convoys of soldiers travelling on the roads.

By the end of 1987 the press was writing of Sri Lanka as "India's Vietnam." For "the Indian Army had never seen a war like this: in an alien land, against a foreign enemy that wore no uniforms, knew no Geneva convention on ethics of war, yet carried deadly modern weapons and fought routinely from behind the cover of women and children."[60] An Indian commander was slightly more generous: while deploring the LTTE's "senseless, mulish, destructive insistence" on armed struggle, he nonetheless saluted their "discipline, dedication, determination, motivation and technical expertise."[61]

As the bodies of soldiers returned in bags to the mainland, pressure mounted to recall the IPKF. From the summer of 1989 the troops began coming back, although the final pull-out was not accomplished until the spring of 1990. More than 1,000 Indian soldiers had died in the conflict.

The decision to send troops to Sri Lanka was consistent with India's growing perception of itself as the "rightful regional hegemon in South Asia."[62] In demographic and economic terms it dominated the region; and it was now determined to express this dominance in terms of military preparedness as well. In January 1987, Indian infantry units mounted a large exercise on the Pakistan border, ostensibly to test new equipment, but really to display to the old enemy a new-found power.[63] Then, in March 1988, India tested its first surface-to-surface missile, capable of attacking targets up to 100 miles away. A year later it successfully tested a more sophisticated device, which could carry a load ten times higher and reach targets 1,500 miles away. Indian missile scientists had taken their country into an exclusive club whose only other members were the United States, the Soviet Union, France, China, and Israel.[64]

These developments caused apprehension in the smaller countries of South Asia. People were talking of the "Ugly Indian," as those in other parts of the world spoke of the "Ugly American." India, admitted a weekly in Calcutta ruefully, "is regarded as the bad boy of the region."[65]

X

Rajiv Gandhi had come to power with an impressive mandate in the elections held after his mother's death. As the general elections of 1989 approached, however, the prospects for his party were uncertain. As in 1967 and 1977, the once regnant Congress was being hard-pressed to maintain its position.

There was, first of all, the ever more serious challenge of regional parties. Through much of Rajiv Gandhi's time in office, the Asom Gana Parishad had ruled in Assam, the Telugu Desam in Andhra Pradesh (where N. T. Rama Rao had come back to power in 1985), and the Akalis in the Punjab. In January 1989 the DMK was returned to power in Tamil Nadu. More robust than all these parties was the CPM in West Bengal, which in 1989 had been in office for twelve years on the trot. During this time its leader and chief minister, Jyoti Basu, had "grown phenomenally in stature." Basu was held in great esteem in the countryside for the agrarian reforms his party had brought about. Unusually for a communist, he was also respected by industrialists, who admired his pragmatic approach to investment and his tempering of the trade unions' militancy.[66]

A second challenge came from the Hindu right. The old Jana Sangh, since renamed the Bharatiya Janata Party (BJP), had won only two seats in the elections of 1984. But it had now hitched its wagon to the campaign for a Ram temple in Ayodhya. As that movement gathered popularity, the party's fortunes rose. The BJP's workers joined those of VHP and RSS in carrying out Ram Shila pujans, ceremonies to worship and consecrate bricks that they hoped would be used in the construction of the Ram temple. To force the issue, the VHP announced that it would organize a formal *shilanyas*, or foundation ceremony, at the disputed site in Ayodhya on 2 November. Bricks from different districts reached the site on the appointed day. The Congress government in Delhi was advised to stop the *shilanyas*, but eventually let it go ahead, for fear of offending Hindus before the general election. The VHP chose a Dalit labourer from Bihar to lay the first brick of what they claimed would, one day soon, be a glorious temple dedicated to Lord Ram.[67]

The brick worship ceremonies led to religious conflict in several towns in northern India. The worst was in the city of Bhagalpur, in Bihar, where Hindus and Muslims battled each other for a week in November. The conflict spilled over into the countryside, where RSS activists led groups in smashing looms and homes owned by the region's celebrated Muslim weavers. Several hundred Muslims died, and many more were rendered homeless. The homeless were gathered into relief camps run not by the government but by Muslim merchants and Islamic relief organizations. The riots in Bhagalpur, and the aftermath of the Ram pujans generally, further polarized the communities. The Muslims felt betrayed by the Congress, and a large section of the Hindu middle class was drawn into open support of the BJP.[68]

A third challenge to the prime minister came from his erstwhile colleague in the cabinet, V. P. Singh. As finance minister, Singh had conducted a series of raids on industrial firms accused of tax evasion. This was seen as exceeding his brief; he was shifted to the defence portfolio, and later dropped from the cabinet altogether. Not long afterwards, a storm broke out over revelations that commissions had been paid to middlemen in a deal involving the sale of the Swedish Bofors gun to the Indian army. The news was first announced over Swedish radio in April 1987. Over the next two years, the press and opposition politicians kept up the pressure on the government, demanding that it name and punish the offenders. The government stonewalled, encouraging speculation that the middlemen were somehow linked to the prime minister himself. The fact that there had been corruption in a defence transaction provoked widespread outrage, which was intensified when it came out that army experts had preferred a French gun to the Bofors, but were overruled by the politicians.[69]

In the public mind, the controversy over the Bofors gun was, rightly or wrongly, linked to the departure of V. P. Singh from the cabinet. The appellation "Mr. Clean" was transferred from Rajiv Gandhi to him. Singh left the Congress, and in June 1988 ran for office, and won, as a candidate of the combined opposition in a parliamentary by-election in Allahabad. By now he had become the focal point of a growing anti-Congress sentiment. In October 1988 his Jan Morcha was merged with the old Janata Party to form the Janata Dal. This new party then joined hands with regional groupings to create a National Front, launched at Madras's Marina Beach and hailed by one of its members, the ever-ebullient N. T. Rama Rao, as a chariot "drawn by seven horses [that] will dispel the gloom and shadows that thickened through the passage of the last few decades of national history."[70]

In the last year of his government's tenure, Rajiv Gandhi embarked on four initiatives that aimed at reversing his declining popularity. In September 1988 he introduced a bill to check the freedom of the press. Under its terms, editors and proprietors could be sent to jail if they were guilty of "scurrilous publication" or "criminal imputation," terms whose definition would be the privilege of the state alone. The bill was evidently a response to the spate of recent stories on corruption; it was a "belated preemptive strike before more damage could be done to the government's image." It prompted a collective protest by editors across the country and a walkout in Parliament, and was eventually dropped.[71]

Then, in January 1989, Rajiv Gandhi visited China, the first Indian prime minister to do so in more than three decades. This was, among other things, an attempt to recast himself as an international statesman. In talks with Chinese leaders the border question was delicately sidestepped. However, New Delhi ceded ground on Tibet, while Beijing for its part said it would not aid insurgents in India's north-east. Rajiv Gandhi had a ninety-minute conversation with the eighty-four-year-old Deng Xiaoping, at which he was told, "You are the young. You are the future."[72]

Next, in March 1989, Rajiv Gandhi reversed the outward-looking, growth-oriented economic policies of his first years in office. In the last budget presented by his government, he increased the taxes on consumer durables and introduced new surcharges on airline tickets and luxury hotels. At the same time, a new scheme to generate employment was introduced for rural areas. With the elections beckoning, Rajiv

Gandhi was "going back to the kind of populism that his mother specialized in."[73]

Finally, in the summer of 1989, the government started a series of high-profile programmes to celebrate the centennial of Jawaharlal Nehru's birth. Seminars, photo exhibitions, television quizzes, poetry festivals, musical concerts, and even skating competitions were held in Nehru's name, all paid for by the state and publicized by state radio and television. On the face of it, these programmes merely honoured India's first prime minister, but "at another, more subconscious level, the blitz repeatedly and subtly whispers the real but hidden message: that there has been no better guardian of the nation than the Nehru family and letting the family down would, in the ultimate analysis, amount to spurning a sacred legacy and inviting the forces of chaos."[74]

Still, Rajiv Gandhi was leaving nothing to chance. In his campaign for re-election he addressed 170 meetings in different parts of the country. As in 1984, he was advised by Rediffusion to stress the threats to the country's unity, which were stoked and furthered by a sectarian opposition and could be overcome by the Congress alone.[75] This time, however, the message did not resonate nearly as widely. For one thing, the accusations of corruption had gravely hurt the government's credibility. For another, the opposition was far better organized. The three main groups had worked out seat adjustments, so that in most constituencies the Congress candidate faced one main opponent—from the National Front, the BJP, or one of the communist parties.

The elections, held in November 1989, were a body blow to the Congress party. It won only 197 seats, down more than 200 from its previous tally. On the other hand, the opposition couldn't quite claim victory either. The Janata Dal won 142 seats, the BJP eighty-six, and the left a few more than fifty. V. P. Singh was sworn in as head of a National Front government, with the left and the BJP choosing to support it from outside. Thus, the second non-Congress prime minister of India was someone who, like the first (Morarji Desai), had spent most his political career in the Congress party.

The general elections of 1989 were the first in which no single party won a majority. That they constituted a watershed is not merely a retrospective reading; some observers said so at the time. "India was in for a period of political instability," wrote Vir Sanghvi. "The days of strong governments ruled by dictatorial Prime Ministers were over. This election was the inauguration of an era of uncertainty."[76]

XI

Even by the standards of Indian history, the 1980s were an especially turbulent decade. The republic had always been faced with dissenting movements; but never so many, at the same time, in so many parts of India, and expressed with such intensity. Two challenges were especially worrying: the continuing insurgency in Punjab, the first such situation in a state considered part of the heartland of India (unlike those old trouble spots, Nagaland and Kashmir); and the unprecedented mobilization of radical Hindus across the country, which threatened the secular identity of the state. Adding to the violence, large and small, was the growing political and administrative corruption, which was highlighted and also made more troubling by an alert press. Outside the country's borders, national prestige had been greatly damaged by the bloody nose given to the Indian army by the LTTE in Sri Lanka.

In the summer of 1985, the weekly *Sunday* in Calcutta, then at the height of its importance and influence, ran a cover story on the "uncontrollable wave of violence" in the country. "Tension and frustration everywhere—social, economic and political," said *Sunday*, was "giving way to sporadic terror and mass protests." "Acts of sabotage, arson, killings and destruction are breaking out all over India like an ugly rash." Thirty-seven years after independence, "India finds itself at a crucial point in its history."

Sunday posed the question, "What is happening to the country and why?" and asked a roster of eminent Indians to answer it. The editor Romesh Thapar remarked that the violence and anger showed that "no one is in command at any level. . . . [T]he fear is growing that we are moving beyond the point of no return, to use a phrase from the jargon of airline pilots. The breakdown is becoming too visible." The columnist Kuldip Nayar quoted a series of newspaper headlines on riots and killings, which recorded "trouble of varying intensity in areas thousands of miles apart," the work of people who "for a long time lived on the edge of disaster" but whose "discontent seems [now] to have reached a bursting point." The policeman K. F. Rustomji noted grimly that Indian politics and administration were now captive to the "fanatic and the demagogue," who "claim the right to organise the deaths of thousands under the guise of democratic dissent." "Forget the dead, count the votes," said Rustomji; this was a withering but not inaccurate characterization of the political purpose of those fanatics and demagogues. Then he added, "In a few years even the votes may not be worth counting because we may have killed democracy by then."[77]

These were recurrent themes in the press commentary of the period: that India would break up into pieces or give up on democracy altogether. Writing in April 1987, *Sunday*'s own political editor, Kewal Verma, issued this dire warning:

> If Rajiv Gandhi continues to slip and no alternative emerges (. . . none is in sight yet), it will lead to political destabilisation with disastrous consequences. For, Khalistan could become a reality. Already in the rural areas of Punjab, Sikh extremists are running a parallel administration. Also, the Rama Janmabhoomi-Babari Masjid issue could lead to large-scale communal war in north India. A prolonged state of political uncertainty and instability would be an invitation to adventurous forces to intervene in the situation. For instance, if the President dismisses the Prime Minister, it may be [the Chief of Army Staff] Gen. Sundarji who will decide who should stay.[78]

The writers quoted in this section were all Indians in their late fifties or early sixties, who had grown up in the warm glow of the Nehru years and remembered the hopes with which the new nation was forged. Their sentiments were no doubt coloured by nostalgia, at least some of which was merited. For the politicians of Nehru's day had worked to contain social cleavages rather than deepen or further them for their own interests. But in other ways the nostalgia was perhaps misplaced. The churning, violent and costly though it undoubtedly was, could be more sympathetically read as a growing decentralization of the Indian polity, away from the hegemony of a single region (the north), a single party (the Congress), and a single family (the Gandhis).

One must reserve final comment on whether the gloom was really justified. As the many forecasts previously quoted in this book have shown, every decade since independence had been designated the "most dangerous" thus far. If there was a novelty about these latest predictions, it was merely that they came from Indians rather than foreigners.

XII

With the end of the present chapter, this book moves from "history" to what might instead be called "historically informed journalism." Part V, which follows, deals with the events of the last two decades, that is, with processes still unfolding. Given our closeness to what is being written about, it adopts a thematic rather than a chronological approach. To ground the narrative, however, each chapter starts with a prediction from the past that in some way anticipated the future.

In a study of the Assam movement published in 1983, the author remarked that the book was "almost contemporary history and contemporary history will not have the logic, the neatness in understanding, the conformity to patterns, that the passage of years gives to things."[79] In a book on Operation Bluestar published in 1994, the author argued that "a decade or so is perhaps the right amount of time to have elapsed before attempting to document contemporary history. It is also the time when one can indulge in the luxury of introspection because events have ceased to colour one's judgement emotionally."[80]

Most archives around the world follow a "thirty-year" rule, keeping closed documents written in the past three decades. That seems just about right, for once thirty years have passed any new "disclosures" are unlikely to materially affect those still living.

In my experience, to write about events as a historian one also needs a generation's distance. That much time must elapse before one can place those events in a pattern, to see them away and apart from the din and clamour of the present. Once roughly three decades have gone by, much more material is at hand—not just archives that are now open, but also memoirs, biographies, and analytical works that have since been published.

When writing about the very recent past, one lacks the primary sources available for earlier periods. Besides, the historian is here writing about times that are close to him as well as his readers. He, and they, often have strong opinions about the politicians and policies of the day. In the chapters that follow, I have tried to keep my own biases out of the narrative, but my success in this respect may be limited—or at any rate, more limited than in other parts of the book. For these decades have been as rich in incident and controversy as any other time in the history of independent India.

PART V

A HISTORY
of EVENTS

26

RIGHTS

In India you do not cast your vote; you vote your caste.

V. N. GADGIL, Congress politician, speaking in 1995

I

IN THE SECOND WEEK of January 1957, India's leading anthropologist, M. N. Srinivas, addressed the annual Science Congress in Calcutta on the subject of "Caste in Modern India." "My main aim in this address," he began,

> is to marshal evidence before you to prove that in the last century or more, caste has become much more powerful in certain respects, than it ever was in pre-British times. Universal adult franchise and the provision of safeguards for backward groups in our Constitution have strengthened caste appreciably. The recent strengthening of caste contrasts with the aim of bringing about a "caste and classless society" which most political parties, including the Indian National Congress, profess.

Srinivas then went on to show how Indian politics was shot through with caste rivalries. In the state of Andhra Pradesh, one major peasant caste, the Kammas, usually supported the Communist Party of India (prompting the witticism that the party's ideology was really "Kammanist"), whereas its rival, the Reddy caste, backed the Congress. In neighbouring Mysore, where the Congress was in power, the Lingayats and Okkaligas fought for control of the party. In Maharashtra and Madras, the main axis of political conflict was Brahman versus non-Brahman. In Bihar, the landowning castes, Bhumihars and Rajputs, battled with the literate Kayasths for the top jobs in the Congress organization. In neighbouring Uttar Pradesh, where the lower castes were better organized, "the tussle between the Rajputs and Chamars for political power is likely to get keener in the near future."

Although the constitution of India pledged itself to a casteless society, said Srinivas, in fact "the power and activity of caste [have] increased in proportion as political power passed increasingly to the people from the rulers." Thus caste was "everywhere the unit of social action." There were, however, some regional variations. It was "not unlikely that the absence of powerful Brahmin groups in the North has prevented the rising of an anti-Brahmin movement and this has probably led to the popular impression that caste is more powerful south of the Vindhyas than to the north." Srinivas continued: "There are signs, however, that caste is becoming stronger in the North. Whether caste conflict will ever become as strong as it is in the South today, remains to be seen."[1]

This talk was delivered in absentia, since Srinivas was away in the United States. Nonetheless, it attracted a stream of excited commentary in the English-language press. For the second general elections were just around the corner. Would people vote according to their individual preference, as democratic theory urged them to do? Or would they vindicate Srinivas by simply voting according to their caste?[2]

II

The subsequent decades were to provide a resounding confirmation of M. N. Srinivas's thesis. Far from disappearing with democracy and modernization, caste continued to have a determining influence in (and on) Indian society. In town or village, at leisure or at work, most Indians were defined by the endogamous group into which they were born.

True, the caste system was by no means unaffected by the economic and social changes unleashed by independence. "Inter-dining," once strictly prohibited, was quite common in the cities; and among the professional classes there were now many marriages between members of different castes. The association between caste and occupation, once so rigid, was also weakening.[3]

Set against this was the growing salience of caste and caste identities in the modern domain of electoral politics. The most striking feature of Indian politics in the 1960s and 1970s was the rise of the "backward castes," groups intermediate between the Scheduled Castes at the bottom and the Brahmans and Rajputs at the top. Yadavs in Uttar Pradesh and Bihar, Jats in Punjab and Haryana, Marathas in Maharashtra, Vokkaligas in Karnataka, and Gounders in Tamil Nadu—these were in Srinivas's phrase, the "dominant caste" in their localities: large in numbers,

well organized, exercising economic and social power. At election time—
to use another of his concepts—they acted as a "vote bank," lining up
solidly behind a politician of their caste.

In Indian law, these groups are known as the Other Backward Castes
(or Classes)—OBCs—to distinguish them from the Scheduled Tribes
and Scheduled Castes. These OBCs formed the social base and provided
the leadership of the parties that were to successfully challenge the dominance of the Congress party. The DMK, which came to power in Madras after the elections of 1967, and the SVD governments of the states
in the north were in essence OBC parties. Ten years later, the backward
castes asserted themselves emphatically on the national stage. Of the
four components of the Janata collective, at least two—the Lok Dal and
the Socialists—were also, in essence, OBC parties.[4]

Economic power had come to the OBCs through land reforms and
the green revolution; political power through the ballot box. What was
lacking was administrative power. Thus the Janata government had appointed the Backward Classes Commission, known then and after as
the Mandal Commission after its proactive chairman. The commission
concluded that caste was still the main indicator of "backwardness." It
identified, on the basis of state surveys, as many as 3,743 specific castes
that were still "backward." These, it estimated, collectively constituted
more than 50% of the Indian population. Yet these castes were very
poorly represented in the administration, especially at the higher levels.
By the commission's calculations, as of about 1980 the OBCs filled only
12.55% of all positions in the central government, and only 4.83% of
Class I jobs.

To redress this anomaly the Mandal Commission recommended that
27% of all positions in the central government be reserved for these
castes, to add to the 22.5% already set apart for Scheduled Castes and
Tribes. For "we must recognise," said the commission,

> that an essential part of the battle against social backwardness is to be
> fought in the minds of the backward people. In India Government ser-
> vice has always been looked upon as a symbol of prestige and power.
> By increasing the representation of OBCs in Government services, we
> give them an immediate feeling of participation in the governance of
> this country. When a backward caste candidate becomes a Collector or
> Superintendent of Police, the material benefits accruing from his posi-
> tion are limited to the members of his family only. But the psychologi-
> cal spin off of this phenomenon is tremendous; the entire community

of that backward class candidate feels elevated. Even when no tangible benefits flow to the community at large, the feeling that now it has its "own man" in the "corridors of power" acts as morale booster.[5]

By the time the Mandal Commission submitted its report, the Janata government had fallen. The Congress regimes that followed, headed by Indira and Rajiv Gandhi successively, sought to give it a quiet burial. But when a National Front government came to power in the general elections of 1989, the report was disinterred. The new prime minister, V. P. Singh, was sensible of the rising political power of the OBCs, and of his less than solid position as head of a minority coalition. Thus on 13 August 1990 a four-paragraph government order was issued implementing the basic recommendation of the Mandal Report. Henceforth, 27% of all vacancies in the government of India would be reserved for candidates from the "Socially and Educationally Backward Classes" identified by the commission.

This order set off a lively debate in intellectual circles. Some scholars argued that the criteria for job reservation should be family income, rather than membership in a particular caste. Others deplored the extension of affirmative action in the first place; allocating one job in two on considerations other than merit would put the efficacy and reliability of public institutions at risk. However, there were also scholars who welcomed the implementation of the Mandal Report as a corrective to the dominance of upper castes, and especially Brahmans, in the public services. They pointed to the states of south India, where more than two-thirds of government jobs were allocated on the basis of caste, without (it was argued) affecting the efficiency of the administration.[6]

In September 1990, a case was brought before the Supreme Court of India, contesting the constitutional validity of the Mandal Commission's recommendations. Three principal arguments were made by the petitioner: that the extension of reservation violated the constitutional guarantee of equality of opportunity; that caste was not a reliable indicator of backwardness; and that the efficiency of public institutions was at risk. While it deliberated on the case, the bench issued a stay on the government order of 13 August.

As is so often the case in India, arguments about public policy were conducted in newspapers and courts, and also spilled over into the streets. On 19 September, a student at Delhi University named Rajiv Goswami set himself on fire in protest against the acceptance of the Mandal Commission report. He was badly burned, but he survived. Other students were inspired to follow his example. These self-immolators were all upper-caste, and their own hopes for obtaining a government job were now being undermined. All together, there were nearly 200 suicide attempts—and sixty-two students succumbed to their injuries.

Other protests were collective. Across northern India, groups of students organized rallies and demonstrations; shut down schools, colleges, and shops; attacked government buildings; and battled with the police. The guardians of the law sought to defend themselves, sometimes to deadly effect. Incidents of firing by the police were reported from as many as six states, and these incidents claimed more than fifty lives.[7]

The conflicts sparked by the Mandal Commission's recommendations were far more intense in northern India. For one thing, affirmative action programmes had long been in existence in the south. For another, the south also had a thriving industrial sector; thus educated young men were no longer as dependent on government employment. Again, while in the south the upper castes constituted less than 10% of the population, the figure in the north was more than 20%. Since there was more at stake all around, the battles, naturally, were fiercer.

Among the strongest supporters of the Mandal Commission were two rising politicians: Mulayam Singh Yadav, who had become chief minister of Uttar Pradesh late in 1989; and Lalu Prasad Yadav, who became chief minister of Bihar early in 1990. Both were born in poor peasant households, and both became politically active at university, joining the socialist movement, which was then still influential. Both were jailed during the emergency, and both joined the Janata party after the emergency was over.

As their common surname indicated, Mulayam and Lalu were from a caste of farmer-herders scattered across north and western India. In colonial times Yadavs had often acted as *lathials* (strongmen) of upper-caste landlords. After independence, now with lands of their own, they had steadily gained economic strength, social prestige, and political power. Both Mulayam and Lalu actively reached out to the Muslims, another very numerous (if much poorer) community in Uttar Pradesh and Bihar. The arithmetic of this move was electoral, for Yadavs and Muslims were each about 10% of the population. In multi-cornered contests—the norm in India—40% of the vote was usually enough. So if one had sewn up both Yadavs and Muslims, and persuaded sections of other "backward" groups to join up, then one had a very good chance of winning.[8]

As India's most populous states, Bihar and Uttar Pradesh together sent 139 members to Parliament. General elections were often decided here. In the first four elections the Congress won a majority of seats in Uttar Pradesh and Bihar. In 1977, following the emergency, the party was wiped out; but in 1980 and 1984 it recovered, winning eighty-one seats in 1980 and 131 in 1984. The number for 1984 was an aberration, a consequence of the martydom of Indira Gandhi. In 1989 the Congress fared disastrously, winning only nineteen seats in the two states. When midterm elections were held two years later, it fared even worse, winning five seats in Uttar Pradesh and only one in Bihar.

When V. P. Singh announced the implementation of the Mandal Report, the Congress—which was then the opposition—was lukewarm. In the elections of 1991 the party returned to power, despite its poor showing in Uttar Pradesh and Bihar, which was compensated for by a strong performance in the south. Now, the numbers set out in the preceding paragraph forced a quick rethink. Were the Congress ever to regain ground in the north, it had to woo back the backward castes. Accordingly, the new Congress prime minister, P. V. Narasimha Rao, issued a new government order on 26 September 1991, endorsing the Mandal Report but adding the rider that in alloting 27% of jobs to OBCs "preference shall be given to candidates belonging to poorer sections" among them.

Meanwhile, the Supreme Court continued its hearings on the petition placed before it. It finally gave its verdict on 16 November 1992. Seven judges dismissed the petition, upholding the constitutional validity of the Mandal Commission and the orders which sought to implement it. Three others dissented. The judgements were characteristically prolix, filling nearly 500 closely printed pages. The dissenting judges argued that "caste-collectivity" was "unconstitutional"; that in deciding who was disadvantaged, impersonal criteria like income should be used instead. On the other side, speaking for the majority, Justice Jeevan Reddy referred to past judgements in which caste had been used as a proxy for backwardness. He invoked the example of affirmative action for blacks in the United States, a precedent worthy of emulation in the present case. For

it goes without saying that in the Indian context, social backwardness leads to educational backwardness and both of them together lead to poverty—which in turn breeds and perpetuates the social and educational backwardness. They feed upon each other constituting a

vicious circle. It is a well-known fact that till independence the administrative apparatus was manned almost exclusively by members of the
"upper" castes. The Shudras, the Scheduled Castes and the Scheduled
Tribes and other similar backward social groups among Muslims and
Christians had practically no entry into the administrative apparatus.
It was this imbalance which was sought to be redressed by providing
for reservation in favour of such backward classes.[9]

In upholding the government orders the Supreme Court added two qualifications: that reservations should not exceed 50% of the jobs in government; and that caste criteria would apply only in recruitment, not in
promotions.

The Janata party had constituted the Mandal Commission in 1978;
its new avatar, the Janata Dal, implemented the recommendations in
1990. Its enthusiasm was not at first shared by rival parties. The CPI
and CPM traditionally saw class, not caste, as the major axis of political
mobilization. The Bharatiya Janata party gave pride of place to (the
Hindu) religion. As for the Congress, it presumed to speak for the nation as a whole. However, by the time the Supreme Court passed its
judgement, these parties were all prepared to endorse it. For they very
quickly realized the political implications of the Mandal Report and the
political costs of opposing it.

The controversy surrounding the Mandal Commission is reminiscent in some ways of the debate, during the 1950s, over the report of the
States Reorganization Commission. As a marker of identity, caste was
as primordial as language—as likely to be deplored by modernizing intellectuals, and as likely to be successfully used for social and political
mobilization. Then, as now, the force of argument was powerless when
faced with the logic of numbers. Then, as now, what began as a contentious and many-sided debate ended with an all-party consensus.

Most reports commissioned by the government of India are read by
few people and discussed by even fewer. The reports of the States Reorganization and Mandal Commissions were altogether exceptional. They
were read by many, debated by many more, and actually even implemented. They may even be—if only because of the number of people
they affected—the two most influential reports ever commissioned by a
government anywhere.

The influence exercised by the States Reorganization Commission
was direct: it led to the redrawing of the administrative map of India on
linguistic lines. The Mandal Commission's influence, however, was mostly

indirect. By its terms only a few thousand government jobs came up for allotment to OBCs. But the debate the report inspired, and its eventual acceptance, provided a tremendous fillip to OBC pride and solidarity. Among the beneficiaries were the two Yadavs, Lalu and Mulayam. Both left the Janata Dal and set up their own parties, and very successfully too. Lalu's Rashtriya Janata Dal stayed in power in Bihar for more than a decade (until 2005); Mulayam's Samajwadi party was in power in Uttar Pradesh for much of the 1990s, and Mulayam is once more chief minister of the state as I write.

III

The 1990s also witnessed an upsurge by Dalits, as the formerly "untouchable" castes were now known. This was led by the Bahujan Samaj Party (BSP), which was founded by a brilliant political entrepreneur, Kanshi Ram.

After the death of Dr B. R. Ambedkar in 1956, the most prominent untouchable leader was Jagjivan Ram. He was in the Congress, and it was in good part because of him that the lowest castes were regarded as a captive "vote bank" by the party. The claim was challenged only in Maharashtra, first by the Republican party that Ambedkar had founded, and later by the militant Dalit Panther organization. One consequence was that "Dalit," meaning "oppressed," replaced the official Scheduled Caste or the Gandhian Harijan as the preferred self-appellation for the low castes. But, from the 1950s through the 1980s, they mostly voted for the Congress nonetheless.

For decades, Jagjivan Ram had "carried the banner of the downtrodden and stood for their interests." His death in 1988, said an obituarist, "left a void" which would be almost impossible to fill. "Scattered, unorganised, leaderless and oppressed, the fate of the scheduled castes, who form 15 per cent of the country's population, . . . hangs precariously in the balance."[10]

As it happened, by this time Kanshi Ram (who was not related to Jagjivan Ram) had been active for more than a decade. He was born in 1932 in the Punjab, and joined the government service after university, working in a laboratory in Maharastra, where he was introduced to the writings of B. R. Ambedkar. Thus radicalized, he quit his job in 1971 and began an organization to represent government employees from a disadvantaged background. This was called the All India Backward and Minority Communities Employees Federation (BAMCEF). For the next decade Kanshi Ram travelled across India, building district and state chapters of the organization. By the early 1980s BAMCEF had a membership of 200,000, many of them graduates and postgraduates. This was a trade union of the Scheduled Caste elite, which, in the leader's words, would form the "think tank," "talent bank," and "financial bank" for the depressed classes as a whole.[11]

BAMCEF's growth area was north India, and particularly Uttar Pradesh, where its rallies regularly attracted audiences of 100,000 or more. The organization's success emboldened Kanshi Ram to start a political party. Several names were tried, but finally it came to be called the Bahujan Samaj party, Bahujan being a more inclusive category than Dalit. Whereas the latter represented the Scheduled Castes or former untouchables, the former contained within it backward castes and Muslims as well.

Four decades of affirmative action had created a strong and articulate middle class among the Scheduled Castes. In the beginning, the SCs were mainly recruited at the bottom of the state machinery, filling menial jobs; over time, they came to be better represented at the higher levels, working as Class I magistrates and officers in the secretariat. The numbers in Table 8 are telling indeed.

A government job provided both economic security and social prestige. By 1995, more than 2 million Dalits were thus advantaged. Of course, the majority of them continued to have lives that were economically

TABLE 8: EMPLOYMENT PROFILE OF SCHEDULED CASTES IN THE GOVERNMENT OF INDIA

GROUP	NUMBER OF SCHEDULED CASTES EMPLOYED		SC JOBS AS % OF TOTAL JOBS	
	1965	1995	1965	1995
Class I	318	6,637	1.64	10.12
Class II	864	13,797	2.82	12.67
Class III	96,114	378,172	8.88	16.15
Class IV	101,073	2,221,380	17.75	21.60
Total	198,369	2,619,986	13.17	17.43

Source: Niraja Gopal Jayal, "Social Inequality and Institutional Remedies: A Study of the National Commission for Scheduled Castes and Scheduled Tribes," paper presented at NETSAPPE Conference, Bangalore, June 2003.

impoverished as well as socially degrading—as agricultural labourers, sweepers, and construction workers.[12] Still, there was now a sizeable middle class to take their case forward. This was the class which staffed BAMCEF, and which then assumed leading roles in Kanshi Ram's Bahujan Samaj party. In this respect, the path the SCs followed was very nearly the reverse of the OBCs. Having tasted political power, the OBCs sought to claim administrative power through the Mandal Report. The SCs, however, first acquired a stake in the administration, before seeking a greater role in party politics.

The BSP made its debut in the general elections of 1984. It garnered more than 1 million votes but won no seats. In subsequent elections it was more successful, winning, for example, eleven seats in 1996 and fourteen in 1999. But it really made an impression in the state elections in Uttar Pradesh. Here, the party activists successfully wooed the Dalit masses, warning them that the Congress wanted only pliant *chamchas* (sycophants) from their ranks. The BSP, on the other hand, stood for "social justice," even "social transformation." Only a party of their own could enhance the dignity, pride, and prospects of the Dalits.[13]

The message was carried by Dalit lawyers, teachers, and officers to their less privileged brethren. Apart from holding meetings and rallies, these intellectuals published a series of tracts providing the lower castes with a heroic history of their own. These tracts were driven by the conviction that "till now Indian history is mostly written by brahmins." Now, an alternative narrative was constructed, which claimed that it was actually the Dalits who "created cultures such as Harappa and Mohenjodaro." But then the invading Aryans "took away their land, alienated them forcibly, hijacked their culture, and subjected them to a state of slavery." Throughout history this suppression had been stoutly resisted, by Dalit workers, peasants, singers, and poets. Their deeds—real as well as mythic—were commemorated in booklets printed and distributed in the hundreds of thousands in Uttar Pradesh during the 1990s.[14]

Political organization and consciousness-raising, working hand in hand, enabled the BSP to take impressive strides in Uttar Pradesh. Between 1989 and 2002 five assembly elections were held in the state. The seats won in these polls by the BSP were, successively, thirteen, twelve, sixtynine, sixty-seven, and ninety-eight. By the end it was winning a steady 20% of the popular vote. The BSP's gains were mostly at the expense of the Congress. This party powered by Dalits had emerged as one of the three major political groups in the state, the others being Mulayam's Samajwadi party and the Hindu-oriented Bharatiya Janata party.

By this time, Kanshi Ram had been supplanted as the BSP's main leader by a one-time protégé. Her name was Mayawati. She was born in 1956 in New Delhi, the daughter of a government clerk. Her ambition was to join the prestigious Indian Administrative Service, but an encounter with Kanshi Ram at a BAMCEF rally made her enter politics instead. At public meetings she attracted attention by her oratorical skills, with her slashing wit aimed mostly at the rival Congress party. By the early 1990s she had become the public face of the BSP. Realizing that the Dalits could never come to power on their own, she sought to build cross-caste and cross-party alliances. She had three brief terms as chief minister; as the head of coalition governments formed in collaboration either with the Samajwadi party or the BJP.[15]

Writing in the 1970s, the journalist and old India hand James Cameron pointed out that the prominent women in Indian public life all came from upper-class, English-speaking backgrounds. "There is not and never has been a working-class woman with a function in Indian politics," remarked Cameron, "and it is hard to say when there ever will be." Within two decades there was an answer, or perhaps one should say a refututation, when a woman born in a Dalit home became chief minister of India's most populous state.[16]

In other parts of the country the Dalit voice was also being heard. The "most significant feature of the Scheduled Castes in contemporary India," wrote the sociologist André Béteille, "is their increased visibility." They were "still exploited, oppressed and stigmatized; but their presence in Indian society could no longer be ignored."[17]

Once submissive as well as suppressed, the Dalits now knew of their rights under the Indian constitution, and were prepared to fight for them. Indeed, the man who piloted that constitution, B. R. Ambedkar, had become the symbol and inspiration for Dalits everywhere. One anthropologist writes that "across Tamil Nadu, statues, portraits, posters and nameplates bearing the image of Dr. Ambedkar proliferate. Halls, schools and colleges named after him abound and even his ideological opponents feel obliged to reproduce his picture and lay claim to his legacy."[18] Pretty much the same was true of most other states of the Union. Wherever Dalits lived or worked, photographs of Ambedkar were ubiquitous: finely framed and lovingly garlanded, placed in prominent positions in hamlets, homes, shops, and offices. Meanwhile, owing to pressure from Dalit groups, statues of Ambedkar were put up at public places in towns and cities—at major road intersections, outside railroad stations, in parks. The leader was portrayed standing proud and erect, clutching in his right hand a copy of the constitution he had written.

Fifty years after his death, B. R. Ambedkar is worshipped in parts of India that he never visited and where he was completely unknown in his own lifetime. Wherever there are Dalits—that is, in almost every district in India—Ambedkar is remembered and, more important, revered.[19]

IV

The rising self-consciousness of the Dalits was accompanied by an escalation of caste conflict. Through the 1990s, there were a series of violent clashes in the countryside, in which Dalits were usually on the receiving end. The root of the conflict was material—the fact that it was the OBCs or upper castes who owned the land and the Dalits who cultivated it. But the form in which this conflict was expressed was often ideological. That Dalits could ask for better wages or for more humane treatment was seen by their presumed superiors as a sign that they needed to be quickly, and if necessary brutally, put back in their place.

One theatre of this conflict was the southernmost districts of the southern state of Tamil Nadu. The clashes here were between the Thevars, a rising middle caste of landowners, and the landless Dalits. They could be sparked by disputes over wages, or by pique that a community once condemned to scavenging was now sending members to the Indian Administrative Service. The Dalits, emboldened, were refusing to be served tea in a separate glass at village cafés (a long-standing custom). And for each statue built by the Thevars of their revered leader Muthuramalinga Thevar (1908–1965), the Dalits would build a statue of Ambedkar in reply. (Indeed, some of the bloodiest clashes were provoked by the demolition by one side of a statue erected by the other.) The rows were material as well as ideological, they were frequent, and they were costly. In a single decade, caste conflicts in Tamil Nadu resulted in more than 100 deaths.[20]

There were comparable conflicts in northern India. We may take as representative an incident in the Haryana village of Jhajhar, where, on the evening of 15 October 2002, a group of Dalits were beaten to death. Earlier that day, the victims were travelling to the market, to sell cowhides that they had collected. According to one account, they were halted by the police, who asked them for proof of how they had come by the hides. According to another (and less likely) account, the Dalits stopped to kill a cow walking by the road and then skin it. This latter version was the one that gained currency. The rumour that a cow had been slaughtered spread through the vicinity, provoking anger because the cow is regarded as holy by upper-caste Hindus. A large mob descended on the police station and dragged out the "violators" while the police looked on. The Dalits were flogged and killed, right on the main road.[21]

Atrocities against Dalits were by no means the preserve of caste Hindus alone. In the Punjab, the landowning Jat Sikhs resented the growing self-confidence of the labouring and artisanal castes. From the early twentieth century, Dalit Sikhs had struggled for a share of the land and access to shrines (both controlled by Jats). Some Dalits sought escape in a religion of their own, Adi-Dharm. More recently, the prosperity fuelled by the green revolution had opened up new possibilities for low castes: work in towns and factories, and opportunities to start their own businesses. There was also a growing Sikh diaspora, and the emigrants sent money back to their kinsmen in the villages.[22]

Again, one conflict may be taken as representative. This was over control of a shrine in the village of Talhan, on the outskirts of the industrial city of Jalandhar. The shrine was in memory of an artisan-turned-saint named Baba Nihal Singh. Sikhs of all castes worshipped there, and in such numbers that their offerings made the temple one of the richest in the district. (The collection was estimated at 50 million rupees annually.) However, the temple committee was controlled by the Jats. They decided how the money was to be spent, whether on the beautification of the shrine, or on building roads to the village, or on feasts. The Dalits had long asked, and long been denied, representation in the management committee. At last they decided to take the matter to court. In January 2003, while the case was being heard, the Jats announced a social boycott of the Dalits. The Dalits, in turn, organized a series of protest strikes. Six months later, the groups clashed violently at a village fair. The administration then intervened to work out a compromise; two Dalits were inducted into the management committee, but they had to maintain Sikh tradition by keeping their hair and beards unshorn.[23]

V

Nowhere were the Dalits as oppressed as in the state of Bihar; nowhere were they better organized to resist; nowhere were caste conflicts so frequent, so bitter, and so bloody.

Historically, the agrarian system of eastern India had been grossly feudal. In neighbouring West Bengal similar inequalities had been attenuated by land reforms, but in Bihar they persisted down into the present. The middle and upper castes owned the land, and the Dalits tilled it. From the 1970s, however, Maoist radicals had taken up the Dalits' cause. Although they had more or less disappeared from West Bengal, where their movement had begun a decade previously, these Naxalites had steadily gathered strength in the districts of central Bihar. They formed agricultural labour fronts that demanded higher wages, shorter hours, and an end to social coercion (which, in some areas, included the right of the landlord to a low-caste bride on her wedding night). They also demanded a share of village common land, and access to natural resources such as freshwater fish, theoretically owned by the community as a whole, but usually the preserve of the upper castes alone.[24]

Mobilization by left-wing radicals had instilled a great deal of self-respect among the lowliest in central Bihar. Travelling through the state in 1999, the journalist Mukul noticed a new confidence among the Dalits. Visitors were treated as social equals and were met with the salutation *Namaskar, bhaijee* ("Greetings, brother"). Departing from the past, the Dalits "do not fold their hands. They do not bend their body. They do not call anybody 'huzur,' 'sahib,' 'sir,' or anything like this. This newfound word [*bhaijee*], is heard repeated all over the region in village after village and haunts the heart."[25]

The anthropologist Bela Bhatia writes that "this sense of dignity is one of the principal achievements of the Naxalite movement." Other achievements included an end to forced labour and a significant increase in the wage rate. Normally paid in kind, this had doubled; besides, the quality of the grain was much better than before. Once made to work twelve hours non-stop, labourers were now allowed regular breaks. And, for the first time in recorded or unrecorded history, women were paid the same as (and treated the same as) men.

The long-term aim of these radicals, however, was the overthrow of the Indian state. Open, hidden, legal, and illegal activities were carried on side by side: processions and strikes on the one hand, the collection of weapons and attacks on their enemies on the other. The Naxalites had their own Lal Sena (Red Army), whose members were trained in the use of rifles, grenades, and landmines. They also had their *safaya* (clean-up) squads, whose marksmen were trained to assassinate particularly oppressive landlords.[26]

In response, the ruling elite had formed *senas* of its own. Each of the landowning castes maintained a private army. The Bhumihars had a Ranbir Sena, the Kurmis a Bhoomi Sena, the Rajputs a Kunwar Sena, the Yadavs a Lorik Sena. The history of Bihar from about 1980 to the present is marked by gruesome massacres perpetuated by one caste or class against another. Sometimes, a Bhumihar or Yadav *sena* would round up and burn a group of Dalits. At other times, the Naxalites would raid an upper-caste hamlet and shoot its inhabitants. According to one list (which is certainly incomplete), in 1996 and 1997 there were thirteen such incidents, in which more than 150 individuals died.[27] Behind this violence lay a savage and sometimes almost incomprehensible hatred. *Mera itihaas mazdooron ki chita par likhi hogi*, claimed one Bhumihar landlord—"My biography will be written around the funeral pyres of [Dalit] labourers." *Aath ka badla assi se lenge!* shouted the Naxalites—"If you kill eight of ours we will kill eighty in revenge."[28]

By the mid-1990s, in much of Bihar the state had no visible presence at all. As one upper-caste gunman told a visiting journalist, "The police are hijras [hermaphrodites]. They should wear bangles and saris. . . . If a murder took place in front of their eyes anywhere hereabouts, they wouldn't have the guts to file a F[irst] I[nformation] R[eport]. There is no government or police. Just us Ranvirs and the M-Lvadis [i.e., Naxalites]."[29]

The growing power of the Naxalites in Bihar was spectacularly underlined by an attack on the town of Jehanabad in November 2005. Hundreds of armed gunmen stormed the town, rained down bombs on government offices, and attacked the jail. They freed 200 inmates, mostly of their own party, among them their area commander. The operation was made easier by the fact that a large part of the district police force was away on election duty. Still, the act underlined the fragility of the legally constituted state in Bihar. Jehanabad is only sixty kilometres from the provincial capital, Patna.[30]

VI

The Naxalites were also active among the Scheduled Tribes (or Adivasis), the other group recognized by the Indian constitution as historically disadvantaged. The Adivasis lived in the areas of India that were richest in resources—with the best forests, the most valuable minerals, and the freest-flowing rivers. Over the years, they had lost many of these resources to the state or to outsiders, and struggled hard to keep what remained.

A particular target of tribal ire was the Forest Department, which restricted their access to wood and to non-timber forest produce such as honey and herbs, which they collected and sold for a living. In the state of Madhya Pradesh, the trade in tendu leaves (used for making bidis, or cheroots) was particularly lucrative. The government had handed over the trade to private contractors, but the actual collection was done by the tribals. The rates were niggardly: thirty rupees for 5,000 leaves. In the early 1990s, the tribals demanded higher rates; when this demand was denied, they stopped traffic on major highways in the state.[31]

Various activists were working in Adivasi areas: some Gandhian, others Marxist. The issues they took up included access to land and forests and the provision of decent schools and hospitals. These were, surely, the groups most neglected by the Indian state, and also the most condescended to. The colonial regime had designated an array of tribal communities as "criminal"—their crime being that they did not live in settled villages but moved around in search of a living. After independence, these tribes had been formally "denotified," but the prejudice against them remained. Officials assigned to tribal districts were known for their disdain toward those whom they were paid to serve. Once quiescent, the tribals were now, under activist influence, moved to protest; the consequence was a series of clashes with the police.[32]

The most celebrated tribal assertion in the 1990s was the Narmada Bachao Andolan (Save the Narmada Movement). Its leader, Medha Patkar, was not herself a tribal; she was a social worker raised and radicalized in Bombay. The movement aimed at stopping a massive dam on the Narmada River that would make homeless some 200,000 people, a majority of them Adivasi in origin. Patkar organized the tribals in a series of colourful marches: to the dam site in Gujarat; to the city of Bhopal (capital of Madhya Pradesh, the state to which most of the people being ousted belonged); to the national capital, Delhi, there to demand justice from the mighty government of India. The leader herself engaged in several long fasts to draw attention to the sufferings of her flock.[33]

Patkar's struggle was unsuccessful in stopping this particular dam, but it did draw wide attention to the government's disgraceful record in resettling the millions displaced by development projects. Official acknowledgement of the Adivasis' long history of suffering, meanwhile, came through the creation in 2000 of two new states of the Union: Jharkhand and Madhya Pradesh, carved out of the tribal districts of Bihar and Chattisgarh, respectively. Also formed was the state of Uttarakhand, from the hill districts of Uttar Pradesh, likewise rich in natural resources subject to exploitation by powerful external interests.

VII

From conflicts in the heartland of India we now move to conflicts in the extremities. Pre-eminent here was that old sore spot, Kashmir. After a quiet decade or two, the Valley erupted during the first months of 1989. In November of that year, Rajiv Gandhi was replaced as prime minister by V. P. Singh. Singh appointed a "mainstream" Kashmiri politician, Mufti Mohammed Sayeed, to the crucial post of home minister. This was a gesture meant to please the Muslims of India in general and the Muslims of the Valley in particular. With one of their kind in charge of law and order, surely the police would bear down on them less heavily than before.

The experiment was very soon put to the test. On 8 December 1989, a young woman doctor was kidnapped as she walked to work in Srinagar. But she was no ordinary doctor; she was Rubaiya Sayeed, the daughter of the home minister. She had been abducted by militants of the Jammu and Kashmir Liberation Front (JKLF). They demanded that, in exchange for her release, five specified JKLF activists be freed from detention. The chief minister, Farooq Abdullah, did not want to yield to the threat. He was overruled by the prime minister in Delhi. On 13 December, the jailed militants were released; a large crowd welcomed them, and marched them triumphantly through the streets of Srinagar. Among the slogans they shouted, one was especially ominous: *Jo kare khuda ka kauf, utha le Kalashnikov*—"If you wish to do God's work, go pick up a Kalashnikov." Later that day, Rubaiya Sayeed was reunited with her family.[34]

The government's capitulation was regarded as a major victory by the militants. Further kidnappings followed: of a BBC reporter, of a senior official, of another daughter of a prominent politician. There were also assassinations: those killed included the vice chancellor of Kashmir University and the head of the local television station.[35]

At this stage, circa 1989–1990, Indian intelligence reported that as many as thirty-two separatist groups were active in the Valley. Of these, two were especially important. The first was the JKLF, which stood for an independent, non-denominational state of Jammu and Kashmir, in which Hindus and Sikhs would have the same rights as Muslims. Its goal was captured in the popular cry *Hame kya chhaiye, azaadi, azaadi.*

("What do we want? Freedom! Freedom!") The second was the Hizb-ul Mujahideen, which (as its name suggests) veered more toward an Islamic regime and was not averse to a merger of the state with Pakistan. The Hizb-ul was led by Syed Salauddin, the nom de guerre of a once-democratic politician who had run in the elections of 1987 but had lost because of a blatant rigging of the votes. It was then that he turned to the gun, and to Pakistan, taking many other young men with him.[36]

Both the JKLF and Hizb-ul had collected a wide variety of arms. With these they killed soft and hard targets, looted banks, and dropped grenades in front of police stations. Their acts grew more daring; in November 1990, they even launched a rocket at the broadcasting station of All India Radio. The government now decided to take a tougher stance, moving in paramiliary forces and some army units to help maintain order. By 1990, there were 80,000 Indians in uniform in the Valley. Thus "the attempt to find a political solution was put aside in favour of a policy of repression."[37]

The situation in Kashmir is tellingly reflected in the following newspaper headlines, all from 1990:

YOUTH TO THE FORE IN SECESSION BID

BLASTS ROCK KASHMIR

KASHMIRI MILITANTS HANG POLICEMAN IN SRINAGAR

PAKISTAN BLAMED FOR REBELLION IN JAMMU AND KASHMIR

ARMY JOINS BATTLE AGAINST MILITANTS IN KASHMIR

TROOPS CALLED OUT IN ANANTNAG, CURFEW IMPOSED

SECURITY FORCES KILL 81 MILITANTS

3 DIE IN FIRING ON J&K PROCESSION

TOTAL BANDH IN KASHMIR, HEADLESS BODIES FOUND

J AND K TROUBLE CLAIMS 1,044 [LIVES] TILL SEPT[EMBER]

"PEOPLE POWER" IN SRINAGAR: CURFEW LIFTED, SHOPS SHUT

TRICOLOUR BURNT AT UN OFFICE

5 LAKH ATTEND J&K "FREEDOM" RALLY

"INDEPENDENCE ALONE CAN HEAL KASHMIR'S WOUNDS"[38]

The inhabitants of the Kashmir Valley were caught in the crossfire, although, as the last few headlines suggest, their sympathies lay more with the militants than with the security forces. Those who might have been neutral were persuaded to take sides following the murder in May 1990 of the respected cleric Mirwaiz Mohammed Farooq. A huge crowd of mourners accompanied his body to the burial ground. Somewhere, somehow—the details remain murky—they got into an altercation with a platoon of the Central Reserve Police Force (CRPF). The CRPF men, in panic, fired on the mourners, killing thirty and injuring at least 300 others. The Mirwaiz's assassins were apparently in the pay of Pakistan; but by the day's end the propaganda war had been decisively lost by India.[39]

The alienation of the Kashmiris was deepened by the behaviour of those sent, apparently, to protect them. Indian soldiers, particularly the CRPF men, were prone to treat most civilians as sympathetic to terrorism. The actions of the CRPF were documented by Amnesty International,[40] and also by Indian human rights activists. In the spring of 1990, a team led by the respected jurist V. M. Tarkunde travelled through the Valley, talking to government officials, militants, and ordinary villagers. Many cases of "excesses" committed by the police and army were reported: beatings (sometimes of children), torture (of men innocent of any crime), extrajudicial (or "encounter") killings, and the violation of women. "It is not possible to list all the cases which were brought to our notice," commented Tarkunde's team:

> But the broad pattern is clear. The militants stage stray incidents and the security forces retaliate. In this process large numbers of innocent people get manhandled, beaten up, molested and killed. In some cases the victims were caught in cross-fire and in many more cases they were totally uninvolved and there was no crossfiring. This tends to alienate people further. The Muslims allege that they are being killed and destroyed because they are Muslims.[41]

VIII

In 1990, as in 1950, radicals in Kashmir were giving politicians in Delhi a severe headache. So too, and perhaps predictably, were radicals in the north-east.

There was good news from the largest state in the region, Assam, where an accord had been reached with the Bodos, allowing for an "autonmous council" to be formed in those districts where the Bodos were a majority.[42] The bad news was that the secessionist United Liberation Front of Assam (ULFA) was very active. Some parts of the state were securely under the control of the official administration; in other parts it was the writ of ULFA that ran. Practically every tea garden paid the rebels an annual sum, based on the numbers of workers the estate employed, and on its profitability. To further augment their coffers the insurgents mounted raids on banks. Army units were sent in to restore order; they captured and killed some top ULFA cadres, while others crossed over the border into Bangladesh.[43]

The 1990s were also a turbulent decade for the state of Tripura. Armed groups fighting for tribal rights regularly attacked settlements of immigrant Bengalis. Here, too, insurgency was sometimes hard to distinguish from sheer criminality. As one researcher wrote in 2001, "innocent deaths, kidnappings and extortions are a regular part of life in Tripura and have been for many years now." Nearly 2,000 killings were reported between 1993 and 2000—of security men, insurgents, and, most of all, civilians.[44]

The gun was also ubiqitous in Manipur, another tiny state that had once been an independent chiefdom. The violence was chiefly a product of ethnic rivalries. The majority Meities, who lived in the valley, clashed with the tribals in the uplands. In the hills also there were divisions, principally between the Thangkul Nagas and the Kukis. In May 1992 Naga militants burned Kuki villages, starting a deadly cycle of massacres and counter-massacres. While fighting among themselves, these groups were all opposed to the Indian state. Some Kukis, and more Thangkuls and Meities, dreamed of forming independent nations of their own.[45]

In several towns in the region, separatists had banned the showing of Hindi films, that hugely popular conduit of the culture of the subcontinent. This was part of a defiant definition of themselves as "not-Indian." In this negative identification, ULFA, the Tripura National Volunteers, the Kuki National Army, and the Meitei rebels all took inspiration from the Nagas, creators of the mother of insurgencies in the north-east. In 1962 one Naga faction had made its peace with the government of India, as did another faction in 1975. But there remained a group stubbornly committed to the idea of an independent, sovereign Nagaland. This was the National Socialist Council of Nagaland (NSCN), led by Isak Swu and T. Muivah.

The NSCN had a solid core of several thousand well-trained fighters. They operated from bases in Burma, making raids across the border and engaging the Indian army. Within Nagaland the rebels commanded support, respect, and perhaps also fear. At any rate, they were sustained by collections made from the public. Even government officials paid a monthly "tax" to the underground. This was a curious if typically Indian paradox—the subsidizing by the state of a group committed to its destruction.

In the mid-1990s, however, a collective of church groups and civil society organizations called the Naga HoHo persuaded the rebels and the government to declare a ceasefire. In 1997 the guns fell silent, and the two sides began to talk. At first the conversations were held in Bangkok and Amsterdam, but eventually Muivah and Swu agreed to visit India. They met the prime minister and travelled to the north-east, but failed to reach an agreement. There were two stumbling blocks: the rebels' insistence that a settlement had to be outside the framework of the Indian constitution; and their demand that parts of Manipur, Assam, and Arunachal Pradesh, where Naga tribes lived, be merged with the existing state of Nagaland into a "Greater Nagalim."

As of November 2007, the ceasefire had held for nine years. Yet a mutually satisfactory solution remained, if not out of reach, at least out of sight. The government of India says it will give the Nagas the fullest possible autonomy, but within the Indian constitution. The NSCN insists that any solution must acknowledge Naga sovereignty, for—it claims— "Nagaland was never a part of India either by conquest by India or by consent of the Nagas."[46] It also asks for the retention of a separate Naga army; anything less would be a betrayal of the memory of those who died for the cause. In Phizo's native village, there is a stone memorial with the inscription: "These men and women of Khonoma gave their lives for the vision of a Free Naga Nation. We remember them and still hold fast to their vision."[47]

The calls for a Greater Nagalim have been resisted by states that would have to cede territory to this new entity. The Meities of Manipur have militantly opposed the proposal, claiming that their state had existed as an independent and integrated territory for over 1,000 years. In the summer of 2001, Meitei radicals torched government buildings and attacked police posts in protest against talks with the Nagas. Posters were pasted on the walls of homes and offices, proclaiming, "Do not break Manipur/No compromise on our territory."[48]

The north-east is a region of violence and conflict, and hence also of migration. Some of the migration is across national borders, as in the continuing immigration from Bangladesh. Other people move within the region—some in search of jobs, some fleeing ethnic persecution. There are also a growing number of "environmental refugees." In the 1960s, a high dam in the Chittagong Hill Tracts of East Pakistan displaced some 60,000 Chakmas. Since they were second-class citizens anyway (as Buddhists in a state dominated by Muslims), they sought refuge in the Indian state of Arunachal Pradesh, where they live on, still second-class, denied passports by the Indian government. Meanwhile, a series of dams being built in Arunachal and Nagaland will render up to 100,000 villagers homeless. These too will have to move elsewhere, in search of an essential resource that is very scarce everywhere in South Asia: cultivable land.[49]

There is a massive military presence in the north-east. The states of the region variously border China, with which India has fought a costly war; Bangladesh, with which India has a profoundly ambivalent relationship; and Burma. But it is not merely for external security that the Indian army has so many men here. They are also needed to maintain the flow of essential goods and services; protect road and rail links; and, not least, suppress rebellion and insurgency. "We have no say vis-à-vis the army," says a long-serving chief minister in Manipur: "They have their own way of working, they will not tell us or listen to us, although they are supposed to be aiding the civil administration."[50]

In the north-east, the army operates under the Armed Forces Special Powers Act (APSPA), which allows its officers and soldiers immunity from prosecution by civil courts, unless specifically permitted by the central government. Since the act also grants permission to "fire upon or otherwise use force even to the extent of causing death" to anyone suspected of breaching the law, it has encouraged aggressive behaviour.

For many years now, human rights groups have asked for the repeal of the APSPA. In the lead are the women of Manipur, long active in opposing male violence of all kinds. The state has dozens of local groups called Meira Paibis, "women torch-bearers." These campaigned successfully against alcoholism, before turning their attention to the excesses of the security forces. The Meira Paibis have demanded that troops leave schools and marketplaces, that they stop picking up young boys at will, and that they open up their prisons and detention centres to public scrutiny.[51]

These demands were renewed in July 2004, when a Manipuri housewife was picked up from her home on the charge of abetting terrorism. She was tortured, raped, and killed, and her body left to rot by the roadside. The incident set off a wave of angry protests in the Manipur Valley. A group of women marched to the army base in Imphal, where they took off their clothes and covered themselves with a white banner carrying the legend "Indian Army, Take Our Flesh." A student leader set himself on fire on Independence Day, leaving a note that read, "It is better to self-immolate than die at the hands of security forces under this Act. With this conviction I am marching ahead of the people as a human torch." A girl student went on an indefinite fast; taken away to a hospital, she still refused to eat. Several years later she lay in her bed, force-fed by the state because she said she would rather die than live under a regime run by the military.[52]

IX

In May 2000, the population of India reached 1 billion. The government chose Aastha Arora, a girl born in Delhi, as the official "billionth baby." Her arrival drew an excited mob of press and television cameramen, who clambered onto beds and tables to get a better shot. "The billionth baby," noted one reporter, "was greeted by a zillion flashlights and doctors say her skin could have been affected."[53]

The choice of Aastha was politically correct, since the United Nations had recently observed the Year of the Girl Child. Yet it was flagrantly at odds with how girls—born or unborn—were treated in many parts of India, not least the countryside around Delhi. Through the twentieth century the sex ratio had been steadily falling: from 972 females to 1,000 males in the year 1901, it had dropped to 947 in 1951 and 927 in 1991. Child mortality was highly variable by gender. In most Indian homes, boys were treated better than girls—boys were given more nutritious food, had better access to health care, and were sent to school while their sisters laboured in field and forest. From the 1980s, advances in medical technology had worked to make more lethal an already deadly prejudice. The new sex determination tests allowed parents to abort female fetuses. Although banned by law, these tests were widely available in clinics throughout India.

By the turn of the twenty-first century, demographers were releasing chilling data. For 1981–2001, and the age group birth to six years, the number of females per 1,000 males had fallen from 992 to 964 in Andhra Pradesh, 974 to 949 in Karnataka, 967 to 939 in Tamil Nadu, and 970 to 963 in Kerala. The changes were even more dramatic in northern India. In Haryana, the ratio had fallen from 902 to 820 between 1981 and 2001. In Punjab, the decline had been even greater, from 908 to 793.[54]

The falling sex ratio in Haryana and Punjab had led to a "crisis of masculinity." According to the traditional rules of marriage, one's spouse had to be from one's caste and linguistic group, though not usually from one's village. As boys grew into men, an increasing number found that brides were simply unavailable in their locality. So they contracted unions with girls from hundreds of miles away, belonging to other states, castes, and linguistic groups. Through the 1990s and beyond, women from the states of Assam, Bihar, and West Bengal were being sought—and, occasionally, bought—by men from Haryana and Punjab. These cross-region liaisons were sometimes informal but at other times legalized through the rites of marriage. Questions remained about how the offspring of these highly unusual unions would be treated by a society still bound, in most other respects, by the ties of caste and kinship.[55]

The variations in gender relations were spatial as well as cultural.[56] Indian women were treated better (or less badly) in the south and in the cities. In the urban context, they were somewhat more free to go to school, take a job, and choose a life partner. There was a rising class of women professionals, making their mark—sometimes a considerable mark—in the law courts, in hospitals, in the universities. There were also successful women entrepreneurs, running advertising agencies and pharmaceutical companies.

There was also a vigorous feminist movement. This was based in the cities and was led by writers and activists, who produced a steady stream of high-quality essays and books on the lives and struggles of women in modern India.[57] After years of lobbying politicians, these feminists were able to bring about a change in the law that would principally benefit their less fortunate rural-based sisters. This was an amendment to the Hindu Succession Act of 1956, which, for the first time, brought agricultural land under its purview, allowing women the same inheritance rights here as men. Another amendment made female heirs equal to males with regard to Hindu joint families (in which sons had previously had claim to a greater share than daughters). The economist Bina Agarwal, whose own work on gender and agriculture had been a critical influence, said of these changes that "symbolically, this has been a major step in making [Hindu] women equal in the eyes of the law in every way."[58] Sadly, social practice remained another matter.

X

A teacher of mine used to say, "India is a land of grievance collectors." The characterization is incomplete, for Indians do not merely collect grievances; they also articulate them. In the 1990s, as before, a variety of rights were being asserted by a variety of Indians, and in a variety of ways. However, as before, while some conflicts were being expressed in more intense and violent forms, other conflicts were being attenuated and even, at times, resolved.

There was, for instance, the return of peace to the state of Mizoram. The leaders of the Mizo National Front (MNF) had made a spectacularly successful transition; once insurgents in the jungle, they were now politicians in the secretariat, put there by the ballot box. Peace had brought its own dividend in the form of water pipelines, roads, and, above all, schools. By 1999 Mizoram had overtaken Kerala as India's most literate state. Integration with the mainland was proceeding apace. Mizos were learning the national language, Hindi: and watching and playing the national game, cricket. And since they also spoke fluent English (the state's own official language), young Mizos, men as well as women, found profitable employment in the growing service sector, particularly in hotels and airlines. Mizoram's chief minister, Zoramthanga, was speaking of making his territory the "Switzerland of the East." In his vision, tourists would come from Europe and the Indian mainland, and the economy would be further boosted by trade with neighbouring Burma and Bangladesh. The Mizos would supply these countries with fruit and vegetables, and buy fish and chicken in exchange. Zoramthanga was also canvassing for a larger role in bringing about a settlement between the government of India and the Naga and Assamese rebels. It was easy to forget that this visionary had once been a radical separatist, seeking independence from India and serving as the "defence minister" and "vice president" of the "Mizo Government-in-Exile."[59]

The troubles had also been resolved, more or less, in the state of Punjab. Here the process had been more tortuous. In 1987 President's Rule was imposed on the state, and repeatedly extended for six months at a time. Without elected politicians to report to, the police energetically chased the militants, by means fair and foul. Gun battles were common, quite often around police stations but also in the countryside. In 1990 the army was called in to help; a year later it was withdrawn. In 1992 elections to the state assembly were at last held. The Akali Dal boycotted the polls, and the elected Congress chief minister, Beant Singh, was killed by a suicide bomber not long after he took office.

In 1993, however, the Akalis returned to democratic politics by taking part in elections to local village councils. Four years later they won an emphatic victory in the voting for the assembly. By this time militancy was perceptibly on the wane. Some terrorists had become extortionists, squeezing money from Sikh professionals and from ordinary peasants. The popular mood had turned away from the idea of a separate state of

Khalistan. Sikhs once more saw the advantages of being part of India. Agricultural growth had slowed down, but trade was flourishing, and the state's languishing industrial sector was being primed for revival.[60]

A sign of normality was that the Akalis, now in power, were fighting among themselves; individuals and factions were vying for control of particularly prestigious or profitable ministries. The chief minister, Prakash Singh Badal, sought to transcend these squabbles by celebrating the three-hundredth anniversary of the proclamation by the tenth guru, Gobind Singh, of the Khalsa, or Sikh brotherhood.[61] His government alloted 3 billion rupees for the festivities, and the Centre granted a further 1 billion rupees. New memorials to Sikh heroes were built, along with new sports stadiums, shrines, and guest houses. At the great gurdwara of Anandpur Sahib, Sikh intellectuals and writers were honoured, in a colourful ceremony attended by the chief minister and by the prime minister as well. One of those felicitated, the novelist and journalist Khushwant Singh, noted with satisfaction that this once "alienated community" had "regain[ed] its self-esteem and resume[d] its leading role in nation-building."[62] The costs, however, had been heavy. By one reckoning, more than 20,000 lives were lost in the Punjab between 1981 and 1993— 1,714 policemen; 7,946 terrorists; and 11,690 civilians.[63]

In February 2005 I visited Punjab for the first time in three decades. At the time, the prime minister of India was a Sikh; so was the chief of army staff and the deputy chairman of the Planning Commission. That Sikhs commanded some of the most important jobs in the nation was widely hailed as a sign of Punjab's successful reconciliation with India. Travelling through the state myself, I could not tell that the insurgency had ever happened, or that the troubles had lasted so long. A spate of fresh investments suggested that things were now very stable. There were signs everywhere of new schools, colleges, and factories. There was even a spanking new "heritage village" on the highway, where one could eat "traditional" Punjabi food to the sound of Punjabi "folk" music.

I drove the entire breadth of the state, from the town of Patiala to the city of Amritsar. My last stop, naturally, was the Golden Temple. The temple was as tranquil as a place of worship should be; spotlessly clean, with orderly lines of pilgrims whose eyes shone with devotion, and music wafting in from the great golden dome in the middle.

Only when I entered the Museum of Sikh History, located above the main entrance to the temple, was I reminded that this was, within living memory, a place where much blood had been shed. The several rooms of the museum run chronologically, the paintings depicting the sacrifices of the Sikhs through the ages. Many martyrs are commemorated on its walls, the last of these being Shaheeds Satwant, Beant, and Kehar Singh. Below them lies a picture of the Akal Takht in tatters, with the explanation that this was the result of a "calculated move" by Indira Gandhi. The text notes the deaths of innocent pilgrims in the army action, and then adds, "However, the Sikhs soon had their revenge." What form this took is shown not in words but in pictures: those of Satwant, Beant, and Kehar.

To see the killers of Indira Gandhi ennobled was unnerving. However, down below, in the temple proper, there were numerous contrary indications, to the effect that the Sikhs were now thoroughly at ease with the government of India. A marble slab was paid for by a Hindu colonel, in grateful memory of the protection granted to him and his men while they were serving in the holy city of Amritsar. Another slab was more meaningful still; this had been been endowed by a Sikh colonel, on the "successful completion" of two years of service in the Kashmir Valley.

27

RIOTS

The language of the mob was only the language of public opinion cleansed of hypocrisy and restraint.

HANNAH ARENDT

I

IN OCTOBER 1952, the chief of the Rashtriya Swayamsevak Sangh (RSS), M. S. Golwalkar, wrote a rare signed article in the English-language press. "Cut from its moorings, regeneration of a nation is not possible," he insisted. It was, therefore,

> necessary to revive the fundamental values and ideas, and to wipe out all signs that reminded us of our past slavery and humiliation. It is our first necessity to see ourselves in pristine purity. Our present and future has to be well united with our glorious past. The broken chain has got to be re-linked. That alone will fire the youth of free India with a new spirit of service and devotion to our people. There cannot be a higher call of national unity than to be readily prepared to sacrifice our all for the honour and glory of the motherland that is the highest form of patriotism.

How could one give shape and meaning to this very general ideal? What specific issue would charge the youth to sacrifice all? "Such a point of honour in our national life," Golwalkar believed,

> is none else but MOTHER COW, the living symbol of the Mother Earth—that deserves to be the sole object of devotion and worship. To stop forthwith any onslaught on this particular point of our national honour, and to foster the spirit of devotion to the motherland, [a] ban on cow-slaughter should find topmost priority in our programme of national renaissance in Swaraj.[1]

In the opinion of Guru Golwalkar and his Sangh, India was a "Hindu" nation. But the Hindus themselves were divided—by caste, sect, language, and region. From the time it was founded in 1925, the mission of the RSS had been to make the Hindus a strong, cohesive fighting force. For its members, as for the organization as a whole, religious sentiment went hand in hand with political ambition. We may not doubt Golwalkar's own personal devotion to the cow. Yet his call to make cow-slaughter a national priority stemmed from a much larger goal: uniting the Hindus.

The cow was found all over India; Hindus too were found all over India; and Hindus worshipped the cow—whereas Muslims and Christians liked to butcher and eat it. That was the logic on which the RSS sought to build a nationwide campaign. Fourteen years after Golwalkar's article, a large crowd marched on Parliament to demand a countrywide ban on cow-slaughter. That was the campaign's high point: its appeal steadily declined thereafter. Even at its zenith, its main attractions were to Hindu holy men, and to RSS workers—it never quite achieved the popular support its promoters had hoped for.

In the 1980s, however, a single holy spot in a single small town was able to accomplish what a ubiquitous holy animal could not. The campaign to build a temple where a mosque stood in Ayodhya generated a widespread appeal. Many Hindus across India, and of different castes, were beginning to see this as a "point of honour in our national life." To these people, the Babri Masjid in Ayodhya was indeed a reminder of "our past slavery and humiliation." To put a temple to Ram in its place had become the "sole object of devotion and worship" for thousands of Hindu youths. This was energy expended in a cause that Golwalkar himself had not anticipated. Were he alive, he might have been surprised, and certainly would have been pleased.

II

In 1984, the Bharatiya Janata Party (BJP), successor to the old Jana Sangh, won only two seats in the eighth general elections. Five years later its tally went up to 86. A major reason for this rise was its involvement in the campaign in Ayodhya.

Anxious to keep the Congress out of power, the BJP now supported V. P. Singh's National Front without joining the government. However, the decision to implement the Mandal Commission's report, announced in August 1990, threw the party into a tizzy. Some leaders thought this a diabolical plan to break up Hindu society. Others argued that the extension of affirmative action was a necessary bow to the aspirations of the backward castes. Within the party, and within RSS *shakhas*, the debate raged furiously—should the Mandal Commission's recommendations be endorsed or not?

Rather than take a position, the BJP chose to shift the terms of political debate away from the Mandal Commission and caste and back toward religion and the question of the disputed site of Ayodhya. The party announced a *yatra*, or march, from the ancient temple of Somnath in Gujarat to Ayodhya. The march would be led by L. K. Advani, an austere, unsmiling man reckoned to be more of a hardliner than his colleague Atal Behari Vajpayee. Advani would travel in a Toyota van fitted up to look like a *rath* (chariot), stopping to hold public meetings on the way.

Starting on 25 September 1990, Advani's *rath yatra* planned to reach Ayodhya five weeks later, after travelling 10,000 kilometres through eight states. Militants of the Vishwa Hindu Parishad flanked the van, flagging it off from one town and welcoming it at the next. At public meetings they were complemented by saffron-robed sadhus, whose "necklaces of prayer beads, long beards and ash-marked foreheads provided a strong visual counterpoint" to these armed young men. The imagery of the march was "religious, allusive, militant, masculine, and anti-Muslim." This was reinforced by the speeches made by Advani: he accused the government of "appeasing" the Muslim minority and of practising a "pseudo-secularism" that denied the legitimate interests and aspirations of the Hindu majority. The building of a temple to Ram in Ayodhya was presented as the symbolic fulfilment of these interests and aspirations.[2]

Advani's march through north-western India was a headache for V. P. Singh's government. The procession "posed a provocation that could not be ignored. Growing disorder, riots, and a final destruction of the mosque loomed ahead. Yet there would be serious consequences to stopping it. Not only would Singh have to act against [the revered god] Rama, but he would also bring down his own ruling coalition and risk serious disorder."[3] The *yatra* reached Delhi, where Advani camped for several days, daring the government to arrest him. The challenge was ducked, and the procession started up again. However, a week before it was to reach its final destination, the van was stopped and Advani was placed under preventive detention. The arrest had been ordered by the chief minister of Bihar, Lalu Prasad Yadav, through whose state the march was then passing.

While L. K. Advani cooled his heels in a government guest house in Bihar, his followers were making their way to Ayodhya. Thousands of *kar sevaks* (volunteers) were converging from all parts of the country. The chief minister of Uttar Pradesh, Mulayam Singh Yadav, was—like his Bihari namesake—a bitter political opponent of the BJP. He ordered the mass arrest of the visitors from out of state. Apparently, as many as 150,000 *kar sevaks* were detained, but almost 75,000 still found their way to Ayodhya. There, 20,000 security personnel were already in the temple town: some regular police, others from the paramilitary Border Security Force (BSF).

On the morning of 30 October, the police intercepted a large crowd of *kar sevaks* at a bridge on the Sarayu River, which divided Ayodhya's old town from the new town. The volunteers pushed their way past the police and surged toward the Babri Masjid, where they were met by BSF contingents. Some *kar sevaks* managed to dodge the BSF, too, and reach the mosque. One planted a saffron flag on the mosque; others attacked the structure with axes and hammers. To stop a mass invasion the BSF *jawans* used tear gas and, later, live bullets. The *kar sevaks* were chased through narrow streets and into temple courtyards. Some of them resisted, with sticks and stones—and they were supported by angry residents, who rained down improvised missiles on the police.[4]

The battle between the security forces and the volunteers raged for three whole days. At least twenty *kar sevaks* died in the fighting. Their bodies were later picked up by Vishwa Hindu Parishad (VHP) activists and cremated, and the ashes were stored in urns. The urns were then taken around the towns of northern India, inflaming passions wherever they went. Hindus were urged to take revenge for the blood of these "martyrs." The state of Uttar Pradesh was rocked by a succession of religious riots. Hindu mobs attacked Muslim localities, and—in a manner reminiscent of the grisly massacres during partition—stopped trains to pull out and kill those who were recognizably Muslim. In some places the victims retaliated, whereupon they were set upon by the Provincial Armed Constabulary (PAC), long notorious for its hostility toward the minority community.[5]

As one commentator put it, L. K. Advani's *rath yatra* had, in effect, become a *raktyatra*, a journey of blood.[6]

III

Among the casualties of the *rath yatra* was Prime Minister V. P. Singh. In November 1990 he resigned, unable to sustain his minority government without the support of the BJP. As in 1979—when Morarji Desai resigned—the Congress allowed a lame duck prime minister (in this case, Chandra Shekhar) to take charge while it prepared for midterm elections. These elections were held in the summer of 1991. In the middle of the campaign Rajiv Gandhi was assassinated, while speaking in a town in Tamil Nadu. The assassin, who was also blown up by the bomb she was carrying, was later revealed to have been a representative of the Liberation Tigers of Tamil Eelam (LTTE). The killing was an act of vengeance: the LTTE had not forgiven Rajiv Gandhi for sending troops against them in 1987.

Notwithstanding the murder of Rajiv Gandhi, the elections went ahead on schedule. Pollsters had predicted a hung Parliament, with no party anywhere near a majority. However, the sympathy generated by the assassination allowed the Congress to win 244 seats. With support from independents, it was in a position to form a majority government. P. V. Narasimha Rao, a congressman from Andhra Pradesh who had held important positions in Rajiv Gandhi's cabinet, was sworn in as prime minister.

In these parliamentary elections of 1991, the BJP won 120 seats, thirty-five more than in the last election. Meanwhile, it also won the elections for the assembly in Uttar Pradesh. It was now in power in four states in northern India, Madhya Pradesh, Rajasthan, and Himachal Pradesh being the others. Clearly, the Ram campaign was paying political dividends. Riots were being effectively translated into votes. At the same time, these successes had led to a crisis of identity. Was the BJP a political party, or was it a social movement? Some leaders thought the party should now put the controversy between mosque and temple on the back burner. It should instead raise broader questions of economic and foreign policy, and work also to expand its influence in south India. On the other side, the VHP and the RSS were determined to keep the spotlight on the disputed territory in Ayodhya. In October 1991, they acquired the land around the mosque, and began levelling the ground, preparing to construct the temple.

In July 1992, the central government sent a team to study the situation. The team found that there had been "large-scale demolition" on the disputed site, and a "large concrete platform" had been built, both in clear contravention of court orders asking for the status quo to be maintained. To the team's dismay, the Uttar Pradesh government, headed by the old RSS hand Kalyan Singh, had turned a blind eye to these activities. There was, in sum, "flagrant violation of the law" in Ayodhya.

Worried that the trouble would escalate, the Home Ministry in New Delhi had prepared a contingency plan, allowing for the imposition of President's Rule in Uttar Pradesh and a takeover of the mosque-temple complex by the central government. However, the prime minister, Narasimha Rao, still hoped the matter could be resolved by dialogue. He had several meetings with VHP leaders, and also consulted with the opposing Babri Masjid Action Committee. The possibility of having the matter referred to the Supreme Court was also discussed.[7]

Meanwhile, the VHP announced that 6 December had been chosen as the "auspicious" day when work on the temple would commence. From the middle of November, volunteers began streaming into Ayodhya, encouraged by the fact that the state government was now in the hands of the BJP. The chief minister, Kalyan Singh, was summoned to New Delhi. The prime minister, P. V. Narasimha Rao, urged him to allow the Supreme Court to decide on the case. Singh answered that "the only comprehensive solution to the Ayodhya dispute was to hand over the disputed structure to the Hindus."[8]

Kalyan Singh had instructed his government to house and feed the thousands of volunteers coming from outside the state. Reports of this large-scale influx alarmed the Home Ministry. It prepared a new contingency plan, under which paramilitary forces would be sent to Ayodhya. By the end of the month, some 20,000 troops had been stationed at locations within an hour's march of the town, ready to move in when required. This, claimed the home secretary at the time, "was the largest mobilisation of such forces for such an operation since Independence."[9]

On the other side, more than 100,000 *kar sevaks* had reached the temple town "complete with *trishuls* [tridents] and bows and arrows." On the last day of November, during a press conference in Delhi at which he announced his own departure for Ayodhya, L. K. Advani said, "I cannot give any guarantee at the moment on what will happen on 6 December. All I know is that we are going to perform *kar seva*."[10]

On the morning of 6 December, a journalist at the site found that "straddling the security wall [around the mosque] were PAC constables armed with batons and RSS volunteers with armbands." The central government forces stationed around Ayodhya had not been asked to move into the town. The job was left to the Uttar Pradesh police and its constabulary. The VHP had planned to begin prayers at 11:30 a.m., on the raised platform constructed beforehand. However, by this time some *kar sevaks* had begun making menacing moves toward the mosque. The RSS workers and police constables tried to stop them, but were met instead by a hail of stones thrown by the crowd, which was getting more charged by the minute. *Mandir yahin banayenge*, they shouted, pointing at the Babri Masjid—"We will build our temple at that very spot." An intrepid youngster scaled the railing ringing the mosque and climbed on top of one of its domes. This was the signal for a mass surge toward the monument. The police fled, allowing hundreds of *kar sevaks* to charge the mosque, waving axes and iron rods.

By noon, volunteers were crawling all over the masjid, holding saffron flags and shouting slogans of victory. Hooks attached to ropes were anchored to the domes, while the base was battered with hammers and axes. At 2 p.m., one dome collapsed, bringing a dozen men down with it. *Ek dhakka aur do, Babri Masjid tor do!* screamed the radical preacher Sadhvi Ritambara ("Shove some more, and the whole thing will collapse"). At 3:30, a second dome also gave way. An hour later, the third and final dome was also demolished. A building that had seen many rulers and dynasties come and go, that had withstood the furies of 400 or more monsoons, had in a single afternoon been reduced to rubble.[11]

Was the demolition of the Babri Masjid planned beforehand? Or was it simply the result of a spontaneous display of popular emotion and anger? To be sure, some BJP leaders were taken aback by the turn of events. Despite his threatening talk the week before, when he saw volunteers rushing the monument, L. K. Advani asked them to return. As the domes came crashing down, he got into an argument with the senior RSS functionaries H. V. Seshadri and K. S. Sudarshan. They thought that now the deed was done, the RSS and the BJP should claim credit for it. "The course of history is not pre-determined," Sudarshan said to Advani. "Accept what has happened." Advani answered that he would instead "publicly express regret for it."[12]

In press conferences after the event, the term most often used by BJP's spokesmen to describe the happenings at Ayodhya was "unfortunate." They knew that in a democracy ostensibly bound by the rule of law, an act of vandalism by the main opposition party could scarcely be condoned. When he met the press at the party's headquarters in Delhi on the evening of 6 December, the ideologue K. R. Malkani "made it clear that we did want the old structure to go, but that we wanted it gone through due process of law. The regret was that it had been demolished in an irregular manner." Seeking to distance the BJP from the act, he claimed that the *kar sevaks* who attacked the mosque were most likely from the Shiv Sena, since they had been heard speaking in Marathi.[13]

The radicals within the movement were less coy. One VHP leader boasted that, as early as September, engineers had been asked to identify the structure's weak spot, and volunteers had been trained on how best to bring it down. "Without this planning how do you think we razed the masjid in six hours?" he said to a reporter. "Do you think a group of frenzied kar sevaks could have gone about it so systematically?"[14] And in a speech in Madras soon after the demolition, the polemicist Arun Shourie noted that "while the BJP leaders tried to disown and distance themselves from what had happened, the Hindus of India appropriated the destruction; they owned it up." The events at Ayodhya, said Shourie, demonstrated "that the Hindus have now realised that they are in very large numbers, that their sentiment is shared by those who man the apparatus of the state, and that they can bend the state to their will." His own hope was that "the Ayodhya movement has to be seen as the starting point of a cultural awareness and understanding that would ultimately result in a complete restructuring of the Indian public life in ways that would be in consonance with Indian civilisational heritage"— a somewhat roundabout way of saying that the demolition of the Babri Masjid should, and perhaps would, be a prelude to the reshaping of India as a Hindu state.[15]

One cannot be certain that all Hindus shared these sentiments, as Shourie assumed they did. But those Hindus who brought down the mosque on 6 December had certainly bent the Indian state to their will. The forces to stop them were at hand, yet the order telling these forces to act never came. Worried that it would be charged with being anti-Hindu, the government of Prime Minister Narasimha Rao "came to perceive the lesser evil in the demolition of the mosque." Only after the deed was done was action taken—in the shape of the dismissal of the Uttar Pradesh government and the imposition of President's Rule.[16]

IV

When the domes of the Babri Masjid fell, they brought those atop them down too. More than fifty *kar sevaks* were injured, some very seriously. At least six deaths were reported. The aftermath of the event was more deadly still. The main leaders of the BJP, such as L. K. Advani, were taken into protective custody; yet riots broke out in town after town, in an orgy of violence that lasted two months and claimed more than 2,000 lives.

The trouble began in the vicinity itself. An influential local priest had expressed the desire that Ayodhya should become the "Vatican of the Hindus." To cleanse the town of the minorities was one step toward that larger goal. *Kar sevaks* celebrated the felling of the mosque by setting fire to Muslim homes and neighbourhoods. In other towns, riots were a consequence of processions organized by the Vishwa Hindu Parishad. Elsewhere, it was Muslims who came out into the streets to protest the demolition, by attacking police stations and attempting to burn government buildings.

Sometimes started by triumphant Hindus, at other times by defiant Muslims, the riots covered large parts of northern and western India; 246 died in Gujarat, 120 in Madhya Pradesh, 100 in Assam, 201 in Uttar Pradesh, sixty in Karnataka. The weapons used by the mobs ranged from acid and slingshots to swords and guns. Children were burned alive; women were shot dead by the police. In this epidemic of violence, "every possible refinement in human unkindness . . . [was] on display."[17]

The city worst hit was India's commercial capital, Bombay. On the morning of 7 December, in a Muslim neighbourhood, Muhammad Ali Road, there was an outpouring of collective anger in which Hindu shops were raided and BJP leaders were burned in effigy. A temple was also razed to the ground. When constables arrived on the scene, the crowd was undaunted. "Police in Ayodhya just stood by and let the mosque be demolished," the people shouted: "We're going to get you now." Through that day and the next, mobs battled police in the area. At least sixty people died in the violence.

Meanwhile, to the north of the city, the shanty town of Dharavi was suffering from an excess of Hindu triumphalism. A "victory rally" organized by the BJP and Shiv Sena ended in attacks on Muslim homes and shops. In retaliation, Muslims stabbed a priest and set his temple on fire. In other places, anger was vented not on the rival community but on the state. Dozens of government buses were trashed or burned, as were at least 130 bus shelters.[18]

On 9 December, the Shiv Sena and the BJP announced a citywide strike to protest the arrest of their leaders in Ayodhya. This, recalled a journalist in Bombay, "was a signal for their followers to go on the rampage. They attacked mosques and Muslim establishments. In one locality, the Shiv Sena put up a notice announcing an award of Rs 50,000 to anyone pointing out a Muslim house."[19]

The Shiv Sainiks were encouraged on by their leader and mentor, Balasaheb Thackeray. In an editorial in the party newspaper, *Saamna*, published on 10 December, Thackeray insisted that the violence of the past few days was merely

> the beginning of an era of retaliatory war. In this era, the history and geography of not only this country but the entire world is going to change. The dream of the Akhand Hindu Rashtra [United Hindu State] is going to come true. Even the shadow of fanatical sinners [i. e., Muslims] will disappear from our soil. We will now live happily and die happily. . . . No revolution is possible by shedding tears. Revolution needs only one offering, and that is the blood of devotees![20]

A curfew was imposed, and the army was called in. It still took ten days for the city to get back to normal, for the commuter trains to be up and running, for offices and factories to be working as before. For three weeks the peace held, but then at the beginning of January another riot broke out. On the morning of 5 January, two Hindu dock workers were stabbed to death in a Muslim neighbourhood. The cause was not clear— it might have been a union rivalry—but the story that Hindus were killed in a Muslim area spread through the city, provoking more violence. In Dharavi, angry Hindus looted shops and warehouses owned by Muslims. In another slum area, Jogeshwari, a Hindu family were burned to death. For a week the fires raged, till Bal Thackeray announced in an editorial in *Saamna* that the attacks could stop, "since the fanatics had been taught a lesson." It was, indeed, the minorities who had borne the brunt of the violence. Of the nearly 800 people who died in the riots, at least two-thirds were Muslim, although Muslims were only 15% of the city's population.

Once more the city limped back to normal. This time the peace held for two months. On 12 March 1993, a sequence of bombs went off in south Bombay: one outside the stock exchange, others in front of or inside luxury hotels and corporate offices. The intention was to cause the maximum damage, for the explosions occurred in the early afternoon, the busiest time in the richest part of the city. More than 300 people died in the blasts. The material used to blow them up was the powerful explosive RDX. The operations had been directed by two Mafia dons based in Dubai, in apparent revenge for the killings of their co-religionists earlier in the season.

The rise of the Shiv Sena had, over the years, somewhat dented Bombay's reputation as a cosmopolitan, multicultural city. That image was dealt a body blow by the riots and bomb blasts of 1992–1993. This was now a "permanently altered city," a "deeply divided city," even a "city at war with itself."[21]

The demolition of the Babri Masjid was depressing enough, but, as the columnist Behram Contractor wrote, "the bigger tragedy, perhaps, is not that India is no longer a secular country, but that Bombay is no longer a cosmopolitan city. Whatever happens henceforth, whether the Ram Janmabhoomi issue is resolved, whether Hindus and Muslims relearn to live together, Bombay's reputation as a free-living and high-swinging city, absorbing people from all communities and all parts of India, is gone for ever."[22]

V

In 1994, the VHP leader Ashok Singhal remarked that the destruction of the Babri Masjid was "a catalyst for the ideological polarization which is nearly complete."[23] Two years later, the Bharatiya Janata party reaped the rewards in the eleventh general elections. It won 161 seats, emerging as the largest single party in Parliament. The Congress was relegated to second place, twenty-one seats behind. The BJP leader Atal Behari Vajpayee was invited to form the government, but after two weeks he resigned, failing to put together a majority. For the next two years the BJP sat in the opposition, while the country was governed by a motley coalition of regional parties calling itself the National Front. When a midterm election was held in 1998, the BJP improved its position further, winning 182 seats. This time, the support of smaller parties and independents gave it the numbers to govern. However, within a year it called another election, hoping to do better still. As it happened, the BJP won the same number of seats (182), but the Congress hit an all-time low of 114 seats. A strong performance by its allies allowed the BJP to govern for a further five years. Thus, the BJP's Atal Behari Vajpayee became the country's longest-serving non-Congress prime minister, remaining in office for six years all together.

In the first years of Indian independence, the wounds of partition had provided an excuse for a vigorous assertion by the Hindu right. The

RSS was particularly active. But when the Jana Sangh won only three seats in the elections of 1952, commentators were ready to write an epitaph for a party that, in a modern, secular, democratic state, dared to base its politics on religion. The socialist politician Asoka Mehta wrote that Hindu communalism "has proved to be weak twice, once in [the elections of] 1946 and again in 1951–2." He was confident that "its ghost is now laid for good."[24] "The Hindu is too tolerant," remarked the writer-couple Taya and Maurice Zinkin. The election results had shown that "Hindu communalism has been utterly defeated," indeed, that "communalism has thus failed, probably finally."[25]

Other observers, the Kashmiri leader Sheikh Abdullah among them, thought that it was mostly Jawaharlal Nehru who kept the Indian state and Indian politics on a secular path. They worried about what would happen after he was gone. After Nehru's death the Jana Sangh slowly gained in influence. It won twenty-five seats in the Lok Sabha in 1967 and twenty-two in 1971, more or less holding its own despite the "Indira wave" of 1971. Later, its participation in the JP movement, its leaders' incarceration during the emergency, and its role in the Janata government raised its profile and its presence. Then it fell away again. Under a new name—the Bharatiya Janata party—it won two seats in the elections of 1984. Even Atal Behari Vajpayee, who had been a member of Parliament since 1957, failed to win re-election. Once more, obituaries were written for politics based on religion. Once more, it was claimed that the Hindu would not tolerate bigotry among his kind. "The most striking feature of Indian politics is its persistent centrism," wrote two American political scientists. Apart from the natural Indian tendency toward moderation, the BJP also had to contend with the fragmentation of the electorate along lines of caste and region—hence the conclusion that "the support base for a national confessional party, [representing] the Hindu majority, is illusionary."[26]

The events of the 1990s confounded these predictions. The big story of this decade was in fact the rise of Hindu communalism, as manifested most significantly in the number of seats won by the BJP in successive general elections. Beyond the formal theatre of party politics, there was also a transformation occurring on the ground. In towns and villages across northern India, relations between Hindus and Muslims were being redefined. Once, members of the two communities had lived next to one another, traded with one another, even befriended and played with one another. True, they also competed and came into conflict. Each community thought itself theologically superior; each had memories—real or imagined—of being scorned or victimized by the other. However, the compulsions of living together meant that these divisions were deflected or subsumed by activities conducted in common. But with the riots sparked by the Ayodhya movement, ambivalence had been replaced by unambiguous animosity. Hostility and suspicion were now the governing— some would say sole—idiom of Hindu-Muslim relations.[27]

Smaller in numbers, and generally poorer in economic terms, the Muslims had more to lose from a souring of relations. In most riots, more Muslims than Hindus died, and more Muslim than Hindu homes were burned. The whole Muslim community had become prey to deep insecurity. The taunts of Hindu chauvinists that Muslims should move to Pakistan made them feel vulnerable and victimized. The sentiments of the ordinary Indian Muslim, circa 1995, were movingly expressed by the Telugu poet Khadar Mohiuddin. On the one hand, he wrote, the Muslim is told by the Hindus to think that

> My religion is a conspiracy
> My prayer meetings are a conspiracy
> My lying quiet is a conspiracy
> My attempt to wake up is a conspiracy
> My desire to have friends is a conspiracy
> My ignorance, my backwardness, a conspiracy.

On the other hand, said Khadar:

> It's no conspiracy
> [for the Hindu] to make me a refugee
> in the very country of my birth
>
> It's no conspiracy
> to poison the air I breath
> and the space I live in
>
> It's certainly no conspiracy
> to cut me to pieces
> and then imagine an uncut Bharat.

The Muslim was being continually asked to prove his loyalty to India. As Khadar Mohiuddin found, "cricket matches weigh and measure my patriotism." When India played against Pakistan, it was demanded of Muslims that they display the national flag outside their homes, and that they loudly and publicly cheer for the national side. In the poet's words: "Never mind my love for my motherland/What's important is how much I hate the other land."[28]

The polarization of the two communities was a victory for the Sangh Parivar, the collective name by which the family of organizations built around the RSS and the BJP is known. Through the first five decades of Indian independence, the ideology of the Sangh Parivar had remained pretty much constant. To my knowledge, the best summation of this ideology appears in D. R. Goyal's authoritative history of the RSS. In Goyal's rendition, the core beliefs of what the Sangh Parivar calls "Hindutva" are as follows:

> Hindus have lived in India since times immemorial; Hindus are the nation because all culture, civilisation and life is contributed by them alone; non-Hindus are invaders or guests and cannot be treated as equal unless they adopt Hindu traditions, culture, etc.; the non-Hindus, particularly Muslims and Christians, have been enemies of everything Hindu and are, therefore, to be treated as threats; the freedom and progress of this country is the freedom and progress of Hindus; the history of India is the history of the struggle of the Hindus for protection and preservation of their religion and culture against the onslaught of these aliens; the threat continues because the power is in the hands of those who do not believe in this nation as a Hindu Nation; those who talk of national unity as the unity of all those who live in this country are motivated by the selfish desire of cornering minority votes and are therefore traitors; the unity and consolidation of the Hindus is the dire need of the hour because the Hindu people are surrounded on all sides by enemies; the Hindus must develop the capacity for massive retaliation and offense is the best defence; lack of unity is the root cause of all the troubles of the Hindus and the Sangh is born with the divine mission to bring about that unity.[29]

Goyal adds that "without fear of contradiction it can be stated that nothing more than this has been said in the RSS shakhas during the past 74 years of its existence."

Although its ideology was unchanged, in time the organization of the RSS grew enormously in strength and influence. Once an all-male body, it opened a separate women's wing, which schoolgirls and housewives were encouraged to join. Once limited to northern India, it set up active branches in states where it previously had no presence at all. Everywhere, the core ideology of the Sangh was adapted to the local context. Thus in Gujarat the rebuilding of the ancient Somnath temple was celebrated as a manifestation of a united and assertive Hinduism. In Orissa, the focus was on the great Jagannatha temple, used by the RSS to build bridges between the local and pan-Indian Hindu identities. There was a particular emphasis on work in tribal areas, on "reclaiming" the Adivasis and "returning" them to the Hindu fold. Schools were opened where tribal boys were taught Sanskrit and acquainted with Hindu myths and legends. The RSS worked hard in times of natural calamity, bringing grain when the rains failed and rebuilding homes after an earthquake.[30]

As its organization grew, the RSS's ideology found even fuller expression through a new campaign strategy. M. S. Golwalkar had thought that cow-slaughter was the issue on which the Sangh Parivar would begin a countrywide struggle. That failed, but then the egregious mistakes of the Congress delivered an even more emotional issue into their lap. When Rajiv Gandhi's government appeased Muslim fanatics and overturned the Supreme Court verdict in the Shah Bano case, the Hindu radicals could claim, more convincingly than ever, that (*pace* D. R. Goyal's words above) the present rulers were "motivated by the selfish desire of cornering minority votes," that to counter this "the unity and consolidation of the Hindus is the dire need of the hour." That "non-Hindus are invaders or guests" was also proved by the stubborn reluctance of Muslims to hand over the Babri Masjid. The monument itself was a standing insult to Hindu pride, a nasty reminder of the slavery of past times, which had not yet been fully overcome. That they were not allowed to construct a shrine to their beloved Lord Ram was only because "the Hindu people are surrounded on all sides by enemies": enemies within, such as the politicians who appeased Muslims; and enemies without, such as the malevolent Muslim nation (Pakistan), which had fought three wars against them. To build the Ram temple, but also to protect themselves more generally, the Hindus had to "develop the capacity for massive retaliation," to realize that "offence is the best defence."

To the phrases already quoted from D. R. Goyal's summation, let us now add the critical last line: "lack of unity is the root cause of all the troubles of the Hindus and the Sangh is born with the divine mission to bring about that unity."

In the Ram movement, the RSS's mission was furthered by its sister organizations, particularly the Vishwa Hindu Parishad, which had taken up the issue in the first place. Then there was the Bajrang Dal, named after Ram's great monkey devotee Hanuman (who was also called Bajrang Bali). This was composed of angry youths, equipped not so much to "protect" their idol (as Hanuman is supposed to have done) as to beat up anyone who stood in their way. Finally, there was the Shiv Sena, actually another party altogether, whose ideas and methods were even more extreme than those of the VHP and the Bajrang Dal. The members of Shiv Sena were prone to calling Muslims "poisonous snakes" and "traitors" and advising them to move to Pakistan.[31]

By the 1980s, the RSS could no longer be called a male or north Indian body; it had reached out to women and to other parts of the country. However, only through the Ram movement did it throw off the label of being a "Brahman-Bania" organization, led and dominated by the elite, traditionally literate Hindu castes. For the first sixty years of its existence it had been guided by a Maharashtrian Brahman—first K. B. Hedgewar, then M. S. Golwalkar, finally Balasaheb Deoras. Then in March 1994 a non-Brahman from Uttar Pradesh, Rajendra Singh, was appointed head of the organization. This was not only a bow to the debate over the Mandal Commission, but also an acknowledgement of the major role played by the backward castes in the Ayodhya movement. The members of the Shiv Sena and the VHP were mostly drawn from the middle castes, and there were a fair number of Dalits as well.

Through this broadening of the base—in terms of region, gender, and above all caste—was created what might justly be called the "mother of all vote banks." In the early days of the Ayodhya controversy, 1985–1986, VHP leaders were apt to refer to the issue as one which affected the "sentiments of sixty crore [600 million] Hindus." As time went on, and the issue remained unresolved, demographic change caused a natural inflation in numbers: "sixty crore" became "seventy crore," even "eighty crore." This was of course a conceit. The VHP and the RSS did not speak for the majority of Hindus. But apparently, they spoke for enough Hindus to allow their political front, the BJP, to emerge as the largest single party in the Indian Parliament.

In the 1990s, the BJP came to define the political agenda in a way the Congress once did in the 1950s and 1960s. Thus a property dispute in a small north Indian town took on overwhelming importance in the life of the nation. And thus political discourse in general came to be obsessed with questions of religious identity rather than economic development or social reform. Losing its hold on the government, winning ever fewer seats in Parliament, the Congress was now merely reacting to debates initiated by the BJP. In desperation, it called upon Rajiv Gandhi's widow, Sonia, then living in seclusion with her family in Delhi, to head the party. After she took charge as the president of Congress in 1998, Sonia Gandhi worked overtime to dispel the image of her party as "anti-Hindu." She regularly visited temples, and even went so far as to participate in the great Kumbh Mela, a congregation held every twelve years in which tens of millions of Hindus take a dip in the Ganges at Allahabad.[32]

While the dispute at Ayodhya remained its focus, the Sangh Parivar also took up other campaigns in the 1990s. More sites were identified where, it was alleged, Muslims had usurped a Hindu shrine—in Mathura, in Banaras, in the Madhya Pradesh town of Dhar, in the Baba Budan hills of Karnataka's Chikmagalur district. Movements were initiated, with varying success, to "reclaim" these places from the "intruders." Simultaneously, there were atacks on Christian missionaries, particularly those working in tribal areas. Churches were burned and priests were beaten up in both Gujarat and Madhya Pradesh. An Australian missionary was burned alive in Orissa, along with his two sons; the arsonist was later identified as a member of the Bajrang Dal named Dara Singh.[33] Hindus were a considerable majority in India, yet the RSS insisted that their pre-eminence was threatened on the one hand by Christian proselytization and on the other by the larger family size of Muslims, attributed to the practice of polygamy.[34]

These campaigns occurred in different parts of India, sometimes led by the RSS, at other times initiated by the VHP or the Shiv Sena, but there was nonetheless an underlying pattern to them. In every case, a religious minority—Muslim or Christian—was targeted, and accused of having hurt Hindu sentiment or of being in the pay of a foreign power. The demonizing of the other was a necessary prelude to mobilizing one's own forces, and thus to fostering a collective spirit of solidarity in a long-divided Hindu community. Usually, there was much malice aforethought. Sometimes, however, the issue taken up was farcical rather than diabolical. In the summer of 2000, for example, the RSS journal, *Panchjanya*, complained that the three leading male actors in the Hindi film industry (Shah Rukh Khan, Aamir Khan, and Salman Khan) were all Muslim. The journal saw in this coincidence a dark conspiracy by (apparently) Mafia dons who funded these actors' films and multinational corporations whose products the actors endorsed. To thwart the conspiracy, *Panchjanya* called on its readers to promote an up-and-coming actor named Hrithik Roshan, the lone "Hindu" challenger to the monopoly of the Khans.[35]

VI

As a rule, the Muslims in India were poorer than the Hindus, and less educated. There were a few Muslim entrepreneurs, but there was no real Muslim middle class. Muslims continued to be under-represented in the professions and in government service. Forty per cent of Muslims in cities lived below the poverty line; the situation in the countryside was not much better. The literacy rate for Muslims was well below the national average, and the gap between them and the other communities was growing. Few Muslim girls were sent to school, and Muslim boys were often placed in madrasas whose archaic curricula did not equip them for jobs in the modern economy. Meanwhile, the taunts of the Sangh Parivar had inculcated a defensive mentality, almost a siege mentality, among the Muslim intelligentsia. The young men, especially, sought succour in religion, seeing in a renewed commitment to Islam an alternative to poverty and persecution in the world outside. Nor was this turn to faith always quietist. A Students Islamic Movement of India had arisen, whose leaders argued that threats from the rival religion could be met only through force of arms.[36]

The rise of Hindu fundamentalism in the 1990s put an already vulnerable minority even more on the defensive. In the border state of Jammu and Kashmir, however, the roles were reversed. Here, the Muslim majority was increasingly expressing its aspirations in religious terms, with the Hindu minority suffering as a consequence.

The popular revolt that broke out in the Valley in 1989 was at first led by the Jammu and Kashmir Liberation Front (JKLF). Within a year, however, the JKLF had ceded ground to the Hizb-ul Mujahideen, whose own commitment to a multi-religious Kashmir was much less certain. The cry of *azaadi* (freedom) was being replaced by that of jihad (holy war). A popular slogan of the Hizb-ul was *Na guerrilla jang, na qaumi jang: al jihad, al jihad.* ("This is neither a guerrilla war nor a national liberation struggle; this is jihad, jihad.")[37]

One consequence of this turn to religion was that the community of Kashmiri Pandits became suspect in the eyes of the militants. They were Hindus, but in other respects akin to their Muslim brethren: speaking the same language, eating the same kind of food, partaking of the same syncretic culture of the Valley. In the past, there had been economic rivalry between Hindus and Muslims. Sheikh Abdullah, for example, had resented and then brought to an end Pandit control of cultivable land and of the state administration. But the social harmony was more or less complete. Even in the partition riots of 1947 Kashmir was untouched, an oasis of peace lauded by Mahatma Gandhi himself.

In the winter of 1989–1990, as the Hizb-ul supplanted the JKLF, the Pandits became a target of attack. Because they were Hindus, and for no other reason, they were seen as agents of a state that had long oppressed the Kashmiris. Several hundred Pandits were killed during 1989–1990, in ways that made the ones who survived deeply insecure. A reporter who documented these murders later wrote:

> These women and men were not killed in the cross-fire, accidentally, but were systematically and brutally targeted. Many of the women were gang-raped before they were killed. One woman was bisected by a mill saw. The bodies of the men bore marks of torture. Death by strangulation, hanging, amputations, the gouging out of eyes, were not uncommon. Often their bodies were dumped with notes forbidding anyone—on pain of death—to touch them.[38]

In panic, Pandit families began leaving the Valley for the Hindu-majority Jammu region. Others fled further afield, to Delhi and even to Bombay.

There were an estimated 200,000 Pandits living in the Kashmir Valley. By the summer of 1990, at least half had left. They lived in refugee camps, some run by the government, others by the RSS. At first, the state's hope, and their own, was that the migration was temporary, and that once peace returned they would return to the Valley. But as it happened they stayed on and on.[39]

Through the 1990s, there were further attacks on Pandits who had chosen to remain. Sometimes entire hamlets were set on fire. By the end of the decade, less than 4,000 Pandits were left in the Valley, a melancholy reminder of the centuries in which they had lived side by side with their compatriots.[40]

The growing militancy in Kashmir was actively aided by Pakistan. The Pakistani Inter-Services Intelligence (ISI) ran camps where terrorists were trained in the use of arms and provided with maps of the region. With the ISI's help, Kashmiri activists moved freely across the border, into India to kill or bomb, then back to Pakistan for rest and replenishment. By now, indigenous militants had been joined by foreign mercenaries—Arabs, Chechnyans, Uzbeks—who had cut their teeth in the war against

the Soviet puppet regime in Afghanisthan. When that war ended and
Russian troops had returned, defeated, to their homeland, these fighters
found another holy cause in the liberation of Kashmir.

By the mid-1990s, the Hizb-ul had been joined by many hundreds of *mehmani* mujahideen (guest freedom fighters). These owed
allegiance to different groups, all of which had headquarters in Pakistan, and all of which practised the austere, fundamentalist version of
Islam taught in that country's many religious schools. Through the
1980s, the Islamicization of Pakistani society had proceeded apace.
At its birth, in 1947, Pakistan had only 136 madrasas; by 2000 it had
30,000. These madrasas, writes Tariq Ali, were "indoctrination nurs-
eries designed to produce fanatics." Pakistan now boasted of as many
as fifty-eight Islamic political parties and twenty-four armed religious militias, whose members were mostly products of the madrasa
system.[41]

The intensification of religious sentiment in Pakistan deepened its
commitment to the "liberation" of Kashmir. Preachers in mosques and
madrasas spoke repeatedly of Indian *zulm* (terror) in the Kashmir Valley, urging their followers to join the jihad there. Youths so swayed entered groups like the Lashkar-i-Toiba, which was rapidly assuming a
leading role in the armed struggle. The proximate aim was the uniting
of Kashmir with the Pakistani nation; this was "a religious duty binding
not only on the people of Pakistan, but, in fact, on the entire Muslim
ummat [brotherhood]." A wider ambition was to catalyze a civil war in
India. As the chief of the Lashkar, Hafiz Mohammed Saeed, boasted,
they were aiming to "set up a mujahideen network across India," which,
when it was running, would spell "the start of the disintegration of India."[42] "Revenge is our religious duty," said Saeed to an American journalist. "We beat the Russian superpower in Afghanisthan; we can beat
the Indian forces too. We fight with the help of Allah, and once we start
jehad, no force can withstand us." Speaking to a Pakistani reporter, the
Lashkar chief claimed that "our struggle will continue even if Kashmir
is liberated. We still have to take revenge [against India] for [the loss of]
East Pakistan."[43]

This animosity and hatred were perhaps not unexpected. For the jihadis, India was the land of the Kafirs, or unbelievers. But as it happened
their wrath was being visited on some co-religionists as well. There were
killings of activists from the National Conference, which wanted autonomy within India; of the JKLF, which wanted independence rather than
merger with Pakistan; and of the People's Conference, which advocated

non-violence.[44] The fundamentalists also came down hard on the pleasures of the people. Movie theatres and video arcades were closed, and drinking and smoking were banned. Militant groups distributed leaflets ordering women to cover themselves from head to toe by wearing the long black veil, or burka. The burka was contrary to Kashmiri custom—here many women did not even wear head scarves. Besides, burkas cost 2,000 rupees apiece. Cynics suggested that tailors and cloth merchants were behind the move. There were, nonetheless, savage attempts to enforce the ban, and acid was thrown on women who disregarded it.[45]

The main target of the fundamentalists' ire, however, was the Indian state and its symbols. Scarcely a week passed without a suicide attack on an army post or police camp. To stop or stem these attacks, even more troops were moved into the Valley. There were now bunkers on every street corner in Srinagar. The Indian army had become "an imposing and ubiquitous presence" in Kashmir, even a "parallel government." It was expected not merely to maintain law and order, but also to run hospitals, airports, bus stations, and tourist centres. The state government had abdicated most of its duties. By about 1995, there were only two functioning institutions in Kashmir—the Indian army on the one side and the network of jihadi groups on the other.[46]

As the Valley came to resemble a zone of occupation, popular sentiment rallied to the jihadi cause. Terrorists mingled easily with the locals, and were given refuge before or after their actions. When their men were killed in bomb attacks, the reprisals of the Indian security forces could be murderous. Soldiers dropped in unannounced in remote villages, searching for terrorists—when they did not find any, they beat up the peasants instead. A large number of custodial deaths were also reported.

The costs of this apparently unending war were colossal. According to government figures, between January 1990 and August 2001 some 12,000 civilians died unnatural deaths—three-fourths at the hands of militants, the rest in the crossfire. Security forces claimed to have killed 13,400 militants, while losing 3,100 of their own. Given the low population densities, this number of deaths in Kashmir was the equivalent of 4 million Indians being killed in the country as a whole.[47] The casualties were spread all across this lovely if increasingly desolate valley. However, they were mostly young men, Kashmiris who came of age in this cursed decade. The journalist Muzamil Jaleel, who almost became a militant himself, later visited a graveyard near his native village. Twenty-one tombstones were those of his friends and classmates.[48]

As James Buchan has written, in the years since 1990,

> the Kashmiri Muslims and the Indian government conspired to abol-
> ish the complexities of Kashmiri civilization. The world [it] inhabited
> has vanished: the state government and the political class, the rule of
> law, almost all the . . . Hindu inhabitants of the valley, alcohol, cine-
> mas, cricket matches, picnics by moonlight in the saffron fields,
> schools, universities, an independent press, tourists and . . . banks. In
> this reduction of civilian reality, the sights of Kashmir . . . are rede-
> fined: not the . . . lakes and Mogul gardens . . . or the storied triumphs
> of Kashmiri agriculture, handicrafts and cookery, but two entities
> that confront each other without intermediary: the mosque and the
> army camp.[49]

Through the 1990s, as Hindu fundamentalism gathered strength in
the rest of India, Islamic fundamentalism was on the ascendant in Kashmir. The two processes began independently, yet each legitimized and
furthered the other. With every communal riot provoked by the Ayodhya movement, radicals in the Valley could more easily portray India as
a state run for and by Hindus. With every killing of innocent civilians or
Indian soldiers in the Valley, the RSS could point to the hand of Pakistan in fomenting trouble within India. There were two critical events
that, as it were, defined this epoch of competitive fundamentalisms: the
destruction of the Babri Masjid and the exodus of the Kashmiri Pandits.
Would one trust a state that could not honour its commitment to protect
an ancient place of worship? Would one trust a community that so brutally expelled those of a different faith? Such questions resonated across
the subcontinent, asked by countless Indians not previously known to
think along lines of religion and faith.

VII

After the Babri Masjid came down, Hindu radicals hoped to build a
grand temple in its place. Architects were commissioned to design an
edifice in marble, and craftsmen engaged to cut the stone and polish it.
However, the site itself remained in the custody of the state. Cases
were being heard in the Allahabad high court and the Supreme Court,
to decide whether a Ram temple had ever existed here, and whether
the VHP had (as it claimed) the legal rights to the land surrounding the
old mosque. Attempts were also made to find a solution outside the

courts. The influential Shankaracharya of Kanchi met with the Babri Masjid Action Committee, and urged them to hand over this one site, in exchange for which no further demands would be made on the Muslims.

The BJP remained committed to the construction of a temple in Ayodhya. When it came to power in 1998, it said it would seek a national consensus on the issue, failing which it would enact enabling legislation. The prime minister, Atal Behari Vajpayee, said, "Rama occupies an exalted place in Indian culture," and claimed that "the entire country wants a Rama temple at Ayodhya," the issue being "how to make it and where."[50]

However, at the site itself the status quo prevailed. The courts took their time disposing of the matter, and no compromise could be reached outside them. Meanwhile, the Vishwa Hindu Parishad organized tours of Ayodhya for *kar sevaks* from all over the country. It also held religious ceremonies in anticipation of the building of the temple. One such *yagna*, held in the last week of February 2002, was attended by hundreds of volunteers from the state of Gujarat. On their way back home by train, these *kar sevaks* got into a fight with Muslim vendors at the Godhra railroad station. The vendors were asked to chant slogans in homage to Lord Ram; when they refused, their beards were pulled. Word of the altercation spread; young men from the Muslim neighbourhood outside the station joined in. The *kar sevaks* clambered back into the train, which started moving even as stones were being thrown. However, the train stopped on the outskirts of the station, when a fire broke out in one of its coaches. Fifty-eight people perished in the conflagration.

Godhra was a town with a long history of communal violence; it had experienced serious riots in 1949, and again in 1981. That Hindus and Muslims had not always been on the best of terms, and that the problem in Ayodhya had strained relations further, is clear. It is also beyond dispute that the incident at the station was started by *kar sevaks* taunting Muslim vendors. What remains unclear is the cause of the fire afterwards. The VHP claimed that it was the work of a Muslim mob. On the other hand, forensic evidence suggests that it originated inside the train, probably when a gas cylinder or kerosene stove accidentally caught fire.[51]

Word that a group of *kar sevaks* had been burned to death at Godhra quickly spread through Gujarat. A wave of retributory violence followed. This was at its most intense, and horrific, in the cities of Ahmedabad and Baroda. Once known for their philanthropic industrialists and progressive intellectuals, once centres of technical innovation and artistic excellence, both places had experienced a prolonged period of economic decline. With this came a deterioration in inter-community relations. Hindus and Muslims now rarely worked or played together, a separation that had in the recent past expressed itself in bouts of communal violence.[52]

These latest riots in Baroda and Ahmedabad were unprecedented in their savagery. Muslim shops and offices were attacked, mosques torched, and cars vandalized. Muslim women were raped. Muslim men were killed, and bonfires were made of their bodies. The mobs were often led by activists of the VHP, with the local administration in collusion. Their weapons included swords, guns, gasoline bombs, and gas cylinders. The vandals had lists of voters that allowed them to identify which homes were Muslim and which were not. Ministers of the state government were camped in police control rooms, directing operations. The police had been instructed to give "free run of the roads to VHP and Bajrang Dal mobs."[53]

Beyond Baroda and Ahmedabad, the violence also reached smaller towns and rural settlements. In the district of Sabarkantha, mobs roamed the countryside in tractors and jeeps, targeting properties owned by Muslims. The numerical record of their activities is available: "2161 houses, 1461 shops, 304 smaller enterprises, . . . 71 factories, 38 hotels, 45 religious places, and 240 vehicles were completely or partially destroyed."[54] What was true of Sabarkantha was broadly true of the state as a whole. The VHP had made clear its desire to render the Muslims hopeless as well as homeless. Thus in Ahmedabad, weeks after the riots had subsided Muslims still found it difficult to get loans from banks, gas and phone connections, and admission to school for their children. Muslims who had fled their villages were told they would have to drop charges against the rioters if they wished to return. Sometimes their safety was made conditional on their conversion to Hinduism.[55]

The chief minister of Gujarat at the time of the riots of 2002 was Narendra Modi, a Hindutva hardliner who had grown up in the unforgiving school of the RSS. Now, he justified the violence against Muslims by citing the burning of the coach in Godhra, which, he said, had set in motion a "chain of action and reaction." In truth, the reaction was many times greater than the original action. More than 2,000 Muslims were killed, and at least 100,000 were made homeless and were living in refugee camps in pitiable conditions that were noticed by the prime minister and the president themselves.[56]

The Oxford English Dictionary defines "pogrom" as "an organized massacre of a particular ethnic group." By this definition, although there have been hundreds of religious riots in independent India, there have been only two pogroms: that directed against the Sikhs in Delhi in 1984, and that directed against the Muslims of south Gujarat in 2002. There are some striking similarities between the two. Both began as a response to a single, stray act of violence committed by, as it were, members of the minority community. Both proceeded to take a generalized revenge on the minorities as a whole. The Sikhs who were butchered were in no way connected to the Sikhs who killed Mrs. Gandhi. The Muslims who were killed by Hindu mobs were completely innocent of the crime at Godhra.

In both cases, the pogroms were made possible by a wilful breakdown of the rule of law. The prime minister in Delhi in 1984 and the chief minister in Gujarat in 2002 issued graceless statements that in effect justified the killings. And serving ministers in their government went so far as to aid and direct the rioters.

The final similarity is the most telling, as well as perhaps the most depressing. Both parties, and leaders, reaped electoral rewards from the violence they had legitimized and overseen. Rajiv Gandhi's party won the general elections of 1984 by a very large margin. And in December 2002, Narenda Modi was re-elected as chief minister of Gujarat after his party won a two-thirds majority in the elections for the assembly.

                                VIII

The rise of the Hindu right in general and the events at Ayodhya in particular were followed by a wave of gloomy forebodings about the future of India. "The secular fabric of the country has been seriously damaged," wrote *Frontline*, a periodical in Madras, adding, "India will never be the same again." For the "events of December 6 and 7 gave India a taste of what things would be [like] if and when the *Hindutva* combine's *Hindu Rashtra* [Hindu state] comes into existence. It became clear . . . [that] the minority communities would have no right to live, not to speak of social interaction; that freedom of expression would be non-existent; and that truth would be only what the rulers perceive." "In the week that followed [6 December 1992], India changed, perhaps forever," commented *Sunday*, a weekly in Calcutta. With the breakdown of authority and the rule of law, "in the eyes of the world, India moved one step closer to being perceived as a tinpot African 'republic.'" The "forces let loose by the vandalism at Ayodhya," lamented *India Today*, a magazine in New Delhi, "have begun not just to take a ghastly toll of human lives, but also to reduce to rubble the edifice of our hopes and aspirations as a people and as a nation."[57]

These worries were shared by the western press. "Like the three domes that crowned the 464-year-old Babri mosque," wrote *Time* magazine, "the three pillars of the Indian state—democracy, secularism and the rule of law—are now at risk from the fury of religious nationalism."[58] The day after the mosque came down, The *Times* of London carried a story with the headline "Militants Bury Hope of Harmony in Rubble of Indian Mosque." The next day's issue quoted the views of the Labour politician Jack Straw, then on a visit to Bombay. Straw thought that there was a real danger that India would slide "into the abyss of sectarianism." The same issue carried a leading article by the Irish intellectual Conor Cruise O'Brien, who confidently proclaimed, "India's history as a secular state appears to be coming to an end." O'Brien now expected a mass flight of Muslims into Pakistan, and the emigration of educated Hindus to Europe and North America.[59]

These were the immediate, so to say knee-jerk, responses of excitable journalists and professional cynics. (O'Brien had previously predicted that the fall of the Berlin Wall would lead to the revival of a cult of Hitler and of a party based on Nazi ideals.) But writers trained to take the long view also echoed these fears. A British author who had written many affectionate books about the subcontinent remarked that "all who care about that country must tremble for the future of its secular democracy."[60] And an American scholar, Paul Brass, who had spent a lifetime studying India, went so far as to compare the Sangh Parivar to the Nazis: "It is past time to note that Indian politics and society display many of the symptoms of a murderous pre-fascist stage which has already produced a multiplicity of localized *Kristallnachts* in numerous urban sites." The "spread of violence, lawlessness and disorder at the local level," Brass thought, might prompt the central government (then controlled by the Congress) into "another venture into authoritarian practices." And so the "Indian state may yet disintegrate in this clash between secular opportunists and chauvinist nationalists equally tied to the pursuit of illusions and chimeras, 'symbols and shadows' of national unity and greatness pursued by all the tyrannical regimes of the twentieth century."[61]

As of November 2007, these dire predictions had not come to pass. In theory, if less assuredly in practice, India remains a secular state. The rule of law is not what it might be, but the writ of the central government still runs over most of India. India has not (yet) become either a tinpot dictatorship of the African kind or a fascist dictatorship modelled on European examples.

Citizens waiting outside All India Radio to watch the general elections return, New Delhi, 1971. *(Press Information Bureau)*

Street graffiti in Bombay, circa 1970, mixing and matching India's two great popular passions: elections and films. *(Press Information Bureau)*

Indira Gandhi with U.S. president Richard Nixon, the foreign leader who most cordially disliked her, Washington, 1971. *(Press Information Bureau)*

Indira Gandhi's most doughty domestic opponent, the socialist and social worker Jayaprakash Narayan. *(The Hindu)*

Indira Gandhi and her favoured son, Sanjay Gandhi, circa 1975.
(Press Information Bureau)

Big Mother/Newspeak: Indira Gandhi at a conference on "democracy" held during the emergency. *(Press Information Bureau)*

RIGHT: C. N. Annadurai, the gifted orator who led India's first successful regional party, the Dravida Munnetra Kazhagam. *(The Hindu)*

The London-educated lawyer-turned-communist Jyoti Basu being sworn in
as the chief minister of West Bengal, Writers Building, Calcutta, 1977. Basu stayed in
the job for twenty-three years, and his party, the Communist Party of India (Marxist),
is in power yet. *(Ananda Bazar Patrika)*

FACING PAGE, BOTTOM:
The great film star
M. G. Ramachandran, a
follower of Annadurai,
who likewise became
chief minister of Tamil
Nadu. *(The Hindu)*

The cartoonist-turned-
demagogue Balasaheb
Thackeray, whose party,
the Shiv Sena, has been
episodically in power
in Maharashtra and
whose cadres have been
responsible for a series
of attacks on Muslims.
(The Hindu)

The austere Morarji Desai, caught with a rare smile on his face, circa 1977. A Congressman for over four decades, Desai became the first non-Congress prime minister of India in 1977, after the ending of the emergency. *(The Hindu)*

Prime Minister Indira Gandhi inspecting the guard at Delhi's Red Fort on
15 August, Independence Day. The year is 1980; her son Sanjay's recent death
seems marked on her face. *(Press Information Bureau)*

The Golden Temple in Amritsar photographed in May 1984,
shortly before the army attack. The fortifications being prepared by the Sikh
militants are clearly visible. *(The Hindu)*

Rajiv Gandhi, the third member of his family to become prime minister of India, the first to take the job not entirely willingly. *(The Hindu)*

Indian soldiers capturing a crucial vantage point during the Kargil conflict of 1999.
(Prashant Panjiar/Outlook)

Protests against the construction of a dam in Maheswar,
Madhya Pradesh, circa 2000. *(The Hindu)*

Atal Behari Vajpayee, the Hindu politician and orator, whose many decades in Opposition were finally rewarded by a full five-year term as prime minister of India. *(The Hindu)*

The Dalit politician Mayawati, celebrating her birthday as chief minister of Uttar Pradesh, with her mentor, Kanshi Ram *(to her right)*, looking on. *(The Hindu)*

Women in Manipur protesting atrocities committed by the Indian army, July 2004. *(Amrita Bazaar Patrika)*

Muslim separatists in Kashmir, circa 2000. *(Associated Press)*

A protester against caste quotas setting himself on fire, New Delhi, 1990.
(Associated Press)

Hindu radicals atop the Babri Masjid in Ayodhya, preparing to bring it down,
6 December 1992. *(The Hindu)*

Amitabh Bachchan in Manmohan Desai's 1977 film *Amar Akbar Anthony*,
a story of three brothers separated in childhood and brought up as Hindu, Muslim,
and Christian respectively. Naturally, the brothers are reunited in the end.
(Courtesy of Nasreen Munni Kabir)

The great classical singer M. S. Subbulakshmi (1916–2004), adorning the cover of a Madras magazine, which sees no need to introduce her. *(Author's collection)*

28

RULERS

I know that most Members of Parliament see the Constitution for
the first time when they take an oath on it.

PRAMOD MAHAJAN, Union minister, speaking in 2000

The current resurgence of identity politics, or the politics of caste
and community, is but an expression of the primacy of the group
over the individual. It does not augur well for liberal democracy
in India.

The sociologist ANDRÉ BÉTEILLE, writing in 2002

I

IN JULY 1958, India's leading journal of public affairs carried an
anonymous essay with the intriguing title, "After Nehru . . ." At the
time, Jawaharlal Nehru had been prime minister of India for eleven
years. He was nearly seventy, and the last representative of the old guard
within the Congress party. Vallabhbhai Patel and Maulana Azad were
dead, Govind Ballabh Pant was ailing, and Chakravarti Rajagopalachari
was sulking in retirement in Madras. The party and the nation were being willed along by the moral authority of the prime minister. There was
no obvious successor among the next generation of congressmen. What
would happen after Nehru was gone?

The essay that posed the question in July 1958 provided this answer:
"The prestige that the party will enjoy as the inheritor of the mantle of
Tilak, Gandhi and Nehru will inhibit the growth of any effective or
healthy opposition during the first few years. In later years as popular
discontent against the new generation of party bosses increases, they
will, for sheer self-preservation, be led to make increasing attempts to
capture votes by pandering to caste, communal and regional interests
and ultimately even to 'rig' elections."

In this situation, the essayist argued, the Congress party would find
it hard to resist the allure of commerce. For "in a politico-economic system of mixed economy, in which the dividing line between mercantilism

and socialism is still very obscure and control over the State machinery can give glittering prizes to the business as well as the managerial classes, the monied interests are bound to infiltrate sooner or later into the ruling cadres of the party in power."

Finally, the writer predicted that the growth of caste, communal, and regional caucuses would lead to an "increasing instability of Government first in the States and later also at the Centre." This instability, in turn, might lead to a competitive patriotism among the different parties. "For instance, the Congress Party may try to unite the nation behind it by warning of the dangers of 'balkanisation,' the Jan Sangh by playing up the fear of aggression from Pakistan, the P[raja] S[socialist] P]arty] by emphasising the competition between India and China and the Communist Party by working up popular indignation against dollar imperialism."[1]

Of all the predictions quoted in these pages, this one has best withstood the passage of time. The elections of 1967, the first after Nehru's death, produced instability at the Centre as well as in the states. There was a growth of popular sentiment along the axes of region, religion, and caste, which found expression within the ruling party and—which the writer did not anticipate—in new parties organized along sectarian lines. As politics became more competitive, the Congress under Indira Gandhi played up the fear, real or imaginary, of balkanization; the Jana Sangh played up the threats, real or imaginary, from Pakistan; and the Communists pointed to the diabolical designs (real or imaginary) of the United States. There was an increasing infusion of money into politics, and there were various attempts to rig elections.

Who was this gifted political astrologer, whose forecasts have been so largely vindicated by later events? He might have been a western political scientist, constrained to write anonymously about a controversial subject concerning another country. Or perhaps he was a civil servant working within the government of India, precluded by his job from speaking out in his own name—this possibility is suggested by his remark that "senior civil servants are hoping that they will retire before Nehru goes," so as not to work under what was likely to be a less broadminded as well as less competent successor.[2]

II

While Jawaharlal Nehru was alive, the Congress always ruled at the Centre. And of all the opposition parties, only the Communists in Kerala had wielded power in the states. Beginning with the elections of

1967, the political landscape of India became more variegated. An increasing number of state governments fell into the hands of non-Congress parties. In 1977 the first non-Congress government came to power in New Delhi. The 1980s saw Congress regain power in the Centre, but at the end of the decade it lost power again.

This growing decentralization of the political system has manifested itself in the rise of coalition governments. The Janata party that came to power in 1977 was itself a coalition of four different parties. The next non-Congress government was the National Front, which came to power in 1989. This had seven distinct components and was still a minority government. Since then no government in New Delhi has been ruled by a single party.[3]

These coalitions have been of three types. The first kind has been dominated by the Bharatiya Janata Party (BJP), successor to the old Jana Sangh. For two weeks in 1996, and then for six years between 1998 and 2004, the BJP headed coalition governments. In this National Democratic Alliance, the BJP kept the post of prime minister and the important portfolios of Home, Finance, and External Affairs, while alloting other ministries to its coalition partners, mostly regional groupings.

The BJP took to coalition politics in the well-founded belief that it could never come to power on its own. With its roots so strongly in northern India, its expansion depended heavily on alliances with other parties, each based in a particular state. With the exception of the Shiv Sena in Maharashtra, these parties did not subscribe to the Hindutva (or "Hindu-first") ideology. Thus, when forming alliances the BJP had to promise to put to one side such contentious issues as the Ram temple in Ayodhya and the abrogration of Article 370 (which gave special status to the state of Jammu and Kashmir).[4]

The second kind of coalition was initiated by the socialist remnants of the Janata experiment. These led the National Front government of 1989–1991 and the United Front government of 1996–1998. They were both minority governments, which encouraged a wider dispersal of ministerial responsibilities. While the prime minister came from the Janata Dal, important portfolios such as Home and Defence were alloted to partners in the alliance.

The third type of coalition has been dominated by the Congress party. In 1991, in the elections held after Rajiv Gandhi's assassination, the Congress won 244 seats. It was by some distance the largest single party, but still fell nearly thirty seats short of a majority. However, the support—brought about by persuasion or other means—of independents and the Jharkhand Mukti Morcha allowed it to remain in power for a full five-year term.

In the elections of 1996 the tally of the Congress fell to 140 seats. P. V. Narasimha Rao resigned as prime minister and, shortly afterwards, as party president. Now the party bosses turned to Sonia Gandhi, Rajiv's widow. Born in Italy, a Catholic by upbringing, Sonia had married into India's top political family but had no political ambitions herself. In 1981, she had been deeply resistant to the idea of her husband's entering politics. After his death ten years later, she retreated into her home and her family.[5]

Before the elections of 1998, however, Sonia Gandhi yielded to pressure from former colleagues of her husband and mother-in-law, and joined the campaign. When the party won only 141 seats, the incumbent president, Sitaram Kesri, was replaced by Rajiv's widow. A year later, midterm elections were held, in which the Congress's tally dropped further, to 114 seats. At this stage pundits were ready to write off the housewife turned politician. However, Sonia Gandhi kept her job and campaigned energetically in a series of assembly elections. Her persistence was rewarded: at one stage, although the National Democratic Alliance (NDA), led by the BJP, was in power at the Centre, as many as fifteen state governments were headed by the Congress.[6]

In early meetings held under Sonia Gandhi's leadership, the Congress had scorned the idea of entering a wider alliance. The old guard held that, in the future as in the past, they would come to power under their own steam. But reality compelled a change of orientation. Before the elections of 2004, the Congress put in place alliances with a variety of other parties. The Congress won 145 seats, but its United Progressive Alliance (UPA) won 222 in all. Since the NDA, led by the BJP, had won only 189, the UPA formed the government with the support, from outside, of the Communists. Sonia Gandhi declined the post of prime minister, which went instead to her trusted colleague Manmohan Singh. Following the NDA model, the Congress kept the Finance, Home, and Foreign ministries. However, important economic ministries such as Information Technology and Agriculture were ceded to partners in the alliance.[7]

The year 1989 marks a watershed in Indian political history. Before that date, the Congress was a mighty colossus; after that date, single-party dominance gave way to a multi-polar system. In the past, some 40% of the national vote had allowed the Congress to win some 60% of the seats in Parliament. Now, behind the fall in the number of seats won by the Congress lay a steady decline in its vote share, as Table 9 makes clear.

TABLE 9: PARTY VOTE SHARES, 1989–2004						
VOTE SHARE OF	1989	1991	1996	1998	1999	2004
Congress	39.5	36.5	28.8	25.8	28.3	26.4
BJP	11.5	20.1	20.3	25.6	23.8	22.2

Between 1989 and 2004, the vote share of the Congress declined by more than ten percentage points; over this period, the vote share of the BJP increased by roughly the same. However, in the last few elections these two major parties have garnered only 50% of the vote between them. Where does the other 50% go? The Communist parties, concentrated in West Bengal and Kerala, generally win about 8% of the vote. The backward caste and Dalit parties, strong in north India, together win about 16% of the vote. The regionalist parties, which have a marked presence in southern and eastern India, get about 11% of the vote.

The decline of the Congress has come in two phases. During the first phase, which began in Kerala in 1957 and peaked in Andhra Pradesh in 1983, the hegemony of Congress was challenged by parties based on identities of region, language, and class. During the second phase, which began in north India in 1967 and has peaked in the same region in the last decade, the Congress has lost ground to parties basing themselves on the identities of caste and religion. On the one hand, the upper castes in particular and Hindus in general have deserted the party and gravitated toward the BJP. On the other hand, the lower castes have preferred to throw their weight behind parties such as Mayawati's Bahujan Samaj party and Mulayam's Samajwadi party. Even the Muslims, traditionally among the Congress's strongest supporters, reacted against the demolition of the Babri Masjid by voting for other parties.

This fragmentation of the party system lies behind the rise of coalition governments. These coalitions are truly multi-hued: whereas the BJP-led NDA government of 1999–2004 brought together sixteen separate parties, the Congress-led UPA alliance which fought (and won) the last general elections had as many as nineteen. And because they are so variegated, these coalitions are also unstable. Between 1947 and 1989, India was ruled by ten different governments and had six different prime ministers. Between 1989 and 2004, the country was ruled by seven different governments and had six different prime ministers. In the first period, the average term of each government was more than four years and that of each prime minister was as much as six years. The corresponding figures for the second period are two years and two and a half years, respectively.[8]

The rise of coalition governments is a manifestation of the widening and deepening of democracy in India. Different regions and different groups have acquired a greater stake in the system, with parties that seek to represent them winning an increasing number of seats—usually at the expense of the Congress, which for the first two decades of independence had claimed, rather successfully, to be a party that represented no section of India in particular but all in general.

This deepening of democracy has come at a cost—a steady loss of coherence in public policy. The wide-ranging policies of economic and social development that Jawaharlal Nehru crafted in the 1950s—among them the boost to heavy industrialization, the reform of archaic personal laws, and an independent foreign policy—would not have been feasible in the fragmented and divided polity of today. Even programmes focused on specific sectors, such as the thrust to agricultural development that Lal Bahadur Shastri and Indira Gandhi provided in the 1960s, would now be difficult to bring to fruition. In the past, when portfolios were allotted to ministers their relevant experience and abilities were taken into account. Now, the distribution of ministries is dictated more by having to please partners in an alliance, who demand portfolios seen as either prestigious or profitable. And in the execution of their duties, cabinet ministers are prone to think more of the interests of their party or their state, rather than of India as a whole.

III

From parliamentary elections, let us move now to the dynamics of party politics in the states. Despite its declining fortunes, the Congress remains a genuinely national party, a force to be reckoned with in most parts of the Indian Union. In many states, there is a stable two-party system, with the Congress providing one pole and the BJP, the Communists, or a regional party the other pole. However, in the massive states of Bihar and Uttar Pradesh, the Congress has been reduced to insignificance. Here the main players are caste-based parties and the BJP.

State elections over the past two decades have been marked by a great deal of volatility. The phenomenon of "anti-incumbency," the voting out of the party in power, is very nearly ubiquitous. Thus, in the states of Himachal Pradesh, Madhya Pradesh, and Rajasthan, Congress governments alternate with BJP governments. In Andhra Pradesh the

Congress alternates with the Telugu Desam; in Kerala it alternates with the Communists. Rarely does a party have even two successive terms in office. One exception was the Rashtriya Janata Dal in Bihar, which held office more or less continuously from 1989 to 2005. More striking still has been the success of the CPM-led Left Front in West Bengal, which has been in power since 1977.

For the first two decades of Indian independence, the Congress was in power in the Centre as well as in virtually all the states. Then, from 1967 to 1989 (except for the brief Janata interregnum), the Congress ran the central government in New Delhi while sharing power with its rivals in the states. In the current period, the Congress has been out of power for long stretches at the Centre as well.

These changes have radically altered the form and functioning of Indian federalism. Now, before a general election, the smaller parties, each powerful in a single state, need to be cajoled and placated before joining an all-India coalition. Thus, "the two aspirants to be 'national parties,' the Congress and the BJP, now must behave like fast-food franchises. They sell their brand to local agents, who choose, reject, bargain or change sides on the basis of local conditions."[9] Ideology plays no part in this bargaining—it is all based on strategic calculation, on what one can extract from the national party by way of ministerships at the Centre or subsidies to one's state. Thus, the DMK and AIADMK have each been part of both Congress and BJP-led alliances, and the Telugu Desam has been with the BJP as well as the National Front.

The alliance in power in New Delhi tends to favour those state governments run by their own people. According to a World Bank study for 1972–1995, states that were ruled by parties which were also in office in Delhi received 4% to 18% more of Central funds than other states. Another study, by two Indian economists, and for a more recent period, estimated that grants were 30% higher when the same party was in power in the state as well as the Centre.[10]

Another consequence of this fragmentation is that the writ of the Centre does not run as authoritatively as it once did. When all chief ministers were of the same party as the prime minister, it was easier to make them sacrifice the interests of their states in favour of what was perceived to be the wider national interest. Now, chief ministers are less likely to do the prime minister's bidding. Once, a dispute between two states could be amicably settled after a word to the two chief ministers from Nehru or Indira Gandhi. Now, a dispute once begun becomes increasingly hard to resolve.

Illustrative here is the dispute between the states of Karnataka and Tamil Nadu over the waters of the Cauvery (or Kaveri) River. The Cauvery originates in Karnataka, flows through the state and into Tamil Nadu, and there it merges with the Indian Ocean. The lower parts of the delta have for centuries had a sophisticated irrigation network, allowing farmers to grow high-value paddy. In contrast, irrigation works in Karnataka are of recent origin; the first canals were built in the early twentieth century, and there was another spurt of canal building after the 1970s.

In 1928, the Cauvery's waters irrigated 11 million acres of farmland in what is now Karnataka, and 145 million acres in what is now Tamil Nadu. By 1971 the gap had increased; the figures then were 44 million acres in Karnataka and 253 million acres in Tamil Nadu. However, by the end of the twentieth century the figures were nearly even: 213 million acres for Karnataka and 258 million acres for Tamil Nadu. This large expansion of irrigation facilities has generated much wealth for the farmers of the Mandya and Mysore districts of Karnataka. Once dependent on a single harvest of a low-value crop (usually, millet), they can now enjoy two or even three harvests a year of high-value crops such as rice and sugar cane.

Through the 1970s and 1980s, the central government convened a series of discussions to work out a mutually acceptable distribution of the Cauvery waters. Twenty-six ministerial meetings were held between 1968 and 1990, but all failed to arrive at a consensus. Tamil Nadu feared that the frenetic canal building in the upper reaches threatened its farmers downstream. Karnataka argued that its late start should not preclude the fullest development of the waters in its territory.

In June 1990, by an order of the Supreme Court, a Cauvery Water Disputes Tribunal was established. It consisted of three presumably impartial judges. On 25 June 1991, the tribunal issued an interim order, directing Karnataka to release 205 million cubic feet of water per year to Tamil Nadu, pending final disposal of the matter. Ten days later, the Karnataka assembly passed a unanimous resolution rejecting the tribunal's order. The Karnataka government then passed its own order, which mandated its officials to "protect and preserve" the waters of the Cauvery for the state's farmers.

The matter went to the Supreme Court, which held that the Karnataka directive was ultra vires of the constitution. The central government now made the tribunal's interim order official by publishing it in the *Gazette*. The chief minister of Karnataka, S. Bangarappa, responded by declaring a bandh in the state. All schools and colleges were closed and, with the administration looking on, protesters were allowed to go on a rampage in Tamil neighbourhoods of the state capital, Bangalore. The violence continued for days, and an estimated 50,000 Tamils were forced to flee the state.

Karnataka's defiance drew angry words from the chief minister of Tamil Nadu, J. Jayalalithaa. Her administration, in turn, encouraged the targeting of Kannada homes and businesses in Tamil Nadu. All together, property worth more than 200 million rupees was destroyed.

In ordering the establishment of the Cauvery Water Disputes Tribunal, the chief justice of the Supreme Court had noted that "disputes of this nature have the potentiality of creating avoidable feelings of bitterness among the peoples of the States concerned. The longer the disputes linger, more the bitterness. The Central Government as the guardian of the interests of the people in all the States must, therefore, on all such occasions take prompt steps to set the Constitutional machinery in motion."

However, while the central government could set the machinery in motion, it no longer had the power to compel the states to accept its recommendations. Fifteen years after it was formed, the Cauvery Water Disputes Tribunal has yet to come up with a final resolution. When the monsoon is good, Karnataka has no problem releasing 205 million cubic feet to Tamil Nadu. But if the rains fail, panic sets in all around. Tamil film stars lead demonstrations and go on fasts to compel Karnataka to see "reason." In her most recent term as chief minister, Jayalalithaa went on a fast herself, surely a less than constitutional method of pressing her state's demands on the Centre. Meanwhile, peasant leaders in Karnataka warn their government that if water is released without their consent, the administration will have to face the consequences.

In bad years, between the months of June and September the question of Cauvery rarely strays off the front pages of the newspapers in Karnataka and Tamil Nadu. Protest and counter-protest are followed by the Centre's ordering Karnataka to release x cubic feet of water to save standing crops in Tamil Nadu. The chief minister of Tamil Nadu demands more than x; her counterpart in Karnataka says he can release only so much less than x. A team from the central government rushes to the Cauvery valley to supervise operations. The precise amount of water eventually released is never made public. One can, however, be certain that it is determined more by the fluid dynamics of inter-party politics than by the logic of science or the letter of the law.[11]

Meanwhile, at the other end of the country, in July 2004 the Punjab assembly passed a resolution abrogating its agreements on sharing water with other states. It would, it said, appropriate as much of the Ravi and Beas rivers as it chose before allowing them to flow on to Haryana and Rajasthan. The resolution was clearly at variance with the spirit of Indian federalism. Moreover, it was piloted by a Congress chief minister at a time when the Congress was also in power at the Centre.

The act of the Punjab assembly was possibly unethical, probably illegal, and certainly unconstitutional.[12] It might, nevertheless, come to be viewed by other states as an encouraging precedent. Water, more than oil, is the resource most crucial for India's economic development—crucial both for agriculture and for sustaining the burgeoning population of the cities. With the increasing fragmentation of the polity, and the declining capacities of the central government, more states might be tempted to take such unilateral action.

IV

In 1993, Parliament passed the Seventy-third and Seventy-fourth Amendments to the constitution. The Seventy-Third mandated the creation of local government institutions at the level of the village, *taluk* (county), and district; the Seventy-fourth did the same for towns and cities. Office holders were to be chosen by universal adult franchise. Everywhere, one-third of the seats were reserved for women, with additional reservations for Scheduled Castes and Scheduled Tribes.

Panchayati raj, or village self-governance, had been an abiding concern of Mahatma Gandhi's. However, both Jawaharlal Nehru and Indira Gandhi were hesitant to devolve power to lower levels, if for different reasons: the former because he felt it would be inimical to economic development, the latter because of a general preference for centralization. In the 1960s, Rajasthan and Maharashtra had both experimented with village and district councils. However, the first serious attempts to create village panchayats were in West Bengal, after the Left Front came to power there in 1977. The process was taken further by the Janata government in Karnataka, which between 1983 and 1987 devolved significant responsibilities to local institutions.

As prime minister between 1984 and 1989, Rajiv Gandhi sought to create an all-India system of local self-governance. His interest was in part a genuflection to the rise of local autonomy movements, which called for a wider sharing of power and authority. But it was also based on political calculation—the fact that while the Congress ruled at the Centre, state governments were dominated by parties hostile to it. *Panchayati raj* would allow New Delhi to bypass these parties and deal directly with the grass roots, allocating it a portion of the funds previously transferred to the state administration.[13]

The process initiated by Rajiv Gandhi bore fruit after his death, when the Congress regained power at the Centre. During the discussions leading up to the amendments, state governments had expressed concern about the undermining of their authority. The legislation as finally passed gave individual states the discretion to specify the functions and powers of the panchayats in their territory. The provincial acts varied widely in intent and consequence. Some states gave panchayats responsibility over all aspects of development work—irrigation, education, health, road building, etc.—and transferred funds appropriately. Other states upheld a more parsimonious view of the functions and finances of their local institutions.[14]

Through the 1980s, West Bengal had been in the forefront of *panchayati raj*; afterwards, the lead was taken by the other state with a strong communist presence, Kerala. When it came to power in 1996, the Left Democratic Front (LDF) decided to allocate 35% to 40% of plan funds for programmes designed and executed by local institutions. Across the state, panchayats were encouraged to hold meeetings, at which villagers interacted with officials and technical experts to set their own priorities. Hundreds of locality-specific plans were prepared; these tended to highlight the careful management of natural resources such as soil, water, and forests.[15]

In Kerala, as in Bengal, the promotion of *panchayati raj* is based on an unstable mixture of idealism and opportunism. On the one hand, left-wing intellectuals and activists believe that by devolving power, villagers can spend public monies on projects relevant to their needs, instead of being subject to directives from above. There is also some evidence that decentralization reduces leakages in the system, that there is less corruption, and thus that more money is actually spent on development projects. On the other hand, in the original Gandhian vision, *panchayati raj* was to be a "party-less democracy," in which the most respected (or able) villagers would be elected regardless of political affiliation. In practice, the process has been thoroughly politicized. In Kerala, and even more so in West Bengal, the CPM has seen in *panchayati raj* an instrument to tighten its hold on the countryside. The power of the panchayat, and its officials, is used not merely in and for themselves but, crucially, to mobilize votes during assembly and parliamentary elections.[16]

These caveats notwithstanding, the Seventy-third Amendment has set in motion a process with possibly profound implications for the future of Indian democracy. A decade after its enactment, there were more than 3 million elected representatives—of whom 1 million were women—in local institutions. The representatives were chosen through a very competitive process, with voter turnout at panchayat elections generally exceeding 70%.

One subject of great interest, and even greater importance, is the impact that *panchayati raj* will have on relations between castes. In Uttar Pradesh, where the Dalits are vocal and organized, the dominant castes are now forced to share power at the local level with those historically less advantaged. In Orissa, where the Dalits are more submissive, they have been excluded from participation in many panchayats (in violation of the law). In Tamil Nadu, the formation of village councils has sharpened existing conflicts between the landed Thevars and the Dalits. About one-fifth of the presidents of panchayats have to be Dalits, but these often find their authority eroded by the upper castes. Likewise, although some women presidents act autonomously, others are mouthpieces for the men in their family or caste.

Notably, members of Parliament and of the various state legislatures are often hostile to the *panchayati raj* experiment. So are many members of the civil service, who argue that this experiment will merely lead to the "decentralization of corruption." Supporters of the new system answer that such criticism is selfishly motivated, emanating as it does from groups that would be hard hit if administrative and financial authority were to be more widely distributed than is now the case.[17]

V

Through the 1990s, Indian politics became more complex at the domestic level, with greater competition between parties and the introduction of a third tier of government. However, when it came to India's dealings with the rest of the world there was a noticeable convergence of views. Whether led by the BJP or the Congress, the ruling alliance was committed to enhancing the country's military capabilities, and to a more assertive foreign policy in general.[18]

One manifestation of this new strategy was a growth in the size and power of the military. India was rapidly moving "from a defence dependent upon diplomacy to a diplomacy strengthened by a strong defence."[19] Military expenditure rose steadily throughout the decade, from the equivalent of $7 billion to $12 billion (U.S. dollars) between 1991 and 1999. Some of this money went on salaries—there were now more than 1 million Indians in uniform, working in the army, navy, or air force, with another 1 million staffing the various paramilitary outfits.

Some of the money also went to buy state-of-the-art weaponry. And some went to manufacturing, indigenously, instruments of war that the richer western countries were not willing to sell to India. In addition to the Agni and Prithvi missiles developed in the 1980s, India now had an intercontinental ballistic missile, Surya (with a range of up to 12,000 kilometres), and another missile, Sagarika, that could be launched from ships. Indian scientists had also developed a range of defensive options, designing shorter-range missiles to be aimed at any the enemy might throw at them.[20]

These missiles were designed by the Defence Research and Development Organization (DRDO), one of two scientific institutions in the vanguard of the defence sector. The other was the Atomic Energy Commission (AEC), which had responsibility for the production of nuclear power and nuclear weapons. An atomic device had been tested in 1974, and in subsequent years the AEC's scientists were able to make it considerably more sophisticated and destructive. From the early 1990s they pressed the government to allow them to test their improved bombs.

In his history of India's nuclear programme, George Perkovich traces the persistent efforts of the scientists. Those who led the missile and nuclear programmes told successive prime ministers that in the absence of tangible results, talented young scientists would prefer high-paying jobs in the commercial sector to the service of the state. "Without full-scale tests," they argued, "morale would fall and the nation would not find replacements for the aging cohort that had produced the first device in 1974." In late 1995, Prime Minister Narasimha Rao approved tests, but he backed off when American satellites revealed the preparations, provoking a strong warning from the U.S. government. When a United Front government came to power in 1996, the scientists urged the new prime minister, H. D. Deve Gowda, to give them the green light. Gowda demurred: he didn't care about the Americans' opinion, he said; it was only that his priority was economic development rather than a show of military strength.[21]

The National Democratic Alliance, led by the BJP, took office in March 1998. The next month Pakistan tested a medium-range missile, provocatively named Ghauri, after a medieval Muslim warrior who had conquered and (according to legend) laid waste to much of northern India. A quick answer was called for, if only because "the BJP's historic toughness on national security would have seemed hollow if the government did not respond decisively to the new Pakistani threat."[22] The heads of the AEC and the DRDO insisted that a nuclear test would be the most fitting response. Their calls were endorsed by the atomic physicist Raja Rammana, who had enormous prestige as the man who had "fathered" the tests of 1974. Ramanna met Prime Minister Vajpayee, who—he assured Ramanna—wanted "to see India as a strong country and not as a soft one." To this the physicist added, "Also, you can't keep scientists in suspended animation for twenty-four years. They will simply vanish."[23]

In the second week of May 1998, the Indians exploded five nuclear devices in the Rajasthan desert. Three kinds of bombs were tested: a regular fission device, a thermonuclear bomb, and a "sub-kiloton" device. Before and after the tests senior members of the NDA government made provocative statements aimed at India's neighbours. The defence minister, George Fernandes, described China as India's "number one threat." The home minister, L. K. Advani, said that India was prepared to pursue across the border any terrorists that Pakistan might send to make trouble in Kashmir.

Opinion polls conducted immediately after the tests suggested that a majority of the urban population supported them. The most enthusiastic acclaim, however, came from the BJP's sister organizations, the VHP and the RSS. They announced that they would build a temple at the test site, and take the sand, contaminated by radioactivity but nonetheless "holy" for them, across India to be worshipped. The chief of the Shiv Sena, Bal Thackeray, saluted the scientists for showing that Hindu men were "not eunuchs." The scientists themselves, clad in military uniforms, posed triumphantly for the news cameras.[24]

Two weeks later this balloon of patriotic pride was punctured and deflated. On 28 May, Pakistan tested its own nuclear device. Their atomic programme had been based on designs and materials stolen from a Dutch laboratory by the scientist A. Q. Khan, supplemented by technical help from the Chinese. The Indian bomb was wholly indigenous. But these distinctions became meaningless when six atomic blasts (deliberately, one more than the other side) disturbed the Chagai Hills in

Baluchistan province. The Pakistani public greeted the news by dancing and singing in the streets. The "father" of this bomb, A. Q. Khan, told interviewers that "our devices are more consistent, more compact, more advanced and more reliable than what the Indians have."[25]

The Pakistani achievement was described as an "Islamic" bomb, in part because at this time no other Muslim nation had one. In India, too, both supporters and opponents of the tests tended to see them as "Hindu." In truth, although the BJP was in power in May 1998, the preparations had been made under successive Congress regimes. The policy of nuclear ambiguity—we have the bomb, but we won't test it—was becoming unsustainable. Pressed by the West to sign the Comprehensive Test Ban Treaty (CTBT), India decided to make its nuclear status a matter of public record.[26]

The BJP naturally tried to make political capital out of the tests, but faced with signing the CTBT and thus relinquishing all nuclear ambitions, a Congress regime would have acted likewise. Indeed, in the past it had been Congress prime ministers who had most insistently claimed "great power" status for India. These claims became more persistent after the end of the cold war. Indian leaders demanded that in deference to its size, democratic history, and economic potential, India be made a permanent member of the United Nations Security Council. That the claim was disregarded made nuclear tests all the more urgent. Across party lines, strategic thinkers argued that an open declaration of nuclear weapons would make the western powers sit up and take notice. Reason and argument having failed, India had necessarily to "blast" its way to world attention.[27]

VI

The only countries acknowledged as nuclear powers were the five permanent members of the UN Security Council—the United States, Russia, China, France, and the United Kingdom. It was also known that Israel had nuclear bombs. When, in the summer of 1998, India and Pakistan simultaneously entered this exclusive club, they created some disquiet among the older members. It was feared that the dispute over Kashmir could lead to the first atomic war in history. Pressure was put on both countries to sort out their differences at the negotiating table.

In February 1999, the Indian prime minister travelled by bus to Lahore to meet his Pakistani counterpart. Atal Behari Vajpayee and Nawaz Sharif spoke of increasing trade between the two countries, and of liberalizing visas. No progress was made on Kashmir, but the fact that the two sides were talking was, to the subcontinent eyes as well as the West, a most reassuring sign.[28]

Barely three months after Vajpayee and Sharif's summit, relations were once more on a short fuse. The provocation was the infiltration into the Kargil district of Jammu and Kashmir of hundreds of armed men, some Kashmiri in origin but others unambiguously citizens of Pakistan. The operation had been planned by the Pakistani army, and the civilian prime minister had been told about it only when it was well under way. The idea was to occupy the mountaintops that overlooked the highway linking Srinagar to Leh, the only all-weather road connecting two towns of crucial importance. The Pakistani generals apparently believed that their nuclear shield provided protection, inhibiting the Indians from acting against the intruders.[29]

The Indian army was first alerted to the infiltration by a group of shepherds. Scanning the mountains with binoculars, in search of wild goats to hunt, they spotted men in Pathan dress digging themselves into bunkers. They conveyed the information to the nearest regiment. Soon, the army found that the Pakistanis had occupied positions across a wide swathe of the Kargil sector, from the Mushkoh valley in the west to Chorbat La in the east. The decision was made to shift them.[30]

The shepherds saw the Pathans on 3 May 1999. Two weeks later the Indians began an artillery bombardment of enemy positions. Air force planes screamed overhead, while on the ground jawans made their way laboriously up the mountain slopes. Men reared in tropical climes had now to fight in cold and treacherous terrain. "In battle after decisive battle Indian infantry battalions clambered up near perpendicular cliffs the entire night in freezing temperatures before lunging straight into battle at first light against the intruders."[31]

The exchanges were fierce and, on both sides, costly. Dozens of peaks, each defended by machine guns, had to be recaptured, one by one. A major victory was the taking of Tiger Hill, in the Drass sector. The battles raged all through June. By the end of the month, the Pakistanis had been cleared from 1,500 square kilometres of Indian territory. The areas reoccupied included all the vantage points overlooking the Srinagar-Leh highway.[32]

In the last week of June, President Bill Clinton of the United States received an unexpected phone call from the prime minister of Pakistan. The two countries were close allies, and now the junior partner was asking to be helped out of a jam of its own creation. More than 2,000

Pakistanis had already died in the conflict, and Nawaz Sharif was in search of a face-saving device to allow him to end hostilities. Clinton granted him an appointment on 4 July, American Independence Day. At that meeting, Sharif promised to withdraw Pakistani troops if America would put pressure on India to resolve the dispute over Kashmir. Clinton agreed to take an "active interest" in the question. With this assurance, Sharif returned to Islamabad and formally called off the operation.[33]

Approximately 500 Indian soldiers died in the Kargil conflict. They came from all parts of the country, and when their coffins returned home the grief on display was mixed with a large dose of pride. The bodies were kept in public places—schools, colleges, even stadiums—where friends, family, and fellow townsmen came to pay their last (and often first) respects. A cremation or burial with full military honours followed, attended by thousands of mourners and presided over by the most important dignitary on hand—often a state's chief minister or governor. The men being honoured included both officers and soldiers. Many hailed from the traditional catchment area of the Indian army (the north and the west of the country), but many others had been born in places not previously known for any martial tradition, such as Ganjam in Orissa and Tumkur in Karnataka.[34] And some who died defending India came from regions long thought to be at odds with the very idea of India. A critical role in recapturing the Kargil peaks was played by soldiers of the Naga regiment. Their valour at the other end of the Himalaya, one army general hoped, would allow the "brave Nagas [to] finally get their Indian identity." Their bravery was certainly saluted by their kinsmen; when the body of a Naga lieutenant returned home to Kohima, thousands thronged the airport to receive it.[35]

The clashes over Kargil also furthered the reintegration of the Punjab and the Punjabis. Farmers along the border insisted that if the conflict became a full-fledged war, they would be at hand to assist the Indian army, providing food and shelter and even, if required, military help. "We shall fight with the jawans," said one Sikh peasant, "and teach the Pakistanis a bitter lesson for violating our territory."[36]

Across India, the conflict with Pakistan unleashed a surge of patriotic sentiment. Thousands volunteered to join the men on the front—so many, in fact, that in several places the police had to fire to disperse crowds surrounding army recruitment centres.[37] The war with China had elicited a similar response, with unemployed youths seeking to join the forces. Yet there was a significant difference. On that occasion, the intruders had overrun thousands of square miles before choosing on their own to return. This time the intruders had been thrown out by the use of force.

In this respect the Kargil war was cathartic for the men in uniform, and for their compatriots as a whole. The Indian army had finally redeemed itself. It had removed, once and for all, the stigma of having failed to repulse the Chinese in 1962. At the same time, the popular response to the conflict bore witness to the birth of a new and more assertive Indian nationalism. Never before had bodies of soldiers killed in battle been greeted with such an effusion of sentiment. It appeared as if each district was determined to make public its own contribution to the national cause. The mood was acknowledged and further encouraged by reporters in print and on television, whose competitive jingoism was surprising even to those familiar with that profession's hoary record of making truth the first casualty of war.

VII

In October 1999, Pakistan's brief flirtation with parliamentary democracy ended. Prime Minister Nawaz Sharif was deposed in a coup led by the chief of army staff, Pervez Musharraf. The Indians were not pleased with these developments, for Musharraf was believed to have masterminded the Kargil operations.

In March 2000 President Clinton visited South Asia. He spent five days in India and five hours in Pakistan, in a historic reversal of the traditional American bias toward the smaller country. This was an acknowledgement of India's rising economic strength, and also a comment on Pakistan's return to military rule. The day after Clinton landed in New Delhi, terrorists dressed in Indian army uniforms descended on the village of Chittisinghpora in Kashmir, pulled Sikh men out of their homes, and shot them. In a village of 300 homes, "nearly every house . . . lost a relative, neighbour, or friend." The tragedy was compounded when the security forces shot five men who they claimed had committed the crime, but who were later found to be innocent.[38]

The killers at Chittisinghpora were probably freelancers who did not have the backing of the Pakistani government.[39] Still, there was little question that the issue of Kashmir continued to divide the two nations most deeply. President Musharraf issued periodic reminders of Pakistan's undying commitment to the "liberation struggle" of the Kashmiris. The Indian prime minister chastised his counterpart for adhering to the "pernicious two-nation theory that brought about the partition."[40]

Neither country was prepared to accept the other's position on Kashmir. However, a dialogue was resumed, perhaps motivated by the need to act as responsible nuclear powers in the eyes of the world. In July 2001 President Musharraf visited Agra at the invitation of the Indian government. He and his wife were put up in a luxury hotel overlooking the Taj Mahal. The general and Vajpayee talked for many hours, with and without aides. The meeting ended inconclusively, when a draft communiqué left both sides dissatisfied. India wanted a greater emphasis to be placed on cross-border terrorism, and Pakistan asked for a more explicit acknowledgement of the democratic aspirations of the Kashmiri people.

While General Musharraf was in Agra, terrorists struck again in the Valley. In a dozen separate attacks at least eighty people were killed. This was becoming a pattern—whenever dignitaries visited New Delhi, the violence in Kashmir would escalate. When the U.S. secretary of state, Colin Powell, came in October 2001, terrorists launched a grenade assault on the Jammu and Kashmir assembly. Two months later, they undertook an even more daring action. Four suicide bombers entered the Indian Parliament in a car and attempted to blow it up. They were killed by the police, who later identified them as Pakistanis.[41]

The assembly building in Srinagar was a symbol of the state's integration with India. The Parliament building in New Delhi was the symbol of Indian democracy itself. Within its portals met elected politicians representing 1 billion people. The attacks on these two places brought an end to the diplomatic dialogue. India accused Pakistan of abetting the terrorists. Appeals were made to the U.S. government to rein in its old ally. While sympathizing with the United States after the incidents of 11 September 2001, India added that its sympathy was made the more sincere by the fact that it had long been a victim of terrorist violence.

In the spring of 2002 exchanges between Indian and Pakisani troops became more frequent. As spring turned to summer, and the troop build-up intensified, the concerns of 1998 returned—would the subcontinent be the site of the first nuclear exchange? A respected Nepali monthly thought that the region was "poised on the cusp of war once again." A leading American analyst believed that "the crisis between India and Pakistan is the most dangerous confrontation since Soviet ships steamed towards the U.S. naval blockade of Cuba in 1962."[42]

In the end, war was averted, although perhaps war had not even been planned. Within India, attention shifted to the coming assembly elections in Kashmir. The state had, as a newspaper in Delhi bluntly put it, a "long history of rigged elections," the elections of 1977 being the exception to the rule.[43] In the past, the Election Commission had, in Kashmir at any rate, "always appeared to be in the company of, and therefore in collaboration with, security forces and partisan state government functionaries." Now it worked overtime to redeem its reputation. The chief election commissioner ordered a complete revision of the voters' list, which was unchanged since 1988. An extensive survey of all houses led to a new, comprehensive list, covering 350,000 pages in the elegant but hard-to-print Urdu script. Copies of the electoral rolls were then distributed to all political parties, and displayed in schools, hospitals, and government offices across the state. A further precaution was the import of 8,000 electronic voting machines, to prevent rigging.[44]

The assembly elections were held in September 2002. The militants killed a prominent moderate just beforehand and urged the public to boycott the elections. Despite these threats, about 48% of eligible voters turned out, somewhat less than was usual in other parts of India, but far in excess of what had been anticipated. International observers were on hand to confirm that the election was fair. The ruling National Conference was voted out of power; the winners were an alliance comprising the Congress and the People's Democratic party. The election of 2002 in Jammu and Kashmir, wrote two long-time students of the state's politics, could "be seen as a reversal of [the] 1987 assembly elections which by eroding the democratic space had become [the] catalyst for separatist politics. . . . This election has brought about a change in the regime through the popular verdict and to that extent it has become instrumental in providing a linkage between the people and the government."[45] The new chief minister, Mufti Mohammed Saeed, expressed these sentiments more crisply, saying, "this is the first time since 1953 that India has acquired legitimacy in the eyes of the [Kashmiri] people."[46]

In the summer of 2003 tourists from other parts of India flocked to Kashmir for the first time in more than a decade. Fifty thousand came in May and June, filling hotels across the Valley and houseboats on Srinagar's Lake Dal. Indian Airlines announced an extra daily flight from Delhi to Srinagar. Provoked by these developments, terrorists made a series of strikes, throwing grenades in shopping centres, kidnapping civilians, and suicide-bombing the chief minister's house.[47] But even more tourists came the next year, and more airlines announced flights to Srinagar.

In January 2005, civic elections were held in Jammu and Kashmir for the first time in almost three decades. An impressive 60% of voters cast their ballots in these local elections, despite threats by terrorists and the assassination of several candidates. Those who voted said they wanted the new councillors to provide new roads, clean water, and better sanitation. A shopkeeper in the town of Sopore—a stronghold of pro-Pakistani militants—was quoted as saying, "We can't wait for civic amenities till *azaadi* [independence]."[48]

According to official figures, the number of "violent incidents" in Jammu and Kashmir decreased from 3,505 in the year 2002 to less than 2,000 in 2005.[49] The state could by no means be said to be at peace. But for the first time in many years, the claim of the Indian government over this territory did not seem altogether hollow. In talks with Pakistan, New Delhi could urge "confidence-building measures," such as a bus linking the two halves of Kashmir. The first bus was scheduled to leave from Srinagar for Muzaffarabad on 7 April 2005. On the afternoon of 6 April, terrorists stormed the tourist complex where the passengers were staying. They were repulsed, and the next day two buses left as planned. A reporter who travelled on one of the vehicles described what happened when it crossed the newly built Aman Setu ("Peace Bridge") and entered Pakistani territory:

> Divided families were reunited, tears and rose petals flecked their faces. The significance of this extraordinary moment lay perhaps in the ordinariness of the backdrop: two buses with 49 passengers had crossed over—and blurred a line that has divided Kashmir for over five decades in blood and prejudice.[50]

There were, however, some people who would rather that the prejudice persisted and the blood continue to be spilt. On 11 July 2006, there were two terrorist attacks against tourists in Kashmir. Eight Bengali visitors were killed. On the same day, deadly bombs went off simultaneously in seven different commuter trains in Mumbai (Bombay). More than 200 innocent civilians were killed, and more than 1,000 injured. It was one of the worst terrorist incidents in history. While the perpetrators remain unidentified, their aims needed no clarification—they wanted to pit Hindu against Muslim, Kashmir against the rest of India, and India against Pakistan.

VIII

The great German sociologist Max Weber once remarked that "there are two ways of making politics one's vocation: Either one lives 'for' politics or one lives 'off' it."[51] The first generation of Indian leaders lived mostly for politics. They were attracted by the authority they wielded, but also often motivated by a spirit of service and sacrifice. The Indian politicians of the current generation, however, are more likely to enter politics to live off it. They are attracted by power and prestige, and also by the opportunities for financial reward. Control over the state machinery, they know, can give glittering prizes to those in charge.

Political corruption was not unknown in the 1950s, as the Mundhra scandal and the Kairon administration in the Punjab demonstrate. But it was restricted. Most members of Nehru's cabinet, and even Shastri's, did not abuse their position for monetary gain. Some Congress bosses did, however, gather money for the party from the business sector. In the 1970s, politicians began demanding a commission when contracting arms deals with foreign suppliers. The money—or most of it—went into the party's coffers to be used in the next elections. By the 1980s, however, political corruption had shifted from the institutional to the personal level. Thus an increasing number of ministers at the Centre and in the states were making money from government contracts, from postings of officials, and by sundry other means.

The evidence of political corruption is, by its very nature, anecdotal rather than documentary. Those who take or give commissions rarely leave a paper trail. However, in the 1990s the Central Bureau of Investigation (CBI) laid charges against a number of prominent politicians for having assets "disproportionate" to their position. The leaders charged included the chief ministers of Bihar and Tamil Nadu, Lalu Prasad Yadav and J. Jayalalithaa. Each was accused of amassing hundreds of millions of rupees from the allocation of government contracts. In another case, the CBI raided the house of Sukh Ram, the Union minister for communications, and found 36 million rupees in cash. It was alleged that this represented the commission on licenses awarded to private telecom companies.

In all these cases, the charges did not lead to convictions, sometimes because of lack of evidence, at other times because of the timidity of the judiciary. There is also a sense of honour among thieves. In the time preceding an election, the opposition makes a hue and cry about corruption in the ruling administration, but if it is elected it does not pursue cases against the previous regime, trusting that it will be similarly rewarded when it loses power.[52] Indeed, politicians from different parties and different states often exchange favours. In one documented case, a Haryana chief minister approved the sale of a plot of public land to the son of a Punjab chief minister—although the market value of the land was 500 million rupees, the price actually paid was 25 million.[53]

In the words of the political scientist Peter deSouza, corruption is Indian democracy's "inconvenient fact." Governments in power in New Delhi take kickbacks on purchases from abroad, especially defence deals. The amount taken on foreign contracts is about 20%. In most states the majority of ministers are on the take, skimming money off licenses to companies, postings of top officers, land deals, and much else. The Planning Commission estimates that 70% to 90% of rural development funds are siphoned off by a web extending up from the panchayat head to the local member of Parliament, with officials too claiming their share. One reason city roads are in such poor shape is that much of the money allocated to them is spent elsewhere. Of every 100 rupees allocated to road building by the Bangalore City Corporation, for example, 40 rupees will go into the pockets of politicians and officials, and another 20 rupees will be the contractor's profit margin. Only 40 rupees will be spent on the job, which is done either badly or not at all.[54]

Because being in power is so profitable, there is now an increasing trade in politicians. To make up the numbers and obtain a majority, legislators are bought and sold for a (usually high) price. In the era of minority and coalition governments the trade is especially brisk. Legislators routinely cross the floor and change parties. This has become so common that in times of political instability, it is not unknown for the assembly members of a particular party to be taken en masse for a "holiday" in Goa, lest they defect to the other side. Here these men—sometimes up to fifty of them—are kept in a hotel, drinking and playing cards, while armed guards watch out for furtive phone calls or unknown visitors. The holiday extends until the crisis has passed, which could take several weeks.

Because politics is such good business, it has also become a dirty business. In 1985 the weekly *Sunday* ran a cover story, "The Underworld of Indian Politics," describing how, especially in the states of Uttar Pradesh and Bihar, candidates with criminal records were running in elections, sometimes winning, and sometimes being made ministers as well. Among the crimes these men were charged with were "murder, abduction, rape, molestation, gangsterism."[55] Over the next decade, a larger number of criminals entered politics—so many, in fact, that a citizens' group filed a public interest litigation (PIL) in the Supreme Court demanding that parties release details about their candidates. In May 2002, the Supreme Court made it mandatory for those running in state or national elections to make public their assets and their criminal record (if any).

The group that had filed the original PIL then set up election watch committees in the states, comprising local lawyers, teachers, and students. The affidavits filed by candidates in five state elections held in 2002–2003 were collated and analysed. In the major political parties—such as the BJP, the Congress, Uttar Pradesh's Samajwadi Party (SP), and Bihar's Rashtriya Janata Dal (RJD)—between 15% and 20% of candidates had criminal records. A detailed study of Rajasthan's Vidhan Sabha election of 2003 showed that roughly half the candidates were very rich by Indian standards—they had a declared wealth of more than 3 million rupees each. And as many as 124 candidates had criminal records. Of these, 40% were charged with crimes that qualified as "serious"—including armed robbery, attempted murder, defiling a place of worship, and arson.[56]

Equally revealing was an analysis of the affidavits of the 541 members elected to Parliament in 2004. The Congress had the wealthiest candidates—their members each had, on the average, assets of 31 million rupees. Most members had assets in excess of 10 million rupees; those who ranked lowest on this scale were the Communists. On the matter of criminal charges, the lead was taken by parties powerful in Uttar Pradesh and Bihar. Many members of Parliament had been "charge-sheeted": 34.8% of RJD, 27.8% of the Bahujan Samaj party, and nearly 20% of the SP. The Congress and the BJP came out slightly cleaner, having only 17% and 20% of their members, respectively, charged with crimes. However, the situation was reversed regarding money owed to public financial institutions. Of all such debts, Congress members of Parliament accounted for 45%, and the BJP members for 23%. Again, it was Communist members who came out best—they reported virtually no debts at all.[57]

From these figures we may conclude that while in power at the Centre, the Congress and the BJP have systematically milked the system—the Congress to a greater extent, since it has been in power longer. Meanwhile, to get to power in the states, and to retain it, parties such as the SP, the BSP, and the RJD had come to rely heavily on criminals.[58]

Along with corruption and criminalization, Indian politics has also increasingly fallen victim to nepotism. Once, most parties had a coherent ideology and organizational base. Now, they have degenerated into family firms.

The process was begun by and within that grand old party, the Indian National Congress. For most of its history, the Congress was a party run by and for democrats, with regular elections to district and state bodies. After splitting the Congress in 1969, Indira Gandhi put an end to elections within the party organization. Henceforth, Congress chief ministers and state unit presidents were to be nominated by the leader in New Delhi. Then, during the emergency, Mrs. Gandhi dealt a second and more grievous blow to Congress tradition, when she anointed her son Sanjay as her successor.

After Sanjay's death, his elder brother Rajiv was groomed to take over the party and, in time, the government. When, in 1998, the Congress bosses asked Sonia Gandhi to head the party, they acknowledged that the party had completely surrendered to the claims of the dynasty. Sonia, in turn, asked her son Rahul to enter politics in 2004, alloting him the safe family borough of Ameth. If the party retains power in 2009, Rahul Gandhi will have precedence over every other congressman if he wishes to become prime minister.

Apart from its corrosive effects on the ethos of India's pre-eminent political party, Indira Gandhi's dynastic principle has served as a model for others to follow. With the exception of the cadre-based parties of left and right, the CPM and the BJP, all political parties in India have been converted into family firms. The DMK was once the proud party of Dravidian nationalism and social reform; its members are now resigned to the fact that M. Karunanidhi's son, or else his nephew, will succeed him. For all his professed commitment to Maharashtrian pride and Hindu nationalism, when picking the next Shiv Sena leader Bal Thackeray could look no further than his son Udhav. The Samajwadi party and Rashtriya Janata Dal claim to stand for "social justice," but Mulayam Singh Yadav has made it clear that only his son Akhilesh will succeed him. When Lalu Prasad Yadav was forced to resign as chief minister of Bihar (after a corruption scandal), his wife Rabri Devi was chosen to replace him, although her previous experience was limited to the home and the kitchen. The practice has been extended down the system, so that if a sitting member of Parliament dies, his son or daughter is likely to be nominated in his place.

Conducting research in a Bengali village, a Norwegian anthropologist found that the term most often used to describe politics was *nungra* (dirty). Politicians were described as those who promoted "abusive exchanges" (*galagali*), caused "fist-fights" (*maramari*), and promoted "disturbances" (*gandagol*). In sum, politics served only to fill society with "poison" (*bish*). This was not always so, said the villagers. Once, soon after independence, politicians were honest, hard-working, and dedicated, but now every party was peopled with "scheming, plotting [and] unprincipled individuals."[59]

These statements are fairly representative of the country as a whole. A survey conducted by Gallup in sixty countries found that lack of confidence in politicians was highest in India, where 91% of those polled felt that their elected representatives were dishonest.[60]

Some consolation can perhaps be found in statements by scholars writing about other societies in other times. Jorge Luis Borges writes of his own country in the 1940s that "the State is impersonal; the Argentine can conceive only of personal relations. Therefore, to him, robbing public funds is not a crime. I am noting a fact; I am not justifying or excusing it." And, speaking of his own continent, Europe, in centuries past, R. W. Southern remarks that "nepotism, political bribery, and the appropriation of institutional wealth to endow one's family, were not crimes in medieval rulers; they were part of the art of government, no less necessary in popes than in other men."[61]

IX

Corruption in contemporary India is widespread not merely in the legislature but also in the executive branch. In past times, it manifested itself more in the lower echelons of the bureaucracy, with minor officials taking bribes to allot housing sites, approve electricity connections, or short-list candidates for jobs.[62] In recent years it has become widespread among higher officials too. The CBI has charged even secretaries to the government of India and chief secretaries of states with having assets "disproportionate" to their income. The lifestyle of some of these officials certainly suggests as much—with private farmhouses and family holidays in exotic locations whose cost must many times exceed their lifetime earnings.[63]

In Jawaharlal Nehru's time, the civil service was shielded from politics; transfers, promotions, and the like were decided within the executive branch itself. From the 1970s, however, individual bureaucrats came increasingly to ally themselves with individual politicians or political parties. When the party they allied with was in power, they got the best postings. In return, they energetically implemented the partisan agenda of the politicians. On deals high and low, officials now work closely with their ministers, and are rewarded with a share of the proceeds. The rot runs deep down the system—thus, every member of a legislative assembly has his own favoured district magistrate, police officer, and so on.

As P. S. Appu points out, the founders of the Indian nation state respected the autonomy and integrity of the civil services. Vallabhbhai Patel insisted that his secretaries should feel free to corect or criticize his views, so that the minister, and his government, could arrive at a decision that was the best under the circumstances. However, when Indira Gandhi started choosing chief ministers purely on the basis of their loyalty to her, these individuals would pick their subordinates by similar criteria. Thus, over time, the secretary of a government department has willingly become an extension of his minister's voice and will.[64]

In a letter to the prime minister, the retired civil servant M. N. Buch has highlighted the consequences of this politicization of the administration. Because of the way the government is now run, he writes, "the disciplinary hierarchy of the civil services (including the police) has completely broken down. A subordinate who does not measure up and is pulled up by his superior knows that he can approach a politician, escape the consequences for his own misdeeds and cause harm to his superior." Since failure cannot be punished, "there is no accountability, there is no monitoring of work, there is no financial discipline and there is a visible breakdown of the system."[65]

Particularly in northern India, the alliances between politicians and civil servants are often made on the basis of caste. In Uttar Pradesh, for example, when the Samajwadi party is in power, backward caste and especially Yadav officials seem to get the most influential and lucrative assignments. If the Bahujan Samaj party were to win the next election, however, then many of these Yadavs would make way for Dalits. If corrupt acts are sometimes undertaken on the basis of caste, they are often justified on the basis of that other great and enduring Indian institution, the family. The money made by illegal means is spent on educating children at expensive schools and colleges abroad, and generally in feathering the nest for future generations.

Oddly enough, the corruption of the Indian state has been mimicked by actors that aim at its destruction. Across the north-east, insurgent groups have found in kidnapping and extortion a profitable alternative to fighting for ethnic or national freedom. In the tiny state of Tripura, 1,394 abductions were reported between 1997 and 2000—an average of over 300 a year. The ransom demanded could be as low as 20,000 rupees for a child or as high as 3 million for the manager of a tea garden.[66]

At a press conference in January 1997, the former chief minister of Meghalaya, B. B. Lyngdoh, lashed out at the media for "lionising" the guerrillas. "They're cowards, petty thieves, robbers and extortionists," insisted Lyngdoh. "Insurgency in the north east died two decades ago."[67] Other politicians have been less brave. A BJP leader in Manipur had fallen afoul of an insurgent group called the KYKL; when he decided to run in a parliamentary election, he placed an advertisement in the newspapers apologizing for his past "mistakes" and appealing to the KYKL to forgive him. Apart from this public apology, a private understanding was also reached between the politician and the militants. Reporting the incident, the columnist Harish Khare grimly observed that like everything else in the north-east, "clemency from an insurgent group is also on sale."[68]

X

There are, of course, still many upright officers in the Indian administrative and police services. Anecdotal evidence, again, suggests that the percentage of corrupt officials is probably considerably lower than the percentage of corrupt politicians. What, then, of the third arm of government, the judiciary? Although here too corruption and negligence are not unknown, "ordinary people look up to judges in a way in which they no longer look up to legislators, ministers or civil servants." This comment is by the distinguished sociologist André Béteille, who adds that "judges, particularly of the higher courts, are by and large believed to be learned, high-minded, independent, dutiful and upright, qualities that one no longer associates with either ministers or their secretaries."[69]

When politicians can no longer be trusted, and when the sectarian identities of caste and religion determine so much of what passes for public policy, the high courts and the Supreme Court receive a spate of public interest litigations, aimed at stopping violations of the law or of the constitution. Such a PIL forced candidates to declare their wealth and criminal records. Other PILs have spanned a wide gamut of issues. Some are aimed at protecting the environment from industrial pollution, others at protecting the rights of disadvantaged social groups such as tribals, the disabled, and the homeless.

The Supreme Court is usually a court of last resort, appealed to when protest and persuasion have failed. Some of its judgements have been socially emancipatory, enabling bonded labourers to be freed and India's notoriously dirty and badly run prisons to be opened up for public scrutiny. Others have curbed political corruption, cancelling licenses issued under dubious justifications or retrieving land grabbed by members of Parliament and ministers. However, the Supreme Court has sometimes exceeded its brief, pronouncing judgements on complex technical matters—the building of a dam, for example—on which its own competence is open to question.

Some judges have taken their "activist" role too seriously, creating rights that cannot be enforced and ordering a stoppage of economic activities without a thought for the unemployment and discontent this would generate. Some other judges have shown an unfortunate penchant for showmanship, such as a judge in Madurai who, while allowing anticipatory bail to an assembly member charged with criminal intimidation, instructed him to spend five days in the city's Gandhi Museum, reading Gandhian literature.[70]

XI

In so far as it holds regular elections, has multiple parties, and has a free press, India is emphatically a democracy. But the nature of this democracy has profoundly changed over the years. In the first two decades of independence, India was more or less a *constitutional* democracy, with laws passed and enacted after due deliberation in Parliament, by political parties that were themselves run on deliberative lines. The third and fourth decades were a period of transition, as the ruling Congress sought to reshape the constitution to give itself more power. At the same time, it led the move away from inner-party democracy toward the anointing of a supreme leader. The opposition answered by moving outside the constitution itself, through a countrywide agitation that sought to delegitimize elected governments and their authority to rule.

In 1949, in his last speech to the Constituent Assembly, B. R. Ambedkar had urged that disputes in India be settled by constitutional means, not by recourse to popular protest. He had also warned against the dangers of bhakti, or hero worship, of placing individual leaders on a pedestal so high that they were always above criticism.

Ambedkar's warnings have been disregarded. As shown dramatically by, for instance, Ayodhya, political disputes have been sought to be settled in the streets rather than in the legislature. This process has been encouraged by the rise of identity politics, with groups organizing themselves on the basis of caste or religion, and seeking to assert themselves by force of numbers rather than by the quality of their arguments. Once, parliamentary debates were of a very high order; now, they have degenerated into exchanges of insults and abuse. At the slightest excuse, political parties organize strikes, shutdowns, marches, and fasts, seeking to have their way by threat and intimidation rather than by reason or argument. The lawmakers of India are, more often than not, its most regular lawbreakers.

The decline of Parliament, and of reasoned public discourse in general, has meant that

> government forces are swarmed by the opposition almost instantly after an electoral mandate. There is no patience, either on the part of the government or the opposition, to respect the authenticity of the mandate to rule given by the voter to a parliament or legislature. Unbending postures adopted by government even in defiance of persistent and legitimate demands of parliamentary oppositions lead to cynicism and a tendency to take to the streets. Having tasted the tumult and mighty disharmonies of plebiscitary mass mobilizations, the opposition gets addicted to it and never wants to return to the mundane task of rational parliamentary debates and ventilation of grievances.[71]

At the same time, most political parties have become extensions of the will and whim of a single leader. Political sycophancy may have been pioneered by the Congress party under Indira Gandhi, but it is by no means restricted to the Congress. Regional leaders like Mulayam, Lalu, and Jayalalithaa revel in a veritable cult of personality, encouraging and expecting craven submission from their party colleagues, their civil servants, and the public at large. Tragically, even Ambedkar has not been exempted from this hero worship. Although he is no longer alive, and is not associated with any particular party, the reverence for his memory is so total and extreme that it is impossible any more to have a dispassionate discussion of his work and his legacy.

Sixty years after independence, India remains a democracy. But the events of the last two decades call for a new qualifying adjective. India is no longer a constitutional democracy but a *populist* one.

29

RICHES

Meet the pissed-off [American] programmer. . . . He's the guy—and, yeah, he's usually a guy—launching websites like yourjobisgoingto-india.com and nojobsforindia.com. He's the guy telling tales—many of them true, a few of them urban legends—about American programmers being forced to train their Indian replacements.

Article in Wired magazine, February 2004

I

IN 1954, AN ECONOMIST in Bombay, A. D. Shroff, began a Forum of Free Enterprise, whose ideas on economic development were somewhat at odds with those then articulated by the influential Planning Commission of the government of India. Shroff complained about the "indifference, if not discouragement" with which the state treated entrepreneurs. He believed that "if the Government of India shed some of their impractical ideologies and extend their active support to the private sector, very rapid industrialisation can be brought about within the next 10 years."[1]

At the same time as Shroff, but independently of him, a journalist in Bangalore, Philip Spratt, was writing a series of essays in favour of free enterprise. Spratt was a Cambridge communist who was sent by the party in the 1920s to foment revolution in the subcontinent. He was arrested and spent many years in an Indian jail. The books he read in prison, and his marriage to an Indian woman afterwards, inspired a steady move rightwards. By the 1950s he was editing a pro-American weekly called *MysIndia*. There he inveighed against the economic policies of the government of India. These, he said, treated the entrepreneur "as a criminal who has dared to use his brains independently of the state to create wealth and give employment." The state's chief planner, P. C. Mahalanobis, had surrounded himself with western leftists and with academicians from the Soviet Union, who reinforced his belief in "rigid control by the Government over all activities." The result, said Spratt, would be "the smothering of free enterprise, a famine of consumer goods, and the tying down of millions of workers to . . . soul-deadening techniques." His own preference was for a plan that would create "the psychological and economic conditions needed for a forward march by private enterprise."[2]

The voices of men like Spratt and Shroff were drowned in the chorus of popular support for a model of heavy industrialization funded and directed by the government. The 1950s were certainly not a propitious time for free marketeers in India. But from time to time their ideas were revived. After the rupee was devalued in 1966 there were some moves toward freeing the trade regime, and hopes that the licensing system would also be liberalized.[3] However, after Indira Gandhi split the Congress party in 1969, her government took its "left turn," nationalizing more industries and returning to economic autarky. Then, in the late 1970s, the socialists in the Janata regime spectacularly affirmed India's economic independence by expelling foreign firms such as IBM and Coca-Cola.

In 1980, Mrs Gandhi returned to power. The next year, the head of the Tata Group of companies gave a long interview to a leading newspaper. J. R. D. Tata said that "the performance of the Indian economy from the mid-fifties to the mid-sixties reflected the soundness of the mixed economy as originally conceived." Industrial production grew at an impressive 8% a year. Then, in the late 1960s, the opportunity arose to open up the economy to competition. Had this been done, Tata thought, "employment would have grown more quickly in all sectors; production would have increased considerably and shortages removed; and Government revenues too would have materially increased, which in turn could have been utilized for developmental programmes." What actually happened, however, was that the government embarked on "the nationalization of major industries on an expropriatory basis."

Moving on from history to the present, Tata urged the government now "to free the economy and see the difference." The recent economic success of countries such as South Korea, Spain, Singapore, and Taiwan was attained because these "newly industrializing countries rely mainly on private enterprise [which] their Government's economic policies are geared to encouraging and supporting."[4]

II

In the 1980s the government of India did lose some of its antipathy toward business. Greater encouragement was given to private enterprise, with key sectors no longer having to be licensed. These were pro-business policies that enabled Indian industry to become more productive and profitable. However, they stopped short of being pro-market policies that would remove impediments to entry and exit by Indian or foreign firms, thus encouraging competition and expanding consumers' choices.[5] It took a major crisis for the Indian state to work toward a fuller liberalization of the economy.

This crisis was linked to the growing external debt of the government. India had long taken aid from multilateral institutions such as the World Bank. In Rajiv Gandhi's regime borrowings from the market also increased rapidly. In the summer of 1991 the debt had reached $70 billion, of which 30% was owed to private creditors. At one stage, foreign exchange reserves were down to two weeks of imports.

The prime minister in 1991 was P. V. Narasimha Rao, a quiet, unemphatic man who had lived and served in the shadow of Indira Gandhi and her elder son. Thrust into the top job after Rajiv Gandhi's death, he revealed a boldness altogether at odds with what was previously known of his character. He appointed as his finance minister Dr. Manmohan Singh, an apolitical economist whose previous jobs included finance secretary and governor of the Reserve Bank. Moreover, Rao gave Manmohan the freedom to carry out economic reforms as he saw fit.

Before he became a public servant, Manmohan Singh had written a doctoral thesis at Oxford, suggesting that India move toward a more open trade regime. His thesis was written in the 1960s; now, three decades later, he seized the chance to put its recommendations into practice. The rupee was devalued, quotas for imports were removed, tariffs were reduced, exports were encouraged, and foreign direct investment was welcomed. The domestic market was also freed; the "license-permit-quota-raj" was substantially done away with, and the public sector was discouraged from expanding. Finally, the reforms sought to curb the profligacy of the government. Measures were introduced to reduce the fiscal deficit, which was running at an alarming 8% of gross domestic product (GDP).[6]

A new industrial policy, framed in July 1991, made it clear that "industrial licensing will henceforth be abolished for all industries, except those specified, irrespective of levels of investment." The exceptions were industries critical to the country's defence, and industries hazardous to the environment and to human health, such as cigarette and alcohol manufacture. This was a dramatic reversal of the existing policy, which had reserved many industries for the state, and many others for the small-scale sector.[7]

There was also a liberalization of the services sector, with private players being encouraged to invest in insurance, banking, telecommunications, and air travel—sectors previously under more or less complete state control. Some economists thought that the reforms did not go far enough, noting, for instance, that the labour laws remained rigid (making it almost impossible for managers to fire workers), and that, while barriers to entry had been removed, barriers to exit remained (thus entrepreneurs still needed government permission to close unprofitable units). The bureaucratic regime had been undermined but not completely dismantled. It still took weeks or months to start a business in India, whereas in China or Malaysia it took a matter of days.[8]

Nonetheless, the changes introduced under the new regime constituted a major departure from past policies. Even a year or two before they were undertaken, such reforms had been considered unlikely or even impossible. In a book published in 1989, a professor at the Harvard Business School identified the vested interests that kept the command economy going—including politicians, bureaucrats, and indigenous entrepreneurs. The apparently permanent hold of this alliance of interests, he wrote, had "served to diminish prospects for fundamental reforms of the nation's economic policies." In countries like South Korea, the discipline of the market and openness to foreign capital had led to a surge of wealth and productivity. In India, however, the state was "paralyzed," and local entrepreneurs were "blind" to the need for reform. The prospect was grim: "the 'miracle' growth achieved by these other industrializing countries will continue to elude India."[9]

III

For years, the Indian economy had expanded at what was derisively called the "Hindu rate of growth." The pro-business reforms of the 1980s had increased the growth rate, and the pro-market reforms of the 1990s increased it further. The steadily improving performance of the Indian economy is captured in Table 10.

Naturally, growth has been uneven, with some parts of the economy doing better than others. The most significant expansion has been in the services sector, which grew at an average of 8.1% a year through the 1990s. Much of this growth was contributed by the software industry, whose revenues grew from only $197 million in 1990 to $8 billion in 2000. In some periods this industry grew at more than 50% a year. Much of this expansion was aimed at the overseas market. In 1990 the exports of the Indian software industry were valued at $100 million, but by the end of the decade the figure had jumped to $6.3 billion.

	TABLE 10: ECONOMIC GROWTH IN INDIA, 1972–2002	
PERIOD	GROWTH IN GROSS DOMESTIC PRODUCT	GROWTH IN PER CAPITA INCOME
1972–1982	3.5%	1.2%
1982–1992	5.2%	3.0%
1992–2002	6.0%	3.9%

Source: Vijay L. Kelkar, *India: On the Growth Turnpike*, K. R. Narayan Oration (Canberra: Australian National University, 2004).

In the year 2000, there were 340,000 software professionals in India, with some 50,000 new engineering graduates being recruited annually. About 20% of these professionals were women. In the first years of the twenty-first century the industry grew at an even faster rate. By 2004, it was employing 600,000 people and exporting $13 billion worth of services.

Both in India and abroad, the software industry is commonly recognized as the "poster boy" of the reforms. The industry is largely indigenous, with firms big and small owned by Indian entrepreneurs, employing Indian engineers trained at Indian universities. Yet the work they do is mostly for foreign clients, who include many of the Fortune 500 companies. Some of this work is routine—maintaining accounts and employee records, for example. Other work is more innovative, such as designing new software, which is then patented and sold overseas. (I-Flex, a financial package developed by an Indian company, is now used in more than seventy countries.) In its early years, the industry focused on "body shopping," sending engineers on short-term visas to work on-site in European and American companies. However, with the development of satellite communications and the World Wide Web, and the increasing sophistication of the work being done, the emphasis has shifted to outsourcing: the codes are written within India and then sent back overseas.

Software firms such as Wipro, TCS, and Infosys are now household names in India. But they are also known and widely respected in business circles abroad. They are listed on the New York Stock Exchange, and they own and operate subsidiary companies in many parts of the world. But there are also many small and medium-size companies in the business, and the market share of the largest firms has steadily declined over the last decade.[10]

The software enterprises are clustered around a few major cities: Delhi, Madras, Hyderabad, and above all Bangalore, which has acquired the sobriquet "India's Silicon Valley." Bangalore is home to India's finest research university, the Indian Institute of Science, set up in 1909. After independence, the city became a hub of industrial units, with large, state-owned factories set up to manufacture machine tools, aircraft, telephones, and electronic equipment. When one adds to this rich scientific tradition Bangalore's mild, Mediterranean climate and cosmopolitan culture, one understands why it has emerged as such an attractive investment destination. Wipro and Infosys both have headquarters here, as do several other important players in the software industry.

To explain the rise of the software sector one must invoke factors both proximate and distant. Success, said John F. Kennedy, has many fathers. In this particular case, all the claimants have truth on their side. Some credit is certainly due to the reforms of 1991, which opened up the foreign market for the first time. But some credit must also be taken by Rajiv Gandhi's government, which gave special emphasis to the then nascent electronics and telecommunications industries. Moving back a decade further, the Janata government's expulsion of IBM allowed the development of an indigenous computer manufacturing and maintenance industry. But perhaps the story should really begin with Jawaharlal Nehru's government, which had the foresight to set up a chain of high-quality engineering schools and the wisdom to retain English as the language of higher education and of interstate and international communication. As one respected analyst of the IT sector comments, "India's greatest asset is a large, educated, English-speaking workforce that is willing to work at relatively low wages."[11] This is a delicious irony: a showpiece of market liberalization was made possible by a man committed to a state-sponsored path of economic development.

In addition to these other factors, a geographical accident has also contributed enormously to the boom—the fact that India is the other side of the globe from the United States, so that work done during the day is ready by the time the client wakes up from his sleep.

Facility with English, and the luck of being five or ten hours ahead of the prosperous West, has led the outsourcing of other forms of work to India. At the higher end of the value chain, medical tests of patients in U.S. hospitals are sent to be analysed by Indian radiologists and pathologists. At the lower end are the mushrooming call centres, where young Indians stay up all night to take calls from holders of western credit cards, or to book seats on western planes and trains. Many of the employees in these centres are women, who can speak grammatical English in an accent of the client's choice, and who work harder than their American counterparts at one-tenth the cost. In 2002 there were more than 300 call centres in India, employing 110,000 people. The industry was growing at a staggering 71% per year. It was estimated that by 2008 it would employ 2 million people and generate $25 billion, amounting to as much as 3% of India's GDP.[12]

The outsourcing of western work to Indian workers is taking ever more varied forms. English teachers in Kerala tutor American kids over the Internet in grammar and composition. Catholic priests in the United States and Canada send prayer requests to their Indian counterparts. One can have a thanksgiving prayer said for 40 rupees (roughly $1) in an Indian church, whereas in an American church it would cost five times that amount.[13]

If less spectacularly, the reforms of the 1990s have also had an impact on the manufacturing sector. Increased competition and the entry of foreign firms have led to greater productivity and lower prices, benefiting the domestic consumer. Some Indian industries have seized on opportunities offered by the opening of international markets. Thus, top clothing brands like Gap, Polo, and Tommy Hilfiger all increasingly have their products made in India. India now exports about 500,000 motor vehicles a year, as well as many sophisticated components used in vehicles assembled elsewhere (one out of every two American trucks uses an axle made by an Indian firm). Another growth area is pharmaceuticals. Medicines exported by Indian companies were valued at $1 billion in 2003. These included drugs made according to the modern pharmacoepia as well as those following the indigenous Ayurveda system.[14]

The opening of the economy also led many foreign firms to come in and tap the Indian market. Between 1991 and 2000, the government approved more than 10,000 investment proposals by foreign companies; if all had come to fruition, they would be worth $20 billion. They ranged from telecommunications to chemicals, from food processing to paper products. Of the projects that actually got off the ground, the most visible brands were in the consumer sector, such as cars made by Ford and Honda, televisions by Samsung, phones by Nokia, and soft drinks by Pepsi and Coca-Cola, whose advertisements and showrooms were now a noticeable presence in the major Indian cities. Less visibly, companies such as Philips, Microsoft, and General Electric had also begun establishing research stations in India, which employed local as well as expatriate engineers in developing cutting-edge technologies for the global market.[15]

The importance of foreign trade to the Indian economy grew steadily through the 1990s. Exports increased from 4.9% to 8.5% of GDP and imports from 7.9% to 11.6% of GDP. Yet, in the aggregate, this remained a relatively closed economy. In 1980, India accounted for 0.57% of world trade; twenty years later the figure had inched up to 0.71%.[16]

IV

One less noticed aspect of recent economic history is the change in the social composition of the entrepreneurial class. Once, the leading capitalists in India came from the traditional business communities— Marwaris, Jains, Banias, Chettiars, Parsis. However, in the past three decades, a range of peasant castes have moved into the industrial sector. Some of the most successful entrepreneurs of late have been from castes who for centuries have worked the land—Marathas, Vellalas, Reddys, Nadars, and Ezhavas. Again, some of the best known software start-ups, such as Infosys, have been initiated by Brahmans, from families who traditionally served the state or the academy and regarded commerce with disdain. There have also been some very successful Muslim entrepreneurs, such as Azim Premji of the software giant Wipro.[17]

Meanwhile, the surge in economic growth has led to an expansion in the size and influence of the Indian middle class. The emergence of this stratum, writes E. Sridharan, "has changed India's class structure from one characterized by a sharp contrast between a small elite and a large impoverished mass, to one with a substantial intermediate class." How substantial it actually is remains a matter of definition and interpretation. Defined most broadly, to include all households with an annual income in excess of 70,000 rupees a year (at 1998–1999 prices), the middle class consists of as many as 250 million Indians. Defined most narrowly, to exclude those who earn less than 140,000 rupees a year, it consists of only 55 million Indians.[18]

This new middle class is the prime target of the new products and services that have entered the Indian market in recent years. There are now more than 50 million subscribers to cable television in India, and at least 100 million Indians who own mobile phones. These services spread widely and rapidly, as does the artefact most typical of the modern consumer economy, the motor vehicle. Bangalore, for example, has as many as 2 million vehicles on its roads, with 20,000 new ones being added every month.

In the early years of Indian independence, an ethic of Gandhian austerity hung heavily over the Indian middle class. In a poor country, one was not supposed to have much wealth, and certainly not supposed to display it. Even those inclined toward hedonism were stalled by the absence of choice. With the opening of the economy in the 1990s, the guilt formerly associated with consumerism has rapidly disappeared. Whether it be cigarettes, cars, whisky, or sunglasses, foreign brands previously unavailable in India now flood the market. Commercial television carries appealing images of the goods being offered; and banks and credit card companies rush in to help one buy—and consume—them.[19]

Although most characteristic of the big cities, the new consumption is not restricted to them. A recent ethnography of rural Kerala describes how consumers in this age of liberalization exercise their choices with care and discrimination, with one eye on their pocket and the other on their neighbour. Rural Kerala, of course, is anything but characteristic of rural India as a whole. For one thing, the villages blend seamlessly into the towns; for another, many villagers have spent time working in the Middle East, making the kind of money that takes them straight into the middle class. Among these new consumers,

> styles and tastes are hierarchically arranged, brand-names acting as markers of distinction: a Keltron (Kerala Electronics; a state enterprise) television confers less prestige than an Onida, Indian made, which, in turn, is not as good as a Sony made under license in India, with maximum prestige attached to foreign-made, imported televisions. . . . Sometimes people leave their labels on consumer durables to emphasise their origins.[20]

As with televisions, so too with a whole range of products from facial creams to cars—the Indian consumer is now spoiled for choice. Once, the only automobiles locally available were a 1950s model Morris and a 1960s model Fiat; now, if one has the money one can buy the latest Mercedes-Benz. Middle-class Indians, once focused on saving for the future, are now much more present-minded. Twenty years ago, only a few Indians had credit cards; now more than 20 million have them. This was once a risk-averse culture, but now millions of Indians invest in property and the stock market.

These changes in production and consumption have led to a fundamental transformation of the urban landscape. Modest homes have given way to grand apartment buildings; one-story offices have been replaced by imposing structures in glass and concrete. There are still traditional bazaars, whose little stalls sell locally made pots and pans or locally grown fruits and vegetables; but there are now also large malls, which display, under one roof, such international brands as Levi's, Estée Lauder, Sony, and Baskin-Robbins.

V

A second consequence of the recent economic growth has been a decline in the percentage of Indians who live below the official poverty line. There is a vigorous scholarly debate on precisely how many poor people there are in India. Some statisticians have concluded that only 15% live below the poverty line, while more pessimistic estimates put the figure as high as 35%. The government of India's own estimate, 26%, lies between these two extremes. Although the precise numbers are in dispute, virtually all scholars accept that in both absolute and relative terms poverty declined in the 1990s. At the beginning of the decade, nearly 40% of Indians were "poor"; by the end of the decade, the figure was 30% or less.[21]

Still, there are huge numbers of poor people in India—close to 300 million, if one sticks to the official estimate. Many of them are in the cities. Beyond the glitzy malls and new office buildings lie the slums and shanty towns where the majority of urban residents live. These are the people who service the middle class yet will never be part of it. They "sell newspapers they will never read, sew clothes they cannot wear, polish cars they will never own and construct buildings where they will never live."[22] Other slum dwellers labour long hours at low wages, in jobs perilous to their health, such as cutting metal and separating chemicals. They are usually unorganized, liable to be laid off without notice, and without insurance or pension benefits.[23]

The majority of the poor people in India, however, live in the villages. The effects of economic liberalization have scarcely percolated into the countryside. Agricultural growth was painfully slow during the 1990s. There were some attempts to diversify crops, and to grow fruits and vegetables for the domestic market and flowers for export. Yet these attempts had only limited success, largely because of deficiencies in infrastructure: a lack of electricity to process crops or keep them in storage, and a lack of roads to take them to the market.[24]

Even regarding the most basic resource, food, the picture was less cheering than it might have been. Taking the country as a whole, there was a modest food surplus. Buffer stocks of 10 million to 20 million tons were being maintained in government godowns (warehouses). Yet the mechanisms for distribution were seriously inadequate; in times of scarcity, stocks did not move quickly enough to communities that needed them. The targeting was inefficient; grain from the Public Distribution System (PDS) more easily reached towns than rural areas, and rich states than poor ones. And there was terrific corruption; according to one estimate, only 20% of the grain released through the PDS actually reached the intended recipients; the rest was sold on the black market. Hunger and malnutrition remained endemic in many parts, and deaths from starvation were reported when the rains failed.[25]

In much of the country, life and livelihood remained dependent on the availability of water. Sixty years after independence, only 40% of cultivated areas was under irrigation. For most farmers, the uncertainties caused by the year-to-year fluctuation in rainfall were compounded by the pre-emption of perennial water sources by the cities. Delhi took its supplies from the Tehri dam, 200 miles away; Bangalore took its from the Cauvery, 100 miles distant. Home to the privileged and the powerful, the cities got the water they demanded at a generously subsidized rate. Scarcity and discrimination sometimes provoked desperate acts. When the journalist P. Sainath was travelling in Tamil Nadu in 1993, his train was stopped in the dead of night by peasants, who then took all the water they could find. Ten years later, when a drought hit northern Rajasthan, herders in Bikaner had to buy water in the open market to save their livestock from dying. The price they paid was 166 times the price a consumer in Delhi was paying for his water.[26]

In the last years of the twentieth century, the first suicides among farmers were reported. This was a disturbingly novel phenomenon, for although hunger and poverty had existed in the subcontinent for centuries, never before had so many rural people gone so far as to take their own lives. Suicide, as the pioneering studies of the French sociologist Émile Durkheim had argued, was a product of the anomie and alienation caused by modern urban living. It increased in France during the late nineteenth century, among migrants to cities who were dislocated from the protective care of the family and community; and it also increased in Bangalore during the late twentieth century, among young software professionals stressed out by the long hours of work or the rapid success of their colleagues.

Indian anthropologists had previously reported high rates of suicide among some isolated mountain tribes.[27] But what was now happening among settled peasant communities was unprecedented. Between 1995 and 2005 there were at least 10,000 suicides by farmers, in states as dispersed as Andhra Pradesh and Rajasthan. Usually, it was the male heads of households who killed themselves, most often by swallowing pesticides, but at other times by hanging or electrocution. In many cases, they took this extreme step because of an inability to pay off debts accumulated over the years—debts owed to banks, cooperatives, or private moneylenders. But indebtedness had also been a pervasive feature of rural life; why, now, did it lead so often to this tragic outcome? No systematic studies exist yet to answer this question, but some preliminary speculation might be in order. *Pace* Durkheim, the suicides among farmers are perhaps related to the rapidity of social change in contemporary India. The new consumer society, its images carried into the villages by television, does place a very high premium on success. Thus when crops fail, or a new crop does not give the yield it promised, the personal humiliation felt is greatly in excess of what it might have been in an earlier, more stable, and less acquisitive time.[28]

VI

One reason for the continuing poverty is the government's poor record in providing basic services such as education and health care. In 1991, the year the reforms began, only 39% of Indian women and only 64% of the men could read and write. Here, India lagged behind not merely the developed nations of the West but also some of its Asian neighbours. Sri Lanka had educated 89% of its women and 94% of its men; and the corresponding figures for China were 75% and 96%, respectively.

The inability—some would say unwillingness—to educate all or even most of its citizens counted as independent India's greatest failure.[29] In the 1990s, however, the government initiated a number of schemes to universalize education. First, there was the District Primary Education Programme, which focused on 250 districts where female literacy was less than the national average. A little later, this was superseded by Sarva Shiksha Abhiyan (Programme to Educate All). The public funds devoted to primary education were increased, and there was also an inflow of money from foreign donors.

The government was pushed to be more proactive by an order of the Supreme Court directing all state governments to provide cooked midday meals in schools. Many children who entered primary school dropped out well before they got to high school. A high proportion of these dropouts were girls, who were withdrawn by their families to help with household tasks such as cooking, cleaning, and collecting firewood. In Tamil Nadu, where midday meals had first been introduced, they had helped considerably in increasing enrolment. It was hoped that a countrywide extension would encourage parents to send their children to school and keep them there.[30]

A number of innovative non-governmental organizations (NGOs) also entered the educational field in the 1990s. One NGO, active in the poorer districts of Andhra Pradesh, was able to place every child in 400 villages in school. The NGO ran a "bridge" course for those who entered school late (most of whom were girls)—giving them six months of intensive coaching before placing them in the regular curriculum. Another NGO was following similar methods among the slum dwellers of India's largest city, Mumbai. It had opened 3,000 *balwadis*, or preschools, where children between the ages of three and five were taught to read and write. In the densely crowded slums, with space at a premium, all kinds of sites were used for preschools—temple courtyards, school verandas, public parks, even offices of political parties. From the *balwadis* the children were sent on to regular municipal schools. By 1998, some 55,000 children had passed through this process, which was now being extended to other cities and towns of northern and western India.[31]

Within the state system, there were considerable variations in implementation and effectiveness. Schools in Bihar and Uttar Pradesh were very badly run, with poor or non-existent facilities—no blackboards, no chairs, no toilets for girls. The teachers were uninterested—absenteeism was high—and the parents apathetic. Among the better-performing states were Kerala and Tamil Nadu in the south and Himachal Pradesh in the north. The educational progress in Himachal Pradesh was both rapid and unexpected. Himachal was dominated by the Rajputs, a caste who had traditionally kept their women at home. It was also a hilly state, with widely dispersed hamlets, making schools hard to situate and harder to get to. However, these natural and cultural disadvantages were overcome by the state's administration, led by the dynamic chief minister, Dr Y. S. Parmar. After Himachal was carved out of Punjab in the late 1960s, Parmar made elementary education a pivotal element of public policy. Public expenditure on education was twice the national average, and the teacher-child ratio was far higher than in other parts of India. Parents were quick to realize the benefits of sending both their boys and their girls to school. Concerned families and capable administrators worked to ensure that the schools were well maintained and the teachers properly motivated. The results were impressive: in 1961, only 11% of girls in these hill districts had been literate; by 1998, the figure had jumped to 98%.[32]

Although no other state performed nearly as well as Himachal Pradesh, the data suggested that the education sector was not as somnolent as it had once been. By the end of the 1990s, the female literacy rate had risen from 39% to 54% and the male literacy rate from 64% to 76%. Behind these changes in quantity lay a fundamental change in mentality. Once, many poor parents had chosen to put their children to work rather than send them to school. Now, parents wished to place children in a position from which they could, with luck and enterprise, escape a life of menial labour for a job in the modern economy. As the educationist Vimala Ramachandran wrote in 2004, "the demand side had never looked more promising. The overwhelming evidence emanating from studies done in the last 10 years clearly demonstrates that there is a tremendous demand for education—across the board and among all social groups. Wherever the government has ensured a well-functioning school within reach, enrolment has been high."[33]

Whereas developments in education called for cautious optimism, the outlook in the health sector remained bleak. Hospitals owned and run by the central government and state governments were in a pathetic state: crowded, corrupt, without basic facilities or qualified doctors. And the political class seemed unconcerned. In fact, public expenditure on health was on the decline. In 1990 it had constituted 1.3% of GDP, but by 1999 the figure had dropped to 0.9%. At the same time, there was a tremendous expansion of privatized health care, which by 2002 accounted for nearly 80% of all health expenditure. This, however, was aimed at servicing the growing middle class. In some areas the poor were served by committed NGOs, but for the most part they were left to their own devices, going to indigenous medicine men or village quacks to treat their illnesses.

Some statistics may be in order here. Average life expectancy in 2001 was only sixty-four years. In many states, infant mortality rates remained high. In Meghalaya, for example, it was eighty-nine deaths per 1,000. India had 60% of the world's leprosy cases (about 500,000). Fifteen million Indians suffered from tuberculosis, a number that rose by 2 million every year. To these older diseases was added a new one—AIDS. By 2004, more than 5 million Indians were HIV-positive.[34]

In the popular mind, Africa is most seriously threatened by AIDS. But in August 2005, in a cover story in the prestigious *Financial Times* weekend magazine, a British journalist wrote that this perception was mistaken, and that "it will be in India, home to one-sixth of humanity, that the global fight against AIDS will be won or lost." There were already several localized epidemics at work; the worry was these would "mesh and contribute to a terrifying steepening of the infection curve." Were that to happen, "all bets were off" on India's joining the league of the world's economic powers. Besides, HIV/AIDS was "not only a growing economic nightmare, but also a growing national security issue," with military personnel five times as likely as civilians to contract the infection. The article's concluding paragraph ran as follows:

> India's precarious public finances and under-resourced public system are in no state to cope with the colossal burden of a sub-continental AIDS pandemic similar to that afflicting parts of Africa. India is at a crossroads in its fight against AIDS and the path it takes now will be decisive for nothing less than the future of the world.[35]

One is tempted to dismiss this as merely the latest in the long line of apocalyptic scenarios by western journalists, except that this time it was not famine or riots or a political assassination that would ruin India, but a lethal virus. However, there is indeed a health crisis in the country, and it is not restricted to AIDS. In the more sober but not necessarily contradictory words of an Indian journalist, "India has stopped thinking about public health and has paid a very heavy price for that."[36]

VII

Economic liberalization has improved the lives of many millions of Indians but has left millions more untouched. And there are also some Indians who have been adversely affected by the freeing of the market and the opening of the economy to the outside world.

Among those who have suffered from economic liberalization, the tribals of Orissa are perhaps foremost. Orissa is divided into a coastal region, dominated by caste Hindus, and a series of mountain ranges in the interior, where live a variety of Adivasi communities. In the state as a whole the Hindus are in a majority, and they wield most of the political and administrative power. In 1999 Orissa overtook—if that is the word—Bihar as India's poorest state. And among the residents of Orissa the upland tribals are the poorest and most vulnerable. Whether in terms of land, income, health facilities, or literacy rate, they lag behind the state as a whole. The tribals are heavily dependent on the monsoon and on the forests for survival. With the woods disappearing, and the rains sometimes failing, they have plunged deeper into poverty, as manifested periodically in deaths from starvation.[37]

The wealth in these highlands is mostly under the ground. Orissa has 70% of the country's bauxite reserves, and also substantial deposits of iron ore. These minerals are concentrated in the tribal districts of Rayagada and Koraput. In the past, these ores were worked by Indian public-sector companies, but in the last decade they have been supplanted by private firms, domestic as well as foreign. The state government has signed a series of leases, offering land at attractive prices to companies that want to mine these hills.[38]

One of the more ambitious projects was floated in 1992 by Utkal Alumina, a consortium that brought together Canadian and Norwegian firms with the Aditya Birla Group. This consortium had its eye on the Baphlimani hills of the Kashipur block of Rayagada district, under which lay a deposit of 200 million tons of bauxite. The proposal was to mine this ore and transport it to a newly built refinery, which would process the material and export the refined product.

Some of the land to be used for these operations was owned by the government; but some 3,000 acres were cultivated by tribals. They saw no benefit in the project, which would dispossess them of their fields and give them nothing in return. In 1993 a delegation of tribal activists met the chief minister and demanded that he cancel the lease. Their request was refused; instead, the government sent a team to survey the land preparatory to its acquisition. Over the next few years the tribals tried a variety of strategies to stop the project from getting off the ground. Employees of Utkal Alumina were prohibited from entering the villages. Roads were blockaded, and marches were organized to raise consciousness about the environmental damage that mining would cause. When the company constructed a model of the kind of house in which it intended to relocate the tribals, the prospective beneficiaries simply demolished the structure.[39]

But the administration was determined to go ahead with the project, seeing it as a source of revenue for the exchequer, some of this intended also for parties and the pockets of politicians. In March 1999, a group of social scientists from Delhi visited Rayagada and wrote a report warning the government of Orissa that "unless the popular discontent among local tribals over the acquisition of land was properly addressed this peaceful district may turn into a hotbed of Naxalite [Maoist] activity."[40] A year and a half later, the environmental journalist Darryl D'Monte came from Mumbai to study the situation. He found the tribals resolute in their opposition. The mines, they told him, would "destroy the ecosystem of the Baphlimani plateau." One Adivasi leader said they would stop all vehicles from entering the area. "We are prepared for any consequences," he insisted, adding, "In a conflagration, anyone ought to be prepared to get singed." D'Monte noted that the government was equally determined to push the project through. "Over the past five years the district administration, in tandem with the police and politicians, has almost acted like the advance guard of the companies."[41]

The conflagration came two months later, and it was the tribals who got singed. On 15 December, the ruling Biju Janata Dal organized a meeting in the area, to win support for the project. Angry villagers refused to allow it to hold the meeting. Three platoons of police arrived to disperse the protesters, but were held up by a group of women. When the police lathi-charged, men arrived to help the women. At some stage the police opened fire, killing three tribals.[42]

The firing in Kashipur did not deter the state government. Encouraged by a growing international demand, they signed a series of agreements with Indian and foreign companies, aimed at mining 3 billion tons of iron and 1.5 billion tons of bauxite over the next twenty-five years. No thought was given to the likely environmental and social consequences.[43] As these projects began to take shape, they too encountered popular resistance. To allow Tata Steel to build a factory processing iron ore for the Chinese market, the government acquired land in Kalinganagar at much less than the market rate. The protests of the local villagers were overruled, the land was handed over, and construction began. In the first week of 2006, a group of tribals demolished the boundary wall, provoking the police to open fire. Twelve people died in the incident. The tribals placed the bodies of these martyrs on the highway and held up traffic for a week. Among the first to express solidarity with them were Maoist revolutionaries.[44]

VIII

It is tempting to view Bangalore as the *benign* face of economic liberalization. There, the opening of foreign markets has generated skilled employment and enormous wealth, shared fairly widely among the population. It is also tempting to see tribal Orissa as the *brutal* face of economic liberalization. The wealth accruing from mining will go to the mine owners and the political class that works in league with them. Those losing out will be the villagers beneath whose land the veins of bauxite run. They will be rendered homeless and assetless, and also left to cope with the degradation of the ecosystem that will be the inevitable consequence of open-cast mining.

Of course, even before 1991 India was marked by sharp inequalities. Some regions and some social groups were noticeably less poor than others. However, the market-oriented reforms have tended to accentuate these inequalities. The states that were poorest grew most slowly during the decade, while the states that were already better off grew faster. Through the 1990s Bihar registered an annual growth rate of 2.69%; Uttar Pradesh, 3.58%; and Orissa, 3.25%. On the other side, Gujarat had a growth rate of 9.57%; Maharashtra, 8.01%; and Tamil Nadu, 6.22%. Broadly speaking, the states that did well were in the south and west of the country, while the states that fared indifferently were in the north and east. At the very bottom were the very populous states of Bihar and Uttar Pradesh. In 1993, these two states accounted for 41.7% of India's poor; in 2000, 42.5%.[45]

It appeared that economic performance was crucially dependent on initial endowments of human capital and physical infrastructure. The states that had better schools and hospitals and hence a more skilled and healthier workforce were usually also the states that had better roads, more reliable electricity, and less corrupt administrations.[46] Naturally, it was to these locations that investment and investors gravitated. In the pre-reform era, the central government often chose to situate industries in areas deemed "backward." But private entrepreneurs were under no such obligation. They looked to areas where they would get the best return on their capital. These were the southern and western states, which surged further ahead as a consequence.

That said, even in the most prosperous states it was not the entire population that prospered. The capitals of Karnataka and Andhra Pradesh—Bangalore and Hyderabad, respectively—were leaders in the software boom, but their own hinterlands had been left far behind. Between 1994 and 2000, per capita consumption expenditure in rural Karnataka grew at 9.5% annually; in urban Karnataka it grew at 26.5%. The corresponding figures for Andhra Pradesh were 2.8% (rural) and 18.5% (urban). Taking India as a whole, expenditure grew at 8.7% per year in the countryside, but at 16.6% in the cities.[47]

As the economist T. N. Srinivasan observes, these wide disparities meant that "if one is poor in India," then

one is more likely to live in rural areas, more likely to be a member of
the Scheduled Caste or Tribe or other socially discriminated groups,
more likely to be malnourished, sick and in poor health, more likely to
be illiterate or poorly educated and with low skills, more likely to live
in certain states (such as . . . Bihar, Madhya Pradesh, Rajasthan and
Uttar Pradesh, and also Orissa) than in others.[48]

One consequence of these disparities is the growing migration from
poorer areas to richer ones. Once, most Indians lived, worked, and died
in the vicinity of their place of birth. Now, they increasingly travel long
distances in search of a living. Labourers from Orissa come to work on
coffee plantations in the Coorg district of Karnataka, 1,000 miles away.
Many of the wheat fields of Punjab and Haryana are harvested by labourers shipped in from Bihar and Jharkhand. But there is also a great
deal of migration into the cities. Many plumbers in Delhi, for example,
come from Orissa, and many taxi drivers in Mumbai from Uttar Pradesh.
Nor is the outflow of artisanal or unskilled labour alone. Thus doctors
and engineers trained in Bihar increasingly seek work elsewhere.[49]

Economic growth in contemporary India is marked by considerable disparities of region and class. The economist Amartya Sen worries that as these inequalites intensify, half of India will come to look
and live like California, the other half like sub-Saharan Africa.[50] Already, prosperity coexists with misery, and technological sophistication with human degradation. The paradoxes of life in India were tellingly
captured in a conversation between the prime minister and villagers in
Orissa that took place in September 2001. From his home in New
Delhi, Atal Behari Vajpayee spoke by satellite to tribals in Kashipur,
whose kinsmen had died eating mango kernel because their crops had
failed. "It is extremely unfortunate that in today's world people die by
eating poisonous material," said the head of a government that could
speak to its citizens by videophone, yet not supply them with wholesome
food.[51]

                              IX

The strategy of economic development followed in the 1950s was backed
by a strong consensus. There were critics, but these were marginal figures, lacking influence and without a social base. By contrast, the strategy of economic development adopted since the 1990s has been subject
to a searing critique within and outside the political system.

The economic debate in contemporary India is conducted between two schools, which the columnist T. N. Ninan calls the reformists and the populists.[52] The reformists ask for a freeing of market forces, the abolition of subsidies, the removal of restrictive labour laws, the full convertibility of the rupee, and a general retreat of the state from the economy. Some would even want health care and education to be privatized. The populists, on the other hand, demand restrictions on foreign investment, the retention by the state of basic industries, and the protection of the interests of labourers and small entrepreneurs. In addition, they demand that the state implement land reforms, fund programmes to end rural poverty, and provide subsidized food, housing, and energy to the urban as well as rural poor.

The arguments between these two groups are very vigorous, and conducted in different forums—in the press, in Parliament, on television, and in the streets. Intriguingly, political parties tend to be in favour of economic reforms when in power, and against them when out of power. Between 1998 and 2004, the Bharatiya Janata party promoted the opening of the economy and the disinvestment of publicly owned industries. These policies were opposed by the Congress party, which had of course originally introduced market-friendly reforms in 1991. Forgetting (or annulling) its own recent history, the Congress led a countrywide strike in March 2000, in protest against liberalization in general and against the rolling back of subsidies in particular.[53]

The BJP fought the elections of 2004 on the promise of bringing prosperity to all through market-led growth. To its slogan, "India shining," the Congress opposed the claims of the *aam aadmi* (common man). However, after winning power, the coalition led by Congress chose the original architect of the reforms, Dr. Manmohan Singh, as prime minister. He, in turn, appointed two well-known reformists as finance minister and deputy chairman of the Planning Commission, respectively. Now it was the turn of the BJP to cry foul. It dusted off the old nationalist slogan *swadeshi* (self-reliance), claiming that the new government's policies were undermining India's sovereignty and independence.

Most curious is the behaviour in and out of power of the Communist Party of India (Marxist), or CPM. In Delhi, CPM intellectuals—many associated with the prestigious Jawaharlal Nehru University—are in the populist vanguard, opposing any move to cut subsidies, sell inefficient state enterprises, or invite foreign capital. And trade unions led by the CPM organize strikes and bandhs whenever a public utility is privatized. In West Bengal, however, the CPM chief minister Buddhadeb Bhattacharya is actively canvassing for investment from foreign and indigenous capitalists. He has chastised trade unions for their excessive militancy, and banned strikes in the software sector. He once went so far as to say that his administration is guided by the slogan "Reform or perish!"

In an era of minority governments and coalition politics, there must necessarily be some give and take, the seeking of a common ground between reformists and populists. One such compromise was worked out in 2005 over the implementation of an Employment Guarantee Scheme (EGS), under which the state would commit itself to providing gainful employment to those who needed it, by putting them to work on schemes for soil and water conservation, road building, and the like. The EGS was promoted by left-wing economists, who thought it would be valuable for the rural poor, and also create badly needed infrastructure in the countryside. But it was opposed by market-oriented economists, who felt it would be an unnecessary drain on the exchequer and would also foster corruption. Predictably, the EGS scheme eventually approved by Parliament was regarded as too radical by the reformists, but as not radical enough by the populists.[54]

The dismantling of the "license-permit-quota-raj" has closed many avenues of corruption. Yet the process of privatization has opened some new ones. When public-sector factories are sold, there are possibilities of favouring a particular bidder in exchange for a financial consideration. Crucially, the state retains the power to acquire and dispose of land—a power abused in the present, as in the past, to allot land to private firms at well below market cost.[55]

Perhaps the most notorious case of corruption in post-reform India concerns a power plant that the American firm Enron wanted to set up in Maharashtra. In June 1992, the state government, which was then controlled by the Congress, signed a deal with Enron guaranteeing the company an inordinately large annual rate of return, 16%, on its investment. The details were leaked to the press, and a popular campaign was launched to stop the project. The Shiv Sena party, then in the opposition, also joined in the protests. The project was temporarily shelved, but when the Shiv Sena won the state elections in 1995, it reversed its stand and resumed negotiations with Enron. There were new protests, this time with the Congress seeking to support them.

The Enron project never materialized, in part because of the intensity of the protests, and in part because of the troubles that the company was facing in the United States (it was finally forced to declare bankruptcy). However, while the controversy was at its height, the head of

Enron in India revealed that it had spent $20 million on "publicity" for the project—a term widely (and almost certainly correctly) seen as a euphemism for bribery. If the negotiations alone involved so much money changing hands, one can only speculate on how rich the pickings would have been when the project was up and running.[56]

X

The growing size of the Indian economy has prompted some noticeable shifts in foreign policy, among them a growing friendship with the United States. As we have seen in this book, these countries did not always or even usually have cordial relations. During the cold war the Americans tilted markedly toward India's hostile neighbour, Pakistan; and India tilted somewhat toward the United States' rival superpower, the Soviet Union.

After 1991 the provocation of the Soviet Union did not exist; but Pakistan did. It was only near the end of the 1990s that the United States moved toward a position of equidistance between India and Pakistan. In the early years of the twenty-first century it even seemed to favour India. The reason for this was chiefly economic: a sense that here was a large market for American goods. (In 1990, trade between India and the United States was worth $5.3 billion; by the end of the decade it had nearly tripled.) President Clinton came to India in 2000, and President Bush came six years later; these visits merely confirmed what had become a fundamental change in attitude. As Stephen Cohen has observed, for many decades Washington tended to treat India as an "insignificant pawn" in the cold war, but by the end of the twentieth century it had become a "natural ally."[57]

In a speech to the Asia Society in Washington on the eve of his visit, George W. Bush described India as a "global leader" and a "strategic partner" and "good friend" of the United States.[58] This anointing of India as a natural ally marked a decisive victory of the American Congress and the White House over the Pentagon. As the former senator Larry Pressler points out, the generals in Washington warmed to Pakistan not only because they could sell it arms,

> but also because the Pentagon would often rather deal with dictatorships than democracies. When a Pentagon official goes to Pakistan, he can meet with one general and get everything settled. On the other hand, if he goes to India, he has to talk to the Prime Minister, the Parliament, the courts and, God forbid, the free press.[59]

For its part, the Indian government took time to realize the significance of the end of the cold war. The nuclear tests of 1998 were in some
measure a continuation of an "independent" foreign policy. However,
after the United States overcame its initial distaste and accepted India's
nuclear capability, New Delhi worked seriously to improve relations. In
a unipolar world it made sense to ally with the most powerful nation.
Indian leaders took to speaking of the "common values" that linked
these two "great democracies." There was also economic self-interest at
work, for the United States was by far the greatest outlet for the software industry. In 2001 relations became so cosy that the BJP foreign
minister even offered to send troops to help the Americans in Afghanisthan. The proposal was overruled by the prime minister, but that it had
been made at all was a sign of how close the political establishments of
the two nations had now become.[60]

As with economic policy, here too the leading parties behave differently in and out of power. In opposition, the Congress harked back to
Nehru's "non-alignment" whenever the BJP government proposed to
move closer to the United States. Since it came to power in 2004, the
Congress has vigorously promoted trade ties, sided with America on nuclear proliferation, and sought American aid on the transfer of nuclear
technology.

The recent coming together of India and America runs contrary to
historical trends; so, and even more emphatically, does the growing concord between India and China. Here too the motor of change is economic. In 2002, the trade between India and China was valued at $5
billion (a decade previously it had been close to zero). Chinese electronic
goods were an increasing presence in shops in India; Indian drugs and
cosmetics were an increasing presence in shops in China. Besides, Beijing had followed Washington in distancing itself from too close an
identification with Pakistan. During the Kargil conflict in 1999, for example, China stayed neutral; by contrast, during the wars of 1965 and
1971 it had come out openly on the side of Islamabad.[61]

In July 2003, Prime Minister Atal Behari Vajpayee spent a week in
China. In Beijing he signed an agreement affirming India's recognition
of Tibet (conquered in 1950) as an integral part of China. The Chinese
returned the compliment, by accepting that Sikkim (annexed in 1974)
was part of India. In Shanghai, Mr. Vajpayee focused on economics,
calling for an alliance between Indian software firms and Chinese man-
ufacturers of computer hardware. It seemed that the two previously hostile

countries were now "taking a new road" and moving "towards a cooperative partnership."[62]

Two years later, the Chinese prime minister, Wen Jiabao, came to India. Remarkably, he chose to visit the city of Bangalore before the national capital, New Delhi. His 100-member delegation was composed mostly of businessmen, and their meetings were mostly with Indian chambers of commerce. In a speech in Bangalore, Wen Jiabao echoed Vajpayee's call for an alliance between Indian software and Chinese hardware, thus ensuring, as he said, that the twenty-first century would be an "Asian century." Speaking for a television channel, the Chinese ambassador to India remarked that to China "the 'B' of business [cooperation] is more important than the 'B' of boundary [disputes]."[63]

XI

In 2004, the Indian economy became a subject of debate in the American presidential election. This was unprecedented; and even more strikingly, it was not the poverty of Indians but their wealth that was being discussed. In several campaign speeches, the Democratic challenger, John Kerry, stoked fears that more American jobs would be shipped east if President Bush was re-elected. Kerry promised that if he was elected, he would reinstate a protectionist regime to save American jobs from being "Bangalored." This too was another first—the first time that a presidential candidate had singled out an Indian city by name as a threat to American interests.

Other American politicians had gotten into the act before Kerry. In 2002, a computer programmer from Florida ran for Congress on a one-point programme: an end to "outsourcing." The same year, a woman member of the New Jersey senate introduced a bill forbidding the outsourcing of state contracts to foreign firms. Like her counterpart in Florida, she complained mainly about Indian computer firms and professionals. These politicians were responding sympathetically to the "pissed off programmers," the Americans who had lost their jobs to Indians and wanted them back.[64]

In December 2003, the influential magazine *BusinessWeek* ran a cover story, "The Rise of India." It noted that there were now more IT engineers in Bangalore than in the whole of Silicon Valley. And they were mostly doing work for American clients, for giant corporations like GE that wanted complex engineering problems solved, as well as for farmers in Kansas who wanted merely to have their tax returns filled out. This "techno take-off is wonderful for India," commented *BusinessWeek*, "but terrifying for many Americans." The local workers laid off by foreign substitutes would face "wrenching change"; few would ever land a job as well paid as the one they had just lost. "No wonder India [was] at the center of a brewing storm in America." State legislatures were under pressure to ban outsourcing; some succumbed, like Indiana, which cancelled contracts awarded to Indian firms.[65]

It must be added at once that these concerns are expressed throughout the western world; they are by no means confined to America. When British Rail outsourced train enquiries to India, there were protests in the United Kingdom, although some saw the outsourcing as poetic justice, a case of the empire's victims striking back. In the summer of 2006, both French and Belgian politicians expressed concern at the possible sale of their biggest steel firm, Arcelor, to Mittal Steel, a company owned and run by Indians. Although the sale finally went through, both popular prejudice and state power were invoked to try to thwart the takeover. The new buyers, it was said, would not adequately appreciate the "culture" of the firm and its workers.

Some commentators on India's economic rise write in paranoid terms; others out of admiration. In April 2004, *Newsweek* informed its readers that India was no longer a poor, benighted Third World country; it was now "a good place to do business," indeed, "an investment-worthy partner" for Americans and American business.[66] Two years later, to mark President George W. Bush's visit to India, the same magazine wrote a breathless celebration of what it called "Asia's Other Powerhouse." "In India, the individual is king," *Newsweek* claimed. Although the credit card industry grew at 35% a year, and personal consumption made up 67% of GDP,

> statistics don't quite capture what is happening. Indians, at least in urban areas, are bursting with enthusiasm. Indian businessmen are giddy about their prospects. Indian designers and artists speak of extending their influence across the globe. . . . It is as if hundreds of millions of people have suddenly discovered the keys to unlock their potential.[67]

In a widely noticed book that was published in 2005, the *New York Times* columnist Thomas Friedman wrote that twenty years ago India "was known as a country of snake charmers, poor people, and Mother

Teresa. Today its image has been recalibrated. Now it is also seen as a country of brainy people and computer wizards."[68] In another much publicized book that appeared the same year, the economist Jeffrey Sachs of Columbia University celebrated "India's historic escape from poverty." He also said that "the return of China and India to global economic prominence" would "reshape global politics and society" in the twenty-first century.[69]

This was a coupling that was becoming increasingly common, with the implication generally that China was "the tiger in front."[70] However, some strategic analysts argued that although India was the "newest Asian tiger," it might in the course of time become the biggest. Its democratic traditions and younger population meant that while China would be "the big winner between now and 2040, India is now driving fast and will pick up all the marbles in the latter half of this century." The United States, the United Kingdom, France, and the South-east Asian countries were all seeking better relations with India. And "with all competing for its favor, India may find itself the kingmaker or perhaps make itself king."[71]

The predictions come thick and fast—that Indians will take away American and European jobs; that India, with China, will become the global superpower of the twenty-first century. Whether such forecasts stem from fear and paranoia, or from wonder and admiration, it must be reckoned a miracle that they are made at all. Through most of its history as an independent nation, India has heard altogether different tunes being sung. After every communal riot, it was said that India would break up into many fragments. After every failure of the monsoon, it was predicted that mass starvation and famine would follow. And after every death or killing of a major leader, it was forecast that India would abandon democracy and become a dictatorship.

Those earlier prophecies also stemmed from a variety of motives—some were made with concern, others out of pity or contempt. They prompted anger and embarrassment among educated Indians. These newer predictions, however, have led to a rising tide of self-congratulation. Indian newspapers and magazines run stories headed "Global Champs" and "On the Way to Number One." A columnist in Delhi was so certain that India was becoming the world's titan that he feared it would repeat the errors of those it had replaced. Whereas the West in its heyday had callously exploited its colonies, he urged "Indian business to establish a loving and friendly relationship with other countries." The important thing, he said, was "to ensure that India is not seen as a cruel imperial power in the world of tomorrow." That India would indeed soon be an imperial power was, however, taken for granted.[72]

Those older anticipations of India's demise were greatly exaggerated. For the constitution forged by the nation's founding fathers allowed cultural hetereogeneity to flourish within the ambit of a single (and democratic) nation state. However, the celebrations of India's imminent rise to power are premature as well. Despite the manifest successes of the new economy, there remain large areas of poverty and deprivation. Only purposive state intervention can correct these imbalances; and the state as it exists now is too corroded and corrupted to act with much purpose. It was mistaken, then, to see India as swiftly going down the tube; and it is mistaken, now, to see it as soon taking its place among the elect of the earth.

30

A PEOPLE'S ENTERTAINMENTS

We have to see that our pictures are spun into the web of national
life, that they sculpt and reflect the real India.
                    The film director V. SHANTARAM, speaking in 1940

There is no Pakistan in Indian music at least.
                    The sociologist D. P. MUKERJI, writing in 1945

I

THE CHAPTERS of this book have explored the labours and struggles of the citizens of free India. But how have they *entertained*
themselves? What do Indians do when they are not working or
fighting or raising a family?

The short answer to this question is that most of them go to the
movies. Feature films are the great popular passion of India, cutting
across the social divides featured in this book—the divides of caste,
class, region, religion, gender, and language.

In the last week of 1895 the Lumière brothers opened the first cine-
matograph in Paris. Soon, intrepid Indian photographers were shooting
and showing films on such topics as *Poona Races '98* and *Train Arriving
at Bombay Station*. The first Indian feature was made in 1913 by a printer,
Dadasaheb Phalke, who was inspired by a pictorial life of Jesus to film the
life of a legendary prince, Raja Harishchandra. Eighteen years later the
first Indian sound feature appeared, Ardeshir Irani's *Alam Ara*.

Through the 1920s and 1930s, Indian films had to compete with pictures made in Europe and North America. But after the Second World War
the number of films made in India increased greatly. In 1945, ninety-nine
feature films were produced; two years later, by the time of independence,
the number had jumped to 250, two-thirds of these made by first-time venture capitalists.[1]

Some early films had devotional or romantic themes; other were influenced by the social and political currents of the time. A classic of the

1930s, *Achhut Kanya*, was about the love of a Brahman man for an untouchable girl. The movies of the interwar period were redolent with patriotic imagery, and love for the nation in the making was manifest in
their dialogue and songs. While film directors and actors were influenced
by the national movement, that movement was supremely indifferent to
them. The producer of *Achhut Kanya* was unable to get the lifelong crusader against untouchability, Mahatma Gandhi, to watch his film. (Apparently, the only film Gandhi saw—and that not till its end—was a
mythological work, *Ram Rajya*.)[2] Nor is there any record of other leaders like Jawaharlal Nehru and Vallabhbhai Patel visiting movie theatres.

Whereas some nationalists ignored the movies, others more actively
proselytized against them. There was always a puritanical streak in the Indian freedom movement, which was repelled by the colourful costumes,
the love stories, and the song-and-dance routines of popular film. After independence, some puritans assumed high office, from which they spoke
out against an industry they did not like. In September 1950 the chief minister of Rajasthan rued the "baneful influence" of motion pictures, while
admitting that he had seen only one film himself. Three years later the chief
minister of Madras complained that the sex and murders in films were cor-
rupting youth. He urged film-makers to "reduce the sex appeal in pictures," and think instead of "the production of puranic [religious] pictures
in colour." "How can we progress in other matters if every young man is
thinking of this [sex] stuff all the time?" he complained. He especially
"asked the poor wage-earners not to see cinemas, not because he disliked
the cinema trade, but because he felt that they could find better use for the
money. The rich could afford to go to pictures and ruin themselves."[3]

In truth, such sentiments were not restricted to the political class. In
December 1952, a committee appointed by the Syndicate of the Calcutta
University found that a major reason for the high failure rate in examinations was that students spent too much time at the movies.[4] Two years
later, a petition was sent to the prime minister claiming that films threatened the "moral health of the country"; apparently, they were "a major
factor in incitement to crime and general unsettlement of society."[5] The
petition was signed by 13,000 housewives, whose cause was taken up in
Parliament by Lilavati Munshi, the wife of a well-known puritan politician, K. M. Munshi. Speaking in the Rajya Sabha in November 1954,
Mrs. Munshi argued that "the cinema can make or mar the whole generation and the entire nation." She thought the latter more likely, since (in her
view) the celebration of crime and sex was encouraging young Indians
to repeat these acts in real life. She was especially worried about "the

showing of the flesh of girls in an unseemly way to excite the crowds." She
was answered in the House by the great actor Prithviraj Kapoor, who insisted that in a free society art could not be throttled. From the artist's
point of view, he added, "sunshine and shadow went hand in hand."[6]

To address these objections, a Censor Board was established, which
saw every film before granting it an approval certificate. Scenes that
were sexually suggestive were prohibited, and films with scenes of violence were granted just an "adults only" certificate. Even so, the industry grew at a terrific pace after independence. By 1961, more than 300
films were made annually and were shown in 4,500 theatres across the
country. By 1990 the number of movie houses had doubled, and the
number of films made more than tripled.

By the 1950s, the city of Bombay had become the acknowledged centre of the film industry. Here were made the most popular films, which
used Hindi, a language understood across much of the country. There
were also thriving industries in the other languages. In 1992, for example, while 189 films were made in Hindi, 180 were made in Tamil, 153
in Telugu, ninety-two in Kannada, ninety in Malayalam, forty-two in
Bengali, and twenty-five in Marathi.[7]

By 1980, India had surpassed the United States as the country that
made the most films in the world. In 1997, the fiftieth year of independence, it was estimated that 12 million Indians—more than the population of many a member state in the United Nations—were going to the
cinema every day.

The growth of the film industry has had a noticeable impact on the
physical landscape of urban India. In the smaller towns, movie theatres
dominate the town centre; in larger metropolises, these theatres are
strung across the city locality by locality. And film posters are ubiquitous, exhibited in vivid colours and various sizes, some small enough to
be stuck on the side of a wayside shop, others gigantic billboards that
tower above the road. Some 70,000 posters are printed for a big-budget
film; pasted wherever a blank wall is available, these stay on in their
faded glory well after the film itself has passed into history.[8]

II

"The ingredients of the average Hindi film," writes Satyajit Ray,

> are well known; colour (Eastman preferred); songs (six or seven) in
> voices one knows and trusts; dance—solo and ensemble—the more

frenzied the better; bad girl, good girl, bad guy, goody guy, romance (but no kisses); tears, guffaws, fights, chases, melodrama; characters who exist in a social vacuum; dwellings which do not exist outside the studio floor; [exotic] locations in Kulu, Manali, Ooty, Kashmir, London, Paris, Hong Kong, Tokyo. . . . See any three Hindi films, and two will have all the ingredients listed above.[9]

Satyajit Ray's own films had no dances and few songs. He took his viewers into his characters' homes, showing the clothes they wore and the food they ate. The lives his protagonists led were utterly and compellingly real. Still, while his films have their (undeniably elevated) place, the popular Indian film has its place, too. Ray might dismiss this as a "synthetic, non-existent society," a "make-believe world." But it was precisely because the world they depicted was unreal that these films appealed. And those who made the most popular movies knew as much. A successful film director of the 1970s, Manmohan Desai, said of his work, "I want people to forget their misery. I want to take them into a dream world where there is no poverty, where there are no beggars, where fate is kind and God is busy looking after his flock."[10]

Peasants and workers in independent India went to the movies for the same reason as, in the nineteenth century, the newly literate working class in Britain chose to read stories of the rich and the famous. As a character in a novel by George Gissing remarks, "nothing can induce working men and women to read stories that treat of their own world. They are the most consummate idealists in creation, especially the women. . . . The working classes detest anything that tries to represent their daily life."[11]

Only farce and melodrama, wrote Gissing, appealed to the British working classes. Such is also the case in India, where, however, farce and melodrama have been suitably indigenized. Some recurrent themes make less sense outside the Indian context—a son's devotion to his mother, for example; or a mother-in-law's contentious relationship with her daughter-in-law; or the difficulties (and glories) of choosing one's life partner in defiance of caste and family custom. Again, in the Indian film the "bad guy" and the "bad girl" are more central roles than in the typical Hollywood melodrama—these are the villain and the vamp, malevolent characters in opposition to whom the hero and heroine appear even purer than one would have thought humanly possible.[12]

A celebrated film director once described his productions as "pageants for peasants."[13] These pageants were set in locations the peasants could only dream of. Sometimes the location was a mythic past, when men flew on horses and conversed with gods; at other times, in places on earth that the viewers would never get to. Indian films were—and are—shot on the French Riviera, in the Swiss Alps, and on the South African coastline, with the characters wearing clothes not worn in India and driving cars never seen here. This was a "wholly voyeuristic cinema, where the object of desire could be anything from Dutch tulips to fancy telephone instruments," and through which the viewer "lived at second hand a lifestyle lived Elsewhere."[14]

Where the Indian film rises above stock themes and stereotypes, and becomes truly original, is in its music. Traditional Indian plays and dramas all had songs of some sort. This custom was carried over to the cinema: each film has about half a dozen songs, sung off-screen by a voice not the actor's; who merely lip-syncs the sung words.

In a historic accident, or perhaps an accident made possible only by history, these songs of love and despair came to be written by some of the finest poets of the age. At the time of independence, and for perhaps a century before that, the pre-eminent language of poetry was Urdu. Before and after partition, many Muslim writers—and not a few Hindus—found refuge in the Bombay film industry. Their noms de guerre—Sultanpuri, Jaipuri, Ludhianvi, Azmi, Badayuni, Bhopali—evoked the towns of north India where Urdu had flowered, as a syncretic language spoken with exquisite refinement by Muslims and Hindus alike.

One reason film songs were so popular was their lyrics. These were rich in puns, wordplay, and historical or political allusion. And they were set to music that was no less appealing. The melodies drew from classical music and folk songs, and their orchestration also borrowed heavily—and for the most part, innovatively—from western exemplars. The sitar and the tabla mixed more or less harmoniously with the saxophone and violin. "Long before fusion music became fashionable," wrote one student of the subject, "it was being performed every day in Bombay's film studios." This was a heady brew, which mixed folk melodies from the Ganges delta with "slivers of Dixieland stomp, Portuguese fados, Ellingtonesque doodles," the whole set to the strict structure of a classical Hindustani raga.[15]

Traditionalists dismissed the film song as "a degraded—even degenerate—form of Indian classical or folk genres." But, as Ashraf Aziz points out, this was neither folk nor classical, but "a new genre of song obligatorily created for the cinematic narrative." It was "a new synthesis resulting in an entirely new form of music."[16] One might add that this form was more widely and intensely loved than its predecessors. As a classical vocalist once complained, the songs of the films were "on the tongues of high society ladies of Calcutta as well as the tongawallahs of Peshawar."[17]

Indian audiences, writes the film historian Nasreen Munni Kabir, are "resigned to stock characters and predictable dialogue." But they know, and hope, that these "tired old stories" can yet "be brought back life by good looking stars and six or eight great songs." These audiences "can accept repetition in storylines," but "they will reject a film's music if it has no originality."[18]

III

From the 1940s to the 1980s, films were watched by two kinds of Indians—young men in all-male groups and families. An anthropologist working in northern India found that "many unmarried men are intensive users of film culture." They liked films as entertainment, and for providing an escape from the family. The theatre was a place where these men could smoke cigarettes (prohibited at home), and joke and play around with their friends. Whereas young women rarely went to the movies, older men sometimes took along their wives and parents. The two groups tended to prefer different kinds of films. Young men liked those with "unrestrained dance and fight scenes," but mixed groups chose to watch films depicting the joys and troubles of family life.[19]

The passion for films was even more intense in south India. Here, male movie-goers formed fan clubs, each club devoted to celebrating a particular male star. The town of Madurai in Tamil Nadu, for example, had 500 such clubs, whose members were mostly in their late teens or early twenties. They included tailors, rickshaw pullers, vegetable sellers, and students. A club's activities were aimed at promoting its star, by putting up posters of his films, buying tickets to watch them, and generally singing his praises in public and in private. Occasionally, the club took a more civic turn, by donating blood in the hero's name or raising money for disaster relief.[20]

In earlier chapters we have met M. G. Ramachandran (MGR) of Tamil Nadu and N. T. Rama Rao (NTR) of Andhra Pradesh, movie stars who became chief ministers of their state on the strength of their acting careers alone. Equally adored in Kannada was the film actor Rajkumar, although he did not seek to convert this adoration into political advantage. In all cases, veneration was a consequence of the fact that in this part of India, film was a prime vehicle for the articulation of linguistic nationalism. The people of the south saw their languages under threat from Hindi; mobilizing to ward off the threat, they sought hope and support from the actors who spoke their own beloved tongue most eloquently. In their films, these stars enacted the essential themes of human existence—life and death, romance and betrayal, prosperity and misery—in phrases and idioms drawn from the rhythms and cadences of everyday speech. Literally as well as metaphorically, NTR and his fans, MGR and his fans, and Rajkumar and his fans spoke the same language.

In the Hindi heartland, the love of films was not so closely tied in with one's social identity. (As it was spoken by more Indians than any other language, Hindi was scarcely seen as being under threat.) Still, because their catchment was bigger, the Hindi stars could command wider—though not necessarily deeper—appreciation. Arguably the most popular film star of all time has been the Hindi actor Amitabh Bachchan. I speak here not merely of India but of the world as a whole—Bachchan was voted most popular in an online poll conducted by the British Broadcasting Corporation in 2001.

Amitabh Bachchan was born in 1942, the son of a famous Hindi poet of Allahabad, and joined films after a stint in the corporate world. He was very tall and fairly dark—in both respects at odds with the popular heroes who preceded him. These handicaps were soon overcome, because of his imperious manner and his magnificent deep voice. Bachchan rose to stardom in the early 1970s—a time of cynicism with regard to the political system, which was being challenged by such extraparliamentary forces as the Naxalites and Jayaprakash Narayan's Bihar movement. Bachchan's roles were in keeping with the times. He played the angry young man, pitted against but always overcoming the system—as a militant worker against unfeeling capitalists, as an honest police officer against corrupt superiors, and even as an underworld don whose wicked manner hid (not very successfully) a golden heart.[21]

In 1982, Bachchan was hospitalized after an accident suffered on the set. Millions prayed for his recovery. He did recover, and three years later he became a Congress member of Parliament from Allahabad, at the invitation of his childhood friend Rajiv Gandhi. "Who will replace the angry young man?" asked the popular press, plaintively.[22] But Bachchan and Rajiv Gandhi then fell out, and the actor left Parliament to return to the screen. As he grew older, his roles changed. He is astonishingly versatile—in his sixties, he can play the stern father as well as the quirky policeman (as in *Bunty and Babli*, 2005). In the first years of the new millennium he played what was his most popular role yet, as the host of *Kaun Banega Crorepati*, the Indian version of *Who Wants to Be a Millionaire?* The show was spectacularly successful, in part because it was in tune with the get-rich-quick temper of post-liberalization India, but also because of the fame and manner of the host. Bachchan was brilliant—by turns gentle and sharp, and superbly bilingual, his improvisations worthy of his father, the Hindi poet who was also a professor of English literature.

A sixtieth-birthday tribute to Bachchan described how his career had "traversed emotions and generations."[23] Perhaps the only other figure who has done this so successfully is the singer Lata Mangeshkar. She too had a gifted father: the singer, actor, and composer Dinanath Mangeshkar. He died in 1942, when Lata was only thirteen. She had spent the better part of her life learning music from her father. As the eldest of five siblings, she very quickly became the family's main breadwinner. She sang at first in Marathi films but soon moved to the more popular and better-paying Hindi arena.

Lata Mangeshkar recorded her first song as a playback performer in 1947. By the end of the 1940s she had become the best-known singer in India. She was also the most sought-after; no producer or director could think of a film without a song by her. In a career spanning five decades, she has recorded more than 5,000 songs.[24]

Before Lata Mangeshkar, women singers in films had husky voices. Her own voice was toward the higher end of the scale. Shrill to some, her voice became to others the very expression of soft femininity. It was the "voice to which the road-side vendor in Delhi has transacted his business, the long-distance trucker has sped along the highway, the Army jawan in Ladakh has kept guard at his frontier bunker and to which the glittering élite have dined in luxury hotels."[25] Her appeal cut across classes and across the political spectrum. The nationalist Jawaharlal Nehru was an admirer, not least because Lata made famous a song (*Ae mere vatan ke logon*) saluting the martyrs of the Chinese invasion in 1962. Much later, another admirer was the chauvinist Bal Thackeray, who upheld Lata as a splendid exemplar of Marathi womanhood.

IV

One feature of the film industry has been its capacious cosmopolitanism. Parsi and Jewish actors have rubbed shoulders with Hindus, Muslims, and Christians. Some of the greatest film directors have been from Bengal or south India.

A representative example is one of the most successful films ever made, *Sholay* (1975). Its director was a Sindhi; its lyricist and one male lead were Punjabi. Other male leads were from Uttar Pradesh, Gujarat, and the North-West Frontier. (Another, who was dropped at the last moment, was from Sikkim.) Of the two main woman stars, one was a Tamil, the other a Bengali living in Madhya Pradesh. The music director was a Bengali—from Tripura.[26]

It was not just in Bombay that the film industry was socially inclusive. In the Madras studios of the Tamil director S. S. Vasan, the "make-up department was first headed by a Bengali who became too big for a studio and then left. He was succeeded by a Maharashtrian who was assisted by a Dharwar Kannadiga, an Andhra, a Madras Indian Christian, an Anglo-Burmese and the usual local Tamils." As one of Vasan's script-writers was to recall, "this gang of nationally integrated make-up men could turn any decent-looking person into a hideous crimson-hued monster with the help of truck-loads of pancake and a number of other locally made potions and lotions."[27]

Above all, the film industry provided a generous refuge to India's largest and often very vulnerable minority, the Muslims. Many of the best lyricists, as already noted, were Muslim; so were some popular script-writers. Some of the best male singers were Muslim. So too were some top directors and, even more strikingly, some top actors. When, during the year of India's first general elections, a magazine in Bombay asked its readers to choose their favourite actor, a Muslim man received the most votes, and a Muslim woman came in second.[28] Interestingly, both had assumed non-Muslim names—Yusuf Khan becoming the Hindu-sounding Dilip Kumar, and Fatima Rashid taking the neutral name Nargis (after the narcissus flower). As Muslim actors and actresses became more established, they no longer needed to resort to such subterfuge. A star of the 1950s and 1960s was the actress Waheeda Rahman. Much later, in the 1990s, the top male stars in Hindi films were three Muslims with a common surname, Khan.

The novelist Mukul Kesavan writes of his childhood in Delhi that in his school and at home he never came across a Muslim name. Then he adds, "The only place you were sure of meeting Muslims was the movies."[29] Notably, the content of the movies also reflected their presence and contribution. Because so many scriptwriters and lyricists were Muslim, the language of the Bombay film—spoken or sung—was quite unlike the stiff, formal, Sanskritized Hindi promoted by the state in independent India. Rather, it was closer to the colloquial Hindustani that these writers spoke, a language suffused with Urdu words and widely understood across the Indian heartland.[30] Again, although most films featured Muslim characters, these were "rarely shown in an unfavourable light. They were honest friends, loyal soldiers, good policemen, bluff Pathans, friendly uncles."[31] There remained one significant taboo—against romantic relationships between Hindus and Muslims. This taboo was partially breached by the hit film of 1995, *Bombay*, which showed a Hindu boy falling in love with a Muslim girl. However, the reverse was not conceivable: no film could go so much against the grain as to show a Muslim man marrying a Hindu girl.

In the world of Indian film Muslims have occupied an honorable place. The leading Malayalam film actor Maamooty remarks, "I have been in this business for the last two decades and a half and I don't remember even a single occasion in which my Muslim identity stood in my way."[32] Would that we could say the same about other spheres of life in independent India.

V

For "an Indian world full of strife, tension and misery," writes one critic, popular film provides "just the right escapism the country needed."[33] While most films took their viewers into a fantasy world, there was also a significant strain of realism. In the first years of independence, three film-makers in particular (partially) bucked the populist trend. These were Bimal Roy, whose *Do Bigha Zamin* (1953) sensitively portrayed the sufferings of the rural poor; Mehboob Khan, whose *Mother India* (1957) interwove the story of a heroic mother with the story of a new nation coming into its own; and Guru Dutt, who in a series of remarkable films explored the darker side of life, as experienced especially by artists shunned by a crassly materialistic society.

The pre-eminent representative of an "alternative" tradition of film-making in India, however, was the Bengali giant Satyajit Ray (1921–1992). The son and grandson of writers, Ray himself was very variously gifted. An accomplished short-story writer in Bengali, he was knowledgeable about classical music (western and Indian), and for many years made a living as an artist and designer. His debut film, *Pather Panchali*, released in 1955, was the first of a trilogy that followed a boy named Apu from childhood into manhood, in the process delineating, with great sensitivity and skill, social changes in the Bengal countryside. Over the next three decades Ray made virtually a film a year, and all,

with one exception, were set in Bengal. Several were based on novels by
Rabindranath Tagore, whose scepticism about nationalism as well as his
aesthetic sensibility deeply influenced Ray. Ray received an Oscar for
"lifetime achievement" in 1992; in the same year, he was awarded India's highest civilian honour, the Bharat Ratna.

Ray's films dealt with an astonishing range of subjects. *Jalsaghar*
(1958) was a paean to music; *Mahanagar* (1963), a portrait of his own
city, Calcutta; *Nayak* (1966), an exploration of an actor, his art, and his
public; *Aranyer Din Ratri* (1970), a juxtaposition of the worlds of the
urban middle class and the forest-dwelling tribal. Other films deal
with politics, though without being "political"; one was set during the
Swadeshi movement of 1905–1906, another at the time of the Naxalite
movement of the late 1960s. Ray made some marvellous children's films,
based on stories written by his grandfather, as well as several detective
films, based on his own novels. In his films, women play strong and often pivotal roles; they are intelligent, artistically gifted, and above all
independent.[34]

Satyajit Ray was an iconic figure in his native Bengal; his films were
discussed by writers in newspapers and magazines, and by passengers in
trains and buses as well. He was also greatly admired abroad; his films
were regularly shown at Cannes and other festivals, and his work was
handsomely praised by his peers, notably Akira Kurosawa. Within India, however, he could attract criticism, as when the actress Nargis alleged in Parliament that he showcased Indian poverty to attract attention
in the West. The charge was petty, not to say petulant; it was probably
provoked by Ray's own less than flattering remarks about Hindi film.

Among Ray's distinguished contemporaries were two fellow
Bengalis—Ritwik Ghatak (1925–1976) and Mrinal Sen (born in 1923).
Both were influenced by the communist movement and their films were
often sharply political, dealing with such themes as peasant protest,
partition, and the great Bengal famine of 1943. The leading radical film-
makers of the next generation were Shyam Benegal (born in 1934) and
Adoor Gopalakrishnan (born in 1941), whose movies took up such issues as the reform of the caste system and the prudery and hypocrisy of
the Indian middle class.[35]

Known sometimes as "art cinema" and at other times as "parallel
cinema," the movies made by Ray, Ghatak, Benegal, and others had a
subtlety of method and an attention to social realism that distinguished
them from the escapist fantasies of the formulaic Bombay film. Although
art films were rarely successful at the box office, they were acclaimed by

critics and won numerous prizes at film festivals. And they often had a long afterlife, circulating and being shown at film clubs—many run by college students—in the major cities of India, and abroad.

VI

Apart from the cinema, Indians have also taken succour in various forms of live entertainment. One is theatre. The subcontinent had a rich tradition of classical Sanskrit drama; besides, each region had its own folk theatre, in which dialogue was usually interspersed with song and dance. Known as *jatra* in Bengal, *natya* in Maharashtra, and *yaksha-gana* in Karnataka, these folk forms skilfully adapted to the modern world. The costumes remained traditional, but the themes of the plays now squarely addressed the debates of the time—the uplift of women: the reform of caste; the conflict between economic development and environmental sustainability.

The creation of linguistic states gave a fillip to regional theatres. They now had a captive audience, so to speak: 30 million or 40 million speakers of the language in which the plays were performed. New groups and movements took shape, working within the linguistic state, but with an eye open to the wider world.

Among these groups was Ninasam, established in 1949 by an areca nut farmer, K. V. Subanna, in his native village in north Karnataka. Subanna studied at the University of Mysore, where he was inspired by his teacher, the poet Kuvempu (K. V. Puttappa), to combine farming with artistic creation. On returning home to Heggodu, he first started a theatre group; this was followed, in time, by a newspaper, a publishing house, a film club, a drama school, and a full-fledged repertory company.

Fifty years after it started, Ninasam is thriving, run now by Subanna's son K. V. Akshara, a graduate of the National School of Drama and of Leeds University. Ninasam organizes "culture camps" where peasants and artisans interact with distinguished scholars from all over the world. But their main activity remains the theatre. Ninasam runs a drama school, many of whose graduates join its travelling repertory.

Every year, during the annual culture camp in Heggodu, three plays are premiered in an auditorium named for the Kannada writer and polymath Shivarama Karanth. The plays are all performed in the local language; one is usually an original Kannada play, the second a translation of a play written in another Indian language, the third a translation of a classic western work. On successive days, the village audience might see plays, for example, by Girish Karnad, Mohan Rakesh, and Anton Chekhov. After being premiered in Heggodu, the plays are taken by the Ninasam repertory company to other towns and villages in the state.[36]

In an average year, the company performs some 150 plays, watched by about 300,000 people. And "so you found farmers who grew areca, rice and sugarcane in daytime turn themselves into connoisseurs of Sophocles, Shakespeare, Molière and Ibsen at night."[37]

Another innovator who has successfully blended folk and classical forms is the director Habib Tanvir. A product of the radical Indian People's Theatre Association of the 1940s, Tanvir later studied at the Royal Academy of Dramatic Arts in London before returning home to Chattisgarh. There he worked with local singers and actors to create superb plays in which song and dance were used to satirize the petty corruption of the village elite and the more brutal corruption of the state. His repertory company consisted chiefly of local actors, who spoke the local dialect. Yet their skill allowed them to present his ideas to audiences well beyond Chattisgarh.[38]

Subanna might be described as a progressive and Tanvir as an activist, but neither explicitly aligned himself with a political party or movement. Other theatre groups have been more directly propagandistic. They include the Jana Natya Mandali, which is closely identified with the Naxalite movement in Andhra Pradesh. The Mandali's star performer is the folk singer Gaddar, a sometime engineering student from a Dalit home who has been active in left-wing politics for more than thirty years. In 1971 he composed a song about the rickshaw pullers of Hyderabad; since then, he has composed and performed many songs celebrating the stoicism of the poor or savaging their oppressors. These songs make offerings to the victims of police brutality or contrast the hard work of the peasants with the opulent lifestyle of the propertied classes. In his songs, says Gaddar, "life is people, people's suffering, their tunes." Often underground, sometimes in jail, detested by the police but revered by the peasantry, Gaddar is a nearly legendary figure, and not just in Andhra Pradesh. When he gave a concert in Bangalore, for example, 20,000 people attended it.[39]

VII

The most sophisticated form of entertainment in modern India is classical music, which is performed in two major styles: the Hindustani and the Carnatic. Traditionally, classical music flourished in courts and temples and was patronized by maharajas and nawabs. During British rule, the princes continued to maintain musicians in their courts, but other patrons also began to emerge—merchants and professionals in cities such as Bombay, Madras, and Calcutta.[40]

The musician whose career best exemplifies these larger shifts in social history is the singer M. S. Subbulakshmi, known as MS. She was born in 1916 in Madurai, into a family of temple musicians and courtesans, and was taken by her musician mother to Madras to further her career. Her exquisite voice was matched by her beauty, and she became a much sought-after figure in the musical circles of the city. In 1940 she married the entrepreneur T. Sadashivam, who managed her subsequent career with great skill. In the 1940s, MS also acted in several films, most notably *Meera*, in which she played the great medieval singer Mirabai.

Subbulakshmi was rigorously trained in the classical style, and took pains to learn from the leading teachers of the time, but she also worked on expanding her repertoire. It was as a singer of *bhajans* (popular religious hymns) that she attracted the attention of Mahatma Gandhi. Another and perhaps even more influential admirer was Jawaharlal Nehru, who attended the premiere of *Meera* at Plaza Cinema in New Delhi, and later named her the "queen of song." An admirer as well as a close friend was C. Rajagopalachari, who served as governor general of India and as chief minister of Madras.

Although the endorsement of such prominent figures was helpful, Subbbulakshmi's claim to greatness was independent of them. She was a remarkable singer, with a very wide range and a dignified and gracious personality. Her many recordings of classical and folk compositions made her well known throughout India. She was very willing to sing for other than metropolitan and elite audiences, and to raise money for worthy causes. One scholar has listed 244 charity concerts that she gave between 1944 and 1987. The towns and causes indicate both her popularity and her concerns: in Jamshedpur, she sang for a women's group; in Bombay, in memory of the Hindustani woman vocalist Kesarbai Kerkar; in Hassan, for a hospital; in Madras, for Little Sisters of the Poor (a Christian charity); in Jaffna, for the Ramakrishna Mission (a Hindu social service organization); in Trichy, for workers in a public-sector factory; in Thanjavur, for a tuberculosis sanatorium named after Mahatma Gandhi.[41]

Subbulakshmi took classical music to all corners of India, but the man who most effectively took Indian music overseas was the sitar player Ravi Shankar. He was born in 1920 in Benares, the younger brother of the famous dancer Uday Shankar. He joined his brother's troupe as a boy, touring Europe with it before he was sent back to train under the musician Allauddin Khan. Allauddin was a legendary disciplinarian, and seven years with him made Ravi Shankar one of the two rising stars of his generation, the other being his guru's son, the sarod player Ali Akbar Khan.

By the time of independence, Ravi Shankar was well established as a concert artist. He usually played solo, but he and Ali Akbar Khan also popularized the duet, or *jugalbandhi*, a form previously unknown in classical instrumental music. Like M. S. Subbulakshmi, he did not restrict himself to the purely classical form. For instance, he created a ballet based on Jawaharlal Nehru's *Discovery of India*, and also composed music for several films made by Satyajit Ray.

In 1956, Ravi Shankar went on the first of what would become annual overseas tours. Of a concert he gave in New York in 1961, the city's newspaper of record wrote that it "created a whole new aural landscape," "evocative of a musical mystique, rich in religion and philosophic traditions." By now Ravi Shankar had begun playing and recording with western musicians—John Coltrane, Yehudi Menuhin, André Previn, and others. His fame increased after the Beatle George Harrison took lessons with him, and began to refer to him as his guru.

In 1967 Ravi Shankar shifted his base to California. He became a regular presence at music festivals at Monterey and elsewhere, and had a leading role in the famous "Bangladesh" concert in 1970. He adapted well to his new audience—introducing each composition in his immaculate English, and taking care to alternate formal ragas with lighter compositions. (Indian audiences could listen to a single raga for four hours at a stretch.) He made his tradition altogether more palatable to the western world, paving the way for younger Indians to take their music to places where it had never been heard before. In the 1990s he returned to India, making New Delhi his base, but he continued to regularly visit the West. Now in his ninth decade, he is still spruce and fit, still capable of presenting a high-quality concert extending for two hours and more.[42]

M. S. Subbulakshmi and Ravi Shankar were not necessarily the greatest musicians of their generation. But they became the best-known because they were great enough, because of their charming personalities, and because through their careers one could trace larger processes of social change. They were splendid ambassadors for their ancient art, helping it adjust to and indeed win acclaim in an impatient and often unforgiving world. They helped expand the audience and support base for their music, thus, in the long run, benefiting numerous performers apart from themselves.[43]

VIII

The form of entertainment most typical of urban-industrial society is, of course, spectator sport. All modern sports are played and watched in India, along with traditional games such as *kho-kho* and *kabaddi*. In terms of achievement, two sports stand out: billiards, in which India has produced several world champions; and field hockey, in which the Indian team was undefeated between 1928 and 1956, winning six Olympic gold medals in succession.

In terms of spectators, the two main sports are football (soccer) and cricket. As in the West, football has been very popular among the working classes. The great industrial centres—Bombay, Delhi, and Bangalore— all have active leagues that include clubs sponsored by industrial firms. The game is also widely followed, and actively played, in Goa, Kerala, and the Punjab.

The capital city of Indian football, however, is Calcutta. Here, sporting rivalry has gone hand in hand with political competition. There are three leading teams; one, Mohammedan Sporting, traditionally represented the Muslims; a second, Mohun Bagan, was started and supported by the Bengali *bhadralok*, or upper classes; a third, East Bengal, was favoured by the more plebeian classes from the other side of the province. These and other teams play each other on the Calcutta Maidan, a vast expanse of green grass in the heart of the city.

From the 1930s to the early 1980s, football was probably the most passionately discussed topic in Calcutta, even more so than politics or religion. The leading clubs each had thousands of followers, whose emotional investment in their team fully equalled that of European football fans. Violence during and after matches was not uncommon. However, after the World Cup of 1982 popular interest in the sport began to wane. This was the first World Cup telecast live in India; alerted to the gap between their own local heroes and the great international stars, men in Calcutta began to turn away from their clubs. The slide has continued; twenty years later, soccer ranks a poor second to cricket in Bengal.

This is true in the rest of India as well. Cricket is a game that relies on wrist work rather than size or physical fitness; to be small and stocky is not always a disadvantage. Thus, Indians can compete with the best players in the world. The slow pace of cricket and the interrupted play also suit Indians, who like to go in groups to matches, there to engage in chatter and banter among themselves and with the players.

In 1983, India won cricket's World Cup. The victory coincided with the spread of satellite television, which took the game to small towns and working-class homes. Through the 1980s and beyond, cricket steadily gained in popularity. Two Indians, Sunil Gavaskar and Sachin Tendulkar, broke world batting records; and Kapil Dev was for a time the bowler with most wickets in Test cricket. The social base of the game widened—more players were coming into the national team from smaller towns, and women particularly were watching the game in large numbers.

By the turn of the twenty-first century, cricket had come to equal film in mass attention and popularity. Some cricketers were as wealthy and as well-known as film stars. They were ubiquitous on television, either playing the game or advertising all manner of products from toothpaste to luxury automobiles.

Much of the sentiment that went into the sport was nationalistic. Two opponents were most disliked, or even hated: the old colonial power, England; and the new rival on the subcontinent, Pakistan. Victory over one or the other guaranteed the players handsome cash prizes, a huge public reception, and an audience with the prime minister.

In the aftermath of the demolition of Babri Masjid, the war in Kargil, and the insurgency in Kashmir, cricket matches between India and Pakistan were far more intensely fought, not just by the players but equally in the minds of those who followed and supported them. The television audience for an India-Pakistan match was about 300 million, and for most of the viewers the match was war minus the shooting. An ugly aspect of this rivalry was that it drew hostile attention to Indian Muslims, who were accused by Hindu fundamentalists of secretly supporting Pakistan. When India defeated Pakistan in the World Cup of 2003, for example, the residents of Bangalore poured out into the streets, "bursting firecrackers, whooping, whistling, cheering aloud with the shouts of *Bharat mata ki jai* [glory to Mother India] rending the air." In Ahmedabad, however, the victory celebration turned into a communal riot, after revellers accused some Muslim students of celebrating the fall of an Indian wicket.[44]

The next year, cricket figured in a curious way in the general elections. At the time of the campaign the Indian team was playing, and winning, in Pakistan, where one of its leading players was Mohammed Kaif, a Muslim from Uttar Pradesh. With seventy-nine seats, Uttar Pradesh was the key to the elections, but its large population of Muslims had rarely voted for the Bharatiya Janata party. For a party trying to shed its Hindu chauvinist image, this victory in cricket came as a gift from the gods. In his speeches in Uttar Pradesh, the prime minister, Atal Bihari Vajpayee, praised the "splendid job done by one of your sons, Mohammed Kaif." "God knows how big a person he [Kaif] would be in future," Vajpayee predicted—before appealing to the Muslims in the audience to vote for his party. He urged the Muslims to trust the BJP, for, he claimed, "we are in a position to protect them."

In the end, the Muslims did not vote for the Mr. Vajpayee's party, which was duly turned out of office. But that the prime minister sought to enlist a cricketer for his cause testifies to the extraordinary importance accorded the game by India and Indians.[45]

IX

Crucial aids to these varied forms of entertainment have been the radio and, more recently, television. The first broadcasting companies started operating in India in the 1920s. These were soon subsumed by the state-owned All India Radio, which for many decades had a monopoly. AIR commanded a far-flung network of stations, collectively serving nearly the whole subcontinent, with only the jungles, deserts, and mountains excluded.

The state's hopes for radio were expressed by a leading nationalist politician as "not only to give entertainments but to give such programmes as will give enlightenment and elevation of spirit to the villagers."[46] Most stations began broadcasting at dawn, with a hymn of invocation, and ended at midnight with a weather report. The programmes inspersed music—classical, film, and folk—with stories, plays, news bulletins, and special shows for women, children, and rural listeners. Education in health and farming methods was also provided. It was a very mixed brew, allowing listeners to pick and choose according to their tastes and needs.

In the year of independence, 1947, the Indian radio industry manufactured only 3,000 sets a year. The number went up to 60,000 in 1951; and up to 150,000 in 1956. By 1962, All India Radio was broadcasting from over thirty stations, and for about 100,000 hours annually. A decade later there were an estimated 15 million radio sets in operation; many of these, of course, listened to by more than one listener.[47]

For a decade after independence, the minister in charge of Information and Broadcasting was Dr. B. V. Keskar, a scholar with a deep interest in classical Indian culture combined with a lofty disdain for its modern variants. In a speech in 1953 he noted:

> Classical music has fallen on bad days and is on the point of extinction in North India. Classical music has lost touch with the masses, not due to the fault of the public, but because of historical circumstances. In the past, it was patronized by Princes and Sardars, but that support has almost ended. During the last 150 years we were under the British who would not understand and support Hindustani music. . . . The main problem before musicians and All India Radio is to revive public contact with classical music. We must make them familiar with our traditional music, and make them more intimate with it.[48]

In the late 1930s All India Radio had already begun employing classical musicians on its staff. The artistes were ranked as A, B, C, etc., according to their age, ability, and experience. They were assigned to the station nearest their home and were expected to advise on programming as well as give regular recitals themselves. By the late 1950s about 10,000 musicians were on the state's payroll. They were from both the Hindustani and the Carnatic style, and they included some of the greatest artists then living, among them Ali Akbar Khan, Bismillah Khan, Mallikarjun Mansur, and Emmani Shankar Sastri.

Most stations on All India Radio played several hours of classical music a day. Saturday night featured the prestigious National Programme, when a single artist played or sang for a full ninety minutes. Every year AIR organized a Radio Sangeet Sammelan, a festival of live concerts held in towns and cities across India. Recordings of these concerts provided material for a month-long celebration of Indian music over the radio.

Along with his love of the classical genres, Dr. B. V. Keskar also had a particular distaste for films and film music. For the first few years of his tenure, popular music was banned on the airwaves. Fortunately, better sense prevailed, and AIR then began a special channel, Vividh Bharati, devoted exclusively to film music. This channel soon found its way into millions of homes, and attracted commercial advertisements that made it self-supporting.[49]

Without All India Radio, Indian classical music might not have survived the death of the princely order. But AIR also played a wider role in national integration, by linking popular culture with high culture, and region with nation. The least appealing part of AIR was its news bulletins. These reported all events—national or international—from the perspective of the party in power, and the propaganda was made even less palatable by the monotonous drone in which it was offered.

From the early 1970s, television began supplementing radio as a major source of entertainment and propaganda. It was the latter objective which at first predominated; programming on the state-owned Doordarshan focused on the government's achievements and urged citizens to grow more food and forge more steel. By the 1980s the channel had discovered the delights of programmes sponsored not by the state but by the market. The serials *Ramayan* and *Mahabharat* were trailblazers, attracting millions of viewers as well as millions of rupees in advertisements. These were followed by soap operas which presented the saga of a family over fifty or more episodes. (An early success was Ramesh Sippy's *Buniyaad*, about a family from Lahore making a new life in India after partition.) While viewers were entertained, the state was being enriched; in just a decade, 1975–1985, the revenues of Doordarshan increased sixtyfold.[50]

In the 1990s, the airwaves were opened up to private operators. Although FM stations sprang up in the cities, the main beneficiaries of this liberalization were television channels. These proliferated at an amazing rate, operating in all the languages of India. By 2000 there were more than one hundred private channels in operation. Some were very specialized, covering only sport, business, film, or news; others were more catholic in their approach, covering all these subjects and more besides. This was a ferociously competitive market, with a high rate of mortality for new entrants and much poaching of staff. The consumers themselves were spoiled for choice—where once there existed a single state-owned channel, now there was a dazzling variety of alternatives on offer.

X

The critic Chidananda Dasgupta once said, "India's popular cinema . . . speaks not in the international language of cinema, but in a local dialect which is incomprehensible to most countries in the world."[51] Dasgupta may have been speaking here as a friend and biographer of Satyajit Ray, and for Bengal, whose artistic standards have tended to be different from (or superior to) those in other parts of the country. In fact, from very early on, Indian film has also appealed to (and resonated with) audiences that were not Indian.

A pioneer in this regard was Raj Kapoor, scion of India's most celebrated film family. (His father, Prithviraj Kapoor, was a celebrated stage and cinema actor; his two brothers, Shashi and Shammi, were notable film stars, as have been his two sons and their children.) Raj Kapoor was a sort of Indian Chaplin, playing a tramp in films directed by himself.[52] He formed a memorable partnership with Nargis, a beauty with whom he acted in seventeen films. When they arrived at a premier in Calcutta, they were mobbed by "hordes of autograph-hunting juveniles."[53] They had the same reception in the Soviet Union: when they went there in 1954 and again in 1956, old veterans of the tsar's wars lined up to shake their hands, and pregnant women told them that they would call their child Raj if it was a boy, or Nargis if it was a girl.[54]

Raj Kapoor's breakthrough film was *Awara*, released toward the end of 1951, in which he played a lovable rogue forced by family circumstances to turn to a life of crime. The reviewer in an upscale English-language newspaper wrote sniffily about the "stilted artificiality" of the film, and about how its "continuous contrivance for effect" had "shatter[ed] realism in the story and rob[bed] the picture of its most essential quality."[55] But the masses flocked to it nonetheless—and not just in India. When the scriptwriter visited the Soviet Union, he discovered that "all bands and orchestras were playing tunes from this film, Russian and Ukranian and Georgian teenagers were singing the *Awara* songs in chorus, and one met people who boasted that they had seen the film twenty or thirty times. In the whole history of the Soviet cinema no film had ever won such popularity, and no film or stage star had won such renown in so short a time."[56]

Hindi films have been popular across Africa, in the Middle East, and in Southeast Asia. An anthropologist doing fieldwork in a Malay village had to take his respondents every week to the nearest cinema, to see what they called simply "a Hindi."[57] And in Japan, the films of the Tamil star Rajnikanth were, for a time, all the rage.

Less surprising has been the popularity of Hindi films in countries that share the same broad culture. An American tourist in Pakistan found that in both public buses and private homes, the music one was most likely to hear was Hindi film music. Pirated cassettes abounded, as did pirated DVDs of the latest films, which were officially banned in Pakistan to protect the domestic film industry.[58] Farther to the west, in Afghanistan, music of all kinds had been banned by the Taliban. But when that regime fell, it was reported that the briskest business was done by barbers who cut beards and by vendors who sold photos of Indian film stars. Songs by Lata Mangeshkar and Mohammad Rafi once more blared out of homes in Kabul. More daringly, young men and women were inspired by Hindi films to choose their own life partners, in violation of family custom and tradition. A court in Kabul was besieged by cases brought by such couples, who pleaded that they be allowed to marry without the permission of their parents.[59]

More recently, Hindi films have found a market in western Europe and North America, chiefly among what are now substantial and wealthy communities of the Indian diaspora. In 2000, four Hindi films were among the top twenty releases of the year in the United Kingdom.[60] Three years later, *Time* magazine reported that the worldwide audience for Indian films greatly exceeded the audience for Hollywood—at 3.6 billion, it was 1 billion people more.[61]

Because of this growing audience overseas, and in keeping with changing mores within India, film characters and themes were undergoing subtle shifts. Western clothes were now more common, and "love marriages" were more acceptable. The vamp had become superfluous, since the heroine was now no longer pure and virginal but capable herself of intrigue and seduction. And the films indulged in an unabashed celebration of wealth. In the past, even if the hero was not poor or unemployed, he tended to identify with the downtrodden. Now, however, it was "a party of the rich," with the audience "invited to watch, from a distance."[62]

In the first year of the millennium a wax image of Amitabh Bachchan was unveiled at Madame Tussaud's in London. This was an even greater honour than being chosen "actor of the century" by the BBC, in a poll biased by frenetic mass voting among Indians. Still, it was not Bachchan but some younger Indians who were emerging as the face of the industry in its new, globalized phase. One was the actress Aishwarya Rai, a former Miss World whom Julia Roberts considered "the most beautiful woman in the world." Rai appeared on the cover of *Time* magazine's Asian edition, served on international film juries, and was wooed by prominent Hollywood directors. A second was the actor Shahrukh Khan, the most successful film hero of his generation. His speaking and singing tours across Europe and North America were wild hits, attended by thousands of Indians, Iranians, Afghans, and Arabs, and by a growing number of Caucasians as well.

Another international success was the composer A. R. Rahman. A child prodigy who composed his first film songs when he was not yet in his teens, Rahman first made a name in Tamil cinema before moving on to Hindi films. His training (by his musician father) was in the classical Carnatic style, which he was adept at blending with rhythms and instruments from other parts of the world. In 2002, Rahman was invited by Andrew Lloyd Webber to compose the music for Webber's *Bombay Dreams*. After the musical's success on the West End, he was commissioned to co-write the music for the first major stage adaptation of J. R. R. Tolkien's *Lord of the Rings*, a production whose budget was 27 million pounds, one-tenth of this being the fee of the composers. Then, in 2004, Rahman was invited to conduct the Birmingham Symphony Orchestra, whose first conductor had been Sir Edward Elgar.[63]

One who would have gloried in Rahman's success was his fellow Tamil, S. S. Vasan. In 1955, Vasan had pleaded with an audience of puritans in Delhi to abandon their "prejudice against film-men." "Recreation and entertainment," he argued, "are almost as important as food, clothing and shelter." If "public men work for the good of the public," Vasan said, then "showmen do, as a matter of fact, work for the pleasure of the public."[64] At the time, both parts of the statement were true, for the public men then active included Jawaharlal Nehru and B. R. Ambedkar. Fifty years later only the latter part holds good. Whereas public men now work mostly for private gain, the "showmen" of India—among whom we must include singers and composers as well as actors, and women as much as men—still work creatively for the pleasure of their ever-growing public.

Epilogue

WHY INDIA SURVIVES

The Sikhs may try to set up a separate regime. I think they
probably will and that will be only a start of a general
decentralization and break-up of the idea that India
is a country, whereas it is a subcontinent as varied as Europe.
The Punjabi is as different from a Madrassi as a Scot is from an
Italian. The British tried to consolidate it but achieved nothing
permanent. No one can make a nation out of a continent of many
nations.

GENERAL CLAUDE AUCHINLEK, writing in 1948

Unless Russia first collapses, India—Hindustan, if you will—
is in grave danger of becoming communist in the not distant
future.

SIR FRANCIS TUKER, writing in 1950

As the years pass, British rule in India comes to seem as remote as
the battle of Agincourt.

MALCOLM MUGGERIDGE, writing in 1964

Few people contemplating Indira Gandhi's funeral in 1984 would
have predicted that ten years later India would remain a unity but
the Soviet Union would be a memory.

ROBIN JEFFREY, writing in 2000

I

IN ITS ISSUE FOR FEBRUARY 1959, the American magazine *Atlantic Monthly* carried an unsigned report on the state of Pakistan. General Ayub Khan had recently taken power in a military coup. What was missing in Pakistan, wrote the correspondent, was "the politicians. They have been banished from public life and their very name is anathema. Even politics in the abstract has disappeared. People no longer seem interested in debating socialism versus free enterprise or Left versus Right. It is as if these controversies, like the forms of parliamentary democracy, were merely something that was inherited willy-nilly from the West and can now be dispensed with."

The *Atlantic*'s reporter believed that "the peasants [in Pakistan] welcome the change in government because they want peace." He saw law and order returning to the countryside, and smugglers and black marketeers being put in their place. "Already the underdog in Pakistan" is grateful to the army, he wrote, adding, "In a poor country . . . the success of any government is judged by the price of wheat and rice," which, he claimed, had fallen since Ayub took over.

Foreign correspondents are not bashful about making generalizations, even if these are based on a single, brief visit to a single, unrepresentative country. The reporter for the *Atlantic* was no exception. From what he saw—or thought he saw—in Pakistan he drew this general lesson: "Many of the newly independent countries in Asia and Africa have tried to copy the British parliamentary system. The experiment has failed in the Sudan, Pakistan and Burma, while the system is under great stress in India and Ceylon. The Pakistan experiment [with military rule] will be watched in Asia and Africa with keen interest."

Forty years later, the *Atlantic Monthly* carried another report on the state of Pakistan. By then, Pakistan had passed from dictatorship to democracy and then back again to rule by men in uniform. It had also been divided, with its eastern wing seceding to form the sovereign state of Bangladesh. And it had been involved in three wars, all initiated by the generals who the peasants had hoped would bring them peace.

This new report was signed by Robert D. Kaplan, who is something of a travelling specialist on ethnic warfare and the breakdown of nation states. Kaplan presented a very negative portrayal of Pakistan: its lawlessness, ethnic conflicts (Sunni versus Shia, Mohajir versus Sindhi, Balochi versus Punjabi, etc.), and economic disparities, and of the training of jihadis and the cult of Osama bin Laden.

Kaplan quoted a Pakistani intellectual who said, "We have never defined ourselves in our own right—only in relation to India. That is our tragedy." The reporter himself thought that Pakistan "could be a Yugoslavia in the making, but with nuclear weapons." Like Yugoslavia, Pakistan reflected an "accumulation of disorder and irrationality that was so striking." Kaplan's conclusion was that "both military and democratic governments in Pakistan have failed, even as India's democracy has gone more than half a century without a coup."[1]

Kaplan may not have read the very different prognosis of Pakistan offered in the *Atlantic* forty years previously. What remains striking is the difference in the assessments of India. In 1959, the *Atlantic* pitied India for being a democracy when it might be better off as a military dictatorship. In 1999, the *Atlantic* thought that democracy had been India's saving grace.

Two years later the World Trade Center in New York fell. As attempts were made by western powers to foster democracy by force in Afghanisthan and Iraq, India's record in nurturing democracy from within gathered renewed appreciation. When, in April 2004, India held its fourteenth general elections, the contrast with Pakistan was highlighted by Pakistanis themselves. "India goes to the polls and the world notices," wrote Ayaz Amir, a columnist in Karachi. "Pakistan plunges into another exercise in authoritarian management—and the world notices, but through jaundiced eyes. Are we so dumb that the comparison escapes us?" "When will we wake up?" he continued. "When will we learn? When will it dawn on us that it is not India's size, population, tourism or IT industry [that is] making us look small, but Indian democracy?"[2]

II

In the elections of 2004, 400 million voters exercised their franchise. The ruling alliance, led by the Bharatiya Janata party, was widely expected to win by a significant margin, and this prediction aroused fears of a renewal of the "Hindutva" agenda. As it happened, the United Progressive Alliance, led by the Congress, defied the pollsters and came to power. The outcome was variously interpreted as a victory for secularism, a revolt of the *aam admi* (common man) against the rich, and an affirmation of the continuing hold of the Nehru-Gandhi dynasty on the popular imagination. In the larger context of world history, however, what is important is not why Indians voted as they did but the fact that they voted at all. The elections of 1952 were described as the "biggest gamble in history," and ever since then, obituaries have been written for Indian democracy. It has been said, time and again, that a poor, diverse, divided country cannot sustain the practice of (reasonably) free and fair elections.

Yet India has done so. In those first general elections voter turnout was less than 46%. Over the years this percentage has steadily increased;

from the late 1960s, about three of five eligible Indians (60%) have voted on election day. In assembly elections the percentage has tended to be even higher. When these numbers are disaggregated, they reveal even more. In the first two general elections, less than 40% of eligible women voted; by 1998 the figure was more than 60%. Besides, as surveys found, women increasingly exercised their choice *independently*—that is, regardless of their husband's or father's views. Also voting in ever higher numbers were Dalits and tribals, the oppressed and marginalized sections of society. In north India in particular, Dalits turned out in far greater numbers than high castes. As the political analyst Yogendra Yadav points out, "India is perhaps the only large democracy in the world today where the turnout of the lower orders is well above that of the most privileged groups."[3]

The Indians' love of voting is well illustrated by a cluster of villages on the Andhra-Maharashtra border. Issued voting cards by the administrations of both states, the villagers seized the opportunity to vote twice.[4] It is also illustrated by peasants in Bihar, who go to the polls despite threats by Maoist revolutionaries. Dismissing elections as an exercise in bourgeois hypocrisy, the Maoists have been known to blacken the faces of villagers campaigning for political parties, and to warn potential voters that their feet and hands would be chopped off. Yet, as an anthropologist working in central Bihar found, "the overall effect of poll-boycott on voter turnout seems to be negligible." In villages where Maoists had been active for years, "in fact, election day was seen as an enjoyable (almost festive) occasion. Women dressed in bright yellows and reds, their hair oiled and adorned with clips, made their way to the polling booth in small groups."[5] Likewise, in parts of the north-east where the writ of the Indian state runs erratically or not at all, insurgents are unable to stop villagers from voting. As the chief election commissioner wryly put it, "the Election Commission's small contribution to the integrity of the country is to make these areas part of the country for just one day, election day."[6]

That elections have been successfully indigenized in India is demonstrated by the depth and breadth of their reach—across and into all sections of Indian society—by the passions they evoke, and by the humour that surrounds them. There is a very rich archive of electoral cartoons, poking fun at promises made by prospective politicians, their desperation to get a party ticket, and much else.[7] At other times the humour can be gentle rather than mocking. Consider the career of a cloth merchant from Bhopal, Mohan Lal, who ran against five different prime ministers.

Wearing a wooden crown and a garland made by himself, he would walk the streets of his constituency, ringing a bell. He unfailingly lost his deposit, thereby justifying his own, self-inflicted sobriquet *Dhartipakad*, or "he who lies, humbled, on the ground." His idea in running, he said, was "to make everyone realise that democracy was meant for one and all."[8]

That elections allow all Indians to feel part of India is also made clear by the experience of Goa. When it was united—or reunited—with India by force in 1961, there was much adverse commentary in the western press. But whereas in 400 years of Portuguese rule the Goans had never been allowed to choose their own leaders, within a couple of years of coming under the rule of New Delhi they were able to do so. The political scientist Benedict Anderson has compared India's treatment of Goa with Indonesia's treatment of East Timor, another Portuguese colony "liberated" by armed nationalists:

> Nehru had sent his troops to Goa in 1960 (sic) without a drop of blood being spilt. But he was a humane man and the freely elected leader of a democracy; he gave the Goanese their own autonomous state government, and encouraged their full participation in India's politics. In every respect, General Suharto was Nehru's polar opposite.[9]

Considering the size of the electorate, it is overwhelmingly likely that more people have voted in Indian elections than in any other democracy. India's success in this regard is especially striking when compared with the record of China. China is larger, but far less divided on ethnic or religious lines, and far less poor. Yet there has never been a single election held there. In other ways too China is much less free than India. The flow of information is highly restricted—when the search engine Google set up shop in China in February 2006, it had to agree to submit to state censorship. The movement of people is regulated as well—the permission of the state is usually required to change one's place of residence. In India, on the other hand, the press can print more or less what it likes, and citizens can say exactly what they feel, live where they want, and travel to any part of the country.

Comparisons between India and China have long been a staple of scholarly analysis. Now, in a world that becomes more connected every day, these comparisons have become common in popular discourse as well. In such a comparison, China might win economically but will lose politically. Indians like to harp on their neighbour's "democracy deficit," sometimes directly and at other times by euphemism or allusion. When asked to put on a special show at the World Economic Forum of 2006, the Indian delegates never failed to describe their land, whether in speech or in print or in posters, as the "world's fastest-growing *democracy*."

If we look at what one might call the hardware of democracy, then this self-congratulation is certainly merited. Indians enjoy freedom of expression and of movement, and they have the vote. However, if one examines the software of democracy, the picture is less cheering. Most political parties have become family firms. Most politicians are corrupt, and many come from a criminal background. Other institutions central to the functioning of a democracy have also declined precipitously over the years. The percentage of truly independent-minded civil servants has steadily declined, as has the percentage of completely fair-minded judges.

Is India a proper or a sham democracy? When asked this question, I usually turn to an immortal phrase of the Hindi comic actor Johnny Walker. In a film in which he plays the hero's sidekick, Walker answers every query with the remark, "Boss, *phipty-phipty*." When asked what prospect he has of marrying the girl he loves, or of getting the job he desires, the sidekick tells the boss that the chances are roughly even, 50% of success and 50% of failure.

Is India a democracy then? The answer is, well, *phipty-phipty*. It mostly is a democracy as regards holding elections and permitting freedom of movement and expression. It mostly is not as regards the functioning of politicians and political institutions. However, that India is even 50% a democracy flies in the face of tradition, history, and conventional wisdom. Indeed, through its own experience it is rewriting that history and that wisdom. Thus Sunil Khilnani remarked of the elections of 2004 that they represented "the largest exercise of democratic election, ever and anywhere, in human history. Clearly, the idea of democracy, brought into being on an Athenian hillside some 2,500 years ago, has travelled far— and today describes a disparate array of political projects and experiences. The peripatetic life of the democratic idea has ensured that the history of Western political ideas can no longer be written coherently from within the terms of the West's own historical experience."[10]

III

The history of independent India has amended and modified theories of democracy based on the experience of the West. However, it has even more frontally challenged ideas of nationalism emanating from the western experience.

In an essay summarizing a lifetime of thinking on the subject, Isaiah Berlin identifies "the infliction of a wound on the collective feelings of a society, or at least of its spiritual leaders," as a "necessary" condition for the birth of nationalist sentiment. For this sentiment to become a more widespread political movement, however, requires "one more condition": the society "must, in the minds of at least some of its most sensitive members, carry an image of itself as a nation, at least in embryo, in virtue of some general unifying factor or factors—language, ethnic origin, a common history (real or imaginary)." Later in the same essay, Berlin comments on the "astonishingly Europocentric" political thought of the nineteenth century and the early twentieth century: where "the people of Asia and Africa are discussed either as wards or as victims of Europeans, but seldom, if ever, in their own right, as peoples with histories and cultures of their own; with a past and present and future which must be understood in terms of their own actual character and circumstances."[11]

Behind every successful nationalist movement in the western world has been a unifying factor, a glue holding the members of the nation together. This has been provided by a shared language, a shared religious faith, a shared territory, or a common enemy—and sometimes all of the above. Thus the British nation brought together people huddling on a cold island—people who were mostly Protestant and who detested France. In the case of France, language combined powerfully with religion. For the Americans, a shared language and a widely shared faith worked in tandem with animosity toward the colonists. As for the smaller east European nations—the Poles, the Czechs, the Lithuanians, etc.—their populations have been united by a common language, a mostly common faith, and a shared and very bitter history of domination by German and Russian oppressors.[12]

By contrast with these (and other examples), the Indian nation does not privilege a single language or religious faith. Although the majority of its citizens are Hindus, India is not a Hindu nation. Its constitution does not discriminate between people on the basis of faith; nor, more crucially, did the nationalist movement that lay behind it. From its inception the Indian National Congress was, as Mukul Kesavan observes, a political Noah's ark that sought to bring every species of Indian on board.[13] Gandhi's political programme was built on harmony and cooperation between India's two major religious communities—Hindus and Muslims. Although, in the end, his work and example did not prevent the division of India, this failure made his successors even more determined to construct independent India as a secular republic. For Jawaharlal Nehru and his colleagues, if India was anything at all, it was *not* a "Hindu Pakistan."

Like Indian democracy, Indian secularism is also a story that combines success with failure. Membership in a minority religion is no bar to advancing in business or the professions. The richest industralist in India is a Muslim. Some of the most popular film stars are Muslim. At least three presidents and three chief justices have been Muslim. At the time of writing, the president of India is a Muslim, the prime minister a Sikh, and the leader of the ruling party a Catholic born in Italy. Many of the country's most prominent lawyers and doctors have been Christians and Parsis.

On the other hand, there have been periodic episodes of religious rioting, in the worst of which (as in Delhi in 1984 and Gujarat in 2002) the minorities have suffered grievous losses of life and property. Still, for the most part the minorities appear to retain faith in the democratic and secular ideal. Very few Indian Muslims have joined terrorist or fundamentalist organizations. Even more than their compatriots, Indian Muslims feel that their opinions and votes matter. One recent survey found that whereas 69% of all Indians approved of and endorsed the ideal of democracy, 72% of Muslims did so. And the turnout of Muslims at elections is higher than ever before.[14]

Building democracy in a poor society was always going to be hard work. Nurturing secularism in a land recently divided was going to be even harder. The creation of an Islamic state on India's borders was a provocation to those Hindus who themselves wished to merge faith with state. My own view—I am speaking as a historian rather than a citizen—is that as long as Pakistan exists there will be Hindu fundamentalists in India. In times of stability, or when the political leadership is firm, they will be marginal or on the defensive. In times of change, or when the political leadership is irresolute, they will be influential and assertive.

The pluralism of religion was one cornerstone of the Indian republic. A second was the pluralism of language. Here again, the intention and the effort predated independence. In the 1920s, Gandhi reconstituted the provincial committees of the Congress on linguistic lines. The party had promised to form linguistic provinces as soon as the country was free. The promise was not fulfilled immediately after 1947, because the creation of Pakistan had aroused fears of further Balkanization. However, in the face of popular protest the government yielded to the demand.

Linguistic states have been in existence for fifty years. In that time they have deepened and consolidated Indian unity. Within each state, a common language has provided the basis of administrative unity and efficiency. It has also led to an efflorescence of cultural creativity, as expressed in film, theatre, fiction, and poetry. However, pride in one's language has rarely been in conflict with a broader identification with the nation as a whole. The three major secessionist movements in independent India—in Nagaland in the 1950s, in Punjab in the 1980s, and in Kashmir in the 1990s—have affirmed religious and territorial, not linguistic, distinctiveness. For the rest, it has proved possible—indeed, desirable—to be Kannadiga and Indian, Malayali and Indian, Andhra and Indian, Tamil and Indian, Bengali and Indian, Oriya and Indian, Maharashtrian and Indian, Gujarati and Indian, and, of course, Hindi-speaking and Indian.

That, in India, unity and pluralism are inseparable is graphically expressed in the country's currency. On one side of the paper money is a portrait of the "father of the nation," Mahatma Gandhi; on the other side is a picture of the Houses of Parliament. The denomination—5, 10, 50, 100, etc.—is printed in words in Hindi and English (the two official languages), and also, in smaller type, in all the other languages of the Indian Union. In this manner, seventeen different scripts are represented. Each language, and each script, represents a distinct culture and regional ethos, here nesting more or less comfortably with the idea of India as a whole.

Some western observers—usually Americans—believed that this profusion of tongues would be the undoing of India. On the basis of their experience in their own country, where English had been the glue binding several waves of immigrants, they thought that a single language—Hindi or English—had to be spoken by all Indians. Linguistic states they regarded as a grievous error. Thus, in a book published as late as 1970, at the end of his stint as the *Washington Post*'s man in India, Bernard Nossiter wrote despairingly that this was "a land of Babel with no common voice." The creation of linguistic states would "further divide the states from each other [and] heighten the impulse toward secession." From its birth the Indian nation had been "plagued by particularist, separatist tendencies," wrote Nossiter; and "the continuing confusion of tongues . . . can only further these tendencies and puts in question the future unity of the Indian state."[15]

That, to survive, a nation state had necessarily to privilege one language was a view that the Soviet dictator Joseph Stalin shared with

American liberals. Stalin insisted that "a national community is inconceivable without a common language," and that "there is no nation which at one and the same time speaks several languages."[16] This belief came to inform the language policy of the Soviet Union, in which the learning of Russian was made obligatory. The endeavour, as Stalin himself put it, was to ensure that "there is one language in which all citizens of the USSR can more or less express themselves—that is Russian."[17]

Like Bernard Nossiter, Stalin might have feared for the future of the Indian nation state because of its encouragement of linguistic diversity. In fact, exactly the reverse has happened—linguistic pluralism has worked to tame and domesticate secessionist tendencies. A comparison with neighbouring countries might be helpful. In 1956, the year the states of India were reorganized on the basis of language, the parliament of Sri Lanka (then Ceylon) introduced an act recognizing Sinhala as the sole official language of the country. The intention was to make Sinhala the medium of instruction in all state schools and colleges, in public examinations, and in the courts. Potentially the hardest hit were the Tamil-speaking minority who lived in the north, and whose feelings were eloquently expressed by their representatives in the parliament. "When you deny me my language," said one Tamil member, "you deny me everything." "You are hoping for a divided Ceylon," warned another, adding, "Do not fear, I assure you [that you] will have a divided Ceylon." A left-wing member, himself Sinhala-speaking, predicted that if the government did not change its mind and insisted on passing the act, "two torn little bleeding states might yet arise out of one little state."[18]

In 1971, two torn medium-size states arose out of a single large one. The country being divided was Pakistan, rather than Sri Lanka, but the cause of the division was the same—language. The founders of Pakistan likewise believed that their state had to be based on a single language as well as a single religion. In his first speech in the capital of East Pakistan, Dhaka, Mohammad Ali Jinnah warned the listeners that they would have to take to Urdu sooner rather than later. "Let me make it very clear to you," said Jinnah to his Bengali audience, "that the State Language of Pakistan is going to be Urdu and no other language. Anyone who tries to mislead you is really the enemy of Pakistan. *Without one State language, no nation can remain tied up solidly together and function.*"[19]

In the 1950s, bloody riots broke out when the Pakistani government tried to force Urdu on recalcitrant students. A sense of being discriminated against on the grounds of language persisted, and ultimately resulted in the formation of the independent state of Bangladesh.

Pakistan was created on the basis of religion, but divided on the basis of language. And for more than two decades now, a bloody civil war has raged in Sri Lanka, the disputants divided somewhat by territory and faith but most of all by language. The lesson from these cases might well be: "One language, two nations." Had Hindi been imposed on the whole of India the lesson might well have been: "One language, twenty-two nations."

That Indians spoke many languages and followed many faiths made their nation unnatural in the eyes of some lay and academic western observers. In truth, many Indians thought so too. They believed that the only way for independent India to survive and prosper would be to forge a bond, or bonds, that overlay or submerged the diversity lying below. The glue, as in Europe, could be provided by religion, language, or both. Such was the nationalism once promoted by the old Jana Sangh and promoted now, in a more sophisticated form, by the BJP. This reaches deep into the past to invoke a common (albeit mostly mythical) "Aryan" ancestry for the Hindus, and a common history of suffering at the hands of (mostly Muslim) invaders, with the suffering tempered here and there by resistance by valiant Hindu chieftains such as Rana Pratap and Shivaji.

A popular slogan of the original Jana Sangh was "Hindi, Hindu, Hindustani." The attempt was to make Indian nationalism more *natural*, by requiring—or persuading—all Indians to speak the same language and worship the same gods. In time, the attempt to impose a uniform language was dropped. But the desire to impose the majority religion persisted. That has led, as we have seen in this book, to much conflict, violence, rioting, and death. Particularly after the Gujarat riots of 2002, which were condoned and to some extent even approved by the central government, fears were expressed about the survival of a secular, democratic India. Thus, in a lecture delivered in the university town of Aligarh, the writer Arundhati Roy went so far as to characterize the BJP regime as "fascist." In fact, she used the term "fascism" eleven times in a single paragraph in describing the actions of the government in New Delhi.[20]

Here again, Indian events and experiences were being analysed in terms carelessly borrowed from European history. To call the BJP "fascist" is to diminish the severity and seriousness of the murderous crimes committed by the original fascists in Italy and Germany. Many leaders of the BJP are less than appealing, but to see the party as "fascist" would be both to overestimate its powers and to underestimate the democratic traditions of the Indian people. Notably, the BJP now vigorously promotes linguistic pluralism. No longer are its leaders from the Hindi heartland alone; and it has expanded its influence in the southern states. Also, it is obliged to pay at least lip service to religious pluralism. One of its general secretaries is a Muslim; even if he is dismissed as a showboy, the ideology he and his party promote goes by the name "positive secularism." The qualifier underlines the larger concession—that even if some leaders of the BJP privately wish for a theocratic Hindu state, for public consumption they must endorse the secular ideals of the Indian constitution.

Finally, despite all its best efforts the BJP was not able to disturb the democratic edifice of the Indian polity. A month after Arundhati Roy delivered her speech, the BJP alliance lost power in a general election that it had called. Its leaders moved out of office and allowed their victors to move in instead. When was the last time a "fascist" regime permitted such an orderly transfer of power?

The elections of 1977 (called by an individual who had proven dictatorial tendencies) and the elections of 2004 (called by a party unreliably committed to democratic procedure) both testified to the deep roots that democracy had put down in the soil of India. In this respect, the country was fortunate in the calibre of its founding figures, and in the fact that they lived as long as they did. Few nations have had, living and working *at the same time*, leaders of such acknowledged intelligence and integrity as Jawaharlal Nehru, Vallabhbhai Patel, and B. R. Ambedkar. Within a few years of independence, Patel had died and Ambedkar had left office; but by then the one had successfully overseen the political integration of the country and the other the forging of a democratic constitution. As Nehru lived on, he was accompanied by outstanding leaders in his own party— K. Kamaraj and Morarji Desai, for instance—and in the opposition, in whose ranks were such men as J. B. Kripalani and C. Rajagopalachari.

Jawaharlal Nehru served three full terms in office, a privilege denied comparable figures in the countries of South Asia, where, for example, Aung San was murdered on the eve of the British departure from Burma, Jinnah died within a few years of Pakistan's freedom, Mujib died within a few years of Bangladesh's independence, and the Nepali democrat B. P. Koirala was allowed only a year as prime minister before being dismissed (and then jailed) by the monarchy. What might those men have done if they had held power as long as Nehru, and if they had the kind of supporting cast that he did?[21]

Of course, there has been a rapid, even alarming, decline in the quality of the men and women who rule India. In a book published in 2003, the political theorist Pratap Bhanu Mehta wrote feelingly of "the corruption, mediocrity, indiscipline, venality and lack of moral imagination of the [Indian] political class." Within the Indian state, he continued, "the lines between legality and illegality, order and disorder, state and criminality, have come to be increasingly porous."[22]

This said, the distance—intellectual or moral—between Jawaharlal Nehru and Indira Gandhi, or between B. R. Ambedkar and Mulayam Singh Yadav, is not necessarily greater than that between, say, Abraham Lincoln and George W. Bush. It is in the nature of democracies, perhaps, that while visionaries are sometimes necessary to make them, once made they can be managed by mediocrities. In India, the sapling was planted by the nation's founders, who lived long enough (and worked hard enough) to nurture it to adulthood. Those who came afterwards could disturb and degrade the tree of democracy but, try as they might, could not uproot or destroy it.

IV

Indian nationalism has not been based on a shared language, religion, or ethnic identity. Perhaps one should then invoke a common enemy: European colonialism. The problem here is the methods used to achieve India's freedom. The historian Michael Howard claims that "no Nation, in the true sense of the word, . . . could be born without war . . . no self-conscious community could establish itself as a new and independent actor on the world scene without an armed conflict or the threat of one."[23] Once again, India must count as an exception. Certainly, it was the movement against British rule that first united men and women from different parts of the subcontinent in a shared endeavour. However, their (eventually successful) movement for political freedom eschewed violent revolution in favour of non-violent resistance. India emerged as a nation on the world stage without an armed conflict or, indeed, the threat of one.

Gandhi and his followers have been widely praised for preferring peaceful protest to armed struggle. However, they should be equally commended for having the wisdom to retain, after the British left, such aspects of the colonial legacy as might prove useful in the new nation.

The colonialists were often chastised by the nationalists for promoting democracy at home while denying it in the colonies. When the British finally left, it was expected the Indians would embrace metropolitan traditions such as parliamentary democracy and cabinet government.

More surprising perhaps was their endorsement and retention of a quint-essentially colonial tradition—the civil service.

The key men in British India were the members of the Indian Civil Service (ICS). In the countryside they kept the peace and collected the taxes, while in the Secretariat they oversaw policy and generally kept the machinery of state well oiled. Although there was the occasional rotten egg, these were mostly men of integrity and ability.[24] A majority were British, but there were also a fair number of Indians in the civil service.

When independence came, the new government had to decide what to do with the Indian members of the ICS. Nationalists who had been jailed by them argued that they should be dismissed or at least demoted. The home minister, Vallabhbhai Patel, however, felt that they should be allowed to retain their pay and perquisites, and in fact be placed in positions of greater authority. In October 1949 a furious debate broke out on the subject in the Constituent Assembly of India. Some members complained that the ICS men still had the "mentality [of rulers] lingering in them." They had apparently "not changed their manners," "not reconciled themselves to the new situation." "They do not feel that they are part and parcel of this country," insisted one nationalist.

Vallabhbhai Patel had himself been jailed many times by ICS men. But this experience had actually confirmed his admiration for them. He knew that without them the Pax Brittanica would, simply, have been inconceivable. And he understood that the complex machinery of a modern, independent nation state needed such officers even more. As he reminded the members of the assembly, the new constitution could be worked only "by a ring of Service which will keep the country intact." He testified to the ability of the ICS men, and also to their sense of service. As Patel put it, the officers had "served very ably, very loyally the then Government and later the present Government." Patel was clear that "these people are the instruments" of national unity. "Remove them and I see nothing but a picture of chaos all over the country."[25]

In those first, difficult years of Indian freedom, the ICS men vindicated Vallabhbhai Patel's trust in them. They helped integrate the princely states, resettle the refugees, and plan and oversee the first general elections. Other tasks assigned to them were more humdrum but equally consequential—such as maintaining law and order in the districts, working with ministers in the Secretariat, and supervising famine relief. In 1967, Patel inaugurated a new organization modelled on the ICS but with a name untainted by the colonial experience. This was the Indian Administrative Service (IAS).

As of this writing there are some 5,000 IAS officers in the employment of the government of India. The IAS is complemented, as in British days, by other "all India" services, among them the police, forest, revenue, and customs services. These are an essential link between the Centre and the states. Officers are assigned to a particular state; they spend half or more of their service career in that province, and the rest in the Centre. To the older duties of tax collection and the maintenance of law and order have been added numerous new responsibilities. Conducting elections is one; supervising development programmes is another. In the course of his career an average IAS officer would acquire at least a passing familiarity with such different and divergent subjects as criminal jurispudence, irrigation management, soil and water conservation, and primary health care.

The IAS, like its predecessor, is truly an elite group. The competition to enter the higher civil services is ferocious. In the year 1996, 120,712 candidates appeared for the examination, of whom only 738 were finally selected. Their intelligence and ability are of a very high order. However, there are complaints of increasing corruption among members of the IAS, and of their succumbing too easily to their political masters. Perhaps if the IAS is abolished at one stroke the country will not descend into chaos. But as things stand, IAS officers play a vital role in maintaining its unity. In times of crisis they tend to rise to the challenge. After the tsunami of 2004, for example, IAS officers in Tamil Nadu were commended for their outstanding work in relief and rehabilitation.[26]

An ICS man, Sukumar Sen, laid the groundwork for elections in India, and IAS men have kept the machinery going. The chief election commissioners in the states are drawn from the service. Junior officers supervise elections in their districts; those on the middle rungs serve as election observers, reporting on violations of procedure. More generally, the civil services are a bridge between state and society. In the course of their work, these administrators meet thousands of members of the public, from all walks of life. Living and working in a democracy, they are obliged to pay close attention to what people think and demand. In this respect, their job is probably even harder than that of their predecessors in the ICS.

A colonial institution that has played an equally crucial role is the Indian army. Its reputation took a battering after the war with China in 1962, before it redeemed itself in successive wars with Pakistan. The blows inflicted by Tamil insurgents in Sri Lanka in 1987–1988 dented

the army somewhat, but then honour was restored by the ousting of the
Kargil intruders a decade later. Although its reputation as a fighting force
has gone up and down, as an agency for maintaining order in peacetime
the Indian army has usually commanded the highest respect. In times of
communal rioting, the mere appearance of soldiers in uniform is usually
enough to make the rioters flee. And in times of natural disaster the
army brings succour to the suffering. When there is a flood, famine, cy-
clone, or earthquake, the army is often first on the scene, and always the
most efficient and reliable actor around.

The Indian army is a professional and wholly non-sectarian body. It
is also apolitical. Almost from the first moments of independence, Jawaharlal Nehru made it clear to the army top brass that in matters of
state—both large and small—they had to subordinate themselves to the
elected politicians. At the time of the transfer of power the army was
still headed by a British general, who had ordered that the public be kept
away from a flag-raising ceremony to be held on the day after independence. As prime minister, Nehru rescinded the order, and wrote to the
general as follows:

> While I am desirous of paying attention to the views and susceptibili-
> ties of our senior officers, British and Indian, it seems to me that there
> is a grave misunderstanding about the matter. In any policy that is to
> be pursued, in the Army or otherwise, the views of the Government of
> India and the policy they lay down must prevail. If any person is un-
> able to lay down that policy, he has no place in the Indian Army, or in
> the Indian structure of Government. I think this should be made per-
> fectly clear at this stage.[27]

A year later, it was Vallabhbhai Patel's turn to put a British general
in his place. When the government decided to move against the Nizam,
the commander-in-chief, General Roy Bucher, warned that sending troops
into Hyderabad might provoke Pakistan to attack Amritsar. Patel told
Bucher that if he opposed the action in Hyderabad he was free to resign.
The general backed down, and sent the troops as ordered.[28]

Shortly afterwards Bucher retired, to be succeeded by the first Indian commander-in-chief, General K. M. Cariappa. At first, Cariappa
restricted himself to military matters, but as he grew into the job he began to offer his views on such questions as India's preferred model of
economic development. In October 1952, Nehru wrote advising him
to give fewer press conferences, and at any rate to stick to safe subjects.

Nehru also enclosed a letter from one of his colleagues in the cabinet, who complained that Cariappa was "giving so many speeches and holding so many Press Conferences all over the country," giving the impression that he was "playing the role of a political or semi-political leader."[29]

The message seems to have gone home, for when Cariappa left office in January 1953, in his farewell speech he "exhorted soldiers to give a wide berth to politics." The army's job, he said, was not "to meddle in politics but to give unstinted loyalty to the elected Government."[30] Nehru knew, however, that the general was something of a loose cannon, who could not be completely trusted to follow his own advice. Within three months of his retirement, Cariappa was appointed high commissioner to Australia. The general was not entirely pleased, for, as he told the prime minister, "by going away from home to the other end of the world for whatever period you want me in Australia, I shall be depriving myself of being in continuous and constant touch with the people." Nehru consoled the general, saying that as a sportsman he was superbly qualified to represent India to a sporting nation. But the real intention, clearly, was to send him as far away from the people as possible.[31]

As the first Indian to head the army, Cariappa had a certain cachet, which lost its lustre with every passing month after he had left office. By the time he came back from Australia, Cariappa was a forgotten man. Nehru's foresight was confirmed, however, by the statements the general made from time to time. In 1958 he visited Pakistan, where army officers who had served with him in undivided India had just effected a coup. Cariappa publicly praised them, saying that it was "the chaotic internal situation which forced these two patriotic Generals to plan together to impose Martial Law in the country to save their homeland from utter ruination."[32] Ten years later, he sent an article to the *Indian Express*. In it, he argued that the chaotic internal situation in West Bengal demanded that President's Rule be imposed for a minimum of five years. The recommendation violated the letter and spirit of the constitution. Fortunately, the piece was returned by the editor, who pointed out to the general that "it would be embarrassing in the circumstances both to you and to us to publish this article."[33]

The pattern set in those early years has persisted into the present. As Lieutenant General J. S. Aurora notes, Nehru "laid down some very good norms," which ensured that "politics in the army has been almost absent." "The army is not a political animal in any terms," remarks Aurora, and the officers especially "must be the most apolitical people on earth!"[34] It is a striking fact that no army commander has ever run in an election. Aurora himself became a national hero after overseeing the liberation of Bangladesh, but neither he nor other officers have sought to convert glory won on the battlefield into political advantage. If army men have held public office after retirement, it has been at the invitation of the government. Some, like Cariappa, have been sent as ambassadors overseas; others have served as governors of states.

The army, like the civil services, is a colonial institution that has been successfully indigenized. The same may be said about the English language. In British times the intelligentsia and professional classes communicated with one another in English. So did the nationalist elite. Patel, Bose, Nehru, Gandhi, and Ambedkar all spoke and wrote in their native tongue, but also in English. To reach out to regions other than one's own, English was indispensable. Thus a pan-Indian, anti-British consciousness was created, in good part, by thinkers and activists writing in the English language.

After independence, among the most articulate advocates for English was C. Rajagopalachari (Rajaji). The colonial rulers, he wrote, had "for certain accidental reasons, causes and purposes . . . left behind [in India] a vast body of the English language." But now that it had come, there was no need for it to go away. For English "is ours. We need not send it back to Britain along with Englishmen." He humorously added that, according to Indian tradition, it was a Hindu goddess, Saraswati, who had given birth to all the languages of the world. Thus English "belonged to us by origin, the originator being Saraswati, and also by acquisition."[35]

On the other hand, there were some very influential nationalists who believed that English must be thrown out of India with the British. In Nehru's day, fitful attempts were made to replace English with Hindi as the language of inter-provincial communication. But English continued to be used within and outside the government. Visiting India in 1961, the Canadian writer George Woodcock found that despite India's strangeness, its "immense variety of custom, landscape and physical types," this was "a foreign setting in which one's language was always understood by someone nearby, and in which to speak with an English accent meant that one was seen as a kind of cousin bred out of the odd, temporary marriage of two peoples into which love and hate entered with equal intensity."[36]

After Nehru's death the efforts to extinguish English were renewed. Despite pleas from the southern states, on 26 January 1965 Hindi became the sole official language of inter-provincial communication. As we have seen, this provoked protests so intense and furious that the order was withdrawn within a fortnight. Thus English continued as the language of the central government, of the superior courts, and of higher education.

Over the years, English has confirmed, consolidated, and deepened its position as the language of the pan-Indian elite. The language of the colonizers has, in independent India, become the language of power and prestige, the language of individual as well as social advancement. As the historian Sarvepalli Gopal observes, "that knowledge of English is the passport for employment at higher levels in all fields, is the unavoidable avenue to status and wealth and is mandatory to all those planning to migrate abroad, has meant a tremendous enthusiasm since independence to study it." But, as Gopal also writes, English "may be described as the only non-regional language in India. It is a link language in a more than administrative sense, in that it counters blinkered provincialism."[37]

Those, like Nehru and Rajaji, who sought to retain English sensed that it might help consolidate national unity and further scientific advance. It has done so, but its role in economic growth has been largely unanticipated. For behind the spectacular rise of the software industry lies the proficiency of Indian engineers in English.

V

If India is roughly 50% democratic, it is approximately 80% united. Some parts of Kashmir and the north-east are under the control of insurgents seeking political independence. Some forested districts in central India are in the grip of Maoist revolutionaries. However, these areas, large enough in themselves, constitute considerably less than one-fourth of the total land mass claimed by the Indian nation.

In four-fifths of India, the elected government exercises legitimate power and authority. Throughout this territory the citizens of India are free to live, study, take employment, and invest in businesses.

The economic integration of India is a consequence of its political integration. These act in a mutually reinforcing loop. The greater the movement of goods and capital and people across India, the greater the sense that this is, after all, *one* country. In the first decades of independence, the public sector did most to further this sense of unity. In plants such as the great steel mill in Bhilai, Andhras laboured and lived

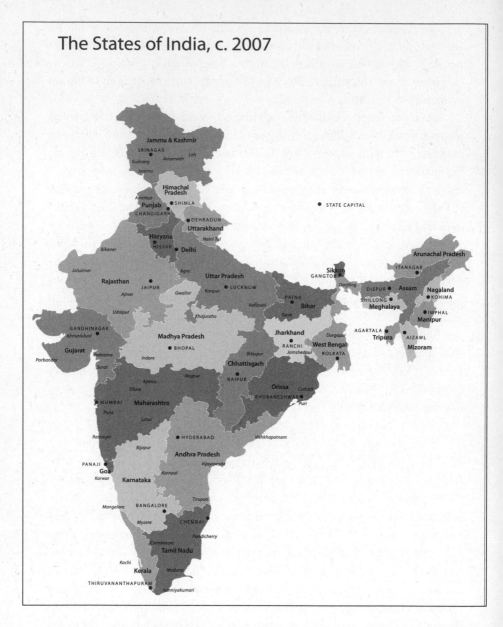

The States of India, c. 2007

alongside Punjabis and Gujaratis. This arrangement fostered appreciation of other tongues, customs, and cuisines, while underlining the fact
that they were all part of the same nation. As the anthropologist Jonathan Parry remarks, in Nehru's imagination "Bhilai and its steel plant
were seen as bearing the torch of history, and as being as much about
forging a new kind of society as about forging steel." The attempt was

not unsuccessful; among the children of the first generation of workers, themselves born and raised in Bhilai, provincial loyalties were superseded by a more inclusive patriotism, a "more cosmopolitan cultural style."[38]

More recently, the private sector, if with less intent, has furthered the process of national integration. Firms with headquarters in Tamil Nadu set up cement plants in Haryana; doctors born and educated in Assam establish clinics in Bombay. Many of the engineers in Hyderabad's IT industry come from Bihar. Migration is not restricted to the professional classes; there are barbers from Uttar Pradesh working in the city of Bangalore, as well as carpenters from Rajasthan. However, it must be said that the flow is not symmetrical. While the cities and towns that are booming become ever more cosmopolitan, economically laggard states sink deeper into provincialism.

                                VI

Apart from elements of politics and economics, cultural factors have also contributed to national unity. Pre-eminent here is the Hindi film. This is the great passion of the Indian people, watched and followed by Indians of all ages, genders, castes, classes, religions, and linguistic groups.

The lyricist Javed Akhtar says of the formally recognized states of the Union that "each has its different culture, tradition and style. In Gujarat, you have one kind of culture, then you go to Punjab, you have another, and the same applies in Rajasthan, Bengal, Orissa or Kerala." He adds, "There is one more state in this country, and that is Hindi cinema."[39]

This is a remarkable insight, which asks to be developed further. As a separate state of India, Hindi cinema acts as a receptacle for all that (in a cultural sense) is most creative in the other states. Thus its actors, musicians, technicians, and directors come from all parts of India. These, in turn, draw ecumenically from cultural forms prevalent in different regions. For example, a single song may feature both the Punjabi folk dance called the *bhangra* and its Tamil classical counterpart, *bharatanatyam*.

Having borrowed elements from here and there and everywhere, the Hindi film then sends the synthesized product out to the other states of the Indian Union for appreciation. The most widely revered Indians are film stars. Yet cinema does not merely provide Indians with a common pantheon of heroes; it also gives them a common language and universe

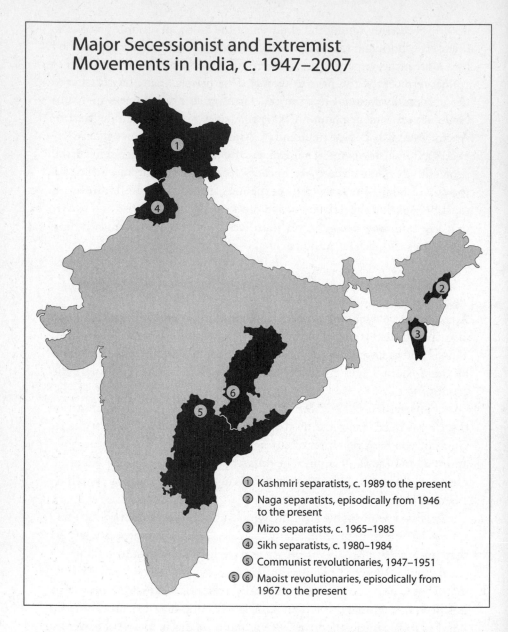

Major Secessionist and Extremist Movements in India, c. 1947–2007

① Kashmiri separatists, c. 1989 to the present

② Naga separatists, episodically from 1946 to the present

③ Mizo separatists, c. 1965–1985

④ Sikh separatists, c. 1980–1984

⑤ Communist revolutionaries, 1947–1951

⑤ ⑥ Maoist revolutionaries, episodically from 1967 to the present

of discourse. Lines from film songs and snatches of film dialogue are used in conversations in schools, colleges, homes, and offices, and on the street. Because it is one more state of the Union, Hindi cinema also speaks its own language—this, however, is understood by all the others.

The last sentence is meant literally as well as figuratively. Hindi cinema provides a stock of social situations and moral conundrums that resonate widely with the citizenry as a whole. But, over time, it has also made the Hindi language more comprehensible to those who previously never before spoke or understood it. When imposed by fiat by the central government, Hindi was resisted by the people of the south and the east. When conveyed seductively by cinema and television, Hindi has been accepted. In Bangalore and Hyderabad, Hindi has become the preferred medium of communication between those who speak mutually incomprehensible tongues. Finally, one may cite the banning of Hindi films, DVDs, and videos by insurgents in the north-east: this, in its own way, is a considerable tribute to the part played by the Hindi film in uniting India.

In 1888, John Strachey wrote that he could not imagine Punjab and Madras ever forming part of a single political entity. But in 1947 they did, along with many other provinces that Strachey regarded as distinct "nations." In 1947 the unity might have been mostly political, but in the decades since then it has been shown also to be economic, cultural, and, it must be said, emotional. Perhaps many Kashmiris and Nagas still feel alien and separate. And perhaps some revolutionaries believe that India is a land of many nationalities. But most of those who are legally citizens of India are happy to be counted as such. About four-fifths of the population, living in about four-fifths of the country, feel themselves to be part of a single nation.

VII

One might think of independent India as being Europe's past as well as its future. India is Europe's past in that it has reproduced, albeit more fiercely and intensely, the conflicts of a modernizing, industrializing, urbanizing society. But it is also Europe's future, in that it anticipated, by some fifty years, the European attempt to create a multilingual, multireligious, multi-ethnic political and economic community.

Or one might compare India with the United States, a country that has been described as "the planet's first multiethnic democracy."[40] Born nearly two centuries later, the Republic of India is today the world's *largest* multiethnic democracy. However, the means by which it has regulated (and moderated) relations between its constituent ethnicities have been somewhat different. For, as Samuel Huntingdon has argued, the American nation has been held together by a "creedal culture" whose "central elements" have included "the Christian religion, Protestant values and moralism, a work ethic, the English language, British traditions of law, justice, and the limits of government power, and a legacy of European art, literature, philosophy, and music." Indeed, "America was created as a Protestant society just as and for some of the reasons Pakistan and Israel were created as Muslim and Jewish societies in the twentieth century."

The United States is of course a nation of immigrants. For much of its history the new groups that came in merged with the dominant culture. "Throughout American history," writes Huntingdon, "people who were not white Anglo-Saxon Protestants have become Americans by adopting America's Anglo-Protestant culture and political values." Of late, however, newer groups of immigrants have tended to maintain their distinct identities. The largest of these are the Hispanics, who live in enclaves where they cook their own food, listen to their own kind of music, follow their own faith and—most important—speak their own language. Huntingdon worries that if these communities are not quickly brought into line, they will "transform America as a whole into a bilingual, bicultural society."

The older American model of assimilation was called a melting pot. Individual groups poured all their flavours into the pot, then drank a single, uniform—or uniform-tasting—drink. Now it appears that the society, and nation, are coming to resemble a salad bowl, with each group starkly standing out, different and distinctive in how it looks and behaves.

Huntingdon himself is less than enthusiastic about the idea of a salad bowl. For him, America has long been, and must always be, a "society with a single pervasive national culture." He observes that Americans identify most strongly with that culture when the nation is under threat. War leads not merely to national consolidation but also to cultural unity. The original American creed was formulated as a consequence of the wars against the Native Americans, the English colonists, and the southern states. The events of 9/11 once more brought patriotism and national solidarity to the fore. Concerned that these energies may dissipate, Huntingdon urges a more thoroughgoing return to the creed that, in his view, was responsible for "the unity and strength of my country."[41]

Interestingly, Huntingdon's views are echoed in statements by the prime minister of Australia, John Howard. Australia too has been subject to waves of immigration, mostly or wholly European to begin with, but more recently of a markedly Asian character. Howard rejects the possibility of multiple cultures coexisting in Australia. "You've got to have a dominant culture," he says, adding, "Ours is Anglo-Saxon—our language, our literature, our institutions."[42]

Huntingdon and Howard's argument is, of course, quite familiar to students of Indian history. It has been made here by political thinkers such as M. S. Golwalkar, and by political parties such as the Jana Sangh and the BJP. They have believed that India has "got to have a dominant culture," and that this culture is "Hindu." As it happened, these views were not endorsed by the founders of the Indian nation—those who wrote the Indian constitution and led the first few governments of independent India. Thus India became a salad bowl rather than a melting pot.

And it has stayed that way. It has sustained a diversity of religions and languages—precisely what Howard, Huntingdon, and some others deem inimical to national survival and national solidarity. India has resisted pressures to go in the other direction, to follow Israel and Pakistan by favouring citizens who adhere to a certain faith or speak a particular language.

VIII

The most eloquent tribute to the idea of India that I have come across rests in some unpublished letters of the biologist J. B. S. Haldane. Haldane was a figure of considerable fame and some notoriety. In 1956, already past sixty, he decided to leave his position at University College, London, and take up residence in Calcutta. He joined the Indian Statistical Institute, became an Indian citizen, wore Indian clothes, and ate Indian food. He also travelled energetically around the country, engaging with its scientists and also with the citizenry at large.[43]

Five years after Haldane had moved to India, an American science writer described him in print as a "citizen of the world." Haldane replied:

> No doubt I am in some sense a citizen of the world. But I believe with Thomas Jefferson that one of the chief duties of a citizen is to be a nuisance to the government of his state. As there is no world state, I cannot do this. . . . On the other hand I can be, and am, a nuisance to the government of India, which has the merit of permitting a good deal of criticism, though it reacts to it rather slowly. I also happen to be proud of being a citizen of India, which is a lot more diverse than Europe, let alone the U.S.A., U.S.S.R., or China, and thus a better model for a possible world organisation. It may of course break up, but it is a wonderful experiment. So I want to be labelled as a citizen of India.[44]

On another occasion, Haldane described India as "the closest approximation to the Free World." An American friend protested, saying his own impression was that "India has its fair share of scoundrels and a tremendous amount of poor unthinking and disgustingly subservient individuals who are not attractive."[45] To this Haldane responded:

> Perhaps one is freer to be a scoundrel in Indian than elsewhere. So one was in the U.S.A. in the days of people like Jay Gould, when (in my opinion) there was more internal freedom in the U.S.A. than there is today. The "disgusting subservience" of the others has its limits. The people of Calcutta riot, upset trams, and refuse to obey police regulations, in a manner which would have delighted Jefferson. I don't think their activities are very efficient, but that is not the question at issue.[46]

Forty years down the line, what Haldane called a "wonderful experiment" might be counted as a modest success. Poverty persists in some (admittedly broad) areas, yet one can now be certain that India will not go the way of sub-Saharan Africa, and experience widespread famine. Secessionist movements are active here and there, but there is no fear anymore that India will follow the former Yugoslavia and break up into a dozen fratricidal parts. The powers of the state are sometimes grossly abused, but no one seriously thinks that India will follow neighbouring Pakistan, where the chief of army staff is generally also the head of government.

As a modern nation, India is simply sui generis. It stands on its own, different and distinct from alternative political models such as Anglo-Saxon liberalism, French republicanism, atheistic communism, and Islamic theocracy. In 1971, at the time of the crisis over Bangladesh, when India found itself simultaneously at odds with communist China, Islamic Pakistan, and America, an Indian diplomat captured his country's uniqueness in this way:

> India is regarded warily in the West because she is against the concept of Imperialism and because she "invented" the "Third World."
>
> India is looked on with suspicion in the "Third World" because of her (subversive) sentiments for democracy, human rights, etc.; the Muslim world is wrathful because of our secularism.
>
> The Communist countries regard India as insolent—and potentially dangerous—because we have rejected Communism as the prime condition for Progress.
>
> We are, of course, on the side of God. But is God on our side?[47]

The writer whose lines open this book, the nineteenth-century poet Ghalib, thought that God was indeed on the side of India. Conflict and privation were all around him, but doomsday had not yet come. "Why does not the Last Trumpet sound?" asked Ghalib of a sage in the holy city of Benares. "Who holds the reins of the Final Catastrophe?" he continued. This was the answer he got:

> The hoary old man of lucent ken
> Pointed towards Kashi and gently smiled.
> "The Architect," he said, "is fond of this edifice
> Because of which there is colour in life; He
> Would not like it to perish and fall."

Ghalib and his interlocutor were speaking then of India the civilization. Speaking now of India the nation state, one must insist that its future lies not in the hands of God but in the mundane works of men. So long as the constitution is not amended beyond recognition, so long as elections are held regularly and fairly and the ethos of secularism broadly prevails, so long as citizens can speak and write in the language of their choosing, so long as there is an integrated market and a moderately efficient civil service and army, and—lest I forget—so long as Hindi films are watched and their songs sung, India will survive.

ACKNOWLEDGEMENTS

IN NEARLY FIVE DECADES as a citizen of India I have had plenty of opportunity to discover that this is sometimes the most exasperating country in the world. However, only while working on its modern history did I find that it was at all times the most interesting. My friend Peter Straus set me off on the journey, by suggesting that I write a book on independent India. And a selfless tribe of archivists and librarians made the journey an adventure rich in thrills and unexpected discoveries.

My greatest thanks are owed to the staff of the Nehru Memorial Museum and Library, a capacious repository of private papers, periodicals, microfilms, and books about modern India. For weeks on end, I had Shri Jeevan Chand and Shri Rautela of the Manuscripts Division as my kindly companions, who brought file after file up from a large, dark corridor into the sunny reading room where I worked. Outside, in the Main Section, the members of the library staff were unfailingly courteous. In sourcing manuscripts, I also received much help from the library's deputy director, Dr. N. Balakrishnan, and his sterling assistant, Deepa Bhatnagar.

Next in order of importance is that other—and more famous—public repository, the British Library in London. My base here was the old India Office Library and Records, which—while I worked there—was called the Oriental and India Office Collections (it now functions under the label Asian and African Studies). By any name it remains a happy place to work in, with its brisk and efficient staff, its close links to other collections, and—not least—the serendipitous meetings it allows with scholars from around the world.

Among the other libraries and archives where I collected material for this book are those maintained by the National Archives of India, New Delhi; the Centre for South Asian Studies, Cambridge; the University of California, Berkeley; Stanford University; the University of Michigan, Ann

Arbor; the University of Georgia, Athens; Cornell University; Friends House, Euston; the India International Centre, New Delhi; the National Library of Scotland, Edinburgh; the Imperial War Museum, London; Oslo University; the Madras Institute of Development Studies, Chennai; Tata Steel, Jamshedpur; and the Lal Bahadur Shastri National Academy of Administration, Mussoorie. I owe special thanks to the Centre for Education and Documentation in Bangalore, from whose fabulously comprehensive collection of news clippings I have extensively drawn.

Aside from private papers and periodicals, this book also draws on other books old and new, as well as pamphlets. Not many of these could I find in libraries (at least not the libraries in my hometown, Bangalore, which is a great centre of science but not, alas, of the humanities). The bulk were bought from bookshops known and unrecognized. I am grateful, in particular, to the Premier Bookshop, Bangalore; the Select Bookshop, Bangalore; Prabhu Booksellers, Gurgaon; the New and Secondhand Bookshop, Mumbai; and Manohar Booksellers, New Delhi. As handy and helpful were the unnamed pavement stalls in Mumbai's Flora Fountain and Delhi's Daryaganj—from whom and where, over the past two decades and more, I have obtained so much of the material for my work as a historian.

The photographs that I have used here come principally from four collections: those maintained by the Press Information Bureau, the Nehru Memorial Museum and Library, and The Hindu and Ananda Bazaar Patrika group of newspapers. I thank these institutions for their assistance, and my wife Sujata for advice on the final selection.

For help of various kinds, I would like to thank Chinmoyee Agarwal; Kanti Bajpai; Suhas Baliga; Rukmini Banerji; Nupur Basu; Millicent Bennett; Stanley Brandes; Vijay Chandru; Shruti Debi; Kanak Mani Dixit; Zafar Futehally; Jagadev Gajare; Amitav Ghosh; my parents, S. R. D. and Visalakshi Guha; Supriya Guha; Wajahat Habibullah; Rajen Harshe; Radhika Herzberger; Trevor Horwood; Shreyas Jayasimha; Robin Jeffrey; Bhagwan Josh; Nasreen Munni Kabir; Devesh Kapur; Mukul Kesavan; Soumya Keshavan; Nayanjyot Lahiri; Nirmala Lakshman; Edward Luce; Lucy Luck; Raghu Menon; Mary Mount; Rajdeep Mukherjee; Rudrangshu Mukherjee; Anil Nauriya; Nandan Nilekani; Mohandas Pai; Sriram Panchu; Prashant Panjiar; Shekhar Pathak; Srinath Raghavan; Nitya Ramakrishnan; Ramesh Ramanathan; Jairam Ramesh; my nephew Karthik Ramkumar; Mahesh Rangarajan; Anuradha Roy; Tirthankar Roy; John Ryle; P. Sainath; Sanjeev Saith; Rajdeep Sardesai; Jalpa Rajesh Shah; Rajbhushan Shinde; K. Sivaramakrishnan; Arvind Subramanian; Nandini Sundar; R. Sudarshan; M. V. Swaroop; Shikha Trivedy; Siddharth Varadarajan; A. R. Venkatachalapathy; Rajendra Vora; Amy Waldman; and Francis Wheen.

Some friends deserve special mention, for their long-term help in matters professional and personal. These good souls are Rukun Advani, André

Béteille, Keshav Desiraju, Gopal Gandhi, David Gilmour, Ian Jack, Sanjeev Jain, and Sunil Khilnani. André and David also provided detailed comments on a draft of the book. And I was kept going by the memory of my friend Krishna Raj, editor for thirty-five years of the *Economic and Political Weekly*, the journal whose own life is so closely bound up with the life of the Republic of India—as the footnotes to this book testify.

I thank, for their support, encouragement, criticism, and chastisement, my editors, Richard Milner of Macmillan and Dan Halpern of Ecco/HarperCollins. I promise to be less tardy with the books that might follow! In fact, without my agent Gill Coleridge even this one would not have been finished. On more than one occasion I have been tempted to take an extended vacation, or drop the book altogether. Each time, it was Gill who brought me back, showing me ways in which it might be continued and, in the end, completed.

My greatest debt, as expressed in the dedication, is to the always interesting and occasionally exasperating Indians with whom I am privileged to share a home.

NOTES

Key to Abbreviations

Archer, "Journal": Mildred Archer, "Journal of a Stay in the Naga Hills, 9 July to 4 December 1947," MSS. Eur. F. 236/362.

CAD: *Constituent Assembly Debates—Official Report* (New Delhi: Lok Sabha Secretariat, 1988).

CWMG: *Collected Works of Mahatma Gandhi* (New Delhi: Government of India, 1958—).

EW: *Economic Weekly.*

HT: *Hindustan Times.*

LCM: Jawaharlal Nehru, *Letters to Chief Ministers,* 5 vols., ed. G. Parthasarathi (New Delhi: Oxford University Press, 1985–1989).

NMML: Nehru Memorial Museum and Library, New Delhi.

OIOC: Oriental and India Office Collections, British Library, London.

SPC: Durga Das, ed., *Sardar Patel's Correspondence, 1945–1960,* 10 vols. (Ahmedabad: Navijan, 1971–1974).

TOI: *Times of India*

TOP: Nicholas Mansergh, ed. in chief, *Constitutional Relations between Great Britain and India—Transfer of Power, 1942–1947,* 12 vols. (London: Her Majesty's Stationery Office, 1970–1983).

WP I, WP II, etc.: White Papers, government of India, 1959–1962.

PROLOGUE: UNNATURAL NATION

1. Translation by Qurratulain Hyder.
2. See Ralph Russell and Khurshidul Islam, eds. and trans., *Ghalib, 1797–1869: Life and Letters* (1969, reprint Delhi: Oxford University Press, 1994), ch. 7.
3. John Strachey, *India* (London: Kegan, Paul, Trench, 1888), pp. 2–5.
4. The best single-volume treatment remains Sumit Sarkar, *Modern India: 1885–1947* (London: Macmillan, 1985). For a more up-to-date account see Sekhar Bandopadhyay, *From Plassey to Partition* (Hyderabad: Orient Longman, 2004), an additional merit of which is its excellent bibliography.

5. Interview in *Adelaide Advertiser*, November 1891, quoted in the "N. B." column of *The Times Literary Supplement*, 9 March 2001.

6. E. H. D. Sewell, *An Outdoor Wallah* (London: Stanley Paul, 1945), p. 110, emphasis added. These words were written in 1934.

7. Winston Churchill, *India: Speeches and an Introduction* (London: Thornton Butterworth, 1931), pp. 38, 120, 125, etc.

8. These quotes are taken, with permission, from Devesh Kapur, "Globalization and the Paradox of Indian Democracy," mimeograph, Department of Political Science, University of Texas at Austin, December 2005.

9. Don Taylor, "This New, Surprising Strength of Mrs. Gandhi," *Evening Standard*, 21 August 1969, emphasis in original.

10. *Statesman* (New Delhi), 10 August 1998.

11. Adam Przeworski et al., quoted in Kapur, *Globalization*.

12. Sunil Khilnani, *The Idea of India* (New York: Farrar, Straus and Giroux, 1997), p. 4.

13. Krishna Kumar, *What Is Worth Teaching?* 3rd ed. (Hyderabad, Orient Longman, 2004), p. 109.

14. Tony Judt, *Postwar: A History of Europe since 1945* (London: William Heinemann, 2005), p. xiii.

15. Marc Bloch, *French Rural History: An Essay on Its Essential Characteristics* (1931, reprint London: Routledge and Kegan Paul, 1978), preface.

CHAPTER 1: FREEDOM AND PARRICIDE

1. *Collected Works of Mahatma Gandhi* (New Delhi: Government of India, 1958—; hereafter cited as CWMG), Vol. 42, pp. 398–400.

2. Jawaharlal Nehru, *An Autobiography: With Musings on Recent Events in India* (1936, reprint London: Bodley Head, 1949), p. 209.

3. *Indian Annual Register, 1930*, Part I (January–June), p. 23.

4. This account of the ceremonies is based on Jim Masselos, " 'The Magic Touch of Being Free': The Rituals of Independence on 15 August," in Jim Masselos, ed., *India: Creating a Modern Nation* (New Delhi: Sterling, 1990); Tai Yong Tan and Gyanesh Kudesia, *The Aftermath of Partition in South Asia* (London: Routledge, 2000), ch. 2; *Statesman*, 15 August 1947; reports in Philip Talbot Papers, Centre for South Asian Studies, Cambridge; reports and correspondence in Mountbatten Papers (MSS. Eur. F. 200), Tyson Papers (MSS. Eur. F. 341), and Saumarez Smith Papers (MSS. Eur. C. 409), all in the Oriental and India Office Collections, British Library, London (hereafter OIOC).

5. Actually, as Salman Rushdie once remarked, half the world had not yet gone to sleep, and the other half was already awake. This witticism did not stop Rushdie from including Nehru's speech in an anthology of Indian writing that he edited—the only piece of non-fiction to find a place in the volume.

6. As related in Rajmohan Gandhi, *The Good Boatman: A Portrait of Gandhi* (New Delhi: Viking, 1993).

7. This section on Gandhi and the period just preceding independence draws on D. G. Tendulkar, *Mahatma: Life of Mohandas Karamchand Gandhi,* 2nd ed. (1963, reprint New Delhi: Publications Division, 1990), Vols. 7 and 8; N. K. Bose, *My Days with Gandhi* (1953, reprint Hyderabad: Orient Longman, 1990);

N. K. Bose and P. H. Patwardhan, *Gandhi in Indian Politics* (Bombay: Lalvani, 1967); and relevant volumes of the CWMG.

8. The words of the then viceroy, Lord Linlithgow, speaking on 8 August 1940.

9. B. R. Nanda, "Nehru, the Indian National Congress, and the Partition of India, 1935–1947," in C. H. Philips and Mary Doreen Wainwright, eds., *The Partition of India: Policies and Perspectives* (London: George Allen and Unwin, 1970), p. 183.

10. *Statesman*, 16 August 1947.

11. The new governor was R. F. Mudie, a British member of the Indian civil service who had chosen to stay on and work for the government of Pakistan. The quote is from a typescript in the Mudie Papers, OIOC (MSS. Eur. F. 164/12).

12. Quoted in Gyanendra Pandey, *Remembering Partition: Violence, Nationalism, and History in India* (Cambridge: Cambridge University Press, 2002), p. 98.

13. See L/P and J/8/575, OIOC.

14. Robin Jeffrey, "The Punjab Boundary Force and the Problem of Order, August 1947," *Modern Asian Studies*, Vol. 8, No. 4, 1974.

15. "Partition" (1968) in W. H. Auden, *Collected Poems*, Edward Mendelson, ed. (New York: Vintage, 1991), pp. 803–804.

16. Quoted in Urvashi Butalia, *The Other Side of Silence: Voices from the Partition of India* (Delhi: Viking, 1998), p. 65. Before he left India Radcliffe burned all his notes and papers, and he never wrote about his experiences in the subcontinent. Auden was cynical about this silence, saying that "he quickly forgot the case, as a good lawyer must."

17. This and subsequent quotes from Rees are from his papers deposited in the OIOC (especially files MSS Eur. 274/66 to MSS. Eur. 274/70).

18. Quoted in H. M. Seervai, *Partition of India: Legend and Reality* (Bombay: Emenem, 1989), p. 148.

19. Nehru to Rees, 3/9/1947, MSS. Eur. F. 274/73, OIOC.

20. Baroo, "Life in the Punjab Today," *Swatantra*, 4 October 1947.

21. See MSS. Eur. 200/129, OIOC.

22. Donald F. Ebright, *Free India: The First Five Years: An Account of the 1947 Riots, Refugees, Relief, and Rehabilitation* (Nashville, Tenn.: Parthenon, 1954), p. 28. Later estimates have put the number of dead at 1 million or more.

23. Note by Major William Short, dated 17 October 1947, in MSS. Eur. F. 200/129, OIOC.

24. As reported by Pyarelal, "In Calcutta," *Harijan*, 14 September 1947.

25. This quote and much of the preceding two paragraphs draw from Dennis Dalton, *Mahatma Gandhi: Nonviolent Power in Action* (New York: Columbia University Press, 1993), ch. 5, "The Calcutta Fast."

26. See Richard Symons, *In the Margins of Independence: A Relief Worker in India and Pakistan, 1942–1949* (Karachi: Oxford University Press, 2001).

27. The violence against the Meos is described in Shail Mayaram, *Resisting Regimes: Myth, Memory, and the Shaping of a Muslim Identity* (New Delhi: Oxford University Press, 1997).

28. Tendulkar, *Mahatma*, Vol. 8, pp. 112–131.

29. "To Members of the R. S. S.," *Harijan*, 28 September 1947.

30. Nehru to Patel, 30 September 1947, in Durga Das, ed., *Sardar Patel's Correspondence, 1945–1950*, 10 vols. (Ahmedabad: Navjivan, 1971–1974, cited hereafter as SPC), Vol. 4, pp. 297–299.

31. Entry dated 13 September 1947, in Alan Campbell-Johnson, *Mission with Mountbatten* (New York: Dutton, 1953), p. 189.
32. "A. I. C. C. Resolutions," *Harijan*, 23 November 1947.
33. M.S. Golwalkar, *We, or Our Nation Defined* (Nagpur, Bharat Prakashan, 1947, first published in 1938), pp. 55–56; quoted in Mohan Ram, *Hindi against India: The Meaning of DMK* (New Delhi: Rachna Prakashan, 1968), p. 64.
34. *Hindustan Times* (Delhi—hereafter cited as HT), 8 December 1947.
35. Tendulkar, *Mahatma*, Vol. 8, pp. 246–266.
36. Robert Payne, *The Life and Death of Mahatma Gandhi* (New York: Dutton, 1969), pp. 637–641; see also Ashis Nandy's fascinating essay on Gandhi and Godse in his *At the Edge of Psychology and Other Essays* (New Delhi: Oxford University Press, 1980).
37. Patel spoke in Hindustani. The English translation here is from *Statesman*, 31 January 1948.
38. Quoted in Sucheta Mahajan, *Independence and Partition: the Erosion of Colonial Power in India* (New Delhi: Sage, 2000), pp. 320–321.
39. See the correspondence between Nehru and Patel in SPC, Vol. 6, pp. 8–31.

CHAPTER 2: THE LOGIC OF DIVISION

1. Khizar Hayat Tiwana to Major Short, 15 August 1947, Short Papers, OIOC (MSS. Eur. 189/19).
2. There is a massive literature on partition, which includes: (1) memoirs by key civil servants and military officials who served in the government at the time; (2) biographies of the important politicians involved in the negotiations—Nehru, Gandhi, Jinnah, Patel, Mountbatten, etc.—(3) regional studies of partition in the Punjab and in Bengal; and (4) wider analytical overviews. To this must be added the volumes of original documents published both in England (the Transfer of Power project) and in India (the Toward Freedom Project plus the published correspondence of Nehru, Patel, Gandhi, and others). A fine recent overview, citing much of the relevant literature, is Sucheta Mahajan, *Independence and Partition: The Erosion of Colonial Power in India* (New Delhi: Sage, 2000). An earlier work representing most of the competing points of view is C. H. Philips and Mary Doreen Wainwright, eds., *The Partition of India: Policies and Perspectives* (London: George Allen and Unwin, 1970).
3. See the revealing portrait in the memoir of Jinnah's former junior, M. C. Chagla, *Roses in December: An Autobiography* (1973, reprint Bombay: Bharatiya Vidya Bhavan, 1994), ch. 5.
4. Lord Birkenhead to Lord Reading, quoted in John Grigg, "Myths about the Approach to Indian Independence," in Wm. Roger Louis, ed., *More Adventures with Britannia: Personalites, Politics, and Culture in Britain* (Austin: University of Texas Press, 1998), p. 211.
5. See Khalid bin Sayeed, *Pakistan: The Formative Phase, 1857–1948,* 2nd ed. (Karachi: Oxford University Press, 1969), especially ch. 6. Two magisterial treatments of Muslim consolidation during late colonial rule are C. S. Venkatachar, "1937–1947 in Retrospect: A Civil Servant's View," in Philips and Wainwright, *The Partition of India*; and Hamza Alavi, "Misreading Partition Road Signs," *Economic and Political Weekly*, 2–9 November 2002.

6. Kenneth O. Morgan, *Labour in Power, 1945–1951* (Oxford: Clarendon, 1984), p. 221.

7. "The Pakistan Nettle," in Moon Papers, OIOC (MSS. Eur. F. 230/39).

8. This account of the 1946 elections is largely based on Sho Kuwajima, *Muslims, Nationalism, and the Partition: 1946 Provincial Elections in India* (New Delhi: Manohar, 1998), supplemented by the following: David Gilmartin, *Empire and Islam: Punjab and the Making of Pakistan* (Berkeley: University of California Press, 1988); David Gilmartin, "A Magnificent Gift: Muslim Nationalism and the Election Process in Colonial Punjab," *Comparative Studies in Society and History*, Vol. 40, No. 3, July 1998; I. A. Talbot, "The 1946 Punjab Election," *Modern Asian Studies*, Vol. 14, No. 1, 1980.

9. See Peter Clarke, *The Cripps Version: The Life of Sir Stafford Cripps, 1889–1952* (London: Allen Lane, 2002), part V.

10. Faiz Ahmad Faiz, "Subh-e-Azadi" (Freedom's Dawn), trans. from the Urdu by V. G. Kiernan in *Poems by Faiz* (1958, reprint Delhi: Oxford University Press, 2000), pp. 123–124.

11. Humayan Kabir, "Muslim Politics, 1942–1947," in Philips and Wainwright, *The Partition of India*, p. 402.

12. Philip Ziegler, *Mountbatten* (London: Collins, 1985), p. 439.

13. Andrew Roberts, "Lord Mountbatten and the Perils of Adrenalin," in *Eminent Churchillians* (London: Weidenfeld and Nicholson, 1994).

14. Jenkins to Mountbatten, 3 May 1947, in MSS. Eur. F. 200/125, OIOC.

15. Jenkins to Mountbatten, 30 July 1947, in MSS. Eur. F. 200/127, OIOC.

16. J. D. Tyson to "Dear Folk," 5 May 1946, MSS. Eur. E. 341/40, OIOC.

17. Note by Sir Francis Burrows, dated 14 February 1947, MSS. Eur. F. 200/24, OIOC.

18. See Malcolm Darling, *At Freedom's Door* (London: Oxford University Press, 1949).

19. Nicholas Mansergh, ed. in chief, *Constitutional Relations between Great Britain and India: Transfer of Power, 1942–1947,* 12 vols. (London: Her Majesty's Stationery Office, 1970–1983; hereafter TOP), Vol. 12, items 200, 209, 389, 489.

20. Quoted in Symons, *In the Margins of Independence*, p. 3.

CHAPTER 3: APPLES IN THE BASKET

1. Pothan Joseph, "Mountbatten Quits India," *Swatantra*, 19 June 1948.

2. Brian Hoey, *Mountbatten: The Private Story* (London: Pan, 1995), pp. 3, 4, 201.

3. Denis Judd, ed., *A British Tale of Indian and Foreign Service: The Memoirs of Sir Ian Scott* (London: Radcliffe, 1999), p. 147.

4. See Penderel Moon, ed., *Wavell: The Viceroy's Journal* (London: Oxford University Press, 1973).

5. The books I have in mind are Alan Campbell-Johnson, *Mission with Mountbatten* (New York: Dutton, 1951); H. V. Hodson, *The Great Divide: Britain-India-Pakistan* (London: Hutchinson, 1969); Dominique Lapierre and Larry Collins, *Freedom at Midnight* (New Delhi: Rupa, 1975); and Philip Ziegler, *Mountbatten: The Official Biography* (London: Collins, 1985). For an early

revisionist view, see Leonard Mosely, *The Last Days of the British Raj* (New York: Harcourt, Brace and World, 1961).

6. Ziegler, *Mountbatten*, p. 424.

7. There have been some fine studies of individual princely states, and of British policy toward the maharajas. However, no one since Menon has attempted an analytical overview of the demise of the princely order, with its (often profound) implications for the history of independent India. See V. P. Menon, *The Story of the Integration of the Indian States* (New York: Macmillan, 1956).

8. For a brilliant brief survey of British relations with princely India, see K. M. Pannikar, *Indian States*, Oxford Pamphlet on Indian Affairs, No. 4 (Bombay: Oxford University Press, 1942). See also the essays in Robin Jeffrey, ed., *People, Princes, and Paramount Power: Society and Politics in Indian Princely States* (Delhi: Oxford University Press, 1978).

9. Quoted in Mario Rodrigues, *Batting for the Empire: A Political Biography of Ranjitsinhji* (New Delhi: Penguin India, 2003).

10. Ian Copland, *The Princes of India in the Endgames of Empire* (Cambridge: Cambridge University Press, 1999), p. 227.

11. W. H. Morris-Jones, "The Transfer of Power, 1947: A View from the Sidelines," *Modern Asian Studies*, Vol. 16, No. 1, 1982, pp. 17–18.

12. Gopal, *Nehru*, Vol. 1, p. 359.

13. See Rajmohan Gandhi, *Patel: A Life* (Ahmedabad: Navjivan, 1991), pp. 408–411; SPC, Vol. 5, passim.

14. The phrase was coined by K. M. Pannikar, and is the underpinning of his classic *Asia and Western Dominance* (London: George Allen and Unwin, 1959).

15. "Maharaja of Bikaner's Appeal to the Princes," SPC, Vol. 5, App. 2, pp. 518–524. This appeal was almost certainly drafted by K. M. Pannikar.

16. Penderel Moon to Major Billy Short, dated 29 March 1947, in MSS. Eur. F. 179/16, Short Papers, OIOC.

17. A representative view is that of the last head of this department, Sir Conrad Corfield. See his "Some Thoughts on British Policy and the Indian States, 1935–1947," in Philips and Wainwright, ed., *The Partition of India*, pp. 527–534.

18. Menon to Sir P. Patrick (undersecretary of state for India), 8 July 1947, in TOP, Vol. 12, pp. 1–2.

19. SPC, Vol. 5, pp. 536–538.

20. TOP, Vol. 12, pp. 36, 51.

21. Campbell-Johnson, *Mission*, p. 140.

22. "Press Communiqué of an Address by Rear-Admiral Viscount Mountbatten of Burma to a Conference of the Rulers and Representatives of Indian States," TOP, Vol. 12, pp. 347–352.

23. See TOP, Vol. 12, pp. 585–588, Hodson, *The Great Divide*, pp. 369f.

24. The words are those of Vallabhbhai Patel, from his statement to the princes of 5 July 1947. See SPC, Vol. 5, p. 537.

25. "Satyagraha Movement in Mysore," *Swatantra*, 27 September 1947; H. S. Doreswamy, *From Princely Autocracy to People's Government* (Bangalore: Sahitya Mandira, 1993), ch. 9.

26. V. P. Menon, *Integration of the Indian States* (1956, reprint Hyderabad: Orient Longman, 1997), pp. 153–154, 179.

27. See E. M. S. Nambooodiripad, "Princedom and Democracy," *New Age*, August 1956 (a review article on V. P. Menon's *Integration of the Indian States*).

28. Robert Trumbull, *As I See India* (London: Cassell, 1952), pp. 76–77.

29. Speeches at Jaipur, Gwalior, and Bikaner in *Time Only to Look Forward: Speeches of Rear Admiral the Earl Mountbatten of Burma, as Viceroy of India and Governor-General of the Dominion of India, 1947–1948* (London: Nicholas Kaye, 1949), pp. 76–78, 91–93, 102–104.

30. These paragraphs summarize a story told over several hundred pages in Menon, *Integration*.

31. Menon to V. Shankar (private secretary to Vallabbhai Patel), 9 August 1949, in G. M. Nandurkar, ed., *Sardar's Letters—Mostly Unknown: Post-Centenary*, Vol. 2 (Ahmedabad: Sardar Vallabhbhai Patel Smarak Bhavan, 1981), pp. 74–76.

32. As told to me by C. S. Venkatachar, who succeeded V. P. Menon as secretary of the ministry of states.

33. Hodson, *The Great Divide*, pp. 367–368.

34. The Travancore story has been principally reconstructed here from TOP, Vol. 12, pp. 76–77, 203–204, 232–233, 281–282, 298–299, 335–336, 414, 421–422, 453; supplemented by A. Sreedhara Menon, *Triumph and Tragedy in Travancore: Annals of Sir C. P.'s Sixteen Years* (Kottayam: Current Books, 2001), especially pp. 231–253. See also A. G. Noorani, "C. P. and Independent Travancore," *Frontline*, 4 July 2003; and K. C. George, *Immortal Punnapra-Vayalar* (Thiruvananthapuram: Communist Party of India, 1975).

35. The best, presumably, was Jawaharlal Nehru.

36. Draft letter dated 18 July 1947 from Lord Mountbatten to nawab of Bhopal, in MSS. Eur. D. 1006 (Major A. E. G. Davy Papers), OIOC.

37. My account of the Bhopal case is based on TOP, Vol. 12, pp. 144–145, 291–297, 436–438, 644, 671–672; Copland, *The Princes of India* , pp. 235–236, 253; Hodson, *The Great Divide*, pp. 365, 375; Menon, *Integration*, pp. 118–119;

38. TOP, Vol. 12, pp. 603–604, 659–662, 767; Menon, *Integration*, pp. 116–118; K. M. Pannikar to Vallabhbhai Patel, undated, but probably from late July 1947, in G. M. Nandurkar, ed., *Sardar's Letters—Mostly Unknown, II: Birth Centenary*, Vol. 5 (Ahmedabad: Sardar Vallabhbhai Patel Smarak Bhavan, 1978), pp. 55–56.

39. R. M. Lala, "Junagadh," *Current*, 27 September 1950; Campbell-Johnson, *Mission*, pp. 191–192; Mosley, *Last Days*, pp. 181–183.

40. Shah Nawaz was the father of Zulfiqar Ali and grandfather of Benazir, both future prime ministers of Pakistan.

41. Patel's feelings about Junagadh are described in Malcolm Darling to Guy Wint, 7 December 1947, in Box 60, Darling Papers, Centre for South Asian Studies, University of Cambridge.

42. "Report by Secretary, Ministry of States, on Junagadh," in SPC, Vol. 7, pp. 688–695.

43. This account is principally based on Menon, *Integration*, pp. 124–149; and Hodson, *The Great Divide*, pp. 427–440.

44. Rafi Ahmed, "Hyderabad Politics," *Swatantra*, 29 November 1947.

45. K. M. Munshi, *The End of an Era: Hyderabad Memoirs* (1957, reprint Bombay: Bharatiya Vidya Bhavan, 1957), pp. 10–11.

46. TOP, Vol. 12, pp. 31–32, 87; "Viswamitra," "Monckton and Mountbatten," *Swatantra*, 15 May 1948.
47. Coupland, quoted in V. B. Kulkarni, *K. M. Munshi* (New Delhi: Publications Division, 1983), p. 117; Patel, quoted in Munshi, *End of an Era*, p. 1.
48. Lucien D. Benichou, *From Autocracy to Integration: Political Developments in Hyderabad State, 1938–1948* (Hyderabad: Orient Longman, 2000), especially ch. 5.
49. Amit Kumar Gupta, *The Agrarian Drama: The Leftists and the Rural Poor in India, 1934–1951* (New Delhi: Manohar, 1996), pp. 291–317, 412–422, etc.
50. See Swami Ramananda Tirtha, *Memoirs of Hyderabad Freedom Struggle* (Bombay: Popular Prakashan, 1967), pp. 181–182.
51. Benichou, *From Autocracy to Integration*, p. 178.
52. See TOP, Vol. 12, pp. 613–615.
53. Benichou, *From Autocracy to Integration*, pp. 230, 235; "Viswamitra," "Monckton and Mountbatten."
54. See TOP, Vol. 12, p. 121.
55. Benichou, *From Autocracy to Integration*, pp. 208–210.
56. "Conflict in Hyderabad," *Times*, April 1948, clipping in Theodore Tasker Papers, MSS. Eur. D. 798/30–36, OIOC. (Date is not shown.)
57. Wilfrid Russell, *Indian Summer* (Bombay: Thacker, 1951), p. 210.
58. C. H. V. Pathy, "A Close-Up of Syed Kasim Razvi," *Swatantra*, 29 May 1948.
59. A vivid account of the society and politics of Hyderabad c. 1947–1948 is contained in Asokamitran's novel *The Eighteenth Parallel*, translated from the Tamil by Gomathi Narayanan (Hyderabad: Orient Longmans, 1993).
60. O. V. Ranga Rao, "Exodus of C. P. Muslims to Hyderabad," *Swatantra*, 11 October 1947; Lanka Sundaram, "Nizam's Acts of War and India's Duty," *Swatantra*, 1 November 1947.
61. Gopal, *Nehru*, Vol. 2, pp. 40–41; SPC, Vol. 5, pp. 236–239; SPC, Vol. 7, pp. 150–151, 186–187, etc.
62. See Mirza Ismail, *My Public Life: Recollections and Reflections* (London: George Allen and Unwin, 1954), pp. 105–128.
63. Quoted in Munshi, *End of an Era*, p. 176.
64. Ibid., pp. 230–231; Gandhi, *Patel*, pp. 482–483; Benichou, *From Autocracy to Integration*, pp. 236–237.
65. Sri Prakasa, *Pakistan: Birth and Early Days* (Meerut: Meenakshi Prakashan, 1965), p. 122.
66. Pattabhi Sitaramayya, "The Hyderabad Tangle," *Swatantra*, 12 June 1948.
67. K. A. Abbas, "Three Days in Hyderabad," *Swatantra*, 24 June 1950.
68. P. J. Griffiths, "India and the Future," *Nineteenth Century*, August 1947.
69. See editorial in *Economic Weekly*, 8 January 1955.
70. *Democracy on the March* (New Delhi: Publications Division, 1950), pp. 1, 9–10, etc.
71. Menon, *Integration*, p. 493.

CHAPTER 4: A VALLEY BLOODY AND BEAUTIFUL

1. From now on, I shall use "Kashmir" to refer to the state of Jammu and Kashmir as a whole, and "Valley" to refer to the vale of Kashmir specifically.

2. Karan Singh, *Autobiography*, rev. ed. (Delhi: Oxford University Press, 1994), pp. 18–19.
3. Abdullah, quoted in Ajit Bhattacharjea, *Kashmir: The Wounded Valley* (New Delhi: UBS, 1994), p. 67.
4. V. K. Chinnammalu Amma, "Sheikh Mohammad Abdullah," *Swatantra*, 22 May 1948; Trilok Nath Moza, "Sher-i-Kashmir Sheikh Abdullah," *Swatantra*, 5 June 1948.
5. These paragraphs on politics in Kashmir in the 1930s and 1940s draw largely from Bhattacharjea, *Kashmir*, pp. 65–76; and from Alastair Lamb, *Kashmir: A Disputed Legacy, 1846–1990* (Karachi: Oxford University Press, 1992), pp. 89–95.
6. Malika Pukhraj, *Song Sung True: A Memoir*, ed. and trans. Saleem Kidwai (New Delhi: Kali for Women, 2003), pp. 200–201.
7. Gopal, *Nehru*, Vol. 1, pp. 322–323.
8. SPC, Vol. 1, pp. 13–15.
9. TOP, Vol. 9, p. 71.
10. SPC, Vol. 1, pp. 29–30; Hasan Zaheer, *The Times and Trials of the Rawalpindi Conspiracy, 1951: The First Coup Attempt in Pakistan* (Karachi: Oxford University Press, 1998), pp. 72–73.
11. Mountbatten to Sir Akbar Hydari (governor of Assam), 17 June 1947, Mountbatten Papers, MSS. Eur. F. 200/13, OIOC.
12. See Ramchandra Kak's note, "Jammu and Kashmir in 1946–1947," written in 1960 as a retrospective defence of the idea of independence. Copy in R. Powell Papers, MSS. Eur. D. 862, OIOC.
13. TOP, Vol. 11, p. 592.
14. TOP, Vol. 12, pp. 3–5, 368.
15. Tendulkar, *Mahatma*, Vol. 8, pp. 67–68.
16. Michael Brecher, *The Struggle for Kashmir* (New York: Oxford University Press, 1953), pp. 23–24.
17. Gandhi, *Patel*, p. 439.
18. SPC, Vol. 1, pp. 45–47.
19. See Josef Korbel, *Danger in Kashmir*, 2nd ed. (Princeton, N.J.: Princeton University Press, 1966), pp. 70–71.
20. SPC, Vol. 1, pp. 56, 62.
21. Quoted in Prem Shankar Jha, *Kashmir, 1947: Rival Versions of History* (Delhi: Oxford University Press, 1998), pp. 32–33.
22. R. B. Batra, quoted in Sisir Kumar Gupta, *Kashmir: A Study in India-Pakistan Relations* (Bombay: Asia Publishing House, 1966), p. 106.
23. Alastair Lamb's book is the best case for Pakistan; Jha's book is an answer from the Indian point of view.
24. See Richard Symons, *In the Margins of Independence: A Relief Worker in India and Pakistan, 1942–1949* (Karachi: Oxford University Press, 2001), pp. 78–79.
25. This and the next few paragraphs are based on Lamb, *Kashmir*, pp. 122–134; Brecher, *Struggle*, pp. 25–33; Gupta, *Kashmir*, pp. 110–115; and Zaheer, *Rawalpindi Conspiracy*, pp. 82–87, 94–96, etc.
26. Lieutenant General L. P. Sen, *Slender Was the Thread: Kashmir Confrontation, 1947–1948* (New Delhi: Orient Longmans, 1969), pp. 34–38.

27. Stanley Wolpert, *Jinnah of Pakistan* (New York: Oxford University Press, 1984), p. 348.

28. Untitled typescript dated 3 November 1947 by Major J. E. Thomson, in Powell Papers, MSS. Eur. D. 862, OIOC; extracts from report in *Daily Express*, 11 November 1947, in *White Paper on Jammu and Kashmir* (New Delhi: Government of India, 1948), pp. 24–25.

29. Lamb, *Kashmir*, p. 143.

30. Amar Devi Gupta, typescript, "A 1947 Tragedy of Jammu and Kashmir State: The Cleansing of Mirpur," in MSS. Eur. C. 705, OIOC.

31. Lord Birdwood, "Kashmir," *International Affairs*, July 1952.

32. See the eyewitness accounts in Dewan Ram Prakash, *Fight for Kashmir* (New Delhi: Tagore Memorial, 1948), pp. 34–39.

33. This account is based on Menon, *Integration*, pp. 397–400; and Gandhi, *Patel*, pp. 442–444. However, Prem Shankar Jha (*Kashmir*, pp. 63–64) claims that the Instrument of Accession was signed by Maharaja Hari Singh in Srinagar on the night of 25–26 October, that is, before he fled to Jammu.

34. S. N. Prasad and Dharm Pal, *History of Operations in Jammu and Kashmir, 1947–1948* (New Delhi: Ministry of Defence, 1987), pp. 28f, 379.

35. Major L. E. R. B. Ferris, quoted in Lieutenant Colonel Maurice Cohen, *Thunder over Kashmir* (1955, reprint Hyderabad: Orient Longman, 1994), pp. 3–4.

36. Nehru to Vijayalakshmi Pandit, 28 October 1947, Vijayalakshmi Pandit Papers, NMML.

37. As told by the veteran Punjab politician Khizr Hyat Tiwana to the former Punjab civil servant Malcolm Darling. See diary note of 9 January 1948, Box 60, Darling Papers, Centre for South Asian Studies, University of Cambridge.

38. Baroo, "Kashmir Interlude," *Swatantra*, 29 November 1947.

39. Bhattacharjea, *Kashmir*, pp. x–xii.

40. Lord Mountbatten, "Note of a Discussion with Mr. Jinnah in the Presence of Lord Ismay at Government House, Lahore, on 1 November 1947," in SPC, Vol. 1, pp. 73–81.

41. Prasad and Dharm Pal, *History of Operations*, pp. 39–40.

42. Ibid., p. 60; Sen, *Slender Was the Thread*, pp. 111–112.

43. Nehru to Hari Singh, 13 November 1947, in S. Gopal, ed. *Selected Works of Jawaharlal Nehru*, Second Series, Vol.5 (New Delhi: Nehru Memorial Fund, 1987), pp. 324–327.

44. CWMG, Vol. 90, pp. 122–123.

45. C. Dasgupta, *War and Diplomacy in Kashmir, 1947–1948* (New Delhi: Sage, 2002), p. 78.

46. Nehru to Hari Singh, 1 December 1947, in SPC, 1, pp. 100–106.

47. Hodson, *Great Divide*, pp. 466–467; Lamb, *Kashmir*, pp. 164–165.

48. Brecher, *Struggle*, pp. 55–75; *Reports of the United Nations Special Commission for India and Pakistan, June 1948 to December 1949* (New Delhi: Ministry of External Affairs, 1950), pp. 53f, 281f.

49. Korbel, *Danger in Kashmir*, p. 109.

50. Gopal, *Nehru*, Vol. 2, pp. 26–27; Dasgupta, *War and Diplomacy*, pp. 17, 111, 134. See also Rajbans Krishen, *Kashmir and the Conspiracy against Peace* (Bombay: People's Publishing House, 1951).

51. H. V. Hodson to Philip Noel-Baker, 2 March 1948, copy in Short Papers, MSS. Eur. F. 189/1, OIOC.

52. See Hodson, *Great Divide*, pp. 469–470.

53. Untitled note by Major-General T. W. Rees, in Rees Papers, MSS. Eur. F. 274/72, OIOC.

54. Dasgupta, *War and Diplomacy*, pp. 144–151, 167–168, 177–183.

55. Air Chief Marshal P. C. Lal, *My Years with the IAF* (New Delhi: Lancer International, 1987), pp. 58–67.

56. Sen, *Slender Was the Thread*, p. 242; Prasad and Dharm Pal, *History of Operations*, pp. 276–277.

57. Penderel Moon to Major Billy Short, 18 October 1948, in Short Papers, MSS. Eur. F. 189/22, OIOC. (Emphasis added.)

58. Korbel, *Danger in Kashmir*, pp. 146–149. Korbel was the father of Madeleine Albright, who would herself deal with the Kashmir question in the 1990s, when she was secretary of state in President Clinton's administration.

59. See material in File No. 74, C. Rajagopalachari Papers, Fifth Instalment, Nehru Memorial Museum and Library, New Delhi (hereafter NMML).

60. *Swatantra*, 14 August 1948.

61. Anon., "South India and Kashmir," *Swatantra*, 25 February 1950.

62. Sheikh Abdullah to C. Rajagopalachari, 27 April 1948, in C. Rajagopalachari Papers, Fifth Instalment, NMML.

63. J. K. Banerji, *I Report on Kashmir* (Calcutta: Republic, 1948), pp. 9–10.

64. Y. D. Gundevia, ed., *The Testament of Sheikh Abdullah* (Dehra Dun: Palit and Palit, 1974), pp. 90–91.

65. V. V. Prasad, "New Delhi Diary," *Swatantra*, 9 October 1948.

66. P. N. Kaula and K. L. Dhar, *Kashmir Speaks* (Delhi: S. Chand, 1950), p. 71.

67. K. A. Abbas, "The Enchanted Valley," *Swatantra*, 23 April 1949.

68. "Marching through Kashmir," *Time*, 10 October 1949.

69. Korbel, *Danger in Kashmir*, p. 25.

70. Kingsley Martin, "Kashmir and UNO," and "As Pakistan Sees It," *New Statesman and Nation*, 21 and 28 February 1948.

71. Quoted in Ram Parkash, *Fight for Kashmir*, p. 99.

72. A. Lakshmana Rao, "Brigadier Usman," *Swatantra*, 10 July 1948.

73. Ram Parkash, *Fight for Kashmir*, p. 174.

74. K. A. Abbas, "Will Kashmir Vote for India?" *Current*, 26 October 1949.

75. Wares Ishaq, "Kashmir Will Vote for Pakistan," *Current*, 2 November 1949.

76. Representative here are the interpretations in Dasgupta, *War and Diplomacy*.

77. On Gurdaspur see Lamb, *Kashmir*, especially pp. 115–116; and, for a rebuttal, Jha, *Kashmir*, p. 81.

78. Zaheer, *Rawalpindi Conspiracy*, pp. 144–145.

79. The quotes that follow are taken from Brecher, *Struggle*, pp. ix–x.

CHAPTER 5: REFUGEES AND THE REPUBLIC

1. Donald F. Ebright, *Free India: The First Five Years—An Account of the 1947 Riots, Refugees, Relief, and Rehabilitation* (Nashville, Tenn.: Parthenon, 1954), pp. 46–47, 62–63, etc.

2. A. N. Bali, *Now It Can Be Told* (Jalandhar: Kashvani Prakashan, 1949), especially ch. 9.

3. V. V. Prasad, "New Delhi Diary," *Swatantra*, 25 December 1947.

4. This section is principally based on M. S. Randhawa, *Out of the Ashes: An Account of the Rehabilitation of Refugees from West Punjab in Rural Areas of East Punjab* (Bombay: Author, 1954); and Gyanesh Kudaisya, "The Demographic Upheaval of Partition: Refugees and Agricultural Resettlement in India, 1946–1947," *South Asia*, Vol. 18, No. 1, 1995. Of the roughly 2.5 million farmers who came from West Punjab, about 80% were resettled in East Punjab. Others were given land in the Ganganagar area of the former Bikaner state, and in the Terai regions of Uttar Pradesh. In both places there are now flourishing communities of Sikh farmers.

5. Ian Stephen, "A Day in Qadian," *Statesman*, 9 January 1949. Mohammad Zafrullah Khan, Pakistan's eloquent spokesman in the UN on the Kashmir question, was an Ahmadiya. So was the physicist Abdus Salam, the only Pakistani to be awarded a Nobel Prize. In the 1980s, under the regime of General Zia-ul-Haq, the Ahmadiyas were declared heretics (for their belief in a living Prophet), and they have since faced discrimination and persecution.

6. See L. C. Jain, *The City of Hope: The Faridabad Story* (New Delhi: Concept, 1998), which also describes the corrosion of the cooperative spirit by the bureaucracy. See also "Experiments in Living: Faridabad—Nilokheri—Etawah," *Times of India*, 14 February 1952.

7. Dorothy Jane Ward, *India for the Indians* (London: Arthur Barker, 1949), pp. 187–189.

8. See V. N. Dutta, "Punjabi Refugees and the Urban Development of Greater Delhi," in R. E. Frykenberg, ed., *Delhi through the Ages* (Delhi: Oxford University Press, 1993).

9. Anon., "A Glimpse into Crowded Bombay," *Swatantra*, 7 August 1948.

10. H. L. Mansukhani, "The Resettlement of Sind Refugees," *Swatantra*, 11 September 1948.

11. Anon., "A Glimpse."

12. R. M. Lala, "Kolwada: Landmark of Swaraj," *Current*, 3 May 1950.

13. Gardner Murphy, *In the Minds of Men: The Study of Human Behavior and Social Tensions in India* (New York: Basic, 1953), pp. 170–175.

14. Taya Zinkin, *Reporting India* (London: Chatto and Windus, 1962), pp. 25–26, 31.

15. Prafulla K. Chakrabarti, *The Marginal Men: The Refugees and the Left Political Syndrome in West Bengal* (Calcutta: Naya Udyog, 1999), p. 33.

16. Joya Chatterji, "Right or Charity? The Debate over Relief and Rehabilitation in West Bengal, 1947–1950," in Suvir Kaul, ed., *The Partitions of Memory: The Afterlife of the Division of India* (Delhi: Permanent Black, 2001), p. 99.

17. Sir Jadunath Sarkar, "Brothers from Over the River: The Refugee Problem of India," *Modern Review*, September 1948.

18. Chakravarti, *Marginal Men*, ch. 3.

19. See letters and statements of 1948–1950 in *A Tale of Woes of East Pakistan Minorities* (Calcutta: Voice of New India, 1966), pp. 13–51.

20. *Current*, 4 February 1953.

21. "Squatters' Colonies," *Economic Weekly* (hereafter cited as EW), 5 June 1954.

22. See undated Memorandum (c. 1954?) in File No. 6, Meghnad Saha Papers, Seventh Instalment, NMML.

23. See "Report of a Tour of Inspection of Some of the Refugee Homes in North-West India" (1955), reproduced in *Seminar*, No. 510, February 2002.

24. "Congress May Lose West Bengal—If Refugees Remain Unsettled," EW, 10 July 1954. There is now a growing literature of memoirs written (or spoken) by Bengali refugees. For a sampling of works in English, see Jasodhara Bagchi and Subhoranjan Dasgupta, eds., *The Trauma and the Triumph: Gender and Partition in Eastern India* (Kolkata: Stree, 2003); Gargi Chakravartty, *Coming Out of Partition: Refugee Women of Bengal* (New Delhi: Bluejay, 2005); Manas Ray, "Growing Up Refugee," *History Workshop Journal*, No. 53, 2002.

25. See R. M. Lala, "Refugees," *Current*, 29 March 1950.

26. S. Gopal, ed., *Selected Works of Jawaharlal Nehru*, Second Series, Vol. 4 (New Delhi: Nehru Memorial Fund, 1986), pp. 115–117. (The original broadcast was in Hindi.)

27. Aparna Basu, *Mridula Sarabhai: Rebel with a Cause* (Delhi: Oxford University Press, 1996), ch. 8.

28. Ritu Menon and Kamla Bhasin, *Borders and Boundaries: Women in India's Partition* (New Delhi: Kali for Women), pp. 91–93, 97–98. See also Urvashi Butalia, *The Other Side of Silence: Voices from the Partition of India* (New Delhi: Viking, 1998), ch. 4.

29. See Chitra Bhanu, "Food Situation Getting Worse in Malabar," *Swatantra*, 29 July 1947; "Famine Conditions in East Godavari," *Swatantra*, 4 October 1947; P. V. C. Rao, "The Food Debacle," *Swatantra*, 7 August 1948; P. V. C. Rao, "Lesson of Gujerat Famine," *Swatantra*, 12 February 1949.

30. Clare Wofford and Harris Wofford, *India Afire* (New York: John Day, 1951), pp. 105–106, 113–115; "Communists in Hyderabad," *Swatantra*, 28 May 1949.

31. Ananth Rao Kanangi, "Communists in Andhra," *Current*, 3 May 1950.

32. Quoted in John H. Kautsky, *Moscow and the Communist Party of India* (New York: Wiley, 1956), p. 49.

33. G. S. Bhargava, "Balchandra Triambak Ranadive," *Swatantra*, 22 April 1950.

34. D. Jayakanthan, *A Literary Man's Political Experiences*, trans. from Tamil by M. S. Venkataramani (New Delhi: Vikas, 1976), pp. 19–22.

35. Gene D. Overstreet and Marshall Windmiller, *Communism in India* (Berkeley: University of California Press, 1959), ch. 13.

36. Quoted in M. R. Masani, *The Communist Party of India: A Short History* (Bombay: Bhavan's Book University, 1967), pp. 78–79.

37. *Pravda*, 25 November 1949, quoted in Mahavir Singh, *Soviet View of the Indian National Congress* (New Delhi: Sanchar, 1991), p. 22.

38. Penderel Moon to his father, 5 February 1949, Moon Papers, MSS. Eur. F. 230/23, OIOC.

39. Anon., "Rounding Up of Communists in Hyderabad," *Swatantra*, 4 June 1949; Wofford and Wofford, *India Afire*, pp. 118–119.

40. Gupta, *The Agrarian Drama*, pp. 464–465.

41. Gopal, *Selected Works of Jawaharlal Nehru*, Vol. 4, pp. 52–53.

42. See correspondence in G. M. Nandurkar, *Sardar's Letters—Mostly Unknown—Post-Centenary*, Vol. 2 (Ahmedabad: Sardar Patel Smarak Bhavan, 1981), pp. 20–22; and *Post-Centenary*, Vol. 3 (1983), pp. 42–43.

43. Baroo, "Enter the Sangh," *Swatantra*, 10 September 1949. For a sympathetic contemporary portrait of the RSS, see Jagat S. Bright, *Guruji Golwalkar and R. S. S.* (Delhi: New India, 1951).

44. Letter quoted in *Current*, 19 October 1949.

45. N. S. Muthana, "Golwalkar's Climb on Congress Ladder," *Current*, 9 November 1949.

46. News report in *Current*, 16 November 1949.

47. Dewan Chaman Lall, quoted in Tai Yong Tan and Gyanesh Kudesia, *The Aftermath of Partition in South Asia* (London: Routledge, 2000).

48. R. G. Casey, *An Australian in India* (London: Hollis and Carter, 1947), p. 114.

49. Albert Mayer, *Pilot Project, India: The Story of Rural Development at Etawah, Uttar Pradesh* (Berkeley: University of California Press, 1958), p. 13.

CHAPTER 6: IDEAS OF INDIA

1. HT, 10 and 11 December 1946.

2. Description by an independent Anglo-Indian member, Frank Anthony. *Constituent Assembly Debates: Official Report* (reprint, New Delhi: Lok Sabha Secretariat, 1988—hereafter cited as CAD), Vol. 8, p. 329.

3. K. Santhanam, quoted in Granville Austin, *The Indian Constitution: Cornerstone of a Nation* (1966, reprint New Delhi: Oxford University Press, 2002), p. 13. The varied ideologies and political trends represented in the Assembly are discussed in S. K. Chaube, *Constituent Assembly of India: Springboard of Revolution* (second edition: New Delhi, Manohar, 2000), especially chs. 8 to 10.

4. Churchill, quoted in CAD, Vol. 2, pp. 267, 271.

5. See "Summary of Representations Received in Office Regarding 'Rights of Minorities,'" in File No. 37, C. Rajagopalachari Papers, Fifth Instalment, NMML.

6. Austin, *The Indian Constitution*, p. 71.

7. CAD, Vol. 1, pp. 59–61. That Nehru would mention the Russian revolution along with the other two may be considered by some characteristic of his broadmindedness, by others as characteristic merely of his lack of discrimination.

8. See CAD, Vol. 4, pp. 737–762.

9. Austin, *The Indian Constitution*, pp. 314–315.

10. The words are those of Ambedkar. See CAD, Vol. 9, p. 974. The contributions of Munshi, Aiyar, and Rau to the making of the constitution were immense. They prepared dozens of notes and minutes on specific subjects, the more important of which are reproduced in B. Shiva Rao, ed., *The Framing of India's Constitution: Select Documents*, 4 vols. (New Delhi: Indian Institute of Public Administration, 1968). On K. M. Munshi's role, see also N. H. Bhagwati, "An Architect of the Constitution," in *Munshi at Seventy-Five* (Bombay: Dr. K. M. Munshi's Seventy-Sixth Birthday Celebration Committee, 1962).

11. In the preface to the 1999 edition of his book, Austin amends this slightly, speaking of unity, social revolution, and democracy as "the three strands of a seamless web." Austin's work is indispensable; but see also the long critique by Upendra Baxi, "'The Little Done, the Vast Undone'—Some Reflections on Reading Granville Austin's *The Indian Constitution*," *Journal of the Indian Law Institute*, Vol. 9, 1967, pp. 323–430.

12. CAD, Vol. 7, p. 39.
13. Ibid., pp. 219, 285, 350, 387, etc.
14. Ibid., p. 305.
15. For a good discussion of how this choice was made, see E. Sridharan, "The Origins of the Electoral System," in Zoya Hasan, E. Sridharan, and R. Sudarshan, eds., *India's Living Constitution* (New Delhi: Permanent Black, 2002). See also "Report by the Constitutional Adviser on His Visit to U. S. A., Canada, Ireland, and England," in Rao, *Select Documents*, Vol. 3, pp. 217–226.
16. Nehru, quoted in Austin, *The Indian Constitution*, p. 121.
17. The phrase is that of Granville Austin's. See *The Indian Constitution*, p. 50.
18. An excellent discussion of the framing of the Fundamental Rights section is contained in B. Shiva Rao, ed., *The Framing of India's Constitution: A Study* (New Delhi: Indian Institute of Public Administration, 1968), ch. 7.
19. Austin, *The Indian Constitution*, p. 56.
20. CAD, Vol. 4, p. 769.
21. CAD, Vol. 11, pp. 711–713.
22. CAD, Vol. 7, p. 360.
23. CAD, Vol. 11, p. 616.
24. Intervention by Shibban Lal Saxena, CAD, Vol. 11, pp. 705–706.
25. Ibid., p. 212.
26. Interventions by Loknath Misra and K. Hanumanthaiya, CAD, Vol. 11, pp. 799, 617.
27. CAD, Vol. 5, pp. 54–55.
28. Intervention by Balkrishna Sharma, CAD, Vol. 5, pp. 74–76.
29. Speech of 17 December 1946, CAD, Vol. 1, p. 102. (Emphasis in original.)
30. CAD, Vol. 4, p. 546.
31. Ibid., p. 859.
32. CAD, Vol. 5, pp. 211–213.
33. Ibid., p. 271.
34. CAD, Vol. 7, p. 306; Vol. 8, p. 300.
35. Intervention by Naziruddin Ahmad, CAD, Vol. 8, pp. 296–297.
36. CAD, Vol. 1, p. 138.
37. CAD, Vol. 4, p. 668.
38. CAD, Vol. 7, p. 356.
39. CAD, Vol. 5, pp. 202–203; Vol. 11, pp. 608–609.
40. CAD, Vol. 9, pp. 667–669.
41. Intervention by Brajeshwar Prasad, CAD, Vol. 10, p. 239.
42. CAD, Vol. 8, pp. 344–345.
43. CAD, Vol. 5, p. 210.
44. Regrettably, there is no biography of Jaipal Singh. See, however, P. G. Ganguly, "Separatism in the Indian Polity: A Case Study," in M. C. Pradhan et al., eds., *Anthropology and Archaeology: Essays in Commemoration of Verrier Elwin* (Bombay: Oxford University Press, 1969).
45. CAD, Vol. 1, pp. 143–144.
46. CAD, Vol. 7, pp. 559–560.
47. Intervention by Brajeshwar Prasad, CAD, Vol. 9, p. 281.
48. CAD, Vol. 1, pp. 26–27.
49. HT, 11 December 1946.

50. CAD, Vol. 8, p. 745.
51. CAD, Vol. 7, pp. 20–31.
52. See Suniti Kumar Chatterji, *Languages and the Linguistic Problem*, Oxford Pamphlet on Indian Affairs, No. 11 (Bombay: Oxford University Press, 1943); Alok Rai, *Hindi Nationalism* (Hyderabad: Orient Longman, 2000).
53. Jawaharlal Nehru, "The Question of Language" (1937), in *The Unity of India: Collected Writings, 1937–1940* (London: Lindsay Drummond, 1941), pp. 241–261.
54. letter to Krishnachandra, 12 May 1945, in CWMG, Volume 80, p. 117.
55. See letters in CWMG, Vol. 80, pp. 181, 317–318; Vol. 81, pp. 33–34, 332.
56. Austin, *The Indian Constitution*, p. 267.
57. See interventions by B. Pocker Sahib Bahadur and Jaipal Singh, CAD, Vol. 4, pp. 553, 554.
58. CAD, Vol. 7, p. 235.
59. Article 343, Constitution of India.
60. This section is based on Ambedkar's last speech to the Constituent Assembly: CAD, Vol. 11, pp. 972–981.
61. John W. Dower, *Embracing Defeat: Japan in the Wake of World War II* (New York: Norton, 1999), p. 347. The making of the Japanese constitution is discussed in chs. 12 and 13.
62. Courtney Whitney, quoted ibid., p. 373.
63. Austin, *The Indian Constitution*, pp. 308, 309–310, 328.

CHAPTER 7: THE BIGGEST GAMBLE IN HISTORY

1. Vignhneswara (V. Raghunathan), *Sotto Voce: A Social and Political Commentary*, Vol. 1, *The Coming of Freedom* (Madras: B. G. Paul, 1951), p. 203.
2. Quoted in *Current*, 18 July 1951.
3. "Disintegration of the Congress," *Current*, 9 May 1951.
4. See S. H. Desai, "Sardar Patel," *Current*, 14 August 1948; A. S. Iyengar, *All through the Gandhian Era: Reminscences* (Bombay: Hind Kitabs, 1950), pp. 289–295 (section titled "Nehru and Patel"); V. Shankar, *My Reminiscences of Sardar Patel*, Vol. 2 (New Delhi: Macmillan, 1975), pp. 20–3.
5. Prasad had a greater following than Rajaji because he was a Hindi speaker from north India (like the majority of congressmen at the time), and because unlike Rajaji he had actively participated in the "Quit India" movement of 1942. See Rajmohan Gandhi, *The Rajaji Story, 1937–1972* (Bombay: Bharatiya Vidya Bhavan, 1984), pp. 190–194.
6. *Statesman*, 26 January 1950. Left-wing critics complained about the pageantry, saying it was a colonial hangover. They were reminded that "pomp and pageantry were Indian before they became British, and the British used them because they understood the Indian mentality." See "Shridharani in Delhi," *Swatantra*, 8 January 1950.
7. The verdicts, respectively, of Michael Brecher, *Nehru: A Political Biography* (London: Oxford University Press, 1959), p. 43; K. A. Abbas, "Rajarshi Tandon—the New President," *Swatantra*, 9 September 1950; and *Current*, 13 September 1950.
8. Nehru to Rajagopalachari, letters of 26 and 27 August 1950, File No. 189, C. Rajagopalachari Papers, Fifth Instalment, NMML.

9. Nehru, "Statement to the Press," 13 September 1950, copy in File No. 24, C. Rajagopalachari Papers, Fifth Instalment, NMML. This statement has not been reproduced in S. Gopal's *Selected Works of Jawaharlal Nehru* (New Delhi: Nehru Memorial Fund, 1986).

10. Letter of 28 March 1950, in SPC, Vol. 10, p. 19.

11. Gandhi, *Patel*, pp. 526–527.

12. 5. Gopal, *Nehru*, Vol. 2, p. 309.

13. Gandhi, *Patel*, p. 530.

14. "Vallabhbhai Patel," in S. Gopal and Uma Iyengar, eds., *The Essential Writings of Jawaharlal Nehru*, Vol. 1 (New Delhi: Oxford University Press, 2003), p. 633.

15. Gopal, *Nehru*, Vol. 2, p. 155.

16. See K. Mukherjee, "The Resurrection of Somnath," *Indian Review*, July 1951.

17. Nehru to Rajendra Prasad, 2 March 1951, copy in Subject File 46, C. Rajagopalachari Papers, Fourth Instalment, NMML.

18. Speech in Hindi at Somnath, 11 May 1951, in Valmiki Choudhary, ed., *Dr. Rajendra Prasad: Correspondence and Select Documents,* Vol. 14 (New Delhi: Allied, 1991). I am grateful to Professor Bhagwan Josh of Jawaharlal Nehru University for this reference. This and other translations from the Hindi in this book are mine.

19. Editorial in *Swatantra*, 8 September 1951.

20. Gopal, *Nehru*, Vol. 2, p. 155.

21. Richard L. Park, "India's General Election," *Far Eastern Survey*, 9 January 1952.

22. This description of the mechanics of the election is based on Sukumar Sen, *Report on the First General Elections in India, 1951–1952* (New Delhi: Election Commission, 1955). That source was supplemented by Park, "India's General Election"; and Irene Tinker and Mil Walker, "The First General Elections in India and Indonesia," *Far Eastern Survey*, July 1956.

23. *Times of India* (Bombay—hereafter cited as TOI), 5 November 1951.

24. See, for example, Asoka Mehta, *The Political Mind of India* (Bombay: Socialist Party, 1952).

25. News report in *Searchlight* (Patna), 22 November 1951.

26. See Craig Baxter, *The Jana Sangh: A Biography of an Indian Political Party* (Bombay: Oxford University Press, 1971), pp. 87–88, etc.

27. Reports in HT, 12 October 1951; TOI, 9 November 1951; Mehta, *The Political Mind*, p. 61.

28. TOI, 9 November 1951; Manikuntala Sen, *In Search of Freedom: An Unfinished Journey* (Calcutta: STREE, 2001), pp. 220–221; Ravi Narayan Reddy, *Heroic Telengana: Reminiscences and Experiences* (New Delhi: Communist Party of India), pp. 71–72.

29. Lord Birdwood, *A Continent Decides* (London: Robert Hale, 1953), p. 103; TOI, 22 January 1952 (news report, "Bovine Election Propaganda").

30. TOI, 1 January 1952.

31. S. Borzenko, "Before the Elections in India," originally published in *Pravda*, 25 October 1951; translated in *Swatantra*, 1 December 1951.

32. Park, "India's General Election."

33. Prakash, "Lalaji," *Shankar's Weekly*, 6 January 1952.

34. This and the following paragraphs on Nehru's all-India election tour are based on newspaper reports in TOI and HT, supplemented by Anon., *The Pilgrimage and After: The Story of How the Congress Fought and Won the General Elections* (New Delhi: All India Congress Committee, 1952).

35. See Ajit Bhattacharjea, *J. P. : His Biography* (New Delhi: Orient Longman, 1975), pp. 254, 256. Indira Gandhi based her allegations on the fact that one Socialist leader, Rammanohar Lohia, had recently returned from a speaking tour in the United States; and another, Jayaprakash Narayan, had once studied there.

36. Frank Moraes, *Jawaharlal Nehru: A Biography* (New York: Macmillan, 1956), p. 413.

37. Anon., *The Pilgrimage and After*, p. 23.

38. D. F. Karaka, *Nehru: The Lotus Eater from Kashmir* (London: Derek Verschoyle, 1953), pp. 96–98.

39. Nehru to Lady Mountbatten, 3 December 1951, quoted in Gopal, *Nehru*, Vol. 2, p. 161.

40. The account of voting and voters' behaviour is largely based on contemporary newspaper accounts, especially in TOI and HT.

41. HT, 26 October 1951.

42. Irene Tinker Walker, "The General Election in Himachal Pradesh, India, 1951," *Parliamentary Affairs*, Vol. 6, No. 3, Summer 1953.

43. "General Elections," EW, 5 January 1952.

44. Jean Lyon, *Just Half a World Away: My Search for the New India* (London: Hutchinson, 1955), pp. 125–130.

45. Sen, *Report*, p. 135.

46. Personal communication from Professor Rajen Harshe of Hyderabad University, 21 May 2002.

47. Park, "India's General Election."

48. C. R. Srinivasan, "The Elections Are On," *Indian Review*, January 1952. (Emphasis added.)

49. Clare Wofford and Harris Wofford, Jr., *India Afire* (New York: John Day, 1951), p. 25.

50. Letter in MSS. Eur. F. 230/26, OIOC.

51. *Organiser*, 7 January 1952, quoted in Margaret W. Fisher and Joan V. Bondurant, eds., *The Indian Experience with Democratic Elections*, Indian Press Digests, University of California, Berkeley, No. 3, December 1956, p. 60.

52. *Tribune* (Ambala), 22 December 1951; and *Hitavada*, 30 December 1951, both quoted ibid., pp. 56–57, 58.

53. This paragraph is based on press reports, ibid., pp. 61f; Nehru's remarks are quoted in W. H. Morris-Jones, "The Indian Elections," EW, 28 June and 5 July 1952.

54. Chester Bowles, *Ambassador's Report* (New York: Harper, 1954), ch. 11.

55. Ahmed Emin Yalman in TOI, 21 February 1951. (He was the editor of the *Daily Vatan* in Istanbul.)

56. D. P. Mukerji, "First Fruits of General Elections," EW, 26 January 1952.

57. Jawaharlal Nehru, *An Autobiography: With Musings on Recent Events in India* (1936, reprint London: Bodley Head, 1949), p. 598 (quote taken from the postscript dated Badenweiler, 25 October 1935).

CHAPTER 8: HOME AND THE WORLD

1. Nirad C. Chaudhuri, "After Nehru, Who?" *Illustrated Weekly of India*, 10 May 1953.
2. Arthur Lall, *The Emergence of Modern India* (New York: Columbia University Press, 1981), p. 128. (Lall was a high-ranking member of the Indian Foreign Service and had worked closely with Nehru.)
3. The *Autobiography* was Nehru's second book-length work. The first, whose title (*Glimpses of World History*) is testimony to his global outlook, was written initially as a series of letters to his daughter from jail. His third major book was published in 1946; its title is also revealing—it was called *The Discovery of India*, suggesting that perhaps this man was an internationalist well before he became a patriot, that he had discovered the world before he had discovered India.
4. "Peace and Empire," in Jawaharlal Nehru, *Peace and India* (London: India League, 1938).
5. See Nehru to S. K. Datta, letters of 20 June 1939 and 24 December 1941, Datta Papers, MSS. Eur. F. 178/28, OIOC.
6. See Jawaharlal Nehru, *India's Foreign Policy: Selected Speeches, September 1946–April 1961* (New Delhi: Publications Division, 1961), pp. 3, 24, 28–29, 31–32. It is important to remember here that Nehru wrote his speeches himself.
7. Quoted in K. P. S. Menon, "India and the Soviet Union," in B. R. Nanda, ed., *Indian Foreign Policy: The Nehru Years* (Delhi: Vikas, 1976), p. 134.
8. James Cameron, *Point of Departure* (London: Arthur Barker, 1967), p. 247.
9. See *Asian Relations: Being a Report of the Proceedings and Documentation of the First Asian Relations Conference, New Delhi, March–April 1947* (New Delhi: Asian Relations Organization, 1948).
10. Quoted in Parsa Venkateshwar Rao, Jr., "The Misty Origins of NAM," *New Sunday Indian Express*, 26 January 2003.
11. CWMG, Vol. 87, pp. 190–193.
12. Quoted in "The Asian Conference, 1947," in Diana Mansergh, ed., *Independence Years: The Selected Indian and Commonwealth Papers of Nicholas Mansergh* (New Delhi: Oxford University Press, 1999), p. 81.
13. Jawaharlal Nehru, *Glimpses of World History* (1934, rev. ed. London: Lindsay Drummond, 1949), p. 930.
14. *Time*, 17 October 1949.
15. P. P. Kumaramangalam to C. Rajagopalachari, 22 December 1947, in File No. 82, Fifth Instalment, C. Rajagopalachari Papers, NMML. Kumaramangalam went on to become the highest-ranking military officer in India, chief of army staff.
16. Harold Isaac, *Images of Asia: American Views of China and India* (1958, new ed. New York: Harper and Row, 1972), especially Part III.
17. Quoted in Gopal, *Nehru*, Vol. 2, p. 59.
18. These speeches are reproduced in Jawaharlal Nehru, *Visit to America* (New York: John Day, 1950).
19. Quoted in J. J. Singh, "The Triumph of Nehru," *Indian Review*, January 1950.
20. See Gopal, *Nehru*, Vol. 2, p. 61.
21. *Time*, 14 November 1949.
22. Dean Acheson, *Present at the Creation: My Years in the State Department* (London: Hamish Hamilton, 1970), pp. 334–336.

23. See Vijayalakshmi Pandit's comments on Dean Acheson in *The Scope of Happiness: A Personal Memoir* (New Delhi: Orient Paperbacks, 1981), pp. 235-236.

24. Bowles, *Ambassador's Report*, ch. 9.

25. Saunders Redding, *An American in India: A Personal Report on the Indian Dilemma and the Nature of Her Conflicts* (Indianapolis, Ind.: Bobbs-Merrill, 1954), p. 47.

26. Quoted in *Hindu*, 30 October 1953.

27. Walter Crocker, *Nehru: A Contemporary's Estimate* (New York: Oxford University Press, 1966), p. 114.

28. Keith Callard, *Pakistan: A Political Study* (London: George Allen and Unwin, 1957), p. 321.

29. See untitled note enclosed with letter from Winston Churchill to Lord Mountbatten, 21 November 1947, in MSS. Eur. F. 200/39, OIOC; Kissinger, quoted in Aslam Siddiqi, *Pakistan Seeks Security* (Lahore: Longmans, Green, 1960), p. 109.

30. See Baldev Raj Nayar, *Superpower Dominance and Military Aid: A Study of Military Aid to Pakistan* (New Delhi: Manohar, 1991); Anon., "U. S.-Pak Pact: An American View," *Swatantra*, 27 February 1954.

31. E. Stanley Jones, quoted in *Hindu*, 25 December 1953. Jones was the author of a number of books on Indian themes, among them a sympathetic study of Mahatma Gandhi.

32. Taya Zinkin, "Indo-American Relations," *Economic Weekly*, Annual No., January 1956.

33. Letter of 21 May 1954, Birla Papers, NMML.

34. "Interview with Hon. John Foster Dulles," ibid.

35. Letter of 6 February 1956, ibid.

36. "Dulles Press Conference in India" (New Delhi: United States Information Service, 1956).

37. See Denis Kux, *India and the United States, 1941-1991: Estranged Democracies* (Washington, D.C.: National Defense University Press, 1993).

38. Jawaharlal Nehru, *Soviet Russia: Some Random Sketches and Impressions* (Allahabad: Allahabad Law Journal Press, 1928).

39. Gopal, *Nehru*, Vol. 1, p. 108.

40. See David Caute, *The Fellow Travellers* (New Haven, Conn.: Yale University Press, 1987).

41. Robert H. Donaldson, *Soviet Policy towards India: Ideology and Strategy* (Cambridge, Mass.: Harvard University Press, 1974), pp. 109-112.

42. See Mikhail Gorbachev, *Memoirs* (London: Doubleday, 1996), pp. 52-53: "Obviously, we [students] were still very far from understanding the principles of democracy. Yet, the simplified black-and-white picture of the world as presented by our propaganda was even then considered rather sceptically by the students. Jawaharlal Nehru's visit to Moscow in June 1955 was an unexpected stimulus for me in this respect. . . . This amazing man, his noble bearing, keen eyes and warm and disarming smile, made a deep impression on me."

43. K. P. Menon, *The Flying Troika* (London: Oxford University Press, 1963), pp. 110-119.

44. Anon., "Soviet Leaders' Visit and After," EW, 24 December 1955.

45. N. A. Bulganin and N. S. Khrushchev, *Visit of Friendship to India, Burma, and*

Afghanistan: Speeches and Official Documents, November–December 1955 (Moscow: Foreign Languages Publishing House, 1955).

46. A. D. Gorwala, "As Nehru Leaves for Moscow," *Current,* 1 June 1955.
47. For example, C. Parameswaran, *Nehru's Foreign Policy X-Rayed* (New Delhi: Author, 1954).
48. For representative views, see L. Natarajan, *American Shadow over India* (Bombay: People's Publishing House, 1952); Romesh Thapar, *India in Transition* (Bombay: Current Book House, 1956). Louis Fischer, travelling through India in 1953–1954, commented that the prevailing understanding of non-alignment "tended to close minds to criticisms of Russia while stimulating a less-than-friendly attitude towards the Western democracies." Fischer, *This Is Our World* (London: Jonathan Cape, 1956), pp. 142–143.
49. "The Bandung Conference," in A. Appadorai, *Essays in Politics and International Relations* (Bombay: Asia Publishing House, 1969), pp. 79–113.
50. *Lok Sabha Debates,* Vol. 1955, col. 8962 to 8974.
51. Gopal, *Nehru,* Vol. 2, pp. 277–290.
52. "Aggression in Egypt and Hungary," *Swatantra,* 10 November 1956.
53. See Nehru, *India's Foreign Policy,* pp. 534f.
54. See Escott Reid, *Envoy to Nehru* (Delhi: Oxford University Press, 1981), ch. 11.
55. L. N. S., "Double-Think," *Swatantra,* 17 November 1956.
56. Gopal, *Nehru,* Vol. 2, pp. 291–299.
57. Frank Moraes, *India Today* (New York: Macmillan, 1960), pp. 198–199.
58. See T. J. S. George, *Krishna Menon: A Biography* (London: Jonathan Cape, 1964).
59. Vincent Sheean, *Nehru: The Years of Power* (London: Victor Gollancz, 1960), pp. 144–145.
60. See news report in *Current,* 15 February 1956.
61. *United Nations World,* quoted in *Current,* 21 April 1954.
62. Sisela Bok, *Alva Myrdal: A Daughter's Memoir* (Reading, Mass.: Addison-Wesley, 1991), p. 252.
63. K. M. Pannikar, *In Two Chinas: Memoirs of a Diplomat* (London: George Allen and Unwin, 1955), pp. 80–82.
64. Nehru, *India's Foreign Policy,* pp. 302–303.
65. Nehru to Vijayalakshmi Pandit, 1 November 1953, Vijayalakshmi Pandit Papers, NMML.
66. SPC, Vol. 10, pp. 335–341. See also Marc C. Feer, "Tibet in Sino-Indian Relations," *India Quarterly,* Vol. 9, No. 4, 1953.
67. D. K. Karaka, "Nehru's Neutralism Brings Mao to Our Frontier," *Current,* 29 November 1950.
68. SPC, Vol. 10, pp. 342–347.
69. Vijayalakshmi Pandit to Jawaharlal Nehru, 16 May 1952, copy in File No. 123, C. Rajagopalachari Papers, Fifth Instalment, NMML.
70. John Rowland, *A History of Sino-Indian Relations: Hostile Co-Existence* (Princeton, N.J.: Van Nostrand, 1967), ch. 7.
71. Bajpai to Subimal Dutt, 18 October 1954, letter in possession of Dr. Supriya Guha. It has been claimed that Patel's famous letter to Nehru on Tibet was actually drafted by Bajpai (personal communication from his son, K. S. Bajpai).

72. Gopal, *Nehru*, Vol. 2, pp. 227–230; Moraes, *India Today*, p. 191. Among the topics discussed by Nehru and Mao was the possibility of an atomic war between the superpowers. When Nehru said he dreaded the prospect, Mao answered that he welcomed it, because while western imperialism would be destroyed the more populous socialist bloc would still have some men standing; these would then reproduce themselves, and in time "the whole world would become socialist." See Stuart Schram, *Mao Tse-tung* (Harmondsworth: Penguin, 1967), p. 291 and n.

73. TOI, 3 November 1954.

74. Notes in File No. 6, Subimal Dutt Papers, NMML; George N. Patterson, *Tragic Destiny* (London: Faber and Faber, 1959), pp. 160–163.

75. Letters to "R," dated 8 December 1956, in File No. 46, C. Rajagopalachari Papers, Fourth Instalment, NMML.

76. Sir Charles Bell, quoted in Dorothy Woodman, *Himalayan Frontiers: A Political Review of British, Chinese, Indian, and Russian Rivalries* (London: Barrie and Rockcliff, 1969), p. 179. Woodman's book remains the best historical account of the origins of the border dispute between India and China. But see also Hsiao-Ting Lin, "Boundary, Sovereignty, and Imagination: Reconsidering the Frontier Disputes between British India and Republican China, 1914–1947," *Journal of Imperial and Commonwealth History*, Vol. 32, No. 3, 2004.

77. On Elwin, the IFAS, and their work in NEFA, see Ramachandra Guha, *Savaging the Civilized: Verrier Elwin, His Tribals, and India* (Chicago, Ill.: University of Chicago Press, 1999), ch. 11.

78. Woodman, *Himalayan Frontiers*, p. 66.

79. "Indo-Pakistan Clash of Ideologies," TOI, 26 January 1952.

80. Gopal, *Nehru*, Vol. 2, pp. 82–88; Chakravartty, *Coming Out of Partition*, pp. 15–25.

81. I have simplified and summarized a complex story told in detail in A. A. Michel, *The Indus Rivers: A Study of the Effects of Partition* (New Haven, Conn.: Yale University Press, 1967).

82. See J. B. Das Gupta, *Indo-Pakistan Relations, 1947–1955* (Amsterdam: Djambatan, 1958), pp. 51–52.

83. "Feelings in the Capital about the Trade Pact with Pakistan," unsigned note dated 28 February 1951, in File No. 61, C. Rajagopalachari Papers, Fourth Instalment, NMML. A year before this, when Nehru signed his agreement with Liaqat Ali Khan, a critic complained that he "represents the beatific school which believes in self-flagellation in reconciliation [with] the enemy." "Shridharani from New Delhi," *Current*, 12 April 1950.

84. *Dawn*, 19, 24, 25, and 28 January 1955.

85. N. V. Rajkumar, *The Problem of French India* (New Delhi: All India Congress Committee, 1951); Governor of Madras to President of India, 16 April 1954, in File 215, C. Rajagopalachari Papers, Fifth Instalment, NMML; *Dawn*, 27 January 1955.

86. TOI, 2 November 1955.

87. Quoted in *Goa and the Indian Union* (Lisbon: Secretariado Nacional da Informaco, 1954).

88. See *Portuguese India: A Survey of Conditions after 400 Years of Foreign Colo-*

nial Rule (Bombay: Goa Congress Committee, 1939); Juliao Menezes, *Goa's Freedom Struggle* (Bombay: Author, 1947).

89. R. M. Lala, "Report on Daman," *Current*, 22 November 1950.

90. Aloysius Soares, *Down the Corridors of Time: Recollections and Reflexions,* Vol. 2, *1948–1970* (Bombay: Author, 1973), pp. 45ff; *Current*, 25 August 1954.

91. Homer A. Jack, *Inside Goa* (New Delhi: Information Service of India, 1955); P. D. Gaitonde, *The Liberation of Goa: A Participant's View of History* (London: C. Hurst, 1987).

92. Y. D. Gundevia, *Outside the Archives* (Hyderabad: Sangam, 1984), pp. 18–19.

93. Letter of 22 January 1953, in Nehru correspondence, Y. D. Gundevia Papers, NMML.

94. C. Rajagopalachari to Edwina Mountbatten, 5 September 1950, File 189, C. Rajagopalachari Papers, Fifth Instalment, NMML.

95. See Carlo Feltrinelli, *Secret Service* (London: Granta, 2002).

96. Bok, *Alva Myrdal*, p. 243.

CHAPTER 9: REDRAWING THE MAP

1. CWMG, Vol. 89, pp. 312–313.

2. "The Question of Language" (1937), in Nehru, *The Unity of India: Collected Writings, 1937–1940* (London: Lindsay Drummond, 1941), pp. 232–233.

3. Quoted in Robert D. King, *Nehru and the Language Politics of India* (Delhi: Oxford University Press, 1997), p. 102.

4. CWMG, Vol. 90, p. 86.

5. Ibid., p. 494.

6. See letter of 8 June 1948 to Tushar Kanti Ghosh, in Subject File 82, C. Rajagopalachari Papers, Fifth Instalment, NMML.

7. *Report of the Linguistic Provinces Commission* (New Delhi: Constituent Assembly of India, 1948), paragraphs 146 and 147.

8. King, *Nehru and Language Politics*, pp. 107–108, passim.

9. See Baldev Raj Nayar, *Minority Politics in the Punjab* (Princeton, N.J.: Princeton University Press, 1960), chs. 2 and 3.

10. Satindra Singh, "Master Tara Singh: A Born Rebel," *Thought*, 9 December 1967.

11. Nayar, *Minority Politics*, p. 143.

12. Quoted ibid., p. 36.

13. The best account of the history of the Andhra movement, on which the preceding paragraphs largely draw, is K. V Narayana Rao, *The Emergence of Andhra Pradesh* (Bombay: Popular Prakashan, 1973).

14. *Current*, 2 January 1952. See also Selig Harrison, *India: The Most Dangerous Decades* (Princeton, N.J.: Princeton University Press, 1960), pp. 234–235.

15. *Congress Sandesh*, quoted in Narayana Rao, *Emergence of Andhra Pradesh*, p. 241.

16. See TOI, 24 February 1952.

17. See "Kowshika," *The Boundaries of Andhra Province* (Pudukottai: Anbu Nilayam, 1947).

18. Narayana Rao, *Emergence of Andhra Pradesh*, p. 243.

19. *History of Andhra Movement,* Vol. 2 (Hyderabad: Committee for History of Andhra Movement, 1985), p. 496.

20. Gandhi to T. Prakasam, 4 January 1947, in *History of Andhra Movement,* pp. 496–497; also CWMG, Vol. 86, p. 242.

21. Interview with Professor Béteille, New Delhi, December 2001.

22. See Subject File 123, C. Rajagopalachari Papers, Fifth Instalment, NMML.

23. See P. R. Rao, *History of Modern Andhra* (New Delhi: Sterling, 1984), p. 130.

24. Letter of 18 August 1953 to General Sir Roy Bucher, Subject File 124, C. Rajagopalachari Papers, Fifth Instalment, NMML.

25. Gopal, *Nehru,* Vol. 2, p. 259.

26. *Memorandum Submitted to the States Reorganization Commission* (Bombay: Bombay Citizens' Committee, 1954).

27. The activities of the committee, including its strategies for fund-raising and public relations, can be followed through the mass of material in File No. 383, Purushottamdas Thakurdas Papers, NMML.

28. Golwalkar, quoted in TOI, 8 November 1951.

29. Report in TOI, 24 May 1954.

30. Gadgil and Deshmukh are both quoted in Robert W. Stein, *The Process of Opposition in India* (Chicago, Ill.: University of Chicago Press, 1970), p. 46.

31. Samyukta Maharashtra Parishad, *Memorandum to the States Reorganization Committee,* May 1954. (Copy in the library of the Gokhale Institute of Politics and Economics, Pune. D. R. Gadgil was the chief draughtsman of this memorandum.)

32. See report of meeting of 20 June 1954 in File No. 383, Purushottamdas Thakurdas Papers, NMML.

33. This section is based on *Report of the States Reorganization Commission* (Delhi: Manager of Publications, 1955).

34. See *Lok Sabha Debates,* Vol. 10, 1955.

35. *Current,* 4 January 1956.

36. The name change was effected toward the end of 1955.

37. Taya Zinkin, *Reporting India* (London: Chatto and Windus, 1962), p. 108.

38. *Current,* 25 January 1956. See also V. M. Bhave, "Struggle for Maharashtra," *New Age,* September 1956.

39. Letter of 23 January 1956, Subject File No. 68, C. D. Deshmukh Papers, NMML.

40. See papers in Subject File No. 67, C. D. Deshmukh Papers, NMML.

41. See letters and papers in Subject File No. 4, N. V. Gadgil Papers, NMML.

42. As reported in alarm to the home minister, G. B. Pant, by Sir Purushottamdas Thakurdas. See letter of 20 January 1956, in File No. 383, Purushottamdas Thakurdas Papers, NMML.

43. *Current,* 15 and 29 February, 1956.

44. Y. D. Phadke, *Politics and Language* (Bombay: Himalaya, 1979), ch. 6.

45. See Baburao Patel, *Burning Words: A Critical History of Nine Years of Nehru's Rule from 1947 to 1956* (Bombay: Sumati, 1956), pp. 106–108.

46. Ravi Kalia, *Bhubaneshwar: From a Temple Town to a Capital City* (Carbondale: Southern Illinois University Press, 1994).

47. Janaki Nair, " 'Past Perfect': Architecture and Public Life in Bangalore," unpublished manuscript. I am grateful to Dr. Nair for showing me a copy of this manuscript, which was to form part of her history of Bangalore. That has since

been published as *The Promise of the Metropolis: Bangalore's Twentieth Century* (New Delhi: Oxford University Press, 2005).

48. TOI, 26 February 1952.
49. Anon., "Andhra Answers Dulles," EW, 5 March 1955.

CHAPTER 10: THE CONQUEST OF NATURE

1. W. Burns, ed., *Sons of the Soil: Studies of the Indian Cultivator*, 2nd ed. (Delhi: Manager of Publications, 1944), Introduction.

2. Gyanendra Pandey, *The Ascendancy of the Congress in Uttar Pradesh, 1926–1934: A Study in Imperfect Mobilization* (Delhi: Oxford University Press, 1978); Peter Reeves, *Landlords and Governments in Uttar Pradesh: A Study of Their Relations until Zamindari Abolition* (New Delhi: Oxford University Press, 1991).

3. Chitra Bhanu, "Food Situation Getting Worse in Malabar," *Swatantra,* 29 July 1947.

4. For illuminating contemporary analyses, see Z. A. Ahmad, *The Agrarian Problem in India: A General Survey* (Allahabad: All India Congress Committee, 1936); S. Y. Krishnaswami, *Rural Problems in Madras* (Madras: Government of Madras, 1947). Valuable surveys of the economic history of colonial India include V. B. Singh, ed., *Economic History of India: 1857–1956* (Bombay: Allied, 1965); Dharma Kumar, ed., *The Cambridge Economic History of India: Vol. 2, c. 1757–c. 1970* (Cambridge: Cambridge University Press, 1983); and Tirthankar Ray, *The Indian Economy, 1857–1947* (New Delhi: Oxford University Press, 2006).

5. See, inter alia, Dwijendra Tripathi, ed., *Business and Politics in India: A Historical Perspective* (Delhi: Manohar, 1991); Medha M. Kudaisya, *The Life and Times of G. D. Birla* (New Delhi: Oxford University Press, 2003).

6. John Kenneth Galbraith, "Rival Economic Theories in India," *Foreign Affairs,* Vol. 36, No. 4, 1958, p. 591.

7. See Meghnad Saha, "The Problem of Indian Rivers" (1938) and "Technological Revolution in Industry—How the Russians Did It" (1943), in Santimay Chatterjee, ed., *Collected Works of Meghnad Saha,* Vol. 2 (Bombay: Orient Longman, 1986).

8. Lala Lajpat Rai, *The Evolution of Japan and Other Papers* (Calcutta: Modern Review, 1922).

9. K. T. Shah, "Principles of National Planning," in Iqbal Singh and Raja Rao, *Whither India?* (Baroda; Padmaja, 1948). Shah was a economist from Bombay who served as secretary of the NPC. See also R. Chattopadhyay, "The Idea of Planning in India, 1930–1951," unpublished PhD dissertation, Australian National University, Canberra, 1985.

10. See, for example, *National Planning Committee: Report of the Sub-Committee on Power and Fuel* (Bombay: Vora, 1949).

11. *Memorandum Outlining a Plan of Economic Development for India,* Parts 1 and 2 (Harmondsworth: Penguin, 1945), emphasis added. The signatories to the Bombay Plan included G. D. Birla, Kasturbhai Lalbhai, Lala Shri Ram, J. R. D. Tata, and Purushottamdas Thakurdas.

12. The intellectual climate of the time, as it pertained to economic policy, is cap-

tured in Tirthankar Ray, "Economic History and Modern India: Redefining the Link," *Journal of Economic Perspectives*, Vol. 16, No. 3, 2002; Nariaki Nakatozo, "The Transfer of Economic Power in India: Indian Big Business, the British Raj, and Development Planning, 1930–1948," in Mushirul Hasan and Nariaki Nakatozo, eds., *The Unfinished Agenda: Nation-Building in South Asia* (Delhi: Manohar, 2001); Pranab Bardhan, "A Note on Nehru as Economic Planner," in Milton Israel, ed., *Nehru and the Twentieth Century* (Toronto: University of Toronto Press, 1991).

13. Speech in Lok Sabha on 15 December 1952, in *Planning and Development: Speeches of Jawaharlal Nehru, 1952–1956* (New Delhi: Publications Division, n.d.), pp. 7–8. See also R. Ramadas, "Report on the Draft Five Year Plan," *Swatantra*, 1 December 1951.

14. See TOI, 4 November 1954.

15. See A. H. Hanson, *The Process of Planning: A Study of India's Five Year Plans, 1950–1964* (London: Oxford University Press, 1966), pp. 111–120.

16. Sunil Khilnani, *The Idea of India* (New York: Farrar, Straus and Giroux, 1997), p. 83. Mahalanobis was an intimate of Rabindranath Tagore's—it was said that he had a better knowledge of Tagore's poems and plays than did the poet himself.

17. For details, see Ashok Rudra, *Prasanta Chandra Mahalanobis: A Biography* (Delhi: Oxford University Press, 1996).

18. This and the following two paragraphs draw on Mahalanobis's letters to Pitambar Pant, June–July 1954, Pitambar Pant Papers, NMML. See also Khilnani, *Idea of India*, pp. 83f.

19. Mahalanobis wrote he was "in favour of seeking the help of both USA and USSR (and of UK and other countries) in developing the industrial production of India" (letter of 7 July 1954, in Pitambar Pant Papers). He was in this respect genuinely non-partisan. In the years to come, his ISI was host to top economists from both sides of the Iron Curtain—Simon Kuznets, Oskar Lange, Charles Bettelheim, Jan Tinbergen, and many others. For details, see Rudra, *Prasanta Chandra Mahalanobis*, ch. 14.

20. "Recommendations for the Formulation of the Second Five Year Plan" and "The Approach of Operational Research to Planning in India," both written in 1955, both reprinted in P. K. Bose and M. Mukherjee, eds., *P. C. Mahalanobis: Papers on Planning* (Calcutta: Statistical Publishing Society, 1985). Along with these narrative papers, Mahalanobis also framed two mathematical models of economic growth. These are discussed in T. N. Srinivasan, "Professor Mahalanobis and Economics," in Rudra, *Prasanta Chandra Mahalanobis*, ch. 11.

21. Hanson, *Process of Planning*, pp. 128–130. See also K. N. Raj, "Model-Making and the Second Plan," EW, 26 January 1956.

22. Government of India, *The Second Five Year Plan* (New Delhi: Planning Commission, 1956), p. 6.

23. P. C. Mahalanobis, "Draft Plan Frame for the Second Five Year Plan," *Economic Weekly*, Special No., 18 June 1955.

24. Hanson, *Process of Planning*, pp. 459–462.

25. Haldane to Mahalanobis, 16 May 1955, quoted in Gopal, *Nehru*, Vol. 2, pp. 305–306.

26. Letter of 22 December 1952, in Jawharlal Nehru, *Letters to Chief Ministers*, 5 vols., ed. G. Parthasarathi (New Delhi: Oxford University Press, 1985–1989, hereafter cited as LCM), Vol. 3, pp. 205–207.

27. Letter of 22 December 1952, LCM, Vol. 3, p. 205; letter of 14 February 1956, LCM, Vol. 4, p. 346.

28. Letter of 13 January 1955, LCM, Vol. 4, p. 123.

29. See "Triangular Contest for Steel Plant," EW, 19 December 1953; Taya Zinkin, *Challenges in India* (New York: Walker, 1966), ch. 7.

30. The friend was Joe Miller, the late, legendary librarian of the Yale School of Forestry and Environmental Studies.

31. See Subject File No. 5, K. P. S. Menon Papers, NMML.

32. Ved Mehta, *Portrait of India* (New York: Farrar, Straus and Giroux, 1970), pp. 285–297.

33. S. Bhoothalingam, "Rourkela Steel Plant," *Indian Review*, April 1956.

34. See Meghnad Saha, *My Experiences in Soviet Russia* (Calcutta, 1945); publisher unknown. See also K. L. Rao, *Cusecs and Candidates: Memoirs of an Engineer* (New Delhi: Metropolitan, 1978).

35. Daniel Klingensmith, "One Valley and a Thousand: America, India, and the World in the Image of the Tennessee Valley Authority, 1945–1970," unpublished PhD thesis, Department of History, University of Chicago, 1999, p. 228.

36. A. N. Khosla to C. Rajagopalachari, 30 August 1953, in Subject File 124, C. Rajagopalachari Papers, Fifth Instalment, NMML.

37. Henry C. Hart, *New India's Rivers* (Bombay: Orient Longmans, 1956), pp. 97–100.

38. "India Marches On: Bhakra-Nangal Project," *MysIndia*, 28 November 1954. Much smaller was the complementary Nangal project, a low concrete dam located eight miles downstream from the Bhakra.

39. *Indian Journal of Power and River Valley Development*, Bhakra-Nangal No., 1956.

40. This portrait of Slocum is based on J. D. Sahi, *Odd Man Out: Exploits of a Crazy Idealist* (New Delhi: Gitanjai, 1991), pp. 55–69, 133; M. S. Randhawa, *A History of Agriculture in India*, Vol. 4, 1947–1981 (New Delhi: Indian Council of Agricultural Research, 1986), pp. 92–93.

41. Hart, *New India's Rivers*, p. 225; *Current*, 14 July 1954.

42. Obaid Siddiqi, *Science, Society, Government, and Politics: Some Remarks on the Ideas of Jawaharlal Nehru*, Zaheer Memorial Lecture, Indian Science Congress, Cochin, February 1990.

43. See Shiv Visvanathan, *Organizing for Science: The Making of an Industrial Research Laboratory* (New Delhi: Oxford University Press, 1985).

44. On Bhabha, see Robert S. Anderson, *Building Scientific Institutions in India: Saha and Bhabha*, Occasional Paper, Centre for Developing-Area Studies, McGill University, 1975.

45. George Greenstein, "A Gentleman of the Old School: Homi Bhabha and the Development of Science in India," *American Scholar*, Vol. 61, No. 3, 1992, p. 417.

46. HT, 3 October 1952. The Community Development programmes were inspired by, and to a great extent modelled on, the work of Albert Mayer in eastern Uttar Pradesh in the late 1940s. See Mayer, *Pilot Project*; Alice Thorner, "Nehru,

Albert Mayer, and Origins of Community Projects," *Economic and Political Weekly*, 24 January 1981.

47. S. C. Dube, *India's Changing Villages* (London: Routledge and Kegan Paul, 1958), pp. 157–163, 192–216, etc.

48. T. S. Epstein, *Economic Development and Social Change in South India* (Manchester: Manchester University Press, 1962), especially pp. 27–47.

49. For details, see B. H. Farmer, *Agricultural Colonization in India since Independence* (London: Oxford University Press, 1974).

50. See, inter alia, R. P. Masani, *The Five Gifts* (London: Collins, 1957); Hallam Tennyson, *Saint on the March: The Story of Vinoba* (London: Victor Gollancz, 1961); Geoffrey Ostergaard and Melville Currell, *The Gentle Anarchists: A Study of the Leaders of the Sarvodaya Movement for Non-Violent Revolution in India* (Oxford: Clarendon, 1971). There is a characteristically acid portrait of Bhave in V. S. Naipaul's *A Wounded Civilization* (Penguin: Harmondsworth, 1977).

51. See Ronald J. Herring, *Land to the Tiller: The Political Economy of Agrarian Reform in South Asia* (New Haven, Conn.: Yale University Press, 1983); "Slow Pace of Land Reforms," *Economic Weekly*, 30 May 1953; S. K. Dey, *Power to the People? A Chronicle of India 1947–1967* (Bombay: Orient Longmans, 1969), pp. 232f.

52. The climate of economic policy in the post-war world is usefully sketched in Daniel Yergin and Joseph Stanislaw, *The Commanding Heights: The Battle for the World Economy* (New York: Simon and Schuster, 2002), chs. 2 and 3.

53. Hanson, *Process of Planning*, p. 128.

54. See "A Note on Dissent on the Memorandum of the Panel of Economists" (1955), in Mahesh P. Bhatt and S. B. Mehta, *Planned Progress or Planned Chaos? Selected Prophetic Writings of Prof. B. R. Shenoy* (Madras: EastWest, 1996), pp. 3–24.

55. Milton Friedman, "A Memorandum to the Government of India, 1955," in *Friedman on India* (New Delhi: Centre for Civil Society, 2000), pp. 27–43.

56. Note of 10 October 1955, reprinted in V. N. Balabubramanyam, *Conversations with Indian Economists* (London: Macmillan, 2001), pp. 198–201.

57. It is noteworthy that the essays of Shenoy, Krishnamurti, and Friedman were not printed for public distribution until the 1990s—by which time, of course, the political and intellectual climate was far more congenial to their views.

58. Anon., "Not a People's Plan," EW, 18 June 1955.

59. I have written elsewhere, and at greater length, about these "green Gandhians." See Ramachandra Guha, *Environmentalism: A Global History* (New York: Addison Wesley Longman, 2000), pp. 23–24, 67–68; Guha, *Mahatma Gandhi and the Environmental Movement*, Parisar Annual Lecture, Pune, 1992.

60. *Current*, 11 June 1952 and 8 June 1955.

61. For the consensus among economists, see I. G. Patel, *Glimpses of Indian Economic Policy: An Insider's View* (New Delhi: Oxford University Press, 2002), especially ch. 2.

62. *Memorandum*, p. 92.

63. "A Correspondent," "On Revisiting the Damodar Valley," EW, 28 February 1953.

64. Letter of 2 October 1952, LCM, Vol. 3, pp. 114–115. Nehru was speaking here of the Tungabhadra Dam, which he visited about a month before coming to Bokaro.

CHAPTER 11: THE LAW AND THE PROPHETS

1. André Malraux, *Antimemoirs*, trans. from the French by Terence Kilmartin (London: Hamish Hamilton, 1968), p. 145. The conversation took place sometime in 1958.
2. CAD, Vol. 8, pp. 543–546, 722–723 (emphasis added).
3. Ibid., pp. 551, 781.
4. For an analysis of the Rau Committee, see Chitra Sinha, "Hindu Code Bill (1942–1956) and Feminist Consciousness in Bombay," unpublished PhD dissertation, Department of History, Mumbai University, 2003.
5. See, for example, Bina Agarwal, "A Bill of Her Own?" *New Indian Express*, 23 December 2004.
6. Ambedkar's speeches on the bill are reprinted in Valerian Rodrigues, ed., *The Essential Writings of B. R. Ambedkar* (New Delhi: Oxford University Press, 2002), pp. 495–516.
7. Dhananjay Keer, *Dr. Ambedkar: Life and Mission,* 3rd ed. (1971, reprint Bombay: Popular Prakashan, 1995), p. 417.
8. The correspondence between Prasad and Nehru has been reproduced in SPC, Vol. 6, pp. 399–404.
9. SPC, Vol. 9, pp. 109–111.
10. This account of the All India Anti-Hindu-Code Bill Committee is based on the reports and documents in Subject File No. 106, D. P. Mishra Papers, Third and Fourth Instalments, NMML.
11. J. D. M. Derrett, *Hindu Law Past and Present* (Calcutta: A. Mukerjee, 1957), pp. 69–70. For a sampling of the conservative legal opposition to the code, see K. S. Hajela, "The Draft Hindu Code, Its Exposition, Comment, and Criticism," *All India Reporter (Journal)*, 1949, pp. 64–67. For a modernist view, see Lahar Singh Mehta, "Some Implications of the Hindu Code Bill, 1948," *All India Reporter (Journal)*, 1950, pp. 26–29.
12. The debates on the Hindu Code in the Provisional Parliament are reproduced in Vasant Moon, ed., *Dr. Babasaheb Ambedkar: Writings and Speeches,* Vol. 14 (Bombay: Government of Maharashtra, 1995).
13. See Files 422, 423, 424, and 430, Delhi Police Records, Ninth Instalment, NMML.
14. Rajendra Prasad to Nehru, 15 September 1951, copy in Subject File No. 189, C. Rajagopalachari Papers, Fifth Instalment, NMML.
15. Nehru to Rajendra Prasad, 15 September 1951; secret note to cabinet by Nehru, dated 25 September 1951, both in Subject File No. 46, C. Rajagopalachari Papers, Fourth Instalment, NMML.
16. Derrett, *Hindu Law,* p. 71.
17. The text of Ambedkar's resignation speech was reproduced in the *Hindustan Times,* 12 October 1951. See also Vasant Moon, ed., *Dr. Babasaheb Ambedkar: Writings and Speeches,* Vol. 15 (Mumbai: Government of Maharashtra, 1997), pp. 825–828.
18. See File 127, Delhi Police Records, Sixth Instalment, NMML.
19. See statement by law minister, *Lok Sabha Debates,* 26 April 1955.
20. The most significant of Nehru's parliamentary interventions on the subject are collected in *Jawaharlal Nehru's Speeches,* Vol. 3, *March 1953–August 1957*

(New Delhi: Publications Division, n.d.), pp. 438–454. Section entitled "Changing Hindu Society."

21. Nehru to K. N. Katju, 13 June 1954; and to R. Venkataraman, 30 September 1954, in S. Gopal, ed., *Selected Works of Jawaharlal Nehru* (New Delhi: Nehru Memorial Fund), Second Series, Vol. 26, pp. 173, 180.

22. See, for example, the speeches of K. C. Sharma, B. D. Shastri, and Nand Lal Sharma, *Lok Sabha Debates*, 29 April, 2 May, and 13 December 1955 respectively; speech of H. C. Mathur, *Rajya Sabha Debates*, 11 December 1954.

23. *Rajya Sabha Debates*, 9 December 1954.

24. Interventions of Seeta Parmanand and M. P. N. Sinha, *Rajya Sabha Debates*, 8 and 6 December 1954. To placate the orthodox, the law minister changed the title of the bill from the Hindu Marriage and Divorce Bill to the Hindu Marriage Bill. This was done to put the accent "not on the dissolution of marriage" but on the "maintenance of marriage [which] is more important" (*Lok Sabha Debates*, 26 April 1955). The change, needless to say, was cosmetic.

25. *Lok Sabha Debates*, 29 April 1955. Others opposed the clause not out of logic, but out of envy. As S. Mahanty sourly noted, "it makes a discrimination in favour of the Muslims who may marry four wives under the Shariat law and not incur any of the offences under this Act" (*Rajya Sabha Debates*, 6 December 1954).

26. *Lok Sabha Debates*, 2 May 1955.

27. Ibid., 26 and 29 April 1955.

28. Intervention by H. J. Khandekar, ibid., 29 April 1955.

29. Ibid., 29 April 1955; *Rajya Sabha Debates*, 8 December 1954.

30. Intervention by M. Muhammad Ismail, *Rajya Sabha Debates*, 11 December 1954.

31. *Lok Sabha Debates*, 29 April 1955.

32. Intervention by Nand Lal Sharma, ibid., 13 December 1955.

33. Ibid., 13 December 1955.

34. Intervention by S. S. More, ibid., 2 May 1955.

35. Marc Galanter, *Law and Society in Modern India*, ed. Rajeev Dhavan (Delhi: Oxford University Press, 1997), p. 29; J. D. M. Derrett, *Religion, Law, and the State in India* (London: Faber and Faber, 1968), p. 326.

36. See *Rajya Sabha Debates*, 11 December 1954, where Dr. P. Subbarayan gave his "special meed of tribute to Dr. Ambedkar who is not here but who laboured hard to push through the Hindu Code before the last Parliament but circumstances did not permit of this measure going through."

37. *Lok Sabha Debates*, 6 December 1956.

38. For a fine discussion of these questions, see Lotika Sarkar, "Jawaharlal Nehru and the Hindu Code Bill," in B. R. Nanda, ed., *Indian Women: From Purdah to Modernity* (New Delhi: Nehru Memorial Museum and Library, 1976).

39. Quoted in D. E. Smith, *India as a Secular State* (Princeton, N.J.: Princeton University Press, 1963), p. 290.

40. See *Parliamentary Debates*, 17 September 1951, excerpted in *Eminent Parliamentarians Monograph Series: Dr. Syama Prasad Mookerjee* (New Delhi: Lok Sabha Secretariat, 1990), pp. 82f.

41. On the workings of the new laws in the several decades they have been in operation, see J. D. M. Derrett, *A Critique of Modern Hindu Law* (Bombay: N. M.

Tripathi, 1970); Satyajeet A. Desai, *Mulla's Principles of Hindu Law*, 18th ed. (New Delhi: Butterworths India, 2001). The caveat "somewhat" is in deference to feminist arguments that while the new bills removed many of the disabilities suffered by Hindu women, they did not bestow "radical equality." See Archana Parashar, *Women and Family Law Reform in India* (New Delhi: Sage, 1992), pp. 79–134.

CHAPTER 12: SECURING KASHMIR

1. Gupta, *Kashmir*, p. 365.
2. See Brecher, *The Struggle for Kashmir*, p. 111.
3. Lionel Fielden, "India Revisited: Indo-Pak Problems," *Indian Review*, May 1950.
4. Note by Nehru on Kashmir, dated 9 January 1951, in Subject File No. 62, C. Rajagopalachari papers, Fourth Instalment, NMML.
5. See Jawaharlal Nehru Correspondence, Vijayalakshmi Pandit Papers, NMML.
6. Cable to State Deparment by Henderson, quoted in Bhattacharjea, *Kashmir*, pp. 196–197.
7. See Abdullah to Gopalaswami Ayyangar, dated 16 January 1951; and note on file by the latter, both in Subject File No. 62, C. Rajagopalachari papers, Fourth Instalment, NMML.
8. See Balraj Puri, "Leaderlessness of Jammu" (March 1950), in *Jammu—A Clue to the Kashmir Tangle* (Delhi: Author, 1966), pp. 20–23.
9. Baburao Patel, *Burning Words*, pp. 147–148.
10. The sheikh's speech is printed in extenso in Gupta, *Kashmir*, pp. 367–370.
11. Prem Nath Bazaz, *The History of Struggle for Freedom in Kashmir, Cultural and Political: From the Earliest Times to the Present Day* (New Delhi: Kashmir Publishing, 1954), pp. 569–571.
12. Ian Stephens, *Horned Moon: An Account of a Journey through Pakistan, Kashmir, and Afghanistan* (London: Chatto and Windus, 1953), pp. 212–213. From Stephens's book we learn that he was in the Valley in April 1952—exact dates are not given, so we can't say whether he talked to the sheikh before or after the speech at Ranbirsinghpura. The speech had also hinted that perhaps Kashmir's place in India was "unnatural." This might have been a coincidence in thinking. On the other hand, if Abdullah met Stephens *before* Ranbirsingh-pura, his speech might very well have been influenced by someone who cynically saw "an anti-Muslim substructure" in "Pandit Nehru's new secular Republic" (*Horned Moon*, p. 267).
13. Gupta, *Kashmir*, pp. 371–372.
14. Speeches of 11 and 19 August 1952, copies in Subject File No. 4, Y. D. Gundevia Papers, NMML.
15. See Daniel Thorner, "The Kashmir Land Reforms: Some Personal Impressions," EW, 12 September 1953.
16. See Richard L. Park, "India Argues with Kashmir," *Far Eastern Survey*, 2 July 1952.
17. See *Eminent Parliamentarians . . .*, pp. 18–19, 109–123.
18. Balraj Madhok, *Portrait of a Martyr: Biography of Dr. Shyama Prasad Mook-erji* (Bombay: Jaico, 1969), pp. 159–161.

19. Karan Singh, *Autobiography* (New Delhi: Oxford University Press, 1989), pp. 149–150.

20. *Current*, 10 and 24 December 1952.

21. The letters between Mookerjee on the one side and Nehru and Abdullah on the other were later published by the Jana Sangh in *Integrate Kashmir: Mookerjee-Nehru and Abdullah Correspondence* (Lucknow: Bharat, 1953).

22. See File Nos. 12, 127, and 164, Delhi Police Records, Eighth Instalment, NMML.

23. *Current*, 26 August 1953.

24. Quoted in Gopal, *Nehru*, Vol. 2, p. 131, fn. 65.

25. For a contemporary interpretation along these lines, see Sadiq Ali and Madhu Limaye, *Report on Kashmir* (New Delhi: Praja Socialist Party, 1953). According to this report, the sheikh "was often heard to remark in his private talks that if Jammu wanted to go out of Kashmir it was welcome to do so; in fact it would be good riddance. Its merger in India would serve just the purpose he had in view, namely an Independent Kashmir" (p. 5).

26. Madhok, *Portrait of a Martyr*, pp. 147–165.

27. See correspondence between Mookerjee and C. Rajagopalachari in Subject File No. 124, Rajagopalachari Papers, Fifth Instalment, NMML.

28. Madhok, *Portait of a Martyr*, pp. 240–242.

29. Letter of 2 July to C. Rajagopalachari, Subject File No. 123, Rajagopalachari Papers, Fifth Instalment, NMML.

30. *Current*, 1 July 1953.

31. See File 164, Delhi Police Records, Eighth Instalment, NMML.

32. See reports and correspondence, File 166, Delhi Police Records, Ninth Instalment, NMML.

33. Gopal, *Nehru*, Vol. 2, pp. 130–131. Nehru's letters to Abdullah are also excerpted here.

34. Nehru to Rajagopalachari, 31 July 1953, Subject File No. 123, Rajagopalachari Papers, Fifth Instalment, NMML.

35. See B. N. Mullik, *My Years with Nehru: Kashmir* (Bombay: Allied, 1971), ch. 3.

36. *Current*, 26 August 1953. Three years later, a copy of the Eid speech that Abdullah was to have made surfaced. This did not call directly for independence, but it reopened the question of accession to India, and also, for the first time, asked that Pakistan be made a party to the dispute. See Mridula Sarabhai, ed., *Sheikh-Sadiq Correspondence, August to October 1956* (New Delhi: privately printed, 1956), App. 1, "Id Speech."

37. Karan Singh, *Autobiography*, pp. 156–164.

38. See reports in File No. 73, Delhi Police Records, Sixth Instalment, NMML.

39. Gopal, *Nehru*, Vol. 2, pp. 132–133; Mullik, *My Years with Nehru: Kashmir*, pp. 42–47.

40. P. N. Kaula and K. L. Dhar, *Kashmir Speaks* (Delhi: S. Chand, 1950), pp. 189–190. An American journalist wrote of the *Bakshi* that he was a "realist [who] can run a party machine and keep its joints oiled," adding that he seemed to be "constituted chiefly of iron or steel" (Sheean, *Nehru*, pp. 109–110). This likewise brings Patel to mind, not least because he was known as the "Iron Man of India."

41. *Hindu*, 25 August 1953, 14 and 29 September 1953.

42. *Current*, 31 March, 25 August, and 6 October 1954; and 12 October 1955.

43. *Current*, 14 November 1955. See also Sheikh Abdullah, *Flames of the Chinar: An Autobiography*, abridged and trans. from Urdu by Khushwant Singh (New Delhi: Penguin India, 1993), ch. 18.

44. See File No. 73, Delhi Police Records, Sixth Instalment. NMML.

45. General Roy Bucher to C. Rajagopalachari, 14 August 1953, in Subject File No. 124, Fifth Instalment, Rajagopalachari Papers, NMML.

46. Bhattacharjea, *Kashmir*, p. 205.

47. See Spratt's unsigned column "The World This Week," *MysIndia*, 13 July, 3 and 17 August, and 9 November 1952.

CHAPTER 13: TRIBAL TROUBLE

1. This account of the early years of the Naga National Council is based on Mildred Archer, "Journal of a Stay in the Naga Hills, 9 July to 4 December 1947," MSS. Eur. F. 236/362 (hereafter cited as Archer, "Journal"). The wife of the last deputy commissioner in the Naga Hills, W. G. Archer, she had interviewed a cross section of the NNC membership and also collected their journal. She was herself to become, in later years, an authority on British art in India.

2. Charles Chasie, *The Naga Imbroglio* (Kohima: Standard, 1999), pp. 33–36.

3. The Crown Colony scheme is discussed in a forthcoming book by Professor David Syiemlieh of the North-Eastern Hill University, Shillong.

4. A. R. H. Macdonald to P. F. Adams (secretary to the governor of Assam), dated 23 March 1947, copy in MSS. Eur. F. 236/76, OIOC.

5. See A. Z. Phizo, *The Fate of the Naga People: An Appeal to the World* (London: Author, July 1960).

6. CWMG, Vol. 88, pp. 373–374. The context makes it clear that Gandhi was against the Nagas' using guns and tanks, though of course he would also have opposed the Indian Army's using them.

7. See J. H. Hutton, *The Angami Nagas* (London: Macmillan, 1921), p. 11 and passim.

8. Archer, "Journal," 30 August 1947. The invocation of God, and the recourse to American heroes, were a consequence of the deep influence on the Nagas of the Baptist missionaries who had converted them.

9. Ibid., 27 September and 23 August 1947.

10. CAD, Vol. 4, pp. 947–948.

11. Useful studies of the tribal predicament include G. S. Ghurye, *The Scheduled Tribes* (Bombay: Popular Prakashan, 1959), first published under a different title in 1943; C. von Fürer Haimendorf, *Tribes of India: The Struggle for Survival* (Berkeley: University of California Press, 1982); Verrier Elwin, *The Tribal World of Verrier Elwin: An Autobiography* (Bombay: Oxford University Press, 1964); and K. S. Singh, *Tribal Society in India* (New Delhi: Manohar, 1985). See also André Béteille, "The Concept of Tribe with Special Reference to India," in *Society and Politics in India: Essays in a Comparative Perspective* (London: Athlone, 1991).

12. See Agapit Tirkey, *Jharkhand Movement: A Study of Its Dynamics* (New Delhi: Other Media Communications, 2002), ch. 2.

13. Memorandum dated 1 May 1947, in Subject File No. 37, C. Rajagopalachari Papers, Fifth Instalment, NMML.

14. For Jaipal's speech, see Ram Dayal Munda and S. Bosu Mullick, eds., *The Jharkhand Movement: Indigenous Peoples' Struggle for Autonomy in India* (Copenhagen: IWGIA, 2003), pp. 2–14.

15. This paragraph is based on an anonymous three-part report on the Naga situation in *Current*, 4, 11, and 18 July 1956; and on Nirmal Nibedon, *Nagaland: The Night of the Guerrillas* (New Delhi: Lancers, 1983), pp. 24–25.

16. Letter to Jairamdas Daulatram, governor of Assam, dated 11 December 1950, in Subject File No. 188, C. Rajagopalachari Papers, Fifth Instalment, NMML.

17. A. Lanunungsang Ao, *From Phizo to Muivah: The Naga National Question in North-East India* (New Delhi: Mittal, 2002), pp. 48–49.

18. "No Independence for Nagas: Plain Speaking by Mr. Nehru," TOI, 1 January 1952.

19. "Demand for Naga State: Delegation Meets Nehru," TOI, 12 February 1952.

20. Report by Krishnalal Shridharani in *Current*, 19 March 1952.

21. "The Tribal Folk," in *Jawaharlal Nehru's Speeches*, Vol. 2 (New Delhi: Publications Division, 1954), pp. 576f.

22. Nehru to C. Rajagopalachari, 26 October 1952, in Subject File No. 107, C. Rajagopalachari Papers, Fifth Instalment, NMML

23. The report on the NEFA tour is reprinted in LCM, Vol. 4, pp. 147–165.

24. NNC letter of 24 October 1952, quoted in *Current*, 15 April 1953.

25. Guha, *Savaging the Civilized*, p. 285.

26. Archer, "Journal," 10 July 1947.

27. Arthur Swinson, quoted in Nibedon, *Nagaland*, p. 26.

28. Asoso Yonuo, *The Rising Nagas: A Historical and Political Study* (Delhi: Vivek, 1974), pp. 210–213.

29. This account of the rift between Phizo and Sakhrie is based on Nibedon, *Nagaland*, pp. 57–68.

30. Ibid., pp. 80–82.

31. Lieutenant General S. P. P. Thorat, *From Reveille to Retreat* (New Delhi: Allied, 1986), ch. 15, "The Nagas." As the commanding officer of the Eastern Command, General Thorat was in charge of operations against the rebels.

32. See clippings in MSS. Eur. F. 158/239, OIOC.

33. Dr. S. R. S. Laing to Charles Pawsey, letters of ? June 1956 and 13 August 1956, in Box I, Pawsey Papers, Centre for South Asian Studies, University of Cambridge.

34. *Lok Sabha Debates*, 23 August 1956.

35. *India News*, 8 December 1956; *Manchester Guardian*, 18 December 1956; both in MSS. Eur. F. 158/239, OIOC.

36. Ignes Kujur, "Jharkhand Betrayed," in Munda and Bosu Mullick, *The Jharkhand Movement*, pp. 16ff.

37. *Lok Sabha Debates*, 22 November 1954; *Current*, 16 February 1955.

38. Letter of 9 March 1955, in T. T. Krishnamachari Papers, NMML.

39. Nehru to Bishnuram Medhi, 13 May 1956, reprinted as App. 7 in Udayon Misra, *The Periphery Strikes Back: Challenges to the Nation-State in Assam and Nagaland* (Shimla: Indian Institute of Advanced Study, 200), pp. 203–204.

CHAPTER 14: THE SOUTHERN CHALLENGE

1. *Report on the Second General Elections in India, 1957* (New Delhi: Election Commission, 1958).
2. Feroze Gandhi was also from the Nehrus' hometown, Allahabad. A Parsi by faith, he at first spelled his surname "Ghandy." However, after he joined the national movement as a young man, he changed the spelling to bring it in line with that of Mahatma Gandhi. The amended surname proved to be of incalculable significance to his wife, because most foreigners, and not a few Indians, assumed that she was in some way related to the Mahatma.
3. See Katherine Frank, *Indira: A Life of Indira Nehru Gandhi* (London: Harper-Collins, 2001), pp. 240–241.
4. Indira Gandhi to Brijkrishna Chandiwala, 11 November 1957, Chandiwala Papers, NMML.
5. Nehru to Vijayalakshmi Pandit, 12 March 1957, quoted in Nayantara Sahgal, *Indira Gandhi: Her Road to Power* (New York: Frederick Ungar, 1982), pp. 1–2.
6. The data in this and the subsequent paragraphs are chiefly derived from the excellent statistical supplement on Indian elections printed as an appendix to *Journal of the Indian School of Political Economy*, Vol. 15, Nos. 1 and 2, 2003.
7. For the rise of the DMK in the 1950s, see Marguerite Ross Barnett, *The Politics of Cultural Nationalism in South India* (Princeton, N.J.: Princeton University Press, 1976).
8. The social history of modern Kerala has been treated with authority and insight in several books by Robin Jeffrey. See specially *The Decline of Nair Dominance*, 2nd ed. (New Delhi: Manohar, 2003), originally published 1975 and *Politics, Women, and Well-Being: How Kerala Became a "Model"* (New Delhi: Oxford University Press, 1992).
9. See Dilip M. Menon, *Caste, Nationalism, and Communism in South India: Malabar, 1900–1948* (Cambridge: Cambridge University Press, 1994).
10. Khrushchev, quoted in *Communist Double Talk at Palghat* (Bombay: Democratic Research Service, 1956), p. 112.
11. "Communist Manifesto for Stable Government, Prosperous Kerala," quoted in Victor M. Fic, *Kerala: Yenan of India* (Bombay: Nachiketa, 1970), pp. 68–69.
12. Like Abdullah, Phizo, and others, EMS has yet to find a serious biographer.
13. E. M. S. Namboodiripad, *Twenty-Eight Months in Kerala* (New Delhi: People's Publishing House, 1959), especially pp. 5–6, 22–23.
14. P. N. Sampath, "Red Government in Kerala," *Indian Review*, July 1957.
15. *Current*, 8 May 1957. Krishna Iyer was actually an Independent member of the Kerala legislature, a fellow-traveller rather than a card-carrying communist. He was later a judge on the Supreme Court.
16. Herring, *Land to the Tiller*, p. 163.
17. This paragraph draws on Herring, *Land to the Tiller*, ch. 6; and T. J. Nossiter, *Communism in Kerala: A Study in Political Adaptation* (Delhi: Oxford University Press, 1982), pp. 149–157.
18. *Current*, 24 April 1957.
19. Anon., "Letter from Kerala: Bloodsuckers Still Thrive," EW, 19 April 1958.
20. Ibid.

21. *Kerala Mail*, quoted in *Current*, 28 August 1957.

22. George Mikes, *East Is East* (London: André Deutsch, 1958), p. 153.

23. For a useful summary, see S. C. Joseph, *Kerala: The "Communist" State* (Madras: Madras Premier, 1959), ch. 8.

24. See Anon., "Who Supported the Communists in Kerala? An Analysis of the 1957 Election Results," EW, 1 August 1959.

25. See "Kerala Letter: Co-Existence in Peril," EW, Special No., July 1959. It is not clear whether these excerpts were originally in English or are translated here from the Malayalam.

26. Rajni Kothari, "Kerala: A Post-Mortem," EW, 28 November 1959.

27. "Kerala Letter: Congress Misalliance with the Congress Church," EW, Annual No., January 1958.

28. Nossiter, *Communism in Kerala*, p. 145.

29. "Red Rule in Kerala," statements by E. M. S. Namboodiripad and Panampilli Govinda Menon, *Illustrated Weekly of India*, 25 January 1959.

30. Kamla Chopra, "Indira Gandhi: A Profile," *Illustrated Weekly of India*, 22 February 1959.

31. Gopal, *Nehru*, Vol. 3, p. 66.

32. Profiles of Mannath in *Illustrated Weekly of India*, 28 June 1959 and in *Current*, 16 September 1959; Anon., *The Agitation in Kerala* (Trivandrum: Department of Public Relations, 1959), pp. 9–12.

33. W. H. Morris-Jones, "India's Political Idioms," in C. H. Philips, ed., *Politics and Society in India* (London: George Allen and Unwin, 1963).

34. For a good description of the protests, see George Woodcock, *Kerala: A Portrait of the Malabar Coast* (London: Faber and Faber, 1967), pp. 270ff.

35. See the letters from Nehru to the prominent Kerala congressman R. Sankar, quoted in Robin Jeffrey, "Jawaharlal Nehru and the Smoking Gun: Who Pulled the Trigger on Kerala's Commmunist Government in 1959?" *Journal of Commonwealth and Comparative Politics*, Vol. 29, No. 1, 1991.

36. See Gopal, *Nehru*, Vol. 3, p. 68.

37. Quoted in "Mrs. Indira Gandhi's Election," undated, unsigned typescript in Pupul Jayakar Papers, held by Mrs. Radhika Herzberger (emphasis supplied). See also *Statesman*, 27 July 1959.

38. Kannikara Padmanabha Pillai, *The Red Interlude in Kerala* (Trivandrum: Kerala Pradesh Congress Commmittee, 1959), pp. 183ff.

39. Woodcock, *Kerala*, p. 272.

40. Nehru to Namboodiripad, 30 July 1959, quoted in Gopal, *Nehru*, Vol. 3, pp. 71–72.

41. See K. P. Bhagat, *The Kerala Mid Term Election of 1960* (Bombay: Popular Book Depot, 1962).

42. Gopal, *Nehru*, Vol. 3, p. 73.

43. See correspondence and papers in Subject File No. 34, C. Rajagopalachari Papers, Fifth Instalment, NMML.

44. The article is reprinted in C. Rajagopalachari, *Satyam Eva Jayate* (The Truth Alone Shall Triumph), Vol. 1 (Madras: Bharathan, 1961), pp. 149–153. See also "Rajaji on Need for Strong Opposition," *Swarajya*, 9 March 1957.

45. C. Rajagopalachari, "Some Thoughts on the Budget," *Current*, 17 August 1957.

46. See "Statement of Principles of the Swatantra Party," EW, Special No. July 1959, p. 894.
47. C. Rajagopalachari, "The Case for the Swatantra Party," *Illustrated Weekly of India*, 16 August 1959.
48. See H. L. Erdman, *The Swatantra Party and Indian Conservatism* (Cambridge: Cambridge University Press, 1967).
49. Gopal, *Nehru*, Vol. 3, p. 120.
50. See Tarun Kumar Mukhopadhyaya, *Feroze Gandhi: A Crusader in Parliament* (New Delhi: Allied, 1992), pp. 109–123.
51. For a useful summary of the controversy, see M. C. Chagla, *Roses in December: An Autobiography* (1973, rev. ed. Bombay: Bharatiya Vidya Bhavan, 1994), pp. 203–211. Justice Chagla headed one of the commissions; Justice Vivian Bose the other. But see also A. D. Gorwala, *The Lies of T. T. K.* (Bombay: R. V. Pandit, 1959).
52. Quoted in Motilal C. Setalvad, *My Life: Law and Other Things* (Bombay: N. M. Tripathi, 1970), p. 282.

CHAPTER 15: THE EXPERIENCE OF DEFEAT

1. George N. Patterson, *Tragic Destiny* (London: Faber and Faber, 1959), p. 187.
2. "Record of Prime Minister's Talk with Dalai Lama" (24 April 1959), in File 9, Subimal Dutt Papers, NMML.
3. See Ramesh Sanghvi, *India's Northern Frontier and China* (Bombay: Contemporary, 1962), pp. 1–2.
4. *Notes, Memoranda, and Letters Exchanged and Signed between the Governments of India and China, 1954–1959* (New Delhi: Ministry of External Affairs, 1959), pp. 26–27, 46. This was the first of nine similarly titled White Papers issued by the government of India between 1959 and 1962, subsequently referred to here as WP I, WP II, etc. Unless otherwise stated, the rest of this section is based on the notes and correspondence in this first White Paper.
5. Schram, *Mao Tse-tung* (New York: Simon & Schuster, 1966), p. 282.
6. George N. Patterson, *Peking versus Delhi* (London: Faber and Faber, 1963), pp. 162–163.
7. For JP's views see *The Tragedy of Tibet: Speeches and Statements of Jayaprakash Narayan* (New Delhi: Afro-Asian Committee on Tibet, 1959); for the Jana Sangh's position, see "India's Stake in Tibet's Freedom," *Organiser*, 27 April 1959, reprinted in Pandit Deendayal Upadhyaya, *Political Diary* (Bombay: Jaico, 1968), pp. 97–101.
8. See Subject File No. 16, Thimayya Papers, NMML.
9. He was the first, and remains the only, Indian military man to be the subject of a biography by a western author: Humphrey Evans, *Thimayya of India* (New York: Harcourt, Brace, 1960).
10. Lall, *Emergence of Modern India*, p. 119.
11. See Wells Hangen, *After Nehru, Who?* (London: Rupert Hart-Davis, 1963), ch. 9. Kaul's alleged closeness to Nehru is also extensively mentioned in his memoirs; Kaul claims that he was a confidant of and sounding board for the prime minister. See Lieutenant General B. M. Kaul, *The Untold Story* (Bombay: Allied, 1967), pp. ix–x, 81–82, 86 fn., 87, 97, 114, 118, etc.
12. Major General D. K. Palit, *War in High Himalaya* (New Delhi: Lancer International, 1991), p. 76.

13. See Thimayya to Nehru, letters of 31 August and 3 September 1959, Thimayya Papers, NMML.

14. Press Clippings File No. 16, Thimayya Papers. This file has a cover note, almost certainly in the general's own hand, summarizing its contents: "If a poll was to be taken outside Parliament, opinion both inside and outside would have found favour with Thimayya."

15. Letters of Ashutosh Lahiri and Sheodatt, Subject File No. 15, Thimayya Papers.

16. H. V. Kamath, "The Sino-Indian Border Dispute," *Illustrated Weekly of India*, 18 October 1959.

17. *Current*, 14 and 28 October 1959.

18. Shiva Rao to Nehru, 3 December 1959, B. Shiva Rao Papers, NMML.

19. Chou to Nehru, 8 September 1959; and Nehru to Chou, 26 September 1959, in WP II, pp. 27–46.

20. The "forward policy" is described in the memoirs of one of its chief architects: B. N. Mullik, *My Years with Nehru: The Chinese Betrayal* (Bombay: Allied, 1971), especially chs. 14 and 19. Mullick was the chief of the Intelligence Bureau, and privy to most of the crucial decisions regarding the border dispute.

21. Latifi to Nehru, 27 November 1959, copy in Subject File No. 423, P. N. Haksar Papers, Third Instalment, NMML. (Emphasis in original.)

22. Quoted in Neville Maxwell, *India's China War* (Harmondsworth: Penguin, 1972) p. 152.

23. *Hindu*, quoted in Dorothy Woodman, *Himalayan Frontiers* (London: Barrie and Rockliff, 1969), p. 245.

24. Steven A. Hoffman, *India and the China Crisis* (Delhi: Oxford University Press, 1990), pp. 67, 73, 82–83, etc. The origins and trajectory of the India-China dispute are, as one can imagine, the subject of a huge and very motivated literature. On the one side are various self-serving memoirs by Indian generals and officials, which seek to blame China for "betraying" India's trust. These are collectively answered by Neville Maxwell's *India's China War*, a well documented book that, however, sees everything, big and small, from the Chinese point of view. Hoffman's is an admirably detached and comprehensive account of the dispute, perhaps the best there is.

25. Chou to Nehru, letters of 7 November and 17 December 1959; Nehru to Chou, letters of 16 November and 21 December 1959, in WP III, pp. 45–59.

26. Owen Lattimore, "India-Tibet-China: Starting Principle for Frontier Demarcation," *Economic Weekly*, Annual No., January 1960. Steven Hoffman, *India and the China Crisis*, pp. 86–87, explains that Chou's offer to "barter" could not be acceptable to India because "it was being asked to accept the clandestine and forceful seizure of parts of its territory [in the west], in return for a worthless assurance that another part of the frontier [in the east] would not be menaced."

27. "Pragmatist," "The Political Economy of Defence," EW, Annual No., January 1960.

28. Presidential address of Pitambar Das, in Girja Kumar and V. K. Arora, eds., *Documents on Indian Affairs, 1960* (Bombay: Asia Publishing House, 1965), pp. 22f.

29. See Gyanvati Darbar, *Portrait of a President: Letters of Dr. Rajendra Prasad*, Vol. 2 (New Delhi: Vikas, 1976), pp. 85–86.

30. Unless otherwise stated, this and the following paragraphs are based on reports and comments in *Indian Express*, 10 March through 27 April 1960.

31. Kumar and Arora, *Documents*, pp. 493–494. The signatories to this letter included J. B. Kripalani, M. R. Masani, A. B. Vajpayee, and N. G. Goray.

32. *Current*, 27 April 1960.

33. "Record of Talks between Prime Minister of India and Prime Minister of China, 20 to 25 April 1960," in Subject File No. 24, P. N. Haksar Papers, First and Second Instalments, NMML. The transcripts of the talks run to over 100 foolscap pages.

34. Copies of the transcripts of Chou En-lai's talks with Desai, Pant, Radhakrishnan, and other leaders are in Subject File No. 26, P. N. Haksar Papers, First and Second Instalments, NMML. Desai was right in spirit but not in substance; it was Karl Marx who sought asylum in the United Kingdom, whereas Lenin lived in exile in that other bourgeois nation, Switzerland.

35. This paragraph is based on Margaret W. Fisher, Leo E. Rose, and Robert A. Huttenback, *Himalayan Battleground: Sino-Indian Rivalry in Ladakh* (London: Pall Mall, 1963), especially ch. 11.

36. The transcripts of the talks are reproduced in App. 11 of Parshotam Mehra, *Negotiating with the Chinese, 1846–1987* (New Delhi: Reliance, 1989).

37. Interview in *Look* Magazine, 18 October 1960, reprinted in Edgar Snow, *The Other Side of the River: Red China Today* (New York: Random House, 1963), pp. 762–763.

38. Nayar, *Minority Politics*, especially pp. 248–260; *Current*, 16 August and 23 August 1961; correspondence between Nehru, Rajaji, and Tara Singh in Subject File No. 82, C. Rajagopalachari Papers, Fourth Instalment, NMML.

39. Nehru to Jayaprakash Narayan, 10 October 1961, Brahmanand Papers, NMML.

40. See E. N. Mangat Rai, *Commitment My Style* (Delhi: Vikas, 1973), ch. 10. For five of Kairon's eight years in power, Mangat Rai was his chief secretary.

41. *Current*, 9 December 1959, 6 January 1960, and 14 September 1963.

42. A. G. Noorani, *Ministers' Misconduct* (Delhi: Vikas, 1973), p. 42.

43. Nibedon, *Nagaland*, pp. 88–90.

44. Phizo, *The Fate of the Naga People*.

45. See, for example, the clippings in the W. G. Archer Papers, MSS. Eur. F. 236, OIOC.

46. Anon, *The Naga Problem* (New Delhi: Ministry of External Affairs, 1960). As many as 2,000 copies of this pamphlet were printed.

47. This memorandum is reproduced in Kumar and Arora, *Documents*, pp. 91–95.

48. Ibid., pp. 101–105.

49. Clipping from *Times*, 21 September 1962, in MSS. Eur F 158/239, OIOC.

50. See Daniel Thorner, "Ploughing the Plan Under: Ford Team Report on Food 'Crisis,'" EW, Special No. July 1959.

51. See *Report of Non Official Enquiry Commission on Cachar* (Calcutta: N. Chatterjee, 1961); L. P. Singh, *Portrait of Lal Bahadur Shastri: A Quintessential Gandhian* (New Delhi: Ravi Dayal, 1996), ch. 3.

52. *Current*, 8 March 1961.

53. Selig S. Harrison, *India: The Most Dangerous Decades* (Princeton, N. J.: Princeton University Press, 1960).

54. See Grover Smith, ed., *Letters of Aldous Huxley* (London: Chatto and Windus, 1969), pp. 926–927.
55. Arthur Cook, "Nehru," *Daily Mail*, 20 February 1962.
56. For details, see WPs IV, V, and VI, passim.
57. *Lok Sabha Debates*, 11 April 1961.
58. Ibid., 17 August and 28 November 1961, and 14 August 1962.
59. Ibid., 5 December 1961.
60. P. D. Gaitonde, *The Liberation of Goa: A Participant's View of History* (London: C. Hurst, 1987), ch. 18; *Illustrated Weekly of India,* Special Issue, 18 February 1962; D. R. Mankekar, *The Goa Action* (Bombay: Popular Book Depot, 1962).
61. See clippings and papers in File No. 8, Box XVI.18, Richard B. Russell Papers, University of Georgia, Athens; File No. 29, Penderel Moon Papers, OIOC (MSS. Eur. F. 230/29).
62. *New York Times,* 18 and 19 December 1961. There is also a suggestion that sections within the Indian army welcomed the adventure in Goa as an easy victory. It was, recalled one officer, "light relief from the gloom and foreboding of the general strategic scene" along the borders with China. See Major General D. K. Palit, *Musings and Memories,* Vol. 2 (New Delhi: Lancer, 2004), pp. 411–412.
63. My account of the election is based on Aloo J. Dastur, *Menon versus Kripalani: North Bombay Election, 1962* (Bombay: University of Bombay, 1967); supplemented by Norman D. Palmer, "The 1962 Election in North Bombay," *Pacific Affairs,* Vol. 30, No. 1, Spring 1963. See also A. D. Gorwala, *Krishna Menon: Danger to India* (Bombay: Author, January 1962). The Hindi ditty was supplied by Nitya Ramakrishnan.
64. "Seminarist," "Issues in the Election," *Seminar,* July 1962.
65. K. P. Subramania Menon, "The Ramifications"; and General K. S. Thimayya, "Adequate 'Insurance,'" *Seminar,* July 1962. That, even in retirement, Thimayya was seriously worried about the Chinese threat is also indicated by a book which he once owned and which is now in my possession; written by a retired major, it provides a historical overview of the NEFA region that had become central to the border conflict. My copy of the book—Major Sitaram Johri, *Where India, China, and Burma Meet* (Calcutta: Thacker, Spink, 1962)—has "K. S. Thimayya, 9 Feb 62" written on its flyleaf; I bought it in a second-hand store in Bangalore, once the general's hometown and now mine.
66. As the spark that set off the Chinese invasion, the Thag La conflict has been widely written about. My account is based on, among other sources, Brigadier J. P. Dalvi, *Himalayan Blunder* (Delhi: Hind Pocket Books, 1970), chs. 7, 9 to 12; Maxwell, *India's China War,* pp. 357 ff; and Hoffman, *India and the China Crisis,* pp. 130ff.
67. Hoffman, *India and the China Crisis,* p. 149.
68. Dalvi, *Himalayan Blunder,* pp. 262–263.
69. *New York Times,* 21 October 1962.
70. Ibid., 24 October 1962.
71. Dalvi, *Himayalan Blunder,* pp. 80–81.
72. Chou to Nehru, 24 October and 4 November 1962; Nehru to Chou, 27 October and 14 November 1962; printed with enclosures in WP VIII, pp. 1–17.

73. John Kenneth Galbraith, *Ambassador's Journal: A Personal Account of the Kennedy Years* (Boston, Mass.: Houghton Mifflin, 1969), p. 385.
74. *New York Times*, 28 and 30 October 1962.
75. *Lok Sabha Debates*, 8 to 14 November 1962. In his closing speech, Nehru deplored the violence against Chinese shopkeepers in New Delhi, which "brutalises us and gives us a bad name." Like his mentor, Gandhi, he knew how easily nationalism could shade into jingoism. To take revenge on innocent shopkeepers was deeply wrong-headed, for "we should always distinguish between governmental action and the people as a whole."
76. The Walong battle is vividly described in G. S. Bhargava, *The Battle for NEFA* (Bombay: Allied, 1964), ch. 5.
77. Hoffman, *India and the China Crisis*, pp. 180–181.
78. Maxwell, *India's China War*, pp. 398ff. In his memoirs, Kaul argues that Se La was a well-positioned and well-fortified garrison that could have held out for a week or more; he blames its fall and the flight of the troops on the failure of nerve of the man in charge, Major General A. S. Pathania. See Kaul, *The Untold Story*, pp. 413ff.
79. As recalled in B. G. Verghese, "Unfinished Business in the North-East," *Mainstream*, 15 June 2002.
80. A. M. Rosenthal, "War Fever in India," *New York Times*, 3 November 1962.
81. D. R. Mankekar, *The Guilty Men of 1962* (Bombay: Tulsi Shah, 1968), pp. 88–90.
82. Woodman, *Himalayan Frontiers*, p. 293.
83. Maxwell, *India's China War*, p. 465.
84. Palit, *War in High Himalaya*, pp. 225, 231.
85. Quoted in Snow, *Other Side of the River*, pp. 761–762. (Emphasis added.)
86. Allen Ginsberg, *Indian Journals: March 1962–May 1963* (San Francisco, Calif.: City Lights, 1970), p. 50.

CHAPTER 16: PEACE IN OUR TIME

1. John Kenneth Galbraith, *Ambassador's Journal* (Boston, Mass.: Houghton Mifflin, 1969), pp. 405–412.
2. Robert Sherrod, "Nehru: The Great Awakening," *Saturday Evening Post*, 19 January 1963.
3. Galbraith to Kennedy, 29 January 1963, copy in Dean Rusk Papers, University of Georgia, Athens. Was it the economist in Galbraith that made him identify China rather than Russia as the greater long-term threat to American interests?
4. See Richard Parker, *John Kenneth Galbraith: His Life, His Politics, His Economics* (New York: Farrar, Straus and Giroux, 2005), p. 400.
5. See clippings in Files 9 and 10, Box XVI.18, Richard B. Russell Papers, University of Georgia, Athens. The rest of this section is likewise based on material in these files.
6. There was also a letter, too crazy, perhaps, to quote in the text, which urged a cheaper method of disposing of the Chinese threat than arming the Indians. S. B. Crowe of Sanford, Florida, recommended that the Americans drop boxes of atomic waste, each with an explosive charge, on the Chinese side of the Himalaya. The communists would be told of this, so that they would "stay out of Ti-

bet and India." However, "if Mao wishes to conduct an experiment in genetics and send 150 million through this radiation hazard, it would be an interesting experiment." Estimating that this would save the American taxpayer "about a billion dollars," Mr. Crowe signed off as follows: "Yours for more economy in Government. The barrel isn't bottomless, inspite of Mr. Keynes and his theories."

7. "Transcript of Prime Minister's Press Conference held on June 15, 1963, in New Delhi," issued by Press Information Bureau, Government of India; copy in Subject File No. 189, P. N. Haksar Papers, Third Instalment, NMML. See also *Statesman*, 16 June 1963.

8. See Stanley Kochanek, *The Congress Party of India; The Dynamics of One-Party Democracy* (Princeton, N. J.: Princeton University Press, 1968), pp. 79 ff.

9. Ibid., pp. 78–80.

10. H. V. Kamath, *Last Days of Jawaharlal Nehru* (Calcutta: Jayashree Prakashan, 1977), pp. 1–2.

11. Wells Hangen, *After Nehru, Who?* (London: Rupert Hart-Davis, 1963).

12. These quotes are from an article by Tom Stacey, originally published in the *Sunday Times* of London, and reprinted under a different title in *Current*, 1 January 1964.

13. Indira Gandhi to Mridula Sarabhai, 4 September 1963, Reel No. 57, Mridula Sarabhai Papers, on microfilm, NMML.

14. See Kanji Dwarkadas to Lord Scarborough, 16 January 1964, MSS. Eur. F. 253/53 (Lord Lumley Papers), OIOC.

15. For the different ways the creation of the state was received, see P. N. Luthra, *Nagaland: From a District to a State* (Shillong: Directorate of Information and Public Relations, 1974), pp. 1–16; A. Lanunungsang Ao, *From Phizo to Muivah: The Naga National Question in North-East India* (New Delhi: Mittal), pp. 81–82.

16. *Currrent*, 4 January 1964.

17. Ibid., 20 April 1963.

18. C. P. Srivastava, *Lal Bahadur Shastri: A Life of Truth in Politics* (Delhi: Oxford University Press, 1995), pp. 71–74; Rajeshwar Prasad, *Days with Lal Bahadur Shastri: Glimpses from the Last Seven Years* (New Delhi: Allied, 1991), pp. 27–29.

19. Mountbatten's conversations with Nehru are reported in the correspondence in Subject File No. 52, T. T. Krishnamachari Papers, NMML.

20. Aparna Basu, *Mridula Sarabhai: Rebel with a Cause* (Delhi: Oxford University Press, 1996), ch. 9, "Kashmir"; HT, 9 April 1964.

21. *Dawn*, 18 November 1960.

22. Nehru to Vijayalakshmi Pandit, 3 October 1953, Vijayalakshmi Pandit Papers, NMML.

23. Nehru to Tikaram Paliwal, 17 July 1955, in H. Y. Sharada Prasad and A. K. Damodaran, eds., *Selected Works of Jawaharlal Nehru: Second Series*, Vol. 29 (New Delhi: Jawaharlal Nehru Memorial Fund, 2001), pp. 452–453.

24. These paragraphs on Abdullah's release and his triumphant return to the Valley are based principally on HT, issues of 6 April to 24 April 1964.

25. See letters and papers in Subject File No. 28 ("Indo-Pakistan Conciliation Group"), Brahmanand Papers, NMML.

26. Jayaprakash Narayan, "Our Great Opportunity in Kashmir," HT, 20 April 1964.
27. C. Rajagopalachari, "Am I Wrong?" *Swarajya*, 25 April 1964.
28. HT, 23 April 1964. In the rest of this section, quotes not given specific attributions come from this newspaper.
29. Telegram dated 29 April 1964, in Subject File No. 92, C. Rajagopalachari Papers, Fourth Instalment, NMML.
30. Ibid., letter of 29 April 1964. As some other letters in this file show, most members of the Swatantra party opposed Masani and Rajaji in their support of the talks between Nehru and Abdullah. K. M. Munshi said that Sheikh Abdullah should be put back in jail. Dahyabhai Patel (son of Vallabhbhai Patel) said that the only solution to the problem of Kashmir was to settle the Valley with Hindu refugees from East Pakistan.
31. Ibid., Abdullah to Minoo Masani, 16 April 1964.
32. Ibid., Shastri to Rajaji, 4 May 1964.
33. "Kashmir—Talk with Sheikh Abdullah on 8 May 1964, at PM's House," Subject File No. 4, Y. D. Gundevia Papers, NMML.
34. Shiva Rao to Rajaji, 10 May 1964; Rajaji to Shiva Rao, 12 May 1964; both in Subject File No. 92, C. Rajagopalachari Papers, Fourth Instalment, NMML.
35. HT, 23 May 1964.
36. Y. D. Gundevia to V. K. T. Chari (attorney-general, Madras), 13 May 1964, Subject File No. 4, Y. D. Gundevia Papers, NMML. A confederation as a solution to the Kashmir problem was apparently first proposed by the journalist Arthur Moore as early as January 1948. Moore believed that "India, Pakistan and Kashmir should become a federated commonwealth state, with common foreign affairs, common defence, and such finance as concerned these subjects, but otherwise all three to be self-governing States." He spoke about it to Mahatma Gandhi, and later also appears to have broached the topic with the prime minister. Moore also wrote about it in a volume of tributes on Nehru's seventieth birthday, calling this issue the "greatest test for Nehru's statesmanship . . . [for] there will never be satisfactory relations between India and Pakistan till the Kashmir issue is settled." See Arthur Moore, "My Friend's Son," in Rafiq Zakaria, ed., *A Study of Nehru*, 2nd ed. (Bombay: Times of India Press, 1960; originally published 1959), especially pp. 175–176. It seems very likely, considering where Moore's article appeared, that Nehru had read this essay.
37. Letter of 20 May 1964, in Subject File No. 92, C. Rajagopalachari Papers, Fourth Instalment, NMML. In Parliament, Masani was one of the fiercest critics of the prime minister. But, like his mentor Rajaji, he saw that in progress on Kashmir lay the future of the subcontinent. On this subject at least he was willing to support Nehru.
38. HT, 25 May 1964. Unless otherwise indicated, the rest of this section is based on HT, 25 to 30 May 1964.
39. *Dawn*, quoted in HT, 27 May 1964. (Emphasis added.)
40. Walter Crocker, *Nehru: A Contemporary's Estimate* (New York: Oxford University Press, 1966), p. 178.
41. S. Gopal gives the matter three paragraphs; Nehru's more recent biographer, Judith Brown, allows it one. The recent works on the Kashmir dispute—for

instance those by Schonfield, Bose, and Ganguly—do not mention these events at all.

42. Romesh Thapar, "Behind the Abdullah Headlines," EW, 30 May 1964.

43. V. K. T. Chari to Y. D. Gundevia, 16 May 1964, in Subject File No. 4, Y. D. Gundevia Papers, NMML.

44. HT, 26 May 1964.

45. Quoted in HT, 29 May 1964.

CHAPTER 17: MINDING THE MINORITIES

1. Austin's diary entry of 28 May 1968 was published thirty years later in *Hindu*, 29 May 1994.

2. See correspondence between H. S. Suhrawardy, Chaudhry Khaliquzzaman, Jawaharlal Nehru, M. A. Jinnah, and M. K. Gandhi, reprinted in A. G. Noorani, ed., *The Muslims of India: A Documentary Record* (New Delhi: Oxford University Press, 2003), pp. 40–52. See also Chaudhry Khaliquzzaman, *Pathway to Pakistan* (Lahore: Longmans, Green, 1961).

3. Jawaharlal Nehru to J. R. D. Tata, 23 October 1947; Tata to Nehru, 4 November 1947, letters in Tata Steel archives, Jamshedpur.

4. Murphy, *In the Minds of Men*, pp. 144–147.

5. See "You Cannot Ride Two Horses," in *For a United India: Speeches of Sardar Patel* (1949: reprint, New Delhi, Publications Division, 1982), pp. 49–52; emphasis added.

6. "Top secret" letter dated 17 July 1948 from H. V. R. Iengar, home secretary, to Dr. Tara Chand, education secretary, in File No. 6/228/48 ("Information Regarding Government Servants Whose Family Is Still Staying in Pakistan"), Records of the Archaeological Survey of India, New Delhi. The rest of this section is based on this file, a copy of which was kindly passed on to me by Professor Nayanjyot Lahiri of the University of Delhi.

7. The superintendent was Pandit Madho Sarup Vats. We know no more of his biography, but Vats is a Punjabi Hindu surname, and it is possible that his vendetta was influenced by direct or indirect knowledge of the massacres in the Punjab.

8. Quoted in Farhana Ibrahim, "Defining a Border: Harijan Migrants and the State in Kachchh," *Economic and Political Weekly*, 16 April 2005.

9. Nehru to Patel, 20 February 1950, SPC, Vol. 10, p. 5.

10. Nehru's letters to Patel, 6 October and 21 November 1947, SPC, Vol. 4, pp. 362–364, 399–401.

11. Letter of 15 October 1947, LCM, Vol. 1, pp. 32–33.

12. Ibid., letter of 2 October 1949, pp. 478–479.

13. Letters of 29 September 1953 and 15 June 1954, LCM, Vol. 3, pp. 375–376, 570. (Emphasis added.)

14. Speech in Lok Sabha on Azad's death, reprinted in *Maulana Azad: A Homage* (New Delhi: Publications Division, 1958), pp. 30–31.

15. On Muslim support to the Congress in national and state elections through the 1950s, see Sisir K. Gupta, "Moslems in Indian Politics, 1947–1960," *India Quarterly*, Vol. 18, No. 4, 1962.

16. Saif Faiz Badruddin Tyabji, *The Future of Muslims in India* (Bombay: Writers' Emporium, 1956). Tyabji's forward-looking agenda makes an interesting contrast

with the nostalgic lament of the Lucknow divine S. Abul Hasan Ali Nadwi, *Muslims in India*, trans. (from Urdu) Mohammad Asif Kidwai (Lucknow: Academy of Islamic Research and Publications, 1961). Tyabji died shortly after making a speech in the Lok Sabha in 1958; his death, at age forty, was described to me (by the distinguished conservationist Zafar Futehally) as "a great tragedy for the Muslims of India."

17. See reports in File Nos. 78 and 79, Delhi Police Records, Fifth Instalment, NMML.
18. Quoted in W. H. Morris-Jones, *Parliament in India* (London: Longmans, Green, 1957), p. 27, fn.
19. "Daily Diary" dated 19 February 1954, in File No. 138, Delhi Police Records, Sixth Instalment, NMML.
20. See Noorani, *The Muslims of India*, pp. 99–100.
21. For details, see Theodore P. Wright, Jr., "The Effectiveness of Muslim Representation in India," in D. E. Smith, ed., *South Asian Politics and Religion* (Princeton, N. J. : Princeton University Press, 1966).
22. W. C. Smith, *Islam in Modern History* (1957, reprint New York, Mentor, 1959), pp. 263–264.
23. Ibid., pp. 268–274.
24. J. D. Tyson to his family, 9 August 1947, in MSS. Eur. D. 341/40, OIOC.
25. See Farida Abdulla Khan, "Other Communities, Other Histories: A Study of Muslim Women and Education in Kashmir," in Zoya Hasan and Ritu Menon, eds., *In a Minority: Essays on Muslim Women in India* (New Delhi: Oxford University Press, 2005).
26. See the essays and evidence in M. K. A. Siddiqui, *Muslims in Free India: Their Social Profile and Problems* (New Delhi: Institute of Objective Studies, 1998).
27. *Current*, 5 September 1956.
28. D. E. Smith, *India as a Secular State* (Princeton, N.J.: Princeton University Press, 1963), especially pp. 412–413.
29. Smith, *Islam in Modern History*, p. 267.
30. Mushirul Hasan, *Legacy of a Divided Nation: India's Muslims since Independence* (Delhi: Oxford University Press, 1997), p. 161.
31. Taya Zinkin, *Challenges in India* (New York: Walker, 1966), pp. 147ff.
32. Mohamed Raza Khan, *What Price Freedom: A Historical Survey of the Political Trends and Conditions Leading to Independence and the Birth of Pakistan and After* (Madras: Author, 1969), pp. 503f.
33. See the studies collected in M. N. Srinivas, ed., *India's Villages* (1955, reprint Bombay: Media Promoters and Publishers, 1985), pp. 28–29, 94, 100, etc. See also McKim Marriot, ed., *Village India: Studies in the Little Community* (Chicago, Ill.: University of Chicago Press, 1955), pp. 45, 47, 51, 68, 70–72, etc.
34. Vijay Prashad, *Untouchable Freedom: A Social History of a Dalit Community* (New Delhi: Oxford University Press, 2000), pp. 156–163.
35. Among the autobiographies and memoirs available in English, see especially Omprakash Valmiki, *Joothan: A Dalit's Life*, trans. from Hindi by Arun Prabha Mukherjee (Kolkata: Samya, 2003); Narendra Jadhav, *Outcaste: A Memoir*, trans. from Marathi by the author (New Delhi: Viking, 2003); Vasant Moon, *Growing Up Untouchable in India*, trans. from Marathi by Gail Omvedt (Lan-

ham, Md.: Rowman and Littlefield, 2001); Siddharth Dube, *Words Like Free-dom: The Memoirs of an Impoverished Indian Family, 1947–1997* (New Delhi: HarperCollins India, 1998); and a pioneering anthology, Arjun Dangle, ed., *Poisoned Bread: Translations from Modern Marathi Dalit Literature* (Hyder-abad: Orient Longman, 1992).

36. Harold R. Isaacs, *India's Ex-Untouchables* (New York: John Day, 1965), pp. 80–81.

37. This paragraph is based on the following essays: Lelah Dushkin, "The Back-ward Classes: I: Special Treatment Policy; II: Removal of Disabilities," EW, 28 October and 4 November 1961. Lelah Dushkin, "Backward Caste Benefits and Social Class in India, 1920–1970," *Economic and Political Weekly*, 7 April 1979. See also Marc Galanter, *Competing Equalities: Law and the Backward Classes in India* (Delhi: Oxford University Press, 1984).

38. Quoted in Owen M. Lynch, *The Politics of Untouchability: Social Mobility and Social Change in a City of India* (New York: Columbia University Press, 1969), p. 89.

39. See Bernard S. Cohn, "The Changing Status of a Depressed Caste," in Marriot, *Village India*, especially pp. 70–72.

40. J. Michael Mahar, "Agents of Dharma in a North Indian Village," in J. Michael Mahar, ed., *The Untouchables in Contemporary India* (Tucson: University of Arizona Press, 1972), p. 29.

41. Isaacs, *India's Ex-Untouchables*, p. 126.

42. Dube, *Words Like Freedom*, p. 53.

43. Lynch, *The Politics of Untouchability*, ch. 3 and passim.

44. Nehru to C. Rajagopalachari, letters of 5 May and 25 June 1952, in Subject File No. 123, Rajagopalachari Papers, Fifth Instalment, NMML.

45. Oliver Mendelsohn and Marika Vicziany, *The Untouchables: Subordination, Poverty, and the State in India* (Cambridge: Cambridge University Press, 1998), pp. 207–208, 252; Devendra Prasad Sharma, *Jagjivan Ram: The Man and His Times* (New Delhi: Indian Book Company, 1974).

46. This account of Ambedkar's last days is based on Vasant Moon, *Dr. Babasaheb Ambedkar*, trans. from Marathi by Asha Damle (New Delhi: National Book Trust, 2002), pp. 203–219. The best treatments of Ambedkar's thought (includ-ing his conversion to Buddhism) are Eleanor Zelliot, *Untouchable to Dalit: Essays on Ambedkar Movement* (Delhi: Manohar, 1992); and Jayashree Gokhale, *From Concessions to Confrontation: The Politics of an Indian Un-touchable Community* (Bombay: Popular Prakashan, 1993). See also Valerian Rodrigues, ed., *B. R. Ambedkar: Essential Writings* (New Delhi: Oxford Uni-versity Press, 2004).

47. Moon, *Growing Up Untouchable*, pp. 52, 107–111, 127, 160–161, etc.

48. Valmiki, *Joothan*, pp. 71f.

49. Jadhav, *Outcaste*, p. 231.

50. Rameshwari Nehru, *Gandhi Is My Star* (Patna: Pustak Bhandar, 1950), pp. 110ff.

51. *Current*, 8 February 1956.

52. N. D. Kamble, *Atrocities on Scheduled Castes in Post Independent India* (New Delhi: Ashish, 1981), pp. 8–46. Kamble's sources were newspaper acccounts in English, Hindi, and Marathi. I have simplified and summarized his wording.

53. Aldous Huxley, *Jesting Pilate: The Diary of a Journey* (London: Chatto and Windus, 1927), pp. 116–117.

54. Speech by H. J. Khandekar, 21 November 1949, in CAD, Vol. 11, pp. 736–737.

55. Aga Khan to Jawaharlal Nehru, 25 January 1951, copy in Subject File No. 61, C. Rajagopalachari Papers, Fourth Instalment, NMML.

56. D. F. Karaka, in *Current*, 11 November 1959. Karaka went on to list Nehru's failures, among them an inability to root out corruption and nepotism, and the foolishness of trusting communist China.

CHAPTER 18: WAR AND SUCCESSION

1. V. K. Narasimhan, *Kamaraj: A Study* (Bangalore: Myers Indmark, 1967); Duncan B. Forrester, "Kamaraj: A Study in Percolation of Style," *Modern Asian Studies*, Vol. 4, No. 1, 1970; J. Anthony Lukacs, "Meet Kumaraswamy Kamaraj," *Illustrated Weekly of India*, 22 May 1966.

2. This account is based on Michael Brecher, *Succession in India: A Study in Decision Making* (London: Oxford University Press, 1966), chs. 2 and 3. See also Stanley Kochanek, *The Congress Party of India: The Dynamics of One-Party Dermocracy* (Princeton, N.J.: Princeton University Press, 1968), pp. 88f.

3. Brecher, *Succession*, pp. 115–117.

4. *Guardian*, 3 June 1964, clipping in MSS. Eur. F. 158/1045, OIOC.

5. Patrick Keatley, "A Sparrow's Strength," reprinted in *The Bedside Guardian 13: A Selection from "The Guardian" 1963–1964* (London: Collins, 1964), pp. 200–203.

6. J. H. Hutton to Charles Pawsey, 29 May 1964, in Box II, Pawsey Papers, Centre for South Asian Studies, Cambridge.

7. M. Aram, *Peace in Nagaland: Eight Year Story, 1964–1972* (New Delhi: Arnold-Heinemann India, 1974), pp. 20–38: A. Paul Hare and Herbert H. Blumberg, eds., *A Search for Peace and Justice: Reflections of Michael Scott* (London: Rex Collings, 1980), ch. 11 ("Nagaland Peace Mission").

8. Narayan to J. J. Singh, dated Kohima, 11 September 1964, J. J. Singh Papers, NMML.

9. See V. K. Nuh, comp., *The Naga Chronicle* (New Delhi: Regency, 2002), pp. 274ff.

10. Dr. Bhabha's speech was quoted in extenso in *Lok Sabha Debates*, 27 November 1964.

11. Ibid., 27 November and 11 December 1964. Both Kachwai and Shastri spoke in Hindi.

12. See K. S. Ramanathan, *The Big Change* (Madras: Higginbothams, 1967), ch. 6.

13. A. S. Raman, "A Meeting with C. N. Annadurai," *Illustrated Weekly of India*, 26 September 1965.

14. See Robert D. King, *Nehru and the Language Politics of India* (New Delhi: Oxford University Press, 1997); Mohan Ram, *Hindi against India: The Meaning of DMK* (New Delhi: Rachna Prakashan, 1968).

15. This account is principally based on news reports in *Hindu*, 27 January to 15 February 1965. See also the four-page photo spread "Language Riots in Madras," *Illustrated Weekly of India*, 28 February 1965.

16. Eric Stracey, *Odd Man In: My Years in the Indian Police* (New Delhi: Vikas, 1981), pp. 209–227.

17. See Morarji Desai, "National Unity through Hindi," *Current*, 30 January 1965.

18. See *Selected Speeches of Lal Bahadur Shastri* (New Delhi: Publications Division, 1974), pp. 119–122.

19. *Lok Sabha Debates*, 18 February 1965.

20. Ghosh to Alexander, 3 March 1965, File No. 60, Horace Alexander Papers, Friends House, Euston.

21. Sir Morrice James, *Pakistan Chronicle* (London: Hurst, 1993), pp. 123–126; G. S. Bhargava, *After Nehru: India's New Image* (Bombay: Allied, 1966), pp. 260–263, 276, 439–441. The ceasefire agreement was signed by officials representing the respective foreign ministries—both Muslims, they were, as it happened, first cousins, one of whom had chosen to be a citizen of India.

22. Letter of 24 May 1965, File No. 60, Horace Alexander Papers, Friends House, Euston.

23. James, *Pakistan Chronicle*, pp. 128–131.

24. See letters of the chief secretary of Jammu and Kashmir, August 1965, in Nayantara Sahgal and E. N. Mangat Rai, *Relationship: Extracts from a Correspondence* (New Delhi: Kali for Women, 1994), pp. 134–139.

25. This account of the hostilities is principally based on Brian Cloughley, *A History of the Pakistan Army: Wars and Insurrections* (Karachi: Oxford University Press, 2006), pp. 68–72, 84–85, 102–106; Air Chief Marshal P. C. Lal, *My Years with the IAF* (New Delhi: Lancer, 1987), pp. 126–134; Lieutenant General Harbaksh Singh, *In the Line of Duty: A Solider Remembers* (New Delhi: Lancer, 2000), pp. 334–353.

26. Singh, *In the Line of Duty*, p. 353.

27. Lal, *My Years*, p. 134.

28. See C. P. Srivastava, *Lal Bahadur Shastri: A Life of Truth in Politics* (New Delhi: Oxford University Press, 1995), pp. 273–275.

29. See Bhargava, *After Nehru*, pp. 300–303.

30. Herbert Feldman, *From Crisis to Crisis: Pakistan, 1962–1969* (London: Oxford University Press, 1972), p. 146.

31. John Frazer, "Who Can Win Kashmir?" *Reader's Digest*, January 1966.

32. As told to me by K. S. Bajpai, who was then the Indian consul general in Karachi.

33. Lieutenant General Jahan Dad Khan, *Pakistan Leadership Challenges* (Karachi: Oxford University Press, 1999), p. 51.

34. Quoted in Feldman, *From Crisis to Crisis*, pp. 139–140.

35. Quoted in Cloughley, *A History*, p. 71.

36. For an acute analysis, see the untitled note on Kashmir by Prem Nath Bazaz, dated 24 October 1965, in Subject File No. 46, C. Rajagopalachari Papers, Fourth Instalment, NMML.

37. Alastair Lamb, *Kashmir: A Disputed Legacy, 1846–1990* (Karachi: Oxford University Press, 1992), p. 263.

38. Nayantara Sahgal, "What India Fights For," *Illustrated Weekly of India*, 3 October 1965; Anon., *The Fight for Peace* (New Delhi: Hardy and Ally India, 1966), especially pp. 260ff.

39. T. V. Kunhi Krishnan, *Chavan and the Troubled Decade* (Bombay: Somaiya, 1971), pp. 99–115; R. D. Pradhan, *Debacle to Revival: Y. B. Chavan as Defence Minister* (Hyderabad: Orient Longman, 1999), pp. 182–187, 207–212, 238–242.

40. Shastri to Jayaprakash Narayan, 21 July 1965 (in Hindi), in Subject File No. 28, Brahmanand Papers, NMML.

41. The speech is reprinted in D. R. Mankekar, *Lal Bahadur: A Political Biography* (Bombay: Popular Prakashan, 1965), App. 3. Unlike Nehru, Shastri was a practising Hindu. But when asked by an interviewer to speak about his faith, he answered that "one should not discuss one's religion in public." Interview in *Illustrated Weekly of India*, 18 October 1964.

42. Singh, *Portrait of Lal Bahadur Shastri*, pp. 87–88.

43. See B. Sivaraman, *Bitter Sweet: Governance of India in Transition* (New Delhi: Ashish, 1987), especially ch. 11, "Green Revolution."

44. John P. Lewis, *India's Political Economy: Governance and Reform* (Delhi: Oxford University Press, 1995), ch. 4; Gilles Boquérat, *No Strings Attached? India's Policies and Foreign Aid, 1947–1966* (Delhi: Manohar, 2003), ch. 15.

45. Srivastava, *Lal Bahadur Shastri*, ch. 31.

46. "Shastri's Last Journey," *Life*, 21 January 1966.

47. Letter to Dorothy Norman, 13 March 1965, in Dorothy Norman, ed., *Indira Gandhi: Letters to an American Friend, 1950–1984* (San Diego, Calif.: Harcourt Brace Jovanonich, 1985), p. 111.

48. Vijayalakshmi Pandit to A. C. Nambiar, letters of 31 July 1964 and 26 January 1966, copies in Pupul Jayakar Papers, in the possession of Radhika Herzberger, Mumbai.

49. Anand Mohan, *Indira Gandhi: A Personal and Political Biography* (New York: Meredith, 1967), pp. 20–37.

50. Nehru to C. D. Deshmukh, 16 April 1956, in Subject File No. 67, C. D. Deshmukh Papers, NMML.

51. "A Fitful Improvization," *Thought*, 22 January 1966.

52. Nirmal Nibedon, *Mizoram: The Dagger Brigade* (New Delhi: Lancers, 1980), especially pp. 30–51.

53. Sajal Nag, *Contesting Marginality: Ethnicity, Insurgency, and Subnationalism in North-East India* (New Delhi: Manohar, 2002), pp. 217–224; Sajal Nag, "Tribes, Rats, Famine, State, and the Nation," *Economic and Political Weekly*, 24 March 2001. See also *Thought* (New Delhi), 2 April 1966, and 7 and 14 October 1967.

54. Unsigned, undated letter to I. A. Bowman, postmarked 13 March 1966, in MSS. Eur. F. 229/62, OIOC.

55. Jayaprakash Narayan to Marjorie Sykes, 24 February 1966, copy in J. J. Singh Papers, NMML. See also Jayaprakash Narayan, *Nagaland Mein Shanti Ka Prayas* (Varanasi: Sarva Seva Sangh, 1966). The title translates as "The Quest for Peace in Nagaland."

56. See clippings in MSS. Eur. F. 158/239, OIOC.

57. Guy Wint to I. A. Bowman, 16 September 1966, in MSS. Eur. F. 229/24, OIOC.

58. Nirmal Nibedon, *Nagaland: The Night of the Guerrillas* (New Delhi: Lancers, 1983), pp. 137–145.

59. Subject File No. 136, D. P. Mishra Papers, Third and Fourth Instalments, NMML; Nandini Sundar, *Subalterns and Sovereigns: An Anthropological History of Bastar, 1854–1996* (Delhi: Oxford University Press, 1997), ch. 7.

60. Singh, *In the Line of Duty*, p. 357.

61. See clippings in MSS. Eur. F. 158/295. The creation of the new Punjab and Haryana was approved in March 1966, but the decision did not go into effect until November, after the borders were delimited. See HT, 2 November 1966.

62. See C. Subramaniam, *Hand of Destiny: Memoirs*, Vol. 2, *The Green Revolution* (Bombay: Bharatiya Vidya Bhavan, 1995), ch. 11 and passim.

63. Mrs. Gandhi's trip to the United States is described in K. A. Abbas, *Indira Gandhi: Return of the Red Rose* (Delhi: Hind Pocket Books, 1966), pp. 147–157.

64. Chester Bowles, *Promises to Keep: My Years in Public Life, 1941–1969* (New Delhi: B. I. Publications, 1972), pp. 525–535. See also Howard B. Schaffer, *Chester Bowles: New Dealer in the Cold War* (New Delhi: Prentice-Hall India, 1994), pp. 280ff.

65. Anon., "India's Food Crisis, 1965–1967," in File 7, Box 32, Thomas J. Schonberg Files, Dean Rusk Papers, University of Georgia, Athens.

66. Memorandum to President Johnson from Orville Freeman, dated 19 July 1966, in File 6, Box 32, Thomas J. Schonberg Files, Dean Rusk Papers, University of Georgia, Athens.

67. This acccount of the devaluation in 1966 is based on Rahul Mukherji, "India's Aborted Liberalization—1966," *Pacific Affairs*, Vol. 73, No. 3, 2000; supplemented by Kuldeep Nayar, *Between the Lines* (Bombay: Allied, 1969), ch. 3.

68. Indira Gandhi to Jayaprakash Narayan, 7 June 1966, copy in J. J. Singh Papers, NMML.

69. *Thought*, 11 June 1966.

70. Jayaprakash Narayan to Indira Gandhi, dated Sarvodaya Ashram, Sokhodeora (Gaya), 23 June 1966, copy in J. J. Singh Papers, NMML.

71. Indira Gandhi to Jayaprakash Narayan, 6 July 1966, copy in J. J. Singh Papers, NMML.

72. *Thought*, 15 October 1966.

73. HT, issues of 31 October through 5 November 1966.

74. Ibid., 5 and 6 November 1966.

75. Ibid., 7 November 1966; *Thought*, 12 November 1966.

76. "Indians Becoming Increasingly Hostile to West," *Sydney Morning Herald*, 13 December 1965.

77. Ronald Segal, *The Crisis of India* (Harmondsworth: Penguin, 1965), pp. 171, 227, 255–257, 172, 309–310.

78. Michael Scott, quoted in Ursula Betts to Ian Bowman, 25 May 1966, MSS. Eur. F. 229/24, OIOC.

79. Paul Ehrlich, *The Population Bomb* (New York: Ballantine, 1968), Preface.

80. William and Paul Paddock, *Famine—1975! America's Decision: Who Will Survive?* (Boston: Little, Brown, 1975), pp. 60–61, 217–218.

81. S. Mulgaokar, "The Grimmest Situation in 19 Years," HT, 3 November 1966.

CHAPTER 19: LEFTWARD TURNS

1. Sol W. Sanders, "India: A Huge Country on the Verge of Collapse," *U.S. News and World Report*, 28 November 1966.

2. Neville Maxwell, "India's Disintegrating Democracy," The *Times*, 26 and 27 January and 10 February 1967.

3. See Yogesh Atal, *Local Communities and National Politics* (Delhi: National, 1971); A. M. Shah, ed., *The Grassroots of Democracy* (New Delhi: Permanent Black, 2007.).

4. E. P. W. da Costa, *The Indian General Elections 1967: The Structure of Indian Voting Intentions, January 1967—A Gallup Poll with Analysis* (New Delhi: Indian Institute of Public Opinion, 1967).

5. *Thought*, 4 March 1967.

6. These paragraphs on MGR and the DMK are based on Robert L. Hardgrave and Anthony C. Neidhart, "Films and Political Consciousness in Tamil Nadu," *Economic and Political Weekly*, 11 January 1975; and N. Balakrishnan, "The History of the Dravidian Munnetra Kazhagam, 1949–1977," unpublished PhD dissertation, School of Historical Studies, Madurai Kamaraj University, 1985, especially pp. 278–286.

7. Narendra Subramanian, *Ethnicity and Populist Mobilization: Political Parties, Citizens, and Democracy in South India* (New Delhi: Oxford University Press, 1999), pp. 204–210; Sagar Ahluwalia, *Anna—The Tempest and the Sea* (New Delhi: Young Asia, 1969), pp. 51–57, 82–84.

8. Jyoti Basu, *Memoirs: A Political Autobiography* (Calcutta; National Book Agency, 1999), pp. 195–209.

9. Bhabani Sengupta, *Communism in Indian Politics* (New York: Columbia University Press, 1972).

10. Marcus F. Franda, *Radical Politics in West Bengal* (Cambridge, Mass.: M.I.T. Press, 1971), ch. 6.

11. See Rabindra Ray, *The Naxalites and Their Ideology* (New Delhi: Oxford University Press, 1992).

12. *Mainstream*, 8 July 1967, quoted in Franda, *Radical Politics*, p. 171.

13. Shanta Sinha, *Maoists in Andhra Pradesh* (New Delhi: Gyan, 1989), chs. 4 to 7; Sumanta Banerjee, *In the Wake of Naxalbari: A History of the Naxalite Movement in India* (Calcutta: Subarnarekha, 1980), ch. 5.

14. See clippings and papers in Subject File No. 3, Dharma Vira Papers, NMML.

15. Sankar Ghosh, *The Disinherited State: A Study of West Bengal, 1967–1970* (Calcutta: Orient Longman, 1971), ch. 3.

16. See clippings in MSS. Eur. F. 158/456, OIOC.

17. Ghosh, *The Disinherited State*, pp. 248ff.

18. See Subject File No. 99, P. N. Haksar Papers, Third Instalment, NMML.

19. See IB report in Subject File No. 212, P. N. Haksar Papers, Third Instalment, NMML.

20. See Ranjit Gupta, *The Crimson Agenda: Maoist Protest and Terror* (Delhi: Wordsmiths, 2004), pp. 105, 110–111, 157–159, etc.

21. Inder Malhotra, "Naxalites Put City in Fear of Bombs," *Guardian*, 19 August 1970.

22. For the (very long) list of charges, see S. N. Dwivedy, *The Orissa Affair and the C.B.I. Inquiry* (New Delhi: Author, 1965).

23. Sunit Ghosh, *Orissa in Turmoil* (Bhubaneshwar: Bookland International, 1991), pp. 149-157; Sukadev Nanda, *Coalition Politics in Orissa* (New Delhi: Sterling, 1979), pp. 70-77.

24. Special Branch report marked "Top Secret," 26 February 1967, Subject File No. 25, DP Mishra Papers, Second Instalment, NMML.

25. Ibid., Mishra to Kamaraj, 21 June 1967.

26. See R. C. V. P. Noronha, *A Tale Told by an Idiot* (New Delhi: Vikas, 1976), ch. 8.

27. Prem Shankar Jha, "Telengana: Language Is Not Enough," *Illustrated Weekly of India*, 3 August 1969.

28. S. K. Chaube, *Hill Politics in North-East India* (Bombay: Orient Longman, 1973), chs. 7 and 8.

29. See letters and notes in Subject File No. 142, P. N. Haksar Papers, Third Instalment, NMML.

30. Dipankar Gupta, *Nativism in a Metropolis: The Shiv Sena in Bombay* (Delhi: Manohar, 1982), pp. 39-40, 82-83, etc.; Vaibhav Purandare, *The Sena Story* (Mumbai: Business Publications, 1999), pp. 22-24, 42-44, etc.

31. *Thought*, 11 February 1967.

32. See notes in Subject File No. 128, P. N. Haksar Papers, Third Instalment, NMML.

33. *Thought*, 16 March, 6 July, and 19 October 1968; *Daily Telegraph*, 27 June 1968.

34. See news clippings in MSS. Eur. F. 158/239, OIOC.

35. See Letters and papers in File No. 61, Alexander Papers, Friends House, Euston.

36. *Thought*, 7 June 1968.

37. A. G. Noorani, "How Does a Riot Begin and Spread?" *Illustrated Weekly of India*, 9 November 1969; N. C. Saxena, "The Nature and Origins of Communal Riots in India," in Asghar Ali Engineer, ed., *Communal Riots in Post-Independence India*, 2nd ed. (Hyderabad: Orient Longman, 1991); K. D. Malaviya to Fakhruddin Ali Ahmad, 30 March 1967, in Subject File No. 128, P. N. Haksar Papers, Third Instalment, NMML.

38. Ghanshyam Shah, "The 1969 Communal Riots in Ahmedabad: A Case Study," in Engineer, *Communal Riots*. See also untitled report on the Ahmedabad riots by a group of Congress members of Parliament, dated 7 October 1969, in Subject File No. 142, P. N. Haksar Papers, Third Instalment, NMML.

39. Khushwant Singh, "Learning Geography through Murder," *Illustrated Weekly of India*, 31 May 1970.

40. Editorial, *Thought*, 2 March 1968; see also S. E. Hassnain, *Indian Muslims: Challenge and Opportunity* (Bombay: Lalwani, 1968).

41. This sketch is based on Bidyut Sarkar, ed., *P. N. Haksar: Our Times and the Man* (New Delhi: Allied, 1989); a conversation with Professor André Béteille, Delhi, February 2005; and material in the P. N. Haksar Papers, NMML.

42. Frank, *Indira*, p. 314.

43. Note dated 21 January 1968, in Subject File No. 198, P. N. Haksar Papers, Third Instalment, NMML.

44. Speech by S. S. Dhawan, London, March 1969; copy in Subject File No. 197, P. N. Haksar Papers, Third Instalment, NMML.

45. Inder Malhotra, *Indira Gandhi: A Personal and Political Biography* (London: Hodder and Stoughton, 1989), pp. 108f.

46. *The Years of Challenge: Selected Speeches of Indira Gandhi, January 1966–August 1969,* 2nd ed. (New Delhi, Publications Division, 1985), pp. 25–28, 34–39, 172–174, 268–269.

47. *Thought,* 8 and 29 March 1969.

48. Uma Vasudev, *Indira Gandhi: Revolution in Restraint* (Delhi: Vikas, 1974), p. 502.

49. Malhotra, *Indira Gandhi,* p. 116.

50. *Thought,* 23 December 1967; Morarji Desai, *The Story of My Life,* Vol. 2 (Delhi: Macmillan India, 1974), pp. 243f.

51. The speech is reprinted in A. Moin Zaidi, *The Great Upheaval, 1969–1972* (New Delhi: Orientalia India, 1972), pp. 103–106.

52. *Thought,* 19 July and 16 August 1969.

53. For details, see Subject File No. 153, P. N. Haksar Papers, Third Instalment.

54. Trevor Drieberg, *Indira Gandhi: Profile in Courage* (Delhi: Vikas, 1972), ch. 7.

55. S. Nijalingappa to Indira Gandhi, 11 November 1969, in Zaidi, *The Great Upheaval,* p. 231.

56. Sukumar Muralidharan and Ravi Sharma, "A Congressman from Another Age: S. Nijalingappa, 1902–2000," *Frontline,* 1 September 2000.

57. See drafts of speeches in Subject File no. 143, P. N. Haksar Papers, Third Instalment, NMML.

58. N(ikhil) C(hakravartty), "Syndicate at Waterloo," *Mainstream,* 16 August 1969.

59. Sahgal, *Indira Gandhi,* p. 53.

60. Note by P. N. Haksar dated 16 September 1967, Subject File No. 118, P. N. Haksar Papers, Third Instalment, NMML.

61. Subject File No. 121, P. N. Haksar Papers, Third Instalment, NMML; Rajinder Puri, *India 1969: A Crisis of Conscience* (Delhi: Author, 1971), pp. 67–73.

62. See letters in Subject File No. 145, P. N. Haksar Papers, Third Instalment, NMML.

63. This account of the parliamentary and judicial interventions in the controversy over the privy purse is based on D. R. Mankekar, *Accession to Extinction: The Story of Indian Princes* (Delhi: Vikas, 1974), chs. 18 to 20.

64. For details, see M. S. Randhawa, *A History of Agriculture in India,* Vol. 4, *1947–1981* (New Delhi: Indian Council of Agricultural Research, 1986), chs. 30 to 32.

65. Don Taylor, "This New, Surprising Strength of Mrs. Gandhi," *Evening Standard,* 21 August 1969.

66. *New York Times,* 26 January 1970.

67. "Is India Cracking Up?" *Thought,* 4 January 1967. (Editorial.)

68. "The Meaning of Naxalbari," *Thought,* 17 June 1967.

69. Kathleen Gough, "The Indian Revolutionary Potential," *Monthly Review,* February 1969. (Based on an essay originally published in *Pacific Affairs,* Winter Issue, 1968–1969.)

70. Lasse Berg and Lisa Berg, *Face to Face: Fascism and Revolution in India,* trans. from Swedish by Norman Kurtin (Berkeley, Calif.: Ramparts, 1971), pp. 23–24, 28, 31, 56, 125, 162, 209–210.

CHAPTER 20: THE ELIXIR OF VICTORY

1. *Thought*, 22 November 1969.
2. *Election Manifestos 1971* (Bombay: Awake India, 1971).
3. Rajaji to Minoo Masani, 2 January 1971, in Subject File No. 142, C. Rajago-palachari Papers, Fourth Instalment, NMML.
4. Indira Gandhi to Dorothy Norman, 23 April 1971, in *Letters to an American Friend*, p. 132.
5. *Thought*, 20 May 1972.
6. "A Special Correspondent," "The Making of Fifth Lok Sabha," *Thought*, 20 March 1971.
7. Khushwant Singh, "Indira Gandhi," *Illustrated Weekly of India*, 14 March 1971.
8. See Mankekar, *Accession to Extinction*, ch. 21.
9. D. N. Dhanagare, "Urban-Rural Differences in Election Violence," in S. P. Varma and Iqbal Narain, eds., *Fourth General Elections in India,* Vol. 2 (Bombay: Orient Longman, 1970).
10. This section is based on Election Commission of India, *Report on the Fifth General Elections in India, 1971–1972* (New Delhi: Manager of Publications, 1973), passim. The CEC was S. P. Sen Varma; his report—the mystical Preface apart—was clearly modelled on the first such, written by his great predecessor, Sukumar Sen.
11. This and the following paragraphs are principally based on Herbert Feldman, *The End and the Beginning: Pakistan 1969–1971* (London: Oxford University Press, 1975), chs. 7 to 9. See also D. R. Mankekar, *Pak Colonialism in East Bengal* (Bombay: Somaiyya, 1971).
12. Lieutenant General A. A. K. Niazi, quoted in Muntassir Mamoon, *The Vanquished Generals and the Liberation War of Bangladesh* (Dhaka: Somoy Prakashan, 2000), p. 159.
13. R. K. Dasgupta, *Revolt in East Bengal* (Calcutta: G. C. Ray, 1971), pp. 4, 7, 9, 21, 24–25, 29, 39, 52, 61, etc. For the colonial treatment of East Pakistan by the West Punjab elite, see also Anthony Mascarenhas, *The Rape of Bangla Desh* (Delhi: Vikas, 1971).
14. See reports by eyewitnesses collected in Anon., *Bangla Desh Documents* (Madras: B. N. K., 1972), ch. 6.
15. Jyoti Sen Gupta, *History of Freedom Movement in Bangladesh, 1943–1973* (Calcutta: Naya Prokash, 1974), pp. 314–316, 325–326. The major who made the announcement was Zia-ur-Rahman, later president of Bangladesh.
16. State Department telegram dated 2 July 1971, reproduced in Roedad Khan, comp, *The American Papers: Secret and Confidential India-Pakistan-Bangladesh Documents, 1965–1973* (Karachi: Oxford University Press, 1999), pp. 613–615.
17. Major General Hakeem Arshad Qureshi, *The 1971 Indo-Pak War: A Soldier's Narrative* (Karachi: Oxford University Press, 2002), pp. 60, 71. The sentences quoted could as easily have been written by an Indian army commander, about Nagaland c. 1957.
18. Werner Adam, "Pakistan's Open Wounds," *Washington Post*, 6 June 1971; *New York Times*, 25 June 1971; World Bank team report, Subject File No. 171, P. N. Haksar Papers, Third Instalment, NMML.

19. Anon., *Bangla Desh Documents*, ch. 7.
20. K. C. Saha, "The Genocide of 1971 and the Refugee Influx in the East," in Ranabir Samaddar, ed., *Refugees and the State: Practices of Asylum and Care in India, 1947–2000* (New Delhi: Sage, 2003).
21. Iqbal Akhund, *Memoirs of a Bystander: A Life in Diplomacy* (Karachi: Oxford University Press, 1997), p. 201.
22. "Threat of a Military Attack or Infiltration Campaign by Pakistan," RAW, January 1971, copy in Subject File No. 220, P. N. Haksar Papers, Third Instalment, NMML.
23. Dhar to Haksar, 18 April 1971, in Subject File No. 220, P. N. Haksar Papers, Third Instalment, NMML.
24. See reports in Subject File No. 169, P. N. Haksar Papers, Third Instalment, NMML.
25. The letter is reprinted in F. S. Aijazuddin, ed., *The White House and Pakistan: Secret Declassified Documents, 1969–1974* (Karachi: Oxford University Press, 2002), pp. 129–130.
26. "Record of PM's Conversation with Dr. Kissinger," dated 7 July 1971, in Subject File No. 225, P. N. Haksar Papers, Third Instalment, NMML.
27. Indira Gandhi to Richard Nixon, 7 August 1971, copy in Subject File No. 220, P. N. Haksar Papers, Third Instalment, NMML.
28. See the documents in Louis Smith, ed., *Foreign Relations of the United States, 1969–1976*, Vol. 11, *South Asia Crisis, 1971* (Washington, D.C.: Department of State, 2005), pp. 28, 35, 164, 167, 288–289, 303, 316, 324, 557, etc.; and the documents in Aijazuddin, *The White House*, pp. 242–246, 258–262.
29. For the broader context of India's changing relations with the superpowers in the early 1970s, see T. V. Kunhi Krishnan, *The Unfriendly Friends: India and America* (New Delhi: Indian Book Company, 1974); Shashi Tharoor, *Reasons of State: Political Development and India's Foreign Policy under Indira Gandhi, 1966–1977* (New Delhi: Vikas, 1982); and Linda Racioppi, *Soviet Policy towards South Asia since 1970* (Cambridge: Cambridge University Press, 1994).
30. This paragraph is based on letters and papers in Subject Files No. 163, 225, and 229, P. N. Haksar Papers, Third Instalment, NMML.
31. "Top secret" note of 5 June 1971 in Subject File No. 89, P. N. Haksar Papers, Third Instalment, NMML.
32. "Record of conversations between Foreign Minister and Mr. A. A. Gromyko, Minister of Foreign Affairs, USSR, on 7 June 1971," in Subject File No. 203, P. N. Haksar Papers, Third Instalment, NMML.
33. The text of the treaty is printed in A. Appadorai, ed., *Select Documents on India's Foreign Policy and Relations, 1947–1972*, Vol. 2 (Delhi: Oxford University Press, 1985), pp. 136–140.
34. *The Speeches and Reminiscences of Indira Gandhi, Prime Minister of India* (London: Hodder and Stoughton, 1975), pp. 162–164.
35. See Aijazuddin, *The White House*, pp. 313, 336–339.
36. Robert Jackson, *South Asian Crisis: India–Pakistan–Bangla Desh* (London: Chatto and Windus, 1975), p. 102.
37. Letter of 23 November, in Aijazuddin, *The White House*, pp. 364–365.
38. Jackson, *South Asian Crisis*, pp. 106–107; Brian Cloughley, *A History of the Pakistan Army: Wars and Insurrections* (Karachi: Oxford University Press, 2006), pp. 148–149.

39. B. G. Verghese, *An End to Confrontation: Restructuring the Sub-Continent* (New Delhi: S. Chand, 1972), pp. 35–50.
40. Cloughley, *A History of the Pakistan Army*, p. 222.
41. Lieutenant General A. A. K. Niazi, *The Betrayal of East Pakistan* (Delhi: Manohar, 1998), p. 132.
42. Ibid., p. 114.
43. D. R. Mankekar, *Pakistan Cut to Size* (New Delhi: Indian Book Company, 1972), pp. 54–63.
44. Jackson, *South Asian Crisis*, pp. 137–138.
45. Telegram quoted in Niazi, *Betrayal*, p. 180.
46. See Aijazuddin, *The White House*, pp. 447, 449–450.
47. Niazi, *Betrayal*, pp. 187ff.
48. *Lok Sabha Debates*, 16 December 1971.
49. Living not far from the border then, I heard Yahya's speech as it was delivered—he had (as Pakistani accounts also suggest) consumed a goodly amount of whisky before taking up the microphone.
50. Air Chief Marshal P. C. Lal, *My Years with the IAF* (New Delhi: Lancer International, 1986), p. 321.
51. Smith, *South Asia Crisis*, pp. 439, 499, 594, 612, 674, etc. See also the letters exchanged between Mrs. Gandhi and Nixon after the end of the war, reproduced in Aijazuddin, *The White House*, pp. 476–480.
52. *Time*, 3 January 1972; James Reston, "India's Victory a Triumph for Moscow," *New York Times*, c. 20 December 1971, clipping in Subject File No. 217, P. N. Haksar Papers, Third Instalment, NMML.
53. *Thought*, 29 January 1972.
54. Quoted in C. M. Naim, *Ambiguities of Heritage: Fictions and Polemics* (Karachi: City Press, 1999), p. 139.
55. See "India after Bangla Desh: A Symposium," *Gandhi Marg*, Vol. 16, No. 2, 1972.
56. Letter of 8 December 1971, in Carol Brightman, ed., *Between Friends: The Correspondence of Hannah Arendt and Mary McCarthy, 1949–1975* (New York: Harcourt Brace, 1995), p. 303.
57. Vajpayee, quoted in *Thought*, 20 May 1972.
58. Ranajit Roy, *The Agony of West Bengal: A Study in Union-State Relations*, 3rd ed. (Calcutta: New Age, 1973), pp. 3–4; Sajal Basu, *West Bengal—The Violent Years* (Calcutta: Prachi, 1974), p. 78.
59. "Message to Mrs. Gandhi from Sir Alec Douglas-Home," dated 20 March 1972, in Subject File No. 179, P. N. Haksar Papers, Third Instalment, NMML.
60. Quoted in S. R. Sen to I. G. Patel, letter dated 2 March 1972, in Subject File No. 225, P. N. Haksar Papers, Third Instalment, NMML.
61. Untitled note in Subject File No. 236, P. N. Haksar Papers, Third Instalment, NMML.
62. Sajjad Zaheer to P. N. Haksar, 23 March 1972, in Subject File No. 243, P. N. Haksar Papers, Third Instalment, NMML (emphasis in original). Mazhar Ali Khan was the father of the student radical Tariq Ali, who later became a prolific author.
63. A. Raghavan, "Five Days That Changed History," *Blitz*, 8 July 1972.
64. Note by Dhar dated 12 March 1972, in Subject File no. 235, P. N. Haksar Papers, Third Instalment, NMML.

65. The text of the Simla Agreement is printed in Appadorai, *Select Documents,* pp. 443–445.
66. The text of the speech is in Subject File No. 93, P. N. Haksar Papers, Third Instalment, NMML.
67. Ibid., annotations.

CHAPTER 21; THE RIVALS

1. See *India: The Speeches and Reminscences of Indira Gandhi,* pp. 215–216.
2. *Hindu,* 16 August 1972.
3. A. Vaidyanathan, "The Indian Economy since Independence (1947–1970)," in Dharma Kumar, ed., *The Cambridge Economic History of India,* Vol. 2. (Cambridge: Cambridge University Press, 1983).
4. This paragraph summarizes several longitudinal studies of rural India. See G. Parthasarathy, "A South Indian Village after Two Decades," EW, 12 January 1963; Kumudini Dandekar and Vaijayanti Bhate, "Socio-Economic Change during Three Five-Year Plans," *Artha Vijnana,* Vol. 17, No. 4, 1975; Robert W. Bradnock, "Agricultural Development in Tamil Nadu: Two Decades of Land Use Changes at Village Level," in Tim P. Bayliss-Smith and Sudhir Wanmali, eds., *Understanding Green Revolutions: Agrarian Change and Development Planning in South Asia* (Cambridge: Cambridge University Press, 1984).
5. These studies are summarized in M. L. Dantwala, *Poverty in India: Then and Now* (Madras: Macmillan India, 1971); and M. Mukherjee, N. Bhattacharya, and G. S. Chatterjee, "Poverty in India: Measurement and Amelioration," in Vadilal Dagli, ed., *Twenty-Five Years of Independence—A Survey of Indian Economy* (Bombay: Vora, 1973). Dandekar and Rath's study was first published in *Economic and Political Weekly* in January 1971.
6. J. P. Naik, "Education," in S. C. Dube, ed., *India since Independence: Social Report on India, 1947–1972* (New Delhi: Vikas, 1977); Amrik Singh, "Twenty-Five Years of Indian Education: An Assessment," in Jag Mohan, ed., *Twenty-Five Years of Indian Independence* (New Delhi: Vikas, 1973).
7. "Indian Economic Policy and Performance: A Framework for a Progressive Society" (1973), in Jagdish N. Bhagwati, *Essays in Development Economics* (Cambridge, Mass.: M.I.T. Press, 1985).
8. Anon., "Mummy Knows Best," *Thought,* 2 October 1971.
9. *Thought,* 5 May 1971; D. R. Rajagopal, "Sanjay Gandhi," *Illustrated Weekly of India,* 11 July 1971.
10. Letter of 2 February 1971, Indira Gandhi Correspondence, P. N. Haksar Papers, NMML.
11. *Current,* 28 July 1973.
12. *Star,* 12 August 1973, clipping in Subject File No. 93, P. N. Haksar Papers, Third Instalment, NMML.
13. Ibid., note of 29 June 1971.
14. See notes and correspondence in Subject Files Nos. 242 and 243, P. N. Haksar Papers, Third Instalment, NMML.
15. Unless otherwise stated, this section is based on the synthesis report of those seventy-five studies: *Status of Women in India* (New Delhi: Indian Council of Social Science Research, 1974). Many of the data quoted there, and here, come from the 1971 census of India.

16. D. R. Gadgil, *Women in the Working Force in India* (London: Asia Publishing House, 1965); Bina Agarwal, "Women, Poverty, and Agricultural Growth in India," *Journal of Peasant Studies*, Vol. 13, No. 2, 1985–1986.

17. Radha Kumar, *The History of Doing: An Illustrated Account of Movements for Women's Rights and Feminism in India, 1860–1990* (New Delhi: Kali for Women, 1993), ch. 6.

18. For more details, see P. G. K. Pannikar and C. R. Soman, *Health Status of Kerala* (Trivandrum: Centre for Development Studies, 1984).

19. Ronald J. Herring, "Abolition of Landlordism in Kerala: A Redistribution of Privilege," *Economic and Political Weekly, Review of Agriculture*, June 1980; P. Radhakrishnan, "Land Reforms and Changes in Land System: Study of a Kerala Village," *Economic and Political Weekly, Review of Agriculture*, September 1982.

20. See *Lok Sabha Debates*, 30 November 1971.

21. Justice K. S. Hegde, "Perspectives of the Indian Constitution," Rajendra Prasad Memorial Lecture, Bharatiya Vidya Bhavan Bombay, March 1972; copy in Subject File No. 220, P. N. Haksar Papers, Third Instalment, NMML.

22. Letter from Indira Gandhi to Jayaprakash Narayan of 9 June 1973 and his reply of 27 June 1973, both in Jayaprakash Narayan Papers, NMML.

23. A. G. Noorani, "Crisis in India's Judiciary," *Imprint*, January 1974.

24. Malhotra, *Indira Gandhi*, pp. 152–153, etc.

25. *Thought*, 1 January 1972.

26. Ibid., 8 July 1972.

27. *Current*, 8 July 1972; *Thought*, 23 September 1972.

28. The minutes of these talks are unavailable, but for clues about what might have been discussed, see Subject Files Nos. 183 and 235, P. N. Haksar Papers, Third Instalment, NMML.

29. These paragraphs on Nagaland in the early 1970s are based on reports in the Kohima weekly *Citizens Voice*. Issues are in Box VIII, Pawsey Papers, Centre for South Asian Studies, Cambridge.

30. *Thought*, 2 March 1974.

31. See Ajit Bhattacharjea, *Unfinished Revolution: A Political Biography of Jayaprakash Narayan* (New Delhi: Rupa, 2004), pp. 193ff.

32. The previous three paragraphs draw on Ghanshyam Shah, "Revolution, Reform, or Protest? A Study of the Bihar Movement," *Economic and Political Weekly*, 9, 16, and 23 April 1977.

33. The correspondence between Narayan and Mrs. Gandhi, very rich but unexplored by their biographers, is in the Jayaprakash Narayan Papers, NMML. The correspondence between JP and Nehru—also less intensely mined than it might have been—is scattered between this collection and the Brahmananda Papers, also at the NMML.

34. Quoted in Bhattacharjea, *Unfinished Revolution*, pp. 205–206.

35. See reports in Subject File No. 272, Jayaprakash Narayan Papers, Third Instalment, NMML.

36. English translation of speech in *Everyman's Weekly*, 22 June 1974.

37. Robert Jay Lifton, *Revolutionary Immortality: Mao Tse Tung and the Cultural Revolution* (Harmondsworth: Penguin, 1967). I offer this comparison knowing that it will be dismissed both by Marxists, who will see JP as a lily-livered re-

formist in comparison with Mao, and by the Gandhians, who will profess shock at the lumping together of a man of non-violence with one known to have caused so many deaths.

38. Anon., "Railway Strike in Retrospect," *Economic and Political Weekly*, 18 January 1975.
39. S. Nihal Singh, *Indira's India: A Political Notebook* (Bombay: Nachiketa, 1978), pp. 215–216.
40. George Perkovich, *India's Nuclear Bomb: The Impact on Global Proliferation* (Berkeley: University of California Press, 1999), pp. 170–180; *Thought*, 25 May 1974; Aziz Ahmad (foreign minister of Pakistan) to Horace Alexander, 15 June 1974, in Alexander Papers, Friends House, Euston.
41. These paragraphs are based on the letters between Mrs. Gandhi and JP in the Jayaprakash Narayan Papers, NMML.
42. Bhattacharjea, *Unfinished Revolution*, pp. 211f; *Everyman's Weekly*, 21 September 1974.
43. See correspondence between Acharya Ramamurti and JP in Subject File No. 273, Jayaprakash Narayan Papers, Third Instalment, NMML.
44. Letter of 14 October 1974, in Subject File No. 277, Jayaprakash Narayan Papers, NMML. Patil's letter—to which JP's reply, if there was one, is untraceable— is reminiscent of the warnings uttered along these lines in the Constituent Assembly by his great fellow Maharashtrian, B. R. Ambedkar.
45. Bhattacharjea, *Unfinished Revolution*, pp. 216–217.
46. *Everyman's Weekly*, 16 and 23 November 1974.
47. See B. S. Das, *The Sikkim Saga* (New Delhi: Vikas, 1983).
48. Letter to JP dated 18 July 1974 from M. Shah, Adoni, Kurnool District, A.P., in Subject File No. 273, Jayaprakash Narayan Papers, Third Instalment, NMML.
49. See statements in Subject File No. 272, Jayaprakash Narayan Papers, Third Instalment, NMML.
50. For a sampling of the former view, see *Everyman's Weekly*, 1974–1975; for the latter view, see *Illustrated Weekly of India* for the same period.
51. Frank, *Indira*, p. 368; Christopher Andrew and Vasili Mitrokhin, *The World Was Going Our Way: The KGB and the Battle for the World* (New York: Basic Books, 2005), pp. 322–323.
52. Unless otherwise indicated, the rest of this section is based on reports and comments in *Indian Express*, 1 February to 21 March 1975.
53. Anon., "The South Poses a Problem for JP," *Everyman's Weekly*, 4 May 1975.
54. Granville Austin, *Working a Democratic Constitution: The Indian Experience* (New Delhi: Oxford University Press, 1999), pp. 314–316.
55. *Indian Express*, 20 March 1975.
56. Unless otherwise stated, the rest of this section is based on reports in *Indian Express*, 10 to 28 June 1975.
57. Prashant Bhushan, *The Case That Shook India* (New Delhi: Vikas, 1978), pp. 98ff.
58. Ibid., p. 94.
59. Quoted in Dom Moraes, *Indira Gandhi* (Boston: Little, Brown, 1980), p. 220.
60. Danial Latifi, "Indira Gandhi Case Revisited," undated typescript in Subject File No. 225, P. N. Haksar Papers, Third Instalment, NMML.

CHAPTER 22: AUTUMN OF THE MATRIARCH

1. *Democracy and Discipline: Speeches of Shrimati Indira Gandhi* (New Delhi: Minstry of Information and Broadcasting, 1975), pp. 1–2.
2. The note is reproduced in Pupul Jayakar, *Indira Gandhi: An Intimate Biography* (New York: Pantheon, 1993), pp. 202–203.
3. K. R. Malkani, *The Midnight Knock* (New Delhi: Vikas, 1978), p. 37.
4. *Democracy and Discipline*, pp. 18–19, 61, etc. This volume prints eleven interviews given in the first three months of the emergency—almost one a week, by a prime minister never known to be overfond of the press.
5. See D. V. Gandhi, comp., *Era of Discipline: Documents on Contemporary Reality* (New Delhi: Samachar Bharati, 1976), p. 254.
6. *Consolidating National Gains: Speeches of Shrimati Indira Gandhi* (New Delhi: Ministry of Information and Broadcasting, 1976), p. 29. The speech was originally delivered in Hindi; I have used the official translation.
7. Joe Elder, "Report on Visit to India. August 11–22, 1975," in File No. 78, Horace Alexander Papers, Friends House, Euston.
8. Ibid., Sharada Prasad to S. K. De, 16 September 1975, in File No. 78, Horace Alexander Papers, Friends House, Euston.
9. P. N. Dhar, *Indira Gandhi, the "Emergency," and Indian Democracy* (New Delhi: Oxford University Press, 2000), pp. 307–311.
10. Narayan to Sheikh Abdullah, 23 September 1975, reprinted in M. G. Devasahayam, *India's Second Freedom—An Untold Saga* (New Delhi: Siddharth, 2004), pp. 351–354.
11. For the circumstances of JP's release, see ibid., chs. 29 and 30.
12. See table reproduced in Gangadharan, Koshy, and Radhakrishnan, *The Inquisition: Revelations before the Shah Commission* (New Delhi: Path, 1978), p. 260.
13. Note of 14 January 1976, in "Emergency File," Hari Dev Sharma Papers, NMML.
14. Indira Gandhi to Verrier Elwin, 14 January 1963, letter in the possession of the Elwin family, Shillong.
15. See Mehta, *Portrait of India*, pp. 545–546.
16. Austin, *Working a Democratic Constitution*, pp. 319–324.
17. Ibid., pp. 334–341.
18. *New York Times*, 30 April 1976.
19. Austin, *Working a Democratic Constitution*, pp. 373–374. See also Nani Palkhivala, "Reshaping the Constitution," *Illustrated Weekly of India*, 4 July 1976.
20. "Notes on a Meeting with Indira Gandhi, 1, Safdarjung Road, 14 March 1976," in MSS. Eur. F. 236/269, OIOC.
21. See the detailed list of forbidden subjects in Sajal Basu, ed., *Underground Literature during Indian Emergency* (Calcutta: Minerva Associates, 1978), pp. 102–114.
22. Prakash Ananda, *A History of the Tribune* (New Delhi: Tribune Trust, 1986), pp. 165–166.
23. Ram Krishan Sharma to Penderel Moon, 25 November 1975, in MSS. Eur. F. 230/36, OIOC.
24. *Guardian*, 2 August 1976.

25. John Dayal and Ajay Bose, *The Shah Commission Begins* (New Delhi: Orient Longman, 1978), p. 208; Michael Henderson, *Experiment with Untruth: India under Emergency* (Delhi: Macmillan India, 1977), p. 89.
26. G. S. Bhargava, *The Press in India: An Overview* (New Delhi: National Book Trust, 2005), pp. 53, etc.
27. Dayal and Bose, *Shah Commission*, pp. 280–293; Henderson, *Experiment with Untruth*, p. 89.
28. See K. K. Birla, *Indira Gandhi: Reminscences* (New Delhi: Vikas, 1987), pp. 50–51.
29. Bhargava, *The Press in India*, pp. 65–66.
30. Quoted in Ved Mehta, *The New India* (Harmondsworth, Penguin, 1978), pp. 63–64.
31. Report by Jonathan Dimbleby in the *Sunday Times*, reprinted in Amiya Rao and B. G. Rao, eds., *The Press She Could Not Whip: Emergency in India as Reported by the Foreign Press* (Bombay: Popular Prakashan, 1977), pp. 20–21.
32. Malhotra, *Indira Gandhi*, p. 182.
33. Report by J. Anthony Lukacs in the *New York Times*, reprinted in Rao and Rao, *The Press She Could Not Whip*, pp. 186–198.
34. See Basu, *Underground Literature*, pp. 7–11.
35. P. G. Mavalankar, *"No, Sir": An Independent M. P. Speaks during the Emergency* (Ahmedabad: Sannistha Prakashan, 1979), pp. 20–25, 29–30, etc.
36. *Economist*, 24 January 1976. This is almost certainly an overestimate, based on figures supplied by the underground newspaper *Satya Samachar*.
37. *Satya Samachar*, 20 September 1976, in "Emergency File," Hari Dev Sharma Papers, NMML.
38. Translated by Sugata Srinivasaraju, and printed as an epigraph to his translation of Chi Srinivasaraju's *Phoenix and Four Other Mime Plays* (Bangalore: Navakarnataka, 2005).
39. Basu, *Underground Literature*, pp. 27, 29, 65; Henderson, *Experiment with Untruth*, p. 21.
40. These paragraphs on George Fernandes's activities during the emergency are principally based on C. G. K. Reddy, *Baroda Dynamite Conspiracy: The Right to Rebel* (New Delhi: Vision, 1977). See also "Emergency File," Hari Dev Sharma Papers, NMML; and Snehalata Reddy, *A Prison Diary* (Mysore: Karnataka State Human Rights Committee, 1977).
41. Henderson, *Experiment with Untruth*, p. 27.
42. I regret that I cannot provide a precise reference for this story. I cannot remember where I first heard or read it, whether from a friend who knew Kripalani or in an obituary printed in the newspapers when he died. Like so many remarkable characters who figure in these pages, Kripalani has yet to find a biographer.
43. "The Emergency: A Needed Shock," *Time*, 27 October 1975.
44. *Sydney Morning Herald*, 1 September 1976.
45. *Times*, 3 and 14 July 1976.
46. "Indira Gandhi's Year of Failure," *Observer*, 27 June 1975. (Editorial.)
47. The only serviceable biography of Sanjay Gandhi remains Vinod Mehta, *The Sanjay Story* (New Delhi: Vikas, 1978).

48. The interview is reprinted in full in Uma Vasudev, *Two Faces of Indira Gandhi* (New Delhi: Vikas, 1977), pp. 193–208. Vasudev, who conducted the interview, was the editor of *Surge*.

49. Ibid., pp. 108–110; Dhar, *Indira Gandhi*, pp. 325–329.

50. *Illustrated Weekly of India*, 25 January 1976.

51. Ibid., 15 August, 14 October, and 7 and 14 November 1976.

52. Dayal and Bose, *Shah Commission*, pp. 189, 229; Mehta, *The Sanjay Story*, p. 139.

53. Janardhan Thakur, *All the Prime Minister's Men* (New Delhi: Vikas, 1977), p. 57; Satyindra Singh, "Pleasing the Crown Prince," *Sunday Pioneer*, 25 June 2000; Mehta, *The Sanjay Story*, pp. 87, 97, 165.

54. Mehta, *The Sanjay Story*, p. 81.

55. See Emma Tarlo, *Unsettling Memories: Narratives of India's "Emergency"* (Delhi: Permanent Black, 2003), pp. 80–82, 98, and map after p. 148.

56. Jagmohan, *Island of Truth* (New Delhi: Vikas, 1978), pp. 9–10, 182–183, etc.

57. Mehta, *The Sanjay Story*; Thakur, *All the Prime Minister's Men*; and Vasudev, *The Two Faces*, all deal at some length with this coterie and its doings.

58. Tarlo, *Unsettling Memories*, p. 140.

59. This account of the incident at Turkman Gate is principally based on John Dayal and Ajoy Bose, *For Reasons of State: Delhi under Emergency* (Delhi: Ess Ess, 1977), ch. 2. See also Mehta, *The Sanjay Story*, pp. 90–95; and Inder Mohan, "Turkman Gate, Sanjay Gandhi, and Tihar Jail," *PUCL Bulletin*, Vol. 5, No. 8, August 1985. Dayal and Bose, as well as Mehta, write that Jagmohan's determination to clear Turkman Gate was in part motivated by the fact that the residents were Muslims—he saw them, apparently, as Pakistani fifth columnists. Jagmohan's own account of the incident is in *Island of Truth*, pp. 144–149.

60. Mohammad Yunus, *Persons, Passions, and Politics* (New Delhi: Vikas, 1980), pp. 251–252.

61. *Satya Samachar*, 12 June 1976, in "Emergency File," Haridev Sharma Papers, NMML.

62. There is an extensive literature on this subject, to which the summary here by no means does justice. For an introduction to the complex issues involved, see Pravin Visaria, "Population Policy," *Seminar*, March 2002.

63. *Illustrated Weekly of India*, 15 August 1976.

64. Mehta, *The Sanjay Story*, p. 112.

65. Ibid., pp. 117–129; Tarlo, *Unsettling Memories*, pp. 80–82, 98, 140, 150–151.

66. Lee I. Schlesinger, "The Emergency in an Indian Village," *Asian Survey*, Vol. 17, No. 7, July 1977.

67. *Satya Samachar*, 26 September 1976; news bulletin of *Lok Sangharsh Samiti* dated 23 November 1976, both in "Emergency File," Hari Dev Sharma Papers, NMML.

68. Basu, *Underground Literature*, p. 36; Gangadharan et al., *Inquisition*, pp. 130–133.

69. The locus classicus of this view is the book by her former secretary P. N. Dhar on the emergency. But the argument haunts virtually all the biographies of Mrs. Gandhi. See Dhar, *Indira Gandhi*, as well as the biographies by Jayakar, Malhotra, Moraes, and Vasudev.

70. *Times*, 26 August 1976.

71. John Grigg, "Tryst with Despotism," *Spectator*, 21 August 1976.
72. See the correspondence between Alexander and Mrs. Gandhi in File No. 78, Horace Alexander Papers, Friends House, Euston.
73. Levin's articles are reprinted in full in Rao and Rao, *The Press She Could Not Whip*, pp. 124–131, 268–276.
74. Dhar, *Indira Gandhi*, p. 344.
75. Henderson, *Experiments with Untruth*, p. 153; Kuldip Nayar, *The Judgement: Inside Story of the Emergency in India* (New Delhi: Vikas, 1977), p. 55.
76. A. M. Rosenthal, "Father and Daughter: A Remembrance," *New York Times*, 1 November 1984.
77. See Jawaharlal Nehru, *Glimpses of World History*, 4th ed. (London: Linsday Drummon, 1949; originally published 1934).

CHAPTER 23: LIFE WITHOUT THE CONGRESS

1. S. Devadas Pillai, ed., *The Incredible Elections, 1977: A Blow-by-Blow Document as Reported in the Indian Express* (Bombay: Popular Prakashan, 1977), pp. 19–22, 37–38, 43.
2. Ibid., pp. 74–76, 107–111.
3. *Illustrated Weekly of India*, 6 March 1977.
4. Bhattacharjea, *Unfinished Revolution*, pp. 282–283.
5. Pillai, *The Incredible Elections*, pp. 196, 198, 237, 244–245, 247.
6. Inder Malhotra, "The Campaign That Was," *Illustrated Weekly of India*, 20 March 1977; Javed Alam, *Domination and Dissent: Peasants and Politics* (Calcutta: Mandira, 1985), pp. 63, 65, 98, 168–169.
7. Pillai, *The Incredible Elections*, pp. 419–422.
8. S. L. M. Prachand, *The Popular Upsurge and the Fall of Congress* (Chandigarh: Abhishek, 1977).
9. See Theodore P. Wright, Jr., "Muslims and the 1977 Indian Election: A Watershed?" *Asian Survey*, Vol. 17, No. 12, December 1977.
10. Indira Gandhi to Fory Nehru, 17 April 1977, copy in Pupul Jayakar Papers, Mumbai.
11. Khushwant Singh, "Editor's Page," *Illustrated Weekly of India*, 27 March 1977.
12. See Janardhan Thakur, *All the Janata Men* (New Delhi: Vikas, 1979), p. 148.
13. *Himmat*, 30 June 1978.
14. *New York Times*, 22 March 1977, and *Washington Post*, 19 April 1977, both quoted in Baldev Raj Nayar, "India and the Super Powers: Deviation or Continuity in Foreign Policy?" *Economic and Political Weekly*, 23 July 1977.
15. Ajit Bhattacharjea, "Janata's Foreign Policy," *Himmat*, 30 December 1977.
16. See press clippings on Carter's visit in File No. 77, Horace Alexander Papers, Friends House, Euston.
17. *Times*, 7 November 1977.
18. "When Zia Complimented Vajpayee," *New Indian Express*, 21 February 1999.
19. *Himmat*, 4 November 1977.
20. Ibid., 20 January 1978.
21. K. A. Abbas, *Janata in a Jam?* (Bombay: Jaico, 1978), p. 84.

22. Ajit Roy, "West Bengal: Not a Negative Vote," *Economic and Political Weekly*, 2 July 1977.

23. Sunil Sengupta, "West Bengal Land Reforms and the Agrarian Scene," *Economic and Political Weekly, Review of Agriculture*, June 1981; Atul Kohli, *The State and Poverty in India: The Politics of Reform* (Cambridge: Cambridge University Press, 1987), ch. 3; Prabir Kumar De, *The Politics of Land Reform: The Changing Scene in Rural Bengal* (Calcutta: Minerva, 1994).

24. Subramanian, *Ethnicity and Populist Mobilization*, pp. 283–286; K. Mohandas, *MGR: The Man and the Myth* (Bangalore: Panther, 1992), pp. 11–12, 33–34.

25. *Guardian*, 12 November 1977.

26. D. D. Thakur, *My Life and Years in Kashmiri Politics* (Delhi: Konark, 2005), p. 277.

27. Shamim Ahmed Shamim, "Kashmir," *Seminar*, April 1978. See also Mir Qasim, *My Life and Times* (New Delhi: Allied, 1992), pp. 154–155.

28. Gilbert Etienne, *India's Changing Rural Scene, 1963–1979* (Delhi: Oxford University Press, 1982).

29. See Martin Doornbos and K. N. Nair, eds., *Resources, Institutions, and Strategies: Operation Flood and Indian Dairying* (New Delhi: Sage, 1990); and Shanti George, *Operation Flood: An Appraisal of Current Indian Dairy Policy* (Delhi: Oxford University Press, 1985).

30. Ashutosh Varshney, *Democracy, Development, and the Countryside: Urban-Rural Struggles in India* (Cambridge: Cambridge University Press, 1998), ch. 4.

31. See Varshney, *Democracy*; and Ashok Mitra, *Terms of Trade and Class Relations* (London: Frank Cass, 1977).

32. Neerja Chowdhury, "Sharpening the Battle Lines," *Himmat*, 23 March 1979; Harry W. Blair, "Rising Kulaks and Backward Classes in Bihar: Social Change in the Late 1970s," *Economic and Political Weekly*, 12 January 1980.

33. Kalpana Sharma, "Bihar—The Ungovernable State?" and Rajiv Shankar, "Why Bihar Remains Poor," *Himmat*, 6 October 1978.

34. Sachidananda, "Bihar's Experience," *Seminar*, November 1979.

35. Arun Sinha, "Class War, Not 'Atrocities' Against Harijans," *Economic and Political Weekly*, 10 December 1977; Pravin Sheth, "In the Countryside," *Seminar*, November 1979.

36. Atyachar Virodh Samiti, "The Marathwada Riots: A Report," *Economic and Political Weekly*, 12 May 1979.

37. Owen M. Lynch, "Rioting as Rational Action: An Interpretation of the April 1978 Riots in Agra," *Economic and Political Weekly*, 28 November 1981.

38. Jayakar, *Indira Gandhi*, pp. 253–254, 263–264.

39. Madhu Limaye, *Janata Party Experiment: An Insider's Account of Opposition Politics* (Delhi: B. R. Publishing, 1994), Vol. 1, p. 451.

40. *New York Times*, 30 October 1977.

41. *Himmat*, 10 March 1978.

42. James Manor, "Pragmatic Progressives in Regional Politics: The Case of Devaraj Urs," *Economic and Political Weekly*, Annual No., February 1980.

43. Ramesh Chandran, "The Battle for Chikmaglur," *Illustrated Weekly of India*, 5 November 1978.

44. Austin, *Working a Democratic Constitution*, pp. 463–464.
45. This account of the conflicts within Janata and the party's split is based on Arun Gandhi, *The Morarji Papers: Fall of the Janata Government* (New Delhi: Vision, 1983); Limaye, *Janata Party Experiment*, Vol. 2; Terence J. Byres, "Charan Singh, 1902–1987: An Assessment," *Journal of Peasant Studies*, Vol. 15, No. 2, 1987–1988; and *Himmat*, 1978 and 1979.
46. *Opinion*, 16 October 1979.
47. Indira Gandhi to Fory Nehru, 17 April 1977, in Jayakar Papers, Mumbai. Jayakar, *Indira Gandhi*, p. 303, quotes this letter but leaves out the crucial last sentence.
48. *Himmat*, 20 July 1979.
49. Jag Parvesh Chandra, *Verdict on Janata* (New Delhi: Metropolitan, 1979), pp. 26, 96; Thakur, *All the Janata Men*, pp. 148–150.
50. *Himmat*, 6 January and 10 February 1978.
51. Sharad Karkhanis, quoted in Gandhi, *The Morarji Papers*, pp. 97–98.
52. Austin, *Working a Democratic Constitution*, pp. 403–404.
53. *Illustrated Weekly of India*, 6 March 1977.
54. This account is based on Austin, *Working a Democratic Constitution*, pp. 409–430. See also Soli Sorabjee, "Repairing the Constitution: The Job Remains," *Himmat*, 23 March 1979.
55. Kumar, *The History of Doing*, especially chs. 6 to 8; Chhaya Datar, *Waging Change: Women Tobacco Workers in Nipani Organise* (New Delhi: Kali for Women, 1989).
56. For details, see Ramachandra Guha, *How Much Should a Person Consume? Environmentalism in India and the United States* (Berkeley: University of California Press, 2006), ch. 2, "The Indian Road to Sustainability."
57. This account is based on my own interactions with these groups over the past three decades. Unfortunately, there is no history of the civil liberties movement in modern India, and there are no studies of its most important groups—such as the People's Union for Civil Liberties and the People's Union for Democratic Rights, both based in Delhi; the pioneering Association for the Protection of Democratic Rights, based in Calcutta; the Committee for the Protection of Democratic Rights, based in Bombay; and the Andhra Pradesh Civil Liberties Committee, based in Hyderabad. Dr. Sitarama Kakarala of the National Law School in Bangalore is currently completing a book on the last-named group.
58. Anil Sadgopal and Shyam Bahadur "Namra," eds., *Sangharh aur Nirman: Shankar Guha Niyogi aur Unka Naye Bharat ka Sapna* (Delhi: Rajkamal Prakashan, 1993). Niyogi was murdered by a hired assassin—hired, most likely, by local industrialists—in 1992. The title of this book translates as "Struggle and Construction: Shankar Guha Niyogi and His Dreams for a New India."
59. Robin Jeffrey, *India's Newspaper Revolution: Capitalism, Politics, and the Indian-Language Press, 1977–1999* (London: C. Hurst, 2000).

CHAPTER 24: DEMOCRACY IN DISARRAY

1. Walter Schwarz, "Two-Party Democracy Faces a Test Run," *Guardian*, 14 May 1977.

2. Clipping from *New York Times*, 4 April 1977; letter to S. K. De, dated 17 June 1977, both in Temp MSS. 577/81, Horace Alexander Papers, Friends House, Euston.

3. Ibid., Horace Alexander to Indira Gandhi, 8 April 1977.

4. These figures on seats and vote shares come from the statistical supplement to *Journal of Indian School of Political Economy*, Vol. 15, Nos. 1 and 2, 2003. This was part of a special issue, "Political Parties and Elections in Indian States: 1990–2003," ed. Suhas Palshikar and Yogendra Yadav.

5. Prabash Joshi, "And Not Even a Dog Barked," *Tehelka*, 2 July 2005; *India Today*, 1–15 January 1980.

6. See Mervyn Jones, *Chances: An Autobiography* (London: Verso, 1987), p. 271.

7. Moin Shakir, "Election Participation of Minorities and Indian Political System," *Economic and Political Weekly*, Annual No., February 1980.

8. Nalini Singh, "Elections As They Really Are," *Economic and Political Weekly*, 24 May 1980.

9. Bashiruddin Ahmad, "Trends and Options," *Seminar*, April 1980.

10. Typescript of interview with Bobby Harrypersadh, dated 31 May 1980, in Pupul Jayakar Papers, Mumbai.

11. *India Today*, 16–31 May 1980.

12. *Hindu*, 24 June 1980.

13. *Tribune*, 27 October 1980, copy in Pupul Jayakar Papers, Mumbai.

14. *India Today*, 16–31 August 1980.

15. M. V. Kamath, "Why Rajiv Gandhi?" *Illustrated Weekly of India*, 31 May 1981.

16. *India Today*, 1–15 December 1981.

17. These paragraphs on the Festival of India are based on clippings and correspondence in MSS. Eur. F. 215/232, OIOC.

18. Rajni Bakshi, *The Long Haul: The Bombay Textile Workers Strike* (Bombay: BUILD Documentation Centre, 1986); Meena Menon and Neera Adarkar, *One Hundred Years, One Hundred Voices: The Millworkers of Girangaon—An Oral History* (Calcutta: Seagull, 2004). The strike, in effect, killed the city's textile industry, with most factories being declared "sick" by the owners or the state. These mill lands are now the subject of much controversy in Bombay; citizens want them to be used for working-class housing or for parks, and real estate speculators hope to turn them into luxury apartments and shopping malls.

19. Jan Myrdal, *India Waits* (Hyderabad: Sangam, 1984).

20. Mahasveta Devi, "Contract Labour or Bonded Labour?" *Economic and Political Weekly*, 6 June 1981.

21. Darryl D'Monte, "In Santhal Parganas with Sibu Soren," *Illustrated Weekly of India*, 8 April 1979; Darryl D'Monte, "The Jharkhand Movement," *Times of India*, 13 and 14 March 1979. For wider historical overviews of the Jharkhand question, see Sajal Basu, *Jharkhand Movement: Ethnicity and Culture of Silence* (Shimla: Indian Institute of Advanced Study, 1984); Susan B. C. Devalle, *Discourses of Ethnicity: Culture and Protest in Jharkhand* (New Delhi: Sage, 1992); Nirmal Sengupta, ed., *Jharkhand: Fourth World Dynamics* (Delhi: Authors Guild, 1982).

22. See Shankar Guha Niyogi, "Chattisgarh and the National Question," in *Na-*

tionality Question in India: Seminar Papers (Hyderabad: Andhra Pradesh Radical Students Union, 1982).

23. Bertil Lintner, *Land of Jade: A Journey through Insurgent Burma* (Bangkok: White Lotus, 1990), pp. 83–84 and passim.

24. "Report of a Fact-Finding Team," in Luingam Luithui and Nandita Haksar, eds., *Nagaland File: A Question of Human Rights* (New Delhi: Lancer International, 1984), ch. 21.

25. Personal communication from P. Sainath, who was covering Andhra Pradesh politics at the time.

26. TOI, 30 March 1982; *Sunday*, 16 January 1983.

27. *Sunday*, 12 December 1982.

28. TOI, 10 January 1983.

29. M. Ramchandra Rao, "NTR—Victim of His Own Charisma?" *Janata*, 24 April 1983.

30. *Indian Express*, 15 September 1983.

31. Myron Weiner, *Sons of the Soil: Migration and Ethnic Conflict in India* (Princeton, N. J.: Princeton University Press, 1978), ch. 3; Alaka Sarmah, *Immigration and Assam Politics* (Delhi: Ajanta, 1999); Anindita Dasgupta, "Denial and Resistance: Sylhet Partition Refugees in Assam," *Contemporary South Asia*, Vol. 10, No. 3, 2001.

32. Amalendu Guha, "Little Nationalism Turned Chauvinist: Assam's Anti-Foreigner Upsurge 1979–1980," *Economic and Political Weekly*, Annual No., October 1980.

33. Sanjib Baruah, *India against Itself: Assam and the Politics of Nationality* (Philadelphia: University of Pennsylvania Press, 1999), especially ch. 5; Tilotomma Misra, "Assam and the National Question," in *Nationality Question in India*; Udayon Misra, *The Periphery Strikes Back: Challenges to the Nation-State in Assam and Nagaland* (Shimla: Indian Institute of Advanced Study, 2000), chs. 4 and 5.

34. Chaitanya Kalbagh, "The North-East: India's Bangladesh?" *India Today*, 1–15 May 1980.

35. *Economic Times*, 3 November 1980.

36. Quoted in TOI, 30 July 1980.

37. See T. S. Murty, *Assam: The Difficult Years—A Study of Political Developments in 1979–1983* (New Delhi: Himalayan, 1983).

38. Devdutt, "Assam Agitation: It Is Not the End of the Tunnel," *Financial Express*, 8 October 1980.

39. A wide-ranging and still valuable collection of essays on Sikh political history is Paul Wallace and Surendra Chopra, eds., *Political Dynamics of Punjab* (Amritsar: Guru Nanak Dev University Press, 1981).

40. There are various versions of the Anandpur Sahib Resolution. I have here used the text as authenticated by Sant Harcharan Singh Longowal and printed in *White Paper on the Punjab Agitation* (New Delhi: Government of India Press, 1984), pp. 67–90.

41. In this account of the Punjab dispute, I have not thought it necessary to give a note for every fact. Among the books and articles I have found helpful are Robin Jeffrey, *What's Happening to India: Punjab, Ethnic Conflict, and the Test for Federalism*, 2nd ed. (Basingstoke: Macmillan, 1994); Chand Joshi,

Bhindranwale: Myth and Reality (New Delhi: Vikas, 1984); Anup Chand Kapur, *The Punjab Crisis* (Delhi: S. Chand, 1985); Ram Narayan Kumar, *The Sikh Unrest and the Indian State* (Delhi: Ajanta, 1997); Mark Tully and Satish Jacob, *Amritsar: Mrs. Gandhi's Last Battle* (London: Pan, 1985); Satinder Singh, *Khalistan: An Academic Analysis* (New Delhi: Amar Prakashan, 1982); Harjot Oberoi, "Sikh Fundamentalism: Translating History into Theory," in Martin E. Marty and R. Scott Appleby, eds., *Fundamentalisms and the State* (Chicago, Ill.: University of Chicago Press, 1996); Hamish Telford, "The Political Economy of Punjab: Creating Space for Sikh Militancy," *Asian Survey*, Vol. 32, No. 11, November 1992.

42. For a provocative analysis of Bhindranwale's sermons, see Mark Juergensmeyer, "The Logic of Religious Violence: The Case of the Punjab," *Contributions to Indian Sociology*, New Series, Vol. 22, No. 1, 1988.

43. Kagal, quoted in Paul Wallace, "Religious and Ethnic Politics: Political Mobilization in Punjab," in Francine R. Frankel and M. S. A. Rao, eds., *Dominance and State Power in India: Decline of a Social Order* (Delhi: Oxford University Press, 1990), Vol. 2, p. 451.

44. See profile of Bhindranwale in *India Today*, 1–15 October 1981; and Murray J. Leaf, *Song of Hope: The Green Revolution in a Panjab Village* (New Brunswick, N.J: Rutgers University Press, 1984), ch. 7, "Religion."

45. Clipping in MSS. Eur. F. 230/36, OIOC.

46. *Indian Express*, 21 September 1981.

47. The verdicts, respectively, of Tully and Jacob, *Amritsar*, p. 71; and Joshi, *Bhindranwale*, p. 90.

48. For an insightful contemporary account of the pressures on the Akalis to become more extreme, see Gopal Singh, "Socio-Economic Bases of the Punjab Crisis," *Economic and Political Weekly*, 7 January 1984.

49. Interview with Madhu Jain in *Sunday*, 4 September 1983; Rajinder Puri, "Remembering 1984," *National Review*, November 2003.

50. Anne Vaugier-Chatterjee, *Historie politique du Pendjab de 1947 à nos jours* (Paris: L'Harmattan, 2001), pp. 158f.

51. On the significance of the Akal Takht, see Madanjit Kaur, *The Golden Temple: Past and Present* (Amritsar: Guru Nanak Dev University Press, 1983), pp. 268–270.

52. Paul Wallace, "Religious and Secular Politics in Punjab: The Sikh Dilemma in Competing Political Systems," in Wallace and Chopra, *Political Dynamics of Punjab*, pp. 1–2.

53. M. J. Akbar, *Riot after Riot: Reports on Caste and Communal Violence in India* (New Delhi: Penguin India, 1988).

54. Achyut Yagnik, "Spectre of Caste War," *Economic and Political Weekly*, 28 March 1981; Pradip Kumar Bose, "Social Mobility and Caste Violence: A Study of the Gujarat Riots," *Economic and Political Weekly*, 18 April 1981.

55. Quoted in Moin Shakir, "An Analytical View of Communal Violence," in Asghar Ali Engineer, ed., *Communal Riots in Post-Independence India*, 2nd ed. (Hyderabad: Sangam, 1991), p. 95.

56. For individual studies of these riots, see Akbar, *Riot after Riot*; Engineer, *Communal Riots*; the reports by civil liberties groups; and articles published in *Economic and Political Weekly* during these years.

57. The following paragraphs, identifying these themes, are based on my own reading of the literature. See also Asghar Ali Engineer, "An Analytical Study of the Meerut Riots," *PUCL Bulletin*, Vol. 3, No. 1, January 1983.

58. George Mathew, "Politicisation of Religion: Conversions to Islam in Tamil Nadu," *Economic and Political Weekly*, 19 June 1982.

59. See M. J. Akbar, *India: The Siege Within* (Harmondsworth: Penguin, 1985), pp. 197ff.

60. Balraj Puri, "Who Is Playing with National Interest?" *Economic and Political Weekly*, 11 February 1984.

61. Lieutenant General K. S. Brar, *Operation Blue Star: The True Story* (New Delhi: UBS, 1987), pp. 35–37. Since Brar led the operation, and since all journalists had been evacuated beforehand, his book is essential in any reconstruction of Operation Bluestar. However, it should be read along with Tully and Jacob, *Amritsar*, which is based on interviews with eyewitnesses and survivors.

62. Brar, *Operation Blue Star*, p. 91.

63. Ibid., pp. 126–127.

64. Lieutenant General J. S. Aurora, "If Khalistan Comes, the Sikhs Will Be the Losers," in Patwant Singh and Harji Malik, eds., *Punjab: The Fatal Miscalculation* (New Delhi: Patwant Singh, 1985), p. 133.

65. J. S. Grewal, *The Sikhs of the Punjab*, 2nd ed. (Cambridge: Cambridge University Press, 1999), p. 227.

66. Shahnaz Anklesaria, "Fall-out of Army Action: A Field Report," *Economic and Political Weekly*, 28 July 1984.

67. Sten Widmalm, "The Rise and Fall of Democracy in Jammu and Kashmir, 1975–1989," in Amrita Basu and Atul Kohli, eds., *Community Conflicts and the State in India* (Delhi: Oxford University Press, 1988); B. K. Nehru, *Nice Guys Finish Second* (New Delhi: Viking, 1997), pp. 627–641.

68. *Week*, 26 August 1984.

69. Indira Gandhi to Erna Sailer, 20 October 1984, copy in Jayakar Papers, Mumbai.

70. Pupul Jayakar, "31 October," typescript, Jayakar Papers, Mumbai.

71. This account of the anti-Sikh riots in Delhi is based on two works deservedly regarded as classics: Anon., *Who Are the Guilty? Report of a Joint Inquiry into the Cause and Impact of the Riots in Delhi from 31 October to 10 November* (Delhi: PUDR and PUCL, 1984); Uma Chakravarti and Nandita Haksar, *The Delhi Riots: Three Days in the Life of a Nation* (New Delhi; Lancer International, 1987). I have also drawn on conversations with friends and colleagues who were active in providing relief after the riots.

72. "The Violent Aftermath," *India Today*, 30 November 1984.

73. "Indira Gandhi's Bequest," *Economic and Political Weekly*, 3 November 1984.

74. Daniel Sutherland, "India Seen Facing Era of Uncertainty," *New York Times*, 1 November 1984; Henry Trewhitt, "U.S. Fears Assassination May Bring Chaos in India, Rivalry in South Asia," *Sun*, 1 November 1984.

CHAPTER 25: THIS SON ALSO RISES

1. TOI, 4 December 1984.

2. Ibid., 14 December 1984.

3. Praful Bidwai, "What Caused the Pressure Build-Up," ibid., 26 December 1984.

4. Radhika Ramaseshan, "Profit against Safety," *Economic and Political Weekly*, 22–29 December 1984; *Indian Express*, 5 December 1984. The tragedy at Bhopal has had a tortured afterlife that is still continuing. The survivors and their families have been ranged against the government (charged with providing insufficient medical relief) and Union Carbide (charged with paying paltry amounts of compensation).

5. Hari Jaisingh, *India after Indira: The Turbulent Years, 1984–1989* (New Delhi: Allied, 1989), pp. 19–20; *Business India*, 17–30 December 1984.

6. Harish Khare, "The State Goes Macho," *Seminar*, January 1985.

7. Mani Shankar Aiyar, *Remembering Rajiv* (Calcutta: Rupa, 1992), p. 53.

8. Harish Puri, "Punjab: Elections and After," *Economic and Political Weekly*, 5 October 1985; *India Today*, 15 September and 15 October 1985.

9. *India Today*, 15 September 1985 and 15 January 1986; *Sunday*, 29 December–4 January 1986.

10. See Lalchungnunga, *Mizoram: Politics of Regionalism and National Integration* (New Delhi: Reliance, 2002), App. D; and *Sunday*, 20–26 July 1986.

11. "Mizoram: Quest for Peace," *India Today*, 31 July 1986.

12. S. S. Gill, *The Dynasty: A Political Biography of the Premier Ruling Family of Modern India* (New Delhi: HarperCollins India, 1996), pp. 394–395.

13. *Business India*, 31 December 1984–13 January 1985.

14. Shubhabrata Bhattacharya, "Rajiv Gandhi's Discovery of India," *Sunday*, 22–28 September 1985.

15. Judgement in Criminal Appeal No. 103 of 1981, decided on 23 April 1985 (Mohd. Ahmed Khan versus Shah Bano and Others), *Supreme Court Cases* (1985), 2 SCC, pp. 556–574.

16. Hutokshi Doctor, "Shah Bano: Brief Glory," *Imprint*, May 1986.

17. Danial Latifi, "Muslim Law," in Alice Jacob, ed., *Annual Survey of Indian Law*, Vol. 21 (New Delhi: Indian Law Institute, 1985).

18. *Lok Sabha Debates*, 23 August 1985.

19. Ritu Sarin, "Shah Bano: The Struggle and the Surrender," *Sunday*, 1–7 December 1985.

20. *Statesman*, 19 December 1985. (Editorial.)

21. *Indian Express*, 21 December 1985.

22. Vasudha Dhagamwar, "After the Shah Bano Judgement–II," TOI, 11 February 1986.

23. *Eve's Weekly*, 29 March–4 April 1986.

24. R. D. Pradhan, *Working with Rajiv Gandhi* (New Delhi: HarperCollins India, 1995), pp. 130–131.

25. Peter Van der Veer, *Gods on Earth: The Management of Religious Experience and Identity in a North Indian Pilgrimage Centre* (London: Athlone, 1988), especially ch. 1; Peter Van der Veer, " 'God Must Be Liberated': A Hindu Liberation Movement in Ayodhya," *Modern Asian Studies*, Vol. 21, No. 2, 1987. Ayodhya's sister town, Faizabad, gives its name to the district. The official who gave the verdict was technically the district judge of Faizabad.

26. Saifuddin Chowdhury, quoted in *Sunday*, 9–15 March 1986.

27. See articles by Neerja Chowdhury in *Statesman*, 20 April and 1 May 1986, re-

printed in A. G. Noorani, ed., *The Babri Masjid Question*, Vol. 1 (New Delhi: Tulika, 2003), pp. 260–266.

28. Inderjit Badhwar, "Hindus: Militant Revivalism," *India Today*, 31 May 1986.
29. Sant Ramsharaan Das of Banaras, writing in May 1989, quoted in Manjari Katju, *Vishwa Hindu Parishad and Indian Politics* (Hyderabad: Orient Longman, 2003), p. 73.
30. *India Today*, 15 March 1986; *Sunday*, 25–31 January 1987.
31. Rajni Bakshi, "The Rajput Revival," *Illustrated Weekly of India*, 1 November 1987.
32. This figure comes from David Page and William Crawley, *Satellites over South Asia: Broadcasting, Culture, and the Public Interest* (New Delhi: Sage, 2001), p. 56.
33. Arvind Rajagopal, *Politics after Television: Religious Nationalism and the Reshaping of the Indian Public* (Cambridge: Cambridge University Press, 2001), p. 84.
34. Sevanti Ninan, *Through the Magic Window: Television and Change in India* (New Delhi: Penguin Books India, 1995), pp. 6–8.
35. Philip Lutgendorf, "Ramayan: The Video," *Drama Review*, Vol. 34, No. 2, 1990, p. 128.
36. Robin Jeffrey, "Media Revolution and 'Hindu Politics' in North India, 1982–1999," *Himal*, July 2001. (Emphasis added.)
37. Interview in *Financial Express*, quoted in Supriya Roychowdhury, "State and Business in India: The Political Economy of Liberalization, 1984–1989," unpublished PhD dissertation, Department of Politics, Princeton University, pp. 100–101. See also Stanley A. Kochanek, "Regulation and Liberalization in India," *Asian Survey*, Vol. 26, No. 12, 1986.
38. See H. K. Paranjape, "New Lamps for Old! A Critique of the 'New Economic Policy,'" *Economic and Political Weekly*, 7 September 1985.
39. See reports in *India Today*, 15 March and 15 April 1985.
40. T. N. Ninan, "Rise of the Middle Class," *India Today*, 31 December 1985. See also "The Rising Affluence of the Middle Class," *Sunday*, 29 October–1 November 1986.
41. Roychowdhury, *State and Business in India*, pp. 73, 122.
42. T. N. Ninan and Jagannath Dubashi, "Dhirubhai Ambani: The Super Tycoon," *India Today*, 30 June 1985; T. N. Ninan, "Reliance: Under Pressure," *India Today*, 15 August 1986; Perez Chandra, "Reliance: The Man behind the Legend," *Business India*, 17–30 June 1985; Paranjoy Guha Thakurta, "The Two Faces of Dhirubhai Ambani," *Seminar*, January 2003.
43. "Crony Capitalism," *Sunday*, 2–8 October 1988; Teesta Setalvad, "Pawar, Politics, and Money," *Business India*, 10–23 July 1989; Sankarshan Thakur, "How Corrupt Is Bhajan Lal?" *Sunday*, 21–27 July 1985.
44. Indranil Banerjie, "The New Maharajahs," *Sunday*, 17–23 April 1988.
45. See Niraja Gopal Jayal, *Democracy and the State: Welfare, Secularism and Development in Contemporary India* (Delhi: Oxford University Press, 1999), pp. 46ff; "The Wretched of Kalahandi," *Sunday*, 19–25 January 1986.
46. R. Jagannathan, "Welcome to Hard Times," *Sunday*, 6–12 September 1987.
47. M. V. Nadkarni, *Farmers' Movements in India* (New Delhi: Allied, 1987);

"New Farmers' Movements in India," *Journal of Peasant Studies*, Special Issue, Vol. 21, No. 2, 1993–1994.

48. Vijay Naik and Shailaja Prasad, "On Levels of Living of Scheduled Castes and Scheduled Tribes," *Economic and Political Weekly*, 28 July 1984.

49. Tanka B. Subba, *Ethnicity, State, and Development: A Case Study of the Gorkhaland Movement in Darjeeling* (New Delhi: Har-Anand, 1992); "Peace in the Angry Hills?" *Sunday*, 24–30 July 1988.

50. *Sunday*, 27 August–2 September 1989; *India Today*, 15 September 1989; *Business India*, 26 June–9 July 1989.

51. *Sunday*, 25–31 January 1987 and 28 August–3 September 1988.

52. Shekhar Gupta, "Punjab Extremists: Calling the Shots," *India Today*, 28 February 1986.

53. See *India Today*, 30 April 1986 and 15 September 1988; and *Sunday*, 3–9 January 1986. The violation of human rights by the police in Punjab through the 1980s and 1990s is extensively documented in Ram Narayan Kumar et al., *Reduced to Ashes: The Insurgency and Human Rights in Punjab* (Kathmandu: South Asia Forum for Human Rights, 2003).

54. *Sunday*, 19–25 May 1985, 19–25 July 1987, and 20–26 March and 1–7 June 1988; *India Today*, 15 June and 31 December 1986.

55. Shekhar Gupta and Vipin Mudgal, "Operation Black Thunder: A Dramatic Success," *India Today*, 15 June 1988.

56. *India Today*, 30 November 1986.

57. Widmalm, "The Rise and Fall of Democracy in Jammu and Kashmir," pp. 167ff.

58. *Sunday*, 9–15 July 1989.

59. See, among other works, A. Jeyaratnam Wilson, *Sri Lankan Tamil Nationalism: Its Origins and Development in the Nineteenth and Twentieth Centuries* (London: C. Hurst, 2000); Sankaran Krishna, *Postcolonial Insecurities: India, Sri Lanka, and the Question of Nationhood* (Delhi: Oxford University Press, 2000).

60. Shekhar Gupta, "Operation Pawan: In a Rush to Vanquish," *India Today*, 31 January 1988.

61. Lieutenant General S. C. Sardeshpande, *Assignment Jaffna* (New Delhi: Lancer, 1992).

62. Krishna, *Postcolonial Insecurities*, p. 154 and passim.

63. See Gill, *Dynasty*, pp. 474–477.

64. *India Today*, 15 June 1989.

65. "The Ugly Indian," *Sunday*, 12–18 July 1987.

66. *Sunday*, 28 September–4 October 1988.

67. Nilanjan Mukhopadhyay, *The Demolition: India at the Crossroads* (New Delhi: HarperCollins India, 1994), pp. 260–262. See also Christophe Jaffrelot, *The Hindu Nationalist Movement and Indian Politics, 1925 to the 1990s* (New Delhi: Penguin India, 1999), pp. 383ff.

68. See People's Union for Democratic Rights, *Bhagalpur Riots* (New Delhi: PUDR, 1990).

69. Chitra Subramaniam, *Bofors: The Story behind the News* (New Delhi: Viking, 1993).

70. *India Today*, 31 March and 15 October 1988; *Sunday*, 30 October–5 November 1988.

71. This Defamation Bill is discussed in M. V. Desai, "The Indian Media," in Marshall M. Bouton and Philip Oldenburg, eds., *India Briefing, 1989* (Boulder, Colo.: Westview, 1989).

72. *India Today*, 15 January 1989.

73. *Sunday*, 12–18 March 1989.

74. Indranil Banerjie, "Mera Dynasty Mahan," *Sunday*, 1–7 October 1989.

75. See *India Today*, 31 October 1989; *Sunday*, 12–18 November 1989.

76. Vir Sanghvi, "A Vote for Change," *Sunday*, 3–9 December 1989.

77. *Sunday*, 16–22 June 1985.

78. Kewal Varma, "The Politics of V. P. Singh," *Sunday*, 19–25 April 1987.

79. T. S. Murty, *Assam: The Difficult Years: A Study of Political Developments in 1979–1983* (New Delhi: Himalayan, 1983), p. vi.

80. Lieutenant General R.S. Brar, *Operation Blue Star* (New Delhi: UBS, 1993), p. 4.

CHAPTER 26: RIGHTS

1. M. N. Srinivas, "Caste in Modern India," Presidential Address to the Section of Anthropology and Archaeology, *Proceedings of the Indian Science Congress, Calcutta, 1957*, Part 2, pp. 123–142.

2. The press reactions to his talk are discussed in M. N. Srinivas, *Caste in Modern India and Other Essays* (Bombay: Asia Publishing House, 1962), Introduction.

3. André Béteille, *Society and Politics in Modern India* (London: Athlone, 1991); Béteille, "Caste and Colonial Rule," *Hindu*, 4 March 2002.

4. The political assertion of the backward castes through the 1960s and 1970s is described in Christophe Jaffrelot, *India's Silent Revolution: The Rise of the Low Castes in North Indian Politics* (Delhi: Permanent Black, 2003). See also D. L. Sheth, "Secularisation of Caste and Making of New Middle Class," *Economic and Political Weekly*, 21–28 August 1999.

5. *Report of the Backward Classes Commission* (Delhi: Controller of Publications, 1980), Vol. 1, p. 57.

6. André Béteille, "Distributive Justice and Institutional Wellbeing," *Economic and Political Weekly*, Special No., March 1991; Dharma Kumar, "The Affirmative Action Debate in India," *Asian Survey*, Vol. 32, No. 3, March 1992; Norio Kondo, "The Backward Classes Movement and Reservation in Tamil Nadu and Uttar Pradesh: A Comparative Perspective," in Mushirul Hasan and Nariaki Nakazato, eds., *The Unfinished Agenda: Nation-Building in South Asia* (Delhi: Manohar, 2001).

7. Jaffrelot, *India's Silent Revolution*, pp. 345–347.

8. See Paranjoy Guha Thakurta and Shankar Raghuraman, *A Time of Coalitions: Divided We Stand* (New Delhi: Sage, 2004).

9. Surendra Malik, comp., *Supreme Court Mandal Commission Case, 1992* (Lucknow: Eastern, 1992), pp. 180, 196, 379, 387, 412, 424, etc.

10. "In Search of the Messiah," *Sunday*, 31 August–6 September 1988.

11. Jaffrelot, *India's Silent Revolution*, ch. 11.

12. Ghanshyam Shah, ed., *Dalits and the State* (New Delhi: Concept, 2002).

13. This account of Kanshi Ram and the rise of the BSP draws on Sudha Pai, *Dalit Assertion and the Unfinished Democratic Revolution: The Bahujan Samaj Party in Uttar Pradesh* (New Delhi: Sage, 2002); and Kanchan Chandra, *Why*

Ethnic Parties Succeed: Patronage and Ethnic Head Counts in India (Cambridge: Cambridge University Press, 2004), ch. 8.

14. Badri Narayan, "Heroes, Histories, and Booklets," *Economic and Political Weekly*, 13 October 2001.

15. Pai, *Dalit Assertion*, pp. 95–97; Shikha Trivedy, "Mayawati," essay to be published in a forthcoming volume on Indian women politicians edited by Malavika Singh.

16. James Cameron, *An Indian Summer* (London: Macmillan, 1974), p. 122.

17. André Béteille, "The Scheduled Castes: An Inter-Regional Perspective," *Journal of Indian School of Political Economy*, Vol. 12, Nos. 3 and 4, 2000.

18. Hugo Gorringe, *Untouchable Citizens: Dalit Movements and Democratisation in Tamil Nadu* (New Delhi: Sage, 2005), p. 112.

19. The posthumous political importance of Ambedkar awaits a serious scholarly analysis. For clues to how important he is to the Dalit consciousness today, see, among other works, Chandra Bhan Prasad, *Dalit Diary: 1999–2003* (Chennai: Navayana, 2004); and Fernando Franco, Jyotsna Macwan, and Suguna Ramanathan, *Journeys to Freedom: Dalit Narratives* (Kolkata; Samya, 2004).

20. See S. Viswanathan, *Dalits in Dravidian Land* (Chennai: Navayana, 2005). See also Haruka Yanagisawa, *A Century of Change: Caste and Irrigated Lands in Tamilnadu, 1860s–1970s* (New Delhi: Manohar, 1996), ch. 7.

21. People's Union for Democratic Rights, *Jhajhar Dalit Lynching: The Politics of Cow Protection in Haryana* (New Delhi: PUDR, 2003).

22. See Mark Juergensmeyer, *Religion as Social Vision: The Movement against Untouchability in Twentieth-Century Punjab* (Berkeley: University of California Press, 1982); Harish K. Puri, "Scheduled Castes in Sikh Community: A Historical Perspective," *Economic and Political Weekly*, 28 June 2003.

23. Ronki Ram, "Limits of Untouchability: Dalit Assertion and Caste Violence in Punjab," in Harish K. Puri, ed., *Dalits in Regional Context* (Jaipur: Rawat, 2004); Surinder S. Jodhka and Prakash Louis, "Caste Tensions in Punjab: Talhan and Beyond," *Economic and Political Weekly*, 12 July 2003.

24. Shashi Bhushan Singh, "Limits to Power: Naxalism and Caste Relations in a South Bihar Village," *Economic and Political Weekly*, 16 July 2005.

25. Mukul Sharma, "The Untouchable Present: Everyday Life of Musahars in North Bihar," *Economic and Political Weekly*, 4 December 1999.

26. Bela Bhatia, "The Naxalite Movement in Central Bihar," PhD thesis, Faculty of Social and Political Studies, Cambridge University, 2000. See also Bhatia, "The Naxalite Movement in Central Bihar," *Economic and Political Weekly*, 9 April 2005.

27. See *Labour File*, Vol. 4, Nos. 5 and 6, 1998, p. 39.

28. Bhatia, "The Naxalite Movement," pp. 134, 87. (My translation.)

29. C. P. Surendran, "On the Run with the Ranvir Sena," *Sunday Times of India*, 26 February 1999.

30. See *Hindu*, 14 November 2005.

31. People's Union for Democratic Rights, *Satpura ki Ghati: People's Struggle in Hoshangabad* (New Delhi: PUDR, 1992).

32. Rahul, "The Bhils: A People under Threat," *Humanscape*, Vol. 8, No. 8, September 2001; and *Budhan: The Denotified and Nomadic Tribes Rights Action Group Newsletter*, various issues.

33. Amita Baviskar, *In the Belly of the River: Adivasi Battles over "Development" in the Narmada Valley* (New Delhi: Oxford University Press, 1995); Jean Dreze, Meera Samson, and Satyajit Singh, eds., *The Dam and the Nation* (New Delhi: Oxford University Press, 1998).

34. *India Today*, 31 December 1999.

35. Manoj Joshi, *The Lost Rebellion: Kashmir in the Nineties* (New Delhi: Penguin, 1999), chs. 1 and 2. See also Tavleen Singh, *Kashmir: A Tragedy of Errors* (New Delhi: Viking, 1995).

36. Smita Gupta, "The Rise and Rise of Terrorism in Kashmir," *Telegraph*, 21 April 1990.

37. Schofield, *Kashmir in Conflict*, p. 147.

38. These headlines are from various news reports filed in the Centre for Education and Documentation, Bangalore.

39. *Telegraph*, 27 May 1990; Joshi, *The Lost Rebellion*, pp. 72–73.

40. Amnesty International, "Urgent Action" Reports Nos. UA 102 and 108, 1991; copies in the files of the Centre for Education and Documentation, Bangalore.

41. V. M. Tarkunde et al., "Report on Kashmir Situation," in Asghar Ali Engineer, ed., *Secular Crown on Fire: The Kashmir Problem* (Delhi: Ajanta, 1992), pp. 210–223.

42. See Chandana Bhattacharjee, *Ethnicity and Autonomy Movement: Case of Bodo-Kacharis of Assam* (New Delhi: Vikas, 1996); Sudhir Jacob George, "The Bodo Movement in Assam: Unrest to Accord," *Asian Survey*, Vol. 34, No. 10, October 1994.

43. Sanjoy Hazarika, *Strangers of the Night: Tales of War and Peace from India's Northeast* (New Delhi: Penguin, 1995), pp. 167–226. See also Sanjib Baruah, "The State and Separatist Militancy in Assam: Winning a Battle and Losing the War?" *Asian Survey*, Vol. 34, No. 10, October 1994.

44. Anindita Dasgupta, "Tripura's Brutal Cul de Sac," *Himal*, December 2001.

45. Bhagat Oinam, "Patterns of Ethnic Conflict in the North-East: A Study on Manipur," *Economic and Political Weekly*, 24 May 2003; U. A. Shimray, "Socio-Political Unrest in the Region Called North-East India," *Economic and Political Weekly*, 16 October 2004.

46. These quotes are from interviews with Muivah in *Times of India*, 2 March 2005, and *Hindu*, 29 April 2005.

47. See J. B. Lama, "Naga Peace: Will the Factions Fall In?" *Statesman*, 18 May 1999.

48. Seema Hussain, "Manipur: Burning Anger," *Week*, 1 July 2001.

49. R. K. Ranjan Singh, "Refugee Problem in Manipur: A Smouldering Volcano," *Grassroots Options*, November–December 1996; Deepak K. Singh, "Stateless Chakmas in Arunachal Pradesh: From 'Rejected People' to 'Unwanted Migrants,'" *Social Sciences Research Journal*, Vol. 9, No. 1, 2001; Walter Fernandes, "IMDT Act and Immigration in North-Eastern India," *Economic and Political Weekly*, 23 July 2005.

50. Rishang Keishing, quoted in Ved Marwah, *Uncivil Wars: Pathology of Terrorism in India* (New Delhi: HarperCollins India, 1995), p. 295.

51. N. Lokendra Singh, "Women, Family, Society, and Politics in Manipur (1970–2000)," *Contemporary India*, Vol. 1, No. 4, 2002.

52. People's Union for Democratic Rights, *Why the AFSPA Must Go* (New Delhi: PUDR, 2005); *Telegraph*, 16 July 2004 (front-page photographs); Sushanta Talukdar, "Manipur on Fire," *Frontline*, 10 September 2004.

53. Nirmala Ganapathy, "Billionth Baby Put through Hell," *New Indian Express*, 12 May 2000.

54. Mahendra K. Premi, "The Missing Girl Child," *Economic and Political Weekly*, 26 May 2001; P. N. Mari Bhatt, "On the Trail of 'Missing' Indian Females," *Economic and Political Weekly*, 21 and 28 December 2002.

55. Ravinder Kaur, "Across-Region Marriages: Poverty, Female Migration, and the Sex Ratio," *Economic and Political Weekly*, 19 June 2004; Prem Chowdhry, "Crisis of Masculinity in Haryana: The Unmarried, the Unemployed, and the Aged," *Economic and Political Weekly*, 3 December 2005.

56. Data collated and analysed in Preet Rustogi, "Significance of Gender-Related Development Indicators: An Analysis of Indian States," *Indian Journal of Gender Studies*, Vol. 11, No. 3, 2004.

57. Although it was published more than a decade ago, Radha Kumar's *A History of Doing* remains the best single guide to the history of the Indian women's movement. One must also mention the magazine *Manushi*, now in its thirtieth year of publication, and the publishing house Kali for Women, which has brought out more than 100 books on themes as varied as the law, the environment, social protest, and the economy.

58. Quoted in *New Indian Express*, 30 August 2005. See also Bina Agarwal, *A Field of One's Own: Gender and Land Rights in South Asia* (Cambridge: Cambridge University Press, 1994); Asha Nayar-Basu, "Of Fathers and Sons," *Telegraph*, 11 October 2005.

59. Anon., "A Blueprint for Mizoram," *Grassroots Options*, Monsoon 1999; Sudipta Bhattacharjee, "How to Be Thirteenth Time Lucky," *Telegraph*, 30 June 1999; Nitin Gokhale, "Meghna Naidu in Aizawl," *Tehelka*, 9 October 2004.

60. Sarabjit Singh, *Operation Black Thunder: An Eyewitness Account of Terrorism in Punjab* (New Delhi: Sage, 2002), especially chs. 22 through 30.

61. See Anne Vaugier-Chatterjee, "Strains on Punjab Governance: An Assessment of the Badal Government (1997–1999)," *International Journal of Punjab Studies*, Vol. 7, No. 1, 2000.

62. "The Dynamic Sikhs," *Outlook*, 29 March 1999.

63. Singh, *Operation Black Thunder*, p. 338.

CHAPTER 27: RIOTS

1. Guru Golwalkar, "Total Prohibition of Cow-Slaughter," *Hitavada*, 26 October 1952. (Emphasis in original.)

2. Richard H. Davis, "The Iconography of Rama's Chariot," in David Ludden, ed., *Making India Hindu: Religion, Community, and the Politics of Democracy in India*, 2nd ed. (New Delhi: Oxford University Press, 1996).

3. Ibid., p. 46.

4. Jaffrelot, *Hindu Nationalist Movement*, pp. 420–422.

5. See Paul Brass, *The Production of Hindu-Muslim Violence in Contemporary India* (New Delhi: Oxford University Press, 2003), pp. 110–123.

6. See Katju, *Vishva Hindu Parishad*, p. 65.

7. Madhav Godbole, *Unfinished Innings: Recollections and Reflections of a Civil Servant* (Hyderabad: Orient Longman, 1996), pp. 344–353.

8. P. V. Narasimha Rao, *Ayodhya: 6 December 1992* (New Delhi: Viking, 2006), pp. 99–100.

9. Godbole, *Unfinished Innings*, p. 363.

10. Quoted in *Sunday*, 6–12 December 1992.

11. This account of the demolition of the Babri Masjid is based mainly on Dilip Awasthi, "A Nation's Shame," *India Today*, 31 December 1992. But see also Harinder Baweja, "Today, 10 Years Ago: What Really Happened," *Asian Age*, 6 December 2002.

12. The conversation was reported in *Sunday*, 13–19 December 1992.

13. K. R. Malkani, *The Politics of Ayodhya and Hindu-Muslim Relations* (New Delhi: Har-Anand, 1993), pp. 3–4.

14. Quoted in Venkitesh Ramakrishnan, "The Wrecking Crew," *Frontline*, 1 January 1993.

15. Arun Shourie, "The Buckling State," in Jitendra Bajaj, ed., *Ayodhya and the Future India* (Madras: Centre for Policy Studies, 1993), pp. 47–70.

16. Francine R. Frankel, *India's Political Economy, 1947–2004: The Gradual Revolution*, 2nd ed. (New Delhi: Oxford University Press, 2005), pp. 714–715.

17. See "Bloody Aftermath," *India Today*, 31 December 1992.

18. Clarence Fernandez and Naresh Fernandes, "The Winter of Discontent," in Dileep Padgaonkar, ed., *When Bombay Burned* (New Delhi: UBSPD, 1993), pp. 12–41.

19. Kalpana Sharma, "Chronicle of a Riot Foretold," in Sujata Patel and Alice Thorner, *Bombay: Metaphor for Modern India* (Delhi: Oxford University Press, 1999), p. 277.

20. Translated from Marathi and quoted in Purandare, *The Sena Story*, p. 369.

21. Clarence Fernandez and Naresh Fernandes, "A City at War with Itself," in Padgaonkar, *When Bombay Burned*, pp. 42–104; Sharma, "Chronicle," pp. 278–286.

22. "Bombay Has Lost Its Character," *Afternoon Dispatch and Courier*, 10 January 1993, reprinted in "Busybee," *When Bombay Was Bombed: Best of 1992–1993* (Bombay: Oriana, 2004).

23. Quoted in Lise McKean, *Divine Enterprise: Gurus and the Hindu Nationalist Movement* (Chicago, Ill.: University of Chicago Press, 1996), p. 315.

24. Asoka Mehta, *The Political Mind of India* (Bombay: Socialist Party, 1952), p. 38.

25. Taya Zinkin and Maurice Zinkin, "The Indian General Elections," *World Today*, Vol. 8, No. 5, May 1952.

26. Susanne Hoeber and Lloyd I. Rudolph, "The Centrist Future of Indian Politics," *Asian Survey*, Vol. 20, No. 6, June 1980.

27. See the evidence and testimony in Peter Gottshcalk, *Beyond Hindu and Muslim: Multiple Identities in Narratives from Village India* (New Delhi: Oxford University Press, 2001).

28. Khadar Mohiuddin, "Birthmark," in Velcheru Narayana Rao, ed. and trans., *Twentieth Century Telugu Poetry: An Anthology* (New Delhi: Oxford University Press, 2002), pp. 221–227.

29. D. R. Goyal, *Rashtriya Swayamsewak Sangh*, 2nd ed., (New Delhi: Ra-

dhakrishna Prakashan, 2000), pp. 17–18. For a fuller expositon of this ideology, as it were, from the horse's mouth, see M. S. Golwalkar, *Bunch of Thoughts* (Bangalore: Vikrama Prakashan, 1966).

30. On the growth of the RSS since 1947, see, among other works, Tapan Basu et al., *Khaki Shorts and Saffron Flags: A Critique of the Hindu Right* (Hyderabad: Orient Longman, 1993); Thomas Blom Hansen, *The Saffron Wave: Democracy and Hindu Nationalism in India* (New Delhi: Oxford University Press, 1999); Pralay Kanungo, "Hindutva's Entry into a 'Hindu Province': Early Years of RSS in Orissa," *Economic and Political Weekly*, 2 August 2003; Nandini Sundar, "Teaching to Hate: RSS's Pedagogical Programme," *Economic and Political Weekly*, 17 April 2004.

31. See Thomas Blom Hansen, *Urban Violence in India: Identity Politics, "Mumbai," and the Postcolonial City* (Delhi: Permanent Black, 2001), p. 85.

32. Neerja Chowdhury, "Sonia Takes a Political Dip at the Kumbh," *New Indian Express*, 20 January 2001.

33. On this last incident, see *Telegraph*, 25 January 1999.

34. On the latter question, see P. N. Mari Bhatt and A. J. Francis Zavier, "Role of Religion in Fertility Decline: The Case of Indian Muslims," *Economic and Political Weekly*, 29 January 2005.

35. See Ashish Sharma, "Losing Their Religion," *Express Magazine*, 9 July 2000.

36. This paragraph draws on, among other works, M. K. A. Siddiqui, *Muslims in Free India: Their Social Profile and Problems* (New Delhi: Institute of Objective Studies, 1998); Abusaleh Shariff, "On the Margins: Muslims in a State of Socio-Economic Decline," TOI, 22 October 2004; Yogendra Sikand, "Lessons of the Past: Madrasa Education in South Asia," *Himal*, Vol. 14, No. 11, November 2001; Yogendra Sikand, "Countering Fundamentalism: The Ban on SIMI," *Economic and Political Weekly*, 6 October 2001; Arjumand Ara, "Madrasas and Making of Muslim Identity in India," *Economic and Political Weekly*, 3 January 2004.

37. Navnita Chadha Behera, *State, Identity, and Violence: Jammu, Kashmir, and Ladakh* (New Delhi: Manohar, 2000), p. 179.

38. Sonia Jabbar, "Spirit of Place," in *Civil Lines 5: New Writing from India* (New Delhi: IndiaInk, 2001), pp. 28–29.

39. Reports in *Telegraph*, 1 April 1990; *Frontline*, 14–27 April 1990; *Illustrated Weekly of India*, 17 June 1990; TOI, 11 February 1991. See also Alexander Evans, "A Departure from History: Kashmiri Pandits, 1990–2001," *Contemporary South Asia*, Vol. 11, No. 1, 2002.

40. See Praveen Swami, "The Nadimarg Outrage," *Frontline*, 25 April 2003.

41. This paragraph is based on Hasan Abbas, *Pakistan's Drift into Extremism: Allah, the Army, and America's War on Terror* (Armonk, N.Y.: Sharpe, 2005), chs. 9 and 10. The quote comes from Tariq Ali, *The Clash of Fundamentalisms: Crusades, Jihads, and Modernity* (London: Verso, 2002), p. 196.

42. Yoginder Sikand, "Changing Course of Kashmiri Struggle: From National Liberation to Islamist Jihad," *Economic and Political Weekly*, 20 January 2001.

43. Pamela Constable, "Selective Truths," in *Guns and Roses: Essays on the Kargil War* (New Delhi: HarperCollins India, 1999), p. 52; Hafiz Mohammed Saeed, interviewed by Amir Mir in *Outlook*, 23 July 2001.

44. See Anil Nauriya, "The Destruction of a Historic Party," *Mainstream*, 17 August 2002; Praveen Swami, "The Killing of Lone," *Frontline*, 21 June 2002.

45. See news report in TOI, 24 January 1990; Joshua Hammer, "Srinagar Dispatch," *New Republic*, 12 November 2001.

46. Reeta Chowdhuri-Tremblay, "Differing Responses to the Parliamentary and Assembly Elections in Kashmir's Regions, and State-Societal Relations," in Paul Wallace and Ramashray Roy, eds., *India's 1999 Elections and Twentieth-Century Politics* (New Delhi: Sage, 2003).

47. Prabhu Ghate, "Kashmir: The Dirty War," *Economic and Political Weekly*, 26 January 2002.

48. Muzamil Jaleel, "I Have Seen My Country Die," *Telegraph*, 26 May 2002.

49. James Buchan, "Kashmir," *Granta*, No. 57, Spring 1997, p. 66.

50. See Noorani, ed., *The Babri Masjid Question*, Vol. 2, pp. 197ff.

51. See Jyoti Punwani, "The Carnage at Godhra," in Siddharth Varadarajan, ed., *Gujarat: The Making of a Tragedy* (New Delhi: Penguin, 2002).

52. Ashutosh Varshney, *Ethnic Conflict and Civic Life: Hindus and Muslims in India* (New Delhi: Oxford University Press, 2002), especially pp. 229–230, 240–241, 275–277; Jan Breman, "Ghettoization and Communal Politics: The Dynamics of Inclusion and Exclusion in the Hindutva Landscape," in Ramachandra Guha and Jonathan Parry, eds., *Institutions and Inequalities: Essays for André Béteille* (New Delhi: Oxford University Press, 1999); Udit Chaudhuri, "Gujarat: The Riots and the Larger Decline," *Economic and Political Weekly*, 2–9 November 2002.

53. Nandini Sundar, "A License to Kill: Patterns of Violence in Gujarat," in Varadarajan, ed., *Gujarat*; Achyut Yagnik and Suchitra Sheth, *The Shaping of Modern Gujarat: Plurality, Hindutva, and Beyond* (New Delhi: Penguin, 2005), ch. 11; report by Ashis Chakrabarti, *Telegraph*, 18 May 2002.

54. Bela Bhatia, "A Step Back in Sabarkantha," *Seminar*, May 2002.

55. Anand Soondas, "Gujarat's Children of a Lesser God," *Telegraph*, 13 March 2002; "Gujarat Villagers Set Terms for Muslims to Come Home," *New Indian Express*, 6 May 2002.

56. Varadarajan, *Gujarat*, pp. 22f. For a profile of Narendra Modi, see Sankarshan Thakur, "The Man Who Could Be Prime Minister," *Man's World*, December 2002.

57. *Frontline*, 1 January 1993; *Sunday*, 13–19 December 1992; *India Today*, 31 December 1992.

58. Michael S. Serrill, "India: The Holy War," *Time*, 21 December 1992.

59. *Times*, 7 and 8 December 1992.

60. Geoffrey Morehouse, "Chronicle of a Death Foretold," *Guardian*, 10 March 2001.

61. Paul R. Brass, *The Politics of India since Independence*, 2nd ed. (Cambridge: Cambridge University Press, 1994), pp. 353–354, 365–366, 348–349.

CHAPTER 28: RULERS

1. Anon., "After Nehru . . . ," EW, Special No. July 1958.

2. When, in a column in the newspaper *Hindu*, I quoted from this prescient essay, correspondents wrote in to suggest who the anonymous writer might be. One who read the essay when it first appeared speculated that the author might have been Nehru himself. Another (and in my view more likely) candidate is Penderel

Moon, the former ICS officer who worked with the government of India for a decade after independence before retiring to All Souls College, Oxford.

3. See M. P. Singh and Rekha Saxena, *India at the Polls: Parliamentary Elections in the Federal Phase* (Hyderabad: Orient Longman, 2003).

4. E. Sridharan, "Coalition Strategies and the BJP's Expansion, 1989–2004," *Commonwealth and Comparative Politics*, Vol. 43, No. 2, 2005.

5. See Rasheed Kidwai, *Sonia: A Biography* (New Delhi: Viking Penguin, 2003).

6. Harish Khare, "Reloading the Family Matrix," *Seminar*, June 2003.

7. E. Sridharan, "Electoral Coalitions in 2004 General Elections: Theory and Evidence," *Economic and Political Weekly*, 18 December 2004.

8. These paragraphs on the changes in the party system draw on, among other works, E. Sridharan, "The Fragmentation of the Indian Party System, 1952–1999: Seven Competing Explanations," in Zoya Hasan, ed., *Parties and Party Politics in India* (New Delhi: Oxford University Press, 2002); Mahesh Rangarajan, "Congress in Crisis," *Seminar*, January 2003; M. J. Akbar, "Prop and Proposition," *Asian Age*, 13 July 2003; Giuseppe Flora, "The Crisis of 1989–1992: Some Reflections," in K. N. Bakshi and F. Scialpi, eds., *India 1947–1997: Fifty Years of Independence* (Rome: Istituto Italiano per l'Africa e l'Oriente, 2002).

9. Robin Jeffrey, " 'No Party Dominant': India's New Political System," *Himal*, March 2002, p. 41.

10. These studies are summarized in Sunil Jain, "Vote Vajpayee," *Business Standard*, 16 February 2004.

11. This account is based on S. Guhan, *The Cauvery River Water Dispute: Towards Conciliation* (Madras: Frontline, 1993), and Ramaswamy R. Iyer, *Water: Perspectives, Issues, Concerns* (New Delhi: Sage, 2003), ch. 3.

12. Ramaswamy R. Iyer, "Punjab Water Imbroglio," *Economic and Political Weekly*, 31 July 2004; Satyapal Dang, "Amrinder Singh and River Water Dispute," *Mainstream*, 4 September 2004.

13. See D. Bandyopadhyay, Saila K. Ghosh, and Buddhadeb Ghosh, "Dependency versus Autonomy: Identity Crisis of India's Panchayats," *Economic and Political Weekly*, 20 September 2003.

14. For details, see Mahi Pal, "Panchayati Raj and Rural Governance: Experiences of a Decade," *Economic and Political Weekly*, 10 January 2004.

15. See T. M. Thomas Isaac and Richard W. Franke, *Local Democracy and Development: People's Campaign for Decentralized Planning in Kerala* (New Delhi: LeftWord, 2000); and Jos Chathukulam and M. S. John, "Five Years of Participatory Government in Kerala: Rhetoric and Reality," *Economic and Political Weekly*, 7 December 2002.

16. Rashmi Sharma, "Kerala's Decentralisation: Idea in Practice," *Economic and Political Weekly*, 6 September 2003; Pranab Bardhan and Dilip Mookherjee, "Poverty Alleviation Efforts of Panchayats in West Bengal," *Economic and Political Weekly*, 28 February 2004; Arild Engelsen Ruud, *Poetics of Village Politics: The Making of West Bengal's Rural Communism* (New Delhi: Oxford University Press, 2003); Nirmal Mukherji and D. Bandopadhyay, "New Horizons for West Bengal Panchayats," in Amitava Mukherjee, ed., *Decentralization: Panchayats in the Nineties* (New Delhi: Vikas, 1994).

17. There is a growing academic literature on these questions. See, inter alia, the

essays by Niraja Gopal Jayal, Bishnu N. Mohapatra, and Sudha Pai in "Democracy and Social Capital," *Economic and Political Weekly*, Special Issue, 24 February 2001; S. Sumathi and V. Sudarsen, "What Does the New Panchayat System Guarantee: A Case Study of Pappapatti," *Economic and Political Weekly*, 20 August 2005.

18. See the critique of Nehru's views in Jaswant Singh, *Defending India* (Bangalore: Macmillan India, 1999), pp. 29, 39, 42-43, 57-58, etc.

19. Stephen P. Cohen, *India: Emerging Power* (New Delhi: Oxford University Press, 2001), pp. 144-145.

20. Anupam Srivastava, "India's Growing Missile Ambitions: Assessing the Technical and Strategic Dimensions," *Asian Survey*, Vol. 40, No. 2, 2000.

21. George Perkovich, *India's Nuclear Bomb: The Impact on Global Proliferation* (Berkeley: University of California Press, 1999), pp. 364-376.

22. Ibid., p. 412.

23. Quoted in Raj Chengappa, *Weapons of Peace: The Secret Story of India's Quest to Be a Nuclear Power* (New Delhi: HarperCollins India, 2000), pp. 51-52.

24. See Paul R. Dettman, *India Changes Course: Golden Jubilee to Millennium* (Westport, Conn.: Praeger, 2001), pp. 41f.

25. Interview in *Newsline* (Karachi), June 1998.

26. Bhumitra Chakma, "Toward Pokharan II: Explaining India's Nuclearisation Process," *Modern Asian Studies*, Vol. 39, No. 1, 2005.

27. For the links between the tests of 1998 and India's wider ambitions, see Hilary Synnott, *The Causes and Consequences of South Asia's Nuclear Tests*, Adelphi Paper 332 (London: International Institute for Strategic Studies, 1999); and Ashok Kapur, *Pokharan and Beyond: India's Nuclear Behaviour* (New Delhi: Oxford University Press, 2001). The arguments of the critics of India's nuclear ambitions are collected in M. V. Ramanna and C. Rammanohar Reddy, eds., *Prisoners of the Nuclear Dream* (Hyderabad: Orient Longman, 2003).

28. *India Today*, 1 March 1999.

29. On why and how Pakistan planned the Kargil operation, see Abbas, *Pakistan's Drift into Extremism*, pp. 169-174; Owen Bennett Jones, *Pakistan: Eye of the Storm* (New Delhi: Viking, 2002), pp. 87ff; Aijaz Ahmad, "The Many Roads to Kargil," *Frontline*, 16 July 1999.

30. Praveen Swami, *The Kargil War*, rev. ed. (New Delhi: LeftWord, 2000), pp. 10-1.

31. Rahul Bedi, "A Dismal Failure," in *Guns and Roses: Essays on the Kargil War* (New Delhi: HarperCollins India, 1999), p. 142.

32. The course of the Kargil war is described in Swami, *Kargil War*; Bedi, "Dismal Failure"; and Srinjoy Chowdhury, *Despatches from Kargil* (New Delhi: Penguin, 2000).

33. Abbas, *Pakistan's Drift into Extremism*, p. 174; interview with Nawaz Sharif in *India Today*, 26 July 2004.

34. See *Asian Age*, 4 July 1999; *Telegraph*, 9 July 1999; *Hindu*, 19 July 1999.

35. *Asian Age*, 6 July 1999; *Hindu*, 4 July 1999.

36. Sarabjit Pandher, "Spirit of Nationalism Eclipses Memories of [Operation] Bluestar," *Hindu*, 16 June 1999.

37. "Army Job Seekers Go Berserk," *Hindu*, 18 July 1999.

38. Sonia Jabbar, "Blood Soil: Chittisinghpora and After," in Urvashi Butalia, ed., *Speaking Peace: Women's Voices from Kashmir* (New Delhi: Kali for Women, 2002), pp. 226f.
39. There has been some dispute about the agents of the Chittisinghpora massacre. For the argument that the killers were recruited by Indian intelligence, which then sought to pin the blame on Pakistan, see Pankaj Mishra, *Temptations of the West: How to Be Modern in India, Pakistan and Beyond* (London: Picador, 2006), pp. 197ff. For the alternative point of view, namely, that the killers were militants who came in from Pakistan, see Praveen Swami, "Iron Veils: Reporting Sub-Continental Warfare in India," in Nalini Rajan, ed., *Practising Journalism: Values, Constraints, Implications* (New Delhi: Sage, 2005).

    My own assessment, that these were most likely freelancers from across the border, is guided, among other things, by a crucial piece of evidence provided by the survivors. This is that the killers spoke both Punjabi and Urdu. Now Urdu is spoken by many Muslims in the Indian State of Uttar Pradesh who, however, do not speak any Punjabi. And the only Punjabis who speak Urdu in the Indian state of Punjab would have had their schooling in that language before partition. They would now be at least seventy years of age, and presumably in no position to trek over high hills to effect a mass murder. On the other hand, there are millions of able-bodied young men in the Pakistan Punjab who speak both their mother tongue and the national language, Urdu.

    As this book must have made quite clear by now, the Indian state has been guilty of many criminal acts in Jammu and Kashmir. But the massacre of the Sikhs in Chittisinghpora does not appear to be among them.
40. See Atal Behari Vajpayee, "Musings from Kumarakom," *Hindu*, 2 January 2001.
41. *Indian Express*, 7 April 2005, lists major terrorist strikes.
42. *Himal South Asian*, June 2002; Michael Krepon, "No Easy Exits," *India Today*, 10 June 2002.
43. HT, 19 May 2002.
44. James Michael Lyngdoh, *Chronicle of an Impossible Election: The Election Commission and the 2002 Jammu and Kashmir Assembly Elections* (New Delhi: Penguin, 2004), pp. 129, 141–142, 149–150, 180–181, etc.
45. Rekha Chowdhury and Nagendra Rao, "Kashmir Elections 2002: Implications for Politics of Separatism," *Economic and Political Weekly*, 4 January 2003.
46. Quoted in TOI, 26 September 2003.
47. See HT, 20 June 2003.
48. Ibid., 30 January 2005; *New Sunday Express*, 30 January 2005.
49. *Hindu*, 17 May 2005.
50. Muzamil Jaleel, in *Indian Express*, 8 April 2005.
51. See "Politics as a Vocation," in Hans Gerth and C. Wright Mills, eds., *From Max Weber: Essays in Sociology* (New York: Oxford University Press, 1946).
52. For an overview of corruption in contemporary India, see Shiv Visvanathan and Harsh Sethi, eds., *Foul Play: Chronicles of Corruption* (New Delhi: Banyan, 1998).
53. B. S. Nagaraj, "Smokescreen Resort," *Indian Political Review*, July 2003.
54. Peter Ronald deSouza, "Democracy's Inconvenient Fact," *Seminar*, November

2004; Prem Shankar Jha, "Keep It Poll-ution Free," *Hindustan Times*, 2 January 2006; TOI (Bangalore), 21 January 2006.

55. *Sunday*, 2–9 March 1985.
56. Reetika Khera, "Monitoring Disclosures," *Seminar*, February 2004. My account of the criminalization of politics also draws on information supplied by Professor Trilochan Sastry, a founding member of the Association for Democratic Reforms, the group which filed the original PIL in the Supreme Court.
57. Samuel Paul and M. Vivekananda, "Holding a Mirror to the New Lok Sabha," *Economic and Political Weekly*, 6 November 2004.
58. For a vivid portrait of one notorious criminal in politics, the Bihari member of Parliament, Mohammad Shahabuddin, see Saba Naqvi Bhowmick, "The Saheb of Siwan: The Tale of an Indian Godfather," in *First Proof: The Penguin Book of New Writing from India 1* (New Delhi: Penguin, 2005).
59. Arild Engelsen Ruud, "Talking Dirty about Politics: A View from a Bengali Village," in C. J. Fuller and Veronique Bénéï, eds., *The Everyday State and Society in India* (New Delhi: Social Science, 2000), pp. 116–118.
60. *International Herald Tribune*, 19 November 2004.
61. Jorge Luis Borges, *The Total Library: Non-Fiction, 1922–1986*, ed. Elliot Weinberger, trans. Esther Allen, Jill Levine, and Elliot Weinberger (London: Penguin, 2001), p. 309; R. W. Southern, *Western Society and the Church in the Middle Ages* (Harmondsworth: Penguin, 1970), p. 154.
62. See Akhil Gupta, "Blurred Boundaries: Corruption and the Local State," originally published in *American Ethnologist*, and reprinted in Zoya Hasan, ed., *Politics and the State in India* (New Delhi: Sage, 2000); Jonathan Parry, "The 'Crises of Corruption' and 'The Idea of India,'" in Italo Pardo, ed., *Morals of Legitimacy: Between Agency and System* (Oxford: Berghahn, 2000).
63. Ashish Khetan, "Taint at the Top," *Tehelka*, 23 April 2005.
64. P. S. Appu, "The All India Services: Decline, Debasement, and Destruction," *Economic and Political Weekly*, 26 February 2005.
65. M. N. Buch to the prime minister of India, 15 March 2003. (I am grateful to Mr. Buch for sending me a copy of the letter.)
66. See Dasgupta, "Tripura's Brutal Cul de Sac."
67. *Grassroots Option*, February 1997.
68. Harish Khare, "Voting the Periphery Out," *Hindu*, 20 March 2004.
69. André Béteille, "The Executive and the Judiciary," *Hindu*, 8 May 2001.
70. These paragraphs on the judiciary are based on S. P. Sathe, *Judicial Activism in India: Transgressing Borders and Enforcing Limits*, 2nd ed. (New Delhi: Oxford University Press, 2002). The example of Madurai is from *New Indian Express*, 23 September 2003.
71. M. P. Singh, "To Govern or Not to Govern: The Dilemma of the New Indian Party System, 1989–1991," in M. P. Singh, ed., *Lok Sabha Elections 1989: Indian Politics in 1990s* (Delhi: Kalinga, 1992), p. 202.

CHAPTER 29: RICHES

1. Quoted in *Current*, 22 September 1954.
2. "The World This Week," *MysIndia*, 23 January 1955; "Towards Totalitarian-

ism," *MysIndia*, 8 May 1955; "A Fatal Economic Policy," *MysIndia*, 8 November 1953.

3. See Jagdish Bhagwati and Padma Desai, *India: Planning for Industrialization: Industrialization and Trade Policies since 1951* (London: Oxford University Press, 1970).

4. J. R. D. Tata, interviewed by Fatma Zakaria, TOI, 12 July 1981.

5. See Dani Rodrik and Arvind Subramanian, *From "Hindu Growth" to Productivity Surge: The Mystery of the Indian Growth Transition* (Washington, D.C.: National Bureau of Applied Economic Research, March 2004).

6. Anne O. Krueger and Sajjid Chinoy, "The Indian Economy in Global Context," in Anne O. Krueger, ed., *Economic Policy Reforms and the Indian Economy* (New Delhi: Oxford University Press, 2002). For an overview of the Indian economy on the eve of the reforms, see Bimal Jalan, ed., *The Indian Economy: Problems and Prospects* (New Delhi: Viking, 1992).

7. Arvind Panagriya, "Growth and Reforms during 1980s and 1990s," *Economic and Political Weekly*, 19 June 2004.

8. Ashok V. Desai, *My Economic Affair* (New Delhi: Wiley Eastern, 1993); Kaushik Basu, "Future Perfect?" HT, 5 May 2005.

9. Dennis J. Encarnation, *Dislodging Multinationals: India's Strategy in Comparative Perspective* (Ithaca, N.Y.: Cornell University Press, 1989), pp. 214–215, 225.

10. Nagesh Kumar, "Indian Software Industry Development: International and National Perspective," *Economic and Political Weekly*, 10 November 2001; Pradosh Nath and Amitava Hazra, "Configuration of Indian Software Industry," *Economic and Political Weekly*, 23 February 2002; Arun Shourie, "Ensuring IT Remains Indian Territory," *New Indian Express*, 3 January 2004.

11. AnnaLee Saxenian, "Bangalore: The Silicon Valley of Asia?" in Krueger, *Economic Policy Reforms*, p. 175.

12. Raj Chengappa and Malini Goyal, "Housekeepers to the World," *India Today*, 18 November 2002; "Outsourcing to India," *Economist*, 5 May 2001.

13. Saritha Rai, "Prayers Outsourced to India" and "U.S. Kids Outsource Homework to India," *New York Times*; reprinted in *Asian Age*, 14 June 2004 and 11 September 2005, respectively.

14. Shankkar Aiyar, "Made in India," *India Today*, 1 December 2003.

15. R. Nagaraj, "Foreign Direct Investment in India in the 1990s: Trends and Issues," *Economic and Political Weekly*, 26 April 2003.

16. Arvind Virmani, "India's External Reforms: Modest Globalisation, Significant Gains," *Economic and Political Weekly*, 9 August 2003.

17. This paragraph is based on Harish Damodaran, *India's New Capitalists* (London: Palgrave Macmillan, 2008).

18. E. Sridharan, "The Growth and Sectoral Composition of India's Middle Class: Its Impact on the Politics of Economic Liberalization," *India Review*, Vol. 3, No. 4, 2004.

19. See William Mazzarella, *Shovelling Smoke: Advertising and Globalization in Contemporary India* (Durham, N.C.: Duke University Press, 2003), pp. 74–76, 240, 258, etc.

20. Filippo Osella and Caroline Osella, *Social Mobility in Kerala: Modernity and Identity in Conflict* (London: Pluto, 2000), p. 127.

21. See, among other works, "Poverty Reduction in [the] 1990s," *Economic and Political Weekly*, Special Issue, 25–31 January 2003; K. Sundaram and Suresh D. Tendulkar, "Poverty in India in the 1990s: An Analysis of Changes in 15 Major States," *Economic and Political Weekly*, 5 April 2003; Angus Deaton, ed., *The Great Indian Poverty Debate* (New Delhi: Macmillan India, 2005).

22. Eduardo Galeano, "The Other Wall," *New Internationalist*, November 1989. (Galeano was actually writing of the Latin American city, which in these respects is of a piece with its Indian counterpart.)

23. See "Footloose Labour," *Seminar*, Special Issue, November 2003; Supriya Roy-Chowdhury, "Labour Activism and Women in the Unorganised Sector: Garment Export Industry in Bangalore," *Economic and Political Weekly*, 28 May–4 June 2005; and, for an overview, Ajit K. Ghose, "The Employment Challenge in India," *Economic and Political Weekly*, 27 November 2004.

24. P. K. Joshi, Ashok Gulati, Pratap S. Birthal, and Laxmi Tewari, "Agriculture Diversification in South Asia: Patterns, Determinants, and Policy Implications," *Economic and Political Weekly*, 12 June 2004; M. S. Sidhu, "Fruit and Vegetable Processing Industry in India: An Appraisal of the Post-Reform Period," *Economic and Political Weekly*, 9 July 2005.

25. Ramesh Chand, "Whither India's Food Policy: From Food Security to Food Deprivation," *Economic and Political Weekly*, 12 March 2005; Jean Dreze, "Praying for Food Security," *Hindu*, 27 October 2003; Madhura Swaminathan, *Weakening Welfare: The Public Distribution of Food in India* (New Delhi: LeftWord, 2000); Ashok Gulati, Satu Kåhkonen, and Pradeep Sharma, "The Food Corporation of India: Successes and Failures in Foodgrain Marketing," in Satu Kåhkonen and Anthony Lanyi, eds., *Institutions, Incentives, and Economic Reforms in India* (New Delhi: Sage, 2000); and, especially, P. Sainath, *Everybody Loves a Good Drought: Stories from India's Poorest Districts* (New Delhi: Penguin Books India, 1996).

26. P. Sainath, "Trains Raided for Water in TN," TOI, 14 May 1993; Sowmya Sivakumar and Eric Kerbart, "Drought, Sustenance, and Livelihoods: 'Akal' Survey in Rajasthan," *Economic and Political Weekly*, 17 January 2004.

27. See Verrier Elwin, *Maria Murder and Suicide* (Bombay: Oxford University Press, 1943).

28. Farmers' suicides are the subject of a remarkable series of field reports published by P. Sainath in *Hindu*. These are too numerous to list individually; see www.thehinduonnet.com. See also R. S. Deshpande and Nagesh Prabhu, "Farmers' Distress: Proof beyond Question," *Economic and Political Weekly*, 29 October 2005; and *Tehelka*, Special Issue, 6 March 2004 (on the farming crisis).

29. See Myron Weiner, *The Child and the State in India* (Princeton, N.J.: Princeton University Press, 1990).

30. Jean Dreze and Aparajita Goyal, "Future of Mid-Day Meals," *Economic and Political Weekly*, 1 November 2003.

31. Sucheta Mahajan, "MVF India—Education as Empowerment," *Mainstream*, 16 August 2003; Rukmini Banerji, "Pratham Experiences," *Seminar*, February 2005.

32. See "The PROBE Team," *Public Report on Basic Education in India* (New Delhi: Oxford University Press, 1999), ch. 9.

33. Vimala Ramachandran, "The Best of Times, the Worst of Times," *Seminar*, April 2004.

34. Subhadra Menon, *No Place to Go: Stories of Hope and Despair from India's Ailing Health Sector* (New Delhi: Penguin, 2004).

35. Jo Johnson, "The Road to Ruin," *Financial Times*, Weekend Edition, 13–14 August 2005.

36. Pamela Philipose, "India Is Seriously Sick," *New Indian Express*, 24 January 2006.

37. Arjan De Haan and Amaresh Dubey, "Poverty, Disparities, or the Development of Underdevelopment in Orissa," *Economic and Political Weekly*, 28 May–4 June 2005; Sanjay Kumar, "Adivasis of South Orissa: Enduring Poverty," *Economic and Political Weekly*, 27 October 2001; Jean Dreze, "No More Lifelines: Political Economy of Hunger in Orissa," TOI, 17 September 2001.

38. Meena Menon, "The Battle for Bauxite in Orissa," *Hindu*, 20 April 2005.

39. Anon., *The Struggle against Bauxite Mining in Orissa* (Bangalore: People's Union for Civil Liberties, 2003); Anon., *How Wrong? How Right?* (Kashipur: Agragamee, 1999).

40. Quoted in Manash Ghosh, "Sins of Development," *Statesman*, 9 March 1999.

41. Darryl D'Monte, "Another Look at 'Backwardness,'" *Lokmat Times*, 13 October 2000; Darryl D'Monte, "Recent Memories of Underdevelopment," www.tehelka.com, 12 October 2000.

42. *The Struggle against Bauxite Mining*, pp. 15–16; *Indian Express*, 18 and 19 December 2000.

43. Bibhuti Mishra, "Patnaik's Industrialisation Killing Orissa's Environment?" *Tehelka*, 19 November 2005.

44. *Hindu*, 4 and 5 January 2006.

45. Montek S. Ahluwalia, "Economic Reform of States in Post-Reform Period," *Economic and Political Weekly*, 6 May 2000; S. Mahendra Dev, "Post-Reform Regional Variations," *Seminar*, May 2004.

46. See K. P. Kannan, "Shining Socio-Spatial Disparities," *Seminar*, May 2004; Jean Dreze, "Where Welfare Works: Plus Points of the T[amil] N[adu] Model," TOI, 21 May 2003.

47. Angus Deaton and Jean Dreze, "Poverty and Inequality in India: A Re-Examination," *Economic and Political Weekly*, 7 September 2002.

48. T. N. Srinivasan, *Eight Lectures on India's Economic Reforms* (New Delhi: Oxford University Press, 2000), p. 31.

49. On migration from rural Bihar in particular, see Gerry Rodgers and Janine Rodgers, "A Leap across Time: When Semi-Feudalism Met the Market in Rural Purnia," *Economic and Political Weekly*, 2 June 2001; and Alakh N. Sharma, "Agrarian Relations and Socio-Economic Change in Bihar," *Economic and Political Weekly*, 5 March 2005.

50. *India Today*, 20 February 2006.

51. *Statesman*, 20 September 2001.

52. T. N. Ninan, "Big Growth, Bigger Debates," *Seminar*, January 2006.

53. See Naushad Forbes, "Doing Business in India: What Has Liberalization Changed?" in Krueger, *Economic Policy Reforms*, p. 131.

54. On the debate over EGS, see Jean Dreze, "Bhopal Convention on the Right to Work: Brief Report and Personal Observations," *Social Action*, Vol. 54, No. 2,

2004; Rinku Murgai and Martin Ravallion, "Employment Guarantee in Rural India: What Would It Cost and How Much Would It Reduce Poverty?" *Economic and Political Weekly*, 30 July 2005.

55. On the links between liberalization and corruption, see Rob Jenkins, *Democratic Politics and Economic Reform in India* (Cambridge: Cambridge University Press, 1999), pp. 87, 90, 93–94, 99, 102–103.

56. See Abhay Mehta, *Power Play: A Study of the Enron Project* (Hyderabad: Orient Longman, 2000).

57. Cohen, *India*, pp. xv, 285–292.

58. News bulletin, CNN/IBN, 22 February 2006.

59. Larry Pressler, "Shun Pakistan, Favour India," *New York Times*, reprinted in *Asian Age*, 23 March 2005.

60. See C. Raja Mohan, *Crossing the Rubicon: The Shaping of India's Foreign Policy* (New Delhi: Viking, 2003), ch. 4; and Strobe Talbot, *Engaging India* (New Delhi: Viking Penguin, 2005).

61. Jairam Ramesh, *Making Sense of Chindia: Reflections on India and China* (New Delhi: India Research, 2005).

62. *Frontline*, 18 July 2003.

63. *Asian Age*, 11 April 2005; news bulletin, NDTV, 9 April 2005.

64. Daniel H. Pink, "The New Face of the Silicon Age," *Wired*, February 2002 (http://www.wired.com/wired/archive/12.02/india_pr.html).

65. Manjeet Kripalani and Pete Engardio, "The Rise of India," *BusinessWeek*, 8 December 2003 (http://www.businessweek.com./magazine/content/03_49/b3861001_mz001.htm).

66. Ron Moreau and Sudip Mazumdar, "An Indian Champion," *Newsweek*, 12 April 2004.

67. Fareed Zakaria, "India Rising," *Newsweek*, 6 March 2006.

68. Thomas Friedman, *The World Is Flat: A Brief History of the Globalized World in the Twenty-First Century* (London: Allen Lane, 2005), p. 459.

69. Jeffrey D. Sachs, *The End of Poverty: How We Can Make It Happen in Our Lifetime* (London: Penguin, 2005), pp. 185–187.

70. See *Economist*, 5 March 2005; and Roger Cohen, "A New Asia's Roar Is Heard," *International Herald Tribune*, reprinted in *Asian Age*, 19 April 2005.

71. Clyde Prestowitz, *Three Billion New Capitalists: The Great Shift of Wealth and Power to the East* (New York: Basic Books, 2005), pp. 101–105, 232–235.

72. Bharat Jhunjhunwala, "Gathering Storm of Indian Imperialism," *New Indian Express*, 10 August 2005.

CHAPTER 30: A PEOPLE'S ENTERTAINMENTS

1. Histories of the Indian film industry include Erik Barnouw and S. Krishnaswamy, *Indian Film*, 2nd ed. (New York: Oxford University Press, 1980), and B. D. Garga, *So Many Cinemas: The Motion Picture in India* (Bombay: Eminence Designs, 1996). Since this chapter is concerned less with individual achievement and more with social history, it is somewhat parsimonious in speaking of the great actors, directors, singers, and composers of Indian cinema. For these, the reader is referred to Ashish Rajadhyaksha and Paul Willemen, eds., *Encyclo-*

paedia of Indian Cinema, 2nd ed. (New Delhi: Oxford University Press, 1999).

2. Amrit Gangar and Virchand Dharamsey, *Indian Cinema: A Visual Voyage* (New Delhi: Publications Division, 1998), p. 90.

3. *Current*, 27 September 1950; *Hindu*, 6 August 1953.

4. *Current*, 24 December 1952.

5. Garga, *So Many Cinemas*, p. 151.

6. *Rajya Sabha Debates*, 26 November and 10 December 1954; *Current*, 22 December 1954.

7. Amrit Gangar, "Films from the City of Dreams," in Sujata Patel and Alice Thorner, eds., *Bombay: Mosaic of Modern Culture* (Bombay: Oxford University Press, 1995).

8. Ranjani Mazumdar, "The Bombay Film Poster," *Seminar*, May 2003.

9. Satyajit Ray, *Our Films, Their Films* (Calcutta: Orient Longman, 1976), pp. 90–91.

10. Quoted in Peter Manuel, *Cassette Culture: Popular Music and Technology in North India* (New Delhi: Oxford University Press, 1993), p. 45.

11. George Gissing, *New Grub Street* (1891, reprint London: J. M. Dent, 1997), p. 354.

12. The best introduction to the narrative structure of the Indian film is Nasreen Munni Kabir, *Bollywood: The Indian Cinema Story* (London: Channel 4 Books, 2001). But see also Panna Shah, *The Indian Film* (Bombay: Motion Picture Society of India, 1950), and Agehananda Bharati, "Anthropology of Hindi Films," *Illustrated Weekly of India*, 30 January and 6 February 1977.

13. S. S. Vasan, quoted in Hardgrave and Neidhart, "Films and Political Consciousness."

14. Mukul Kesavan, "An Undergraduate History of Hindi Cinema," in B. G. Verghese, *Tomorrow's India: Another Tryst with Destiny* (New Delhi: Viking, 2006), p. 323.

15. Naresh Fernandes, "Remembering Anthony Gonsalves," *Seminar*, November 2004. See also Vanraj Bhatia, "Film Music," *Seminar*, December 1961, and Manuel, *Cassette Culture*, ch. 3.

16. Ashraf Aziz, *Light of the Universe: Essays on Hindustani Film Music* (New Delhi: Three Essays Collective, 2003), pp. xvii–xviii.

17. Bade Ghulam Ali Khan, quoted in H. Y. Sharada Prasad, "Ye kaun aaj aaya savere savere," *Asian Age*, 18 May 2005.

18. N. M. Kabir, "Playback Time: A Brief History of Bollywood Film Songs," *FilmComment*, May–June 2002, p. 41. For informative sketches of lyricists, composers, and singers in Hindi film, see Manek Premchand, *Yesterday's Melodies, Today's Memories* (Mumbai: Jharna, 2003).

19. Steve Derné, *Movies, Masculinity, and Modernity: An Ethnography of Men's Filmgoing in India* (Westport, Conn.: Greenwood, 2000), ch. 2. See also Narendra Panjwani, "A Small Town Goes to the Movies," *Hindi*, Vol. 2, No. 2, 2001.

20. Sara Dickey, *Cinema and the Urban Poor in South India* (Cambridge: Cambridge University Press, 1993); Sara Dickey, "Opposing Faces: Film Star Fan Clubs and the Construction of Class Identities in South India," in Rachel Dwyer and Christopher Pinney, eds., *Pleasure and the Nation: The History,*

Politics, and Consumption of Public Culture in India (New Delhi: Oxford University Press, 2001).

21. On Bachchan's career, see, inter alia, Chidananda Das Gupta, *The Painted Face: Studies in India's Popular Cinema* (New Delhi: Roli, 1991), pp. 239ff, and Ashok Banker, *Bollywood* (New Delhi: Penguin, 2001), pp. 67–77.

22. *Sunday*, 24 February–2 March 1985.

23. Kaveree Bamzai, "A Legend Turns 60," *India Today*, 21 October 2002.

24. These biographical details are from Harish Bhimani, *In Search of Lata Mangeshkar* (New Delhi: Indus, 1995), and Punita Bhatt, "The Lata Legend," *Filmfare*, 1–15 June 1987.

25. Sunil Sethi, quoted in Garga, *So Many Cinemas*, p. 192.

26. Anupama Chopra, *Sholay: The Making of a Classic* (New Delhi: Penguin, 2000), p. 29 and passim.

27. Ashokamitran, *My Years with Boss: At Gemini Studios* (Hyderabad: Orient Longman, 2002), pp. 16–17.

28. *Current*, 3 September 1952.

29. Mukul Kesavan, "Cine Qua Non!" *Outlook*, 18 August 1997.

30. Mukul Kesavan, "Urdu, Awadh, and the Tawaif: The Islamicate Roots of Hindi Cinema," in Zoya Hasan, ed., *Forging Identities: Gender, Communities, and the State* (New Delhi: Kali for Women, 1994).

31. Jerry Pinto, "The Woman Who Could Not Care," in *First Proof: The Penguin Book of New Writing from India 1* (New Delhi: Penguin, 2005), pp. 49–50.

32. Quoted in Shajahan Madampat, "Portrait of a Religious Muslim as a Secular Icon," unpublished paper.

33. Bunny Reuben, *Follywood Flashback: A Collection of Movie Memories* (New Delhi: Indus, 1993), p. 267.

34. Among the many studies of Ray, the best are probably Andrew Robinson, *Satyajit Ray: The Inner Eye* (London: Andre Deutsch, 1989), and Chidananda Dasgpupta, *The Cinema of Satyajit Ray*, 2nd ed. (New Delhi: National Book Trust, 2001).

35. The work of these and other directors is discussed in Yves Thorat, *The Cinemas of India, 1896–2000* (New Delhi: Macmillan India, 2000).

36. This account draws on Rustom Bharucha, "Ninasam: A Cultural Alternative," in *Theatre and the World* (New Delhi: Manohar, 1990), ch. 14; various reports published by Ninasam; and my own visits to Heggodu.

37. H. Y. Sharada Prasad, "Subanna," *Asian Age*, 19 October 2005.

38. Sudhanva Deshpande, "Habib Tanvir: Upside-Down Midas," *Economic and Political Weekly*, 13 September 2003.

39. Gaddar's life and work are the subject of a forthcoming book by Venkat Rao. Among many articles by Rao, see especially "Writing Orally: Decolonization from Below," *positions*, Vol. 7, No. 1, 1999.

40. See, among other works, Bonnie C. Wade, *Music in India: The Classical Traditions*, rev. ed. (Delhi: Manohar, 2001), originally published 1979; Mohan Nadkarni, *The Great Masters: Profiles in Hindustani Classical Music* (New Delhi: HarperCollins India, 1999); and Ludwig Pesch, *The Illustrated Companion to South Indian Classical Music* (New Delhi: Oxford University Press, 1999).

41. Indira Menon, *The Madras Quartet: Women in Karnatak Music* (New Delhi: Roli Books, 1999), pp. 173–178. A recent biography of M. S. Subbulakshmi is T.

J. George's *MS: A Life in Music* (New Delhi: HarperCollins India, 2004). I have also drawn on an unpublished essay by the music scholar Keshav Desiraju.

42. There is, as yet, no biography of Ravi Shankar. I have drawn here on his own autobiography, *Raga Mala* (Guildford: Genesis, 1997); on conversations with music lovers; and on my own thirty-year experience of listening to his music.

43. For more on these and other artists, see Kumar Mukherji, *The Lost World of Hindustani Music* (New Delhi: Penguin India, 2006), a fine and richly anecdotal history by a scholar-performer.

44. TOI, 3 March 2003; *Asian Age*, 3 March 2003.

45. The arguments in these paragraphs are elaborated in Ramachandra Guha, *A Corner of a Foreign Field: The Indian History of a British Sport* (London: Picador, 2002). See also Richard Cashman, *Patrons, Players, and the Crowd: The Phenomenon of Indian Cricket* (Bombay: Orient Longman, 1980).

46. C. Rajagopalachari, quoted in Pon. Thangamani, *History of Broadcasting in India: With Special Reference to Tamil Nadu, 1924-1954* (Chennai: Ponnaiah Pathipagam, 2000), pp. 104-105.

47. The spread of the radio in India is described in Thangamani, *History of Broadcasting*; and in Mehra Masani, *Broadcasting and the People* (New Delhi: National Book Trust, 1976). See also David Lelyveld, "Transmitters and Culture: The Colonial Roots of Indian Broadcasting," *South Asia Research*, Vol. 10, No. 1, 1990.

48. *Hindu*, 19 July 1953.

49. David Lelyveld, "Upon the Subdominant: Administering Music on All-India Radio," in Carol A. Breckenridge, ed., *Consuming Modernity: Public Culture in a South Asian World* (Minneapolis: University of Minnesota Press, 1995).

50. Ritu Sarin, "Doordarshan: The Money Machine," *Sunday*, 18-24 August 1985.

51. Chidananda Dasgupta, "Cinema: The Unstoppable Chariot," in Hiranmay Karlekar, ed., *Independent India: The First Fifty Years* (Delhi: Oxford University Press, 1998), p. 442.

52. Wimal Dissanayake and Malti Sahai, "Raj Kapoor and the Indianization of Chaplin," paper presented at a symposium, "Humour in Cinema: East and West," Waikiki, Hawaii, November 29-December 3, 1986.

53. *Current*, 28 September 1955.

54. Bunny Reuben, *Raj Kapoor: The Fabulous Showman* (New Delhi: Indus, 1995), pp. 88f.

55. TOI, 5 January 1952.

56. K. A. Abbas, *I Am Not an Island: An Experiment in Autobiography* (New Delhi: Vikas, 1977), p. 372.

57. Personal communication from Professor James C. Scott of Yale University.

58. Stephen Alter, *Amritsar to Lahore: Crossing the Border between India and Pakistan* (New Delhi: Penguin, 2000), pp. 132-133, 136, 172-173, 178.

59. "Bowled Over by Bollywood," *Guardian Weekly*, 27 May-5 June 2005.

60. "Move Over LA, Here Comes Bombay," The *Times*, 22 June 2000.

61. *Time*, 27 October 2003. See also Raminder Kaur and Ajay J. Sinha, *Bollywood: Popular Indian Cinema through a Transnational Lens* (New Delhi: Sage, 2005).

62. Sudhanva Deshpande, "Hindi Films: The Rise of the Consumable Hero," *Himal South Asian*, August 2001.

63. TOI, 25 February 2004.
64. S. S. Vasan, "Film Production in India Today," in R. M. Ray, ed., *Film Seminar Report 1955* (New Delhi: Sangeet Natak Akademi, 1955), pp. 33–35.

EPILOGUE: WHY INDIA SURVIVES

1. Robert D. Kaplan, "The Lawless Frontier," *Atlantic Monthly*, September 1999.
2. Ayaz Amir, "The Beauty of Democracy," *Dawn*, reprinted in *Asian Age*, 17 May 2004.
3. Yogendra Yadav, "Understanding the Second Democratic Upsurge: Trends of Bahujan Participation in Electoral Politics in the 1990s," in Francine R. Frankel, Zoya Hasan, Rajeev Bhargava, and Balveer Arora, eds., *Transforming India: Social and Political Dynamics of Democracy* (New Delhi: Oxford University Press, 2002), p. 133.
4. *Deccan Herald*, 10 October 2004.
5. Bela Bhatia, *The Naxalite Movement*, pp. 114–120.
6. J. M. Lyngdoh, quoted in TOI, 3 December 2003.
7. See, for instance, the collected works of R. K. Laxman, published by Penguin India. Laxman is the most prolific and (by common consent) the most original of Indian cartoonists, but there have been many other gifted practitioners, who, like him, specialize in political satire.
8. *Telegraph*, 2 January 2003.
9. Anderson, *The Spectre of Comparisons* (London: Verso, 1998), p. 132.
10. Sunil Khilnani, "Democracy and Nationalism in India," lecture delivered at Collège de France, 30 May 2005, p. 2.
11. Isaiah Berlin, "Nationalism: Past Neglect and Present Power" (1979), in *Against the Current: Essays in the History of Ideas*, ed. Henry Hardy (London: Pimlico, 1997), pp. 346–347, 353–354.
12. The modern literature on nationalism will fill a library. For a sampling, see Ernest Gellner, *Nations and Nationalism* (Oxford: Basil Blackwell, 1983); Benedict Anderson, *Imagined Communities: Reflections on the Origins and Spread of Nationalism* (London: Verso, 1983); Anthony D. Smith, *The Ethnic Origin of Nations* (Oxford: Basil Blackwell, 1986); Liah Greenfeld, *Nationalism: Five Roads to Modernity* (Cambridge, Mass.: Harvard University Press, 1992); Eric Hobsbawm, *Nations and Nationalism since 1780* (Cambridge: Cambridge University Press, 1993); Tom Nairn, *Faces of Nationalism: Janus Revisited* (London: Verso, 1997). See also Hans Kohn, *Nationalism: Its Meaning and History* (Princeton, N.J.: Van Nostrand, 1955), a classic early work.
13. See Mukul Kesavan, *Secular Common Sense* (New Delhi: Penguin India, 2001).
14. See Javeed Alam, *Who Wants Democracy?* (New Delhi: Orient Longman, 2004).
15. Bernard D. Nossiter, *Soft State: A Newspaperman's Chronicle of India* (New York: Harper and Row, 1970), pp. 119–123.
16. Joseph Stalin, *Marxism and the National Question* (London: Martin Lawrence, 1936), pp. 5–6.
17. Quoted in Peter A. Blitstein, "Nation-Building or Russification? Obligatory Russian Instruction in the Soviet Non-Russian School," in Ronald Grigor Suny and Terry Martin, *A State of Nations: Empire and Nation-Building in the Age of Lenin and Stalin* (New York: Oxford University Press, 2001), p. 255.

18. See Neil DeVotta, *Blowback: Linguistic Nationalism, Institutional Decay, and Ethnic Conflict in Sri Lanka* (Stanford, Calif.: Stanford University Press, 2004), pp. 89–91.

19. S. M. Burke, ed., *Jinnah: Speeches and Statements 1947–1948* (Karachi: Oxford University Press, 2000), p. 150. (Emphasis added.)

20. Arundhati Roy, "How Deep Shall We Dig?" *Hindu*, 25 April 2004.

21. Hugh Tinker, *Reorientations: Studies on Asia in Transition* (Bombay: Oxford University Press), pp. 71f.

22. Pratap Bhanu Mehta, *The Burden of Democracy* (New Delhi: Penguin India, 2003), pp. 28, 114–115.

23. Howard, quoted in Samuel Huntingdon, *Who Are We? America's Great Debate*, Indian ed. (New Delhi: Penguin India, 2004), pp. 28–29.

24. David Gilmour, *The Ruling Caste: Imperial Lives in the Victorian Raj* (London: John Murray, 2005).

25. CAD, Vol. 10, pp. 43–51.

26. On the history and functioning of the IAS, see David C. Potter, *India's Political Administrators: From ICS to IAS* (New Delhi: Oxford University Press, 1996); K. P. Krishnan and T. V. Somanathan, "Civil Service: An Institutional Perspective," in Devesh Kapur and Pratap Bhanu Mehta, eds., *Public Institutions in India* (New Delhi: Oxford University Press, 2004).

27. Nehru to General Lockhart, 13 August 1947, in Group XLIX, Part I, Cariappa Papers, National Archives of India, New Delhi.

28. See Group XXI, Part II, Cariappa Papers.

29. Nehru to Cariappa, 13 October 1952, in Group XLIX, Part I, Cariappa Papers.

30. *Hindu*, 14 January 1953, reprinted 14 January 2003.

31. See correspondence in Group XLIX, Part I, Cariappa Papers.

32. Note of 12 December 1958, Group XXXIII, Part I, Cariappa Papers. Cariappa went on to claim that for these Pakistani generals "war between India and Pakistan was simply unthinkable."

33. Frank Moraes to General Cariappa, 19 December 1968, Group XLIX, Part I, Cariappa Papers.

34. J. S. Aurora, "If Khalistan Comes, the Sikhs Will Be the Losers," in Patwant Singh and Harji Malik, eds., *Punjab: The Fatal Miscalculation* (New Delhi: Patwant Singh, 1985), pp. 137–138.

35. C. Rajagopalachari, quoted in Guy Wint, *Spotlight on Asia* (Harmondsworth: Penguin, 1955), p. 130.

36. George Woodcock, *Beyond the Blue Mountains: An Autobiography* (Toronto: Fitzhenry and Whiteside, 1987), p. 105.

37. S. Gopal, "The English Language in India since Independence," in John Grigg, ed., *Nehru Memorial Lectures, 1966–1991* (Delhi: Oxford University Press, 1992), pp. 202–203.

38. Jonathan Parry, "Nehru's Dream and the Village 'Waiting Room': Long Distance Labour Migrants to a Central Indian Steel Town," paper to be published in *Contributions to Indian Sociology*.

39. Nasreen Munni Kabir, *Talking Films: Conversations on Hindi Cinema with Javed Akhtar* (New Delhi: Oxford University Press, 1999), p. 35.

40. Martin Walker, *Makers of the American Century* (London: Chatto and Windus, 2000), Preface.

41. Huntingdon, *Who Are We?*, pp. xv–xvi, 12, 40, 61, 63, 171, 232, 316, etc.

42. *Time*, 6 March 2006.

43. Ronald W. Clark, *JBS: The Life and Work of JBS Haldane* (Oxford: Oxford University Press, 1968).

44. Haldane to Geoff Conklin, 25 July 1962, J. B. S. Haldane Papers, National Library of Scotland, Edinburgh.

45. J. Neyman (professor of statistics, University of California, Berkeley) to Haldane, 18 September 1961, in Haldane Papers.

46. Haldane to Neyman, 26 September 1961, in Haldane Papers.

47. D. N. Chatterjee to P. N. Haksar, 6 July 1971, Subject File No. 171, Haksar Papers, Third Instalment, NMML.

INDEX

Page numbers in *italics* refer to maps.